THEODORE REX

THEODORE REX

Edmund Morris

RANDOM HOUSE

NEW YORK

PUBLISHER'S NOTE

The narrative of this book confines itself exclusively to Theodore Roosevelt's presidency, 1901–1909. For compatibility with quotations, many
usages current at that time have been retained, particularly with regard to
place-names. Hence, e.g., *Peking* is used for Beijing and *Port Arthur* for
modern Lushun. Where necessary, such names are clarified in the notes. A
few words spelled differently then, but pronounced the same now, have
been modernized. Hence, *Tsar* for *Czar*. "Simplified spellings" adopted by
Roosevelt in his second term have been retained as idiosyncratic when
quoted. Hence, *thoroly, fixt, dropt.* Ethnic appellations and honorifics reflect the styles of the Roosevelt era, as do occasional references to countries as feminine entities. Superlatives such as *an unprecedented landslide*
apply only as of the date cited. Expectations or intimations of "coming
events" are those of the period. Historical hindsights are confined to the
notes.

LIBRARY OF CONGRESS CATALOGING-IN-PUBLICATION DATA

Morris, Edmund.
Theodore Rex / Edmund Morris.
p. cm.
Sequel to: The rise of Theodore Roosevelt.
Includes bibliographical references and index.
ISBN 0-394-55509-0 (acid-free paper)
1. Roosevelt, Theodore, 1858–1919. 2. Presidents—United States—
Biography. 3. United States—Politics and government—1901–1909. I. Title.

E757 .M885 2001
973.91'1—dc21   2001019366

Printed in the United States of America on acid-free paper

Random House website address: www.atrandom.com

2 4 6 8 9 7 5 3

FIRST EDITION

Book design by Barbara M. Bachman

To my Mother and Father

CONTENTS

THEODORE REX

14–16 September 1901

Saturday

THEODORE ROOSEVELT became President of the United States without knowing it, at 2:15 in the morning of 14 September 1901. He was bouncing in a buckboard down the rainswept slopes of Mount Marcy, in the Adirondacks. Constitutionally, not so much as a heartbeat impeded the flow of power from his assassinated predecessor to himself. Practically, more than four hundred miles of mud and rails still separated him from William McKinley's death chamber in Buffalo, where preparations for an emergency inauguration were already under way.

For all Roosevelt knew, he was still Vice President, yet he already realized that he would soon assume supreme responsibility. Yesterday's telegrams, relayed up the mountain by telephone operators, riders, and runners, had documented the spread of gangrene through his bullet-ridden Chief:

THE PRESIDENT IS CRITICALLY ILL

HIS CONDITION IS GRAVE

OXYGEN IS BEING GIVEN

ABSOLUTELY NO HOPE

The last telegram to reach Roosevelt's vacation cabin in Upper Tahawus had been urgent enough to banish all thought of waiting for clearer weather:

THE PRESIDENT APPEARS TO BE DYING AND MEMBERS

OF THE CABINET IN BUFFALO THINK YOU SHOULD

LOSE NO TIME COMING

So, shortly before midnight, he had kissed his wife and children good-bye and begun the descent to North Creek station—at least a seven-hour drive, even by day.

He was now, at the moment of his accession, halfway through the second stage of this journey, some five miles north of Aiden Lair Lodge, where a new wagon and fresh horses awaited him. He sat alone on the passenger seat, shrouded against splashes of mud in a borrowed raincoat several sizes too big. His favorite hat, a broad-brim slouch pulled well over his ears, kept some of the drizzle off his spectacles—not that he could see anything beyond the buckboard's tossing circle of lamplight. Nor had he much to say: since leaving Lower Tahawus, indeed, he had spoken hardly a word to the lanky youth in front of him. From time to time, he muttered to himself.

Sincere, if slight, grief for McKinley—a cold-blooded politician he had never much cared for—struggled in Roosevelt's breast with more violent emotions regarding the assassin, Leon Czolgosz. In his opinion, those bullets at Buffalo had been fired, not merely at a man, but at the very heart of the American Republic. They were an assault upon representative government and civilized order. Unable to contain his rage, he leaned forward and blurted an excoriation of Czolgosz into the rain. "If it had been I who had been shot, he wouldn't have got away so easily. . . . I'd have guzzled him first."

—⟰—

MEANWHILE, IN WASHINGTON, Secretary of State John Hay sat alone, weeping. For hours, he had heard newsboys shrieking outside his library window: *"Extra! Extra! All about the President dying!"* Aging and increasingly hypochondriachal, Hay had once worked for Abraham Lincoln and James Garfield, and seen them both assassinated. This third assassination, compounded by the recent death of his own son, was enough to extinguish all desire to go on living in an alien century. But duty had to be done. When the final knell sounded across Sixteenth Street, he wrote a telegram officially informing Theodore Roosevelt that McKinley was dead. He ordered it sent to North Creek Station.

—⟰—

AT ABOUT 3:30, the lights of Aiden Lair Lodge appeared in the mist. The landlord, Mike Cronin, was waiting outside with his rig. Roosevelt climbed down onto the wooden landing. "Any news?"

"Not a word." Cronin spoke awkwardly, uncertain how to address his passenger. "Jump in right away, and we'll be off." He fumbled with a lantern. Roosevelt said, "Here, give it to me!" and joined him on the driver's seat.

The new horses, two big black Morgans, started off swiftly. Cronin was an expert whip, and hoped to break his own daylight record of just under two hours to North Creek. The horses knew every curve of the sixteen-mile road, but the descent grew slippery, and one of them stumbled. Conscious of the precious value of his cargo, Cronin dragged on the reins.

"Oh, that doesn't matter!" Roosevelt exclaimed. "Push ahead!"

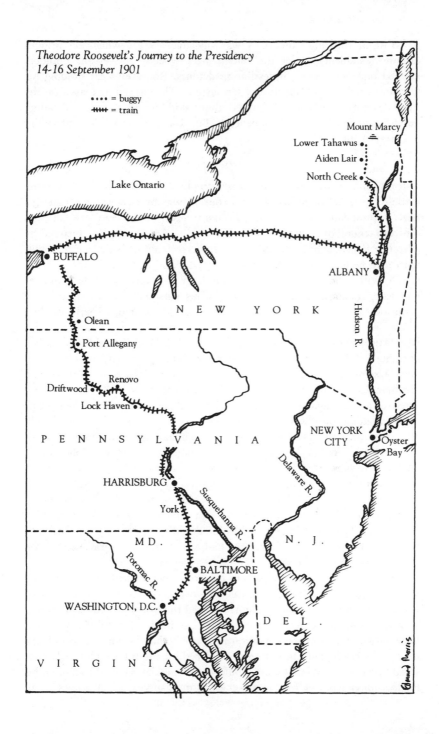

Theodore Roosevelt's Journey to the Presidency
14-16 September 1901

•••• = buggy
++++ = train

Mount Marcy
Lower Tahawus •
Aiden Lair •
North Creek •

Lake Ontario

• BUFFALO

ALBANY •

N E W   Y O R K

• Olean

• Port Allegany

Renovo

Driftwood •

Lock Haven •

Hudson R.

P E N N S Y L V A N I A

NEW YORK
CITY

• Oyster
Bay

Delaware R.

HARRISBURG •

York •

Susquehanna R.

N. J.

M D .

Potomac R.

• BALTIMORE

WASHINGTON, D.C. •

D E L .

V I R G I N I A

Most of the time, the road was invisible, except when log bridges drummed suddenly under the buckboard's wheels, and errant boulders loomed out of the mud, necessitating detours. Roosevelt kept holding his watch to the lantern. "Hurry up! Go faster!" Their speed increased on the steep descent. Cronin worried aloud about skidding off a bend and falling hundreds of feet into the bogs beneath. But Roosevelt was calm. "If you're not afraid I am not."

⟶

SINCE PUBERTY HE had taught himself to pluck the flower safety out of the nettle danger. Although his physical courage was by now legendary, it was not a natural endowment. He had been a timid child in New York City, cut off from schoolboy society by illness, wealth, and private tutors. Inspired by a leonine father, he had labored with weights to build up his strength. Simultaneously, he had built up his courage "by sheer dint of practicing fearlessness." With every ounce of new muscle, with every point scored over pugilistic, romantic, and political rivals, his personal impetus (likened by many observers to that of a steam train) had accelerated. Experiences had flashed by him in such number that he was obviously destined to travel a larger landscape of life than were his fellows. He had been a published author at eighteen, a husband at twenty-two, an acclaimed historian and New York State Assemblyman at twenty-three, a father and a widower at twenty-five, a ranchman at twenty-six, a candidate for Mayor of New York at twenty-seven, a husband again at twenty-eight, a Civil Service Commissioner of the United States at thirty. By then he was producing book after book, and child after child, and cultivating every scientist, politician, artist, and intellectual of repute in Washington. His career had gathered further speed: Police Commissioner of New York City at thirty-six, Assistant Secretary of the Navy at thirty-eight, Colonel of the First U.S. Volunteer Cavalry, the "Rough Riders," at thirty-nine. At last, in Cuba, had come the consummating "crowded hour." A rush, a roar, the sting of his own blood, a surge toward the sky, a smoking pistol in his hand, a soldier in light blue doubling up "neatly as a jackrabbit" . . . When the smoke cleared, he had found himself atop Kettle Hill on the Heights of San Juan, with a vanquished empire at his feet.

From that viewpoint, the path to the presidency looked clear. Returning home a hero, Roosevelt had been elected Governor of New York within two weeks of his fortieth birthday. He had toured the Midwest and been greeted everywhere as if he was a presidential candidate. Dutifully supporting William McKinley for renomination in 1900, he had begun to assemble his own campaign organization for 1904. Everything in his hard philosophy assured him that the White House would be his one day. He had fought all his life for supreme power, for "that highest form of success which comes . . . to the man who does not shrink from danger, from hardship, or from bitter toil."

Yet just when his momentum seemed irresistible, there had come that sickening sideways pull into the Vice Presidency, followed by a political dead halt. And now this even more violent lurch back on course!

His path ran, appropriately, past a cemetery: the churchyard of Minerva. Wet gravestones gleamed as the buckboard raced through the village. Beyond, slopes gave way to swamps, and the road began to flatten out. A pallor in the mist signaled dawn. At five o'clock, Cronin announced that they were only two miles from North Creek. Roosevelt ordered a stop "to let the horses blow." He straightened his tie and smoothed his suit, saying there might be some "notables" waiting at the station.

The final dash was dramatic enough to satisfy Roosevelt's love of stagy arrivals. Sun-reddened cliffs disclosed the racing floodwater of the Hudson River, and Cronin's horses, refreshed by their brief pause, thundered thrillingly over the bridge into town. The noise acted as a drumroll, heralding their entrance onto Main Street. Voices shouted "There he comes!" The buckboard flew past darkened housefronts and stoops still bare of the morning milk. Its wheels had hardly come to rest at the depot when Roosevelt jumped down to discover, if not "notables," at least a small crowd of local citizens and the neat, bespectacled figure of his secretary, William Loeb, Jr. A special train stood waiting. The time on the station clock read twenty-two minutes past five.

Loeb wordlessly handed over John Hay's telegram from Washington. Roosevelt unfolded it. There was a moment of silence, broken only by the impatient hissing of the locomotive. He stared at the eight words in his hand:

THE PRESIDENT DIED AT TWO-FIFTEEN THIS MORNING

Looking suddenly worn and weary, he pocketed the paper and strode across the wet platform. A private car was ready for him. He darted up the steps, turned, and waved once. Loeb followed him inside. The train began to move before the door swung shut behind them.

⟋⟍

ROOSEVELT'S FIRST WORDS, as he settled into his plush seat, were that he wanted to get to Buffalo "as soon as possible." Loeb had anticipated this wish, and secured the fastest locomotive on the Delaware & Hudson Railroad. Three years of experience had taught him that his boss was always in a hurry. That dart up the train steps was typical: he could remember Governor Roosevelt doing the same up all seventy-seven stairs of the State Capitol in Albany.

Mount Marcy's cloud banks began to lift, and the other peaks glowed in the sun as the special raced south toward Albany. But fog lingered in the Hudson Valley, and the crew of the locomotive could only trust in its emergency right-of-way. Roosevelt dictated a series of telegrams, including one to Edith that was as terse as Hay's to himself. "Darling Edie" always knew what to do. She and the children would find their own way down the mountain and home to Oyster Bay. His work finished, he dismissed Loeb and sat staring out into the flying mists.

At about seven o'clock there was a scream of brakes, and a crash that shook the whole train. It jarred to a halt. Word came back that the locomotive had collided with a handcar in the fog: two men were nearly killed.

Roosevelt did not need to be told what might have happened had the handcar been another train. For fifteen minutes, while a gang cleared the track, he had leisure to ponder the mortal vulnerabilities of power. This accident was nothing compared to the threat of another Czolgosz lurking in wait for him. Anarchism, that plague of European government, was a virulent strain in America, fed by social unrest, and fear of it was spreading. Just the other day an old black man had taken him by the hand and said, "Look out they don't get you, Mr. Vice-President."

Personally, Roosevelt was not worried about assassination. If a bullet came from behind, he could do nothing about it, and would "go down into the darkness," that being his fatalistic image of death. If the attack was frontal, as on McKinley, he had confidence in the abnormal speed of his reflexes, and the power of his 185-pound body. Last winter, in Colorado, he had leaped off his horse into a pack of hounds, kicked them aside, and knifed a cougar to death. What a great fight that had been!

His larger concern was the effect of morbid micro-organisms like Czolgosz on the American body politic. As President he intended to "war with ruthless efficiency" against them, just as he had warred against his own diseases in youth. Roosevelt had never hesitated to identify himself with the United States. Personal and patriotic pride throbbed as one in his breast. When, accepting the vice presidency, he saluted "a new century big with the fate of mighty nations," it was clear which nation, and which leader, he believed would ultimately prevail.

Is America a weakling to shrink from the world work of the great world-powers? No. The young giant of the West stands on a continent and clasps the crest of an ocean in either hand. Our nation, glorious in youth and strength, looks in the future with eager eyes and rejoices as a strong man to run a race.

Youth, size, and strength: these things, surely, would render America proof against the anarchic strain. At forty-two, he, Theodore Roosevelt, was the youngest man ever called upon to preside over the United States—itself the youngest of the world powers. The double symbolism was pleasing. He refused to look at the future through "the dun-colored mists" of pessimism. Even now (as his train jerked into motion again), the fog outside was evaporating into a clear sky, and light flooded the Hudson Valley. Black night had given way to bright morning. Soon he would take the oath as President of "the mightiest Republic upon which the sun has ever shone."

⌒

AT TWO MINUTES before eight, the train stopped briefly at Albany. Loeb emerged to tell waiting reporters that Roosevelt was "very tired," and would have no statement to make until after his inauguration. Breakfast was whisked aboard, along with the morning newspapers. Within five minutes, the special was on its way again, accelerating to sixty miles an hour.

Roosevelt, sucking down some badly needed coffee, had as much to learn from DEATH EXTRA dispatches as millions of other Americans that morning. The President's last hours were chronicled in poignant detail. Here was Senator Mark Hanna, who loved McKinley like a brother, dropping onto gouty knees and pleading, "William, William, speak to me!" Here were doctors squirting stimulants into the dying man's heart, to shock him into momentary recognition of his wife. And here, framed in black, were the President's last words, pious enough to heave all the bosoms in Christendom: "Nearer, my God to Thee . . . *His will be done!*"

In rude contrast, other columns celebrated the "Tremendous Energy," "Superb Health," and "Strenuous Life" of McKinley's successor. Roosevelt did not need to read these, nor the potted biographies listing his many qualifications for office. He was more interested in analyses of his political situation.

The New York *World* announced that he had already "definitely fixed in his mind the nomination for 1904." His old foe Senator Hanna, Chairman of the Republican National Committee, would have to be gotten out of the way somehow. The newspaper was silent as to Roosevelt's chances of election. No Vice President succeeding to the presidency through death had yet won another term in his own right.

The New York *Press* predicted that John Hay would resign as Secretary of State, followed by Treasury Secretary Lyman J. Gage. Roosevelt did not like this forecast. No matter how genuine the desire of both Secretaries—ailing, old, and bereaved—to retire, he could not afford to have them decamp before he reached the White House. It would look like a vote of no confidence. There might be serious repercussions on Wall Street, where Hay was seen as an aggressive promoter of American commercial interests abroad, and Gage as guardian of Republicanism's holiest grail, the protective tariff.

A remarkable consensus of Democratic and Republican editorial writers held that Roosevelt would be as "conservative" as McKinley. The very unanimity of this opinion seemed contrived, as if to soothe a nervous stock market. The financial pages reported that "Severe Shocks," "Feverish Trading," and "Heavy Declines" had hit Wall Street on Friday, when the Gold Dollar President began to die. Roosevelt knew little about money—it was one of the few subjects that bored him—but even he could see that one false move this weekend might bring about a real panic on Monday.

⌒

AS THE NEWS of McKinley's death flashed around the world, members of Roosevelt's circle of acquaintance could reflect with grim satisfaction on the many times they had predicted the presidency for him. In Dresden, his German tutor claimed first honors. "He will surely one day be a great professor," she remembered telling his mother. "Or who knows, he may even become President of the United States."

In Albany, an old girlfriend mused on the "strange prophetic quality in Theodore." Ever since her first crush on him, Fanny Parsons had felt a "mystical" certainty that he would lead his country to world power. In Dickinson, North Dakota, the editor of a cowboy newspaper recalled the young Roosevelt's complete lack of surprise at being told that he was destined for the White House. In Indianapolis, Benjamin Harrison's son reread a memo by the late President: "Should Mr. Roosevelt aspire to become President of the United States, I believe that he will be successful." In London, a Member of Parliament checked his diary entry for the day Roosevelt had been elected Vice President: "This can only mean one thing—that the Almighty has decided to promote the good McKinley to the vale of tears." And in arctic Norway, a traveling Henry Adams stared aghast at the wire dispatches from America. "So Teddy is President! Is not that stupendous! Before such a career as that, I have no observations to make."

Minds less fatalistic could view Roosevelt's career only as a crazy trajectory, like that of a bee smacking against many surfaces before buzzing into the open air. Some ward heeler's notion to nominate the young aristocrat for the New York Assembly; the freak tragedy that drove him west; the chance encounter that brought him back; the overnight war that made him Governor; his entrapment into the vice presidency, his liberation by an assassin . . . Horatio Alger could not get away with such a story.

Yet there was no doubt that Theodore Roosevelt was peculiarly qualified to be President of all the people. Few, if any Americans could match the breadth of his intellect and the strength of his character. A random survey of his achievements might show him mastering German, French, and the contrasted dialects of Harvard and Dakota Territory; assembling fossil skeletons with paleontological skill; fighting for an amateur boxing championship; transcribing birdsong into a private system of phonetics; chasing boat thieves with a star on his breast and Tolstoy in his pocket; founding a finance club, a stockmen's association, and a hunting-conservation society; reading some twenty thousand books and writing fifteen of his own; climbing the Matterhorn; promulgating a flying machine; and becoming a world authority on North American game mammals. Any Roosevelt watcher could make up a different but equally varied list. If the sum of all these facets of experience added up to more than a geometric whole—implying excess construction somewhere, planes piling upon planes—then only he, presumably, could view the polygon entire.

—⌒—

THOUSANDS OF PEOPLE were milling on the platform of Exchange Street Station, Buffalo, when Roosevelt's train approached at 1:30 P.M. But the engineer, obeying security instructions, did not slacken speed. He continued west at full steam. Four minutes later, the train drew up at Terrace Station, where a private carriage and twelve mounted policemen stood waiting in the sunshine. Roosevelt was down the steps of his car before the wheels stopped rolling. An hour's rest had cleared the tiredness from his face, but his eyes were troubled. Some onlookers shouted, "Hurrah for Teddy!" He silenced them with a glare, and climbed into the waiting carriage. One of the policemen reached after him. "Colonel, will you shake hands with me?" Roosevelt recognized, and briefly embraced, a veteran of his regiment. Within thirty seconds, the cavalcade was on its way.

Roosevelt's companion in the carriage was Ansley Wilcox, a Buffalo friend who had put him up on earlier, happier visits. Wilcox suggested that they go to his home at 641 Delaware Avenue for a quick lunch. McKinley's body, attended by a quorum of the Cabinet, lay in the Milburn House, one mile farther uptown.

The cavalcade moved too fast for crowds to form, so the sidewalks of Delaware Avenue were practically empty when they reached number 641. Roosevelt remembered the Wilcox Mansion as one of Buffalo's most elegant houses, but today its white pillars were hideously swathed in black, drapes blinded every window, and veils of fading wisteria hung from the walls like widow's weeds. Averting his gaze, he hurried inside.

Over lunch, he said that he had decided where he wanted to be sworn in: "Here." Wilcox protested that arrangements had been made to hold the ceremony at the Milburn House, in a room below McKinley's corpse. "Don't you think it would be far better to do as the Cabinet has decided?" Roosevelt was adamant. "No. It would be far worse."

He would go there, he said, only to pay his respects. First he must make himself presentable. By a fortunate coincidence, Wilcox was of similar size and build, so Roosevelt was able to borrow a frock coat, waistcoat, and striped trousers. His bull-like neck presented no problem, as he had brought

"ITS WHITE PILLARS WERE HIDEOUSLY SWATHED IN BLACK."
The Wilcox Mansion, Buffalo, September 1901

a fresh shirt and collar. The Rooseveltian head, however, proved too large for any of Wilcox's tall silk hats. John S. Scatchard, a macrocephalic neighbor, entered the annals of history by lending his own capacious topper. A satin tie, fine watch chain, gloves, and gold-topped cane completed Roosevelt's furnishings. Bootblacks polished away the last traces of Adirondack mud from his person, and he emerged onto the porch at 2:30, lustrous from head to foot.

Even now, the only spectators in Delaware Avenue were two platoons of mounted police, a knot of reporters, and a teenage girl. Roosevelt exploded with rage at the sight of the troopers. "I told you I did not want an escort!" he roared at the State Inspector General. He was clearly overwrought, and had to be coaxed to accept a few troopers around his carriage.

To swelling cries of "Roosevelt is coming! Roosevelt is coming!" the carriage sped north to Milburn House. He jumped out in precipitate fashion, then, recollecting himself, advanced across the lawn with bowed head. The dapper figure of George Bruce Cortelyou, McKinley's secretary, came out to meet him. Roosevelt removed his hat. They talked gravely for a few seconds. Cortelyou, whose normally sleek, fortyish features were ravaged with grief and exhaustion, explained that an autopsy was being performed upstairs. Roosevelt would not be able to see the body. Mrs. McKinley was too prostrated to receive him. Senator Hanna was nowhere to be seen—he had limped off mumbling something about possible "misconstruction" if he attended the inaugural ceremony. Secretaries Hay and Gage were in Washington, looking after the government. The rest of the Cabinet was waiting in the parlor.

Hat in hand, Roosevelt followed Cortelyou inside.

SIX SOLEMN FIGURES rose to greet him. A voice called out, "The President of the United States." It was the first time he had heard the phrase in reference to himself. But its drama did not register, so intent was he upon behaving correctly.

After formal handshakes, he stood listening to the familiar hoarse murmur of Elihu Root, Secretary of War. How often had this authoritative figure, this severe face under the ridiculous fringe, bent over him in fatherly advice! Root—"the brutal friend to whom I pay the most attention"—had been one of the group of eminent New Yorkers that supported his entry into politics, seventeen years ago. Root, lawyer without peer, had hornswoggled the Saratoga convention into overlooking his technical ineligibility for the gubernatorial nomination. Time and again, the rising politician had submitted hot speeches to Root's icy scrutiny, always with bracing results. He even enjoyed the deadly Root wit, though it bruised his ego.

Now, however, Roosevelt was senior. He politely rejected Root's recommendation of an inauguration on the spot, saying it would be "more appropriate" elsewhere. The Secretary bowed assent.

Returning to his carriage, Roosevelt was driven back the way he had come. Root and the other Cabinet officers followed in separate carriages, with reporters running behind them.

A STRANGE HOTHOUSE glow filled Ansley Wilcox's green library as Roosevelt entered it alone. From now on, he would have to get used to deference whenever he crossed a threshold. The luminescence came from a stained-glass window, fringed with sunny ivy. He chose this bright spot for himself, and watched the Cabinet officers filing in. Cortelyou arranged them in arcs to left and right, while a federal judge, John R. Hazel, stood in the center of the room. Loeb, acting as doorman, admitted a selection of local dignitaries. Among them Roosevelt recognized Senator Chauncey Depew (R., New York), looking humble for once, doubtless regretting how he used to tease "Teddy" about wanting to be President. Next, Loeb beckoned in representatives of the three press agencies, and, in a final relaxation of proprieties, a small party of women.

Some constitutional documents were given to Judge Hazel, who shuffled them into order. Roosevelt gazed around the library. A glint in his spectacles betrayed displeasure. Loeb came up inquiringly, and there was a whispered conversation in which the words *newspapermen* and *sufficient room* were audible. Hurrying outside, Loeb returned with two dozen delighted scribes. They proceeded to report the subsequent ceremony with a wealth of detail unmatched in the history of presidential inaugurations.

The library clock struck 3:30. Elihu Root muttered something urgent to Roosevelt, then took up his position. There was a moment of extreme quietness, broken only by the chirp of a sparrow in the window. Roosevelt half turned, and gazed almost yearningly through the glass, a boy trapped in school. Root's voice reclaimed his attention.

"Mr. Vice President, I—"

The Secretary of War choked, sobbed, and for a full minute struggled to control himself. Roosevelt's face was stern, but as the suspense mounted his cheek muscles began to twitch, and his right foot pawed the floor. At last, Root managed to continue. "I have been asked, on behalf of the Cabinet of the late President . . . to request that, for reasons of weight affecting the administration of the government, you should proceed to take the constitutional office of the President of the United States."

Roosevelt bowed, cleared his throat, and said waveringly, "I shall take the oath at once." He, too, seemed to be fighting tears, but his voice grew rapidly stronger: "And in this hour of deep and terrible national bereavement I wish to state that it shall be my aim—" (here he shook his shoulders and pulled back his head) "—to continue absolutely unbroken the policy of President McKinley for the peace, the prosperity, and the honor of our beloved country."

This speech, the shortest inaugural anybody could remember, created a profound impression. It struck all present as "pledge, platform, and policy all in one." Roosevelt spoke with characteristic passion, punctuating his words with dental snaps, as if biting the syllables out of the air. He seemed to vibrate with force, sincerity, and reverence for the memory of his predecessor. To one observer, he symbolized "the magnificent moral and mental balance of the nation." His statement "instantly solved the political and commercial crisis." Finance, in the person of John G. Milburn, grew calm. Industry, in the person of Chauncey Depew, was comforted. And Government, in the persons of the Cabinet officers, breathed a collective sigh of relief.

Roosevelt was to receive worldwide praise for his few words. Yet they were not original. Elihu Root had suggested, *sotto voce* while the clock was chiming, that he "declare his intention to continue unbroken the policy of President McKinley for the peace, prosperity, and honor of the country." Roosevelt's parrot memory had preserved the words intact.

Judge Hazel clutched an inscribed parchment. "Please raise your right hand and repeat after me: *I, Theodore Roosevelt* . . ." Roosevelt's arm shot up, fully extended. Throughout the oath, his hand remained high and steady, as if carved from marble. His face was drawn, and his eyes glittered. Depew was struck by the "terrible earnestness" with which he articulated every word. Yet even at this moment of ritual fidelity to the text of the Constitution, Roosevelt could not resist adding a personal flourish. "*And thus I swear,*" he concluded, ejaculating the words like bullets. Then he bowed his head.

Two minutes ticked by. The room filled with an almost unbearable tension. Beads of sweat stood on Roosevelt's brow. Not until a third minute elapsed did he look up.

"Mr. President," the judge said, holding out the certificate of oath, "please attach your signature."

Roosevelt's pen scratched across the parchment. Forty-three persons stood in thrall until he dismissed them with a kingly nod. They trooped out dreamy-eyed, as from a perfect theatrical performance. "I have witnessed many of the world's pageants in my time," Senator Depew said afterward, "—fleets and armies, music and cannon, . . . but they all seemed to me tawdry and insignificant in the presence of that little company in the library of the Wilcox house in Buffalo."

━━━━

ROOSEVELT REMAINED BEHIND to shake hands with members of his Cabinet. Asking them to prepare for an immediate meeting, he went into the hall to receive the farewells of departing guests. "God bless you, Mr. President." "The whole country will pray for you, Mr. President." There were tears on many faces, but he seemed unmoved.

A reporter was struck by Roosevelt's "curious nervous tension," so at odds with his usual boyish good cheer. "The cause of it was not at all any sense of the weight of his new position . . . but the reaction of a strong man to the idea that he was entering a domain where assassins lurked in the shadows and the ground might open at any moment under his feet."

The Cabinet meeting proceeded behind closed doors. Afterward Roosevelt came out onto the porch to announce that all six officers had agreed to remain in their positions, "at least for the present." He had similar "assurances" from his two absent Secretaries, John Hay and Lyman Gage. This was true, in the sense that both men had wired messages of support. But until he saw them in Washington, he hardly knew what their "assurances" were worth.

Business completed, Roosevelt put on his borrowed silk hat. "Let's take a walk," he said to Elihu Root. "It will do us both good." A quartet of policemen fell into line behind him on the gravel path. Irritatedly, he shooed them away. "I do not want to establish the precedent of going about guarded." The policemen touched their helmets, retreated a yard or two, and followed as before. Roosevelt headed for the gate like an escaping bull, but found Delaware Avenue blocked by cordoned-off crowds. He was forced to take leave of Root in the street, and marched back to the mansion in frustration.

Refuge was at least available in the morning room, where Cortelyou had laid a desk with pencils, an exercise book, and a copy of *Messages of the Presidents*. Turning to a proclamation of President Arthur, Roosevelt drew the rough pad toward him. He began to scrawl his first presidential order, making 19 September a day of official mourning. *God in his infinite wisdom* . . . The pencil hovered, then slashed back through the cliché. *A great and terrible bereavement,* it wrote instead, *has come upon our nation.* Roosevelt tried to make the last words more personal: *has befallen our people. The President of the United States has been struck down.* . . . How to describe the act of assassination? *A foul and dastardly crime* . . . *the basest of all crimes* . . . *a crime so dastardly* . . .

He struggled to reconcile his love of strong language with the need for dignified expression. It had always been thus with him: conflict between belligerence and civilized restraint, between animal brutality and human decency, between pessimism and optimism, or, as his perceptive friend Owen Wister put it, "between what he knew, and his wish not to know it." In youth, the aggressive impulse had predominated, but in maturity he had strengthened himself to a state of containment, like a volcano sheathed in hardened lava. For three years there had been no serious fissures. At any rate, his struggle today was brief. The sentences began to shape themselves into statesmanlike prose, and soon the pencil was moving confidently. *Now, therefore I, Theodore Roosevelt, President of the United States* . . .

AT FOUR O'CLOCK, word came that Mark Hanna's carriage was outside. Roosevelt hurried onto the porch and watched the old man descend, trembling on a cane. Hanna was clearly broken by the death of his adored "William." He was pallid and stooped, and his piggy feet dragged in the gravel. "The Senator," a reporter scribbled, "seems to have aged ten years in the last twenty-four hours." With spontaneous grace, Roosevelt ran down to meet him, hand outstretched. Hanna was surprised and moved. Shifting his soft white hat and cane, he returned the gesture. "Mr. President, I wish you success and a prosperous administration, Sir. I trust that you will command me if I can be of service." Roosevelt smiled and murmured a few sympathetic words about McKinley. He helped Hanna up the steps, and said, "I want your friendship."

Seated inside, Hanna resisted further blandishment. He said that he would support the Roosevelt Administration only as long as it remained an extension of McKinley's. As to the question of the Republican presidential nomination in 1904, that was "something for the future to decide." Roosevelt replied, "I understand perfectly," and escorted the Senator back to his carriage. Hanna drove away without so much as a wave.

That evening, George Cortelyou announced that there would be a private memorial service for McKinley at the Milburn House the next morning, Sunday. Roosevelt and his Cabinet officers would attend, and remain in Buffalo until Monday morning, when a funeral train would depart for Washington. On Tuesday, there would be further memorial exercises at the Capitol, followed by an interment ceremony Wednesday in Canton, Ohio. Mrs. McKinley would vacate the White House at her convenience. In the meantime, Roosevelt would stay at his sister's house on N Street.

While Cortelyou talked, Roosevelt ate an early dinner, then went exhausted to bed.

SOMETIME AFTER MIDNIGHT in New York City, three hundred miles away, John F. Schrank began to dream. He was twenty-six years old, short, and reclusive. He lay above a saloon that had employed him once, before the Sunday-closing crusade of Police Commissioner Theodore Roosevelt. Since that crusade (and because of it, Schrank believed), he had been unable to get a job.

Now, as he dreamed, his shabby surroundings were transformed into a funeral parlor full of flowers. An open coffin stood before him. President McKinley sat up in it and pointed to a dark corner of the room. Schrank, peering, made out a man in monk's raiment. Under the cowl were the bespectacled features of Theodore Roosevelt.

"This is my murderer," said McKinley. "Avenge my death." Schrank woke, and checked his watch. 1:30 A.M. Almost immediately, he went back to sleep. McKinley did not speak to him again that night. Indeed, the appeal would not be renewed for another eleven years—until the same hour of the same night of the week, in another gruesome September.

Sunday

ROOSEVELT AWOKE REFRESHED early the next morning. "I feel bully!" He went out onto the porch for some air, unaware that he was being minutely observed through the fence. His tanned skin stretched over his jutting jaw. His teeth gleamed through thick, half-parted lips. His neck, too squat for a standing collar, merged with weight-lifter shoulders, sloping two full inches to the tip of his biceps, and his chest pushed apart the lapels of his frock coat. He tugged at his watch chain with short, nervous fingers, shifting his small, square-toed shoes. Here, palpably, was a man of expansive force. When he breathed, the porch seemed to breathe with him.

Breakfast, laced as usual by vast infusions of caffeine, served only to stoke

Roosevelt's energy. A sheaf of congratulatory telegrams further stimulated him: one read simply, VIVE LE ROI. He managed to look solemn on the way to Milburn House, but his mind was seething with politics. During the memorial service, he caught sight of Herman H. Kohlsaat, publisher of the Chicago *Times-Herald,* and whispered urgently, "*I want to see you.*"

Kohlsaat followed him back to the Wilcox Mansion. He was shown into the library, and found Roosevelt exchanging compliments with a beaky, fortyish professor from Princeton. "Woodrow, you know Kohlsaat, don't you? Mr. Kohlsaat, let me introduce you to Woodrow Wilson." The professor bowed out. Roosevelt got straight to the point.

"I am going to make two changes in my Cabinet that I know will please you," he said. Kohlsaat began to preen. He was a journalist of large influence, and even larger vanity. But what he heard next did not please him at all. "I am going to let John Hay go, and appoint Elihu Root Secretary of State," Roosevelt said. "I am also going to ask Lyman Gage for his resignation."

Actually, Roosevelt had no intention of firing either Hay or Gage. On the contrary, he was worried by continued reports that they would resign as soon as he got to Washington. The presence in Buffalo of Kohlsaat, who knew both men well, came as a godsend. Roosevelt had long since perfected the art of manipulating newspapermen. Kohlsaat rose to his herring like a trained seal.

KOHLSAAT   John Hay is an old friend of mine. . . . What have you against Lyman Gage?

ROOSEVELT   (*teeth snapping*) He always gets his back up against the wall, and I can't get around him.

KOHLSAAT   Don't you know I am responsible for Mr. Gage being in the Cabinet? . . . Yesterday, when you were sworn in, you issued a statement that you were going to carry on McKinley's policies, and now you propose to fire his Secretary of State and Secretary of the Treasury!

ROOSEVELT   (*after a pause, falsetto*) . . . Old man, I am going to pay you the highest compliment I ever paid any one in my life. I am going to keep both of them!

Compounding the flattery, he invited Kohlsaat to accompany him to Washington the next day. "The only other friend I have on the train is Elihu Root." Then, casually: "Gage does not like me. I want you to wire him to meet you at your hotel on our arrival and tell him he must stay for a while, at least, and I want you to see the Associated Press man and ask him to send a dispatch that when we reach Washington tomorrow night I am going to ask Hay and Gage to remain in the Cabinet."

Kohlsaat bustled off feeling he had managed to sway the rods of power. Had he understood the subtleties of Rooseveltian press relations, he might have seen that he had been tricked into making a personal appeal to Gage. The AP dispatch would also forestall any possible resignation statement by Hay. Neither man could then quit without appearing disloyal to Roosevelt, and to the unfinished agenda of William McKinley.

Roosevelt's move was well-timed. Even now, in Washington, the Secretary of State was composing a letter that read like a valedictory.

SEPT. 15, 1901

My dear Roosevelt: If the Presidency had come to you in any other way, no one would have congratulated you with better heart than I. My sincere affection and esteem for you, my old-time love for your father—would he could have lived to see where you are!—would have been deeply gratified. And even from the depths of the sorrow where I sit, with my grief for the President mingled and confused with that for my boy, so that I scarcely know, from hour to hour, the true source of my tears—I do still congratulate you, not only on the opening of an official career which I know will be glorious, but upon the vast opportunity for useful work which lies before you. With your youth, your ability, your health and strength, the courage God has given you to do right, there are no bounds to the good you can accomplish for your country and the name you will leave in its annals. My official life is at an end—my natural life will not be long extended; and so, in the dawn of what I am sure will be a great and splendid future, I venture to give you the heartfelt benediction of the past.

God bless you.
Yours faithfully,
JOHN HAY

Monday

16 SEPTEMBER DAWNED so bright that Buffalo's heavy black drapery looked inconsequential, even tawdry, against the overwhelming blueness of lake and sky. A stiff breeze snapped thousands of half-mast flags. At shortly after 8:15, Roosevelt, escorted by a small troop of mounted policemen, rolled down Delaware Avenue on his way to Exchange Street Station. Presently, windblown fragments of music heralded the approach of McKinley's cortege from City Hall. Roosevelt ordered his procession to follow at a respectful distance. He stood watching at the station entrance as soldiers unloaded the coffin and carried it inside. "Nearer My God to Thee" sounded inevitably from the band. Mrs. McKinley was escorted onto the platform, a frail figure almost

hidden by black-clad relatives. Then Roosevelt stepped forward. He seemed surprised at the sight of a huge, mute crowd. Unthinkingly, he waved his hat. Before boarding the train, he groped for Herman Kohlsaat in the press party and hissed again in his ear. *"Did you send that telegram to Gage?"*

~

THE FUNERAL TRAIN, courtesy of the Pennsylvania Railroad, consisted of two black-draped locomotives—one, with a particularly sad whistle, to steam ahead as pilot for the other—plus a baggage car, a saloon car, and five sumptuous Pullmans. Reporters were assigned to the first of these, Senator Hanna and other dignitaries to the second, Roosevelt and his Cabinet to the third. The fourth carried George Cortelyou and members of the McKinley family. Officially speaking, Cortelyou was now Roosevelt's personal secretary, but as long as Mrs. McKinley depended on him, he was pleased to defer to Loeb. The fifth and final car, a glass observation parlor, acted as a catafalque: McKinley's coffin rode inside on a bed of flowers.

At 8:57, the train began to move. Church bells tolled across the city. Thousands of onlookers crowded every platform, stairway, bollard, and bridge. From sheds and warehouses along the track, grimy workmen emerged to squint and stare. The avid scrutiny of all these eyes was too much for Roosevelt. He ordered his blinds drawn—but not so soon as to miss the sight of workmen hurrying back to their jobs after the train had passed them by. For a while he sat alone, waiting for the liberating sense of acceleration into open country.

What he had just observed—evidence of America's passion for work, its impatient refusal to loiter a moment longer than necessary—was pleasing, if not surprising. For several years, both he and the world had been aware that the United States was the most energetic of nations. She had long been the most richly endowed. This first year of the new century found her worth twenty-five billion dollars more than her nearest rival, Great Britain, with a gross national product more than twice that of Germany and Russia. The United States was already so rich in goods and services that she was more self-sustaining than any industrial power in history.

Indeed, it could consume only a fraction of what it produced. The rest went overseas at prices other exporters found hard to match. As Andrew Carnegie said, "The nation that makes the cheapest steel has other nations at its feet." More than half the world's cotton, corn, copper, and oil flowed from the American cornucopia, and at least one third of all steel, iron, silver, and gold.

Even if the United States were not so blessed with raw materials, the excellence of her manufactured products guaranteed her dominance of world markets. Current advertisements in British magazines gave the impression that the typical Englishman woke to the ring of an Ingersoll alarm, shaved with a Gillette razor, combed his hair with Vaseline tonic, buttoned his Arrow shirt, hurried downstairs for Quaker Oats, California figs, and Maxwell House coffee, commuted in a Westinghouse tram (body by Fisher), rose to his office in an Otis elevator, and worked all day with his Waterman pen under the efficient glare of Edison lightbulbs. "It only remains," one Fleet Street wag suggested, "for [us] to take American coal to Newcastle." Behind the joke lay real concern: the United States was already supplying beer to Germany, pottery to Bohemia, and oranges to Valencia.

As a result of this billowing surge in productivity, Wall Street was awash with foreign capital. Carnegie calculated that America could afford to buy the entire United Kingdom, and settle Britain's national debt in the bargain. For the first time in history, transatlantic money currents were thrusting more powerfully westward than east. Even the Bank of England had begun to borrow money on Wall Street. New York City seemed destined to replace London as the world's financial center.

It was hard to believe that the United States had struggled out of a depression only five years before. Prosperity was everywhere for Roosevelt to see—if not through drawn blinds at the moment, then memorably on his recent trip to Minnesota. The weather-stained barns of poorer days, the drab farmhouses and blistered grain elevators, were pristine with new paint. He had seen corrugated dirt giving way to asphalt, rotten boardwalks smoothing to stone, shards of shacks pushed aside by new redbrick houses. Not so long ago, Midwestern towns had glowed dully at night, if they glowed at all. Now they were constellations of electricity, bright enough to wake the sleeping traveler. Equally bright, by day, were silver threads of irrigation in the green fields, and new, steel-roofed sheds and schoolhouses.

Behind Roosevelt now (he could reopen his blinds, as the train gathered speed), Buffalo receded into a cyclorama of modern industrial development. Louis Sullivan's "skyscraper," the Prudential Building, bespoke a modern, defiantly native school of architecture. Scores of dockside cranes dipped and reared like hungry pterodactyls. Horseless carriages trailed plumes of dust and engine smoke in and out of town. Hydroelectric-plant towers loomed against the mists of Niagara, sending invisible thrills of power through the industrial suburbs. Wherever the sun shone, it glinted on countless telephone and telegraph wires, weaving block to block in warps and woofs of copper.

Trees soon barred Buffalo from sight, but the wires pursued the train effortlessly, rising and falling from pole to pole. Already news of Roosevelt's departure had flashed along them, flickering into every corner of the land. Wires like these, connecting with other wires in Albany and yet more wires in the Adirondacks, had summoned him from the peak of Mount Marcy. In about twelve hours, they would broadcast the details of his arrival in Washington.

EMPTY LAKESIDE LAND BEGAN to roll by. Roosevelt relaxed with the morning newspapers. Almost every editor in the country, it seemed, approved of his promise to continue "unbroken" the policies of President McKinley. The New York *Herald* featured an on-the-spot sketch of him taking the oath, hand held high, saying that he deserved "golden praise." *The Albany Journal* and *The Washington Post* contributed their share of fine ounces. The New York *Sun,* banner journal of business conservatism, hailed his "responsible" desire to keep the Cabinet intact. "Nothing so sobers a man as the possession of great power."

The funeral train slowed to ten miles an hour as it approached Aurora, first village on the line. Farmworkers crowded the embankment, doffing their hats to the passing catafalque. Schoolchildren knelt in the cinders, holding up streams of black bunting. Thinly, through the hiss of steam and rumble of wheels, came the sound of their voices singing:

> *Nearer my God to Thee,*
> *Nearer to Thee . . .*

The train did not stop. Accelerating again, it moved out of the flat country into a narrow valley splotched with red maple trees. Roosevelt returned to his newspapers.

The foreign papers indicated that British opinion was in his favor. Even *The Times,* which had been critical of him during his bellicose Navy Department days, said that he had "great gifts" as a leader, and hoped that his "impulsiveness" was a thing of the past. The *Daily Chronicle* welcomed him as a benign, if formidable, new force in world affairs. "He believes in a big America. He is an expansionist and an imperialist, . . . [but] we are safe in thinking that this youngest of Presidents will prove one of the greatest."

Continental comment was reported to be cooler. Misgivings about Roosevelt's peculiar brand of Pan-Americanism had been expressed in both Paris and St. Petersburg. In Berlin, the *Kreuz-Zeitung* feared that the new President might be "anti-German." But the *Neueste Nachrichten* recalled that as a teenager he had lived and studied with a Dresden family. Surely this meant that he would have more sympathy than his predecessors for the Teutonic point of view.

On one thing most nations were agreed: under Theodore Roosevelt, American sea power was sure to burgeon rapidly. The man who had prepared Admiral Dewey for Manila Bay was unlikely to let the United States Navy remain fifth in the world.

❧

LOEB ANNOUNCED THE Secretary of War. Roosevelt willingly cast aside his newspapers. Elihu Root was the one person on the train he felt he could talk to freely. Soon, both men were deep in conversation, swaying in their seats as the train sped south. About 9:30, its momentum slowed so that a farm boy was able to race it through the fields, waving a flag. The outbuildings of Arcade, N.Y., came into view, followed by a little railroad station. Almost reluctantly, the train stopped. About twenty Grand Army veterans snapped to attention on the platform. Their ancient tunics looked pinched and trussed, but they held themselves stiff with respect for a fallen comrade. A few much younger soldiers stood to one side. *Their* uniforms were intimately familiar to Roosevelt: he had worn that khaki himself (hand-tailored by Brooks Brothers) in the Spanish-American War. He drew the blinds, afraid they might salute him rather than McKinley.

For ten minutes, while the locomotive took on water, Roosevelt and Root sat in semidarkness, listening to the sound of a band playing "Nearer My God to Thee." Evidently they were to hear little else on their long way to Washington. Between strophes, there was a crunch of boots in the gravel, and an old soldier's voice called quaveringly: "We're all heartsore for Major McKinley."

Much as Roosevelt coveted the respect of Grand Army veterans, he knew they would never love him as they had loved his predecessor. McKinley had marched with them at Antietam, when "Teedie" Roosevelt had been but a child in a zouave suit. A gulf, not merely of years but of ideology, separated him from these heroes of the past. They had fought to preserve the Union; he had fought to create a world power. The old soldiers had cheered when the young soldiers liberated Cuba, but they fell silent when similar "freedoms" were imposed on Puerto Rico, Guam, and the Philippines. They had watched with worried eyes as the Stars and Stripes rose over Hawaii, Wake Island, and half of Samoa, and Secretary Hay began negotiations to purchase the Danish West Indies. Was their beloved republic, they asked, taking on the trappings of an imperial power?

The ideological gulf had yawned even wider when the young soldiers persuaded McKinley that occupation of Spain's former colonies should continue well beyond armistice. Cuba and Puerto Rico would need two or three years to perfect new constitutions and build independent economies. The Philippines would need much longer, half a century perhaps. Seven million largely illiterate tribesmen could not be left to govern themselves without reverting to the laws of the jungle.

Powerful commercial, strategic, and moral arguments to this effect had been advanced by the young soldiers—Theodore Roosevelt prominent among them—campaigning for McKinley's re-election. They had trumpeted the islands as new markets for America's superabundant production, cited naval research in favor of a global defense system, and looked to Congress to ensure that America would hold on to what the Supreme Court euphemistically called its "unincorporated territories."

The old soldiers remained fiercely opposed to expansionism. They asked how a nation that had won its own independence in a colonial war could force dependence upon others. They rejected McKinley's assurance, "No imperial designs lurk in the American mind." So did most intellectuals, and Democrats looking for an issue to break the Republican Party. As yet this anti-imperialist lobby remained a minority, but its numbers were growing, and its propaganda was powerful. Roosevelt could see the day when it might paralyze his foreign policy.

"World duties," he felt, were the inevitable and welcome consequence of America's aggrandizing power. Old men and "mollycoddles" had no understanding of the huge historical forces at work. Just two weeks ago in Minnesota, he had dismissed the cliché that all great nations come to dust:

> So they have; and so have all others. The weak and the stationary have vanished as surely as, and more rapidly than, those whose citizens felt within them the lift that impels generous souls to great and noble effort. This is only another way of stating the universal law of death, which is itself part of the universal law of life. . . .
>
> While the nation that has dared to be great, that has had the will and the power to change the destiny of the ages, in the end must die, . . . |it| really continues, though in changed form, to live forevermore.

His vision was too grandiose to be merely territorial. He had no interest in square miles as such. Expansion, to him, meant a hemispheric program of acquisition, democratization, and liberation. Cuba, for example, was already eligible for freedom (of sorts) and should have it (in a way) as soon as Congress worked out a policy for tariff reciprocity with the island. Puerto Rico was semi-independent, in the sense that Secretary Root had ended the military government there and given most powers to a native legislature. The real problem was what to do about the Philippines. "Sometimes," Roosevelt confessed, "I feel it is an intensely disagreeable and unfortunate task which we cannot in honor shirk."

Clearly, a vast, primitive archipelago, divided by seven thousand waterways, seventy dialects, and the world's most mutually incompatible religions—Christianity and Islam—needed an authoritarian government to hold it together. If not America's, whose? There were also reasons of strategy to consider. Given half a chance, base-hungry powers such as Germany or Japan would annex and enslave the islands in perpetuity. The United States could at least be trusted not to hold them a day longer than democratic scruples required.

President McKinley's enduring ambition was noble, yet Filipinos seemed ungrateful. Rebellion had been raging on the archipelago for almost two years; Root needed a seventy-thousand-man army to control it. Some measure of peace had at last been achieved. Today's papers were blessedly free of bad news from "over there." But neither Roosevelt nor Root cared to speculate what nice, clean-cut American boys were doing to keep that peace.

<hr/>

THE TRAIN BEGAN to move again. Root took his leave, and Roosevelt finished going through the newspapers. Great Britain offered "sincere expressions of sympathy" to the "bereaved" United States. No doubt the sympathy was sincere—an Anglo-American rapprochement had been under way for at least three years. Moscow confirmed another plot to assassinate Tsar Nicholas II—in Marseilles, of all places. One would have expected it rather in Tokyo: the most dangerous current rivalry in the world was that between Russia and Japan.

Both powers were circling like wolves about that sick mammoth, China. Their first snap and snarl would probably be over the mammoth's Manchurian extremity, Kwangtung Province. Other wolves were on the prowl: German ones trailing the Russian pack, British behind the Japanese. America had its own "Open Door" trade relations with China to protect, and a corollary pledge to "preserve Chinese territorial and administrative integrity." Roosevelt's instinct was to stand watchfully aside for the moment. He might one day have to leap in—as into those hounds in Colorado!—and sort out the predators with his bare hands.

Worldwide, the balance of power was to his advantage. As long as Kaiser Wilhelm II of Germany (his likely enemy, he felt, in any foreseeable war) remained preoccupied with the Tsar, and the Tsar and the Meiji Emperor of Japan continued to mass forces around Kwangtung, the President of the United States could surely perfect a partnership with King Edward VII to control the Western Hemisphere. Of course, he must do most of the controlling. The United States acknowledged Britain's dominion of Canada (what a pity, he always felt, that President Polk had not "taken it all" in 1846!), but he intended to end, once and for all, a languid argument about the southern Alaskan boundary line. "I have studied that question pretty thoroughly and I do not think the Canadians have a leg to stand on." They were entitled to the few miles of coast that were theirs by treaty, and not a pebble more.

This was the only issue dividing the English-speaking powers. Elsewhere, there was benign assent. Britain seemed willing to accept the Monroe Doctrine, which Roosevelt, on the whole, held in greater reverence than the Nicene Creed. Lord Lansdowne's Foreign Office had forsworn any role, strategic or territorial, in the construction of a canal across Central America. The second Hay-Pauncefote Treaty, now at the point of ratification, approved American management of such a project, and granted the United States exclusive right to fortify the canal.

Roosevelt could claim a large share of credit for the latter clause. As Governor, he had been outraged by the first Hay-Pauncefote treaty, which had allowed for neutrality and openness of the canal in the event of war. His criticism had been outspoken, and had hurt John Hay, but the Senate had agreed with him. Now there was this new, tougher treaty. It gave the United States Navy freedom to maneuver through the canal in wartime, while preventing other belligerents from doing so. He looked forward to signing it as soon as Hay laid it on his desk.

There remained the question of where to build the canal: Nicaragua or Panama. Nicaragua was the overwhelming preference of Congress: old John Tyler Morgan, chairman of the Senate Committee on Interoceanic Canals, had been croaking its praises for a decade. Roosevelt privately favored Panama, despite the failure of French engineers there. But his public attitude must be noncommittal. All he could urge now was that the canal be dug by American hands, and the first spade sunk during his Presidency. The stupendous task was uniquely that of the United States: "We must build the Isthmian Canal, and we must grasp the points of vantage which will enable us to have our say in deciding the destiny of the oceans of the east and the west." Otherwise, Germany might start digging. The thought of the Kaiser acquiring land rights anywhere in the Americas was enough to freeze Roosevelt's blood. A presidential commission was studying the choice of route, once and for all. It would probably recommend Nicaragua, and he would abide by its decision.

Even so, Panama remained an attractive alternative. The Isthmus was at its narrowest there—fewer than forty miles from sea to sea—and his nature was to love shortcuts. There were rumors that the entire French operation, both equipment and excavations, would soon be for sale. And the political situation in Panama was promising. That reluctant appendix to Colombia was having one of its annual rebellions against the authority of Bogotá—the forty-eighth or forty-ninth, by Roosevelt's count. Since Colombia was itself waging war against Venezuela, there was a chance that, for once, Panama might succeed. If so, the rebels would surely offer their canal route to the United States, in exchange for a share of revenue and guaranteed independence from Colombia.

⌀

THE ALLEGHENY FOOTHILLS turned black and greasy near Olean. Discarded oil drums dribbled into Cuba Lake. The very ground seemed to ooze. Here, in 1627, Franciscan explorers had discovered a spring of "thick dark water that burned like brandy." Later settlers found this same crude seeping out of rocks all over the Alleghenies. They had cursed it as poison for the soil, until Indians persuaded them it was medicinal. Roosevelt himself came from a generation of children who had been rubbed with evil-smelling "rock oil" whenever they had chest colds.

Olean Valley now was a landscape inconceivable to its discoverers. The slopes bristled with filthy derricks and flaming chimneys. Double-headed pumps toggled crazily, sucking tarry sludge out of the earth. High in the sky floated an oily miasma that seemed to drain the world of color.

Apocalyptic though the scene was, Roosevelt was aware of something more disturbing above and beyond it all, "a new and dark power" that shadowed every prospect in American life. The power had its source in a contract between executives of the industry he looked upon, and the carrier transporting him.

Nearly thirty years before, the Standard Oil Company and the Pennsylvania Railroad had pledged:

The party of the second part will pay and allow to the party of the first part . . . rebates . . . and on all oil transported for others, *drawbacks*.

Those simple words introduced a new concept—un-American to some—of privilege in commerce, bestowing rewards upon the large at the expense of the small. Both parties excused the contract by saying it would prevent "loss or injury by competition." If they thus blasphemed against the gospel of free enterprise, Standard Oil, at least, was unrepentant. What, John D. Rockefeller wanted to know, was so holy about competition? Did it not lead to unrealistic rate-cutting, cycles of overproduction and depression, and needless duplication of services? What interdependent industries needed was less competition, and more "cooperation."

Rockefeller's rebate privilege had been too flagrant to survive under law. But it was followed, over the years, by sophisticated arrangements to the same effect. Standard Oil had engulfed its smaller rivals, while the Pennsylvania Railroad made similar deals with other industries, and became one of the richest transport systems in the country.

Presidents Cleveland, Harrison, and McKinley paid little attention to the phenomenon of Combination. To them, it seemed a natural economic trend. If industries produced vital supplies, if railroads functioned as semipublic utilities, why restrict their profitable development? Only slowly, and locally, had ordinary Americans—workers, consumers, and small businessmen—begun to feel the "dark power" growing. For Combination's irresistible tendency was toward Monopoly; and whatever corporate executives might say about increased efficiency and reduced waste, the historic inclination of Monopoly was to raise prices and lower wages.

Standard Oil had taken early steps to protect itself against common-law suits—and, in doing so, had perverted one of the most sacred words in the legal vocabulary. It reorganized its component corporations into a "trust," whereby all stocks were delivered to an independent board, which then operated the entire combination in unison. Congress had no power to quash this move. Within nine years, John D. Rockefeller had "entrusted" himself with 90 percent of the oil-refining business of the United States.

His profits were so fabulous that other industrial giants had rushed to organize interstate "trusts" of their own. Congress, responding to public concern, had passed the Sherman Antitrust Law of 1890. It declared illegal "every contract, combination in the form of trust, or conspiracy in restraint of trade or commerce among the several States." But the Law was too comprehensive to be particular. Corporate lawyers (Elihu Root prominent among them) elaborated the trust concept into that of a "holding-company" chartered in one hospitable state, yet monopolizing related corporations throughout the nation. Holding-company directors concerned themselves with questions of finance, so the lawyers argued they were unengaged in "trade or commerce." The Supreme Court had agreed reluctantly with this argument, and had ruled in *U.S. v. E. C. Knight Co.* (1895) that a trust controlling 98 percent of the nation's sugar-refining business was legal, since refining was not itself an interstate activity.

The depression of the mid-nineties had cramped trust growth. But combination, aided by the spread of the telephone-telegraph web, resumed with a vengeance after the war with Spain. In 1898, there had been twenty multi-million-dollar industrial trusts; now, there were one hundred and eighty-five. The proliferation evoked an image, in many minds, of a constrictive organism stretching out to every extremity of American civilization. Hence the title of Frank Norris's new antitrust novel: *The Octopus.*

These trackside mourners of Olean Valley, staring blindly at Roosevelt as he whizzed by—how enmeshed were they? The oil trust paid their wages. Other trusts carpeted their houses, papered their walls, piped their water, sluiced away their sewage. Trust ice cooled them in summer, trust wool warmed them in winter—as did trust whiskey. These men chewed trust tobacco, and checked trust watches. These women baked trust flour and cooked trust beef in trust stoves full of trust coal. These children chewed trust gum and scribbled on trust slates. Roosevelt himself had trusts to thank for the starch in his shirt, the type on his newspapers, the glass of his window, the rails under his wheels. Poor dead McKinley, two cars back, was jiggling in a trust coffin: what might a cynic make of *that!*

Ideologically, Roosevelt was committed to a conservative view of the trusts. Personally, he felt a certain ambivalence. He saw "grave dangers" in unrestricted combination, yet he could not deny that the economy functioned better now that the trusts were, in effect, running it. The price of kerosene, for example, had been declining for thirty years, courtesy of Standard Oil. America was no longer a patchwork of small self-sufficient communities. It was a great grid of monopolistic cities doing concentrated business with one another: steel cities and rubber cities, cities of salt and cloth and corn and copper. Just beyond these hills was a place that actually called itself Oil City! American exporters did not need a book of vouchers to dispatch one consignment across a rickety grid of independent railroads, each with its own timetable, rates, and reliability quotient. Now one ticket sped a million tons to either coast on flawlessly synchronized trains. At every port, trust-operated ships were ready to ferry the consignment on. If freight charges were higher than they used to be, so was turnover, and so were profits.

According to a recent survey, at least 65 percent of the national wealth was attributable to the trusts. That statistic did not even include the newest and most gigantic combination of all, Andrew Carnegie's merger of his steel company with nine others. United States Steel, capitalized at almost one and a half billion dollars and feeding more than one million people, was virtually a nation in itself. Its income and expenditures approximated those of the Second Reich. It, too, had a Kaiser, an emperor of finance, and if today's newspapers were to be believed, Wilhelm II might soon cede him a portion of his realm: "Mr. John Pierpont Morgan is trying to get control of the German steamship lines."

⌐◦⌐

ROOSEVELT LIKED MORGAN. The solitary, bottle-nosed banker had been a friend of his father, and on that score alone merited affection. Even so, he did not know him well. Few did. Only Morgan's immediate family, and the half-dozen handsome young aides who stood between him and the world (as if to screen his legendary ugliness) claimed that privilege. Governor Roosevelt had once denied Morgan tax exemptions on two railroads. He had tried to make amends with a testimonial dinner ("an effort on my part to become a conservative man, in touch with the influential classes"), but the financier remained unmollified. Roosevelt's last letter to Morgan had been answered by a secretary.

So far, 1901 had been Morgan's *annus mirabilis*. Along with his new billion-dollar trust, he controlled several banks, including the international House of Morgan, the Western Union Telegraph Company, the Pullman Car Company, Aetna Life Insurance, General Electric, Britain's Leyland Steamship Lines, and twenty-one railroads. Control, indeed, was his passion—not the constant, clashing competition of the free market. As chairman of J. P. Morgan and Company, he handled more wealth than any other man on earth, and was capable of plunging the United States into a depression overnight—or rescuing it from one. Yet his greatest power derived from his integrity of character. One nod of the massive head was security for fifty million; one snort of the carbuncled nose was enough to sweep all opposition from his path. *Review of Reviews* saluted him as "the most masterful personality in the country, perhaps in the world."

But now there was a challenger to that title, riding to Washington on one of the few Northeastern railroads Morgan did not control. Sooner or later, their personal trajectories must intersect, as surely as this Alleghany track was destined to run into those of the Susquehanna Valley. Roosevelt hoped that the confluence would be smooth. To his mind, the real threat posed by financiers such as Morgan lay not so much in their combination policies as in their virtual freedom—thanks to *U.S. v. E. C. Knight*—from federal regulation. Even President McKinley had talked of doing "something about the trusts." Roosevelt himself had publicly warned:

> The vast individual and corporate fortunes, the vast combinations of capital which have marked the development of our industrial system, create new conditions, and necessitate a change from the old attitude of the State and the nation toward property. . . . More and more it is evident that the State, and if necessary the nation, *has got to possess the right of supervision and control as regards the great corporations which are its creatures.*

He now stood committed to those words, uttered only two weeks ago at the Minnesota State Fair. Morgan's philosophy was also on record: "I owe the public nothing."

If they were indeed set on a collision course, Roosevelt was determined not to be the one derailed. Morgan may be master of United States Steel, but *he* was master of the United States Government—surely the greatest combination of all. National stability required that he maintain eminent right-of-way.

⌐⊶

ELSEWHERE IN THE TRAIN, Senator Hanna was slumped, cursing the day that William McKinley accepted Theodore Roosevelt as his running mate. "Now look—that damned cowboy is President of the United States!"

Herman Kohlsaat came back to tell Roosevelt about Hanna's despair. He suggested that the Senator be treated with utmost delicacy, for he had the power to block all White House initiatives during the coming session of Congress.

Roosevelt reacted blankly. "What can I do?" Kohlsaat suggested a flattering supper *à deux* in the presidential car.

⌐⊶

AT FOUR MINUTES past eleven, the funeral train drew into Port Allegany, Pennsylvania, and stopped for a while to allow platform mourners to look at the dead President's bier. Souvenir collectors laid nickels and pennies and flowers on the rails. When the wheels started to roll again, there was a crunching of coins, and the perfume of pressed roses filled the air. In future years, misshapen metal discs and bits of dried petal would remind the citizens of Port Allegany of McKinley's last earthly journey.

◦—⊂◦—

THE STEEP CLIMB up Keating Ridge began. At times the locomotive seemed about to stall. Shortly before noon, it dragged its payload over the crest and with loud puffs of relief entered a winding valley. Hills crowded in on both sides. Then one cut gave way to the shaft of a coal mine, and for a few seconds Roosevelt and his fellow passengers could exchange stares with four hundred filthy coal miners.

Boys, youths, and old men (were they really old, or just toothless?) stood bareheaded, leaning on picks and shovels. Their small, smudged eyes (only the creases showing white), squat bodies, and tape-wrapped shins proclaimed them to be Slavs. It was impossible to tell from their swarthy expressions whether the sight of a presidential cortege moved them or not. Implicit in the stare of those eyes, the power of those knobbly hands, was labor's historic threat of violence against capital.

Roosevelt knew that nowhere in America was the threat more real than in the Pennsylvania coalfields—the bituminous region he had just entered, and the anthracite region to east and south. Valley after valley, as the train snaked through, disclosed communities as squalid as any these people could have fled in Europe. Thousands of sooty shacks on stilts, with pigs tied below; gutters buzzing with garbage; mules clopping to the mineheads, hock-deep in fine gray dust. Beneath that dust, men were scrabbling in wet, gassy gloom, earning a dollar and change for every ton of coal they hacked. If 1901 turned out to be a good year, they might get five hundred dollars apiece—about what Roosevelt had already earned as President of the United States. In cash, they would realize perhaps a third of that—their wage packets were subject to compulsory deductions for rent, fuel, medical bills, and food supplied at inflated prices by the company store. As a group, they aged and ailed faster than any other workers in American industry.

These boys began their careers at eight or nine, picking splinters of slate out of the coal breakers until their hands were scarred for life. These men worked coal ten hours a day, six days a week. They ate coal dust in their bread and drank it in their milk; they breathed it and coughed it. At forty or forty-five, most were so ravaged by black-lung disease that they had to return to the breakers to pick slate with their grandchildren, contracting fresh black scars until they died.

Roosevelt understood enough about social repression to sense that today's contempt for the unskilled worker was tomorrow's likely revolution. Trade-union membership had more than doubled in the last five years. Sullen miners personally fueled most of the nation's industrial machine. In his opinion, "the labor question" was the greatest problem confronting twentieth-century America, "the most far-reaching in its stupendous importance." He had been saying so since the United Mine Workers (UMW) first struck the Pennsylvania anthracite mines in 1900. How worried Hanna had been that bloodshed might prevent McKinley's re-election! The Senator had wheedled both sides to an interim contract. Today's New York *Sun* noted that this *modus vivendi* was to expire in six months. Passion was building in the pits: if the UMW was not soon recognized as a bargaining agent by the mine operators, the next coal strike could be violent enough to obliterate memories of the Haymarket Riot.

Roosevelt had been violently inclined himself in Haymarket days. He had fantasized leading a band of riflemen against the rioters, and shooting them into submission. But middle age, and the democratizing effect of war, had moderated his attitude toward organized labor.

⌒

PILLARS OF HEMLOCK and pine rose on either side of the train, suffusing it in cool gloom. Here and there a shaft of light fell vertically (for the sun stood at noon), disclosing naves and transepts carpeted with needles, cloisters where deer and pheasants sought sanctuary from the hunting season.

Roosevelt was more prone to revere such natural architecture than any Gothic cathedral. Trees were objects of deep spiritual significance to him, especially when they were full of birdsong. He had stocked the bare slopes of Sagamore Hill with elms and chestnuts and oaks and dogwoods, faithful to his family motto, *Qui plantavit curabit.* The jungles of Cuba had made a soldier of him; the forests of Wyoming had brought him solace after the death of his first wife; the piney air of Maine had cut and soothed the asthma in his teenage lungs. Further back still, in boyhood, were memories of summer nights in the woods, and the sound of a beloved, bass voice reading *Last of the Mohicans* under fire-reddened branches.

I am sorry the trees have been cut down. Little Teedie Roosevelt had been nine when he wrote that, after some minor act of vandalism in Georgia. As an adult, what was he to make of the wasteland he now began to see in Pennsylvania? The Allegheny forest receded on both sides, leaving only stumps. Soon there was nothing but a fringe of trees on the highest ridges, beyond reach of any saw. Stumps, stumps, and more stumps perforated the landscape, like arrows snapped off in death agony. Most were blackened. Local lumberjacks wanted white pines only—less profitable trees could be burned like weeds. There were no saplings to be seen. With billions more trees beyond the horizon, replanting was a waste of time.

Descent via Emporium Junction and Driftwood revealed even worse devastation. Roosevelt had foreseen just such sterility when Governor of New York: "Unrestrained greed means the ruin of the great woods and the drying up of the sources of the rivers." These hillsides, which for centuries had absorbed foliage-filtered rainfall, were now bare, gullied by direct precipitation. The courses running off them were choked with mud and dead fish.

A town sign flashed by: RENOVO. Edith had vacationed here as a child. The name—Latin for *I renew*—sounded mocking in these dying uplands of the Susquehanna. About the only renewal Roosevelt could see was a station repair yard, where flatcars were being overhauled to carry away more and more trees. He understood (as most Americans did not) the tendency of transport and industrial combinations to consume the environments they served. United States railroads owned more timberland than all the nation's homesteaders.

To him, *conservation*—a term just becoming politically fashionable— meant "not only the preservation of natural resources, but the prevention of the monopoly of natural resources, so they should inhere in the people as a whole."

⌒

IT WAS NEARLY time for lunch. Roosevelt ordered places laid for himself and the Secretary of War, and went to pay his respects to Mrs. McKinley. Ravaged, almost comatose with grief, she did not detain him long. By 1:30, he was back in his car and the congenial company of Elihu Root.

He felt at home with conservatives. Whether or not the term applied to himself, he owed his political advancement to men of Root's type: wealthy Republicans who belonged to the Union League Club, read the *North American Review,* and were coldly polite to butlers. More conservative rhetoric followed after lunch, as the other Cabinet officers on the train came in one by one to see him. With the exception of Attorney General Philander Chase Knox, a polished little man of forty-eight, they were venerable figures. There was his old boss, Secretary of the Navy John Davis Long, portly and lumbering at sixty-three. Secretary of Agriculture James Wilson was sixty-six, Secretary of the Interior Ethan Allen Hitchcock sixty-five, Postmaster General Charles Emory Smith fifty-nine. Elihu Root was fifty-six. The two absent Secretaries, John Hay and Lyman Gage, were sixty-two and sixty-five respectively.

McKinley had chosen carefully: a more orthodox phalanx of Republicans would be difficult to assemble. To a man, these conservatives believed in the sanctity of property and the patrician responsibilities of wealth and power.

Their eyes were honest, but hard (Knox again the exception, with his veiled, astigmatic stare). They were accustomed to luxury travel on complimentary railroad passes, and a myriad of other corporate privileges. They were prepared, in return, to give trust lords such as J. P. Morgan their favorable support in disputes between capital and labor, or local and interstate commerce. They tacitly acknowledged that Wall Street, rather than the White House, had executive control of the economy, with the legislative cooperation of Congress and the judicial backing of the Supreme Court. This conservative alliance, forged after the Civil War, was intended to last well into the new century, if not forever. Senator Hanna was determined to protect it: "Let well enough alone!"

Roosevelt was too restless and too reform-minded to heed such a motto. On the other hand (to use his favorite phrase), he despised the theorists who advocated radical change. Not for him Eugene Debs's vision of a society purged of aggression, with all citizens pooling their assets in a state of torpid *bonhomie*. He tended toward a biological view of the common man as a brute—albeit capable, with encouragement, of self-refinement. Years of sweaty acquaintance with cowboys, policemen, and soldiers had convinced him that their instincts were benign, that greater social efficiency was as much their desire as his. All they needed was enlightened leadership.

In a fundamental disagreement with Social Darwinist thinkers, Roosevelt condemned "that baleful law of natural selection which tells against the survival of some of the most desirable classes." His own field studies, both scientific and political, had shown him how populous species, whose competition was ferocious, advanced more slowly than those whose selection was determined by reasonable numbers and controlled by certain laws of behavior. As with guinea pigs, so with Slavs; as with lions, so with Anglo-Saxons.

The United States, with seventy-seven million citizens, was still uncrowded and healthily competitive. But its social balance would be threatened if poverty spread in proportion to immigration. (Hundreds of Japanese coolies and thousands of dirt-poor Chinese peasants were arriving every month, boxed in barrels, buried under potatoes, sandwiched between bales of hay.) The worst thing he could do now was "let well enough alone." Somehow he must grant a little leisure, and a little extra money, to the multitudes currently working only to survive. This would enable them to develop those noneconomic virtues—intelligence, unselfishness, courage, decency—which he loosely defined as "character." Character determined the worth of the individual, and "what is true of the individual is also true of the nation."

At the same time, he must persuade Union League Republicans that perpetual, mild reform was true conservatism, in that it protected existing institutions from atrophy, and relieved the buildup of radical pressure. All his life he had preached this doctrine. He would preach it louder now that he had universal attention. He might not have power—yet—to convert his Cabinet, much less the Senate. But youth and time were on his side, and the presidency promised to be "a bully pulpit."

⟨⟩

AS IF TO REASSURE Roosevelt that the America of his dreams could be a reality, the exquisite town of Lock Haven rocked into view. Tall houses glowed white and apricot in the mid-afternoon light. Willows trailed their fronds in the glassy river, quiet lanes divided schools and steeples and shops. Here was Social Order, in the harmonious interdependence of rich and poor. Here was Fecundity, symbolized by the women on every stoop, lifting their babies to bless the new President. Here was Industry, in the form of an immaculate paper mill. And here—palpably, all about—was Morality. The fine white paper from that mill went under contract to Roosevelt's good friend Edward W. Bok, publisher of *Ladies' Home Journal.* Both men believed that the bourgeois domestic environment—efficient, loving, aesthetic, mother-controlled— was the nucleus of a perfect society (although Roosevelt wished the *Journal* would emphasize women's suffrage less, and regular childbearing more).

Girls softly pelted the train with flowers as it steamed through Lock Haven Depot. More girls with more flowers were waiting down the line, at Williamsport. The locomotive stopped there briefly to take on water, and an invitation scrawled in childish capitals was delivered to Roosevelt's car. Unable to resist it, he stepped outside and bowed. A little boy yelled "Hooray!" then burst into tears as an older girl smacked him for irreverence. The train jerked forward again, crossed the Susquehanna, and entered a broad landscape of harvest crops, orchards, and stone farmhouses.

Thickening crowds at every level crossing announced the approach to Harrisburg. Urchins perched like starlings on telephone poles. Soon even haystacks bore teetering human loads. At twenty minutes to five, city buildings closed in. A crescendo of ten thousand voices singing "Nearer My God to Thee" floated out of Union Station. Church bells, steam whistles, and several discordant bands joined in the din.

Governor William Stone of Pennsylvania was waiting on the platform with an honor guard, but Roosevelt stayed aloof behind drawn blinds. Harrisburg was notoriously the most corrupt seat of state government in the nation. It was also a bedrock of orthodox Republicanism. This posed delicate problems of executive strategy. If he wished to preserve his honest reputation, he could not identify too closely with machine politicians here—yet to govern effectively he had to cooperate with the machine's Washington representatives. Only three weeks ago he had mused, "Were I President, I should certainly endeavor to do what the two Pennsylvania Senators wished in matters of patronage—so as I honorably could."

A messenger ran along the train with a telegram for Herman Kohlsaat. It was a favorable reply, from Secretary Gage, to Roosevelt's plea for loyalty. Kohlsaat jumped out and bought the evening papers. Riffling through them, he found the headlines he was looking for. Wall Street had reacted optimistically to the news that Gage and Hay might stay. Opening prices had soared one to six points higher than Friday's closing, and steadiness had prevailed throughout the market. A spokesman for the financial community called these signs "clear and reassuring."

Roosevelt was relieved to hear the good news. "I don't care a damn about stocks and bonds, but I don't want to see them go down the first day I am President!"

The tolling of church bells faded as the train moved on, but the singing did not. Thousands of black-clad mourners crammed around Cumberland Valley Bridge took up the threnody of McKinley's dying hymn. By now the lugubrious tune palled on passengers who had listened to it ever since leaving Buffalo. For days to come, awake or asleep, they would hear voices crooning *"Near-urr, my God to Thee, near-urr to Thee!"* Their nerves, tightened by seventy-two hours of suspense, tragedy, excitement, and fatigue, began to fray in the waning daylight. Women burst into tears. Men grew morose, or in the case of Senator Hanna, profane. "That damn cowboy wants me to take supper with him alone, damn him!"

Ahead, in the press car, a group of reporters sat talking about death. They noticed a country funeral procession crawling darkly up the slope of a hill. It receded into the distance behind McKinley's bier. *"What shadows we are,"* someone quoted softly, *"and what shadows we pursue."*

⌦

THE SUN WAS SETTING, and its rays gilded the misty transpirations of peach orchards and tobacco fields. An old farmer, hearing the onrush of the train, climbed off his harrow and stood to attention, his red shirt incandescent in the horizontal light. Children ran to cluster around him. Their spindly shadows, leaping east, briefly stroked the wheels of Roosevelt's car.

To eyes that had so recently gazed upon oil derricks and steel bridges and Harrisburg's jumbled housing, the little group looked quaintly anachronistic, a vignette of the past century. Though such families still accounted for 60 percent of the American population, their numbers were dwindling as Combination crept across the countryside, leveling hedgerows and quintupling the size of farms. (These very fields were already in fief to the tobacco trust.) Departments of agriculture in state after state boasted the effects of the new "scientific management." Kansas wheat production had increased to such an extent that some farmers there were calling themselves "manufacturers." *Review of Reviews* reported enormous sales of sophisticated agricultural machinery across the nation. An "ultra-new combined header and thresher" was being tested in California. Eight horses were needed to haul it; it advanced across a field of standing grain, miraculously leaving nothing behind but a row of stuffed sacks.

Technological progress for big farmers, however, did not mean that life was any better for small. In the Midwest, nearly three fourths of rural families lived below subsistence level. In the South (looming ever closer as Roosevelt rode), country people sought town jobs through the winter, just to survive on fatback and hoecake.

Roosevelt could see little relief for the rural unemployed in the immediate future. A place like York, Pennsylvania (flashing by redly at a quarter to six), was the typical country town grown too big. There were more than a thousand such cities across the nation. For its new poor, York offered only more poverty. A laborer might trade his hoe for a hammer, for a few extra dollars a week, but the increment was meaningless, given urban costs. His children would still run barefoot through November, and in midwinter their breath would be ice on their bedsheets. Even more wretched than these migrants were the immigrants from unsalubrious parts of Europe further crowding American cities. Since January, nearly half a million had poured in. With their greasy kerchiefs and swollen cheekbones, they seemed content to live in any slum and do any work, for pig's wages. Not surprisingly, the native-born Americans they supplanted felt rage and ethnic contempt. Roosevelt's journalist friend William Allen White spoke for many in his syndicated diatribes against "Hunkies and Italians, the very scum of European civilization."

Roosevelt was not immune to such sentiments himself—his youthful views on the inferiority of various ethnic stocks had been republished with rather embarrassing frequency—yet he believed in America's ability to integrate all comers. One of his favorite stories was that of Otto Raphael, the young Russian Jew he had plucked from the Lower East Side of Manhattan and made a policeman. Roosevelt was the first President ever to be born in a large city; he welcomed the clash of alien cultures, as long as it did not degenerate into mass collision. As such, he saw no paradox in being an opponent of the xenophobic American Protective Association, and strong supporter of the Immigration Restriction League. But he felt that America's first responsibility was to its literate, native-born, working poor.

Several thousand such citizens stood watching his train pass through the industrial outskirts of York—half a mile of humanity silhouetted against the sunset, dinner pails in hand. Then they were gone. Night closed in. For the next half hour Roosevelt sat with his elbow on the window ledge, staring through his own reflection at the speeding darkness.

THE CONSISTENT FEATURES of the political landscape, as he saw it, were fault lines running deeply and dangerously through divergent blocks of power. Potential chasms lurked between Isolationism and Expansionism, Government and the Trusts, Labor and Capital, Conservation and Development, Wealth and Commonwealth, Nativism and the Golden Door. And since the last election, the fault lines had widened. As William Jennings Bryan kept saying, "The extremes of society are being driven further and further apart."

Roosevelt thought he knew what was causing the underlying drift: a crumbling of Government, the national bedrock. Some quick executive reinforcements (such as he always made when taking a new job) would slow the drift until the next election. Then, assuming he was the Republican Party's chosen candidate, he might campaign for more fundamental change. How, in the meantime, to care for those millions of Americans out there in the twilight? How to articulate their vague feelings that despite general peace and prosperity, something deep down was wrong with the United States? Here was his challenge as President: to put into speech, and political action, what they felt in their hearts, but could not express. His appeal must be to neither reactionary nor radical, but to Everyman—the farmer in the red shirt.

Signs were not wanting in September 1901 that Everyman was impatient, inclining toward revolution. From several Western states came demands for direct voter participation in primary elections, direct election of senators, and a referendum system to permit citizens to pass legislation without the consent of their legislators. In Madison, Wisconsin, a Republican insurgent who called himself "Bob" had won the governorship on an antitrust ticket, and was crying hoarsely for regulation of interstate railroad rates. In Cleveland, Ohio, a fat radical nicknamed "Tom" had captured City Hall, and was bellowing threats against its private utility companies.

Far-flung and lonely as these voices might sound to a trainload of Old Guard politicians en route to Washington, one passenger, at least, was acute enough to pay attention. He sensed that they might some day swell into a chorus, the first great political outcry of the twentieth century. He must soon respond to it, or the farmer in the red shirt would vote for somebody else in 1904, and Theodore Roosevelt would go down in history as a President unworthy of power, forcibly retired at forty-six.

⌐☙⌐

ROOSEVELT'S REVERIE WAS disturbed by Senator Hanna arriving for supper. While the two men ate and talked, the funeral train crossed the Mason-Dixon Line. Black faces began to flash by, lit by the glare of watch fires. Up North, earlier in the day, there had been few such faces—maybe one in fifty. Here in Maryland the ratio was one in five; across the South as a whole, one in three.

Census statistics such as these meant various things to marketers, sociologists, and geographers. To Roosevelt and Hanna they reduced down to one vital political fact: whoever commanded the loyalty of Southern blacks commanded the Republican presidential nomination.

The South was Hanna's chief source of political strength. No matter that he himself represented Ohio. No matter either that the Republican Party in Dixie was so weak that in some state legislatures it had no seats at all. What did matter was that the South was disproportionately rich in delegates to national conventions. Hanna's expert cultivation of these delegates, and his control of party funds as Chairman of the Republican National Committee, had guaranteed the two nominations of William McKinley. In his other role as

Senator in charge of White House patronage, he had been a rewarding boss, showering offices and stipends upon the faithful. As long as the South continued to send delegations of these blacks north every four years, Mark Hanna would remain party kingmaker. For a moment—just one moment, two days ago—Hanna had seemed vulnerable. But Roosevelt's vow of fidelity to McKinley's policies reconfirmed his power. The new President must continue to consult him on matters of Southern patronage, as the old had done. And consultation, given Hanna's mastery of the system, implied consent, rather than advice.

Such a partnership might be good for a party weakened by assassination, but it was hardly desirable for Roosevelt as a presidential candidate in 1904. Grotesquely, the next Republican nominee could be Hanna himself. "Uncle Mark" did not look like a vote-getter at sixty-three, with his arthritic limp and huge, melancholy eyes. Yet he was loved and respected by both business and labor. Even Roosevelt found Hanna's "burly, coarse-fibered honesty" attractive.

To consolidate his Presidency, therefore, he must quietly build up a Southern organization of his own. He had in fact already sent an urgent summons to the nation's most influential black leader, Booker T. Washington of Tuskegee, Alabama, asking him to come north for patronage consultations.

"Theodore," said Hanna, perhaps reading his mind, "do not think anything about a second term."

⌒

AT TWENTY PAST SEVEN, the train pulled into Baltimore. Flowers, handkerchiefs, gloves, and Bible pages cushioned the sound of its slowing wheels. The catafalque was gently detached from the rear of Mrs. McKinley's car and shunted forward for the last stage of the journey. As soon as it was coupled, the train began to move again, serenaded by a choir of two thousand Negroes. They sang the inevitable dirge, but the tenderness of their voices was such that both words and melody regained full poignance. At least one passenger felt that it was the sweetest music he had ever heard.

An hour later, the lights of Washington came into view. Loeb helped Roosevelt into a dark Prince Albert coat, and gave him the black kid gloves and silk hat he had worn in Buffalo. Crape was tied around the Presidential sleeve.

There was neither clanging of bells nor singing when the locomotive nosed under the shed of Sixth Street Station at 8:38. Silence filled the cavernous space. Even the crowd outside stood hushed, listening for the final groan of brakes. All personnel on the platform were military or naval, with the exception of two elderly gentlemen in top hats: John Hay and Lyman Gage. Their black clothes made a somber contrast with the glitter of braid and swords all around them. Beside them paced the portly figure of Commander William Sheffield Cowles, Roosevelt's brother-in-law, and host, until such time as Mrs. McKinley vacated the White House.

As usual in moments of high drama, Roosevelt delayed appearing. For nearly a quarter of an hour, the Cabinet waited in a semicircle around his car, and anticipation mounted on the platform and in the street. At last, a few minutes before nine, he came down the steps, jaw set sternly. The military guard presented arms. Roosevelt shook hands with Hay and Gage, and whispered the urgent word *stay* in the former's ear. He made it clear this was an order: Hay "could not decline, nor even consider." Then he marched on, his Cabinet following in double file. Five Secret Service men appeared from nowhere and clustered about him. Ignoring the crowd at the station entrance, he took command with the natural ease of a colonel of cavalry. "Divide off, divide off!" He waved a black-gloved hand at the Cabinet officers. They formed two facing ranks. Roosevelt joined Hay on the right-hand side. There was a pause, and onlookers barricaded behind the gates were able to contrast his features with those of Senator Hanna. Roosevelt's face was lined with fatigue, but looked harsh and strong. Hanna's was pitiful, full of despair.

Soldiers and sailors approached with the coffin on their shoulders. The crowd uncovered, and "Taps" broke the silence. Then, just as the coffin was sliding into the hearse, there was a flash from a window across the street, accompanied by a revolver-like crack. Roosevelt flinched. "What was that?"

"A photographer," said Commander Cowles.

"Something should be done with that fellow," Roosevelt muttered savagely. For a moment, in his nervousness, he forgot he was President, and gestured Hay and Gage into his carriage ahead of him. They demurred. He climbed in, taking the rear right seat. The Secretaries followed, with Commander Cowles. A little colonel jumped up on the box, yellow plumes waving. Ahead, to the sound of trumpets, the hearse began its journey to the White House. Roosevelt's carriage rolled off a few seconds later. Thousands of spectators watched it disappear into the warm Washington night.

THE FIRST
ADMINISTRATION

1901–1904

*The epigraphs at the head of every chapter
are by "Mr. Dooley," Theodore Roosevelt's
favorite social commentator.*

CHAPTER 1

The Shadow of the Crown

*I see that Tiddy, Prisidint Tiddy—here's his health—is th'
youngest prisidint we've iver had, an' some iv th' pa-apers
ar-re wondherin' whether he's old enough f'r th'
raysponsibilities iv' th' office.*

ON THE MORNING after McKinley's interment, Friday, 20 September 1901, a stocky figure in a frock coat sprang up the front steps of the White House. A policeman, recognizing the new President of the United States, jerked to attention, but Roosevelt, trailed by Commander Cowles, was already on his way into the vestibule. Nodding at a pair of attachés, he hurried into the elevator and rose to the second floor. His rapid footsteps sought out the executive office over the East Room. Within seconds of arrival he was leaning back in McKinley's chair, dictating letters to William Loeb. He looked as if he had sat there for years. It was, a veteran observer marveled, "quite the strangest introduction of a Chief Magistrate . . . in our national history."

As the President worked, squads of cleaners, painters, and varnishers hastened to refurbish the private apartments down the hall. He sent word that he and Mrs. Roosevelt would occupy the sunny river-view suite on the south corner. Not for them the northern exposure favored by their predecessors, with its cold white light and panorama of countless chimney pots.

A pall of death and invalidism hung over the fusty building. Roosevelt decided to remain at his brother-in-law's house until after the weekend. It was as if he wanted the White House to ventilate itself of the sad fragrance of the nineteenth century. Edith and the children would breeze in soon enough, bringing what he called "the Oyster Bay atmosphere."

At eleven o'clock he held his first Cabinet meeting. There was a moment of strangeness when he took his place at the head of McKinley's table. Ghostly responsibility sat on his shoulders. "A very heavy weight," James Wilson mused, "for anyone so young as he is."

"A STOCKY FIGURE IN A FROCK COAT."
Theodore Roosevelt walks to work, 20 September 1901

But the President was not looking for sympathy. "I need your advice and counsel," he said. He also needed their resignations, but for legal reasons only. Every man must accept reappointment. "I cannot accept a declination."

This assertion of authority went unchallenged. Relaxing, Roosevelt asked for briefings on every department of the Administration. His officers complied in order of seniority. He interrupted them often with questions, and they were astonished by the rapidity with which he embraced and sorted information. His curiosity and apparent lack of guile charmed them.

The President's hunger for intelligence did not diminish as the day wore on. He demanded naval-construction statistics and tariff-reciprocity guidelines and a timetable for the independence of Cuba, and got two visiting Senators to tell him more than they wanted to about the inner workings of Congress. In the late afternoon, he summoned the heads of Washington's three press agencies.

"This being my first day in the White House as President of the United States," Roosevelt said ingratiatingly, "I desired to have a little talk with you gentlemen who are responsible for the collection and dissemination of the news."

A certain code of "relations," he went on, should be established immediately. He glanced at the Associated Press and *Sun* service representatives. "Mr. Boynton and Mr. Barry, whom I have known for many years and who have always possessed my confidence, shall continue to have it." They must understand that this privilege depended on their "discretion as to publication." Unfortunately, he could not promise equal access to Mr. Keen of the United Press, "whom I have just met for the first time."

Boynton and Barry jumped to their colleague's defense. Roosevelt was persuaded to trust him, but warned again that he would bar any White House correspondent who betrayed him or misquoted him. In serious cases, he might even bar an entire newspaper. Barry said that was surely going too far. Roosevelt's only reply was a mysterious smile. "All right, gentlemen, now we understand each other."

MUCH LATER THAT EVENING, after a small dinner with friends in the Cowles house on N Street, the President allowed himself a moment or two of querulousness. "My great difficulty, my serious problem, will meet me when I leave the White House. Supposing I have a second term . . ."

Commander Cowles, replete with roast beef, sank deep into leather cushions and folded his hands over his paunch. He paid no attention to the cataract of talk pouring from the walnut chair opposite. For years he had benignly suffered his brother-in-law's fireside oratory; he was as deaf to Rooseveltian self-praise as he was to these occasional moments of self-doubt. How like Theodore to worry about moving out of the White House before moving in! The Commander's eyes drooped. His breathing grew rhythmic; he began to snore.

"I shall be young, in my early fifties," Roosevelt was saying. "On the shelf! Retired! Out of it!"

Two other guests, William Allen White and Nicholas Murray Butler, listened sympathetically. Prodigies themselves—White, at thirty-three, had a national reputation for political journalism, and Butler, at thirty-nine, was about to become president of Columbia University—they were both aware that they had reached the top of their fields, and could stay there for another forty years. Roosevelt was sure of only three and a half. Of course, the power given him dwarfed theirs, and he might win an extension of it in 1904. But that would make its final loss only harder to bear.

So Butler and White allowed the President to continue lamenting his imminent retirement. They interrupted only when he grew maudlin—"I don't want to be the old cannon loose on the deck in the storm!"

Undisturbed by the clamor of younger voices, Commander Cowles slept on.

QUIET SETTLED OVER Washington that weekend, as the government resumed its interrupted vacation. With Congress not due back in town until December, there was little to detain anyone who could afford to leave. Lafayette Square was deserted. Office-seekers—those perennial mosquitoes whining around the body politic—were mercifully few, thanks to mass appointments by Hanna and McKinley earlier in the year. Roosevelt waved away unsatisfied applicants, saying that he was in mourning; but he knew that they would return in ever-increasing numbers. Nothing could stop the natural attrition of federal jobs by resignations, retirements, and deaths.

Nervous tension still afflicted him at unguarded moments. "You ought to be ashamed of yourself!" he roared at a boy who tried to photograph him leaving church. Later, on a twilight stroll with Lincoln Steffens, his fantasy about being attacked recurred. He demonstrated just what he would do with his fists, feet, and teeth if another Czolgosz came out of the shadows. "What I sensed," Steffens recalled, "was the passionate thrill the President was finding in the assassination of the assassin."

By Monday morning, Roosevelt had calmed down enough to perform his duties with dignity and dispatch. "Here is the task," he wrote Henry Cabot Lodge. "I have got to do it to the best of my ability; and that is all there is about it. I believe," he added, with the naïveté that had always endeared him to his friend, "you will approve of what I have done and the way I have handled myself so far."

The presidential suite was now ready for occupancy. Reluctant to spend his first night there alone, he sent a telegram to his younger sister, Corinne, inviting her and her husband, Douglas Robinson, to be his guests. They came down by express train from New Jersey, and Commander and Mrs. Cowles joined them for dinner *en famille*. Roosevelt was in a nostalgic mood. His thoughts kept reverting to Theodore Senior. "What would I not give if only he could have lived to see me here in the White House!"

Later, when decorations from the table were distributed as boutonnieres, the President received a saffronia rose. His face flushed. "Is it not strange! This is the rose we all connect with my father." For a moment "Teedie," "Bamie," and "Pussie" were children again, clustering around the broad bright man who had always worn a yellow flower in his buttonhole. "I think," said Roosevelt, "there is a blessing connected with this."

⌐◯⌐

TWO EVENINGS LATER, a carriage drew up outside the White House. The moon had not yet risen. Not until a boy and a girl tumbled into the light of the portico did reporters in Lafayette Square realize that Edith Roosevelt had arrived. True to her reticent fashion, she came under cloak of darkness. There was a moment of hesitation before she emerged, a comely figure draped in black. Her exquisite profile, usually cast modestly downward, tilted as she followed Kermit and Ethel up the steps. She brought no other children. Little Archie and Quentin were coming with their nurse, Ted had gone straight to Groton, and Alice, the eldest and most independent, would find her own way to the capital.

Kermit and Ethel vanished into the vestibule, and reappeared clinging to their father. Careless of watching eyes, he threw his arms around Edith, then escorted her inside for supper.

Over the next few days of official mourning, Washington correspondents were starved of substantive news, and covered Kermit and Ethel as if they were visiting royalty. The latter's negotiations with ground staff on the subject of white rabbits was treated by *The Washington Post* as a diplomatic dispatch. "It is understood that the high contracting parties are about to reach an agreement, the only point of difference being that of the assignment of territory to the rabbits. . . . A protocol is likely to be signed tomorrow."

Official Washington smiled as more children and more animals joined the Roosevelt menagerie. The White House police were particularly disarmed, allowing Archie and Quentin to march in their morning parades, and looking the other way as Kermit carved huge slices out of the lawn on his bicycle.

Alice, naughtily hiding out in Connecticut, kept everybody guessing. At seventeen, she already had her father's instinct for delayed entrances.

DISTRACTED AS THE reporters were with family gossip, they missed the secret visit of a black man to Roosevelt's office late on the night of Sunday, 29 September. It was unlike Booker T. Washington to be so furtive. He was a world-famous figure, revered even by white Southerners, and had visited William McKinley in broad daylight. But fame had made him cautious. Privately, he admitted to "grave misgivings" about Roosevelt's telegram from Buffalo. The President must not expect him to be an automatic ally in any strategy to dismantle the Southern patronage system wrought by McKinley and Hanna.

Washington's resistance did not last long. He was impressed by how frankly Roosevelt stated that he did not intend to appoint "a large number of colored people" to federal office in Dixie. That would only worsen racial tensions there, currently exemplified by a lynch rate of about one hundred hangings per year. Better to name just a few exemplary blacks, concentrating instead—with Washington's approval—on "the very highest type of native Southern white man . . . regardless of political influences." He, Theodore Roosevelt, was the first President to mingle Union and Confederate blood. As such, he wanted "to see the South back in full communion" with the North.

Washington listened, darkly impressed. Here was a candidate desperate for delegates in 1904, yet willing to gamble on a patronage policy of quality rather than quantity—indeed, if Roosevelt was to be believed, to appoint members of the opposite party when necessary. For forty years, Republican executives, aided by Grover Cleveland, had imposed Northern reform on the South, with the result that white Democrats there were almost totally alienated from the federal civil service. Divided as they might be into "Gold" and Bryanite factions, they were united in their fear of the fecund Negro. Only the most rigid segregation, they believed, could save them from all becoming mulattoes.

State by state, Southern legislatures were disfranchising Negroes. By the next presidential election, not one black man in a thousand would be eligible to vote. Washington understood that it made little sense for Roosevelt to elevate many Negroes in areas where they were unwelcome at the ballot box. Every new black postmaster licking stamps, every tax assessor asking uppity questions, would fan the flames of Southern race hatred. And the "flames" were not metaphorical. Just the other day in Winchester, Tennessee, a maddened crowd of whites had burned a black man at the stake and sold slices of his roasted liver.

Washington, whose political agenda was as unsentimental as Roosevelt's (if considerably more veiled), agreed to help create a new Southern majority of moderate white appointees, plus a minority of blacks. The President, in gratitude, promised an identical patronage policy in the North.

This effusion might have bypassed most ears, but Washington caught its significance. No other President had ever appointed a black official above the Mason-Dixon Line. None had considered the feelings of franchised blacks in such states as New York, Ohio, Indiana, and Illinois. Surely this was proof of Roosevelt's enlightenment.

⌒

AFTER LEAVING THE White House, Booker T. Washington headed south via Virginia, where he had been born a slave forty-five years before. One of the first things he could remember was the sight of his uncle being strapped to a tree and screaming under the lash of a cowhide whip, *"Pray, master, pray, master!"* The half-coherent cry still rang in his ears, convincing him of the white man's urgent need to be regarded as superior, and the black man's equally urgent need to accommodate that fantasy, on pain of extinction.

Washington's pale gray eyes and tawny complexion further sharpened his consciousness of white lust, white guilt, and white hatred. As his mother had endured the embraces of some nameless white man—or men—so must he endure the contempt of rednecks, and the paternalism of rich Yankees. Present passivity was future power.

For sixteen years he had been urging his fellow Negroes to accept disfranchisement as inevitable, to concentrate instead on educational and vocational self-improvement. Blacks and whites alike, with the exception of extremists at either end of the color spectrum, accepted this as the only practical solution to "the color problem." Washington's famous simile, "We can be as separate as the fingers, yet one as the hand in all things essential to mutual progress," implied both economic integration and social segregation. But he insisted that the vote would not long be withheld from a race acquiring skills, learning, and property.

Washington's philosophy of accommodation struck many black intellectuals as craven, yet his career showed how it could be turned to advantage. Where once little Booker had crawled on packed dirt, and endured slave shirts that stung his skin, big Booker now summered in wealthy New England resorts, and ruled a multimillion-dollar educational empire. The Tuskegee Normal and Industrial Institute of Alabama, the black teacher-training college he had founded in 1881, was a huge and thriving enterprise, financed by eager philanthropists. Through the "Tuskegee Machine"—his secret fraternity of academics, businessmen, preachers, politicians, and journalists—he controlled most of the nation's Negro newspapers and political platforms. Washington was the most powerful black man in America, and to Theodore Roosevelt (who tended to equate power with creativity) "a genius such as does not arise in a generation."

Exactly what his full ambition was nobody knew. Courteous yet inscrutable, he operated on many levels. Roosevelt, gazing at him with blind patrician eyes, saw only a chunky yellow man of quiet speech and deferential manner. Washington, gazing back, saw himself reflected quite otherwise in the President's spectacles: a double image of anger and power, wholly, bitterly black.

⌒

NO SOONER HAD he returned to Alabama than the patronage agreement he had with Roosevelt was put to the test. A federal district court judge died in Montgomery, not far from Tuskegee. Washington swung into immediate action. The vacancy could best be filled, he wrote the President, by Thomas G. Jones, a former governor of the state. "He stood up in the Constitutional Convention and elsewhere for a fair election law, opposed lynching, and he has been outspoken for the education of both races. He is head and shoulders above any of the other persons who I think will apply for the position." Jones also happened to be a Democrat.

Roosevelt received the last piece of information with modified rapture. He would have preferred a Republican judge to begin with, if only to lull Senator Hanna into a false sense of security. This important appointment would be seen as a prototype of his future patronage policy. Hanna was bound to suggest someone from the "Lily White" wing of the GOP. A dilemma then loomed. If Roosevelt accepted Hanna's recommendation, he would look like a puppet in his first major presidential act, and perpetuate the Southern status quo. If he appointed Governor Jones—a racial moderate who had fought under Lee—he would gratify Negroes, while persuading Southern Democrats that their long exile from political privilege was over.

Morally, his course was clear. Yet the politician in him hesitated. Washington sent an aide, Emmett J. Scott, to the White House to press the appointment. Scott reported that the President was cordial, yet cagey:

> [He] wanted to know if Gov. Jones supported Bryan. . . . I told him No. He wanted to know how I knew. I told him of the letter wherein he (Governor Jones) stated to you that . . . he had not supported Bryan, etc. etc. Well, he said he wanted to hear from you direct.

Washington was forced to investigate and reply with some embarrassment that if Jones had never actively "supported" the Commoner, he had cast a vote for him in 1900.

Scott delivered the telegram to Roosevelt. Surprise and chagrin struggled on the President's face. He paced up and down. "Well I guess I'll have to appoint him, but I am awfully sorry he voted for Bryan."

So was Mark Hanna, when the appointment was announced on 7 October. He heard the news at home in Ohio, and demanded to know why Roosevelt had acted without consulting him. The President replied frankly: "Because my experience has taught me that in such a case a quick decision really prevents bitterness."

Hanna wrote back in the tones of a patient, but miffed, mentor. Roosevelt must "go slow" until he got back to town. There were bound to be many applicants for federal favor in the weeks ahead. "Reserve your decision—unless in cases which may require immediate attention. Then if my advice is of importance, Cortelyou can reach me over the 'long distance.' "

Despite Hanna's concern, praise for the appointment of Judge Jones was both loud and bipartisan. *The Atlanta Constitution* proclaimed itself "electrified . . . with hope of a new day." Three wealthy young white Republicans in Montgomery, Alabama, announced that they were forming a "Roosevelt Club," to "revolutionize and revitalize" GOP politics. *Review of Reviews* declared that Roosevelt had "immensely strengthened the real and permanent interests" of his party.

Encouraged, the President began to indulge some official vanities. He ordered three glossy carriages and five new horses, and commissioned a patriotic new livery, consisting of blue coat, white doeskin trousers, high boots, and top hat with tricolor cockade. He scrapped the old "Executive Mansion" letterhead, with its Gothic curlicues, and replaced it with stationery proclaiming THE WHITE HOUSE in plain sans serif. He made free use of his power of summons. John Hay, hobbling over daily from the State Department, complained that one interview a month had been enough for McKinley.

Roosevelt in any case did not seem to need much help with foreign policy. He was already formulating it. His first diplomatic document was a three-thousand-word set of instructions for delegates to the International Conference of American States.

Behind the show, and the energy, Hay detected incipient signs of *noblesse oblige*. "Stay away if you want to be amused," he wrote Henry Adams in Europe.

Teddy said the other day, "I am not going to be the slave of tradition that forbids Presidents from seeing friends. I am going to dine with you and Henry Adams and Cabot whenever I like." But (here the shadow of the crown sobered him a little), "of course I must preserve the prerogative of the initiative."

Most observers felt that Roosevelt had exercised the prerogative wisely during his first month in office. He had consoled and inspired a stricken country, steadied the stock market, established decent standards of patronage, and tempered the mutual hatreds of race and party. While doing these things in the name of continuity, he had somehow managed to hint at a future bright with possibilities of reform. It remained to be seen whether he was not, perhaps, enjoying too much success too soon.

"For the moment all America praises the new President," a British correspondent wrote. "But trouble is bound to come."

CHAPTER 2

The Most Damnable Outrage

Thousan's iv men who wudden't have voted f'r him
undher anny circumstances has declared that undher
no circumstances wud they vote f'r him now.

ON 16 OCTOBER 1901, the President heard that Booker T. Washington was back in town, and invited him to dine that night in the White House. Roosevelt had a momentary qualm about being the first President ever to entertain a black man in the White House. His hesitancy made him ashamed of himself, and all the more determined to break more than a century of precedent. He received Washington at 7:30 P.M. and introduced him to Edith. The only other non-family guest was Philip B. Stewart, a friend from Colorado.

Dinner proceeded behind closed doors, under the disapproving gaze of a Negro butler. Southern politics was the main topic of conversation. Washington's aloofness precluded friendly chat, as did Edith Roosevelt's sweet uninterest in anyone—black or white—who was not, as she put it, *"de nôtre monde."*

The President felt entirely at ease. It seemed "so natural and so proper" to have Washington wield his silver. Here, dark and dignified among the paler company, was living proof of what he had always preached: that Negroes could rise to the social heights, at least on an individual basis. Collective equality was clearly out of the question, given their "natural limitations" in the evolutionary scheme of things. But a black man who advanced faster than his fellows should be rewarded with every privilege that democracy could bestow. Booker T. Washington qualified *honoris causa* in the "aristocracy of worth."

For those blacks who did not, Roosevelt had little political sympathy. The Georgian blood of his unreconstructed mother persuaded him that the Fifteenth Amendment had been "a mistake," and that, in nine cases out of ten,

"DARK AND DIGNIFIED AMONG THE PALER COMPANY."
Booker T. Washington, 1901

disfranchisement was justified. Blacks were better suited for service than suffrage; on the whole, they were "altogether inferior to the whites."

Yet Roosevelt believed (as most Americans did not) that this inferiority was temporary. The arguments of Charles Darwin, Jean Lamarck, and Gustave Le Bon convinced him that Washington's race was merely adolescent, as his own had been in the seventeenth century. Negro advancement must "necessarily be painful"—witness the scars on Washington's face, his air of swarthy suffering—but equality would come, as black Americans, generation by generation, acquired the civilized characteristics of whites. It was crucial that these voteless millions should begin to feel working for them "those often unseen forces in the national life which are greater than all legislation."

Just how "unseen" should Washington be in his new role as presidential adviser? Even now the secretive Tuskegean was preparing to slip out of town on a midnight train. Could Roosevelt rely on him to spread the word to Negroes that the federal government was on their side?

Sometime during the last moments of the day, after Washington had left and before Roosevelt went to bed, an Associated Press reporter stopped by the White House to ask, routinely, about the day's guest list. By 2:00 A.M. a one-sentence dispatch was humming round the country: "Booker T. Washington, of Tuskegee, Alabama, dined with the President last evening."

⌖

NEITHER ROOSEVELT NOR Washington could complain about Negro reactions to this release when it appeared in the morning newspapers. Untimely congratulations warmed them, like sunbeams before a storm. "Greatest step for the race in a generation," a black man telegraphed from Nashville. "The hour is at hand," another rejoiced, "to make the beginning of a new order." A third, who remembered young Theodore Roosevelt, skinny and shaky, seconding the nomination of a Negro to chair the 1884 Republican convention, told him, "Your act in honoring [Washington] was a masterly stroke of statesmanship—worthy of the best minds this country has produced." And at a humbler level of black opinion, federal messenger boys discussed the dinner in excited whispers.

Whites, too, reacted favorably, at least those of liberal instinct. But during the afternoon, distant rumblings warned that a political hurricane was on its way up from the South. An early thunderclap was sounded by the *Memphis Scimitar*:

> The most damnable outrage which has ever been perpetrated by any citizen of the United States was committed yesterday by the President, when he invited a nigger to dine with him at the White House. It would not be worth more than a passing notice if Theodore Roosevelt had sat down to dinner in his own home with a Pullman car porter, but Roosevelt the individual and Roosevelt the President are not to be viewed in the same light.
>
> It is only very recently that President Roosevelt boasted that his mother was a Southern woman, and that he is half Southern by reason of that fact. By inviting a nigger to his table he pays his mother small duty. . . . No Southern woman with a proper self-respect would now accept an invitation to the White House, nor would President Roosevelt be welcomed today in Southern homes. He has not inflamed the anger of the Southern people; he has excited their disgust.

The word *nigger* had not been seen in print for years. Its sudden reappearance had the force of an obscenity. Within hours, newspapers from the Piedmont to the Yazoo were raining it and other racial epithets on the President's head.

ROOSEVELT DINES A DARKEY

A RANK NEGROPHILIST

OUR COON-FLAVORED PRESIDENT

ROOSEVELT PROPOSES TO CODDLE THE SONS OF HAM

Some of the more sensational sheets expressed sexual disgust at the idea of Edith Roosevelt and Washington touching thighs, so to speak, under the table. The President was accused of promoting a "mingling and mongrelization" of the Anglo-Saxon race. Booker T. Washington was sarcastically advised to send his daughter to the White House for Christmas: "Maybe Roosevelt's son will fall in love with her and marry her."

The storm squalled louder when reporters discovered that Roosevelt had entertained blacks before, in the gubernatorial mansion at Albany and at Sagamore Hill. Hate mail and death threats swamped the White House and the Tuskegee Institute. In Richmond, Virginia, a transparency of the President's face was hissed off the Bijou screen. In Charleston, South Carolina, Senator Benjamin R. Tillman endorsed remedial genocide: "The action of President Roosevelt in entertaining that nigger will necessitate our killing a thousand niggers in the South before they will learn their place again."

Roosevelt was dumbfounded by the violence his invitation had provoked. At first he blamed Bourbon extremists. Yet even the most temperate Southern opinion held him in reproof. "At one stroke, and by one act," the *Richmond News* declared, "he has destroyed the kindly, warm regard and personal affection for him which were growing up fast in the South. Hereafter . . . it will be impossible to feel, as we were beginning to feel, that he is one of us."

⟢

BY TACIT AGREEMENT, Roosevelt and Washington refused to discuss their dinner with reporters. The President sent private word to Tuskegee that he "did not care . . . what anybody thought or said about it." Both men were buoyed, however, by the continuing support of Northern newspapers. The *Springfield Republican* remarked that while Roosevelt's gesture "may have been an indiscretion," it was "splendid in its recognition of the essential character of the presidential office."

⟢

ON 21 OCTOBER, another lightning report flashed through the South. The President and Booker T. Washington were to dine together again, at Yale University's bicentennial. What was more, Miss Alice Roosevelt would probably join them. Yale issued a denial—Dr. Washington was merely scheduled to march behind Roosevelt in the academic procession—but too late to still the uproar in Dixie. "The whole South," a nervous white minister wrote, "has not been so deeply moved in twenty years."

Roosevelt looked calm and purposeful as he traveled through Connecticut on 23 October. The Secret Service, however, was noticeably apprehensive when he reached the Yale campus. In view of what had happened the last time a President had accepted public handshakes, he was was forbidden to work the crowd.

Shocked by this restriction, Roosevelt seemed to realize his personal and political danger for the first time. He averted his eyes from Washington during their march to Hyperion Theater. A revised security plan seated them far apart, with the Negro in the audience and Roosevelt himself on the stage. No reference to their dinner was made during the ensuing speeches. But cheers filled the hall when Supreme Court Justice David J. Brewer invoked the Father of the Nation and remarked, "Thank God, there have always been in this country college men able to recognize a true Washington, though his first name be not George."

Degrees were awarded to a distinguished list of honorees, including John Hay, Elihu Root, Woodrow Wilson, and the white-suited Mark Twain. "One name yet remains—" President Arthur Hadley intoned, and was unable to continue, so loud was the roar for Theodore Roosevelt.

Notwithstanding this expression of support, Roosevelt declined to see Washington later in the day. At a public reception that evening, he sat aloof, kneading his silk hat. He seized on Twain and asked whether it had been "right" to invite a Negro to the White House. The novelist, speaking carefully, said that a President was perhaps not as free as an ordinary citizen to entertain whomever he liked.

Twain's private opinion was that Roosevelt should "refrain from offending the nation merely to advertise himself and make a noise."

A LARGE CROWD awaited the arrival of the presidential train in Washington the next morning. Few eyes followed Roosevelt as he stepped down to the platform; attention was riveted on Alice, pausing prettily behind him. The rumor, false or not, that she had been willing to eat with a Negro was scandalous, and the slenderness of her body, in its wine-colored traveling dress, sent agreeable signals of sex. Newsmen ogled her with pleased anticipation as she followed her father out of the station, a bunch of violets nodding in her belt. Here, manifestly, was copy for many seasons.

ROOSEVELT'S QUERULOUSNESS about his dinner invitation did not abate in the days ahead. While maintaining a public silence, he admitted to friends that he was puzzled and depressed. He had only wanted to show "some little respect" to an esteemed fellow American. White Southerners could abuse him if they chose. "I regard their attacks with the most contemptuous indifference, but I am very melancholy that such a feeling should exist in such bitterly aggravated form." As for Booker T. Washington, "I shall have him to dine just as often as I please."

Some of these remarks may have reached Washington's ears, for a polite letter came from Tuskegee:

> *My dear Mr. President:* I have refrained writing you regarding the now famous dinner which both of [us] ate so innocently until I could get to the South and study the situation at first hand. Since coming here and getting into real contact with the white people I am convinced of three things: In the first place, I believe that a great deal is being made of the incident because of the elections which are now pending in several of the Southern states; and in the second place, I do not believe the matter is felt as seriously as the newspapers try to make it appear; and in the third place I am more than ever convinced that the wise course is to pursue exactly the policy which you mapped out in the beginning; not many moons will pass before you will find the South in the same attitude toward you that it was a few years ago.

That attitude, however, had always been skeptical. Sensing Roosevelt's need for reassurance, Washington wrote again to say that the controversy was "providential," even therapeutic. "I cannot help but feel . . . that good is going to come out of it."

Some good, certainly, accrued to himself. His reception by the President had transformed him into a political force of the first magnitude. Booker T. Washington now commanded the fear, as well as the love, of black Americans. Eventually the former emotion might qualify the latter, but for the time being he was "King of a captive people."

Roosevelt's gains were more negative. He had learned the evanescence of presidential popularity, the complexity of race prejudice, and "the infinite capacity of the newspaper press to manufacture sensations." He had to accept that he had no real constituency in the South, and stood little chance of assembling one, so united were Democrats against him. Perhaps his dream of bipartisan reform had always been quixotic. The most he could hope was that Southern blacks would reward his goodwill at the next national convention.

The summer of 1904, however, seemed far away in the fall of 1901. Roosevelt could only lament his sudden misfortune, and the revival of old doubts about his maturity. A forty-third candle on his birthday cake on 27 October did not console him, nor the gift of a possum from some black admirers. He dutifully announced that he would wait until "the first frosty day" before eating his critter, "well browned, and with sweet potatoes on the side." But his private melancholy persisted through the first week of November:

> I have not been able to think out any solution of the terrible problem offered by the presence of the Negro on this continent, but of one thing I am sure, and that is that in as much as he is here and can neither be killed nor driven away, the only wise and honorable and Christian thing to do is to treat each black man and each white man strictly on his merits as a man. . . . Of course I know that we see through a glass dimly, and, after all, it may be that I am wrong; but if I am, then all my thoughts and beliefs are wrong, and my whole way of looking at life is wrong. At any rate, while I am in public life, however short a time it may be, I am in honor bound to act up to my beliefs and convictions.

As the famous dinner receded into memory and mythology, Roosevelt grew more conciliatory toward his critics, admitting that he might, just possibly, have made a mistake. But only in the political sense; morally speaking, "my action was absolutely proper."

He kept his vow to consult Booker T. Washington on matters of race and patronage, but never again asked him to dinner. And when Washington next visited the White House, George Cortelyou was careful to schedule the appointment at ten o'clock on a regular business morning.

CHAPTER 3

One Vast, Smoothly Running Machine

MR. DOOLEY	*A hard time th' rich have injyin' life.*
MR. HENNESSY	*I'd thrade with them.*
MR. DOOLEY	*I wud not. 'Tis too much like hard work.*

THE NIGHT OF MONDAY, 11 November 1901, was moonless, and shadows drowned the canyons of downtown New York City. Wall Street, darkest canyon of all, was deserted except for a group of carriages waiting outside the House of Morgan. Midnight struck, then one o'clock.

Inside the gloomy building, behind successive ramparts of granite, mahogany, and ground glass, three financiers conferred. James J. Hill and E. H. Harriman habitually shunned the light of day, the flash and glare of publicity. As for J. Pierpont Morgan, the third party to the business at hand, his aloofness was so Olympian that he was not even present. An aide, George W. Perkins, negotiated in his stead.

This common need for seclusion had little to do with shyness, although Morgan's carbuncled nose, Hill's bald pate, and Harriman's wire-spectacled features twitching around a huge damp mustache brought out the worst in small boys and cartoonists. Had the financiers been as gorgeous as gods, their desire would likely still be to operate in private. Combinations, they felt, were best put together quietly.

Decent, driven men, they had enriched themselves beyond imagination by anonymous deals in railroad stocks. They had built up great transportation systems, stimulated interstate commerce, and improved life for uncounted millions of people. Their philanthropies were legion, their senses of social responsibility sincere.

Yet they had learned with chagrin that the wages of large achievement were public scrutiny and malice. This only made them retreat deeper into themselves. At the heights of their careers, they were a bruised, petulant trio, bent on further organization of the economy—its "Morganization," in popular parlance.

Their meeting tonight demanded especial discretion. It marked the climax of a secret seven-month war between Hill's Great Northern and Harriman's Union Pacific railroads for control of Morgan's Northern Pacific. Also at stake was the Burlington & Quincy road, connecting the three systems with Chicago. Mere rumors of this "battle of titans," earlier in the year, had precipitated the worst panic in Wall Street history; Morgan had been obliged to pump sixteen million dollars into the market to save the stock exchange from collapse.

Right now, Hill seemed to be winning. Harriman had managed to amass a majority of Northern Pacific preferred shares, but they were due to be retired by forced exchange for common shares on New Year's Day 1902, and Hill (with Morgan's connivance) owned a majority of those. There was no guarantee, however, that Harriman would not challenge the power of those shares in court. If successful, he would end up controlling four of America's six western rail networks. That thought was enough to whiten what was left of James J. Hill's hair.

At sixty-three, Hill was ten years older than Harriman. The strain of fighting a ruthless adversary had taken its toll. One horizon-filling vision still haunted him: the combination of the Great Northern, the Northern Pacific, and the Burlington into a rail megasystem covering seventeen states and thirty-two thousand miles of track. Harriman alone could prevent that dream from becoming reality. Hill therefore had to seduce "the little man," as he called him, into some sort of partnership.

What lay before them and Perkins was a proposal to create a trust so immense as to absorb the stock of all three railroads—some four hundred million dollars' worth. These securities would be invested in a "holding company," which would act as a conduit for profits, and protect the component roads. Harriman would be rewarded with board seats proportionate to his Northern Pacific holdings, free access to the Burlington system, and a huge sum of cash. Hill proposed calling their new trust "The Northern Securities Company Limited."

Anybody could see from the draft charter that Northern Securities, if incorporated, would be the greatest combination in the world, second only to U.S. Steel. It would earn one hundred million dollars a year. Its commerce would extend from Chicago to Seattle, and thence, via Hill shipping lines, as far as China.

The flaw in this Columbian scheme was that the Great Northern and Northern Pacific were competitive roads. Mutually operated, they might seem to be acting in restraint of interstate trade, as defined by the Sherman Antitrust Act.

But Hill was confident of the legality of his charter. The finest trust attorneys in the country had researched the Supreme Court's interpretation of the Sherman Act, and found no precedent to threaten Northern Securities. Indeed, the decision in *U.S. v. E. C. Knight* seemed to affirm the right of a holding company to acquire competing stocks, whether the result was monopoly or not.

The bells of Trinity Church struck two o'clock. It was time for a decision. Harriman weighed the cost of further warfare against the profits of truce, and pronounced himself "perfectly satisfied" with Hill's offer.

George Perkins agreed to join them on the board of the new trust, as representative of the House of Morgan. The three men voted to file for immediate incorporation. Then they went into the night.

⌒

THE NEXT DAY, Tuesday, 12 November, Roosevelt finished drafting his first Annual Message to Congress. The task had occupied him, on and off, for more than seven weeks. He had taken particular pains with the subsection on trusts, and was looking forward to reading it to his Cabinet.

⌒

SECRECY SURROUNDING THE formation of Northern Securities lasted a further twenty-four hours. Not until Wednesday morning did a prominent but vaguely worded announcement of "a settlement" in "the Northern Pacific matter" appear in the New York *Sun,* Morgan's mouthpiece. There was no hint of the formation of a new trust, but more details were promised later in the day. Clearly, the story was so big Morgan wanted to delay it until after the stock exchange closed.

Roosevelt worked until lunchtime. At 1:15 he called for the White House barber—he had an eccentric fondness for being shaved in the early afternoon—then marched with glowing cheeks into the dining room. He asked the Attorney General of the United States to accompany him.

⌒

ROOSEVELT HAD TAKEN to calling Philander C. Knox his "playmate." At first sight, the little lawyer seemed an unlikely candidate for friendship. He was short, smooth, pale, and expressionless, a porcelain egg of a man, weighted in place, yet tilting to the slightest touch. His dark blue eyes stared in different directions. No spoon could crack him open for inspection. In the words of a frustrated interviewer, "He offers no point of attack."

Knox was the quintessential attorney, ready to argue any brief for a fee. The larger the fee, the better he argued. Happily for him, corporations in his home state of Pennsylvania could afford very large fees indeed. By the time he joined the second McKinley Administration, Knox had argued himself into the highest income bracket of the law, and his client list boasted such names as Carnegie, Mellon, and Frick.

The Attorney General spent his money well, in *nouveau-riche* style. His first gesture on coming to Washington had been to beat the Count of Monte Cristo's price for a pair of high-stepping horses. He established himself in a lavishly redecorated mansion on K Street, wore pearls at cuffs and collar, and entertained all comers to magnums of Moët & Chandon Impérial. Although he affected to be bored by his own splendor, Knox worked behind the biggest desk in town, and was lobbying for a new, palatial Department of Justice building. "I think I shall need a large appropriation. . . . It should be built entirely of marble."

His languid, *laissez-faire* law enforcement so far had earned him the nickname "Sleepy Phil." Cynics noted that Knox had helped organize U.S. Steel. Henry Adams dismissed him as a Wall Street stooge, "sodden with corporate briefs," not realizing that Knox needed instructions in order to function. President McKinley had never supplied them. A friend remarked, "There must be a client—Knox would not know himself without one."

Roosevelt was quick to remedy this deficiency. He had asked Knox to help him draft the trust-control paragraphs of his Message to Congress, with encouraging results. "I am being advised by the best Attorney General this Government has ever had." In just eight weeks the two men had become fast friends. They could often be seen riding together in Rock Creek Park.

Knox, Roosevelt discovered, was a distinguished equestrian. Those high-stepping horses were not just for show. Neither were the thousands of leather volumes in his library; the Attorney General was a perpetual, if monotonous, quoter of verse and historical facts. He was polite without being humble, and could be startlingly outspoken. This further endeared him to his "client." When a visitor asked the Roosevelt children who their father's favorites were, they drummed their spoons and piped in chorus, "Mr. Root and Mr. Knox."

❧

NEITHER THE PRESIDENT nor the Attorney General would reveal what they discussed over lunch on 13 November 1901, but since the Hill-Harriman "settlement" was the day's big news, they probably devoted little time to the weather. Such a truce could portend only one thing: further monopolization of the railroad industry. Roosevelt knew both Hill and Harriman slightly, and Morgan rather better. But he was more concerned with the *Sun*'s revelation that George W. Perkins had been an auxiliary party to the settlement.

Perkins was the brightest of J. P. Morgan's "golden boys"—clever, charming, successful in both insurance and finance, a self-made millionaire at thirty-nine. To Roosevelt, he was a close friend, "one of the men I most re-

"THE BEST ATTORNEY GENERAL THIS GOVERNMENT HAS EVER HAD."
Philander Chase Knox, ca. 1901

spect." Perkins had come to the White House recently to advise him on the corporate section of his Message—along with another Morgan partner, Robert Bacon. (Handsome, godlike "Bob," who so overshadowed pale "Teddy" in the Harvard class of '80!) It was plain now why they had reacted negatively to his antitrust paragraphs, "arguing like attorneys for a bad case."

Whatever doubts the President may have had about trust control, he had none now. "Perkins may just as well make up his mind that I will not make my Message one hair's breadth milder."

❧

MORGAN, HILL, AND HARRIMAN announced the Northern Securities Company late that afternoon. A few evening newspapers carried the story, but its full impact did not register across the country until Thursday, 14 November. By then, a majority of directors named to the board had approved the conversion and combination of their various stocks, and the giant trust was a *fait accompli*. The New York *Sun* praised Hill's charter as "broad and masterly."

The New York *Journal* saw it as yet another step toward universal monopoly. Ordinary citizens had lost their capacity to feel "rage and terror" at such news; all they wanted to know was "whether the concentration shall be in the public interests or against them." With heavy irony, the *Journal* complimented "the best business brains in America" for advancing socialism's concept of a nationalized industrial state:

> They are smoothing out all the difficulties, consolidating staffs, and creating one vast, smoothly running machine. When they have finished, all the Government will have to do will be to assume the debts of the system, exchange national bonds for stock, and give the general manager a commission from the President of the United States.

The irony was lost on George Perkins, who excitedly clipped the column and sent it to Roosevelt. "To me there is a great deal of significance in an editorial of this kind from a paper like the *Journal*."

In due course, both Perkins and Robert Bacon were reported to have joined the board of Northern Securities, balancing the power of Hill and Harriman. Other board members came from the Rockefeller empire, and the Vanderbilt and Gould systems. The complete directorate read like a miniature *Who's Who* of finance capitalism.

The more Roosevelt and Knox looked at Northern Securities, the more they saw it as a symbol of the arrogant beauty of Combination. Unlike U.S. Steel—a smoky picture, to most minds, of ovens and boilerplate—the new trust was imaginable in detail, length, and breadth. Here was a shining necklace of rails, bejeweled with real estate, spread across America's bosom. What it adorned, it monopolized.

Speculators rushed to buy. One of the first was Senator Hanna. "Can I get some of the new 'Holding' Co. stock as an investment," he begged Perkins. "I asked Mr. Hill to give me some and he said he would but I would like more. . . . I wish you would look 'a little out' for me."

Lesser citizens to whom one share, at $110, represented ten weeks' wages wondered how a company purporting to operate in Hoboken, N.J., could do legitimate business halfway around the globe. The popular journalist Ray Stannard Baker, writing for *Collier's Weekly*, noted with what "humdrum monotony" five or six plutocratic names appeared on the rosters of giant corporations. "You can ride from England to China on regular lines of steamships and railroads without once passing from the protecting hollow of Mr. Morgan's hand."

What would happen when these owners of owners began owning one another? Morgan already owned Perkins. Who would be the ultimate ruler of the American economy? "Is it possible," Baker asked, "that the time will come when an imperial 'M' will repose within the wreath of power?"

As if in answer to his question, the Roman initials *T.R.* were emblazoned on the sides of White House carriages.

⌒

IN MID-NOVEMBER, the leaders of the Senate began to return to town, many on complimentary railroad passes signed by Hill or Harriman, and paid courtesy calls on the President. Mark Hanna took a look at his Message typescript, and reacted even more negatively than Perkins. "I see dynamite in it."

He objected in particular to the heated tone of Roosevelt's language against overcapitalization. Phrases such as *baleful evils, despotism,* and *storm centers of financial disturbance* would not go down well on Wall Street, while *inevitable depression, reduced wages,* and *mismanagement and manipulation* might imperil the current détente between capital and labor.

Other senators proposed other changes. None seemed to notice that for every word the President had written in criticism of "bad" trusts, there were five in praise of good. Gradually, reluctantly, he erased adjectives, then sentences, then whole paragraphs. He suppressed his condemnation of price-fixing and preferential rebates. He withdrew a proposal to make corporate records subject to government scrutiny. He even crossed out his wish for a Constitutional amendment "to confer on the National Government the power to supervise great industrial combinations." The Senators were still not satisfied. They were the legislative veterans, he the executive novice, dependent on their support in consolidating his presidency. So he continued to cut, now pages at a time.

⌒

RESTRAINED AS HE might have become on matters of trust policy, Roosevelt remained outspoken on the subject of appointments. His daily public reception, held at noon in George Cortelyou's antechamber, amounted to a patronage mart, and he reveled in the opportunity to show off the decisive speed of his mind. "Tell me what you have to say, quickly, quickly!" No matter how concise the request, he was always ready with a reply—and not always the one hoped for:

SENATOR DEBOE	Mr. President, I have Collector Sapp's resignation in my pocket, but—
ROOSEVELT	You have? I'll take it. Here, Mr. Cortelyou; wire Mr. Sapp that his resignation has been accepted and ask him to turn the office over to his first deputy at once. Have someone telephone the Treasury. . . . (*Over his shoulder, moving on*) That's all right, Senator; everything will be promptly attended to.

He would whirl on round the room, pumping hands and grinning, ejaculating his automatic "Glad to see you!" and "Dee-*lighted*!" like snorts from a steam engine. Office-seekers learned not to trifle with his memory ("Haven't you a jail record?"), nor to present him with trumped-up dossiers of support ("Petition? I could get a petition to have you hanged!").

Those other White House pests, the murmurers of special requests, found Roosevelt impossible to buttonhole. Like an actor, he projected his voice past them, at the crowd. The more furtive his interlocutor, the louder he responded, and he took care to repeat, *fortissimo*, any request that he deemed improper. The effect was of salt poured on slugs. Even as the supplicants melted away, Roosevelt's voice would follow: "Senator Depew, do you know that man going out? Well, he is a crook."

There were days when the visitors besieging him were so numerous that Cortelyou had to empty the antechamber five times before lunch. On such occasions the President could be overstimulated, and his frankness coarsened to rudeness. "I don't give a damn for the Legislature of Texas!" he roared at Senator Joseph Bailey, making a lasting Democratic enemy. He called to an aide, over the heads of Representative John Dalzell and Senator Julius Caesar Burrows: "Come here, Mr. McAneny, and help me with these two gentlemen. They are boring me about appointments." Burrows left the White House angrily, muttering, "This young man won't last long."

Monitors of Roosevelt's Western patronage noticed that an ability to shoot straight seemed to appeal to him more than strict fidelity to the Bill of Rights. Civil Service Commissioner William Dudley Foulke recorded his interview with Pat Garrett, slayer of Billy the Kid and candidate for Customs Collectorship of El Paso, Texas:

ROOSEVELT	How many men have you killed?
GARRETT	Three.
ROOSEVELT	How did you come to do it?
GARRETT	In the discharge of my duty as a public officer.
ROOSEVELT	(*looking pleased*) Have you ever played poker?
GARRETT	Yes.
ROOSEVELT	Are you going to do it when you are in office?

GARRETT   No.

ROOSEVELT   All right, I am going to appoint you. But see you observe the
             civil service law.

The appointment dismayed many Texans, not because of Garrett's bloody
record but because he was an agnostic. "In El Paso," the President said approvingly, "the people are homicidal but orthodox."

⟶⟨⟶

ON 18 NOVEMBER 1901, Secretary of State Hay and the British Ambassador, Lord Pauncefote, signed their long-negotiated treaty granting the
United States exclusive right to build an interoceanic waterway in Central
America. Two days later, the Isthmian Canal Commission, appointed by President McKinley to recommend the "most practicable and feasible" route, reported in favor of Nicaragua. This news was held for release after the opening
of Congress, but William Randolph Hearst got an advance copy of the report,
and splashed it across the pages of his New York *Journal*.

It was a big scoop, if not much of a story. Popular and Congressional sentiment had been in favor of a Nicaragua Canal for so long that the Commission's decision was expected. Panama might possibly have been chosen, but
that fetid little Colombian province was already a monument to the folly of
French canal engineers. After twenty-two years of mismanagement, scandal,
disease, and death, all that was left of Ferdinand de Lesseps's *grand canal du
Panama* was a gang of lethargic workers, some crumbling buildings and rusty
machinery, and an immense, muddy scar reverting to jungle.

Nicaragua, in contrast, offered a virgin landscape, a healthy climate,
one hundred miles of navigable freshwater, and the lowest pass in the
Cordilleras. Its leaders were unanimously eager to reach an agreement with
the United States, whereas those of Colombia were divided by civil war, unable to treat with their own rebels, let alone representatives of a foreign
power.

And yet—this was Hearst's real news—one sentence in the report implied
that the Commission was not wholehearted about its recommendation:

> There are certain physical advantages, such as a shorter canal line, a
> more complete knowledge of the country through which it passes, and
> lower cost of maintenance and operation in favor of the Panama
> route, but the price fixed by the Panama Canal Company for the sale
> of its property and franchises is so unreasonable that its acceptance
> cannot be recommended by this Commission.

Minus that extra compensation—$109 million—a Panama Canal would
cost $156 million, as opposed to $200 million for a Nicaragua Canal. And it

would be finished sooner, thanks to the French excavations. So mere economics had kept the commissioners from endorsing the private preference of the President of the United States.

⚬

ROOSEVELT FINISHED READING his revised Message aloud to the Cabinet on 22 November. All twenty-five thousand words were his own work. Previous Presidents had done little more than to collate and introduce the reports of executive departments. But he was still a writer, with a writer's reluctance to sign prose he had not composed, or at least edited. Feeling a sudden revulsion for the ink-stained typescript, he sent it off to be printed.

Twelve days still intervened before the reassembly of Congress. He decided that he wanted to be alone with his family for a while, somewhere away from Washington. The executive yacht *Sylph* was rigged, and Navy Yard cannons primed for a twenty-one-gun salute. By 3:30 that afternoon, the Roosevelts were on their way up Pennsylvania Avenue. Passersby were touched to see the President kissing four-year-old Quentin, first on one chubby cheek, then the other.

⚬

BACK IN MINNESOTA, James J. Hill saluted his own child, Mary, in his own fashion, with twenty dollars in gold. He had earned them during his first few days as president of the Northern Securities Company. "It is the hardest job I have ever undertaken," he said, in the voice of a man whose ambitions were complete.

⚬

WHILE THE *SYLPH* cruised the lower Potomac, through chill salt mists, Americans browsed a syndicated newspaper article entitled TEDDY'S HOROSCOPE. The astrologist-author noted that Theodore Roosevelt had become President under a remarkable coincidence of Capricorn and Aquarius. This meant that, beginning in 1902, his Administration would bring about many changes, particularly with respect to "laws" and "treaties." He would increase the nation's military power, and go on to handle "vast political problems, the like of which we do not dream of today."

Although Roosevelt was a man much influenced by Mars, he was likely to be peaceable in foreign affairs. His aggression would spill out on the domestic front. (But he would be asking for trouble if he tried to bully Congress.) There was likely to be "a remarkable recrudescence" of social violence soon. While some years of prosperity lay ahead, "a crash is surely coming, and securities will drop to rock bottom."

The President need not worry about ill health or assassination. But he was fated to suffer "the death of some intimate friend . . . or cabinet official, probably the latter."

⌒

JOHN HAY'S AVUNCULAR fondness for Theodore Roosevelt had became almost grandfatherly as he watched him struggle toward statesmanship. The President, he wrote a friend, was "a young fellow of infinite dash and originality."

Although Hay was sometimes embarrassed by Roosevelt's gaucheries, he forgave them as *folies de jeunesse.* Youth, as the President kept saying, was "a curable disease." How boyish of Theodore not to notice, that final freezing Friday before Congress assembled, that the Cabinet Room fire was unlit, and that some of his older officers were still in their overcoats! And how charmingly unpretentious—when he at last *did* notice—to light the logs himself, and coax them to flame!

CHAPTER 4

A Message from the President

On th' wan hand I wud stamp them undher fut;
on th' other hand, not so fast.

SHORTLY BEFORE NOON on Tuesday, 3 December 1901, a committee of senators and representatives called upon the President. They announced that the Fifty-seventh Congress was in session, and "ready to receive any communication" he might want to make. The delegation bowed out, and returned to Capitol Hill by official carriage. After a polite interval, one of Roosevelt's own monogrammed vehicles followed. It drew up outside the House of Representatives, and a White House secretary jumped out with an enormous manila envelope.

Octavius L. Pruden had carried thirty presidential messages up the Capitol steps, but this was the heaviest yet. It consisted of two duplicate eighty-page volumes—one for the House, one for the Senate. Each was silk-lined, leather-bound, gold-stamped, and sealed with the presidential wafer. A Secret Service man, marching beside Pruden, kept guard over the precious cargo.

Actually, the content of Roosevelt's Message was the worst-kept secret since the Declaration of Independence. For at least six weeks, White House guests had been treated to stentorian readings of the author's favorite passages. Newspaper presses across the country held every word in cold type, and in Britain and Europe the Message was already being published and commented on.

Even so, Congress was tense with anticipation when Pruden appeared at the door of the House and announced, "A message from the President of the United States." Speaker David B. Henderson took delivery of the first volume and broke its seal. He was surprised to see printed text, instead of the traditional formal copperplate. A reading clerk took it from him, and flicked through to the end. "Yes, sir, it is signed." Henderson shrugged. The clerk intoned Roosevelt's opening sentence: *"The Congress assembles this year in the shadow of a great calamity."*

There was an immediate reaction. Presidential messages were supposed to begin blandly, with hackneyed phrases about the United States being at peace with mankind. But as the clerk continued to read, it was clear that Roosevelt was all business.

William McKinley, he said, was the victim of a chillingly modern breed of assassin. Lincoln and Garfield had been martyrs for the kind of government they stood for; today's political killer wanted to destroy government itself. Roosevelt began to eulogize his predecessor, but rage against Czolgosz diverted him into a magnificent six-minute tirade against anarchism, and those who abused the First Amendment by inciting it. The reading clerk could not help but perform histrionically: *"The wind is sowed by the men who preach such doctrines, and they cannot escape their responsibility for the whirlwind that is reaped. . . . If ever anarchy is triumphant, its triumph will last for but one red moment, to be succeeded for ages by the gloomy night of despotism."*

The House sat rapt as Roosevelt demanded federal jurisdiction over attacks on the presidential line of succession, and a ban on all politically violent immigrants. *"They and those like them should be kept out of this country; and if found here they should be promptly deported to the country whence they came; and far-reaching provision should be made for the punishment of those who stay. . . . The American people are slow to wrath, but when their wrath is kindled it burns like a consuming flame."*

At this, the spell over the listening representatives broke. The sound of their applause rolled after Pruden as he hurried down the corridor to make his second delivery.

⌒

THE SENATE, in contrast to the brilliantly lit House, was not yet illuminated for business. Dull winter sunshine seeped through the glass roof, too faint to reach the floor. Pruden hesitated in the doorway while senators settled like shadows into their chairs. A page relieved the messenger of his burden. Not until it was placed on the chief clerk's lectern did somebody throw a switch; Roosevelt's first words were heralded by a flood of incandescent light.

For a quarter of an hour, the seated company listened silently. Paperbound offprints of the Message—another novelty—were distributed, and senators began following the text like dutiful pupils.

"During the last five years business confidence has been restored, and the nation is to be congratulated because of its present abounding prosperity."

Mark Hanna sat nodding solemnly at his own revisions. Henry Cabot Lodge, the President's best friend, lounged nearby, looking, as usual, as if he was about to go to sleep. But every now and again he unscrewed his fountain pen and endorsed a passage that appealed to him.

"The captains of industry who have driven the railway systems across this continent, who have built up our commerce, who have developed our manufactures, have on the whole done great good to our people."

As Roosevelt swung into his much-edited subsection on trusts, Senator John Coit Spooner (R., Wisconsin) got up and walked across the room. Spectators in the press gallery watched the small, pigeon-toed figure, guessing that it would stop at one of three desks. These, and Spooner's own, were the four corners of Republican power on Capitol Hill.

SPOONER, AT FIFTY-EIGHT, had the fastest mind, best constitutional knowledge, and most lethal wit in Congress. No senator could match him in debate; he was a scholar of classical rhetoric, and when short of a riposte—which was seldom—he could quote from Cicero or John Wilkes. He was equally dangerous as a listener, specializing in gadfly questions that stung ponderous orators. His very appearance stamped him as unique. In a chamber luxuriant with beards and mustaches, Spooner's clean, chiseled features glowed pale as stone. It was an arresting, almost shocking face, with an imperious twitch to the nostrils. Great waves of hair, polished pince-nez, and oversize cravats softened the cold sculpture. They suggested a frustrated actor. If so, the part Spooner most longed to play was that of President of the United States. But he had always been too spontaneous, and too impatient, for campaign teamwork. Solo improvisation suited him better.

His perambulation ended at the desk of William Boyd Allison (R., Iowa). Stooping, he began to whisper in the old man's ear. Rooseveltian rhetoric continued to echo over their heads:

"Many of those who have made it their vocation to denounce the great industrial combinations . . . known as 'trusts,' appeal especially to hatred and fear. . . . The whole history of the world shows that legislation will generally be both unwise and ineffective unless undertaken after calm enquiry and with sober self-restraint."

Here were cautious words to appeal to Senator Allison—if Spooner's whispering allowed him to hear them. Throughout his political career, "the Old Fox" had counseled due process in lawmaking. His genius was the resolution of discord; his vanity was to affect humility. Not once in his seventy-two years had he expressed a public point of view. Colleagues joked that if the road from Des Moines to Washington was a piano keyboard, "Allison could run all the way without ever striking a note."

This *legerdepied* kept him from being beholden to anybody, while gratifying everybody. When legislation arose to favor the urban East, Senator Allison modified it so as not to alienate the rural West. If Southern Democrats forced bills upon him to benefit their poorer constituents, he attached innocent-looking amendments and profited Wall Street as well. But his moderating did not make him moderate. Like Spooner, Allison was a Hamiltonian fiscal conservative.

Poised in his equilibrium, he was upset by any shock, and could lash out with the sudden bitchiness of old age. Friends forgave him these outbursts. They knew he was tormented by a swelling prostate. Allison's weary shuffle, his dark-brown, nicotinous smell—the very breath of the antebellum— guaranteed deference in a chamber worshipful of seniority.

"All this is true, and yet it is also true that there are real and grave evils."

In the front row of the chamber, beneath the reading clerk, sat a senator even hoarier than Allison. At seventy-four, Orville H. Platt (R., Connecticut) was the *éminence grise* of the Republican leadership. No relation to Thomas C. Platt of New York (Roosevelt's ancient enemy, senescent now in a forgotten corner), he served as the Senate's spiritual mentor, its legislative and ethical conscience.

There was something Lincolnesque about Platt's grooved, bearded face, and the awkwardness of his six-foot-four-inch frame. Scholarly, mild, logical, and reclusive, Platt was almost a caricature of New England bookishness; his idea of an amusing evening was to read Greek to his wife. But the mildness was deceptive. Few senators worked more aggressively on behalf of big business.

"There is a widespread conviction," the clerk declaimed, *". . . that combination and concentration should be, not prohibited, but supervised and within reasonable limits controlled; and in my judgment this conviction is right."*

Spooner returned to his seat. The outburst that none of Roosevelt's advisers had been able to suppress was coming. *"It is no limitation upon property rights or freedom of contract to require that when men receive from government the privilege of doing business under corporate form . . . they shall do so upon absolutely truthful representations. . . . Great corporations exist only because they are created and safeguarded by our institutions; and it is therefore our right and duty to see that they work in harmony with these institutions."*

If Nelson W. Aldrich (R., Rhode Island) deduced that Roosevelt was sounding the keynote of his presidency, he showed no sign. The sixty-year-old "Manager of the United States" looked as he always did: big, handsome, placid, nonchalantly powerful. His brow was calm, his silvery mustache stiff, his black eyes steady on the page before him.

"The first essential in determining how to deal with the great industrial corporations is knowledge of the facts—publicity."

Aldrich's was a classic poker face. Indeed, he was champion of a private poker game at which he, Spooner, Allison, and Platt formulated policy. So elite was this little circle, so doubly dedicated to cards and politics, that its interests tended to fuse; the house would deal tariff schedules, pension bills, and aces of clubs interchangeably. Most evenings, Aldrich collected.

His power derived in part from natural authority, in part from pure memory. Spooner was quicker, and the two senior members were perhaps wiser, but none could match Aldrich's command of information. No matter how raw the data—ore piles of statistics, a rubble of currency regulations—he processed them with the silent efficiency of a kiln. Consequently, he was the Senate's ranking expert on such subjects as paper-money circulation, railroad bonds, and free wool. His actions on these issues did not usually make headlines, but Aldrich never cared for publicity.

Roosevelt, in contrast, seemed to equate it with democracy. *"In the interest of the public, the government should have the right to inspect and examine the workings of the great corporations."*

As far as Aldrich was concerned, news was noise, an intrusive bedlam that disturbed the quiet condominium of government and economy. The more attention public servants enjoyed, the more they would want to be *seen* to be doing, at the expense of free entrepreneurs.

"The nation should, without interfering with the power of the States in the matter itself, also assume power of supervision and regulation over all corporations doing interstate business."

Aldrich believed that, on the contrary, the nation could do with a little "supervision and regulation" by businessmen. He was himself a successful railroad executive. "I would undertake to run this government for three hundred million a year less than it is now run for," he said. Since this was not constitutionally possible, he could at least control the United States Senate to a greater degree than it had ever known. With a majority of 55 to 31, and a supplementary majority of 187 to 151 in the House, he might even manage to control Theodore Roosevelt as well.

"I believe that a law can be framed . . ."

⟶⟶

THE SENATE WAS popularly and inaccurately known as "The Millionaires' Club." Aldrich protested that he, for one, had begun life as a wholesale grocer. Ordinary Americans saw magazine pictures of his palatial house on Narragansett Bay, noted that his daughter had just married John D. Rockefeller, Jr., and doubted that the Senator would recognize a grocery now if he saw one.

Aldrich was indeed extremely rich, but he told the truth about his origins. There were a few other self-made millionaires in the Senate; aristocratic millionaires, like Lodge, formed an even smaller minority. Only sixteen members could be described as wealthy or well-born. Orville Platt was not ashamed to admit that he had never seen more than a hundred spare dollars in his life.

The remaining seventy-four senators were divided evenly between the middle and working classes. Far from representing an "alliance between business and politics"—another popular fallacy—fewer than one in four represented commerce or industry. Most were lawyers of ordinary accomplishment.

What held them together was their collective dedication to politics as a profession. Conscience, not corruption, kept the average senator in office. He worked seven days a week, assisted by one secretary and one typist, for five thousand dollars a year—one tenth of what Roosevelt earned. Venality was a constant temptation, but only the most unscrupulous senators, men such as Matthew Quay and Boies Penrose of Pennsylvania, fattened at the public trough.

Under Aldrich's management, the Senate was disciplined and hierarchical in structure. Younger members rose by patience and labor. Not even such a brilliant upstart as Albert J. Beveridge of Indiana (ardent, golden-haired, Botticellian) could hope for early privilege. Committee seats were rewards for loyalty and efficiency, and Allison dispensed them with a fine eye for political balance. Positions of power were rotated by the Republican leadership. Aldrich chaired Finance, with Spooner, Allison, and Platt sitting to his left and right. The same quartet, but with Allison in the chair, controlled the Republican steering committee, which in turn controlled all legislative business. Aldrich dominated Interstate Commerce and Cuba Relations; Allison, Appropriations; Spooner and Platt, Judiciary. A few other GOP senators— Hanna, Lodge, George Frisbie Hoar of Massachusetts, Eugene Hale of Maine—helped swell the ranks of this conservative elite.

ROOSEVELT BROUGHT HIS trust remarks to an indecisive end, suggesting that if Congress felt debarred from passing a law regulating interstate commerce, it should consider a Constitutional amendment to that effect. He called for a new department to regulate commerce and industry, and new laws to improve conditions for American workers. He granted labor's right to combine for self-advancement, as corporations did, on condition neither threatened the larger rights of society.

By now it was past one o'clock. Bottles of bourbon stood tall and cool in the Senate saloon, and white bean soup bubbled in the restaurant. Members began paging through their copies to see how much Message was left. The survey was discouraging—almost twice as much again. But some of the upcoming issues were too important to walk out on. Roosevelt had shrewdly intermixed them with others of less consequence.

He demanded reform of immigration laws, including a threefold ban on persons of low intellect, low morals, and low wage requirements. He analyzed tariff protectionism and trade reciprocity at length, if not in depth. Clearly, neither subject interested him; he was happy to leave them to Senator

Aldrich, their virtual proprietor. He launched an attack on railroad rebates and rate-fixing. *"The railway is a public servant. Its rates should be just to, and open to, all shippers alike."*

Then, striking a note altogether new in presidential utterances, Roosevelt began to preach the conservation of natural resources. He showed an impressive mastery of the subject as he explained the need for federal protection of native flora and fauna. Urgently, he asked that the Bureau of Forestry be given total control over forest reserves, currently parceled among several agencies, and demanded more presidential power to hand further reserves over to the Department of Agriculture.

The theme of "water-storing" infused his rhetoric as he appealed for the reclamation of arid public lands. He said that the interstate irrigation program he had in mind was so ambitious that only the national government could undertake it. It must not risk the fate of the countless private schemes that Western water speculators had tried, and failed, to get rich on in recent years. Nor should the reclaimed lands benefit anyone other than the settlers willing to farm them. *"The doctrine of private ownership of water apart from land cannot prevail without causing enduring wrong."*

Action on all fronts must begin immediately. Yet—a typical Rooseveltian hedge—it must proceed cautiously: *"We are dealing with a new and momentous question, in the pregnant years while institutions are forming, and what we do will affect not only the present but future generations."*

⎯⎯

FOR ANOTHER HOUR, the Message droned on, while clerk after clerk read himself hoarse, and somnolence gathered in the air like fog. Roosevelt was impassioned on the Navy's need for more battleships and heavy armored cruisers, firm in his defense of the Monroe Doctrine, galvanic in his call for a canal across Central America. He praised the Smithsonian Institution and the Library of Congress as national treasures—something no previous President had thought to do. He was silent on Negro disfranchisement and lynchings, optimistic for the future of free Cuba, and pessimistic about early independence for the Philippines. He was dogged to the point of dullness on rural free mail delivery, national expositions, merchant-marine subsidies, and the need for a permanent census bureau.

By two o'clock, many senators could stand it no longer, and left the chamber to fortify themselves. Even Henry Cabot Lodge showed impatience as he and sixty-six other holdouts waited for the President's peroration.

Roosevelt returned at last to the subject of death, with which he had begun two and a half hours before. He noted that William McKinley had been preceded to the grave by Queen Victoria of England and the Dowager Empress Frederick of Germany. He seemed to be reminding his older auditors that nineteenth-century cobwebs were blowing away all over the world. The twentieth century looked bright for all Americans, yet they would not abandon traditional values.

"*In the midst of our affliction we reverently thank the Almighty that we are at peace with the nations of mankind; and we firmly intend that our policy shall be such as to continue unbroken these international relations of mutual respect and good will.*"

⌒

ALDRICH, ALLISON, SPOONER, and Platt emerged from the chamber smiling like Wagnerites after a slow performance of *Siegfried*. Each had an approving adjective for the President's Message. It was "able," "excellent," "admirable," and "intrepid." Their satisfaction was not surprising, since its caveats and circumlocutions had been dictated by themselves.

Democratic leaders, too, were mostly complimentary, although Senator James K. Jones of Arkansas pointed out that the President's trust control proposals were so nonspecific as to be legislatively worthless. "The Message is in every respect disappointing."

Members of the House reacted with general approbation, as did the nation's press. The adjective *conservative* was used often, as if in relief that the young President had matured so quickly. Only 12 percent of editorial comments were critical of him; a mere half of one percent condemnatory.

That night, Roosevelt entertained the Republican leadership to dinner. He had reason to celebrate. Not since the time of Lincoln had a President's first thoughts received such public attention; congratulatory telegrams were pouring in, and the stock market was surging. Even as he feasted, eighteen of his proposals were being drafted into bills.

Aldrich and Allison saw no immediate threat to the legislative status quo. Yet they sipped Roosevelt's sauterne with a vague sense of unease. Walter Wellman, White House correspondent of the Chicago *Record-Herald,* caught their mood:

It is not so much what he has done as what he may do that fills [them] with anxiety. . . . They have been accustomed to a certain way of playing the game. They know all the rules. . . . Naturally the question arises in many minds: What of the future? What will it all come to? The significance of this great Message, this remarkable piece of writing, is that it has raised up a new intellectual force, a new sort of leader, against whom the older politicians are afraid to break a lance, lest he appeal to the country . . . and take the country with him.

⌒

THE WINTER DAYS shortened toward solstice. Roosevelt returned home from his afternoon rides in ever-thickening darkness. Whether he came from Rock

Creek or the Potomac flats, sooner or later L'Enfant's perspectives disclosed the Capitol ahead of him, high and remote on its wooded hill, twinkling with lights as Congress worked late.

On 7 December, he received his first piece of legislation from the Senate. It was a minor customs waiver, and he signed it impatiently. A bill authorizing construction of the Isthmian Canal would have been more to his taste, but the Senate had yet to ratify the Hay-Pauncefote Treaty. When it eventually did, on 16 December, congressmen were already turning their thoughts toward Christmas. Roosevelt gave up hope of a canal bill before the new year, and turned his energies to building up political strength.

The quickest way to do this was through patronage, so he began to bombard the Hill with as many as thirty appointments a day. A surprise choice was fifty-three-year-old Governor Leslie Mortier Shaw of Iowa to replace Lyman Gage as Secretary of the Treasury. Gage resigned with understandable chagrin, having stayed on—at Roosevelt's request—to give Wall Street a sense of continuity. Now, with stocks rising, he found himself dispensable. Postmaster General Charles Emory Smith also felt a presidential chill, and stepped aside for Henry C. Payne of Wisconsin.

It did not escape notice that the new Cabinet recruits were protégés, respectively, of Senators Allison and Spooner. Those two Republican stalwarts were plagued by party insurgencies back home; Iowa and Wisconsin were notoriously fickle states, receptive to new ideas. Roosevelt's nominations seemed to align him with the Old Guard against reform.

There was further significance in his appointment of Payne, a "Roosevelt Republican" with no love for Mark Hanna. Payne was one of the GOP's top political managers. Life had been lean for him during the McKinley years. At fifty-eight, he hungered for a salaried office with spoils. Roosevelt gave him both, in good measure: the Postal Service was the richest source of patronage in Washington. Mark Hanna's effulgence as party boss began to dwindle with the December light.

Almost simultaneously, Senator Joseph Benson Foraker of Ohio proclaimed himself a Roosevelt Republican, too. Foraker resented his colleague's domination of the Ohio party, and gave notice that he would endorse the President in 1904. Yet another anti-Hanna recruit was Senator Matthew Quay of Pennsylvania. Roosevelt turned a blind eye to Quay's semicriminal record, gave a consulship to one of his cronies, and flattered his intellectual pretensions: "So you're fond of De Quincey, Senator?"

Night after night, he gazed more cheerfully at the Capitol, knowing that some of its lights, at least, twinkled for him.

⟫—

ONE UNSEEMLY INCIDENT marred the week before Christmas: the President's public scolding of Nelson A. Miles, Commanding General of the

United States Army. His treatment of the old soldier was by most accounts brutal. "It is a horrible thing," wrote a former aide to Benjamin Harrison, "to realize that we have a bully in the White House."

Roosevelt had developed an antipathy for the Commanding General during the Spanish-American War, dismissing him as nothing more than "a brave peacock." Miles still loved to parade before admiring eyes. At sixty-one, he was a splendid specimen of bristling military masculinity. If he wore more gold braid, silver stars, and polished leather than seemed necessary for national security, few begrudged him his glitter. He was, after all, a hero of the Indian Campaigns.

What angered Roosevelt now was not so much the preening and strutting as signs that the Commanding General wished to become Commander-in-Chief. He was not particular as to which party should nominate him, but the latest signs were that he was courting the anti-imperialistic vote, with a view to running as a Democrat in 1904.

As Commanding General, Miles had access to all classified dispatches sent to the Secretary of War. Secrets embarrassing to Elihu Root's management of the war in the Philippines were being leaked to senators in the opposition. Roosevelt and Root were sure that he was responsible.

Miles played into their hands on 17 December by telling an interviewer that he disagreed with a naval court investigating a dispute between two admirals. Root informed him, on behalf of the President, that the senior officer of one service had "no business" criticizing legal proceedings in another. Miles hurried to the White House to explain that his remark had been merely "personal." Roosevelt was in the middle of an open reception, and jumped at the chance to humiliate him. His voice rose to a shout, accompanied by jabs of the presidential forefinger: "I will have no criticism of my Administration from you, or any other officer in the Army. Your conduct is worthy of censure, sir."

"You have the advantage of me, Mr. President," Miles said, controlling himself. "You are my host and superior officer." He bowed and left the room. On 22 December, his reprimand was made official. There was much sympathy for him, and criticism of the President for going beyond normal disciplinary decencies. "Mr. Roosevelt," commented *The Army and Navy Register,* "approached General Miles in a manner which, without exaggeration, may be described as savage."

⁓

PURGED, PERHAPS, by his outburst, Roosevelt radiated contentment at pre-Christmas appearances. The approach of the festive season always delighted him. Now that he inhabited the house of his highest desire, his excitement was childlike. "The President," a visitor remarked, "seems to get whole heaps of fun out of the Presidency."

Yet there was something about Roosevelt that gave close observers pause. Was he as naïvely impulsive as he seemed? Why was he so cheerfully equivocal on every possible issue? Why had he sent Philander Knox down to Florida for a month's "rest," and why was the Attorney General carrying such a suspiciously fat briefcase?

"I should say," the last reporter to interview the President in 1901 wrote, "that he has something up his sleeve."

⌒

HOWLS OF MIRTH, mixed with music and hand-claps, were heard in the East Room after dinner on 25 December, as the President led his family and friends in a Virginia reel. The tempo quickened until even Senator Lodge shed his solemnity and joined in. Roosevelt, beaming like a boy, performed a variety of buck-and-wing steps to loud applause. Edith collapsed in tears of laughter, while his children exhorted him to further display. "Go to it, Pop!"

The band swung into the tune the Rough Riders had adopted at training camp in San Antonio. Seizing another partner, Roosevelt stomped out a joyous cakewalk, and the sound of singing voices rolled out into Lafayette Square:

> *When you hear dem-a bells go ding, ling, ling,*
> *All join round, and sweetly you must sing,*
> *And when the verse am through,*
> *In the chorus all join in,*
> *There'll be a hot time in the old town tonight!*

CHAPTER 5

Turn of a Rising Tide

Divvle a bit do I care whether
they dig th' Nicaragoon Canal
or cross th' Isthmus in a balloon.

WALTER WELLMAN, REPORTER, was strolling beside the Potomac one day early in 1902 when a horsewoman rode past at a sedate clip. Presently, another rider followed, cantering to catch up with her. The stiff beard and haughty posture identified him as Senator Henry Cabot Lodge. Then came the noise of a big stallion moving at full gallop. Wellman stepped out of the way as it drummed by in a spray of gravel. The bespectacled rider was waving an old campaign hat and laughing with pleasure. "*Ki-yi!*" he screamed, galloping on. "*Ki-yi!*"

To Wellman and other Washington correspondents, Roosevelt's recreational antics were a welcome diversion from politics. The President was variously reported to have marched twenty miles through heavy rain (in Norfolk jacket, corduroy knickers, yellow leggings, and russet shoes), swum nude across the freezing river, and climbed with fingers and toes up the blast holes of a disused quarry. His habit of forcing luncheon guests to accompany him on afternoon treks did not endear him to those who would have preferred to remain behind with the wine and walnuts.

Foreign offices in Britain and Europe worried that their representatives might not be up to the physical hazards of dealing with Theodore Roosevelt. Junior diplomats campaigned for postings to his court, on the basis of common youth and strength. The essential qualification was perhaps best expressed by Cecil Spring Rice, Roosevelt's former best man and now a British Commissioner in Egypt: "You must always remember that the President is about six."

Charles William Eliot of Harvard University confirmed that Roosevelt "had always been a boy." A former Secretary of State, Richard Olney, was reminded of the prophecy of Ecclesiastes: *Woe to thee, O land, when thy King is a child and thy princes eat in the morning.* He copied the words out, adding, "The last part of the sentence may be regarded as an extraordinary forecast of the present White House lunches."

It was the lunches, indeed, that made Roosevelt exercise so hard. He enjoyed entertaining as much for the food as for the conversation, and shamelessly hogged both. Talking relieved his mind, but eating had no such purgative effect. The Washington social season was at its height, and whatever fat he burned off during the afternoon was restored, even added to, at nightly receptions and gala dinners. The presidential shirtfront continued to swell with flesh and animal vitality. Roosevelt's monologues grew so uninhibited that some guests wondered what the stewards were serving him. "Theodore is never sober," Henry Adams observed, "only he is drunk with himself and not with rum."

Adams was back in town from Europe, gossipy and peevish as ever after a long stay abroad. He was more saddened than amused by a reunion of the old Hay-Adams circle around Roosevelt's table. "None of us have improved," he wrote afterward. Hay seemed slower and more formal, Lodge looked dangerous with ambition, while the President had become increasingly dogmatic. "He lectures me on history as though he were a high school pedagogue."

The Fifty-seventh Congress, Adams predicted, would not reward Roosevelt with any worthwhile legislation. Other, less grudging observers were not so sure. The President was obviously an adroit politician. Speed was his most astonishing characteristic, combined improbably with thoroughness. Four naval officers gave him an oral briefing, then found, on returning to work, that he had forwarded detailed summaries of their testimony for signature.

Roosevelt made it a point of honor to answer all letters upon receipt, dictating with such rapidity that his stenographers had to operate in shifts. Often he did so while hand-correcting documents already in typescript. ("It makes the letter more personal.") He hesitated only when he had replied to someone in anger. Usually, a milder version went forth, while the original was filed for posterity.

The President was also a cornucopia of policy notes, press releases, instructions, and memoranda. A joke went around that if the mutilated remains of his grandmother were discovered in his cellar, Roosevelt would immediately produce written evidence that he was elsewhere at the time of the crime. His documentary caution extended to tracking down letters of his youth, and asking owners to keep them private. Again and again, White House reporters were reminded that the President must never be quoted. Even paraphrases of his remarks had to be submitted for approval.

This managerial compulsion did not surprise old Washington hands. They had long been aware of the "boy's" maturity of purpose, as of his precocious talent. "Roosevelt," declared Grover Cleveland, "is the most perfectly equipped and the most effective politician thus far seen in the Presidency."

⟿

ON FRIDAY, 3 JANUARY, Mark Hanna issued a press statement on "the present status of the canal question." Why Hanna—a member of the Senate Committee on Interoceanic Canals, but not an active one—should suddenly espouse this subject was a mystery to newsmen. They supposed that a man so tied to Great Lakes shipping and transcontinental railroads might work to quash the idea of any Isthmian waterway—as the directors of Northern Securities were said to be doing. Yet here he was proclaiming himself a canal man, and hinting at his own preference.

Hanna said that, contrary to general belief, the Isthmian Canal Commission was "impressed with the superior advantages of the Panama route." It had recommended Nicaragua "to bring the Frenchmen to terms." And indeed, the Compagnie Nouvelle du Canal de Panama now seemed likely to announce a reduced price for its rights and holdings. Accordingly, "a powerful group of Senators" stood ready to transform the pending Canal Bill in Panama's favor.

At least one reporter—the ubiquitous Walter Wellman—already had a shrewd idea of what the price would be. Wellman did not merely represent the Chicago *Record-Herald* in Washington; he was something of a political operator and go-between. Acting on behalf of the "powerful group," he had cabled Philippe Bunau-Varilla, chief negotiant for the Compagnie in Paris: COMMITTEE SENATE PROBABLY ACCEPT OFFER FORTY MILLIONS. IMPERATIVE NOT HIGHER. MOVE QUICKLY.

On the very morning Hanna's statement was published, a return cable confirmed that the Compagnie would sell all rights and assets for forty million dollars. Admiral John G. Walker, chairman of the Isthmian Canal Commission, delivered the offer to the State Department at noon. Secretary Hay received it without comment. Roosevelt, too, remained silent.

⟿

ON 9 JANUARY, the House of Representatives voted overwhelmingly for Nicaragua, 308 to 2. Senator John Tyler Morgan (D., Alabama) announced that his Committee on Interoceanic Canals would consider the House bill at once, with a view to recommending its passage into law.

The old man could barely control his excitement. After twelve years of invoking visions of a blue, all-American canal, closer to home than France's muddy "ditch," he saw his dream trembling on the verge of reality. The South would have its renaissance as ships of a hundred nations, Nicaragua bound, put in at Gulf ports and loaded rich cargoes of Alabama coal, Mississippi cotton, Tennessee lumber, Florida beef, and Georgia peaches.

Mark Hanna jerked him back to reality at a meeting of the Committee on Thursday, 16 January:

HANNA   I want the report on Nicaragua delayed until the Panama offer has been considered.

MORGAN   It is not worth waiting for.

HANNA   Well, the President thinks it is worth waiting for.

MORGAN   What do you mean by that?

HANNA   I mean that the President has asked Admiral Walker to call the Canal Commission together so it can make a supplemental report for him, which he intends to send to Congress.

MORGAN   Don't believe anything of the kind.

HANNA   Suppose you ask the President.

Morgan hurried to the White House. Roosevelt said that in view of France's new offer, the Canal Commission should be given a chance to "reconsider" its original finding.

Shocked and depressed, Morgan tried to get Admiral Walker to appear before his Committee for an emergency briefing on Friday. But Walker said he was too busy. The President wanted a new, unanimous report, deliverable to the White House "not later than tomorrow evening."

Experience had taught Roosevelt that a Saturday press release was sure of front-page treatment on Sunday or Monday morning—papers on those days being traditionally short of news. The supplemental report was delivered and released on schedule. Its impact was all that he could have desired. COMMISSION SAYS PANAMA IS BEST, proclaimed the New York *Herald*.

The commission thinks it has a good bargain. . . . [It] recites the advantages and the disadvantages of the two routes, showing that the Panama route would be 134.6 miles shorter than the Nicaragua route, with fewer locks and less curvature; that the time of transit through Panama would be twelve hours, against thirty-three hours at Nicaragua . . . that there is already a railroad at Panama which would be very servicable in building the canal; that two artificial harbors would have to be constructed at Nicaragua and only one would be necessary at Panama.

The commission . . . finds now that the reduced offer of the Panama company has made the estimated cost of construction of the Nicaraguan canal $45,630,704 greater than Panama, and the estimated cost of maintenance and operation $1,300,000 greater.

White House messengers transmitted the report to Congress on 20 January. A "Panama boom" began in the Senate, with Aldrich, Allison, and Platt joining Hanna, Spooner, and Lodge on the list of converts. But most of their colleagues awaited the recommendation of Senator Morgan's committee. Morgan himself declared that Theodore Roosevelt was the true author of the new report. "I will strive to defeat it."

For the rest of the week, tension prevailed on Capitol Hill. Groups of well-dressed, whispering men gathered in the byways of the Senate, their numbers increasing daily as trains from New York, Chicago, and the South brought fresh infusions of lobbying power. On Wall Street, Edward H. Harriman began to buy up Panama Canal bonds at 6 percent.

Meanwhile, the shock effect of the "boom" reached as far as Panama City. Separatists there panicked, realizing that an American decision to funnel the world's commerce through their territory would bind them forever to Colombia. If they could only break from Bogotá in time, the golden waterway might be theirs in perpetuity.

⌒

OF ALL THE WELL-DRESSED whisperers who thronged the Capitol in the last weeks of January 1902, none wore finer cloth, or whispered more urgently, than William Nelson Cromwell of New York City, and Philippe Bunau-Varilla, of Paris. Although they were but newly acquainted (Bunau-Varilla was just off a transatlantic steamer), they lobbied for Panama like life-long partners.

Cromwell was the more talkative of the two, at ease in an atmosphere of intrigue. Pop-eyed, cherubic, curly-haired, he had a cute dimple in his pink chin, and his speech fanned a soft, silvery mustache. If the silver was deceptive (he was only forty-seven), the gold elsewhere on his person was genuine, betokening a former Brooklyn boy. Cromwell had earned millions as a trust attorney and American counsel for the Compagnie Nouvelle. But these riches were nothing compared to the commissions and fees he hoped to earn, should Congress accept the Compagnie's new offer. Even at the reduced price of forty million dollars, it would still be the biggest real-estate deal in history.

If Cromwell's relations with the Compagnie Nouvelle were mercenary, Bunau-Varilla's were evangelical and censorious. Passionate in his devotion to French canal technology, he could spit at the incompetents who had mismanaged the great scheme in Panama. "*Asines,*" he called them, "—donkeys, absurd people."

It was hard for Americans not to laugh at Bunau-Varilla bristling, so Gallic was he in his gamecock fierceness, all frown and spiked mustaches. Had he stood a foot taller, he might have looked as formidable as he in fact was. He had the bruising willpower and aristocratic intelligence of the best French *education d'élite*. Yet he had earned that privilege through scholarships. His great wealth, like Cromwell's, was self-made. Bunau-Varilla was secretly a bastard of humble birth.

Now forty-two years old, he had been inspired in youth by Ferdinand de Lesseps, architect of Suez, and architect *manqué* of Panama. Bunau-Varilla had gone to the Isthmus as a civil engineer in 1885, and within a year, through sheer drive, had become head of de Lesseps's vast, floundering project. He had resigned early enough to avoid association with the collapse of the old Compagnie Universelle du Canal Interoceanique, and late enough to become a major stockholder in the Compagnie Nouvelle du Canal de Panama.

Bunau-Varilla therefore stood to make even more money, presumably, than Cromwell on the sale of the Compagnie Nouvelle's assets in 1902. But above profit, above even *travail pour la patrie*, Bunau-Varilla cherished "this great Idea" of a canal linking the Atlantic and the Pacific oceans. As an engineer, he was convinced that Panama was the only feasible route. As a lobbyist, he passionately preached its advantages. The New York *Sun* espoused his cause and proclaimed him "an idealist of the first grade."

⌐☞⌐

ON 24 JANUARY, Roosevelt attended his first Gridiron Club dinner as President of the United States. Mark Hanna was another guest of honor. Both men laughed heartily as an actor impersonating an obsequious Frenchman bowed, scraped, and presented the Senator with a gold brick labeled PANAMA.

⌐☞⌐

AT THE END OF the month, there was an ominous delay in Senate action on the Canal Bill. Senator Morgan announced that his committee was not satisfied as to why the Isthmian Canal Commission had changed its recommendation. Furthermore, he would chair an investigation into the legality of the Compagnie Nouvelle's proposed transfer of rights.

It was all very well for French stockholders to offer "their" property to the United States—but what if Congress paid the forty million dollars, then found that they lacked authority to sell? Colombia had only temporarily ceded France the rights to cut a canal across Panama, and the rights might not be transferable to another power. Morgan insinuated that the "Panama boom" was a nuisance tactic, organized by railroad men who wanted no canal at all.

With new hearings scheduled through spring, it became clear that the Canal Bill would not resurface in Congress until shortly before the summer recess. Legislators turned their attention to more immediate issues: tariff adjustments for the Philippines, reciprocity with Cuba, a quixotic resolution for the direct election of senators. Few noticed, as the bill slipped off the calendar, that it had acquired an unobtrusive amendment, giving the President of the United States the final choice of route. Roosevelt was quick to reward the author of the amendment with Washington's most valuable coinage: free White House access. "When you come here," he wrote John Coit Spooner, "always come straight to my room."

With that, Panama faded from the news, and its lobby from the Capitol. Only Cromwell and Bunau-Varilla remained behind to plot future legislative strategy. They believed that the dry words of the Spooner Amendment would flower like seeds in better political weather. Other Panama promoters, less optimistic, felt that the President had tried to bully Congress and failed.

Jokes began to circulate that "Terrible Teddy" was good for nothing but dining with black men and exercising the diplomatic corps. When the jokes reached Princeton, the beaky professor who had interviewed Roosevelt at Buffalo made a public demand that he be treated with more respect. "He really determines an important part of the destinies of the world," Woodrow Wilson said. Americans would discover soon enough that Theodore Roosevelt was "larger" than they knew, "a very interesting and a very strong man."

⌒

THE PRESIDENT CLIMBED carefully up the beanstalk, an ax in his belt. He clenched his teeth as he tried to separate a tangle of branches above him. High in the sky, on a spreading crest of leaves, sat a giant, gorging and grinning. The giant's knife was sharp and eager over an array of heaped platters. Roosevelt, peering through thick lenses, sensed rather than saw what the dishes contained: helpless, trussed human beings.

From outer space, a pen flew in, loaded with ink. It scratched across the giant's belly, THE TRUSTS, and wrote over Roosevelt's head, WILL JACK REACH THE OGRE?

⌒

A FEW DAYS AFTER Edward Kemble's cartoon appeared in *Life,* Roosevelt told a friend, "The time has come when my course has to be definitely shaped."

It was 5 February 1902. He had been in office nearly five months, listening to advice and experimenting with power, not always successfully. His gesture toward Booker T. Washington looked, in retrospect, more courageous than wise; his reform appointments would show only long-term effects; veterans were upset with him over General Miles; and as for the fine phrases of his First Message to Congress, he heard no chinks from masons immortalizing them in marble. Signs of creeping disillusionment were evident in the press, and on Capitol Hill.

Any fool could tell what the public expected of him. Jack must reach, and grapple with, the ogre of Combination. Mail poured daily into the White

House, urging him to prosecute various trusts under the Sherman Act. He had referred possible suits to the Attorney General, but in all cases save one, Knox saw no grounds for legal action. This exceptional case looked strong enough to go all the way to the Supreme Court, yet it was fraught with political risk. Roosevelt and Knox were careful not to identify "it" in their communications. "Am giving it constant attention," the latter had telegraphed from Florida, "to the end that your wishes, with which I am in full sympathy, can be creditably executed."

Now, eight weeks later, Knox was back in town, but still hedging over his opinion. Roosevelt decided to insist upon it. The Attorney General begged one more week. He canceled all his social engagements from 5 February on, citing "a public duty that will admit of no postponement," and plunged, with renewed energy, into research. As far back as A.D. 483, he found, the Emperor Zeno had directed the Praetorian Prefect of Constantinople, *No one may presume to exercise a monopoly of any kind . . . and if anyone shall presume to practice a monopoly, let his property be forfeited and himself condemned to perpetual exile.*

Plunging deep into sociological theory, Knox postulated the "underlying laws" that linked all social and industrial movements, and the common-law "sanctions" that prompted them. Was it rash of the President to seek sanctions of his own? Knox found enlightenment—as Roosevelt himself had done, years earlier—in Benjamin Kidd's *Social Evolution*. The British philosopher argued that *laissez-faire* economics might suit one stage in a nation's development, but not necessarily the next. Some governmental tamping-down should follow a period of explosive growth. Nor was discipline incompatible with democracy. As Knox himself put it, "Uncontrolled competition, like unregulated liberty, is not really free."

What, then, of the Constitution? Knox brooded over Supreme Court rulings on the Sherman Act. *U.S. v. Trans-Missouri Freight Association* (1897) had concluded that combination in restraint of interstate trade was unlawful "whether reasonable or not." Yet *U.S. v. E. C. Knight* (1895) had condoned some monopolistic practices, and made them difficult to prosecute at the federal level. Knox felt that *Knight* had been badly argued. He saw reversal possibilities in Justice John Harlan's lone dissent. ("Combinations, governed entirely by the law of greed . . . threaten the integrity of our institutions.") And Harlan still sat on the Court.

For once in his cautious career, Knox felt impelled to advise a policy of risk. Even if Roosevelt's suit failed, it would point up the "moral dualism" in contemporary American society, whereby big businessmen exhibited one set of values at home, and another set, tending toward barbarism, at the office. If the suit succeeded, it would more or less guarantee the President a second term. And if he, Philander Chase Knox, argued it before the Supreme Court, persuasively and brilliantly . . .

The Attorney General's astigmatism gave some people the impression that his one eye focused on immediate business, while the other contemplated dreamy horizons, visible only to himself. "Sleepy Phil" was indeed looking beyond books and briefs in 1902—toward the Governorship of Pennsylvania, or to a seat in the Senate, if only old Matt Quay would die. Farther off, in 1908 or 1912, Knox saw an even more pleasing prospect: the job of his current client.

Before the week was over, he was ready with a fourteen-page opinion. He delivered it personally to Roosevelt. "If you instruct me to bring such a suit, I can promise you we shall win it."

⌐⊃—

THE PRESIDENT GAVE only one vague hint of his impending action in the days following. "Mr. Hanna," he said after breakfast on Tuesday, 18 February, "what do you think about the Northern Securities Company?"

Hanna, preoccupied with plans for a business trip to New York, replied that the great trust was "the best thing" that could have happened to the Northwest. As a shareholder and old friend of James J. Hill, he could hardly have said less. That evening, he left town.

⌐⊃—

ON THURSDAY, 20 FEBRUARY, the Senator returned to Washington, and found his train full of trust attorneys. He ran into Knox's predecessor, John W. Griggs, in the parlor car, and asked what was taking him to the capital. Griggs realized that Hanna had not yet seen the morning newspapers.

"The government has brought a suit against the Northern Securities Company."

Hanna was thunderstruck. Knox's overnight statement read:

> Within a very short time a bill will be filed by the United States to test the [combination of] the Northern Pacific and Great Northern systems through the instrumentality of the Northern Securities Company. Some time ago the President requested an opinion as to the legality of this merger, and I have recently given him one to the effect that, in my judgment, it violates the provisions of the Sherman Act of 1890, whereupon he directed that suitable action should be taken to have the question judicially determined.

The statement was typical of Knox in its precise, chilly brevity. It was typical, too, of Roosevelt in its timing. A popular but jurisdictionally weak state suit against Northern Securities, initiated by Governor Samuel R. Van Sant of Minnesota, was about to be thrown out of court. By announcing his own federal suit now, Roosevelt would benefit from the likely publicity. Henceforth

he, and not the Governor, would be seen as David battling the Wall Street Go-
liath.

Knox's willingness to invoke the Sherman Act was concussive in its effect
on financial markets. Even as Hanna stood listening to Griggs in the parlor
car, J. P. Morgan was working to avoid a panic on Wall Street. At first, Morgan had refused to believe the news from Washington. But there had been
such a wild rush to sell at 9:00 A.M., accompanied by reports of "demoral-
ized" exchanges in London, Paris, and Berlin, that his instinctive reaction was
to counterbuy. More stocks fell off the board during the first hour than in a
normal day's trading. Morgan bought steadily through lunchtime, and
around three o'clock prices began to rally.

It had been a near thing. The floor was loud with denunciations of
Theodore Roosevelt. Not since President Cleveland's Venezuela Note in 1895
had stockbrokers been so taken by surprise. An investor who knew the Attorney General rang to ask why he had not gotten "a friendly tip in advance."
Back over the line came Knox's curt reply, "There is no stock ticker in the Department of Justice."

Shortly afterward, all telecommunications with Washington were broken.
A violent snowstorm descended over the Atlantic seaboard, coating the
Northeastern grid with ice. Wires snapped by the thousand, hanging from
their poles in tinkling festoons. By the time Hanna and Griggs reached the
capital, Pennsylvania Avenue was muffled with snow.

⌒

BEFORE NIGHTFALL THE following day, seven representatives of the House
of Morgan had arrived in town, including Morgan himself. He marched
through the Arlington Hotel's slushy entrance under a testudo of umbrellas.
A spokesman announced that the chairman had come south to dine with his
old friend Senator Depew and a group of mutual acquaintances prominent in
politics, finance, and industry. Morgan called this occasional fraternity the
"Corsair Club." The name, taken from his yacht, had waggish associations
with piracy, not to mention his image as captain of the United States economy.

If the purpose of the dinner was convivial, it failed miserably. Henry
Adams described the general mood as "black," and reported that "Pierpont
sulked like a child." When, at ten o'clock, a telephone call from the President
invited Depew to bring his guests around for a visit, Morgan had to be
coaxed to go along. Thirteen Corsairs piled into a series of hacks and automobiles and drove four blocks through the still-falling snow. Roosevelt received them with polite formality. Responding in kind, they stayed off the
subject of Northern Securities.

He was intelligent enough to know they came only because a presidential
invitation could not be declined. Until forty-eight hours before, these men

had stood with him. Now they stood shoulder to shoulder against him, legionnaires of the established economic order, bristling with wealth, courteously hostile behind their breastplates of boiled cotton. Depew. Morgan. Perkins. Rockefeller. Steele. Hanna. Cassatt. Their very names spelled power. So did that of Elihu Root—a Corsair too, and no longer Roosevelt's automatic ally.

The Secretary of War was a bitter man that night. It was humiliating for him to have been surprised by Wednesday's announcement. The knowledge that other Cabinet colleagues had been surprised too only emphasized Knox's sudden ascendancy. Root was convinced that Roosevelt must have "some personal reason" for eschewing his counsel.

Either that, or as Henry Adams put it, "Theodore betrays his friends for his own ambition."

—⌾—

SURE ENOUGH, it was Knox, not Root, who sat at the President's elbow when J. P. Morgan returned to the White House alone the next morning, Saturday, 22 February. Aware, perhaps, that lava was rolling his way, Roosevelt needed the protection of a cool, hard legal front.

There was something volcanic about Morgan. The hot glare and fiery complexion, flushing so deep that the engorged nose seemed about to burst, the smoldering cigar, the mountainous shoulders—merely to look at him was to register tremors.

Yet interlocutors soon discovered that Morgan's sparks and smoke were a kind of screen, concealing someone essentially quiet and shy, almost clerical. As a youth, he had dreamed of becoming a professor of mathematics; he was equally attracted to the rituals of the Episcopal Church, in which he had served as a vestryman for forty years. But he was also the inheritor of a family bank, and had a lightning ability to figure large sums of money. These endowments, plus his involuntary power of domination, made him *de ipse* the nation's financial leader. He sought relief from numbers by collecting indiscriminate quantities of great or ghastly art. His Madison Avenue library bulged with uncut volumes. Occasionally, in country homes, Morgan would fumble at a passing woman.

Whatever qualms the President may have had in granting an interview, he had little difficulty handling Morgan. Or at least Roosevelt chose not to remember any, when recounting the conversation afterward. Morgan had seemed less furious than puzzled. Why had the Administration not asked *him* to correct irregularities in the new trust's charter?

ROOSEVELT	That is just what we did not want to do.
MORGAN	If we have done anything wrong, send your man to my man and they can fix it up.

ROOSEVELT	That can't be done.
KNOX	We don't want to fix it up, we want to stop it.
MORGAN	Are you going to attack my other interests, the Steel Trust and others?
ROOSEVELT	Certainly not—unless we find out that in any case they have done something that we regard as wrong.

Alone with Knox later, Roosevelt mused, "That is a most illuminating illustration of the Wall Street point of view." Morgan could think of the President of the United States only as "a big rival operator" with whom to cut a deal.

⌒

THE HOUSE OF MORGAN was reduced to pleading, in the weeks that followed, that its chairman be spared the indignity of public testimony. He was old; his honor was vital to the nation's credit. Roosevelt asked Knox if it was necessary to include Morgan in the suit. "Well, Mr. President, if you direct me to leave his name out I will," the Attorney General said. "But in that case I will not sign my name to the bill."

Knox's formal complaint, dated 10 March 1902, accordingly listed James J. Hill and J. Pierpont Morgan as defendants. E. H. Harriman, who stood to make more out of the merger than both principals, was granted technical anonymity as an "associate stockholder." But Assistant Attorney General James M. Beck, assigned by Knox to brief the Eighth Circuit Court on the case, named Harriman as one of "the great triumvirate" seeking to impose upon the Northwest a monopoly "infinite in scope, perpetual in character."

⌒

OF THE THREE DEFENDANTS, Hill was the angriest and most determined to fight all the way to the Supreme Court. Morgan and Harriman suggested a settlement, in order to protect their other interests. But Hill insisted on contesting the government's suit. "There is nothing in the operation of the Northern Securities Company that violates the Sherman Law or the laws of any other state." The two railroads named by Knox had been cooperating amicably for twenty years. Indeed, in regions where they could have competed, the Great Northern and Northern Pacific had charged mostly identical rates. Was this the "restraint of trade" Roosevelt sought to prosecute? Hill was damned if he was going to dismantle the world's greatest transport combination because of "political adventurers who have never done anything but pose and draw a salary."

Roosevelt's action won support from both sides of the political field alike, as a much-needed check on the ramifications of *U.S. v. E. C. Knight.* Liberals welcomed a blow struck by authority against monopoly. Conservatives were confident that the Supreme Court would reaffirm that holding-company combinations were both legal and benign.

Roosevelt uttered no predictions and made no boasts. He accepted full responsibility for the suit, even excusing the original plaintiffs in Minnesota. "I am rather inclined to think it was as much a surprise to them as to anyone." He was content, after seizing public attention, to let *Northern Securities v. U.S.* have due process. The case was unlikely to reach the Supreme Court before the winter term of 1903–1904; time enough for trumpeting then, if he won. Until another large matter arose to challenge his powers, he could return to routine presidential affairs.

He pretended to be bored by the state visit of Prince Heinrich of Prussia ("I shall take him out to ride in the rain—and I hope it will rain like hell!"), but obviously enjoyed playing host amid pomp and ceremony. Prince Heinrich was the brother of Kaiser Wilhelm II, and an admiral in the German Navy, so Roosevelt was able to pump him on European politics and naval affairs. When a providential downpour came, he was touched by the efforts of "the wretched creature" to gallop at full speed behind him. Heinrich was rewarded with the most elaborate stag dinner ever seen in Washington.

Alice Roosevelt—debutante of the season, and glowing prettier by the day

"ROOSEVELT . . . TOLD THE DISAPPOINTED GIRL
SHE WOULD HAVE TO STAY HOME."
Father and daughter at the launching of the Kaiser's yacht, 25 February 1902

as the richest bucks in town vied for her favor—attracted even more attention than the royal visitor. Gorgeous in white lace and "Alice blue" velvet, she smashed champagne over a new, American-built yacht, which the Prince had come to pick up for his brother. Heinrich, enchanted, returned home and recommended that Fraulein Alice be invited to visit the Kaiser's court. But Roosevelt decided she should go to London instead, as his representative at King Edward VII's coronation.

He regretted the impulse when a British newspaper counseled that Alice be treated as "the oldest daughter of an Emperor." A Washington scandal sheet began to make arch references to "the Crown Prin— beg pardon— daughter of the President." Roosevelt was annoyed by these intimations of antirepublicanism, and told the disappointed girl she would have to stay home.

In the meantime, he basked in popular praise. Previous Presidents had sued the trusts with various success, but none had done so voluntarily, and with such virile force. He had acted, on grounds few lawyers considered valid, at the height of the greatest merger movement in history.

For these reasons, his old friend Owen Wister placed the *Northern Securities* suit "at the top of all Roosevelt's great and courageous strokes in the domain of domestic statesmanship." Whether fated for good or ill, it had excited public optimism at the very moment that public pessimism saw no end to the tyranny of wealth. "I think that to make up his mind to take this first step, to declare this war, on the captains of industry, was a stroke of genius; and I more than think—I know—that it marked the turn of a rising tide."

CHAPTER 6

Two Pilots Aboard, and Rocks Ahead

It looks to me as if this counthry was
goin' to th' divil.

"CHAOS! EVERYWHERE!" Henry Watterson exulted on 13 March 1902. The veteran Democratic pundit was visiting Washington to scout out future opportunities for his party. "For the first time these thirty years," he reported, "it is the Republicans who are at sea."

Rival hands were tugging at the wheel of the ship of state. One pair belonged to President Roosevelt, who was responsible for last month's violent tack to port; the other to Senator Hanna, who wanted to resume the course set by President McKinley. "Both compass and rudder are still intact," wrote Watterson, enjoying his metaphor. "But there are two pilots aboard, and rocks ahead."

On the very day these remarks were published in *The Washington Post*, the *Washington Times* printed a front-page, foot-high photograph of Hanna, captioned THE MAN OF THE HOUR. Since the caption was very large, and the copyright date *1901* very small, readers were persuaded that the Senator was his old self again. Massive, placid, benign, he loomed from the page, dwarfing the masthead. Gone—or at least refined by studio lighting—was his former porcine flabbiness. Here was Statesmanship, glowing on the fine brow and in the magnificent eyes; here was Solidity and Sound Money.

Hanna's presidential stock had been rising on Wall Street since the *Northern Securities* suit. Bankers and industrialists took his candidacy in 1904 for granted. So did Old Guard politicians in Washington. They estimated that he already had enough delegates to be nominated on the first ballot. His mail was thick with appeals for him to declare, and not all were typed on corporate stationery. "While we admire the presidint Theodore Roosevelt," one correspondent scrawled, "there are such things as being to strenuous, what we wan is a man of the people."

Hanna dismissed the campaign talk as "amusing," but did not discourage it. His backers, led by Senator Nathan B. Scott and other probusiness members of the Republican National Committee, were serious. Laugh as he might—"that smile would grease a wagon," a henchman said—he had to be impressed when five hundred members of the Society of Ohio rose in his honor, waving starched napkins and hailing him as "the next President of the United States."

Deep in his soul, Hanna did not want the job. He was sixty-four and ailing. Every ascent of the Capitol steps in the March wind worsened his bursitis and packed more calcium around his knees. Grief for McKinley still tormented him, as did remorse over their occasional quarrels. He was prone to periods of melancholy, lasting weeks at a time; during these fits, he could not recognize his own son in the street. As for ambition, he had only to watch Roosevelt lustily working the crowd at White House receptions to realize that his senatorial seat suited him much better than the Presidency.

That chair, which he filled so amply it seemed a polished, creaking part of him, emanated prestige rather than power. Hanna had been in the Senate only five years, and was thus junior to more than half of his colleagues. Senator Spooner made more brilliant speeches in a week than Hanna had in his whole career. He could never hope to match the parliamentary skills of an Aldrich or an Allison. Henry Cabot Lodge's orations sounded like Greek to him, and indeed some phrases were.

Yet Hanna's web of influence stretched in so many directions—to the grass roots of party politics, to labor unions and trade associations and countless loyal offices in the civil service—that the Senate leaders granted him extraordinary privileges. They could hardly slight a man whom four out of five voters (according to a recent poll) believed to be "the greatest living American." It was understood that "Uncle Mark" called upon nobody, except the President of the United States. He received callers in the Capitol's vice-presidential suite. When he rose to speak on one of the issues he had made his own—shipping subsidies, labor relations, immigration reform—the Senate always filled, and he was listened to with a hush that sounded louder than applause.

Such eminence, plus a fat portfolio and a box of honor in Cleveland's Hanna Theater, were all that he asked from life. But he must soon campaign for re-election. Clearly, presidential rumors would be to his advantage in rallying the Ohio Republican Party; he should not deny them too vehemently. His disclaimer, when it came, was mild: "I am not in any sense a candidate, and trust my friends will discourage any movement looking toward that end."

The newspapers published this statement in small print, while they headlined a more immediate threat to Roosevelt's authority.

AFTER THREE MONTHS, Nelson A. Miles still bore on his cheek the angry red of reprimand. He wanted revenge on the President and the Secretary of War. Thanks to continued access to War Department materials, he thought he now had a lethal weapon: secret reports of atrocities perpetrated by American forces against the *insurrectos* in the Philippines. Here was an issue which could embarrass Roosevelt and Root, rally all anti-imperialists, and make a political hero of himself. Miles took care, however, not to raise the issue in such a way as to risk further charges of insubordination. As a preliminary move, he granted an interview to Henry Watterson.

The Commanding General, Watterson reported, had been refused permission to visit the Philippines, where he wanted to conduct an inquiry into the insurrection, now more than three years old. Watterson did not state what, exactly, Miles supposed the inquiry might reveal. But he implied that dark truths were being suppressed, to Roosevelt's likely political cost. "As events are lining up in Congress, the paramount issue, the issue of issues, in 1904 will be the Philippines."

The White House remained silent as amplifications of the story spread nationwide on 17 March. Then a furious denunciation of Miles appeared in the *Boston Herald*. Nobody familiar with Rooseveltian invective could doubt who was the "very highest possible authority" cited:

> General Miles's most recent effort to recall himself to public attention . . . is so palpably an effort in his own behalf that the mere statement of it ought to suffice to convince the country of his insincerity. . . . His whole effort is to discredit the Administration. He is becoming daily more and more of an intriguer, and therefore more and more useless as the head of the Army. . . . There is absolutely no truth in the statement that the President and Secretary Root fear General Miles, or are personally uneasy because of anything he may do.

Not content with this, Roosevelt dictated an open letter to Miles, full of recriminations. "I do not like the clear implication . . . that brutalities have been committed by our troops in the Philippines." He admitted that there had been "sporadic cases" of violence against prisoners. But these were inevitable in war, as the general must surely remember from the days when he was tracking Geronimo. "In the Wounded Knee fight the troops under your command killed squaws and children as well as unarmed Indians."

The letter was deemed too confrontational to send, let alone publish, so he unbosomed himself in a series of memoranda to Elihu Root. He wanted the record to show that Miles had once approached him in an "utterly fatuous" attempt to run against William McKinley. "To my mind his actions can bear only the construction that his desire is purely to gratify his selfish ambition, his vanity, or his spite."

The memos were classified *Confidential, Private,* and *Personal.* Root filed them, knowing such strictures, in Roosevelt's parlance, usually meant "Hold for Publication." He had hardly done so, indeed, before Congress asked for documents relating to Miles's insinuations, and the President sanctioned their release.

Root wrote separately to Henry Cabot Lodge, whose Senate Committee on the Philippines was considering a transition from military to civil government in the archipelago. He acknowledged forty-four cases of documented cruelty, of which thirty-nine had already resulted in convictions under the military justice system. Aside from these isolated lapses, "the war in the Philippines has been conducted by the American army . . . with self-restraint, and with humanity, never surpassed, if ever equaled, in any conflict."

Root's words masked embarrassment, for he knew that Miles had gotten hold of a secret report that indicated otherwise. It came from the military governor of Tayabas, Major Cornelius Gardener, and described how the *barrios* of that once-peaceful province had been brutalized by American soldiers. Gardener spoke of "deep hatred toward us," and, more disturbingly, of reciprocal prejudice against the Filipinos: "Almost without exception, soldiers, and also many officers, refer to the natives in their presence as 'niggers', and the natives are beginning to understand what 'nigger' means."

So damning was the Gardener Report that Governor William Howard Taft had suppressed it for seven weeks, on the querulous ground that it might be "biassed." Root was guilty of delay himself, having sent his copy back to Manila, by slow sea mail, for "verification." He had done so, however, for sensibly strategic reasons. The insurrection was in fact almost over, and a final surrender by holdout guerrillas was expected within weeks. The honor of American arms, of Republican foreign policy, demanded a clean, decisive victory.

⁂

GENERAL MILES MOVED adroitly during the next few weeks. He made no attempt to leak the Gardener Report, beyond letting Democrats in Congress know it existed. They began to press for its publication. Meanwhile, he set about sabotaging another aspect of Administration policy. Tall and dignified in his coruscating uniform, he dominated the Senate Committee on Military Affairs hearings on the Army Bill.

This measure, the most profound review of American military organization in more than a century, was the fruit of several years' hard labor by Elihu Root. It sought to make line and staff officers interchangeable, to promote by merit rather than seniority, and to create a general staff answerable to the Secretary of War. More to the point, it also sought to abolish the system whereby Root administered, and Miles commanded, the Army on a coequal basis.

Root wanted a vertical structure that sent power down from himself to a Chief of Staff. The office of Commanding General would therefore be abolished. Root counted on the approval of the American people, in view of their "ingrained tendency . . . to insist upon civilian control of the military arm."

Miles reminded the Senate Committee that the American people also had a prejudice against authoritarianism. He glittered to great effect while portraying Roosevelt and Root as executive upstarts who wished to create a monarcho-militarist court, like that of the Kaiser in Germany. The concept of a general staff was "utterly subversive to the interests of the military establishment." Miles hitched back his epaulets and declared in martyred tones that he would rather resign than submit to "despotism" from the White House.

Senator Joseph Hawley, the chairman of the committee, was himself a retired major general. He praised Miles's testimony as "unanswerable," and allowed that the Army Bill, as presently drafted, would receive no further consideration. GENERAL MILES WINS, *The Washington Post* blazed, while Watterson congratulated the American people on escaping "an Act to make the President of the United States a military dictator."

Root's expressionless calm in the face of this defeat boded ill for Miles. Few doubted that the Commanding General would be dismissed for insubordination. Yet day after day went by with no action by the White House. March gave way to April. Miles and Root continued to work in their opposing suites in the War Department, striding past each other in contemptuous silence.

Roosevelt was struggling with contrary impulses of rage and caution. Miles was "a perfect curse," but his huge popularity both inside and outside Congress could not be ignored. To dismiss him now might sabotage the Army Bill forever, and set Miles up as a sentimental favorite for the Democratic presidential nomination.

Perhaps, after all, he should be allowed to visit the Philippines. The thought of Miles having to endure a forty-nine-day ocean voyage was pleasing, and with luck his visit would coincide with the mosquito season. But what atrocities might he uncover there, to the detriment of Roosevelt's own candidacy in 1904? "It is getting to be a case," the President complained, "of whether I can longer permit great damage to the Army for the sake of avoiding trouble to myself."

❦

LODGE'S COMMITTEE ON the Philippines reluctantly published the Gardener Report on 11 April. It caused instant national outrage. Two days later, the Anti-Imperialist League released the even more shocking confession of a Major C. M. Waller, on trial for genocide in Samar:

Q   Had you any orders from General [Jacob H.] Smith to kill and burn? If
     so, state all that he said.
A   "I wish you to kill and burn. The more you kill and the more you burn,
     the better you will please me." Not once only, but several times . . .
Q   Did you ever ask General Smith whom he wished you to kill?
A   Yes. He said he wanted all persons killed who were capable of bearing
     arms, and I asked if he would define the age limit.
Q   What did General Smith say?
A   "Ten years."

Waller also quoted a written order from the general: "The interior of
Samar must be made a howling wilderness."

No sooner had the phrases *kill and burn* and *howling wilderness* registered on the American conscience than a third, *water cure,* came out of the
Committee hearings. Witness after witness testified to widespread use by
American soldiers of this traditional torture, developed by Spanish priests as
a means of instilling reverence for the Holy Ghost:

> A man is thrown down on his back and three or four men sit on his
> arms and legs and hold him down and either a gun barrel or a rifle
> barrel or a carbine barrel or a stick as big as a belaying pin . . . is sim-
> ply thrust into his jaws . . . and then water is poured onto his face,
> down his throat and nose . . . until the man gives some sign of giving
> in or becomes unconscious. . . . His suffering must be that of a man
> who is drowning, but who cannot drown.

Other reports spoke of natives being flogged, toasted, strung up by their
thumbs, and tattooed "facially" for identification.

Amid mounting cries of revulsion, the President swung into action. He
met with his Cabinet on 15 April, and demanded a full briefing on the Philippine situation. Root said defensively that one officer accused of water torture
had been ordered to report for trial. Roosevelt was not satisfied. His entire insular policy was in danger, not to mention his reputation for decent gover-
nance. He directed Root to flash a cable to Major General Adna Chaffee,
Commander of the Philippines Army:

THE PRESIDENT DESIRES TO KNOW IN THE FULLEST AND
MOST CIRCUMSTANTIAL MANNER ALL THE FACTS. . . . FOR
THE VERY REASON THAT THE PRESIDENT INTENDS TO
BACK UP THE ARMY IN THE HEARTIEST FASHION IN EVERY
LAWFUL AND LEGITIMATE METHOD OF DOING ITS WORK,
HE ALSO INTENDS TO SEE THAT THE MOST VIGOROUS
CARE IS EXERCISED TO DETECT AND PREVENT ANY

CRUELTY OR BRUTALITY, AND THAT MEN WHO ARE
GUILTY THEREOF ARE PUNISHED. GREAT AS THE
PROVOCATION HAS BEEN IN DEALING WITH FOES WHO
HABITUALLY RESORT TO TREACHERY MURDER AND
TORTURE AGAINST OUR MEN, NOTHING CAN JUSTIFY OR
WILL BE HELD TO JUSTIFY THE USE OF TORTURE OR
INHUMAN CONDUCT OF ANY KIND ON THE PART OF THE
AMERICAN ARMY.

Roosevelt also ordered the court-martial of General Smith, "under conditions which will give me the right of review." These gestures, which coincided
with the surrender of Miguel Malvar, the last uncaptured Filipino guerrilla
leader, relieved pressure on the White House, if not the War Department.
Tired and depressed, the Secretary sailed for a working vacation in Cuba.

CALLS FOR ROOT'S resignation followed him across the water. When General Smith admitted, on 25 April, to having authorized the slaughter of Filipino boys, even loyal Republicans were revolted. "It is almost incredible,"
the Philadelphia *Press* commented, "that an American officer of any rank
could have issued an order so shameful, inhuman, and barbarous." Root was
accused of a cover-up, or at least a reluctance to prosecute Army cruelty. "If
we are to 'benevolently assimilate' Filipinos by such methods," remarked the
New Orleans *Times-Democrat,* "we should frankly so state, and drop our
canting hypocrisy about having to wage war on these people for their own
betterment."

Roosevelt again made no effort to help his beleaguered Secretary. Relations between them had been strained since the *Northern Securities* suit.
Root's mood was not improved by his awareness that the President had
known at least "the essence" of General Smith's murderous policies for four
months. Their tacit understanding had been that commanders such as Smith
should be allowed to end the war quickly, with not too many questions asked.

Like all conservatives, Root disliked being called a reactionary. He sought
to build policy on "good and essential" truths, historically tested. One such
truth was that democracy had not succeeded in Asia—except, after a fashion,
among the sophisticated Japanese. Most Filipinos were "but little advanced
from pure savagery." For every case of water torture the anti-imperialists
might name, he could cite instances where American boys had been mutilated
and burned alive—sometimes after honoring a white flag. One could no more
trust than treat with the *insurrectos;* they were "Chinese" in their obtuseness.
Miguel Malvar's surrender document stated that all his people wanted was
"independence under a protectorate." This pathetic desire to be both liberated and looked after suggested that Kipling had been right about the White

Man's Burden. America had a moral duty toward her "new-caught sullen peoples, half-devil and half-child." They had been taught the harsh discipline of war, and must now adapt to the milder discipline of civil government.

In formulating his attitude toward Filipinos, Root relied on the dispatches of William Howard Taft. The Governor was a convert to the "moral mandate" philosophy. When first sent to the archipelago in 1900, he had been an anti-imperialist. Massive, patient, capable, radiating goodwill, he had both charmed and reassured the enemy, whom he embraced collectively as "our little brown brother." American soldiers in the field sang over their campfires:

> He may be a brother of Big Bill Taft,
> But he ain't no brother of mine.

Taft had succeeded so well in the Philippines, as diplomat and executive, that his conversion to imperialism passed almost unnoticed. Only recipients of his classified dispatches understood how deeply he despised the people he governed.

Filipinos, Taft wrote, were "the greatest liars it has ever been my fortune to meet." The educated minority were "ambitious as Satan and quite as unscrupulous." The rest—some six and a half million peasants and jungle tribesmen—were inferior to "the most ignorant negro," and "utterly unfit" for self-government. "They need the training of fifty or a hundred years before they shall even realize what Anglo-Saxon liberty is."

These sentiments, while not uncommon, had force coming from a man widely believed to be of presidential caliber. Root chose not to reveal that it had been Taft who had initially delayed the Gardener Report. Silent, stern, and loyal, he expressed no chagrin over Roosevelt's lack of sympathy. Solace was available in the form of a historic task in Havana. Under soothing fans in the Palacio del Gobernador, Root negotiated the final details of Cuban independence.

—◦—

THE PRESIDENT REMAINED oddly optimistic, although he had more reasons than Root to be gloomy. For the first time since his accession to power, he began to feel real opposition building up against him in Congress. Republican conservatives in the House had reacted contemptuously to an Administration measure aimed at giving Cuba tariff reciprocity as a present for independence. Democratic senators were using Root's refusal to resign as an excuse to block passage of the Philippines civil-government bill. And on Wall Street, rumors that Attorney General Knox was going to proceed against the "Beef Trust" had strengthened corporate longings for a President Hanna.

"Theodore is a total, abject, hopeless failure," Henry Adams reported with satisfaction. "He was always what we, in the language of praise, called a damn fool, and he has become a damn nuisance. . . . At this rate, he will bring the government to a standstill in a year."

If so, the members of his Cabinet did not seem too worried. On 24 April they invited him to join them on a stag cruise in celebration of John D. Long's retirement as Secretary of the Navy. Long himself acted as host aboard USS *Dolphin.*

The little white yacht glided down the Potomac on the evening breeze. She gave off sounds of band music, while a huge, air-filled dolphin swung at her masthead. When the boat returned after dinner, Long's guests were seen standing on deck in white ties and tails, drinking brandy and coffee, under strings of colored lights. A Navy fiddler began to play bluegrass tunes. The President seized Philander Knox and began to dance. John Hay, tiny, dapper, and white-bearded, launched into a sedate two-step, while Leslie Shaw and Henry Payne "shook down" with Midwestern skill. At the climax of the reel, James Wilson, an awkward six foot three, disgraced the Department of Agriculture by falling down. Roosevelt's high-pitched laughter could be heard across the water. "Get up, you old cornstalk!"

His good cheer may have been helped by an awareness that the Fifty-seventh Congress was dying, while his Administration was becoming stronger and more Rooseveltian. The appointments of Shaw as Treasury Secretary and Clay Payne as Postmaster General had been political rather than ideological. Long's retirement (which he had accepted "with regret" but alacrity) gave him the opportunity to hire Representative William Henry Moody of Massachusetts, a forty-eight-year-old expansionist and "big navy man," who could be relied on to keep the flag flying over the Philippines.

SPRING CAME TO the capital in an efflorescence of azaleas, dogwood, and magnolia, affecting even the dyspeptic Adams with a sense of rising sap and "restless maternity." Newlywed couples strolled the Mall—Washington now outranked Niagara as a sexual shrine—holding hands and asking directions in a rich variety of accents. The air grew daily warmer. Mockingbirds began to sing on the White House grounds. Roosevelt and his wife took to sitting on the South Portico, talking of the things that had linked them since childhood: flowers, poetry, the tales of Uncle Remus. They breathed the scents of the garden, and watched the moon whitening the Washington Monument.

An especial closeness linked them this season, because Edith felt maternal pangs stirring within her. The President boasted to complete strangers that he expected "a most important event in his household," come October.

ELIHU ROOT RETURNED from Cuba to find a virulent pamphlet making the rounds, entitled "Secretary Root's Record: Marked Severities in Philippine

Warfare." Published by the Anti-Imperialist League, it was more spiteful than accurate, and Roosevelt decided that the time had come for a counteroffensive. He summoned Henry Cabot Lodge and asked him to defend Root on the floor of the Senate.

When Lodge rose to do so on 5 May, every seat in the chamber was taken. He began by admitting "with deep regret" that a number of American soldiers had tortured and killed Filipino guerrillas. No effort would be spared to bring the guilty to judgment. "But why," he asked rhetorically, "did these things happen?"

He began to read an official catalog of horrors that soon had his audience wincing. Some American prisoners of war had had their eyes slashed, their ears cut off, and their bowels hacked out. Others had been slow-roasted, dismembered with axes, buried alive, and stoned to death. Drowning men had been used for target practice. Medics had been knifed in the back as they tended the wounded. Lodge could not bring himself to report publicly, as he did in private, that some captives had been castrated and gagged with their own testicles. "Perhaps," he drawled in his dry voice, "the action of the American soldier is not altogether without provocation."

Over the next few days, a barrage of pro-Administration statements, interviews, and editorials appeared in the Republican press. Reasonable voices were heard suggesting that the Army should be allowed to complete its current investigations, notably that of General Smith, before Elihu Root was held to further account. Groaningly, the big Philippines civil-government bill began to move toward passage. It promised a legislative assembly, an independent judiciary, and an expanding array of civil rights. Senate Republicans closed ranks behind it.

Only George F. Hoar of Massachusetts—stately, white-haired, Ciceronian—joined the Democratic opposition in calling for a declaration of total independence for the Filipinos. His eloquence was such that Roosevelt interrupted a Sunday walk to pluck at his toga. "I sympathize with—I sympathize with you," the President said, stuttering in his earnestness. "I agree with you entirely, but how can I make any declaration just now? You respect Governor Taft? Don't you?"

Hoar evaded the question, but, like Senator Hanna, could not help being beguiled by the questioner. "Everybody that knows President Roosevelt knows his sincerity," he wrote the veteran anti-imperialist Carl Schurz.

⌐⊙⌐

ROOSEVELT'S DESIRE TO hold on to the Philippines, for strategic and idealistic reasons, did not affect his corresponding urge to let go of Cuba, the independence of which he and the Rough Riders had fought for in 1898. What better time to do so than now—and who more fitting to represent him at the transition ceremony than his old comrade, the military governor of the island, Brigadier General Leonard Wood?

A few seconds before noon on 20 May 1902, Wood clicked to attention in Havana's Palacio del Gobernador, before an audience of local dignitaries. "Sirs," he read, "under the direction of the President of the United States I now transfer to you as the duly elected representatives of the people of Cuba the government and control of the island—"

On the roof of the palace, Lieutenant Frank McCoy prepared for flagstaff duty. The Stars and Stripes hung above him, its folds barely heaving. Below, in the Plaza de Armas, a dense crowd sweated with anticipation. Thousands more Cubans jammed the adjoining streets and every balcony, turret, and tree with a view. Even the harbor swarmed. Boats heavy with spectators jostled at anchor, under a shimmer of bunting.

"—and I hereby declare the occupation of Cuba by the United States and by the military government of the island to be ended." Wood saluted President Tomás Estrada Palma and handed over the documents of transfer.

From far across town, the Cayabas cannons boomed. Lieutenant McCoy remained at attention. He had to count forty-five concatenations, one for every state of the Union, before he hauled down a flag that he would have preferred to keep flying. Both he and General Wood felt they were abandoning a "saved" people to perdition.

By any standards, Wood's two-and-a-half-year governorship had been a spectacular success. A trained surgeon, he had transformed Cuba from one of the world's most pestilential countries into one of its healthiest. He had achieved the "miracle" of eliminating *Stegomyia fasciata*. As a result, Cuba was free of yellow fever for the first time in almost two centuries. The miracle had not happened gently. Doors barred against Wood's sanitation teams had been smashed open, *hidalgos* forced to pick up their own litter, and public defecators horsewhipped at the scene of the crime. Buildings in Havana and Santiago de Cuba had been purged with disinfectant so strong that "even insects came out of the ground to die." But, thanks to this draconian treatment, Havana was now a more sanitary city than Washington, D.C.

The cannons continued to thud as the crowd grew restless. Cubans had mixed feelings about what was happening. The old "Cuba-Libre" coalition—intellectuals, radicals, and peasants—welcomed the departure of the *yanquis*. Yet what Wood called the island's "better class"—businessmen, teachers, merchants, plantation owners—regretted the hasty withdrawal of funds and social services. Wood, after all, had built three thousand new schools. He had paved Havana's dirt streets, and transformed its parks from dangerous jungles into safe gardens. He had catacombed the city with new sewer systems, water mains, and conduits for power and communications. He had even protected the Cuban economy from exploitation by American entrepreneurs.

What protection, the "better class" wanted to know, could President Palma guarantee? Who would teach in the new schools, and out of what textbooks? Who would buy the sugar sacks already crowding every warehouse?

The forty-fifth cannon blast sounded. Lieutenant McCoy stepped to the flagstaff and undid the halyards. Old Glory seemed reluctant to descend. It sank a few feet, then the cords snagged, and it briefly rose.

There were groans and catcalls in the plaza. McCoy pulled till the cloth tumbled about him. To thunderous cheers, General José Miguel Gomez, hero of the war against Spain, appeared on the roof to hoist the colors of *Cuba Libre*. But the cords snagged again, and Gomez asked for a lighter flag. It fluttered aloft amid screams, tears, and ragged blasts of artillery.

"IT FLUTTERED ALOFT AMID SCREAMS, TEARS, AND
RAGGED BLASTS OF ARTILLERY."
Independent Cuba raises her flag, 20 May 1902

As soon as protocol permitted, General Wood bade President Estrada Palma farewell. He drove down to the harbor, escorted by troopers of the Seventh Cavalry, and boarded the USS *Brooklyn*. The white cruiser weighed anchor at four o'clock. A hundred thousand pairs of eyes watched it steam north past the wreck of the *Maine,* upon which some grateful islander had tossed a chain of flowers.

CHAPTER 7

Genius, Force, Originality

What's all this about Cubia an' th' Ph'lipeens?
What's beet sugar?

THEODORE ROOSEVELT'S TOTAL lack of inhibition—some said, of decorum—was much discussed at Washington dinner tables in the spring of 1902. Whether exercising, working, or pricking the bubbles of solemnity around him, he seemed unconcerned by his growing reputation as "the strangest creature the White House ever held."

On 28 May, he was seen hanging from a cable over the Potomac, presumably in some effort to toughen his wrists. Owen Wister caught him walking behind John Hay on tiptoe, bowing like an obsequious Oriental. This might or might not have been connected with the fact that Roosevelt was currently studying *jujitsu*. White House groundsmen, unaware that he was a published ornithologist, were puzzled by his habit of standing under trees, motionless, for long periods of time. Hikers in Rock Creek Park learned to take cover when he galloped by, revolver in hand; he had a habit of "popping" shortsightedly at twigs and stumps with live ammunition.

Petitioners visiting the Executive Office learned to keep talking, because the President usually had an open book on his desk, and was quite capable of snatching it up when the conversation flagged. One day, the French Ambassador, Jules Cambon, found Roosevelt supine on the sofa, kicking his heels in the air. Cambon invited him to attend the dedication of an American monument to Comte de Rochambeau, whereupon Roosevelt, still kicking, yelled, "All right! Alice and I will go! Alice and I are toughs!"

On another occasion he appeared in George Cortelyou's antechamber and jumped clean over a chair. He encouraged his big horse, Bleistein, to similar arts of levitation at the Chevy Chase Club. Photographs of them airborne together soon appeared in the *Washington Times*. Roosevelt was delighted—

"THEODORE ROOSEVELT'S TOTAL LACK OF INHIBITION . . .
WAS MUCH DISCUSSED AT WASHINGTON DINNER TABLES."
Graduation ceremony at United States Naval Academy, 1902

"Best pictures I've ever had taken!"—and passed out autographed copies to his Cabinet.

Hay, who as Secretary of State stood next in line to succeed Roosevelt, pretended to be annoyed at Bleistein's easy clearance of the rails. "Nothing ever happens," he complained.

⌒

ROOSEVELT MIGHT HAVE said the same about the Fifty-seventh Congress. Only one of the requests in his First Annual Message had been enacted: the establishment of a permanent Census Bureau. Senators Aldrich and Allison were maddeningly vague about what remained on the calendar. The President despaired of being able to affect them with any sense of social urgency. Friends took the brunt of his impatience. "Get action; do things; be sane," he snapped at a former Rough Rider. "Don't fritter away your time. . . . Be somebody; get action."

Behind the harsh ejaculations lay anger at his failure to "get action" himself—in particular the Philippines civil-government bill, which he needed to show that the Administration's colonial policy in the Far East was as enlightened as it had been in the Caribbean. It galled him that Senator Hoar was still calling for Philippine independence, in tones of majestic condemnation:

You have wasted six hundred millions of treasure. You have sacrificed nearly ten thousand American lives—the flower of our youth. You have devastated provinces. You have slain uncounted thousands of the people you desire to benefit. . . . I believe—nay, I know—that in general our officers are humane. But in some cases they have carried on your warfare with a mixture of American ingenuity and Castilian cruelty.

Hoar was addressing himself to Republican imperialists generally, but the words *you* and *your* sounded uncomfortably specific, as far as Roosevelt was concerned.

At Arlington National Cemetery, on Memorial Day, the President came to the defense of his Philippines policy. "Oh my comrades," he cried at grizzled ranks of Civil War veterans, "the men in the uniform of the United States who have for the last three years patiently and uncomplainingly championed the American cause in the Philippine Islands, are your younger brothers, your sons." They were fighting to impose "orderly freedom" upon a fragmented nation, according to rules of "just severity" sanctioned by Abraham Lincoln. On Mindanao as at Gettysburg, "military power is used to secure peace, in order that it may itself be supplanted by the civil power."

Roosevelt reminded his audience that legislation to that effect was now before Congress. There was scattered applause. "We believe that we can rapidly teach the people of the Philippine Islands . . . how to make good use of their freedom."

The year's first hot sun beat down on bald heads and bright medals. A breeze came off the Potomac, stirring hundreds of flags up the hill, and swaying the oaks over Roosevelt's head. Invisible choirs of seventeen-year cicadas buzzed in counterpoint to his voice. Perhaps Filipinos would govern themselves the next time locusts sang at Arlington. Perhaps not. "When that day will come," Roosevelt shouted, "it is not in human wisdom to foretell."

For the time being, America's global interests mandated a continuing presence in Manila. "The shadow of our destiny . . ."

He had been working on his speech for weeks, in an attempt to make it the first great oration of his Presidency. But another shadow darkened his face, and he improvised a sudden, disastrous apologia for the recent military scandals:

Is it only in the army in the Philippines that Americans sometimes commit deeds that cause all other Americans to regret? No! From time to time there occur in our country, to the deep and lasting shame of our people, lynchings carried on under circumstances of inhuman cruelty and barbarity—cruelty infinitely worse than any that has ever been committed by our troops in the Philippines—worse to the victims, and far more brutalizing to those guilty of it.

Had he spat upon the porch of the Custis-Lee Mansion, he could not have more effectively unified Democratic opposition to the Philippines bill. The ugly word *lynchings,* which he had so far avoided using in public, sounded deliberately provocative. "I do not think the South will care much for Mr. Roosevelt after this," said an outraged Dixie Senator. "He is dead so far as my section is concerned."

Sure enough, when the bill came up for vote on 3 June, the Senate divided along party lines. The Republican majority prevailed (Senator Hoar alone dissenting), but Roosevelt took no credit for the vote. Neither could he console himself with Northern reaction to his outburst: even the New York newspapers called it "indiscreet," "unfortunate," and "in extremely bad taste." Bruised and rueful, he hoped for passage of his Cuban reciprocity bill, as a sign that Congress was not totally hostile toward him.

⟿

ANOTHER MEASURE, HOWEVER, had precedence in the legislative logjam. On Wednesday, 4 June, Senator Morgan called for the reading of House Resolution 3110, "To provide for the construction of a canal connecting the waters of the Atlantic and Pacific Oceans." Despite January's Canal Commission turnaround on Panama, Morgan was confident that the Nicaragua route would prevail. His own Committee on Interoceanic Canals had reported in favor of it, seven to four. Parliamentary rules required a reading of Senator Spooner's half-forgotten amendment to the resolution:

> *Be it enacted & c. That the President of the United States is hereby authorized to acquire, for and on behalf of the United States, at a cost not exceeding $40,000,000, the rights, concessions, grants of lands [etc.] owned by the New Panama Canal Company, of France. . . . The President is hereby authorized to acquire . . . a strip of land, the territory of the Republic of Colombia, ten miles in width, extending from the Caribbean Sea to the Pacific Ocean . . . and to excavate, construct, and to perpetually maintain, operate and protect thereon, a canal, of such depth and capacity as will afford convenient passage of ships of the greatest tonnage and draft now in use.*

Morgan laid down his copy of the amendment with an old man's tremor, and made his final, weary plea for the Nicaragua route. He had no new technological arguments to present. Instead, he spent half an hour condemning Panama as a cesspool of racial and political squalor. He expressed Alabaman disgust for its "low grade" population. Panamanians were not only unclean, but unstable: they lived—always had lived—in "a chronic state of insurrection and violence" against the authority of Bogotá.

Senator Hanna sat listening, the stillest man in the room. Morgan pointed out that the Treaty of New Granada (1846) actually obligated the United States to hold Colombia together, in exchange for railroad rights across the Isthmus. A commitment was a commitment.

Storming on, the withered little Senator waxed prophetic. Should Washington show the least inclination to ignore the treaty, "There is no doubt that Panama would eagerly seek protection under the folds of the flag of the United States." And should an American President be so rash as to extend that flag, "It would poison the minds of the people against us in every Spanish-American republic in the Western Hemisphere."

As soon as Morgan sat down, Hanna was on his feet. "Mr. President, I desire to give notice that I will address the Senate tomorrow at two o'clock on the pending bill."

⟿

WHEN SENATORS RECONVENED on 5 June, they were surprised to find the chamber festooned with maps and diagrams. One twenty-foot projection, hanging from the visitors' gallery, showed red and black dots splotching Central America. The dots represented volcanoes, active and extinct. Those in red were lined up mainly with Nicaragua. Panama was dot-free.

Hanna entered to a whirring of press telephones. Latecomers hurried to their seats as he sorted a mass of books and papers. He began to speak in his customary lackluster style. "Mr. President, the question of transportation is one of the important items of the day."

The chamber settled down to being informed rather than entertained. Not for Hanna the old-fashioned eloquence of Senator Hoar. He deemed it irrelevant to a new, statistical century. Of his eighty-eight listeners, forty-one were for Nicaragua, thirty-five for Panama, and twelve undecided. Data, not dramatics, would get him the ten further votes he needed. "I was once," he admitted, "in favor of the Nicaragua Canal." But after two years of reflection, "I have been forced by stubborn facts and conditions to change my mind."

For the next one and a half hours, Hanna funneled his "stubborn facts" like wheat into the Senate granary. Every dry grain had its kernel of persuasion. "The Panama route is forty-nine miles long, as against one hundred eighty-three miles of the Nicaragua. . . . Trade winds blow every day in the year from sixteen to twenty knots across the Nicaragua route. . . . The annual cost of operating the Nicaragua Canal is one million, three hundred and fifty thousand dollars, or, say one million, three hundred—"

"Oh, do make him sit down," came a woman's voice from the gallery. It was a cry of concern more than boredom: Hanna's arthritis was visibly tormenting him. He said that he would conclude his speech the next day.

Polls in smoke-filled rooms that night indicated that the majority of senators favoring Nicaragua had already diminished. Cromwell and Philippe

Bunau-Varilla lobbied like men possessed, while Senator Morgan's lieu-tenants tried to fight attrition with scandal. They whispered that French shareholders of the Compagnie Nouvelle would not see a dime of the forty-million-dollar transfer fee, and that President Roosevelt, Secretary Hay, and Senator Spooner were the likely beneficiaries, along with Hanna, Cromwell, and Bunau-Varilla. Even "Princess Alice" was rumored to be in on the deal.

༄

HANNA RESUMED HIS speech as soon as the Senate reopened for business on Friday, 6 June. Pointing to the splotched volcanic map, he said he wished to discuss "the burning question" of igneous activity in the Caribbean region. Just the previous month, Mont Pelée in Martinique had erupted, killing forty thousand people. Panama was "exempt" from this kind of danger. Not so Nicaragua, which lay along an almost continuously volcanic tract extending northwest from Costa Rica. Senator Morgan's canal would cut straight across that tract—"probably the most violently eruptive of any in the West-ern Hemisphere." Mount Momotombo, a hundred miles from the proposed route, had blown up only two months prior to Pelée. Had it done so with equal force, it would have precipitated "enough cinders and lava . . . to fill up the basin of Lake Managua."

For another hour, Hanna cited alarming seismological, social, and navi-gational evidence against Nicaragua. Even as he spoke, Mont Pelée was erupting again. Reports of his speech in the evening newspapers jostled news of sky-darkening clouds and six-foot fluctuations of sea level.

༄

AS LONG AS THE canal debate lasted, the President kept his own counsel. Two senators visited him with learned arguments for Nicaragua, and he lis-tened to them solemnly, scribbling on a notepad. Had they been able to look over his shoulder, they would have seen that he was merely doodling the names of his children, over and over again.

༄

MEANWHILE, HIS CUBAN reciprocity bill was being lobbied to death. The House of Representatives had authorized him to grant a 20 percent tariff re-duction on all Cuban exports to the United States—with the exception of re-fined sugar, which could come in free. But this last, seemingly generous provision guaranteed opposition in the upper chamber. Senators beholden to the American refining industry—mainly Easterners, mainly Democrats—objected to foreign favoritism, while Senators from states that produced beet sugar—mainly Westerners, mainly Republicans—condemned the bill as an-tiprotectionist. "I wish," Roosevelt sighed, "that Cuba grew steel and glass."

Common sense suggested that he leave trade policy to such experts as Nelson Aldrich. But his always active conscience ("In this particular case of reciprocity a moral question is concerned") plagued him. And morality aside, he believed that commercial sweets would reconcile Cubans to the sour taste of a United States garrison at Guantánamo.

On 13 June, Roosevelt took the bold step of sending Congress a "Special Message on Cuba." He did so knowing that the Message could well fail, and advertise to the world that he had no power of presidential persuasion. It might even lead to a general tariff battle, a split party, and defeat for himself in 1904. His hope against hope was that the warring senators would be shamed into a compromise. "Cuba is a young republic," he wrote, "still weak, who owes to us her birth, whose future, whose very life, must depend on our attitude toward her."

Some senators detected a note of self-identification in this appeal, and guffawed as it was read aloud. Meanwhile, sugar-heavy freighters wallowed in the island's ports, symbols of prosperity held in check.

ANOTHER CAUSE DEAR to Roosevelt's heart—reclamation of the arid West—was preoccupying the House that same day. He did not want to have a second Special Message laughed at, so he wrote a passionate letter to the chairman of the House Appropriations Committee:

> *My dear Mr. Cannon:* I do not believe that I have ever before written to an individual legislator in favor of an individual bill, but I break through my rule to ask you as earnestly as I can not to oppose the [National Reclamation Bill]. Believe me this is something of which I have made a careful study, and great and real though my deference is for your knowledge of legislation, and for your attitude in stopping expense, yet I feel from my acquaintance with the Far West that it would be a genuine and rankling injustice for the Republican party to kill this measure. I believe in it with all my heart from any standpoint. . . . Surely it is but simple justice for us to give the arid regions a measure of relief, the financial burden of which will be but trifling. . . . I cannot too strongly express my feeling upon this matter. *Faithfully yours,*
>
> THEODORE ROOSEVELT

Representative Joseph ("Not One Cent for Scenery") Cannon was Congress's leading anticonservationist. In Illinois, where he hailed from, well-watered corn thrust tall out of the nation's richest soil. But the President spoke for a harsher, more remote West, where recent settlers struggled to fertilize the desert. He had tasted enough alkali dust as a young rancher in the Badlands to understand the desperation of stockmen unable to breed, farmers unable to reap or sow.

For a quarter of a century, environmental pioneers had urged the construction of vast irrigation systems to collect and distribute Western floodwaters. John Wesley Powell and WJ McGee noted that the arid lands thus reclaimed—one third of the total area of the United States—could be sold to farmers and ranchers, and the profits recycled for further reclamation. But Congress had responded with unenforceable public land laws, allowing a "water monopoly" to grow up in the West. This combination levied extortionate rates where supply was meager, and dried out established communities in order to irrigate speculative tracts elsewhere.

Roosevelt expressed "keen personal pride" in the reclamation measure. It seemed to him properly to combine federal responsibility with private enterprise, in that water rights would be sold, deposit-free and interest-free, to small farmers, who would eventually repay the government out of the profits from their irrigated property. Although it was offered in the appropriate name of Francis G. Newlands (D., Nevada), the President felt that it had grown out of the irrigation proposals of his First Annual Message, and he protested vehemently when Newlands claimed authorship.

Cannon ignored Roosevelt's letter, but a majority of the House, responding to strong White House pressure, voted in favor of the bill. The Senate followed suit. On 17 June 1902, Roosevelt delightedly signed the National Reclamation Act into law. It funded a six-hundred-man civil-engineering force within the National Geological Survey, and conjured up, like some glittering grail of future prosperity, a vision of dams and aqueducts bejeweling the country's unwatered tracts. "They must be built for permanence and safety," the President urged, "for they are to last and spread prosperity for centuries."

Reclamationists spoke almost drunkenly of supporting a new population of one hundred million, and creating such opportunities for American producers as to make the current economy seem like penury. Mark Hanna praised the act as Theodore Roosevelt's first major legislative achievement, and said that its importance would grow with the years. "People have not paid much attention to this business. . . . It's a damn big thing."

◦⌐

DURING THE NEXT two days, the Senator, grumbling "he was two thirds crazy, he was so tired," launched a final blitz for Panama votes. Bunau-Varilla conducted a simultaneous propaganda campaign, sending every Senator a Nicaraguan postage stamp showing the live cone of Momotombo. "An official witness," he typed beneath, "of the volcanic activity of the Isthmus of

Nicaragua." Cromwell lobbied in his own secretive fashion. One by one, the ten votes Hanna needed slipped from the Nicaragua checklist. When it was clear that Panama would prevail, the slippage became an avalanche. The final tally, on 19 June, was 67 to 6 in favor of a Panama canal.

By a margin of 44 to 34, the Senate also approved the Spooner Amendment. Theodore Roosevelt, nine months President of the United States, was handed power to join the world's largest oceans. Forty million dollars—the largest sum in real-estate history, dwarfing the Louisiana Purchase—was placed at his disposal, plus $130 million in construction funds. Exultant, he forecast that the Panama Canal would be "the great bit of work of my administration, and from the material and constructive standpoint one of the greatest bits of work that the twentieth century will see."

⌐⊃—

ROOSEVELT'S EUPHORIA WAS short-lived, because two days later a delegation of Republican leaders informed him that his Special Message on Cuba had failed. Hearteningly, though, Senators Aldrich, Platt, Hanna, Spooner, and Foraker had all backed him up. But the party's endemic inability to agree on tariff reciprocity had defeated even them. He had to take what comfort he could in widespread admiration for his goodwill toward Cuba and "spectacular courage." Even the New York *Evening Post,* not usually complimentary, had called him "a brave man and a real President."

Somewhat cheered, Roosevelt left town on 24 June to accept an honorary degree from Harvard. Early next morning, the sun-tipped spires and elms of his alma mater appeared across the Charles. After a reunion breakfast in Back Bay with members of the Class of 1880, he crossed Harvard Bridge in a plush carriage. He relaxed comfortably against its cushions in his white waistcoat, a Porcellian Club button at his breast, squinting at the bright water. Then the familiar elms of Cambridge dappled his silk hat, and bugle calls and cheers heralded his approach to Harvard Yard. Here, twenty-five years before, he had nursed the first great sorrow of his life; twenty-four years before, wheezed asthmatic over Rhetoric and Comparative Anatomy; twenty-three years before, suffered agonies over a girl from Chestnut Hill. *As long as I live, I shall never forget how sweetly she looked, and how prettily she greeted me. . . .*

Grief; disease; desire. And now, even more privately, Edith's failure to carry her latest baby to term. Only the most masculine activism could dispel these feminine frailties. Roosevelt burst from his carriage like a bear. At the welcoming ceremony in Massachusetts Hall, he stood erect and talkative, his big chest nudging the presidential robes of Charles William Eliot.

Outside in the Yard, the Class of 1902 was yelling for "Teddy." Stimulated by the sound of cheers and press of flesh, Roosevelt began to radiate his

famous electricity. He joined the Commencement procession. Deputy marshals Owen Wister and Woodbury Kane, '82, followed him.

WISTER   When we were in college, you didn't used to like him much.
              How do you feel now?
KANE   If he and I were crossing the Brooklyn Bridge, and he ordered
              me to jump over, I'd do it without asking why.
ROOSEVELT   (*calling*) What are you fellows dangling behind for? Come
              alongside!
WISTER   (*hurrying to catch up*) Unconditional surrender?
KANE   Absolutely, old man.

The President's behavior after receiving his honorary LL.D. was so archetypal as to imprint itself on the eyes and ears of many observers. Dr. Eliot escorted him to a guest suite to change, and watched with fascination as he tore
off his coat and vest and slammed a large pistol on the dresser. Eliot asked if
it was his habit to carry firearms. "Yes, when I am going into public places."

At the Alumni Banquet, Roosevelt spied Senator Hoar and plumped down
beside him like an impulsive boy. He whispered a confession, saying it was his
"dearest wish" to do what the Senator wanted in the Philippines.

Dr. Eliot began to speak, interrupting them. At the first mention of the
word *millions*, so dear to university presidents, Roosevelt's attention wandered. Finance meant no more to him than the music of Chopin. He suppressed a yawn, and swiveled in his seat, staring at pictures on the walls.
When John D. Long introduced him with a joke about his inability to sit still
in any position of power, Roosevelt shook from head to foot with laughter.
Moments later, he was leaning over the high table at an angle of thirty degrees, his teeth still bared, but no longer in mirth.

John Hay, seated nearby, knew what was coming. Harvard, to Theodore,
was a temple defiled by mugwumps, who congregated here to exchange the
dull coins of anti-imperialism. Sure enough, Roosevelt launched into a stentorian defense of his island administrations, and of the public servants who
sacrificed their careers to help "weaker friends . . . along the stony and difficult path of self-government." Clapping his hands for emphasis, he bit three
names out of the air: "Elihu Root . . . Will Taft . . . General Wood!" Root
could be earning fabulous fees as a corporate lawyer in New York, Taft could
be a Justice of the Supreme Court, and Wood, in a more mythologically inclined culture, would be celebrated as "a hero mixed up with a sun god" for
the miracles he had performed in Cuba.

Hay, listening, sensed a thought in many old heads: *He is so young, and
will be with us for many a day to come.* The President's forehead wriggled, his
pince-nez flashed, and his harsh voice skipped from baritone to squeak, as

pent-up loyalties poured out. With a final lunge across the linen, he roared, "I can show my appreciation in no way save the wholly insufficient one of standing up for them and their works, and that I do!"

He dropped back to his seat, drenched with sweat, and got a standing ovation. Hay marveled at his power to transform a skeptical audience. Even Dr. Eliot was moved. "He has genius, force, originality." Old Edward Everett Hale, who had attended more Commencements than any man present, babbled that the President had made "a speech to be remembered . . . for centuries."

Roosevelt had to attend four more functions, and make three more speeches, before he could retire to his private car. Pale with exhaustion, he vomited and went straight to bed. He was asleep before the train left Boston.

WASHINGTON WAS SHUTTERING up for the summer when he got back. Edith and the children had left for Oyster Bay. Even the White House was barred to him, on account of extensive restoration and refurbishment by the architect Charles McKim. Carpenters were busy salvaging historic bits of floorboard, and plaster dust floated out of every window. It would not be habitable again until the fall.

He took up temporary residence a few doors away, at 22 Jackson Place, and signed a last-minute stack of bills, none of them his. Legislation, Roosevelt realized, was not his forte. Public leadership was. Invitations were flooding in for him to address audiences in New England in August, in the Midwest in September, in the far West whenever he cared to come. He ac-

"THE CAPITAL DROWSED INTO ITS ANNUAL DOLDRUMS."
Theodore Roosevelt's White House in summer

cepted them indiscriminately, even a grotesque summons from Los Angeles, singed across the shoulders of a calfskin.

Congress adjourned on the first day of July. The capital drowsed into its annual doldrums. Hardly a hoofbeat disturbed the shimmering pavements, and cicadas hummed in Lafayette Square. Roosevelt, dressed in white from head to foot, had one final, purgative duty to perform: a proclamation of amnesty in the Philippines. It had to be written around the fact that the Moros of Mindanao were not yet subjugated. They were fanatic Muslims, and could be conveniently differentiated from other Filipinos. Elsewhere, *Pax Americana* ruled throughout the archipelago. In a lame attempt to equate civil government with independence, Roosevelt postdated the declaration "July Fourth, 1902."

Only then did he feel free to join his family on the shores of Long Island Sound.

CHAPTER 8

The Good Old Summertime

*Th' capital iv th' nation has raymoved to Eyester Bay,
a city on th' north shore iv Long Island,
with a popylation iv three million clams.*

SUMMER RAIN WAS FALLING as the Oyster Bay special chugged out of Long Island City on 5 July 1902. New York's fringes progressively crumbled from wet factories to brickyards to sodden fields of flowers and vegetables. These in turn gave way to patches of marsh hazy with insects. Presently, the land grew solid enough to support acre after acre of greenhouses, a farm or two, and some new towns still edged with mud. Then white steeples began to prick the horizon—pikestaffs protecting the privileged greens of Nassau County— and the train swung northeast toward the Sound.

Roosevelt had been riding this way for nearly thirty years, first as a teenager lugging rifles, birdshot, and the smelly paraphernalia of taxidermy, now as a President badly in need of a vacation. Familiar station signs flashed by in the drizzle: Roslyn Harbor, Sea Cliff, Glen Cove. The names had a marine ring, yet no hint of sea showed beyond wet roofs and foliage. The train curved eastward again, slowing almost to buggy speed as it descended Locust Valley. Forest closed in, broken only by an occasional duck pond or timber cut, then the valley broadened, and light sliced through thinning trees. The rails leveled out, and suddenly the train was rolling along a little harbor stiff with yachts.

Were it not for the mild, salt-laden air, Oyster Bay might be mistaken for a lake. Green slopes surrounded it at all points of the compass, keeping out both the swell of the sea and the turbulence of the outside world. (New York was not thirty miles away, but could have been three hundred.) At the flattest part of the shoreline, a few sandy roads converged on a post office, an inn, six churches, and ten or twelve squat commercial buildings. Members of the President's official party looked around anxiously for sources of entertainment. They saw only a library and an empty, dripping bandstand. "There are many one-horse towns on Long Island," a reporter noted, "but it is doubtful if there is another as uninteresting as Oyster Bay."

The little community turned out in force to welcome its returning squire. Steam whistles shrilled the President's arrival, and thunder and lightning added extra dramatic effects. A new depot, not quite finished, sheltered Roosevelt as he descended from the train. Kermit, Ethel, and Archie, representing the family, flung themselves upon him, while his Secret Service escort made a wedge through the crowd. Grinning at the shouted familiarities of old-timers—here he was unavoidably "Teddy"—he climbed into an open surrey. Kermit joined the coachman, while the two younger children snuggled close to their father. He threw a protective oilcloth over them. Then, with a final wave at the crowd, he took what cover he could under his rapidly collapsing Panama hat.

The surrey splashed east along Audrey Avenue, past the Oyster Bay Bank building, of which the first-floor office suite—two melancholy brown-painted rooms—had been reserved through September by George Cortelyou. Roosevelt had no desire to visit these headquarters. He intended to put as much distance as possible between himself and White House staff. His destination lay three miles farther on, beyond Christ Episcopal Church and Youngs Cemetery, around the bend of Oyster Bay Cove. As the village fell away, Shore Road became an avenue of moss-hung locust trees winding past the resorts of the rich—white-pillared "cottages" of twenty or forty rooms, lawns sloping to sea level, beached rowboats bearing old names that spoke of power, breeding, and interbreeding: Tiffany, Beekman, Gracie, Roosevelt, Roosevelt, Roosevelt.

Turning north, the surrey left the mainland and followed the line of Cove Neck as it jutted, rising, into the bay. Reeds waved to the left of the road, and saltwater slapped close to the horse's hooves, while on the other side the landscape became more rural, and fields and woods spaced out the mansions of Roosevelt's immediate neighbors. Ahead rose the crown of the peninsula. Its highest house was invisible for trees—trees he had planted himself, in early manhood. *Qui plantavit curabit.*

A private driveway led steeply up the slope, and Sagamore Hill disclosed itself at last, glowing dull red through the rain. Red brick below, red wood above; brown and yellow awnings over the west piazza; streaming shingles the color of old mustard. Roosevelt's eyes, rejoicing in the house's ugliness, noticed only one unfamiliar note: a telephone pole trailing wires back the way he had come. Evidently Cortelyou was determined to keep him in touch with affairs of state.

❧

RAIN GAVE WAY to sun in the days that followed. The hilltop breezes sweetened as catalpa and locust bloomed below, and the birds of Roosevelt's youth saluted his acute ear with remembered calls. Exulting in their clamor, he began to compose his first piece of presidential nature-writing:

Among Long Island singers the wood-thrushes are the sweetest; they nest right around our house, and also in the most open woods of oak, hickory, and chestnut, where their serene, leisurely songs ring through the leafy arches all day long. . . . Chickadees wander everywhere; the wood-pewees, red-eyed vireos, and black-and-white creepers keep to the tall timber, where the wary, thievish jays chatter, and the great-crested flycatchers flit and scream. In the early spring, when the woods are still bare, when the hen-hawks cry as they soar high in the upper air, and the flickers call and drum on the dead trees, the strong, plaintive note of the meadow-lark is one of the most noticeable and most attractive sounds. On the other hand, the cooing of the mourning-doves is most noticeable in the still, hot summer days.

Ovenbirds fluted too, in the heat, but more frequently after dark, when the whippoorwills were calling. Roosevelt spent many moonlit evenings on the piazza in his rocking chair, with Edith beside him, listening to this "night-singing in the air." Despite his mature preoccupation with politics, he was still susceptible to poetic impressions. Musing on the behavior of screech owls, he produced one extraordinary, if ungrammatical, image:

They come up to the house after dark, and are fond of sitting in the elk-antlers over the gable. When the moon is up, by changing one's position, the little owl appears in sharp outline against the bright disk, seated on his many-tined perch.

To the west, beyond Hell Gate, he could see the nimbus of New York City, and, northeast across the Sound, the twinkling lights of Connecticut. At regular intervals, Fall River Line steamers en route to Massachusetts drew chains of gold across the water.

No matter how beautiful the night, the President could never relax entirely, knowing that William "Big Bill" Craig, his bodyguard, lurked in some nearby bush, while other large men prowled the lawns and driveway. Secret Service protection had become a full-time nuisance since McKinley's assassination. Roosevelt disliked it, but the agents were inexorable. They checked their watches when he went upstairs, stared at his window while he slept, and hung yawning around the kitchen at breakfast time. They webbed the estate with trip wires, and treated all visitors as potential anarchists, even a party of dowagers from the Oyster Bay Needlework Guild. On afternoons off, they wandered around town looking for "cranks," their knobby pockets and patent-leather shoes infallibly identifying them as plainclothesmen.

Roosevelt gave up protesting that he could adequately defend himself. (The sight of a gun butt protruding from the presidential trouser-seat caused some consternation in Christ Episcopal Church.) Instead, he used his familiarity with the landscape to shake off his escort as often as possible. One day he managed to escape Big Bill Craig for two hours by galloping Bleistein into the woods. Another of his tricks was to lead unwary officers to Cooper's Bluff, the almost vertical, 150-foot sand cliff at the end of Cove Neck. Talking casually, Roosevelt would arrive at the brink, then drop out of sight like a plummet. The Secret Service men would instinctively follow, and, losing their footing, somersault to the bottom in a choking avalanche. Meanwhile, the President, striding off unscathed, could enjoy a few moments of peace.

Yet had it not been for the cordon that Craig threw about Sagamore Hill, Roosevelt would have enjoyed no peace at all. Every train from "York," as Oyster Bay natives called the metropolis, brought delegations of politicians, office-seekers, and sycophants bent on disturbing his leisure. "I never seed the like of it," said Si Josslyn, veteran clam digger of Cove Neck, "and it ain't no wonder the President has to stan' most of 'em off." Only pilgrims on urgent public business, with a pass signed by Cortelyou, were permitted up the private road.

Cabinet officers and Congressmen found that strange rules of protocol applied in the President's house:

SMALL BOY	(*reproachfully*) Cousin Theodore, it's after four.
ROOSEVELT	By Jove, so it is! Why didn't you call me sooner? One of you boys get my rifle. (*Apologetically*) I must ask you to excuse me. . . . I never keep boys waiting.

Rough Riders, accustomed to instant access to their Colonel, found Sagamore Hill harder to take than the heights of San Juan. They joined the crowds of other rejectees in town, gazing in frustration at the big house and windmill across the bay.

Most disappointed of all were members of the press, who could not reconcile Roosevelt's availability in the White House with his refusal to receive them at home. Starved of news, they mooched unhappily in the village, waylaying every returning visitor for bits of information. About once a week, the President would trot down East Main Street, followed by a procession of children (at least ten Roosevelt cousins lived on Cove Neck, in addition to his own brood). Little Archie, clad in a Rough Rider suit, always brought up the rear. Reporters would run alongside in the dust, bawling questions to which the President was benignly deaf.

One day, he reined in his horse and teased them with a mock bulletin. "I want you to know all the facts, so I shall give them to you at first hand. Teddy [Jr.] is now fishing for tadpoles, but really expects to land a whale. Archie shot three elephants this morning. Ethel at this moment is setting fire to the rear of the house; Kermit and the calico pony are having a wrestling match in the garret, and Quentin, four years old, is pulling down the windmill."

Unamused, the reporters began to concoct their own fantasies of life at Sagamore Hill. Roosevelt took no notice until suggestive accounts of a picnic *à deux* with Edith appeared in several newspapers. The headlines were arch: "PRESIDENT AND MRS. ROOSEVELT STROLL IN ARCADY—Executive Realizes the Poet's Dream—'A Loaf of Bread, a Jug of Wine and Thou, Singing in the Wilderness.' " Worse still were patently sexual references to himself as "a gallant gentleman in knickerbockers," bent on "pleasuring" his "lady," and making "little sallies into the heart of nature."

He traced the stories to the Oyster Bay correspondent of the New York *Sun,* and complained to the paper's editor, Paul Dana:

> It seems to me they are not proper stories to be told about a President or the members of his family. . . . I very much wish you would send instead of your present man at Oyster Bay someone who will tell the facts as they are, and will not try to make up for the fact that nothing is happening here by having recourse to invention. The plain truth of course is that I am living here with my wife and children just exactly as you are at your home; and there is no more material for a story in one case than in the other!

Dana withdrew his correspondent, and the press corps learned to respect the veil that the President drew across his family activities. Both he and Edith held to the Victorian concept of childhood as a state of grace that cameras, and coarse questions, could only profane.

For the younger Roosevelts, the long summer days certainly seemed appareled in celestial light. "It is avowedly the ambition of the President," a visitor wrote, "to make Sagamore Hill ever remain in the eyes of his children, the one spot on earth which is different from every other." The estate, with its forty acres of lawns, gardens, wheat fields, and woodland, its stable, barn, windmill, and well, its molehilly tennis court and turtle pond full of nice green scum, was about as near to Paradise as any child could wish. Best of all, perhaps, was its long stretch of private beach, beyond the heron pools in Cold Spring Harbor. There were two red bathing houses there, some battered boats, and miles of quiet water.

These haunts, Elysian as they were, needed the transforming touch of a Zeus to make them divine. Roosevelt did not disappoint. He gave off a godlike aura of radiance and vitality, and the children luxuriated in it, like bees in sun.

From early morning, when he drummed them downstairs for a prebreakfast game of "bear," until late evening, when he romped them up to bed, their days were spent largely in his company. His burly arms tickled them, swung them shrieking into the sea, steadied their gun barrels, and rowed them around the bay. He was slightly dangerous in his fun. His bulk halfsmothered them—girls as well as boys—in wrestling contests. His playful

"CHILDHOOD AS A STATE OF GRACE."
Quentin Roosevelt in the daisy field at Sagamore Hill

cuffs rang in their ears, his myopia made him a lethal diver. At night in the woods, he enthralled them with harsh, yodeling ghost stories, climaxed with a flash of teeth, a roar, and a pounce, deliciously scary. Later, recovering round the campfire, they would revel in his infamous clams, fried in beef fat and garnished with equal parts pepper and sand.

Only when he climbed wearily into his sleeping bag did their adoration turn to protectiveness, and for as long as possible they would stay awake, guarding the President of the United States as he slept.

NO MATTER WHERE Roosevelt spent the night, his presence was required in the library of Sagamore Hill every weekday at 8:30 A.M. Secretary Cortelyou, oily and purposeful as an otter, would come up the drive with a leather bag full of mail, and for the next few hours "typing machines" would click, and a Morse transmitter rattle, as he and the President dispatched affairs of state. Since the government was in recess, their business was neither copious nor demanding. Cortelyou was usually on his way by noon, and Roosevelt, looking like a large plump urchin in negligee shirt, linen knickers, and canvas shoes, would play a set of tennis before lunch.

With the sun glowing on his awnings, and the table piled with the products of his farm—roast chickens, asparagus, potatoes, corn, fresh rye bread and butter, gooseberries, grapes, peaches swimming in cream—he was tempted to forget that summer must end, that the fecund ripeness of the nation's economy would be susceptible, sooner or later, to cold winds. A new magazine, ironically entitled *World's Work,* reported that more Americans were on vacation, and spending more money, than ever before. After a century of struggle, of wars and assassination and depression and empire-building, the United States felt entitled to bask at last in peace and prosperity. A musical paean to mindlessness lilted round the country. Holidaymakers sang the song on yachts in Bar Harbor, on the roller coasters of Coney Island, on horseback in Colorado, and on streetcars in San Francisco. They bellowed it in chorus from vaudeville boats in the Hudson, and heard it echoing back at them from the Palisades:

> *In the good old Summertime,*
> *In the good old Summertime!*
> *The sun affects some people*
> *In a manner quite divine . . .*

⸺

THE ONLY MEMBER of Roosevelt's family who expressed discontent that summer was eighteen-year-old Alice—brittle, boy-crazy, and by her own admission "bored to extinction" at Oyster Bay. She yearned for the elegant youths of Newport and Saratoga and for her adored maternal grandparents in Boston, and in particular she lusted after money. Her own considerable private income was not enough. "I want more," she scribbled in her diary, "I want everything. . . . I care for nothing but to amuse myself in a charmingly expensive way." She prowled round the dark house, a caged blond cheetah among its skins and stuffed trophies.

Heedless on the piazza overlooking the bay, her father used the long afternoons to catch up with his reading. His "beach book" for the season was Nicolay and Hay's *Abraham Lincoln: A History,* in ten volumes. Unfazed, he read it straight through, along with his usual supply of dime novels and periodicals.

Since Roosevelt was a devotee of *Review of Reviews,* edited by his good friend Albert Shaw, he probably noticed the extraordinary face reproduced in halftone on page 37 of the July issue. Pale eyes absolutely lacking in self-doubt, an unfurrowed brow, haughty nostrils, a long cruel mouth over a tremendous jaw—features both intellectual and tough, adamantine in their cold, smooth pallor: it was the beaky professor who had visited with him in Buffalo the day after his inauguration.

Woodrow Wilson, the magazine reported, was about to become president of Princeton University. "Every great step that he has taken has been one of conscious choice, leading to a definite, logical end." Still only forty-five, Dr.

Wilson had farther yet to go. Already "one of the political parties" wanted to send him to the New Jersey State Senate, "and recently a Western newspaper has pointed him out as the right kind of man to be a candidate for President of the United States."

⎯⎯⎯

ON 14 JULY, Elihu Root delivered to Sagamore Hill the first politically charged document of the season. It was a transcript of General "Kill and Burn" Jake Smith's court-martial in Manila. The general's fellow officers had predictably found him guilty only of excessive zeal, and they "admonished" him to mend his ways.

For a moment Roosevelt was tempted to accept the verdict, in the spirit of his recent amnesty declaration. Military authority no longer applied in the Philippines; ugly memories of the pacification campaign should be encouraged to fade. Part of him sympathized with General Smith. As a former commanding officer himself, Roosevelt had no illusions about the nature of guerrilla warfare. "I thoroughly believe in severe measures when necessary, and am not in the least sensitive about killing any number of men when there is adequate reason."

Smith, however, had condoned the killing of women and children—"shooting niggers," to use the general's own phrase. Roosevelt could not tolerate such genocidal rhetoric, nor could he discount the brutalizing effect it must have had on junior officers. The court-martial, he decided, had been a miscarriage of justice. He ordered Smith's prompt dismissal from the Army.

After dinner, Roosevelt and Root sat up late in their tuxedos working on another Philippines problem: how to buy and secularize Vatican holdings in the archipelago, to the gratification of natives, without alienating American Catholics. Both of them got deep satisfaction out of such chesslike exercises in policy. At 2:00 A.M., they closed the last folder and went out onto the lawn overlooking Oyster Bay. Root puffed a cigar. He had been touched by the President's cry of comradeship at Harvard. Roosevelt, in turn, felt convinced that of all the men in his Cabinet, Root alone had the qualities to succeed him as President.

Friends again, they stood surrounded by the tranquillity of wealth, protected by the trappings of power. Below them, Root's naval transport lay black on the moonlit water. Farther off floated another recent arrival, slender, white, and glistening: Roosevelt's own official vessel, USS *Mayflower*. Personally, he did not much care for yachts. But this 273-foot refitted dispatch boat, with its twelve guns and white-and-gold reception rooms (not to mention its wine cellar, silk paneling, and a solid marble bath), was clearly more suited to his dignity than the *Sylph* or tubby little *Dolphin*. He looked forward to a tour of inspection in the morning.

⎯⎯⎯

ABOUT FIVE HOURS LATER, sailors were swabbing the *Mayflower*'s decks, and its officers were dressing below, when a rowboat began to splash across the bay. Pulling the oars was a stocky man in a sleeveless swimsuit. The sailors paid no attention until there was a creaking of the gangway ladder, and the President appeared beaming in their midst.

"Bully! Bully!" Roosevelt exclaimed, as he rushed around admiring fixtures and fittings. By the time the officers came on deck in their hastily buttoned tunics, he was already rowing back to Sagamore Hill for breakfast.

"ROOT ALONE HAD THE QUALITIES TO SUCCEED HIM AS PRESIDENT."
Elihu Root as Secretary of War

ROOSEVELT'S DECISION TO dismiss General Smith won universal praise. Democrats congratulated him for acknowledging that there had been both cruelty and injustice in the Philippines campaign. Republicans felt that he had upheld the national honor.

Even the Anti-Imperialist League conceded that the President had out-maneuvered them at every turn. His seemingly haphazard actions since General Miles's opening shots in February now looked more like a careful battle plan. First, a broadside against the general's character and reputation; next, a series of aggressive moves that were actually retreats—his acceptance of the Gardener Report, his demand for an investigation, his self-distancing from Root. . . . Each of these feints had coincided with, and neutralized, some strike by the League, Congress, or the press. Then his double dispatch of envoys—Lodge to the Senate with a promise of justice in Manila, Root to Cuba with a grant of independence. Finally, the coup de grâce: Roosevelt had himself invaded Harvard Yard and captured the mugwumps in their own stronghold. Magnanimous in victory, he had offered amnesty to the Filipinos, and buried the hatchet in one of his own generals.

Anti-imperialism, Charles Francis Adams wrote Carl Schurz, was a lost cause, thanks to Theodore Roosevelt. "I think he has been very adroit. He has conciliated almost every one."

⁓

ALMOST UNNOTICED IN the bluster of the President's Harvard speech had been a hint that he would soon have to choose a nominee for the Supreme Court. Justice Horace Gray's resignation letter was now on file. Roosevelt had already offered the seat to William Howard Taft, knowing that the Governor longed, above all things, for a judicial appointment. But Taft had regretfully declined, citing unfulfilled business in the Philippines.

With Justice Gray gone, the Court seemed to stand evenly divided on the status of the Philippines as "unincorporated" American territory. A similar balance of opinion seemed likely to confront the *Northern Securities* suit, currently grinding its way through circuit-court review. Roosevelt therefore had to be sure that whoever he chose to replace Gray shared the Administration's colonial and antitrust philosophy.

He dreamily informed Henry Cabot Lodge, who thought that an ideal candidate was available in Massachusetts, that the next Justice should be a patrician person with enlightened instincts at home and conservative views abroad, somebody who would unite "aloofness of mind" with "broad humanity of feeling." Not only that, this person should have a respectful sense of what the Administration wanted of him:

> Now . . . in the ordinary and low sense which we attach to the words "partisan" and "politician," a judge of the Supreme Court should be

neither. But in the higher sense, in the proper sense, he is not in my judgment fitted for the position unless he is a party man, a constructive statesman, constantly keeping in mind his adherence to the principles and policies under which this nation has been built up and in accordance with which it must go on; and keeping in mind also his relations with his fellow statesmen who in other branches of the government are striving in cooperation with him to advance the ends of government.

Having thus briskly disposed of the doctrine of an independent judiciary, Roosevelt left Lodge to send his candidate down, and went for a cruise on the *Mayflower*.

⌦

FOG DELAYED THE President's return on 24 July. His press detail was marooned with him off Sea Girt, New Jersey, so a tremendously tall stranger was able to arrive at the Oyster Bay station that afternoon, unannounced and unrecognized.

Oliver Wendell Holmes, Jr., Chief Justice of the Massachusetts Supreme Court, was not well-known outside legal circles, but his distinction was obvious to anyone, even in mist. Unabashed by his height, he walked with lean, military grace. A ten-inch mustache, whitening (he was sixty-one), swept like a bow wave on either side of his haughty profile. His gaze, clear gray and cool, projected the most original intelligence in American jurisprudence. It was Holmes who, in 1881, had shockingly suggested that most statutes were obsolete by the time they got between leather covers. "The life of the law has not been logic: it has been experience. . . . At any given time [it] pretty nearly corresponds . . . with what is then understood to be convenient."

In his world there was neither absolute good nor absolute evil—only shifting standards of positive and negative behavior, determined by the majority and subject to constant change. Morality was not defined by God; it was the code a given generation of men wanted to live by. Truth was "what I can't help believing." Yesterday's absolutes must give way to "the felt necessities of the time."

Theodore Roosevelt, too, "felt" things, if more viscerally. After returning to Oyster Bay on the twenty-fifth, he received Holmes (who had stayed over at Sagamore Hill) and saw, or thought he saw, a healthy bias against "big railroad men and other members of large corporations." Here was a man who evidently believed—always had believed—that the executive and legislative branches of government should have precedence over the judiciary in controlling natural democratic developments. Roosevelt agreed with Lodge that Holmes, well-bred, learned, and forceful, was "our kind right through."

⌦

HOLMES RETURNED TO Boston unsure of his fate, but a letter appointing him to the Supreme Court arrived within days. He accepted it neither humbly nor vainly, but as an earned consequence of forty years of hard work. Although he agreed to keep quiet, pending the official announcement, he could not resist teasing his wife about moving to Washington in December. "We shall have to dine with the President. In tails, Fanny, and white satin."

꩜

AS AUGUST APPROACHED, sardonic new verses attached themselves to America's reigning hit, sounding a note of folk concern clearly audible to the President, despite his isolation on Sagamore Hill.

In the good old Summertime,
In the good old Summertime!
The way they've raised the price of coal
I don't like it at all for mine . . .

Grotesque as it was to think of domestic heat when every noon required another trip to the icehouse (crickets crouching in damp nooks; foot-square chunks of frozen pond packed in eelgrass), Roosevelt was aware that a national crisis was building in the coalfields of eastern Pennsylvania. One hundred and forty-seven thousand anthracite miners had quit work early in the spring, vowing not to return to their jobs in the fall unless management agreed to a substantial increase in wages, and recognized United Mine Workers as their legitimate bargaining representative. The mine operators refused to consider either demand. Now, with eighteen thousand bituminous miners striking in sympathy, and fifty thousand coal-road workers laid off for lack of traffic, the total number of idle men approached a quarter of a million.

Ordinary Americans were only just beginning to realize the superlative dimensions of the crisis. Here was the nation's biggest union challenging its most powerful industrial combination—a cartel of anthracite railroad operators and absentee "barons" in total control of an exclusive resource. Already it amounted to the greatest labor stoppage in history. A visiting British economist predicted that if the current standoff lasted until cold weather came, there would be "such social consequences as the world has never seen."

Roosevelt concluded unhappily that he should not intervene in what was essentially a private dispute between labor and management. Only if the public interest was threatened could he assume emergency powers. So far, the strike had been oddly peaceful. Then at the end of July, just as he was about to announce Judge Holmes's appointment, violence erupted in the anthracite country.

CHAPTER 9

No Power or Duty

MR. HENNESSY *What d'ye think iv th' man down in Pinnsylvania*
who says th' Lord an' him is partners in a coal mine?
MR. DOOLEY *Has he divided th' profits?*

FOR ELEVEN WEEKS, the sheriff of Schuylkill County, Pennsylvania, had patrolled the environs of Shenandoah in anticipation of violence. He and his fellow officers sniffed the carbonic gases leaking from untended mines, and avoided the perpetual flames wavering along dark slopes of culm. Valley after anthracite-packed valley seemed to be smoldering with discontent.

What made Sheriff Bedall nervous was the inscrutability of the striking miners. Most were Slavic, and few spoke English, jabbering away instead in incomprehensible dialects and poring over newspapers apparently printed backward. For "foreigners," they were clean-living, almost austere. Tens of thousands had sworn off liquor to solemnize the strike; saloons stood empty from Ashland to Tamaqua. In the strangely clear air, women and girls hoed vegetables—preserving extra supplies for the months to come—while men and boys played baseball. Congregations flocking to Mass had the tranquil expressions of pilgrims sure of deliverance.

Only when a young, priestlike figure in black passed their way did the Slavs betray their suppressed passions. They poured from their shacks waving icons of his face, and crowded the wheels of his carriage like pilgrims around a catafalque. With gap-toothed grins and roars they chanted, *"Johnny! Father! Johnny da Mitch!"*

John Mitchell, the thirty-two-year-old president of United Mine Workers, encouraged this evangelical treatment by wearing his white collar very high, and buttoning his long black coat to the neck. At every stop on his journey he allowed breaker boys to sit at his feet while he preached the gospel of labor organization. A former coal miner himself, he knew that the credulous masses that looked to him for deliverance needed faith to sustain them. Faith, and food: these "anthracite people" would be starving already, had he not persuaded their brethren in the bituminous fields to go back to work and pay extra dues to support them.

Swarthy, silent, introspective, and worn, Mitchell calculated the coefficients of patience and time. The strike was now thirteen weeks old, and Mitchell had risked as many concessions as he dared. He had temporarily held pump men, engineers, and firemen to their jobs, so that mines would not flood or explode; he had offered to arbitrate; he had even hinted to Carroll D. Wright, Roosevelt's Commissioner of Labor, that he would not push union recognition if management agreed to a reduction in the contract workday from ten to eight hours, an equitable system of assessing each miner's output, and an overall wage increase of 10 percent.

Mitchell's concessions had been taken as weakness by the financiers who, through mutual ownership of mines and coal-bearing railroads, operated the greatest industrial monopoly in the United States. Their spokesman, George F. Baer of the Philadelphia & Reading Railroad, declined private communications with Mitchell and addressed him, tauntingly, through the press. "Anthracite mining," he said, "is a business and not a religious, sentimental, or academic proposition."

When the miners responded by calling out their remaining brethren in the pump rooms and firehouses, Baer became truculent. They could stay out "six months, or six years," he blustered. "Cripple industry, stagnate business or tie up the commerce of the world, and we will not surrender."

So the first seepages began underground, and the culm fires flickered freely. Mitchell, accepting voluntary relief contributions from other labor organizations, gave notice that the conciliatory phase of his strike was over.

Roaming the anthracite valleys, he discounted rumors of nonunion labor being hired out of state. Both he and Mark Hanna (worriedly monitoring the situation from Cleveland) agreed that if the operators did try to break the strike, the result would be such violence as to obliterate all memories of previous bloodshed in mining disputes.

George Baer assumed a pose of haughty indifference. "The coal presidents are going to settle this strike, and they will settle it in their own way," he announced on 29 July.

⌐∾⌐

SHENANDOAH WAS QUIET most of the day following his remarks. Blackened willows bent over the stream oozing between colliery and town; gray-black breakers loomed against the sky, silent and smokeless. Spires and domes of Polish and Greek churches caught the afternoon sun. For all its influx of new immigrants, Shenandoah remained a deeply traditional coal town, haunted by memories of the "Molly Maguire" labor terrorists of a generation before. Here, in 1862, America's first coal strike had occurred.

Centre Street was dominated by the Philadelphia & Reading station. This depot represented just one node in the ivylike spread of George Baer's railroad through Schuylkill County. Its steel tendrils linked mineheads and ironworks and slag heaps. Its runner roots carved so deeply into coal seams that the landscape sagged. Every year, it transported some ten million tons of black satiny crystals. Eight other "coal roads" contributed to the anthracite country's annual production of fifty-five million tons, which heated virtually every house, school, and hospital in the northeastern United States.

Shortly before 6:00 P.M., Sheriff Bedall's deputy was seen walking out of Shenandoah in the direction of the colliery. He was accompanied by two strangers, one of whom carried a suspicious-looking bundle. A group of picketing strikers confiscated it, and found it to contain miner's clothing. Screaming "son of a bitch scab!" the strikers beat both strangers unconscious. The deputy took refuge in the Reading depot. Soon five thousand maddened Slavs were besieging him. A bystander tried to go to his aid, and was clubbed to death. Borough policemen managed to bundle the deputy into a locomotive behind the depot. The crowd found out and jammed the rails, whereupon the policemen panicked and began to fire indiscriminately. Waves of Slavs fell wounded. Those with guns of their own fired back. More than one thousand bullets were exchanged before the locomotive churned away. By sunset, Centre Street was in the hands of the mob, and the sheriff sent a desperate telegram to Governor William Stone: BLOODSHED RAN RIOT IN THIS COUNTRY PROPERTY DESTROYED CITIZENS KILLED AND INJURED SITUATION BEYOND MY CONTROL TROOPS SHOULD BE SENT IMMEDIATELY.

THE FIRST DISPATCHES to reach Oyster Bay the next morning were apocalyptic, with stories of policemen being shot through the head and strikers sliced in half by the locomotive. Subsequent accounts reduced the death toll to one, and the list of injured to sixty. Shenandoah was reported to be peacefully under civil control. The guns and bayonets of Pennsylvania's National Guard glinted on the hills around town, but Governor Stone made no immediate attempt to invade the valley. He said that federal assistance was neither necessary nor desirable.

This freed Roosevelt to continue his own vacation, although he confessed to feeling increasingly "uneasy." The Shenandoah riot had made front pages across the country, and editorial comment indicated that sympathy for the miners was beginning to erode. The question was, Were John Mitchell and his men determined enough to bring on a social catastrophe in the fall? And not incidentally, what damage might George Baer and *his* top-hatted cohorts do to Republican prospects in the congressional elections?

Ten thousand bared heads, under beating heat at Scranton on 1 August, indicated that the miners would endure any discomfort in support of their revered leader. "The one among you who violates the law is the worst enemy you have," Mitchell lectured them. "I want to impress on you the importance of winning this strike," he went on, shouting and sweating. "If you win . . . there will be no more strikes."

Few among the audience realized that Mitchell was a profound conservative who privately thought most Slavs were "a drove of cattle" and detested the action he was required to lead. His nature shrank from confrontation. He saw himself as a businessman specializing in the business of labor; he believed in negotiated "adjustments" based on sound economic principles. Just as George Baer was in obvious terror that the strike would bankrupt an aging industry, so did Mitchell fear that the union he had built up might disintegrate from attrition. Every day now saw a few hundred more Slavs sell up and head back to Europe.

"If you lose the strike," he warned, "you lose your organization."

For the next two weeks, calm prevailed in the anthracite valleys. To D. L. Mulford, a visitor from Philadelphia, the calm signified not fear but a rock-like resolve. He sensed an equal hardening in the attitude of management, and saw the two sides as millstones grinding helpless consumers between them.

Roosevelt began to toy with similar images for a series of speeches he had to write on problems of capital and labor. On 22 August, he was due to begin a six-hundred-mile circuit of New England, the first of three tours keyed to the fall congressional campaign. Winter coal, or lack of it, was sure to be on the minds of his northern audiences. Yet he hesitated to make direct reference to the strike.

From what he heard, Americans were still concerned more about combinations in general than about the anthracite combination in particular. "I don't know whether you understand what a feeling there is on the trust question," wrote a friend, puzzled by the President's failure to prosecute more holding companies. (International Harvester had just been capitalized at $120 million, under the same New Jersey law that spawned Northern Securities.)

The feeling went both ways, as Attorney General Knox discovered on 8 August, when he stopped at Atlantic City en route to Oyster Bay. That evening in the Garden Café, Knox entertained a small mixed party. The restaurant's lights were dim, so he was not recognized by three Pennsylvanian trust lords who lurched in for a bottle of wine—evidently not their first of the evening. Millionaires all, they were Charles T. Schoen, of the Pittsburgh Pressed Steel Car Company; Theodore Cramp, of Cramp & Sons, shipbuilders; and Arthur H. Stephenson, of Stephenson Yarns. A boozy male conversation ensued. Schoen's voice was particularly loud. (Some years before,

Knox's law firm had been involved in a suit to oust Schoen from his job.) After a few minutes, the headwaiter brought him a message: "Attorney-General Knox objects to your noise and vulgar language."

"The hell he does," said Schoen, enraged. "I'd like to know what right he has to interfere with us," the drunken executive blustered, and began a tirade against government antitrust policy. Knox stood up, small and bristling in his dinner suit. He said crisply that he would not tolerate any more "objectionable remarks." Cramp and Stephenson at once offered some of their own. Amid jeers and imprecations, Knox escorted his party out.

As he lightly put it to reporters afterward, "I had such a pressing invitation to go back that I couldn't resist." But what ensued had not been funny. According to eyewitnesses, the Attorney General had re-entered the restaurant alone and shaken his finger in Schoen's face. "You are a blackguard, sir!"

Schoen, too sluggish to rise, had roared back, "You are a cur!" Cramp and Stephenson had jumped up, fists flying, but waiters and bystanders pulled them off, and Knox was escorted out, shaken, bruised, and minus several waistcoat buttons.

He tried to make light of the incident at Sagamore Hill, joking that Schoen probably felt worse than he did. But the incident emphasized the passions with which Roosevelt had to contend. A cartoon on the front page of the *Philadelphia North American* showed the President standing thoughtfully beside the battered, bandaged form of his Attorney General, while three retreating toughs jeered, "Hooray for the trusts!"

⌐⊃⌐

AS ALWAYS IN SITUATIONS involving extremes, Roosevelt's instinct was to seek out the center. He drafted a major speech on trust policy for delivery in Providence, Rhode Island, balancing it to appeal equally to paupers and plutocrats. Just to make sure about the latter, he forwarded a copy to E. H. Harriman. "Will you send it back to me with any comments you choose to make?"

The financier, facing years of legal harassment in the *Northern Securities* suit, complied. But he let Roosevelt know what priority a presidential document enjoyed in his office. "My day has been so much occupied I have not had an opportunity until after five o'clock to read it."

Some paragraphs on trust control, Harriman wrote, sounded "a little broad," and might bring on a sudden recession, even depression. A President should work for "understanding and confidence" between Wall Street and the public, not mutual mistrust. Testily, he asked Roosevelt "to have a little patience" and allow the economy to benefit from the recent boom in consolidations, before making "any radical change" in regulatory law.

If Roosevelt needed any further evidence of the arrogance of capital, he got it on 21 August, when newspapers published George Baer's reply to a correspondent urging compromise in the coal strike:

> The rights and interests of the laboring man will be protected and cared for—not by the labor agitators, but by the Christian men to whom God in His infinite wisdom has given the control of the property interests of the country, and upon the successful Management of which so much depends.

This pious protestation touched off a firestorm of ridicule. Baer was accused of blasphemy and hypocrisy. "A good many people think they superintend the earth," *The New York Times* remarked, "but not many have the egregious vanity to describe themselves as its managing directors." The *New York Tribune* gave mock thanks that God would be able to manage the strike "through the kindness of the coal operators."

Roosevelt, about to leave for New England, wistfully asked his Attorney General, "What is the reason we cannot proceed against the coal operators as being engaged in a trust?" Knox replied that until the Supreme Court ruled on *Northern Securities v. U.S.* the Sherman Act was too narrowly drawn to support such a move. As President, he had "no power or duty in the matter."

THE *SYLPH* STEAMED across Long Island Sound in glittering sunshine. Roosevelt lounged in a deck chair astern, enjoying the breeze. He sat staring at the green retreating bulk of Sagamore Hill, while Connecticut grew proportionately. The yacht's wake took with it his last moments of vacation. Thirteen days of campaign duty beckoned, all the way north to Maine: he wanted to get as many Republican congressman as possible elected or re-elected in the fall.

Three traveling aides—George Cortelyou, Assistant Secretary Benjamin F. Barnes, and Captain George A. Lung of the Navy Medical Corps—left the President alone, as did a pool of five reporters, four typists, and two telephonists. But his ubiquitous bodyguard hovered.

Roosevelt had grown fond of William Craig. Time was when Big Bill, an immigrant from Britain, had protected Queen Victoria. Now forty-eight years old, he stood six foot three and was still quick and muscular as a bull. Perhaps his best friend in the world was four-year-old Quentin Roosevelt. They liked to read comics together.

AT NOON THE FOLLOWING day, Saturday, 23 August, Theodore Roosevelt stood on a high platform in front of Providence's City Hall. Twenty thousand people filled the square below, and another thousand sat behind him. Wherever he looked, miniature flags flashed red, white, and blue. Squinting against the scintillations of brass-band instruments and binocular lenses, he began his speech.

> We are passing through a period of great commercial prosperity, and such a period is as sure as adversity itself to bring mutterings of discontent. At a time when most men prosper somewhat some men always prosper greatly; and it is as true now as when the tower of Siloam fell upon all alike, that good fortune does not come solely to the just, nor bad fortune solely to the unjust. When the weather is good for crops it is also good for weeds. (*Applause*)

It was a classic Rooseveltian opening in its complementary positives and negatives, its appeal to every social order, its biblical reference and earthy proverb. Honest industrialists, the churchgoing middle class, the rural poor—all were reassured that the President had their particular interests at heart.

Human law, he went on, encouraged moneymaking, but natural law prevented equal gain. If wealthy men abused their good fortune, or the needy sought to penalize them, both groups would be buried "in the crash of the common disaster." General progress depended on benevolence at every level of society, and "above all things stability, fixity of economic policy."

Roosevelt noticed that the square was becoming too crowded in front of him, and cautioned against the danger of crushing. Then he swung gracefully into his main theme:

> Where men are gathered together in great masses it inevitably results that they must work far more largely through combinations than where they live scattered and remote from one another. . . . Under present-day conditions it is as necessary to have corporations in the business world as it is to have organizations, unions, among wage workers.

E. H. Harriman could scarcely find fault with these measured phrases—nor, for that matter, could Rhode Island's most prominent exemplar of corporate wealth, Senator Aldrich, sitting erect twelve feet away.

"Every man of power," the President said carefully, "by the very fact of that power, is capable of doing damage to his neighbors; but we cannot afford to discourage the development of such men merely because it is possible they may use their power for wrong ends. . . . Probably the greatest harm done by vast wealth is the harm that we of moderate means do ourselves when we let the vices of envy and hatred enter deep into our own hearts."

His audience began to show signs of restlessness. "There is other harm," he quickly added. It was time for him to shout the words Harriman had objected to. He did so with passion:

The great corporations which we have grown to speak of rather loosely as trusts are the creatures of the State, and the State not only has the right to control them, but it is in duty bound to control them wherever need of such control is shown. . . . (*Applause*) The immediate necessity in dealing with trusts is to place them under the real, not the nominal, control of some sovereign to which, as its creatures, the trusts shall owe allegiance, and in whose courts the sovereign's orders may be enforced. (*Applause*) In my opinion, this sovereign must be the National Government.

By now, he was punching his left palm so hard the blows echoed like ricochets. Once, he surprised the people behind him by spinning on his heel and pointing directly at them. Nobody laughed; the President's face was hard and stern. Time and again, his imperious hand rejected applause. A reporter sensed his "almost desperate determination" to be understood.

Yet Roosevelt's equal compulsion to follow every strong statement with a qualifier caused the speech to degenerate into a series of contradictions on the pros and cons of regulatory law. By the time he sat down, much of his audience had wandered off.

THERE WAS SOME EXASPERATED comment in the press on the President's equivocations. "He spent more time in trying to pacify those who criticize the trusts than in pointing out a remedy," William Jennings Bryan wrote in *The Commoner*. Even normally supportive Republican editorials were unenthusiastic. These, however, were but inner-page qualms. Front pages everywhere bore the headlines Roosevelt wanted:

PRESIDENT WOULD REGULATE TRUSTS
In Speech at Providence Says Government Should Control Capital
MIGHT AMEND CONSTITUTION
If Step Were Necessary to Give Controlling Power

Evidently, the use of rhetoric was to make positive points that would cause typesetters to reach for their display faces. Negative dissemblings rated body copy (which he could always cite, when necessary, in self-defense). A few thousand myopic scrutineers of the body text mattered little, if millions of larger vision registered the banner words above.

THE PRESIDENTIAL SPECIAL, a train of rare beauty, puffed north along the Atlantic seaboard. Its press complement, originally set at six, swelled to fifty as reporters realized that Roosevelt was out to make news. Navy Secretary

William H. Moody came aboard at Boston to keep him company. Every stop brought a crescendo of church bells, band music, and calls for "Teddy." On 26 August alone he addressed a quarter of a million people, leaning over the back rail of his Pullman and rasping out little homilies about "the simple life."

At Bangor, Maine, an old loyalty reawakened. "If anyone sees or knows where Bill Sewall of Island Falls, Aroostook, is," Roosevelt yelled from the balcony of Bangor House, "I wish he would tell him that I want him to come in and lunch with me right now." The bewhiskered woodsman who had toughened him as a teenager pressed dazedly through the crowd, and went inside to roars of applause.

As the tour entered its second week, publicity surrounding it grew. So did a general admiration of Roosevelt's courage in making trust control a campaign issue. "Not since the nation hearkened to the words of the Great Emancipator," declared the New York *Press,* "has a Chief Magistrate of the United States delivered to the American people a message of greater present concern."

Even citizens of other countries seemed to be aware of its importance. All Europe, *Literary Digest* reported, was "ringing with Roosevelt," to the extent that Germans had begun to find him more fascinating than their own Emperor.

⌒

THE TRAIN SWUNG south again, then west. Old World place-names were checked steadily off the printed schedule. Portland. Portsmouth. Epping. Manchester. Newbury. Every stop a speech, or two or three. Every bypass a balm for the tired throat, a respite for reading.

To Roosevelt, as to all marathon campaigners, the trip became an accelerating blur, a mélange of whistle-stops, poking hands, curious eyes, and bands, bands, bands, raucously thumping. In between each, a few pages of English medieval poetry. A valley, a gleaming river. Vermont. Evening reception in Burlington. Night cruise on Champlain. Sleep. Lazy lakeside Sunday. Rest for raw throat. Sleep. Monday. September now; the lake chill-blue. Almost a year ago, on an island lying green in that water, a garden party, a shrill summons to the telephone. Czolgosz. McKinley. "Little ground for hope." Dread anniversary approaching. What effect might it have on mad minds? Big Bill extra watchful.

Brattleboro. Girls in white strewing petals. Northfield, Massachusetts. Solemn divinity students. *Ahem!* "Men of righteous living . . . robust, virile qualities." Fitchburg. Roses showering out of a bell of bunting. *Harrumph!* "We must get power . . . use that power fearlessly." Dalton. Japanese lanterns dappling upturned faces. "The government is us . . . you and me!"

"THE GOVERNMENT IS US . . . YOU AND ME!"
Roosevelt during his New England tour, 1902

Wednesday. Last day of tour. 3 September 1902. A glorious morning. Bright, crisp. Too nice to stay on train. Ride in open carriage to Pittsfield. Four elegant grays. Light, well-sprung barouche. Co-passenger: Governor Winthrop Murray Crane of Massachusetts. Opposite: Cortelyou. Up front: Big Bill Craig. Mounted escort. Berkshire hills. Bugles, cheers. Arrive Pittsfield. Two hundred schoolchildren. Songs in the sunlit air. "Friends and fellow citizens . . ." Ten minutes quite enough. Next stop: Pittsfield Country Club.

A smooth, downhill road, grooved in the center with a trolley track. This section of line closed off, presumably. Horses keep to right, just in case. But ahead, track cuts sideways across their path. 10:15 A.M. Behind, over the clatter of hooves, a rumbling. Horses now on curve of track. Louder rumbling behind; Craig half-turning, one great arm outstretched. *"Oh my God!"* A mad crescendo; bells, screams; a sudden, shivering crash. Craig engulfed in a blur of speed and noise. President, Governor, and secretary hurled in different directions, like fragments of a bomb.

⌒

ROOSEVELT LANDED ON his face at the side of the road. He lay still for a moment, as the interspliced carriage and trolley car skidded to a halt nearby. Then, tremblingly, he searched for and found his spectacles unbroken in the grass. The air was full of dust and shouts. Captain Lung came running. "Are you hurt, Mr. President?"

"No, I guess not," Roosevelt grunted through bleeding lips. He stood up and peered about him. Governor Crane was unhurt. Cortelyou looked concussed. The coachman lay unconscious, blood oozing from his ears. Craig was nowhere to be seen. Roosevelt staggered over to the wreckage (the barouche overturned and stove in, the horses kicking feebly in harness). Beneath the trolley car was a mass of blood and bone. All eight steel wheels had passed over his bodyguard.

He saw a man in engineer's uniform staring stupidly, and bunched his fists in his face. "Did you lose control of the car?" The man was too frightened to reply. "If you did," said Roosevelt, voice shaking, "that was one thing. If you didn't, it was a God-damned outrage!"

As his heir apparent mused later, it might also have been a national tragedy. John Hay calculated that Roosevelt had escaped death by just two inches. "Had the trolley car struck the rear hub instead of grazing it and crashing into the front wheel . . . Crane and the President would have been tossed to the left and under the car just as poor Craig was."

At the time, all Roosevelt could think of was vengeance. The engineer became truculent. "You don't suppose I tried to do it, do you?" For a moment he and the President were at the point of blows. Then Roosevelt remembered his dignity and turned back to the wreckage. "Well, I had the right of way anyway," the engineer shouted, as deputies led him off.

Roosevelt did not seem to hear. He knelt beside the reddened wheels. "Too bad, too bad," he murmured. "Poor Craig. How my children will feel."

⌒

QUENTIN WAS INDEED a bereft little boy when Roosevelt got back to Sagamore Hill that evening. But the President, whose face was blue-black and grotesquely swollen, attracted more immediate sympathy. He was also limping slightly from a bruise on his left shin.

In the days that followed, varying explanations of the accident came from Pittsfield. Charges of manslaughter were filed against Euclid Madden, the engineer. One story was that passengers on the trolley car had bribed him to pursue the President; another claimed he had been coming down the slope on schedule, and could not brake fast enough when the barouche got in his way. Madden pleaded guilty. He was sentenced to a heavy fine, plus six months in jail for failing to control his car.

Memories of "poor Craig" faded slowly, like the leaves around Sagamore Hill. The anniversary of William McKinley's death came and went without incident. Next day, 15 September, Roosevelt hosted a garden reception to celebrate his first year in office. Several thousand Nassau County neighbors came to shake the President's hand and sip raspberry shrub from specially engraved glasses. Long Island Sound shimmered through the trees; the air was sweet with the smell of popcorn and banana fritters. Although Roosevelt was still bruised about the face, he seemed healthy and vigorous as he welcomed his guests. "Dee-lighted!" He shook fifty-two hands a minute for three hours.

"It takes more than a trolley accident to knock me out," he boasted, "and more than a crowd to tire me."

Only Edith knew that beneath the neatly pressed flannel trousers, the pain in his shin was beginning to bother him.

The Catastrophe Now Impending

It was different when I was a young man,
Hinnissy. In thim days, Capital an' Labor
were friendly, or Labor was.

THE PRESIDENTIAL EAGLE fluttered bravely at masthead, its golden wings beating the drizzle. Roosevelt and his aides huddled below in raincoats and wraps, waiting for Manhattan to show across the East River. Fall was still three days off, but for party politicians the summer had already ended. A "grave and delicate" question demanded Roosevelt's attention out west, where he was headed on another campaign trip.

The question was one of basic Republican policy. Some ambitious insurgents in Iowa, led by Governor Albert B. Cummins, had forced a revolutionary idea into the state platform for 1902:

We favor such amendments of the Interstate Commerce Act as will more fully carry out its prohibition of discrimination in ratemaking, and [such] modification of the tariff schedules [as] may be required to prevent their affording a shelter to monopoly.

In other words, monopolistic corporations should be controlled by special, punitive taxation. Price-fixing would give way to an equitable redistribution of Wall Street's wealth. Railroad rate regulation would control the tendency of agricultural prices to decline in inverse proportion to manufacturing costs. And fair-trade agreements would reopen overseas markets shut by the impossible cost of doing business with the United States.

This "Iowa Idea" made little sense to Roosevelt (what, for instance, about trusts whose products were already on the free list?), but he could see its appeal to ignorant voters. Before leaving Oyster Bay, he had summoned six Republican leaders to advise him on what to say about the tariff while on tour.

The meeting had been so divided as to confirm his suspicions that the Iowa Idea was a party-splitter. Senators Allison and Spooner and Postmaster General Payne, all Midwesterners, thought he should recommend some discreet modification of rates, to relieve radical pressures beyond the Mississippi. Senators Aldrich, Hanna, and Lodge had objected to any tinkering with a system that worked on behalf of their Eastern industrial constituencies. "As long as I remain in the Senate and can raise a hand to stop you," said Hanna, flushed of face, "you shall never touch a schedule of the tariff act."

Roosevelt inclined to the Western point of view. But Governor Cummins's suggestion that the tariff was "the mother of trusts" was irresponsible. No wonder Hanna, an arch-protectionist, was so disturbed. Already, the Iowa Idea was on the lips of other prairie insurgents: Governors Robert M. LaFollette of Wisconsin and Samuel Van Sant of Minnesota were barking it with the fervor of patent-medicine salesmen. Protection must give way to Reciprocity—had not William McKinley said as much, the day before he was shot?

McKinley's successor remembered being a free-trade man himself once, in hot youth. But he had found it wise to recant that heresy upon entering Republican politics. His failure eighteen years later to win even a minor bill of reciprocity for Cuba proved that protectionism was still the holiest tenet of party faith. Indeed, Speaker David B. Henderson, an Iowan, had announced he would not run for re-election, rather than submit to tariff blasphemies on the stump.

Roosevelt, thinking ahead to 1904, hesitated between risk-taking and caution. He had always been willing to embrace a worthy cause—civil-service reform, for example—if it could be proved legal and representative of vox populi. Tariff reform was beginning to look like just such a mass movement. But the mass, as yet, was still a minority. He did not want to alienate a key constituency—those millions of small businessmen and farmers who traded exclusively within the United States, and relied on tariffs as a bulwark against foreign competition. To them, protection was a right honored by twelve successive Republican administrations, and the Iowa Idea was both an insult and a threat.

During the next eighteen days, Roosevelt intended to drum into Midwestern and Western skulls the basic incompatibility of trust control and tariff reform. He planned major addresses on each issue, at Cincinnati and Indianapolis, before taking his message of strenuous moderation across the heartland of insurgency, from Milwaukee and St. Paul to Sioux Falls and Des Moines. He was setting out, he acknowledged, on an expedition fraught with risk. Every step must be measured carefully, and not just because of the nagging pain in his left shin. "There are a good many worse things than the possibility of trolley-car accidents in these trips!"

DISEMBARKING ON THE East Side, the presidential party proceeded across Manhattan by cavalcade. Secret Service men rode one hundred feet ahead, making sure, this time, that all local traffic was stationary. A Hudson River ferry took Roosevelt on to Jersey City. At 2:14 P.M., his special pulled out of the depot and chugged west through the rain.

When the train crossed the Pennsylvania border, a small, saturnine, droop-eyed man got on. Matthew S. Quay was accustomed to free rides, as senior Senator from the Keystone State, on both public and private transport. Alone with Roosevelt for the next twenty-five miles, he reported on the coal strike. Happily, the miners were about to capitulate. They had abandoned their demand for union recognition. The determination of operators had defeated John Mitchell; management was not mocked.

No sooner had Quay detrained in Philadelphia than another hitch rider got on. This was Frank B. Sargent, Commissioner of Immigration, a former union leader and the Administration's secret observer in anthracite country. Alone with Roosevelt for the next forty miles, he too reported on the coal strike. Happily, the miners were in good moral and financial shape. Recognition mattered less to them than fair wages. The determination of the rank and file gave John Mitchell strength; labor could not be bullied.

Roosevelt sent a wry message back to Senator Quay that he had received some "almost diametrically opposed" information. The truth, as usual, must lie somewhere in between.

⌒

HIS LEFT LEG WAS hurting badly next day at the Music Hall in Cincinnati. But he showed no sign of discomfort, beyond asking a capacity audience not to interrupt him with applause. "I intend . . . to make an argument as the Chief Executive of a nation who is the President of all the people."

It was the first time Roosevelt had invoked the majesty of office, and the crowd listened with appropriate respect. For a while he expounded his familiar formula for trust control: tolerance, mild regulation, and public accountability. All the proposed alternatives, he said, were "ineffective or mischievous." Chief among these was the Iowa Idea, "a policy . . . which would defeat its own professed object." Governor Cummins imagined that tariff penalties would cause trusts to end monopolistic practices. Yet most trusts controlled far less than half of their respective markets. The rare trust with majority control had an advantage of only one or two percentage points. "Surely in rearranging the schedules affecting such a corporation, it would be necessary to consider the interests of its smaller competitors who control the remaining part, and which, being weaker, would suffer most?"

Speaking lucidly and calmly, the President reminded his audience that some trusts might react to tariff penalties by laying off "very many tens of thousands of workmen." Other trusts would escape discipline because their products were tariff-free. "The Standard Oil Company offers a case in point—and the corporations which control the anthracite coal."

By choosing two particularly unpopular trusts to illustrate the inequities of the Iowa Idea, Roosevelt managed to sound both reform-minded and conservative. He mentioned his own "present legislative and constitutional limitations," and ended with a vague promise that in spite of them, he would deal "exact and even-handed justice . . . to all men, without regard to persons."

At last the audience could applaud freely. He listened with an air of abstraction to the roars that followed him into the street. "It's rather peculiar," he remarked, "that everywhere they call for 'Roosevelt' or 'Teddy,' but never say 'Theodore.' "

A REPORTER COVERING Roosevelt's arrival at Detroit on Sunday, 21 September, was impressed with the change in him since his last visit, two years before. No longer was he a young, ruddy-faced Governor, grinning and squinting and pumping hands. He appeared to have aged considerably; his features were sterner. The close-cropped auburn hair glinted with gray, and there was "an indefinable something about his appearance, call it dignity, call it responsibility—that showed he felt the weight resting on his shoulders."

Actually, the main weight Roosevelt felt was on his left leg. He complained of pain, and was unresponsive to press-pool questions about the coal strike. As soon as he reached the Hotel Cadillac, he went to bed.

Early the next morning, the inevitable crowd of gogglers gathered on the sidewalk outside. "Just keep your eye on that little window," a porter said helpfully. "That's his bathroom, and when you see a light in there you'll know that the President is in his tub." The light remained off, to general mystification. His major appearance of the day was at a convention of Spanish-American War veterans. Normally he delighted in such events, but he arrived late and delivered a perfunctory address, grimacing and sweating heavily. During the subsequent parade, he had to stand for four hours. At the end, he looked drained.

Speculation that something was wrong with his health began early on Tuesday, at an outdoor event in Logansport, Indiana. Despite steady rain, he launched into the big speech he had been expected to deliver that afternoon at Indianapolis. He declined applause as he extolled the glories of private enterprise. Beneficiaries of the new prosperity must look to themselves, he said, rather than to government, for the advancement of their welfare. Stressing the word *individual* again and again, he prayed that great issues of the future would be decided by Americans thinking "as Americans first, and party men second."

The tariff, for example—Roosevelt deftly brought it in—should be judged not as a political issue, but "as a business proposition" working in the people's common interest. That interest would only be harmed by "violent and radical changes." Perhaps some subtle regulatory device could be installed to correct the flaws in tariff policy, "without destroying the whole structure."

Standing awkwardly off balance, Roosevelt allowed that his personal preference would be for a board of distinguished and pragmatic tariff commissioners. The concept was Senator Spooner's, although he did not say so.

<hr />

WITH FURTHER ROARS ringing in his ears, he stepped off the platform and saw, sloping away from him at an angle of forty-five degrees, a grassy path slick with rain. He hesitated, then allowed Captain Lung to take his elbow as he descended, slowly and with set face.

From Logansport station, secret telegrams flashed ahead to Indianapolis. Roosevelt reached the state capital on schedule, but begged "fifteen or twenty minutes grace" before attending a reception in his honor at the Columbia Club. He closeted himself with four surgeons in an anteroom, then emerged expressionless for lunch. There were no presidential remarks over coffee; just a grim smile, a wave, and a hurried exit. Bystanders were surprised to see Roosevelt's carriage speed off toward St. Vincent's Hospital, Secret Service men galloping after.

Rumors proliferated. "The President has burst a blood vessel!"

"He's sick!"

"He's been shot!"

At St. Vincent's, the four surgeons were waiting. Before following them into the operating theater, Roosevelt had an intimation of mortality. He called for Elihu Root, who was on tour with him, and asked George Cortelyou to witness their conversation. "Elihu . . . if anything happens, I want you to be Secretary of State."

It took a moment for the meaning of these words to sink in. He was appointing his line of succession. "If John Hay should be President," Roosevelt went on, "he would have nervous prostration within six weeks." In that case, the Constitution might require a third new Chief Executive before Christmas. Only one man, in Roosevelt's judgment, could rise to such an emergency.

Root paced up and down, unable to speak. Finally he managed, "I guess you don't need to disturb yourself in the least about anything of that kind."

The President moved on without comment. Entering the operating theater, he tried to joke with the surgeons. "Gentlemen, you are formal! I see you have your gloves on." He took off his trousers and left shoe, revealing a tumor halfway down his shin. It bulged nearly two inches. He lay down on the table and refused anesthetic. "Guess I can stand the pain."

Dr. George H. Oliver's scalpel pricked and sliced, disclosing a circumscribed accumulation of serum under the shin's periosteum. Syringes punctured the sac and sucked the serum out, drop by drop. Roosevelt muttered to himself occasionally, and when the suction went deep, asked for a glass of water. Three aspirations were needed before the wound was pronounced clean.

At five o'clock, Cortelyou issued a bulletin stating that the President had had a successful operation, and was resting comfortably with his leg in a sling. "It is absolutely imperative, however, that he should remain quiet." Two and a half hours later, a heavily sedated Roosevelt was carried out of the hospital, lying stiff on a stretcher, his face white under the streetlamps. Spectators removed their hats. At eight o'clock, the presidential train left for Washington.

Successive bulletins through the night assured the nation that Roosevelt was in no danger of blood poisoning. (The four surgeons were not so sure.) News of the cancellation of his western trip came as a relief to protectionists. "If it had been completed," said one member of the Indiana Old Guard, "I do not think there would have been anything left of the Republican party. That Logansport speech today was the limit."

PAINTERS AND PLASTERERS were putting the finishing touches to a restored White House when Roosevelt arrived back in Washington on 24 September 1902. But the gleaming halls and new Executive Wing were still bare of furnishings, so he was carried back to his temporary quarters at 22 Jackson Place. An anxious Edith was waiting to nurse him. "I feel a great deal better than I look," he told reporters before she closed the door.

She established him in a second-floor parlor overlooking Lafayette Square. The room was large and sunny and full of well-wishers' flowers. Treetops waved beneath its windows. It was an ideal place to recuperate, but the President, rolling around in a wheelchair, with his leg trussed stiffly in front of him, soon complained of inactivity.

He regretted that he had not been able to discuss tariff policy in the Midwest as fully as he wished. Still, his two big speeches had done much to quash the Iowa Idea. Governor Cummins was disavowing any threat to Republican unity, and other tariff reformers were following suit.

That did not stop Roosevelt from worrying if he had, indeed, gone too far with conservatives in his Logansport address. "I only hope Uncle Mark doesn't mind it." His fears seemed realized on 27 September, when Hanna rose at the Ohio State Convention and scoffed at the notion of a tariff commission. Amid cheers of "Hanna in 1904," the Senator continued: "A year ago I gave you a piece of advice, 'Let well enough alone.' . . . Today I say, 'stand pat.'"

Stand pat. That was it: Old Guard Republicanism in two words. Roosevelt's dilemma, as he plotted his uncertain future, was how to convince reformers that he was their best hope, while standing pat enough to please conservatives.

Right now, he could not stand at all. Ominously, his left leg had begun to throb again.

⟣

ON SUNDAY, 28 SEPTEMBER, the Surgeon General of the Navy, Dr. Presley M. Rixey, decided that a second operation was necessary. The President's temperature was rising, and there was a new swelling, large and shiny as a monocle, on his shin. This time—since Rixey intended to cut to the bone—Roosevelt allowed himself to be semi-anesthetized with whiskey. Cocaine was rubbed around the swelling. Then Rixey, assisted by an orthopedist, made a two-inch incision over the tibia and reopened the periosteum. Serous fluid welled out. It was allowed to drain, revealing a length of white, roughened bone. A few dark spots, the size of knitting-needle points, were visible. Rixey scraped the bone smooth, and left the incision unstitched, so that further fluid could flow out naturally, in the process of healing. Overnight, Roosevelt's temperature subsided. A bulletin listing his condition as "satisfactory" was posted Monday morning, together with orders that he must remain chairbound for at least another fortnight.

⟣

CHILL WEATHER THAT weekend sent the first tremors of panic through coal-dependent states. Northeastern hospitals, alarmed by a rise in the pneumonia rate, competed for reserve anthracite at three or four times last winter's cost. Poor families burned coconut shells, available at fifteen cents a sack from candy companies, to keep warm. From New York, Mayor Seth Low wired the President: "I CANNOT EMPHASIZE TOO STRONGLY THE IMMENSE INJUSTICES OF THE EXISTING COAL SITUATION. . . . MILLIONS OF INNOCENT PEOPLE . . . WILL ENDURE REAL SUFFERING IF PRESENT CONDITIONS CONTINUE."

Henry Cabot Lodge, who viewed all situations politically, whether they were social, sexual, or seasonal, feared that his Bay State constituents might vote Democratic in November. "They say (and this is literal) 'We don't care whether you are to blame or not. Coal is going up, and the party in power must be punished.' " He made a characteristic inquiry. "Is there anything we can appear to do?"

"Literally nothing," Roosevelt wrote back, "so far as I have yet been able to find out." Unless Pennsylvania requested federal aid, the strike remained a state issue.

He suspected that the real issue in anthracite country was one of executive "face." The operators refused to recognize John Mitchell because they associated him with their humiliation in 1900, when Senator Hanna had bullied them into an election-year wage increase. They would never hand labor another victory to help a politician. At least, not *this* politician:

> Unfortunately the strength of my public position before the country is also its weakness. I am genuinely independent of the big monied men in all matters where I think the interests of the public are concerned, and probably I am the first President of recent times of whom this could truthfully be said. . . . I am at my wits' end how to proceed.

Two days later, the Governor of Massachusetts arrived in town, red-eyed with worry. W. Murray Crane felt a bond with Roosevelt since their shared escape from death at Pittsfield, but he did not hesitate to lecture him: "Unless you end this strike, the workers in the North will begin tearing down buildings for fuel. They will not stand being frozen to death."

"Agreed. What is your remedy?"

Crane suggested Roosevelt appeal to both sides simultaneously, in words showing that he favored neither. Perhaps a bipolar conference could be arranged, along the lines of one that had happened almost accidentally during a teamsters' strike in Boston. Then, too, management had refused to meet with labor, but the Governor had been allowed to shuttle between adjacent hotel suites as mediator. This dialogue-by-proxy led to an arbitration agreement in fewer than twenty-four hours. "It worked then," Crane said, "and it will work now."

A crisis-management team collected round Roosevelt as he brooded over what to do. Along with Crane and the essential Knox, there were his Postmaster General, Secretary of War, and Secretary of the Navy. Payne spoke for the electorate; Root for Wall Street; and Moody advised on the probable reactions of Congress.

Crane's idea of a conference was opposed only by Knox. But the other Cabinet officers clearly hoped that somebody else of stature would intervene, as Hanna had done two years before. Roosevelt was not so sanguine, nor had he patience to wait much longer. His moral sense—always abstract, always powerful—persuaded him that the miners were entitled to the tribunal they asked for. He felt that Knox was advocating "the Buchanan principle of striving to find some constitutional reason for inaction."

In the cool morning light of 30 September, he summoned his advisers back for another meeting. "Yes, I will do it," he said, wincing at the pain in his leg. He showed them the draft of an invitation he proposed to send to George Baer. Knox subjected it to close legal review. Crane, Payne, and Moody made further changes. "I am much obliged to you gentlemen," the President growled through set teeth, "for leaving me one sentence of my own."

He got his revenge on the memorandum of action that they, in turn, submitted to him.

> *1st.* We would recommend that a telegram be sent to the leading operators and also to Mitchell, the President of the Miners' Association, substantially in the form of your proposed letter to Mr. Baer. . . .
>
> *2nd.* We would suggest [saying] that upon the one hand the operators, as the owners of the coal mines, entertain certain views upon the basis of their conduct, whereas upon the other hand their workmen claim that certain modifications in the arrangements heretofore existing between them should be made; that these are substantially commercial questions affecting immediately the parties concerned, but the public only indirectly—

Roosevelt reached for a pencil. *"The public also, vitally,"* he scrawled.

> —that so long as there seemed a reasonable hope that these matters could be adjusted between the parties it had not seemed proper on your part to interfere in any way; that you should disclaim your right or duty to interfere upon any legal grounds—

"Legal grounds *now existing,*" Roosevelt rephrased it.

> . . . but that the request has been so general from all classes of people—

Roosevelt struck out line after cautious line, and wrote: "But that the urgency and terrible nature of the catastrophe now impending over a large portion of our people, in the shape of a winter fuel famine, and the further fact that as this strike affected a necessity of life to so many of our people, no precedent in other strikes will be created, impel me, after much anxious thought, to believe that my duty requires me to see whether I cannot bring about an agreement."

THE COAL STRIKE was five months old. Every mail, every newspaper proclaimed an escalation of violence in anthracite country. There had been, by various estimates, six to fourteen murders, sixty-seven aggravated assaults (from eye-gougings to attempted lynchings), and sundry riots, ambushes, and arson. Bridges were being blown up, trains wrecked, mines flooded. Seven counties in northeastern Pennsylvania were under military surveillance. Governor Stone authorized state troops to "shoot to kill" at any provocation.

Mark Hanna wrote from Cleveland to say that the operators had told him

"YOU SEE HOW DETERMINED THEY ARE."
John Mitchell as president of United Mine Workers, ca. 1902

they would not accept even an industry-appointed board of arbitration. "You see how determined they are. It looks as if it was only to be settled when the miners are starved to it." And from Wilkes-Barre came John Mitchell's most emotional public statement yet, vowing that his men would make the ultimate sacrifice, if necessary:

The present miner has had his day; he has been oppressed and ground down and denied the right to live the life of a human being; but there is another generation coming up, a generation of little children prematurely doomed to the whirl of the mill and the soot and the noise and the blackness of the breaker. It is for [them] that we are fighting. We have not underestimated the strength of our opponents . . . but in the grimy hand of the miner is the little white hand of a child, a child like the children of the rich.

Sentimentalities of this kind left Roosevelt unmoved. More than any prophecies of future doom, or loss of congressional seats in November, he dreaded an immediate spread of "socialistic action" through the ranks of labor if his telegram to Baer failed. So he cast it in the form no American could refuse: that of a presidential invitation.

> I SHOULD GREATLY LIKE TO SEE YOU ON FRIDAY NEXT,
> OCTOBER 3ᴰ, AT ELEVEN O'CLOCK A.M., HERE IN
> WASHINGTON, IN REGARD TO THE FAILURE OF THE COAL
> SUPPLY, WHICH HAS BECOME A MATTER OF VITAL
> CONCERN TO THE WHOLE NATION. I HAVE SENT A
> SIMILAR DISPATCH TO MR. JOHN MITCHELL, PRESIDENT
> OF THE UNITED MINE WORKERS OF AMERICA.

Duplicate telegrams went out to six other mine owners and coal-road executives. All agreed to attend, with the exception of the Pennsylvania's A. J. Cassatt, who pleaded noninvolvement in the dispute, and the Delaware & Hudson's aged Robert M. Olyphant, who said he would be represented by his counsel, David Willcox. Mitchell was reluctant to face such a phalanx of management alone, and received permission to bring along three UMW district presidents. Roosevelt made no attempt to explain the curious imbalance of his initial list. To liberals, it betrayed a bias in favor of management; to conservatives, it was a recognition of Mitchell's monopolistic power. "Doesn't that just show," Willcox fumed, "that this one man has got the biggest kind of a trust in labor?"

In an eve-of-conference briefing, Knox and Root cautioned the President against allowing either side to hurl accusations of monopoly and tyranny. The tone of the proceedings must be kept lofty, in the higher interests of millions of innocent Americans without heat.

Roosevelt himself, as he prepared for the greatest challenge of his political career, could take satisfaction in the fact that the operators had already moderated their position. They had actually consented to meet under the same roof as John Mitchell. And in the same room too: a President in a wheelchair could hardly be expected to perform shuttle service.

CHAPTER 11

A Very Big and Entirely New Thing

MR. HENNESSY	*It'll be a hard winther if we don't get coal.*
MR. DOOLEY	*What d'ye want with coal? Ye're a most onraison-able man. D'ye think ye can have all th' comforts of life an' that ye mus' make no sacryfice to uphold th' rights iv property?*

CURIOUS ONLOOKERS BEGAN congregating outside number 22 Jackson Place early on Friday, 3 October 1902. Their ranks were swelled by the largest contingent of reporters and photographers seen in Washington since the beginning of the Spanish-American War. It was an exquisite fall morning. Sun slanted through the open windows of the President's second-floor parlor, at such an angle that people across the street could make out several yards of silk wall-covering, and the tops of fourteen empty chairs. Roosevelt himself was nowhere to be seen.

Just before ten o'clock, the Attorney General, natty in white vest and bowler, skipped up the front steps with his hands in his pockets. Moments later, he reappeared above, suddenly bald. From within came a piping shout, "Hello, Knox!" Roosevelt rolled into view in a blue-striped robe, a bowl of asters in his lap. He placed the flowers on a sunny sill, then, to general disappointment, moved out of sight.

Actually, he had only wheeled himself into a corner between two windows. Flanked thus, he sat in inscrutable shadow, facing a semicircle of seats bathed in light. For once he was not performer, but audience. He could not direct the players who would soon appear before him, yet without him they could not interact: they must throw their speeches his way.

For almost an hour he conferred quietly with Knox and another early arrival, Commissioner of Labor Carroll D. Wright. Outside, police tried to contain the thickening crowd. John Mitchell and his three aides came across the

"FROM WITHIN CAME A PIPING SHOUT."
The temporary White House, no. 22 Jackson Place, 1902

square at six minutes before eleven. Kodaks clicked—probably in vain, because with his swarthy face and dark gray eyes under a black fedora, the union leader was dark enough to defeat any exposure. A black frock coat ballooned slightly behind him as he walked. Such saturninity was to be expected, perhaps, of a former coal miner. But Mitchell's white starched collar, dazzling in the sun, made him also look clean and handsome enough to thrill any woman in the crowd. Only the scarred hands betrayed the years he had spent underground.

While George Cortelyou was receiving the UMW delegation, a plush landau drew up. George F. Baer sat alone opposite two colleagues, his isolation proclaiming him their leader. He had breakfasted in his private railroad car, enjoyed a cigar, and taken a walk, yet his face was drawn and droopy-eyed. With his ascetic features and narrow beard (which he fingered nervously at the sight of the crowd), Baer looked almost French. But from behind, as he stepped down onto the sidewalk, he revealed a fat Teutonic neck, close-cropped and obstinate.

Eben B. Thomas, chairman of the Erie Railroad, and William H. Truesdale, president of the Delaware & Hudson, followed Baer into the house, doffing glossy hats, their silver whiskers flashing. Behind, in another landau, came David Willcox, waspishly elegant in a flowered silk vest. He was accompanied by Thomas P. Fowler of the New York, Ontario, & Western, all clenched mouth and crinkly hair, and John Markle, an independent mine owner, whose jowls and choleric complexion advertised him as the most dangerous man of the six.

"Gentlemen," said Cortelyou, "if you are ready, we will go to the President."

~~

ROOSEVELT RECEIVED HIS guests apologetically. "You will have to excuse me, gentlemen, I can't get up to greet you."

Commissioner Wright performed the introductions.

"Dee-*lighted*," Roosevelt kept saying, snapping the syllables off with his teeth. He indicated the empty chairs. Watchers outside were amused to see fourteen heads dropping simultaneously, like cherries in a slot machine. The President reached for a typescript.

"Gentlemen, the matter about which I have called you here is of such extreme importance that I have thought it best to reduce what I have to say into writing." He began to read with great emphasis, pausing after each sentence to check reactions around the room.

> I wish to call your attention to the fact that there are three parties affected by the situation in the anthracite trade—the operators, the miners, and the general public. I speak for neither the operators nor the miners, but for the general public.

A yard or two beyond the President's propped-up leg, George Baer listened intently. Roosevelt admitted he had no "right or duty to intervene in this way upon legal grounds." He was bound, however, to use what influence he could to end an "intolerable" situation. His guests must consider the consequences of further disagreement.

> We are upon the threshold of winter, with an already existing coal famine, the future terrors of which we can hardly yet appreciate. The evil possibilities are so far-reaching, so appalling, that it seems to me that you [are] required to sink for the time being any tenacity as to your respective claims in the matter at issue between you. In my judgment the situation imperatively requires that you meet upon the common plane of the necessities of the public. With all the earnestness there is in me I ask that there be an immediate resumption of operations in the coal mines in some such way as will without a day's unnecessary delay meet the crying needs of the people.

Laying down his typescript, Roosevelt added, "I do not invite a discussion of your respective claims and positions." John Mitchell stood up in polite disobedience.

Mr. President, I am much impressed with what you say. We are willing to meet the gentlemen representing the coal operators to try to adjust our differences among ourselves. If we cannot adjust them that way, Mr. President, we are willing that you shall name a tribunal who shall determine the issues that have resulted in this strike. And if the gentlemen representing the operators will accept the award or decision of such a tribunal, the miners will willingly accept it—even if it is against their claims.

Roosevelt moved quickly to forestall any response from Baer. "Before considering what ought to be done, I think it only just . . . that you should have time to consider what I have stated as to the reasons for my getting you together." He distributed copies of his opening declaration. "Give it careful thought and come back at three o'clock."

~⊃~

THE OPERATORS RETURNED in frustration to their private train. They had expected a formal hearing, at which they could argue that John Mitchell did not represent the peculiar interests of anthracite labor. He was, in fact, president of a union whose membership was predominantly bituminous. Since soft coal was to a certain extent competitive with hard (and might become more so, with emergency conversion of home heating appliances), Mitchell was a walking conflict of interest.

Roosevelt had discouraged them from expressing this reasonable scruple, while weakly—or deliberately?—allowing Mitchell to pontificate in time for the evening papers. Then, adding insult to injury, he had announced a long recess, which meant *they* would be unable to make any headlines before the next morning.

A typist awaited Baer in his mobile office. Her fingers began to fly as he told her exactly what he thought of the whole proceeding.

~⊃~

A BOWL OF WHITE roses replaced the asters in Roosevelt's window that afternoon, but it stimulated no feelings of truce. The operators were in a mood of heavy, postprandial truculence. "Do we understand you correctly," Baer asked over the President's foot, "that we will be expected to answer the proposition submitted by Mr. Mitchell this morning?"

Roosevelt would have preferred a reply to his own statement. "It would be a pleasure to me," he said, "to hear any answer that you are willing to make."

"You asked us to consider the offer of Mr. Mitchell . . . to go back to work if you will appoint a commission to determine the questions at issue."

"I did not say that!"

"But you did, Mr. President. Or so we understood you."

"I did not say it!" Momentarily forgetting himself, Roosevelt leaned forward. Onlookers below saw his blue-sleeved arm punching the air. "And nothing that I did say could possibly bear that construction."

Cortelyou read back the stenographic record. Baer proceeded in tones of cool insolence.

"We assume that a statement of what is going on in the coal regions will not be irrelevant." Roosevelt, perhaps realizing that he had been unfair during the morning, made no protest.

Some fifteen to twenty thousand nonunion miners, Baer informed him, stood ready to provide the public with anthracite coal. But they had been terrorized by Mitchell and his goons. Free men were unable to trade their labor on the open market without being "abused, assaulted, injured, and maltreated." Operators needed armed guards and police to protect private property—all for fear of a bituminous upstart "whom," Baer scolded the President, "you invited to meet you."

Roosevelt stared out of the window, tapping his fingers.

For five months, Baer complained, there had been rampant violence in eastern Pennsylvania, "anarchy too great to be suppressed by the civil power." Governor Stone's shoot-to-kill order had had a salutary effect. However, anarchy would return if Mitchell's men got any "false hopes."

By now Baer's German blood was up, and he treated Roosevelt to a political lecture. "The Constitution of the United States requires the President, when requested by the Governor, to suppress domestic violence." Brushing aside the fact that Stone had not yet asked for help, he guaranteed that he and his colleagues would produce all the anthracite America needed, if they could be assured of federal protection. "The duty of the hour is not to waste time [but] to reestablish order and peace at any cost. Free government is a contemptible failure—"

The phrase *free government* sounded like a euphemism for *your government.*

"—is a contemptible failure if it can only protect the lives and property, and secure the comfort of the people, by compromising with the violators of the law and the instigators of violence and crime."

Baer concluded with a sarcastic rejection of "Mr. Mitchell's considerate offer to let our men work on terms that he makes." His tone was so bitter that neither Roosevelt nor the UMW men caught the significance of a last-minute counterproposal: that anthracite labor disputes be referred to local courts "for final determination."

Obliquely, Baer was accepting Mitchell's key demand: that the operators submit to the authority of a third power. The line between adjudication and arbitration was thin, and Baer had been forced to choose one side against the other. Contrary to popular impression, he was telling the truth when he said that a 10 percent wage hike would threaten industry profitability. Anthracite mining was a rich but moribund business, vulnerable to extinction if it allowed cheaper, more plentiful bituminous coal to become the Northeast's fuel of choice. By next spring, if the strike lasted through winter or was too expensively settled, Shenandoah could be on its way to ghosthood, and the Philadelphia & Reading's freight cars filled with nothing but air.

Roosevelt felt a twinge of sympathy. Baer was a self-made man who had begun work at thirteen. He rightly believed in capital as "the legitimate accumulations of the frugal and the industrious." Behind his bluster, he could not long deny the necessities of life—work and wages and warmth—to people as desperate as he once had been.

Mitchell, rising to reply, repeated his call for arbitration by a presidential board. He spoke with deliberate softness, looking earnestly into Roosevelt's eyes. Courteous, flattering phrases floated in the air: *much impressed with the views you expressed . . . deferring to your wishes . . . accept your award . . . respectfully yours.* He managed to use the second-person singular eleven times in six sentences.

Roosevelt asked the views of the other operators. E. B. Thomas specifically blamed the UMW for twenty deaths, plus "constant and increasing destruction of dwellings, works, machinery, and railroads." He echoed Baer's adjudication offer. Again it was ignored.

John Markle stood up next, and angrily loomed over Roosevelt's wheelchair. "This, Mr. President, is Exhibit A of the operators." He brandished a newspaper cartoon of the goddess Labor being pursued by hoodlums, while the goddess Justice sat blind and helpless, bound by political cords. "Are you asking us to deal with a set of outlaws?"

Roosevelt was fortunate in being confined to his wheelchair, for he confessed afterward that he would have liked to have taken Markle "by the seat of the breeches and nape of the neck" and thrown him out the window. He stoically endured a further indictment of UMW propaganda by Truesdale, and demands by Willcox for antitrust proceedings against the union. When silence fell at last, he asked Mitchell if he had anything more to say.

It was a crucial moment for the labor leader. Thomas had made serious accusations of homicide, which he must answer for the record. Roosevelt's eye calmed him.

"The truth of the matter," Mitchell said, "is, as far as I know, there have been seven deaths. No one regrets them more than I do." However, three of these deaths were caused by management's private police forces, and no charges had been leveled in the other four cases. "I want to say, Mr. President, that I feel very keenly the attacks made upon me and my people, but I came here with the intention of doing nothing and saying nothing that would affect reconciliation."

The air in the room was chill with failure. Roosevelt formally asked if

Mitchell's arbitration proposal was acceptable. To a man, the operators replied, "No."

⌒

OUTSIDE IN LAFAYETTE SQUARE, shadows were lengthening to dusk. The onlookers, especially those up telephone poles and trees, knew things were not going well. They had seen angry gestures, heard once the crash of a fist— Baer's?—on wood. Now the door of number 22 flew open, and the operators came out grimly en masse. They refused to take press questions. "You may as well talk to that wall," one of them said, "as to us." Upstairs, Mitchell and his deputies remained closeted with Roosevelt. Reporters guessed, correctly, that the most urgent colloquy of the day was taking place.

While doctors hovered to check his blood pressure, the President warned Mitchell that any more atrocities, as detailed in the afternoon's complaints, would warrant federal intervention. In that case he, as Commander-in-Chief of the United States Army, "would interfere in a way which would put an absolute stop to mob violence within twenty-four hours, and put a stop to it for good and all, too."

The bells of Washington struck five as Mitchell went down into the street, his face blank with despair.

"There is no settlement," he announced.

⌒

"WELL, I HAVE TRIED and failed," Roosevelt wrote Mark Hanna after the doctors had gone. "I feel downhearted over the result because of the great misery ahead for the mass of our people." Aides were surprised to find the President not angry. He even tried to find excuses for Baer. As for Mitchell, "I felt he did very well to keep his temper." Roosevelt agreed with Carroll Wright that the strike reflected injustice on both sides. "What my next move will be I cannot yet say."

He wanted to see how the American people would react to the official report of the day's proceedings, which was even now thumping through Government Printing Office presses. It was made available just before midnight. The next morning, Roosevelt sensed such a rush of popular approval as to sweep away any feelings of personal failure.

The national newspapers congratulated him almost unanimously for his courage in calling the conference. Never before, the New York *Sun* remarked, had a President of the United States mediated the contentions of capital and labor. The New York *Mail & Express* said his "happily worded" address was one "that any President might have been proud to utter." John Mitchell won praise for his firmness and good manners, and blame for "lack of patriotism" in bargaining with a vital resource. Most negative comments focused on the "insolent," "audacious," "sordid" behavior of the operators.

Roosevelt tended to agree with the Brooklyn *Eagle* that the fundamental issue now was "coal and not controversy." He was inundated with mail demanding a military invasion of the anthracite fields. Some letters, on heavy corporate stationery, reminded him that President Cleveland had not hesitated to break up the 1894 Pullman railroad strike, in the name of free enterprise and private property. Others, misspelled and querulous, besought him to seize the mines "for the people," under law of eminent domain.

Roosevelt began to empathize with Lincoln at the onset of the Civil War. For the first time in his Presidency, he breathed the alpine air of a great decision. He could not retreat from the height he had assumed on 3 October—not unless he wanted to risk "the most awful riots this country has ever seen." Only one other living American knew what it was like to be so alone at the peak of power. Or was that man too old and fat to remember, much less care?

As if to reassure him, Grover Cleveland wrote from Princeton, New Jersey. "My dear Mr. President, I read in the paper this morning on my way home from Buzzard's Bay, the newspaper accounts of what took place yesterday between you and the parties directly concerned in the coal strike." The patient, spiky, sloping script was the same as it had been when Cleveland had been in the White House, benignly tolerating Roosevelt's activism as Civil Service Commissioner. "I am so surprised and 'stirred up' by the position taken by the contestants that I cannot refrain from making a suggestion."

This was that Baer and Mitchell would welcome a "temporary escape" from their deadlock, if appealed to in such a way as to make them both look humane. They should be asked to postpone their quarrel long enough to allow the production of anthracite for the winter. Then they could "take up the fight again where they left off."

Roosevelt, of course, had already suggested much the same thing. Cleveland had always been a bit slow. Nevertheless, his counsel represented eight years of presidential experience. Here was the brute disciplinarian of 1894 recommending reason over force.

"Your letter was a real help and comfort to me," Roosevelt replied. He declined, however, to issue another appeal, feeling that Baer's attitude precluded it. "I think I shall now tell Mitchell that if the miners will go back to work I will appoint a commission to investigate the whole situation and will do whatever in my power lies to have the findings of such a commission favorably acted upon."

Roosevelt did not say which distinguished private citizen he hoped might chair this commission. He merely ended his letter with a reminder that he had been "very glad" to make one of Cleveland's friends Surgeon General.

⎯◦⎯

JOHN MITCHELL RECEIVED the President's new proposal doubtfully. He said he would consider it. Roosevelt, meanwhile, was put under medical orders to refrain from further work. He expressed his frustration to the Librarian of Congress:

> *Dear Mr. Putnam:* As I lead, to put it mildly, a sedentary life for the moment I would greatly like some books that would appeal to my queer taste. I do not suppose there are any histories or any articles upon the early Mediterranean races. That man Lindsay who wrote about prehistoric Greece has not put out a second volume, has he? Has a second volume of Oman's Art of War appeared? If so, send me either or both; if not, then a good translation of Niebuhr and Momsen [*sic*] or the best modern history of Mesopotamia. Is there a good history of Poland?

Putnam obliged, only to receive a presidential reprimand. "I do not like the Poland. It is too short."

WHILE ROOSEVELT READ and Mitchell pondered, violence continued to roar in the anthracite valleys. At night, military searchlights played nervously around Shenandoah. "Things are steadily growing worse," a state trooper reported, "and the future of this region is dark indeed." A Justice Department spy in Wilkes-Barre reported that he had lost sympathy for the miners. UMW executives were openly inciting mobs to riot. The New York *Sun* demanded that labor thugs be treated like Filipino guerrillas: "without parley and without terms." Governor Stone called out Pennsylvania's entire ten-thousand-man National Guard.

The weather turned cold and wet. Inch by inch, seepage mounted in empty mine shafts. Hills of unsold anthracite lay under the beating rain. Public pressure built on George Baer, who seemed at the point of a nervous breakdown before meeting with J. P. Morgan in New York. "He literally ran to the elevator making frantic motions with his right arm, to ward off the reporters," a UMW observer wrote Mitchell. "He almost hysterically repeated over and over, nothing to say, nothing to say. . . . He shook and trembled and his face was livid."

Mitchell, sensing weakness, turned Roosevelt down. "We believe that we went more than half way in our proposal at Washington, and we do not feel that we should be asked to make further sacrifice." His statement was published on 9 October. Within hours, a striker was shot dead at Shenandoah. Panicking, the mayors of more than one hundred of America's largest cities called for the nationalization of the anthracite industry.

Roosevelt noted that Poland's ancient kings had also been hampered by irresponsible subjects. "I must not be drawn into any violent step which would bring reaction and disaster afterward." He decided to appoint his

commission of inquiry, whether Mitchell liked it or not. Congress was entitled to a full report on the situation before he took the law into his own
hands. A follow-up letter reached Grover Cleveland on 11 October:

> In all the country there is no man whose name would add such weight
> to this enquiry as would yours. I earnestly beg you to say that you will
> accept. I am well aware of the great strain I put upon you by making
> such a request. I would not make it if I did not feel that the calamity
> now impending over our people may have consequences which with-
> out exaggeration are to be called terrible.

Cleveland was sixty-five years old, retired, and chronically short of
money. His only substantial investment was in—of all things—the anthracite
industry. If he accepted Roosevelt's invitation, he would be obliged to sell
these stocks at current, depressed prices. "You rightly appreciate my reluctance to assume any public service," he wrote back. However, "I feel so
deeply the gravity of the situation, and I so fully sympathize with you in your
efforts to remedy present sad conditions, that I believe it is my duty to undertake the service."

Anticipating an early call, Cleveland sold his coal shares and waited for
the President to tell him when he should report for work. But the call never
came. Roosevelt's attention had been diverted by the magic name of J. P.
Morgan.

⟨⟩

IT WAS ELIHU ROOT who suggested that "Pierpontifex Maximus" might be
able to succeed where reason had failed. Morgan was, after all, the financial
gray eminence behind the mine operators. Their coal roads slotted into his
greater northeastern railway combination, and he had a seat on several of
their boards.

Root told the President that he had "some ideas" that Morgan might persuade the operators to accept. Without saying what they were, he requested a
temporary leave of absence, so that he could visit New York unofficially. "I
don't want to represent you; I want entire freedom to say whatever I please."

One of the things Roosevelt liked about Root was his utter self-
confidence. He granted leave, but first summoned Philander Knox and made
his own attitude clear to both men: as soon as it became necessary for him to
send the Army into Pennsylvania, he would do so without consulting them.
He would use full force to reopen the mines, so that "the people on the eastern seaboard would have coal and have it right away." Root and Knox were
welcome to submit formal, written protests, but he intended to act as if the
nation were in a state of siege.

Far from dissenting, the Secretary of War put a force of ten thousand

Army regulars on instant alert. Then Elihu Root, private citizen, took the midnight sleeper to New York.

⟨⟩

WHILE ROOT AND MORGAN conferred aboard the yacht *Corsair,* anchored off Manhattan, John Mitchell sat in his Wilkes-Barre digs, chewing on a cigar and snipping at the Sunday paper. A visitor saw that he was sinking into one of his frequent attacks of depression. All around him lay trashy piles of newsprint and dime novels; on his knees, a child's magazine cutout was gradually forming.

When Mitchell finished his scissor-work, he propped it on the mantelpiece. It depicted Abraham Lincoln and two unshackled black slaves, with a caption reading: "A Race Set Free, And The Country At Peace."

⟨⟩

THE WEATHER TURNED dry and mild, but Roosevelt (semimobile now, on crutches) felt no release of tension. On the contrary, he began to hear rumors of a general strike. That, combined with a sudden frost, would certainly deliver him the greatest crisis faced by any President since April 1861.

Like Lincoln before him, he chose his military commander with care. General John M. Schofield, a veteran of the Pullman strike, was secretly summoned to 22 Jackson Place, and put in charge of Root's reserves. The President did not mince words. "I bid you pay no heed to any other authority, no heed to a writ from a judge, or anything else excepting my commands." Schofield must be ready to move at a half hour's notice, invade Pennsylvania, dispossess the operators, end the strike, and run the mines as receiver for the government.

The old soldier received these orders with equanimity. But Congressman James E. Watson, the House Republican Whip, was aghast when Roosevelt confided the details of his plan. "What about the Constitution of the United States? What about seizing private property without due process of law?" Exasperated, Roosevelt grabbed Watson by the shoulder and shouted, "The Constitution was made for the people and not the people for the Constitution."

Then, late on the evening of 13 October, Elihu Root and J. Pierpont Morgan crossed Lafayette Square and knocked on Roosevelt's door.

⟨⟩

WALTER WELLMAN, as usual the only journalist in town who knew what was going on, watched the door close behind Morgan. He knew the financier was carrying a document capable of ending the strike overnight—a document Root could have proclaimed from the deck of the *Corsair.* Yet here was the great J.P. coming south "to place the fruit of his power and labor before the young President." Capital, it would seem, was tacitly acknowledging the supremacy of Government.

At first, Roosevelt was disappointed with Morgan's "agreement," which was addressed to the American people and bore the signatures of all the operators. It began with several pages of familiar complaints, followed by an arbitration offer not much different from the one George Baer had floated at the conference. There was a stated willingness to accept, alternatively, Roosevelt's commission. But the operators sounded as arrogant as ever in dictating what kind of commissioners he should choose:

1. An officer of the Engineer Corps of either military or naval service of the United States.

2. An expert mining engineer, experienced in the mining of coal and other minerals, and not in any way [still] connected with coal mining properties either anthracite or bituminous.

3. One of the judges of the United States court of the eastern district of Pennsylvania.

4. A man of prominence, eminent as a sociologist.

5. A man, who by active participation in mining and selling coal is familiar with the physical and commercial features of the business.

Anyone could see there was no place for labor here. The word *sociologist* introduced a note of jargon, yet signaled a clear preference: Carroll D. Wright was the author of *Outline of Practical Sociology.* Morgan added verbally that Judge George Gray, of the Third Judicial Circuit, and Thomas H. Watkins, a retired anthracite executive, would be acceptable candidates for slots 3 and 5. Three places on the proposed commission were thus earmarked for conservatives, and union sympathizers were unlikely to qualify for the first two.

Nevertheless, Roosevelt began to see a legal beauty in the document he held in his hands—beauty perfected by Elihu Root via many scratched-out sheets of *Corsair* stationery. Alone among his advisers, Root understood that the coal-strike conference had foundered not on the shoals of arbitration, but on the rock of recognition. The main element in Baer's and Markle's tirades had been their refusal to accredit a union, three fourths of whose members worked outside the anthracite field.

Thus, the language of the agreement pretended that the operators had never been against arbitration per se, only arbitration with the UMW. Their list of desirable commissioners took advantage of Mitchell's willingness to accept any board the President chose. It was also calculated to make Roosevelt seem to be taking their advice, whereas in fact Root's syntax left him plenty of room to negotiate each candidate. Ultimately, the operators hoped to boast that *they* had proposed arbitration, and were making the commission's decision *their* victory. A Pyrrhic one, perhaps—but Mitchell would surely concede it.

As Grover Cleveland remarked, "When quarreling parties are both in the wrong, and are assailed with blame . . . they will do strange things to save their faces."

ROOT AND MORGAN remained closeted with Roosevelt for one and a half hours. At last, the financier came down alone, and emerged into the night. Reporters surged around him. Usually, when confronted by the press, Morgan flinched, or cursed. Sometimes he even struck out with his cane. But now he smiled. A voice called, "Has the strike been settled?"

He stopped under a tree and relit his half-burned cigar, as if pondering an answer. Then, still smiling, he walked wordlessly off.

THE "CORSAIR AGREEMENT" was announced on 14 October. Roosevelt invited John Mitchell to discuss it with him the following day. As he feared, the labor leader objected on the ground that it constrained free power of presidential appointment. Roosevelt asked if, "in view of the very great urgency of the case," the miners would perhaps "defer to the operators' views."

Mitchell was sure they would not—unless the commission was expanded to seven members, with at least two chosen freely. He would "do his best" to sell that notion to the UMW. Roosevelt said that if so, he would push for former President Cleveland in slot 1, instead of the Army engineer. The next four commissioners could be typecast as per the Agreement, while the last two would be selected by Mitchell and himself: a high Catholic ecclesiastic and a representative of labor.

Temptingly, he dropped the names of Bishop L. Spalding, a Baltimore patrician and industrial scholar, and Edgar E. Clark, chief of the Railway Conductors Union. Mitchell showed interest, and allowed that the latter would make an "excellent" commissioner. The first whiff of settlement gathered in the air.

Roosevelt cautioned that he could only "try" to get management to agree to all this. After Mitchell left, he ordered Root to get somebody from the House of Morgan to come south as quickly as possible. Then, feeling a need for fresh air, he laid aside his crutches and went for a long drive out of town.

GEORGE PERKINS AND Robert Bacon reached 22 Jackson Place at seven o'clock, as the President was dressing for dinner with John Hay. They said they had "full power" to represent both Morgan and the operators. He showed them his expanded list of commissioners, then limped the hundred yards to Hay's house. Perkins and Bacon remained behind to huddle on the telephone with Morgan and Baer.

While they conferred, Roosevelt celebrated. He obviously believed the strike was over. Pride in his skills as mediator, and joy in his returning health, bubbled up inside him. "He began talking at the oysters, and the *pousse-café* found him still at it," Hay reported to Henry Adams. "When he was one of us, we could sit on him—but who except you, can sit on a Kaiser?"

⟋⟍

THE STRIKE, HOWEVER, was not over, as Roosevelt found to his chagrin when he got back to Jackson Place at 10:00. Perkins and Bacon said they personally approved the idea of a seven-man commission, but that Baer was driving them mad with objections to the inclusion of Edgar Clark. Under no circumstances would the operators allow "a labor man" power over their future.

Roosevelt privately looked on the next three hours as a "screaming comedy." Yet the evening could well have disintegrated into tragedy. Perkins and Bacon predicted civil warfare if the President did not yield to Baer's objections. Roosevelt saw revolution if he did. Root and Wright joined in the debate, to a jangling counterpoint of long-distance telephone calls. Midnight struck. In two more hours, the morning newspapers would go to press. Roosevelt redoubled his pressure on Perkins and Bacon. Suddenly, the latter said there could be some "latitude" in choosing commissioners, as long as they were put under the right "headings." Roosevelt pounced.

> I found that they did not mind my appointing any man, whether he was a labor man or not, so long as he was not appointed *as a labor man*. . . . I shall never forget the mixture of relief and amusement I felt when I thoroughly grasped the fact that while they would heroically submit to anarchy rather than have Tweedledum, yet if I would call it Tweedledee they would accept it with rapture; it gave me an illuminating glimpse into one corner of the mighty brains of these "captains of industry."

With a straight face, he proposed that Edgar E. Clark be moved to the "eminent sociologist" slot. After all, Mr. Clark must have "thought and studied deeply on social questions" as a union executive. Perkins and Bacon agreed at once. They also said yes to the selection of Bishop Spalding, while Roosevelt approved E. W. Parker of the United States Geological Survey as the scientist.

The President now had five commissioners acceptable to both sides, with one more slot—that of the Army engineer—not yet negotiated. For the seventh, he still hoped to appoint Grover Cleveland. If Clark qualified as a "sociologist," a former Commander-in-Chief could be described as having some military experience.

Suspecting, perhaps, that even mighty brains might jib at this, he said casually that he would like Carroll Wright to serve "as recorder." Perkins and Bacon again agreed, not realizing that the President now had, in effect, a reserve board member, whom he could promote at leisure if any of the seven proved problematic.

Morgan's men adjourned once more to the telephone. Back over the line came consent to the "eminent sociologist" and to the Catholic prelate. But Baer had the satisfaction of rejecting a former President of the United States. This permitted the instant elevation of Wright. And so, as Roosevelt put it, the thing was done. "Heavens and earth, it has been a struggle!"

_____

SOME WEEKS AFTER the Coal Strike Commission had begun its work, and anthracite fires were glowing in forty million grates, George Baer encountered Owen Wister and roared at him, "Does your friend ever think?" The railroad executive was still furious over Roosevelt's "impetuous" intervention between free-market forces. Even the most conservative economic experts were predicting that United Mine Workers would win at least a 10 percent wage increase, plus fairer and safer working conditions and the right to arbitrate all disputes.

"He certainly seems to act," Wister replied.

The rest of the world seemed to agree. Theodore Roosevelt's mediation between capital and labor earned him fame as the first head of state to confront the largest problem of the twentieth century. He was cheered in the French Chamber of Deputies, and hailed by *The Times* of London as a political original. "In a most quiet and unobtrusive manner the President has done a very big and entirely new thing. We are witnessing not merely the ending of the coal strike, but the definite entry of a powerful government upon a novel sphere of operation."

At home, Roosevelt basked in a popular outpouring of admiration and affection that boded well for 1904. And far beyond that, to the end of his days, he could rejoice with falsetto giggles at "the eminent sociologist."

CHAPTER 12

Not a Cloud on the Horizon

In this palace he lives like a king.

"THE PRESIDENT RETURNS to Secretary Hay the two little German brochures on the trust question," said Roosevelt, dictating. "The President has troubles of his own, and positively declines to read these articles in the original. If the enthusiastic consul who sent them will translate them (by preference into verse), the President may or may not look at them."

He was in high good humor as his forty-fourth birthday approached. The late October air was fragrant with political fruit. With arbitration of the coal strike under way, Democratic Congressional candidates were unable to campaign on the theme of labor unrest. Nor could they attack the Republican Party in other vulnerable areas. *Harper's Weekly* noted how deftly the President had neutralized such issues as trust control, Philippine independence, Cuban reciprocity, and tariff reform. If the GOP was rescued from a rout in November, it had Theodore Roosevelt to thank. "The power of one man thus to cover his party with the mantle of his own strength is unprecedented in the history of American politics."

Tributes, in the form of endorsements from state Republican conventions, were already piling up, each gaily wrapped with the ribbon "1904." Political veterans could not remember a time when delegates across the country had pledged themselves to a sitting President so soon. At latest count, Roosevelt had 394 votes from fifteen states. Ninety-eight more votes would give him half of the projected maximum of 984, and he had nineteen months to expand that half into a majority. Wall Street, of course, still wanted Senator Hanna in the White House. Yet J. P. Morgan had shown that it was possible to do business with the President and not burst a blood vessel. Even E. H. Harriman now proclaimed himself a Roosevelt man, and had "come to the front handsomely" with campaign contributions.

Roosevelt's long-term prospects, indeed, were so favorable that he had lost interest in the current campaign. "I feel like throwing up my hands and going to the circus." Secretly, he plotted a postelection hunting trip to Mississippi, and allowed himself several bad puns on the words *Baer* and *bear.*

It was not blood he craved, so much as exercise. His left leg had now healed, but he was lame from the wheelchair, and his girth was increasing. He felt he might turn fat to muscle with a few days' violent activity. The alternative method of losing weight did not seem to occur to him: he continued to eat heartily three times a day. A guest at lunch noticed that waiters "were always moving toward the President."

He had, besides, a sound domestic reason to quit town as soon as possible. The newly restored White House was ready for occupancy—or would be, as soon as it stopped reeking of fresh paint and varnish. Edith was busy choosing fabric and furnishings for some twenty large rooms. Such delicate details were beneath his robust attention. To hunt swatches of chintz was a woman's job; to kill *Ursus horribilis,* a man's.

⬥

ON 4 NOVEMBER, Roosevelt was chagrined to see Oyster Bay fall to the Democrats. Only the traditional Republican vote of northern New York saved his native state from a takeover. Governor Benjamin B. Odell, Jr., won re-election by fewer than ten thousand votes. Nationwide, the Democratic Party gained twenty-six new Congressmen.

Even so, analysis of the results showed that the GOP had performed better than normal for a ruling party in off-year elections. It still had a House majority of thirty seats, ample for legislative purposes, and its margin of dominance in the Senate was unchanged. Some seriously eroded fields of support south of the Mason-Dixon Line could be written off as Democratic territory anyway. Everywhere else, except Nevada, the aggregate of votes cast indicated statewide Republican pluralities.

Roosevelt's hopes for nomination in 1904 were thus extended to probable election as President in his own right, by a margin of nearly 170 electoral votes. No doubt he would never capture Dixie, but the rest of the country offered a dazzling perspective. The only flecks in this kaleidoscope were those of Republican insurgents in the Midwest—Governor LaFollette of Wisconsin looming particularly large. One of these days, that particular crystal would have to be shaken into the pattern, no matter how jarring its color.

⬥

A SIGNBOARD READING SMEDES dripped with the damp of a Mississippi autumn afternoon. On one side of the rails was a depot; on the other, a plantation store. Cotton fields sprawled dully, their extent incalculable behind curtains of mist. About twenty Negroes waited on bales, swinging their legs and staring down the track toward Vicksburg. The President had tried to keep the location of his hunting trip secret, but bush telegraph advised that he would look for bear hereabouts, on the banks of the Little Sunflower River.

Among the bale-sitters, at least, Roosevelt was guaranteed a welcome. Ever since his dinner for Booker T. Washington, Southern blacks had called him "our President" and compared him to Lincoln. They did not care that he had only just announced his first appointment of a Negro to high federal office—Dr. William D. Crum, Collector-designate of Customs in Charleston, South Carolina. It was good enough that he elsewhere favored moderate white Democrats over the "Lily White" extremists of his own party. Had not Dr. Washington himself declared Roosevelt's opposition to any further "drawing of the color line" in Southern politics?

Within the depot, two plantation owners were also waiting. George H. Helm and Hugh L. Foote were not ashamed to show support for the President in a state where so many of his own race despised him. Roosevelt could hardly have chosen a worse time to visit the Yazoo delta. The idea of Dr. Crum (wealthy, cultured, conscientious, but black) seated in a position of power overlooking Fort Sumter was incendiary enough to revive the passions of a year ago—not to mention the passions of 1861. James K. Vardaman, a prominent Mississippi Democrat, had openly advertised for "16 coons to sleep with Roosevelt." Given such propaganda, the President's hosts were worried about a possible assassination attempt. Hence the secrecy surrounding his hunt, and the remoteness of his camp, fifteen miles east of Smedes, in a privately owned forest choked with bud vine and briar. Only one access trail had been hacked. Armed guards were on patrol, ready to stop with buckshot any unauthorized stranger.

Shortly before four o'clock, a locomotive and private car steamed out of the mist and clanked to a halt. Roosevelt emerged in leather leggings, a blue flannel shirt, and a rough corduroy jacket. Around his waist was a cartridge belt, flashing with steel-jacketed and soft-nose bullets. An ivory-handled hunting knife rode on his hip, and he gripped his favorite .40-.90 Winchester. The gun was custom-made, with a crescent cheek-piece that somehow helped alleviate Roosevelt's 8-D myopia. Its walnut butt was scarred with Colorado cougar bites.

He stepped down with a crunch of hobnail boots onto Mississippi soil, followed by George Cortelyou and the rest of his hunting party. Helm and Foote, assuming he wanted to shed his presidential identity, addressed him politely as "Colonel." He shook hands, then heaved himself onto a waiting horse. His companions mounted, too, and they rode off together into the fog.

―――

THE NEXT FIVE DAYS made for the worst hunt of Roosevelt's life: "simply exasperating . . . I never got a shot." Bears were not rare around the Little

Sunflower, just rare wherever he went. His veteran catcher, Holt Collier (lifetime tally, 1,600 specimens), tried to lure game within range of the presidential rifle, yet hunter and prey invariably moved in different directions.

The other men in the party did not dare to bag anything themselves. Roosevelt insisted on first blood. "I am going on this hunt to kill a bear, not to see anyone else kill it." Embarrassingly, he had given representatives of the three press agencies permission to visit camp once a day. The resultant nonstories caused national hilarity. He was obliged to let his companions shoot a bear and a deer, if only to soothe their Southern pride.

Paradoxically, one misadventure worked to his political advantage, and spawned the most enduring of all Rooseveltian myths. Early on the morning of 14 November, Holt Collier's hounds scented bear and began to yelp. Roosevelt and Foote galloped after the pack, but thickening brush cut them off. Collier tactfully suggested that they stake out a nearby clearing, while he rounded up the critter and drove it past them—"same as anybody would drive a cow."

The yelping of the hounds receded into silence. Roosevelt and Foote sat for hours, sweating as the sun climbed and cooked the humidity of the forest. Noon came, and with it boredom and hunger. Eventually they concluded that Collier's bear had gone astray, so they might as well ride back to camp for lunch.

No sooner had they left than a lean black bear burst through the brush with the pack at its heels. Hot and exhausted, it lunged into a pond, and the dogs splashed after it. The bear reared and struck out, crushing one hound's spine. Collier threw a lariat over the shaggy neck and pulled tight. Then he waded in and cracked the bear's skull with the butt of his gun—carefully, because he wanted it to stay alive.

Back at the camp, the hunters heard excited horn calls. A messenger from Collier galloped up. "They done got a bear out yonder about ten miles and 'Ho' wants the Colonel to come out and kill him."

Roosevelt rode back at full speed. He was both disappointed and upset, on reaching the pond, to find a stunned, bloody, mud-caked runt tied to a tree. At 235 pounds, the bear was not much bigger than he. He refused to shoot. "Put it out of its misery," he said. Somebody dispatched it with a knife.

The hunt continued for another three days, but the curse of that tortured bear kept Roosevelt's bullets cold. He did not know, as he crashed vainly through the mists, that the outside world was already applauding his "sportsmanlike" refusal to kill for killing's sake. Clifford Berryman, the *Washington Post* cartoonist, was inspired to make a visual pun linking the incident with the President's race policy. He sketched a very black bear being roped about the neck by a very white catcher, and Roosevelt turning away in disgust, with sloped rifle. The cartoon appeared on the front page of the *Post* on 16 November, captioned DRAWING THE LINE IN MISSISSIPPI.

Whether or not readers got Berryman's pun, they rejoiced in his imagery, and demanded more "bear cartoons" after Roosevelt returned to Washington. Berryman obliged—again and again, as he realized he had hit upon a symbol the public adored. With repetition, his original lean bear became smaller, rounder, and cuter. He drew it as "a poor measly little cub with most of its fur rubbed off, and big ears like prickly pears," and it became the leitmotif of every cartoon he drew of Theodore Roosevelt.

That winter, by one of the mysterious coincidences that yoke inventions, stuffed, plush bear cubs with button eyes and movable joints began to issue from Margarete Stieff's toy factory in Giengen, Germany. Three thousand were ordered by F.A.O. Schwarz of New York City, while in Brooklyn a storekeeper named Morris Michtom began producing something similar at $1.50 each. The competing bears soon fused, along with Berryman's cub, into a single cuddly entity that attached to itself the nickname of the President of the United States. For decades, perhaps centuries to come, uncounted millions of children across the world would hug their Teddy Bears, even as the identities of Stieff, Michtom, Berryman, and Roosevelt himself rubbed away like lost plush.

~

EDITH ROOSEVELT RECEIVED her husband in a White House immeasurably different from the dark, dank mansion they had inherited from the McKinleys. Gone were the executive offices crowding the second floor, and the malignant outgrowth of greenhouses on the west facade. Gone were the sagging floorboards that needed to be shimmed up during receptions, the barroom glass screens and scuffed wooden stairs, the curly wallpaper and wainscots jaundiced with fifty years of tobacco spit. Gone, too, were the mustard carpets, the dropsical radiators, the sad-smelling laundry, the vertical wooden pipes that made flatulent noises in wet weather. Best of all, gone was the china hen, hatching a nestful of china eggs, that had bid a glazed welcome to every visitor to the vestibule since the time of President Hayes.

For this improvement alone, the Roosevelts were entitled to the thanks of a grateful nation. But McKim, Mead & White had done more than strip; they had extensively rebuilt, while remaining faithful to Roosevelt's injunction that the White House should be "restored to what it was planned to be by Washington." Outwardly it was the same, except for fresh paint and the addition of two sweeping pillared pavilions. Even these were not altogether new, for the eastern pavilion rose on the site of one demolished thirty years before, while the western, designed by Benjamin Latrobe and Thomas Jefferson, was simply exposed after decades of being hidden behind greenhouse glass.

The pavilions flanked a spacious basement that had been transformed into reception rooms capable of handling thousands of visitors at a time. In place of pipes and boilers—now sunk out of sight and earshot—there were parlors for ladies and gentlemen entering from the new porte cochere on East Executive Avenue. A separate, oval luxury lounge was provided for diplomats arriving through the south door. The vaulted corridor linking these suites with the central stairway made an art gallery. Edith Roosevelt had graced its white walls with portraits of First Ladies. Now Dolley Madison, "Lemonade Lucy" Hayes, and Edith herself, sumptuously portrayed in white chiffon by Théobald Chartran, could observe the flow of guests strolling up to the ground floor.

"The first impression one gets," an architectural critic wrote of the main vestibule, "is that its size has been greatly increased." Cleared of all clutter, refinished in buff and pure white, soaring above marble slabs that shone like mirrors, the hall seemed to breathe light and air. A delicate screen of wrought iron barred any further ascent of the stairs, while six stately columns invitingly revealed the crimson-carpeted corridor. There was a dramatic feeling of entrance, of access to power.

Thanks to solid reconstruction, it was now possible to walk the length of the corridor without creakings or precautionary detours. A further burst of light heralded the East Room. This great parlor was so changed that only people remembering the days of President Monroe could view it without shock. Charles McKim had scraped, chipped, and burned away eighty-four years' accretion of fust and filigree, leaving nothing but the original walls. New waxed parquet reflected three coruscating chandeliers. Bronze standards glowed in every corner, and marble wainscots and consoles augmented the general radiance. Twelve classical bas-reliefs replaced the dark portraits that used to hang over the doors like guillotine blades. Window drapes and banquette seats were of yellow silk. The room's only baroque decoration was a magnificently carved and gilded grand piano, courtesy of Steinway and Sons.

South of the corridor, the three smaller state parlors had been relined with silks and velvets, but they kept their traditional color schemes, at Roosevelt's command. A pair of exquisitely carved Empire-style mantels adorned the Green and Red Rooms. The Blue Room in between was stiff with corded silk. Two new silver-knobbed side doors allowed for a speedier flow of handshakers past the President at receptions.

The most Rooseveltian—and least authentic—of McKim's restorations was the State Dining Room. Almost two thirds larger than the old, with seating for more than one hundred guests, it was oak-paneled and mahogany-furnished, the chairs padded with tapestry. A disgruntled-looking moose, and some dozen other North American game mammals, stared glassily out from the walls, bracing for years of presidential monologues.

Roosevelt, marching through, did not affect any aesthetic rapture. Subtlety, balance, refinement of line, harmonies of color and texture escaped his eye, as music bypassed his ears. To him, game heads were not decorative statements so much as reassuring tokens that he was (*pace* Mississippi!) a mighty hunter. Gentlemen of his class—McKim included—felt at home dining beneath tusks and antlers, ensconced in oiled wood. Even effete little Henry Adams liked this room.

Breeding, however, saved Roosevelt from the pretensions of the *nouveau riche*. Having deaccessioned the china hen, he felt no urge to replace it with a Japanese miniature tree, or a collection of Bavarian steins. He was too much of a professional himself to venture any amateur design suggestions. Indeed, his only mild criticism was that here and there McKim had not been austere enough.

Upstairs, Edith Roosevelt had fewer scruples. Fortunately, her fondness for brown-and-green upholstery, and pink-and-green garlanded curtains, left intact the structural grand plan. Two big new bedrooms where the executive suite used to be increased the White House's total of domestic apartments to seven. Now that Kermit had followed Ted to Groton, there was plenty of room for houseguests. The oval library had been turned into an elegant parlor, suitable for the entertainment of fashionable ladies. Next door, the former Cabinet Room became Roosevelt's writing "den," with leather chairs, a deep fireplace, and yards of books. Knowing her husband's love of all things nautical, she set an old desk carved from the timbers of HMS *Resolute* in the center of the room. Here, late at night, after she had gone to bed, he could work on the final draft of his Second Annual Message.

⌒

THE DOCUMENT WAS half the length of its predecessor and clearly the work of a cautious Chief Executive. Roosevelt had little to say on matters of domestic policy, except to demand a special fund for antitrust prosecutions, and to insert the word *urgent* into his repeat request for a Department of Commerce. He took a peaceable survey of international affairs, noting that the United States and Mexico had just become the first powers to submit a legal dispute to The Hague.

"As civilization grows," he wrote, "warfare becomes less and less the normal condition of foreign relations." Yet he could not resist pointing out a corollary responsibility for the strong to maintain order. "More and more the increasing interdependence and complexity of international political and economic relations render it incumbent on all civilized and orderly powers to insist on the proper policing of the world."

By this he did not mean to threaten well-behaved Latin American nations. On the contrary, they could look for protection against European aggression, under guarantee of the Monroe Doctrine. The Western Hemisphere was secure. "There is not a cloud on the horizon at present . . . not the slightest chance of trouble with a foreign power."

With these bland words, Theodore Roosevelt revealed—or, rather, further concealed—an unguessed aspect of his character; namely, that of the covert diplomat practicing Louis XV's *secret du roi*. Foreign policy was, he acknowledged, "the subject on which I feel deepest." The very depth of his feeling convinced him that negotiations, in times of crisis, should be private and verbal, hence undocumented.

He had a far-flung network of intermediaries and informants, men of diplomatic or intellectual or social stamp, by no means all Americans. Most of them were globe-trotting friends from prepresidential days, such as Cecil Spring Rice of Berlin, Constantinople, and St. Petersburg; Henry White, *chargé d'affaires* at the American Embassy in London; and Arthur Hamilton Lee, a Tory member of the British Parliament. Their urbane, literate reports kept him up to date with court affairs and privileged gossip. As members of the *secret,* they were able to negotiate without paper, and keep agreements quiet, protecting the sensitivities of parties. They in turn could trust Roosevelt's absolute discretion.

Not until after he left the White House would he reveal, confidentially, that in late 1902 "the United States was on the verge of war with Germany." Even then, his allusions to "the Venezuela business" were to be cryptic and contradictory, enough for a generation of historians to call him a liar. Seven decades had to pass before cohering bits of evidence suggested that the basic facts of the story were accurate, and that Roosevelt had remained silent about it in order to spare the dignity of an emperor.

The full extent of the crisis would have to be inferred circumstantially, from an extraordinary void in the archives of three nations—deletion after deletion hinting at some vanished enormity, a painted-out battle of Titans visible in *pentimento* through layers of pale wash.

⮑

ROOSEVELT HAD SEEN the crisis coming for eleven months. It involved a familiar situation: failure by a Latin American republic to repay European loans. Venezuela, bled white by civil war and corruption, owed some sixty-two million bolivars to an impatient consortium headed by Great Britain and Germany. These powers, acting in unlikely alliance, were now proposing to blockade Venezuela with a multinational armada until Caracas paid up. Both nations had scrupulously assured the United States that they were interested in debt collection only, and had no desire to establish footholds in the Western Hemisphere.

The President sympathized with their frustration. Ever the stern moralist, he blamed Cipriano Castro, *caudillo* of Venezuela, for ignoring honorable obligations. The fact that Castro was only five feet tall, and simian in appearance, confirmed his general prejudice against Latin Americans as political primates, low in the pantheon of nations. To evolve, they must be taught responsible behavior. Or as he robustly advised a contemporary houseguest, the German diplomat Speck von Sternburg: "If any South American country misbehaves toward any European country, let the European country spank it."

Baron von Sternburg, about to return to Berlin, was a charter member of the *secret du roi*. British-born and -educated, married to a pretty blonde from Kentucky, he had known Roosevelt since 1889. He understood that uninhibited private language did not necessarily translate into policy. However, this was no longer the young Civil Service Commissioner blustering away at the Cosmos Club. This was the President of the United States, dominating a new, austere White House that gave off a chilly radiance of power.

When Roosevelt condoned the "spanking" of New World republics, then, one had to remember a significant qualifier in his First Annual Message: *"provided that punishment does not take the form of acquisition of territory by any non-American power."*

Current Anglo-German assurances of benign intent suggested that this qualifier was being heeded. Roosevelt believed, at least, what Britain said. The Hay-Pauncefote Treaty amounted to a guarantee that King Edward's government had no designs on the Western Hemisphere. But a secret memorandum from Rear Admiral Henry Clay Taylor, Chief of the Bureau of Navigation, warned that Germany was otherwise inclined. Taylor wrote that the Kaiser's navy would bombard Venezuela within weeks if President Castro resisted the blockade. She would then "certainly demand indemnity for her expenses." But Castro had no money. Thus, in logical steps:

§Venezuela . . . could offer nothing but territory, or mortgage her revenue in such a way as to place herself in complete political dependence on Germany.

§The United States could not allow either of these, and yet Germany's right to indemnity would be incontestable.

§The only courses open to the United States [would then be] payment of the indemnity, taking such security as she can from Venezuela, or war.

"The first method," Taylor concluded, "is cheapest, the second most probable."

His argument had crude force. Roosevelt was saddened by the whole situation. "I have a hearty and genuine liking for the Germans, both individually and as a nation." His identification with German culture was deep and strong, dating back to his days as a teenage student in Dresden. German blood flowed in his veins. He could recite long passages of the *Nibelungenlied* by heart; Frederick the Great and Otto von Bismarck rated among his personal heroes.

Part of him welcomed the idea of German capital investment in Latin

America, on the ground that countries such as Venezuela would benefit from development by a superior civilization. Another part of him agreed with Taylor that Germany wanted more than dividends in the New World. There was an ominous sentence in her proposal to cosponsor the blockade: "We would consider the temporary occupation on our part of different Venezuelan harbor places and the levying of duties in those places."

The adjective *temporary* reminded him that in 1898 Kaiser Wilhelm II had "temporarily" acquired Kiauchow, China, on a lease that had somehow lengthened to ninety-nine years. Germany's well-known shortage of *Lebensraum*—in Spring Rice's phrase, its "curbed feeling"—translated into an explosive need for new horizons. Burgeoning yet hemmed in, the Reich had to feed a million new mouths a year, and market a gross national product that was doubling every decade. Its army was already the most formidable in the world; now it was building a huge new navy. This combination of social, economic, and strategic aggrandizement, to a President who had recently reread Theodor Mommsen's *History of Rome,* portended the rise of a new, militaristic imperium in Europe, just as the sun was beginning to set on British South Africa.

What better place to establish a collection house today, a colony tomorrow, than lush, crippled Venezuela? Spring Rice and von Sternburg had given Roosevelt, over the years, a shrewd idea of the *Weltpolitik* of Germany's militarist ruling class. Expansionists such as Chancellor Bernhard von Bülow regarded the Monroe Doctrine as an insult, at best a hollow threat. Alfred von Tirpitz, Secretary of State for Naval Affairs, made no secret of his desire to establish naval bases in Brazil (where three hundred thousand Germans lived already), and in the Dutch Caribbean islands.

Germany, therefore, stood isolated in Roosevelt's sights as he braced himself for the shock of foreign aggression in South America. He could not guess that at even deeper levels of secrecy, Wilhelmstrasse strategists were working on a plan for the possible invasion of the United States. The plan called for Tirpitz to dispatch his fleet to the Azores at the first signal of transatlantic hostilities. From that point, the fleet would steam south and take "Puerteriko," then launch surprise attacks along the American seaboard. A likely landing place was Gardiners Bay, on Long Island—which meant that when German troops advanced on New York City, they would march right past Roosevelt's house.

꧁꧂

THE PRESIDENT, lacking precise intelligence, had to rely on intuition as the Venezuelan crisis developed. Fortunately, that intuition, in situations concerning the Monroe Doctrine, was acute. His animal Americanism—a buffalo nervously sniffing the prairie wind—sensed the circlings of a distant predator. As long as Tirpitz held off (there had been no formal blockade announcement yet), he could technically state that the diplomatic horizon was clear. But he gave notice in his Message that the United States was looking to her defenses. "For the first time in our history, naval maneuvers on a large scale are being held under the immediate command of the Admiral of the Navy."

Coincidentally or not, these maneuvers were directed at the same theater as the Anglo-German blockade. On 21 November, four battleships of the North Atlantic squadron arrived off Isla de Culebra, Puerto Rico. Four cruisers and two gunboats of the Caribbean squadron lay in wait for them. From other points in the Western Hemisphere, other white warships put to sea, converging like slow bullets upon the target area.

⌒

SEA POWER, that early obsession of Roosevelt's youth, had returned to haunt him as Commander-in-Chief. Since entering the White House he had been, in his own words, "straining every nerve to keep on with the upbuilding of the Navy." Perhaps his most important achievement in that regard was the appointment of two ardent strategic reformers as Secretary of the Navy and Chief of the Bureau of Navigation. William H. Moody and Admiral Taylor were working to create a larger, more war-ready fleet. They did not lack for funds. Roosevelt's First Message to Congress had generated enough money to finance the construction of two new battleships and two armored cruisers, plus a special appropriation for the maneuvers. The President had also, at the urging of a messianic young lieutenant named William S. Sims, instigated a program to improve fleet marksmanship. With less fanfare, he had approved a six-month survey of the Venezuelan coastline, and had transferred control of Culebra to the Navy Department, "in case of sudden war."

The most recent tables of world naval strength ranked the United States behind Britain, France, and Russia in ships built and building, but ahead of Germany at 507,434 to 458,482 tons. This position would soon improve, since the United States had more tonnage under construction than any country except Britain. Germany, however, had more vessels in commission—especially in the Atlantic, at twelve battleships to eight American. The latter were more heavily armored, with standard twelve- and thirteen-inch guns. But in aggregate fighting mass, Germany enjoyed an advantage of about 50 percent.

For two years, tacticians at the Naval War College had been trying to "combat" this, in maneuvers charted across an ocean of cartographic paper. They sat cross-legged on contoured islands, or perched on mainland stools, and smoked and threw dice while celluloid ships—Blue for the United States, Black for Germany—crept over the grid lines, trailing dotted wakes and firing tiny broadsides of pencil. The results were not encouraging. In almost every engagement, Black's tighter track curves, the sheer range and accuracy of its lead, combined to scatter Blue all over the table.

Germany, the tacticians concluded, could seize key harbors in any

Caribbean confrontation. A more optimistic view was put forward by the General Board of the Navy, the duty of which was to review such findings for the President. It found that if he established another base south of the one at Isla de Culebra, the hemisphere would be secure as far south as the Amazon.

As far as Roosevelt was concerned, the forthcoming maneuvers would show, better than any calculation by college or committee, just how much sea power the United States actually had. Real ships, and real guns, were being committed to this "game." If Germany and Britain wanted to splash in the same water, they must play by American rules, or the game could become deadly.

⟿

HE WAS ABLE TO stage a tableau to this effect at his first dinner in the new Executive Dining Room, on 24 November. Pale, frail Speck von Sternburg was the guest of honor. Elsewhere at the same table sat pale, frail John St. Loe Strachey, editor of the London *Spectator* and another of Roosevelt's cosmopolitan circle. The two foreigners were visiting America for "personal reasons," in response to invitations from the White House. They had opposing rooms upstairs. Each had been vouchsafed a flattering presidential *tête-à-tête*—von Sternburg at dead of night, Strachey on horseback in the rain. Agog at such favors, they could be counted on to return home with the kind of intelligence that, in von Sternburg's phrase, was "better talked over than written." The Baron was well-connected on the Wilhelmstrasse, and Strachey, through his periodical, was one of the most powerful opinion-shapers in Britain.

Between the two foreigners Roosevelt placed the Admiral of the United States Navy, as someone who could not fail to impress them. George Dewey, about to leave for the Caribbean exercises, was America's greatest military hero. He had destroyed the entire Spanish fleet at Manila in '98. (Given permission, he would have bombarded Germany's ships, too.) Blessed by Admiral Farragut and anointed by McKinley, he gave off an almost divine aura. There were people who carried little icons of him at their bosoms. Some Filipinos thought he communed directly with God.

The Admiral was now almost sixty-five. His immaculate mustache was snowy, and his well-pressed uniform did not hang as straight as it had three years before, the day he rolled down Fifth Avenue behind Governor Roosevelt's prancing horse. Too many good lunches at the Metropolitan Club had pinkened the mahogany tan; he tended to nod off in the late afternoon. Awake, however, Dewey still had formidable authority, accentuated by the glitter of four gold stars. As Roosevelt reminded him, in the order sending him back to sea, his "standing" was enough to ensure world attention to the Caribbean maneuvers.

But Dewey had more than prestige to suit the President's current purpose.

He was notoriously the most bellicose Germanophobe in the United States. And if Speck von Sternburg could not see *that,* over the white flowers and wineglasses, he needed a stronger monocle.

⌒

THE NEXT DAY, Britain and Germany officially informed the State Department of their intents to proceed against Venezuela. There would be an ultimatum followed by a blockade, within the bounds of the Monroe Doctrine. Secretary Hay replied that the United States "greatly deplored" any European intervention in the affairs of a South American republic. He conceded, however, that such action was sometimes justifiable.

Meanwhile, the United States armada off Culebra was joined by a flotilla of support vessels, including colliers and torpedo boats. Farther south, two battleships and four cruisers of the European and South Atlantic squadrons met near Trinidad, at a point only 125 miles from the Venezuelan coast.

Finally, on 1 December, Admiral Dewey went down to the Navy Yard in Washington, where Roosevelt's yacht *Mayflower* awaited him as his flagship. He ordered its crew to prepare for the open sea.

CHAPTER 13

The Big Stick

*One good copper with a hickory club is worth all th' judges
between Amsterdam an' Rotterdam.*

ON THE MORNING of Dewey's departure, Roosevelt drained his umpteenth cup of coffee, then spent twenty minutes walking in the garden with Edith. They had come to treasure this early ritual, now that his work took up most of the day and much of the night. The stroll helped him digest three breakfast courses—or rather six, as he usually ordered both choices of each, plus a bowl of fruit or cereal. Edith fondly let him eat as much as he liked. She believed that his intellectual turbine, whirring always at abnormal speed, needed a proportionate supply of fuel. At ten to nine, before going indoors, she would pick a rosebud for his buttonhole. Then, with her kiss warming his cheek, he would march along Jefferson's colonnade toward his office in the new Executive Wing.

It was a treat not to have to operate out of home anymore. This neutral space, full of winter sun, pleasingly separated his work from his private life. As Roosevelt gave all of himself to each, so he disliked to have the one encroach upon the other. Any person with legitimate business to transact could see him where he was going. But in future, only those worthy of intimacy might venture back the way he had come.

The scents of a little flower shop greeted him as he traversed "the President's Passage" and entered a hallway dividing the Cabinet Room, on his right, from the Executive Office on his left. The latter was a spacious, southward-facing chamber, thirty feet square, hung with dark olive burlap and simply but solidly furnished. Behind his massive mahogany desk—unencumbered by a telephone, an instrument Roosevelt deemed suitable only for clerks—three tall windows framed, in triptych, the Washington Monument, a lawn still red with construction mud, and Virginia rising beyond the silver river.

Another set of windows looked east toward the residence. If he caught sight of Archie or Quentin misbehaving in the garden, he had only to heave up a sash and roar at them. Thick doors (and a NO SMOKING sign) insulated him from supplicants and sycophants collecting in Secretary Cortelyou's big office beyond, and from gentlemen of the press, who now had their own den down the corridor. An oil portrait of Lincoln hung over the mantel, where he could see it at all times. Logs glowed in the fireplace; a tiny clock ticked. Polished leather under his cuffs reflected an *art nouveau* lamp and silver bowl of American Beauty roses.

The room's main decoration was a huge globe. Spun and stopped at a certain angle, this orb showed the Americas floating alone and green from pole to pole, surrounded by nothing but blue. Tiny skeins of foam (visible only to himself, as Commander-in-Chief of the United States Navy) wove protectively across both oceans, as far south as the bulge of Venezuela and as far west as the Philippines. Asia and Australia were pushed back by the curve of the Pacific. Africa and Arabia drowned in the Indian Ocean. Europe's jagged edge clung to one horizon, like the moraine of a retreating glacier.

When Roosevelt spoke of the Western Hemisphere, this was how he saw it—not the left half of a map counterbalanced by kingdoms and empires, but one whole face of the earth, centered on the United States. And here, micro scopically small in the power center of this center, was himself sitting down to work.

There was nothing much he could do right now about the Caribbean theater, except wait for an opportunity to invoke the Monroe Doctrine there, once and for all. President Cleveland had attempted to do so definitively against Britain in 1895—also in a matter regarding Venezuela—but Lord Salisbury's government had backed down too soon for any American show of force. Roosevelt held that only "power, and the willingness and readiness to use it" would make Germany understand the Monroe Doctrine fully. If he could send such a forceful message, it would "round out" Cleveland's policy nicely.

Few among the President's callers that morning saw his new globe as anything other than a piece of furniture. Congress was back in town—not the newly elected Fifty-eighth but the same old Fifty-seventh, reconvening for its last winter session. Senators and Representatives paid their usual respects, and declared their usual keen interest in the Message he would be sending them later in the day.

For two and a half hours, Roosevelt pumped hands and exchanged pleasantries. Toward noon, his flow of visitors slackened, as Congressmen and correspondents headed for Capitol Hill. The White House grew quiet. Even Edith and Alice took a carriage to watch the opening ceremonies. Roosevelt remained at his desk. Behind him as he worked, the USS *Mayflower* dropped down the bright river.

⌒

FOR THE NEXT WEEK, he remained closeted in the White House, giving no hint of anxiety about Venezuela. By 4 December, Secretary Moody had authorized a concentration of fifty-three warships—the largest such deployment the Navy had ever seen—compared with twenty-nine Allied vessels. The imbalance signified nothing, of course, since neither armada was contending. Still, Roosevelt had real strength available if he needed it. He knew the historic propensity of blockades toward invasion.

On 7 December, Germany and Britain informed President Castro that they were closing their consulates in Caracas and initiating "pacific" measures to satisfy their claims against him. Admiral Dewey simultaneously took command of the fleet off Culebra, under orders to be ready to move south at an hour's notice. He began an immediate program of dummy landings along stretches of the Puerto Rican shore that resembled Venezuela's.

As if toughening himself for the crisis to come, Roosevelt intensified his latest exercise routine, "singlesticks." Every evening in the residence, he and Leonard Wood donned padded helmets and chest protectors and beat each other like carpets. "We look like Tweedledum and Tweedledee," the President joked.

General Wood noted in his diary that Roosevelt was too excitable a stick-fighter to remember the rules. "It is almost impossible to get him to come to a guard after having been hit or delivering a blow." Despite bruised shoulders and swollen wrists, the two old Rough Riders soon graduated to heavy ash rods.

Speak softly and carry a big stick was a West African proverb Roosevelt had tried out once, as Vice President, and memorized as a personal mantra. Perhaps the current situation would enable him to test its effectiveness, starting with the soft speech. "If a man continually blusters, if he lacks civility, a big stick will not save him from trouble; but neither will speaking softly avail, if back of the softness there does not lie strength, power."

⟨⟩

ON 8 DECEMBER, the German Ambassador, Theodor von Holleben, visited the Executive Office with a party of his compatriots. The appointment was ceremonial. However, it gave Roosevelt a chance to talk to the Ambassador privately, without attracting the attention of reporters. He was adept at drawing callers aside on such occasions, and hissing something forceful through smiling teeth.

The reason for his circumspection was that he had to deal, through von Holleben, with the most dangerous man in the world. Wilhelm II, Emperor of Germany, loomed clear in his imagination—clearer, perhaps, than if they had actually met. (Roosevelt was too good-natured to be a perceptive judge of people in the flesh.) For several years, even before becoming Vice President, he had been receiving apprehensive reports about the Kaiser from mutual acquaintances. Cecil Spring Rice, for one, saw Wilhelm as an economic and military expansionist, with a "definite plan" to consolidate German interests in South America. General Wood, just back from observing the German Army maneuvers at Potsdam, did not know what to be more impressed with: the Kaiser's bewitching personality, or his domination of an inhumanly efficient military machine.

Roosevelt the Germanist admired Wilhelm's finer Teutonic qualities, as he did those of Helmuth Karl von Moltke and Albrecht von Roon. He was also aware of some beguiling similarities between the Kaiser and himself. Only three months separated their respective dates of birth, Wilhelm being the younger. Physically, they were alike in their burly, grinning virility, their hunting prowess, and their conquest of juvenile disability—in the Kaiser's case, a withered left arm. They had the same quick nerves, charm, explosive speech, and weakness for moralizing. They were catholic in intellect, encyclopedic in memory. They shared a passion for things military, identifying particularly with sea power.

However, as Roosevelt pointed out, superficial similarities between men or nations accentuate their serious differences. In contrast to his own steely sense of direction, he saw a brilliant waywardness in Wilhelm, as of running mercury. The Kaiser was vain, coarse, romantic, and often foolish. He was xenophobic in general and anti-Semitic in particular, given to hoarse shouts of *"Ein Reich, ein Volk, ein Gott!"* His fits of rage were so violent as to make onlookers sick.

What made Roosevelt most wary was Wilhelm's inclination toward bejeweled fantasy. "He writes to me pretending that he is a descendant of Frederick the Great! I know better and feel inclined to tell him so." The Kaiser liked to dress up as Frederick; when he posed for photographs in his hero's thigh-boots he revealed rather wide hips. Roosevelt, alive to any hint of effeminacy, understood that in negotiating with Wilhelm he must at all times remember the importance of show. It would be foolhardy to humiliate him in the Caribbean. The Kaiser was enough of a man to stand a tough, confidential message—and enough of a woman, presumably, to retreat if it could be made to look glamorous.

⌐◦⌐

ACCORDING TO ROOSEVELT's later testimony, he spoke to Ambassador von Holleben "with extreme emphasis," and told him

> to tell the Kaiser that I had put Dewey in charge of our fleet to maneuver in West Indian waters; that the world at large should know this merely as a maneuver, and we should strive in every way to appear simply as cooperating with the Germans; but that I regretted to say . . . that I should be obliged to interfere, by force if necessary, if the

Germans took any action which looked like the acquisition of territory in Venezuela or elsewhere along the Caribbean.

The tactfulness of this warning was lost on von Holleben, who doggedly repeated Germany's official position. His Majesty had no intention to take "permanent" possession of Venezuelan territory. With a touch of sarcasm, Roosevelt said that he was sure Wilhelm felt the same about Kiaochow, which was "merely held by a ninety-nine years lease."

Again von Holleben failed to react. Roosevelt politely informed him that he would wait ten days for a total disclaimer from Berlin. If none was forthcoming, Admiral Dewey would be ordered south "to observe matters along Venezuela."

The Ambassador escorted his party out. "You gave that Dutchman something to think about," said William Loeb, who was doing secretarial duty. But Loeb wondered if von Holleben had the courage to transmit an ultimatum. "I don't think he will give the Kaiser a correct picture of your attitude."

꧁

THE "PACIFIC" BLOCKADE turned violent the next morning, 9 December. Four Venezuelan gunboats were seized by the Allies, and three of them destroyed by Germany. President Castro, in a panic, proposed that all claims against his country be arbitrated, and asked the United States to intercede for him.

John Hay relayed Castro's proposal to London and Berlin, while Roosevelt considered the implications of his secret ultimatum to the Kaiser. The sinking of the gunboats struck him as "an act of brutality and useless revenge." If *Der Allmacht* was this willing to lay violent hands on Venezuelan shipping, what price Venezuelan real estate? More than ever, Roosevelt suspected that Germany wanted to establish "a strongly fortified place of arms" near the future Isthmian Canal. He himself was pledged to violence now—unless von Holleben brought him a peaceable message in the nine days remaining.

꧁

MORE THAN EIGHT thousand miles away, the only detached units of the United States Navy steamed to a routine rendezvous at Manila. Neither the Pacific nor the Far Eastern Squadron was needed for Caribbean duty. But Roosevelt had never forgotten that, in 1898, it had taken the battleship *Oregon* sixty-four days to rush from San Francisco to Florida via Cape Horn.

Palpably, between the extremes of his divided fleet, a mirage of locks and water shimmered across Panama.

꧁

IN BERLIN, Speck von Sternburg was reporting to Chancellor von Bülow and State Secretary Olaf von Richtoven on his recent visit to America. He cautioned them against "basking in the illusions" of Roosevelt's extravagant welcome to Prince Heinrich, nine months before. They must be aware of a steady deterioration in United States–German relations.

Expressionless, self-effacing, and cunning, von Sternburg had his own interests in mind. He knew that Roosevelt was uncomfortable with Ambassador von Holleben, and would prefer a more congenial envoy in Washington. "I feel absolutely confident," he wrote the President afterward, "that a radical change must take place. . . . Of course I didn't say a word as regards myself as a candidate."

Roosevelt did not mind members of his *secret du roi* advancing themselves, since by doing so they usually advanced American foreign policy. A little farther down in von Sternburg's letter, he read: "The Venezuelan crisis is causing a considerable stir here."

There seemed to be a similar stir in London, where St. Loe Strachey was railing in the *Spectator* against "one of the most amazingly indiscreet alliances ever made with a foreign power." British popular opinion was generally against shared adventurism. In the United States, newspaper hostility toward Germany rose to such a pitch that von Holleben sent a worried cable to the Wilhelmstrasse.

Von Bülow passed it on to the Kaiser, who scrawled irritatedly in the margin, "Herr Ambassador is over there to take the pulse of the press and to calm it, when necessary, by administering proper treatment." Wilhelm agreed, however, that Germany should refrain from any more unilateral displays of force. "We will allow our flag to follow the lead of the British."

The ink on his superscription was scarcely dry when the British Royal Navy obliged off Puerto Cabello. The captain of an armored cruiser, responding to some "insult" to the Union Jack, bombarded the Venezuelan coast, and a German cruiser joined in, heavily damaging two forts.

Roosevelt continued to believe that Germany was "the really formidable party" in the alliance. Sir Arthur Balfour's government had to find a way out or jeopardize the rapprochement between the two great English-speaking powers. One thing was certain: Britain would declare neutrality in any clash over the Monroe Doctrine.

Sunday, 14 December, dawned gray and bitingly cold in Washington. The White House stood shrouded in weekend quiet. But the clock of war ticked on. Four more such dawns, and Roosevelt's deadline would expire. Then Theodor von Holleben came to see him.

If Roosevelt expected an answer to his ultimatum of 8 December, he was soon disappointed. Von Holleben was a *Diplomat älterer Schule,* a sociable old Prussian with a bachelor's paunch and mild, misty eyes. His booming laugh precluded conversational attack. He preferred to do business in writing, with long delays between dispatch and response. The characteristics of his diplomacy were concern about America's rise to world power, and what John Hay called "mortal terror of the Kaiser."

Today, von Holleben seemed interested in talking about only the weather and, of all things, tennis. When he rose to go Roosevelt asked if his government was going to accept the arbitration proposal transmitted by Secretary Hay. The Ambassador said, "No."

Controlling himself, Roosevelt replied that Kaiser Wilhelm must understand he was "very definitely" threatening war. Von Holleben declined to be a party to such language.

The President said that in that case he would advance his ultimatum by twenty-four hours. Calculating back to 8 December, the deadline would now fall on the seventeenth, rather than the eighteenth. Von Holleben, shaken, insisted that His Majesty would not arbitrate. Roosevelt let him have the last word.

<hr />

WILLIAM LOEB SAW the Ambassador go, but made no log of his visit. Neither did clerks at the State Department or the German Embassy. It suited everybody concerned that blank paper should obliterate the diplomatic record. Wilhelm was still free to end the crisis without evidence of being coerced.

Von Holleben pondered Roosevelt's incredible threat. He could transmit it now (if he dared to transmit it at all) only as a matter of extreme urgency. Contrary to von Sternburg's insinuations, he had long been aware of the rise of anti-Germanism in the United States, to the extent of predicting war, sooner or later, over the Monroe Doctrine. But the Kaiser had scoffed at his qualms. "We will do whatever is necessary for our navy, even if it displeases the Yankees. Never fear!" This ultimatum might well be Rooseveltian bluster. Von Holleben did not want to be dismissed as an alarmist.

But what if the President was serious? Von Holleben decided to consult a German diplomat in New York who knew Roosevelt well—Consul General Karl Bünz. Under cloak of a snowstorm, the Ambassador left town. Late that evening he registered at the Cambridge Hotel, Manhattan.

Sometime during the next twenty-four hours, Bünz assured him that the President was "not bluffing." Nor was Roosevelt's short-term strategy flawed. Whatever the worldwide strength of the Kaiser's Navy, it was currently dispersed. Admiral Dewey was therefore in a position to deal a brutal blow to German prestige in the Caribbean.

As von Holleben struggled with this frightening information, diplomatic strains developed between London and Berlin. Lord Lansdowne, the British Foreign Secretary, found himself in a difficult position, with King Edward VII expressing annoyance at the Venezuelan entanglement, and the German Ambasador, Count Paul von Metternich, insisting the Kaiser would not arbitrate. Lansdowne wondered querulously if the Allies could at least agree on "the principle of arbitration," and "perhaps invite the United States" to weigh some of their claims against Venezuela.

This was the first hint that the British government wanted Theodore Roosevelt to help resolve the crisis. His neutrality, not to mention his recent mediation of the great coal strike, recommended him as an arbitrator. But Metternich would not budge.

It was now Tuesday, 16 December. Fewer than twenty-four hours remained before Roosevelt's deadline. In New York, von Holleben went down to Wall Street to check the latest fluctuations of German-American and Latin American opinion. In London, the British Cabinet approved Lord Lansdowne's proposal to accept arbitration "in principle," thus driving a wedge into the alliance. In Washington, the Roosevelt Cabinet met in closed session. And in San Juan, Puerto Rico, a fast torpedo boat stood ready to rush any emergency orders to Admiral Dewey.

"Such cables," Admiral Taylor alerted naval intelligence, "may be written in cipher . . . and [are] to be considered confidential." He reminded all staff that "there are many matters connected with the business of the fleet here, which are not a proper subject for discussion."

After less than an hour in the Cabinet Room, Secretary Moody hurried back to his office with a presidential order. A White House spokesman said that it concerned Christmas visits that the fleet would make to various Caribbean ports. Reporters soon learned that Dewey's big battleship squadron was headed for Trinidad, only sixty miles from La Guiria. And why was the Navy Department handing out detailed maps of the blockade zone?

Throughout the crisis so far, Roosevelt had pursued a policy of apparent candor and cooperation with the press, issuing regular bulletins about the maneuvers, along with qualified assurances that he was handling the Allies with restraint. "He sees little reason," the Washington *Evening Star* noted that afternoon, "to be throwing out unofficial intimations to Germany and England that this country has fixed a deadline, which they must not cross." The truth or untruth of this statement lay in the adjective *unofficial*.

By now the Ambassador's unexplained absence from town was causing comment along Massachusetts Avenue. He was scheduled to attend an evening reception at the home of the British Ambassador, Sir Michael Herbert. Protocol clearly required that he make an appearance, but darkness came, and von Holleben was not seen. Neither were the German military and naval attachés. They had slipped away to join their leader in New York.

From there, before midnight, certain words flashed to Berlin. Roosevelt was not to know exactly how von Holleben transmitted his threat of war, only that the threat got through—on a night when the Atlantic cable was so electric with communications that even *The Times* of London was denied access. Once read, von Holleben's words were probably burned, in approved German-security fashion. His dispatch of record for 16 December 1902 advised only that

> now the cannons have spoken, and Germany has shown the world it is willing to assert its fair rights, we would make a good impression on all Americans if our government were to accept arbitration in principle.

The reaction in Berlin was immediate. On 17 December, the Reichstag voted secretly to accept arbitration, in such haste that other encouragements, from Hay in Washington and Metternich in London, were redundant on receipt.

⌒

SO THE DEADLINE passed in peace. There could be no end to the blockade until arbitration actually began, but a massive release of tension was felt on both sides of the Atlantic.

Roosevelt's triumph was von Holleben's disgrace. The Ambassador remained in New York while arrangements were made to bring him home on permanent disability leave. "I am a sick man," he told a reporter. "I cannot answer a single question." He had misjudged a President, misled an Emperor, and nearly started a war. His only consolation was that the Wilhelmstrasse could not cite these as reasons for his recall without making the decision to arbitrate seem forced. To save the Kaiser's face, it was necessary to save von Holleben's. Discreet cooperation from the White House made both expedients possible.

On 19 December, Germany and Britain formally invited Roosevelt to arbitrate their claims against Venezuela. He said he would think about it, and left town with his children to spend a day or two in the pinewoods of northern Virginia. Cortelyou announced that the President had been under great strain "both mentally and physically . . . in the Venezuela crisis."

This was the nearest Roosevelt got to a public acknowledgment that there had indeed been a "crisis" involving himself. "I suppose," he wrote privately, "we shall never make public the fact of the vital step."

Overflowing with goodwill, he went out of his way to praise things Teutonic at a meeting with trade representatives of the Kaiser. For twenty minutes he spoke, in vigorous if ungrammatical German, of Goethe, Schiller, Lessing, and Theodor Körner. "He astounded us," one of the group said afterward. "He is as well posted on German affairs as on American. . . . His familiarity with the masterpieces of German literature would amaze even the most exact scholar in the Fatherland."

⌒

ROOSEVELT RESERVED HIS decision on whether to act as arbitrator through the holidays. John Hay felt sure that he would, in the end, resist this chance for easy glory, and refer the case to the International Court of Justice at The Hague. Feeling a surge of tenderness, he put his rusty poetic talents to work and composed a Christmas Eve ode to the President of the United States.

> *Be yours—we pray—the dauntless heart of youth,*
> *The Eye to see the humor of the game—*
> *The scorn of lies, the large Batavian mirth;*
> *And—past the happy, fruitful years of fame,*
> *Of sport and work and battle for the truth*
> *A home not all unlike your home on earth.*

Snow fell as the Secretary wrote. His poem joined the other presents piling around the White House Christmas tree.

"SNOW FELL AS THE SECRETARY WROTE."
Theodore Roosevelt's White House in winter

CHAPTER 14

A Condition, Not a Theory

*We insist that though his happy fellow-citizen may pass us
our vittles, he shall not fork out our stamps.*

"THE EQUILIBRIUM OF the world is moving westwards," a member of the
Institut de France told Jean Jules Jusserand early in 1903.

Jusserand, packing his ambassadorial uniform for Washington, did not
disagree. An intellectual himself (he was a specialist in medieval culture, and
had published several works of literary and social history), he accepted, and
mourned, the decline of French power. Yet it coincided excitingly with the rise
of his own diplomatic fortunes. At forty-seven, he found himself entrusted
with a mission of major importance: to protect France's *entente cordiale* with
her sister republic from increased competition by foreign monarchies. Tunis
and Copenhagen had been nothing next to this. Clearly he had been selected
less for experience than for brains and youthfulness—qualities now much in
demand on Massachusetts Avenue. In Berlin, fifty-year-old Baron Speck von
Sternburg was also packing for transfer. Britain's forty-five-year-old Sir
Michael Herbert had been at his post for three months. All three ambassadors
had American wives.

Equally clearly, Jusserand saw that his life as half-scholar, half-envoy was
over. Washington had little time for historiographical musings. As his friend
at the Institut put it, "You will no longer decipher manuscripts, but men."
Jusserand could write in Latin and read fourteenth-century English with perfect fluency. But could he construe Theodore Roosevelt? The task had been
too much for his predecessor, Jules Cambon, who seemed to doubt the President's sanity.

Speculation about Roosevelt was intense at the Quai d'Orsay. French
foreign-policy experts believed him to be the strongest international personality since Bismarck. Yet they could not reconcile the *impérialiste* who
talked about "the proper policing of the world" with the statesman who

"HE FOUND HIMSELF ENTRUSTED WITH A MISSION
OF MAJOR IMPORTANCE."
Jules Jusserand, anonymous sketch

had just modestly declined to arbitrate the Venezuela matter. Instead, Roosevelt had suggested that all parties to the dispute meet on neutral ground in Washington, in order to negotiate a protocol for referral to The Hague.

Might he be, against original expectations, a man of peace?

THE JANUARY ISSUE of *McClure's* disagreeably reminded Roosevelt that he had problems to confront at home, regardless of foreign powermongering. Never before had an American magazine publisher put out so shocking a number. Absent were the pallid love stories and escapist travelogues that most

readers looked for. In their place were three long articles on trust abuse, political corruption, and union violence. Each one, Samuel S. McClure noted in
his introductory editorial, could be entitled "The American Contempt of
Law."

The frontispiece photograph showed John D. Rockefeller seated, exuding
the security of two hundred million dollars. But his trouser leg, hitched too
high, revealed a hint of flabby calf, a vulnerable length of sock. This documentary note permeated the subsequent articles, which were remarkable for
depth of research, toughness of language, and something fresh to reportage:
a sort of tacit moral disdain.

"The Oil War of 1872," by Ida Tarbell, described the panic that hit Ti-
tusville, Pennsylvania, when the Standard Oil Company announced new
freight rates crippling to independent producers. Only one supplier, under a
hitherto unknown name, was entitled to enjoy special rates: it turned out to
be an alias for Standard Oil. A contemporary blacklist of "conspirators," reproduced in facsimile, prominently featured Rockefeller's name. The man
with the flabby calf had gone on to other, more subtle schemes, inexorably
locking an entire industry in his corporate grip. Tarbell was as meticulous in
documenting Rockefeller's acts of philanthropy as she was in analyzing the
fine print of his contracts. But she noted that "religious emotion and sentiments of charity . . . seem to have taken the place in him of notions of justice
and regard for the rights of others."

Elsewhere in *McClure's*, Lincoln Steffens contributed "The Shame of
Minneapolis: Rescue and Redemption of a City That Was Sold Out." The article, plentifully illustrated with bribery lists and police-file photographs, recounted the slide to corruption of a once-honest mayor. Thanks to the efforts
of a courageous grand juror, Minneapolis was now purged, but Steffens allowed a cynical question to shadow his last paragraph: "Can a city be governed without any alliance with crime?"

The third story, by Ray Stannard Baker, was an equally harsh and factual
survey of conditions in Pennsylvania during the coal strike. Entitled "The
Right to Work," it consisted of interviews with nonunion miners who had
braved bullets and beatings to continue working. One was quoted as saying,
"I believe that a man should have a right, no matter what his reasons are, to
work when and where he pleases." Baker reported that this miner had been
set upon by union vigilantes, and blinded with a rock.

All in all, the January *McClure's* made for ugly reading. But palpably, beneath its flotsam of fact, a new kind of reportage—"torrential journalism,"
Roosevelt called it—was surging from wellsprings of popular discontent.

⌒

THE FIFTY-SEVENTH Congress reconvened for the last time on 5 January,
and Roosevelt moved swiftly to push through the legislative program he had

been talking about for so long. "From now until the 4th of March my hands will be full," he wrote Kermit. The American economy had expanded at such a rate in 1902 (oil production alone was up 27 percent) that he knew there was no hope of controlling trust growth by occasional slow prosecutions under the Sherman Act. What was needed was an overall regulatory system calling for the cooperation, rather than the coercion, of businesses engaged in interstate trade.

He wanted three antitrust weapons: a Department of Commerce with an investigatory Bureau of Corporations, a bill banning railroad rebates to large industrial companies, and an "Expedition Act" that would provide special funds to speed up the Justice Department's prosecution of illegal combinations. (After eleven months, the *Northern Securities* case was still under judicial review.)

These requests, written in English, were passed to Philander Knox, who translated them into language convoluted enough for Congressmen to understand. Even as "Administration bills," they were less ambitious than some other antitrust measures already pending in the House. One such, sponsored by Representative Charles E. Littlefield of Maine, sought to give the Interstate Commerce Commission draconian powers over all monopolistic corporations. Inasmuch as it contained some Rooseveltian ideas, the President let Littlefield know that he could count on him for support. "I am prepared to go the whole distance!" He did not add that he doubted the distance would be very long, legislatively speaking.

The "Bureau of Corporations" clause in his own Department of Commerce bill struck Roosevelt as a more realistic proposal. Corporations would not be forced to open their books if they felt disinclined. All that Knox called for was an information exchange between government and industry, for the common good. Wall Street raised no objections, but corporate representatives congregated in Washington to make sure that the bill did not get stronger in committee. The House of Morgan sent an adroit lobbyist, William C. Beer, to monitor Roosevelt's dealings with Capitol Hill.

"He was jovial—away up," Beer reported to George Perkins, after his first presidential encounter. "I am sure that he feels the Department of Commerce is his baby, and his alone."

⟑

JUSSERAND AND VON STERNBURG, both still in Europe, were unable to attend the President's annual Diplomatic Reception on 8 January. But the rest of their Washington colleagues were there, beribboned and bemedaled, clutching swords, checking the precedence list posted outside the Blue Room. ("Germany" was slashed off the top in pencil: so much for the former doyency of Theodor von Holleben.) Secretary Hay, a diminutive, elegant figure in black, stood behind the President as he shook hands. His snowy beard screened all expression. Only the slanting, hemiopic eyes flashed occasionally with what Henry Adams called his "cosmic cynicism."

One by one the diplomats filed by, bowing at an international variety of angles. Two of the most junior loomed disproportionately large in Roosevelt's spectacles: Don Gonzalo de Quesada, Minister of Cuba, and Dr. Tomás Herrán, the Colombian *chargé d'affaires*. They served as walking reminders that the two treaties he wanted most—respectively granting Cuban trade reciprocity and canal rights in Panama—were still nothing but draft protocols.

Roosevelt's strategy regarding the first measure was simple. Hay assured Quesada that if Congress had not helped his struggling republic by 4 March, the President would call a special session and compel it to sit until "justice was done." The canal treaty presented a more vexing problem, in that Herrán kept getting conflicting instructions from Bogotá. Depending on the vagaries of sea mail and Colombia's chronically faulty telegraph system, he was at times ordered not to sign Hay's protocol, and at others, apparently, authorized to haggle over its monetary terms as if he were negotiating a contract for the sale of coffee.

Downstairs, 1,800 nondiplomatic guests were discovering that the White House's new spaciousness had been bought at the expense of old coziness. The night was blustery, and as group after group crowded through the swing doors into the East Wing lobby, frigid gusts blew through the basement. Footmen confiscated coats and wraps, in exchange for cold metal tabs that some women stored wincingly *en décolletage*. Until all the ambassadors and ministers were received above, there could be no movement of the thinly clad throng. Mothers and daughters huddled together for warmth while the gusts rearranged their coiffures and rattled the portraits of the First Ladies.

Upstairs, in contrast, the modernized heating system worked so well that several embassy ladies grew flushed and faint. Etiquette did not permit them to sit while Mrs. Roosevelt remained standing. Tempers rose along with the temperature, until ushers cracked a few windows in the East Room. The resultant convection only increased the flow of fresh air beneath.

Roosevelt (attended, for the first time in White House history, by military aides) felt a corresponding chill in some of the later hands he shook. His last guests, drawn past him with a brisk "Dee-lighted," proceeded as if catapulted toward the State Dining Room, only to encounter another line for hot punch. At 10:30, a young aide in a cutaway coat shouted that the reception was over, and a band of forty pieces swung into "Bill Bailey, Won't You Please Come Home?" Yet another line jammed the basement as metal tags were redeemed, and the swing doors gave proof that the night was colder than ever. Outside on East Executive Avenue, hundreds of carriages jostled for precedence while porters bawled out names through megaphones.

The President, oblivious, cheerfully entertained a few close friends to a supper of bouillon, champagne, and ice cream.

⟨⟩

AT BREAKFAST THE next morning, one of his houseguests, Owen Wister, said, "I don't believe you should have appointed Dr. Crum."

Roosevelt looked incredulous. "You don't?"

William D. Crum was the black Republican he had named as Collector of Charleston nine weeks before. Although thirteen other Negroes had already won Roosevelt's federal favor, Dr. Crum was the first he had chosen to replace a white incumbent. This alone guaranteed that there would be lively debate in the Senate when the appointment came up for confirmation. Several other factors suggested that the President (for all his air of innocence) was seeking a showdown with Senator Benjamin R. Tillman of South Carolina, the chief articulator of race hatred on Capitol Hill. "Pitchfork Ben" was not likely to vote in favor of a high Negro official in the cradle of the Confederacy—particularly one who had once had the temerity to campaign against him.

Roosevelt turned to Mary Wister, who was known for her good works and enlightened interest in Negro education. But she echoed her husband's criticism.

"Why, Mrs. Wister! Mrs. Wister!" His head swiveled back and forth. "Why don't you see—why you *must* see that I can't close the door of hope upon a whole race!"

The Wisters said that he had, in fact, pushed it farther shut. Thirteen Negro appointments in sixteen months (compared to three thousand white) amounted to something less than a hill of beans. Moreover, most had been to minor posts or "consultancies"—such as the one exploring the idea of wholesale transportation of blacks to the Philippines. President McKinley had been more generous.

Roosevelt's argument was that the quality of his Southern appointments mattered more than their quantity. Blacks were better served in the long run by an enlightened coalition of Gold Democrats and Union League Republicans than by the Hanna-McKinley alliance of "Lily White" bosses and purchasable Negro delegates. Before appointing Dr. Crum, he had awarded four of the most important posts in South Carolina to decent white men, three of them Democrats and two the sons of Confederate soldiers. His fifth nominee represented this same philosophy of merit. Objection to Dr. Crum could be based only on race, and "such an attitude would, according to my convictions, be fundamentally wrong."

Wister, who had lived in Charleston, tried to explain that white Southerners could not be appealed to on the grounds of logic. "It's a condition you have to reckon with, not a theory." The Reconstruction nightmare of a rapacious black majority raised up by Yankee patronage was still vivid enough to make men like Tillman scream. "Your act theoretically ought to do good to the colored race, but actually does them harm by rousing new animosity."

The argument lasted through two more breakfasts. "Here the Negroes are," Roosevelt said despairingly, as the Wisters drank his coffee. "Not by their wish but our compulsion; and I cannot shirk the duty. . . ."

Not until 11 January, when he bade them good-bye, did he admit with outstretched arms, "Well, if I had it to do over again, I—don't—*think*—I'd—do it."

⌒

WISTER FLATTERED HIMSELF afterward that the President had surrendered, "in his completest school-boy manner," to adult reasoning. If so, naïveté soon yielded to impulsiveness again. Roosevelt came to the defense of a belea-guered black postmaster in Indianola, Mississippi, who also happened to be female.

He knew her territory: Indianola stood not far from where he had hunted bear last fall. Appointed by President Harrison and reappointed by McKinley, Mrs. Minnie Cox was by all accounts a worthy citizen. She administered her office efficiently and even charitably, paying overdue box fees herself rather than embarrass white customers short of funds. But she had also invested her federal salary in local businesses, and become prosperous over the years. By local definition, she had therefore become uppity. At a mass meeting, white Indianolans chose to "persuade" her to resign.

Since Mrs. Cox was, as Mississippi's Senator Anselm J. McLaurin al-lowed, "an intelligent Negro," she had needed little persuasion. After hur-riedly resigning, she had left town on vacation—the mayor of Indianola allowing that if she came back too soon "she would get her neck broken in-side of two hours."

Roosevelt's reaction was prompt and precisely articulated. Mrs. Cox was being coerced "by a brutal and lawless element purely upon the ground of color." He declined to "tolerate wrong and outrage of such flagrant charac-ter." Neither would he stop paying Mrs. Cox her full federal salary. "The postmaster's resignation has been received, but not accepted."

In deference to the feelings of white Indianolans, however, he would not reopen her post office. In future, they could pick up their mail at Greenville, thirty miles away by country road.

⌒

ON 12 JANUARY, news leaked that the President had decided to give Boston a black Assistant District Attorney. In living memory, no Negro had ever re-ceived a Northern federal appointment. The report, coinciding with Roo-sevelt's defense of Mrs. Cox and his refusal to back down on Dr. Crum, touched off an explosion of editorial criticism similar to that following his dinner with Booker T. Washington. Only now the complaints were heard from as close to home as his own native city. *The New York Times* accused him of using political operatives to corral black delegates—"not a nice game"—and the New York *Herald* saw danger of "setting the country back a generation in color prejudice and sectional strife." Students at Columbia University debated a resolution "that President Roosevelt's policy of appointing Negroes to offices in states where sentiment is opposed to it, is unwise." Redneck reactionaries again excoriated the "nigger-loving" President, and the sheriff of Sunflower County, Mississippi, called him "a 14-karat jackass."

By now, Roosevelt was used to this kind of invective. More worrying was the prospect of fair-minded Southerners regarding him as socially irresponsible. He pointed out in a letter to the editor of *The Atlanta Constitution* that merit, not color, was his prime patronage concern. On at least three recent occasions in Georgia, he had chosen to replace black men with white. Conversely, the white citizens of Savannah had not protested when he had retained a Negro as their Collector of Customs—the identical position that Dr. Crum was to hold in Charleston.

> Why the appointment of one should cause any more excitement than the appointment of the other I am wholly at a loss to imagine. As I am writing to a man of keen and trained intelligence, I need hardly say that to connect either of these appointments . . . or my actions in upholding the law in Indianola, with such questions as "social equality" and "negro domination" is as absurd as to connect them with the nebular hypothesis or the theory of atoms.

Black leaders tried not to make things worse for him by openly saluting his policies. But William M. McGill, a Tennessee preacher and publisher who knew Mrs. Cox, could not resist issuing a brief statement in her behalf: "The Administration of President Roosevelt is to the Negro what the heart is to the body. It has pumped life blood into every artery of the Negro in this country."

⁓

ROOSEVELT WORKED OFF his political frustrations in typical physical fashion. He chopped down trees on Cathedral Heights, gunned his big horse Bleistein daily through Rock Creek Park, and, when ice made riding dangerous, hiked for miles in hobnailed boots, crashing over saplings like a bear. His singlesticks duels with Leonard Wood continued: after one session he was so whacked about the right arm that he had to greet his evening guests left-handed.

⁓

ALONG EMBASSY ROW, anticipation of the arrival of new ambassadors from Germany and France mounted. Jusserand was an unknown quantity, but Baron von Sternburg's previous postings to Washington, not to mention his closeness to the President, allowed for a good deal of gossip—not all of it friendly. "*Il est plus anglais qu'un anglais,*" sneered the Russian envoy, Count de Cassini, "*et plus américain qu'un américain.*" Insofar as Cassini himself spoke French at home, and was excessively proud of his Italian surname, this was a qualified condemnation.

"I see you are to have Specky again," Cecil Spring Rice wrote enviously from St. Petersburg. "What fun." With the Venezuela arbitration talks not yet under way, Roosevelt remained guarded. Time enough for "fun" when the Kaiser withdrew his warships, which were ostensibly guarding against any breakdown in the peace process. "He thinks he has me because he is sending an intimate friend of mine to Washington. I know what I mean to do. . . . The new Ambassador will not influence me any more than Herr von Holleben could."

This confidence, shared with the French *chargé d'affaires,* Pierre de Margérie, let the diplomatic corps know that Roosevelt had not been merely modest in declining to arbitrate Allied claims against Venezuela. He wanted to use the current negotiatory situation to make a powerful, one-sided point. Since Germany and Britain would not deal directly with their debtor, President Castro had asked Herbert Bowen, the United States Minister in Caracas, to represent him at the talks. This awkward choice played right into American hands.

"Mr. Bowen is a capable man, but his manner is not always, shall we say, diplomatic," the President said to de Margérie. Rambling on half ruminatively, he enunciated for the first time the Roosevelt Corollary to the Monroe Doctrine:

> The debts will be paid. I'll do whatever's necessary to ensure that. There's the Monroe Doctrine to consider. Since we can't, on the one hand, tolerate permanent seizure of territory by a European power in any of the American republics . . . I, on the other, can't let *them* hide behind the Doctrine in order to shirk obligations.

De Margérie speculated that it might have been a delusion to the contrary that caused President Castro to be so cavalier about credit in the first place. "That is precisely what I want no more of," Roosevelt snapped. If Venezuela refused to abide by the arbitration agreement, he would enforce it himself. "I have the means."

~

ON 22 JANUARY, Roosevelt held another conference, this time with Senators Hanna, Spooner, and Shelby M. Cullom, chairman of the Committee on Foreign Relations. They discussed the deadlocked Panama Canal Treaty. Bogotá's latest instructions to Dr. Herrán proposed an annual rent that was at least a half-million dollars more than the United States was prepared to pay for a sea-to-sea strip of jungle six miles wide. Secretary Hay had made a New Year's concession, offering to begin rental payments within nine years rather than fourteen, but this was still not satisfactory to Herrán. After six weeks of argument, negotiations had broken off, and both men were bedridden with frustration.

Under the Spooner Amendment—now enshrined in law—Roosevelt was required to revert to the Nicaragua alternative in the event of failure to negotiate a satisfactory agreement with Colombia. His advisers, Panama partisans all, dreaded such a reversal. Recent events in the Caribbean, they said, indicated that trouble with some major foreign power over the Monroe Doctrine was "inevitable." Prompt construction of a Panama canal was "an absolute vital necessity for the United States."

Roosevelt agreed to offer Bogotá a final concession, more than doubling the original rental figure proposed. The next morning, 22 January, Hay wrote to Herrán:

> I am commanded by the President to say to you that the reasonable time that the statute accords for the conclusion of negotiations with Colombia for the excavation of a canal on the Isthmus has expired, and he has authorized me to sign with you the treaty of which I had the honor to give you a draft, with the modification that the sum of $100,000, fixed therein as the annual payment, be increased to $250,000. I am not authorized to consider or discuss any other change.

Herrán weighed this note for a few hours only. Its finality was unmistakable. Unbeknown to Hay, Herrán had secret instructions to sign the moment he felt "everything might be lost by delay." That moment had now come. According to his calculations, Colombia actually had everything to gain. Indeed, by signing now, she would make a profit of $7.25 million on the original protocol. The loss of a few extra rental millions was nothing compared to the catastrophe of losing all. Colombia might have her canal, and Panama too, forever.

Late in the afternoon, Herrán went to Hay's house.

⟨⌒⟩

NEWS THAT THE Panama Canal Treaty had been signed reached the White House in time to cheer Roosevelt at another disastrous reception. His problem this evening was not with crowd handling, but with the color of certain guests. Four or five Negroes strolled in to shake his hand. They were federal officeholders, so their attendance at an official, stand-up event was not unusual. This time, however, they made so bold as to bring their wives. Southern Congressmen hurried for the exits, swearing never to visit the White House again. No black women, as far as anybody could remember, had ever been entertained at a private function at 1600 Pennsylvania Avenue.

Yet another racial scandal erupted in Dixie.

"'Pears lak us niggers is on top now, Marse Roberts," an old field hand teased his boss in Georgia.

"How's that?"

"H'ain't we got a nigger for President?"

White reactionaries believed the same, but failed to find it funny. James K. Vardaman, running for Governor of Mississippi, went to the limits of public invective. Theodore Roosevelt was nothing but a "little, mean, coon-flavored miscegenationist," while the White House had become "so saturated with the odor of the nigger that the rats have taken refuge in the stable."

This was not the kind of publicity Roosevelt needed, coinciding as it did with Senate Commerce Committee hearings on his nomination of Dr. Crum and floor debate on his closing of the Indianola post office.

He was lucky enough to be defended in the latter case by the fastest mind on Capitol Hill. John Spooner addressed the Senate on 24 January, in an atmosphere more rife with sectionalism than at any time since the "bloody shirt" demagoguery of his youth. Speaking with his usual easy rapidity, he affirmed the President's goodwill toward all law-abiding Southerners. But the principle at stake in Indianola was that for which the Union Army had fought: an unconscionable minority must not be allowed to subvert the sovereignty of the state. Mrs. Cox had been "asked" to resign, after years of exemplary service:

It is as idle as the wind, Mr. President, to cavil upon the proposition that this was not a forced resignation. . . . If it was not duress, what was it? It was the power behind it that constituted the duress; it was the fact that that power was executed by the white citizens of that country, and that this person against whom it was addressed was colored.

Senator McLaurin rose to defend the right of a community to rid itself of *personae non gratae*. Mrs. Cox must submit to the will of her neighbors; that was the way of the South. Why, he himself had known persons who were asked to leave town in twenty-four hours.

"I have no doubt the Senator has," Spooner said.

Goaded by chuckles, McLaurin launched into a rambling correlation of race domination and rape. White Southerners would never forsake their own moral standards. "It will take a hundred thousand bayonets to restrain them if the virtue of their women is assaulted."

Spooner affected polite puzzlement. "Mrs. Cox had not made any improper advances to any woman in Indianola, had she?"

McLaurin ranted on for another forty minutes, but the debate was over.

⌘

ON 25 JANUARY, Dr. Herrán received new and belated instructions not to sign the Panama Canal Treaty. He cabled home that he had already exercised his previous authority to do so. Now it was up to the Colombian and United States Senates to ratify or reject the agreement.

"Gladly shall I gather up all the documents relating to that dreadful canal," he told a friend, "and put them out of sight."

⌘

IN THE LAST DAYS of January, the press began to notice unusual overtime activity in naval yards and stations. Roosevelt, alarmed by new signs of German truculence, had secretly directed that the Caribbean situation, while still under control, "was that which usually precedes war, and all possible preparations were to be made."

The arbitration negotiations, begun in plenary on the twenty-sixth, were not going well. Herbert Bowen was blustering so much about American security that he was neglecting the desperate condition of Venezuela, starved even for bread and salt. Britain was agreeable to a token settlement, but Germany insisted on full retribution. Her envoys now talked of occupying Venezuela's customs houses for the next six or seven years.

That sounded, to Roosevelt, ominously like the beginning of another "ninety-nine year lease." "Are people in Berlin crazy?" he burst out to the German *chargé d'affaires,* Count Albert von Quadt. "Don't they know that they are inflaming public opinion more and more here?"

He did not add that one of his own German informants had told him that war fever was on the rise in the Reich. But he counted the hours until Quadt's new boss arrived at the White House on 31 January.

⌘

BARON VON STERNBURG found the atmosphere along Massachusetts Avenue much changed from the days when he and Sir Michael Herbert had been young men about town together, playing tennis with "Teddy" and courting American girls. Indeed, it had become more formal in the few months since von Sternburg had been the President's houseguest. Now he represented the full majesty of the German state.

After his first formal meeting with Roosevelt, von Sternburg told Sir

Michael ("Mungo" no longer) that the President had not concealed his impatience for a prompt settlement of the Venezuela dispute. Roosevelt had also, disturbingly, suggested that the Anglo-German alliance was weakening. If so, the Kaiser's small squadron might soon be left alone in the Caribbean, facing 130,000 tons of American armor.

Von Sternburg sent a worried cable to the Wilhelmstrasse, just as his predecessor had done in December. He warned that the United States fleet had again been ordered to "hold itself in readiness." Whether it was this threat, or Bowen's bullying, or advices from London that the British Government was in danger of collapse, German intransigence at the arbitration table soon moderated.

⌐◠⌐

ROOSEVELT COULD NOT resist boasting about his sense of burgeoning American power to his next ambassadorial visitor, Jules Jusserand, on 7 February. "I am not for disarmament," he said. On the contrary, he intended to build up the American Army and Navy until they could handle "foes more formidable than Spain ever was."

Relaxing in the silken glow of the Blue Room, the two men took stock of each other. Roosevelt was familiar with Jusserand's writings, in particular a study of *Piers Plowman* that had made him temporarily wistful about the low estate of American literary scholarship. Now he saw a dapper, dark-bearded little diplomat, shorter even than Secretary Hay, yet wiry beneath his weight of gold braid. Jusserand's eyes were a brilliant black, his nose sharply beaked. He had a birdlike habit of cocking his head to one side, and when he did so with his plumed helmet on, Roosevelt had to struggle not to laugh.

The Ambassador's own first impression of "the extraordinary President . . . more powerful than a King," was one of both relief and surprise. He felt himself being swept away by a *joie de vivre* that engulfed all trouble. Unlike Bowen, he sensed no brutality, only the "force of will to do things."

Beaming like a schoolboy proud of his homework, Roosevelt launched into a discussion of Jusserand's books. He related material in *English Wayfaring Life* to the habits of hoboes in Colorado, said he had been reading *Piers Plowman* on his ill-fated trip west, and talked of Chaucer and Petrarch, Shakespeare and Voltaire. Then, perhaps sensing Hay's polite distress, he intoned a few "cordial sentiments" for transmittal to the Quai d'Orsay, and the interview was over.

⌐◠⌐

THAT EVENING, Roosevelt the diplomat reverted to Roosevelt the politician. For several weeks he had been log-walking nimbly from one antitrust bill to another, keeping up with the general flow through Congress, waiting to see which would prove the most buoyant and fastest-moving. Already, almost twenty different such measures had jammed or sunk from sight. Knox's Expedition Bill floated free out front, sure of passage. With a special "antitrust provision" promised out of general appropriations, the Attorney General could now count on the substantial funds and quick process he needed to prosecute rogue corporations. Senator Stephen B. Elkins similarly guaranteed an Anti-Rebate Bill that would satisfy both the Administration and fair-minded railroad executives.

Congressman Charles Littlefield's antimonopoly bill lay ponderously low despite House approval, and its sharpest protuberance—a clause empowering the government to subpoena corporate records—seemed certain to jag at the weir of the Senate. Just behind came what was now known (greatly to Roosevelt's irritation) as the "Department of Commerce and Labor" Bill. Having been subtly reshaped in committee by Senator Knute Nelson, it sought to establish a double agency that would monitor all aspects of industrial production, while giving the President of the United States direct control over the Bureau of Corporations. Thus, Roosevelt alone would decide whether the private workings of trusts should be publicized or not.

In view of this privilege, he decided to step finally from Littlefield's to his own bill. But before doing so, he wanted to get full press attention. Luck and perfect timing gave him a story that made headlines all over the country:

J. D. ROCKEFELLER TRIES TO BLOCK THE TRUST BILL

CHIEF OF STANDARD OIL COMPANY SENDS
PEREMPTORY ORDERS TO SIX U.S. SENATORS

SENSATION IN CONGRESS

NOT THE FIRST TIME BIG COMBINATION
HAS TRIED TO DEFEAT ROOSEVELT PLAN

PRESIDENT THREATENS EXTRA SESSION

Not since his Northern Securities announcement had Roosevelt so effectively provoked a popular outcry. Thanks to *McClure's*, John D. Rockefeller was once again a despised symbol of corporate greed, and Standard Oil stereotyped as the ultimate antigovernment trust. Both impressions were unfair: Rockefeller was semiretired and devoted to charitable works, while his great corporation had operated fairly and lawfully for years. But Roosevelt knew from experience that a public image, once registered, is almost impossible to rephotograph: later exposures only darken the underlying silhouette. Just as *he* was for all time "the Rough Rider," so was Rockefeller "the Robber Baron," and Standard Oil "the Anaconda," constricting democracy in its coils.

By publicizing these three images simultaneously, he simplified the complicated situation in Congress and strengthened support for the "Roosevelt plan." And by identifying six senators as recipients of Standard Oil's "orders," he ensured six votes in favor of the Bureau of Corporations: the honorable gentlemen could hardly reject him now without seeming to be Rockefeller stooges.

Subsequent articles revealed that the name *Rockefeller* had appeared on only two of Standard Oil's germane telegrams, and that it was in any case qualified by the abbreviation *Jr.* This did not save Rockefeller Senior from being accused of "the most brazen attempt in the history of lobbying."

The old tycoon maintained a hurt silence. When the Department of Commerce and Labor Bill got to the Senate, it was approved in thirty seconds flat.

~

ON 8 FEBRUARY, Woodrow Wilson, the president of Princeton, got a big laugh explaining to a meeting of alumni why this year's groundhog had returned to its burrow. It was afraid that Theodore Roosevelt would put a "coon" in.

~

"JUST AT PRESENT," Roosevelt wrote his eldest son, "Congress is doing most of the things I wish."

For the first time since becoming President, he felt real political momentum. In response to his urgent demands, echoed by the General Board of the Navy, the House initiated legislation for four new battleships and two armored cruisers, while the Senate rewarded Elihu Root's long struggle for an Army General Staff. By agreement with Great Britain, Roosevelt and King Edward VII were each empowered to appoint three "impartial jurists of repute" to negotiate the Alaskan boundary dispute. Favorable action on the Panama Canal Treaty was promised—as soon as Senator Morgan stopped filibustering it.

Roosevelt did not like the sound of that filibuster, and he was wary of corresponding tactics to delay the Cuban Reciprocity Treaty through the end of the session. Knowing that his legislative luck might not last, he worked around the clock without intermission, lobbying even as he ate.

On Saturday, 14 February, the Commerce and Labor Act arrived on his desk. He signed it with two pens, one of which went to the man he had decided to appoint as Secretary of the new Department: George Cortelyou. The other pen went to George Perkins of J. P. Morgan and Company. Evidently, Roosevelt expected the future relations of government and business to be amicable rather than antagonistic.

As a final cadence to these resolving harmonies, news came before nightfall that Herbert Bowen and his fellow negotiants at the Venezuela conference had agreed on a protocol to be submitted to The Hague. The last foreign battleships were steaming out of the Western Hemisphere.

~

THE NEXT MORNING'S newspapers proclaimed the double achievement: BLOCKADE ORDERED RAISED and THE PRESIDENT'S ANTITRUST PROGRAM COMPLETED.

Roosevelt let the first news story speak for itself. He was reluctant to draw personal attention to Wilhelm II's large-bottomed retreat: "It always pays for a nation to be a gentleman." About the second he was oddly defensive, fearing that it might not look like much of a triumph to readers studying the details. How were they to know he had had "a regular stand-up fight" with Senators Hanna and Aldrich before getting any trust legislation at all?

It was a fact, though, that he had negotiated only a modest, discretionary program. The powers invested in him had more to do with publicity than direct discipline. To forestall any radical discontent, he decided to issue a victory statement through the Attorney General's office, emphasizing the cooperative nature of his plan. J. P. Morgan and George Perkins happened to be in town, so he summoned them to the White House after dark, along with Aldrich and Hanna.

Soon Aldrich was on his way to Knox's house with scribbled instructions from the President: *"Say what has been done: practically substantially everything asked for. . . . Not only has a long stride in advance been taken; not only have all the promises of last fall been made good, but Congress has now enacted all that is practicable and all that is desirable to do."* It was unclear whether these sentiments were those of sender or bearer, but Knox duly announced that the legislation just passed by Congress was "highly gratifying" to the Administration, and represented the concerted wisdom "of many earnest and thoughtful men."

The result was another batch of positive headlines. They helped counteract negative editorials, such as one in the *Philadelphia Ledger* mocking the Roosevelt plan as "a lame and impotent conclusion to so much ferocious talk." Few Republican papers went as far as the Philadelphia *Press* in claiming that "no such revolution in the operations of trusts and railroads has been worked since the Interstate Commerce Act was passed."

Nevertheless, Roosevelt had brought about the first strengthening of federal regulatory authority in more than a decade, and unlike any Chief Executive before him, identified himself with antitrust policy. In the words of the Washington *Evening Star,* "The President of the United States is the original 'trust-buster,' the great and only one for this occasion."

Whether this would redound to his future glory was uncertain. There were signs that yesterday's great wave of combination was slowing, even as competition thrived, and the nation's wealth swelled. Memories of hard times were growing dim. The American people were bored with antitrust, as they were tired of winter. Like their President, they looked forward to a summer of new issues. For now, "trust-busting" could safely be left to Knox, Cortelyou, and the courts.

⌒

GEORGE BRUCE CORTELYOU had a habit of carefully straightening his spectacles whenever anything was laid in front of him, whether a memorandum on his desk or sheet music on his piano. Each new challenge had to be focused twenty-twenty, in center lens, as he dealt with it. This self-protective gesture was the legacy of boyhood years when demands and deprivations came from unexpected directions, leaving him a young stenographer of impeccable ancestry but common education. Yet there had been, even then, a slithering efficiency about Cortelyou (associates used such words as *oiled, smooth, eel-like* to describe him) that sped him to high position, if not wealth, under Presidents Cleveland and McKinley. Now, still poor, he was raised to Cabinet rank under President Roosevelt.

Exulting, he straightened his spectacles and contemplated the future. "I am not going into this new department with the idea of staying indefinitely," he wrote a friend. "I have refused many advantageous business offers. . . . If I am successful, and I think I shall be, the returns will be immediate and liberal within a very short time after I retire." Just at the moment, however, he needed five thousand dollars to repay a debt of honor. A check for six thousand came by return mail. At forty, Cortelyou felt for the first time the luxurious correlation of money and power.

Political gossips doubted that the thirty-seven-year-old Commissioner of Corporations would accept much of Cortelyou's authority. James Rudolph Garfield was the son of President Garfield, and Roosevelt's former protégé at the Civil Service Commission. Although he was foppish enough to care passionately about silk hats, his lean good looks were those of a privately educated sportsman. As such he qualified for the elite company of exercise companions whom Roosevelt delighted to abuse with cliff-crawls and frigid swims.

Cortelyou, despite seventeen months of almost daily proximity to the President, had never been so privileged.

⌒

ON 18 FEBRUARY, Roosevelt invited Speck von Sternburg to join him for a horseback trot in Rock Creek Park. Snow had fallen and frozen the night before; wedges of white lay in the trees, and the stream growled between ice-roughened banks. The skinny German bobbed along looking correct but cold in afternoon dress, while Roosevelt relaxed warmly in fur coat and cap.

Now that Germany's battleships were at last clear of the Caribbean, a soothing signal to Wilhelm II seemed called for. He discounted the seriousness of the naval threat posed by Admiral Dewey, and said that His Majesty's representatives had made "the best impression imaginable" during the recent negotiations.

The President's words again showed a respect for diplomatic face. As "a gentleman," he was in honor bound not to embarrass Wilhelm any more than he had already. So was John Hay. So were loyal archivists. On both sides of the Atlantic, defoliation of the records began. Nine crisis-period telegrams from Sir Michael Herbert disappeared from the British Foreign Office. Three sets of State Department instructions to London and Berlin were suppressed; a fourth was pruned of urgent adverbs. The German "U.S.–Venezuela Relations" series, fifty-one pages thick for 1901, thinned to a mere nine pages for 1902–1903. Hay apparently felt only two insignificant items of his December correspondence were worth preserving. The 1902 dossier of notes sent to the Wilhelmstrasse by the American Embassy in Berlin ends midsentence in a note dated 17 October. Nearly four hundred pages of blank paper followed.

And so, by polite agreement, the Venezuelan crisis faded from history. When Admiral Dewey thoughtlessly boasted that his deployment in the Caribbean had been "an object lesson to the Kaiser," Roosevelt summoned him to the White House for a reprimand. The sight of the old warrior in medals melted his anger, but he wrote seriously afterward, "Do let me entreat you to say nothing that can be taken hold of by those anxious to foment trouble between ourselves and any foreign power, or who delight in giving the impression that as a nation we are walking about with a chip on our shoulder. We are too big a people to be able to be careless in what we say."

⤙⤚

THE FIFTY-SEVENTH Congress pushed on toward adjournment, shuddering against brakes applied by four determined Senators. John Tyler Morgan fanatically filibustered the Panama Canal Treaty; Quay filibustered a banking bill, to punish Aldrich for filibustering *him;* and Benjamin Tillman filibustered everything in sight.

Roosevelt's "tyrannical and unconstitutional" attempts at race reform provided the big Southerner with plenty of material for harangues (one eye fiery beneath black brows, the other horribly missing; fists flailing from worn sleeves, as his voice screeched higher and higher). He had managed to bully the Senate Commerce Committee into a negative report on Dr. Crum, and threatened social violence if the full Senate overrode it: "We still have guns and ropes in the South."

Of that Roosevelt was aware. But he also understood the tendency of most lawmakers to exaggerate their emotions:

To the Secretary of War:
This [enclosure] is austerely called to your attention by the President, who would like a full and detailed explanation, if possible with inter-jectional musical accompaniment, about the iniquity of making a pro-motion for the senior Senator from Maine and refusing to make one for the junior Senator.

Especial attention is directed to the pathos of the concluding sen-tence of the junior Senator's letter. An early and inaccurate report is re-quested.

T.R.

March began, and the big clock in the upper chamber ticked away the last sixty hours of the session. Matters more urgent than patronage backed up against continuing filibusters: the unratified Cuban and Colombian treaties, and several vital spending measures, including the four-battleships bill. Soothsayers predicted a last-minute rush of legislation on the morning of the fourth. Surely not even "Pitchfork Ben" would allow the government to go bankrupt at noon.

Treaties were another matter. Roosevelt saw now that the Senate was cravenly going to let the clock postpone any vote on Cuban reciprocity until the next Congress. So he acted while he still had time. *"I, Theodore Roo-sevelt, President of the United States of America, do hereby proclaim that an extraordinary occasion requires the Senate of the United States to convene at the Capitol in the city of Washington, on the fifth day of March at 12 o'clock noon."*

He had hardly finished dictating when complaints about his "precipitous and unnecessary action" resounded in the upper chamber. Evidently he had acted just in time. He responded by threatening to call back the House of Representatives as well, if funds were not voted in support of his naval buildup. If that meant he had to postpone his promised Western tour yet again, postpone it he would, "and keep Congress here all summer."

A House-Senate conference hastily recommended that the President be given enough funds to build not four but five big new battleships. But at 10:00 P.M. on 3 March, Senator Tillman, his face ugly with anger, vowed to filibuster every cent in funds not yet appropriated unless South Carolina was bought off with pork-barrel money. "I'll stand here and read Byron till I drop dead in my tracks." At 2:00 A.M., he got his way. He yielded the floor to Sen-ator Quay, who promptly embarked on another set of dilatory tactics.

Outside, the moon was setting, and the Capitol dome was obscured with shadow. In the tobacco-stale House, legislators snored at their desks. Word of Tillman's victory came to the chairman of the Appropriations Committee. He got to his feet in sudden agitation, a bony, bearded, goatlike figure. "Mr. Speaker, if the House will bear with me . . ."

Joseph Gurney Cannon was sixty-six, and had been enduring Senate filibusters for nearly half his life. He had seen the House's power decline steadily, till it functioned as almost a legislative bureau of supply to the Senate, sending money and parchment down the corridor on demand. Only last fall, Roosevelt and the Republican "leaders" had not even bothered to include Speaker Henderson in their tariff conference at Oyster Bay. To Cannon's proud sensibility, the night just ending marked the nadir of what had once been the greatest deliberative body in the world.

Yet in this dark hour he felt dawn coming for himself. Later today, the retiring Speaker would lay down the gavel, and he—"Uncle Joe" of Danville, Illinois, the tightest wad and toughest talker in Congress—would take it up. Long years of frustration against the Senate surged in Cannon's breast. His face reddened, and he began to shout, rousing his colleagues from sleep:

> I am in earnest, with a message to the House touching this bill. . . . We have rules, sometimes invoked by our Democratic friends and sometimes by ourselves—each responsible to the people after all's said and done—by which a majority, right or wrong, mistaken or otherwise, can legislate.
>
> In another body, there are no rules. In another body, legislation is had by unanimous consent . . . and in the expiring hours of the session we are powerless without that unanimous consent. *Help me Cassius, or I sink!*

When Cannon lost his temper, he made even Senator Tillman seem tame. His body jerked in spasms, and he grew so hot he would tear off his coat and collar and douse himself with ice water. Now, however, he fought for his dignity, and for that of the House of Representatives:

> I am getting to be a somewhat aged man. I pray God that my life may be spared until an intelligent and righteous sentiment, north and south, pervading both the great parties, will lash anybody into obedience to the right of the majority to rule.

Applause roared and rolled out of the chamber into the marble hall. Nobody in the Senate heard it: that body had voted itself a short recess. The House followed suit. Congressmen emerged blearily into the chill air and dispersed in quest of beds, breakfast, and fresh clothes. A pallor tinged the sky beyond East Capitol Street. One by one, the naphtha lamps winked out.

THEODORE ROOSEVELT'S CARRIAGE rolled up the Hill shortly after 10:00. He found both assemblies back in session. As tradition required, he went to the President's Room to sign late bills. But the green baize table was bare. He sat waiting in a plump leather chair, his Cabinet officers ringed around him. George Washington and *his* Cabinet looked down from the walls. A black bust of McKinley stared into space. Finally, bills began to come in. He scrutinized and signed them to the ticking of a grandfather clock. The naval-construction appropriation was satisfying, but he still saw no confirmation of his choice for Collector of Charleston. He was not downcast, having long since decided to put Crum in office, if necessary, by means of interim and recess executive power. Perhaps the next Senate would be less obstructive than this one.

As the hands of the clock narrowed toward noon, his companions tiptoed across the lobby to watch the Fifty-seventh Congress die. Roosevelt sat alone except for his new secretary, William Loeb, Jr. Through the swinging door, in snatches, came the final drones of senatorial oratory—something about *snuffboxes?* The hands of the clock merged. "May God's benediction abide with you all," a voice called.

Far away, at the other end of the building, members of the House began singing "God Be with You Till We Meet Again" to the former Speaker, while the next Speaker smiled, a red carnation bright in his buttonhole. Joseph Cannon always looked amused; it had something to do with the cut of his mouth; but his eyes were hooded and hard. In the months and years ahead, Roosevelt would have a new force to reckon with on Capitol Hill.

CHAPTER 15

The Black Crystal

*We're a gr-reat people. We ar-re that. An' th' best
iv it is, we know we ar-re.*

LATE ON THE AFTERNOON of 1 April 1903, a stranger in a slouch hat got off a train waterstopping at Altoona, Pennsylvania, and crunched up the wrong side of the track. Six gleaming private cars screened him from the crowd on the platform. Tilting his head back as he approached the locomotive, he called in a harsh, yodeling voice, "Will you take a passenger in there?"

The fireman stared down stupidly, so the stranger appealed to higher authority. "Mr. Engineer, I'd like to ride with you a few miles." This time there was no mistaking the command in his voice. A second or two later, Theodore Roosevelt was in the cab, receiving sooty handshakes. He seated himself where he could pretend to be driving, and gazed eagerly ahead at the Alleghenies. The whistle blew, the throttle dipped, and the Pacific Coast Special clanked into motion, while the crowd waved and cried "Godspeed!" at its curtained caboose.

Free at last of Washington and the special session of the Senate (which had taken fifteen days to give him the treaty ratifications he demanded), Roosevelt was embarking on his much-delayed tour of the West. While in postponement, it had grown to the most ambitious presidential itinerary yet undertaken. During the next eight weeks, he was scheduled to travel fourteen thousand miles through twenty-five states, visiting nearly 150 towns and cities and giving an estimated two hundred speeches. Five major addresses, forming a review of his legislative and administrative achievements to date, lay snug in his traveling desk, along with something more formal to say at the dedication ceremonies of the Louisiana Purchase Exposition. All the other speeches, unwritten, he would leave to inspirations of time and place. Twenty years of public speaking had taught him that provincial audiences would listen to anything as long as it was seasoned with local references.

The challenge awaiting him beyond the Alleghenies was enough to daunt a fit man, and Roosevelt was far from fit. His long struggle with Congress over race, regulation, and reciprocity, the emotional drain of Edith's latest miscarriage, and the stress of entertaining fifteen thousand guests in the White House since last November had brought about a return of his childhood bronchial wheezings. He was further weakened by recent influenza and laryngitis. He longed for the dry healthfulness of the West, which had restored him so often in the past. As soon as he had delivered his five policy addresses, he planned a short vacation in Yellowstone National Park.

Reveling already in feelings of liberation, Roosevelt breathed coal smoke and mountain air for forty-nine miles. At Seward, he thanked the engineer for a "bully" trip, descended, and marched back down the length of his train. First, a baggage car; then the *Atlantic,* a club car heavy with wood and leather, plus a fully equipped barbershop; then the *Gilsey* diner, stocked with champagne and cigars; then the *Senegal,* a big Pullman carrying reporters, photographers, telegraphers, and Secret Service men; then the *Texas,* a compartmental sleeper for White House staff, and any guests Roosevelt might ask to ride along.

Last came the President's own *Elysian,* seventy feet of solid mahogany, velvet plush, and sinkingly deep furniture. It had two sleeping chambers with brass bedsteads, two tiled bathrooms, a private kitchen run by the Pennsylvania Railroad's star chef, a dining room, a stateroom with picture windows, and an airy rear platform for whistle-stop speeches. Whatever austerities Roosevelt looked forward to at Yellowstone, he would not lack for creature comforts now or later.

AT 8:50 THE FOLLOWING NIGHT, he stood in black tie and silk lapels on the stage of the Chicago Auditorium, waiting for a long roar of welcome to subside. "Mr. Chairman—Mr. Chairman, ladies and gentlemen—" But the roar went on. President McKinley had never been cheered like this. Five thousand people overcrowded the hall. Even when they calmed, another horde outside the doors continued to shout, creating a bizarre echo effect as Roosevelt began to speak. His text, an affirmation of the Monroe Doctrine with special reference to Cuba, Venezuela, and Colombia, featured his favorite "West African proverb," except now the source was obscured, to make it more memorable and quotable:

> There is a homely old adage which runs, *Speak softly and carry a big stick: you will go far.* If the American nation will speak softly, and yet build, and keep at a pitch of the highest training, a thoroughly efficient navy, the Monroe Doctrine will go far.

This generated such loud applause as to suggest that the audience took his "adage" as aggressive, rather than cautionary. Actually, Roosevelt was trying to say that soft-spoken (even secret) diplomacy should be the priority of a civilization, as long as hardness—of moral resolve, of military might—lay back of it. Otherwise, inevitably, soft speech would sound like scared speech.

He reiterated his distaste for national "boasting and blustering." In liberating Cuba and defusing the Venezuela crisis, the United States had proved herself to be idealistic rather than imperialistic, independent yet global-minded. Treaties negotiated by his Administration guaranteed that Americans alone would build and defend the Panama Canal; bills initiated by him had provided the necessary money and warships. But true, hemispheric security in a rearming world would require a much larger fleet than that currently envisaged by Congress. "If we have such a Navy—if we keep on building it up—we may rest assured . . . that no foreign power will ever quarrel with us about the Monroe Doctrine."

THE PRESIDENT INVITED some of his old Chicago cronies to join him for supper at his hotel. Herman Kohlsaat and the financier Charles G. Dawes arrived first, and were at once irradiated in Rooseveltian warmth. But as the reception proceeded and more and more "friends" crowded the room, they found themselves edged toward the crockery and spoons. Roosevelt continued to beam indiscriminately upon all comers, a searchlight picking out vessels of any size. Later, Dawes the diarist wrote:

> His hearty greetings are simply the natural results of his own good spirits and splendid vitality. . . . He has no "blind side." . . . He seeks to wield power—not to avoid wielding it. He apparently loves everybody and nobody—both at once—everything and everybody being subordinated to his desire to keep the approbation of the public—not simply for the sake of that approbation but for the sake of that right-doing as well, which brings it.

The *Chicago Tribune*'s front-page headline the next morning ran: SPEAK SOFTLY AND CARRY A BIG STICK, SAYS ROOSEVELT. Within hours, baseball bats and rough-hewn clubs waved over the heads of onlookers along the presidential trail.

In Milwaukee's Plankinton House, Roosevelt reviewed his trust policy at a dinner for local merchants and manufacturers. Heavy with sausages and *schnapps*, they tried to guess where he stood on the conservative/radical issues now dividing Wisconsin Republicans. His balanced phrases gave them no help. "We are not in the least against wealth . . . nor yet for the demagogic agitator . . . on the contrary . . . on the other hand . . . the alternative is . . ."

The grinning equivocations went on and on, wreathing through cigar smoke and sweet wine fumes, while smilax, asparagus vines, and American Beauty roses intertwined above his head, and a thousand lightbulbs drowsily heated the room. Champagne was served. Now the President was beating time to a German *Trinklied,* and joining in chorus after chorus:

> *Er lebe hoch! Er lebe hoch!*
> *Hoch! Hoch! Hoch!*

Further roars of "*Hoch!*" followed him as his train pulled out of the station. "Good song, that!" he shouted, and waved till darkness swallowed him up.

⌐⊙⌐

TARIFF POLICY IN ST. PAUL. Labor policy in Sioux Falls. Philippines policy in Fargo. . . . Roosevelt arrived at Bismarck, North Dakota, toward sunset on 7 April, and saw, opening out beyond the Missouri, the windswept landscape of his youth. Great balls of thistle spooled across the prairie. He gazed around him, visibly relaxing. "Good to breathe this free Western air again."

He ate a barbecued-ox sandwich and drank a mug of cider, then returned to his train. Two of his old Badlands buddies, Sylvane and Joe Ferris, were waiting on the other side of the water, at Mandan. They climbed aboard the *Elysian,* their faces solemn with excitement.

For the next two hours, Roosevelt entertained them as the flat grassland swayed in his windows. He effortlessly recalled places and scenes, even the names of horses and dogs they had forgotten. At Dickinson, he manifested himself as a sort of *deus ex machina* to people who remembered him as a reedy young ranchman, running along the tops of cattle cars and jabbing at steers with a pole.

When the train drew near the Badlands, darkness already had descended. The President went onto his rear platform and watched coulees etch themselves into the grassland, black out of silver, like a giant printer's block. Medora lay in the deepest cut of all, a clutch of houses by the sand-choked Little Missouri. Here, twenty years before, he had come to shoot his first buffalo, and found himself "at heart as much a Westerner as an Easterner." But this time he did not have to drag his duffel bag alone across the sage. And the entire population of the Badlands, as far as he could see, had gathered to welcome him.

Joe Ferris was upset that Roosevelt would not take his old pony, Manitou, for a gallop through the buttes; security forbade it. The President stayed in Medora no longer than it took to say a few words, shake every hand, and endure some fond, erroneous reminiscences. Then he was on his way again, leaving the disappointed populace to cheer itself up with a dance. Why had he looked so stern, why had he not stayed the night?

Perhaps he sought to protect some dreamy nostalgia from present scrutiny. The free range of twenty years before was gone. He did not have to dwell on its eroded green and barbed-wire entanglements. Nor need he ever return.

Night shrouded the Château de Morès, home of his long-dead ranching rival; shrouded the ruins of his log house in the Elkhorn bottom; shrouded Nolan's Hotel in Wibaux, Montana, where he had once knocked out the drunken bully who had called him "Four Eyes." The train sped across Montana, hauling him away from what he still thought of as "Dakota." No North and South then!

It was still the Wild West in those days, the Far West. . . . It was a land of vast silent spaces, of lovely rivers, and of plains where the wild game stared at the passing horseman. It was a land of scattered ranches, of herds of long-horned cattle, and reckless riders who unmoved looked in the eyes of life or of death. In that land we lived a free and hardy life, with horse and with rifle. We worked under the scorching midsummer sun, when the wide plains shimmered and wavered in the heat; and we knew the freezing misery of riding night guard round the cattle in the late fall round-up. In the soft springtime the stars were glorious in our eyes each night before we fell asleep; and in the winter we rode through blinding blizzards, when the driven snow-dust burnt our faces. . . . We knew toil and hardship and hunger and thirst; and we saw men die violent deaths as they worked among the horses and cattle, or fought in evil feuds with one another; but we felt the beat of hardy life in our veins, and ours was the glory of work and the joy of living.

Shortly after noon on 8 April, Roosevelt found himself in Gardiner, Montana, at the entrance to Yellowstone Canyon. The park was not yet open for the season. Ten-foot drifts of snow glared in the Rockies. He looked forward to spending two therapeutic weeks here, before continuing with his tour.

When he emerged from his car, he was already wearing full riding gear and a Western hat. He was followed by a short, white-bearded, instantly recognizable figure: the wildlife writer John Burroughs, revered by millions of Americans for his sentimental essays on nature. Affable, placid, and malleable, "Oom John" had been invited along as a walking advertisement that the President would kill no animals in Yellowstone.

They were greeted by the park superintendent, Major John Pitcher, a small escort of cavalrymen, and some mule carts loaded with camping equipment. Roosevelt swung joyfully up onto a waiting gray stallion, while Burroughs, who had not ridden a horse in forty years, was helped into one of the carts.

"By the way, Mr. President," Pitcher said as they rode through the gates, "an old friend of yours named Bill Jones has been very anxious to see you, but I am sorry to say that he has got so drunk that we had to take him out into the sage brush."

Hell-Roaring Bill Jones! He of the happy triggers, the alkali thirst, and the transcendental cussing!

"I will try to have him meet you before we leave the park," Pitcher promised. A guide led the way down the canyon, and Roosevelt passed out of sight. Reporters, forbidden to follow, were left hanging round the sidelined train, wondering what stories they could file for the next fifteen days.

⟡

A FEW HOURS AFTER the President disappeared, flash news reached Gardiner. Four judges of the United States Eighth Circuit Court in St. Louis had just upheld Roosevelt's suit against the Northern Securities Company. The opinion came as a shock to most Americans, after more than a year of languid legal proceedings. It showed how the new Expedition Act had strengthened antitrust law. The court had ruled unanimously, in an astonishingly narrow interpretation of the Sherman Act, that mere *power* of a combination to restrain trade was earnest of intent, whether or not the power was exercised by its holding company.

"If this decision is upheld by the Supreme Court," James J. Hill was quoted as saying, "no less than eighty-five percent of the railroad systems of the United States will be up in the air."

William Loeb asked a soldier to hurry word of the court's ruling along the President's trail. No reply came back from the silent mountains.

⟡

THE NORTHERN SECURITIES opinion was Roosevelt's fourth political victory in fewer than four weeks. He had also succeeded in winning reciprocity for Cuba, digging rights in Panama, and an equitable arbitration award for last winter's striking miners. (Their wages had, as expected, been raised 10 percent by the Anthracite Coal Commission.) All these decisions, except the Commission's, were subject to review: the Cuban treaty by the House of Representatives, the Panama Canal Treaty by the Colombian Senate, and the Circuit Court ruling by the Supreme Court. But America's perennial flux and reflux of power from the executive branch to the legislative and back again seemed to have turned in his favor.

That did not mean it was anywhere near a full resurgence. His unpopularity on Capitol Hill and Wall Street—as a Chief Executive prone to rash impulses, self-advertisement, and fiscal irresponsibility—was extreme. Remarkably, though, the nation at large (outside the white South) regarded him quite differently, as political observers were everywhere conceding, not without bemusement. One of the most articulate attempts to explain this dichotomy of opinion was that of Henry Herzberg, a New Yorker writing for the Charleston *News*. He ascribed the paradox to Roosevelt's own "psychology of inconsistency," illogically reflecting both an aristocratic will and a democratic desire to please. Hence, the President was both coordinated and conflicted, inimitable yet representative of a wide range of new, hard-to-define trends:

> Such a bosom of necessity must surge with overleaping ambition. There are passions ever impelling some righteous action and promptings which ever restrain these moral impulses.
>
> Mr. Roosevelt is bold and fearless yet timid and wary; he is ambitious and striving, but circumspect and cautious. He is imperious in mind, but thoughtful and considerate in action. Whether or not these temperamental traits of Mr. Roosevelt give us a picture of the typical President of the future is doubtful, but certain it is that the nervous energy, the irrepressible ambition, the fascinating elements which predominate in Mr. Roosevelt's nature represent the American character now in the making.

⟨⚭⟩

ROOSEVELT WAS NO stranger to Yellowstone, having first visited it in 1886. As founder of the Boone & Crockett Club, he had worked to save it from vandalism and exploitation, and he took pride in having been a motive force behind the National Park Protective Act of 1894. Only last year he had won an appropriation that made the Yellowstone bison wards of the federal government. Now he could enjoy the benefits of his work in solitude.

Or near solitude. John Burroughs caught cold the first day, and remained behind at Mammoth Hot Springs; but Major Pitcher stuck tight. Roosevelt bided his time. He passed several sociable nights with the superintendent, eating sardines and hardtack round the campfire, and helping wash up in the icy river. Each day, he rode deeper into the park, while snow dust boiled in the peaks and mountain sheep stared down at him, half veiled by their own breath. He feasted his eyes, long starved for the sight of game, on pronghorns and buffalo and black-tailed deer. A giant herd of elk enthralled him for four hours. His ear caught the counterpoint between a solitaire singing at the top of a canyon, and a water-ouzel perched a thousand feet below.

On 12 April, he suddenly said that, as it was Sunday, he wished to "take a walk alone." Pitcher felt unable to deny a President's desire for private devotion, so Roosevelt marched happily off and for six hours worshiped God in his own fashion.

There were rumors, later on, of rifle shots echoing in the park, and Roo-

sevelt was definitely seen with a cartridge bruise on his cheek. But Pitcher announced that the President had merely indulged in "a little target shooting"
back at camp and been wounded by an ejected shell.

Burroughs, who had rejoined the party, confirmed this. Roosevelt was
sincere in his vow not to kill local wildlife, even such permissible prey as coy-
otes and cougar. He still lusted, or thought that he lusted, after big game, but
nowadays it was the pursuit, rather than the quarry, that interested him. A
new protective sensibility was notable in his account of these days in Yellowstone:

> Every man who appreciates the majesty and beauty of the wilderness
> and of wild life, should strike hands with the far-sighted men who
> wish to preserve our material resources, in the effort to keep our
> forests and our game-beasts, game-birds, and game-fish—indeed, all
> the living creatures of prairie and woodland and seashore—from wan-
> ton destruction. Above all, we should recognize that the effort toward
> this end is essentially a democratic movement. It is entirely within our
> power as a nation to preserve large tracts of wilderness, which are val-
> ueless for agricultural purposes and unfit for settlement, as play-
> grounds for rich and poor alike. . . . But this end can only be achieved
> by wise laws and by a resolute enforcement of the laws.

Roosevelt expressed contempt for "the kind of game butcher . . . who
leaves deer and ducks and prairie chickens to rot," worse still market hunters
and rich dilettantes who hunted by proxy.

Only once did he weaken, when a four-inch meadow mouse hopped
across his path. He slew it in the interest of science, and sent the skin and
skull, with tabulations, to the United States Biological Survey.

⎯⎯

BACK IN GARDINER, bored members of the White House press detail fished,
scavenged for elk antlers, and got drunk with mountain men. Their thirdhand
reports of Roosevelt's activities began to sound slightly testy. When word
came that the President had watched Old Faithful erupting and its mist turning to hail as it fell, the New York *World* man called it "his only rival in in-
termittent but continuous spouting."

Finally, on 24 April, a cloud of dust in the foothills signaled the President's
return. The train was shunted out of its siding, and Hell-Roaring Bill Jones
brought in from the sagebrush, stark sober for the first time in years, for a
quick reunion. Before leaving, Roosevelt dedicated a new arched gateway to
the park, calling Yellowstone a "veritable wonderland," and noted that Europeans seemed more interested in visiting it than were most Americans. He

spoke feelingly about forest reserves, buffalo breeding, and Yellowstone's "essential democracy." Then, with a flash of teeth (his face dark tan with snow burn, his nose peeling), he swung aboard the *Elysian* and was gone. The train moved northeast, then southeast, descending to levels of hotter, thicker air.

On the flatland, it accelerated to maximum speed, crossing the Wyoming, South Dakota, and Nebraska state lines in a single day. The succession of prairie hamlets blurred into a dreary pattern to travelers on board. Always a long, low depot, red-painted and sand-coated, with wide, rakish eaves; always a concentration of buggies and carts, iron filings magnetized on the papersheet plain; Roosevelt running out onto his platform and waving, sometimes with his table napkin. ("Those children wanted to see the President of the United States, and I could not disappoint them.") Then the cheers suddenly stifled, as if a door had been slammed, and in dwindling retrospect, the sight of families turning their backs against whorls of white dust.

At whistle-stops, always the local dignitaries, with their furrowed eyes and crooked medals and drooping trousers, silver cornets playing "Hail to the Chief," whiskery veterans of the Grand Army of the Republic, a bobbing sea of bowlers and bonnets, and invariably, boys on telegraph poles screeching, "How are you, Teddy?"

Just as invariably, the President would rehearse his litany of McGuffey Reader virtues ("If I might give a word of advice to Omaha . . .") until reporters no longer bothered to transcribe them. Only Roosevelt found new stimulation eight or ten times a day, thundering every platitude with the pleased air of having just discovered it. He was quite unapologetic: "Platitudes and iteration are necessary in order to hammer the truths and principles I advocate into people's heads."

Indistinguishable as the whistle-stops soon became, even to him, each was supreme drama to a little audience that had been looking forward to it for weeks. Some buggy travelers had come one hundred miles to perch on the platform and peer endlessly at the horizon, waiting for a smudge of smoke to signal that "Teddy" was imminent. Then a speck growing in the smoke, a crescendo of wind and wheels, a great locomotive advancing—too fast, surely, to stop? Despair as it indeed keeps moving. Relief when it halts, after all, under the water tank one hundred yards down the track. A general stampede toward the *Elysian,* where Roosevelt stands grinning in frock coat and vest. He leans over the rail, pumping hands and tousling cowlicks. "Dee-lighted!" Rearing back, he begins to orate, punctuating every sentence with palm-smacks and dental percussion, while his listeners stand mesmerized. The engine bell rings; the train jerks forward. Another grin, and a farewell wave. The Cheshire-cat flash of those teeth floats in the sky long after the train is a speck again.

"WHEREVER HE WENT, INFANTS WERE BRANDISHED AT HIM."
The President on his cross-country tour, 1903

THE "ESSENTIAL DEMOCRACY" of Yellowstone—its lesson that government can both serve and conserve, and that future generations had as much right to natural resources as contemporaries—remained on Roosevelt's mind as he journeyed through America's heartland. No longer was he the patrician politician addressing high affairs of state in Eastern cities. He was, at least for the moment, a man of the earth, a cuddler of babies. Wherever he went, infants were brandished at him, wiggling representatives of the next generation. His robust views on childbearing ("Three cheers for Mr. and Mrs. Bower and their really satisfactory American family of twelve children!") were bolstered by spaces so wide and soil so deeply fertile. With the irrigation schemes he had signed into law, these plains might one day support a hundred million people.

In Iowa's fecund fields, glistening with spring rain, women in faded Mother Hubbard gowns crowded around his car, their arms bursting with progeny. A platoon of boys and girls hoisted a banner over their heads: NO "RACE SUICIDE" HERE, TEDDY! It was another of Roosevelt's catchphrases, broadly biological rather than ethnic in its implications. Bachelors declining to marry, urban women repressing their natural reproductive function, denied America the seed she needed to grow and be great. Ripeness was all. "I congratulate you upon your crops," he said, smiling around at clustered families, "but the best crop is the crop of children."

Some of his new democracy, and all of his charm, was evident in the west Kansas cow town of Sharon Springs, where on 3 May he attended divine service:

> There were two very nice little girls standing in the aisle beside me. I invited them in and we all three sang out of the same hymn book. They were in their Sunday best and their brown sunburned little arms and faces had been scrubbed till they almost shone. It was a very kindly, homely country congregation . . . all of them looking well-to-do and prosperous in a way hardly warranted as it seemed to me by the eaten-off, wired-fence-enclosed, shortgrass ranges of the dry plains round-about. When church was over I shook hands with the three preachers and all the congregation, whose buggies, ranch wagons, and dispirited-looking saddle ponies were tied to everything available in the village. I got a ride myself in the afternoon, and on returning found that all the population that had not left had gathered solemnly around the train. Among the rest there was a little girl who asked me if I would like a baby badger which she said her brother Josiah had just caught. I said I would, and an hour or two later the badger turned up from the little girl's father's ranch some three miles out of town. The little girl had several other little girls with her, all in clean starched Sunday clothes and ribbon-tied pigtails. One of them was the sheriff's daughter, and I saw her nudging the sheriff, trying to get him to make some request, which he refused. So I asked what it was and found that the seven little girls were exceedingly anxious to see the inside of my car, and accordingly I took them all in. The interior arrangements struck them as being literally palatial—magnificent. . . . I liked the little girls so much that I regretted having nothing to give them but flowers; and they reciprocated my liking with warm western enthusiasm, for they hung

about the car until it grew dark, either waving their hands to me or kissing their hands to me whenever I appeared at the window.

The baby badger, which reminded Roosevelt of "a small mattress, with a leg at each corner," was christened Josiah, and given well-ventilated accommodations on the *Elysian*'s front platform. From this vantage point he was able to survey an unrolling landscape as the train proceeded to Denver and then bent south along the line of the Rockies.

⎯⎵⎯

NEW MEXICO TERRITORY opened up ahead, and Roosevelt began to encounter a wilder species of western fauna: Rough Rider veterans. Importunate, noisy, and side-armed, they demanded preferential access to their Colonel, even in small desert towns at 3:00 in the morning.

1ST VOICE   Why don't the son of a gun come out? *(Bang! Bang! Bang! Bang! Bang!)*

2ND VOICE   Three cheers for President Roosevelt! *(Bang! Bang! Bang!)*

At Santa Fe, he was corralled by his former Mexican-American sergeant into serving as godfather at the baptism of Theodore Roosevelt Armijo in an old adobe church. Candle in hand, looking at the back of the father's swarthy neck, he reflected that "his ancestors and mine had doubtless fought in the Netherlands in the days of Alva and Parma, just about the time this mission was built and before a Dutch or English colonist had set foot on American soil."

In the plaza afterward, Roosevelt spoke seriously on his new theme, the conservation of natural resources. "This is a great grazing state. Because of the importance of the grazing industry I wish to bespeak your support for the preservation in proper shape of the forest reserves of the state." He was conscious of opposition in his audience, many of whom were sheep farmers, and guiltily aware that their flocks destroyed forest growth. He tried to make them understand that forest pasturage, properly restricted and supplemented by irrigation schemes, could be self-renewing. They stood quietly in the hot square, cowboys in pale sombreros, muscular Mexican women in lace tea gowns, bandy-legged soldiers in khaki, priests in black-and-red cloaks, plump, prosperous-looking shepherds, and stockmen frowning at his words.

A similar audience awaited Roosevelt on the edge of the Grand Canyon. The stupendous chasm, which he had not seen before, powerfully affected him. "I don't exactly know what words to use in describing it. It is beautiful and terrible and unearthly." He was relieved to hear that the Santa Fe Railroad had rejected a plan to build a hotel at Rowe's Point. "Leave it as it is," he implored the crowd. "You cannot improve on it. The ages have been at work on it, and man can only mar it—keep it for your children, your children's children, and for all who come after you."

Those last words were to become a recurrent theme in Roosevelt's speeches as he crossed the Sierras and descended the Pacific slope. All the landscape was new to him now. He exulted in California's lush, feminine fertility. Here, literally blossoming around him, was desert made flowerland by irrigation: houses embowered with roses and grapevines, deep orchards, acres of golden poppies, wildflowers speckling the sage in pointillistic patterns. Here, he told himself, "a new type" of American child was growing up, indigenous as the flowers, half familiar yet exotic. New York seemed impossibly far away; Europe a historical memory. "I felt as if I was seeing Provence in the making—that is, Provence changed by, and in its turn changing, a northern race."

Fifteen hundred children and millions of flowers greeted him at Redlands on 7 May. The roadway under his carriage was so thick with rose petals that he rolled along soundlessly and fragrantly. When he arrived in front of the Casaloma Hotel, the children serenaded him; they pelted him with blossoms as he stood up to speak. Again he talked of irrigation, of conservation, and of procreation. There were yet more children, and roses, at San Bernardino and Riverside and Pasadena (their upthrust arms, holding bouquets, seemed to undulate in the breeze of his rhetoric). Roosevelt became slightly incoherent, as if drunk on the scented air: "this plain tilled by the hand of man as you have never tilled it until it blossomed like the rose . . . blossomed as I never dreamed in my life that the rose could blossom . . ."

But the horticultural climax to his visit was yet to come. He reached Los Angeles on 8 May, in time for the final parade of the Fiesta de Flores. Looking dazed, he sat on the reviewing stand as marshals rode by, perched on saddle blankets apparently woven from carnations and roses. They were followed by a barren float piled with sand and bones: the desert as cadaver, unlamented. Then came a tableau of efflorescent California: waterworks spraying mist over seedlings and grain; harsh sunflowers yielding to lilies and pansies; citrus and olive groves jiggling with fruit. The floats, drawn by ropes and chains of flowers, became ever more extravagant: a thirty-foot mobile garden, courtesy of the Los Angeles Parks Department; an eight-foot pyramid of white carnations, symbolizing the purity of organized labor; a submarine of scarlet geraniums; and a flower globe of the Earth, with the United States picked out in yellow daisies, between oceans of undulating fern. Amid all the color and luxuriance, nubile girls in white waved prettily, to the President's obvious pleasure.

For four hours, the child California bloomed like a rose before him.

THE SIGHT OF AN enormous redwood towering above Santa Cruz three days later was expected also to enchant the President. But he frowned at its petticoat of calling cards and advertising posters. "Those cards pinned up on that tree give an air of the ridiculous to this majestic grove," he said angrily. He began to lecture bystanders. "Do keep these trees, keep all the wonderful scenery of this wonderful state unmarred by vandalism or the folly of man." Refusing an official escort, he went to cool off in a nearby grove. When he came back, the cards had been taken down.

"There is nothing more practical in the end than the preservation of beauty," Roosevelt declared the next day. He was speaking at Stanford University, whose architecture and setting, half Pacific, half Mediterranean, enhanced his impression of California as the loveliest of states.

In a major conservation address, he urged the students to respect their natural heritage. "I feel most emphatically that we should not turn into shingles a tree which was old when the first Egyptian conqueror penetrated to the valley of the Euphrates." This was not to say that most of the North American forest could not be "used" scientifically and efficiently, if government exerted its just powers. Properly protected, woodlands and grasslands would function forever as spongelike sources of water for irrigation, making immense tracts of arable land available to homesteaders under the national reclamation program. "Water speculation"—rentals charged by the private owners of dams and streams in semidesert areas—would dwindle as public reservoirs swelled. Monopoly, whether of wood or water, would be confounded, and land laws refined to their original democratic purpose.

"We have a right to expect that the best trained, the best educated men on the Pacific Slope, the Rocky Mountains and great plains states will take the lead in the preservation and right use of the forests," Roosevelt roared. He did not add that he had quietly expanded the federal woodland by one third in his first year as President. Such a boast would only antagonize western reactionaries.

⌒

CONCERN MOUNTED, MEANWHILE, behind boardroom doors on Wall Street that Theodore Roosevelt was "an extremely dangerous man." For all his lip service at Milwaukee and St. Paul to *laissez-faire* ways, he seemed to stand, in the eyes of Henry W. Taft, for "a pretty pronounced type of socialism." He had shown prejudice against railroad owners, beef packers, and coal-mine operators; he had won a referral of Knox's *Northern Securities* suit to the Supreme Court, and stirred up hell in the South; now he was protecting foliage and threatening to strengthen the public-land laws. His professed truce with the trusts was likely to last as long as it took him to win the Presidency in his own right. Once he got the executive bit between those grinning, biting teeth, there would be no holding him.

A group of financiers, asked whom they would prefer to see as the Republican nominee in 1904, replied almost unanimously, "Somebody like Hanna."

⎯⎯⎯⎯⎯

MORE THAN 2,500 MILES, and a greater distance between prejudice and perception, prevented Roosevelt's capitalist critics from seeing him address a conservative audience of "citizens of the Golden State" at the Palace Hotel in San Francisco on 12 May. Had they done so, they might have been reassured as to his fiscal soundness. Standing in white tie over a table spread with cloth of gold, beneath hanging golden garlands two feet thick, he accepted a gold loving cup and reverently invoked the need for "a gold basis" for the nation's currency. His subsequent call for a more elastic money supply could have been written by Senator Aldrich, and indeed probably was.

The next morning, at Mechanics Pavilion, Roosevelt changed guises, reverting to the exultant imperialism of his prepresidential days. He looked toward the Orient and saw nothing but an American ocean, veined with American cables and crisscrossed by American freighters, the largest in the world:

> Before I came to the Pacific Slope I was an expansionist, [*applause*] and after having been here I fail to understand how any man, convinced of his country's greatness . . . can be anything but an expansionist [*applause*]. In the century that is opening the commerce and the command of the Pacific will be factors of incalculable moment in the world's history.

He reviewed the rise and fall of seagoing civilizations from the Phoenicians and Carthaginians to the more recent navies and the merchant marines of northern conquerors. California—America's new Greece—must now rise to the commercial and cultural challenges of "the greatest of all the seas." The United States as a whole must follow its westward destiny until West and East merged. This meant a new global strategy:

> In the South Seas the great commonwealth of Australia has sprung into being. Japan, shaking off the lethargy of centuries, has taken her rank among civilized, modern powers. European nations have seated themselves along the eastern coast of Asia, while China by her misfortunes has given us an object-lesson in the utter folly of attempting to exist as a nation at all, if both rich and defenseless.

The audience understood Roosevelt's last reference very well. He was bringing his historical survey right up-to-date. Current newspapers agitatedly reported a crisis situation in the Chinese province of Manchuria. Tsar Nicholas II, whose forces had occupied that industrialized region for five years, had failed to honor a promised withdrawal timetable. Now Russian officials were conspiring to keep Manchurian ports closed to foreign trade—a clear breach of Secretary Hay's Open Door policy in the Far East—while profiting themselves from mining and shipping concessions. And much to Japanese alarm, the Trans-Siberian Railway, with its seemingly limitless capability to bring in military reinforcements, was nearing completion.

In other disturbing Russian news, dispatches reported a mass killing of Jews in the Bessarabian city of Kishinev. Casualty figures "worse than the censor will permit to publish" were leaking out. *The American Hebrew*'s estimate was one hundred and twenty killed and five hundred injured in anti-Semitic riots; the Tsar himself was rumored to have ordered the slaughter.

For the first time, popular unease was palpable about the ever-burgeoning empire in the East. It loomed beyond the haze of the Pacific horizon, menacing primarily Japan. American hearts warmed to that warlike little power, if only because it stood as a bulwark for the Philippines.

Roosevelt was constrained, as President, from criticizing the domestic policies of another sovereign state. But he made clear that he would not tolerate Russian aggression in the Pacific. "The inevitable march of events gave us the control of the Philippine Islands at a time so opportune that it may without irreverence be called providential," he said. "Unless we show ourselves weak, unless we show ourselves degenerate sons of the sires from whose loins we sprang, we must go on with the work we have undertaken—" Applause interrupted him. "We infinitely desire peace, and the surest way of obtaining it is to show that we are not afraid of war."

After making his standard calls for muscular morality at home and a big navy abroad, he concluded on a note of exaltation rare even for him:

> Our place as a nation is and must be with the nations that have left indelibly their impress on the centuries. . . . Those that did not expand passed away and left not so much as a memory behind them. The Roman expanded, the Roman passed away, but the Roman has left the print of his law, of his language, of his masterful ability in administration, deep in the world's history, deeply imprinted in the character of the races that came after him. I ask that this people rise level to the greatness of its opportunities.

TWO EVENINGS LATER, Roosevelt lay high in Yosemite, on a bed of fragrant pine needles, looking up at the sky. On all sides soared the cinnamon-colored shafts of sequoia trees. He had the feeling that he was "lying in a great solemn cathedral, far vaster and more beautiful than any built by the hands of man."

"A PLACE OF WORSHIP."
Roosevelt at Glacier Point, Yosemite, May 1903

Birdsong filled the arches as the sky darkened. He identified the treble *tessitura* of hermit thrushes, and thought it "an appropriate choir for such a place of worship."

His companion was John Muir, the glaciologist, naturalist, and founder of the Sierra Club. Since early youth, Muir had roamed Yosemite, carrying little more than "some bread and tea in an old sock," returning to civilization as infrequently as possible. At sixty-five, he knew more about the park, and loved it more passionately, than any other American. Roosevelt had booked his exclusive services well in advance: "I want to drop politics absolutely for four days, and just be out in the open with you."

The President was disappointed to find that Muir had no ear for bird music. He was Wordsworthian rather than Keatsian, revering only "rocks and stones and trees." Garrulous, erudite, and wall-eyed, he talked a pure form of preservation that Roosevelt was not used to hearing. He had no patience with the utilitarian "greatest good for the greatest number" policy of Chief Forester Gifford Pinchot, the President's very good friend. *Conservation* favored business at the expense of nature, and property rather than beauty. "The 'greatest number' is too often found to be number one."

Whatever resonance such views found in the President's own developing awareness of the "democracy" of national parks, he would have preferred to hear less of Muir and more of the hermit thrushes. Eventually he fell asleep, in the piney air. Another bird chorale saluted him at dawn.

For the next forty-eight hours, the boy in Roosevelt, never quite suppressed, reveled in his wild surroundings. "This is bully!" he yelled, when Muir burned a dead tree for him and the sparks hurtled skyward. After another night out, he awoke at Glacier Point, and was intrigued to find himself buried under four inches of snow. "This is bullier!"

On 17 May he came down from the peaks in dusty khakis, his eyes sparkling. "I never felt better in my life!" Muir, too, was elated, having confessedly fallen in love with the President's "interesting, hearty and manly" personality. The substance of their camping conversations remained tacit, suggesting some philosophical difference on the subject of Gifford Pinchot. Muir won at least an immediate presidential order to extend the California forest through the Mount Shasta region, and a promise that Yosemite's over-commercialized valley would be ceded back to the national park system. Roosevelt's next conservation statement, on 19 May, was obstinately utilitarian, yet an eloquent plea later that day echoed the preservationist sentiments he had expressed at the Grand Canyon. Speaking in Sacramento, he begged Californians to preserve their "marvelous natural resources" unimpaired. "We are not building this country of ours for a day. It is to last through the ages."

ON THE MORNING of 23 May, Roosevelt sailed across Puget Sound toward Seattle, the apogee of his great swing across the nation. "Well, thank heaven," he wrote Henry Cabot Lodge, "tomorrow I turn my face toward the East." He suddenly, with a returning traveler's sense of anticlimax, felt as spent as the fireworks fizzling in the sun over Alki Point. "I am so jaded and nerve-weary and bored that it almost seems as if I *could not* go through the remainder of the speech-making."

Seattle neither knew nor cared about the President's tiredness. From the moment he stepped ashore, inexorable hands nudged him from platform to platform, and fifty thousand worshipers drained him with their adoration. It was late at night before he fell into bed at the Hotel Washington, only to be shaken awake by William Loeb. He had forgotten to address a banquet group downstairs: he must get up, don full evening dress, step out on the balcony, apologize, and "say a few words." When he retired for the second time, Roosevelt had to struggle with a problem new to him: insomnia.

Fortunately for his rest, a telegram dispatched that afternoon from Cleveland did not reach him until the next morning:

> THE ISSUE WHICH HAS BEEN FORCED ON ME IN THE
> MATTER OF OUR STATE CONVENTION THIS YEAR
> ENDORSING YOU FOR THE REPUBLICAN NOMINATION NEXT
> YEAR HAS COME IN A WAY WHICH MAKES IT NECESSARY
> FOR ME TO OPPOSE SUCH A RESOLUTION. WHEN YOU
> KNOW ALL THE FACTS I AM SURE YOU WILL APPROVE MY
> COURSE.
>
> M. A. HANNA

Roosevelt, fatigue forgotten, pondered this telegram excitedly as his train wound east to Walla Walla. He felt in the mood for "a knockdown and dragout fight with Hanna and the whole Wall Street crowd." Fate had placed a big political stick in his hands.

Fate—or Joseph B. Foraker. Ohio's wily, irascible senior Senator had for years been plotting to wrest control of the state Republican Party from Hanna. That organization was about to have its annual convention, and Foraker had issued a surprise demand that the state party endorse Theodore Roosevelt for President, one year early. This put Hanna in the impossible position of having to deny the resolution without seeming to be against the President's nomination. Alternatively, if he confirmed it, he would seem to be engineering an endorsement for himself. Either way, he stood to lose presidential favor, while Foraker would gain power and prestige—and a possible chance at the GOP nomination in 1908.

Roosevelt saw an irresistible chance to play one Senator off the other. Hanna was clearly appealing for help. He was not in good health. If Wall Street was not so determined to have "somebody like Hanna" in the White House, he would surely have disclaimed any presidential ambition whatsoever. Roosevelt dictated a curtly formal reply, and released it to the press at Walla Walla:

> YOUR TELEGRAM RECEIVED. I HAVE NOT ASKED ANY MAN
> FOR HIS SUPPORT. I HAVE HAD NOTHING WHATEVER TO
> DO WITH RAISING THE ISSUE. INASMUCH AS IT HAS
> BEEN RAISED OF COURSE THOSE WHO FAVOR MY
> ADMINISTRATION AND MY NOMINATION WILL FAVOR
> ENDORSING BOTH AND THOSE WHO DO NOT WILL OPPOSE.
>
> THEODORE ROOSEVELT

Hanna had no choice but to wire back that "in view of the sentiment expressed" he would not after all oppose the resolution.

Thus the President added a fifteenth endorsement to the list of states already committed to him, forced neutrality upon Hanna, gratified Foraker, and banished his own "nerve-weariness." Benisonlike, the lilacs and locusts of Walla Walla enveloped him in their fragrance. "This whole incident," he wrote to Lodge, "has entirely revived me."

~~~

ROOSEVELT ARRIVED AT BUTTE, Montana, on 27 May to find that mining city divided, like the Ohio GOP, into two warring political factions. Neither bore much relation to national party lines, and both were eager to welcome him. He saw at once that the crowd "was filled with whooping enthusiasm and every kind of whiskey," and that a riot might ensue if either camp felt slighted. Modeling his conduct on that of Mr. Pickwick at Eatanswill, he presented an equable face to both Buffs and Blues, addressing the former in the afternoon and the latter in the evening. He solved the problem of apportioning dinner tickets by asking Butte's enormous top-hatted mayor to issue exactly one hundred seats on a fifty-fifty basis. Satisfied, the factions respectively presented him with a silvered copper vase and a silver loving cup. Roosevelt was touched by a third gift, a pair of silver scales from Butte's black minority. "This," he said, lifting it delicately aloft, "comes in the shape I appreciate—the scales of justice held even."

He waited until the applause died. "I fought beside the colored troops at Santiago, and I hold that if a man is good enough to be put up and shot at then he is good enough—" Again he paused, while the crowd held its breath, wondering whether he was going to risk violence with a racially charged remark. Scattered Negroes, some Swedes, two Austrian families, a Chinese, and an Australian jostled with polyglot miners, Rough Riders, and dangerous-looking "rednecks" from the Coeur d'Alene. Roosevelt's old friend Seth Bullock of Deadwood, South Dakota, stood guard with a long .44.

"—for me to do what I can to get him a square deal," said the President. The phrase sank in, and the crowd relaxed.

"Nobody made a motion to attack me," Roosevelt wrote John Hay afterward.

My address was felt to be honor enough for one hotel, and the dinner was given in the other. When the dinner was announced the mayor led me in—or to speak more accurately, tucked me under one arm and lifted me partially off the ground, so that I felt as if I looked like one of those limp dolls with dangling legs carried around by small children, like Mary Jane in "The Golliwogs," for instance. As soon as we got in the banquet hall and sat at the head of the table the mayor hammered lustily with the handle of his knife and announced, "Waiter, bring on the feed!" Then in a spirit of pure kindliness he added, "Waiter, pull up the curtains and let the people see the President eat!"—but to this I objected. The dinner was soon in full swing. . . . Of the hundred men who were my hosts I suppose at least half had killed their man in private war, or had striven to encompass the assassination of an enemy. They had fought one another with reckless ferocity. They had been allies and enemies in every kind of business scheme, and companions in brutal revelry. As they drank great goblets of wine and sweat glistened on their hard, strong, crafty faces. They looked as if they had come out of the pictures in Aubrey Beardsley's Yellow Book.

Roosevelt left prudently early. He stood on the rear platform of the *Elysian* as his train pulled out of town, and the citizens of Butte howled and fired shots into the air. They would doubtless continue to celebrate all night.

After recanvassing Idaho, the train headed south to Salt Lake City, then east, recrossing the plains of Wyoming, Nebraska, Iowa, and Illinois. May turned to June. Day after day, freak rainstorms beat down. On either side of the tracks, the vast Midwest lay flat and flooded, halved by Roosevelt's trajectory. Here, in the heartland of the country, was his political center of gravity. Ahead of him in the baggage car sat his silver scales, effortlessly maintaining their balance. The Negroes of Butte had chosen well. Nothing appealed to him more than the concept of equilibrium. Justice separating good and evil, power—"my hand on the lever"—regulating the conflicting interests of blacks and whites, Buffs and Blues, tycoons and tradesmen, the born and the unborn. The phrase he had coined en route, *a square deal,* was potent. He tried it again on 4 June, standing in the drizzle by Lincoln's tomb. Cheers and applause resounded in the wet air.

He created one further magnificent image at Springfield Armory, as the sun lowered on the last day of his tour. Rhetorically, it was too strange, too poetic, to register on his audience; he seemed hardly to notice it himself, and never used it again. But after eight weeks of travel and 262 speeches, he could think of no more slogans, no positive platitudes. Blinking with exhaustion, he found only a compressed, negative metaphor for himself and the social forces he sought to mediate.

"Envy and arrogance," said Roosevelt, "are the two opposite sides of the same black crystal."

WHATEVER PRIVATE PERPLEXITY this suggested (did he see the Presidency, for all his efforts to fire it up, as something cold and dark at heart, merely reflecting outside passions?) was negated by male buffoonery that evening, as the train sped across Indiana. Roosevelt was sitting in his parlor with the Hoosier State's quarrelsome senators, Charles W. Fairbanks and Albert J. Beveridge, when two reporters marched in, waggishly attired in top hats and frock coats. "Mr. President, we desire to present you the keys of our great and beautiful car. The freedom of the *Gilsey* is yours, sir."

Roosevelt recalled that he had promised to accept the hospitality of the press on the final night of his tour. "My fellow Americans," he cried, his voice choked with fake sobs, "I am deeply affected by this spontaneous welcome, this unparalleled and unprecedented greeting." He allowed himself to be escorted forward. Fairbanks and Beveridge joined the general exodus of White House staff to the *Gilsey.*

As Roosevelt passed through the *Senegal,* two grinning black porters snapped to attention, saluting him with brooms. Hideous caricatures of "Teddy" lined the walls. A small group of cordoned-off reporters, pretending to be a welcoming crowd, cheered and clicked Kodaks. Roosevelt shook with laughter. "Well, this is bully!" He proceeded under an arch of spread trousers to his table in the *Gilsey,* where the menu sent him into further convulsions. It advertised "Haunch of Snow-fed Cinnabar Mountain Lion" and "Purée of Yosemite Mule," and was footnoted: "Guests who find their wine too warm will notice an improvement after placing their glasses between any two Senators from the same state who happen to be present."

The subsequent dinner was private, but leaks indicated that the President "talked a string and ate like a farmhand."

He was in bed by midnight. Ohio rumbled by unseen in the small hours. Ahead, Pennsylvania's hills waited for dawn. Barreling through blackness, the train twisted now left, now right.

CHAPTER 16

White Man Black and Black Man White

Th' black has manny fine qualities. He is joyous,
light-hearted, an' easily lynched.

SENATOR BEVERIDGE AND others getting off Roosevelt's train in Washington on 5 June 1903 were amazed to see a multitude jamming Pennsylvania Avenue all the way downtown from Sixth Street Station. Normally the capital paid little attention to executive comings and goings, but this looked like an almost royal welcome. Apparently, the President's forceful oratory on tour, his widely reported disappearances into the wilderness, and his haughty suppression of Mark Hanna—in Walla Walla, of all places!—had caught the public's imagination, and strengthened him as the likely ruler of America for six more years. Roosevelt now enjoyed the endorsement of sixteen state Republican organizations, and seventeen more were expected to follow suit. "He will be nominated by acclamation," Beveridge predicted, "and elected by the greatest popular majority ever given a President."

For the moment, Roosevelt was interested in the acclamation of only an intimate minority. He addressed a few words to the crowd in Lafayette Square, then rasped, "I thank you again, my friends, but now I am going in to my own folks."

Edith had been busy with landscapers during his absence. The White House grounds, winter-bare when he saw them last, and littered with construction rubble, were elegantly lush. The north lawn was a sheet of velvet, its beds bejeweled with pansies. Blossoms dense as ermine lay on the shrubbery. Fountains rose above the new terraces to east and west, separated by plantings of boxwoods and Dutch bays.

Although the President could not see it yet, there was a surprise tennis court waiting for him just south of his office window. Perhaps Edith had read about his prodigious eating over the last eight weeks (ox steaks on rye in North Dakota; dozens of fried grayling at Yellowstone; lamb and white bread

"THERE WAS A SURPRISE TENNIS COURT WAITING FOR HIM JUST
SOUTH OF HIS OFFICE WINDOW."
View of the renovated White House, ca. 1903

spread with cream in Nebraska; *pluvier au cresson* and *petits fours* at St. Louis; a two-hour chuckwagon breakfast on the Colorado prairie; T-bones and broilers at Yosemite; and always, between stops, presidential command of the *Elysian*'s kitchen). He was aware of having gained seventeen pounds en route to the Pacific. There would be inevitable comparisons with "stout Cortez," and Elihu Root was bound to ask archly for a copy of his remarks on expansionism.

A younger, slimmer, oil-painted Roosevelt greeted him in the vestibule. Edith had hung Fedor Encke's portrait there, rather than the more recent rendering by John Singer Sargent, knowing that her husband loved to see himself in Rough Rider uniform. "I cannot say that I think it looks particularly like me," he commented, but admitted that it was the image he wanted his children to have of him.

Roosevelt's vanity was oddly leavened with modesty. He never failed to take the bait when Root drawled, "Mr. President, I would like so much to have you give us an account of the fight at San Juan Hill," yet he deferred to all Civil War veterans. He lectured some of the finest minds in America on their own specialties, while protesting his own intellectual ordinariness: "I am but the average man." Living in a White House more formal than any in history, he nevertheless entertained cowboys and backwoodsmen there, on equal terms with Cabinet officers and diplomats.

Although political analysts were beginning to use the word *genius* to describe his political sleight of hand, he scoffed at such hyperbole. Genius was what drove Frank Jarvis in the hundred meters, or John Keats in "Ode on a Grecian Urn": "power to do what no one else has the power to do." His own power, idiosyncratic as it seemed, was the same given to all Presidents. Democratically won, it could be democratically lost, as soon as he failed to please.

Yet his wife, watching him swig Apollinaris from his Golden State loving cup "as if he were a King of Thule," noticed a new, almost placid confidence in his attitude toward affairs of state. Less intimate observers, such as former Senator David B. Hill, feared the development of "demagogical and dangerous tendencies." There was little anyone could do to restrain Roosevelt for the next half year, until the new Congress was sworn in. Three current issues offered him much opportunity for executive rashness: Jewish demands to protest the Kishinev pogrom; allegations of spoilsmanship, forgery, bribery, and fraud in the Post Office Department; and reports that resistance to the Panama Canal Treaty had developed in Colombia.

To all of these challenges the King of Thule felt equal. He would receive the Jews and make the Post Office's own internal investigation (relating, fortunately, to matters predating his presidency) an essay on open government. But the third matter required urgent attention

~⌒~

ONE OF HIS FIRST acts on returning to his desk was to ask the State Department for a copy of the 1902 Canal Bill, which spelled out his powers in the event of nonratification. John Hay cautioned him that there was no immediate crisis. The Colombian Congress had not yet assembled to debate the treaty. And President José Manuel Marroquín was constitutionally authorized to override any negative vote.

There was no guarantee, though, that Marroquín *would* so override. Roosevelt discovered that Hay had been keeping quiet about a sharp deterioration in Colombian-American relations. Cables from the American Minister in Bogotá, Arthur M. Beaupré, quoted angry local protests against any "surrender of sovereignty" in the canal zone, and described a general feeling that the treaty prescribed a "loss of the national honor." (Apparently this feeling related to the ten-million-dollar fee negotiated by Hay and Herrán. Beaupré said he had received "private" assurances that Colombia's honor would be restored if the United States agreed to pay "a much greater sum of money.")

Hay, a poet's soul in a diplomat's body, reacted with sulky distress to any criticism of his treaties. An instrument like this—the painstakingly worded distillation of months of gentlemanly conversation, of late-night *pourparlers* and next-morning "memorials," calligraphed at last on crisp parchment—

"A POET'S SOUL IN A DIPLOMAT'S BODY."
Secretary of State John Hay, 1904

was as dear to him as any sonnet. Wholesale rejection was apt to aggravate his chronic depression.

Roosevelt moved quickly to restore the diplomatic offensive, and Hay's wilting morale. One of the most important conventions in the history of the Americas demanded a resolute State Department. He saw the Secretary briefly, behind closed doors, on the afternoon of 8 June. Whatever transpired, Hay returned to work as if galvanized. The next morning, new instructions went out to Beaupré, couched in language of unusual force:

THE COLOMBIAN GOVERNMENT APPARENTLY DOES NOT
APPRECIATE THE GRAVITY OF THE SITUATION. THE CANAL
NEGOTIATIONS WERE INITIATED BY COLOMBIA, AND
WERE ENERGETICALLY PRESSED UPON THIS GOVERNMENT
FOR SEVERAL YEARS. THE PROPOSITIONS PRESENTED BY
COLOMBIA, WITH SLIGHT MODIFICATIONS, WERE FINALLY
ACCEPTED BY US. IN VIRTUE OF THIS AGREEMENT OUR
CONGRESS REVERSED ITS PREVIOUS JUDGMENT AND
DECIDED UPON THE PANAMA ROUTE. IF COLOMBIA
SHOULD NOW REJECT THE TREATY OR UNDULY DELAY ITS
RATIFICATION, THE FRIENDLY UNDERSTANDING BETWEEN
THE TWO COUNTRIES WOULD BE SO SERIOUSLY
COMPROMISED THAT ACTION MIGHT BE TAKEN BY THE
CONGRESS NEXT WINTER WHICH EVERY FRIEND OF
COLOMBIA MIGHT REGRET.

Hay acted like a new man in the days that followed. Town gossip had it that twenty-one months of "strenuous Teddy" had enfeebled him—that he was being kept on only as a venerable symbol, Washington's last link with the administration of President Lincoln. There was some truth to both rumors, although Hay was still capable of inspired diplomacy. And his relationship with Roosevelt was genuinely affectionate, rooted in a mutual memory of Theodore Senior introducing them nearly thirty-three years before—reedy boy and young diplomat shaking hands to the roar of the Hudson Valley thunderstorm.

At sixty-four, Hay was still as elegant as he had been then. The severe cut of his Savile Row clothes gave line to his five-foot-two-inch figure, while a slight fullness of silk under the winged collar focused attention on his unforgettable face. In youth, when merely mustached, Hay had looked almost mandarin, with his high cheekbones and Ming-smooth brow. Now the mustache floated over a magnificent whitened Vandyke, while the skin above was slashed with creases, two of the deepest plummeting in a frown so anguished that photographers felt obliged to retouch them.

The Secretary was, by common consent, one of the great talkers of his time, holding forth in a quiet, beautiful voice. Like a well-resined viola, it poured forth suave melodies, lapsing instantly into accompaniment whenever the presidential trumpet sounded. Even more than Root, Hay was a master of the sly *mot juste* that inspired Roosevelt to go too far. His inert pose and hazel stare gave no hint of the hilarity suppressed beneath his waistcoat.

Although Hay found the President amusing, he never savaged him as Adams did. He recognized that Roosevelt had "plenty of brains, and a heart of gold," not to mention a gift for storytelling that rivaled his own. Curious to hear about the great cross-country trip, he invited Roosevelt to dinner on 12 June, along with Ambassador and Madame Jusserand.

With very little encouragement, the President launched beaming into an account of his adventures. Big sticks and badgers and midnight fusillades, rose-petaled streets and redwoods, golden gifts and glistening Beardsleyesque faces held the table entranced. As he talked on and on, Roosevelt began to free-associate earlier western memories: of sharing a bed with the judge who jailed Calamity Joe, of Hell-Roaring Bill Jones chasing a lunatic across the prairie, of bandy-legged Frank Brito "shooting at his wife the time he killed his sister-in-law." To Jusserand, such stories sounded as remote and strange as any in *Piers Plowman*. Roosevelt's extraordinary frankness, his high-pitched mirth (punctuated with table thumps and chortles of "*Hoo! Hoo!*"), and perpetual discharge of energy were such that the Ambassador could conclude only that France was being vouchsafed some sort of privileged audience.

After dinner, Hay displayed some of the rarities in his library. Roosevelt took up an autographed page proof of the Gettysburg Address, then, his mind leaping to other subjects, began to talk and gesticulate. The precious sheet flapped in the air, to Hay's silent agony. Rescuing it, he begged Roosevelt to endow him with a typed transcript of his western monologue, to preserve for posterity.

Roosevelt, flattered, promised to oblige.

‑‑‑‑‑‑‑

THE COLOMBIAN MINISTER for Foreign Affairs was mystified by Hay's cable. What was this threatened "action" by the United States—something directly aggressive, or just reversion to a Nicaragua Canal? Beaupré did not know, and the State Department sent no clarification. Thirty years of foreign-policy experience had taught Hay to keep his opponents guessing. "There are three species of creature," he liked to quip, "who when they seem coming, are going: diplomats, women, and crabs."

That same day, 13 June, Roosevelt sat in private conference with William Nelson Cromwell. It was not his habit to receive lobbyists. But Mark Hanna had strongly urged the meeting, and after Walla Walla he wanted to be accommodating. The glossy little lawyer had made himself indispensable in all canal matters, darting with bright-eyed, bumblebee quickness among every possible source of pollen. Cromwell had spies in Bogotá, paid agents in Colón and Panama City, political supporters in Washington, and financial backers in Paris and New York. Every infusion of news, every fresh pledge of funds was more honey in his hive. Roosevelt's stiff petals yielded to his fervor.

For a half hour before lunch, and two hours that afternoon, they went over every aspect of the canal situation. Cromwell thought that President

Marroquín favored the treaty, but did not have enough political strength to oppose the will of the Colombian Congress. If Marroquín recommended ratification, there might be a coup by antitreaty forces; if he advised against, he risked the secession of Panama.

Roosevelt told Cromwell that he was "determined" to build a Panama Canal, and would tolerate no trickery by Colombia; if the treaty was rejected, and Panama seceded, he would "strongly favor" dealing with the new republic.

This was all the lobbyist needed to hear. He walked out into the fresh June evening. White sails crept down the Potomac; somewhere a baseball crowd was roaring. Washington had shut for the summer. Only its insatiable press corps lingered. Cromwell felt that pleasant loosening of the lips known to all Executive Office visitors, particularly those who think they have prevailed on the President. Full as he was of news, he did not dare to leak it directly. Instead, he briefed an aide who had close connections to the New York *World*. Overnight, an uncannily prophetic article ground out of the Pulitzer press:

NEW REPUBLIC MAY ARISE TO GRANT CANAL

*The State of Panama Ready to Secede
If the Treaty is Rejected by the Colombian Congress*

ROOSEVELT IS SAID TO ENCOURAGE THE IDEA

Washington, June 13 — President Roosevelt is determined to have the Panama Canal route. He has no intention of beginning negotiations for the Nicaragua route.

The view of the President is known to be that as the United States has spent millions of dollars in ascertaining which route is most feasible; as three different Ministers from Colombia have declared their Government willing to grant every concession for the construction of a canal, and as two treaties have been signed granting rights of way across the Isthmus of Panama, it would be unfair to the United States if the best route be not obtained.

Advices received here daily indicate great opposition to the canal treaty at Bogotá. Its defeat seems probable. . . . Information has also reached this city that the State of Panama, which embraces all the proposed canal zone, stands ready to secede from Colombia and enter into a canal treaty with the United States . . . giving this Government the equivalent of absolute sovereignty over the canal zone. The city of Panama alone will be exempted. . . . In return the President of the United States should promptly recognize the new Government, when established, and at once appoint a Minister to negotiate and sign a canal treaty.

The article went on to report that Roosevelt's Cabinet fully supported his plan, as did congressional leaders. Apparently the President was prepared to wait "a reasonable time" for ratification of the treaty, but if there was any hint of deliberate delay, he would quickly "make the above plan operable."

One detail missing from the article was Cromwell's private prediction that the Panamanian revolution would occur on the third day of November.

Roosevelt issued no denial of the *World* article, nor of similar scenarios in the Washington *Evening Star* and New York *Sun*. He was known to be a quick repudiator of his own faux pas, so evidently he was sending Bogotá a message. Herrán sent one, too, also predicting that Panama might secede.

Cromwell, for his part, smoothly assured reporters that he "still expected ratification."

⎯⎯

ON 15 JUNE, six solemn gentlemen waited on the President: Leo N. Levi, Jacob Furth, Solomon Sulzberger, Joseph D. Coons, Adolf Moses, and Simon Wolf. They were escorted by John Hay, courteously veiling his usual jocular anti-Semitism. ("The Hebrews—poor dears!") One could not mock their present distress. All over America, Christians as well as Jews were collecting funds to help the surviving victims of the Kishinev pogrom. Ten thousand refugees were still homeless, and an equal number dependent on relief.

Roosevelt wanted to contribute one hundred dollars. "Would it do any good for me to say a word in behalf of the Jews?" he asked Hay and Root before receiving the delegation. "Or would it do harm?" He knew the answer in advance. They objected even to his sending money, on grounds of diplomatic propriety. "I suppose," Roosevelt conceded, "it would be very much like the Tsar spreading his horror of our lynching Negroes."

Hay tried to explain to the delegation, representing the executive committee of B'nai B'rith, that there were only two "motives" that might justify Administration criticism of Russia's domestic policy. The first was national self-interest, and the second (hardly imaginable) an expressed willingness in St. Petersburg to listen. "What possible advantage would it be to the United States, and what possible advantage to the Jews of Russia, if we should make a protest against these fiendish cruelties and be told that it was none of our business?"

Leo Levi, the group's spokesman, awkwardly addressed himself to the first consideration. He said that it was indeed in the national interest to prevent a diaspora of persecuted Russian Jews to America. The anti-Tsarist "propaganda" such immigrants would bring with them was sure to under-

mine "amity between Russia and the United States." Something must be
done "to allay the fears of the Jews in Russia, and thus stem their rush to this
country."

Having thus expressed the traditional disdain of Western for Eastern
Jews, Levi went on to read a petition to Nicholas II, the language of which
was enough to make Hay blanch. It spoke of "horror and reprobation
around the world" at the carnage in Kishinev, accused Russian authorities of
tolerating "ignorance, superstition, and bigotry," and concluded: "Religious
persecution is more sinful and more fatuous even than war."

Hay responded first, in unctuous but negative tones. He said that the
United States deplored all "acts of cruelty and injustice" but had to "carefully
consider" whether she had any right to question the internal affairs of another sovereign power. The Tsar in any case was an "enlightened sovereign"
who would surely never permit another Kishinev.

Roosevelt spoke much more sympathetically. "I have never in my experience in this country known of a more immediate or a deeper expression of
sympathy," he said. It was natural that the United States, with her large Jewish population, should have "the most intense and widespread" reaction
against the pogrom. He recited some lines from Longfellow's "The Jewish
Cemetery at Newport," and paid tribute to the American Jews who had
fought in the Revolution and Civil War.

Inevitably, mention of the word *war* reminded him of his charge up San
Juan Hill. "When I was myself in the army, one of the best colonels among
the regular regiments who did so well on that day, who fought beside me, was
a Jew!" As regimental commander, he had personally promoted five men:
"two Protestants, two Catholics, and one Jew."

Ingenuous protests like this, half boyish, half calculating, always made
Hay's whiskers twitch, but the committee listened with respect. Soon Roosevelt was well away:

> You may possibly recall—I am certain some of my New York friends
> will recall—that during the time I was Police Commissioner, a man
> came from abroad—I am sorry to say, a clergyman—to start an anti-
> Jewish agitation in New York, and announced his intention of holding
> meetings to assail the Jews. The matter was brought to my attention.
> Of course I had no power to prevent these meetings. After a good deal
> of thought I detailed a Jewish sergeant and forty Jew policemen to pro-
> tect the agitator while he held his meetings. So he made his speeches
> denouncing the Jews, protected exclusively by Jews!

It was a story he loved to tell. "Now let me give you another little
example. . . ."

After an hour of such confidences, the committee trooped out glowing with satisfaction. Questioned by reporters, they had to admit that they had failed in their mission. However, the President had promised to read the petition "most carefully."

◦―◦

HIS EXCELLENCY Arturo Paul Nicolas, Count de Cassini and Marquis de Capizzucchi de Bologna, Russian Ambassador Extraordinary and Minister Plenipotentiary to the United States, told Roosevelt that some four hundred anti-Semitic rioters had been arrested in Kishinev, and the local governor dismissed for failing to prevent the pogrom.

Hay cautioned that Cassini could not be trusted. For all his Italian nomenclature, he was as Russian as *borscht*, and lied with fabled virtuosity. The Ambassador, who mysteriously depended on his teenage daughter, Marguerite, for social purposes, introduced her around town as "Princess Cassini," when she was neither a princess nor, according to rumor, a Cassini. His numberless jeweled decorations may not all have been earned in the Tsar's service, but they were the glittering envy of Embassy Row. When he stood under a chandelier at receptions, he looked like a section of the Milky Way.

Cassini's assurances regarding Kishinev were nothing compared to his obfuscations about when, if ever, Russia intended to withdraw from Manchuria. He would say only that the ports there were now open to United States trade. This came as news to American observers in China, who reported that the Russian Bear had also begun to prowl Korea.

"Dealing with a government with whom mendacity is a science is an extremely difficult matter," Hay complained.

Roosevelt cared little for Korea, a little, impotent kingdom that fancied itself an empire—and even less for China. But he was aware that the latter was potentially the world's greatest market. If the Open Door was not so blocked by Russia, the United States could easily export everything the Chinese wanted to buy. "We wish for our people the commercial privileges which Russia again and again has said we shall have," Roosevelt wrote to Lyman Abbott, the editor of *Outlook*. "It is very irritating. I do not know what action may be necessary in the future."

As a strategic pragmatist, he felt that Russia had some "legitimate aspirations" to fulfill in Manchuria, providing China was not partitioned, and the Far Eastern balance of power maintained. He agreed with Frederick W. Holls, one of his private foreign-policy advisers, who had written: "*You cannot keep an Empire of one hundred and twenty million away from a harbor* [Port Arthur] *which is not frozen up in winter. . . . No Empire would build a stupendous work like the Siberian railroad, to end anywhere but in an ice-free harbor under its own control.*"

Cassini expressed the same thought to his daughter in the privacy of the Russian Embassy. "Try to understand this, Margot," he said, running a long forefinger down the map of Manchuria to Port Arthur. "To possess the East, Russia must possess the Liaotung peninsula."

⟳

ROOSEVELT PUT ASIDE HIS foreign-policy troubles on the new White House tennis court. He played with intense concentration, quite unaware of the strangeness of his style. When serving, he grasped the racket stem halfway, forefinger pointing upward. His myopia kept him close to the net, but his reflexes were so quick that he nevertheless covered the court well, chasing the balls that got past him. After smashing a winning shot, he would rejoice with falsetto shrieks, and hop around on one foot, singing and laughing. Washington's tour guides began driving their vehicles down West Executive Avenue, with megaphoned commentary: "To the left you will see the famous tennis court. On most any pleasant afternoon you may see the President there, reaching for a high ball."

Roosevelt's favorite opponents were Gifford Pinchot and James Garfield. Although they were younger and more lithe than he, he could manage three sets with either of them. Speck von Sternburg, his old partner from Civil Service Commission days, still played a decent game, and Henry Cabot Lodge returned serves from all positions consonant with senatorial dignity. But the season's real surprise was Jules Jusserand. Looking not unlike a Mont Blanc chamois, with his pointy beard and neat, precise leaps, the little ambassador darted about as nimbly as he ranged the field of medieval literature. Roosevelt beamed at him with increasing favor, much to the envy of Count Cassini, who received no invitations.

⟳

ON 22 JUNE, the President received a letter from his first Southern appointee, Judge Thomas G. Jones of Alabama. He was pleased to read that Jones had, true to Booker T. Washington's recommendation, condemned peonage as the modern equivalent of slavery, and sentenced several white racists to prison for holding black "employees" against their wills. Roosevelt sent a copy to Lyman Abbott (his most consistently reliable editorial supporter). "Unfortunately," he wrote, "there is in the South a very large element . . . which hates and despises the Negro but is bent upon his continuing in the land."

The "element" was larger than he thought, and not confined to the South. One hundred miles northeast of the White House that evening, quiet groups of white men began to collect around a penitentiary near Wilmington, Delaware. The building was a massive structure, representing the latest in prison engineering. Wilmington's police chief, whose name was Black, had chosen it to shelter a Negro murder suspect, whose name was White. Black felt that White needed all the security he could get, because the murder victim—who had identified him before dying—was a white teenage girl.

White sat now deep within the penitentiary, in a steel cell in a steel gallery in a steel chamber, sheathed behind brick walls, each with its own steel door, then a thicker wall, with a bigger door of wood and steel, then a yard, then another brick wall, and the biggest door of all, beyond which the quiet groups were forming.

Daylight faded. Still more quiet men came from the city, and from the fields, until there were no spaces left between the groups waiting for dark. The communal mood was disciplined, almost professional. Marksmen checked their rifles; boilermakers armed themselves with freshly sharpened saws and cold-steel chisels; quarriers counted out sticks of dynamite; ship-yard workers readied a huge launch ram.

At sunset, electric lights went on in the yard. The marksmen took aim. Quickly, methodically, every bulb was shot out. Inside, the warden took his wife and children upstairs and locked them in the women's chamber. Chief Black and two deputies arrived, stood against the yard door, and pleaded that the law be allowed to take its course. A short man in a red sweater listened, smiling, then said, "Come on boys, get to one side, you're bothering us." Out of the darkness came the ram, and the big door split like balsa. The crowd, four thousand strong now, surged roaring into the yard.

Guards on the penitentiary roof fired high. There was an answering fusillade, so heavy that the guards dropped out of sight. The boilermakers came forward and began to saw through the door of wood and steel bars. In twenty minutes, it was down. Beyond lay a door of solid steel. That took a half hour. The crowd waited patiently. A flight of stairs led down to yet another steel door. The boilermakers took new saws and cold chisels, and set to work.

Prison staff inside pushed a firehose through the door's speaking hatch and shot out a high-pressure blast. This momentarily delayed progress, but the marksmen fired bullets down the hose until its handlers withdrew. Soon the door was open. Tunnel-like passages receded in several directions. The mob explored them and reported back to the man in the red sweater. Attention focused on a third door of solid steel. The boilermakers crouched down again.

By then the rumble of thousands of voices, and the steady rasp of sawing, must have penetrated to the inmates, who had not heard the initial tumult in the yard. Most were Negroes. By the time the third door fell, and the mob entered the prison chamber, they were hysterical with fear. "He's in cell thirteen!" one man screamed. "On the second gallery!"

That meant two more barriers of steel. Afterward, when experts came to assess the damage, they had nothing but praise for the skill of the boilermakers. Every plate, bar, and bolt was sliced as smoothly as cheddar. The last filament snapped at 11:00 P.M., and cell thirteen revealed itself. It was empty.

There was a moment's hesitation, then: "Shove back the panel!" Hard as it was to believe that a six-foot Negro could squeeze himself into a shallow closet measuring four feet by two and a half feet, when the door slid open White burst out like a bull. Viselike hands secured him. Then, as joyful shouts echoed through the passages into the yard, the prisoner was escorted outside.

"I did it!" White jabbered in half-praying, half-confessional tones. "O Christ save my soul! I did it!" His mantra continued nonstop, even when the man in the red sweater calmed the waiting crowd: "Let nobody strike or hurt him. We are going to take him to the place where he committed the crime, and we are going to burn him alive."

An oddly ecclesiastical procession began. A man on a white horse rode his mount in slow circles to clear the way. Next came an old farmer in blue overalls, carrying a lantern on a long forked stick. Then came White, weaving as if drunk between his two escorts. Six other horsemen flanked him, and the crowd fell into place behind.

As the procession moved out into open country, along a mud road pleached with maple trees, its joy increased. Someone struck up "There'll Be a Hot Time in the Old Town Tonight," to roars of laughter. Then massed voices joined in "Marching Through Georgia." Young men jumped through the trees and fanned out across the fields. But they stayed abreast of the swaying lantern and the white horse.

Around midnight, the scene of White's crime came into view: a notched hedge by a plowed field. He stood talking to himself as carpenters cut fence rails into faggots. A youth in a Panama hat chopped slats into kindling. Soon a neat pyre arose, its interstices stuffed with straw. Ceaselessly moving, the man on the white horse shaped the crowd into a circle, and ordered the inner ring to hold hands. Centripetal pressure made the ring wreathe and sway. Oddly, those nearest the pyre seemed disposed to kick it down. "For God's sake," a voice called, "don't do this! Shoot the man! Hang him . . . don't burn him!"

The man in the red sweater shouted, "We're going to burn the nigger alive, and we're going to do it right here and now." He produced a rope. White was brought inside the ring and bound from the ankles up, like a papoose. His confession moaned on—"Then I gave her a hack in the throat with my knife and asked her again. . . ." The rope began to cramp his chest. "You would not do this to me if I was a white man. . . ." A few more coils silenced him. It was 1:30 in the morning.

Suddenly, White was seized at head and foot and tossed onto the pyre. A match lit the straw. "Give it to him!" "Burn him up!" The yells sounded scattered and uncertain. Then flames climbed over White's body. Several watchers turned away, gagging.

Some of the Negro's bonds burned loose, and he managed to writhe off the pyre, screaming "O God forgive me!" He was tossed back, head foremost, and the fire, fierce now, engulfed him. Incredibly, White writhed off again. Before he could be picked up, an exasperated bystander hoisted a long-handled hammer, arched it through the air, and shattered his skull. "That settles it!"

There was a chorus of disappointment from the incendiarists, led by the old farmer with the lantern. They returned the corpse to the pyre, which burned all night. By dawn, a few pale bones were all that remained of the black man, White. Vendors hawked them in the streets of Wilmington as souvenirs.

CHAPTER 17

No Color of Right

*I'll tell ye . . . 'tis a gr-reat mistake to think that
annywan ra-aly wants to rayform.*

THE DELAWARE LYNCHING was not, as some shocked headlines claimed, the first to occur north of the Mason-Dixon Line. But it was the first there with a motive that was explicitly racial, and its sadism revolted even Southerners. Roosevelt, child of a Georgian mother, was torn in his heart between "the horror that such savagery aroused" and concern that if he spoke out against it now, as passions still surged (fresh mobs were roaming the streets of Wilmington, protesting Sheriff Black's arrest of the man in the red shirt), he might touch off worse and wider demonstrations. His one public reference to lynching, in front of the Custis-Lee Mansion, had badly damaged him politically. There was no question he must say something soon—but when, and how best for moral effect?

He poured out his distress to Jules Jusserand, who was fast becoming a confidant. What really worried him, he said, was "the demoralizing effect of mob executions" on young minds. He had heard of boys of twelve taking part. "They will be brutalized for life."

The Delaware affair came as a particular shock to Roosevelt, because the national lynch rate had been dropping since he had taken office. If, now, four thousand hitherto peaceful whites living on Union soil were capable of such barbarity, what price Judge Jones's manumission of a few peons in the South?

❧

AS SUMMER SETTLED DOWN over Washington, the President, deserted by his wife and children, waited impatiently for some positive news from Bogotá. On 24 June, he gave a bachelor dinner for Hay and Jusserand. He said he was studying the *War Reports* of Prince Eugene of Savoy, that most self-confident and impetuous of monarchs, and was not fazed by James J. Hill's angry determination to take the *Northern Securities* case to the Supreme Court. "He detests me, but I admire him," Roosevelt said. "He will detest me much more before I have done with him."

Hay, much of whose wealth derived from railroad stocks, disapproved of the Administration's antitrust policy. "Where will it begin, and where will it stop?" he complained to Jusserand afterward. "Where is the limit, the line of demarcation?"

The next morning, a cable arrived from Arthur Beaupré, saying that the Colombian Congress had at last convened to debate the treaty, but did not appear to be intimidated by Hay's ultimatum. A good sign, perhaps, was that President Marroquín had not specifically recommended against ratification. That guaranteed many weeks—if not months—of leisurely debate.

Hay and Roosevelt agreed to await further developments in their respective watering places. With that, they separately left town. Assistant Secretary of State Francis B. Loomis remained behind to stay in wire contact with Beaupré.

"Out of consideration for my feelings," the President advised Hay, "pray go as little to Washington this summer as possible—otherwise I shall feel too poignantly that I am neglecting my own duty."

CANNONS CRASHED AND a school choir sang "God Save the President" when Roosevelt stepped down under the white gull-wings of Oyster Bay station on 27 June 1903. He listened smiling, his hand resting on a child's small golden head. The face beneath suffused in bliss. His own children stood outside the circle of attention, waiting to escort him to his carriage. They felt no sense of deprivation, for what he gave, he gave without stint. Only Alice, still the family "orphan" at nineteen, yearned for more. Haunted by the ghost of her namesake, hurt by his denial of that ghost, contemptuous of his guilt, she fought the maddening smile as best she could, with her own income, with cigarettes and flashy clothes. She begged him to let her buy a red automobile like Marguerite Cassini's. Rebuffed, she "chauffeured" the cars of other friends at desperate speeds up to twenty-five miles an hour. She kept dynamite caps and pet reptiles in her purse, stuck silver butterflies in her hair, and—knowing how Roosevelt despised arrogant wealth—flaunted her popularity with the Four Hundred. But she remained his "blessed girl." It was also what he called dowdy little Ethel.

"Father doesn't care for me," Alice scratched angrily in her diary. "That is to say, one eighth as much as he does for the other children. . . . We are not in the least congenial. . . . Why should he pay any attention to me or things that I live for, except to look upon them with disapproval."

The most Roosevelt would say, to Ted, was, "I wish she had some pronounced serious taste."

Ted, now fifteen, understood the word *serious* very well. He had all of his

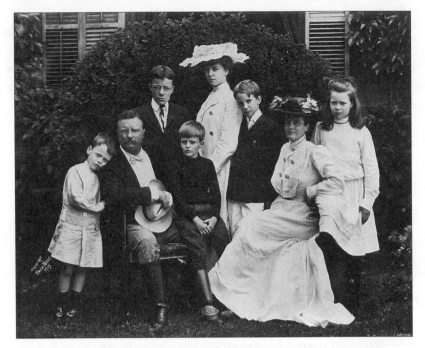

"WHAT HE GAVE HE GAVE WITHOUT STINT."
The President and his family, summer 1903

father's purposeful force, but imagination and intellect were denied him. Small, nervous, grim, plug-ugly, he made plenty of the best blood flow at Groton. "He is a regular bull terrier," Roosevelt noted proudly. "In a game last year he broke his collar bone, but finished the game without letting anyone know what had happened."

Kermit, thirteen, was a grave, fine-eyed, clumsy adolescent, whom Edith adored. Roosevelt was aware of a solitariness and bookishness not unlike his own in youth. But Kermit also had a yielding quality: if not exactly soft ("He seems to hold his own well with boys"), he was pliable and easy to bruise.

Ethel, nearly twelve, was already the family *hausfrau*—a heavy-legged, blunt-featured girl who bossed the servants and took no nonsense from horses. Roosevelt thought her "gloomy," but she was in reality shy, intimidated both by his power and by her half-sister's glamour.

The two smallest boys, aged nine and five, were still too much in a state of perpetual motion, on banisters, bicycles, ponies, stilts, or swaying trees, to register on anyone with precise definition. Out of the noisy scurry that was Archie there poked occasionally a fierce, hawklike face, and sharp bony extremities much bitten by Josiah the badger. When the dust clouds around Quentin thinned, a miniature Theodore Roosevelt was revealed, dome-headed and wheezily garrulous, with mild, rather abstracted blue eyes.

⌐⌐

"WASHINGTON IS NOW quite deserted," Speck von Sternburg noted at the end of June, "and the men who are pushing the world seem to be taking a short and well-deserved nap." One of the pushiest, however, remained in town long enough to disturb the rest of both President and Secretary of State. "The Russian Government," Count Cassini announced on 1 July, "most positively and absolutely denies the reports that it has offered any official explanations to the American Government . . . regarding the Kishinev incident."

Roosevelt was mystified. No explanation had been demanded. He and Hay had decided, on second thought, to allow the B'nai B'rith leaders to proceed with their petition, on the understanding that it was nongovernmental, and almost certainly a waste of ink. Cassini confirmed the latter point: "The Russian Government has categorically refused to receive any petitions, communications, or representations from any power regarding Russian internal affairs."

Behind this statement Roosevelt sensed shame over the pogrom, as well as fear of publicity that might further hurt Russian prestige—already damaged by the occupation of Manchuria. He saw how he might exploit the Tsar's embarrassment to his own advantage, winning the gratitude both of Jews and of American exporters hungry for Far Eastern trade. A peremptory telegram went forth from Oyster Bay to Acting Secretary of State Loomis, ordering him "in the absence of Secretary Hay" to respond publicly to Cassini's statement. He must express "the deep sympathy felt not only by the Administration, but by all the American people for the unfortunate Jews who have been the victims of the recent appalling massacres and outrages." Loomis was further authorized to quote "another official" as saying, in tones recognizably Rooseveltian, that "it seemed somewhat strange, to say the least," for the Russian government to make such a statement at such a time, "when by methods which are certainly the reverse of friendly to the United States, it has sought to make China join in breaking the plighted faith of all the powers as to the open door in Manchuria."

Throwing all semblance of impartiality aside, Roosevelt urged Loomis to expedite the Jewish petition (still gathering signatures), and prepare it for immediate transmission to St. Petersburg. Cassini was about to sail home on vacation; Russia must feel America's displeasure before he arrived and smoothed things over.

John Hay, unaware of what was going on, wrote Roosevelt to say that Cassini's "extraordinary" statement reinforced his earlier doubts about the petition. Better simply for B'nai B'rith to publicize its rejection in advance. "We can then all of us say what we think proper, and Russia cannot complain of anything we say among ourselves."

His letter came too late to influence the telegrams and telephone calls buzzing back and forth between the summer White House and Washington. Whether Hay liked it or not, Roosevelt was beginning to act more and more as his own Secretary of State.

⟡

A DAY OR TWO LATER, Hay received a summons to Sagamore Hill, amid rumors that he would soon resign. It was assumed—correctly—that he felt the United States was becoming too confrontational in its foreign policy, not only *vis-à-vis* Russia and Germany, but also toward Canada and Great Britain in the Alaska boundary dispute. (Roosevelt's three "impartial jurists," Elihu Root, Henry Cabot Lodge, and former Senator George Turner, were busy polishing their prejudices for an upcoming tribunal in London.)

Hay was not so much disenchanted as weary of the strain of working for "Theodore the Sudden." He packed his bags, wondering if this was to be the first of many summer interruptions. McKinley had never called for him without reason. Roosevelt tended to call first and think of reasons afterward. "I always find TR engaged with a dozen other people, and it is an hour's wait and a minute's talk—and a certainty that there was no necessity of my coming at all."

Sure enough, when he rolled under the porte cochere on 7 July, the President was entertaining three senators, a Quaker financier, a poet, and a playboy. "Will you excuse me till I play a game of tennis with Winty Chanler, I have had no exercise all day." Hay went off for a stroll around the estate, and did not see Roosevelt again that afternoon. In spite of himself he was charmed by Sagamore Hill. He admired its high panorama of trees and water—no other houses visible in any direction—and liked its air of dignified simplicity. At six o'clock, out of long habit, he dressed in black tie for dinner, and noticed that Roosevelt did the same. "The President was so cordial and hospitable," he wrote his wife, "that I felt ashamed of my surly crossness at having to go there."

When they did have their discussion, over coffee on the porch, it was long and businesslike. Hay abandoned all thought of resignation. Aside from Manchuria and the Kishinev petition, there were encouraging developments in Bogotá. President Marroquín had privately begun to pressure the Colombian Congress to ratify the Panama Canal Treaty. Members of the lower chamber were reported to be in favor. Senate opposition was still stiff, but if Marroquín was as powerful as Beaupré believed, the treaty might yet prevail, and Panamanians withdraw their threat of secession.

President and Secretary talked far into the night, while their imagined world ordered itself pleasingly, obediently, beyond the twinkling horizons of Oyster Bay.

HAY SAID GOOD-BYE the next morning, then continued south to Washington. His surprise arrival in the broiling city served notice to both Loomis and Roosevelt that he was still boss of the State Department, and would monitor all their future communications. Yet he could not forget the latter's graciousness at Sagamore Hill. "It is a comfort to work for a President who, besides being a lot of other things, happened to be born a gentleman."

On 12 July, a sobering cable arrived from Arthur Beaupré. He reported that only now, after five weeks, had Hay's ultimatum at last been communicated to the Colombian Congress. It was "construed by many as a threat of direct retaliation against Colombia," in the event of nonratification of the treaty. Delegates from the province of Panama were capitalizing on that threat, and talking openly of secession.

By a coincidence unsurprising to intimates of William Nelson Cromwell, the New York *World* prophesied the next morning that there would be a revolution in Panama on 3 November. Later in the day, a desperate message from Colombian liberals reached the State Department. The treaty might be saved if the United States would consent to two amendments: one requiring the Compagnie Nouvelle to pay a ten-million-dollar rights-transferral fee, and the other increasing the zone's acquisition price from ten million to fifteen million dollars.

Hay prepared a note of refusal. "Make it as strong as you can to Beaupré," Roosevelt ordered him. "These contemptible little creatures in Bogotá ought to understand how much they are jeopardizing things and imperiling their own future."

THE KISHINEV PETITION finally wound its way up Sagamore Hill on 14 July. It was carried by Leo Levi and Simon Wolf, who did not know what to make of the President's sudden urgency. Levi suppressed the cynical thought that Roosevelt might use a human tragedy in Bessarabia to shame the Tsar into opening up Manchuria. Wolf was embarrassed at how few signatures they had been able to collect on such short notice. The names of influential Gentiles were especially elusive in the vacation season. Unavoidably, the list still looked like a Jewish petition, rather than a mass interdenominational declaration.

Oscar Solomon Straus, a prominent Jew with diplomatic experience, and Albert Shaw, editor of *Review of Reviews,* joined the company for lunch in the President's paneled dining room. When Roosevelt heard that the petition bore "only two or three thousand" signatures, he agreed that it was hardly worth submitting in physical form. Then he made an inspired suggestion. Secretary Hay should dispatch an official cable to Count Vladimir Lamsdorff, the Tsar's Minister of Foreign Affairs inquiring whether or not an unofficial petition "relating to the condition of the Jews in Russia" would be acceptable to His Majesty. The cable would quote the entire text of the petition. Of course, Lamsdorff would say no. But he would have to file the cable as a formal message, while its senders published it around the world. Americans would have made their moral point, and Russians could not complain of any breach of diplomatic etiquette.

Everyone approved of this idea. The President led the way to his library, adapted a previous draft prepared by Hay, and pinned the petition to it. Straus, stoop-shouldered and frail, undertook to deliver the precious document to the State Department for immediate dispatch.

Long before he got to Washington, the Russian Embassy announced that "certain cities in Manchuria" were open to foreign commerce. This was less a coincidence, perhaps, than the consequence of Roosevelt's earlier blast against the Tsar's domestic and foreign policies. Evidently Russia did, after all, worry about her inflexible world image. Hated by China, threatened by Japan and Japan's ally Britain, she did not need to add the United States to her list of enemies.

Nicholas II's rejection of the petition cable the next day thus came as neither a disappointment nor a surprise. Roosevelt authorized the B'nai B'rith leaders to publicize the rejection as they chose, and accepted congratulations from John Hay. "You have done the right thing in the right way, and Jewry seems really grateful," the Secretary wrote.

An exuberant Roosevelt was less inclined to call the matter quits. "If only we were sure that neither France nor Germany would join in, I should not in the least mind going to 'extremes' with Russia!"

THE CRESCENT SELF-CONFIDENCE Edith Roosevelt had noticed after her husband's return from the West continued to energize him. He seemed to delight in juggling as many political and diplomatic balls as possible. To the annoyance of his children, carriages full of ponderous adults kept creaking through the chestnut trees. One such vehicle on 15 July discharged Treasury Secretary Leslie Shaw, Herman Kohlsaat of the Chicago *Record-Herald*, Charles J. Bonaparte, special counsel for the Justice Department in the Post Office investigation, and Ray Stannard Baker, reporter at large for *McClure's*. Baker's briefcase was especially bulky with notes, maps, and memoranda. The President had asked him to substantiate charges of corruption in the Salt River Valley, Arizona, reclamation project.

A servant showed the visitors into the library. Roosevelt was nowhere to be seen. They sat for a while under the varnished gaze of Theodore Senior, absorbing an aura of well-handled books, oak, and mahogany. On the desk, radiant with sun slanting in through gauze curtains, there lay a gold-miner's pan, a silver dagger, and an inkwell ornamented with a little bust of Abraham Lincoln. Bearskins snarled silently on the floor. Somewhere a clock was ticking: it was well past noon.

Like a sudden explosion, the President blew in through the door. He looked ruddy and healthy in knickerbockers, worn gray shirt, and scuffed hiking shoes, and was bursting with mirth. In his hand he carried a note and newspaper clipping.

"I want to read you something I have just got," he said, "in connection with conditions in the South."

He shot a gleeful glance at Bonaparte, who owned a Maryland plantation. The note was from Booker T. Washington. "My dear Mr. President, the enclosed is a true story." Roosevelt turned to the clipping, from the Baltimore *Herald*:

An old Florida colonel met Booker T. Washington and in a bibulous burst of confidence said to the Negro educator: "Suh, I am glad to meet you. Always wanted to shake your hand, suh. I think, suh, you're the greatest man in America."

"Oh no," said Mr. Washington.

"You are, suh," said the colonel, and then, pugnaciously, "who's greater?"

"Well," said the founder of Tuskegee, "there's President Roosevelt."

"No, suh," roared the colonel. "Not by a jugful; I used to think so, but since he invited you to dinner I think he's a [---] scoundrel."

The library rang with presidential laughter. A gong sounded, and Roosevelt led the way into the dining room. Baker left a bemused account of the subsequent proceedings:

It was a very simple lunch, served by a maid. At first the President talked postal affairs with Mr. Bonaparte, asserting over and over again that he wanted the investigation to be thorough.

"I don't care who it hits!" he said. "We must get to the bottom of these scandals." He then turned abruptly to me and said, "Baker, who is the chief devil down there in the Salt River Valley?"

Since I had never considered the situation in terms of devils, I hesitated a moment—and the President burst into a vigorous, picturesque, and somewhat vitriolic description of the situation, implying that if he could catch the rascals who were causing the trouble he would execute them on the spot. Several of the statements he made seemed to me to be inaccurate, or at least exaggerated, but when I tried to break into the conversation—boiling inside with my undelivered articles and memoranda (one of which indeed I tried to draw from my pocket)—the President put one fist on the table beside him, looked at me earnestly, and said: "Baker, you and I will have to get together on these subjects."

He instantly turned aside, leaving me—I think—with my mouth open, and began telling in a loud voice and with great unction of his lunch [with] a committee of prominent Jews interested in the Kishinev petition. He even imitated Oscar Straus by a hitch of the shoulders and laughed heartily when somebody asked if he had provided boiled ham for his guests. Once he said:

"Do not all these things interest you? Isn't it a fine thing to be alive when so many great things are happening?" . . .

As the time drew near for leaving, I began to wonder when the President would ask me for the information upon which I had spent so much time and hard work. I had my heavy briefcase in hand when I went up to say goodbye—and my grand plans for enlightening the Government of the United States vanished in a handshake.

Mr. Bonaparte, Mr. Kohlsaat, and I walked down together, some three miles, to Oyster Bay. I carried my heavy case, filled with my memoranda, and papers, and maps and pictures—and the sun was hot.

Behind his jocularity on Southern race relations, the President was giving serious thought to an "utterance" on lynching. He admitted that long-term justice for the Negro concerned him more than any other issue. One of his least-noticed guests that July was Rollo Ogden, sometime Presbyterian missionary, editor of the New York *Evening Post,* and a crusader against mob justice. They met amid reports that anti-Negro vigilantes were menacing a jail in Evansville, Indiana. Governor Winfield T. Durbin had sent in state troops, who killed six rioters; even so, hundreds of terrified blacks were quitting town. The parallels to both the Wilmington lynching and the Kishinev pogrom were obvious. (A cartoon in *Literary Digest* showed Nicholas II tearfully rejecting the B'nai B'rith petition: "Excuse me, I'm too busy weeping over this Delaware affair.") Roosevelt promised Ogden that he would say something soon.

For political reasons, he could not do so immediately. A Democratic primary campaign of extreme virulence was approaching its climax in Mississippi, with two racists, Hernando Money and James K. Vardaman, respectively fighting two Administration-backed moderates for the senatorial and gubernatorial nominations. Since there was no effective Republican op-position in that state, selection was as good as election. Much invective was being lavished on the "nigger-loving gang in Washington," particularly Roo-sevelt for his support of Minnie Cox. Governor Andrew H. Longino, running for re-election, was blamed for involving the President in Mississippi politics during his 1902 visit to the Little Sunflower. Any move now by the detested "Teddy" against lynching, which Longino had himself condemned, would en-sure the Governor's defeat.

⟳

SO ROOSEVELT REMAINED SILENT, as midsummer heat mounted across the nation. The sun shone strong on western corn, ripening what looked, to James Wilson's expert eye, like bumper crops. A good harvest was gold in Re-publican coffers, the Secretary of Agriculture wrote from South Dakota: "This people is very prosperous and so enthusiastic for you that they will con-tribute just as freely to next year's campaign as to build a church."

Temperatures—and tempers—rose less encouragingly at labor conven-tions in many cities. So far in 1903, there had been a record three and a half thousand strikes nationwide, and not only Wall Street held Roosevelt respon-sible. In a severe blow to his popular image, the National Association of Let-ter Carriers endorsed William Randolph Hearst for President as "a true friend of the plain people." Union after union berated Roosevelt for the low pay in-crease awarded the anthracite miners, and for his more recent, precedent-setting enforcement of an open shop in the Government Printing Office.

James S. Clarkson, his chief patronage lieutenant outside Washington, grew nervous. He bombarded Sagamore Hill with statistics showing "the alarming growth of the Socialist vote in this country." Hearst, he wrote, was a real threat, with enough funds and newspapers (three hundred at last count) to alienate every trade union from the Republican Party. He begged Roosevelt to avoid any further gestures toward free labor.

This was not the right thing to say to a President who prided himself on being fair. "Of course I will not for one moment submit to dictation by the labor unions any more than by the trusts," Roosevelt shot back, "and that no matter what the effect on the presidential election may be." Three times in one sentence, he reminded Clarkson that he stood for "a square deal."

The sun beat down ever more fiercely, turning Southern plantations white, Western farms gold, Northern fields yellow and silver. It bleached the pale Percherons working Roosevelt's own forty-seven acres. Farmers every-where looked forward to an autumn bounty. But in the shadowed enclave of Wall Street, bears prowled. On 22 July, Jefferson Seligman, a banker friend, came out to see the President, warning of an imminent financial "panic."

Roosevelt had never understood the ebb and flow of money, through his own hands or anyone else's. "Every morning Edie puts twenty dollars in my pocket, and to save my life I can never tell her afterward what I did with it." So he listened with more patience than comprehension as Seligman expounded the need for currency-reform legislation.

The problem, apparently, was an "inelastic currency," combined with a seasonal need for cash to move America's crops to market. Toward the end of summer, demand greater than supply caused cash to flow from Wall Street banks to the rural heartland, leaving behind depleted vaults and falling stock prices. Late in the fall, the money began to flow back. But promoters, stock-jobbers, and other speculators trembled while it was gone, lest banks call their loans. This summer, the risk looked greater than usual. Continued combination and overcapitalization—not to mention worry over the Northern Securities Company's appeal to the Supreme Court—had created a vast surplus of vulnerable stocks. "Undigested securities," J. P. Morgan called them.

Roosevelt referred Seligman to Leslie Shaw, who had an emergency plan to transfer government gold into the national reserves. Then he braced for the strong views his next guest was bound to have on any such corrective measure. Joseph G. Cannon famously knew more about finance than anybody else in Congress, even Senator Aldrich. A profound conservative, of the Midwestern, small-town variety, Cannon was unlikely to be disturbed by the current situation. Eastern trust lords had been too grandiose in their capitalizations: they needed a short, sharp slump (affecting millionaires primarily) to teach them fiscal responsibility.

"Uncle Joe wants no legislation," Roosevelt dictated to a secretary, while waiting for Cannon to arrive. "It seems to me we ought to have some."

When the Speaker climbed out of his carriage, it was clear he was playing the defiant hayseed. He wore a seersucker jacket with tails that floated on the breeze, and salt-and-pepper trousers ballooned round his bony legs. The accepted uniform for waiting on the President was a dark frock coat, irrespective of season. But Cannon declined to apologize for his appearance. It was too "damn hot," he said.

CANNON'S RUMPLED APPEARANCE, his scraggy white beard, perpetual half-chewed cigar, and folksy profanities were all part of a calculated image to disguise one of the most disciplined forces in government. Close inspection revealed his clothes to be of fine quality (a daily fresh pink in his lapel suggested the private dandy), while the beard was kept short and the cigar, when puffed, gave off mellow evidence of Havana leaf. As for the profanities, they were carefully mild. Cannon was actually more at home quoting Shakespeare and the Bible, which he studied every day along with the *Congressional Record*. His wire-puppet jerkiness was caused by an unusually fast reflex system, mental and physical. Not even Roosevelt was quicker to react to the occasional signals of intent or flexibility that politicians flash in conversation.

And back of the quickness was an instant obstinacy whenever any tenet of orthodox Republicanism was threatened. The thin grin would vanish, the blue stare freeze, the long bony forefinger tap with suppressed fury. He was, in the President's not unaffectionate opinion, "a hard, narrow old Boeotian."

After a two-hour lunch, officially described as "social," Cannon left Sagamore Hill smiling, hinting that he might consider some currency reform in a future session. But when he stopped off in New York, en route to his home in Illinois, he showed no inclination to reassure Wall Street further on that score. "I could not get him to visit a single banker," Congressman Lucius Littauer wrote Roosevelt. "His constant reiteration was that a time of financial panic was not one in which to discuss the necessity of financial legislation."

No sooner had Cannon left town on 23 July than a serious collapse in share values began on Wall Street. Banks canceled credit, and syndicates unloaded their reserve investments of high-grade securities. U.S. Steel common dropped by more than 50 percent. Frantic for more funds, the syndicates put up their newer, underwritten offerings, and got almost nothing for them. J. P. Morgan's United States Shipbuilding Company went bankrupt, as did the hundred-million-dollar Consolidated Lake Superior. Four major brokers went out of business.

Like ripples round a dropped stone, waves of desperation ringed outward, but shallowly, failing to shake the calm depths of general investment. Cannon had gotten—perhaps even brought on—the "rich man's panic" he wanted. Secretary Shaw wrote to reassure Roosevelt, as did James Clarkson: "The country is prosperous every place else except Wall Street, and perhaps the Street is all the better for this experience."

So while stockbrokers raged, blaming the Administration's antitrust policies—"This is a market on which John D. Rockefeller could not borrow on Standard Oil"—Roosevelt kept cool in white flannels. He had discovered a new sport, cricket, and spent many hours with a British professional, learning the difference between topspins, long-hops, and silly mid-ons.

⌐☙⌐

A THOUSAND MILES SOUTH, the white Democrats of Mississippi prepared to cast their primary votes for Governor and Senator. James K. Vardaman's vicious rhetoric had somehow turned the contest into one between "Rooseveltism" and racism. On 9 August, the President decided to issue his long-delayed "utterance," in the form of a public letter to Winfield T. Durbin of Indiana.

"My dear Governor Durbin," he wrote, "permit me to thank you as an American citizen for the admirable way in which you have vindicated the majesty of the law by your recent action in reference to lynching." (Durbin had not only dispelled rioters with troops, but proclaimed the right of a black murderer to a fair trial.) "All thoughtful men," Roosevelt continued, "must feel the gravest alarm over the growth of lynching in this country, and especially over the peculiarly hideous forms so often taken by mob violence when colored men are the victims—on which occasions the mob seems to lay most weight, not on the crime but on the color of the criminal."

In a minority of cases—fewer than one in four—lynch victims were guilty of rape, "a crime horrible beyond description." Yet rape's very bestiality required that society respond to it in a civilized fashion. Roosevelt was at his most impassioned when he commented on the sadistic quality of lynchings:

> There are certain hideous sights which when once seen can never be wholly erased from the mental retina. The mere fact of having seen them implies degradation. . . . Whoever in any part of our country has ever taken part in lawlessly putting to death a criminal by the dreadful torture of fire must forever after have the awful spectacle of his own handiwork seared into his brain and soul. He can never again be the same man.

Rollo Ogden congratulated him after the letter was published. "One of your happiest inspirations in the public service." Other liberal-minded editors praised the strength, if not the promptness, of the President's statement. They did not see how delaying it had improved Mississippi's political situation, where Vardaman and Hernando Money both won decisively.

Roosevelt concluded that for the time being he had done all he could, rhetorically and practically, to help the American Negro. He would not risk his political future by seeming to endorse, in Vardaman's phrase, "the black wave of ignorance, superstition, and immorality with which the South is perpetually threatened."

BY NOW, THE State Department was seriously concerned over Arthur Beaupré's silence. The Minister to Colombia was notorious for the frequency and verbosity of his cables. Three wordless weeks had given the impression he had been garroted. On 12 August, however, a thousand dollars' worth of prose suddenly came over the wire. Beaupré summarized no fewer than nine amendments that had been attached to the Panama Canal Treaty in committee. The Colombian Senate now proposed at least five million dollars more in cash, plus huge kickbacks from the Compagnie Nouvelle and the Panama Railroad. The United States would be granted "tenancy" only in the canal zone, and would have to endure Colombian standards of law enforcement and sanitation. Beaupré begged John Hay, who was back in New Hampshire, "for an emphatic statement . . . or instructions" before the amendments were adopted by the Colombian Senate.

Hay was enraged. He had sent at least two sets of instructions over the past month, making plain that the United States would accept no amendments whatever. Evidently, Beaupré had not received them. Colombia's cable service, Hay noticed, malfunctioned with curious regularity whenever the text of the treaty was undergoing serious scrutiny.

Now there arrived at Sagamore Hill a letter written by a longtime American resident of Bogotá. It described antitreaty sentiment in the capital as increasingly raucous and bitter. Politicians, merchants, planters, and common citizens were complaining that the United States wanted them to make a sacrifice "of untold millions belonging, by right, to their children." One agitator was quoted as excoriating the "dirty American pigs" already wallowing in Panama mud.

Neither Roosevelt nor Hay had any public comment or prediction. "I am totally in the dark as to what the outcome in the Isthmus will be," the President told Senator Morgan.

The first indication that he was losing patience came on Friday, 14 August, when Shelby M. Cullom, Chairman of the Senate Committee on Foreign Relations, emerged from a lunchtime conference at Sagamore Hill. Speaking with obvious authority, Cullom told reporters that no matter what happened in Bogotá, the Administration remained committed to a Panama Canal.

Q   How can the canal be built without the treaty?
A   Well, we might make another treaty, not with Colombia, but with Panama.
Q   But Panama is not a sovereign state. . . .
A   Intimations have been made that there is great discontent on the Isthmus over the action of the Congress of the central government, and Panama might break away and set up a government which we could treat with.
Q   Is the U.S. prepared to encourage such a schism in a South American republic?
A   No, I suppose not. But this country wants to build that canal and build it now.

Whatever "action" Cullom was referring to—or anticipating—he could not have more clearly signaled Senate support for any executive powers Roosevelt might avail himself of in the near future.

That weekend, an extraordinary naval panoply spread across Long Island Sound. Twenty-two white warships could be seen lying in parallel rows off the entrance to Oyster Bay, a spectacle, in the eyes of one observer, "almost overwhelmingly suggestive of America's newly-born sea power." Monday dawned bright and mirror-calm. The sun picked out thousands of white-clad sailors stationing themselves in geometric shapes on decks and in rigging. Oyster Bay bristled with pleasure boats come to witness the President's review of the fleet.

Roosevelt came down from Sagamore Hill after breakfast and boarded the USS *Mayflower*. Nine and a half hours later, he returned home, eyes bloodshot from the glare of white metal and water, buffeted by the roar of continuous twenty-one-gun salutes—sixty-three thousand rounds in all. Hanging smoke thickened the dusk as he walked through the woods. An urgent cable from Beaupré awaited him.

BOGOTÁ, AUGUST 12, 7 P.M. THE TREATY WAS REJECTED BY THE SENATE TODAY IN ITS ENTIRETY.

ROOSEVELT WAS STILL digesting this news—"We may have to give a lesson to those jack rabbits"—when a note arrived from John Hay. The Secretary, who had never been a Panama enthusiast, reminded him that he could now revert to "the simple and easy Nicaraguan solution," rather than press ahead with "the far more difficult and multifurcate scheme" articulated by Senator Cullom.

Before replying, Roosevelt studied the text of a startlingly aggressive memorandum by John Bassett Moore, the reigning American authority on international law. It had been forwarded to him by Francis B. Loomis, who was fast becoming his preferred contact at the State Department.

Professor Moore's memorandum argued that Panama was the only place in the Americas to build a canal "for the world." The question of Colombian sovereignty was therefore a global rather than a regional one. All nations had a right to benefit from the opening of this great "gate of intercourse" between East and West. One nation could not delay, or demand an exorbitant fee for, that constructive advance. Moore recalled that in 1846, Colombia—then known as New Granada—had guaranteed the United States free transit across the Isthmus "*upon any modes of communication that now exist, or that may hereafter be constructed.*" This "sort of supportive partnership" (Washington promising in return to protect both Colombian integrity and neutrality of the transit zone) must have been contracted in order to bring about, ultimately, a canal. Otherwise, as President Polk had pointed out, the United States had no direct interest in preserving the Colombian federation.

For almost six decades, successive administrations had honored the Treaty of New Granada, saving Colombia many times from outside attack and internal revolt. The Panama Railroad, designed and built by Americans, had operated continuously, to the profit of both countries. "Colombia has again and again claimed," Moore wrote, "that it was our duty to protect the route . . . thus construing the treaty more broadly than we have done and less favorably to her own sovereignty." This claim in effect "approached the point of making us responsible on the Isthmus."

Moore noted, further, that the language of the 1846 treaty guaranteed passage across Panama not only to American citizens, but also to their "Government." This by definition included military personnel and matériel. As early as 1852, indeed, President Fillmore had deployed troops on the Isthmus with neither permission nor protest from Bogotá. There had been other deployments since, with the express concurrence of the Colombian Senate.

Throughout the long special relationship, Americans had never "enjoyed the full benefit . . . that the treaty was intended and expected to secure"— namely, a canal. In view of the fact that Colombians had gotten their own side of the bargain—rail transit and armed protection—Washington could now reasonably "require" Bogotá to ratify the Hay-Herrán Treaty. All other considerations, including last-minute amendments, were superfluous and irrelevant. "The United States in constructing the canal would own it; and after constructing it, would have the right to operate it. The ownership and control would be in their nature perpetual."

The effect upon Roosevelt of this vehement document was to make him strangely cautious. He referred it to Hay, suggesting that the Administration "do nothing," at least not right away. "If under the treaty of 1846 we have a color of right to start in and build the canal, my offhand judgment would favor such proceeding. . . . What we do now will be of consequence, not merely decades, but centuries hence, and we must be sure that we are taking the right step before we act."

⁓

NOT SURPRISINGLY, news of revolutionary activity on the Isthmus came within days. "The fathers at Bogotá are eating sour grapes," Assistant Secretary of State Alvey A. Adee wrote Hay, "and the teeth of the children of Panama are getting a fine edge on to 'em."

Hay was pleased that the President wanted to wait "a reasonable time" before deciding what to do next. He warned him against an outright seizure of Panama, which Moore's memorandum seemed to justify. "The fact that our position, in that case, would be legal and just, might not greatly impress the jack-rabbit mind. I do not believe that we could *faire valoir* our rights in that way without war—which would, of course, be brief and inexpensive."

Gradually, a partial understanding of Colombia's behavior emerged, together with hopes that President Marroquín might yet save the situation by executive action. Beaupré seemed to feel some responsibility, having deeply offended the Colombian Senate with his imperious notes demanding ratification. He pleaded that the proposed treaty be given its full legal term to expire—some thirty more days.

"The President will make no engagement as to his action in the canal matter," Hay replied. From then on, the wires from Oyster Bay and Washington were silent. Apprehension mounted in Bogotá.

"For the first time I must tell you," Tomás Herrán wrote William Nelson Cromwell, "that I have lost all hope."

⟶

AUGUST DROWSED TO an end. Inland, the weather turned cool, but Oyster Bay was reluctant to yield its summer heat. Geese continued to laze in the mudflats, and, when the breeze shifted landward, their guttural conversation could be heard at the top of Sagamore Hill. Other sounds were audible now, as the air sharpened: the distant tolling of a bell buoy, sometimes even the thrum of a steamer out to sea. Evening brought the less welcome whine of mosquitoes. For some reason, they avoided Roosevelt, as he sat on the piazza reading Euripides, and fanned out in search of Secret Service men hiding in the grape arbor.

Toward the end of the first night watch, about 10:15 P.M. on 1 September, a buggy rolled silently up the driveway's grass shoulder. Clouds covered the moon. Nobody saw the little vehicle until it got within fifty yards of the house. Then Roosevelt, working behind blinds in his library, heard sounds of scuffling and swearing outside.

Unthinking, he stepped onto the piazza, and stood with the light behind him. Two of his guards were struggling with a youth in the buggy. "There he is!" the youth screamed, and brandished a revolver. It was knocked to the ground, while other agents rushed out of the dark and shoved Roosevelt back inside.

"I came to kill the President," the youth admitted, as manacles were snapped on his wrists. At Oyster Bay police station later, he rambled about Roosevelt's action in the Government Printing Office matter. "Why doesn't the President do something for organized labor? He's said a lot about it, but he hasn't bettered the condition of the working man."

The security detail at Sagamore Hill was increased to a twelve-man, twenty-four-hour alert, while Roosevelt, shaken, reflected on his sudden unpopularity among unions. By insisting that all GPO employees swear obedience to the civil-service law, he had disillusioned thousands of radicals who had come to count on his "partiality" during the great coal strike. Even more damagingly, he had issued an executive order mandating an open-shop policy in every government department. The influential Central Labor Union of Washington, D.C., declared in a nationwide mailing, "The order of the President cannot be regarded in any but an unfriendly light."

A providential invitation came for him to review the Labor Day parade in Syracuse, New York. He accepted, to the delight of the little city: it had not been so honored in many years.

His speech there on 7 September was so utopian that Jules Jusserand accused him of parroting Sir Thomas More. Actually Roosevelt was identifying with Euripides—like himself, an upper-class celebrant of middle-class virtues—as he mused at length on the vulnerability of republics that failed to preserve their social equipoise. Whichever class arose to dominate others—whether high, low, or bourgeois—always made disproportionate claims on the government:

> Again and again in the republics of ancient Greece, in those of medieval Italy, and medieval Flanders, this tendency was shown, and wherever the tendency became a habit it invariably and inevitably proved fatal to the state. . . . There resulted violent alternations between tyranny and disorder, and a final complete loss of liberty to all citizens—destruction in the end overtaking the class which had for the moment been victorious as well as that which had momentarily been defeated. The death-knell of the republic had rung as soon as the active power became lodged in the hands of those who sought, not to do justice to all citizens, rich and poor alike, but to stand for one special class and for its interests as opposed to the interests of others.

Uniquely, the checks and balances of American democracy worked to prevent any such lodgment. National unity was a moral challenge, rather than an economic one:

> The line of cleavage between good and bad citizenship lies, not between the man of wealth who acts squarely by his fellow and the man who seeks each day's wage by that day's work, wronging no one. . . . On the contrary, [it] separates the rich man who does well from the rich man who does ill, the poor man of good conduct from the poor man of bad conduct. This line of cleavage lies at right angles to any arbitrary line of division as that separating one class from another, one locality from another, of a man with a certain degree of property from those of a less degree of property.

A civilized commonwealth, enjoying "the true liberties which can only come through order," depended on square dealing between representatives of capital and labor. Just as the former had accepted a limited degree of public scrutiny, so must the latter face up to their own public duty. In any recession acerbated by strikes and union violence, "the first and severest suffering would come among those of us who are least well off at present."

William Jennings Bryan would not have used the last two words. It was little touches like that—innocent, optimistic—that endeared Roosevelt to his audiences, even when he was trying to be severe.

BY MID-SEPTEMBER, predictions of Panamanian independence were being published almost daily in American and European newspapers, and voiced aloud even in Bogotá. Isthmian delegates to the Colombian Congress began to pack their bags and head for home. Senator José Domingo de Obaldía called out to the secretary of the American legation, "We'll meet within a few weeks in the new Republic of Panama."

Desperate to keep Colombia intact, President Marroquín ignored Obaldía's open rebelliousness and appointed him Governor of Panama. Tomás Herrán, in Washington, was reminded of Spain's panic just before the loss of Cuba. Only a last-minute ratification of the treaty, he cabled his minister, could save Colombia now. Otherwise, the Colossus of the North would "indirectly" favor the coming revolution, and would doubtless jump to recognize an independent Panama. "President Roosevelt is a decided partisan of the Panama route, and hopes to begin excavation of the canal during his administration. Your excellency already knows the impetuous and vehement character of the President, and you are aware of the persistence and decision with which he pursues anything to which he may be committed."

Proposals for a "resumption of negotiations" came by return of wire. Some last-chancers in the Colombian Senate were under the impression that the United States would pay forty million dollars, rather than ten, for canal rights, in exchange for a legislative finding that canceled the Compagnie Nouvelle's extended concession. Hay ignored this transparent attempt at fraud. "It is altogether likely," he wrote the President, "that there will be an insurrection on the Isthmus against that regime of folly and graft that now rules in Bogotá. It is for you to decide whether you will (1) await the result of that movement, or (2) take a hand in rescuing the Isthmus from anarchy, or (3) treat with Nicaragua."

Roosevelt had already opted for the first choice, but made plain his perfect willingness "to interfere when it becomes necessary so as to secure the Panama route without further dealing with the foolish and homicidal corruptionists in Bogotá."

As the Panama Canal Treaty died, so did summer. Around Cove Neck, lilies and pale beach rosemary gave way to goldenrods and coarse asters, bristling against fresher breezes. Edith Roosevelt put away her white dresses. Archie and Quentin started wearing shoes again. Ted and Kermit braced themselves for another year at Groton. Their father industriously chopped wood.

The thudding ax and sprays of chips did not quite work off an onset of autumnal melancholy. A harvest of tart political fruits awaited him when he returned to the White House. Relations with Russia and Colombia had deteriorated sharply. His Syracuse speech did not seem to have reduced tensions between business and labor. Government antitrust policies were being blamed for the "rich man's panic." The Postal Service's corruption probe had spread into his own state. Local Republicans warned that if the upper house in Albany were implicated, he would "certainly" lose New York in 1904.

These problems were complicated by another, more painful and personal. Elihu Root (currently representing him at the Alaska Boundary Tribunal in London) wanted to return to the practice of corporate law, after four and a half years as Secretary of War. Roosevelt had long dreaded this resignation as "the worst calamity that could happen to me officially." But he could not deny his old friend's need to recoup lost income. Fortunately, Root was willing to stay on until an adequate successor could be found.

Roosevelt took one last daylong row with Edith, down to the salt marsh at the end of Lloyd's Neck. They ate their lunch there and watched the white sails of coasters passing up and down the Sound. Then he pulled home, exulting in the opposition of the wind and tide. "Next Monday I go back to Washington," he wrote his sister Corinne on 23 September, "and for the thirteen months following there will be mighty little letup to the strain."

He was confident of nomination to another term in his own right, but not at all sure of election. "I suppose few Presidents can form the slightest idea of whether their policies have met with approval or not—certainly I cannot. . . . As far as I can see these policies have been right, and I hope that time will justify them. If it does not, why, I must abide the fall of the dice, and that is all there is about it."

CHAPTER 18

The Most Just and Proper Revolution

*An autocrat's a ruler that does what th' people wants
an' takes th' blame f'r it.*

THE PRESIDENT'S FIRST visitor when he returned to his desk on 29 September 1903 was Secretary of the Navy William Henry Moody. With the expected retirement of Elihu Root, the forty-nine-year-old Moody was seen as the new "strong man" of the Administration, remarkable for ambition, breeding, and intelligence. As a young Massachusetts lawyer, Moody had caught the favorable attention of Judge Oliver Wendell Holmes, Jr. Later, as a member of the House of Representatives, he had also impressed—and sometimes infuriated—Assistant Secretary of the Navy Theodore Roosevelt. Although Moody had not been willing, in those days, to "whoop to war" with Spain, he now felt as grandly as the President about America's future as a world power. Her principal engine of advancement must be an ever-expanding navy, in whose wake freedom would spread like foam.

Since joining the Cabinet sixteen months before, Moody had been much at Roosevelt's elbow—on his ill-fated tour of New England, as an adviser during the coal strike and the Venezuelan crisis, a fellow passenger on the presidential train to California. The two men looked like brothers: stocky, hard-chested, ruddy, with big strong heads and ragged mustaches. They shared Harvard manners, blunt speech, and a constant heartiness. But whereas Roosevelt's warmth was genuine, there was a core of coldness in Moody, a Puritanism none could thaw. He was the only bachelor member of the Cabinet, walking home alone every night with a slight, rheumatic limp.

Emerging from the White House, he made an official statement of policy on the canal situation. He said that Roosevelt would refrain from action "as long as there was the least possible hope" of a change of mind by the Colombian Congress. The President, Moody stressed, "takes the ground that this is a most important question, and the final decision is a decision for centuries."

⟳

HAVING THUS TRIED to dispel rumors that he wished to use force against Colombia, Roosevelt braced himself for a showdown with Samuel Gompers and other executives of the American Federation of Labor. He scheduled their visit for an unusually late hour—after dinner—and made a thorough study of the Government Printing Office case, which was sure to be an item on the agenda. His instinct was to give Gompers "a good jolt." Labor must be made to understand that it was subject to the same Square Deal as capital, in the Rooseveltian scheme of things.

> In this particular matter I would be as incapable of considering my own personal future as if I were facing foreign or civil war, or any other tremendous crisis. It is a sheer waste of time for these people . . . to threaten me with defeat for the Presidency next year. Nothing would hire me even to accept the Presidency if I had to take it on terms which would mean a forfeiting of self-respect. Just as I should refuse to accept it at the cost of abandoning the Northern Securities suit, or of repealing the trust regulation of last [sic] year, or of undoing what I did in the anthracite coal strike, so I should refuse to take it at the cost of undoing what I did in this matter of Miller and the labor unions.

William A. Miller was the GPO foreman whose dismissal he had overridden as an unjust reprisal for increasing the productivity of the bindery division. Now the bookbinders were trying to get Miller out on morals charges, saying that he kept three wives. Roosevelt, embarrassed, could argue only that the foreman's morals, or lack thereof, constituted "a new case," subject to routine review.

This apparent sanction of both the open shop and open marriage was bringing in some of the most hostile mail he had ever received. Unions in more than a dozen states had pledged opposition to his candidacy in 1904. Plainly, he risked losing his most hard-won constituency if he failed to satisfy the AFL delegates. He drafted a "reply" to what he guessed they were going to say, asked Moody, Garfield, and Cortelyou to check it, then had it typed pending release. This document was in his dinner-jacket pocket when Gompers came to the White House at 9:15, accompanied by four aides.

One of them was John Mitchell, shockingly changed from the handsome union executive of one year before. Mitchell's eyes were hollow from drink, his body had thickened, and a hernia stiffened his gait. For all the fame he had won in the great strike, his miners were still unrecognized and overworked, their 10 percent raise already eroded by inflation.

Roosevelt sized Gompers up as "a sleek article," and found that he could handle him with ease. The AFL leader was plainly anxious to avoid a confrontation in threatening economic times. Not until toward the end of a general review of labor matters did Gompers drop the name *Miller,* enabling Roosevelt to produce his statement.

"I thank you and your committee for your courtesy," the President read aloud, "and I appreciate the opportunity to meet with you." They had to hear him out.

> I ask you to remember that I am dealing purely with the relation of the government to its employees. I must govern my action by the laws of the land, which I am sworn to administer, and which differentiate any case in which the government of the United States is a party from all other cases whatsoever. These laws are enacted for the benefit of the whole people. . . . I can no more recognize the fact that a man does or does not belong to a union as being for or against him, than I can recognize the fact that he is a Protestant or a Catholic, a Jew or a Gentile, as being for or against him.

Miller's habits at home were irrelevant to his freedom, as a federal employee, to take an antiunion stance on principle. Reinstating him was a matter of executive privilege. "And as to this my decision is final."

The delegation trooped out, looking grim under the lights of the porte cochere. Secretary Loeb distributed copies of Roosevelt's statement to reporters. Gompers, aware that he had been scooped by a master of press relations, refused any comment. "It would not be respectful," he said, and strode down the dark driveway.

Editorial opinion the next morning almost unanimously supported the President. Radical unions remained resentful, but Gompers bowed to the popular mood, and saw to it that anti-Roosevelt resolutions were defeated at the AFL convention. The open shop became official government policy. "It seems to me that this was the greatest act of your administration," gushed Ray Stannard Baker. Baker did not realize that the President was already working on something that better deserved that superlative.

―❧―

"YOU MAY HAVE noticed that I have not said a word in public about the canal," Roosevelt wrote Mark Hanna on 5 October. "I shall have to allude to it in my Message." He had decided to call a special session of Congress in November, ostensibly to secure bicameral approval of the Cuban-reciprocity treaty, but also to have legislative support at hand, in case emergency action was needed in Panama.

There was no doubt now that the province would soon—must—secede from the Colombian federation. Bogotá's rejection of the canal treaty, and Washington's apparent acceptance of that rejection, amounted to dual death-blows to the *Istmusenos*. Not only had they lost their long-dreamed water-way, spilling wealth on both sides forever, but their railroad, too, would become redundant, once the Nicaragua Canal opened for business. With no paved highways, no bridges, little industry, and less commerce, they might just as well revert to jungle living.

The President could not help feeling sympathetic. Here was a little ridge of country, about as wide as southern Vermont, a half-drowned hogback of mostly impenetrable rain forest, walled off from the rest of Colombia by mountains. Geographically, it belonged to Central America. Its only surface communications with the southern continent were by sea or mule train. Let-ters took fifteen days to get to Bogotá, if they got there at all; about the only reliable deliveries were those carrying tax money out of the Isthmus.

Panama's political status as a *provincia* of Colombia was equally tenuous. It had spontaneously joined the New Granadian Federation in 1821, and se-ceded with its disintegration in 1830. Bogotá had reasserted control twelve years later, and from then on Panama had alternated stormily between semi-autonomy and subjugation. Roosevelt counted no fewer than fifty-three isth-mian insurrections, riots, civil disturbances, and revolts since 1846. None had been perpetrated with any American help. On at least ten occasions (six times at Bogotá's request, twice during his own presidency), Washington had blocked rebel movements and shipments along the Panama Railroad.

In doing so, it had argued that it sought only to protect the railroad's neu-tral right-of-way, which civil war might compromise. Now an infinitely greater right—that of all trading nations to enjoy the benefits of a Panama Canal—had been denied by the "corruptionists" of just one government. "This does not mean that we must necessarily go to Nicaragua," Roosevelt wrote. "I feel we are certainly justified in morals, and therefore justified in law, under the treaty of 1846, in interfering summarily and saying that the canal is to be built and that they must not stop it."

The *therefore* was characteristic, an example of the Rooseveltian ratio-nality that so often amused Root and Knox. It did not amuse Hanna. The Senator's only suggestion was that the Compagnie Nouvelle should be paid to continue its halfhearted excavations in Panama, while Congress thought up some new way of settling with Colombia.

This advice contrasted with the roarings of Albert Shaw in *Review of Re-views,* the nation's most influential journal of opinion. Bogotá's "blackmailing adventurers" had insulted the United States by demanding a ten-million-dollar "bribe," Shaw wrote. Washington should "look with favor" upon sep-aratists in Panama, with a view toward supporting their revolution.

Roosevelt tried to calm the editor down, informing him that "as yet, the people of the United States are not willing to take the ground of building the canal by force." But the theme of blackmail, like King Charles's head, could not be kept out of his draft Message to Congress:

It is out of the question to submit to extortion on the part of a beneficiary. . . .

The interest of international commerce generally and the interest of this country generally demands that the canal should be begun with no needless delay. The refusal of Colombia properly to respond to our sincere and earnest efforts to come to an agreement, or to pay heed to the many concessions we have made, renders it in my judgment necessary that the United States should take immediate action on one or two lines: either we should drop the Panama Canal project and immediately begin work on the Nicaraguan canal, or else we should purchase all the rights of the French Company, and, without any further parley with Colombia, enter upon the completion of the canal. . . . I feel that the latter course is the one demanded by the interests of this Nation and I therefore bring the matter to your attention for such action in the premises as you may deem wise.

He was careful not to predict any "misconduct" that might be to America's advantage on the Isthmus. William Nelson Cromwell bustled in to see him on 7 October, and bustled out none the wiser—"a typical revolutionist," in Roosevelt's opinion, "mysterious, and in it for the fun of the game." Three days later, however, the President received someone much harder to deflect.

Philippe Bunau-Varilla was escorted by Assistant Secretary of State Loomis. Tiny as the Frenchman was—he barely reached his companion's sternum—Roosevelt saw at once that he was a shrewd and aggressive personality. The globular head bulged with intelligence, and the eyes—"duellist's eyes"—were as chill as glass. Most people were overawed when they entered the Executive Office for the first time, but Bunau-Varilla was calm. Roosevelt felt himself being sized up.

He knew that there was "an underlying motive" for the visit, which would not be stated directly. Loomis introduced Bunau-Varilla as the new co-owner of *Le Matin* in Paris. For a while they all made polite conversation about French journalism, avoiding any reference to Panama. Then Loomis mentioned the Dreyfus affair. Bunau-Varilla took the cue:

BUNAU-VARILLA Mr. President, Captain Dreyfus has not been the only victim of detestable political passions. Panama is another.

ROOSEVELT Oh yes, you have devoted much time and effort to Panama, Mr. Bunau-Varilla. Well, what do you think is going to be the outcome of the present situation?

BUNAU-VARILLA Mr. President, a revolution.
ROOSEVELT A revolution . . . Would it be possible? (*To Loomis*) But if it became a reality, what would become of the plan we had thought of?

Loomis remained rigidly mute. The President, for all his air of fake surprise, was referring to John Bassett Moore's proposal to "require" Colombia to sign the canal treaty. Roosevelt asked what made Bunau-Varilla think that a revolution was coming.

"General and special considerations, Mr. President." Bunau-Varilla spoke with careful vagueness, not wanting to embarrass Roosevelt with details. But he could not resist asking if the United States would be supportive of an armed uprising in Panama.

Roosevelt ignored the question.

"I don't suppose you can say."

"I cannot."

"Will you protect Colombian interests?"

"I cannot say that."

All that the President *would* say was that Colombia, in rejecting a treaty she herself had proposed, had forfeited any further consideration by the United States. "I have no use for a government that would do what that government has done."

Both men were anxious for the interview to end. They perfectly understood each other. Roosevelt saw that if anyone was capable of bringing about the revolution, it was this tremendous little foreigner. Bunau-Varilla, in turn, was convinced that the United States would find a way to support him.

⟶

THE PRESIDENT'S FAUX PAS about a "plan" may not have been involuntary. When receiving officers and gentlemen—Bunau-Varilla was, like himself, a colonel—he was sure that his confidence would not be abused. (It might, however, be discreetly *used*.) With advisers, Roosevelt was even franker, telling Professor Moore that he would recognize Panama if it revolted and set up an independent government "under proper circumstances."

In the same spirit, he now informed Albert Shaw that he would be "delighted" to hear of an uprising on the Isthmus. "But for me to say so publicly would amount to an instigation of a revolt, and therefore I cannot say it." With his current unpopularity among unionists, white Southerners, and Wall Street bankers, he dared not risk any word or deed that might revive old images of him as a rash, rough-riding imperialist.

John D. Long could not have chosen a worse time to publish an article in *Outlook* jocularly recalling the days when the President, as Assistant Secretary of the Navy, had wanted "to send a squadron across the ocean to sink . . . the Spanish fleet while we were still at peace with Spain." Roosevelt angrily denied the allegation, but critics of his Administration thought that Colombia should take it as a forewarning. "He is the most risky man the United States has had in the Presidency," declared the *Philadelphia Record.*

Another article, by Henry Watterson in the Louisville *Courier-Journal,* alleged that half of the forty million dollars that American taxpayers were paying to the Compagnie Nouvelle for canal rights would be kicked back to various American senators, lobbyists, engineers, and columnists—the "thieves" behind the original switch to Panama. While nobody believed that Roosevelt had any "share of the stealage," he was being importuned by too many unscrupulous parties. There was only one honest alternative: to opt for Nicaragua, and quickly. "Time's up, Mr. President!" Watterson taunted. "Will you act . . . or will you continue to play politics?"

Philippe Bunau-Varilla demolished Watterson's claims in a letter to the New York *Sun.* He noted that "not one cent" of the canal-rights money could be disbursed illegally, since the Compagnie Nouvelle was in receivership, and thus managed by the courts of France. As for the Nicaragua route, "it has all the advantages over Panama except the technical ones."

Watterson was reduced to weak taunts aimed at "Mr. Vanilla Bean." The nickname stuck, to Bunau-Varilla's fury, but the charges of corruption did not.

❧

MANUEL AMADOR GUERRERO, an elderly physician accredited by the Panamanian revolutionary *junta,* met with Bunau-Varilla in New York. An American intermediary, known only as "W," had led him to believe that the Roosevelt Administration would contribute at least six million dollars of unspecified secret funds to his cause. The money was needed to buy gunboats that would prevent Colombia from landing reinforcements on the Isthmus when revolution broke out. Bunau-Varilla told him to forget about any such subsidy.

A more realistic hope, based on Roosevelt's hints in the Executive Office, was that the United States Navy would provide such protection, under Roosevelt's treaty obligations to keep traffic across Panama clear. Amador said that in that case the *junta* had no worries about the five hundred Colombian troops garrisoned in Panama City. They had been so long neglected and underpaid by Bogotá that they could certainly be bribed to join the revolution.

Bunau-Varilla grandly promised to raise one hundred thousand dollars for this purpose. If he could not borrow it from a New York bank, "I can provide it, myself, from my own personal fortune."

Downtown, as the conspirators shook hands, William Nelson Cromwell prepared to decamp for Paris. "The fun of the game" was rapidly becoming too fraught for him. He was terrified that President Marroquín would find out that he, too, had been plotting with Panamanians, and cancel the Compagnie Nouvelle's remaining rights.

And there was still the dread prospect that Roosevelt might yet decide to dig in Nicaragua. Obsequiously, Cromwell sent him a final appeal before sailing:

YOUR VIRILE AND MASTERFUL POLICY WILL PROVE THE SOLUTION OF THIS GREAT PROBLEM.

⌐⌐

BUNAU-VARILLA, having invested so heavily in Panama's future, returned to Washington on 15 October to see if John Hay would tell him anything more than Roosevelt had. The Secretary of State received him at home, and put on a dazzling display of diplomatic obtuseness. He waited for Bunau-Varilla to raise the subject of Panamanian unrest, then agreed that a revolution was likely. "But," he added in his silky voice, "we shall not be caught napping."

He mentioned that a squadron of Navy ships was coaling up in San Francisco, and would next "sail towards the Isthmus." There was some talk about the propensity of Latin American nations for political violence. Then Hay changed, or seemed to change, the subject. "I have just finished reading a charming novel, *Captain Macklin*."

He picked up Richard Harding Davis's latest adventure story and said that it was about an American soldier of fortune who visits Central America and enlists in a revolutionary army, under the command of an idealistic Frenchman. "Take it with you," Hay urged. "It will interest you."

That evening, on the train back to New York, a wildly excited Bunau-Varilla pored over *Captain Macklin*. Every page furthered his idealistic identity with the French general, fighting in the jungle for "justice and progress." But the book also made him worry about *mañana*. When he next saw Dr. Amador, he behaved with Napoleonic briskness, handing over a plan of military action, a declaration of independence, a draft republican constitution, and "a code with which to correspond with me." The United States, he guaranteed, would move to protect Panama within forty-eight hours of the revolution.

Amador accepted both the documents and the promise. But he was much less willing to accede to Bunau-Varilla's airy follow-up, "Nobody knows better than I the final aim, which is the completion of the canal and the best way to attain it. It will, therefore, be necessary to entrust me with the diplomatic representation of the new Republic at Washington."

All Amador could say was that he would discuss the matter with his colleagues. Bunau-Varilla, elated, began to design a national flag.

⌐⌐

THAT NIGHT, two young Army officers, Captain Chauncey B. Humphrey and Lieutenant Grayson Murphy, visited the White House to report secretly on a tour they had just made of Panama. Roosevelt listened with interest, having sent them south himself, to survey strategic approaches to the canal zone.

They confirmed Bunau-Varilla's predictions of a revolution, saying it would probably occur late that month, or in early November. While crossing by train from Colón to Panama City, disguised as English tourists, they had found themselves in the same car as José de Obaldía. The Governor and his aides, assuming that the foreigners spoke no Spanish, had openly—but unenthusiastically—talked about a break from Bogotá. Captain Humphrey got a feeling of general gloom, based on the failure of Panamanian revolutions in the past.

He and Murphy also heard that a German lobbyist had influenced the Colombian Senate's rejection of the canal treaty, that votes had been sold—either way—at seven to ten thousand gold dollars apiece, and that an American railroad man with "a remarkably attractive wife" had bought a number of nays.

Casting aside his disguise, Captain Humphrey had later met with leaders of the *junta*. They proved to be so desperate for military aid that they actually offered him command of their forces. If successful in winning Panama's freedom, he and Lieutenant Murphy would get a quarter of the ten million dollars that Washington would then (surely) pay for canal rights.

Humphrey had declined appointment, explaining that he was an American Army officer and served only one flag. But he had not scrupled to give free tactical advice (including how to seize a Colombian gunboat lying off Panama City), and a list of Texan arms suppliers. In exchange, he had gotten an indication of the *junta*'s current assets: five hundred troops, 2,500 arms, and $365,000 in cash and pledges.

The President was not a passive auditor of Humphrey and Murphy's tale. He impressed them with his topographical and political knowledge of the Isthmus. They half hoped he would say that the United States must avoid any military role there, so that they could resign their commissions and become real-life Captain Macklins. But he made no such disclaimer, and they were shown out into the night. "There goes our revolution," Murphy muttered sadly.

ROOSEVELT SPENT THE weekend brooding over the Humphrey-Murphy report, identifying to an almost comical degree with President Andrew Jackson. "*There* was an executive who realized not only the responsibilities, but the opportunities of the office," he told a lunch group including George Haven Putnam. Old "King Andrew" was no saint, but he had never hesitated "to cut any red tape that stood in the way of executive action. . . . Now, Haven, I hear you chuckling. I know what you are thinking about."

On Monday, crisp cables began to issue from the White House and the

Navy Department. The *Dixie* was loaded with a battalion of Marines and ordered to Guantánamo, Cuba, arrival date 29 October. Moody ordered the *Boston* to steam secretly, "with all possible dispatch" to San Juan del Sur, Nicaragua, within striking distance of Panama City, while the *Marblehead, Concord,* and *Wyoming* proceeded (as per Hay's alert to Bunau-Varilla) to Acapulco. The only maverick movement in this slow concentration of forces was that of the gunship *Nashville,* which had only just left Colón. To wheel her round would excite Colombian suspicions, so she was allowed to continue to Caimanera, Cuba.

In coincidental, yet related movement, the steamer *Yucatán* sailed for Colón from New York. Dr. Amador was on board, looking rather portly, because he wore under his vest the silk flag of Panamanian independence, stitched by Madame Bunau-Varilla. He was probably unaware that five years before, "Roosevelt's Rough Riders" had headed south on this same dilapidated vessel, with equal dreams of glory.

On 23 October, in further irony, Roosevelt had a recurrence of the malarial fever that had stayed in his system since the Santiago campaign. He spent the afternoon lying on a sofa by a bright fire, with Edith knitting and rocking beside him.

On 26 October, the New York *Herald*'s Panama correspondent, whose brother was a *junta* member, reported that seventy anti-Colombian insurgents had "invaded" the Isthmus. Governor Obaldía dispatched one hundred men to meet this imaginary force, conveniently weakening the garrison in Panama City.

On 27 October, Roosevelt turned forty-five, and Dr. Amador was welcomed home. While the President, well again, celebrated with an eighteen-course dinner, Amador had to confess that the only aid he had won in *el Norte* was pledged by a Frenchman five feet four inches tall.

⟨⟩

BUNAU-VARILLA, HOWEVER, was as good as his word. He had already transferred one hundred thousand dollars in personal funds from Paris to New York. But, as a hard man, he set hard conditions on Amador. The money would not be sent on until he received a cable confirming the success of the revolution and appointing him Panama's Minister Plenipotentiary in Washington. He would then press the Roosevelt Administration to protect and quickly recognize the new republic. "The only dangerous period for you will be from the moment the revolution begins to forty-eight hours after the telegram is handed to me."

Judging from his "trigonometrical" projections of the various movements involved—of United States warships, of Colombian reinforcements (already deploying), of *junta* agents throughout the Isthmus—the earliest likely date for such news was 29 October. When a cable from Amador arrived on that date, Bunau-Varilla congratulated himself. But the coded message was not what he expected:

FATE NEWS BAD POWERFUL TIGER. URGE VAPOR COLON.
SMITH

Some of it, at least, he could decipher. *Fate:* Bunau-Varilla. *News:* Colombian troops arriving. *Bad:* Atlantic side. *Powerful:* in five days. *Tiger:* more than two hundred men. *Smith:* Amador. But *urge vapor Colón* seemed more language than code. *Urge* must be English, *vapor* either American English or Spanish. *Vapor:* steam. Steamer!

He was being asked to arrange the dispatch of an American warship to Colón before the Colombian troops got there on 2 November. Bunau-Varilla grabbed a valise and rushed for a Washington train.

Francis B. Loomis received him at home, coldly and noncommittally. The next morning, Bunau-Varilla hung around Lafayette Square, wondering whether to knock on John Hay's door, when Loomis chanced, or contrived, to bump into him. Now the Assistant Secretary was confidential, if cryptic: "It would be terrible if the catastrophe of 1885 were to be renewed today."

Riding back to New York on the Congressional Limited, Bunau-Varilla deduced that Loomis had told him that the United States did *not* intend to permit the burning of Colón by government troops, as she had the last time Panama seriously rebelled. Which must mean that naval force of some sort was on its way. Newspapers aboard the train reported that the *Nashville,* last seen off Cuba, had arrived in Kingston, Jamaica—en route, surely, to the Isthmus. Five hundred nautical miles at ten knots an hour worked out to two days' steam. About twelve extra hours would be necessary for preparations. Bunau-Varilla jumped out of the train at Baltimore.

It was ten minutes past noon, 30 October 1903. He sent a wire to "Smith" in Panama City.

ALL RIGHT. WILL REACH TON AND A HALF.

Ton and a half: two and a half days. Calculating from now, that meant the *Nashville* should arrive off Colón in the small hours of 2 November. The revolution might be slightly delayed, but not compromised. Bunau-Varilla waited for another train, knowing there was little more he could do for the moment. He had urged a vapor to Colón. Now everything depended on Smith.

⌐⊃~

ROOSEVELT SWATTED AWAY the late-October light on the White House tennis court. Despite twinges of gout and a thickening waistline, he triumphantly took a set from James Garfield. Then he put his racket away and prepared for humiliation in the November polls.

It was his habit to be gloomy about elections, even in a year as "off" as this. Some thirteen states were due to choose governors, mayors, and local legislatures. Of these, only three gave him real cause to worry, because of Republican infighting. In New York, the party was badly split, boding ill for the state's all-important electoral-college vote. In Delaware, he was accused—with some justice—of being equivocal between two GOP factions, one of which was corrupt. And in Ohio, Tom L. Johnson's run for Governor was threatening the legislative majority that Mark Hanna would need for re-election. Roosevelt hoped that Johnson would be beaten, because a Hanna happily back in the Senate would be a Hanna less likely to think of running for the presidency in 1904.

At least there was good news from London, where Elihu Root, Henry Cabot Lodge, and George Turner won a near-total victory at the Alaska Boundary Tribunal. Canada was left with a few token islands. Lodge, over-joyed (insofar as a Brahmin could feel joyful about anything), wrote to say that Roosevelt should not worry about temporary setbacks to his domestic policy. Such things only "looked" bad, in contrast to his general popularity and success. "I think you are fundamentally just as strong as you ever were."

If so—and Tuesday's vote would tell—that political strength was secondary to the strength of will Roosevelt felt surging in himself with regard to coming events on the Isthmus. Now was the time to fulfill "not only the responsibilities, but the opportunities of the office." Indeed, "Opportunity" was the title of his favorite Washington poem, by the late Senator John J. Ingalls, framed on the wall opposite his desk:

> *Master of human destinies am I!*
> *Fame, love, and fortune on my footsteps wait;*
> *Cities and fields I walk; I penetrate*
> *Deserts and seas remote, and passing by*
> *Hovel and mart and palace, soon or late*
> *I knock unbidden once at every gate!*
> *If sleeping, wake; if feasting, rise before*
> *I turn away. It is the hour of fate,*
> *And they who follow me reach every state*
> *Mortals desire, and conquer every foe*
> *Save death; but those who doubt or hesitate,*
> *Condemned to failure, penury and woe,*
> *Seek me in vain and uselessly implore.*
> *I answer not, and I return no more!*

Whatever happened in Colón or Panama City over the next few weeks—or days, or hours—he must, if necessary, occupy the canal zone and start the digging by main force.

⟋⟋⟍

ALL DAY LONG on Monday, 2 November, *junta* scouts scanned the sea northeast of Colón for signs of Bunau-Varilla's promised gunboat. But they sighted nothing—not even the Colombian troop transport reportedly on its way. If the latter arrived first, their revolution would be much less sure of success.

The *Nashville* was, nevertheless, approaching at full speed, and Secretary Moody knew all about the troopship. In a series of orders approved by Roosevelt, the *Dixie* had been dispatched to follow in the *Nashville*'s wake, while the *Boston, Marblehead, Concord,* and *Wyoming* were cleared for Panama City.

The coordinated grace of these trajectories on Moody's map board was deceptive. Straight lines could not render the communications errors, coaling delays, and bureaucratic blocks that slow any naval mobilization. The *Dixie,* now in Kingston, could not sail immediately, while the Pacific squadron, laboring down the Mexican coast, had yet to bypass Nicaragua. Meanwhile, the Isthmus remained quiet. Neither Bunau-Varilla (anxiously awaiting Amador's confirmation cable in New York) nor Loomis were aware that the *junta* had postponed the revolution by forty-eight hours.

Now the plot was to wait until dawn on 4 November, giving the United States time to establish a strong naval presence off both coasts, before the pro forma arrest of Governor Obaldía in bed. All other government officials of any consequence would be jailed at the same time, with the exception of General Esteban Huertas, commander of the Panama City garrison and a willing, if expensive, recruit. Huertas's battalion, plus two thousand veterans of earlier revolutions, three hundred railroad workers, and a like number of firemen, should establish order without much difficulty. A rocket would signal their success, and summon the liberated people of Panama City to the Plaza de Santa Ana. Then a declaration of independence (not Bunau-Varilla's) would be read, and a new flag (not Bunau-Varilla's) raised above the palm trees. Meanwhile, in Colón, the chief of police, Porfilio Meléndez, would proclaim the revolution there. By nightfall, all or most of Colombia's three hundred thousand *Istmusenos* should be celebrating their new identities as Panamanians.

Two uncertainties, however, complicated this *zarzuela* scenario: Would the American gunboat arrive before the Colombian troopship? And could it be relied on to control events in Colón?

⟋⟋⟍

ROOSEVELT'S LAST TACTICAL move of the day was to approve a "secret and confidential" cable that addressed both questions. It ordered Commander

John Hubbard of the *Nashville* to "maintain free and uninterrupted transit" across the Isthmus. If the transit seemed threatened by "any armed force with hostile intent," he was to "occupy" the railroad line. Then, with repetitive emphasis:

PREVENT LANDING OF ANY ARMED FORCE WITH HOSTILE
INTENT, EITHER GOVERNMENT OR INSURGENT. . . .
GOVERNMENT FORCE REPORTED APPROACHING COLÓN IN
VESSELS. PREVENT THEIR LANDING IF IN YOUR
JUDGMENT THIS WOULD PRECIPITATE A CONFLICT.

A similar order went out to Hubbard's fellow commanders on the Pacific side.

Darkness settled over Washington. Two thousand miles south, in a warmer twilight, the *Nashville* dropped anchor off Colón.

⌒

INSTEAD OF RETIRING with Edith after dinner, Roosevelt boarded a special sleeper to New York. It was his habit every election eve to head homeward to vote. He enjoyed the ritual. If Panama chose to revolt now, it would have to do it without him.

He was awakened at 6:00 to prepare for transfer across Manhattan. At the same hour in Colón, first light disclosed another overnight arrival in the harbor: the Colombian troopship *Cartagena*. While the President bathed and breakfasted, Commander Hubbard sent an inspector aboard the *Cartagena* and found her to be swarming with *tiradores*, select sharpshooters of the Colombian Army. None of them seemed to have a clear idea of why they had been sent to the Isthmus—only that they had been ordered by General Juan Tovar to debark quickly.

On shore, Chief Meléndez and other *junta* agents braced for trouble. Colonel James Shaler, the sympathetic superintendent of the Panama Railroad, agreed that at all costs the *tiradores* must be kept from crossing over to Panama City. Yet Commander Hubbard, inexplicably, raised no objection to the debarkation.

Hubbard's problem was that he had not yet received his secret orders from Washington. He had no more clue than the captain of the *Cartagena* as to why he had been ordered back to Colón. At 8:20 A.M., therefore, the troopship nosed up to the Panama Railroad dock, and five hundred *tiradores* came ashore, bristling with weaponry.

Simultaneously, Roosevelt crossed the East River in bright fall sunshine. Behind him, the towers of Manhattan scintillated. Electoral bunting flapped in the streets, and huge crowds—too huge for Republican comfort—lined up to vote. At 8:30 he reached the Long Island Rail Road pier, settled into a waiting "special," and its whistle blew for Oyster Bay.

Another, very short private train prepared to depart Colón for Panama City. Colonel Shaler had rigged it to accommodate the Colombian battalion's sixteen senior officers. As he seated them, he explained that Governor Obaldía was anxious to see General Tovar as soon as possible. The *tiradores* would follow later in the day, as soon as more rolling stock could be procured. Shaler's courtly urgency overcame Tovar's doubts, and the train pulled out of the depot, leaving behind five hundred puzzled soldiers. The wooden houses of Colón slipped by at increasing speed. Jungle crowded in, and vegetation slapped at the sides of the car. Tovar and his aides rode over the saddle of hills Roosevelt wanted to divide, swaying in chlorophyllous gloom, suspended between two oceans.

⌒

THE PRESIDENT VOTED above Yee Lee's Laundry in Oyster Bay at five minutes before ten. Then he drove out along Cove Neck for a quick look at Sagamore Hill. The big house was shuttered and dark, ghostly with sheeted furniture. A heavy fume of camphor balls discouraged entry. He walked

"THE BIG HOUSE WAS SHUTTERED AND DARK."
Sagamore Hill in winter

around the estate, and noticed that the old barn, where he had romped with so many of his children, was beginning to give way. Two dogs greeted him; a third stared indifferently. Japanese maples trembled in full, scarlet leaf, but most other trees were bare, exposing a wider panorama of Long Island Sound than he had seen all summer.

After about a half hour fighting desolate emotions, he returned to his carriage and was driven back to Oyster Bay station.

⌐⊙⌐

AS ROOSEVELT DID SO, Commander Hubbard agonized over yesterday's orders, which had at last come through to the *Nashville*. He did not quite understand them, still having no knowledge of the prerevolutionary situation in Panama. The *tiradores* did not look like a "force with hostile intent," now that they had lost their leaders. They squatted under the arcades of Colón, chatting with women. Nor was there any sign, as far as Hubbard could see, of the "insurgent" threat Washington seemed to anticipate. He went ashore to interrogate Colonel Shaler about it, and quickly lost his innocence. Returning to the *Nashville*, he sent a cable to Washington:

IT IS POSSIBLE THAT MOVEMENT MAY BE MADE TONIGHT
AT PANAMA TO DECLARE INDEPENDENCE, IN WHICH CASE
I WILL PROTEST AGAINST TRANSIT OF TROOPS NOW HERE.

A certain lack of urgency at the railroad yard in collecting the cars necessary for such transit suggested that Hubbard would not have to do much protesting. Around 11:30, Shaler received a call confirming that General Tovar's party had arrived in Panama City. It had been welcomed by an impressive delegation of civic leaders, headed by Governor Obaldía, and by General Huertas and the garrison guard, glittering in full dress uniform. The first order of business, of course, was to have the Governor's office arrange for delivery of the *tiradores*—but while this was being done, Tovar and his staff were invited to join Obaldía for lunch and a *siesta*.

⌐⊙⌐

AT 2:34 P.M., ROOSEVELT'S special train pulled out of Jersey City for Washington. Facing six hours of travel, he remembered that Nicholas Murray Butler had asked him for a list of recommended books. It seemed like a strange request, coming from the President of Columbia University, yet deserving of a full answer. He cast his mind back over what he had read since taking the oath of office, and began to scribble.

Parts of Herodotus; the first and seventh books of Thucydides; all of Polybius; a little of Plutarch; Aeschylus' Orestean Trilogy; Sophocles'

Seven Against Thebes; Euripides' *Hippolytus* and *Bacchae;* and Aristophanes' *Frogs.* Parts of *The Politics of Aristotle.*

All these had been in translation. However, he had read, in French, the biographies of Prince Eugene of Savoy, Admiral Michiel de Ruyter, Henri Turenne, and John Sobieski. He had also browsed, if not deeply studied, Froissart on French history, Maspero on the early Syrian, Chaldean, and Egyptian civilizations, "and some six volumes of Mahaffey's *Studies of the Greek World.*" What else?

The *Memoirs* of Marbot; Bain's *Life of Charles the Twelfth;* Mahan's *Types of Naval Officers;* some of Macaulay's *Essays;* three or four volumes of Gibbon and three or four chapters of Motley. The battles in Carlyle's *Frederick the Great;* Hay and Nicolay's *Lincoln,* and the two volumes of Lincoln's *Speeches and Writings*—these I have not only read through, but have read parts of them again and again; Bacon's *Essays . . . Macbeth; Twelfth Night; Henry the Fourth; Henry the Fifth; Richard the Second;* the first two cantos of Milton's *Paradise Lost;* some of Michael Drayton's *Poems*—there are only three or four I care for; portions of the *Nibelungenlied. . . .*

~

ROOSEVELT HAD BARELY settled in his seat before the first hint of trouble in Panama reached the State Department. Hubbard's early-morning dispatch from Colón had gone astray; this one came from Oscar Malmros, the United States Consul in Colón.

REVOLUTION IMMINENT . . . GOVERNMENT VESSEL
CARTAGENA, WITH ABOUT 400 MEN, ARRIVED EARLY
TODAY, WITH NEW COMMANDER IN CHIEF, TOVAR . . .
NOT PROBABLE TO STOP REVOLUTION.

Washington was ill prepared to deal with such sudden news, since most of its top officials, including Root, Moody, and the President himself, were out of town on election trips. Assistant Secretary Loomis cabled Felix Ehrman, the United States Vice Consul in Panama City, ordering him to keep the State Department apprised of the situation in Panama City. Ehrman could reply only that it was "critical," but not yet violent. Some sort of uprising was expected "in the night."

Had the Vice Consul been better informed, he might have noticed the curious frequency with which deadlines of "five o'clock" recurred in local communications. Governor Obaldía had promised the increasingly desperate Tovar that his battalion would be delivered at that hour. The fire brigade was on notice to be ready for action then, and a freelance scribe assigned to write an important public proclamation had his contract amended accordingly. Word spread that there would be "a great mass meeting" in Plaza de Santa Ana at 5:00 P.M., and certain key citizens were told to bring guns.

⌒

. . . Church's *Beowulf;* Morris' translation of the *Heimskringla,* and Dasent's translation of the sagas of Gisli and Burnt Njal; Lady Gregory's and Miss Hull's *Cuchulain Saga* together with *The Children of Lir, The Children of Turin, The Tale of Deirdre,* etc.; *Les Précieuses Ridicules, Le Barbier de Séville;* most of Jusserand's books, of which I was most interested in his studies of the *Kingis Quhair;* Holmes' *Over the Teacups;* Lounsbury's *Shakespeare and Voltaire;* various numbers of the *Edinburgh Review* from 1803 to 1850; Tolstoi's *Sebastopol* and *The Cossacks;* Sienkiewicz's *Fire and Sword,* and parts of his other volumes; *Guy Mannering; The Antiquary; Rob Roy; Waverley; Quentin Durward;* parts of *Marmion* and the *Lay of the Last Minstrel;* Cooper's *Pilot;* some of the earlier stories and poems of Bret Harte; Mark Twain's *Tom Sawyer; Pickwick Papers; Nicholas Nickelby; Vanity Fair; Pendennis; The Newcomes; Adventures of Philip;* Conan Doyle's *White Company.* . . .

⌒

WHEN ELISEO TORRES, the young colonel whom General Tovar had left in command of the *tiradores,* asked Colonel Shaler when his men might expect to cross the Isthmus, he received a variety of answers. At first Shaler repeated Obaldía's promise of delivery by five, but when that hour drew near, the railroad suddenly demanded advance payment of all fares. Torres, who had no money, was quick-thinking enough to insist on the government of Colombia's right to transport troops on credit. Consul Malmros, overhearing, confirmed that such a right was written into the railroad's concession. Shaler did not contest this, but noted that the concession also called for the Governor of Panama's signature on all military travel requisitions. Also there was still the question of a shortage of available cars, most of the railroad's rolling stock unfortunately being on the other side of the Isthmus.

Torres waxed more and more angry. Shaler had to admit, quietly to Chief Meléndez, that the railroad could not stall much longer without jeopardizing its treaty privileges. Torres could probably be held off until sunset, when trains stopped running anyway. But some cars were going to have to be laid on in the morning, unless Shaler received "written orders of the United States Government to refuse the transportation."

⌒

ROOSEVELT RECALLED PLOWING through Charles Lever's *Charles O'Malley* and some Brockden Brown novels with little real enjoyment, during the period when he was confined by his leg injury. Keats, Browning, Poe, Tennyson, Longfellow, Kipling, Bliss Carmen, Lowell, Stevenson, Allingham, and Leopold Wagner were more to his taste, and he had spent many enjoyable hours in their literary company. He had read aloud to his children ("and often finished afterwards to myself") the stories of Hans Christian Andersen, the Brothers Grimm, and Howard Pyle. As for Joel Chandler Harris, "I would be willing to rest all I have done in the South as regards the negro in his story 'Free Joe.' "

⌒

FIVE O'CLOCK CAME and went in Colón without any word of a disturbance in Panama City. The cable and railroad offices prepared to shut down for the night. Commander Hubbard came ashore again from the *Nashville,* and heard with concern that Shaler was resigned to transporting the government battalion in the morning. But before he could object, at 5:49 P.M., a call came through from Herbert G. Prescott, Shaler's deputy at the Pacific terminus. Strangely, Prescott wanted to speak to Chief Meléndez. His message was a coded one—indicating that Prescott, too, was an agent of the *junta,* and saying that the revolution was "about to begin."

Subsequent calls made clear that General Tovar and his senior staff had already been arrested at the order of General Huertas. Governor Obaldía was next (surrendering with the utmost equanimity), and by 6:00 P.M. the *junta* had started reorganizing itself as a "Provisional Government." Its official documents and proclamations showed that the elderly Dr. Amador held little real power. The executive signatures were always those of José Augustin Arango, Federico Boyd, and Tomas Arias.

One of their first official acts was to send Shaler a telegram warning him, in the strongest terms, "not to accede" to any request for transportation of the *tiradores.* "This act would be of grave consequences for the company you represent."

⌒

KENNETH GRAHAME. *Somerville and Ross. Conrad. Artemus Ward. Octave Thanet. Viljoen. Stevens. Peer. Burroughs. Swettenham. Gray. Janvier. London. Fox. Garland. Tarkington. Churchill. Remington. Wister. White. Trevelyan* . . .

By the time Roosevelt tired of jotting, he had listed 114 author names. "Of course I have forgotten a great many." His catalog did not strike him as impressive. "About as interesting," he concluded, "as Homer's Catalogue of the Ships."

He dozed off several times as the train raced south. Night fell. The weather was still mild and clear. Democratic weather. Faceless stations whizzed by in the dark. Sooner than expected, Washington loomed ahead. At 8:14 he alighted at Sixth Street Station. A reporter pushed an election dispatch into his hand. He stopped and read it under the bright platform lights. The Republican Party had suffered a landslide defeat in New York.

Refusing comment, Roosevelt shook hands with the locomotive crew, then climbed into a waiting White House carriage. It rolled down Pennsylvania Avenue past the *Evening Star* and *Post* buildings, only half noticed by crowds peering up at giant, illuminated stereopticon screens. Preliminary polling figures alternated with celebrity portraits and comic "moving pictures." By 9:00, Roosevelt had arrived in the West Wing telegraph room to check on further results. But Loomis was there with a cable that drove all thoughts of the election from his mind. It was Vice Consul Ehrman's nervous message of five hours before. Now, Ehrman cabled again:

UPRISING OCCURRED TONIGHT, SIX. NO BLOODSHED.
ARMY AND NAVY OFFICIALS TAKEN PRISONERS.
GOVERNMENT WILL BE ORGANIZED TONIGHT, CONSISTING
OF THREE CONSULS, ALSO CABINET. SUPPOSED SAME
MOVEMENT WILL BE EFFECTED IN COLÓN. ORDER
PREVAILS SO FAR. SITUATION SERIOUS. FOUR HUNDRED
SOLDIERS LANDED TODAY. BARRANQUILLA.

Roosevelt sent at once for his top State and Navy Department aides. Hay arrived within minutes, accompanied by Loomis. Moody was still out of town, so his second in command, Charles H. Darling, came instead, followed by Admiral Taylor, Chief of the Bureau of Navigation, and two assistant officers. A crisis conference began in the President's office.

Ehrman's "no bloodshed" was good news, and Arango, Boyd, and Arias seemed to be going about their business efficiently so far. But the presence of those soldiers in Colón was indeed "serious" (and would look even more so when Roosevelt found out there were five hundred, not four). The *Nashville* was so far the only American presence on either side of the Isthmus. Hubbard's guns and Marines might, or might not, be enough to stop the government battalion from crossing over and quashing the revolution.

All the more reason, therefore, to keep Tovar's troops on the Caribbean side. But "reason" of a legal nature must be found in the treaty of 1846. Roosevelt was aware that early in his own presidency, the State Department had blocked a shipment of rebel arms along the railroad, on the ground that they might be used to prevent further transport of anything. Could the same scruple now justify blocking a shipment of government soldiers, whose only mission was to maintain the integrity of the Colombian federation?

Apparently, it could. Roosevelt authorized a draft set of instructions for the Navy Department to set in cipher, and cable immediately:

For NASHVILLE. In the interests of peace do everything possible to prevent government troops from proceeding to Panama [City]. The transit must be kept open and order maintained.

Direct the ATLANTA to proceed with all speed to Colón.

Also the BOSTON [to Panama City].

Repeat all of yesterday's orders.

Remarkable in this document was its lack of any reference to the "strict neutrality" imposed upon American commanders in earlier Isthmian crises.

By 10:30 P.M., the specific order to Commander Hubbard was ready for transmission and signed by Hay. Further cables went to the other ships involved, although their urgency was largely symbolic. The *Atlanta* had to finish stoking up in Kingston before it could join the *Nashville*; the *Boston* had not yet cleared Honduras; the rest of the Pacific Squadron would need three more days to get to Panama City. At least the *Dixie* was nearing Colón, where Hubbard could doubtless use it.

Up Pennsylvania Avenue, the stereopticon watchers were roaring, as result after result flickered onto the screens. Mayor Seth Low of New York City had conceded defeat. A Democratic rout was announced in Maryland. Especially loud cheers, around eleven o'clock, signaled a triumph for "Hanna Republicans" in Ohio.

The White House conference broke up fifteen minutes later, after another cable from Panama City announced that a government gunboat had tossed five or six shells into the city, "killing a Chinaman in Salsipuedes street and mortally wounding an ass." If that was the extent of Colombia's rage so far, a tired President could get some sleep.

꩜

THE BIG WORD *REVOLUTION* crowded election results on the right-hand side of the front page of *The Washington Post* the next morning. Most other newspapers, however, treated the story from Panama City as if it were the final, entirely predictable installment of a serial that had begun well but lost its power of suspense. In any case, the New York *World* had given away the ending nearly four months before—even forecasting yesterday's date. This temporary lack of interest (the story being by no means over) enabled Roosevelt, Hay, Loomis, and Darling to concentrate on the worsening crisis in Colón.

Commander Hubbard, by triple authority of the White House and the State and Navy Departments, had issued a denial of rail transport to the *tiradores*. (They were free to march across the Isthmus, if they liked, on a mud trail two feet wide, through one of the wettest jungles in the world.) Hubbard informed Colonel Shaler in writing that any redistribution of troops, loyal or revolutionary, "must bring about a conflict and threaten that free and uninterrupted transit of the Isthmus which the Government of the

United States is pledged to maintain." He had sent an early copy of this order to Colonel Torres, emphasizing that it applied to both sides, and trusting in his "cordial" cooperation.

Torres reacted with cordial fury. He was still unaware of what had happened in Panama City, but he had grown increasingly nervous since the departure of his commanding officers. Their silence was suspicious, as was Hubbard's cryptic reference to a possible "conflict." Did the commander mean a clash with *insurrectos* inland, or an international battle right here on the Colón waterfront? Torres knew only that an American naval officer was denying him the right to cross his own country.

The mid-morning train from Panama City arrived, bringing the first unofficial news of yesterday's uprising. Porfirio Meléndez offered to buy Torres a drink. Under soothing fans at the Astor Hotel, he confirmed that Panama had seceded from Colombia. The new republic's security had been guaranteed by the United States, which was sending more warships. General Tovar was in jail, along with his fellow officers, and so was Governor Obaldía. All Panamanians supported the revolution, so resistance was "entirely useless." If Colonel Torres would be so good as to order his men to surrender their arms, the *junta* would provide rations and passage back to Barranquilla.

Torres went in a frenzy to the prefect of Colón and told him to deliver an ultimatum to Consul Malmros. Unless Tovar and Amaya were freed by 2:00 P.M., he would open fire on the town "and kill every U.S. citizen in the place."

When Commander Hubbard heard of this threat, shortly after one o'clock, he took it as tantamount to "war against the United States." All male Americans in Colón were ordered to take cover in Shaler's stone depot, while their women and children were rushed aboard steamers in the harbor. Forty-two heavily armed Marines simultaneously came ashore to defend the railroad, while the *Nashville* patrolled the waterfront. Its guns covered the town at boardwalk level.

Undeterred, Torres's five hundred men surrounded the railroad yard.

⌒

IN WASHINGTON, the President lunched with Justice Oliver Wendell Holmes — "one of the most interesting men I have ever met" — and Sir Frederick Pollock, Professor of Jurisprudence at Oxford University. Roosevelt enjoyed their company, yet remained temperamentally unable to understand the workings of minds more concerned with reason than power.

In New York, Philippe Bunau-Varilla decoded a cable from his friend "Smith" in Panama City. It was not, as he expected, his appointment as the new republic's Minister Plenipotentiary, but a pressing demand for one hundred thousand pesos. He decided to send half that amount. Fifty thousand pesos equaled about twenty-five thousand dollars, or one quarter of his total pledge. If *junta* members wanted the rest, they would have to make good on the ministership—and certify that they held both coasts. The United States was not likely to dig a canal on only one side of the continental divide.

"With all the insistence possible," he cabled back, "I recommend you to seize Colón."

~

COLONEL TORRES, closeted with Chief Meléndez, let his 2:00 P.M. deadline pass. For another hour and a quarter, Colombians and Americans continued to draw beads on each other across the railroad yard. The tension increased as the *Cartagena,* which had raised anchor after the *Nashville* lowered its guns, steamed toward the horizon at a speed suggesting she sought safety beyond it. Now that they had lost their troopship, the *tiradores* were more than ever compelled to stand and fight.

Then Torres approached the depot, smiling. Evidently there had been some pecuniary progress in his negotiations with Chief Meléndez. He told Colonel Hubbard that he now felt "most friendly" toward the United States. But he needed an authorization from his captive leader before he called off his men. Colonel Shaler undertook to transport a pair of Colombian envoys to Panama City for that purpose, and Commander Hubbard promised them safe conduct. After their special train had puffed off, Torres and Hubbard agreed to a mutual, modified fallback. The Marines would retire to the *Nashville,* and the battalion would camp on a hill outside town, while Colón would be left under the control of Chief Meléndez.

A state of unnatural calm settled over the shabby little port, even as Panama City, where the first revolutionary bonuses had just been paid out in silver, abandoned itself to wild celebrations. In Bogotá, mobs raged through the streets and stoned President Marroquín's house. And in Washington, Roosevelt and Hay worried over a cable from Malmros: PANAMA IN POSSESSION OF COMMITTEE WITH CONSENT OF ENTIRE POPULATION. . . . COLON IN THE POSSESSION OF THE GOVERNMENT.

And in New York, a naval emissary boarded a steamer of the Panama Railroad Company with a secret package addressed to the commander-in-chief of the North Atlantic Fleet. It contained war plans for an emergency occupation of the Isthmus.

~

COLONEL HUBBARD WENT ashore early on Thursday, 5 November, to find the *tiradores* (rendered irritable by mosquito bites) about to re-enter town. Torres said he had to be ready for the orders of General Tovar, due when his envoys arrived on the mid-morning train. Hubbard, infuriated, once more landed Marines, mounted cannons around the depot, and sent American women and children to safety. The *Nashville* resumed its sweep of the waterfront.

To popular relief, the envoys brought no orders, written or oral, from General Tovar. He declined to command from the depths of a jail cell; he merely expressed confidence that Colonel Torres "would always do his duty." Chief Meléndez, scenting capitulation, reappeared at Torres's elbow. The colonel blustered bravely all day; then, shortly before sunset, he agreed to accept an "indemnity" of eight thousand dollars advanced by Colonel Shaler. The money was counted out in cash. For another thousand dollars' credit (guaranteed by Colonel Hubbard), the captain of the Royal Mail Company steamship *Orinoco* agreed to transport the *tiradores* home. Torres plodded aboard with his sacks of American gold. Four hundred and sixty men and thirteen women followed him up the gangplank. Shaler sent a farewell gift of two cases of champagne.

Just then, at 7:05 P.M., the *Dixie* arrived in Colón harbor. It docked rapidly, undeterred by a violent rainstorm, and disgorged four hundred Marines. But their services were not needed. The *Orinoco* was already under way, and the Panamanian flag rose above Casa Meléndez.

⌐☉⌐

ROOSEVELT'S CABINET MEETING on the morning of Friday, 6 November, was devoted exclusively to Panama. Hay and Moody presented their latest consular dispatches, inaccurately reporting peace, stability, and rejoicing all over the Isthmus. A cable from Arango, Boyd, and Arias confirmed that "*Señor* Philippe Bunau-Varilla" had been appointed their "envoy extraordinary" in Washington, "with full powers to conduct diplomatic and financial negotiations." (For Bunau-Varilla, sitting on his money in New York, that title was not yet good enough.)

There was no doubt what the *junta* wanted: diplomatic recognition of the Republic of Panama. Roosevelt and Hay were willing to extend such courtesy, now that the entire width of the Isthmus had been secured. The delicate question was when. A prompt announcement might forestall any attempt by Colombia to reclaim the Isthmus with a much larger military force. Panama, organized and recognized, could legitimately ask for American aid in repelling "foreign" invaders—and seven American warships were on hand to comply. All the same, there was such a thing as indecent haste. Questions were being asked in British newspapers about Commander Hubbard's denial of transit rights to the *tiradores*.

Roosevelt did not feel the world as a whole would long deplore their repatriation to Barranquilla. All his readings in history and geography, all his thrusting Americanism, "every consideration of international morality and expediency," told him that after four hundred years of dreams and twenty years of planning, the Panama Canal's time had come. Colombia was clearly guilty of fatal insolence. Panama deserved the thanks—and support—of other self-determinant nations for her "most just and proper revolution."

Shortly before lunch, the Cabinet meeting broke up. Hay returned to the State Department and cabled a message to Consul Ehrman in Panama City.

THE PEOPLE OF PANAMA HAVE, BY AN APPARENTLY UNANIMOUS MOVEMENT, DISSOLVED THEIR POLITICAL CONNECTION WITH THE REPUBLIC OF COLOMBIA AND RESUMED THEIR INDEPENDENCE. WHEN YOU ARE SATISFIED THAT A DE FACTO GOVERNMENT, REPUBLICAN IN FORM, AND WITHOUT SUBSTANTIAL OPPOSITION FROM ITS OWN PEOPLE, HAS BEEN ESTABLISHED IN THE STATE OF PANAMA, YOU WILL ENTER INTO RELATIONS WITH IT.

The time was 12:51 P.M.; the infant republic had been in existence not quite sixty-seven hours.

⌐

ROOSEVELT ADJOURNED TO LUNCH. One of his guests was Oscar Straus, whose understanding of international law, commerce, and diplomacy increasingly impressed him. Musing aloud, Roosevelt wondered about the validity of the 1846 treaty, in that it had been contracted with New Granada. Did American obligations to an extinct federation still apply in 1903?

Straus suggested that the treaty was contracted only with the legitimate "holders" of the Isthmus. American rights related to the territory, which was unchangeable. "Our claim must be based upon what is known in law as 'a covenant running with the land.' "

Roosevelt seized upon the words with delight. That evening, an announcement of provisional recognition of Panama, issued by the Secretary of State, quoted Straus's dictum. Hay was careful to add the phrase *as lawyers say,* and equally careful to eschew any reference to himself. His first words were, "The action of the President in the Panama matter," and he identified Theodore Roosevelt no fewer than sixteen times in the next twenty paragraphs. "The imperative demands of the interests of civilization required him to put a stop . . . to the incessant civil contests and bickerings which have been for so many years the curse of Panama."

Professor John Bassett Moore was pleased to see some of his own language in the announcement, and sent Straus a note of mutual congratulation. "Perhaps, however, it is only a question . . . of the 'covenant running *away* with the land'!!"

CHAPTER 19

The Imagination of the Wicked

A man can be r-right an' be prisidint, but he can't
be both at th' same time.

AFTER TWENTY-TWO years in politics, Theodore Roosevelt was used to critical noise, but the uproar following the recognition of Panama threatened
even his robust eardrums. Loudest of all were the cries of Oswald Garrison
Villard in the New York *Evening Post*.

> This mad plunge of ours is simply and solely a vulgar and mercenary
> adventure, without a rag to cover its sordidness and shame. . . . At one
> stroke, President Roosevelt and Secretary Hay have thrown to the
> winds the principles for which this nation was ready to go to war in
> the past, and have committed the country to a policy which is ignoble
> beyond words.

If Villard meant the strictures of Abraham Lincoln against secession, Roosevelt could cite an earlier principle, fought for by George Washington. Panamanians now, as Americans then, were tired of paying taxes to a remote,
autocratic government that invested nothing in return. He would have
counted himself "criminal, as well as impotent," had he not defended the revolution. But a time to reply would come. For the moment, his protesters had
the floor.

In tones approaching libel, Villard denounced the "indecent haste" with
which Roosevelt had betrayed trust, "just for a handful of silver." Colombia
had not rated so much as a warning:

> It is the most ignominious thing we know of in the annals of American
> diplomacy. . . . And this blow below the belt is dealt by the vociferous
> champion of fair play! This overriding of the rights of the weaker is

the work of the advocate of "a square deal"! The preacher to bishops
has shown that, for him at least, private morality has no application to
public affairs. . . . If the President is careless of the national honor, and
ready at a word to launch us upon unknown seas, the duty of Congress is but the more imperative. Let this scandal be thrown open to
the public gaze.

Villard's attacks continued for several days, until even the doubtful demurred. "I rather hope you will continue to pitch in to Roosevelt," one reader
wrote, "[but] as a matter of constitutional and international law, he was fully
justified in all he did last week." Colombia had received ample warning—
from Panamanians, if not from Roosevelt. She had been too cowardly, or too
corrupt, to fight. Roosevelt was bound to recognize her usurper, as other
Presidents had accepted the obsolescence of New Granada. Nor could he be
blamed for moving quickly, along with Britain, France, and Germany: "Nations must strike when irons are hot."

Anti-imperialists, who had been starved of an issue since the end of the
Philippines war, would not be quieted. "Nothing that Alexander or Nero ever
did had a coarser touch of infamy," William Henry Thorpe wrote in *The
Globe*. "And all the depredations of England in Ireland, in Africa, or India
have been gentlemanly compared with this sleek and underhanded piece of
national bank robbery." The Chicago *Chronicle* worried about "the distrust
which we shall hereafter inspire among South and Central American countries." Homer Davenport, cartoonist for the *New York American,* sketched a
majestic eagle with a tiny, isthmus-shaped animal dangling from its claw.

However, 75 percent of the nation's more conservative (if less strident)
newspapers supported Roosevelt. "Colombia has simply got what she deserved," the *Pittsburgh Times* commented, in words echoed by many. The
Chicago Tribune agreed with John Hay that "the action of the President . . .
was the only course he could have taken in compliance with our treaty rights
and obligations." Roosevelt's new vision of the Isthmus, said the *Baltimore
American,* would "inure to the advantage of the whole world." Democratic
and independent editors vied with Republican ones for expressions of relief
and satisfaction, albeit qualified. "Even if the United States fomented the
revolution," the *Buffalo Express* remarked, "it acted in the interests of the
governed."

South American reactions turned out to be surprisingly muted, with fears
of "a foreign protectorate" in Panama tempered by pleasure at the prospect
of a new commercial age. Very few newspapers saw evidence of United States
involvement in the revolution. "The change is to be welcomed, no matter
how it has been brought about," said the Chilean *Times*. Even in Bogotá, *El
Relator* published a litany of Colombia's sins against her separated citizens:

We have converted the lords and masters of that territory into pariahs of their native soils. We have cut their rights and suppressed all their liberties. We have robbed them of the most precious faculty of a free people—that of electing their mandatories: their legislators, their judges.

In Europe, as in the United States, there was a preponderance of praise over dismay. *The Times* of London called Roosevelt's attitude "studiously correct," and expressed little sympathy for Colombia, "the most corrupt and retrograde republic in Central America—which is saying a good deal." Conservative newspapers in both Britain and France marveled that the legislators of Bogotá had tried to milk a treaty that would have brought one fifth of the world's trade to their shores. Only in Germany was fear expressed of Roosevelt the "master" expansionist. "He is the type of advancing Americanism, as clever as he is unscrupulous, as powerful as he is sly."

The President himself remained unruffled by all the fuss. A British visitor to the White House on 11 November found him absorbed in *Tittlebat Titmouse*.

<hr />

ON 13 NOVEMBER, a small man in brand-new diplomatic uniform paid a visit to the Blue Room. Secretary Hay presented him to Roosevelt as "His Excellency M. Philippe Bunau-Varilla, Envoy Extraordinary and Minister Plenipotentiary of the Republic of Panama." Bunau-Varilla bowed, handed over his credentials, and begged permission to read a short *discours* of his own composition. It owed its brevity to Hay, who had edited out many Gallic metaphors likely to threaten the President's composure. But Bunau-Varilla managed to mix a few more after Roosevelt joked, "What do you think, Mr. Minister, of those people who print that we have made the Revolution of Panama together?"

"It is necessary patiently to wait," Bunau-Varilla replied, "until the spring of the imagination of the wicked is dried up, and until truth dissipates the mist of mendacity."

Afterward, with Hay, Bunau-Varilla was all business. The United States must take advantage of his accreditation, as he would be unable to represent Panama for long. Already a delegation headed by Dr. Amador was reported to be en route to Washington for treaty "consultations." That could mean endless Hispanic haggling.

Hay understood. "I shall send it to you as soon as possible."

What Bunau-Varilla received, two days later, was a slightly altered version of the old Hay-Herrán Treaty, allowing for a ten-million-dollar indemnity and an annual rental of $250,000. Although these amounts were clearly fab-

298 • THEODORE REX

ulous to an impoverished little isthmian republic, the terms struck Bunau-Varilla as otherwise being not generous enough toward the United States. He wanted the quick approval of the United States Senate, and felt that he should add inducements, such as "a concession of sovereignty *en bloc.*" A presidential election year loomed; Democrats and anti-Roosevelt Republicans were looking for an opportunity to humiliate the Administration.

Working through the night, with only two hours' sleep, Bunau-Varilla sent Hay the next day a new protocol, markedly more in the interest of the United States. "Simply a suggestion to enable you to decide," he wrote. On 18 November, he received a return message: "Will you kindly call at my house at six o'clock today?"

The Secretary was unwontedly formal when Bunau-Varilla presented himself. "I have requested Your Excellency to be so good as to keep this appointment in order to sign, if it is agreeable to Your Excellency, the Treaty which will permit the construction of the Interoceanic Canal." He produced two beautifully typed copies, and waved aside "an insignificant question of terminology" in article 2. "If Your Excellency agrees to it, the Treaty will now be read, and we will then sign it."

Conscious that Dr. Amador might at any minute knock on Hay's door, Bunau-Varilla was quite willing to forgo the reading. He had not thought to bring a seal, so the Secretary offered him a choice of sealing rings. Bunau-Varilla chose one embossed with the Hay coat of arms. The clock stood at 6:40 P.M. Pens scratched across parchment. Wax melted on silk. Two oceans brimmed closer, ready to spill.

$\backsim$

BUNAU-VARILLA WAS at Sixth Street Station three hours later to greet the diplomatic delegation. "The Republic of Panama is henceforth under the protection of the United States," he announced as Dr. Amador stepped down, followed by Pablo Arosamena and Federico Boyd. "I have just signed the canal treaty."

Amador reeled with shock. Bunau-Varilla felt obliged to support him. "Cherish no illusion, Mr. Boyd, the negotiations are closed."

$\backsim$

THANKSGIVING APPROACHED WITH lowering skies and shortening days. But Capitol Hill was lit up again, weeks earlier than usual. The Fifty-eighth Congress had convened in special session, at Roosevelt's request.

That looked like the extent of its obedience, at least until its regular session began in December. The dragging, eighteen-month-old question of Cuban reciprocity, incredibly not yet resolved by last March's treaty approval, lacked the romantic appeal of "gunboat diplomacy" on the Spanish Main. Yet for political scientists, usually more interested in data than drama, there was much logistical fascination in the increased power of the House. Thanks to the census of 1900 and the election of 1902, a record apportionment of 386 representatives now crowded the lower chamber. One hundred and twenty were freshmen, and more than half of those were Democrats. But the Republican total was still large enough for the new Speaker to wield a formidable majority. Moving fast while Senate leaders took up the Panama treaty, Joseph Cannon played host to a stream of callers, lavishing them with large confidences and small cigars. "I believe in consultin' the boys," he said in the hayseed accent he liked to affect, "findin' out what most of 'em want and then goin' ahead and doin' it."

What "the boys" (i.e., Uncle Joe himself) wanted was to remind the Senate of his famous threat about "the right of the majority to rule." On 19 November, the House voted overwhelmingly in favor of a reciprocity bill for Cuba, based on the Senate's own treaty terms. Nothing remained but due process to make it law, whereupon the senatorial beet-sugar lobby maneuvered for adjournment, in order to mount a filibuster during the regular session.

Cannon pointed out that if two houses were needed to pass a bill, two houses were also needed to vote for adjournment. As far as he was concerned, the special session could run on through its statutory limit on 7 December. Senators from remote states were thus denied a Thanksgiving vacation, while the Speaker laughed at their discomfiture, ash peppering his vest.

MARK HANNA, who had been noticeably subdued since coming back to town, went to spend the holiday in New York, at the home of J. P. Morgan.

His uncharacteristic quietness was caused partly by exhaustion and partly by a new strain on his relations with the White House. The President had offended him by asking him to "manage" the Roosevelt campaign of 1904. If that was a ploy to head off any last chance of a Hanna candidacy, it was a remarkably obvious one, insulting to the Senator's intelligence. All Hanna wanted to do was enjoy the afterglow of his triumphant re-election. If the glow was intensified, for the moment, by electric lightbulbs spelling out HANNA FOR PRESIDENT in Cleveland and New York, he saw no harm in a little celebrity before making a final disclaimer. Roosevelt should know by now that he had no further ambitions. He was tired, he told George Cortelyou, of going to the White House with his hand over his heart "and swearing allegiance."

Morgan, no less perceptive than the President, talked throughout Thanksgiving dinner of Hanna's "duty to the country." He spoke not only for himself, but for all the Wall Street moneymen still recovering from the summer panic. The Pennsylvania Railroad's yards were crowded with empty cars. Morgan's pride, U.S. Steel, had reduced wages sharply. As a result, millworkers and boilermen from Rhode Island to California faced an impoverished winter. Miners were rioting in Colorado. Theodore Roosevelt—seeking with one hand to constrict capital and with the other to throttle organized labor—was to blame. Financiers mistrusted what Oswald Garrison Villard called Roosevelt's "terrifying habit of 'suddenness,' " demonstrated so recently in Panama. They looked to Hanna—a businessman as well as a Senator, an employer well respected by workingmen—to save the Republican Party from schism.

When the Senator remained silent, Morgan appealed to Mrs. Hanna. It would be "easy" to nominate her husband, he said, "if he would only give the word." She replied with feminine forthrightness: nothing would induce Mark to run.

This did not stop Hanna from joshing reporters afterward. "You can say what you damn please," he told them, grinning and thumping his cane.

⌐⊷

THE SENATOR'S CONTINUING conservative appeal exasperated Roosevelt, who thought it had been disposed of at Walla Walla. He saw trouble with Hanna in the months ahead, particularly with regard to party patronage. There was the vexed question of Dr. Crum, and a much newer one concerning Leonard Wood. Roosevelt wished to make his old Rough Rider commander a Major General at forty-three. Unfortunately, Wood had once jailed one of Hanna's political cronies for postal fraud in Cuba. The Senator was now bent on revenge. Nothing would better demonstate his renewed legislative clout than blocking an obvious piece of presidential favoritism.

In a last-minute effort to negotiate a truce, Roosevelt summoned Hanna to the White House on the evening of 4 December. They sat up till nearly midnight. Hanna won the right to say what he liked about Wood on the floor of the Senate, in exchange for permitting the appointment. Roosevelt also promised not to force the Senator to serve another term as Chairman of the Republican National Committee. In theory, this cleared Hanna to run for the presidency. But Roosevelt could see at close quarters that he was an exhausted man.

Another party elder who had to be wooed before the regular session began was the priestly George F. Hoar. Roosevelt needed him to bless the Administration's Panama policy as a sign to anti-imperialists (a dwindling but still powerful faction in Congress) that God had not been mocked on the Isthmus. He invited the Senator to take an advance look at his Third Annual Message. Hoar began to read the Panama section, then stood up in disgust. "I hope I may never live to see the day when the interests of my country are placed above its honor," he said, and walked out of the White House.

Roosevelt turned to his two closest aides for counsel, and got only wisecracks. "I think," Philander Knox teased, "it would be better to keep your action free from any taint of legality." Elihu Root was even more sarcastic. "You have shown that you were accused of seduction, and you have conclusively proved that you were guilty of rape."

Both men rallied behind him, however. Knox provided a written opinion, "Sovereignty over the Isthmus, as Affecting the Canal," which showed that the United States had legal grounds for her recognition of Panama. And Root came up with an ingenious argument to protect recess appointments from Speaker Cannon's forelengthening of Congress. Since the special session was by definition different from the regular, there must be a moment, no matter how infinitesimal, between them. This interval could be defined as a "constructive recess," occurring neither before nor after but precisely *at* noon on 7 December 1903. As long as the President specified that time and date on all his commission sheets, he could reappoint Dr. Crum without Senate approval. Senator Tillman might fight the case all the way to the Supreme Court; in the meantime, Charleston would keep its black collector.

It was counsel like this that Roosevelt dreaded losing in the new year. "Whenever I see you or Root under the weather," he told Knox, "I sympathize with Mr. Snodgrass when he beseeched Mr. Winkle for his sake not to drown."

⌒

I AM ENABLED TO lay before the Senate a treaty providing for the building of the Canal across the Isthmus of Panama.

The section of the President's Message that George Hoar had bridled at was read aloud to Congress on 7 December. Roosevelt wrote with evident confidence that Hoar's colleagues would ratify the Hay–Bunau-Varilla Treaty, already endorsed (albeit angrily and reluctantly) by the Panamanian government.

He reviewed United States–Colombian relations since 1846, showing how successive secretaries of state had interpreted the old Treaty of New Granada, always in the interest of free, neutral transit across the Isthmus. He quoted Lewis Cass: "Sovereignty has its duties as well as its rights, and none of these local governments [should] be permitted, in a spirit of Eastern isolation, to close the gates of intercourse on the great highways of the world." With no hint of irony, he also quoted William Henry Seward on the need of the United States to "maintain a perfect neutrality" in connection with political disturbances south of the border. He cited Attorney General James Speed's opinion that Washington was obliged to defend the Isthmus "against other and foreign governments."

For more than half a century, the United States had behaved honorably toward Colombians—favoring them, indeed, by electing not to dig in Nicaragua, and in drawing up the first canal treaty at their request. The

Colombians had then repudiated it in such a manner as to make plain that "not the scantiest hope remained of ever getting a satisfactory treaty from them." As a result, the people of Panama had risen "literally as one man."

"Yes, and the one man was Roosevelt," said Senator Edward Carmack.

The President proceeded with his usual list of local riots and rebellions since 1850. He noted that on ten occasions—four times at Colombia's request—American soldiers had been obliged to protect transit, life, and property. He scornfully quoted yet another request, just received, for the United States to crush the Panamanian revolution, so that President Marroquín could declare martial law and approve the old treaty "by decree."

> Under such circumstances the government of the United States would have been guilty of folly and weakness, amounting in their sum to a crime against the nation, had it acted otherwise than it did when the revolution of November 3 last took place in Panama. This great enterprise of building the interoceanic canal cannot be held up to gratify the whims, or . . . the even more sinister and evil peculiarities, of people who, though they dwell afar off, yet, against the wish of the actual dwellers on the Isthmus, assert an unreal supremacy over the territory. The possession of a territory fraught with such peculiar capacities as the Isthmus in question carries with it obligations to mankind. The course of events has shown that this canal cannot be built by private enterprise, or by any other nation than our own; therefore it must be built by the United States.

The comments of congressmen afterward suggested that they were waiting to see how the American people reacted to the President's Message. "I don't know what's in it," said Representative William P. Hepburn of Iowa, dodging reporters.

Within a few hours, a largely favorable wind of opinion had begun to blow, and both parties adjusted sail. Senator Hoar alone refused to join his Republican colleagues in supporting the Hay–Bunau-Varilla Treaty. He cited the recent remark of another former Secretary of State, Richard Olney: "For the first time in my life I have to confess that I am ashamed of my country."

Roosevelt, congenitally unable to question the rightness of his own decisions, did not understand what Hoar and other moralists meant when they talked of "conscience" in foreign-policy making. If conscience was something more lasting than emotion, more flexible than intellect, he could do without it. He did not regret what he had done, because it was done. Second thoughts were like grief; they inhibited the vital onrush of life, of the world's work. He only knew that opportunity—Senator Ingalls's "master of human destinies"—had knocked unbidden at his gate:

It is the hour of fate,
And they who follow me reach every state
Mortals desire, and conquer every foe,
Save death . . .

"In this Panama business," Roosevelt exploded to his son Ted, "the *Evening Post* and the entire fool mugwump crowd have fairly suffered from hysterics, and a goodly number of Senators, even of my own party, have shown about as much backbone as so many angleworms." Quick to emasculate his critics, he dismissed the liberals of New York and Massachusetts as "a small body of shrill eunuchs."

He kept such expressions private, yet the violence of his language betrayed fear that the eunuchs would revive his old reputation for impulsiveness. Since the *Northern Securities* suit, he had worked hard to persuade party professionals that he was both conservative and cautious. His impartiality in the coal strike, his quiet management of the Venezuela crisis, his voluntary abandonment of antitrust activities, his insistence on the open shop in government—these were hardly the policies of a radical. Yet here was Villard still berating him as "a rash young man," and a Wall Street consortium pledging one million dollars to make Mark Hanna President of the United States.

The Republican National Committee was about to meet in Washington to make its first plans for 1904; then Philander Knox and attorneys representing the Northern Securities Corporation were to present their final arguments before the Supreme Court. Should either of these confrontations embarrass the Administration, Roosevelt's hopes of another term could crash.

⟨⟩

ON 9 DECEMBER, Walter Wellman was admitted to the Executive Office and given a major scoop. He reported it the next day, in front-page articles in the Philadelphia *Press* and Chicago *Record-Herald*:

> *Washington, Dec. 9*—President Roosevelt has refused to make peace with the trust and railway corporation leaders of New York. They approached the President with an offer to withdraw their opposition to him if he would give them certain assurances as to his future course. The President declined point-blank. Angered by this rejection . . . the big financiers started a last desperate movement designed to bring Senator Hanna forward as a candidate for the Republican nomination for President. This, too has failed. Mr. Hanna is not willing to become a candidate with the backing of Wall Street and the support of the Lily Whites of the South. These important disclosures, *which I am able to*

make on the highest authority, explain much that has been going on above and beneath the surface during the past month.

Wellman said that the President's importuners had represented J. P. Morgan, E. H. Harriman, James J. Hill, and "the Rockefeller-Gould combination." They were afraid he was a warmonger as well as a trustbuster: "He might wreck the country any morning before breakfast." Hanna, fortunately, was no alarmist. As for Roosevelt and Administration leaders, "they do not believe the judgment and level-headed common sense of the American people can be upset by such methods."

The article, reprinted widely, was the talk of Washington on 11 December, when fifty-two Republican bosses convened at the Arlington Hotel. Hanna escorted them to the Green Room of the White House after lunch. "Mr. President, I have the honor to present *en masse* the members of the Republican National Committee."

He and Roosevelt stood side by side, with a mirror behind them, facing a semicircle of respectful faces. The committeemen could see the bald back of Hanna's head in the glass, his arthritic stoop beside the President's bursting virility. There was an awkward pause.

HANNA	You had better pass around the room, Mr. President, and shake hands with each one.
ROOSEVELT	All right, I was just wondering which was the best way to get at them.
HANNA	You will have no trouble. . . . They are all anxious to see you.
ROOSEVELT	(*bowing*) I have sat at the feet of Gamaliel.

Laughter warmed the room as he made his circuit.

Two days later, the committee came out of conference and expressed almost unanimous support for the President. As an endorsement, it was neither binding nor, indeed, expressed with any particular enthusiasm. But clearly Gamaliel had laid down his staff.

❦

ON 14 DECEMBER, Knox put on a brilliant performance before the Supreme Court. Edith Roosevelt was there to watch and listen for her husband, along with Lodge, Spooner, and Moody. The little Attorney General spoke calmly, piling premise upon premise with plump smacks of fist into palm. He argued that any obstruction to interstate commerce, "whether it be a sandbar, a mob, or a monopoly," could and should be removed by the government. The Northern Securities Company was obstructive in that it had the effect, if not the technical title, of a "trustee arrangement" uncontrollable by individual states. Although the Justices listened impassively (Oliver Wendell Holmes

"MR. PRESIDENT, I HAVE THE HONOR TO PRESENT . . ."
Mark Hanna and members of the Republican National Committee, 11 December 1903

slouching, silky-mustached, on the extreme left of the Bench), most observers felt that Knox's argument was unanswerable.

Roosevelt was overjoyed. This boded well for a favorable decision in the spring. In other good news, Nicaragua became the first Latin American nation to recognize Panama. All the world's major powers had already done so except Britain and Japan, and their announcements were due at any moment.

Further presents crammed his presidential stocking. The Senate voted for Cuban reciprocity, 57 to 8. G. P. Putnam's Sons confirmed a thirty-thousand-dollar contract for the publication of a new edition of *The Works of*

Theodore Roosevelt in fourteen volumes. Another thirty thousand dollars was deposited to his account in New York as the bequest of a deceased uncle. Although the most cash the President generally saw was what Edith put in his pocket, he understood that in his forty-sixth year, he was beginning to be rich.

Better than money, his greatest dream in life seemed more and more realizable. According to the New York *Herald,* twenty-three states had already pledged him 496 votes at next June's Republican National Convention— eleven more than he needed to be nominated. And ten months remained for him to persuade the American people that he was no longer "His Accidency," but a substantial statesman deserving their vote of confidence.

THE SEVENTEENTH OF December 1903 was a workday much like any other for Roosevelt. He faced, at carefully timed intervals through the morning, a newspaper owner from upstate New York, a counsel to the Hague tribunal, a consul from Shanghai, an aspirant postmaster from Missouri, an old hayseed from Oklahoma, the secretary of the Postal Progress League, the Attorney General of the United States, two doctors, three reverends, six senators, fifteen railway inspectors, and uncounted congressmen. At one o'clock, he was to conduct his usual barbershop *levée.* Root, Lodge, and Cortelyou were scheduled to join him for lunch, along with Winthrop Murray Crane. There would be precious little time for exercise in the afternoon, since he had bills to sign and letters to dictate, and appointments every hour until six o'clock. Then he must play bear with Archie and Quentin, spend some time with Edith, and dress for the Cabinet dinner. And the Odells and Mellens would be staying the night.

While Roosevelt talked to the consul from Shanghai, two brothers on a windswept beach in North Carolina shook hands. Then one of them lay down beside some covered ribs in front of a propeller motor. It sparked to life. Tremulous and spindly, a matchbox of spars and muslin accelerated along a rail, and stepped into the air. Its wings rippled on an invisible swell, like wet leaves on water. The swell surged to ten feet, then fifteen feet, before gently subsiding. Ecstatic, the flying machine kicked off and soared, again and again and again.

CHAPTER 20

Intrigue and Striving and Change

Whin he does anny talkin'—which he sometimes does—he talks at th' man in front iv him. Ye don't hear him hollerin' at posterity. Posterity don't begin to vote till after th' polls close.

HENRY ADAMS ATTENDED Roosevelt's annual Diplomatic Reception on 7 January 1904, and was disturbed by signs of a developing autocracy—to say nothing of a nervous system that seemed to be beyond self-discipline. The President accosted him with a war whoop and ordered him upstairs for supper:

> I was stuffed into place at the imperial table, opposite Joe Chamberlain's daughter. . . . Root sat at the end of the table between us. . . . We were straws in Niagara. Never have I had an hour of worse social *malaise*. We were overwhelmed in a torrent of oratory, and at last I heard only the repetition of I-I-I—attached to indiscretions greater than one another until only the British female seemed to survive. How Root stands this sort of thing I do not know, for it is mortifying beyond even drunkenness. The worst of it is that it is mere cerebral excitement, of normal, or at least habitual, nature. It has not the excuse of champagne, the wild talk about everything—Panama, Russia, Germany, England, and whatever else suggested itself—belonged not to the bar-room but the asylum. . . . When I was let out and got to bed, I was a broken man.

Another veteran of quieter times visited Washington that month and found that it was no longer the genteel city he remembered. "I am glad to leave," Charles G. Dawes wrote in his diary, after seeing both Mark Hanna and the President. "The air is full of intrigue and striving and change."

ON THE AFTERNOON of 27 January, Roosevelt sent a White House carriage and a company of cavalry to Sixth Street Station. Crowds collected along Pennsylvania Avenue. Such trappings usually heralded a visiting head of state, although none had been announced. When the procession clattered and jingled back downtown, the carriage rode much lower on its springs. Inside sat an enormously corpulent man of forty-six, his jowls tanned and his mustache bleached by years of Pacific sun. He smiled with enchanting sweetness, waving a cushioned palm, his pale blue eyes squeezed between chuckling rolls of fat. He was the retiring Governor of the Philippines, and now the successor to Elihu Root as Secretary of War: William Howard ("Big Bill") Taft.

Merely to look at him was to be warmed and impressed. Taft had none of Root's austerity or Roosevelt's restless energy. He lounged comfortably at any angle, and spoke calmly in all circumstances. At 330 pounds, he was periodically drowsy from too much food. Yet he was not lazy; once he got under way, he had the ponderous momentum of an elephant. His gestures were slow, but full of power. He bore with no complaint huge loads of work, and produced commensurately. Whether he dictated a document or wrote it by hand, the words flowed in their hundreds and thousands, bland but never specious, unsparkling yet clear. His was not the vocabulary of a calculating politician. Taft wrote, thought, and acted like a judge.

The Supreme Court was his admitted dream. "As far back as I can remember, I believe my ambitions were of a judicial cast," he told a reporter, after checking into the Arlington Hotel. He did not mention that Roosevelt had twice offered him a seat on the Bench, and that he had declined only out of a sense of "duty" in the Philippines. Still less would the elephant allow that Mrs. Taft (perched small and determined in his howdah) was nudging him in another direction.

The reporter, Kate Carew of the New York *World,* asked, "Which would you rather be, Chief Justice of the United States, or President of the United States?"

Taft quaked with self-protective laughter. "Oh, ho, ho! Of course I couldn't answer that question." He flushed with merriment, while she thought, *He must have been a very pink and white baby.*

"Who do you suppose," Miss Carew pursued, when the heavings subsided, "will be the Republican candidate for President this year?"

"PRESIDENT THEODORE ROOSEVELT!" Taft boomed, puffing out his cheeks.

"And who in 1908?"

"Oh," he said, smiling, "that is too far ahead."

"But I had read somewhere that perhaps you would be."

Taft began to talk about golf.

TWO DAYS LATER, the outgoing Secretary of War attended his last Cabinet meeting. He appeared to be struggling with his composure as Roosevelt thanked him for staying on until Taft could relieve him. Root had a public reputation of being "the coldest proposition that ever came down the pike." But friends knew the warmth of his bottled-up emotions and the precision of his wit, which Owen Wister nicely described as "humor in ambush." The crack about the President's culpability for "rape" was already part of Administration lore, as was the cable Root had sent to Manila, after hearing that Taft had taken a twenty-five-mile ride: HOW IS THE HORSE?

Roosevelt rambled on affectionately until Root stood up, unable to bear more. He crossed to Taft's left, symbolically shedding power. "Mr. President," he said. His eyes filled, and he stopped.

It was the little parlor in Buffalo all over again. Then, however, Root had been taking charge of a young and nervous beneficiary. Now he was quitting a leader who could do without him. "I thank you for what you have been good enough to say, Mr. President. This, of course, has been the great chapter in my life. . . ." He could not go on. "You know, sir, what I would say."

The following evening, Root attended a Gridiron Club dinner in his honor at the Arlington. Roosevelt was there, along with the full Cabinet; even Senator Hanna limped downstairs. A performance group threw satiric barbs. Taft (giggling and guffawing, prodigiously duplicated in mirrors around the room) was warned that he might catch cold in Root's chilly aura. If so, he must stand close when Mark Hanna finally swore allegiance to Theodore Roosevelt. The President's glow of joy would thaw him.

Roosevelt and Hanna, separated by white linen and bowls of roses, laughed with the rest. But the latter looked far from happy. He ate and drank nothing, and there were dark smudges under his eyes.

"How is your health, Senator?" somebody asked.

"Not good."

HANNA DID NOT leave his bed the next morning, Sunday, nor on Monday, the first of February. The jingling cavalrymen rode down the avenue again, below his windows, escorting Elihu Root to the station. Taft was sworn in. An order went out for an extra large Cabinet chair to be built for the new Secretary.

Day followed upon icy day. It had been the whitest winter in decades; Washington lay locked under a glaze of hard snow. Children skated on the streets. Alice Roosevelt and her friend Marguerite Cassini went bobsledding together and competed for the attentions of Congressman Nicholas Longworth, rich, youngish, and sexily balding.

Something about Alice's laugh, when she asked if "Nick" had ever proposed, made Marguerite say, "Yes, he has." The two girls began to see less of each other.

Roosevelt took a new course of *jujitsu,* lunched with Buffalo Bill, and sent a long tirade against the demoralization of scientific historiography to his latest intellectual "playmate," Sir George Otto Trevelyan. He heard with relief that Mrs. Cox, the black postmaster of Indianola, Mississippi, had decided not to seek another term. In her place, he quietly appointed a white man.

The newspapers reported that Elihu Root had made a powerful speech to an audience of New York Republicans, warning them that Theodore Roosevelt was "not safe":

> He is not safe for the men who wish to prosecute selfish schemes for the public's detriment. He is not safe for the men who wish the Government conducted with greater reference to campaign contributions than to the public good. [*Applause*] He is not safe for the men who wish to drag the President of the United States into a corner and make whispered arrangements. . . . I say that he has been, during these years since President McKinley's death, the greatest conservative force for the protection of property and our institutions in the city of Washington.

When Root used the adjective *conservative,* conservatives listened. Private word came that Wall Street opposition was at last diminishing. "It has become almost flat for me to express to you my realization of all you have done for me," the President wrote Root.

Late on the evening of 4 February, George Cortelyou came in with a shock bulletin. Senator Hanna had been diagnosed with typhoid fever. Roosevelt was at the Arlington Hotel well before nine the next morning. Doctors barred entry to the sickroom, but he stayed ten minutes with Mrs. Hanna. The afternoon papers noted his pilgrimage, as did Hanna, who scrawled a trembly note:

> *My dear Mr. President:*
> *You touched a tender spot old man when you call personaly [sic] to inquire after this a.m. I may be worse before I can be better But all the same such "drops" of kindness are good for a fellow*
>
> > *Sincerely Yours*
> > *M.A. Hanna*
> > *Friday PM*

The Senator lay comatose for several days, then surprised Mrs. Hanna by reaching for her hand. "Old lady," he said, "you and I are on the home stretch."

HALF A WORLD AWAY, the Far East exploded into war. For months, State Department officials had known that Japan would not long tolerate Russia's expansionism in Manchuria and her designs on Korea. However, even John Hay was surprised by the ferocity and speed of the first attack, on 8 February. Dispatches confirmed that Admiral Heihachiro Togo had virtually annihilated the Russian Oriental fleet in a single swoop on Port Arthur. On the ninth, reports of further naval attacks followed like claps of thunder. In under twelve hours, Russia's two biggest battleships were sunk, another seriously damaged, and four cruisers disabled or destroyed. Japan was now the superior power in the Yellow Sea. Minister Kogoro Takahira could hardly conceal his elation as he delivered the Mikado's proclamation of war to Hay. On 11 February, Roosevelt announced that the United States would remain neutral.

Count Cassini, the Russian Ambassador, was not consoled by Hay's expressions of sympathy. He knew that the President personally favored Japan. Marguerite and Alice became even more estranged.

UNCONSCIOUS, MARK HANNA drifted toward death. He had never paid much attention to the world at large. Panama was merely a crossroads of American commerce, the oceans but highways for American ships. The cosmopolitan curiosity of a Theodore Roosevelt (currently reading a study of Indo-European ethnicity, in Italian) was beyond him. All he had learned in life was that industry created wealth, and wealth subsidized good government. He had not done badly in either field; he had made seven million dollars, and a President of the United States.

Hanna's horizon contracted. He knew nothing of the vigilants in the lobby below, the constantly shrilling telephone booth, the letter from Roosevelt: "May you soon be with us again, old fellow, as strong in body and as vigorous in your leadership as ever."

Inert on the pillow, he looked as formidable as ever, porcine features firm, skin tanned from oxygen treatment. But in the small hours of Monday the fifteenth his heart began to fail. Doctors worked all morning to stimulate life. They blew ether up his nose, poured champagne and whiskey and nitroglycerine down his throat, and pumped brandy into his abdomen in eight-ounce shots. Washington's political activity slowed to a halt. Congressmen quit their desks and joined the crowd in the Arlington lobby. At 3:00 P.M., when Roosevelt walked over again from the White House, Hanna's pulse rate was scarcely perceptible. It fluttered for three and a half more hours, then stopped.

Governors, generals, Cabinet officers, and senators pressed sobbing out of the lobby into the freezing night. Even Nelson Aldrich cried, his face contorted with sorrow.

ON 23 FEBRUARY, after nine weeks of debate, the Panama Canal Treaty came up for ratification. By now, most of the world agreed with John Hay that Roosevelt had followed a "perfectly regular course" in recognizing Panama. The little republic had just constituted herself into a tripartite democracy, and elected Manuel Amador as its first President. Encouraged by these developments, and by a positive legal argument by Elihu Root published in that morning's newspapers, the Senate voted in favor of the treaty, 66 to 14.

Roosevelt and his successors were given power "in perpetuity" over the Canal Zone, ten miles wide, dividing Panama into two provinces and extending three miles out to sea each way. The power, though not technically absolute, was what "the United States would possess and exercise *if it were the sovereign of the territory* . . . to the entire exclusion of the exercise by the Republic of Panama of any such sovereign rights, power or authority."

It was dread of such provisions that had caused old Amador to totter in Bunau-Varilla's arms. The original Hay-Herrán Treaty had called for a ninety-nine-year renewable lease and a much narrower Canal Zone. But Bunau-Varilla had been so anxious to achieve ratification that Panamanians already felt he had mortgaged their future. Instead of becoming a hero of the people he had helped liberate, he incurred their lasting resentment.

Bunau-Varilla triumphantly resigned as Panamanian Minister, stating that he would accept no salary for his services. It was enough that the Great Idea could now be realized, "for the honor of Panama and for the glory of France and of the United States."

Few Americans imagined, as Secretary Shaw prepared to disburse ten million dollars as down payment on the Zone (J. P. Morgan & Co., agents), that Amador could be anything but pleased.

⟨⦁⟩

AN ENORMOUS MAP in the White House enabled Roosevelt to keep pace with the Russo-Japanese War. He pinned it with little flags to show the movement of forces ("Japan is playing our game"), browsed weekly bulletins from the Office of Naval Intelligence, and wondered if he might not have to mediate a peace settlement one day. At present, the belligerents simply wanted to destroy each other. Japan, flush with naval success, was ready for a land battle. Russia would soon strike back. The world waited.

Cecil Spring Rice, now Secretary of the British Embassy in St. Petersburg, wrote to say that Russia was obsessed with expanding eastward as well as westward. "There has been nothing like it since Tamurlane. The whole of Asia and half Europe!" He foresaw problems with Muslims one day, but who could ultimately resist a Bear so big, so blindly driven?

Roosevelt, replying, looked instead to a victorious Japan as the "great new force" in the Far East. Should Korea and China proceed to develop themselves along Japanese lines, "there will result a real shifting of the center of equilibrium as far as the white races are concerned." He was philosophical about this. "If new nations come to power . . . the attitude of we who speak English should be one of ready recognition of the rights of the newcomers, of desire to avoid giving them just offense, and at the same time of preparedness in body and in mind to hold our own if our interests are menaced."

⎯⌒⎯

ON MONDAY, 14 MARCH, both Wall Street and the White House opened nervously for business. The Supreme Court was expected during the course of the day to announce its decision in *U.S. v. Northern Securities*. Reports were that the decision would be "very drastic," perhaps worse for railroad interests than last year's lower-court ruling.

"All I can do is hope," Roosevelt told friends.

Of one Justice, at least, he could be sure. Oliver Wendell Holmes, Jr., had so far proved a grateful supporter of Administration policies. During the Alaska boundary negotiations in London, Holmes had worked discreetly to soothe British sensibilities riled by the President's official commissioners. He called at the White House more often and less formally than any other Justice, and was quite capable of teasing Roosevelt for self-righteousness: "The King, of course, can do no wrong."

Justice William Rufus Day, Roosevelt's second appointee to the Bench (in place of the wistful Taft), was a self-effacing little man of mild liberal tendencies. He, too, could be relied on. Justice David J. Brewer certainly could not, being an ultraconservative, patrician ideologue. The other Republicans on the Bench were less predictable. Noisy old John Marshall Harlan ("the last of the tobacco-spitting judges," Holmes fondly called him) was a libertarian and a maverick. He had been against monopoly in the past, dissenting in *U.S. v. E. C. Knight*, but was wary of too much federal power. Justice Henry Brown was such a cold-blooded legal theorist, analyzing the statute books as if they were so many volumes of algebra, that he was capable of finding that x equaled y in the face of unanimous sentiment for z. Justice Joseph McKenna was an austere plodder, ill trained in law, and crotchety on issues he could not understand.

On the Democratic side, Chief Justice Melville W. Fuller and Justices Rufus Peckham and Edward D. White were conservatives of uncertain persuasion. They seemed likely to vote against the government—although Roosevelt had hopes of the affable White.

By noon, the Court Chamber in the Capitol was crowded with representatives of all three government branches. Attorney General Knox sat directly in front of the bench, exuding his usual porcelain impassivity. William Howard Taft sprawled nearby, a beached whale. Senators Spooner and Lodge conferred in low voices at the bar. "*Oyez, oyez!*" the clerk cried. Silence fell as nine Justices filed in, silk robes rustling. The attendance of Justice Brown, who was ill, emphasized the importance of the proceedings.

Chief Justice Fuller seated himself and waited until the chamber had settled. Two dozen reporters standing at the back of the chamber craned to see which way his white head would swivel. He turned to the right, and nodded at Oliver Wendell Holmes.

Holmes proceeded to read, in his clear, sharp voice, a decree reversal of no popular interest whatever. The audience slumped disappointedly. After about five minutes, silence fell again. Fuller gave a second nod, and Justice Harlan announced, "Case Number 277." Instantly there was a scurrying of shoes, as messengers rushed off to alert congressmen that *Northern Securities* was "up." Within minutes, the corridor was jammed all the way to the Rotunda.

"Let us see what are the facts disclosed by the record," Harlan began. He showed how in 1901 "defendant Hill" and "defendant Morgan" had combined the Great Northern and Northern Pacific railroads into a holding company headquartered in New Jersey—thus making the interests of all stockholders identical. "No scheme or device could more certainly come within the words of the [Sherman] Act . . . or could more effectively and certainly suppress free competition." Harlan's strong, measured voice continued to rise and fall, but evidently the Administration had won its case. The messengers scurried off again, this time to telegraph and telephone offices. Harlan was still reading when they got back. He did not reach his summation until twenty past one: "The judgment of the Court is that the decree below be, and hereby is, affirmed."

Cables flashed across the country: NORTHERN SECURITIES DECISION AFFIRMED. It was five minutes before someone thought to telephone the President, who was just sitting down to lunch with John Hay. Roosevelt was overjoyed, but declined to comment. William Loeb told reporters that the President felt the victory belonged to Knox.

The dimensions of that victory were still unclear. Back in court, Justice Brewer struck an encouraging note as he concurred with the decision, then a discouraging one as he rejected Harlan's opinion. But he offered another of his own, proposing a "rule of reason" that would prevent wholesale antitrust proclamations. Justices Day, Brown, and McKenna joined the majority; Fuller, Peckham, and White opposed, making the verdict so far five against three. Only one vote more was needed to make Roosevelt's victory decisive.

Justice Holmes dissented.

"Great cases," he lectured the stupefied audience, "like hard cases, make bad law. For great cases are called great, not by reason of their real importance in shaping the law of the future, but because of some accident of immediate overwhelming interest which appeals to the feelings and distorts the judgment."

He seemed to be implying that an "accident of immediate overwhelming interest" named Theodore Roosevelt had made an emotional issue of *Northern Securities,* and was exaggerating its legal significance.

> The statute of which we have to find the meaning is a criminal statute . . . of a very sweeping and general character. It hits "every" contract or combination of the prohibited sort, great or small, and "every" person who shall monopolize or attempt to monopolize, the sense of the act, "any part" of the trade or commerce among the several states. There is a natual inclination to assume that it was directed against certain great combinations and to read it in that light. It does not say so. On the contrary, it says "every," and "any part." Still was it directed specially against railroads. . . .
>
> If the act before us is to be carried out according to what seems to me to be the logic of the argument for the Government, which I do not believe that it will be, I can see no part of the conduct of life with which on similar principles Congress might not interfere [and] . . . hardly any transaction concerning commerce between the states that may not be made a crime by the finding of a jury or a court.

Holmes pointed out that the Sherman Act forbade only combinations in restraint of trade, not combinations in restraint of competition. He saw no evidence that the Northern Securities Company had "attempted to monopolize some portion of the trade or commerce of the realm," nor had it discriminated against "strangers" to its charter. He rejected Knox's plea that mere power to discriminate was as culpable as discrimination itself. What was monopoly anyway? A single railroad running down a narrow valley could be said to monopolize local traffic. "Yet I suppose," Holmes scoffed, "no one would say the statute forbids a combination of men into a corporation to build and run such a railroad in the United States." Neither could the sheer size of Northern Securities be equated with monopoly. "Size has nothing to do with the matter."

The Justice concluded with a sarcastic reference to the narrowness of today's verdict.

> I am happy to know that only a minority of my brethren adopt an interpretation of the [Sherman] Law which in my opinion would make eternal the *bellum omnium contra omnes,* and disintegrate society so far as it could into individual atoms. If that were its intent I should regard calling such a law a regulation of commerce as a mere pretense. It would be an attempt to reorganize society. I am not concerned with the wisdom of such an attempt, but I believe that Congress was not entrusted by the Constitution with the power to make it, and I am deeply persuaded that it has not tried.

So by a margin of just one concurring vote, case number 277 sank to the footnotes of history.

⌐⌐

JOHN HAY, who personally disapproved of antitrust actions, was struck by the bitterness of the President's remarks about Holmes in the days following. "I could carve out of a banana a judge with more backbone than that," Roosevelt raged. Holmes had not behaved like "a party man, a constructive statesman." For a while it seemed that the Justice was going to become *persona non grata* at the White House, but Roosevelt's sudden storms were short. "I have such confidence in his great heartedness," Holmes wrote a friend, "that I don't expect for a moment that after he has had time to cool down it will affect our relations."

Knox and Taft joined in lamenting the closeness of the decision. Popularly, however, it was perceived as a big victory for democracy over monopoly. Nine out of ten national newspapers congratulated the President. The case both dramatized and demonstrated the latent strength of the Sherman Act. As the New York *Evening Post* remarked, the fundamental question of *Northern Securities v. U.S.*—to what extent might combination freely proceed?—was answered: not much, without popular approval. "Surely the most far-reaching benefit of the decision is the vindication of national control."

The New York *World* agreed, but worried about placing such control in the hands of Theodore Roosevelt. He had already broadened the use of executive power in labor mediation, in foreign policy, and in federal patronage. Now he had dissolved the world's second-largest trust. "Imagine the Demagogue as President, armed with all the legitimate power of an office grown greater than man had dreamed was possible . . . ! He is Everything. He is Power. He is Patronage. He is Privilege."

The three men most affected by the decision reacted with surprising equanimity. J. P. Morgan puffed serenely on a cigar, smiled, and waggled his great head at reporters. E. H. Harriman turned defeat into victory by suing for his old Northern Pacific stock, at a huge profit. James J. Hill put on a brave public face, saying, "The three railroads are still there, earning good money." Only in private was he critical of the President as an aspirant king, surrounded by "gilded flunkies."

Roosevelt persuaded himself that the case had ended happily, in spite of Justice Holmes's dissent. If he had not achieved the historic review he dreamed of, he had won a temporal accord that redressed the balance between government and free enterprise. Washington resounded with praise, and predictions of four more Rooseveltian years. "As far as I can see," Joseph Bucklin Bishop wrote in the *Commercial Advertiser,* "there is no need of an election."

⌐⌐

BY 1 APRIL, Washington was efflorescent with cherry blossom. A million and a quarter new bulbs splotched parks and roadsides. To Roosevelt, who since Groundhog Day had been hopefully snapping twigs for signs of sap, the warming sunshine felt especially pleasant. Mrs. J. Borden Harriman, remembering him as a boy, found him boylike still, "the embodiment of spring . . . bubbling with life and hope." An Administration bill to set up American government in the Panama Canal Zone was set for passage, and the nation's economy was improving. So were his *jujitsu* skills. Indeed, he had just shown how the latter could be adapted to politics, by grabbing a pension measure right out of the hands of Congress and flipping it into an executive order of his own. Veterans now found that they were eligible for benefits at the early age of sixty-two, and their gratitude was sure to translate into a huge number of votes in November.

As always when the President was happy, his happiness touched those around him. "He is a very sweet and natural man and a very trusting man," William Howard Taft wrote. ". . . I am growing to be very fond of him."

Even so, Roosevelt's bright spring was not entirely cloudless. William Randolph Hearst seemed intent on a populist campaign for the presidency. Meanwhile, Old Guard Republicans were insisting that lanky, awful Charles W. ("Icicle") Fairbanks be nominated for Vice President. He was the senior Senator from Indiana, a tireless speaker, and Wall Street's darling. "Who in the name of Heaven else is there?" Roosevelt asked, not expecting any answer.

A long-simmering foreign-policy crisis also threatened to embarrass him, at a time when he did not want any more accusations of "gunboat diplomacy." It was virtually a repeat of the Venezuelan affair of 1902–1903, transposed to the Dominican Republic. Again, an impoverished Caribbean nation could not pay its debts; again, Germany was an impatient creditor; again, the United States Navy had conducted "exercises" off Isla de Culebra, in a choreographed evocation of the Monroe Doctrine. So far, Wilhelm II had sent in no warships—only a fulsome letter to Roosevelt, unfortunately not reproducible at the Republican National Convention:

> Your unlimited power for work, dauntless energy of purpose, pureness of motives moving towards the highest ideals, this all crowned by an iron will, form qualities which elicit the highest admiration from everybody over here. They are the characteristics of a "man," and as such most sympathetic to me. The 20th century is sadly in want of men of your stamp at the head of great nations. . . . Thank Heaven, the Anglo-Saxon Germanic Race is still able to produce such a specimen. You must accept it as a fact that your figure has moved to the foreground of the world, and that men's minds are intensely occupied by you.

"As always when the President was happy,
his happiness touched those around him."
Theodore and Edith Roosevelt receiving at a White House garden party

The Kaiser could yet turn nasty if Roosevelt did not make good his own
Corollary to the Monroe Doctrine, and place Santo Domingo under American receivership. Juan Franco Sanchez, the Dominican Minister of Foreign
Affairs, was in Washington practically begging for annexation. Roosevelt saw
political problems if he agreed. Any new protectorate, coinciding with his acquisition of the Canal Zone, was likely to reactivate the pesky Anti-
Imperialist League, and give the Democrats a major campaign issue. Cuba
was *libre* and the Philippines, thanks to Taft, pretty well pacified; his own
youthful appetite for empire was gone.

He searched for a simile strong enough to express his distaste for another insular possession: "I have about the same desire to annex it as a gorged boa constrictor might have to swallow a porcupine wrong end to."

⌒

TWO MONTHS AFTER Mark Hanna's death, the question of who should be the new chairman of the Republican National Committee had not been resolved. Elihu Root, prospering hugely as a Wall Street attorney, declined to serve. Three other candidates pleaded ill health: Henry Clay Payne of Wisconsin, Winthrop Murray Crane of Massachusetts, and the septuagenarian Cornelius N. Bliss of New York. The last, a veteran of McKinley's first Cabinet, had such excellent corporate connections, not to mention "stainless honor and purity," that Roosevelt urged him to reconsider. Bliss said he would think about it.

In the meantime, the President felt free to set his own Republican agenda, in a series of indiscretions calculated to heave fresh sod on Hanna's grave. He preached conservation to the National Wholesale Lumber Dealers' Association, and political morality to Republican professionals. He meddled in the gubernatorial politics of New York and Missouri, ordered a draft platform for the convention, considered and approved a mysterious proposal to translate American campaign literature into Bohemian, and grossly flattered the first national assembly of American periodical publishers: "It is always a pleasure for a man in public life to meet the real governing classes."

Hearing that some desperate Democrats were trying to persuade Grover Cleveland to run against him, he circulated among newspaper editors ("for your private use") a note from the former President that appeared to support his labor policies during the coal strike. Cleveland fumed with rage: "I am amazed at Roosevelt. . . . There are some people in this country that need lessons in decency and good manners."

"Theodore thinks of nothing, talks of nothing, and lives for nothing but his political interests," Henry Adams noted. "If you remark to him that God is Great, he asks naïvely how that will affect his election."

Old Guard Republicans worried about the undignified spectacle of a President campaigning for his own office. He was supposed to put himself in the hands of party professionals. McKinley had successfully sat out two campaigns at home in Canton, Ohio; here was "Teddy" virtually setting up preconvention headquarters in the White House.

The most that conservatives could do, until the party organized itself at the national convention in June, was beg Roosevelt not to go public with his spring exercise schedule, lest tabloid newspapers beholden to William Randolph Hearst depict him as a clown, or worse still, a snob. Skinny-dipping in Rock Creek Park, rough-riding on Bleistein, and tennis—that effete, Anglophile pastime of the rich—all carried a high degree of political risk. Aides shuddered at the memory of last year's tour-bus megaphones on West Executive Avenue.

Reluctantly, in view of the marvelous weather, the President continued to exercise indoors. After some vain efforts to strangle his Japanese wrestling instructor, he managed three new throws that were "perfect corkers." As a result, he was mottled all over with bruises, and lame in both big toes, the right ankle, left wrist, and thumb.

⌒

HIS SIGNATURE FINGERS still worked, however. On 28 April he scrawled *Theodore Roosevelt* at the bottom of the last sheet of legislation to come his way before Congress adjourned: "An Act to Provide for the Temporary Government of the Canal Zone at Panama, the Protection of the Canal Works, and Other Purposes." Simultaneously in Paris, documents confirming the sale and conveyance of French rights were signed. Thus, as the largest real-estate transaction in history was consummated, the largest engineering project in history was begun.

Philippe Bunau-Varilla, who had waited in New York for this moment, sailed for France. His last request of Panama was that the diplomatic salary he had declined should be put toward a monument to Ferdinand de Lesseps, the canal's progenitor. For better or worse, the completed waterway (he could see it already, blue and brimming from Gatun to Balboa) would be identified with a more contemporary hero. Both men would always, for him, merit the supreme adjective *great*.

⌒

"I HAVE TAKEN possession of, and now occupy, on behalf of the United States, the Canal Zone and public land ceded by the Republic of Panama," Roosevelt announced.

By terms of treaty and act, he could exercise as much military, civil, and judicial authority as he liked in the Zone. But he immediately delegated this authority to his Secretary of War. Taft was a proven, brilliant colonial administrator, sensitive to native pride. The Panamanians, who showed early signs of being temperamental neighbors, would be soothed by him. "A more high-minded and disinterested man does not live," Roosevelt wrote fondly.

He sent Taft an official letter, stipulating a government and constitution for the Zone in precise, peremptory language. Power was to be invested in a new, seven-man Isthmian Canal Commission, already appointed. This would be chaired, as the old commission had been, by Admiral John G. Walker. Major General George W. Davis, USMC, was appointed Governor of the Zone. All but one of the other Commission members were engineers.

Roosevelt ordered Taft to "supervise and direct" this body, as he had the Philippines Commission. On the plainly administrative level, it could be trusted to regulate, recruit, survey, purchase, and disburse. The basic privileges of the Bill of Rights were guaranteed to all inhabitants of the Zone, except—as he robustly specified—"idiots, the insane, epileptics, paupers, criminals, professional beggars [and] persons afflicted with loathsome or dangerous contagious diseases." For good measure, he threw in felons, anarchists, and *insurrectos.*

Sanitary reform along the lines of General Wood's pioneering work in Havana was "a matter of first importance," the President wrote. "I desire that every possible effort be made to protect our officers and workmen from the dangers of tropical and other diseases, which in the past have been so prevalent and destructive in Panama."

⌒

ON 10 MAY, Cornelius Bliss formally declined the party chairmanship. A few days later, J. Hampton Moore, leader of the youth-oriented National Republican League, hurried to Washington to press the name of Senator Boies Penrose of Pennsylvania. Roosevelt could not see Moore until the late afternoon.

"You might as well know," the President said, "that I shall recommend George B. Cortelyou."

Shadows stole across the lawn outside, darkening the Executive Office windows. Moore stared at Roosevelt, trying to gauge his expression. Was that a smile, or a grin? Perhaps he was baring his teeth in anticipation of a fight, because this appointment was sure to upset the Republican Old Guard. They would want to know how an impoverished ex-stenographer, not quite forty-two, could possibly raise millions of dollars from the likes of J. P. Morgan, let alone manage the immense complexity of a national campaign.

Roosevelt seemed to have no such doubts. He rambled on about how young Republicans might help him win in November. Both he and Moore were aware that, even as they talked, an Old Guard stalwart lay near death in the reddening hills of western Pennsylvania. Senator Matthew Quay, master manipulator of so many national conventions, had bought his last delegate. So had Mark Hanna, already nothing more than a name set in stone in Cleveland.

Farther west still, in Wisconsin, the political careers of John Coit Spooner and Henry Clay Payne were in decline. Governor LaFollette had completed his takeover of that state's organization, and was threatening to send a radical delegation to Chicago. "The last consignment of Great Captains of the Republican Party are passing into the twilight," the New York *Sun* mourned. Even that venerable newspaper, expositor of corporate conservatism for so many years, had had its day. Its famous symbol—an orb half hidden behind a black mountain—looked more like dusk than dawn.

The President beamed at his visitor, showing no regret for *temps perdu.* Few people realized it, but Roosevelt loved Quay, probably the most despised politician of the last twenty years. He had made a secret pilgrimage to say good-bye, and been moved by Quay's lament, "I do wish it were possible for me to get off into the great north woods and crawl out on a rock in the sun and die like a wolf!" Public men of the future must face a brighter, more businesslike light, the shadow-free light of Cooper-Hewitt lamps and popping press bulbs and Luxfer office windows. George Cortelyou—stenographer, scheduler, filer, colorless as onionskin, the quintessential modern bureaucrat—did not blink at this kind of light. Neither did Moore's young Republicans.

"Go see Cortelyou as soon as you can," the President said. "And tell him," he added ingratiatingly, "I want him to work with you."

CHAPTER 21

The Wire That Ran Around the World

"I hope ye're satisfied," he says. "I am," says Jawn Hay.

AT SIXTY-FOUR years of age, Ion Perdicaris—"Jon" to boyhood friends in New Jersey—felt that he had found his final home in Tangier, Morocco. His dividends from United States cotton and gas stocks financed a palatial villa outside of town, on the slopes of Djebal Kebir.

This did not mean that Mr. Perdicaris had severed all American ties. Cultured and suave, he made a point of entertaining visiting compatriots, and enjoyed his role as dean of Tangier's little English-speaking colony. When the mood struck him, he was capable of crossing to New York, renting the Fifth Avenue Theatre, and putting on a show scripted by himself, with sets by "I. Perdicaris," and his own stepdaughter as star. Such shows might open on Monday and close the following Thursday; but Mr. Perdicaris was wealthy enough to be philosophical, returning always to the peace of his Moroccan retreat.

He sat there now on the cool evening of 18 May 1904, relaxed in dinner jacket and pumps, surrounded by his family and the luxurious jumble of a cosmopolitan life. Tiny amphorae on the mantel testified to his birth in Athens, where his father had been United States Consul General. Oriental rugs and American skins bestrewed the floor; Moorish tables and shelves displayed a collection of *objets d'art* from three continents; William Morris wallpaper hinted that the lady of the house was an Englishwoman. Mrs. Perdicaris, however, was as happily expatriate as her husband. She liked to cuddle two Brazilian monkeys, who ate orange blossoms out of a pouch slung round her waist.

The other male member of the party was her son, Cromwell Varley. He was younger than his stepfather by some twenty years. But when sudden screams came from down the hallway, the old man lithely beat him to the door.

Mr. Perdicaris supposed, as he ran, that his French chef was quarreling with the German housekeeper as usual. Not until he reached the servants' quarters, with Varley following, did he realize that bandits had invaded his property. Armed Moors approached him, pausing only to club his butler to the floor with rifle butts. Mr. Perdicaris tried to intervene. He was instantly beaten and bound with palmetto cords. Varley leaped forward, enraged, whereupon his hand was slashed and he, too, taken prisoner. The rifles prodded both men toward the guardhouse, where a handsome, short, pale, turbaned Berber intoduced himself.

"I am the Raisuli."

Mr. Perdicaris was not encouraged. Ahmed ben Mohammed el Raisuli was a notorious insurgent, ruling three of the most violent hill tribes in Morocco—the Er Riff Mountain *kabyles,* whom Sultan Mulay Abd al-Aziz IV had never been able to subdue. Captured once by the Pasha of Tangier, Raisuli had spent four years chained to a wall. Since then, his hatred of the French-dominated sultanate had become compulsive. Yet his voice tonight was low and unthreatening.

"I swear by all we hold sacred," Raisuli said, indicating Mr. Perdicaris's other servants, "that if there is no attempt to escape or rescue, no harm shall come to these people. But they must mount and ride with us!"

Mr. Perdicaris saw his own horses being saddled for travel. He had no idea why he was being abducted. "I accept your assurance, Raisuli," he replied in Arabic. He and Varley were made to mount, too. A small caravan formed, and trotted out into the darkness.

Helpless and hysterical, Mrs. Perdicaris remained behind. Then she discovered that Raisuli had neglected to cut the villa's telephone cord. Just before eleven o'clock, Samuel Gummeré, the American Consul General in Tangier, rode up through the cork trees to comfort her.

⟋⟍

THE FIRST CABLE from Gummeré did not reach the State Department until early afternoon of the next day, 19 May.

MR. PERDICARIS, MOST PROMINENT AMERICAN CITIZEN
HERE, AND HIS STEPSON MR. VARLEY, BRITISH SUBJECT,
WERE CARRIED OFF LAST NIGHT FROM THEIR COUNTRY
HOUSE, THREE MILES FROM TANGIER, BY A NUMEROUS
BAND OF NATIVES HEADED BY RAISULY [*sic*]. . . . I
EARNESTLY REQUEST THAT A MAN-OF-WAR BE SENT AT
ONCE. . . . SITUATION MOST SERIOUS.

John Hay was out of town, so once again Assistant Secretary of State Francis B. Loomis had to handle a foreign crisis with the President.

Conveniently, Roosevelt had just dispatched sixteen white warships on a "goodwill cruise" of the Mediterranean. His response was quick, and more forceful than Gummeré could have hoped. Loomis cabled back that some of these ships would be sent to Tangier, as soon as possible. "May be three or four days before one can arrive."

His estimate was somewhat optimistic. The nearest ships to Morocco were those of Rear Admiral French E. Chadwick's South Atlantic Squadron, comprising the fast cruiser *Brooklyn,* a protected cruiser, and two gunboats. About one day behind steamed four big battleships of the North Atlantic Fleet, under Rear Admiral Albert S. Barker. Bringing up the rear was Rear Admiral Theodore F. Jewell's European Squadron of three protected cruisers.

The last seven units were scheduled to rendezvous in the Azores before proceeding to Portugal and the Rivieras. Chadwick's four were due to visit Gibraltar, and then tour the North African coast. These were the vessels Roosevelt chose to divert to Tangier. But he overestimated the speed at which even the *Brooklyn* could move. The Navy Department advised that Chadwick would not reach Tangier much before the end of May.

⌒

RAISULI'S CARAVAN JOGGED inland all day, under the staring sun. Mr. Perdicaris and his stepson stifled under Moorish *haiks,* wrapped around them for disguise. Toward evening, they ascended into the Riff Mountains—tribal country, forbidden to Christians and coastal Arabs alike. Mr. Perdicaris's horse slipped on some rocks. The old man, still bound, was thrown off, dislocating a thighbone. He lay quivering until Varley and Raisuli lifted him back onto the saddle. For hours, the climb continued up a wet, dark gorge. Shortly before midnight, Raisuli called a halt at the village of Tsarradan, on the spur of Mount Nazul. Mr. Perdicaris was escorted to a hut that reeked of stagnant water. Unable to stand on his throbbing leg, he lay down on the clay floor, and someone threw a blanket over him. He could not sleep. The hut's thatch was half open to the sky. Rain began to fall, softening the clay to paste.

In all his wandering life, Mr. Perdicaris had never felt so remote from help or hope.

⌒

ROOSEVELT'S ARMADA STEAMED on across the Atlantic, leaving the Caribbean basin unguarded. As if to remind its citizens that out of sight was not out of mind, the President chose 20 May—the second anniversary of *Cuba libre*—to make an official statement of his Corollary to the Monroe Doctrine. Once again Elihu Root served as his spokesman. Addressing the Cuba Society of New York that evening, Root asked permission to read a letter from the President of the United States.

Its first two paragraphs were blandly congratulatory, but there was a passing clause that caught attention: "It is not true that the United States has any land hunger or entertains any projects as regards other nations, *save such as are for their welfare.*"
The third paragraph moved quickly from reassurance to threat.

If a nation shows that it knows how to act with decency in industrial and political matters, if it keeps order and pays its obligations, then it need fear no interference from the United States. Brutal wrongdoing, or an impotence which results in a general loosening of the ties of a civilized society, may finally require intervention by some civilized nation, and in the Western Hemisphere the United States cannot ignore this duty; but it remains true that our interests, and those of our southern neighbors, are in reality identical.

The letter ended as it began, with polite clichés, but its message was clear: Caribbean and Latin American countries must in future match their "interests" to those of the Colossus of the North. If not, they would be policed.
In sending such a message at such a time—little more than four weeks before the Republican National Convention—Roosevelt took a calculated risk. Better, with mere rhetoric, to arouse a chorus of criticism from anti-imperialists than to court much wider outrage by actually implementing the Corollary, if things got any worse in Santo Domingo. His statement should at least reduce the latter possibility through November.
Congressman David DeArmond of Missouri accused him in the New York *World* of "jingoism run mad." The same newspaper also used the word *mad,* along with *patronizing, menace, knight-errantry,* and *bumptiousness.* Yet most commentators north and south of the border praised the President's good intentions. Memories of German and British gunboats bombarding Venezuela still rankled. For better or worse, the Roosevelt Corollary was now a permanent feature of hemispheric policy.

"I ASK NOTHING from you," Raisuli told Mr. Perdicaris, much to the latter's relief. However, Raisuli clearly intended to ask a great deal from the Sultan of Morocco before he released so valuable a pair of hostages, and was content to let international pressure build for their release. At his leisure, he sent Abd al-Aziz a list of his demands, and settled down to the life of a village celebrity. He strolled around Tsarradan, accepting the adoration of youths who kissed the hem of his burnoose.
When Mr. Perdicaris asked what he wanted from Fez, Raisuli mentioned five specific concessions: an end to harassment of the Er Riffs by government forces; release of all *kabyle* political prisoners; dismissal of the Pasha who had

chained him; a ransom of seventy thousand Spanish silver dollars; finally, elevation to overlordship of two of Morocco's richest districts.

Mr. Perdicaris was aghast and depressed at the extravagance of these terms. Raisuli showed him a plait braided under his turban. "This will disappear only when my wrongs are avenged—mine and those of my people!"

A few days later, word came that Sultan Abd al-Aziz was not interested in bargaining for foreign hostages. Raisuli promptly had the imperial messenger's throat slit.

⌒

ROOSEVELT'S REDEFINITION OF the Monroe Doctrine and his dispatch of warships to the Mediterranean were the gestures of a palpably confident executive. "I had much rather be a real President for three years and a half," he told George Otto Trevelyan, "than a figurehead for seven years and a half." The odds on renewed "real" power were in his favor: with 708 out of 988 convention delegates pledged to him, his nomination was now a certainty. Democrat campaign planners were in such despair over his popularity that, having failed to persuade Grover Cleveland to run, they seemed likely to settle for Alton B. Parker—a New York State judge who, as Elihu Root remarked, "has never opened his mouth on any national question."

Reticence and its political cousin, caginess, were in Roosevelt's opinion weaknesses to be taken advantage of. When a deputation of conservative senators, including Aldrich and Spooner, visited the White House to protest his selection of the "inexperienced" Cortelyou as Chairman of the Republican National Committee, he was unsympathetic. "I held this matter open for months, and allowed plenty of time to make selections, and none of you had a word to say."

Ironically, he was quite capable of being closemouthed himself, but only when the sensibilities of other people or governments had to be considered, or important announcements delayed. And sometimes—as now—he preferred the quick efficiency of a news leak. A White House "source" informed reporters that George B. Cortelyou would become Postmaster General after the election, in place of Henry Clay Payne. This was a strategic move aimed at enhancing the former's authority as party chairman. Campaign workers were sure to obey Cortelyou if they knew he would soon inherit the government's richest patronage agency.

Roosevelt assembled the rest of his second-term Cabinet at leisure and mostly in secret. "He wants us all to resign—" John Hay noted in his diary, "but he wants to reappoint me." Agriculture Secretary James Wilson might be kept on, Hay thought; Treasury Secretary Leslie Shaw, who had presidential ambitions for 1908, probably not. "Taft he wants to keep either where he is, or as Attorney-General if Knox goes."

This was the first recorded indication that Knox's astigmatic gaze had begun to focus beyond the Administration. Like Taft, his dearest wish was to sit at center bench on the Supreme Court. But Chief Justice Fuller, at seventy-one, remained annoyingly healthy. Meanwhile, the passing of Matthew Quay gave Knox an irresistible chance to represent his home state in the Senate.

In any case, the President's latest preference for a Supreme Court appointment was William H. Moody. To that end, Roosevelt decided definitely to shift Moody to the Justice Department as soon as Knox resigned. He had other, long-range plans for Taft.

With less than a month to go before the convention in Chicago, he became obsessive about controlling every last detail. He plotted the Coliseum's seating plan, insisting that "every Republican editor in the country" be accommodated. He selected the speakers and edited the speeches. "For all we know," the New York *Evening Post* jibed, "he may have designated the men who are to lead the cheering." Representatives of state committees were amazed at his knowledge of what they were doing and whom they were hiring.

"Mr. President, I have come for your final answer," Albert J. Beveridge said one day, crowding his desk like an earnest schoolboy. "Am I, or am I not, to be temporary chairman of the Chicago convention?"

As tactfully as possible, Roosevelt mentioned the name of somebody taller. Beveridge stiffened. "Root? Elihu Root! What can he say that the country will listen to?"

Unconsoled, the little Hoosier performed one of his imitations of Napoleon retiring to Elba. "Very well, Mr. President, so be it. I am once more alone. . . . Alone at school, alone at the Bar, alone in the Senate, alone in the party! Good morning, Mr. President."

Roosevelt's next visitor found the President convulsed with laughter.

⌒

ROOSEVELT DID NOT read Raisuli's list of demands until 28 May. He sent for Hay in a hurry, and asked what the State Department thought of them. Hay said they were "preposterous." The United States could not possibly force their acceptance on the Sultan. Personally, he would like Mr. Perdicaris's life to be saved. "But a nation cannot degrade itself to prevent ill-treatment of a citizen."

The President seemed to agree. However, that afternoon a Navy Department cable went out to Admiral Jewell's European Squadron, east of the Azores, ordering it to proceed to Tangier at once. With the South Atlantic Squadron already dispatched, some thirty thousand tons of American gunmetal should soon persuade the Sultan to start negotiating.

⌒

AT 5:30 A.M. on 30 May the white turrets of the *Brooklyn* appeared off Tangier. Her big guns boomed a long salute. Moroccan cannons politely boomed back. Admiral Chadwick's other three ships, the *Atlanta, Castine,* and *Marietta,* glided in at intervals through the day. Each in turn sent its salute, and the cannons answered. The prolonged, stately thudding was music to Samuel Gummeré's ears.

That night, four Marines armed only with pistols slipped ashore to guard the Consul and Mrs. Perdicaris. More thudding on 1 June announced the arrival of Admiral Jewell's cruisers, *Olympia, Baltimore,* and *Cleveland.* Unnoticed in all the excitement, one of Raisuli's agents left town and galloped to Tsarradan, in the mountains. He breathlessly reported the arrival of the American warships, "one after the other." Tangier was *mkloub,* "upside down."

Mr. Perdicaris listened, his heart surging with patriotic gratitude. His only fear was whether this messenger, too, would have his throat slit. But Raisuli seemed pleased at the pressure building up on Abd al-Aziz.

"The presence of these vessels," he said, "may result in his acceding to my demands, and then you will be able to return to your friends."

⟁

SEVEN DAYS AFTER the arrival of the last American warship in Tangier Bay, Gummeré was able to communicate only an unofficial, preliminary hint that the Sultan might deal with Raisuli. Roosevelt's patience began to run out, and Hay cabled:

PRESIDENT WISHES EVERYTHING POSSIBLE DONE TO
SECURE THE RELEASE OF PERDICARIS. HE WISHES
IT CLEARLY UNDERSTOOD THAT IF PERDICARIS IS
MURDERED, THIS GOVERNMENT WILL DEMAND THE LIFE
OF THE MURDERER. . . . YOU ARE TO AVOID IN ALL YOUR
OFFICIAL ACTION ANYTHING WHICH MAY BE REGARDED
AS AN ENCOURAGEMENT TO BRIGANDAGE OR BLACKMAIL.

Before nightfall, Tangier advised that the Moroccan government had formally accepted Raisuli's terms, except the huge ransom, which would have to be "reasonably negotiated."

⟁

ON 10 JUNE, Governor Samuel Pennypacker announced that Philander Chase Knox had been appointed to succeed Matthew Quay as Senator. Roosevelt accepted the Attorney General's resignation, but no longer with Dickensian emotions. He wrote effusively, carelessly. Knox was replaceable—as Root had proved to be. Even so, the President's words were sweet enough for Knox to paste them in his scrapbook:

Many great and able men have preceded you in the office you hold; but there is none among them whose administration has left so deep a mark. . . . You have deeply affected for good the development of our entire political system in its relations to the industrial and economic tendencies of the time.

Behind the exchange of courtesies lay some personal disillusionment. Roosevelt had grown impatient with the Attorney General's obsessive legalism. Knox was critical of the President's autocratic tendencies, particularly in the area of executive prerogative. And he was quick to reject press speculation that he would be an antitrust crusader on Capitol Hill. "President Roosevelt's policies are his own," he told reporters. "I have been no more than the exponent of his ideas."

⌒

JOHN HAY FORWARDED another demand from Raisuli to Roosevelt on 15 June. The Berber now wanted control of four more Moroccan districts. "You see there is no end to the insolence of this blackguard," Hay wrote. "I feel that it would be most inexpedient to surrender to him. We have done what we can for Perdicaris. . . . Who knows what he will ask next?"

The Secretary's desire to disengage betrayed a secret embarrassment. Researchers at the State Department were beginning to suspect that Mr. Perdicaris might not be an American citizen after all. Hay was anxiously awaiting their final report. How would delegates to the Chicago convention react if the President was found to have bombarded Morocco in behalf of a fraudulent old Greek?

Roosevelt, unsuspecting, asked Hay to explore the possibility of a joint military expedition with Britain and France. "Our position must be to demand the death of those who harm him if he is harmed."

Hay unhappily consulted with the envoys of both countries. Neither liked Roosevelt's idea. Jules Jusserand was particularly wary: an American landing at Tangier might threaten France's own program for total acquisition of Morocco—"pacification," as it was called on the Quai d'Orsay. He was astute enough to sense that Hay did not really want him to agree.

"The President's will is, more and more, predominant in public affairs," Jusserand informed Foreign Minister Théophile Delcassé. "And he hesitates less and less to follow it, despite the advice of his Cabinet officers. They, to tell the truth, resist only very weakly."

Similar complaints came from Chicago, where the Republican National Committee was already meeting. Senator Nathan B. Scott, the acting Chairman, objected bitterly to the way George Cortelyou had been foisted upon the party. Roosevelt, hearing that the Old Guard was plotting a last-minute revolt, responded forcefully, by telegram: PEOPLE MAY AS WELL UNDERSTAND

THAT IF I AM TO RUN FOR PRESIDENT THEN CORTELYOU IS TO BE CHAIR-
MAN. . . . I WILL NOT HAVE IT ANY OTHER WAY. He asked for the names of the
intriguers, whereupon their opposition faded, but not their resentment.
"Your Uncle Theodore knows how to run things," Scott growled at a newspaperman.

—❧—

ON MONDAY, 20 JUNE, the mass of Republican delegates arrived in
Chicago. They looked languorous, almost bored under their straw hats. As
Henry Cabot Lodge wrote Roosevelt, "Excitement is impossible where there
is no contest."

Old-timers talked nostalgically about the last really fought-out Republican convention, in 1884. Some remembered twenty-five-year-old Theodore
Roosevelt of New York, standing on a chair and yelling for a roll call in his
high, harsh voice. They remembered drunken roars for James G. Blaine, glee
clubs bellowing the praises of President Arthur, and that softest yet most pen-
etrating of noises, the rustle of "boodle," as Southern blacks sold and resold
their votes.

Now, two decades later, Chicago could have been hosting a temper-
ance chautauqua. No bunting brightened the streets. Sidewalks were bare of
button-hawkers and barkers: every fakir with anything to sell had decamped
to the World's Fair in St. Louis. Dull clouds scudded over Lake Michigan. The
wind felt heavy and wet.

—❧—

THAT EVENING, Roosevelt dictated a letter to Kermit. "Tomorrow the National Convention meets, and barring a cataclysm I shall be nominated. . . .
How the election will turn out no one can tell." The possibility, however remote, that he might be beaten caused an access of pride and gratitude for
nearly three years of power:

> From Panama on down I have been able to accomplish certain things
> which will be of lasting importance in our history. Incidentally, I don't
> think that any family has ever enjoyed the White House more than we
> have. I was thinking about it just this morning when Mother and I
> took breakfast on the portico and afterwards walked about the lovely
> grounds and looked at the stately historic old house. It is a wonderful
> privilege to have been here and to have been given the chance to do
> this work, and I should regard myself as having a small and mean
> mind if in the event of defeat I felt soured at not having had more, in-
> stead of being thankful for having had so much.

—❧—

"AN ENORMOUS PAINTING OF MARK HANNA ...
HUNG OVER THE SPEAKER'S PLATFORM."
The Republican National Convention, Chicago, June 1904

LONG BEFORE PROCEEDINGS began on Tuesday, word spread that the President would monitor every minute of every session, via a special telephone line running direct from his office to the basement of the Coliseum. Delegates began to get uneasy feelings of remote control. A disgusted Pennsylvanian decided not to attend. "The boss has fixed it all up and we might as well go home."

One thing Roosevelt had neglected to "fix," however, was the Coliseum's decor. As a result, it was not his portrait that greeted people entering the hall at noon. An enormous painting of Mark Hanna, seven feet wide and twenty feet tall, hung over the speakers' platform. Twenty-eight other Hannas looked down somberly from various angles. In further evidence of Old Guard aesthetics, a black-draped chair was "set aside" for Senator Quay, and the dead features of President McKinley appeared on every admission ticket. "In every corner of the hall there is a ghost," a reporter observed. Even some of the living looked sepulchral when they sat under tobacco-blue sunbeams slanting down from the skylight.

A question buzzed from aisle to aisle: "Where is Roosevelt's picture?" Sharp eyes eventually noticed a few small steel engravings, spaced around the upper gallery and almost smothered in festoons.

At 12:14, another pallid figure—Postmaster General Payne, clearly not long for the world—approached the rostrum and gaveled the Thirteenth Republican National Convention to order. Elihu Root rose to respectful applause, and began his keynote speech. In the vast space, his husky voice failed to carry. "The responsibility of government rests upon the Republican Party. The complicated machinery through which eighty million people—"

"Louder!" a voice called. "Louder!"

IN WASHINGTON, it was an hour later by the clock, and the President was having lunch. He knew exactly what themes were being sounded in Chicago. Root had promised to trumpet (insofar as quiet Elihu could trumpet anything) the achievements of the last four years, "from an administration rather than from a personal standpoint." There would be solemn fanfares on the names of McKinley and Hanna, rising scales of economic statistics, a canon on Party and Patriotism, and always the reassuring *basso ostinato* of Continuity. Root may not be a virtuoso performer, but nobody could match his mastery of political polyphony.

IN TANGIER, it was nearly five hours further on. Late-afternoon sun beat on the seven white warships in Tangier Bay. They made a deceptively peaceful picture. Today, 21 June, was supposed to have seen the release of Mr. Perdicaris and his stepson—or so Consul Gummeré had been led to believe, after the Sultan's latest yielding to Raisuli's demands. But the trail down from Tsarradan had remained quiet: Morocco, as Gummeré complained, was "a country of delays."

Aboard the *Brooklyn,* he and Admiral Chadwick had decided that the United States could not tolerate any more "double dealing and treachery," either on the part of Raisuli or the Moroccan government. "We have come to a point when our position has now become undignified and humiliating," Gummeré cabled Hay. Chadwick joined him in suggesting "an ultimatum immediately for large indemnity for every day's further delay and that Marines will be landed and customs seized."

BY NOW, Root's voice had strengthened, and most delegates were with him. They applauded his depersonalized summary of the Administration's fiscal, antitrust, agricultural, and foreign policies. They received in silence the news that five battleships, four cruisers, four monitors, and thirty-four torpedo destroyers and torpedo boats had joined the Navy since 1900, while another thirteen battleships and thirteen cruisers were under construction. As Root approached his peroration, the applause grew louder and more frequent. He began to refer delicately to William McKinley's "successor." He quoted the honest pledge of "unbroken" continuity given at Buffalo on 14 September 1901, to further cheers. "Our President," he declared with a sweeping gesture, "has taken the whole people into his confidence."

"All except the members of the National Committee," Senator Scott murmured.

Root did not enunciate the words "Theodore Roosevelt" until his final sentence, at 1:18 P.M. There was a gratifying roar, but it died in thirty seconds. At 2:10 P.M., the convention adjourned for the day, and Henry Cabot Lodge's Committee on Resolutions began to write the party platform. Simultaneously, Consul Gummeré's cable arrived in Washington.

⌐∽

HAY PONDERED THE cable overnight. More and more, he dreaded an American show of force. European reactions would be negative, and could turn hostile when—as now seemed certain—Mr. Perdicaris was revealed to be a Greek. A report from Athens confirmed that one "Ioannis Perdicaris" had applied for Greek citizenship there, at the start of the American Civil War. *Ioannis* certainly sounded similar to *Ion*.

Unable to confront Roosevelt with this news, Hay asked a deputy, Gaillard Hunt, to take the Perdicaris file over to the White House, along with a recommendation that Raisuli and the Sultan be given a final warning. As Commander-in-Chief (not to mention political candidate) Roosevelt must consider the risks.

Hunt came back and said that the President had not been at all pleased with the contents of the file. However, he had authorized Hay's suggested ultimatum. Rightly or wrongly, Raisuli believed Mr. Perdicaris to be American; he had therefore done deliberate violence to the whole concept of American citizenship. For that he must be held responsible, and the Sultan responsible for him.

⌐∽

ONCE AGAIN IT was afternoon in Morocco as Roosevelt conducted his mid-morning audience, and delegates in the Chicago Coliseum awaited the noon opening gavel.

Hay, drafting his ultimatum, hit upon "a concise impropriety" to gratify the aggressive Gummeré. It nicely balanced the more cautious phraseology that followed:

WE WANT PERDICARIS ALIVE OR RAISULI DEAD. FURTHER
THAN THIS WE DESIRE LEAST POSSIBLE COMPLICATIONS
WITH MOROCCO OR OTHER POWERS. YOU WILL NOT
ARRANGE FOR LANDING MARINES OR SEIZING CUSTOM
HOUSE WITHOUT SPECIFIC DIRECTIONS FROM THE
DEPARTMENT.

Hay could not resist showing his draft to Edwin M. Hood, the veteran State Department correspondent for the Scripps-McRae news service. "Think I'll send it," he said, as one old newspaperman to another.

"Then I will too," Hood replied. The message went out over government and news wires simultaneously. But by the time it reached Morocco, Gummeré had no need for it. An up-country sheik announced that he would make his village available for the exchange of hostages and ransom on the next morning, 23 June.

HOOD'S DISPATCH REACHED Chicago at about 3:00 P.M., and a copy was delivered to the permanent chairman of the convention, Joseph Cannon. He let it lie on his desk while Henry Cabot Lodge read the Republican Party platform for 1904.

"We declare our constant adherence to the following principles," Lodge shouted. His voice rang with the earnestness of a politician determined to say as little as possible. He was noncommittal on the tariff, trust control, labor relations, and foreign policy. The future of the Philippines was left vague. Disfranchised Negroes got a few words of sympathy, insurgent Republicans none. There was no call for railroad rate regulation, no acknowledgment of the Iowa Idea, no mention of the power war between Governor LaFollette and Senator Spooner. (The latter's Old Guard delegation doggedly occupied Wisconsin floor space, courtesy of the Committee on Credentials.)

When Lodge finished, Cannon called for acceptance of the platform. There was a unanimous, if apathetic, chorus of ayes. Cannon, smiling, took up his slip of paper. "With the consent of the Convention, the Chair will direct the Clerk to read a dispatch from Washington . . . received through the courtesy of the Scripps-McRae Newspaper Association."

"*Bulletin,*" the clerk read. "*Washington, June 22. Secretary of State Hay has sent instructions to Consul General Samuel R. Gummeré, as follows: 'We want either Perdicaris alive or Raisuli dead.'*"

After two days of procedural torpor, the convention reacted galvanically to Hay's "concise impropriety." Delegates jumped on their chairs and shouted with delight. "Roosevelt and Hay know what they are doing," a Kansan exulted. "Our people like courage. We'll stand for anything those men do."

Cannon quickly adjourned the session, content to let enthusiasm build for the nominations.

⌐◦⌐

A FEW MINUTES before eleven o'clock on Thursday, 23 June, Frank S. Black, a former Governor of New York, rose to nominate the President. Immensely tall and craggy, he glared through professional spectacles and shook a boyish thatch of hair. "From every nook and corner of the country," he orated, "rises but a single choice to fill the most exalted office in the world." Applause welled up, as if echoing his metaphor. Roosevelt had chosen well. Black—his predecessor in Albany—was the party's best speaker, more poetic than Spooner, less preachy than Hoar.

After some more flights of populist imagery, Black got down to the personal. He reminded the convention that Roosevelt, for all his fame as a soldier, was by nature a writer and scholar. "A profound student of history, he is today the greatest history maker in the world." However, "the fate of nations is still decided by their wars." The peace that scholars craved was probably illusory, certainly temporary:

Events are numberless and mighty, and no man can tell which wire runs around the world. The nation basking today in the quiet of contentment and repose may be still on the deadly circuit and tomorrow writhing in the toils of war. This is the time when great figures must be kept in front. If the pressure is great, the material to resist it must be granite and iron. Whether we wish it or not, America is abroad in this world. Her interests are on every street, her name is on every tongue. Those interests so sacred and stupendous should be trusted only to the care of those whose power, skill and courage have been tested and approved. (*Applause*) And in the man whom you will choose, the highest sense of every nation in the world beholds a man who typifies as no other living American does, the spirit and purposes of the twentieth century.

It was just eleven o'clock. "Gentlemen," Black roared, "I nominate for President of the United States . . . Theodore Roosevelt of New York!"

An elemental din built and built, and for twenty-one minutes the convention rocked in pandemonium. Three sergeants at arms carried in Roosevelt's portrait, crudely rendered in crayon, yet big enough to blot out most of Mark Hanna's. They swung the President from side to side, while he gazed with waxy eyes at the party he could at last call his own.

⌐◦⌐

THE REAL ROOSEVELT received the news of his nomination, along with that of Fairbanks for Vice President, and confirmation of Cortelyou as Chairman, just after lunch, as he sat with Edith and Alice on the White House portico. His secretary, Loeb, brought the telegram. The vote had been unanimous, but every state from Alabama to Wyoming had insisted on recording its tally separately, making 994 votes out of 994.

With kisses on his cheeks, he walked happily to his office and met a congratulatory crowd of newsmen. He invited them in for "an Executive session," and tilted back laughing in his big chair as they fired questions at him. Prophecies, jokes, reminiscences, and indiscretions poured out freely, enchantingly. Roosevelt asked that nothing he said be printed. And nothing ever was.

⌒

THAT EVENING, Mr. Perdicaris strolled for the last time on the village green at Tsarradan. His hurt leg had long since healed. Yesterday's messages, to the effect that "His Chereefian Majesty was most graciously pleased to accede to the demands" of Raisuli, had come too late for quick departure. But the ransom caravan was definitely on its way, and a descent from the mountains was planned for the morning.

Mr. Perdicaris slept no better than he had on his first night, five weeks before. At 4:00 A.M. on 24 June, horses and pack mules were made ready, and soon a long cortege was snaking north to Mount Nazul. Raisuli rode beside the hostages on a gray charger. Dark cords of camel hair twisted about his turban, and a cartridge belt slapped his broad chest: "Every inch," Mr. Perdicaris thought enviously, "a man of daring deeds."

They crested Nazul just as the sun did, and in the bursting light, all the peaks and ridges around them, wreathed in lower mists, turned amethyst and rose, crimson and lilac. The old man reined to a halt, enraptured by one of the most gorgeous displays of color he had ever seen. Raisuli, grinning, asked if he "regretted" his involuntary mountain vacation.

Keeping to the ridge, they continued north and eventually sighted a white fleck in the blue distance, which Raisuli said was Tangier. Around noon they found themselves looking down on the town of El Zellal, where the meeting with the Sultan's emissaries was to take place.

Many hours later, when the last stacks of silver coin had been counted and the political prisoners handed over and two ceremonial luncheons eaten, Raisuli took Mr. Perdicaris aside and said good-bye. He promised that if anyone tried to harm him, "I . . . will come with all my men to your rescue."

Mr. Perdicaris was more inclined to cry than laugh. Affectionately drawn to Raisuli even as he rejoiced for himself, he mounted his black horse and rode off with the Sultan's party. Other emotions struggled in his breast toward midnight, when Tangier came into view, and he saw in the harbor the mastheads of Admiral Chadwick's ships, twinkling the news of his return.

As a youth, Mr. Perdicaris had thought little of his American citizenship, and bartered it away to avoid taxation during the Civil War. Too much money and travel had made him complacent and careless of formalities; there would be many awkward questions asked soon enough, before the State Department decided to forgive him; but he had no doubt now where, and to whom, his allegiance belonged.

"Thank Heaven," he said to himself, "it is that flag, and that people—aye, and that President, behind those frigates, thousands of miles away, who have had me dug out from amongst these *kabyles*! That flag and no other!"

CHAPTER 22

The Most Absurd Political Campaign of Our Time

*I think a lot iv us likes Tiddy Rosenfelt that wuddn't
iver be suspected iv votin' f'r him.*

THE DIFFICULTY OF MOUNTING a serious challenge to Theodore Roosevelt's candidacy in 1904 became apparent when the Prohibition Party gave its backing to a man named Silas Swallow. To the regret of satirists and cartoonists, Mr. Swallow was unable to choose the General Secretary of the Methodist Conference, Ezra Tipple, as his running mate. Tipple was a Roosevelt supporter.

So, by late June, were such reluctant converts as J. P. Morgan and E. H. Harriman. James J. Hill remained adamantly opposed, as did George F. Baer of coal-strike infamy. But many conservative Democrats, including George J. Gould, James Speyer, and Jacob H. Schiff, let Cornelius Bliss (who had agreed to serve as Republican campaign treasurer) know that he could rely on them for money. For such men, memories of William Jennings Bryan's two disastrous "Free Silver" campaigns were worse than their apprehensions of Roosevelt's Square Deal.

There was no chance that the Democratic National Convention—assembling in St. Louis as Roosevelt headed home from Washington in early July—would nominate Bryan again. When Bryan himself arrived at the local Coliseum, he found himself seated about two thirds of the way down the aisle, about where he had sunk in party esteem. Yet faded as the Commoner now seemed, with his balding head and resonant, empty voice, he was more vivid a personality than the likely nominee. Alton Brooks Parker, Chief Justice of the New York Court of Appeals, was gray enough to defeat the new science of autochrome photography. Drably decent, colorlessly correct at fifty-two, Parker dressed by habit in a gray cutaway coat and gray cutaway trousers. He lived in a gray house overlooking the gray waters of the Hudson, and was the author of many gray legal opinions, so carefully worded that neither plaintiffs nor defendants knew what he really felt on any given issue. Even the heart of Alton B. Parker was a gray area.

Roosevelt had foreseen the judge's candidacy for years. He knew Parker from gubernatorial days, and feared him precisely because he *was* colorless. "The neutral-tinted individual," he wrote George Otto Trevelyan, "is very apt to win against the man of pronounced views and active life."

Personally, he liked Parker very much. The judge was attractive on close acquaintance. Big and solid as an upstate lumberman, he exuded healthy, untroubled self-confidence. No furrow of doubt marred the smooth brow; his jaw was forceful; and his mustache (graying, but still tinged with auburn) curved easily and often into a thick-lipped grin. If his conversation was bland, tending toward boring, that was no novelty in a politician—and Parker was a politician, for all his judicial demeanor.

Eighteen years of public nonpartisanship had not erased Republican memories of Parker managing David B. Hill's landslide campaign for Governor in 1884. Even Hill, the arch-Democrat, had jibbed against supporting Bryan in 1896; yet Parker had tranquilly voted for Free Silver and "toilers everywhere" before accepting the most privileged seat on the New York bench. As a result, he could look Western miners in the eye and say that he had never deserted them, and behave with equal complacency at Gold Dollar banquets hosted by August P. Belmont. No wonder Hill—still state boss, and anxious to return old favors—saw him as the potential unifier of the Democratic Party.

And so did most of the 962 other delegates who took their seats in St. Louis on Wednesday, 6 July. About one hundred conservatives would have supported Grover Cleveland, had the former President agreed to run, and about two hundred radicals were pledged or beholden to William Randolph Hearst. All Hill had to do was marshal a majority that was two thirds greater than these minorities to nominate Parker. But first, all factions had to agree on a platform.

⌒

ON FRIDAY, a little knot of newsmen gathered outside Parker's house in Esopus, New York, waiting for the hall telephone to ring with good news for him. It remained silent all day. Around sunset, a press dispatch arrived, saying that ideological squabbling in St. Louis was preventing any progress toward the judge's nomination. William Jennings Bryan had waged such a fanatic battle against any mention of gold in the platform that the Committee on Resolutions might recommend no currency plank at all.

There was an instant clamor for Parker. He came onto the porch, genial and impassive, and listened to the dispatch. "I thank you, gentlemen, for the opportunity to comment." Pencils bristled eagerly, and he pointed at a sail-boat on the Hudson. "It's a pretty sight, isn't it?"

With this witticism he retired for the evening. A reporter called after him, asking sarcastically when he would be available, if more news came. "The usual hour," said Parker, and waved good-night.

That meant early the next morning, when he took his regular swim. Fog rolled up from the river and blanketed the moon. The newsmen smoked and dozed in rocking chairs. Eventually the fog began to whiten, but it did not burn away with dawn. Dew dripped from three thousand apple trees.

At 6:35 A.M., the *New York Times* man saw Parker slip out of the back of the house bare-legged, in an old rubber raincoat. He was tempted to follow him downhill, but decided to stick near the telephone. It shrilled just thirteen minutes later. Parker's secretary came out to announce that the judge had been nominated unanimously, on the first ballot.

Only one reporter knew where Parker was. He ran down the slope and encountered a big wet man at the water's edge. "Judge, you've got it!"

"Oh, is that so?"

A foghorn bleated on the river. Parker pulled on his raincoat and walked up the hill, shivering slightly. The other reporters saw him coming, and took off their hats. He shook hands with them all. Somebody handed him the tele-phone message, and he read it with drops of water trickling down his face.

Even at this moment, Parker could not express his emotions. "No," he said, "I will reserve anything I have to say until I am officially notified."

He stepped onto the porch, tall, cold, glowing with health, clutching the achievement of his life in his hand. Inside, breakfast awaited him, and the Democratic newspapers. They were full of disapproving accounts of Bryan's currency-plank abandonment. One especially angry editorial caught his eye:

> At this hour of writing, before the taking of the ballot, we are assum-ing the nomination of Judge Parker. He must at once declare, sound-money Democrats will demand that he declare, that the gold monetary standard, as now established by law, is permanent. . . . Judge Parker must understand that, making his canvass on this plat-form without a public profession of his personal belief, . . . he cannot expect to receive the support and votes of the sound-money Demo-crats of the East. They will desert him by the tens of thousands. . . . Better another term of Roosevelt, better Roosevelt indefinitely, than one term of a President incapable of yielding in the slightest degree to the dangerous demands of a party which confesses itself to be still in-sane and unsafe.

Parker ate and drank and thought, then changed into riding clothes and went out alone on horseback. Shortly before noon he returned, summoned his secretary, and dictated a telegram to William F. Sheehan, leader of the New York delegation at St. Louis.

The telegram was so blunt that Western Union called for verification. It reached the convention hall just as delegates were assembling to nominate a vice-presidential candidate. Sheehan instantly suppressed it, but he and Hill could not hide their panic, and a wave of rumor swept the Coliseum. Had Judge Parker refused to run? "The Democratic party," Senator Tillman shouted, "can always be relied on to make a damn fool of itself at the critical time."

After four hours, the telegram was finally read aloud from the rostrum:

> I REGARD THE GOLD STANDARD AS FIRMLY AND IRREVOCABLY ESTABLISHED, AND SHALL ACT ACCORDINGLY IF THE ACTION OF THE CONVENTION SHALL BE RATIFIED BY THE PEOPLE. AS THE PLATFORM IS SILENT ON THE SUBJECT, MY VIEW SHOULD BE MADE KNOWN TO THE CONVENTION, AND IF IT IS PROVED TO BE UNSATISFACTORY TO THE MAJORITY, I REQUEST YOU TO DECLINE THE NOMINATION BEFORE ADJOURNMENT.
>
> ALTON PARKER

Parker's words were rather less surprising than his tone, which came as a cold slap in the convention's hot, weary face. Sheehan and other leaders worked desperately to assure delegates that the judge meant no "dictation." He was just merely behaving like a man "of rectitude and honor." There was no move to withdraw the nomination, but the rest of the proceedings were anticlimactic. An eighty-year-old multimillionaire, Henry G. Davis of West Virginia, was endorsed for Vice President, in hopes that he might contribute to the campaign. Then a thousand uninspired Democrats headed for their hotel rooms.

ROOSEVELT WAS FULL of admiration for Parker's telegram. "It was a bold and skillful move," he wrote Henry Cabot Lodge. He doubted that the judge had any personal principles on the subject of gold. In waiting until the last minute to instruct the convention, Parker had "become a very formidable candidate and opponent."

Professionals in both parties were similarly impressed. As Roosevelt predicted, the New York *Evening Post* endorsed Parker in near-adulatory terms. Other New York newspapers to support him were the *Times, Herald, World,* and *Staats-Zeitung.* The Brooklyn *Eagle, Boston Herald, Detroit Free Press,* Milwaukee *Journal,* and—worryingly—the *Springfield Republican* followed suit. Every one had supported McKinley in 1900.

Time would tell if the Parker wave represented a temporary swell, or some real shifting of the political current. Many warm, placid weeks lay ahead, before political activity picked up again in September. Almost all of the official campaigning would be done by the two national committees and their treasurers and copywriters and speakers. Roosevelt and Parker were required to do nothing, except make one acceptance speech and write one acceptance letter apiece.

Both candidates were expected to sit out the planning phase of the campaign in their respective retreats—although Roosevelt had scheduled a midsummer visit to Washington, to confer with party tacticians. In the meantime, clams were spouting in Cold Spring Harbor, and the corn was green on Sagamore Hill; distant picnic spots beckoned, and the waters of the bay cried out for the splash of oars.

Even from the austere heights of Esopus, New York, the Hudson showed more than a hint of blue.

ON 27 JULY, fifty-four solemn Republicans creaked up Sagamore Hill in a dusty procession of buggies. Despite the heat, they all wore neckties and stiff

"FIFTY-FOUR SOLEMN REPUBLICANS."
Roosevelt being notified of his nomination, 27 July 1904

collars, and their trousers were ironed to knife-edges—even, incredibly, those of Speaker Cannon. One and all were solemn, for they were enacting the party's most hallowed ritual: a formal notification of nomination to its presidential candidate.

Roosevelt awaited them on the broad porch, surrounded by his wife and a clutch of children. He wore a frock coat and white waistcoat. The visitors respectfully banged the dust from their hats before mounting the steps to shake his hand. William Loeb brought out a low stool for Cannon to stand on. The Speaker teetered awkwardly, and drew a typed speech from his pocket. "It's seven minutes long," he apologized.

As he read a condensed version of the Chicago platform, the sea breeze brought up scents of hay. Flags snapped on the house's high roof. Roosevelt swayed with pleasure, patting one of his nephews on the head. He kept glancing toward Edith, aloof in filmy white lace. "That's perfectly true," he interrupted at one point, "perfectly true."

When the President's turn came, Alice Roosevelt, unnoticed till now, eased through the crowd and stood slightly behind him, where he could not see her. Her eyes never left his face. He spoke for twelve minutes, and used the word *power* a lot. She laughed with delight at every burst of applause. Later, as the younger Roosevelts served croquettes, ice cream, and lemonade on the lawn, she moved gracefully about, beguiling man after man with her twenty-year-old body and gray-blue, almost phosphorescent eyes. Something flickered at her wrist. A bright green snake twined round her fingers and wriggled up the front of her dress.

Roosevelt paid no attention. He was more interested in checking whom Governor Odell was talking to, on a secluded bench in the garden. Alice was not the only one of his children to wear reptiles next to the skin. She was, however, the only one who resented him—though loving him with equal violence. Her attitude toward herself was equally confused. "I feel that I want something, I don't know what." At times, in her padlocked diary, she fantasized symbols of escape: a roadster, a rich husband, a world tour, a London season. Roosevelt's "political" reasons for refusing to indulge her drove her to such paroxysms of rage that her handwriting degenerated into a near-maniacal scribble. At other times, like this, she luxuriated in his aura of power, much as the snake enjoyed the warmth of her own bodice.

"When I come down to bed rock facts," Alice told herself, "I am more interested in my father's political career than anything in the world. Of course I want him re-elected . . . but there again, I am afraid it is because it would keep me in my present position."

⌐◯⌐

ROOSEVELT'S THOUGHTFUL OBSERVANCE of Governor Odell (parchment-pale, rumpled, and glowering) in the garden betrayed his worry that the dour

"BEGUILING MAN AFTER MAN WITH HER TWENTY-YEAR-OLD
BODY AND . . . ALMOST PHOSPHORESCENT EYES."
Alice Roosevelt, 1904

politico might prove a liability in the election. Since both presidential candidates happened to be New Yorkers, the Empire State's vote was bound to be unusually partisan.

Odell had proved to be a gifted administrator, pushing through wider reforms than Roosevelt himself had done, saving more money, and overhauling the party machinery. Politically, however, the Governor was being overtaken by accelerating trends that he was powerless to understand, much less control. He still thought that labor should defer to capital, that New York City and New York State had more things in common than not, that party discipline guaranteed straight-ticket voting. These nineteenth-century notions were challenged by evidence that New York State's independent vote was growing and might well return a Democrat to Albany, if not to Washington, D.C.

After two terms, Odell was not popular enough to run again. But having painstakingly made himself party boss, he wanted to remain so. Much to the disgust of Democrats, he had forced the state Republican Committee to elect him its chairman. This brazen mixing of executive politics and electioneering was sure to be a campaign issue, particularly if Odell tried to choose his own successor. Roosevelt dreaded the prospect of having to carry a heavy puppet, should the presidential race become close. New York State represented the nation's largest block of electoral votes.

It was vital, therefore, to find a gubernatorial candidate who would be perceived as a Roosevelt Republican. Odell did not object, as long as he was consulted. He agreed with the President that one New Yorker, above all others, had the integrity and stature to sweep the state. Unfortunately, Elihu Root was adamant about remaining in private life. "I must ask my friends to accept as final the refusal of the nomination." To make things doubly plain, he stayed away from Sagamore Hill.

The press noted Root's absence from the notification ceremony, as did other national strategists. At their behest, Roosevelt wrote his old friend and proffered the most glittering of grails:

> The Republicans of this country are turning their eyes towards you as being the man who, by present appearances, would, if elected Governor of New York, become the foremost Republican in the land, and the natural leader of the party. . . . You would become the man likely to be nominated by the Republicans for the Presidency in 1908.

Root politely declined. He told Henry Cabot Lodge that after serving at the national level he had developed a "perfect loathing and disgust" for the "sordid details of state politics." He suspected that Governor Odell's inheritance might be corrupt. Five years of overwork under two Presidents had left him drained. He was almost sixty. Even if the grail were offered him, he would be sixty-three before he could hold it. More to the point, he simply did not want it.

⌒

ON THE DAY AFTER the notification ceremony, Roosevelt returned to the capital he had so recently quit. With what John Hay described as "cheery cruelty," he insisted that his Cabinet officers break their vacations and join him. Questions of labor and monetary policy had to be discussed before he could issue his acceptance letter, and another potential Mediterranean crisis, this time in Turkey, required group attention. Mrs. Roosevelt's added presence indicated that he was in no hurry to go home.

Washington sweltered and stagnated. Dust settled on doorsteps in the northwest sector, etching the panels of barred doors. For block after block, blinds filled every window, giving the city an empty, eyeless look. John Hay took afternoon drives in vain search of breezes. Eastward along Pennsylvania Avenue, the air boiled silently over the sidewalks. Capitol Hill floated like a mirage about to slide over the horizon. It was too hot for birds to sing. The trees around the White House rang with beetles.

Inside, the big stone mansion was cool and fragrant with cut flowers. Roosevelt worked mornings only, debating what to do about a meat workers' strike in Chicago, and about a treaty-breaking refusal by Turkey to grant American missionaries the same privileges enjoyed by those from European nations. The first question was easy to answer in an election year: he would do nothing. But the second begged comparisons with Perdicaris's kidnapping, in that it involved a desperate envoy, a languid Sultan, and conveniently available units of the United States Navy. Roosevelt decided on 5 August to dispatch Admiral Jewell's three fast cruisers to the Levant in a further demonstration of "goodwill."

Freed for a few weeks from the demands of fatherhood, and reveling in the luxury of being alone with his "sweetest of all sweet girls," he wrote to his sister Bamie:

> Edith and I are having a really lovely time in Washington. The house is delightful. We breakfast on the portico, and then stroll in the garden; and at night we walk through the garden or on the terraces. Tomorrow we intend to cut church, and to ride out to Burnt Mills to spend the day, walking through the gorge. . . . The next three months will be wearing at times. I have no idea what the outcome will be, and I know that, as I shall hear little but what is favorable, it will be impossible for me to tell. However, come what may, I have achieved certain substantial results, have made an honorable name to leave the children, and will have completed by March 4th next pretty nearly seven years of work (dating from the time I became lieutenant colonel of my regiment) which has been of absorbing interest and of real importance. So, while if defeated, I shall feel disappointed, yet I shall also feel that I have had far more happiness and success than fall to any but a very few men; and this aside from the infinitely more important fact that I have had the happiest home life of any man whom I have ever known.

In New York, where the summer heat was only a degree or two less intense, George B. Cortelyou moved into a modern suite of offices at 1 Madison Avenue. Old Guard visitors used to the noisy disorder of earlier campaign headquarters felt that they had stumbled into the premises of a small, efficient corporation. "The brass band has departed," James Clarkson remarked, with a touch of sadness. Polite young men sat at neat desks and spent a great deal of time on the telephone. There was not a spittoon to be seen.

The chairman himself occupied a big room on the fourth floor, overlooking Madison Square. Somehow, the sunbeams angling in left him cool. He wore a stiff white vest at all times, and his handshake was dry. He slapped no backs and never went into a huddle, as Hanna used to do; the contrast with his burly, lapel-gripping predecessor was total. Cortelyou diffused a quieter authority, no less potent. Success became him: he had lost the drawn, intense look of his thirties. A female reporter admired his geometric grooming, the tie precisely pinned, the dark, silver-streaked hair brilliantined back.

Also unlike Hanna, Cortelyou left the responsibility of soliciting contributions to professional money men. Cornelius Bliss was given responsibility for eastern fund-raising; Charles Dawes collected west of the Mississippi. The chairman made it clear that Roosevelt must be elected "upon an absolutely clean and business basis." To that end, he abolished the old "bureaus"—ethnic, industrial, religious, and social—that used to serve as two-way conduits between the Republican National Committee and special-interest groups. The only bureau he kept was that of speakers, awarding it to his enemy, Nathan B. Scott.

The Senator softened, as did other members of the Old Guard, who realized that they had misjudged Cortelyou. The contacts he had built up in eighteen months as Secretary of Commerce and Labor were not inconsiderable; even the great J. P. Morgan was said to admire him. "Cortelyou is a splendid executive—resourceful and tactful and masterful," Dawes wrote in his diary. "Am delighted with the way he takes hold of things."

Roosevelt tried once to issue a set of moral instructions, but when he tried a second time, Cortelyou courteously lost his temper. "If I did not know you as well as I do I should resent you sending me such a communication," the chairman wrote. "Whatever may be my shortcomings—and they are many—I think I have a fair degree of moral fiber. . . . I am conducting this campaign for your reelection on as high a plane as you have conducted the affairs of your great office."

⁓

ROOSEVELT HAD LONG wanted to "smash" the Ottoman Empire as a passé power, opulent and corrupt. While not exactly violating the terms of her most-favored-nation agreement with the United States, Turkey had for more than a year been so discriminatory toward American missionaries and schoolteachers, and so obstructive in dealing with American diplomats throughout the Ottoman Empire, that the treaty might as well have been written in water.

John G. Leishman, the United States Minister in Constantinople, reported that the Sublime Porte, as Sultan Abd al-Hamid's government was called, had closed on him once too often. He demanded a military response. On 8 August, Hay, who was an adroit politician behind his courtly whiskers, suggested to Roosevelt that Leishman should knock on the Porte just once more, just as Admiral Jewell's squadron arrived at Smyrna. If the Sultan then reacted as obligingly as His Chereefian Majesty had in Tangier, and granted all the Minister's claims, Roosevelt would be congratulated on a brilliant diplomatic victory, without having landed a single Marine. If, however, the Sultan pleaded one of his usual excuses—fatigue, indisposition, a prior engagement in the harem—Leishman should come away in one of the ships, and the matter be referred to Congress. Roosevelt would then look like a responsible Commander-in-Chief, while all danger of bloodshed would be postponed until after the election.

The President agreed, and Hay sent new instructions to Leishman.

AS HEADLINES ON the Turkish crisis grew larger, and European diplomats hurried back to Washington from vacation, Democratic National Committee officials competed for attention by notifying Alton B. Parker of his nomination for the Presidency.

Their high hopes were dampened in more ways than one on Wednesday, 10 August, the day set for the ceremony. Once more, fog shrouded Esopus, and rain fell in sheets on Parker's steep lawn, bleeding mud into the river.

At midday, a small steamer brought the committeemen north from New York City. They disembarked at the pier and looked askance at the slippery path up to the house. An authoritative escort aligned them two abreast and shouted "Forward march." Almost immediately, their formation broke up as they floundered and lost traction. One toiler, bent almost double, was heard to say that the hero of San Juan himself "couldn't climb this hill." August Belmont's shoes raced on a patch of slime, and he tumbled backward. Fortunately, someone caught him, or the party's richest benefactor would have ended up in the Hudson.

Parker waited on the porch until they came up, drenched and puffing, to shake his hand. He led the way to an open dais in the garden. About two thousand friends and townspeople sat patiently under low umbrellas. Congressman Champ Clark of Missouri made the notification address, and handed over a moist copy of the St. Louis platform. Camera bulbs popped in the drizzle. Then the judge, bareheaded, made his first political address in nearly two decades.

His declamation came as a surprise to the sodden crowd. He spoke confidently, incisively, like his rival, with little risings of the voice and sideways jabs of the arm. Yet somehow the Rooseveltian air of command was missing. At one point he broke from his text to urge an exposed group of listeners to take shelter under the trees: "You can hear just as well, and you won't get wet." Nobody moved.

The speech itself was uninspiring. Like Roosevelt, Parker summarized his party's campaign philosophy, but apologetically, as if he was embarrassed by the limp envelope in his pocket. He attacked the President's refusal to name a date for Philippine independence, without suggesting a date himself. He seemed unable to utter the words *Morocco* and *Turkey* when he harrumphed, "I protest against the feeling, now far too prevalent, that by reason of the commanding position we have assumed in the world we must take part in the disputes and broils of foreign countries."

Parker received his longest burst of applause when he announced that if elected he would serve only one term. Fate conspired to spoil even his final accolade. Just as cold hands began to clap, a photographer yelled for quiet. Down came umbrellas and hats, and everybody posed motionless in the sifting rain.

⌒

AFTERWARD, LOYAL COMMENTATORS hailed Parker's speech as a workmanlike synthesis of all that the Democratic Party stood for. Only the most fervent found anything to admire in his literary style and stage presence. Adjectives such as *impersonal, sober, labored,* and *heavy* recurred in editorial columns from Boston to San Francisco. If politics was supposed to be interesting, then Theodore Roosevelt was elected already.

An educated electorate would presumably, however, concentrate on the issues that divided the two candidates. Their acceptance speeches, plus the party platforms and convention proceedings, could now be published in "campaign textbooks" for editors and other speakers to expound on.

Cortelyou's textbook presented the Republican Party as the guardian of prosperity, the guarantor of high tariffs, the resolver of labor disputes, and the original upholder of the gold standard. It boasted of the emancipation of Cuba, the Philippines Armistice, the Panama Canal Act, and the Hay–Bunau-Varilla Treaty. It reminded Northeasterners that the President had settled the coal strike, and Southwesterners that he was making the desert blossom. Without actually using the word *Negro*, it said that any states guilty of "special discrimination" in suffrage should be penalized by reduced representation in Congress.

The Democratic textbook, much thinner, noted that Republican "prosperity" benefited Wall Street more than Main Street, while protectionism made American goods cheaper abroad than at home. It accused Roosevelt of disrespect for the Constitution—and promised that President Parker would "set his face sternly against Executive usurpation of legislative and judicial functions." *His* Administration would not be "spasmodic, erratic, sensational, spectacular, and arbitrary." Abroad, Democrats were for Philippine independence, and against jingoism, imperialism, and "the display of great military armaments." At home, they deplored what they saw as Roosevelt's attempts "to kindle anew the embers of racial and sectional strife."

Neither party had anything specific to say about trust control, labor policy, or tariff reform. Both candidates agreed that the Panama Canal would be of vast benefit to mankind. Parker said nothing about lynchings—still occurring at a rate of one every four days—and Roosevelt, having courageously raised the subject in 1903, was content to let it rest.

Major press endorsements were not expected until the fall. Yet the most eagerly awaited came with devastating suddenness on 11 August, fewer than twenty-four hours after Parker's speech. For as long as anyone could remember, the New York *Sun* had visited its wrath on any politician, Republican or Democrat, who presumed to interfere with the free workings of capital—as Roosevelt had done during the coal strike. But the paper's editors compared his record with Parker's rhetoric, and announced their decision in five weary words:

THEODORE! with all thy faults—

⟨⟩

WITHIN DAYS OF the arrival of Admiral Jewell's squadron at Smyrna, Minister Leishman advised that Abd al-Hamid had promised, in an informal memorandum, that there was to be "no discrimination between American schools and those of other nationalities" anywhere in his Sultanate. Clearly, Turkey's willingness to negotiate was related to the weight of armor on her doorstep.

Leishman would have preferred something more binding than a note scribbled by a secretary, but Roosevelt hastened to proclaim victory without violence. He ordered Leishman to accept the Sultan's word without question, adding, INFORM ADMIRAL THAT FLEET CAN NOW LEAVE.

Thanks to Hay's restraint, Roosevelt the candidate was able to bask in praise of his statesmanship. He wished that the election could be held "next Tuesday." Even critical commentators were reduced to grudging admiration. The Brooklyn *Eagle* suggested that he had aimed his naval guns "at the Democratic enemy, not the Sultan," pointing out that Jewell could have been sent east immediately after the Perdicaris affair. But Roosevelt had obviously delayed his grand gesture to coincide with Judge Parker's notification ceremony. "The power to seize the psychological moment is the essence of genius in politics, and if anybody doubts that Theodore Roosevelt is a genius he should reverse himself on this further evidence."

⟶

THE PRESIDENT WAS now free to resume his summer vacation. But he did so aware that a much more serious crisis was burgeoning in the Far East.

For almost a month now, Japanese naval and ground forces had been consolidating themselves around Port Arthur, redoubt of the Liaotung Peninsula and strategic key to both Korea and Manchuria. The Russian-held fortress still stood, but without naval protection, leaving Japan in complete command of the sea approaches. On 20 August, General Maresuke Nogi began a "final" assault on Port Arthur. Wave after wave of seemingly berserk little infantrymen broke bloodily on the fortress walls for two nights and days. But the walls held, and the waves receded, carrying a flotsam of fifteen thousand dead and wounded. Nogi's army settled down to what looked like a long winter of siege.

Farther inland, three other Japanese columns converged on Liao-yang, where Russia's main army lay entrenched. On 23 August, there began nine days of what *Review of Reviews* called "perhaps the most desperate fighting of modern times." Three hundred thousand soldiers tried to kill one another on roads and fields and hills. The Russians, who fought bravely but unimaginatively, fell back mile by mile, battered by Japanese frontal pressure and harassed by surprise attacks on their rear communications. They summoned ten thousand reserves to stay their retreat, in vain. Even behind breastworks, they lost more men than the enemy did. For forty-eight hours the air was so loud with artillery blasts, at sixty shots a minute, that men wondered if they would ever hear again.

"The Russians think only with half a mind," Roosevelt wrote Hay, as birds sang in the quiet woods of Sagamore Hill. "I think the Japanese will whip them handsomely."

⟶

SENATOR BEVERIDGE TOOK a similar view of the President's own political battle. "Unless I am in a chloroformed state and merely dreaming, you are going to have the greatest victory since the Civil War."

The "speaking phase" of the campaign got under way as August turned to September. Orators from all parties spread out across the land with prepared texts and throat lozenges. The loudest voice, at first, was that of the Socialist presidential candidate, Eugene Debs. ("The capitalists made no mistake in nominating Mr. Roosevelt. They know him well. . . . He [has] nothing in common with the working class.")

A quieter voice eventually proved to have more effect than any other. From the moment of his selection as Roosevelt's running mate, the fifty-two-year-old Charles W. Fairbanks had been caricatured as a "stuffed club" and "Wall Street puppet." He was mocked for his spindly height, his triple-strand baldness, his prim manners and paper-dry personality. The New York *Sun* compared him unfavorably to a table of logarithms, while the *Evening Post* opined that he had been nominated for national-security reasons. "The maddest anarchist would never think of killing Roosevelt to make Fairbanks President."

The puppet comparison worked best. At six foot four, Fairbanks moved and spoke as if he had no life of his own. His voice seemed to emanate from some inner Edison cylinder, and his gestures were correct but mechanical, as if jerked by hidden wires. At exhortatory moments, his fist would clench, always in the same upheld position. Whenever he delivered a warning, a lank forefinger would shoot up, and he would rock back on his heels. From time to time, both hands would snap open like fans, and remain open until he shook them shut.

This awkwardness was oddly compelling on the hustings. But what made Fairbanks so effective was what had made him a millionaire at forty, a quiet power in the Senate, and a presidential possibility for 1908: he simply could not be stopped. The voice droned on relentlessly, the arms kept pumping, and the long legs kept striding, wherever Nathan B. Scott sent him, from White River Junction, Vermont, to Spokane, Washington. Hundreds were amused; thousands bored; hundreds of thousands convinced. If Roosevelt demonstrated the power of personality in American politics, Charles Fairbanks showed the benefit of persistence.

The first tests of their combined appeal came on 6 and 13 September, when voters in Vermont and Maine went to the polls to elect governors. August Belmont, who seemed to be managing Parker's campaign over the head of the Democratic National Committee, did not conceal his anxiety. Both states were Republican strongholds, but if the GOP margin was significantly reduced in either, Democrats could take heart for November. In Vermont, however, the Democratic candidate was defeated by a margin greater than even Cortelyou hoped for, and another Republican surge was registered in Maine.

"Unless we throw it away, we have the victory," a satisfied President declared.

Nothing was heard from the gray house at Esopus but Parker's usual booming silence. The judge—now retired from the Court of Appeals—remained as inscrutable as if he were still wearing silk. Joseph Pulitzer, the strident owner of the New York *World*, began to have second thoughts about him. "The people need a judicial Chief Magistrate, but not too judicial a candidate."

THE PRESIDENT CHOSE this moment to issue his long-awaited acceptance letter, a twelve-thousand-word enlargement upon his acceptance speech, covering every aspect of Republican policy. At least twelve close advisers—including Root, Cortelyou, Spooner, and a cross-section of lawyers and journalists—had added their own contributions, but the letter's clarity and comprehensiveness were pure Roosevelt, as were its ideological blows at Parker. Coinciding as it did with the GOP triumph in Maine, it had the dizzying effect of a follow-up punch.

Its basic theme was the self-contradiction of the St. Louis platform, which failed to reconcile Cleveland's urban conservatism with Bryan's agrarian radicalism. "Our opponents . . ." Roosevelt wrote, "seem at a loss, both as to what it is that they really believe, and as to how firmly they shall assert their belief in anything." After eight years of screaming for free silver, they now called for gold—but only because Judge Parker told them to. They solemnly endorsed the civil-service law, "the repeal of which they demanded in 1900 and 1896." As for the issue of Philippine independence, "they have occupied three entirely different positions within fifty days."

He proclaimed his own consistency, emphasizing that if elected he would proceed "on exactly the same lines" in national defense, insular administration, tariff policy, and management-labor relations. Without even a pass at modesty, he listed his eighteen proudest executive achievements, including the coal-strike settlement, arbitration of the Venezuela crisis, establishment of the Department of Commerce and Labor, dispatch of the Kishinev petition, and "decisive actions" in Panama, Tangier, and Smyrna. "There is not a policy, foreign or domestic, which we are now carrying out, which it would not be disastrous to reverse or abandon."

Sonorously he concluded: "We have striven both for civic righteousness and for national greatness; and we have faith to believe that our hands will be upheld by all who feel love of country and trust in the uplifting of mankind."

The President's letter was greeted rapturously by Republicans and ruefully by Democrats. Even *Harper's Weekly,* usually his bitter critic, praised it as "a masterful and extraordinarily able document." John Hay wrote to say that Judge Parker must regret ever quitting the state bench.

⌒

"WELL, MY PART is pretty nearly ended," Roosevelt had to acknowledge, as the Republican National Committee took full charge of his campaign in mid-September. After three years of bossing George Cortelyou, he faced eight weeks of being bossed in return—a novel sensation for any President.

Cortelyou's first priority was fund-raising, now that Wall Streeters were returning to New York from their country places. So for a while the chairman ceded initiatives to the treasurer. Silver-whiskered, avuncular, discreet, Cornelius Bliss went calling on old friends downtown. In office after paneled office, he was welcomed as a money man among money men, someone who knew the dollar's political worth as well as its purchasing power. Speaking the language of money, he had little difficulty in getting financiers to admit that Roosevelt had not harmed the workings of *laissez-faire*. The *Northern Securities* suit looked, in retrospect, like a necessary check on illegal combination—"salutary from every point of view," as *The Wall Street Journal* conceded.

Most of Bliss's visits ended with the scratch of a pen writing many zeros on a slip of paper, or with the even more satisfying sound of banknotes being counted out. Few donors demanded favors in return. When one did, asking to be appointed Ambassador to Belgium, Cortelyou returned his check. Bliss was not quite so fastidious, provided understandings were kept vague.

"Now, Mr. Bliss, we want to make this contribution," said John D. Archbold of the Standard Oil Company, handing over $100,000. "But"—he chose his words carefully—"we do not want to do it without its being known and thoroughly approved of by the powers that be."

Bliss smiled. "You need have no apprehension about it whatever," he said.

AT 10:00 A.M. ON 22 SEPTEMBER, Judge Parker drove unrecognized through the streets of lower Manhattan. He entered the Hoffman House by a side door and was at once closeted with Democratic campaign planners. As they urgently and gloomily conferred, a bedlam of steam whistles signaled the passage down the East River of an important vessel. It was the USS *Sylph,* the smaller of Roosevelt's two official yachts, cruising white and silver between crowds lining either bank. The President strolled on deck accompanied by a bulldog pup and waving a black slouch hat. He was on his way back to Washington.

The bedlam continued as the *Sylph* rounded Battery Point. Admiral Barker, back from the Mediterranean on the *Kearsarge,* saluted the Commander-in-Chief with twenty-one thunderous guns. (Meanwhile, Parker was trying to have a working lunch with the chairman of the Democratic National Committee.) Roosevelt, enjoying himself, ordered the *Sylph* to proceed up the West Side. The steam whistles followed him north as far as Grant's Tomb, before he doubled back and crossed to the railroad dock at Jersey City. Cheers of two thousand welcomers rolled across the Hudson. Finally, at 1:27 P.M., his six-car special got under way, carrying the presidential party, Mr. and Mrs. William Loeb, Jr., six Secret Service men, a governess, the entire summer White House complement of secretaries, stenographers, clerks, and messengers, plus a stallion, a bay mare, a calico pony, Josiah the badger, the bulldog pup, and other pets.

Parker's next interlocutor was Representative William Cowherd, who informed him that the Democratic congressional campaign was critically short of funds. He would of course need a majority in the House if he expected to prevail as President.

The judge spent another day and night in Manhattan, and by the time he left town on 24 September he was so depressed he would not talk to reporters even about the weather. As soon as he got back to Esopus, he ordered his horse, and rode off alone. For the rest of the afternoon he cantered aimlessly through the countryside.

_⌒_

WHEN ROOSEVELT GOT back to Washington, the little flags on his wall map of the Russo-Japanese War needed repositioning. There now had to be a cluster so close as almost to hide Port Arthur, where the Russian garrison was still under siege. Nearly two hundred miles inland, the Battle of Liao-yang was inconclusively over, with more than forty thousand dead. General Kuropatkin's army was in retreat on the plains south of Mukden. Marshal Oyama's forces were extended along the mountain slopes opposite.

This new pattern of flags pleased the President more than it did John Hay, who saw nothing but blood and snow for the rest of the winter, and, trampled underfoot, his cherished Open Door policy for China. "War grows more frightful to me as I grow older," he confessed. Roosevelt, younger and less sentimental, saw the possibility of a favorable balance of power developing in the East. He was prepared to let the Island Empire colonize Korea—but not Manchuria.

"I would like to see the war ending with Russia and Japan locked in a clinch, counterweighing one another, and both kept weak by the effort," he told Jules Jusserand. This would safeguard the security of Hawaii and the Philippines. He noticed signs of Japanese exhaustion, as evinced by General Nogi's failure to take Port Arthur: "Look how long they've been predicting its surrender!"

Jusserand, whose own government was allied with the Tsar's, reported "_un notable changement_" in Roosevelt's views to the Quai d'Orsay.

_⌒_

ACCORDING TO ALL THE laws of political navigation, the Democratic campaign vessel, split along ideological lines and commanded by a man who would not steer, should by now have sunk. Amazingly, however, she began to ride higher in the last week of September, and on the first day of October gave off a blast of live steam.

Joseph Pulitzer complained, in an open letter spread across two pages of the New York _World,_ "You have not kept the faith, Mr. President, in your promise of publicity as to the affairs of the corporations. . . . Why?" Roo-

sevelt's much-vaunted Bureau of Corporations had been in existence for eighteen months, but Americans still knew nothing of how trust lords such as
E. H. Harriman and J. P. Morgan operated. Both men, Pulitzer reported, were
giving huge sums to the Republicans. (He did not mention that August Belmont and James J. Hill were doing the same for the Democrats.) "When they
give something to Mr. Cortelyou for your campaign . . . they regard your acceptance of their tribute as an implied promise of protection."

Pulitzer proceeded to ask ten bold-face questions.

1. How much has the beef trust contributed to Mr. Cortelyou?
2. How much has the paper trust contributed to Mr. Cortelyou?
3. How much has the coal trust contributed to Mr. Cortelyou?
4. How much has the sugar trust contributed to Mr. Cortelyou?
5. How much has the oil trust contributed to Mr. Cortelyou?
6. How much has the tobacco trust contributed to Mr. Cortelyou?
7. How much has the steel trust contributed to Mr. Cortelyou?
8. How much have the national banks contributed to Mr. Cortelyou?
9. How much has the insurance trust contributed to Mr. Cortelyou?
10. How much have the six great railroads contributed to Mr. Cortel-
    you?

The aggregate answer—which Cortelyou declined to give—was: less than
half of what Hanna and McKinley had collected from such sources in 1900.
Corporate contributions were actually tapering off, since the President
seemed such a cinch for election.

Cortelyou's friends knew him to be a man of almost ludicrous probity. He
had spent the last fourteen years paying off debts of honor at maximum interest, despite the forgiveness of his creditors. But these were private matters.
Pulitzer's "Ten Questions" (shrewdly aimed at him, rather than at the well-
respected Bliss) amounted to ten very public slurs on Cortelyou's reputation.
Soon Democratic campaign speakers were shouting his name over and over
again, along with *How much? How much? How much?*, until the chorus resounded throughout New York State. Judge Parker alone maintained an austere silence.

All Cortelyou said in response was that the next Administration was
going to be "unhampered by a single promise of any kind." Roosevelt chafed
with frustration. He was beginning to have doubts about his choice for
chairman. The fighter in him longed to push Cortelyou aside and lead "the
most savage counterattack possible." Bliss wrote urging him to have faith.
"Mr. Cortelyou is proving to be all we anticipated, and more: his grasp of the
details of the business in hand is remarkable."

Roosevelt was not soothed. One needed to be more than a detail man to
see that winning the White House was not enough: it had to be won in such

a way that state houses were won, too—at least those vital to one's future executive effectiveness. Cortelyou did not seem to "grasp" the necessity of a Republican victory in New York's gubernatorial contest.

After Elihu Root's refusal to run, the state GOP had compromised by nominating Lieutenant Governor Frank W. Higgins. Unfortunately, Higgins was a listless candidate whose first reaction to being dubbed "Odell's stooge" had been to stop campaigning and sulk. The Democratic National Committee, sensing weakness, had begun to lavish money on its own local ticket. If Cortelyou—or someone more forceful—did not immediately kick some fight into Higgins, the second Roosevelt Administration might have to deal with a broken Odell machine and a Tammany Hall governor.

An even worse scenario, not inconceivable in the event of a foreign emergency or major scandal, was that Roosevelt's current popularity could decline nationwide, to the point that defeat in New York might cost him his Presidency. "Pray get out and put yourself into the canvass at the earliest possible moment," Roosevelt wrote Higgins. "You and I are in the same boat. We shall sink or swim together."

Higgins continued to sulk. By the second week of October, gloom over his candidacy was so great that contributions to both the presidential and gubernatorial campaigns dwindled further. "The drift here seems to be against us," William Dudley Foulke wrote Roosevelt.

At 1 Madison Avenue, the telephone rang for Cortelyou. He was out. Staff rushed in search of Bliss: it was the President calling. But the treasurer was out, too. Senator Scott came on the line.

ROOSEVELT	Who is this?
SCOTT	Mr. Scott.
ROOSEVELT	What is this I hear about Higgins? I hear there is some danger of his being defeated.
SCOTT	Well, if the election was now, I fear he would be defeated.
ROOSEVELT	What is the trouble?
SCOTT	The [state] committee claim that they have no funds. . . .
ROOSEVELT	Well, can't Mr. Bliss settle that . . . can't the state committee raise the funds?

Scott explained that Bliss and Cortelyou had budgeted a quarter of a million dollars for the gubernatorial campaign. Now, just when Odell needed to bolster Higgins's sagging ratings, the campaign was in default. The President exploded.

ROOSEVELT	I would rather lose the election in the country than be defeated in my own state.
SCOTT	There is no danger, Mr. President, . . . no danger whatever of

your not carrying the state. If the funds were furnished . . . I
have no doubt we can elect Mr. Higgins.

ROOSEVELT   I will send for Mr. Harriman.

E. H. Harriman was a heavy investor in the New York State Republican
organization, and therefore wanted to avoid a Higgins defeat. He was also,
according to rumor, keen to see his good friend Benjamin B. Odell in the
United States Senate. Roosevelt needed to harness the energies of all three
men: financier, candidate, and boss.

"In view of the trouble over the State ticket in New York, I should much
like to have a few words with you," he wrote Harriman on 10 October. "Do
you think you can get down here within a few days and take either lunch or
dinner with me?" Harriman accepted the invitation, but found that his schedule would not allow him to come south in less than a week.

The President detected a whiff of coquettishness, and turned coy himself.
"Now, my dear sir, you and I are practical men," he wrote again. "If you
think there is any danger of your visit to me causing trouble, or if you think
there is nothing special I should be informed about . . . why of course give up
the visit for the time being."

Harriman was thus put in the awkward position of having to push for a
meeting he had postponed. Roosevelt casually added that there were "certain
government matters not connected with the campaign" he had hoped to discuss. The implication was clear. If elected, he would be embarking on a program of railroad rate reform, such as a wise tycoon might want to know
about in advance.

When Harriman called for an appointment, he was politely asked what he
wanted to see the President about. In the event, he did not get down to Washington until the twentieth, by which time the "October scare" was moderating. Twelve thousand New Yorkers rah-rahing for Roosevelt at Madison
Square Garden indicated that the President was still strong in the Empire
State, even if Higgins was not.

Roosevelt received Harriman—small, curt, dark, quick—late in the afternoon, alone except for William Loeb, who was soon excused. That evening,
the financier returned to the White House for dinner. There were no other
guests. Roosevelt spent most of the time talking about New York politics.
Whatever else was said, Harriman went back north committed to raising
$260,000 on behalf of New York GOP candidates. He had a pleased sense of
usefulness and high importance. "They are all in a hole," he boasted to an
aide, "and the President wants me to help them out."

HARRIMAN PROVED AS good as his word, personally contributing fifty thousand dollars and leaning on several of his Wall Street colleagues. J. P. Morgan,

who had once said that Roosevelt would be lucky to raise more than a four-figure sum in the whole financial district, gave one hundred thousand dollars, following up with fifty thousand more. Millionaires virtually stood in line as realization spread that the President was likely to be elected by a historic majority. Chauncey Depew doffed his Senatorial hat, put on that of chairman of the New York Central Railroad, and gave $100,000. Henry Clay Frick gave $50,000, saying that he would be amenable to further requests. George Perkins wrote three separate checks totaling $450,000, with the good wishes of himself, the House of Morgan, and the New York Life Insurance Company. George J. Gould, of Western Union and the Great Northern Railway, gave fully half a million dollars. Other donations came in from executives of Standard Oil, National City Life, General Electric, American Can, and International Harvester.

The flood became an embarrassment for Roosevelt. Did all these men imagine they were buying him? "Corporate cunning has developed faster than the laws of nation and state," he remarked to the reporter Lindsay Denison. "Sooner or later, unless there is a readjustment, there will come a riotous, wicked, murderous day of atonement." Born to wealth, with an inherited sense that it must be repaid with public service, he found himself increasingly repelled by those who went after money for money's sake, or used it to buy power. Unless wealth was chastened by culture or regulated by government, it was at worst predatory, at best boring. He did not care how little time he spent in future with E. H. Harriman. "It tires me to talk to rich men. You expect a man of millions, the head of a great industry, to be a man worth hearing; but as a rule they don't know anything outside their own businesses."

⸺

DEMOCRATIC CAMPAIGN OFFICIALS could not hide their disappointment in Alton B. Parker. Although James J. Hill and George F. Baer had been generous supporters of his candidacy, their primary desire was obviously to stop Roosevelt rather than support Parker. His refusal to do or say anything partisan was irritating reporters and alienating voters. As one workingman complained, "The Jedge hain't quite riz to the occasion."

On 22 October, in New York, the veteran strategist Daniel S. Lamont tried to shock Parker's complacency. "Well, you are going to be licked, old fellow, but brace up and make the best fight you can, and when it is over, come down here and practice law."

Like most presidential candidates, Parker could not believe bad news. "How do you know I am going to be defeated?"

"Why, they have underwritten it, just as they would underwrite building a railroad to San Francisco."

The judge returned stunned to Esopus. He decided that if he could not win, he could at least speak out against the "menace" of corporate campaign funds.

As luck would have it, he was visited the next afternoon by a delegation of supporters. He managed to startle them with some semispecific allegations of "debasing and corrupt" payments to the GOP by "individuals of corporations . . . who would control the results of election contests." His remarks made modest headlines on 24 October.

John Hay, whose memories went back to the hellfire days of American political oratory, was not impressed by Parker's tepid outrage. "We are at the fag end of the most absurd political campaign of our time," he wrote Henry Adams, "and it looks like Roosevelt to the gamblers and the Jews."

~

ALICE LIKED TO TEASE her father about his habit of writing "posterity letters" whenever anything occurred that might affect his historical reputation. It was a habit that went back to the earliest days of his political career, when he would write solemn screeds to Bamie and portentously sign them "Theodore Roosevelt," as if she were unaware of his surname.

Some instinct warned him, on the eve of his birthday, that the Democrats might return to the theme of corporate contributions in the closing days of the campaign. The instinct was triggered when a reporter from New York mentioned seeing a check made out to the Republican National Committee by an executive of Standard Oil—still the most hated trust in popular mythology. Another reporter confirmed this, and said the check had been written after Cornelius Bliss intimated that a failure to be generous would be to the "disadvantage" of the Rockefeller interests.

Roosevelt's reaction was to dictate not only a posterity letter, but a posterity telegram and posterity memorandum as well. The letter went to Cortelyou:

> I have just been informed that the Standard Oil people have contributed one hundred thousand dollars to our campaign fund. This may be entirely untrue. But if true I must ask you to direct that the money be returned to them forthwith. . . . It is entirely legitimate to accept contributions, no matter how large they are, from individuals and corporations on the terms on which I happen to know that you have accepted them: that is, with the explicit understanding that they were given and received with no thought of any more obligation . . . than is implied by the statement that every man shall receive a square deal, no more and no less, and this I shall guarantee him in any event to the best of my ability.

He did not explain why a check from John D. Archbold should be any less acceptable than one from E. H. Harriman, except to say that "in view of my past relations with the Standard Oil Company," the transaction might be construed "as putting us under an improper obligation."

By telegram, he demanded that Cortelyou confirm the refund, and by memo, he explained at length how he had heard about the check. Then, forsaking pomposity for his normal boyish good cheer, he celebrated his birthday.

Elihu Root, who over the years had developed an almost paternal tenderness for him, sent a note to the White House: "I congratulate you on attaining the respectable age of 46. You have made a very good start in life and your friends have great hopes for you when you grow up."

IN THE LAST DAYS of October, Parker unexpectedly yielded to the pleas of the Democratic National Committee and undertook a speaking tour. He confined himself to a few pivotal counties in New York and New Jersey, but adopted an aggressive tone that kept him in the national headlines. His theme—"The trusts are furnishing the money with which they hope to control the election"—focused on the hapless Cortelyou, who was once again portrayed in yellow newspapers as a Wall Street toady.

Roosevelt was at first sympathetic, then nervous when the chairman failed to respond adequately to his letter about Standard Oil. He telegraphed again: "Has my request been complied with? I desire that there be no delay."

There was no reply. Loeb made a follow-up call to New York and got through only to Bliss, who said with distinct irritation, "No contribution has been received from the Standard Oil Company and none will be received."

Roosevelt had to accept this denial. But restraint became more and more difficult as Parker began to repeat the "Ten Questions," and suggest that Cortelyou's rapid rise from presidential aide to Secretary to party chief had been engineered with the precise intent of dunning captains of industry. No man in the country, the judge implied, enjoyed such equal access to privileged information in his former fiefdom, the Bureau of Corporations. Hence his success in "demanding" support from tycoons too scared to resist him. "Although this may be satisfactory to the conscience of Republican leaders," Parker said, without actually naming the President, "it must, I firmly believe, be condemned as a shameless exhibition of a willingness to make compromise with decency."

When Cortelyou again said nothing, Roosevelt lost patience. "I have never seen him so troubled," his wife wrote. The question was no longer one of whether he should enter the campaign, but when. With Election Day looming on Tuesday, 8 November, he decided that the Saturday morning prior would be the best moment to hit Parker, and "hit him hard." That way, the judge would suffer a repeated onslaught of headlines throughout the weekend, and would be unable to publish much of a reply before Monday—too late, probably, to regain the initiative.

Parker was tempted into a final indiscretion on Thursday, 3 November, when he accused the Republican National Committee of "blackmail" and threats to leak secret data from the Bureau of Corporations. This was going too far, as he himself seemed to realize the following day, when he hedged on the source of his information in a lame speech in Brooklyn.

Shortly before twelve o'clock that night, the President released his statement. Old-time journalists had to look back to the 1880s for a political utterance that packed more force. It was long—over a thousand words—but passionate enough to compel thorough reading. He began by rephrasing Parker's charges and innuendos, making them sound at once more extreme, yet easier to refute. His prose in answer was shotgunned with characteristic repetitions and alliterations that lodged in anyone's memory the points he wanted to make.

> Mr. Parker's accusations against me and Mr. Cortelyou are monstrous. If true, they would brand both of us forever with infamy, and inasmuch as they are false, heavy must be the condemnation of the man making them. . . .
>
> The assertion that Mr. Cortelyou had any knowledge gained while in any official position whereby he was enabled to secure and did secure any contributions from any corporation is a falsehood. The assertion that there has been any blackmail, direct or indirect, by Mr. Cortelyou or by me is a falsehood. The assertion that there has been made in my behalf and by my authority by Mr. Cortelyou or by anyone else any pledge or promise . . . in recognition of any contribution from any source, is a wicked falsehood.
>
> That Mr. Parker should desire to avoid the discussion of principles I can well understand, for it is but the bare truth to say that he has not attacked us on any matter of principle or upon any action of the government save after first misstating that principle or that action.

Roosevelt asked all voters to check his record as the prosecutor of *Northern Securities* and the mediator of the coal strike, and then ponder Parker's cozy relations with the "great corporate interests" that had financed the *Democratic* campaign. With a sarcastic pun, he compared the judge's "trusted" advisers to his own roster of Root, Knox, Crane, Moody, Garfield, and Cortelyou—all of whom must be corrupt, if one was.

"The statements made by Mr. Parker," he again declared, "are unqualifiedly and atrociously false."

⤝⤞

"VICTORY. TRIUMPH. My Father is elected," Alice wrote in her diary for 8 November 1904. "Received Parker's congratulatory telegram at 9. Carried New York State by over 200,000. Higgins elected Governor. An unprecedented landslide. It is all colossal."

Her last adjective was no girlish exaggeration. Although the full dimension of the President's majority would take days to tabulate, he had been returned to power by thirty-three of the forty-five states, even managing to detach Missouri from the historically solid "South." He seemed certain to amass at least as large a popular vote as McKinley's in 1900, and to outscore every one of his twenty-five predecessors in the electoral college.

Purged by his last-minute blast at Parker, astounded at the extent of his sweep, and reverential to the memory of George Washington, he dictated a quick statement to reporters at 10:30 P.M. in the White House vestibule, while Alice Roosevelt stood by, not quite believing her ears.

"On the fourth of March next I shall have served three and a half years, and this three and a half years constitutes my first term. The wise custom which limits the President to two terms regards the substance and not the form. Under no circumstances will I be a candidate for or accept another nomination."

Interlude

ON THE DAY AFTER Roosevelt's election, Wilbur and Orville Wright took their flying machine on a series of long, celebratory hops over Ohio. Farther west, other aviators vied for the St. Louis World's Fair Grand Prize for Aeronautic Achievement. With less than a month to go before the exposition formally closed, the award—one hundred thousand dollars—seemed impossible of attainment, a chimera not unlike the nightly glow of one hundred thousand fairground lights trying to hold back the encroachment of the prairie.

Since the Brazilian birdman Alberto Santos-Dumont had arrived in St. Louis in June, only to have his long silk gasbag slashed while in storage, American "aero-planes," airships, ornithopters, gliders, balloons, and kites had been lifting off in wobbly attempts to make three flights over a fifteen-mile, L-shaped course. Metallic lighter-than-air cylinders, pterodactyl-like contraptions flapping bamboo wings, aluminum-and-silk sky-cycles, and huge cigars and saucers and tetrahedrons defied gravity with varying success—most triumphantly the *California Arrow,* a dirigible that floated for thirty-seven minutes over the exhibition's fluttering flags. If unable to perform the requisite L, it described many graceful Os, wheeling careless of the wind, and releasing, at two thousand feet, a pigeon that tired of flight long before it did.

Nobody won the Grand Prize, but various ascents advanced the frontiers of science. Three men in a balloon soared almost two miles high and sent down wireless messages in the first American demonstration of air-to-ground telegraphy. Two airship distance records were broken. And throughout the final weeks of the Fair, as the President of the United States prepared to visit, an effervescence of meteorological balloons rose until they burst, dropping little basketfuls of data under cones of silk.

∽

HENRY ADAMS, who loved expositions as much as he hated politics, had visited St. Louis at the earliest opportunity. Stooped and sedentary at sixty-six, he was inspired less by the Fair's awkward attempts at levitation than by its horizontal dynamic, the almost contemptuous way a small Midwestern city had turned its back on the Mississippi and scattered palaces across the plain, gilding them with dollars and bathing them with light, daring the distant world to come and save it from insolvency.

Adams saw such thin crowds, and such a consequent emptiness of exhibits and promenades, that he doubted the city fathers would recoup a third of their twenty or thirty million. Yet they seemed "quite drunk" with expectations of profit, as Roosevelt had been earlier in the year, at the height of his unpopularity with Congress. The Fair was *schwärmerisch*—visionary—and above all paradoxical in its crass commercialism and unstudied beauty. "One asked oneself whether this extravagance reflected the past or imaged the future; whether it was a creation of the old America or the promise of the new one."

Both coming and going, Adams (who had not been that far west in a decade) was struck by the raw power pulsating from landscapes once agricultural, now industrial—steam engines and smokestacks dirtying the air and surrounding each town with a no-man's-land of "discards." Ever since confronting an enormous, silently whirring dynamo at the last World's Fair—in Paris, four years before—he had been trying to formulate a dynamic theory of history that would index man's progress (or regress) to the curve of power production. But the curve was now becoming so steep, and the progress (or, again, regress) so fast that Adams saw nothing ahead but an acceleration that threatened the law of inertia.

He had tried to show, in his just-completed study of medievalism, *Mont Saint-Michel and Chartres,* that the "conservative Christian" civilization of the preceding nineteen hundred years had been dominated by one centripetal, feminine, fertile image, the Virgin. She had erected all of Europe's great cathedrals, humanized its laws, and inspired its family and social values. One did not have to be a Catholic, or for that matter a European, to look to her for comfort. But now the centrifugal, masculine, destructive dynamo threatened the Virgin—and, more personally, Henry Adams's whole worldview.

The settled life, the *vis inertiae* he had enjoyed since boyhood, whose blue blood and classical education gave him a sense of stability at rest, and of steady direction when advancing himself, must soon, apparently, change to a perpetual motion that was not so much forward as omnidirectional, and favored the less weighted members of society: the young, the rudely opportunistic, above all the nimble Jews. In which case, he and his beloved John Hay were bound to be thrown off while Roosevelt, the very personification of dynamism (and with something of a "Jew look," come to think of it, in a strong light), spun St. Louis, and Washington, and the world, into a maelstrom beyond Adams's power to control.

"The devil is whirling me round, in the shape of a grinning fiend with tusks and eye-glasses . . . faster and faster, and I can't get off."

ROOSEVELT GOT TO the World's Fair just in time, on 26 November, as the commissioners were preparing to douse its lights. He came at the behest of Henry Adams—or rather, at the behest of Edith, whom Adams had urged to see the white palaces before they reverted to prairie.

"We really had great fun, although we only spent one day at the Fair," Roosevelt reported to Kermit. Unconsciously using Adams's own language, he described his visit as "a perfect whirl." He stomped through the display halls so fast that even Alice had to run to catch up. His hurry was less a matter of urgency than camouflage: unbeknownst to reporters, he was nursing several boxing and riding injuries, including a burst blood vessel that had spread a bruise "big as two dinner plates" across the inside of his thigh.

He was impressed by the beauty of the illuminations, but only one exhibit spoke to him personally. It was his own Maltese Cross ranch cabin from 1884, reverently presented by the State of North Dakota.

The presidential train did not depart St. Louis until after midnight on 28 November. Edith, exhausted, retired to her stateroom, but Roosevelt still had some energy to work off. He called for a stenographer and dictated a thousand-word letter-review of James Ford Rhodes's five-volume *History of the United States from the Compromise of 1850*. Inevitably if naïvely, the great theme of North versus South made him think of his own recent Appomattox at the polls, and he segued into a jovial reflection that Democratic cartoonists had played into his hands by representing him as the eternal Rough Rider, "carrying a big stick and threatening foreign nations." This had only made a "kind of *ad captandum* appeal on my behalf," especially to younger voters.

A couple of midnights later, as November gave way to December, the president of the World's Fair turned a rheostat at the base of the Louisiana Purchase Monument, and the illuminations began to fade as one hundred thousand spectators applauded. They had some reason to cheer. Nearly nineteen million visitors from around the world had helped replenish the city's coffers, if not those of the exposition itself. Clearly "the spirit of St. Louis"—a new expression, already popular—was more potent than the pessimistic whinings of Henry Adams.

As if in earnest of that spirit, the little meteorological balloons continued to rise for the rest of the year, shining and swelling and bursting.

⁓

MARGUERITE CASSINI HAD just dressed in satin and chinchilla for a ball on 2 January 1905 when she came across her father in the vestibule of the Russian Embassy. His hands held a batch of telegrams, and were shaking. "Go back upstairs and take off those clothes!" he growled at her. "You're going nowhere tonight. Port Arthur has been surrendered!"

The Ambassador's choler concealed, perhaps, his embarrassment at having first heard about the surrender a few hours earlier, during the White

House New Year's reception. John Hay had discreetly murmured the news before Theodore Roosevelt trumpeted it to other diplomats. Only a lifetime's training in court politesse had enabled Cassini to move on, and greet Minister Takahira as if nothing had happened.

While Europe reacted in shock—Roosevelt's ten-month certainty that Japan would win the war had been shared by only the French—rumors ran along Embassy Row that the United States would press for a peace settlement. Hay denied them all. Rheumatic, perpetually coughing, seizing every chance to stay in bed, the Secretary had lost his appetite for hard work. More and more since the election, Roosevelt was taking the controls, and accelerating the pace, of foreign policy.

Hay had been Secretary of State for six years now. Working with characteristic quietness and dedication—qualities that had endeared him in youth to Lincoln—he had built a series of agreements and alignments that peacefully buttressed the United States against the rivalries of Europe, Central Asia, and the Far East. The current Anglo-American rapprochement was largely his, as was the Open Door in China, and the reaffirmed Alaskan boundary, and the Paris and Panama Canal Treaties. He brought a high moral tone to the often mendacious business of diplomacy, without compromising any of his country's commercial interests. All that remained for him to complete his life's work (for he knew himself to be dying) was to negotiate a peace in Manchuria that would keep the Open Door ajar and save Russia from revolution.

However, Count Cassini seemed confident that the Tsar's endless military reserves would humble Japan sooner or later. Those twenty-four thousand troops lost at Port Arthur were as replaceable as grapes in the Trubetskoy vineyard. The Russian Baltic Fleet was on its way around the world to wreak revenge on Admiral Togo. But Cassini may have been merely posturing; before the war, he had seemed to favor a peaceful Russian foreign policy, especially *vis-à-vis* China. But, as Hay reminded Roosevelt, "dealing with people to whom mendacity is a science is no easy thing."

All *he* knew in January 1905 was that if the belligerents did not soon agree to a cease-fire, his heart would give out in the attempt to negotiate one. Along with all his Cabinet colleagues, Hay had handed in his resignation. But this was a formality, returning to Roosevelt the power of appointment—or reappointment. The Secretary could only hope against hope that he would not be needed in the new Administration.

Politely disapproving, he stood by as two junior members of the *secret du roi* arrived from overseas for White House consultations. One was the President's Harvard classmate Baron Kentaro Kaneko, and the other his former best man, Cecil Spring Rice, still attached to the British Embassy in St. Petersburg.

MEANWHILE, HENRY ADAMS tried again and again to plot the power curve of 1901 through 1904, and relate it to force fields other than Roosevelt's personality. He wanted to include his Dynamic Theory of History in an intellectual memoir he had begun to write, provisionally entitled "The Education of Henry Adams: A Study of Twentieth-Century Multiplicity." Adams figured that he would need about two years to finish the book, which he would then publish privately, in a limited edition, for members of his immediate circle. John Hay would be the first to see it—if Hay lived long enough—and of course the President must get a copy, too.

What would Roosevelt make of Adams's Roosevelt, the godlike perpetrator of "pure act"? Insofar as he *was* pure act, he might be amused but not particularly interested. The President was not a speculative, nor a spiritual man. He was in too much of a hurry to make the world over, today or preferably yesterday, to care what Adams (or for that matter Hay) might think of him. They were both of them sixty-six; he twenty years younger. "With him wielding unmeasured power with immeasurable energy in the White House," Adams wrote, "the relation of age to youth—of teacher to pupil—was altogether out of place; and no other was possible."

Unless, of course, one continued one's own education by watching the sometimes disorientating spectacle of youth in flight from the past. Roosevelt's *Energetik,* his dirigible ability to change course at a moment's notice, his tendency to write exuberant Os in the air, made Adams doubt his own trail across "the darkening prairie of education." To a historian born in 1838, "always and everywhere the Complex had been true and the Contradiction certain." Here was Roosevelt trumpeting either-or banalities, lecturing intellectuals as though they were children, and yet repeatedly prevailing in the most intricate political situations. Might the President's simplicity be that of an *idiot savant* who instinctively understood how Complexity worked, even to the point of using Contradiction to generate extra energy? If so, he was certainly not simplistic. He was, on the contrary, formidable: twentieth-century in his eager embrace of Chaos, eighteenth-century in his utter self-certainty. To Roosevelt, as to Kant, "Truth was the essence of the 'I.' "

ANOTHER HENRY WHO had long observed Roosevelt with bemusement visited the White House that January and was taken aback by its new splendor and protocol. Henry James attended the annual Diplomatic Reception, not inappropriately, as America's most distinguished expatriate writer. Like Adams before him, he was swept upstairs afterward for "supper" in a sea of velvet-and–gold lace uniforms and found himself sitting one dowager away from Roosevelt.

"The President is distinctly tending—or trying—to make a 'court,' " he wrote later. Yet he could not help being flattered at his placement above so many representatives of empires. Elsewhere, at a point hardly less privileged, next to Mrs. Roosevelt, sat the sculptor Augustus Saint-Gaudens. Democracy still reigned at the heart of the Republic; art mattered here as much as politics.

"Theodore Rex," James allowed, "is at any rate a really extraordinary creature for native intensity, veracity, and *bonhomie*—he plays his part with the best will in the world and I recognize his amusing likability."

⤚

THE IMAGINATION MUST *be given not wings but weights.* Francis Bacon's dogged dictum, which Adams had so long thought salutary, seemed negated by this new century with its young men impatient of gravity and its young powers—America, Japan, Germany—pushing back the borders of old empires. The only constant now was change. Here was Roosevelt, whose main responsibilities were to keep the United States safe and solvent, collaring Capital and Labor in either hand and splicing oceans more than one thousand miles south of Key West. Here was Arthur Balfour, at last report the Prime Minister of Great Britain, embracing a New Theory of Matter, and informing the world that all of human history, "down to say, five years ago," was nothing but an illusion. Here was Kaiser "Willy" suddenly facing west, and leaving "Nicky," his poor little *crétin* cousin, to face Red revolution at home and Yellow Peril in the Far East.

Adams belonged to the minority of Washington intellectuals that dreaded a Japanese victory. Russia was, he acknowledged, a moribund empire, but at least its crown and its army held the peasants at bay, not to mention the new Mongols crowding Port Arthur. If the Tsar was deposed, "I foresee something like a huge Balkan extending from Warsaw to Vladivostok; an anarchy tempered with murders." Nearer home, France—Russia's ally—could become vulnerable to German imperialism. Hay's attitude was frustratingly ambivalent: while aware of the ruin Russia's defeat would visit upon his Open Door policy, he nevertheless worked for Theodore Roosevelt, and the President's proclamation of neutrality compelled him to be discreet.

What tormented Adams was the possibility that Roosevelt's electoral triumph—which the world had gasped at—might persuade one or the other power to ask the President to mediate a peace settlement. Surely the Virgin, if she still had any say in world affairs, would allow Hay that final honor.

⤚

BOTH KANEKO AND Spring Rice made social calls on the ailing Secretary of State. They were politely vague about their conversations with the President, Kaneko saying only that Roosevelt kept insisting that Japan should not be "exorbitant" in her demands for a price to end the war. The Baron was in no hurry to return home, and hinted at the possibility of "important news" from his government in the spring.

Hay looked out his window and saw nothing but the frozen gray of early February. "The weather remains gloomy," he wrote in his diary, "*et moi aussi.*"

Heart pain kept him awake at night, and when he slept he was often plagued by nightmares. Once he dreamed he was going to be hanged. Mrs. Hay conspired with Adams to ship him to Bad Nauheim, Germany, for a cure, but he would not hear of leaving town until after the President's Inauguration. That was more than a month away. Congress was still in session, and he had to calm the agitation of Takahira and Cassini, both of whom visited on him what they could not properly communicate to Roosevelt.

Cassini waved aside Japan's recent victories as "*éphémères.*" The American people should know that Russia had four hundred thousand soldiers in Manchuria, not to mention Admiral Zinovi Rozhdestvenski's "fine fleet," still desperately steaming toward the war theater. "Russia is neither defeated nor ruined."

The President also showed signs of rising agitation. Those who knew him understood that he was merely working up steam for the Inauguration. Henry James thought the Rooseveltian machine was "destined to be over-strained" one day. He had to admit that, at present, "it functions astonishingly, and is quite exciting to see."

With that, James left town. So did many Democrats wanting to put as much distance as possible between themselves and "Theodore the First" on the day of his coronation. "Roosevelt has the world in a sling right now," Henry Watterson wrote from a cruise ship in the Mediterranean. "But, wait a little."

THE SECOND ADMINISTRATION

1905–1909

CHAPTER 23

Many Budding Things

Onaisy lies th' head that wears a crown.

THEODORE ROOSEVELT TOOK his second oath of office in sharp, cold sunshine on 4 March 1905. Exactly four years before, he had stood on this same Capitol platform, watching President McKinley being sworn in by this same little Chief Justice. Then, heavy rain and a dogged phalanx of mostly incumbent Old Guard Republicans had reinforced his sense of having been forced

"THE WHOLE SCENE . . . WAS ONE OF CONSTANT MOVEMENT."
Roosevelt's Inauguration, 4 March 1905

into political immobility. Now, a blustering wind tore at his hair and speech cards as he stepped forward to address the crowd. It tossed the dozens of flags rising to either side of him, so violently that some wrapped around their staffs in tight spirals of red, white, and blue. Other flags, suspended between the marble columns behind him, whipped and cracked. The caps of several Annapolis and West Point cadets went spinning through the air. Women clutched at their hats (none more determinedly than Alice Roosevelt, who wore a flimsy white-and-black satin wheel, undulant with ostrich plumes), while men jammed their toppers down. The whole scene, from the ten-acre crush of spectators in the plaza to hundreds more onlookers perched dangerously on every one of the Capitol's upper protuberances (not to mention boys clambering in trees, and a whirl of pigeons around the dome), was one of constant movement, as if Roosevelt's energy had animated the entire body politic.

"My fellow citizens, no people on earth . . . with gratitude to the Giver of Good . . . under a free government . . . things of the body and the things of the soul . . . justice . . . power . . ." The wind snatched at his shouted phrases, now muffling them, now hurling them at one group of listeners, while others heard not a word.

Roosevelt read with difficulty, his silk pince-nez ribbon slapping the side of his face. Nobody, with the exception of his wife and Dr. Rixey, knew that he was losing sight in his left eye—the legacy of a recent boxing blow. He was obliged to keep a tight grasp on his cards with both hands. Close observers noticed a strange, heavy gold ring on his left third finger. It contained a strand of Abraham Lincoln's hair. John Hay had given it to him with a request that he wear it when he was sworn in: "You are one of the men who most thoroughly understand and appreciate Lincoln."

Hay could not have made a gesture more certain to move Roosevelt, whose worship of the Emancipator was admixed with pride that Theodore Senior had once been an habitué of Lincoln's White House—indeed, had met the young John Hay there. The effect of the gift was to imbue the President, at least temporarily, with a Lincolnesque devotion to the Constitution as "a document which put human rights above property rights."

Unremarked in Roosevelt's letter of thanks to Hay (which had expressed "love" for the first time in his male, non-family correspondence) was the fact that some sort of valediction was implied: if not from President to President, then at least from the man who had served them both, in youth and age, and was now palpably ceding his last responsibility as Secretary of State. Roosevelt had declined Hay's pro forma resignation, but clearly any settlement of the Russo-Japanese War was going to have to be put into younger, stronger hands—hands calmed, one hoped, by this precious token of statesmanship.

"Much has been given us," the President bellowed, leaning forward into the wind, "and much will rightfully be expected of us."

THE LENGTH OF HIS Inaugural Address was in reverse proportion to the size of those expectations. He spoke for no more than six minutes, employed few rhetorical flourishes, and said nothing of substance. Thousands of spectators cheered with some bewilderment, not understanding that the President, with a new Senate convening in special session and foreign ministries looking to him to mediate the Russo-Japanese War, was deliberately presenting as bland a public face as possible.

Afterward, Roosevelt joked to Henry Cabot Lodge, "Did you see Bacon turn pale when he heard me swear to uphold the Constitution?" Senator Augustus Bacon of Georgia, a strict constructionist, overheard this remark, as intended. "On the contrary, Mr. President, I never felt so relieved in my life."

Count Cassini led the diplomatic corps offstage, his chest virtually armor-plated with gold and silver orders. A commensurate glittering defensiveness had begun to characterize St. Petersburg's attitude toward any peace overture that might be construed as further meddling by the United States in Russian affairs. So impregnable was this breastwork that John Hay could not answer when Minister Takahira asked if Cassini believed external peace might help Russia achieve internal peace, or vice versa.

At two o'clock, the President entertained two hundred guests at lunch in the White House, while thirty-five thousand Rough Riders, Negro Republicans, Harvard alumni, anthracite miners, Indians (Chief Geronimo prominent in war paint and feathers), cowboys, Grand Army veterans, ward heelers, Filipino scouts, Oyster Bay neighbors, and bandsmen massed at the eastern end of Pennsylvania Avenue. High above the banners and placards being readied for display (WE HONOR THE MAN WHO SETTLED OUR STRIKE) floated an enormous and not very threatening Big Stick.

During the ensuing parade, which lasted three and a half hours, Roosevelt scorned his glass-enclosed reviewing stand and stood alone in the constant wind, waving his tall hat, bowing, clapping, and laughing. Whatever tomorrow's newspapers might say about him being still the youngest of Presidents, he was now the same age Theodore Senior had been when he had died—a sobering thought to his sisters, if not to himself. Four more years of strenuous responsibility loomed. Nor was he as constantly healthy as he pretended to be. The "Cuban fever" he shared with so many of these Rough Riders (trotting by with rebel yells) had to be kept down with drugs; his joints were stiffening, no matter how much he exercised; and his blood pressure, always abnormally high, was being worsened by hardening arteries.

"The President will of course outlive me," Hay wrote in his diary, "but he will not live to be old."

⌒

ON 10 MARCH, Roosevelt decided it was time "to let the Japanese Government understand that we should be glad to be of use" in any effort to arrive at a negotiated settlement. He cautioned Hay that this stated willingness must not sound too much like an "offer." If he was to be a peacemaker, he could not let the Tsar think he had solicited the job. Hay obediently bypassed Takahira and gave Lloyd C. Griscom, the young United States Minister to Japan, carte blanche to leak the President's availability.

The leak coincided with the Japanese capture of Mukden, after weeks of savage fighting. Even Count Cassini had to admit to feelings of despair. He came to see Hay, who was preparing to leave for Europe, and spoke at such length about Russia's "tremendous sacrifices and misfortunes" in wartime that the Secretary, losing patience, asked, "When will come the time of your diplomats?"

Cassini sank into even deeper gloom. "We are condemned to fight. We cannot honestly stop."

Hay left Washington on 17 March and journeyed north to New York. So, by a separate train, did Roosevelt. The Secretary went to stay overnight in his daughter's suite at the Lorraine Hotel. He had no sooner settled in than a crescendo of hooves in the street below signaled the approach of the presidential cavalcade. Hay got to a window in time to see his employer sweep by, en route to Delmonico's restaurant.

Roosevelt was in town to give away his niece Eleanor to his fifth cousin Franklin, in a Roosevelt-Roosevelt marriage sure to elicit press wisecracks about "King Theodore's" proliferating dynasty. He seemed sublimely unconscious of the young man's hero-worship of him. (Franklin had sat unnoticed, a handsome and angular figure, among the crowd of special guests at the Inauguration.) Nor did he realize—or care—that in giving Eleanor away, he inevitably attracted more attention than she did. His presidential gravitas was by now so charged that he took for granted a centripetal clustering wherever he moved or stood.

To that end, he had authorized the construction of a vast new salon at Sagamore Hill. It was to be big enough to accommodate the many delegations who came to see him every summer, and grand enough to impress the envoys of emperors.

THE PRESIDENT TOOK a midnight train back to Washington. He was back at his desk before John Hay, too weak to walk, could be wheeled aboard the SS *Cretic*. For the next few crucial months, Theodore Roosevelt would be in sole charge of the foreign policy of the United States.

A situation of extraordinary complexity presented itself. Morocco had suddenly become a factor in the Russo-Japanese War. Kaiser Wilhelm II was again using a small state's weakness to aggrandize his own empire. This time, however, *der Allmächtige* had cloaked his power play in the guise of an initiative seemingly in the interest of Sultan Abd al-Aziz. He proposed to Roosevelt, in a letter delivered by Ambassador von Sternburg, that the United States and Germany "combine to compel" France to observe an open-door policy in North Africa. Such a combination would amount to a direct challenge to the Franco-British "Entente Cordiale," which in effect shut Germany out of both Morocco and Egypt.

France, of course, was Germany's traditional enemy (as Mr. Perdicaris had discovered in his own household), and currently very vulnerable because her ally, Russia, was distracted with war elsewhere. In singling out France's efforts to obtain a commercial and military monopoly in Morocco, Wilhelm cleverly made her seem no less greedy than Russia in Manchuria. This put Roosevelt in the difficult position of having to agree with him, or seem hypocritical in demanding free trade elsewhere. If the President did so agree—to the detriment of Théophile Delcassé's most cherished strategic dream, a "Triple Entente" among London, Paris, and St. Petersburg—Germany could not only strengthen its own North African presence, but also woo France away from Russia, and gain immensely in European influence. Great Britain, in turn, might begin to bristle for war, since the English were convinced that the Kaiser had designs on their homeland.

Roosevelt's first instinct was to stall. He did not want to seem ungrateful for help France had given him in his own little Moroccan adventure, ten months before. More seriously, he felt his peacemaking credentials with the Japanese would be compromised if they saw him being manipulated by the Tsar's cousin. Then, on 31 March, Wilhelm made a surprise visit to Tangier and aggressively repeated his demand for an international solution to the Moroccan problem.

"The Kaiser has had another fit," Roosevelt wrote Hay. "What a jumping creature he is, anyhow!"

Von Sternburg was fobbed off with a noncommittal note that was more applicable to the Far Eastern situation. When, inevitably, Wilhelm jumped again, Roosevelt was prepared to say that the United States would not agree to any parley on Morocco without France's consent.

April came with no sign of willingness by either Russia or Japan to take the first formal step toward peace. Both sides were afraid of "losing face." However, they kept hinting, mainly through French intermediaries, that they were weary of war. Envoy of the various alliances besieged Roosevelt. In just one week he had to listen to Takahira, Cassini (twice), von Sternburg (three times), Jusserand, and Sir H. Mortimer Durand, a "worthy creature of mutton-suet consistency" who to his annoyance had been appointed Great Britain's latest ambassador, instead of Cecil Spring Rice. None would commit their own countries to anything, yet they expected him to squeeze commitments out of others. Exasperated—"I wish the Japs and Russians could settle it between themselves"—Roosevelt decided to go ahead with a long-planned hunting trip in search of western wolves and bears. He needed to satisfy his ebbing yet still compulsive blood-lust. Presumably nothing decisive would happen in the Far East until Russia's Baltic Fleet struck the blow St. Petersburg so counted on. That might not be until May.

Rather than leave the White House in charge of Vice President Fairbanks, who had been relegated to near-total obscurity since the Inauguration, Roosevelt assigned crisis-management powers to William Howard Taft. "I am not entirely satisfied with the foreign situation," he admitted to Hay, "but there isn't anything of sufficient importance to warrant my staying."

Rumors proliferated that Taft was the President's chosen successor. Edith Roosevelt worried about the growing fondness of each man for the other. When Theodore asked Taft for advice, what he usually got was approval. "They are too much alike." She felt that her husband had been better served during his first term by the cool counsel of Philander Knox and Elihu Root. His natural ebullience tended toward explosiveness unless periodically checked. He might joke about having Big Bill around to "sit on the lid," but politically speaking Root had packed more weight. Taft wanted to love and be loved. Consequently, he was easy to push, easy to hurt. Already Roosevelt showed a cheery tendency to bully him. "Here, Will, look at this . . ." (a flattering portrait of old Chief Justice Fuller) ". . . looks as if you might have to wait a long time."

At any rate, Taft could be relied on. The President stayed in Washington just long enough to hand him a new, reorganized Isthmian Canal Commission. Then he quit town, leaving instructions that he be wired at any change in the international situation.

⌒

THE FIRST IMPORTANT telegram to reach him at "Camp Roosevelt," outside New Castle, Colorado, was dated 18 April. It reported that Minister Takahira had been to see Taft, and dropped the merest hint that Roosevelt would be acceptable to the Japanese government as a mediator. Apparently, Delcassé was trying to insinuate himself into the negotiatory process. He had undertaken to bring the belligerents together, "provided that Japan would consent to eliminate from the negotiations certain conditions humiliating to Russia." These included cession of territory and the payment of any indemnity.

Tokyo did not feel confident in the French Minister's impartiality, since France was allied with Russia, and had ambitions in China herself. But the news that St. Petersburg was now willing to talk peace had prompted Takahira to say to Taft that his government recognized "that the friendly offices of some Power might be necessary" to initiate a peace conference. At the same time, the President of such a Power must understand that the Japanese would negotiate directly, or not at all, and under no advance pledges whatsoever.

Roosevelt wired back to Taft his agreement with Tokyo's scruples, but added two of his own: Japan must continue her support of the Open Door in Manchuria, and press for full restoration of that province to China. He said nothing about "friendly offices," since he had not yet been asked to provide them.

While awaiting Takahira's reaction, he brooded upon an urgent letter von Sternburg had sent him about the Morocco matter. Wilhelm II, unaware that Roosevelt was high in the Rocky Mountains, cut off from the nearest telegraph office by thirty miles of snowdrifts and greasy mud, was asking him to find out if the British government intended to back up France in her attempt to dominate North Africa. Roosevelt detected a note of querulousness, familiar to him from the days of the Venezuela crisis, but was not unsympathetic to the Kaiser's request. France certainly was abusing the independence of Morocco, as guaranteed by the 1880 Madrid Conference, and Britain, in his opinion, grossly overestimated German Foreign Office aims in Europe.

"I do not care to take sides between France and Germany in the matter," he wrote Taft on 20 April. "At the same time, if I can find out what Germany wants, I shall be glad to oblige her if possible." He authorized the Secretary to sound out Sir Mortimer Durand, if "the nice but somewhat fat-witted British intellect will stand it."

With that, Roosevelt returned to the purpose of his presence in Colorado: the pursuit of bears. He had already killed a big black one (exactly the same weight as Secretary Taft), breaking both its hips with one bullet, and its back with another. In a departure for him, he was hunting with hounds and terriers, some of whom were so mauled by bobcats and lynxes that they could do little afterward but lie around and bleed. It was interesting to watch the pack get revenge when a cat fell off a dead branch, right into a circle of snapping jaws: the Tsar's imminent predicament.

One little dog, a black-and-tan runt named Skip, adopted Roosevelt and took to sleeping at the foot of the presidential bed, growling at all comers.

The country was wild and steep and, because of its altitude, still in the grip of winter. White peaks massed above the camp—a clutch of tents and one log cabin, pitched in a grove of bare aspens and great spruces beside a rushing, ice-rimmed brook. Each day, Roosevelt and his hunting companion, Dr. Alexander Lambert of New York, rode out after an early breakfast, accompanied by guides and twenty or thirty dogs, and remained ten or twelve hours in the saddle, returning ravenous to the cook tent and falling into bed afterward in the cabin.

Roosevelt had been pleasantly surprised, during his earlier wolf hunt in Oklahoma, to find that he still had plenty of physical vitality. ("One run was nine miles long and I was the only man in at the finish except the professional wolf hunter Abernathy.") Going without lunch for weeks had reduced his weight, while leaping and sliding down mountain ravines gave him the exultant, if illusory, sense of being young again. On 24 April, he killed another bear, and on 25 April yet another, a small female, breaking her neck with a single bullet. Then he began to feel ill.

Late that evening, a telegram in cipher from Taft arrived by special messenger at the White House communications center in Glenwood Springs. After it was decoded overnight, William Loeb found that it contained the text of a secret cable from Baron Jutaro Komura, the Japanese Foreign Minister, to Takahira.

> You are hereby instructed to convey to the President through the Secretary of War cordial thanks of the Imperial Government for his observation and at the same time to declare that Japan adheres to the position of maintaining the Open Door in Manchuria and of restoring that province to China. Further you will say that the Imperial Government, finding that the views of the President coincide with their own on the subject of direct negotiations, would be highly gratified if he has any views of which he is willing or feels at liberty to give . . . in order to pave the way for the inauguration of such negotiation.

Taft added, in a postscript to Roosevelt: "Letter from Griscom today says Denison of Japanese Foreign Office says they are anxious to effect peace through you. . . . Cassini has sulked ever since your departure. Would it be wise to suggest beginning through him or through Jusserand?"

Loeb felt unable to trust any messenger with such a document, and decided to deliver it himself. He took a train to New Castle, then hired a mustang and a horse wrangler and ascended the mountain there. Arriving at Roosevelt's camp late that afternoon, he handed the telegram over.

The President read it, and at once became deeply thoughtful. At dinner, Loeb and Lambert both noticed that Roosevelt was not himself. He said little and had no appetite. The telegram was clearly weighing on him. Before going to bed, he wrote a letter to Philip B. Stewart, the organizer of his hunt, saying that he was not well and would be returning to Washington earlier than planned.

At 9:00 P.M., Loeb accompanied him and Lambert to the log cabin. The night was cold, and clouds obscured the mountain. Snowdrifts covered the creek bottom. Loeb was assigned a bunk with thick blankets. Before blowing out his candle, he saw Skip snuggling against the President for extra warmth.

Around midnight, Loeb was awakened by the sound of footfalls scrunching in the drifts outside. Roosevelt's bunk was empty. Fresh snow was falling outside the cabin's open door. Not for several moments did Loeb make out the pajama-clad figure of the President of the United States walking barefoot to and fro in the whiteness, with Skip clasped in his arms.

Incredulous, Loeb called out. Roosevelt stopped and turned. "Is that you, Billy?"

Loeb could see that he was completely disoriented with Cuban fever. The President allowed himself to be led back inside, but held fast to Skip. Loeb silently prodded Lambert awake. They treated Roosevelt with lemon juice, calomel, and quinine, then tucked him into bed like a child, the dog still close to his chest.

The next morning at eight, he was dressed and ready for breakfast. He looked seedy, but talked for an hour about the Japanese proposal, as if not quite sure how to respond. Certainly he did not intend to come running back. He dictated a telegram for Loeb to send Taft from Glenwood Springs:

Am a good deal puzzled by your telegram and in view of it and the other information I receive I shall come in from my hunt and start home Monday, May eighth instead of May fifteenth as I had intended. This will be put upon ground of general condition of public business in Washington, so as to avoid talk about the Russian-Japanese matter. Meanwhile ask Takahira if it would not be advisable for you to see Cassini from me and say that purely confidentially, with no one else to know at all, I have on my own motion directed you go to him and see whether the two combatants cannot come together and negotiate direct.

A spell of bad weather set in. Roosevelt spent the next few days recovering from his malaria and reading Pierre de La Gorce's *Histoire du Second Empire*. Jules Jusserand, who understood better than anyone else in Washington that the key to the President's heart was his mind, had made sure that he packed all seven volumes, along with Albert J. M. de Rocca's *Mémoires sur la guerre des Français en Espagne*.

Roosevelt read at less than his usual breakneck speed, hampered by rusty French and the occlusion of his left eye. In the process, he pondered every word, and was "struck by certain essential similarities in political human nature, whether in an Empire or a Republic, cis-Atlantic or trans-Atlantic."

This was not quite the reaction Jusserand had hoped for. It was altogether too large-minded for a President whose sympathy France needed in Morocco and the Far East. At least, though, Roosevelt was not reading Clausewitz, or samurai sagas, or Ieronim Pavlovich Taburno's *Pravda o Voine*.

WHAT NONE OF THE diplomats appreciated, as they obeyed their instructions, was Theodore Roosevelt's lifelong obsession with balance. He loved the poised spin of the big globe in his office, the rhythm of *neither-nor* sen-

"THE KEY TO THE PRESIDENT'S HEART WAS HIS MIND."
Roosevelt reading with Skip in Colorado, May 1905

tences, the give-and-take of boxing, the ebb and flow of political power play. His initial tilt in the Russo-Japanese War ("*Banzai!* How the fur will fly when Nogi joins Oyama!") had straightened like the needle of a stepped-off scale. He instinctively sought neutrality now, as more and more potentates yielded to parochial fears: the Tsar of defeat and deposition, the Mikado of impoverishment, the Kaiser of encirclement, King Edward VII of invasion, Sultan Abd al-Aziz of serfdom, Delcassé an end to *la glorie de la France*—not to mention whatever Korea's impotent Emperor and China's aged Empress must be feeling.

Although Roosevelt had plainly been irresponsible in heading west at such a time, his isolation had the effect of making him seem all the more "above" the fray, eminently desirable as a peacemaker. And in *remaining* aloof, at least for a while longer, he kept all parties guessing as to how he would proceed.

⤶

ROOSEVELT HAD BEEN interested to discover, after killing his third black bear, that "in her stomach . . . there were buds of rose-bushes." His task now was to corner the biggest bear of his career, badly worried by yellow hounds, and bring forth the flowers of peace. He had already tried, and failed, to do so through George von Lengerke Meyer, his new ambassador to St. Petersburg. Meyer had managed to see Nicholas II and present an offer of mediation worded almost as delicately as Hay's earlier murmurings to Takahira. But Tsarina Alexandra had monitored the interview, and Nicholas, cowed by her fierce stare, had changed the subject without committing himself.

The Tsarina's problem with peace was a *double* loss of face for Russia, if her husband was seen as suing for peace out of weakness. Not only would Japan look like an external victor, but Russia's peace party, dominated by the formidable Count Sergei Witte, would gain great power within the Empire. And there was always the imponderable of revolutionary discontent, seething among intellectuals and the peasantry.

"Did you ever know anything more pitiable than the condition of the Russian despotism in this year of grace?" Roosevelt wrote Hay. "The Tsar is a preposterous little creature as the absolute autocrat of 150,000,000 people. He is unable to make war, and he is now unable to make peace."

The only Russian left who might still effectively make both was Admiral Rozhdestvenski. His fleet was stronger than Japan's, and Roosevelt noted that France had given him a base in Eastern waters. But in the coming battle, "my own belief is that Japanese superiority in morale and training will more than offset this."

A steady succession of snowstorms and blizzards made Roosevelt rather regret his self-enforced sojourn on New Castle Mountain. On 6 May, he was at last free to descend to Glenwood Springs. As he subsequently recorded in "A Colorado Bear Hunt," his first piece of published nature writing as President,

> As we left ever farther behind us the wintry desolation of our high hunting-grounds we rode into full spring. The green of the valley was a delight to the eye; bird songs sounded on every side, from the fields and from the trees and bushes beside the brooks and irrigation ditches; the air was sweet with the springtime breath of many budding things.

CHAPTER 24

The Best Herder of Emperors
Since Napoleon

*Thim was th' modest days iv the raypublic, Hinnissy.
It's different, now that we've become a wurruld power.*

ROOSEVELT'S SOJOURN IN the mountains had understandably caught the
attention of the popular press. Humorists such as the poet Wallace Irwin
made the most of it—noting that Dr. Lambert had been invited along as much
for his camera as for his company:

> *"Come hither, Court Photographer,"*
>   *The genial monarch saith,*
> *"Be quick to snap your picture-trap*
>   *As I do yon Bear to death."*
> *"Dee-lighted!" cries the smiling Bear,*
>   *As he waits and holds his breath.*

The fact that an urgent telegram had been delivered by William Loeb was
also noted. But Roosevelt so adroitly concealed its content that the message
was thought to be about further mischief-making by Cipriano Castro:

> *But as he speaks a messenger*
>   *Cries, "Sire, a telegraft!"*
> *Which he opens fore and aft,*
>   *And reads, "The Venezuelan stew is boiling over—TAFT."*

Irwin did not doubt, therefore, that the President had decided to return
home early to "spank" a Latin American republic, as lustily as he had done
in 1903. This misperception suited Roosevelt's purposes. The longer the press

thought he was concerned only with Monroe Doctrine matters (Santo Domingo would prove to be the first test of his Corollary), the better he could secretly answer the biggest challenge of his career.

> So backward, backward from the hunt
> The monarch lopes once more.
> The Constitution rides behind
> And the Big Stick rides before
> (Which was a rule of precedent
> In the reign of Theodore).

THE BATTLE OF Tsu Shima on 27 May 1905 was the greatest naval engagement since Trafalgar. Russia's Baltic Fleet was annihilated in a holocaust of two thousand shells per minute. Japan sank twenty-two Russian ships, including four new battleships, and captured seven others. She lost only three torpedo boats in the process, and killed four thousand men. Admiral Rozhdestvenski was taken prisoner. The Tsar's humiliation was complete. Only his limitless supply of military manpower, and the nearly eight thousand miles separating Tokyo from St. Petersburg, served to protect the Romanoff dynasty from rout.

Roosevelt was awed by how decisively Japan had proved herself "a civilized, modern power"—civilization, to him, being synonymous with strength. Although he confessed to Cecil Spring Rice that he loathed the Tsarist form of government, he felt a deep sympathy for ordinary Russians and their culture, so much more congenial to him than that of Nippon. If this culture was to survive Tsu Shima, and not regress into some dark age of the Russian soul, Nicholas II must be coaxed at once into the peace process.

His cousin Wilhelm would seem the likeliest agent to prevail on him, except that the Kaiser, currently obsessing about France and Great Britain, was not averse to having Nicholas tied up in Manchuria a while longer. Ambassador Cassini did not seem to know what was going on in St. Petersburg, insofar as he could be trusted: "What I cannot understand about the Russian," Roosevelt complained, "is the way he will lie when he knows perfectly well that you know he is lying." Jusserand was both adorable and adoring, and certainly influential on the Quai d'Orsay—which in turn exerted great influence upon the Russian Foreign Ministry. But France, right now, was preoccupied with the frightening prospect of war with Germany over Morocco. Théophile Delcassé could hardly be expected to lean on a weak but friendly Emperor in the East when a strong and extremely hostile one was demanding his resignation in the West.

So the diplomatic whirlpool spun its rounds.

ROOSEVELT PUT ALL his hopes on George von Lengerke Meyer. Although the United States Ambassador had been in St. Petersburg only seven weeks, he was already irreplaceable, the kind of man Kipling envisaged as being able to "walk with kings." The way Meyer bore himself had much to do with his effectiveness. No aristocratic American rode a horse better, with so straight a back and so poised a top hat. All the Brahmin airs—Beacon Hill, Harvard, Essex County; oars and polo, cigars and buckshot, severity and solemnity—emanated from his manly person. He had worked for the right shipping companies, married the right woman, and sat on the right committees in the Massachusetts Legislature. After four years as Ambassador to Italy, Meyer already had the desired "envoy" look: sleek fine brow, clipped mustache, a face at once open and noncommittal. Only the overlarge, long-fingered hands were strange, more suited to a cellist, or masseur. But cello-playing and massage arts were not incompatible with royal diplomacy. He was just old enough to have graduated one year ahead of Theodore Roosevelt, and just enough inferior, in whatever imponderables determine clubmanship, to have made the A.D., but not the Porcellian. Decent, discreet, comfortingly dull, he lacked the imagination to be afraid of anything except failure to do his duty.

Roosevelt had already spelled that duty out, in detail:

> I want a man who will be able to keep us closely informed, on his own initiative, of everything we ought to know; who will be, as an Ambassador ought to be, our chief source of information about Japan and the war—about the Russian feeling as to the continuance of the war, as to the relations between Russia and Germany and France, as to the real meaning of the movement for so-called internal reforms, as to the condition of the army, as to what force can and will be used in Manchuria . . . and so forth.

In other words, the President wanted Meyer to look at the war through *Russian* eyes. He, Roosevelt, already had his own American take on it, communicated frankly enough to whiten Hay's last gray whiskers:

> I am not inclined to think that Tokyo will show itself a particle more altruistic than St. Petersburg, or for the matter of that, Berlin. I believe that the Japanese rulers recognize Russia as their most dangerous permanent enemy, but I am not sure that the Japanese people draw any distinctions between the Russians and other foreigners, including ourselves. I have no doubt that they include all white men as being people who, as a whole, they dislike, and whose past arrogance they resent; and doubtless they believe their own yellow civilisation to be better. . . .

For years Russia has pursued a policy of consistent opposition to us in the East, and of literally fathomless mendacity. She has felt a profound contempt for England and Japan and the United States, all three, separately and together. It has been impossible to trust to any promise she has made. On the other hand, Japan's diplomatic statements have been made good. Yet Japan is an oriental nation, and the individual standard of truthfulness in Japan is low. No one can foretell her future attitude. We must, therefore, play our hand alone. . . . Germany and France for their own reasons are anxious to propitiate Russia, and of course care nothing whatever for our interests. England is inclined to be friendly to us and is inclined to support Japan against Russia, but she is pretty flabby and I am afraid to trust either the farsightedness or the tenacity of purpose of her statesmen; or indeed of her people.

After only two meetings with the Tsar, Meyer was unable to convey anything more "Russian" than the fact that nobody knew what His Majesty was going to do. This was not enough for Roosevelt. Tsu Shima afflicted him with a new sense of urgency in saving Russia from double collapse, abroad and at home. Even the Japanese seemed to be in a hurry, dropping their usual circumlocutions when they asked, on 31 May, if the President would "directly and entirely of his own motion and initiative . . . invite the two belligerents to come together for the purpose of direct negotiation." Roosevelt guessed that Tokyo's resources were depleted, after fifteen months of all-out war.

At all costs, Nicholas II must be prevailed upon before his generals divined the same thing. Moving with a secrecy so extreme that only Edith and William Loeb knew of Japan's request, Roosevelt summoned Cassini. He told him to convey to the Tsar his frank opinion that the war was "absolutely hopeless for Russia." If His Majesty would agree to the idea of a peace conference, he thought he "would be able to get" the assent of Japan.

The move was pro forma, because he doubted that Cassini would have the courage to transmit such a message. His next step was to order Meyer to call on the Tsar "at once," and express the same sentiments even more forcefully.

Count Lamsdorff, the Russian Foreign Minister, fussed when Meyer asked for an immediate audience with the Tsar. His Majesty was in the country, at Tsarsköe Selò; the royal family was about to celebrate Her Majesty's birthday; His Majesty never received diplomats on such occasions; the imperial calendar for the next few days was full. Meyer then used the plainest possible language. The President of the United States had cabled him that morning with a proposition that only the Emperor and Autocrat of All the Russias could receive. And since Her Majesty's birthday was not until tomorrow, 7 June, he, Meyer, was quite ready to take a train to Selò now.

Lamsdorff did not like being hustled, but at two o'clock the following afternoon, Meyer found himself alone with Nicholas II. After thanking the gravely courteous monarch for receiving him "on such a day," he presented an oral paraphrase of Roosevelt's cable.

This was a mistake. The Tsar, with no formal language to react to, merely said that he needed time to "ascertain what his people really wanted." He continued to laud the *uma* of Mother Russia as if unaware that the Empire's revolutionary movement now included representatives of every social class. Meyer listened patiently, then asked, "Will Your Majesty allow me to read my instruction?"

Now it was the Tsar's turn to listen, sentence by sentence, to Roosevelt's actual words:

> It is the judgment of all outsiders, including all of Russia's most ardent friends, that the present contest is absolutely hopeless and that to continue it would only result in the loss of all of Russia's possessions in East Asia. To avert trouble, and as he fears, what is otherwise inevitable disaster, the President most earnestly advises that an effort be made by . . . representatives of the two Powers to discuss the whole peace question themselves, rather than for any outside Power to do more than endeavor to arrange the meeting—that is, to ask both Powers whether they will not consent to meet.

As Meyer read on, stressing Roosevelt's principal points—complete secrecy, an unprompted invitation, no outside participants—the Tsar listened in silence. From somewhere on an upper floor came the piping sounds of the Romanoff children playing. Outside in the palace gardens, lilacs bloomed in the full beauty of Russian spring.

> If Russia will consent to such a meeting the President will try to get Japan's consent, acting simply on his own initiative and not saying that Russia has consented . . .

Meyer was able to read this sentence with sincerity because he did not know, any more than Nicholas did, that the initiative had in fact already come from Japan.

> . . . and the President believes he will succeed. Russia's answer to this request will be kept strictly secret, as will all that has so far transpired, nothing being made public until Japan also agrees. The President will then openly ask each Power to agree to the meeting, which can thereupon be held. As to the place of the meeting, the President would sug-

gest some place between Harbin and Mukden; but this is a mere suggestion. The President earnestly hopes for a speedy and favorable answer to avert bloodshed and calamity.

Meyer finished reading, but no answer came. Nicholas sat mute through a series of further appeals, improvised by the increasingly desperate Ambassador. He showed emotion only once, when Meyer remarked that if Japan proved obstinate or greedy at the conference table, Russians would unite behind their sovereign. At this, the Tsar made a half gesture, as if wanting to touch him.

"That is my belief, and I think you are absolutely right," Nicholas said.

Meyer made much of his own friendship with Roosevelt, extending back to Harvard days, and said that the President was acting, as he always had, "from the highest motives." He understood that it was agonizing for a Commander-in-Chief to put aside "pride and ambition" in a time of national adversity, but that the saving of "possibly hundreds of thousands of lives" would justify it, and win His Majesty world respect. The alternative was to go on fighting a horde of fanatic Orientals who, unlike "Christian" soldiers, had no fear of death—indeed, had an obsessive worship of it.

Protocol required that the Tsar, not Meyer, signal the end of the interview. Three o'clock approached, but Nicholas still made no move. At last he said, "If it will be absolutely secret as to my decision, should Japan decline, or until she gives her consent, I will now commit to your President's plan. . . . Do you suppose," he added, "that President Roosevelt knows, or could find out in the meantime and let us know, what Japan's terms are?"

MEYER'S JOYFUL BOMBSHELL hit the White House the next day with no outside reverberation whatsoever. Not until 10 June, after both belligerents had accepted Roosevelt's formal "invitation," did the press get official word of what had been going on, and who was responsible for the sudden decrease in international tension. The London *Morning Post* hailed the emergence of a new world peacemaker:

> Mr Roosevelt's success has amazed everybody, not because he succeeded, but because of the manner by which he achieved success. He has displayed not only diplomatic abilities of the very highest order, but also great tact, great foresight, and finesse really extraordinary. Alone—absolutely without assistance or advice—he met every situation as it arose, shaped events to suit his purpose, and showed remarkable patience, caution, and moderation. As a diplomatist Mr Roosevelt is now entitled to take high rank.

Strangely, the President was nowhere to be seen at the time of the announcement. He had, in fact, left town the day before on a mysterious trip to
Rapidan, Virginia, allegedly to spend the weekend with some friends. His real
destination was a nearby *dacha* in dense forest that Edith Roosevelt had acquired as a hideaway for them both. The Tsar and Tsarina would have found
it somewhat confining, since it consisted of one rough-cut, stone-chimneyed
boarded box, with two smaller boxes upstairs. The pitched roof was overlong
in front, creating a shaded "piazza" at mosquito level. Edith called the place
Pine Knot, after the most noticeable feature of its interior decoration.

Here, as the news of the forthcoming peace conference reverberated
through Europe and Asia, the President and his wife relaxed in solitude, hearing nothing but birdsong and the trickle of a spring. "It really is a perfectly
delightful little place," Roosevelt wrote Kermit. "Mother is a great deal more
pleased with it than any child with any toy I ever saw, and is too cunning and
pretty, and busy for anything." Since Edith's culinary industry extended
mainly to boiling water for tea, he served a breakfast of fried eggs and bacon,
a dinner of two fried chickens with biscuits and cornbread, plus cherries and
wild strawberries for dessert. The following morning, by way of variety, he
fried eggs and beefsteak. Roosevelt noted, almost with surprise, that two such
meals a day were "all we wanted," and he worked off some of the effects by
cutting down trees.

⌒

HIS UNCHARACTERISTIC CIRCUMSPECTION lasted after he returned to
work on 12 June. "The President is usually a very outspoken personage, but
for ten days he has been absolutely dumb," complained George Smalley, the
Washington correspondent of *The Times* of London. "The State Department
has not known what is going on. The Cabinet does not know—Taft ex-
cepted."

What was "going on" was a new phase of negotiations so delicate as to
make the previous ones seem easy. Russia and Japan each felt that they had
lost face in agreeing to talk peace, and each now sought to regain it by dis-
agreeing as much as possible on all follow-up details, such as where to meet
and when, and how to ensure equal negotiatory strength. Roosevelt was by
no means "dumb" in his official communications with both foreign ministries, addressing them in a third-person style that nicely mixed courtesy and
contempt for their posturing:

> The President feels most strongly that the question of the powers of
> the plenipotentiaries is not in the least a vital question, whereas it is
> vital that the meeting should take place if there is any purpose to get
> peace. . . . The President has urged Russia to clothe her plenipoten-
> tiaries with full powers, as Japan has indicated her intention of doing.

But even if Russia does not adopt the President's suggestion, the President does not feel that such failure to adopt it would give legitimate ground to Japan for refusing to do what the President has, with the prior assent of Japan, asked both Powers to do.

There was a world of sensitivity in his use of the words *assent* and *asked*. He did not want even to hint on paper that he considered the war to have been "the triumph of Asia over Europe." But in plain speech to Cassini, he did not hesitate to state that he had not sympathized with Russia from the start of the war, and considered her entire military effort to have been "a failure." She would lose no matter how long she kept on fighting, so she had better start making concessions now. To Takahira, he said that obstinacy over peace terms would prolong the war at least another year and cost Japan untold "blood and money." Japan had already won so much, "the less she asked for in addition the better it would be."

Smalley was wrong about Taft being well-informed on the President's current diplomacy. Since coming back from Colorado, Roosevelt had confided only in members of his *secret du roi:* Edith, Henry Cabot Lodge, Speck von Sternburg, and Jules Jusserand. Even to such intimates, he told only what he wanted to tell. Like a mirror-speckled sphere at a prom, sending out spangles of light, he beamed fragmentary particulars at different dancers. They circled beneath him (or did *he* revolve above them?) in movements of accelerating, apparently random intricacy. The resultant sweep and blur was enough to make any bystander dizzy, because it looked centrifugal; Roosevelt, however, felt only a centripetal energy, directed inward.

As he mediated between Russia and Japan, he was secretly doing the same between Germany and France. Wilhelm II had become so strident in calling for a conference on the Moroccan question (ranting about a Franco-British plot to contain the Reich) that Roosevelt saw the danger of a "world conflagration" that would make the war in the Far East look like a border skirmish. The French government must accept the idea of a conference. He was accepting it himself, if only to make Wilhelm feel wanted. "Let not people in France take it amiss if I am found particularly flattering toward the Emperor," he told Jusserand, before handing Speck von Sternburg a memo of near-Levantine obsequiousness.

The French Ambassador himself needed stroking, because his superior and patron, Delcassé, had just resigned over the Morocco problem. Roosevelt made a point of consulting Jusserand as if he were an honorary Cabinet officer, and told a bewildered congressman, "He has taken the oath as Secretary of State."

Another—and surprised—recipient of presidential confidences was Sir Mortimer Durand, unaware that Roosevelt privately rated his intelligence at "about eight guinea-pig power." A summons to the White House at 10:00 P.M.;

the Washington Monument dark against the full moon; fireflies striking sparks over the lawn; magnolia blossoms stirred by the southern breeze. A long wait, then one of the President's patented sudden entrances. Two cane chairs drawn up on the porch. A torrent of Rooseveltian talk.

"He told me," Sir Mortimer informed Lord Lansdowne, "that he wished me to know the exact course of the recent negotiations, England being the ally of Japan. . . . He had told no single person except Taft [*sic*]—Hereafter a month or so hence, he might tell Lodge and one or two others, i.e. everyone."

The British Ambassador might have been less beguiled by this frankness had he been aware that Roosevelt had already given Lodge almost a mirror version of it. ("You are the only human being who knows . . . except Edith, though I shall have to in the end tell both John Hay and Taft.") Lodge, in turn, did not know some of the things that Sir Mortimer now knew: that the President had "lashed out savagely" when Count Cassini implied that Russia was going along out of sheer magnanimity, and had told Takahira to be content with the Tsar's willingness to appoint plenipotentiaries, because the very word meant "persons with full powers."

So with speech both soft and hard, white lies and colorful confidences, Roosevelt coaxed the peace process along. Durand noted how happy he was that June, how proud of his quiet game, and how "perfectly confident of success."

⌒

JUSSERAND HAD NO sooner gotten used to being teasingly addressed as "John Hay" than the real owner of the name sailed home to claim it. "Cordial congratulations on your peacemaking," Hay wrote after disembarking in New York. "You do not need any Secretary of State."

The weather in the capital was already hot, and Roosevelt urged Hay to go straight on to his place in New Hampshire. Hay, however, seemed determined to come south.

"I suppose nothing will keep John away from Washington," the President wrote Clara Hay. "But he must not stay here more than forty-eight hours. . . . He must rest for this summer."

She knew as well as Roosevelt that Hay would not see another. His German "cure" had been ineffectual, and he hardly had the strength to walk, let alone work. Some obscure desire to reconnect with the scenes of his youth in the nation's capital drove him. In the mid-Atlantic, he had dreamed of reporting back to the White House and being greeted not by Theodore Roosevelt, but by Abraham Lincoln. The vision had filled him with an overpowering melancholy.

"I am going to Washington simply to say *Ave Caesar* to the President," Hay wrote, in the last of his letters to Henry Adams.

A White House dinner invitation awaited him when he got in on 19 June. He declined, but crossed the square later and found the Roosevelts still at the table. Refusing to be tempted by ice cream, fruit, and coffee, he joined the President on the same porch that had recently accommodated Durand. Roosevelt was in cordial humor, and gave Hay a full report on the peace negotiations. As they talked, there was a strange guttural sound in the darkness, and an owl flew over their heads. It perched on a window ledge and looked down on them with an expression that struck Hay as wise, yet also full of scorn.

⌐∽

NEWS OF THE SECRETARY'S death on 1 July from a coronary thrombosis reached Roosevelt that day, just after he had moved to Sagamore Hill for the summer. Simultaneously, William Howard Taft headed to San Francisco, accompanied by Alice Roosevelt and a large Congressional party, to embark on a slightly mysterious "goodwill tour" of the Far East.

Taft's renewed assignment to diplomatic business underlined a need, now critical, for a strong Secretary of State—someone who could be relied on to restore morale at the State Department after more than two years of moribund leadership. "Elihu," the President said after Hay's funeral, "you have got to come back into my Cabinet."

Root sat silent, eyes downcast. In his seventeen months away from the government, he had attained happiness and wealth at the New York bar. His wife, who hated Washington, was re-established in Manhattan society, and Thomas Hastings was building them both a splendid town house on Park Avenue. Listening to the President's words, Root felt nothing but an immense tiredness.

He exchanged glances with Roosevelt, then heard himself accepting.

⌐∽

ROOSEVELT WAS QUITE willing to ease Root's return to service by relieving him of responsibility for the current peace negotiations. Apart from an emerging consensus that the conference might possibly be held in Washington, as more neutral than any other major world capital, Russia and Japan seemed more determined than ever to find reasons to go on fighting.

A sense gathered among scholars of foreign policy that more had passed than the last nineteenth-century Secretary of State, and more was coming than the mere settlement of a Far Eastern quarrel. Other current developments presaged ill for world peace: a sudden decline in French diplomatic prestige, triggered by Delcassé's resignation; a reciprocal increase in the strategic power of Germany; mutiny aboard the battleship *Potemkin* at Odessa, along with enough riots and strikes elsewhere in Russia to convince George Meyer that the Tsar's subjects were in a prerevolutionary state; a loss of imperial will in Britain, in the wake of the Boer War debacle (to Roosevelt's exasperation, Lord Lansdowne would not even lean on Japan, his Far Eastern ally, to moderate her peace terms, as Delcassé had done on *his* ally, Russia). Flabby Sir Mortimer, with his disinclination to shin up large, steep obstacles in Rock Creek Park, struck Roosevelt as a pretty good symbol of a culture that had lost its force.

Wilhelm II seemed to feel differently. In a manipulative letter, dated 13 July, he warned Roosevelt that the British were opposed to "the great work that the President is so ardently pursuing for the benefit of the whole world." They sought an indefinite prolongation of the war, in order to weaken both belligerents and ultimately bring about the partition of China.

Roosevelt was reinforced in his own opinion that Lord Lansdowne did not really want peace. Cecil Spring Rice tried to make him understand that the Foreign Minister could not force an ally into accepting peace terms contrary to that ally's interest. Had Lansdowne done so, "we would have broken our word." But this did not mean Britain looked for a settlement so humiliating for the Tsar that it would amount to a military defeat. "If Russia is excluded from the Pacific she must seek an exit for her energies elsewhere—in Persia, Afghanistan, or in the Near East."

"Now, oh best beloved Springy," Roosevelt replied, "don't you think you go a little needlessly into heroics when you say that . . . 'honor commands England to abstain from putting any pressure whatever on Japan to abstain from action which may eventually entail severe sacrifices on England's part?' " He did not notice the French having any such shrinking scruples about *their* alliance with Russia, even though they had more to worry about in eastern Europe than the British in Asia Minor.

> My feeling is that it is not to Japan's real interest to spend another year of bloody and costly war in securing eastern Siberia, which her people assure me she does not want, and then to find out that she either has to keep it and get no money indemnity, or else exchange it for a money indemnity which, however large, would probably not more than pay for the extra year's expenditure and loss of life. . . . Practically the only territorial concession they wish from Russia is Sakhalin [Island], to which in my judgment they are absolutely entitled.

Knowing he could rely on Spring Rice's discretion, he wrote that Lord Lansdowne and Prime Minister Balfour "ought to know" that it had been Japan, not any other power or person, that had first asked him to intervene in the crisis. Their precious ally, therefore, was probably in a less advantageous position than they imagined.

Roosevelt's admiration for Japan had by now passed its peak. He was still amazed that the little Island Empire had managed to humiliate Russia on land and sea, while actually increasing her exports and building up her industrial might. The very efficiency with which she had accomplished such miracles, however, made him wonder what future expansion Japan was capable of. Eight years before, in a strategic question posed to planners at the Naval War College, he had written, *Japan makes demands on Hawaiian Islands. This country intervenes. What force will be necessary to uphold the intervention, and how should it be employed?* Now, he was even more convinced that the United States had to commission more warships, build them bigger, and launch them faster. Or what had happened at Tsu Shima might happen in Pearl Harbor—and not too far ahead, either:

> In a dozen years the English, Americans and Germans, who now dread one another as rivals in the trade of the Pacific, will have each to dread the Japanese more than they do any other nation. . . . I believe that Japan will take its place as a great civilized power of a formidable type, and with motives and ways of thought which are not quite those of the powers of our own race. My own policy is perfectly simple, though I have not the slightest idea whether I can get my own country to follow it. I wish to see the United States treat the Japanese in a spirit of all possible courtesy, and with generosity and justice. . . . If we show that we regard the Japanese as an inferior and alien race, and try to treat them as we have treated the Chinese; and if at the same time we fail to keep our navy at the highest point of efficiency and size— then we shall invite disaster.

The oracular tone of this "posterity letter," addressed to Spring Rice, betrayed anger and embarrassment over an upsurge of anti-Japanese prejudice in California. Members of the state legislature had officially declared all immigrants from Japan to be "immoral, intemperate, [and] quarrelsome." Roosevelt considered this resolution, passed unanimously, to be "in the worst possible taste." He was afraid that it might compromise his image as a neutral broker between what Ambassador Cassini was pleased to call the "white" and "yellow" parties to the peace conference. He asked Lloyd Griscom to inform the Japanese Foreign Office that the vote in Sacramento did not represent American popular feeling.

⊂⊃

HAPPILY, THE PRESIDENT could rely on two more effective emissaries to communicate this message in a way certain to beguile Prime Minister Taro Katsura's government. Alice, now twenty-one, and Taft were an odd couple to send halfway around the world on a steamer named, significantly enough,

"FLOATY-HATTED, BUTTERFLY CHARM AND . . . JOVIAL PURPOSEFULNESS."
Alice Roosevelt and William Howard Taft en route to Japan, 1905

the *Manchuria.* But her floaty-hatted, butterfly charm and the Secretary's jovial purposefulness (as palpable, yet unbruising, as his embonpoint) had captivated huge crowds in Honolulu.

A complement of about thirty members of Congress and their wives, plus staff and servants, gave Taft's party the air of a presidential delegation—which in fact it almost was. He insisted that his main purpose was to take the congressmen on a tour of the Philippines (putting paid, presumably, to any lingering illusions they might have about the readiness of islanders for independence), but Roosevelt had asked him to visit Japan first, for public as well as secret reasons.

Alice was by now an assured celebrity, inured to the flare and smell of press photography, and incessant speculation about her romantic intentions. She was, if anything, wilder than ever, smoking cigarettes whenever she felt like it, mastering the abdominal jiggles of the *hula,* and occasionally firing impromptu fusillades with her pocket revolver. Taft felt obliged to remind her that he was responsible to the President for her conduct abroad.

When they arrived in Tokyo on 25 July, Alice dazzled the Japanese to such an extent that the Congressional wives might just as well not have disembarked. For all her independent Western ways, she took to the local culture at once, lunching with the Mikado, posing prettily with Princesses Nashimoto and Migashi-Fushimi, and sitting cross-legged for hours without fatigue.

She was also present when Taft dined with Prime Minister Katsura, but had no idea that the two men were engaged in business that directly affected her father's peacemaking. On 27 July, they agreed on a "memorandum of conversation," which Taft thought important enough to flash to the White House, in a cable of Brobdingnagian length.

Although the memorandum was only agreed *on,* not agreed *to,* it was plainly an informal declaration of intent regarding the security concerns of Japan in East Asia, and of the United States in the eastern Pacific. Since the conversation enjoyed executive privilege—Taft representing his President, Katsura his Emperor—legislators in neither country were required to ratify it, or even know about it. Unenforceable yet morally binding, friendly yet wary, its importance lay in its timing, just weeks before the presumed negotiation of a peace treaty that would recognize Japan as a power of the first rank. Taft wanted a statesman's assurance that Hawaii and the Philippines would not be menaced in future years. Katsura wanted Korea.

As the Prime Minister observed, Korea had been "the direct cause" of the Russo-Japanese War. Japan was entitled to suzerainty over the peninsula as "the logical consequence" of her military successes. Allowing Koreans to mismanage their destiny, as they had in the past, would merely invite further wars, or an indefinite extension of this one.

Regarding the Philippines—which Katsura understood was a subject of peculiar importance to Taft—Japan's "only interest" would be to see the archipelago governed "by a strong and friendly nation like the United States." If the word *like* conveyed a slight hint of ambiguity, Taft did not seem to notice it, so encouraged was he by the Prime Minister's emphatic tone.

Taft said that, in his judgment, "President Roosevelt would concur" with Japan's views on Korea. However, he cautioned that he had no authority to nullify the American-Korean protection treaty of 1882. The most he could do, if the Prime Minister needed further evidence of concurrence, would be to communicate the substance of their conversation to Roosevelt and Elihu Root—who had just been sworn in as Secretary of State, and whom he felt some "delicacy" in supplanting.

"If I have spoken too freely or inaccurately or unwittingly," Taft wired Root afterward, "I know you can and will correct it. . . . Is there any objection?"

Roosevelt answered with two terse sentences.

YOUR CONVERSATION WITH COUNT KATSURA ABSOLUTELY CORRECT IN EVERY RESPECT. WISH YOU COULD STATE TO KATSURA THAT I CONFIRM EVERY WORD YOU HAVE SAID.

As far as Roosevelt was concerned, Korea was better off as a Japanese colony than a Russian one, or even a Chinese one. And American interests were greatly enhanced. Unless Count Katsura was as big a liar as Count Cassini, he knew now that Japan would not take advantage of the fragility of the Philippines' civil government. Hawaii, too, was safe. Japan's postwar development of Korea should create another immigrant market, and slow the "yellow" influx that Californians were objecting to. Last, a gratified Japanese delegation to the peace conference must surely, now, listen to his pleas for magnanimity toward the Russians.

⌒

ALICE, UNAWARE OF why Katsura smiled at her with such satisfaction, passed her five days in Tokyo in a daze half ecstatic and half erotic. Her philandering *idée fixe,* Congressman Nicholas Longworth, was a member of Taft's party, and dancing with him on warm nights aboard ship had reduced her to a state of almost desperate lust. "Oh my heart my heart. I can't bear it. I don't know what's the matter with me. . . . He will go off and do something with some horrible woman and it will kill me off. . . . Oh my blessed beloved one my Nick." She kept reminding herself that he was bald and had a roll of fat at the back of his neck, but in vain; one moment alone with him in some dark corner, and she was again in raptures.

At a dinner entertainment at the Maple Club, she tapped Lloyd Griscom on the shoulder. "Do you see that old, bald-headed man scratching his ear over there?"

"Do you mean Nick Longworth?"

"Yes. Can you imagine any young girl marrying a fellow like that?"

Since her father had never once mentioned her mother to her, she had no way of knowing that Theodore Roosevelt had had a similar conversation, at a similar event, when he, too, had been twenty-one, despairingly in love with Alice Hathaway Lee. Her determination was as great now as his had been then.

"Why, Alice, you couldn't find anybody nicer," Griscom said.

On the night of 29 July, she stood with Taft on the balcony of Shimbashi station and waved good-bye. Her last impression of Tokyo was a medley of thousands of paper lanterns, densely packed people, grinning—or snarling— teeth, and barking roars of "*Banzai! Banzai! Banzai!*" The roars were interspersed with a chant that, so far as Alice could make out, meant, "Japan a thousand years, America a thousand years."

ALTHOUGH ROOSEVELT, on the whole, breathed more freely when Alice was in another hemisphere, he missed her company. Of all his children, she was the only one with an original intelligence. He identified with her quirky reading tastes, her strong passions, her ravenous curiosity. Vicariously, half enviously, he lived through "Alice's Adventures in Wonderland" (as the press kept reporting them), and sent her one of his quaint "picture letters," a mix of deliberately naïve drawings and allusive prose. It included a sketch of his daughter and the Empress Dowager of China exchanging ceremonial puffs of opium.

At the top of the page, over another drawing of Alice being pursued by bicycle cops, he depicted himself as a toothily grinning, vaguely Oriental sun flapping two beneficent wings:

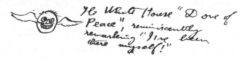

At the time of the sketch, his wings were still beating in vain with regard to an armistice between Russia and Japan, and also to the fraught issue of an indemnity, which Katsura's government seemed determined to demand. But July had otherwise seen a heartening *accelerando* of diplomatic developments, as if the peace conference, so long discussed and dreamed of, was suddenly so urgent that it had to take place at once. In short order, the two powers appointed their full delegations, separately confided (to Roosevelt only) the extent of their possible concessions, and announced that they would meet in early August on American soil—the United States being, at least symbolically, halfway between Europe and Asia. The initial introductions would be performed at Oyster Bay by President Roosevelt.

Washington was, of course, no longer a suitable location for the conference proper. Tempers were likely to be hot enough without the aggravating factor of Potomac humidity. Roosevelt volunteered to find "some cool, comfortable and retired place," where there would be "as much freedom from interruption as possible." Many East Coast seaside towns made bids to host the conference. Only one met his stipulations, while also offering the security and communications facilities necessary for a major diplomatic event: Portsmouth, New Hampshire.

The pretty, little town boasted a navy yard—strictly speaking, in Kittery, across the bay in Maine—and ample hotel accommodations for both delegates and press. Authorities at the yard made available a big, dignified, vaguely Petrovian building with its own railway siding, and plenty of exposure to sea breezes. Its oblong design, centering on a pedimented entrance facade, was symmetrical enough to satisfy the most stickling insistence on equal space. It was the architectural equivalent of a joint communiqué.

Kogoro Takahira, who had been named as Japan's junior plenipotentiary to the conference, approved Portsmouth without hesitation. So did his opposite number and new colleague on Embassy Row in Washington, Baron Roman Romanovich von Rosen. (Count Cassini, having lied to Roosevelt once too often, had been tactfully recalled by the Tsar.) Their respective governments followed up with such alacrity that Alice, steaming west on her first crossing of the Pacific, had bypassed the Japanese delegates steaming east; and long before her father's self-portrait reached her, the Russian team had arrived in New York from Cherbourg.

◦—

AT SIX AND A half feet tall, Russia's senior plenipotentiary was a delight to cartoonists, who imagined him crushing, or bear-hugging, his tiny Japanese adversaries to death. Yet Sergei Iulievich Witte was more adept at commercial negotiations than at the often dangerous business of ending a war. He was a former finance minister and railroad man, convinced that gold, not gunpowder, was the final arbiter of all questions. As such, he had become so identified with the "peace party" in his homeland that Nicholas II at first absolutely declined to appoint him. Only when two other nominees quailed before the challenge had the Tsar yielded to the urgings of Witte's supporters.

Henry Adams had met Witte in St. Petersburg a few years before and recognized him as an archetypal Slav, except for an inherited streak of Dutch phlegmatism. "He is quite ignorant. Of the world outside Russia, and especially of America, he knows little. He fears Germany, detests England, and clings to France. He is a force; a rather brute energy, a Peter-the-Great sort of earnestness." More recent reports described Witte as the ablest man in Russia, a "most bitter enemy" of reform, and a likely leader of the government, were the Tsar not so afraid of him.

Roosevelt had hoped that Marquis Hirobumi Ito would head the Japanese delegation, since he was a revered former statesman, and had the same pragmatic views about peace as Witte. But to the further joy of cartoonists, Katsura appointed the puniest-looking officer in his government, Baron Jutaro Komura. The Foreign Minister was delicately boned and wizened, although he was only forty-eight, with eyes black as calligrapher's ink, and nervous, jerky gestures, as if swatting at imaginary gnats. He had the pallid look of a man who lived largely on seaweed. Lloyd Griscom had learned not to underestimate him. Komura was, like Takahira, a Harvard graduate, and he had the advantage over Witte in that his mind was "remarkably Western in its comprehension of world affairs." Not only that, he had served as a diplomat in St. Petersburg, Washington, Peking, and Seoul—the power centers in the current war. If he had any weakness as a negotiator, it was the common Japanese one of being "apprehensive lest somebody might get the better of him."

The four plenipotentiaries were each assisted by six accredited aides, of economic, diplomatic, or military persuasion. Together with their clerical staffs, security officers, and countless hangers-on, they invested New York City with an unusual amount of diplomatic pomp as the fifth of August, the day they were to meet at Oyster Bay, drew near.

That solemn engagement did not prevent first Komura and Takahira, then Witte and Rosen from paying advance visits to the President at Sagamore Hill. The Japanese party came an hour earlier than arranged, in their high silk hats and frock coats. They waited for a while on the porch until they heard a shouted greeting from the trees far below and saw their host approaching in knickerbockers and a collarless brown shirt. He was waving an ancient hat.

After Roosevelt had changed, he escorted them into the "North Room," a new adjunct to the house, designed by C. Grant LaFarge for the reception of important visitors. It had been completed just six weeks before: a space both deep and high, sunken four steps down from the first-floor walkway, and stretching forty polished feet to its farther windows (a spread eagle cawing silently between them). Although the woodwork and vaulted ceiling were of heavy Philippine hardwoods and the walls lined with simulated leather, there was plenty of natural light, thanks to two other west-facing windows. These were set into a square, bookshelved reading alcove. Two black bison heads glowered on either side of the east fireplace, and extrusions of horn and fur elsewhere reminded Komura that the President was a man who liked blood. Ionic columns subtly evoked his statesmanship; flags and military mementos his heroism in Cuba; a blurry painting by P. Marcius Simons, entitled *Where Light and Shadow Meet*, his sense of universal harmony; and three small carved initials, paired with his own, signaled the presence of a woman in the house.

"Framed" thus in Komura's view, Roosevelt said frankly that he was concerned that Japan might ask for too much at Portsmouth. Russia should be given some opportunity to negotiate. The Baron replied by reading him a list of demands, many of which were nonnegotiable. Russia must recognize Japan's "paramount" interests in Korea, withdraw all troops from Manchuria, and sacrifice her trade and transport privileges there. Russia should also pay an indemnity for war costs. The Liaotung Peninsula must become Japanese, as must Sakhalin Island—Japan's latest territorial prize—and the railroad to Port Arthur. Russia must never again maintain a large naval fleet in "the Extreme East," and must sacrifice to Japan her few remaining warships, stuck in neutral ports. She should allow Japanese fishing boats into her home waters.

Arrogant though these terms may have sounded in a large quiet room, with Sergei Witte thirty miles away, they were not as harsh as they could have been. Komura indicated the possibility of some flexibility on some points. His idea of generosity, however, was not to insist that Russia level every last brick of her fortifications around Vladivostok. Roosevelt suggested that the latter port did not need to be disarmed, if Japan was going to take over the Port Arthur railway. As for the indemnity, he said he had heard "from France" that Witte would not hear of it. Komura and Takahira should perhaps propose reparation in principle at first, rather than rapping out hard numbers of yen.

The Baron did not object to any of Roosevelt's comments, saying only that Japan had a right to be indemnified. The possibility of a compromise at Portsmouth floated faintly in the air, like one of Alice's peace puffs. But it lasted about as long. After Komura and Takahira had taken their leave, Roosevelt heard again from his French source (Philippe Bunau-Varilla, of all people, communicating through Francis B. Loomis) that Witte had vowed to "break off" the peace conference within ten days if Japan did not make acceptable concessions. On the other hand, Russia "would consider paying at least part of Japan's expenses in the war."

Roosevelt was worried enough by Witte's semantics to write his friend Kentaro Kaneko—not a member of the Japanese delegation, but actively fronting for it in New York—and urge "that great care be used about the word indemnity and that it possibly be avoided." Doubtless remembering how he had persuaded George Perkins and Robert Bacon to accept an "eminent sociologist" on the Coal Strike Commission, he added, "If he does not object to reimbursing Japan . . . it does not make the slightest difference to you whether it is called an indemnity or not."

The Russian plenipotentiaries, less courteous than the Japanese, did not deign to visit Sagamore Hill until 4 August—or, by their calendar, 27 July. To them, it was the name day of the Empress Marie Feodorovna. All Roosevelt knew was that in fewer than twenty-four hours, he had to introduce both delegations at a welcoming ceremony aboard the *Mayflower*. And he still did not know officially what Witte's terms were going to be.

His guests arrived straight from an emotional service at the Russian Orthodox Church in Manhattan. Roosevelt had no way of knowing whether the Slavonic melancholy that Witte discharged like fog over the Volga was endemic, or merely a reaction to the uninspiring send-off from their priest: "May God help you and grant you wisdom. Just now we all feel lost and do not know what to do or what the future will bring."

Still less could he guess that Witte and Rosen felt "lost," too, torn diplomatically between personal awareness that Russia was beaten in the war, and Nicholas II's insistence that she was not. Their country was in the first throes of a slow revolution that they knew to be unstoppable. At best, the revolution could be postponed if they could negotiate a foreign peace that would enable the Tsar's ministers to deal undistractedly with the war developing in streets and basements back home. Failure at Portsmouth would mean a contraction of Russia's borders, even as her social structure rotted. Just afew days ago, Sakhalin Island had been occupied by Japanese forces. That made one of the most explicit of their instructions—not under any circumstances to give up Sakhalin—already redundant, and enhanced their sense of doom.

Paradoxically, the sense persuaded them that they were "one man with one mind, one will and one heart beating for our country." To save Russia, or at least preserve *their* Russia for another decade or two, they faced a task that transcended even the dictates of the Tsar. Fatalism—and Baron Rosen's suspicion that it had been Japan, not Theodore Roosevelt, that had pressed for this conference—made them formidable.

Witte was enormous enough, with his double-jointed, oncoming gait, to convey a sense of careless power. His gaze was not so much to be returned as endured, and he spoke bad French with torrential rapidity. Roosevelt could not help being impressed. They lunched and talked for two and a half hours, the ambassador (a polished and vapid presence) translating. "We are not conquered," Witte said, "and can therefore accept no conditions which are not suitable to our position. Consequently, first of all, we shall not agree to pay any indemnity."

This was not a promising beginning. However, Witte handed over a letter from Nicholas II that at least allowed for some concessions, such as recognition of modified rights for Japan in Korea, and transfer of the Liaotung Peninsula, providing China agreed. Russia's "interior condition," Witte allowed, was serious, but "not such as it is thought to be abroad." Her plenipotentiaries were willing to negotiate what she had lost so far, in a fair fight, as long as the Japanese did not gamble on more of the same. If they did, "We shall carry on a defensive war to the last extremity, and we shall see who will hold out the longest."

Witte watched Roosevelt closely as he responded. He could see that the President, like most Americans, was pro-Japanese, and confident that Baron Komura would prevail at Portsmouth. Yet some doubts gradually began to show—Roosevelt was not a good concealer—along with some embarrassment at having misjudged the validity and force of Russian feelings.

Roosevelt said that he was convinced that peace was in the interest of both belligerents. Therefore, at the last resort, Russia should agree to pay an indemnity. He had personally tried to get Japan to moderate her demands, but the choice appeared to be war or money.

The plenipotentiaries went back to New York even more pessimistic than they had been in the morning. "It was clear that the President has very little hope of a peace treaty," Witte cabled Count Lamsdorff, "and he therefore expresses the opinion that it is necessary in any case to arrange matters in such a manner that, in the future, when either of the parties wishes it, it will be possible to begin negotiations anew without difficulty."

THE FUNDAMENTAL EQUIVALENCE, yet fighting differences, between Tweedledum and Tweedledee had occurred to Roosevelt in previous apparently irreconcilable disputes. By the time the sun rose over Long Island Sound the next morning, he knew that the powers he was about to bring together were both financially drained and split internally, for all their shows of solidarity, by "war" and "peace" factions. So much for twinship. But, as they would soon discover at Portsmouth, a monstrous crow was bearing down upon them. All the more reason then for him to treat them today with such impartial courtesy as to make them aware that from next Wednesday on they must resolve their own quarrel.

He sent two identical cruisers to New York to pick up the delegations. Oyster Bay began to tremble with the activity of small craft—cutters, yachts, gigs, wherries, skiffs—jiggling for vantage points around the *Mayflower*, anchored white and aloof about a quarter of a mile offshore. Nearby stood the *Dolphin, Sylph,* and *Galveston.* For connoisseurs of marine display, it was the spectacle of 17 August 1903 re-enacted, but minus the overmastering presence of battleships: a panoply of peace rather than war. The weather was sunny and humid, the bay soon filling with hazy light as the shadow of Cove Neck withdrew and crept up the slope of Sagamore Hill.

Shortly after noon, a concatenation of cannon fire announced the President's arrival aboard the *Mayflower.* He climbed the gangway in his usual statesman's frock coat and silk hat, with only a white waistcoat conceding the heat. The deck of the yacht glittered like a ballroom with bemedaled uniforms and polished brass fittings. From then on, the cannon salutes were almost continuous, as first the Japanese and then the Russian plenipotentiaries left their own ships and approached Roosevelt's via a lane of open water. To general surprise, Witte was bowing and grinning as spectators yelled his name. Precisely as each party came up the side of the *Mayflower,* its flag joined the Stars and Stripes lolling aloft.

The President did not welcome his guests above, but waited below, flanked by admirals and adjutants, in a paneled salon while protocol officers conducted the formalities on deck. Since Komura and Takahira had arrived in the United States before Witte and Rosen (and also gotten out to Sagamore Hill sooner), they were escorted down first, trailed by their suite. Roosevelt greeted them, then left them seated in an anteroom as Witte and Rosen descended into the salon.

Inevitably, Assistant Secretary of State Herbert H. Peirce mispronounced some of the Russian names. Roosevelt, smiling and ejaculating his famous "*dee*-lighted," at least recognized that of Fedor Fedorovich Martens, a St. Petersburg law professor whose works he knew and praised. After presenting his own aides, he told Witte that he would like to introduce the members of the opposing delegation.

The door to the other salon opened, and fifteen black-coated Japanese filed in. Witte felt the moral pain of an envoy, invested with the dignity of the world's largest empire, being confronted by his betters in war. An observer was struck by the absolute expressionlessness of the faces on either side. "Baron Komura," Roosevelt said, "I have the honor to present you to Mr. Witte and Baron Rosen."

As the President handled the plenipotentiaries, the other delegates shook hands, then retired to opposite sides of the room in awkward silence. Roosevelt alone seemed at ease, talking warmly and incisively, nudging his guests by degrees toward an open door, through which was visible a buffet table and no chairs. Then, briskly, like a Park Avenue hostess, he said, "Mr. Witte, will you come in to lunch with Baron Komura?"

Asia and Russia crossed the threshold together, escorted by the United States.

⟶

THE LUNCH, eaten standing up by everybody except the President and plenipotentiaries, was cold. So was the wine—refreshingly so, on a day so hot. Problems of precedence were negated by the general absence of seats. Those set aside for Roosevelt were grouped so casually in a corner that nobody sitting with him seemed to notice who faced left, and who right. To Komura, he spoke English, and to Witte, his own variety of French, loose in grammar yet fluid and comprehensible.

Other guests conversed less easily. They kept talking, however, until champagne was served (by Chinese waiters substituting for the *Mayflower*'s normal staff of Japanese). The President rose, raised his glass, and said loudly to everybody in the room, "Gentlemen, I propose a toast to which there will be no answer and which I ask you to drink in silence, standing."

The last stipulation, at least, was bound to be obeyed.

Roosevelt went on, staring hard at Witte. "I drink to the welfare and prosperity of the sovereigns and to the peoples of the two great nations whose representatives have met one another on this ship. It is my most earnest hope and prayer, in the interest not only of these two great powers, but of all civilized mankind, that a just and lasting peace may speedily be concluded between them."

After the requisite hush and sipping, conversation continued with gradually increasing *bonhomie*. ("How is Madame Takahira?" "I hope the Baroness is well.") A young reporter from the *Sun* syndicate, to whom Roosevelt had awarded one of the most prized exclusives in journalism, realized that all belligerents were human.

> For the first time it was borne in upon me that wars were not only not necessary, but even ridiculous; that they were wholly man-made. . . . [I] questioned Socrates' conclusion that to know the good is to practice it. Humanity is simply not built like that. Except for a few savage or half-savage tribes, we all know that war profits no one, that its only result in the world, in the words of Croesus, is that "In war the fathers bury their sons, whereas in peace the sons bury their fathers,"—the normal course. But we are no more normal than we are certain to practice the good if we know it. Those bits of wisdom from the Greek world are two and a half millennia old, but they only emphasize our persistent unwisdom.

When lunch was over, Roosevelt and his chief guests posed for a formal photograph. Some of the chagrin he had seemed to feel the previous day, for misjudging the Russians, made him place Witte and Rosen on his right. Or was it, more subtly, his intuition that when the dread indemnity question was raised, Witte would be the only negotiator wise enough to give in? Throughout the reception, he had been more amiable to Witte than to Komura.

The latter, dwarfed and sickly looking on the President's left, remained impassive. But a camera caught an expression of real hurt on Takahira's face.

⏤◠⏤

AT TWENTY MINUTES to three, Roosevelt bade farewell to everyone, put his silk hat back on, and left the *Mayflower*, to another twenty-one-gun salute.

"WHEN LUNCH WAS OVER, ROOSEVELT AND HIS CHIEF GUESTS POSED
FOR A FORMAL PHOTOGRAPH."
*Left to right: Sergei Witte, Baron Rosen, the President, Baron Komura,
and Ambassador Takahira, 5 August 1905*

His preliminary diplomatic work was done. The Japanese exited next, and
were ferried to the *Dolphin*. Their counterparts remained aboard the much
larger host ship, which hoisted Russian colors and prepared to sail for
Portsmouth. A change in the displacement of the delegations would seem to
have occurred. But the much smaller *Dolphin* weighed anchor first, as if determined to establish precedence. The *Mayflower* let her go, then followed at
leisure. Witte and his aides reappeared on deck in light summer clothes.

That evening, a guest at Sagamore Hill thought the President looked weary but content. "I think we are off to a good start," Roosevelt said, admitting that he had been afraid of making a slip during the day. "I know perfectly well that the whole world is watching me, and the condemnation that will come down on me, if the conference fails, will be world-wide too. But that's all right."

_⌒_

THE FIRST INDICATION that something had gone seriously wrong at Portsmouth came on Friday, 18 August, when Kentaro Kaneko hurried out to Oyster Bay from New York. The self-important Baron, who served as a messenger from Komura, was beginning to irritate reporters with his almost daily pilgrimages up Sagamore Hill. They suspected that Kaneko was none too bright. He could hardly order a cup of tea without mentioning his Harvard education, and reverently quoted the President's aphorisms ("The railroad train is doubtless stronger than a bull, but that doesn't say the train wants a bull on the track") as if he understood them.

His news today, however, was urgent. The peace negotiations were on the verge of deadlock. Witte, whose overbearing garrulousness (and clever cultivation of American press opinion) grated more and more on Komura, was insisting that Russia would give up no territory and pay no indemnity. Japan had moderated her peace terms at Roosevelt's suggestion, dropping Vladivostok and changing the word *indemnity* to *reimbursement,* but Witte was plainly hardening, rather than commensurately softening, Russian attitudes. He refused in particular to concede Sakhalin, which he described as "a watchman at our gates." All he was willing to consider was some sort of arrangement recognizing Japanese economic interest in the island.

Later that evening, Roosevelt received related news from George Meyer in St. Petersburg. It indicated that Witte was acting on royal authority. Nicholas II, who had made plain at Tsarsköe Selò how precious Sakhalin was to Russia, was increasingly under the sway of war advocates. To them, an indemnity under any name would be an admission that the Motherland was conquered. No Japanese jackboot had yet trodden her soil—unless one counted the non-continental mass of Sakhalin.

Roosevelt detected a resurgence of the Russian lack of logic that had so infuriated him with Count Cassini. His Majesty would not give up Sakhalin, yet Sakhalin was already occupied by the Japanese. Russia was not conquered— she had merely been beaten in every land battle of the war, and lost almost all of her navy. Her soil was undefiled, but if she did not soon treat with Japan, she could say good-bye to eastern Siberia.

A fantasy began to grow in him. He would like to march the Tsar and his ministers to the end of Cove Neck, and "run them violently down a steep place into the sea." But reality beckoned. The peace conference would soon founder if Russia could not be persuaded to sacrifice some of her "honor." He told Kaneko that he would appeal, if necessary, to the Tsar, and enlist the aid of the Kaiser and President Loubet of France as well.

The courier returned home satisfied. That night, Roosevelt, having heard from Speck von Sternburg that Britain and France were conspiring to step in as peacemakers, sent a telegram to the Russian delegation in Portsmouth, in care of Herbert H. Peirce. It was galvanizing enough for the Assistant Secretary to wake Baron Rosen up at 2:00 A.M. and tell him he was expected at Sagamore Hill in the early afternoon.

All diplomatic niceties, evidently, were being waived in this hour of crisis. The President of the United States was no longer a neutral mediator between belligerents. He was prepared to intervene, and to do so peremptorily. Rosen had no choice but to obey his summons.

Roosevelt was playing tennis in white flannels when Rosen found him at four o'clock. Disconcertingly, he kept returning to the game at pauses in their conversation, as if to mime the serves and returns of diplomatic dialogue. He said that three of Russia's principal concerns at Portsmouth—imprisoned war vessels, naval limitation, and Japanese control of Sakhalin—were resolvable, in his opinion. Japan would back down on the first two, and the Tsar must accept the last as a fait accompli. Occupied ground was enemy ground.

"We Americans," Roosevelt said, by way of example, "are ensconced at Panama and will not leave."

It was not the most fortunate comparison, but Rosen was more interested in what the President proceeded to say about Sakhalin. Roosevelt seemed to know that Witte had reluctantly begun to talk about dividing the island—the northern half to be Russian and strategic, the southern Japanese and commercial.

He asked Rosen if his delegation would transmit a proposal to the Tsar as "an idea expressed in private conversation" with the President. This was that Russia should buy her half from Japan, as holders of the real estate in question. Without even mentioning the word *indemnity,* a negotiable quantity of money would begin to flow in Tokyo's direction. The talks would be reanimated, tempers would cool, and the unmentionable could perhaps be submitted to allies for arbitration.

Rosen, politely masking his resentment at being manipulated, agreed to carry the proposal back north for his chief to relay to St. Petersburg. Witte reluctantly obliged on 21 August, advising Count Lamsdorff, "If it is our desire that in the future America and Europe side with us, we must take Roosevelt's opinion into consideration." On Monday, the President felt uneasy enough about Russian duplicity to cable Meyer and ask him, once again, to read a personal message to Nicholas II:

I earnestly ask your Majesty to believe in what I am about to say and to advise. I speak as the earnest well-wisher of Russia and give you the advice I should give if I were a Russian patriot and statesman. . . . I find to my surprise and pleasure that the Japanese are willing to restore the northern half of Sakhalin to Russia, Russia of course in such case to pay a substantial sum for this surrender of territory by the Japanese and for the return of Russian prisoners. It seems to me that if peace can be obtained substantially on these terms, it will be both just and honorable. . . . If peace is not made now and war is continued, it may well be that, though the financial strain upon Japan would be severe, yet in the end Russia would be shorn of those east Siberian provinces which have been won by her by the heroism of her sons during the last three centuries. The proposed peace leaves the ancient Russian boundaries absolutely intact. The only change will be that Japan will get that part of Sakhalin which was hers up to thirty years ago. As Sakhalin is an island it is, humanly speaking, impossible that the Russians should reconquer it in view of the disaster to their navy; and to keep the northern half of it is a guarantee for the security of Vladivostok and eastern Siberia to Russia. It seems to me that every consideration of national self-interest, of military expediency and of broad humanity makes it eminently wise and right for Russia to conclude peace substantially along these lines, and it is my hope and prayer that your Majesty may take this view.

Roosevelt used the words *substantial* and *substantially* with little consideration for an Emperor whose idea of conciliation was "not an inch of land, not a rouble of indemnities." The cable went off, coded to cheat Russian surveillance, with carbon copies referred to the ambassadors of Germany and France. He sent a much colder message to Baron Kaneko: "I think I ought to tell you that I hear on all sides a good deal of complaint expressed among the friends of Japan as to the possibility of Japan's continuing the war for a large indemnity." Then, putting his trust in the hands of Meyer, he soothed himself by reflecting that Ramses II had not scrupled to treat with the Hittites in 1272 B.C., after years of militant blustering.

"I cannot trust myself to talk about the Peace Conference," Henry Adams wrote Elizabeth Cameron from Paris. "I am too scared. Literally I am trembling with terror. . . . The general *débâcle* must now begin."

⏤

THE SIGHT OF Sergei Witte standing huge and rumpled to the right of the President of the United States did not beguile Nicholas II, when, on 23 August, Meyer showed him a batch of photographs from the *Mayflower*. Nor was the Tsar disposed to be reasonable, as he had been during their last interview. He remarked rather peevishly that his cousin Wilhelm had just sent him a letter urging peace, and added that it was "quite a coincidence" that such missives always seemed to precede audiences with the American Ambassador.

"Russia is not in the position of France in 1870," Nicholas said, refusing again to pay any indemnity. Meyer had to argue for two hours before he consented to pay at least "a liberal and generous amount" for the care and maintenance of Russian prisoners of war. This encouraged the Ambassador to press him on Sakhalin, and he at last said that Japan could keep "that portion" of the island she had once had clear title to.

On the same day, Roosevelt, who by now had become a one-man electrical storm of cables to St. Petersburg, Peking, Paris, London, and Tokyo, again wrote Kaneko. Dropping all diplomatic politesse, he went to the edge of brusqueness in implying that Japan was being both greedy and inconsiderate at the conference table. Another year of war would merely "eat up more money than she could at the end get back from Russia." Then followed a moral lecture, in language a Nipponese aristocrat was not used to hearing:

> Ethically it seems to me that Japan owes a duty to the world at this crisis. The civilized world looks to her to make peace; the nations believe in her; let her show her leadership in matters ethical no less than matters military. The appeal is made to her in the name of all that is lofty and noble; and to this appeal I hope she will not be deaf.

The letter was wired to Tokyo, while Meyer, at Roosevelt's insistence, kept pressuring the Tsar for further concessions. Both initiatives failed, or seemed to fail. In the absence of changed instructions, the peace conference went into recess.

ON FRIDAY, 25 August, Roosevelt shocked most of his countrymen by dropping to the floor of Long Island Sound in one of the Navy's six new submarines, appropriately named the *Plunger.* He remained beneath the surface (lashed with heavy rain) long enough to watch fish swim past his window. Then, taking the controls, he essayed a few movements himself, including one which brought the ship to the surface rear end up.

Once again, he seemed to be miming, albeit unconsciously, the progress of negotiations at Portsmouth, where the issue of the indemnity had become a dead weight. The afternoon following his dive marked the low point of the conference, with Witte and Komura staring at each other in silence, smoking cigarette after cigarette, for eight minutes. Rumors spread over the weekend that the Russians were asking for their hotel bills. On Monday, Roosevelt concluded that he could do nothing more. According to Meyer, Japan's fa-

natic insistence on compensation—at a scarcely conceivable 1.2 billion yen—
had so enraged the Russian people that "even the peasants" supported their
sovereign's refusal to pay.

On Tuesday, 29 August, Witte suddenly placed a sheet of paper on the
table. He said it contained Russia's final concessions. They were less, not
more, generous than the concessions Japan could have accepted a week before, from the hands of the Tsar. Russia would pay no indemnity. Japan might
have south Sakhalin, but only if she gave up the north, "*sans aucune compensation.*"

Komura sat impassive. Silence grew in the room. Witte took up another
piece of paper and began to tear bits off it—a habit, intolerable to Japanese
sensibilities, that he had indulged throughout the conference. Eventually, Komura said in a tight voice that the Japanese government wanted to restore
peace, and bring the current negotiations to an end. He consented to the division of Sakhalin and withdrew the claim for an indemnity.

Witte accepted this acceptance, and said that the island would be cut at
the fiftieth degree of latitude north. The Russo-Japanese War was over.

⁓

HENRY J. FORMAN, the young reporter whom Roosevelt had permitted on
board the *Mayflower,* had accompanied the President on a quick trip to
Wilkes-Barre, Pennsylvania, earlier in the summer of 1905. The occasion had
been a routine appearance before coal miners, in a parklike square cut across
by ropes, like a giant spider's web. For some extraordinary reason, as John
Mitchell addressed the crowd, bound around by the ropes, it had begun to
sway from side to side, in an almost hydraulic movement that gathered force
frighteningly. Mitchell, sweating, begged the crowd to keep still, lest the ropes
break and people be trampled to death. But the swaying continued. Alarm
was visible on the faces of those in front of the speaker stand, as if they could
not help themselves.

Then Roosevelt was announced. Holding up his arms to a roar of acclaim,
he began to speak. Forman could not remember what he said, only that the
crowd all at once "froze to attention."

The peace the President had made possible at Portsmouth was the result
of just such an inexplicable ability to impose his singular charge upon plural
power. By sheer force of moral purpose, by clarity of perception, by mastery
of detail and benign manipulation of men, he had become, as Henry Adams
admiringly wrote him, "the best herder of Emperors since Napoleon."

After the Treaty of Portsmouth was signed on 5 September, he allowed
himself a characteristic moment of self-congratulation. "It's a mighty good
thing for Russia," he allowed, "and a mighty good thing for Japan." And,
with a thump of his chest, "a mighty good thing for *me,* too!"

CHAPTER 25

Mere Force of Events

*Ye see, th' fact iv th' matter is th' Sinit don't know what th'
people iv th' Far West want, an' th' Prisidint does.*

CROWNED HEADS AND columnists around the world hastened to praise
Theodore Roosevelt in September 1905. "Accept my congratulations and
warmest thanks," Nicholas II cabled, adding, "My country will gratefully
recognize the great part you have played in the Portsmouth peace conference." An overjoyed Wilhelm II declared, "The whole of mankind must unite
and will do so in thanking you for the great boon you have given it." Emperor Mutsuhito wrote in the careful language of the Japanese court, "To
your disinterested and unremitting efforts in the interests of peace and humanity, I attach the high value which is their due."

Roosevelt was pleased enough with these pro forma expressions to copy
them into a posterity letter to Henry Cabot Lodge. He did not notice, or
bother to notice, the subtler signals they sent forth: the Tsar's unconscious
separation of himself from his subjects, the Kaiser's readiness to speak for
every person on the planet, the Mikado's enigmatic formality. But neither did
he let the praise go to his head. As he wrote to Alice (still touring the Far East
with Nick):

> It is enough to give anyone a sense of sardonic amusement to see the
> way in which the people generally, not only in my own country but
> elsewhere gauge the work purely by the fact that it succeeded. If I had
> not brought about peace I should have been laughed at and con-
> demned. Now I am over-praised. I am credited with being extremely
> longheaded, etc. As a matter of fact I took the position I finally did not
> of my own volition but because events so shaped themselves that I
> would have felt as if I was flinching from a plain duty if I had acted
> otherwise. . . . Neither Government would consent to meet where the

other wished and the Japanese would not consent to meet at The Hague, which was the place I desired. The result was that they had to meet in this country, and this necessarily threw me into a position of prominence which I had not sought, and indeed which I had sought to avoid—though I feel now that unless they had met here they never would have made peace.

Alice had returned to Japan after visiting China and the Philippines and had been taken aback by the sudden coolness of the Japanese people toward her. Evidently, Komura's agreement with Witte was seen as a humiliating retreat after one and a half years of military triumph. She heard that there had been riots in Tokyo when news of the treaty signing came in.

This did not mean that high officials in the Katsura government were not secretly satisfied with the treaty. It gave Japan peace at just the moment she would have had to stop fighting anyway, through sheer exhaustion of resources. Nor was Roosevelt under any illusion as to what Portsmouth meant in terms of future Pacific strategy. After Tsu Shima, he had seen the war as "the triumph of Asia over Europe," and mused, almost with complacency, on

"SHE HEARD THAT THERE HAD BEEN RIOTS IN TOKYO."
Alice in the Far East, late summer 1905

America's geopolitical position between the belligerents. Now, as he studied a report he had commissioned on the immigration scare in California, he again began to worry about what agitators there called "the Yellow Peril." He admired the Japanese too much to use such language himself, but saw that for the rest of his presidency he was going to have to monitor with extreme caution the ambitions of these "wonderful people." While he did so, Secretary of State Root (even now immersed in a major re-examination of Canadian and Latin American policy) would have to be relied on to maintain the security of the Western Hemisphere.

So could a new recruit to the Administration, whom Roosevelt had long wanted to woo away from the House of Morgan: his old Harvard classmate Robert Bacon. As First Assistant Secretary of State, replacing Francis B. Loomis, the handsome and athletic Bacon also rated inclusion in the presidential "tennis crowd"—more and more jealously dubbed "Teddy's Tennis Cabinet" by unsuccessful aspirants to it.

⌒

FOR ALL THE CONSENSUS that Roosevelt had proved himself a master diplomat, he could not boast, or even agree, that the world was demonstrably safer as a result of his efforts. Socialism was spreading like dry rot in Russia, even through the ranks of the army, with consequent weakening of authority and strengthening of authoritarianism. Morocco remained a potential flash point of war among the European powers. At least the commitments that Wilhelm II had managed to coax from Britain, France, Austria-Hungary, and a reluctant United States to address the problem in conference had tamped down on the fuse for a few more months: talks were scheduled to begin in Algeciras, Spain, early in the new year. Roosevelt took further comfort in the fact that Nicholas II, no longer troubled by Japanese ambitions, could now look west again, and help curb those of the Kaiser.

Freed from global responsibility himself, for the first time in eight months, he was able to start preparing for what promised to be the biggest legislative season of his presidency. Indeed—sobering thought—it would effectively be his last. The "odd year" and "even year" disequilibrium of congressional sessions meant that only the first and third of any presidential term were long enough for the passage of major bills. And, inevitably, the third tended to be wary of anything radical, because it preceded another general election. So Roosevelt had until early December to write the defining Message of his second term.

One issue above all others that he was determined to fight for "as a matter of principle" was that of railroad rate regulation. Ever since his election, he had sensed a rising, almost populist rage against the power of trusts (uninhibited, apparently, by the Elkins Anti-Rebate Law of 1903) to fix interstate shipping charges. The rage was not *entirely* populist, in that it rose above white collars rather than blue, and expressed itself, articulately and persuasively, in the pages of middle-class magazines such as *McClure's* and *Everybody's*. And it had persisted since the articles by Ida Tarbell, Lincoln Steffens, and Ray Stannard Baker that had caught Roosevelt's eye in January 1903—articles that had made *McClure's* the most influential magazine in the country.

Roosevelt had been warned during the summer, by S. S. McClure himself, that the fall of 1905 would be a time of renewed journalistic calls for—what? McClure could only write, rather clumsily, "law-abidingness and uprightness in political matters." Doubtless somebody with less money and more style would find a compact term for the new movement, inchoate as yet but definitely gathering force: a social current that sooner or later must politicize itself—if it had not done so already in the "Iowa Idea" and Roosevelt's own huge electoral mandate.

What particularly characterized the movement, McClure reported, was the evangelical fervor of its practitioners. As yet, they lacked a leader, even a liturgy. But their fervor, patent wherever the publisher traveled in the United States, "almost correspond[ed] to the passion that one finds in a country when it is on the eve of a righteous war."

Now here, in the President's hand, were page proofs of a new article by Baker, "Railroad Rebates." It was scheduled for publication in *McClure's* in December, coincident with the opening of the Fifty-ninth Congress. Second of a five-part series, it assailed the "secret, underhand" dealings and "piggish" greed of "the oil-barons, beef-monopolists, the steel-trust millionaires, the sugar magnates, the banana kings and their like." Baker, who was apparently paid by the word, decried rebates as "wrong, wrong morally, wrong economically, wrong legally."

This was carrying fervor too far, but Roosevelt saw no harm in encouraging political rhetoric more extreme than any he would use on Congress himself. Let Baker, Steffens, et al. do what advance guards had always done in battle: draw enemy fire from both sides while Caesar advanced down the middle. He responded to the page proofs, therefore, with the utmost delicacy:

> I haven't a criticism to suggest about the article. You have given me two or three thoughts for my own message. It seems to me that one of the lessons you teach is that these railroad men are not to be treated as exceptional villains but merely as ordinary Americans, who under given conditions are by the mere force of events forced into doing much of which we complain. I want so far as I can to free the movement for their control from all rancor and hatred.

Just how "far" he would, in fact, go to keep the public temper sweet remained to be seen. For the moment, he was still exulting in the afterglow of

Portsmouth. On 30 September, Oyster Bay collected at the depot to cheer him back to Washington. The little sheet of water beyond the rails lolled in its bowl, careless of the cannon fire (and submarine plunges) that had shaken it so thrillingly during the summer. Roosevelt's fellow villagers, however, seemed determined not to forget the glory he had visited upon them eight weeks before. A large shield, starred and striped, hung over the station entrance, framed to right and left by the flags of Russia and Japan, and surmounted by a banner image of a white dove with olive leaves in its beak.

The President approached this portal between two cordons of young women in white dresses. To general surprise—since he was famous for self-control—he had tears in his eyes when he turned to say good-bye.

⌒

RAY STANNARD BAKER'S proofs were not the only ones Roosevelt had to check that fall. Two articles of his own, "Wolf-Coursing" and "A Colorado Bear Hunt," were due out in consecutive issues of *Scribner's Magazine,* followed by a collection of wildlife pieces in book form at the end of October. Somewhat redundantly entitled *Outdoor Pastimes of an American Hunter,* this volume was the fourth in a series begun with *Hunting Trips of a Ranchman* (1885) and continued with *Ranch Life and the Hunting Trail* (1888) and *The Wilderness Hunter* (1893). It supplemented an already bewildering variety of different editions of *The Works of Theodore Roosevelt,* which had begun to come out in 1900 and bulked as large as fifteen-volume sets of history, natural history, biography, criticism, memoir, and political philosophy.

His sudden return to authorship after four years of self-imposed silence, coupled with his current celebrity as peacemaker, prompted the first serious attempt by a foreign intellectual—for that matter, *any* intellectual—to make political and literary sense of the President of the United States. Léon Bazalgette, France's ranking authority on Whitman and Thoreau, published a *livre broché* entitled simply *Théodore Roosevelt.* Although it was based only on close study of the Roosevelt canon, its thirty-five pages packed more perceptions into the President's character than any current full-length biography of him.

Bazalgette admitted that, as a nonpolitical person, he preferred Roosevelt's nature writings to the histories and social commentaries. They were more beguiling and more self-revealing. A paradoxical sweetness and love of life, in no way mitigating the author's blood lust, emanated from such books as *The Wilderness Hunter* (whose title, in French, hauntingly became *Le Chasseur des solitudes*). Despite many dogged pages, and a deliberate avoidance of fine prose, these works charmed "with their simplicity and acute sense of realism." They were imbued with a poignant nostalgia for the free western way of life, which had passed away even as Roosevelt had participated in it. The plainness of his style enabled him to achieve special effects "more intense than those of professional writers." (Bazalgette seemed to be unaware that the President had once earned a living with his pen.) Perhaps the most remarkable of these effects derived from his uncanny ear for sounds, which, combined with scientifically precise observation, often enabled him to achieve "a communion with all that breathes in Nature."

Roosevelt the modern statesman clearly owed much to his youthful cultivation of, and acceptance by, frontiersmen of the hardest and most violent sort. A man who could earn the respect of such "desperadoes," and write about them with such unsentimental empathy, was unlikely to be fazed by eruptions of the primitive in the behavior of senators, or, for that matter, of plenipotentiaries. His youth in the Badlands had been an education in essentials:

> He was able to observe there, in its absolute nakedness, the perpetual phenomenon of existence on this planet: human life consisting of the rhythm and friction of two parallel dynamics, inextricably interlaced, twin instincts eternally directing its course, the struggle for existence and the acceptance of existence. Both of them are positive forces, fertilizing and appropriate, the complete and final fusion of which will probably coincide with the ruin of humanity and the reign of silence around the world.

Out of his lessons in man and nature, Roosevelt had evolved a Darwinian philosophy that was harsh, yet wholly altruistic. No one reading his volumes of political and social essays, *Administration—Civil Service, American Ideals,* and *The Strenuous Life (La Vie intense),* could have doubted what sort of President he would be. An anarchist had ironically elevated to power "the supreme political personality of our time, of all contemporary statesmen the one surest of his mission, and most capable of achieving it."

What these didactic works lacked in charm, they made up for in exhortatory effect. Old World sensibilities might recoil, at first, from the extraordinary aggression of Roosevelt's attacks on "that most dangerous of all classes, the wealthy criminal class," as well as on all who put private gain, or cloistered security, or machine loyalty before their larger social obligations.

> The tone is resolute, affirmative, maybe even brutal. He is pitiless toward hypocrites and rogues, whom he always identifies by name. Rare, in a man of his station, is the audacity, vehemence, and hasty decisiveness with which he exposes and denounces the corruption of the political world around him. . . . To live, for him, has no meaning other than to drive oneself, to act with all one's strength. An existence without stress, without struggle, without growth has always struck him as

"OF ALL CONTEMPORARY STATESMEN, THE ONE SUREST OF HIS MISSION."
Roosevelt in his Sagamore Hill study, September 1905

mindless. Those who remain on the sidelines he sees as cowards, and consequently his personal enemies.

There was, nevertheless, "a contagious force" to Roosevelt's moral energy, which no foreign sophisticate could resist. "One feels braced by the presence of a reformer, in the full sense of the word. . . . He shakes our delicacies, repeats to us the healthy, grand lesson that no refinement can compensate for rugged virtues."

Braced thus, one was pleasantly shocked when Theodore Roosevelt stopped preaching and started affirming. At such times, Bazalgette wrote,

Roosevelt was possessed of an almost evangelical urgency, campaigning for political and social reform with the "ineradicable conviction" of a John Knox or a Martin Luther:

> Such is the magnetism of his utterance, so forceful is his advocacy, that he persuades us to understand him and love him, even though we—I speak of such [Europeans] as myself—flinch and protest, and refuse to suit our instincts to his. When, for example, the excess which is part of his nature moves him to the point of "spread-eaglism," formidably increasing the vibration of patriotic and warlike strings, I am not with him, and turn instead to his noble dream that "justice will rule, not only between man and man, but also between nation and nation." It is the dream, more than any others I might cite, he has done the most to bring about.

In political prose as in political speech, the President's most characteristic weapon was the rhythmically beating fist. Every beat punched home an idea or part of an idea, and he never stopped punching.

> He has only one limiting and devouring ambition, which is to move and convince. He has too much to say not to dispense altogether with artifices of style, too much faith and force to need anything else. He is a workman who puts the best of his energy into driving rivets. He hammers out understandings.

THE LEGISLATIVE CONSENSUS that Roosevelt wanted to forge during the winter of 1905–1906 was going to require more than huge amounts of energy. He would also have to exercise his gift for delicate negotiation—an attribute Bazalgette did not know about, since it was incommunicable in writing and by its nature discreet. The same landslide that had swept him back into power had elected a Congress with big Republican majorities, so whatever reforms he intended would have to be accomplished within the bounds of party orthodoxy. And prosperity was booming in both farms and factories. With a largely contented populace and a paralyzed political opposition (Parker had been the worst-beaten candidate in the history of the popular vote), he must whip up a moral fervor for his program, rather than the usual economic and social arguments that got difficult bills through.

Having found, during the last session of the Fifty-eighth Congress, that tariff revision was too divisive an issue to wreck his presidency on, he was happy to trade it for legislation addressing the fact that most American business was now conducted across state lines—a phenomenon the framers of the Constitution could not possibly have foreseen. That meant that "the government must in increasing degree supervise and regulate the workings of the railways engaged in interstate commerce." The Sherman Act was no longer enough, nor the Anti-Rebate Law. The Bureau of Corporations could only monitor business malfeasance, not control it. What was needed was a larger, stronger Interstate Commerce Commission.

Here Roosevelt parted company with radicals demanding that the ICC be empowered to fix rates. As his letter to Baker showed, he believed that railroad executives justifiably took advantage of the free-enterprise system, and that a President's job was to keep the system fair. The most he was prepared to ask Congress for was a maximum rate, to be imposed by the ICC only in cases of dispute.

Another law he was looking for was in the area of employer's liability. This was not a new cause for him. As Governor of New York, he had signed a bill mandating it, and as President he had called for the protection of federal employees in the District of Columbia. Immediately after the last election, he had called for a comprehensive Congressional study of the subject, "with a view of extending the provisions of a great and constitutional law to all employments within the scope of Federal power." That call had been mainly propaganda, since the lame-duck Fifty-eighth Congress had soon after quacked its last; but this time around, his intent was sincere. So was his desire for an investigation into child-labor abuses, legislation to maintain sanitary standards in the food industry, and governmental supervision of insurance corporations.

ONE OF THE FIRST things Roosevelt did after returning to Washington was to dedicate his forthcoming book to John Burroughs. He was greatly amused when Scribner's mistakenly advertised the title as *Outdoor Pastimes of an American Homer.* "I am hurt and grieved at your evident jealousy of my poetic reputation," he wrote Professor James Brander Matthews, who had sent him a note of mock inquiry from Columbia University. "If you saw my review of Mr. Robinson's poems you may have noticed that I refrained from calling him 'our American Homer.' This was simply due to the fact that I hoped some discerning friend would see where the epithet ought to go."

The allusion was to Edwin Arlington Robinson, the reclusive and poverty-stricken northeastern balladeer, whose collection *The Children of the Night* had come his way earlier in the year. Kermit Roosevelt had studied some of the poems at Groton and been transfixed by their chilly beauty. The President had read them too, at his son's urging, and agreed that Robinson had "the real spirit of poetry in him."

Kermit had found out that Robinson was living in New York City, drinking heavily, and so desperate for money he was working ten hours a day as a time-checker in the Manhattan subway system. Clearly, such an existence was not conducive to the production of more verse. The President, in strict secrecy waiving all civil-service rules, had offered Robinson jobs in the immigration service or the New York Customs House, which latter the poet accepted. A tacit condition of employment was that, in exchange for his desk and two thousand dollars a year, he should work "with a view to helping American letters," rather than the receipts of the United States Treasury.

In further generosity, Roosevelt had written a review of *The Children of the Night,* comparing Robinson's prosody to "the coloring of Turner," and published it in *Outlook* during the Portsmouth peace conference. Léon Bazalgette might have had this enlightened kind of patronage in mind when he approvingly quoted a Roosevelt dictum, "A poet can do much more for his country than the proprietor of a nail factory."

THE PRESIDENT STAYED in Washington just eighteen days, intently plotting railroad-legislation strategy, before embarking on a nine-day tour of the South. His ostensible purpose was to generate favorable publicity for the GOP, in advance of the November elections. But he also wanted to try out some of the centralized-government rhetoric of his upcoming Message in an area of the country that cherished the notion of states' rights. If his ideas won favor there, it would be much more difficult for Congressional conservatives to challenge them in December.

Tensions were high when he arrived in Raleigh, North Carolina, on 19 October to make an announced address on railroad rate legislation. Lieutenant Governor Francis D. Winston did not appreciate being frisked by agents before being allowed to shake the President's hand, and the "peanuts 'n pickle" lunch laid on at the state fairground came close to a denial of hospitality. Hunger, or anger, made Roosevelt orate with persuasive effect. ("The new highway, the railway, is in the hands of private owners, whereas the old highway . . . was in the hands of the state.") He was rewarded with considerable applause.

The following day he made a pilgrimage, poignant to him, to Bulloch Hall, the white-columned mansion in Roswell, Georgia, where his mother had grown up and married his father. The floors were no longer polished by corn shucks tied to the feet of a mulatto slave boy, as they had been then, and only the Union flag flew in the little park down the avenue. But he knew the place so vividly in his imagination, from listening to his mother and aunt talk about it, that he felt he was revisiting it.

"It is my very good fortune," Roosevelt told the villagers of Roswell, "to have the right to claim that my blood is half southern and half northern."

The farther south he went, the more heartening it was for him to see that white Southerners seemed disposed to forgive him for his "Negrophilist" behavior in 1902 and 1903. Some of his welcomes were almost royal in their tri-umphalism. He avoided the question of black disfranchisement in his speeches, and made only one unscripted reference to lynching, when Gover-nor Jeff Davis of Arkansas suggested to his face that the "only good Negro is a dead Negro." This Roosevelt could not tolerate. "Above all other men, Governor, you and I [as] exponents and representatives of the law, owe it to our people, owe it to the cause of civilization and humanity, to do everything in our power, officially and unofficially, directly and indirectly, to free the United States from the menace and reproach of lynch law."

⟶

ROOSEVELT WAS SO pleased with his Southern trip that he invited the histo-rian James Ford Rhodes to the White House to hear about it. Rhodes arrived on 16 November and found Root and Taft among his fellow guests. The Pres-ident recounted his put-down of Governor Davis with the meticulousness of an actor analyzing a *coup de théâtre*. He said he had controlled his displea-sure at first, and proceeded with his own speech until he felt the crowd was "in sympathy" with him. Then he had marched up to Davis, looked him in the eye, and issued his reprimand, gesticulating in such a way that both Gov-ernor and audience thought he was going to throw a punch. The cheering had been "enthusiastic and genuine."

It was clear to Rhodes that the President's brave stand had been made not out of compassion, but out of concern for due process. Roosevelt, encouraged by Root and Taft, proceeded to give robust evidence that he and Davis were not far apart on phylogenetic matters. The Fifteenth Amendment had been "very unjust and bad policy." Lincoln's dream of a graduated extension of suffrage, as more and more black men qualified for it, was all very well, but the Yazoo Delta offered proof that a people could regress. Negroes, Roosevelt said, were "two hundred thousand years behind."

Rhodes suggested "a million," and the President agreed. He cheerfully went on to castigate the Irish, who struck him as a good argument for An-glophilia. Not that there were many other justifications. The English were by nature undemocratic, and were not even good at governing themselves any-more: Prime Minister Balfour and his Cabinet were "a set of split carrot-heads" who might "answer perfectly well for a pink tea." He did not believe in sending American boys to Oxford, and would "dislike exceedingly" to have one of his daughters marry a foreigner. (At least Alice, just back from her marathon junket to the Far East, would spare him that pain: she and Nick were now unofficially engaged.) English girls, on the other hand . . .

Léon Bazalgette could only dream of listening to Roosevelt talk, as Rhodes was now. But the Frenchman understood that these floods of appar-ent aggression, half fierce, half humorous, were more indicative of energy than of serious thought. They were part of *l'outrance qui est dans sa nature,* the excess that was part of Roosevelt's nature. The weir had constantly to spill, to keep the deep water behind clear and calm.

⌒

A SURPRISE RESULT of the elections that month was that machine candidates of either party were punished in what *Outlook* called "the Rout of the Bosses." Even Henry Cabot Lodge, who was not machine-made but seemed to personify orthodox Republicanism in Massachusetts, nearly lost his senatorial seat. New York, New Jersey, Maryland, Pennsylvania, Ohio, and Indiana favored "Reform" or "New Idea" tickets over ones labeled "Stalwart" or "Old Guard." Evidently, there was a schism developing in the GOP, and the force driving it apart was the same fervor S. S. McClure had tried to describe earlier in the summer. Only now it was less vague, more political, easier to define—as Ray Stannard Baker did, in the first article of his railroad series:

> We are at this moment facing a new conflict in this country, the importance of which we are only just beginning to perceive. It lies between two great parties, *one a progressive party seeking to give the government more power in business affairs,* the other a conservative party striving to retain all the power possible in private hands. One looks toward socialism, the other obstinately defends individualism. It is industrialism forcing itself into politics. And the crux of the new conflict in this case, recognized by both sides, is the Railroad Rate.

Baker might have used a less distracting word than *party,* with its inevitable overtones of registration and organization. But *progressive,* an adjective hitherto only generally indicative of forward social movement, had been transformed into a label, and might in time (depending on how effectively conservatism resisted it) rate the ultimate dignity of a capital *P.*

Roosevelt could not have wanted a louder fanfare of trumpets to proclaim the importance of his Fifth Message to Congress. But Baker, never one for restraint, gave him an extra trombone blast all to himself: "Out of hopelessness of justice has arisen the present widespread demand, voiced by President Roosevelt, for some tribunal which is at once impartial and powerful enough to do justice as between the Railroad and the Citizen."

⌒

THE MESSAGE ITSELF, published on 5 December, was quieter and more rationally argued than readers of *McClure's* might have expected. Indeed, its opening section, subheaded "Control of Corporations," was written in a lucid, unemotional style that belied what Bazalgette had said about the President's tendency toward rhetorical "roughness."

In our industrial and social system the interests of all men are so closely intertwined that in the immense majority of cases a straight-dealing man who by his efficiency, by his ingenuity and industry, benefits himself must also benefit others. Normally the man of great productive capacity who becomes rich by guiding the labor of many other men does so by enabling them to produce more than they could produce without his guidance; and both he and they share in the benefit, which comes also to the public at large. The superficial fact that the sharing may be unequal must never blind us to the underlying fact that there is this sharing, and that the benefit comes in some degree to each man concerned.

Roosevelt was clearly addressing himself to Speaker Cannon and the conservative Senate leadership still managed by Nelson Aldrich—Republicans whose votes, and control of votes, he would need in the months ahead. He had to persuade them, without melodramatics, that unless they began to respond to the demands of the Progressives (some of whom were now members of Congress), the Grand Old Party was likely to become two parties, and sooner rather than later.

The Department of Justice, he wrote, was devoting too much of its time to prosecuting antitrust cases on an individual basis. And experience had shown that individual states lacked the power, in an age of combination, to stop the abusive practices of trusts operating across their borders. What was needed was a regulatory and supervisory law enacted by the only body as big as the biggest trust—"that is, by the National Government." The need was so great that if Congress would not move, the Constitution would have to be amended.

He emphasized that the law should be positive rather than prohibitory, monitoring growth rather than slowing it, and imposing discipline only when the growth became destructive of competition. Its prime focus must be on railroad rates, and in particular on rebate rates, which were discriminatory and should be forbidden "in every shape and form." A commission should be created (or the ICC empowered) to establish a maximum reasonable rate whenever a rate was shown to be unfair—and unfairness meant "minimum" rates for big shippers as well as excessive ones for small. In the former instance, "the commission would have the right to declare this already established minimum rate as the maximum; and it would need only one or two such decisions by the commission to cure the railroad companies of the practice of giving improper minimum rates."

The President kept reiterating that he was asking for an administrative agency, not an enforced partnership between government and private business. His Message proceeded to spin itself out, as usual, to prodigious length, and contained no fewer than seventy-three requests for moderately progressive new laws. But already he had issued the war call most sure to bring him into direct conflict with Senator Aldrich: he had challenged free enterprise's right to set its own prices in the competitive marketplace. To Aldrich, Depew, Hale, Foraker, even to Senator Elkins, this was a blasphemy, however quietly uttered, against one of the fundamental tenets of the Constitution.

Roosevelt had until Christmas to work with a reform-minded legislator— probably that jovial Methodist bison Senator Jonathan P. Dolliver of Iowa— on the language of his railroad bill, and concentrate all the political momentum he had built up as President. Then in the new year, force must meet with force.

CHAPTER 26

The Treason of the Senate

But now whin I pick me fav-rite magazine off th' flure,
what do I find? Ivrything has gone wrong. Th' wurruld is
little better thin a convict's camp.

"YOU AND I, of course, can never believe in the *benevolent despot*."

George F. Baer, president of the anthracite-carrying Philadelphia & Reading Railroad, had as much reason as his addressee, Senator Stephen B. Elkins, to view Theodore Roosevelt's current ascendancy with misgivings. As an industrialist privately engaged in interstate commerce, he saw any governmental intrusion upon his right to set his own shipping rates, such as the President was now proposing, in the light of flames licking around the last copy of the Constitution.

Elkins—affable, unreliable, energetic, a chronic schemer personifying the West Virginian notion that all scenes and situations could be profitably mined—had been happy to sponsor Roosevelt's Anti-Rebate Bill in 1903, if only because men like Baer wanted it. The railroads were weary of handing out special favors to a widening roster of not-so-special customers. But the chairman of the Senate Committee on Interstate Commerce was considerably less willing to endorse the idea of railroad rate regulation. Apart from opposing it on principle, he resented the way the President had chosen a junior Senator, Dolliver of Iowa, to draft the legislation.

Roosevelt did not see how Elkins could expect to be consulted on a bill that, in effect, proclaimed the failure of the Elkins Law. Three years before, the "accidental" President had to take what weak measures he could coax from the Senate; now he had power enough to get almost anything he wanted. That did not mean getting it would be easy, or quick. For the sake of future harmonious relations with the Upper House, he could only hope that Elkins and Aldrich and other stalwarts would accept the fact that he represented the will of the people.

The truth of the situation was that most Americans supported him unconditionally. Even "Pitchfork Ben" Tillman was forced to acknowledge that Theodore Roosevelt was "the most popular President the country has ever had." Speaking on the floor of the Senate, Tillman berated his colleagues for their subservience to Roosevelt's public relations:

> The newspapers are the men who have made him what he is, as far as the public knows, because he has never had the opportunity in all his journeyings and speeches to meet more than one in a thousand of his fellow-citizens, and it is through the great instrumentality represented in that press gallery that he has become puffed to such a degree that he "strides the world like a colossus, and we smaller men"—you, thank God, not I—"crawl around between his legs hunting for yourselves dishonorable graves or a piece of pork."

It was not the most fortunate literary allusion from a senator who generally displayed a public appetite for pork such as the Armour Brothers meatpacking company might fail to satisfy. But Tillman made a valid point: the President had Washington correspondents working on his behalf as if they were in his employ, and he had the added support of the new investigatory journalists. More than any other previous occupant of the White House, Roosevelt understood that the way to manipulate reporters was to let them imagine they were helping shape policy. A "consultation" here, a confidence shared there, and the scribe was transformed into a pen for hire.

Another weapon in Roosevelt's negotiatory arsenal was the Antitrust Division of the Justice Department, revitalized by (now Senator) Philander Knox. Within days of the Message, Attorney General Moody had ordered wholesale prosecutions of shippers and conveyors still linked by concessionary arrangements. Indictments had already been returned against some of the most eminent corporate names in America, including the Great Northern Railway and three members of the notorious "beef trust"—concurrently the unwilling subjects of a series of articles in *Collier's* investigating the food industry. The Justice Department's own press releases further helped to whip up public support for the President's program.

In consequence of all these factors, Roosevelt now commanded a bipartisan, proregulatory majority in the House of Representatives. Senator Elkins's committee looked like an increasingly lonely redoubt as it braced to do battle with "progressives" both within and without the Capitol.

⟁

ONE OF THE earliest aspirants to the new label loomed shock-headed among the President's hand-shakers at a White House reception on 4 January 1906. Robert M. LaFollette of Wisconsin, just elevated from Governor to Senator, was an insurgent even as to hairstyle. Dense and irrepressible, a pompadour did what it could to add to LaFollette's height. He was fifty years old and five feet five inches tall, opaque except for his facial flush: inside, he was all dark, dour aggression.

Roosevelt recognized him at once, and held up the reception line to recall their first meeting, seventeen years before in Washington. It had also been a formal occasion; Civil Service Commissioner Roosevelt had accidentally spilled some coffee on Mrs. LaFollette's white satin gown.

"When I wake up in the dark, and think about that, I blush!" Roosevelt said.

Such naïve naturalness of expression was hard to resist. "Mr. Roosevelt is one of the most likable men that I am acquainted with," Mark Twain remarked a few days later, dictating his autobiography. The President was "the most popular human being that has ever existed in the United States," by virtue of his "joyous ebullitions of excited sincerity." Twain was nevertheless moved to express the misgivings of not a few thoughtful observers who wondered if a Roosevelt unrestrained might not become a Roosevelt moving too fast for his own good. "He flies from one thing to another with incredible dispatch. . . . each act of his, and each opinion expressed, is likely to abolish or controvert some previous act or expressed opinion."

In private correspondence and conversation, the President gave quite the opposite impression. He was deliberate about his intent to use railroad rate reform as a switch between two different stages on the American economic journey. It was not he, but the outdated system of *laissez-faire*, that was accelerating out of control. Elihu Root, a conservative for life (and a favored member of the Aldrich poker circle), saw that "the central fact" for Theodore was that the last decades of the nineteenth century had been a period of risk for capital—risk demanding great courage from entrepreneurs, and rightly rewarding them with enormous wealth if their new modes of production paid off. When those modes became established modes, however, and risk declined in consequence, there would have to be "a surrender by capital . . . of its high percentage of profit." Unfortunately, today's conservatives—self-made men like Elkins and Aldrich, both of them railroad board members—believed with complete sincerity in the stand-pat values embodied by President McKinley and Mark Hanna. Roosevelt understood that a "profound reconstitution [had] taken place in modern industrial society," and that change was in the direction of economic redress.

He also believed something else with complete sincerity, too: that unless capital consented to some redistribution of profits, piling up beyond reason now that times were stable and competition was often turning to complicity, "the radical elements in society" would resort to violence.

In a rare admission of this fear, Roosevelt confided to Sir Mortimer Durand that he was "dreadfully worried" about the fate of the Dolliver bill. Durand repeated his words to Sir Edward Grey, Foreign Secretary of the new Liberal government in Great Britain:

> He told me that when he woke up at night and the remembrance of it all came to him he had to force himself to think of bear shooting and other things more agreeable than Senators or he could never get to sleep again. He said that he had made a careful study of Cromwell and was convinced that Cromwell never meant to become a dictator, but had been forced to do so against his will by the persistent folly and obstructiveness of his parliaments. "If I had the power to dissolve parliaments, and the will to override the Constitution, I should be tempted to do the same." However a man here had to live his life "under representative institutions."

The trouble with the Senate in 1906 was that it was *not* a representative institution, except insofar as state legislatures elected its members—often at the command of party machines, or at the behest of corporate contributors. Aldrich and most of his colleagues were so sure of continued incumbency that Roosevelt doubted he would be able to get "coherent—that is, effective—action from them" by invoking voter displeasure.

As if on cue, *The Cosmopolitan* magazine proclaimed on 15 January that it would publish a major new "exposure" series by David Graham Phillips, entitled "The Treason of the Senate." The first article would focus on Chauncey M. Depew and Thomas Collier Platt as "New York's Misrepresentatives."

Roosevelt was not charmed by this announcement, nor by heavy hints, in the current *Arena,* that Senators Depew and Platt took orders from Standard Oil, along with Aldrich, Bailey, Elkins, Gorman, Lodge, Penrose, and Spooner. He needed the votes of such men. Ray Stannard Baker's less vindictive railroad series, still running in *McClure's,* might yet persuade them to accept his bill. But vulgar abuse could only stiffen their resistance to reform—the instinct of stand-patters under attack, after all, is to stand even more pat.

⌐⌐

IN ALGECIRAS, ON 16 January, Wilhelm II's longed-for conference on the status of Morocco got under way. This time around, Roosevelt, with no direct interest in the south Mediterranean theater, was happy to leave American peacemaking efforts to others—specifically, to a delegation of professional diplomats headed by Henry White, now United States Ambassador to Italy. "I want to keep out of it if I possibly can." The stakes at the conference table were much less fraught than they had been six months before, since the Kaiser had been unable to secure an alliance against France with his war-weary cousin, Nicholas II. In a sense, Wilhelm had already won what he had blustered for in 1905: the humiliation of France and the resignation of Théophile Delcassé.

White was under instructions to press for nothing more controversial than stability and security in Morocco, with occasional vague references to an "open door" there. The bulk of the negotiating could be left to more interested parties. Their wranglings would no doubt be interminable. If the situation ever got ugly, Roosevelt could always be consulted by cable.

⟳

SENATOR ELKINS TOOK no immediate umbrage at the President's apparent cooperation with the progressive press. He even worked up a regulation bill of his own, to see if it would satisfy him. Inevitably, however, it called for private rather than public rate control. Roosevelt remained committed to Senator Dolliver's bill.

On 27 January, Dolliver sent that measure to the House. It was quickly and favorably reported by that body's Committee on Interstate and Foreign Commerce, and it received the sponsorship of Elkins's counterpart chairman, Congressman William P. Hepburn (R., Iowa). Although all the world knew who had demanded the legislation and who had drafted its language, it forthwith became "the Hepburn Bill," and thereby gained prestige. Tall and stately at seventy-two, Hepburn was the House's best debater, admired for his strength of character and legal acumen. Roosevelt, who affectionately called him "Colonel Pete," could wish for no more effective sponsor. Nor could Hepburn himself wish for a bigger piece of legislation to crown his long career. Railroad rate regulation was the greatest challenge handed to Congress in forty years. More precisely, to the Senate—the House voted to approve the bill on 8 February by an astounding margin, with only seven negative votes. But the forces of reaction were confident that Old Guard delay tactics down the corridor would eventually make this victory Pyrrhic. "No railway rate bill," the New York *Sun* declared, "will be passed by the Fifty-ninth Congress."

At one o'clock the following afternoon, a triumphant Roosevelt received Ray Stannard Baker at his daily shaving *levée*. Invitations to this ritual were coveted in Washington, and Baker was particularly flattered to find no other guests in attendance.

"How are you, Baker? I haven't seen you since our correspondence in November."

The President unclipped his pince-nez and sat down in a light chair that seemed threatened by his bulk. The barber applied a layer of lather while Roosevelt launched straight into an analysis of the Hepburn Bill. Baker, who had heard reports that Roosevelt was wavering on some clauses provocative to the Senate, was surprised how determined he was to give the ICC power over disputed rates.

Roosevelt recognized that for "the railroad Senators," the great question was going to be over the role of courts in regulation—whether they should judge only the fairness of the ICC's rates, or (as Elkins preferred) judge the actual disputes. He said that he and Attorney General Moody stood together in holding that the bill should say nothing specific about jurisdictional limits. Each court should be allowed "to find—as it were—its own level." Taft and Philander Knox were both in favor of strict language.

Baker discovered, as Steffens had before him, that the only time to interrupt Roosevelt *à toilette* was when the razor made further loquacity perilous. He waited until the presidential chin was being scraped before venturing that the railroad bill was "the most important" Roosevelt could ever claim credit for.

"Yes, but not the most important administrative action. That was Panama."

Since being out-maneuvered by Roosevelt in the summer of 1903, Baker had learned how to keep a presidential interview on track. He suggested that the Hepburn Bill was "only a first step." It could not accomplish all the American people wanted; they would surely ask for more.

Roosevelt's head began to swivel in protest. The barber had to match strokes with his gyrations.

"If this is a first step, where do you think we are going?"

"You may not agree with me, Mr. President, but I believe that we cannot stop short of governmental ownership of the railroads."

Roosevelt became vehement. He said that he knew, better than anyone else, how "inefficient and undependable" federal employees were. It would be "a disaster" to have them in charge of free enterprises.

Waiting for another razor opportunity, Baker reported that he had just been in Kansas, where there was much social discontent. "The people out there are getting beyond you on these questions."

"Here is the thing you must bear in mind," Roosevelt said, clearly irritated. "I do not represent public opinion: I represent the public. There is a wide difference between the two, between the real interests of the public, and the public's opinion of these interests. I must represent not the excited opinion of the West, but the real interests of the whole people."

Even as he spoke, the Hepburn Bill was being considered by the Elkins Committee. Its basic provisions were the same as those Roosevelt and Dolliver had hammered out the previous December. The ICC would be authorized to set reasonable rates, whenever rates were justifiably challenged; railroads would have thirty days to appeal such decisions in court; private car lines were, for the first time, placed under ICC control; and all of them would have to adopt a uniform and open system of bookkeeping.

Baker and Lincoln Steffens, not being practical politicians, were disappointed in the Hepburn Bill, and Roosevelt had patiently to tolerate their complaints. But the bill was already too strong for Aldrich, who was casting around for some means to defeat it. One of the Senator's few legislative liabilities was that he had no controllable majority on the Elkins Committee.

Knowing how ruthlessly Aldrich operated, Roosevelt did not put it past him to allow the bill to be strengthened excessively, and then passed—aware that it would alarm the Supreme Court. "The one thing I do not want is to have a law passed and then declared unconstitutional."

⌒

THE COSMOPOLITAN'S SERIES "The Treason of the Senate" began to run in earnest in mid-February. It attacked Senator Depew for being rich, and worse still, jovial. David Graham Phillips's literary style exemplified what was emerging as a common characteristic of the progressives: their fierce, preachy, perpetual grimness. They could no more convey the humor of a situation than they could view a perquisite without frowning. For fifteen minutes or a thousand words, they bracingly commanded attention, even admiration; then they lost it. They simply went on too long and too loudly. LaFollette noticed that when he got up to speak, his colleagues drifted out of the chamber.

Perhaps the fiercest of the young progressives making headlines in February 1906 was a socialist. Upton Sinclair, a bony, driven twenty-seven-year-old, proclaimed himself as dedicated to the equalization of wealth. Yet in the past year, he had managed to sell the same novel to four different publishers—an achievement any capitalist might envy. His book was entitled *The Jungle*. It detailed unsanitary practices in Chicago's meatpacking houses with a relish verging on the pathological. First serial rights went to *The Appeal to Reason*, a socialist sheet with an enormous readership. The quarterly journal *One Hoss Philosophy* followed up with longer extracts, minus only an episode in which a female meatpacker, forced to give birth on the job, inadvertently allows her baby to be made into sausages.

Macmillan and Company, meanwhile, had bought book rights to the novel, before allowing Sinclair to move it to Doubleday, Page. Now, at last, *The Jungle* was between hard covers and selling as fast as clerks could count change. Sinclair had shortened, sanitized, and sentimentalized the plot, but it still presented a nauseating picture of the largest unregulated industry in the United States.

Doubleday had cannily timed its release to coincide with Senate debate on a pure-food bill. But the book's success was so great that proponents of the legislation used it to drum up public support. Senator Beveridge sent a copy to the White House. Roosevelt hardly needed to be reminded of the bill, having initiated it himself in his Fifth Message. That document read quaintly now, to eyes scorched by Upton Sinclair's prose:

I recommend that a law be enacted to regulate interstate commerce in misbranded and adulterated foods, drinks, and drugs. Such law would protect legitimate manufacture and commerce, and would tend to secure the health and welfare of the consuming public. Traffic in foodstuffs which have been debased or adulterated so as to injure health or to deceive purchasers should be forbidden.

In requesting such legislation, Roosevelt was merely echoing a regulatory sentiment that had been growing on Capitol Hill during his presidency—growing, indeed, as fast as the American population was outgrowing its dependence on local and seasonal meats, fruits, and vegetables. The railroad age had brought the phenomenon of factory foods refrigerated for distant transport and sale, scientifically preserved for longer shelf life, artificially flavored for better taste. Mechanized techniques transformed large animals into rows of cans, reduced whole orchards to juice, or, even more efficiently, made juice out of nonfructile chemicals—would wine out of water be next? The ancient triple unit of man, horse, and plow became the single "combine harvester," an inexorably advancing, all-too-obvious symbol of combination in the American economy.

Sinclair was but the most recent and passionate of the radical protesters against all this cutting up and churning out. Poverty-stricken for most of his young life, he saw himself as one of the straws that the combine compressed into bales and tossed aside. His real motive in writing *The Jungle* was political, as the English MP Winston Churchill saw at once: from its dedication "To the Workingmen of America" to its concluding cries of "Organize! Organize! Organize!" it was a declaration of war against capital.

⌒

ALICE ROOSEVELT HAD no such socioeconomic prejudice. Newspaper articles heralding her imminent wedding to Congressman Nicholas Longworth degenerated into endless catalogs of gold and silver gifts, every one of which, gorgeous or garish, she accepted with glee. White House aides complained that Miss Roosevelt would accept "anything but a red-hot stove," and that the accumulating pile of treasure, requiring a special room and twenty-four-hour security, was "entirely too much to be given to one person."

"Trinkets," Alice said, when asked if she was still short of anything. "Preferably *diamond* trinkets."

King Edward VII's gift fit that category, being a gold snuffbox with a diamond-encrusted lid. The Kaiser sent a diamond bracelet. Cuba invested part of her reciprocity income on a spectacular pearl necklace. Ambassador Jusserand delivered, on behalf of his government, a magnificent Gobelin tapestry, and the Dowager Empress of China sent enough brocaded silk to keep Alice in dinner gowns for decades. A cornucopia of crystal, china, and jewelry poured in from congressmen and other aspirants for presidential favor.

The President gave away his daughter in the East Room at noon on 17 February, before a capacity congregation of family members and the Washington establishment—many women wearing brilliant accents of "Alice Blue." Outside, the White House grounds jostled with the most frenzied press activity the capital had ever seen. Roosevelt seemed oddly subdued in his white waistcoat, and answered the Bishop of Washington's question "Who giveth this woman?" in an inaudible voice. Posing with Alice afterward for a photograph of notable stiffness, he stood leaning away from her slightly, his face devoid of expression. She held herself erect, almost as tall as Nick, in white satin trimmed with old lace, a frozen Niagara of white and silver brocade cascading from her waist and down the carpeted dais.

Did Roosevelt's masked look, and his apparent scruple not to touch Alice with his shoulder, convey an awareness that the lace covering her shoulder and sweeping in a graceful crescent across her breasts had been worn, long ago, by another Alice? And did Edith Roosevelt, who also remembered that lace with pain, have it in mind when she kissed her stepdaughter good-bye and said, not entirely jokingly, "I want you to know that I'm glad to see you leave. You have never been anything else but trouble"?

The bride, heading off to Cuba on honeymoon, was missed at least by her Mexican yellow-head parrot. For days after her departure, the White House resounded with despairing calls of "Alice—Alice—Alice."

⌐

ROOSEVELT READ THE Depew/Platt profile in *The Cosmopolitan* and began to wonder if the literature of exposure was not becoming a destructive force. He approved of public attacks on corruption and fraud, but not this kind of "hysteria and sensationalism." The double tendency of subjective journalism, he felt, was toward "suppression of truth" and "assertion or implication of the false."

What bothered him particularly about the current series was that its publisher, William Randolph Hearst, was a member of Congress. Here was an elected representative of the people using the fourth estate to malign and manipulate his colleagues, probably with intent to destabilize. "I need hardly tell you what I feel about Hearst," the President wrote to the Attorney General of New York State, "and about the papers and magazines he controls and their influence for evil upon the social life of this country."

The pity was that honest exposure writing, even the fact-filled fiction of Sinclair, could still be an influence for the good—witness Senator Aldrich's sudden withdrawal of opposition to the Pure Food Bill after the publication of *The Jungle.* A man with extensive interests in the food industry, Aldrich believed that government had no right to prevent consumers from poisoning themselves. But he abstained from voting when the bill passed the Senate on 21 February, by a vote of 63 to 4.

Although speculation arose that the Senator was working secretly to defeat the bill later in the House, Roosevelt could congratulate himself on another legislative victory. "The tone of the Republican Senators is not so defiant as it was a few weeks ago," Sir Mortimer Durand reported to London, "and one hears on all sides predictions that Mr. Roosevelt will carry all the various measures upon which he was to have been overthrown." The British Ambassador thought that fear of Depew's fate might be the reason Old Guard solidarity had begun to erode. Roosevelt, whose contempt for "business in politics" was well known, looked more and more like a tribune of morality as the exposure journalists went about their work.

If so, the tribune had his sword shattered two days later. Aldrich's negotiatory cunning revealed itself when the Senate Committee on Interstate Commerce deadlocked over amendments to the Hepburn Bill. Senator Dolliver had managed to override the nay votes of Elkins and four other Republicans, and got an agreement to report the bill as written. But after seeming to accept defeat, Aldrich enlisted Democratic support to empower all non-Committee members of the Senate to amend the bill freely later. Violent arguments broke out as to which "friend of the measure" would report it. Aldrich bided his time, then proposed Benjamin R. Tillman—a name so unexpected that the committee voted in favor almost out of shock.

Senator Tillman was neither a Republican nor, notoriously, a "friend" of anything to do with Theodore Roosevelt. His only qualification as sponsor of a federal regulatory measure was his near-paranoid obsession with states' rights. This, plus the Hepburn Bill's popularity outside Congress, meant that reform was still a possibility. But Aldrich had at one stroke rendered Dolliver impotent, made the bill look regional rather than national, and severely embarrassed the President of the United States. Debate opened on the Senate floor on 28 February.

Now began a series of blows which Roosevelt could not at first parry. His oldest political ally, Senator Lodge, spoke out against regulation. So did Senator Knox, apparently forgetful of the days when he and the President had prosecuted illegal railroad combinations across state lines. So did Senator Spooner, author of the language that had facilitated the Panama Canal. So did every Republican of any legislative weight in the upper chamber. Joseph B. Foraker, emerging as the most aggressive of the "railroad senators," made no fewer than eighty-seven speeches in defense of free enterprise.

The issue of court power, again forced by Aldrich, became the main threat to the railroad bill. Roosevelt, Hepburn, and Dolliver had imagined that debate would focus on *administrative* power—the rate-fixing authority of the

ICC. They wanted, at worst, a "narrow review" amendment, which would permit the courts to rule only on procedural questions.

So, amid dry clouds of legalistic dust, the battle dragged on.

⟶

WAS ONE TO believe that there was nowhere a god of hogs, to whom this hog-personality was precious, to whom these hog-squeals and agonies had a meaning? Who would take this hog into his arms and comfort him, reward him for his work well done, and show him the meaning of his sacrifice?

As prose, *The Jungle* left something to be desired, and Upton Sinclair's ear for dialogue (*"Eik! Eik! Uzdaryk-duris!"*) was perhaps best appreciated in Lithuania, but Roosevelt was both fascinated and repulsed by the book Senator Beveridge had sent him. Although disguised as fiction, it had the tang— in this case the reek—of fact. He drew it to the attention of his Secretary of Agriculture, James Wilson, along with a letter Sinclair had written him, calling for an investigation of the meatpacking industry. "I would like a first-class man to be appointed to meet Sinclair, as he suggests; get the names of witnesses, as he suggests; and then go to work in the industry, as he suggests." The investigation, he stressed, must be kept "absolutely secret." Attorney General Moody had already learned, from prosecuting the beef trust, that Packingtown was capable of any venality in defending its interests. "We don't want anything perfunctory done in this matter."

Roosevelt's was a mind in which literary images and political priorities floated interchangeably. Whether or not Sinclair's description of immigrant workers bending over stinking masses of blood and offal and bits of bone under lights "like far-off twinkling stars" reminded him of Bunyan, he chose to cite a parallel passage in *Pilgrim's Progress* when he addressed a white-tie dinner of the Gridiron Club on 17 March. It represented his current opinion of investigative journalists, and was fortunately articulated after the squab stuffed with chestnuts *sur canapé*.

. . . the Man with the Muckrake, the man who could look no way but downward with muckrake in his hand; who was offered a celestial crown for his muckrake but who would neither look up nor regard the crown he was offered but continued to rake to himself the filth of the floor.

Roosevelt's subsequent remarks about "a certain magazine" that he had just read "with great indignation" could not be reported, due to the Gridiron's tradition of confidentiality. He spoke for nearly three quarters of an hour over a white, twelve-foot model of the Capitol, glowing with internal lights. According to one member of the audience, he "sizzled" with moral disdain. Since his listeners represented all of official Washington, and since *The Cosmopolitan* had just published another installment of "The Treason of the Senate," it was not long before the Man with the Muckrake was identified as David Graham Phillips.

Nor was it long before the Man became plural—denoting all writers of Phillips's type—and the noun a verb, as in *muckrakers, muckraking, to muckrake.* A new buzzword was born. Ray Stannard Baker reacted to it as if stung. Opprobrium cast on all investigative journalists, he wrote Roosevelt, might discourage the honest ones, leaving the field to "outright ranters and inciters." Roosevelt's reply indicated a determination to give the Gridiron speech again, in some more public forum. "People so persistently misunderstand what I said that I want to have it reported in full."

⟺

THE LAST THING Roosevelt needed, as he prepared for the final stages of debate on the Hepburn Bill, was escalation of the Algeciras Conference into another full-scale diplomatic crisis. But any proceedings involving the Kaiser seemed to slide toward war at some point, and this one was no exception. After six weeks of talk and translation, the conferring powers (most actively, Germany, France, Austria-Hungary, and Great Britain) had deadlocked in a dangerous squabble about how Morocco was to be policed. France wanted gendarmes in control of all port cities. Wilhelm II objected, because German traders might then be denied access to the interior. His negotiants suggested that a multinational force, equally representing all parties to the conference, might keep order more peaceably.

Roosevelt felt the first, distinct tuggings of a foreign entanglement absolutely contrary to his inclinations. With some asperity, he told an informal emissary from the Kaiser that Germany had "perhaps fourteen times less interests" in Morocco than France.

"We do not admit that anyone except ourselves be the judge of our interests," the German replied.

"Then I do not understand this insistence upon having a conference. Why take the opinion of others if only your own counts for you?"

Roosevelt repeated this exchange to Jusserand afterward, along with the alarming information that Germany's ruling trinity—the Kaiser, Count von Bülow, and Admiral Alfred von Tirpitz—apparently all believed that the Reich was now omnipotent in Europe.

"Never have I seen the President so upset," Jusserand reported to the Quai d'Orsay.

Austria was now backing Germany at Algeciras, while Britain sided with France. As the confrontation worsened, both camps turned to Roosevelt to bring about another successful mediation. Jusserand and Speck von Sternburg plagued him with warnings and cajolements. He resisted them as he could. They did not seem to understand, or care, that he was more interested in trying to figure out why Senator Knox had so tersely rejected his offer of an appointment to the Supreme Court. (Justice Brown had resigned at the beginning of March; now Taft was considering the position.)

Unwilling as he was to intervene over White's head, Roosevelt saw a definite if distant threat looming at Algeciras. He suspected that what the Kaiser really wanted was "the partition of Morocco"—followed by the establishment of a German or German-friendly port, too far west for American comfort. Von Sternburg was reminded that the conference would never have taken place if Wilhelm had not begged the United States to push for it, nine months before. As a return favor, Roosevelt suggested, His Majesty might consider fashioning a compromise out of existing proposals. The policing issue could be solved if Germany accepted a Moorish force in all ports, commanded by French and Spanish "instructing officers." The force would be paid for by all conferees, and France and Spain would unequivocally declare an open door to all Morocco.

In a letter of unusual frankness, Roosevelt told the Kaiser that though Germany would not get the multinational police it wanted, France was going to have to accept a considerable reduction of its current authority in Tangier.

> If the conference should fail because of Germany's insisting upon pressing France beyond the measure of concession described in this proposed arrangement . . . Germany would lose that increase of credit and moral power that the making of this arrangement would secure to her, and might be held responsible, probably far beyond the limits of reason, for all the evils that may come in the train of a disturbed condition of affairs in Europe.

Wilhelm responded by translating this proposal—with variations minor and not so minor—into German for Austria's benefit, then retranslating it into English as a proposal of his own. Roosevelt was reminded, as so often in his presidency, of Tweedledum's need to trump Tweedledee, and decided not to accept it. He told von Sternburg that he suspected Germany really did want a war with France. If so, the Kaiser would have to live with the consequences, and a severe decline in American goodwill.

Secretary Root added his own grave opinion, which the Ambassador cabled to the Wilhelmstrasse: that Germany's conduct at the conference was "paltry and unworthy of a great power."

On 19 March, White cabled that yet another proposal, described as "Austrian" but more largely the President's own, had been laid on the table at Algeciras. Again with feelings of *déjà vu*, Roosevelt allowed Wilhelm to retreat in glory. "Communicate to His Majesty," he instructed Speck von Sternburg, "my sincerest felicitation on this epochmaking political success at Algeciras. The policy of His Majesty on the Morocco question has been masterly from beginning to end."

⁓

THE ARTICLE IN *The Cosmopolitan* that had so exercised Roosevelt's wrath was a portrait of Senator Aldrich as "The Head of It All." If that muck-spattered gentleman was grateful to him for returning the attack, there was no apparent lessening of Old Guard opposition to the railroad rate bill in the last days of March. Twenty-four implacable conservatives stood pat between Roosevelt and regulation. Many lesser items of presidential legislation, such as a statehood bill for Arizona and New Mexico and a tariff bill for the Philippines, were held up too, while in the House, Speaker Cannon had emerged as an eloquent spokesman for impure food. Sir Mortimer Durand revised his recent positive predictions. "At the present moment it seems as if the session were likely to close with a series of defeats for Mr. Roosevelt. . . . Some of the strongest men in the Republican party are at the head of the malcontents."

One of the weakest men in the Republican Party, influentially speaking, visited Roosevelt late at night to urge him to demand rates that were reasonable as well as nondiscriminatory. Robert LaFollette had been studying railroad finance for thirty years, and thought that the President might listen to him on the subject.

"But you can't get any such bill as that through Congress."

"That is not the first consideration, Mr. President."

A fault line instantly ran between the idealist and the practical politician. LaFollette did not see—or, seeing, did not understand that it was already unbridgeable, and must one day become a chasm.

"But I want to get something through," Roosevelt said.

To do so, he needed forty-six of the Senate's ninety votes. Assuming he got none of the Old Guard block of twenty-four, he would have to build a majority out of seventy-six votes, thirty-three of which belonged to the opposing party. Senator Tillman undertook to deliver only twenty-six Democrats, since not all his colleagues liked the idea of rate regulation, and very few liked Roosevelt. Washington insiders delighted in the paradox that "Teddy" now depended on the parliamentary tactics of "Pitchfork Ben."

A small group of proregulatory senators from the Plains states came to the President's rescue on 31 March. There was something symbolic about their solidarity: they represented the old agrarian values of grain and grassland, eternally resisting the spread of smoke and steel. But they saw that Roosevelt, unless he compromised on the issue of court review, would never get the Hepburn Bill through the Senate. Some language had to be included to check and balance the ICC's proposed rate-making power. This would persuade more Republicans to vote for the measure. Senator Chester I. Long of Kansas suggested adding an amendment that was "broad" enough to please more Republicans, yet still "narrow" in the sense that the ICC would retain plenty of regulatory power. Courts should be allowed to rule on whether any disputed order was "beyond the authority of the Commission," or in violation of the constitutional rights of railroad operators.

The President was agreeable to this idea, which he thought might yield fifteen or even twenty votes on top of Tillman's twenty-six. But he was embarrassed by the fact that he could not discuss it with his legislative lieutenant. Tillman and he were not on speaking terms. In 1902, the Senator had been banned from the White House for punching out a colleague, mid-debate. That disinvitation was now canceled, but Tillman showed no inclination to drop by. He had never forgiven Roosevelt for some prepresidential wisecracks about Populists. ("A taste for learning and cultivated friends, and a tendency to bathe frequently, cause them the deepest suspicion. . . . Senator Tillman's brother has been frequently elected to Congress upon the issue that he wore neither an overcoat nor an undershirt.")

Somebody suggested that the President enlist the aid of a distinguished former Senator, William Eaton Chandler, who was close to Tillman and presumably proregulatory, having been lobbied out of office by a railroad company some years before. Chandler was summoned to the White House that evening, massaged into complicity, and sent on to Tillman with secret expressions of Roosevelt's wrath against the "lawyers" impeding reform in the Senate.

Tillman knew he was being manipulated, but agreed to help build a bipartisan majority in favor of what he genuinely felt was "a great legislative bill." For the next two weeks, he and Senator Bailey labored over the amendment with Attorney General Moody, while Roosevelt polished prose of his own. It was a restatement of the "Muckrake" speech, scheduled for delivery at the most public ceremony on his upcoming schedule, the dedication of the House Office Building on 14 April.

⌒

BUNYAN'S NOISOME FIGURE, more interested in piling up dirt than stargazing, duly made every major newspaper in the country. But the very potency of the image, and the speed with which it became a cliché, distracted popular attention from the rest of Roosevelt's address, which had ominous implications for the very rich.

He noted that the United States was passing through a period of "social, political, and industrial unrest." So far as the unrest took the form of a struggle between the "haves" and "have-nots," those essential counterbalances of a capitalist economy, it was to be condemned. But where it was moral, and sought to punish evildoers of any stamp, it was a "sign of healthy life" that government should welcome.

> It is important to this people to grapple with the problems connected with the amassing of enormous fortunes, and the use of those fortunes, both corporate and individual, in business. . . . No amount of charity in spending such fortunes in any way compensates for misconduct in making them. As a matter of personal conviction, and without pretending to discuss the details or formulate the system, I feel that we should ultimately have to consider the adoption of some such scheme as that of a progressive tax on all fortunes, beyond a certain amount, either given in life or devised or bequeathed upon the death of any individual—a tax so framed as to put it out of the power of the owner of one of these enormous fortunes to hand on more than a certain amount to any one individual.

If conservatives in the audience could believe their ears, the President was proposing that government should profit from, and even confiscate, the rewards of private enterprise. His subsequent warning that railroad rate regulation was but "a first step" toward greater federal control of the economy sounded a declaration of ideological war.

Was it, though? Roosevelt's by now compulsive habit of following every statement with a counterstatement (positives neutralizing negatives and *on the other hand* used as a kind of conjunction) muted the overall effect of his speech. Those who had heard him off the record at the Gridiron were disappointed. He sounded progressive one minute and reactionary the next, as he alternately scowled and smiled at muckraking and moneymaking, allowing that there were good and bad varieties of each.

Reporters got plenty of quotes, but their editors were not too sure which way, ideologically, the President was headed. If in the direction of restraint of free speech, he would sooner or later collide with Justice Holmes. If he wanted more and more centralized government, then Senator LaFollette would be quick to march behind him, as would Upton Sinclair and a lengthening line of socialists and communists.

Men with muckrakes continued their work—some, such as Baker, decently and doggedly, others, like David Graham Phillips, with waning fervor. Good investigative reporting was simply too expensive for most editors, and too slow for journalists paid by the piece. Baker felt betrayed by Roosevelt, who had seemed so encouraging of his work, yet had now twice trivialized it by association. He still admired the President's "remarkable versatility of mind," if not the seeming versatility of his principles.

SENATORS TILLMAN AND Bailey learned a similar lesson on 4 May, the day after they introduced their Roosevelt-backed "narrow review" amendment to the Hepburn Bill. After five weeks of secret negotiations conducted through William E. Chandler, Tillman felt in honor bound to let the White House know that he was, as yet, one vote short of the twenty-six he had promised.

At 3:00 that afternoon, Roosevelt called a press conference and announced, as if the Tillman-Bailey Amendment had suddenly ceased to exist, that he had decided to support a "broad review" amendment crafted by Senator Allison. Rambling for almost a half hour, he imputed his own switch to the Republican leadership, which had accepted the will of the American people.

A disillusioned progressive reporter interrupted him. "But Mr. President, what we want to know is why you surrendered."

Tillman and Bailey wanted to know, more basically, how any self-respecting politician could yield to the embrace of the opposition for five weeks, then to that of his own party at the merest whiff of a winning vote. At any rate, their loss was Roosevelt's gain. Republicans fell into line behind him like stock cars on the Santa Fe. Even Senator Elkins endorsed the Hepburn Bill, saying with a straight face that although he owned a large quantity of railroad stock, he was "ten times" more sympathetic toward shippers than toward carriers. The most ambitious legislative initiative since Reconstruction could now move to passage as a co-achievement of the White House and the Republican leadership. Democrats seeking re-election in the fall would have to find another law to boast about.

"I love a brave man," Bailey said, "I love a fighter, and the President of the United States is both—on occasions; but he can yield with as much alacrity as any man who ever went into battle."

⤙⤙⤚

ROOSEVELT TRANQUILLY RECEIVED the British writer H. G. Wells at the White House on 6 May. They lunched and strolled the grounds together. Wells, who was on assignment for the London *Tribune,* noted that the President had none of the usual stiffness of politicians afraid of being quoted. He talked in the manner of Arthur Balfour, another intellectual who had risen to supreme eminence. But unlike that unhappy statesman, recently deposed, Roosevelt had the "power of overriding doubts in a sort of mystical exaltation." He seemed more representative than patrician:

> He is the seeking mind of America displayed. . . . His range of reading
> is amazing; he seems to be echoing with all the thought of his time, he
> has receptivity to the point of genius. And he does not merely receive,
> he digests and reconstructs; he thinks. . . . He assimilates contempo-

"A COMPLEX MINGLING OF WILL
AND CRITICAL COMPLEXITY."
Theodore Roosevelt in mid-sentence.

rary thought, delocalizes it and reverberates it. He is America for the first time vocal to itself.

Having read extensively in Roosevelt's earlier writings, Wells had expected "Teddy" the Rough Rider, all slouch hat and swordsmanship. Instead, he found himself dealing with a friendly, gray-clad statesman, whose voice was more confidential than strenuous, and whose clenched fist waved almost absentmindedly. The President's screwed-up, bespectacled face conveyed "a complex mingling of will and critical perplexity." There again, Roosevelt was representative. "Never did a President so reflect the quality of his time."

⟨⟨⟨⟩⟩⟩

IF BY "QUALITY of his time" Wells was alluding to the progressive impulse behind Roosevelt's current regulatory proposals, its force burgeoned in the days immediately following. Tillman railed against the President for treachery and manipulation of muckrakers, but his language was oddly muted, as if he had to acknowledge that the Hepburn Bill deserved bipartisan support.

On 18 May, the Senate approved the bill with only three dissenting votes—two by gentlemen from Alabama, and one from the lone Republican who still hoarsely declaimed the right of railroads to regulate themselves: Joseph B. Foraker of Ohio. Even though the original Roosevelt-Dolliver measure's simplicity was now complicated by the Allison Amendment, its sheer accumulation of legislative weight, from a motion few supported to a majority measure only extreme conservatives opposed, was evidence that the President had started something very big.

Railroad rate regulation was not yet a reality, since the bill now had to be reported to a joint committee of the House and Senate. This did not stop early words of praise from flowing Roosevelt's way. The most moving were uttered by the man most disposed to choke on them. "But for the work of Theodore Roosevelt in bringing this matter to the attention of the country, we would not have had any bill at all," Benjamin R. Tillman said. "Whatever success may come from it will largely be due to him."

AS THE WEATHER WARMED, so did the attitude of both Houses toward other items of progressive legislation. Joseph Cannon grudgingly relaxed his opposition to the Pure Food Bill. Senator Beveridge introduced a separate meat-inspection bill based on the President's secret investigation of Packingtown practices—a probe that not only vindicated everything Upton Sinclair had written in *The Jungle,* but supplied extra details so disgusting that Roosevelt could not bring himself to release them. He did not scruple, however, to let congressional leaders know what was in the report. Apprehensive that some details might leak, the Senate voted unanimously to make Beveridge's bill an amendment to the Agricultural Appropriations Bill. That gave food-industry advocates in the House the task of explaining why meat shipped across state lines should not be inspected and dated by federal agents.

James W. Wadsworth, Chairman of the House Committee on Agriculture, rose to the challenge with such determination that Roosevelt sent Congress the results of his probe on 8 June, warning, "My investigations are not yet through." Wadsworth did not seem fazed even by an account of a hog carcass falling from its hook and sliding halfway into a packinghouse men's room, whence it was retrieved and sent on to its destination, unwashed.

Again, Roosevelt saw a need for compromise. The Congressman was a stockbreeder and as fanatically opposed to regulation of his industry as Foraker was on behalf of the railroads. Beveridge was ordered to sacrifice can-dating (which Wadsworth believed would hinder sales) in exchange for the more important principle of mandatory inspection. Again, a majority in favor materialized, and the principle moved toward passage.

On 8 June, the President signed into law "An Act for the Preservation of American Antiquities," the first of an accelerating series of measures deriving from his Fifth Message. It empowered him to proclaim national monuments and historic and prehistoric sites on federal ground, without resort to Congress. Then came twin measures establishing the liability of federal agencies and common carriers for negligence-caused job accidents. A pleasedly firm presidential signature, inscribed with an eagle quill, granted Oklahoma statehood. The last two days of the month, and of the session, brought protection for Niagara Falls from hydroelectric despoilment, immunity for witnesses in antitrust cases, stricter standards for alien naturalization, a lock system for the Panama Canal, and the three major laws Roosevelt most wanted: the Railroad Rate Regulation Act on the twenty-ninth, and the Meat Inspection and Pure Food and Drug Acts on the thirtieth.

That afternoon, the temperature in Washington rose to one hundred degrees. Government buildings seemed to explode with released tension as limp-collared legislators and administrators emerged from every doorway and headed out of town. Roosevelt, looking relatively cool in a white suit, was in as much a hurry as any. But he had to wait until the House dispatched a final bill to him at 9:30 P.M., via the fastest automobile in town. By then he had had more than his fill of the Fifty-ninth Congress, and could be sure that most of its members—Senator Foraker in particular—hoped his vacation would be long.

Still, it had been an historic session, he felt, one that had greatly extended the authority of centralized government. Over railroads alone, that reach now embraced passenger rates, pipeline fees, freight bills, storage and refrigeration contracts, and a plethora of other surchargeable services, from switch and spur facilities to dockyard terminals. Already, Packingtown was scrubbing down, food inspectors sharpening their pencils, and pigs being kept out of privies. The Man with the Muckrake was chastised, and the rule of Burke—movingly cited by Ray Stannard Baker—affirmed as a guiding principle of progressivism: "Society cannot exist unless a controlling power upon will and appetite be placed somewhere."

CHAPTER 27

Blood Through Marble

I'm not so much troubled about th' naygur whin he lives
among his opprissors as I am whin he falls into
th' hands iv his liberators.

EDITH KERMIT ROOSEVELT was waiting in the yellow-wheeled family wagon when her husband's train steamed into Oyster Bay station on 1 July 1906. She positioned herself, as always, slightly aloof, letting a width of cinder road intervene between the carriage door and the door of the depot, where the usual crowd of villagers was jostling.

The President emerged, caught sight of Kermit first, and kissed him. Then he began to shake hands while Edith sat with Quentin beside her, wrapped in her private role as wife and mother.

She was not quite forty-five and not quite slender, a calm, contented woman who had gotten what she wanted by simply waiting for it—as she waited now for the only man she had ever loved. The fact that she was not the only person in his romantic history had long since ceased to hurt her, as far as anyone knew, but with Edith, "far" was not much. The averted gaze, the set mouth, the careful expressionlessness she gave to the world outside her world revealed little and invited nothing. To children other than her own, she appeared as "a remote goddess . . . as calm and imperturbable as a Buddha." Born into the same wealthy *haut-bourgeois* circles as Theodore, and having become, at age four, his intimate friend, she had acquired a sense of privilege that never left her, even though her alcoholic father's money had dissipated with such quickness that she remembered a childhood more shabby than genteel.

There had never been any question in her mind, as she grew up, that "Teedie" would marry her. When he chose someone prettier and richer, Edith had simply counted the days until fate would return him to her. She would have counted fifty years, if necessary. In the event, five were enough. Edith had reacted to Theodore's aberrant liaison much as she had to her father's

"A REMOTE GODDESS . . . CALM AND IMPERTURBABLE AS A BUDDHA."
The President's favorite photograph of Edith Kermit Roosevelt

drinking, by simply editing it out of her book of life. The name of Alice Hath-away Lee was not to be mentioned, even in the index; no illustrations of that sweet, blank face were necessary; a quick cut from 1880 to 1885 would speed the narrative nicely. There had remained the awkward subplot of a step-daughter, but at last, thanks to Nick Longworth, it was part of another tale.

Episcopalian, erudite, conservative, intensely private, and—when her serenity was threatened—a formidable adversary, Edith struck most strangers as snobbish. The impression was in part correct (Archie and Quentin had to research the antecedents of all their would-be friends) but caused mostly by her New England reserve. She did not consider herself superior, so much as separate from *hoi polloi*. In receiving lines, she let the President do the glad-handing, while she stood clutching a nosegay, smiling only slightly, her sap-phire eyes cool. What they saw, they saw without mercy. Mediocrity bored her, as did class resentment. "If they had our brains," she was wont to say of servants, "they'd have our place."

Yet within a silken web of family, social, and political connections, almost all spun about her by Theodore, Edith was frank, warm, unassuming, and loyal. Henry Adams found her "sympathetic" and greatly preferred her company to that of the President. "She has bad taste, and that too is a comfort." To Ray Stannard Baker, she was "a singularly attractive woman, of rare refinement and charm of manner." Jules Jusserand informed his government that she was "certainly adorned with most precious and charming qualities"—adding, by way of explanation, that she was of French descent.

Edith was well-read enough to hold her own in conversation with Adams and Henry Cabot Lodge. "She is not only cultured, but scholarly," Roosevelt boasted. Her intellectual interests were more sophisticated than his, inclining toward *belles-lettres* and aphoristic essays, and she loved the theater, to which he reacted as if caged. Whereas his idea of a sublime musical experience was "The Stars and Stripes Forever," played by the full Marine band, hers was a recital in the East Room by Ernestine Schumann-Heink. Edith did not equate such occasions with fashion; her taste in clothes was at best severe, and she cared little for intermission gossip. Yet she enjoyed entertaining, whether brilliantly at diplomatic dinners in Washington, or messily at mosquito-infested picnics with her children, the largest and worst of whom, she joked, was Theodore.

His attitude toward her—beyond the fact, clear to all, that they personified every syllable of the marriage vow—was one of doglike adoration. He looked to her for porch company, for approving pats and hugs, and sometimes, guiltily, for discipline when he had done something wrong. She could bring him up short, during one of his indiscreet monologues, by giving off a special quietness that he could sense within seconds. "Why, *Ee*-die, I was only going to say . . ."

Her attitude toward him was complementary, yin to his yang. Theodore represented "the fire of life" (an image from Walter Savage Landor that she often cited), and she warmed both hands at him. Deeply domestic, she accepted his compulsive need for public attention, knowing that he could stay home only so long before the urge to hunt or fight or orate would take him away again. She had enough quiet humor to suffer his idiosyncrasies—the yodels of falsetto laughter, the mad rock-climbs, woodsmen and their wives invited to stay over in the White House—even though he often outraged her sense of propriety.

"You only have to live with me," she periodically reminded him, "while I have to live with *you*."

⬿

HE DID NOT LOOK well this July day, with his limp and obvious need for rest after seven months of legislative wrangling. Edith had thought him "jaded" a month before, and others had noticed even earlier signs of exhaustion. Whenever he was tired, his internal pressure tended to spew, geyserlike. There had been an outburst, to Sir Mortimer Durand's face, about the "damned little Jew" of a British journalist who had accused him of paying court to the Kaiser. William E. Chandler had also been scalded, after politely asking if the White House had shown "good faith" in negotiating with both parties during the rate-bill fight. And Norman Hapgood, a journalist guilty of suggesting that Roosevelt sometimes denied his own press leaks, was currently in receipt of a presidential letter that came close to a demand for armed satisfaction.

Nervous fatigue could be allayed in the soothing environs of Sagamore Hill. But Roosevelt had more chronic physical problems to face up to—or more accurately, to play down. He admitted to Kermit and Ethel that his steadily dimming left eye was causing him "a little difficulty," and that his ankle sprain was complicated by rheumatism. His weight hovered obstinately around two hundred pounds, no matter how much he exercised.

"He is certainly the most enduring man I have ever known," Gifford Pinchot reported to Irving Fisher, a concerned fitness expert, "and it seems to me equally certain that his endurance can have little to do with his diet." The President consumed whatever was put before him, with a partiality for meat over vegetables: "I should say that he ate nearly twice as much as the average man."

Fisher, who had been studying the nutritional theories of Russell H. Chittenden, replied, "It is clear to me that the President is running his machine too hard. . . . In another decade or two . . . I would almost risk my reputation as a prophet in predicting that he will find friction in the machine, which will probably increase to almost the stopping point."

Edith sweetly served cakes, ice cream, and lemonade on the Fourth of July. The Oyster Bay *Pilot* thereafter noticed an unprecedented number of presidential rowing excursions. Roosevelt was also seen haying with his farmworkers, sweating hugely in white clothes and forking loads so large he had to center himself underneath before lifting them.

"*J'ESSAIE DE FAIRE circuler le sang à travers le marbre,*" Auguste Rodin declared in August 1906, after getting permission to sculpt the President on a forthcoming visit to America. "I try to make the blood circulate through the marble."

Theodore Roosevelt was sanguine in every sense of the word, physiological and psychological. He was ruddy and excitable, flush-faced, susceptible to cuts and grazes. ("Theodore," Edith remarked, after he collided with the Sagamore Hill windmill, "I wish you'd do your bleeding in the bathroom.") The medieval humor *sanguis* expressed his character exactly: courageous, optimistic, affectionate, ardent. His apparent fatigue in the summer of 1906 was the result of overstimulation rather than overwork. For more than a year now, he had prevailed too easily against too many opponents, and found himself more than equal to the largest tasks. As a result, he had begun to receive regular boosts of journalistic hyperbole, intoxicating enough to contravene the Pure Food and Drug Act. "It is now universally recognized by experienced politicians of all parties," *The Washington Post* reported, ". . . that he has more political acumen in one lobe of his brain than the whole militant tribe of American politicians have in their combined intelligence; that his political perception, so acute as to amount almost to divination, is superior to that of any American statesman of the present or immediate past era."

With so much success in his system, and nothing—for the moment—to restrain him, Roosevelt was fast approaching a level of executive hypertension. His reaction, then, was more or less predictable on 16 August, when he received a telegram from the mayor and citizens of Brownsville, Texas, a depressed, dust-baked outpost on the Rio Grande:

> At a few minutes before midnight on Monday, the 13th, a body of United States soldiers of Twenty-fifth United States infantry (colored), numbering between 20–30 men, emerged from the garrison inclosure, carrying their rifles and abundant supply of ammunition, also begun [*sic*] firing in town and directly into dwellings, offices, stores, and at police and citizens. During firing, one citizen, Frank Natus, was killed in his yard, and the lieutenant of police, who rode toward the firing, had his horse killed under him and was shot through the right arm, which has since been amputated at the elbow. After firing about 200 shots, the soldiers retired to their quarters. We find that threats have been made by them that they will repeat this outrage. We do not believe their officers can restrain them. . . . Our condition, Mr. President, is this: our women and children are terrorized and our men are practically under constant alarm and watchfulness. No community can stand this strain for more than a few days. We look to you for relief; we ask you to have the troops at once removed from Fort Brown and replaced by white soldiers.

Roosevelt ordered a full report on the incident from the War Department. Supplementary details were already appearing in the press. The black battalion—three companies minus a fourth on separate assignment—had arrived in Brownsville fewer than three weeks before, and racial tensions had been rising ever since. Soldiers had been denied access to local bars, shoved off sidewalks, beaten, and warned that their brains might be blown out. On the eve of the riot, the usual "large" Negro had tried to force himself on the usual "respectable" white woman. She could not describe his face, but had total recall of his khaki trousers.

As a result of warnings from downtown, Major Charles W. Penrose, the battalion's white commander, had placed all his men under curfew the following night. Yet about fifteen of them had allegedly found a key to the barracks and gone on their murderous rampage downtown—even though a call to arms, begun while the bullets were still flying, found all soldiers present or accounted for. The culprits must have sprinted back as soon as they heard the bugle and snuck into line in time to holler "Present" when the roster was read.

Only one voice of authority expressed doubt as to such a scenario. Brigadier General William S. McCaskey, commander of the Army's Southwestern Division, cautioned the War Department in a telegram received on 18 August:

CITIZENS OF BROWNSVILLE ENTERTAIN RACE HATRED TO AN EXTREME DEGREE . . . PROVOCATION GIVEN THE SOLDIERS NOT TAKEN INTO ACCOUNT.

Some damaging hard evidence, however, indicated that the allegations were not altogether fanciful. Major Penrose reported that he had been presented with seventy or more Army-rifle shell casings that matched those clean rifles. Exhibit B was a dropped soldier's cap. Regretfully but unanimously, Penrose and his four white junior officers concluded that men of the Twenty-fifth Infantry must be guilty.

Roosevelt waited no longer than 20 August before deciding, on the basis of a second appeal from the Brownsville citizens' committee, that Fort Brown should be "temporarily abandoned." He ordered the battalion to march to nearby Fort Ringgold, pending a full investigation by the Capitol Army Chief of Staff. No sooner had he done so than a preliminary report from the Assistant Inspector General of the Southwestern Division persuaded him to move them much farther, beyond posse range. Major Augustus P. Blocksom confirmed most of Major Penrose's findings, and unequivocally described the rioters as "soldiers." Blocksom allowed that no positive identifications had been made, but, in words not calculated to delay the President's action, warned of possible "mob violence" if the soldiers were not moved soon.

Roosevelt then sent the bulk of the battalion to quarantine in Fort Reno, Oklahoma. Twelve suspects fingered by another Army inspector were to be held in the guardhouse at San Antonio, while he awaited further evidence of their guilt from Major Blocksom.

It came on 29 August, and was unequivocal. "That the raiders were soldiers of the Twenty-fifth Infantry cannot be doubted," Blocksom wrote.

Their commanding officers were not responsible for permitting the violence, since at first sound of gunfire downtown they had imagined the fort was being attacked, and issued a defensive call to arms. Only when the mayor of Brownsville showed them the casings the next morning had they realized their misapprehension. Major Penrose was now conscientiously trying to identify the perpetrators himself, but could not get a single black interviewee to name names. It was clear to Blocksom that the men, veterans and juniors alike, were engaged in a conspiracy to obstruct justice. If they did not break ranks soon, they should all "be discharged from the service and debarred from reenlistment in the Army, Navy and Marine Corps."

Blocksom added a personal observation that "the colored soldier is much more aggressive in his attitude on the social equality question than he used to be."

<hr />

THE SAME COULD BE said of Theodore Roosevelt. Over the last year and a half, his Negro policy had noticeably hardened. He remained incapable of the race hatred of Benjamin R. Tillman, or even the patrician disdain of Owen Wister. Yet he had no quarrel with those whites in Brownsville who believed that blacks were "inferior socially." Nor, with another round of congressional elections looming, did he want to jeopardize his new popularity in the South. That region's white voters had welcomed him extravagantly last fall, in part because he had atoned for his early radicalism. His one outburst against "lynch law" was forgiven, if only because it had been provoked by the Governor of Arkansas.

More ominously, he had begun to sound a theme that played well in Brownsville: "The colored man who fails to condemn crime in another colored man . . . is the worst enemy of his own people, as well as an enemy to all the people."

<hr />

THE PRESIDENT'S *SANGUIS* was again in evidence on 3 September, when a fighting fleet three miles long saluted him in Long Island Sound. "By George! Doesn't the sight of those big warships make one's blood tingle?"

It was the greatest naval display of his presidency so far. Three out of every four of these white leviathans had been built since the war with Spain. During his first term alone, Congress had authorized thirty-one new vessels, including ten battleships. Two new all-big-gun battleships were due to begin construction in the fall. The United States Navy, fifth in the world when he took office, was now third. Admittedly, that ranking had been rendered academic by Great Britain's recent introduction of HMS *Dreadnought*, a tengun, turbine-driven monster stronger, quicker, and smoother than anything else afloat. But the mere fact that sea power was entering a new age augured well for Roosevelt's future defense proposals. Already, thanks to *Dreadnought,* he had been authorized by Congress to build a battleship of unlimited displacement, and guns as heavy as it could carry.

He looked forward to sailing on the newest of his completed battleships, the *Louisiana,* in a couple of months' time. Construction of the Panama Canal was well under way, and he wanted to see "the dirt fly" with his own eyes. In the meantime, he braced for the likelihood that a few of these white ships might soon be required for active duty in Cuba—exactly the last place he wanted to send them, at a time when the Democratic Party was looking round for a fall campaign issue.

An uprising by "liberals" had taken place on the island eighteen days before, in protest against alleged election-rigging by President Tomás Estrada Palma and his regime of "moderates." The fighting since then had been fierce enough to make both party names jokeworthy. But what was less funny was the obligation of the United States to intervene in any such dispute, under an amendment attached years before to a bill long since forgotten, by Senator Orville Platt of Connecticut. The Platt Amendment in effect made Cuba an American protectorate, should she ever become unable to govern herself, and thus invite the greedy interest of foreign powers.

Having fought for the liberty of Cubans in 1898, bestowed it himself in 1902, and preached the "moral" virtues of a reciprocity treaty with them, Roosevelt was unwilling to see any more cartoons of himself in Rough Rider uniform. For a day or two after the naval review, an amnesty offer by Estrada Palma encouraged hopes of peace. But the insurrection could not be quelled, and on 8 September came the inevitable request for naval intervention by the United States.

Roosevelt authorized the dispatch of two warships, along with a harsh warning by Assistant Secretary of State Robert Bacon that the President considered intervention to be "a very serious thing." Before landing any Marines, he would have to be "absolutely certain" that the Cuban government was indeed helpless.

"Just at the moment I am so angry with that infernal little Cuban republic that I would like to wipe its people off the face of the earth," he wrote to Henry White on 13 September. "All that we wanted from them was that they would behave themselves and be prosperous and happy so that we would not have to interfere." It was particularly galling to be called back there just after Elihu Root, who had made the improvement of North-South relations his priority as Secretary of State, had told Latin Americans: "We wish for no victories but those of peace; for no territory except our own; for no sovereignty except the sovereignty over ourselves."

Roosevelt's annoyance reflected the fact that both Cuban factions were gambling on seeing the Stars and Stripes rise again over Havana—the moderates because they hoped to be kept in power, the liberals because they believed they would consequently get a free and fair election. Thus, he was presented with a paradox of foreign policy. By not intervening, he would encourage civil war; by intervening, he would strengthen both sides, and therefore have to stay.

To his further annoyance, he heard that Bacon had, against instructions, authorized the landing of a party of Marines in Cuba. The Assistant Secretary was the best-looking man in the Administration, if not its brightest. "You had no business to direct the landing of those troops without specific authority from here . . . ," Roosevelt furiously cabled him. "Unless you are directed otherwise from here the forces are only to be used to protect American life and property."

Hoping still to avoid direct intervention, he summoned Bacon and Taft to Oyster Bay for a crisis meeting. His latest Secretary of the Navy, Charles J. Bonaparte, joined them. Bonaparte was a small man with a large signature, fully six inches long, proclaiming that the blood of the great Emperor flowed in his veins. He was therefore something of an expert on foreign adventures, and, as a lawyer well-read in history, qualified to warn of their consequences. Bonaparte had not approved of Roosevelt's youthful jingoism, but otherwise identified with him as a fellow patrician bent on reform.

It was agreed that the President should make a final appeal to Cubans to "sink all differences" and "remember that the only way they can preserve the independence of their republic is to prevent the necessity of outside interference." Roosevelt sent a letter to this effect to the Cuban minister in Washington, and released it to the press. He announced also that Bacon and Taft were being dispatched immediately to Havana, in the hope that they could broker some sort of truce.

—❧—

THE FIRST DAY of fall found the President in limbo at Sagamore Hill. A final week of vacation stretched ahead, with no visitors on his calendar, and no news yet of any break in the Brownsville investigation—except that a grand jury in San Antonio had failed to indict any of the twelve main suspects. Roosevelt consequently had time to ponder three important replacement problems.

That of a successor to Justice Brown was the most urgent, with the Supreme Court due to reconvene in October. Once again, Taft had turned him down. Or rather, Helen Taft had begged Roosevelt not to appoint her husband. She was already mentally redecorating the White House. Taft sounded sincere in protesting a continued sense of obligation toward the Philippines (where an Army unit commanded by General Leonard Wood had recently slaughtered six hundred of his "little brown brothers," against a resurgence of Moro violence). Yet he sounded just as sincere in saying that he would jump at the job of Chief Justice. Behind Taft's jolly-fat-man facade, there lurked a love for titles.

For much of the summer, Roosevelt had hesitated between appointing William Henry Moody and Horace H. Lurton, a Democrat recommended by Taft. He favored the Attorney General, except that Moody came from the same state as Oliver Wendell Holmes, Jr. Not only that, the Antitrust Division of the Justice Department was just beginning what promised to be an exciting prosecution of the Standard Oil Company; any move of Moody would seem either precautionary or defensive. So Lurton had loomed as the next Justice until Henry Cabot Lodge, to whom all Democrats were lepers, entered a passionate protest against him. The President, accordingly, remained undecided.

He was much more certain of the absolute necessity of getting a new British Ambassador to replace Sir Mortimer Durand. During last year's peacemaking efforts, and again during the Algeciras Conference, he had been maddened by Durand's disinclination to unbend in private conversation. He interpreted it as stupidity. (Actually, the Ambassador was a shy but perceptive man, well aware that Roosevelt equated "privacy" with persuasion.) Sir Mortimer also disliked slogging through the thickets of Rock Creek Park, another essential locale for diplomatic dialogue. Without doubt, the British government must recall him. But how, and how soon, could such a delicate matter be arranged? And what chance was there of Cecil Spring Rice being sent instead? Answers would not be forthcoming until the arrival in early October of a possible intermediary, Arthur Lee, MP, secretly summoned from England.

The least urgent yet most momentous question Roosevelt had to consider was that of his own successor. Mrs. Taft did not know it, but his personal preference always had been for Elihu Root. "I would walk on my hands and knees from the White House to the Capitol to see Root made President. But I know it cannot be done. He couldn't be elected." The Secretary of State was considered by many who knew him to be a great man—something never said of Taft. Intellectually formidable, tireless, brave, unbeatable in any negotiation, Root was hampered by his identity as a corporate lawyer. However honorable, that was simply the wrong thing to be at a time when Roosevelt himself had declared war on *laissez-faire*.

Taft was warm dough to Root's cold iron. He presented no hard edge to the public, or indeed to the President, who imagined that the dough could be permanently imprinted "T.R." There were other possible Republican candidates, of course, such as Speaker Cannon and Senator Foraker on the right, and Senator Beveridge on the left. Roosevelt was not averse to flattering any of them in front of reporters, but as long as Chief Justice Fuller stayed alive, he saw his successor in Taft.

The Washington Post joked that he did not really need one. "There is but one man who can prevent the Republican party from nominating Theodore Roosevelt for re-election in 1908, and that man is Theodore Roosevelt himself."

⟳

JOSEPH B. FORAKER gave early notice of being as much a presidential scourge in the next session of Congress as he had been during the last. In an unctuous telegram received just before Roosevelt's departure from Oyster Bay on 28 September, he wrote, "I fear it may be unwelcome to call your attention to the fact that under our treaty with Cuba . . . consent is given to the United States, not to the President, to intervene on certain specified grounds." Congressional approval was required before troops could be sent and local authority usurped. "Pardon me for saying this is an awfully serious matter, with far-reaching serious consequences."

Roosevelt could not deny the treaty, nor the serious view Foraker took of everything, even jokes. He replied with polite restraint. "I am sure you will agree with me that it would not have been wise to summon Congress to consider the situation in Cuba, which was changing from week to week and almost from day to day. . . . You, my dear Senator, are the last man to advocate my playing a part like President Buchanan or failing to take the responsibility that the President must take if he is fit for his position." So far, he had taken only "tentative" steps toward intervention, and would look to Congress for a "permanent policy" in December. In the meantime, he reserved his right to intervene directly if necessary. There had been a near-total breakdown of government in Havana, with Estrada Palma insisting on full American control rather than any power-sharing with the *insurrectos.*

Privately, Roosevelt seethed at the censorious tone of Foraker's telegram. The Senator had known him since his first participation in a Republican presidential convention, at Chicago in 1884. They had been fellow sponsors of a resolution nominating a black man as temporary chairman of the proceedings. Since then, their relations had been formal rather than friendly, although Foraker had supported Roosevelt's nomination for the vice presidency and publicly praised him for entertaining Booker T. Washington. Now, however, Foraker had presumed to question his authority as Commander-in-Chief.

"He is a very powerful and very vindictive man," Roosevelt wrote Lodge, "and he is one of the most unblushing servers and beneficiaries of corporate wealth within or without office that I have ever met. It is possible that he has grown to feel so angry over my course, that is, over my having helped rescue the Republican party and therefore the country from the ruin into which, if he had his way . . ."

Lodge was so used to Theodore's eruptions that he did not notice, or choose to notice, incipient signs of executive paranoia. He was more concerned with protecting the President in the event of any open clash with Foraker. After many years of side-by-side service in the Senate, Lodge knew that "Fire Alarm Joe" could be a dangerous adversary.

Foraker was now sixty years old. Tall and spare, with steel-gray hair and more steel, apparently, infusing his spine, he personified the railroads he defended. As a result, he was often caricatured as the ultimate Old Guard reactionary. If Roosevelt's predominant humor was blood, Foraker's was phlegm: his coldness repelled as much as it intimidated. Only in oratory, at which he excelled, did he live up to his nickname. He was primarily a negative force, resistant to change.

⟋⟍

IN ONE OF THE few light moments of a grim summer, the President responded to a request from Attorney General Moody as to the correct orthography of Justice Department press releases. "I can only advise you to follow the example of the younger Mr. Weller just prior to the moment when he was in such unseemly fashion advised by the elder Mr. Weller how to spell his own name—and this to the great scandal of the court."

"Simplified Spelling" was now, by presidential edict, compulsory usage in all Administration documents. Roosevelt had become a convert of a philological reform movement emanating from Columbia University. An impressive phalanx of academics with letters trailing after their names sought to remove as many letters as possible from words that only a typesetter could love. They cited the carefree irregularities of spelling in past centuries (pointing out that the Swan of Avon himself never seemed to know how to spell *Shakespeare*), and asked why contemporary stylists had become so obsessed with standardization. The answer was, of course, that unpronounced letters caused confusion—hence, incredibly, 1,690 variants of the noun *diarrhea*, a word of common significance if there ever was one. Spelling, free of ambiguities, they argued would do away with the need of standardization, and schoolchildren and civil servants could take exams without fear.

In its Circular number 6 for the summer of 1906, Columbia's Simplified Spelling Board, flush with a gift of ten thousand dollars from Andrew Carnegie, declined to propose "any change in the spelling of proper names, especially of surnames," thus ensuring that their donor would not feel obliged to sign any future checks *Andru Karnegi*. The President, similarly content not to become *Rozevelt,* embraced the Board's recommendations with the enthusiasm of a man of letters who had long since objected to the practice of putting a *u* in *honor.*

It seemed to him that Circular number 6 and its predecessors justified the adoption of some "very moderate and common-sense" spelling reforms, which would keep the government in step with "the ablest and most practical educators of our time"—men such as Thomas R. Lounsbury, Professor of English at Yale University. In a letter to the Public Printer of the United States, Roosevelt ordered simplified spelling of some three hundred frequently used words. Such changes, he argued, were "but a very slight extension of the unconscious movement which has made agricultural implement makers and farmers write *plow* instead of *plough* . . . just as all people who speak English now write *bat, set, dim, sum,* and *fish,* instead of the Elizabethan *batte, sette, dimme, summe,* and *fysshe.*"

There could be little protest against these examples—certainly not by menu writers in Chinatown, where *dim sum* was already approved usage. But Roosevelt's appended list of new spellings caused a sensation in bureaucratic Washington:

> *addresst blusht comprize deprest egis fagot gazel kist partizan phenix pur ript snapt thru vext winkt*

Soon, the nation's newspapers were vying with one another to coin new, sarcastic simplifications, until *Harper's Weekly* complained, "THIS IS TU MUTCH." Members of Congress and the Supreme Court announced their absolute unwillingness to go along. Roosevelt seemed to sense defeat, even as he insisted that he would continue to use the new styles himself. He told the Public Printer that none of his changes should be considered permanent. "If they do not ultimately meet with popular approval they will be dropt, and that is all there is about it."

⌖

ON 29 SEPTEMBER, President Estrada Palma and his entire Cabinet resigned, leaving Taft with no alternative under the Platt Amendment but to issue a declaration of intervention by the United States. He established himself as the temporary executive of a "Cuban" administration, "conforming as far as may be to the Constitution of Cuba," and operating under the Cuban flag. Roosevelt had insisted on that last touch. He told Taft that the role of the United States must simply be to ensure that Cuba stayed solvent and stable until she could once again govern herself. To that end, American troops would guard the island's treasury and maintain order in her towns. A simultaneous agreement with the liberals guaranteed that all insurrectionary activities would cease, pending free and legal elections.

In his last official act before returning to Washington from Oyster Bay, Roosevelt sent Taft six thousand additional troops. "I congratulate you most heartily upon the admirable way you have handled the whole matter," he cabled, adding that he had instructed the State Department to continue Cuban foreign relations "as if no change had occurred." It was crucial that all islanders understood that he had intervened only because the government had collapsed. "I am most anxious that there should be no bloodshed between Americans and Cubans."

Back in the White House on 1 October, he chafed at not having Taft at hand to help him decide finally between Moody and Lurton for the Supreme Court. He did not trust his own judgment on matters of Constitutional import, and in this case could hardly ask the Attorney General for an opinion.

Even more critical was the ugly matter of Brownsville. Ideally, Taft should be in charge of it, as Secretary of War. But until a provisional governor could be installed, somewhere around midmonth, Roosevelt would have to supervise the Army's ongoing investigation. It was fraught with political risk. Color had become an issue in the congressional campaign, after the recent outbreak, in Atlanta, of some of the worst race violence on record. Twenty black men had been killed and hundreds wounded at the hands of a mob crazed by reports of "an unusual number" of Negro assaults on white women. Roosevelt remained silent on the massacre. He did not even mention race relations in his "platform" address of the season, a somewhat repetitive-sounding denunciation of corporate greed, delivered on 4 October in Harrisburg.

Only those with ears attuned to the clang of Rooseveltian clichés detected a new overtone of impatience with executive restraints. He paid homage, for the gratification of his audience, to the Pennsylvanian jurist and Founding Father James Wilson (1742–1798), and cited Wilson's belief that "one uniform and comprehensive system of government and laws" arose in response to frequently conflicting decisions of state and federal judges. That superjurisdiction was, in effect, the will of "the sovereign people" who, in 1906, were determined "to assert their sovereignty over the great corporations of the day."

To Henry Cabot Lodge, knowing Roosevelt's tendency to use the word *sovereign* as if it were a personal pronoun, such statements sounded more like Nietzsche than Wilson. But the Senator worried only that his old friend was bearing down too hard on businessmen as opposed to radical agitators. Had Lodge a deeper knowledge of Wilson's philosophy, he might have come across a ruminative passage that was practically pure Theodore: *"If I am asked . . . how do you know that you ought to do that, of which your conscience enjoins the performance? I can only say, I feel that such is my duty. Here investigation must stop; reasoning can go no farther."*

Propelled by just such a sense of moral certainty, hearing answers rather than questions and inviting no argument, Roosevelt decided it was time to bring the Brownsville affair to a conclusion. He ordered his new Inspector General, Ernest A. Garlington, to proceed to Oklahoma and Texas and interview the quarantined members of the Twenty-fifth Infantry personally. "If the guilty parties cannot be discovered, the President approves the recommendation [by Major Blocksom] that the whole three companies implicated in this atrocious outrage should be dismissed and the men forever debarred from reenlisting in the Army or Navy of the United States."

⚯

WHILE AWAITING GENERAL Garlington's report, the President played host to Arthur Lee. His old friend arrived from England on 12 October, rather mystified at having been summoned across the Atlantic without explanation.

Roosevelt, who made no small talk, immediately broached the subject. "I have had to finally abandon any attempts to do confidential business through the present British Ambassador, and must do it through someone else."

As a member of the government Sir Mortimer Durand represented, Lee was at once put into a delicate diplomatic position. Roosevelt made him understand that something more important than protocol was at stake. The United States and Great Britain "ought to be in specially intimate relations," but had reached a virtual standstill because of Durand's imprisonment in his own culture. "He doesn't begin to understand us."

At present, fortunately, the international situation was quiet, and no difficult negotiations loomed between Washington and London. "I say this, however," Roosevelt went on, "and cannot say it too emphatically, that if any difficult question *does* arise, your government will have to send over, specially, someone with whom we *can* work, to deal with it. This is not merely my view, but that of Root, and also of Taft—who will probably be the next President."

Lee stayed at the White House for several days, during which time he was permitted to read the private correspondence Roosevelt had had with other ambassadors during the Portsmouth and Algeciras conferences. "I cannot help but deplore the gradual waning of British prestige and popularity over here, during the last three years," the President said, knowing that his words would be repeated throughout Whitehall, "and the eclipse of the British Embassy by the French and German missions—both of which are exceptionally well filled."

Edith Roosevelt contributed her own quiet propaganda over dinner. "You remember, of course, that in your time here, and until Sir Michael Herbert died, it was never spoken of in Washington except as '*the* Embassy.' " Lee remembered well, and with nostalgia. In 1899, he had been military attaché to Sir Julian Pauncefote, and engaged to marry an American heiress. It was largely to Ruth Lee's fortune that he owed his current comfortable place in British society. Now Mrs. Roosevelt seemed to be suggesting that the pair of them could restore 1300 Connecticut Avenue to the center of Washington's *haut monde*. "Hardly any of the right kind of people go there," Edith pursued. "The Durands do practically nothing in the way of entertaining—and that little so poorly that people do not care to go."

Lee left the White House with an official note from Roosevelt, practically appointing him to the British foreign service. He did not know that a letter recalling Sir Mortimer was already on its way. Sir Edward Grey had heard so many presidential complaints about Durand from Henry White that a more cerebral Ambassador was being looked for. This did not augur well for Lee—who in any case sat on the wrong side of the House of Commons.

Sir Mortimer was thunderstruck when Grey's letter arrived on 21 October. Twice that night he came down to reopen his dispatch box "to assure myself that I had not dreamt the whole thing." He had not. His diplomatic career was over.

Edith Roosevelt had chosen the right qualifier to describe the way the Durands entertained. Sir Mortimer was not a wealthy man, and for two years had spent dollars as if they were shillings, just to fulfill his mission. He had given up polo, books, hunting, and traded in his life-insurance policy. Even so, he was penniless.

"I must try to take it like a gentleman," he wrote in his diary.

⟋

BY NOW, TAFT was back in Washington, having installed Charles E. Magoon as Provisional Governor of Cuba. The crisis that had so upset Roosevelt seemed to have been resolved without force, and with the happy acquiescence of most islanders. No date was yet set for *Cuba libre segundo,* but Taft and Magoon both understood that it had to occur before the President left office.

Senator Foraker was forced to acknowledge that the Administration had behaved honorably toward a sister republic. Perhaps now, he suggested in a campaign speech, the Administration would find the time to address some problems closer to home, such as that of race relations. "It is important to protect Cubans in Cuba, but it is even more important to protect Americans in America."

Ignoring him, Roosevelt commandeered Taft and Root for five days of tense consultations about the Supreme Court matter. Three sitting Justices and four Senators helped him decide that William H. Moody would be his third appointee to the Bench. The official announcement was delayed, for propriety, until after the elections, but Moody's name was leaked on 24 October, to the great satisfaction of voters from Massachusetts.

General Garlington's Brownsville report reached the War Department around the same time. It was remarkable for a lack of evidence so total as to inculpate him for word-spinning. He stated that during exhaustive interviews with the main suspects in San Antonio, he had encountered nothing but "a wooden, stolid look" as each soldier, in turn, "positively denied any knowledge" of the affair. This, to an investigating officer brought up in Greenville, South Carolina, could mean only the opposite. He had called them all back in groups and made sure they understood the President's ultimatum: if no man confessed or informed, all would be adjudged guilty. They remained silent.

Garlington had then proceeded to Fort Reno and interviewed the troops held in quarantine. Again, he was frustrated by the conspiratorial caginess he took to be typical of black men: "The secretive nature of the race, where crimes to members of their color are charged, is well known." He concluded "that the firing into the houses of the citizens of Brownsville . . . was done by enlisted men of the Twenty-fifth Infantry," and recommended that every man in the battalion be held responsible for the crimes of the few. As the President had stipulated, they should be dishonorably discharged.

On 30 October, Roosevelt summoned Booker T. Washington to the White House, in a clear indication that he was worried about how Negro voters might react. Election Day was just one week away, and the political situation nationwide was volatile. The Democratic Party had recovered from its debacle under Alton B. Parker two years before, and—as Senator Foraker gloomily observed—stood to gain from progressive/conservative infighting among Republicans. Race and labor were key issues, with the Industrial Workers of the World fanning radical discontent among Western miners, and Southern whites wildly agitated by the Atlanta riots. (In Tennessee, rumors circulated of "Negro companies drilling by night.") William Randolph Hearst was showing alarming strength as the Democratic nominee for Governor of New York, against Roosevelt's personal candidate, Charles Evans Hughes, a coldly brilliant Republican lawyer.

Washington listened with misgivings as the President told him that he was about to dismiss 167 Negro soldiers, without honor and without trial. He had just been in Atlanta, and sensed that Roosevelt was making a terrible mistake. American blacks would have trouble understanding why "our friend" (as Washington always called him) should rush to judgment at such a time, without giving a single man of the Twenty-fifth Infantry a chance to testify in court. Even more distressing was the likelihood that redneck racists everywhere would applaud Roosevelt's willingness to act on what passed for evidence in lynch country: unsubstantiated charges of rape, instant identifications of black men last seen in darkness, the "wooden, stolid look" of Negro terror, and a few dozen shell casings ejected from clean rifles.

⌐◠

WASHINGTON'S DISTRESS GREW after leaving the Executive Office. On 3 November, he wrote begging Roosevelt not to do anything precipitous about Brownsville until they could meet again. "There is some information which I must put before you before you take final action." But his letter arrived at the wrong psychological moment. Roosevelt's blood was up, after two days of hunting wild turkey at Pine Knot. It was Election Eve, and he was

"HE WOULD HAVE LOST HIS SEAT, AND VERY LIKELY HIS WIFE."
Mr. and Mrs. Nicholas Longworth, ca. 1906

about to leave for New York, where Elihu Root (speaking on White House authority) had just come within one syllable of saying that the President held William Randolph Hearst responsible for the death of William McKinley.

Root's statement had pulverized the Democratic campaign, not to mention Hearst's chances of running for President in 1908. Roosevelt could not wait to get to a voting booth to add to the rout. He had no interest in belaboring Brownsville any further. "You can not have any information to give me privately to which I could pay heed, my dear Mr. Washington," he wrote, "because the information on which I act came out of the investigation itself."

With that, he left for Oyster Bay by overnight train. His discharge order, dated 5 November 1906, was not released for another thirty-six hours, until after Republicans had gone to the polls to elect Hughes Governor of New York, and re-elect Congressman Nicholas Longworth in Cincinnati. Had just half of Nick's three-thousand-odd black constituents voted against him, he would have lost his seat, and possibly his wife.

Across the nation, Roosevelt's popularity helped contain the Democratic surge. The GOP lost twenty-eight seats in the House, but retained its working majority, and gained four seats in the Senate. It won Massachusetts and Ohio, and Roosevelt was pleased to see Frank R. Gooding, Idaho's antiradical Governor, re-elected in a rebuff to the Western Federation of Miners. Representative James Wadsworth was punished for opposing last spring's Meat Bill, and sent back to the farm to inspect his own beeves at leisure. Sales of *The Jungle* notwithstanding, socialist candidates suffered everywhere.

"Well, we have certainly smitten Ammon hip and thigh," Roosevelt wrote to Alice.

Meanwhile, blacks fresh from the polls pondered his Special Order number 266, as transmitted by the War Department:

> By direction of the President, the following-named enlisted men [in] Companies B, C, and D, Twenty-fifth Infantry, certain members of which organizations participated in the riotous disturbance which occurred in Brownsville, Tex., on the night of August 13, 1906, will be discharged without honor from the Army by their respective commanding officers and forever debarred from reenlisting in the Army or Navy of the United States, as well as from employment in any civil capacity under the Government.

There followed 167 names, including that of First Sergeant Mingo Sanders, who had fought in Cuba in '98, and remembered dividing rations of hardtack and bacon with Colonel Roosevelt after the Battle of Las Guasimas; Corporals Solomon P. O'Neil, Temple Thornton, and Winter Washington; Cooks Leroy Horn and Solomon Johnson; Musicians Joseph Jones, Henry Odom, and Hoytt Robinson; and Privates Battier Bailey, Carolina De Saussure, Ernest English, Thomas Jefferson, Willie Lemons, Joseph Shanks, John Slow, Zacharia Sparks, William Van Hook, and Dorsie Willis.

⌒

BOOKER T. WASHINGTON was not surprised by the swiftness and unanimity of black reaction. For the last five years, he sadly noted, Theodore Roosevelt had been the idol of America's ten million Negroes. Now, within days—"I might almost say hours"—the President had become a pariah.

Telegrams of protest began to flow into the White House, not all from blacks. Roosevelt replied to one with an arrogance of tone and language that increasingly reflected his attitude to criticism: "The order in question will in no way be rescinded or modified. The action was precisely such as I would have taken had the soldiers guilty of the misconduct been white men. . . . I can only say that I feel the most profound indifference to any possible attack which can be made on me in this matter."

On 16 November, the first dishonorable-discharge papers were served on men of the Twenty-fifth Infantry. Roosevelt's name was mentioned at a black convention that day, and was received in complete silence. But by then the President was in Panama, in the depths of the Culebra Cut, watching the dirt fly.

⌒

HE HAD SEEN CULEBRA looming over the *Louisiana*'s white bow before he saw anything else of the Isthmus. Too low to be a cordillera, too high for any rock-splitters in the world—save those of the United States—it was already carved half open. Imaginations less vivid than his would have no difficulty picturing the day, perhaps no more than six or seven years off, when the continental spine would be snapped, and North and South America, paradoxically, brought closer together by a mutual highway of water. A new age of wealth and Pacific connections was coming to all those invisible Latin republics lying off to his left, while *el Coloseo del Norte* would be able to speed battleships as big as this one, and bigger and bigger, through her own secure conduit!

In the meantime, there was the vital question of yams.

Roosevelt heard about them in the cockpit of a Bucyrus steam shovel, which attracted him so irresistibly that he had stopped his open-sided train and clambered aboard, careless of mud. (Edith watched him seek out the driver's seat, her expression veiled by what looked like a small meatsafe of mosquito netting.) While a cameraman snapped away, the President asked about workforce morale. The shovel operator said it was not good among the nineteen thousand black laborers, mostly British West Indians, who did most of the digging in the cut. No number of monster machines could compensate for the loss of these men, should discontent send them home. (American Negroes were deemed not strong enough to work in tropical heat.)

Food was part of the problem. Panama yams, sold in the labor-camp commissary, did not compare to those of Jamaica. There appeared to be a direct correlation between yam quality and productivity along the line, perilous to the future of world commerce.

Roosevelt proceeded through the cut in rain so torrential that the Mount Hope Reservoir, not yet ready for use, began to fill up. He stopped at the sump to observe the copulatory heavings and thrustings of an excavation plow, but food remained on his mind, and he kept asking workers about their diet. At Rio Grande, he heard that the government-issue vegetables tasted

"HE CLAMBERED ABOARD, CARELESS OF MUD."
Roosevelt mounting a steam shovel, Panama Canal Zone,
November 1906.

worse, and cost more, than those in private stores. Seizing one complainer, he escorted him into the camp commissary. The clerk remained stoic at the sight of a burly President in a white suit and mud-spattered canvas leggings.

"Let me see your yams," Roosevelt said, firing off monosyllables like a repeater rifle. "Here is a yam that does not look right to me. This man says you sell him rotten yams."

"Yes, sir, and it's not surprising," the clerk replied. "Yams may go bad in a few hours in this climate." He explained that yams were susceptible to spoilage in great heat. In Panama, as elsewhere around the globe, the doctrine of caveat emptor applied. If a customer found rot-specks on any purchased yam, he could always bring it back for exchange.

Roosevelt appealed to his informant. "Mr. President," came the reply, in lilting Caribbean English, "I does not incline to demean my personal dignity by comporting myself with such bally, humiliating condescension."

Taking the hint, Roosevelt got back on his train and headed south on the tracks that Colonel Shaler, three years before, had closed to the Colombian *tiradores*. He called halts so often en route that the fingers of Theodore P. Shonts, president of the Canal Zone's governing commission, drummed with nervousness. By the time he got to Panama City, in a cacophony of steam whistles, Roosevelt had been touring sites and asking questions for almost ten hours. His cotton blouse was dark with sweat, and his leggings encrusted enough to make him waddle. But he exulted in everything he had seen and heard.

Much of it had been squalid, rather than magnificent. The black labor force was so disease-prone that Shonts was thinking of bringing in Chinese coolies. Perhaps sanitary and nutritional reforms would help. Certainly, flush toilets would. Roosevelt felt that government mess facilities, run by married couples from Jamaica or Barbados, might eradicate dirt-floor cooking sheds. And if West Indians would only stop sleeping in the same wet clothes they worked in, their alarming mortality rate (eighty-five pneumonia deaths in the last month alone) would surely improve.

The President, as H. G. Wells had noticed, was incapable of seeing negatives except in positive translation. The sheer extremity of Panama's challenges—meteorological, technological, geological, psychological—was wine to his head. He could not wait, the next morning, to get back to the Culebra Cut, even though rain was falling heavier than ever, and a landslide near Paraíso diverted his train. Dynamiters blew the top off a bluff for him. Steam shovels ate rock. A choir of "Zonian" schoolchildren sang "The Star-Spangled Banner." John Stevens, chief engineer, stood him on a hilltop, map in hand, and verbally built a new town in minutes.

All around them, flash *cascadas* ran down the slopes, and villages lay half drowned, as if the canal was already rising. Descending to the floor of Gatun Dam, Roosevelt was struck by the thought that in a few years' time, ocean liners would be floating in water a hundred feet above his head.

⌒

"STEVENS AND HIS MEN," the President wrote Kermit a few days later, "are changing the face of the continent, are doing the greatest engineering feat of the ages, and the effect of their work will be felt while our civilization lasts."

He was returning home on the *Louisiana,* with two other war vessels in convoy, able for the first time to visualize the true enormity of his achievement in Panama. What he had made possible, Stevens was making real. The chief engineer was just his kind of person: "a big fellow, a man of daring and good sense, and burly power."

Kermit, who was expected to keep this letter for posterity, may have recognized the unconscious, if slightly enlarged, self-portrait his father always painted when he described someone he admired. Stevens was actually five years older and an inch taller than the President, but the key words, perhaps, were *daring* and *burly power.*

A newer element in Roosevelt's letter was what the Kaiser might call the *Erdenton,* or earth note. Its implication, again unconscious, seemed to be that Stevens and his technicians, "so hardy, so efficient, so energetic," were not the only Americans changing the face of the world in 1906. Theodore Roosevelt, too, wanted to leave his impress on civilization.

That made the cable that awaited him at Ponce, Puerto Rico, on 21 November all the more annoying:

NEW YORK REPUBLICAN CLUB AND MANY OTHERS
APPEALING FOR A SUSPENSION OF THE ORDER
DISCHARGING COLORED TROOPS UNTIL YOUR
RETURN. . . . MUCH AGITATION ON THE SUBJECT AND
IT MAY BE WELL TO CONVINCE PEOPLE OF FAIRNESS
OF HEARING BY GRANTING REHEARING. TAFT.

If press reports were to be believed, Taft had actually granted such a suspension, pending the President's return. Roosevelt was quick to countermand it. "Discharge is not to be suspended," he wired back, "unless there are new facts of such importance as to warrant your cabling me. I care nothing whatever for the yelling of either the politicians or the sentimentalists."

While he continued his voyage north (bypassing Cuba), Army processors obediently reduced the ranks of the Twenty-fifth Infantry to zero. The last "Brownsville raider" surrendered his uniform on 26 November, a few hours before Roosevelt got back to Washington.

<hr />

BY NOW, A BURGEONING editorial consensus had begun to express dismay at the insubstantiality of the War Department's reports on Brownsville. *The New York Times* noted that there was "not a particle of evidence" in any of them to justify dismissal without honor. Read in sequence, the documents showed that every authority concerned, from Major Penrose to the President, had proceeded on an assumption of guilt and challenged the soldiers to prove their own innocence.

This case was made most forcefully by the Constitution League, a new, progressive, multiracial alliance dedicated to fighting discrimination and disfranchisement. Financed for the most part by the sort of rich white goo-goos Roosevelt despised—men lacking in "burly power"—it found in Brownsville the cause it was looking for, and began an independent investigation.

At the end of November, Gilchrist Stewart, a black attorney for the League, came to Washington to present Roosevelt with a four-page memorandum of reasons why the discharged soldiers might be innocent. William Loeb, forewarned, made the President unavailable, so Stewart presented the memorandum to Joseph B. Foraker instead.

The Senator, too, was looking for a cause, now that railroad rate regulation was a fait accompli and Cuba no longer a scare. He had aspirations to succeed Roosevelt in the White House. If he could find some way of discrediting Taft as presidential heir apparent—for that matter, discrediting Roosevelt, too—he was sure that he was good-looking and eloquent enough, and popular enough in corporate boardrooms, to be nominated in 1908. Brownsville offered him both the means and end of this grand plan.

Beyond ambition, and in contrast to his otherwise negative disposition,

Foraker had a passion for racial justice. As a young Union soldier, he had wanted the Civil War to go on "until slavery is abolished, and every colored man is made a citizen, and is given precisely the same civil and political rights that the white man has." Political opponents accused him of caring only for the Negro voters of Ohio. He certainly never professed any particular fondness for blacks in general. Senator Foraker merely felt the same about the Constitution in 1906 as Private Foraker had felt in 1862.

He was so electrified by the Constitution League's memorandum that he began to amass his own archive of Brownsvilliana at home, muttering as he studied letters and clippings. Julia Foraker recognized the signs: her husband was planning a resolution on the subject as soon as Congress reconvened.

~

ROOSEVELT'S SIXTH ANNUAL Message, delivered on 4 December, was notable for the fervor of its condemnation of race hatred, in particular the "bestial" nature of lynch law.

> The members of the white race . . . should understand that every lynching represents by just so much a loosening of the bands of civilization; that the spirit of lynching inevitably throws into prominence in the community all the foul and evil creatures who dwell therein. No man can take part in the torture of a human being without having his own moral nature permanently lowered. Every lynching means just so much moral deterioration in all the children who have any knowledge of it, and therefore just so much additional trouble for the next generation of Americans.

Unfortunately for the President, these fine words had a hollow ring in the upper chamber, where Senator Foraker had already introduced his Brownsville resolution. It "directed" the Secretary of War to supply the Senate with every official document pertaining to the case, along with the service records of every black man dismissed.

The resolution was approved, giving Taft no choice but to comply. Resentfully, he complained to reporters that the Commander-in-Chief of the United States Army was empowered to dismiss soldiers without honor. Foraker's response, measured and scholarly, made Taft sound like a whiner. Roosevelt indeed had that privilege, but the articles of war did not permit him to inflict it "as a punishment—as though it had been in pursuance of the sentence of a court martial." Taft, as a former judge, must surely remember that "no man can be deprived of life, liberty, or property without due process of law."

Roosevelt remained silent. He closeted himself with the original Brownsville report of Major Blocksom, rereading it carefully. Its findings did not alter his conviction as to the guilt of the men. But after studying another view of the case, by a retired Union Army general, he betrayed the first trace of regret over the hastiness of his action. He wrote Taft a confidential note, saying he was now "uncertain whether or not the officers of the three colored companies . . . are or are not blamable," and asking for "a thoro investigation" to clarify his thinking.

◦━◦

ALL IN ALL, this was not a propitious moment for Theodore Roosevelt to be officially informed that he had just won the Nobel Peace Prize, for his work in ending the Russo-Japanese War. "I am profoundly moved and touched . . . ," he cabled the chairman of the Nobel Committee. "What I did I was able to accomplish only as the representative of the Nation of which for the time being I am President."

He added that, upon reflection, he had decided to donate the prize money—almost thirty-seven thousand dollars—to "a foundation to establish at Washington a permanent Industrial Peace Committee."

To Kermit, he explained that after consultation with Edith, he could not accept as a personal gift a sum of money earned as a public figure. "But I hated to come to the decision, because I very much wisht for the extra money to leave to all you children."

◦━◦

SIR MORTIMER DURAND's last public view of Roosevelt occurred at a Gridiron dinner on 8 December. He thought that the President's laughter seemed strained, and noticed a flash of anger when somebody joked about a possible third term.

"Now don't let us have any damn nonsense," Roosevelt said, raising a hand to quiet the crowd. "When I made that declaration on the night of my election, I knew what I was about."

He continued with his speech, his voice constantly breaking into falsetto. Durand studied the bulldog profile, the bared teeth, and strange neck scar.

> It is not beautiful, but there is nevertheless an undeniable strength about it—It is a vehement, rather vulgar strength—and some allowance must be made for the divinity that doth hedge a king—but there is strength of a kind. He is not quite a gentleman—but he is fitted for success in the world.

A good motto for him, Durand thought, would be *Rem facias rem, si possis recte, si non quocunque modo rem*—"The thing, get the thing, fairly if possible, if not, then however it can be gotten." Roosevelt believed himself to be righteous, and his nature was to believe things with such passion that he took no prisoners when contradicted. "I regard him as a man who might at any time be extremely dangerous, for neither his temper nor his honesty can be trusted."

As if in proof, Roosevelt the righteous attacked on 19 December, with a special message to the Senate totally upholding the Blocksom report. "Scores of eyewitnesses" in Brownsville had established beyond any doubt that "lawless and murderous" Negro soldiers had "leaped over the walls from the barracks and hurried through the town," blasting away with their guns "at whomever they saw moving." The testimony of those who watched in horror was "conclusive," and there was the corroborative evidence of Army-issue "shattered bullets, shells and clips."

As to the shared guilt of all the men he had discharged, there was "no question" of their complicity in "shielding those who took part in the original conspiracy of murder." Roosevelt searched, rather too hastily, for words to communicate the dastardliness of their crime. "A blacker," he wrote, "never stained the annals of our Army."

He used his strongest language in repudiating Foraker's assertion that the dishonorable discharge was not a legitimate punishment. The only thing wrong with it was that it was "utterly inadequate" in this case: "The punishment meet for mutineers and murderers such as those guilty of the Brownsville assault is death; and a punishment only less severe ought to be meted out to those who have aided and abetted mutiny and murder and treason by refusing to help in their detection."

Foraker responded on the floor of the Senate with a speech that limited itself to facts. He said that only eight, not "scores," of witnesses claimed to have seen Negro soldiers rioting. He demonstrated the invalidity of every precedent and legal argument Roosevelt and Taft had cited for the discharges. He looked for hard evidence of a conspiracy, found none, and noted that General Garlington had had no better luck.

Few listening could doubt that a political war was being declared. It would probably last as long as the President continued to bluster and the Senate continued to probe—strife between executive and legislative, impetuosity and due process. Fortunately, Christmas was coming, and New Year's Day with its traditional courtesies, so there was time for both sides to weigh the costs of battle.

⌒

"WHEN YOU TURNED those niggers out of the army at Brownsville," Owen Wister asked Roosevelt, "why didn't you order a court of enquiry for the commissioned officers?"

The two old friends were out walking together, along the shore of the Potomac.

"Because I listened to the War Department, and I shouldn't," Roosevelt replied. He paused. "Of course, I can't know all about everything."

Defensively, he launched into a long disquisition on the fickleness of financial advisers. Wister heard him out.

"And so, the best you can do is to stop, look, and listen—and then jump."

"Yes. And then jump. And hope I've jumped right."

CHAPTER 28

The Clouds That Are Gathering

*We've been staggerin' undher such a load iv mateeryal wealth
that if we can't dump some iv it I don't know what'll happen to
us. We ar-re so rich that if we were anny richer we'd be broke.*

THE NEW YEAR of 1907 found Theodore Roosevelt at the peak of his Presidency. With Cuba peaceful and the Senate irresolute, for the moment, on Brownsville, he could luxuriate in his Nobel Prize and congratulate himself on the fact that if he so much as winked, a popular majority would form to re-elect him in 1908. He was still only forty-eight years old. America was unprecedentedly prosperous. The national product had become so "gross" that railroads were hard put to supply enough cars, and banks enough cash, to move it. As a result, prices were rising—but so were wages.

All this good economic news redounded to the credit of the man in the White House. Attendees at his annual New Year's reception observed only one note of grimness in the smiles and handshakes he exchanged with more than eight thousand visitors. It occurred when he greeted Senator Foraker.

⤙

THE FOLLOWING MORNING, Roosevelt had an hourlong legislative conference with Speaker Cannon and Congressman Longworth. He did not indicate to the press, if indeed he even realized, that exactly one quarter of a century had passed since he first attended such a conference in Albany, as the freshman assemblyman from the Silk Stocking district.

Then, as ever since, his obsession had been to find and hold the center of power. In 1882, he had watched a small group of Tammany mavericks parlay eight votes out of 128 into an operating advantage that had effectively immobilized the state government for more than three weeks. Roosevelt had never forgotten his early lesson in the application of physics to political process. A mass of opinion on one side was quantifiably irrelevant, if balanced by an equal and contrary mass on the other. The same went for any number of masses, large or small, as long as they balanced circularly. Only the slightest pressure, applied by whoever stayed *in medias res,* was necessary to tilt the opposites to and fro, or for that matter hold them still. That was power: operating freedom, not force.

He saw that his legislative balancing act now was going to be especially delicate through 4 March, when the Fifty-ninth Congress would end. With a much more Democratic Congress due in December, he was going to be losing many old allies (most seriously, Senator Spooner) and gaining, if not enemies, at best an equal number of newcomers more likely to cultivate his heir apparent than himself. Those Republicans re-elected would by the same token not have to worry, anymore, about contradicting an enormously popular President. Even the representatives among them now knew that they would see out his second term.

To maintain his centricity, therefore, he was going to have to be less confrontational and more accommodating as his power slowly waned. When decisive action was necessary, he could always resort to a privilege he understood better than any President before him: that of the executive order.

On 14 January, Roosevelt moved to quell a fierce Senate debate over whether he had exceeded his authority in dismissing the Brownsville soldiers. He sent Congress another special message on the subject, much less aggressive than his first. Although he still insisted that he had acted correctly, he allowed for the first time that he was prepared to readmit any dischargee who "shows to my satisfaction that he is clear of guilt, or of shielding the guilty." This was not of much comfort to those who believed that the burden of proof should lie on the other side, but it persuaded a majority of the Senate that the President had not broken any law.

Foraker, undeterred, pressed for, and won, a full investigation.

⎯⎯⎯⎯

NEXT, THE PRESIDENT tried to counter "this belief in Wall Street that I am a wild-eyed revolutionist." He had always jumped at chances to show plutocrats that he had no objection to the formation of trusts of any size, as long as they consented to scrutiny by the Bureau of Corporations.

Such an opportunity presented itself when George W. Perkins arranged for Judge Elbert H. Gary, chairman of U.S. Steel, and Cyrus H. McCormick, president of International Harvester, to meet discreetly with Roosevelt's incoming and outgoing Corporations Commissioners, Herbert Knox Smith and James Garfield. The encounter took place in a New York hotel on 18 January. Perkins, who was fluent in both federal and boardroom English, acted as interpreter.

Judge Gary praised the work of the Bureau of Corporations under Garfield, and said that President Roosevelt's overall supervision had helped make it a bastion of "private rights." He added that he hoped the agency would be as willing to cooperate with International Harvester in the future as it had been with his own company in the past.

This was a discreet allusion to a deal that Gary had concluded with Roosevelt and Garfield more than a year before. Faced with a bureau investigation of U.S. Steel, he had undertaken to open up the giant trust's books, on condition that only the President could decide whether there was anything there worth prosecuting. The agreement had worked well enough to avoid any antitrust action by the Justice Department.

Now Congress was calling for a bureau probe into allegations that McCormick's company was monopolistic. Perkins and Gary asked, as board members, if the President would extend International Harvester the same kind of most-favored-trust status. Garfield was quite sure that Roosevelt would. And so was Roosevelt, when he heard. Gentlemen's agreements were an accepted part of his code of behavior, as was the discretion they entailed. All Americans needed to know, in this case, was that *he* knew all about a giant trust that already controlled 85 percent of the national reaper and harvester market.

⌐∽⌐

IF MEMBERS OF THE Gridiron Club, welcoming Roosevelt to their annual dinner on 26 January, wondered how he could possibly top his previous performances before them, they soon found out. He arrived at the New Willard Hotel looking unusually grim, and the club president, Samuel G. Blythe, saw that entertaining him was not going to be easy.

When Roosevelt took his seat next to Blythe, he saw that by chance or, more likely, design, Joseph Foraker had been placed in front of them, at a table perpendicular to the main table. He thus could look forward to several hours of studying the Senator's haughty profile, while Foraker did not have to look at him.

Oysters were served, then clear green-turtle soup. Between spoonfuls, the President leafed through a souvenir booklet of caricatures of prominent guests. Each sketch was accompanied by jokey captions. One beneath Foraker's portrait arrested his attention:

All coons look alike to me.

Blythe saw the presidential jaw tighten, and got an impression of slowly rising fury. Roosevelt waited for the planked shad to be served, then leaned over and said, "I would like to speak now, if it can be arranged."

Service was halted, and Blythe rose to announce the President of the United States. Diners laid down their forks in surprise.

Roosevelt began cordially enough, with compliments to his hosts, then swung on a "Millionaire's Row" of financiers and lectured them on corporate control. His manner became peremptory. Men of wealth, he said, were going to have to learn to live with the reforms undertaken by his Administration. (J. Pierpont Morgan listened glowering, three places to his left.) The only alternative was a takeover of Wall Street by "the mob, the mob, the mob."

Then, picking up his souvenir program, Roosevelt read aloud, "*J. B. Foraker sez, sez he, 'All coons look alike to me.'* " He threw the booklet down in disgust. "Well, all coons do not look alike to me."

These words were delivered in a near shout. Roosevelt stared straight into Foraker's eyes and launched into a passionate rationale for his Brownsville action. The shad grew cold as he attacked Foraker for questioning an executive decision by the Commander-in-Chief of the United States Army. Senate debate on the subject was "academic," because he had "all power" vested in himself in such matters. And "all" meant what it said. Nobody else had any power of review of the discharges.

Diners from the back of the room stood up and crowded the aisles. Foraker sat fidgeting. After half an hour, Roosevelt ended with a few conciliatory words, and sat down amid cheers.

Blythe was faced with the choice of proceeding with the evening's set program, already in disarray, or honoring the American rule that nobody ever speaks after the President. He elected to abandon form altogether. Once, as a boy, he had driven twenty-nine miles in a springless wagon to hear "Fire Alarm Joe" orate. He had an idea that Foraker might respond if asked to do so with the right combination of wit and suddenness.

"The hour for bloody sarcasm having arrived," Blythe announced, "I take the liberty of calling upon Senator Foraker for some remarks."

Foraker stood up, stark white in the face. He said that he was "embarrassed" at having to follow the President. But, Roosevelt having so clearly singled him out by word and gesture, he would respond.

The sarcasm most people were waiting for did not materialize at once. (Neither did the next course.) Foraker spoke at length in defense of his own hands-off attitude to corporate control, earning napkin waves of approval from Millionaires' Row. Then at last he mentioned the word *Brownsville*, and proceeded to justify his nickname.

Never before, at the Gridiron or anywhere else, had a President been challenged before an audience. Foraker was an unusually handsome man, more than six feet tall, and his unsmiling demeanor and effortless command of language made everything he said sound oracular. Napkins fluttered elsewhere in the room as he observed, in the words of the Fourteenth Amendment, that "all *persons*" looked alike to him, black or white, male or female, old or young.

He noted that the President had said earlier, in reference to big business-men, that "no man was either so high or so low that he would not give him the equal protection of the law if innocent of offense against the law." If so, where was equal protection for the innocents of Brownsville? Roosevelt had himself admitted that many "absolutely innocent" soldiers had been branded as criminals in his discharge order. First Sergeant Mingo Sanders, with twenty-six years of service and a record of bravery in battle, was left depen-dent and disgraced "when he was nearing the time when he would have a right to retire on pay, without honor"—even though Foraker knew, and had reason to believe Roosevelt knew, "that he was as innocent of any offense against the law of any kind whatever as the President himself."

Roosevelt half rose from his seat. Blythe had to restrain him, saying that he would have "a chance for rebuttal" after the Senator finished. Foraker proceeded to squander his great moment, going on so long that Roosevelt again tried to interrupt, and was again held back.

Foraker grew maudlin. There had been a time, as the President well knew, "when I loved him as though one of my own family." He still had "an affec-tionate regard for him," and had for the most part "cordially supported all the measures of his Administration." At last he sat down. Such a hubbub en-sued, with members crowding to congratulate him, that Blythe's gavel was unable to restore calm. Then Foraker heard a familiar high-pitched voice, and saw the President standing, appealing to be heard.

The noise subsided to a buzz that continued throughout Roosevelt's re-buttal. It muted what was, to attentive listeners, an exquisitely lethal mo-ment, when he suggested that Foraker's defense of the Brownsville rioters was consistent with the Senator's enthusiastic backing, some years before, of a convicted double murderer for United States Marshal.

It was now nearly midnight, and 266 uneaten dinners had coagulated in the Willard kitchen. The buzz of conversation continued, but an air of unre-solved disharmony hung over the tables. Uncle Joe Cannon got up in an at-tempt to clear it. "If the floor of this great hall should suddenly cave in, and all the people here be precipitated to the cellar . . . it would not deter the progress of the United States."

There was little applause. Roosevelt sat fiddling with a fork until Blythe called for a concluding song, then declared the Twenty-second Annual Dinner of the Gridiron adjourned.

⌒

WHATEVER SHAKY REPUTATION for confidentiality the club had managed to preserve after Roosevelt's "Man with the Muckrake" speech was demol-ished by the Roosevelt-Foraker clash. A detailed account, with "exit inter-views," was published in *The Washington Post*. The scandal was immense, the political consequences immediate.

"IF THE FLOOR OF THIS GREAT HALL SHOULD
SUDDENLY CAVE IN . . ."
Speaker Joseph Cannon, ca. 1907

Roosevelt jeered at Winthrop Murray Crane's concern that the alienated Foraker would cause "a split" in the Republican Party, big enough to elect a Democrat in 1908.

"I call that a splinter," he said.

Far from aggravating the party's inner tensions, he felt that he had moved at just the right time to prevent a split. Fate had conspired to put in his way a provocative cartoon caption, a row of financiers, and Foraker himself—the man most likely to get Wall Street's vote in 1908, if something lethal was not done to him soon—in front of the most power-packed audience Washington could muster. It had been a rhetorical opportunity irresistible even to a President who loved to eat. His lecture to the plutocrats and *segue* to an attack on Foraker had branded the Senator as an apologist for wealth, if only by association. Conversely, by his reiteration of the War Department's case against the Twenty-fifth Infantry, he had shown *himself* to be someone who stuck to moral principles. Distasteful though the spectacle of a President and Senator squabbling had been to some guests, Roosevelt's "favorite audience"—a mythical grizzled farmer reading a newspaper at fireside—would probably see a confrontation of Right *v.* Wrong, or Executive *v.* Legislative, or Authority *v.* Anarchy, or whatever other antitheses suggested themselves.

Closer to home, political professionals saw an effective blow in favor of Taft against Foraker for the nomination in 1908. The Secretary (who had accompanied Roosevelt to the Gridiron dinner) was actually a reluctant party to the Brownsville discharges. He had been on vacation at the time of the incident, and the first prosecutorial steps had been taken in Oyster Bay. Taft's subsequent attempt to suspend the discharges and get a "rehearing" of the evidence against the soldiers had been prompted by an emotional appeal on their behalf from the president of the National Association of Colored Women. Most recently, he had annoyingly drawn Roosevelt's attention to a conflict in the testimony of the eyewitness who "saw" black soldiers kill Frank Natus, and suggested that the Senate be informed.

These scruples were, however, kept confidential, so Taft had come away from the New Willard looking more than ever a loyal Cabinet officer unbeholden to Wall Street, who just *happened* to hail from the same state as Senator Foraker.

By the time the Senate Committee on Military Affairs began its investigation of Brownsville on 4 February, Foraker was about as welcome at the White House as Benjamin Tillman had been in 1902. He and his wife began to notice signs of social pariahdom. Friends stopped visiting their house by daylight. James Garfield, a regular dinner giver, sent no invitations, complaining that Foraker was "trouble." A "journalist" of strange ubiquity making notes whenever the Forakers went out. Most ominously, Foraker discovered—in an experience, again, not new to Tillman—that his mail was being opened and read.

Roosevelt showed no outward concern about the committee hearings, which promised to last, on and off, for at least a year. He had the assurance of Foraker's colleagues that, whatever new evidence might come to light, he was entitled, as Commander-in-Chief, to uphold his own discharges.

⊶

A VISITOR TO THE White House on 13 February found the President discussing race relations of a far more complex sort with Root and Taft. For the last four months, "Yellow Peril" agitation had been violently resurgent in California, precipitated by the San Francisco Board of Education's decision to segregate Japanese schoolchildren. The order made no distinction between the children of long-term, Americanized Japanese residents and those of immigrant laborers fresh off the boat—currently disembarking, or swimming ashore, at the rate of one thousand per month. Any child with sloe eyes on the West Coast would now learn what it was like to be a black child in Alabama.

Roosevelt sat on the front edge of his chair, talking vehemently, as usual, while Taft lounged, twiddling his thumbs. Root stretched out his legs and gazed, for perhaps the thousandth time in his life, at Theodore over steepled forefingers. The visitor, State Senator Everett Colby of New Jersey, was struck by the quizzical expression on each Secretary's face. Roosevelt was giving his views on immigration, and veering, in a way Root knew only too well, toward a monologue on the "splendid qualities" of Nipponese culture and customs.

Since the Treaty of Portsmouth, Japan had been justifiably proud of its accession to first-power status. Any declaration of prejudice by a Pacific Rim nation (which was how California was viewed through Eastern eyes) was an insult too painful to be borne. In the words of William Sturgis Bigelow, one of the President's principal advisers on Far Eastern affairs, "They don't care— broadly speaking—what is done to them as long as it does not seem to be done to them *as Japanese.*"

Roosevelt had tried, and failed, to make the Golden State observe the Golden Rule. Some of the most passionate language in his last Message to Congress had been devoted to a plea for respect for Japan as "one of the greatest of civilized nations." He noted that San Franciscans had been happy to accept one hundred thousand dollars in earthquake-emergency aid from the Japanese in 1906, before shutting their relatives out of the city school system and abusing them in other ways, simply "because of their efficiency as workers." This last remark had hit home with local labor unions, who were the real agitators in San Francisco, desperate to repatriate every "coolie" in the city. When Roosevelt followed up with a request for a new immigration act, "specifically providing for the naturalization of Japanese who come here intending to become American citizens," the *San Francisco Chronicle* had called him unpatriotic, and the Californian congressional delegation began to act like ambassadors from a besieged country.

Senator Tillman, meanwhile, was seized by an apocalyptic vision of the Administration integrating "Mongolian" schoolchildren with white ones in the West, then doing the same with black schoolchildren in the South. He shouted himself so hoarse on the subject of race that London's *St. James Gazette* seriously questioned his sanity.

Roosevelt decided on a moderation of his attitude, not just to soothe redneck neuroses, but because of the much more dangerous mood of the Japanese government. Tokyo's response to the San Francisco segregation order had been a formal complaint against the "stigma and odium" it entailed. Such language was not to be ignored, coming from a war-hardy Pacific nation at a time when the United States battle fleet was entirely concentrated in the Atlantic. And Culebra was not yet cut.

The result was a gathering war scare in Washington, stirred up by the anti-Japanese rhetoric of Senator George C. Perkins of California. Roosevelt the balancer sought to steady both sides by attaching to a pending immigration bill an amendment that would significantly reduce the number of Japanese arriving in America from Hawaii. Its language, authored by Root, gave him power to deny entry by "any aliens" to both the United States and her insular possessions. The last phrase was vital, because Hawaii had become a cornucopia of coolie labor. Yesterday's pineapple pickers were today's almond hullers and tomorrow's stokers for the Northern Pacific Railroad.

"Why should I have to pay a fireman six dollars a day for work that a Chinaman would do for fifty cents?" James J. Hill asked Finley Peter Dunne, over lunch at Au Savarin in New York. "Let down the bars!"

To win passage, the exclusion amendment needed advance approval from Japan. That authoritarian empire was able to restrict emigration of her nationals by simple denial of exit permits. In fact, she had already discreetly promised Root she would do so, if the San Francisco school ban was rescinded. Once the immigration bill was passed (nowhere citing the Japanese as "Japanese"), Tokyo would cooperate with Washington to keep the flow of cheap labor at an acceptable level.

The only flaw in this commitment was something hard for imperialistic minds to understand: the government of a federal republic, while able to wage war, could not tell a local school board what to do. Negotiation, not coercion, was required. Hence the presence of Roosevelt's two most persuasive Cabinet officers at the White House on 13 February 1907. They were in the midst of an extraordinary six-day series of meetings with Mayor Eugene E. Schmitz of San Francisco, trying to convince him and members of his school board that their action stood, as Root put it, "in the way of an international agreement."

Schmitz, who was currently under indictment for embezzlement and extortion, was not unwilling to make a deal, if he could return home with dignity enhanced. Cowed by the President, beguiled by Taft, and outclassed by Root, he agreed to readmit Japanese children to the San Francisco school system, providing they spoke some English and were not overaged. And he could boast, if he wanted, that he had helped initiate a "Gentlemen's Agreement" between the United States and Japan that would determine Pacific policy for as far ahead as anyone could see.

⟨⊙⟩

SINCE ROOSEVELT'S ADMIRATION of the Japanese was based in large part on their fighting qualities, he did not delude himself that a stately exchange of diplomatic notes was enough to counter the threat posed by Admiral Togo's navy. In the glow of peacemaking at Portsmouth, he had briefly decided that the American fleet was large enough—his first term had seen it double in planned size. One new battleship a year, from 1905 on, seemed all that was necessary to compensate for the attrition of older vessels.

He had even gone along with the Tsar's recent efforts—understandable, in view of the near obliteration of the Russian Navy—to bring about a Second Hague Conference, which might slow the battleship race among Britain, France, the United States, Germany, and Japan. The idea of arms limitation appealed to Roosevelt in theory. However, "I do not feel that England and the United States should impair the efficiency of their navies if it is permitted to other Powers, which may some day be hostile to them, to go on building up and increasing their military strength."

This ambivalence between containment and competition had abruptly modulated toward the negative immediately after the San Francisco school order. In a letter to Sir Edward Grey, Roosevelt wrote that "the race question" was an "immediate source of danger" in Japanese-American relations, and worriedly admitted that "in the event of war we should be operating far from our base." He was thinking of the Philippines, but also of the long-term threat to Hawaii and the West Coast posed by battleships like the *Satsuma*, a dreadnought under construction in the Yokosuka shipyard.

To his current demand for an all-big-gun battleship of "at least eighteen thousand tons," he added a request that Congress fund it along with last year's vessel, funds for which had not yet been appropriated. He released for publication letters to the chairmen of both naval-affairs committees, urgently arguing "the superior value of battleships of large displacement, high speed, and great gunpower."

On 15 February, there was a brief flurry of budgetary protest in the House of Representatives. But with the war scare at its height, few lawmakers wanted to look irresolute. The President got his dreadnoughts. Three days later, the immigration bill was passed with the exclusion amendment intact, trans-Pacific tensions subsided, and Roosevelt handed the by-now-tired subject of arms limitation over to Elihu Root.

AS THE END OF the session approached, Roosevelt had to deal with a new challenge thrown on his desk by Senator Charles W. Fulton, Republican of Oregon. On 22 February, Fulton attached to the Agricultural Appropriations bill an amendment proposing that every public tree, sapling, or sprout in six northwestern states, totaling some sixteen million acres, be withdrawn from the President's protection and placed at the disposal of Congress. Or, as Fulton (infuriated by two years of land encroachment by Chief Forester Gifford Pinchot) put it: *Hereafter no forest reserve shall be created, nor shall any addition be made to one heretofore created, within the limits of the States of*

Oregon, Washington, Idaho, Montana, Colorado, or Wyoming except by act of Congress. On 25 February, the amendment was enacted and sent to the White House for signature.

Roosevelt let it lie on his desk.

The bulk of the American public had probably not noticed that in his last Message to Congress, he had for the first time used the plain word *Conservation* as a subject heading. There had been *Forest Conservation* and *Water Conservation* in his First Message, but they had denoted specific and separate programs, on par with *Reclamation* in 1903 and *Public Lands* in 1905. *Conservation*, by itself, was at once more general and more philosophical— religious even, a writ preaching the common sanctity of wood and water and earth and flora and fauna. It even had its menorah: the many-armed drainage basin, WJ McGee's "harmonious interrelationship of parts," purging the countryside of pollution, restoring the ravages of erosion, imposing order on human settlement, controlling floods, nurturing species, and generating power.

Roosevelt had virtually asked for a fight over forest reserves. It was he— working always with Pinchot, a favored member of the Tennis Cabinet— who had persuaded Congress in 1905 that forest care was a form of crop management, and should be transferred from the Department of the Interior to that of Agriculture. In the process, the Forest Bureau, run by bureaucrats, had become the Forest Service, run by foresters. Pinchot had used its enlarged budget and semiautonomous powers to acquire control of grazing licenses, hydroelectrical leases, and even police summonses in the national parks. He had stretched the meaning of the word *forest* so much that some westerners wondered when the Great Salt Lake was going to need his urgent protection.

The wonder was that the Transfer Act had not precipitated a fight at the beginning, rather than the end, of the Fifty-ninth Congress. But Roosevelt's interim blitz of regulatory legislation, and other distractions such as Brownsville and the Cuba intervention, had enabled Pinchot to slink expertly through government groves, adding twenty million acres to his domain, and a proportionate increase of revenue to the budget of the Forest Service. He left few tracks, until his acquisitions were announced by presidential proclamation.

There was something pantherlike about the Chief Forester, with his long, lean walk and hypnotic stare. Acquaintances differed on the exact quality of that gaze: it was erotic to some women, while men tended to see an idealism bordering on fanaticism. "The eyes do not look as if they read books," Owen Wister wrote, "but as if they gazed upon a Cause." Not that Pinchot was unlettered. He had the right cultural credentials: Exeter, Yale, postgraduate study at the École Nationale Forestière in France, and research spells in the ancient woodlands of Switzerland and Germany. And he was, to Roosevelt's approval, a New England gentleman, rich and well-connected, with a strong social conscience.

The two men had known each other since the 1890s. What the President especially liked was Pinchot's killer instinct, coupled with the fact that he fought cleanly. That made him all the more dangerous, because he was invulnerable to charges of corruption. He did have an Achilles' heel, and Roosevelt recognized it with some amusement: "Pinchot truly believes that in case of certain conditions I am perfectly capable of killing either himself or me. If conditions were such that only one could live, he knows that I should possibly kill him as the weaker of the two, and he, therefore, worships this in me."

President and Forester, fighting together, were an adroit combination. This became evident when Roosevelt, still holding off on the Agricultural Appropriations bill, managed to co-opt all the public lands Senator Fulton thought he had saved from being saved. A forced draft of Administration clerks—some of them working forty-eight-hour shifts—completed by Saturday, 2 March, all the paperwork necessary for the President to proclaim twenty-one new forest reserves, and eleven enlarged ones, in the six states specified.

He immediately signed these executive orders, knowing that Congress had no power to stop them except by a formal vote—which he would at once veto. Thus came into existence, along with others, the national forests of Holy Cross and Montezuma, Colorado; Medicine Bow, Colorado and Wyoming; Priest River, Idaho and Washington; Big Belt, Big Hole, and Otter Forest, Montana; Toiyabe, Nevada; Blue Mountain, Oregon; Olympic Forest, Washington; Rainier, Washington; Cascade, Washington; and Bear Lodge, Wyoming. Only after the last acre was reserved did Roosevelt sign the Agricultural Appropriations Act, allowing Fulton's now worthless clause to float over his proud *Theodore Roosevelt.*

⌒

ON 4 MARCH, the political season whistled to an end, literally, with some sifflation from the rostrum of the House by Representative Frank B. Fulkerson (R., Missouri). James Bryce, the new Ambassador from Great Britain, listened enchanted as the slender stream of sound filled the great hall, and the hands of the clock converged on noon. Then Uncle Joe Cannon reached for his gavel, and banged the Fifty-ninth Congress out of existence.

Simultaneously, a reshuffled Roosevelt Cabinet took office. No names made headlines, since the President had announced his appointments and reappointments before the last election. For the sake of continuity in congressional relations, he had kept most officers in their old jobs until now. One new face was that of Oscar S. Straus as Secretary of Commerce and Labor— the first Jew in Cabinet history. (Washington dinner-table opinion was divided as to whether Roosevelt had chosen Straus as a signal of goodwill toward the business community, or of contempt toward Russia, where the plague of pogroms had become endemic.)

A stranger choice, for the gossips, was that of Ambassador George von L. Meyer to succeed George B. Cortelyou as Postmaster General. Why should so suave and successful a diplomat, who hobnobbed with the Kaiser and the King of Italy, forsake the gilded halls of St. Petersburg for the Post Office's bleary corridors? Cortelyou, who seemed to be promoted every time the President put on weight, was now Secretary of the Treasury. Charles J. Bonaparte continued as Attorney General, his former job at the Navy Department being taken over by Victor H. Metcalf, while James R. Garfield became Secretary of the Interior.

Cortelyou had been at the Treasury only ten days when he was tested even more severely than Leslie Shaw had been during the "rich man's panic" of 1903. Prices on the New York Stock Exchange, rendered unstable by a world-wide overexpansion of credit, plummeted without warning on 14 March. The Dow Jones Industrial Average declined by one quarter. Several big businesses went bankrupt. Doubts that the President's former note-taker could handle such an emergency were swiftly dispelled when Cortelyou deposited twelve million dollars' worth of Treasury gold in New York banks to replenish the money drain. This Morgan-like gesture saved Morgan himself from having to do something similar. It also pre-empted an emergency plan by E. H. Harriman and four other financiers to make twenty-five million available at the first hint of a crash. The speed and certainty with which Cortelyou acted helped to arrest the stock slide and turn it into a slow, but manageable decline. He won instant respect on Wall Street, and no more jokes were made about his stenographic past.

Roosevelt scoffed that the quasi-panic had been "a demonstration arranged by Mr. Harriman to impress the Administration." Few financiers were prepared to believe that the Southern Pacific tycoon would make so expensive a gesture of protest against government regulation. A mild recession did seem to be in the making, though, and Jacob H. Schiff wrote to the President, begging him to do something statesmanlike before things got worse.

Schiff—silver-bearded and courtly, with the accent of his native Germany still heavy on his tongue—was one of Roosevelt's few Democratic supporters, and, as such, not inclined to mince words. "We are confronted by a situation not only serious, but which, unless promptly taken in hand and prudently treated, is certain to bring great suffering upon the country," he wrote. It was not so much a money crisis as a loss of confidence, brought about belatedly by last year's regulatory reforms. Investors were afraid to risk funds in railroad stocks, out of fear that the Sixtieth Congress might be even more amenable to reform than the Fifty-ninth. With no Congress at all sitting for the next eight months, that fear was bound to intensify. Railroad securities would fail to sell, and railway improvement and construction programs would be canceled by nervous executives, causing both devaluation and deterioration. Schiff suggested that Roosevelt "bring together a committee representative of the railroad interests and the Interstate Commerce Commission," along the lines of his successful coal-strike conference of five years before. Its job would be to discuss whatever future regulatory legislation the President had in mind, so that an endorsed program could be presented to Congress. "This will speedily restore confidence and dispel the clouds that are gathering over us in so threatening a manner."

Roosevelt wrote back to say that J. Pierpont Morgan had recently tried to get some railroad executives, including Harriman, to visit the White House, but none had shown. He was therefore disinclined to call a conference. "Sooner or later they will realize that in their opposition to me for the last few years they have been utterly mistaken . . . that nothing better for them could be devised than the laws I have striven for and am striving to have enacted."

Harriman would only say, enigmatically, to reporters, "This has been an unusual winter, both as to politics and as to weather."

~

SO HAD IT BEEN for the President. The perfect conditions, meteorological and political, that had brightened his New Year's Day (excepting always the dark cloud of Brownsville) had become unsettled almost at once. Now Jake Schiff was talking of more and bigger clouds, and a financial storm to come. A phrase in Schiff's latest letter was disquieting: *"your stern and uncompromising attitude in important questions."*

Roosevelt had tried to be more moderate, and restrain his natural force— and indeed succeeded in doing so much of the time. But men such as Foraker brought out the primitive in him. It was a quality lesser men recognized and admired—witness the macabre artifact coming his way (according to *The New York Times*) from deepest Texas: a silver-mounted, jewel-studded big stick, carved by the citizens of Brownsville in his honor.

More rational admirers, including Henry Cabot Lodge and James Garfield, thought they detected signs of exhaustion in the President. On an excursion to Cambridge, he had spoken so mechanically, as if spinning some internal Edison cylinder, as to scotch a nascent campaign by William James to make him president of Harvard in 1909. "Althou' he praised scientific research," the philosopher complained, "there wasn't otherwise a single note of innovation or distinction in anything he said." Few knew that at the very end of winter, the Roosevelts had nearly lost their son Archie to diphtheria. The boy's nine-day struggle for life, including at least one heart failure, took its emotional toll.

Spring came late to the White House grounds, less benignly than Roosevelt had ever seen it, with frigid air coming down from Canada to wither the magnolia blossoms. Every tree bore its dead brown load, and other buds stayed dormant. When Roosevelt ventured his first tennis game of the season, with Pinchot, Garfield, and Jusserand, a snow squall struck. They grimly played four sets. The following day, cold rain fell.

Normally, in short-session years, April and May were pleasant months for the President and his Cabinet, with no congressional liaison to worry about and plenty of time to talk policy. But this change of season brought an unwelcome flowering of bad political news. The Immigration Act seemed to be having no effect on the flow of Japanese coolies into California. Consequently, the Yellow Peril was again being proclaimed in San Francisco. In Ohio, Joseph B. Foraker announced his opposition to Taft's undeclared presidential candidacy. This was tantamount to launching his own campaign for nomination by the state GOP. Disturbingly, he began to court Ohio's black voters, who were enough upset about Brownsville to back him.

In early May, a compromise was advanced by George B. Cox, Cincinnati's former political boss, who offered to unite the party behind Taft for President and Foraker for another term as Senator. Foraker accepted this arrangement, knowing it left him quite free to run for President. Taft rejected it on the ground that he would be seen as a deal maker. The unhappy result for him was to make Foraker a stronger candidate than ever, while fueling rumors that Taft lacked political ambition.

It also revived talk about Roosevelt's own presumed secret agenda. "At the moment," he wrote Kermit on 15 May, "I am having a slightly irritating time with well-meaning but foolish friends who want me to run for a third term." He did not mention his elder daughter, who preferred the phrase *second elective term*. Going along with their plans would make him the virtual overlord of the next Congress, and, probably, the longest-serving President in history (yet by no means the oldest: if he served through to March 1913, he would still be only fifty-four).

Nor did he mention to anybody, unless to Edith Roosevelt in utter privacy, that nine tenths of him wanted to run again. And that nine tenths was reason, not emotion. He could not account for the moral particle that stopped him, except to describe it vaguely as a "still, small voice."

Having thus made, or remade, one of the fateful decisions of his life, Roosevelt left Washington with Edith and Archie for a few days at Pine Knot. The weather, though still crisp, was clear, and he took his field glasses to do some bird-watching.

⌖

HE SAW THEM ON 18 May, for the first time in twenty-five years—another reminder that *tempus fugit*. There were about a dozen, unmistakable with their pointed tails and brown-red breasts, flying in characteristically tight formation to and fro before alighting on a tall, dead pine. He compared them to some mourning doves in the field beyond; and there was no question of the difference between the two species. All his ornithological training told him that he was looking at "the passenger pigeon—*Ectopistes migratoria*—described on page 25 of the 5th volume of Audubon," a bird generally accepted to be on the edge of extinction.

He had collected and cataloged a specimen as a boy, noting even then that it was becoming rare on Long Island. Once it had been the most abundant feathered thing in the world, so prolific that a single flock, in 1832, had been assessed at more than two and a quarter billion birds. Old frontiersmen remembered passenger pigeons literally blotting out the sun. In 1856, the Ohio legislature had declared, "The passenger pigeon needs no protection."

Thus encouraged, hunters had succeeded in obliterating it to such an extent that, by the end of the nineteenth century, shootings became almost as rare as sightings. W. B. Mershon's valedictory *The Passenger Pigeon,* in press even as Roosevelt watched his flock circling and settling, recorded the last bird killed in Wisconsin in 1900.

Twice more that afternoon, the passenger pigeons swooped over Pine Knot. Their large size and rapid, circular movements seemed confirmatory, but they did not perch again, and vanished as quickly as they had come. Roosevelt stayed at the cabin for three more days, walking and riding with Edith through the woods from noon to sunset, and saw no evidence that he had not been dreaming.

CHAPTER 29

Such a Fleet and Such a Day

> Q   *D'ye think he wants a third term?*
> A   *I do not.*

OYSTER BAY. *Oyster Bay. Oyster Bay. Oyster Bay. Oyster Bay. Oyster Bay. Oyster Bay . . .*

The agreeable monotony of Roosevelt's schedule for late June 1907 was interrupted on the twenty-seventh by a captain from the General Board of the Navy and a colonel from the Army War College. They accompanied Victor H. Metcalf, the Secretary of the Navy, and Postmaster General George von L. Meyer, who had definitely not come to discuss rural free delivery. Meyer's presence, indeed, helped explain his real role in the Cabinet, which was to advise the President on questions of extreme diplomatic delicacy.

Five weeks before, after returning to Washington from Pine Knot, Roosevelt had been exasperated to hear that anti-immigrant riots had broken out in San Francisco. "Nothing during my Presidency has given me more concern than these troubles," he wrote Kentaro Kaneko. He argued that what was happening in California was nothing new. Nor was it essentially racial: it had plenty of precedents in European history over the last three centuries. France's Huguenots, for example, had been as white as their coreligionists in Great Britain, but when they immigrated there, they had excited "the most violent hostility," indistinguishable from what had happened at the Golden Gate. Then as now, mobs of workmen caused most of the trouble, expressing labor's chronic fear of being devalued by competition. Now as not then, hope lay in the increased ability of "gentlemen, all educated people, members of the professions, and the like" to visit one another's countries and "associate on the most intimate terms." This was the particular responsibility of elected representatives. "My dear Baron, the business of statesmen is to try constantly to keep international relations better, to do away with the causes of friction, and to secure as nearly ideal justice as actual conditions will permit."

Meyer himself could not have put the case with more finesse. But the fact remained that coolies were still coming, and having their faces beaten in. The Immigration Act was still not working as it should, the San Francisco Police Board had taken up where the school board had left off, reactionary newspapers were screaming, and Japanese opposition leaders were calling for war.

Elihu Root did not take the last threat seriously. He wrote Roosevelt to say that alarmists had their own agenda, but "this San Francisco affair is getting on all right as an ordinary diplomatic affair. . . . There is no occasion to get excited."

Roosevelt was not so sure. Japan had behaved with commendable restraint during the early months of the crisis. Recently, however, he had begun to detect "a very, very slight undertone of veiled truculence" in her communications concerning the Pacific coast. He heard from members of his *secret du roi* that the Japanese war party really did think the United States was beatable. The Office of Naval Intelligence reported evidence of Japanese war preparations, including purchase orders for nearly eighty thousand tons' worth of armored vessels from Europe, and a twenty-one-thousand-ton dreadnought from Britain. (So much for any chance of a disarmament agreement at the Second Hague Peace Conference, now in session.)

His responsibility as Commander-in-Chief was to look to the nation's defenses. Hence the arrival at Sagamore Hill of two top military strategists. He had asked them to bring him contingency plans, "in case of trouble arising between the United States and Japan."

⌒

COLONEL W. W. WOTHERSPOON and Captain Richard Wainwright proved to be little more than messengers, delivering a somewhat obvious finding by the Joint Board of the Army and Navy. The board stated that because Japan's battleships were all in the Pacific, and those of the United States in the Atlantic, the latter power should "take a defensive attitude" in any confrontation, until its heavy armor could be brought around Cape Horn.

Roosevelt said, for the record, that he did not believe there was any real chance of a war with Japan. Then he approved the only controversial aspect of the Joint Board's report: a recommendation by Admiral Dewey that "the battle fleet should be assembled and despatched for the Orient as soon as practicable."

The idea was not new. For at least two years, the Navy had considered transferring the fleet from one ocean to the other as a tactical exercise, but had never managed to decide the extent of the move, or the logistics of support. Fuel supplies were a particular problem, and the West Coast of the

United States was short on bases. Dewey calculated that it would take at least ninety days to mount an emergency battle presence in the Pacific. "Japan could, in the meantime, capture the Philippines, Honolulu, and be master of the sea."

Roosevelt considered the options, and his own as President and Commander-in-Chief. He had just seventeen months left in office, and wanted to make a grand gesture of will, something that would loom as large historically in his second term as the Panama Canal coup had in his first. What could be grander, more inspirational to the Navy, and to all Americans, than sending sixteen great white ships halfway around the world—maybe even farther? And what better time than now, when positive news was in such short supply? Wall Street's stock slide in March had caused many brokerage houses to fail and bank reserves to drop. Foreign markets had also begun a steady decline, with stocks plummeting in Alexandria and Tokyo, Frenchmen hoarding more gold than usual, and even the Bank of England low on cash. Jacob Schiff had said that "uncertainty" lay at the bottom of all distrust. All the more reason, then, to make one highly visible arm of the United States government look quite certain of itself, as it moved from sea to shining sea.

The massive deployment appealed to Roosevelt as diplomacy, as preventive strategy, as technical training, and as a sheer pageant of power. There was also the enormity of the challenge. He had private information that neither British nor German naval authorities believed he could do it. Well, he would prove them wrong. "Time to have a show down in the matter."

He issued a series of orders to Secretary Metcalf. The Subic Bay coal stockpile in the Philippines must be enlarged at once. Defense guns must be moved there from Cavite. Four armored cruisers of the Asiatic Fleet were to be brought back to patrol the West Coast. And finally—Roosevelt's operative order, climaxing ninety minutes of talk—the Atlantic fleet would set sail from Hampton Roads, Virginia, in October, destination San Francisco.

When someone asked how many battleships would make the trip, Roosevelt said that depended on how many there were in service at the time. If fourteen, he would send fourteen; if sixteen, then sixteen. He wanted them "all to go."

Metcalf was authorized to announce the dispatch of the "Great White Fleet"—as it soon became known—appropriately on the Fourth of July. But the news was too big to hold, in view of the tense state of American-Japanese relations. By the time the Secretary issued his statement, Ambassador Aoki had already moved defensively to say that Japan did not regard Roosevelt's gesture as "an unfriendly act."

His Excellency thus avoided sounding overjoyed at the prospect of an enormous alteration in the balance of naval power in the Pacific. And Roosevelt, by intimating that San Francisco would be the fleet's farthest port of call, encouraged Californian alarmists to think it was being dispatched for their protection. They would have been less comforted if they had known that he was privately talking to Henry Cabot Lodge about sending it on "a practice cruise around the world."

⟋⟍

THE CONNECTION JACOB Schiff had tried to draw for Roosevelt earlier in the year, between persecution of men of property and loss of investor confidence, was dramatically demonstrated at the beginning of August, when Judge Kenesaw Mountain Landis of the United States District Court fined the Standard Oil Company of Indiana more than twenty-nine million dollars in an antirebate case. John D. Rockefeller, Sr., said that the judge would be dead before he ever saw a dime of his fine. Within a week, the stock market slumped again.

Conservatives blamed Roosevelt and his "fool Attorney General" for jamming regulatory levers into the American economic machine. *The New York Times* declared that Landis's ruling exemplified "that spirit of vindictive savagery toward corporations that, until recently, possessed the minds of . . . persons in authority." A sheaf of concerned-citizens' letters was delivered to Sagamore Hill, variously accusing the President of orphanicide, old age abuse, cruelty to women, and "Rough Rider methods" sure to bring on hard times. An anonymous postcard asked if he was aware that he had ruined every single industry in the forty-six states.

Roosevelt, who had been enjoying himself with plans for the fleet cruise ("go thru the Straits of Magellan; have thirty days' target practice in the Pacific"), was forced to reply to some of the more important missives. "You say that the verdict against the Standard Oil Company has done great damage," he wrote to Henry Lee Higginson, the Boston banker, "and you advise me to let the public know that the prosecutions will not be pushed. . . . I cannot grant illegal immunity."

He chose to call the economic contraction of 10 August a "flurry," rather than a "panic," and used sensible logic against his accusers, asking why, if Wall Street's disarray was his fault, markets in France, Britain, Germany, and Canada were failing in exactly the same way. "The present trouble is worldwide."

This was true enough, but behind his show of unconcern lay a sense that the money men might be right in predicting a real crash to come. He addressed a letter to his "fool Attorney General," who was preparing to prosecute International Harvester under the Sherman Act. Bonaparte seemed to have forgotten about last January's agreement between the trust and the Bureau of Corporations on a cooperative "investigation," which was even now under way. One such probe by one government agency was surely enough. "Please do not file the suit until I hear from you," Roosevelt instructed.

With that, he resumed his interrupted vacation and a reading of Guglielmo Ferrero's five-volume *The Greatness and Decline of Rome*. He was struck by the similarity of many conditions endemic to ancient imperial and modern industrial civilizations. "As I am fighting hard to better some of these very conditions just at the moment," he wrote George Otto Trevelyan, "the book has a certain grim attractiveness for me, in the present as well as the past tense."

⟋⟍

ONE THING THE ROMANS had understood very well was the role of fresh water in sluicing, sanitizing, irrigating, and beautifying both landscapes and townscapes. Old Father Tiber had been the *fons et origo* of a spreading web of canals, viaducts, underground pipes, and fountains that linked communities more effectively than any system of law.

WJ McGee, the visionary environmental scholar and proponent of the "interrelationship of parts" (as his compressed initials suggested) had long dreamed of a similar water-based network making one massive hydrosystem of the United States. Earlier in the year, he had found Gifford Pinchot a willing ally in persuading Roosevelt to appoint an Inland Waterways Commission that would prepare "a comprehensive plan for the improvement and control of the river systems of the United States." The Commission, chaired by McGee, was due to report within a year. In the meantime, to publicize its work, it was sponsoring inspection trips of major lakes and rivers. Roosevelt delightedly accepted an invitation to cruise down the Mississippi on a paddle steamer with Pinchot and other commission members in the early fall. He thought he might combine it with a bear hunt in the canebrakes of Louisiana, to get himself in shape for dealing with the critters of the Sixtieth Congress.

By the time he came on board at Keokuk, Iowa, on 1 October, the steamer's passenger complement had expanded to include some twenty state governors, and Pinchot and McGee were consumed with a new idea, which they wanted him to articulate en route, at Memphis. It was that a great conference on conservation should be held at the White House in the spring of 1908—the first such gathering in the history of any nation—and that every governor in the country would be asked to attend.

A sense that the President was again about to announce something enormous gathered as the USS *Mississippi*, accompanied by a flotilla of lesser ships, thrashed its way south. Crowds lined both banks, craning for a sight of Roosevelt on deck. At night, when the river's humid mists made navigation difficult, they burned huge bonfires to light his way. They took off their hats as he passed, and refrained from cheering lest they disturb his sleep.

Roosevelt made his announcement at Memphis on 4 October, tersely, in the course of an address to the Deep Waterways Convention. "It ought to be among the most important gatherings in our history," he said, adding that the time had come to make "an inventory of the natural resources which have been handed down to us." The rest of his speech amounted to a summary of

"THE PRESIDENT WAS AGAIN ABOUT TO ANNOUNCE SOMETHING ENORMOUS."
Roosevelt and Gifford Pinchot on the Mississippi River, October 1907

McGee's enviromental philosophy. "There is an intimate relation," he said, "between our streams and the development and conservation of all the other great permanent sources of wealth."

The impact of this statement might have been greater if the New York Stock Exchange, which most Americans associated more clearly with wealth, had not again begun to show signs of deep unrest. Over the next two weeks, as the President lunged after bear in the canebrakes around Stamboul, Louisiana, some prices dropped to record lows, and others jiggled crazily. The initial cause of panic was a failure by two speculators, F. Augustus Heinze and Charles W. Morse, to take over the United Copper Company. They succeeded only in bankrupting two brokerage houses, another mining concern, and a bank. These implosions, headlined across the country, revealed to the Street that Heinze and Morse had been funded in their venture by the august Knickerbocker Trust, the very name of which signaled stability and money old and hard as bedrock.

The bedrock showed signs of crumbling on the afternoon of Friday, 18 October, as panicking Knickerbocker investors hacked out their gold deposits. Over the weekend, J. Pierpont Morgan, working like a tycoon possessed, organized two relief committees of financiers (one headed by the ubiquitous George W. Perkins) to raise funds and decide which trusts, sure to fail over the next few days, merited saving for the stability of the national economy. New York banks were at the height—or rather, the depth—of their annual currency shortage. This contributed to what James Bryce described as "a simultaneous deficiency of capital and confidence."

On Monday, 21 October, as the President headed home with deliberate slowness, to avoid even sharper panic, rumors circulated that the Knickerbocker had only ten million dollars left in cash. With sixty million loaned out, the trust might be unable to issue good checks past midday Tuesday. Well before that hour, Morgan saw its reserve dwindle to two million dollars, and coldly decided to let it collapse. "I can't go on being everybody's goat."

By the time Roosevelt got back to the White House on Wednesday afternoon, money was almost unobtainable on Wall Street, call loan rates had risen to 125 percent, and the entire credit structure of the United States was under siege. Morgan and George Cortelyou (forsaking all governmental dignity to serve as the great man's aide) were holding off hordes of desperate raiders. Overnight, the Secretary agreed to deposit twenty-five million dollars in Treasury funds in national banks—more than twice as much as his pledge of seven months before.

Roosevelt seemed unaware of how acute the situation was. Radiant and purified from his hunt, he patrolled the Executive Office with his hands behind his back, regaling all comers with his exploits in the canebrakes.

"Do I look as though those Wall Street fellows were really worrying me?"

"No, Mr. President, you certainly do not."

"I've got them," he said through his teeth, "on the run."

It was exchanges such as this that persuaded some men that Roosevelt was fiscally retarded.

By now, most of the nation's premier plutocrats were volunteering their help to Morgan, including E. H. Harriman, Henry Clay Frick, and John D. Rockefeller, Sr., who offered, incredibly, half of all his securities. At 1:30 P.M. on Thursday, 24 October—too late for Roosevelt to do anything except try to catch up, in briefing after briefing, with what had happened during his absence—the panic reached a point of almost terminal hysteria. The President of the New York Stock Exchange told Morgan that his institution would have to shut down. Morgan told him to wait, and summoned the chief executives of the city's largest banks. Among them, they pledged twenty-five million dollars to keep the Exchange open through three o'clock. Stocks rebounded at once, and the "Roosevelt Panic of 1907" began to abate.

The President was gracious enough, on Friday, to issue a statement of congratulation to Cortelyou and "those conservative and substantial businessmen who in this crisis have acted with such wisdom and public spirit." He used the words *confidence* and *calm* as often as possible, and managed to allay public nervousness, if not the unavoidable impression that he had been away from his desk, playing in the canebrakes, while conscientious financiers had been saving the American economy. For once they were not—and for a while yet were relieved of being—"malefactors of great wealth."

ALTHOUGH A TOTAL crash had been averted, the crisis on Wall Street was by no means over. The next business week, starting on Monday, 28 October, was equally fraught, with New York City on the verge of defaulting for lack of cash to borrow, and another major financial institution, the Moore & Schley brokerage house, threatening to go the same way as Knickerbocker Trust. Morgan and his men came to the aid of the city, and devised an emergency plan to save Moore & Schley by persuading U.S. Steel to buy it—or rather, to buy the collateral shares for its loans, which were invested in the Tennessee Coal and Iron Company. Elbert H. Gary did not seem to like this idea, which involved trading a large amount of U.S. Steel gold bonds for Tennessee Coal's lower-rated stock. Nor did Frick, who worried that Roosevelt might seize on the acquisition as an excuse for yet another antitrust prosecution. The President had shown himself quite ready to bite the hand that fed him after begging for corporate campaign donations in 1904.

Judge Gary said he would endorse the Morgan plan, but only if Roosevelt endorsed it, too. He liked the President, and believed him to be a pragmatic man, responsive to reasoned argument. Early on Monday, 4 November, he and Frick visited the White House for breakfast. Roosevelt was so impressed by their willingness to consummate an undesirable deal in order to forestall a "general industrial smashup," that he agreed within twenty minutes to let them go ahead. Immediately after their departure, he let Attorney General Bonaparte know that the acquisition had his approval.

The New York Stock Exchange had not yet opened when Gary called George Perkins to advise him of Roosevelt's goodwill. Perkins passed on the news just before nine o'clock. Relief flooded the market, and within hours prices began to rally.

ON 11 NOVEMBER, Roosevelt signed forty-six copies of a document, which more than any other he had ever written could justifiably be called a "poster-

ity letter," in that it addressed itself, with the utmost urgency, to the future. It was his promised call for a national conservation conference. One copy went to each state and territorial governor, and a further five hundred copies to a cross-section of the most influential men in the country, from members of Congress and Justices of the Supreme Court to industrial tycoons and editors of major newspapers.

"It seems to me time for the country to take account of its natural resources," the President wrote, "and to enquire how long they are likely to last."

The suggestion that anything so unquantifiable as the mineral and vegetal and hydrological wealth of one of the world's largest nations might, in fact, be rendered into an "account" was almost as shocking as the cold, hard tone of Roosevelt's last seven words. He wrote with the finality of a man who had, with his own eyes, seen the last few flutterings of a species that had once been capable of blackening the sky.

"We are prosperous now," he continued, not even bothering to qualify his statement. Wall Street's current recession was as trivial, historically speaking, as a waver in one of a redwood's hundreds of growth rings. "We should not forget that it will be just as important to our descendants to be prosperous in their time as it is to us to be prosperous in our time." He repeated what he had said at Memphis about the gravity of the responsibility Americans had to pass on to their children a protected natural heritage. For more than a century, that endowment had been "depleted and in not a few cases exhausted," especially in the northeastern states. The situation was already so serious that it was a matter for all government, not merely the federal government, to face:

I have therefore decided, in accordance with the suggestion of the Inland Waterways Commission, to ask the Governors of the States and Territories to meet at the White House on May 13, 14, and 15 [next], to confer with the President and with each other upon the conservation of natural resources.

It gives me great pleasure to invite you to take part in this conference. . . . I shall also invite the Senators and Representatives of the Sixtieth Congress to be present at the sessions as far as their duties will permit.

The matters to be considered at this conference are not confined to any region of groups of States, but are of vital importance to the Nation as a whole and to all the people. These subjects include the use and conservation of the mineral resources, of the resources of the land, and the resources of the waters in every part of our territory. . . .

Facts, which I cannot gainsay, force me to believe that the conservation of our natural resources is the most weighty question now before the people of the United States. If this is so, the proposed conference, which is the first of its kind, will be among the most important gatherings in our history in its effects upon the welfare of all our people.

⌒

WALL STREET'S currency drought lasted through November. Cortelyou, whose commitment of Treasury funds into the New York banks had increased to $69 million, got presidential permission to raise $150 million more in government and Panama bonds, just to keep the market buoyant. Not for at least a year, in expert opinion, would stocks rise back to pre-1907 levels. But a short recession after seven fat years seemed preferable to seven lean years, such as had followed the depression of 1893.

Roosevelt wrote Kermit to say that blame for the economic downturn would inevitably center on himself and his regulatory policies. He might have to spend the rest of his presidency answering to the two classes of people always most vociferous in hard times: the bewildered and the guilty. However, "I am absolutely certain that what I have done is right and ultimately will be of benefit to the country."

His Seventh Annual Message to Congress, delivered on 4 December, rang throughout with the same unapologetic note. "There may be honest differences of opinion as to many government policies; but surely there can be no such differences as to the need of unflinching perseverance in the war against successful dishonesty."

⌒

BY NO HINT OF a frown, or a yawn, did he ever suggest that such routine work had become boring for him. But his animation whenever he mentioned Admiral Robley Evans's battle fleet, now assembling at Hampton Roads, Virginia, for its pre-Christmas departure, was palpable. With 348,000 tons of white-painted armor and gunmetal ready to sail at his command, and most of the civilized world waiting to see if such an armada could possibly hold together for more than a few days at sea, executive paperwork offered few compensatory charms.

Except, perhaps, the pleasure of striking four names off his annual Christmas-card list: *Mr. E. H. Harriman, Mrs. Harriman, and the Misses Harriman.*

⌒

THE SIXTIETH CONGRESS, dominated even more than the Fifty-ninth by Speaker Cannon and Senator Aldrich, made immediately plain that it intended to stand as a conservative battlement against whatever progressive onslaughts—or Constitution-defying executive orders—Roosevelt might throw against it. Congressmen who prided themselves on their personal rectitude disliked the now habitual preachiness (more bully than pulpit) with which the

President told them what laws to pass. They recalled Tom Reed's famous jibe, "If there is one thing for which I admire you more than anything else, Theodore, it is your original discovery of the Ten Commandments."

Cannon and Aldrich, respectively self-appointed as the protectors of *laissez-faire* on Capitol Hill, had had their worst fears of Roosevelt's financial irresponsibility confirmed by the stock-market slump. Eugene Hale, chairman of the Senate Committee on Naval Affairs, issued a statement saying that Congress would not appropriate funds to send the Great White Fleet on its way. Roosevelt countered by informing him that the Navy already had enough money in hand, and enough coal in store, to transfer its ships at least from one ocean to another—indeed, possibly as far as the Philippines. Congress was welcome to leave the fleet there—halfway around the world—if it wanted. As for his standing order to sail, "I am Commander-in-Chief, and my decision is absolute in the matter."

This early skirmish established what would likely be the style of the two remaining legislative seasons of Roosevelt's presidency: increasing obstructionism on Capitol Hill, more resort to surprise tactics at the other end of Pennsylvania Avenue. Power attrition on both sides was the key factor. Only Senator Allison remained of Aldrich's aging leadership. Orville Platt was dead, and John Spooner retired, a casualty of the LaFollette insurgency in Wisconsin. Cannon's almost complete control of the House could not be denied, but if progressivism continued to change American attitudes toward government, he ran the risk of soon being perceived as a reactionary tyrant, determined to subvert the will of the people.

Roosevelt remained a formidable force, by virtue of his popularity, tactical skill, and unequaled political intelligence. But he had not much more than six months left as the leader of the Republican Party. By next June, a new claimant to that title would be nominated, and in less than a year, a new President elected. Senator Foraker was already a declared candidate, and "Uncle Joe" was not saying no to rumors that he might run, too. Senators LaFollette and Beveridge were separately wondering if they should mount token candidacies, to test the strength of the progressive movement, while William Howard Taft remained an oddly apathetic heir apparent.

Never again—unless Roosevelt withdrew his vow not to seek a third term—would "Theodore Rex" dominate the political scene as completely as he had for the last three years. And on 11 December, he removed all lingering doubts as to the seriousness of his post-election statement that he would not accept another nomination for President. "I have not changed and shall not change the decision thus announced."

⟜⟝

MONDAY, 16 DECEMBER, broke sunny, sharp, and clear over the James River estuary after a weekend of heavy rain. All sixteen ships of the battle fleet lay waiting for him, blindingly white in the eight o'clock light, as the *Mayflower* creamed into the Roads and proceeded past each gold-curlicued bow. The air drummed with 336 cannon blasts, not quite dividing into twenty-one-gun strophes.

"By George!" Roosevelt exulted to Secretary Metcalf. "Did you ever see such a fleet and such a day?"

When the presidential yacht came to anchor, gigs and barges brought aboard "Fighting Bob" Evans—a surprisingly small, fierce-faced man, limping with rheumatism—four rear admirals, and sixteen commanding officers. Roosevelt made no speech after shaking all their hands, only drawing Evans aside for a few minutes and muttering to him with earnest, snapping teeth. Bystanders watched the admiral's cocked hat bobbing like a gull as Roosevelt bit off sentence after sentence. What scraps of dialogue floated on the breeze were mostly banal: "I tell you, our enlisted men . . . perfectly bully . . . best of luck, old fellow."

Less audibly, the President was giving Evans secret orders to stay in the Pacific for several months, then proceed home via the Indian Ocean and Suez Canal. Cameras clicked as the two men bade each other farewell. The commanders returned to their ships, and, as the *Mayflower* got under way for Cape Henry, one by one the battleships weighed anchor and hauled around in stately pursuit. They overtook Roosevelt at the mouth of Chesapeake Bay and ground past him in a perfectly spaced, three-mile-long column. He watched with intent seriousness, periodically doffing his top hat, until the *Kentucky,* the last unit of the Fourth Division, moved by in a vast white wall, all its sailors saluting.

CHAPTER 30

Moral Overstrain

_He's a gr'-reat man, an th' thing I like best about him is that in
th' dark ye can hardly tell him fr'm a Dimmycrat._

"THE REACTION AGAINST ROOSEVELT, socially, is violent," Henry Adams
wrote to a friend as the last tremblings of the great panic subsided. "And, like
all Presidents, he will probably find himself, in his last year, a severely de-
throned king."

When Adams used the adverb _socially_, he tended to restrict its compass
to the community he belonged to with a sense of tranquil entitlement: old-
moneyed, Ivy League, Yankee. The President himself was of this ilk, although
his blood was not as blue as Adams's, and his portfolio nothing like as black.
Yet there were—always had been—"foreign" elements in Roosevelt, differences of will rather than mere quirks of character, disturbing to men and
women who would otherwise have found him congenial. Ever since he had
forsaken his background, at age twenty-three, for what he called the "governing class" of practical politicians, there had been something vaguely trai-
torous about him. It was not the mere fact that he had chosen a career in
which breeding mattered little—Henry Cabot Lodge had done the same, with
no loss of dignity. Nor was it his cultivation of cowboys and locomotive engineers and the occasional black dinner companion. It was that from the very
start, and most disturbingly since October's panic, Roosevelt had never
shown much respect for wealth. As he said himself, "I find I can work best
with those people in whom the money sense is not too highly developed."

Essentially an independent, he mistrusted the tendency of the wealthy to
form tight, self-protective social cliques or (when they went into business)
combinations in restraint of trade. The tighter each formation, the more obsessed it became with its own cohesion, and the more resentful of outside
monitoring. He had noticed a definite increase in this resentment since the
panic, especially along Wall Street, where the rumors that he was an alcoholic

had strengthened into reports that he was insane. At the annual banquet of the New York Chamber of Commerce, a toast to the health of the President of the United States had been met with almost total silence.

To Ambassador James Bryce, scholarly septuagenarian who had followed Roosevelt's career from afar for almost twenty years, there was something medieval about the current politico-economic struggle. ("Combinations in restraint of trade," Bryce reminded his government, "are contrary to common law since Henry II.") The castles of wealth had been owned by "the great trust barons," who in theory owed allegiance to the state, but in truth were beholden only to Money. The only nationally empowered defender of the rights of "their villein consumers" had been Roosevelt, intervening "partly from benevolent disinterestedness, partly from statecraft, much as did the medieval Church." In the process, he had won the devotion of an enormous plebeian following. By March 1907, the struggle had seemed "to be going *à outrance*," leading to the collapse of the stock market in October, and looking more and more like an episode from a knightly chronicle:

> The oppression of the weak, the perversion of justice to private ends, the petty warfare, such as that of Heinze with Amalgamated [*sic*] Copper, fought out from underground forts in Montana mines, excommunications such as those pronounced by the Attorney-General against "bad Trusts": the temporary ascendancy of a strong personality with great authority, without direct means of control, but with the support of public faith in the constitution and sanction of that authority, all find political parallels in the Middle Ages.

Bryce left vague whom he meant by "strong personality with great authority," although he did note that J. Pierpont Morgan had "for a time quite outshone Theodore Roosevelt as a saviour of society." He was definite, though, in saying that 1907 had marked the end of the "individualistic" era of checking combinations—as exemplified by Roosevelt's willingness to make discreet arrangements with the likes of Judge Gary and Cyrus H. McCormick. In the new year of 1908, "the guiding principle has been changed to the socialistic ambition to control and convert them."

ALL THAT WAS NEEDED to precipitate a final, all-out battle was a direct challenge. It came on 6 January, and from an unexpected quarter: the Supreme Court of the United States. One of Roosevelt's proudest legislative achievements, the Employers' Liability Act of 1906, was struck down on the grounds that it applied to intrastate corporations as well as interstate ones—thus unconstitutionally infringing upon states' rights.

The President's initial reaction was to send Justice William R. Day a book on the need for a federal liability law protecting workers, begging him to read what it had to say about two higher-court rulings inimical to bakers and tenement-house cigar makers in New York. "If the spirit which lies behind these two decisions obtained in all the actions of the Federal and State courts, we should not only have a revolution, but it would be absolutely necessary to have a revolution, because the condition of the worker would become intolerable."

Justice Day, who had concurred with the majority opinion of Justice White, was not able to do much more than note the title of the little volume Roosevelt found so alarming: *Moral Overstrain.*

In the three weeks that followed, the President gave evidence of suffering from that condition himself. He became incensed by Congress's obvious reluctance to act on his last Message, which included demands for inheritance and income taxes, national incorporation of interstate businesses, greater federal power over railroad rates, compulsory investigation of major labor disputes, wider application of the eight-hour day, and no fewer than four new battleships.

Not unconnectedly, he also viewed with concern two looming threats to the presidential candidacy of William Howard Taft. First, Senator Foraker had made his own candidacy official, and had called upon the Ohio GOP to choose between its two sons well in advance of the national convention, set for Chicago on 16 June. And in New York, the successful and popular Governor Charles Evans Hughes was showing strength as a national candidate as well.

Roosevelt had tried to help Taft by repeating, forcefully and unequivocally, that he himself would not run for a third term. This had at least allayed lingering doubts about his determination to retire. But how to eliminate Hughes, whom he had backed strongly only fourteen months before? He was quite willing to act, if he could do so without seeming treacherous. The Governor was intelligent but humorless, and exuded such an aura of scraggybearded self-righteousness that Roosevelt had taken to calling him "Charles the Baptist."

An announcement that Hughes was to speak on national issues at the New York Republican Club on 31 January, in a clear bid for party attention, enabled the American people to observe, yet again, that Theodore Roosevelt was the most adroit tactician in American politics. Working at top speed, he wrote a Special Message to Congress, radical enough to excite the admiration of Upton Sinclair, and released it on the day of Hughes's speech. Its first words deceptively suggested that it was a response to the Supreme Court's antilabor ruling, but its later paragraphs, filling twelve and a half columns of dense print in *Congressional Record,* amounted to a rewrite, in much harsher language, of his neglected Message of two months before. As a result, he simultaneously wrested from Hughes all the lead headlines (HOTTEST MESSAGE

EVER SENT TO CONGRESS), put both Court and Congress on the defensive, dulled Morgan's "saviour of society" shine, and by the sheer audacity of his proposals made the progressive/conservative split in the Republican Party permanent, with himself—ambiguous no longer—aligned firmly on the left.

He demanded that the employers' liability law be re-enacted in a form that would satisfy the Supreme Court, yet apply even more strongly to interstate commerce. He declared that congressional unwillingness to write any remedial entitlements for job injuries into the so-called federal worker's compensation law was an "outrage" and "humiliation" to the United States. "In no other prominent industrial country in the world could such gross injustice occur. . . . Exactly as the working man is entitled to his wages, so he should be entitled to indemnity for the injuries sustained in the natural course of his labor." Ultimately, private employers should be compelled to apply federal principles of liability and compensation across the entire industrial landscape.

Roosevelt proudly cited the Anthracite Coal Commission's 1903 strike report as "a chart" for action against the abuse of court injunctions in strikes and walkouts. "Ultra-conservatives who object to cutting out the abuses will do well to remember that if the popular feeling does become strong, many of those upon whom they rely to defend them will be the first to turn against them." The Interstate Commerce Commission's powers should be extended to total financial supervision of railroads, and also physical control of interstate operations and the scheduling of deliveries of perishable products. It was the inadequacy of the Hepburn Act, not its introduction in 1906, that had created an "element of uncertainty" in railroad-stock speculations, and "contributed much to the financial stress of the recent past." Lastly, the Sherman Act should be refocused to distinguish between beneficial combinations and "huge combinations which are both noxious and illegal."

Referring to himself not infrequently in the royal plural, Roosevelt admitted that he was engaged in a "campaign against privilege" that was "fundamentally an ethical movement." His targets were stock gamblers "making large sales of what men do not possess," writers who "act as the representatives of predatory wealth" (among them, probably, the entire editorial staff of the New York *Sun*), and "men of wealth, who find in the purchased politician the most efficient instrument of corruption." He reserved his strongest language for these multimillionaires, not identifying them directly but taking care to repeat, with incantatory frequency, the names of John D. Rockefeller's Standard Oil Company and E. H. Harriman's Santa Fe Railroad. Such men were "the most dangerous members of the criminal class—the criminals of great wealth."

Americans upon whom such men preyed had three choices: to let them flourish without supervision, to control them at the state level, or to regulate them by federal action. He did not doubt that the last option was the only way, as common law no longer had power to deal with uncommon wealth.

These new conditions make it necessary to shackle cunning as in the past we have shackled force. The vast individual and corporate fortunes, the vast combinations of capital, which have marked the development of our industrial system, create new conditions, and necessitate a change from the old attitude of the State and the Nation toward the rules regulating the acquisition and untrammeled business use of property.

⟶

SUBSCRIBERS TO THE theory that Roosevelt was crazy found in his Special Message all the evidence they wanted. Chancellor James Roscoe Day of Syracuse University remarked that "much of it reads like the ravings of a disordered mind." *The New York Times* and New York *Evening Mail* both spoke of the President's tendency toward "delusion," especially with regard to imaginary conspiracies against him, and the New York *Sun* said that his "portentous diatribe" might be referred better to psychologists than to the archivists of Congress. "It is an even more disturbing reflection that the hand which penned this message is the same hand which directs the American Navy, now on its mission toward unknown possibilities. God send our ships and all of us good luck!"

Charles Lanier, of Winslow Lanier & Co., added drugs to the derangement theory. He claimed, in a rumor that tickled Roosevelt enormously, that "the President is crazy, and furthermore . . . indulging immoderately in drink and is an opium fiend." *Current Literature,* in one of its regular roundups of public opinion, noted the curious fact that almost all the questions about Roosevelt's mental health were being asked, loudly and querulously, in his home state. Calmer voices there were few, and none so salutary as that of a progressive judge, William J. Gaynor of Brooklyn: "Every purseproud individual, as well as reactionary dullard, always considers a great character insane. In their littleness of heart, of soul, he seems so to them; but the people know that Frederick the Great was not insane, although he was called so all over Europe, just as well as they know and understand Theodore Roosevelt."

Gaynor's words were borne out by the echolike promptness and fidelity of the response of "Roosevelt Republicans" west of the Hudson. The Philadelphia *North American* placed the Special Message "in the forefront among the really memorable state papers in the history of the nation," and the Chicago *Evening Post* found it "a profoundly conservative document" in its insistence upon basic moral liberties. In remarkable harmony, a chorus of Southern Democratic newspapers praised the President's attack on his own Old Guard, and the *Baltimore Sun* seemed quite serious in proposing that he run for re-election as a Democrat, with William Jennings Bryan as his vice-presidential candidate.

Bryan himself—improbably resurgent after the defeat of Alton B.

Parker—had gracious things to say. "It is a brave message and needed at this time. All friends of reform have reason to rejoice that the President has used his high position to call attention to the wrongs that need to be remedied."

All friends of Roosevelt were not, however, friends of reform, as he discovered when he received a letter from Nicholas Murray Butler early in February. More than six years had passed since Butler had sat listening to the "accidental" President ruminate in Commander Cowles's parlor—years in which Butler's own self-discovery, as president of Columbia University, had hardened into chronic self-importance.

> Of all your real friends perhaps I, alone, am fond enough of you to tell you what a painful impression has been made on the public mind by your Special Message. . . .
>
> Surely the sorry record of Andrew Johnson is sufficient proof that a President, whether right or wrong, cannot afford to argue with his adversaries, after the fashion of a private citizen, other than in a state paper or in a formal public address. If you will read this Message over quietly, and then read any of the most important Presidential Messages which have preceded it, you will, yourself, see exactly what I mean. You will see how lacking it is in the dignity, in the restraint, and in the freedom from epithet which ought to characterize so important a state paper. . . .
>
> My honest opinion is that so far as the Message has had any purely political effect, it is to bring Mr. Bryan measurably nearer the White House than he has ever been before.

Roosevelt declined to accept Butler's censure. "You regret what I have done. To me your regret is incomprehensible."

⌁

ON 7 FEBRUARY, the Great White Fleet, dispatched toward unknown possibilities by an allegedly deranged (William James preferred the term *dynamogenic*) Commander-in-Chief, entered the Strait of Magellan. Since leaving Hampton Roads, it had become a diplomatic phenomenon, attracting worldwide press attention and spreading as much goodwill as foam along the Brazilian and Argentine coastlines. Even Punta Arenas, Chile, a windswept wood-and-iron outpost near the extreme tip of the continent, welcomed Admiral Evans and his sailors with elaborate hospitality and specially hiked prices.

For twenty-two hours, the Chilean destroyer *Chacabuco* led Evans's flagship *Connecticut* through the misty Strait—a surreal *Doppelgänger* of the waterway being carved across Panama—while fifteen other coal-heavy ships wallowed behind at four-hundred-yard intervals. No more than three men-of-war had ever performed this maneuver in convoy, and the going was hazardous even for single units. But the fleet steamed steadily through. It veered off course only once, when a sudden turbulence proclaimed the conflicting levels of two oceans. By the time the last vessel emerged into open sea, the first was already steaming toward Valparaiso, and the Pacific theater had received its largest-ever infusion of battleships.

⟿

ROOSEVELT HAD still not announced his intention to send the fleet around the world—its official destination remained San Francisco. But Japan was aware that another war scare in the United States could quickly alter the fleet's course; Admiral Dewey's "ninety-day lag" no longer applied. This knowledge, combined with mounting diplomatic pressure from Elihu Root, now forced the conclusion of the "Gentlemen's Agreement," on which Tokyo had been politely stalling for nearly a year.

Throughout 1907, the influx of Japanese coolies into the United States had continued to pour unabated, making a mockery of the new immigration law. Root had tired of pointing out that the flow had to be restricted at its source, as per Tokyo's verbal promise. Instead, he had taken advantage of the publicity attending the dispatch of the Great White Fleet to warn Ambassador Aoki that unless there was "a very speedy change in the course of immigration," the Sixtieth Congress was certain to pass an exclusion act, greatly to the detriment of Japanese-American relations.

By 29 February, as the fleet headed north from Callao, Peru, the Gentlemen's Agreement was finally implemented. Coolies were no longer permitted to immigrate to Hawaii, passport restrictions were tightened, and illegal agencies were being prosecuted by Japanese authorities. And at last, the monthly "Yellow Peril" index compiled by the State Department began to decline.

Roosevelt celebrated by confirming that the Great White Fleet, now en route to the Golden Gate, would proceed around the world after a couple of months' rest and refitting. Its itinerary would include Hawaii, New Zealand, Australia, the Philippines, Japan (about two weeks before the presidential election), China, Ceylon, the Suez Canal, Egypt, the Mediterranean, and Gibraltar. Its due date for return to Hampton Roads was 22 February 1909, ten days before he was to leave the White House.

⟿

PULVERIZING AS THE President's Special Message had been to the boomlet for Governor Hughes, and however revealing of Roosevelt's own changing ideology, it merely increased the opposition of congressional conservatives against him. Joseph Cannon in the House and Nelson Aldrich in the Senate vied with each other to deny him the reforms he had begged with such eloquence. However, a small band of progressive Republicans and a larger one of moderate Democrats (who had applauded repeatedly during the reading of the Message) helped him win at least three new laws: a re-enacted Federal Employers' Liability Act, the Workman's Compensation Act for federal employees, and the Child Labor Act for the District of Columbia.

He also won, on 10 March, a nonlegislative victory with fruits that tasted distinctly sour. The Senate Committee on Military Affairs concluded its thirteen-month investigation of the Brownsville affair and found, by nine votes to four, that Roosevelt had justifiably dismissed without honor the soldiers of the Twenty-fifth Infantry. Three thousand pages of testimony, and the congruent opinions of virtually all Army authorities from the Commander-in-Chief on down, were enough to convince five Democrats and four Republicans that the men were guilty. The dissenting members were all Republican, but they were themselves divided, in a way that paradoxically compromised the majority vote. Two found the testimony to be contradictory and untrustworthy, reflecting irreconcilable antipathies between soldiers and townspeople. Senators Foraker and Morgan G. Bulkeley insisted that "the weight of the testimony" showed the soldiers to be innocent.

So did the weight of the only hard evidence in the case: thirty-three spent Army-issue cartridges found at the scene of the crime. Ballistics experts had testified that, while the shells had definitely been fired by Springfield rifles belonging to the Twenty-fifth, the actual firing had occurred during target practice at Fort Niobrara in Nebraska, long before the battalion was ordered to Texas. The mystery of the translocation of the shells to Brownsville was simply explained. Army budget officers frowned on waste of rechargeable ordnance, so 1,500 shells had been recovered from the range, sent south, and stored in an open box on the porch of a barracks hut at Fort Brown, available for any soldier—or passing civilian—to help himself.

Such technical information, however, could not explain away the "wooden, stolid look" that Inspector General Garlington had seen on the faces he interviewed. It was a look so evocative of Negro complicity that the War Department had briskly dispensed with the formality of allowing every soldier his day in court.

Roosevelt's other major legislative request, unsatisfied through the first weeks of spring, was for four new battleships. The House followed the recommendation of its Committee on Naval Affairs and appropriated funds for only two. Unappeased by an extra appropriation to build a naval base at Pearl Harbor, Roosevelt put his hopes in the Senate. Debate there began on 24 April, none too favorably. Senators seemed more inclined to question the legality of his battle-fleet cruise order than to double the battleship quota of the House bill. But they also had to take into account his still phenomenal popularity, and the hold the Great White Fleet had taken of the public imagination. Three days later, Roosevelt won a modified victory: two battleships plus a guarantee that two more would be funded before he left office.

Sounding rather like a small boy, he claimed not to have expected four all at once, but had asked for them only because he wanted to be sure of getting two.

⁓

ROOSEVELT'S ENDORSEMENT of the recommendations of the Inland Waterways Commission was not unallied with his own profound enjoyment of anything rocky, slimy, hardscrabble, and dangerous. In Washington, he had become a confirmed river rat, frequently cruising down the Potomac or up the Anacostia in the *Sylph,* and hiking, wading, and climbing for miles along the wild banks of Rock Creek. Invitations to accompany him on what he was pleased to call "walks" usually bore the cautionary superscript, *Put on your worst clothes.* This gave notice that, sooner or later, he and his companions would end up in water, irrespective of whether it was freezing, mud-choked, or dangerously turbulent.

"But, Mr. President," Jules Jusserand was reduced to saying, "I have no worst clothes left."

Roosevelt was so much at home in the creek that he often walked straight across it, absorbed in conversation, not seeming to notice the water around his hips, even when he was jostling ice floes. He was impervious to cold, and when necessary would start swimming, while his companions succumbed to cramps. "To succeed in such cases," one of his former Rough Riders advised Jusserand, "you must have a good layer of fat under your skin."

The little Ambassador was not well padded, but he was as tough as an Alpine *montagnard* and had become Roosevelt's favorite exercise partner. He even accompanied the President on an excursion across a Potomac water pipe, so high and slimy that they were forced eventually to admit defeat. Roosevelt, who wanted to follow the pipe to its destination on a midriver island, hailed a passing rowboat and asked to be ferried there. As the boat pushed out into the current, Roosevelt put his arm around Jusserand's neck, struck an attitude, and intoned: "Washington and Rochambeau crossing the Delaware."

Shortly after the battleship vote, in warm May weather, the President led Jusserand, Assistant Secretary of State Robert Bacon, and three other hikers on a strenuous, cliff-hanging expedition along the Virginia side of the Potomac, near Chain Bridge. When all were pouring with perspiration, Roosevelt suggested a swim and stripped naked. His party followed suit, but Jusserand absentmindedly kept on his black kid climbing gloves. "Eh, Mr. Ambassador," Roosevelt called from the water's edge, "have you not forgotten something?"

Jusserand shouted back, "We might meet ladies."

The river was still cold, and when the swimmers returned to shore they were obliged to step wet into their clothes, and pull their socks on over mud-

"PUT ON YOUR WORST CLOTHES."
Roosevelt (invisible) leads a Rock Creek Park expedition

plastered feet. A further rock-climb was prescribed to restore body heat. Jusserand admired the President's bearlike ascent of a cliff so precipitous that it defeated everyone else except the athletic Bacon. When, finally, they trooped back to their waiting carriages, the Assistant Secretary's trouser leg was slit from hip to ankle.

⌒

ON 12 MAY, forty-five state and territorial executives dined at the White House on the eve of the Governors' Conference. They were joined by thirty other dignitaries and Roosevelt acolytes at a vast horseshoe table in the State Dining Room. The President sat with Chief Justice Fuller on his right and Speaker Cannon on his left (in a severe sulk at being downgraded). Elsewhere in the room, he could see members of what Owen Wister called his "Concert of Familiars": Gifford Pinchot, hawk-nosed at the extreme south end of the shoe next to Frank McCoy, who had hauled down Old Glory in Havana, six years before; John Mitchell of United Mine Workers, dulled by drink; Justice Holmes, long since returned to presidential favor; handsome James Garfield; Commander William Sims, the Navy reformer, even handsomer; and Justice Moody, clean-shaven now, with a strange aloofness settled upon him, the most interesting-looking man in the room. Faces less intimately familiar looked back at him from among the many anonymous governors: Andrew Carnegie and James J. Hill, millionaires; Captain Archibald Willingham de Graffenreid Butt, his new Georgian military aide; Senator Newlands of Nevada; and William Jennings Bryan, probably the last person any social secretary would expect to see on the President's dinner list, with the exception of Booker T. Washington.

Bryan's presence (and controversial placement next to Moody) signaled the democratic nature of tomorrow's conference "on the conservation of natural resources." When wood and water were endangered, the political differences between men of power dissolved. To Roosevelt's regret, his only living predecessor, Grover Cleveland, was unable to attend because of illness.

Many of the governors had never been in the White House before, and they were noticeably awed by the splendor of their reception. Roosevelt, wanting to stress the conference's momentousness, had ordered that they be presented to him "as for a state dinner." He had welcomed them one by one in the East Room, then led them down the great vestibule with Fuller walking alongside him, in a mimetic show of Power and Justice guiding Procedure.

The dinner seating had been planned with further formality by the State Department, but Roosevelt, looking it over, had decided that enough was enough and rearranged it so that men with things to say to each other, such as James J. Hill and Theodore E. Burton of the Inland Waterways Commission, could sit together—conferring, after all, being the whole point of conferences. To further aid the flow of talk (and sherry, sauterne, and claret), he

"THEY WERE NOTICABLY AWED BY THE
SPLENDOR OF THEIR RECEPTION."
Theodore Roosevelt hosts the first conservation conference, May 1908

elected to have no toasts or speeches. Gentlemen from the West, who tended to eat more than they spoke, were awarded full command of a menu including littleneck clams on the half shell, *coquilles* of fresh caviar, strained gumbo, cold salmon *Bayardère,* squabs *à l'Estouffade,* filet *piqué Richelieu,* ice cream *pralinée,* "fancy cakes," and coffee.

Since the night was warm, cigars and liqueurs were served on the West Terrace. Roosevelt accepted neither, concentrating all his attention on Bryan. The two men talked at a small table for more than an hour. Captain Butt overheard the President saying, "I confess to you confidentially that I like my job." The rest of the company strolled and admired the fragrant garden.

In spite of himself, Roosevelt was impressed by the Commoner. "A wonderful man," he remarked afterward.

⁓

AT ELEVEN O'CLOCK the following morning, Roosevelt called to order a vastly larger assembly in the East Room. Present, along with the governors and their aides, were his entire Cabinet (minus only Taft, who was in Panama, and Metcalf, who was with the fleet in San Francisco); all nine Justices of the Supreme Court; an uncounted number of members of Congress; representatives of sixty-eight professional societies, including those of chemistry, law, medicine, publishing, social and political science, civil engineering, forestry, architecture, mining, scenic and historic preservation, statistics, drainage, farming, lumber, slack cooperage, and hay; twenty-one editors and reporters from technical, news, and popular publications; forty-eight special guests, including academics, geographers, entomologists, biologists, soil experts, and commissioners of labor and Indian affairs. In a major gesture toward universal representation, one seat was assigned to Sarah S. Platt-Decker, president of the General Federation of Women's Clubs.

Allowing for a few invitees not showing, and excluding a constant influx and egress of senators and congressmen, the Governors' Conference totaled some 360 persons. The "Syllabus" prepared for its guidance by WJ McGee intimidatingly comprised ninety-five aspects of conservation, preservation, and planned exploitation under eleven headings: Mineral Fuels, Ores and Related Materials, Soil, Forests, Sanitation, Reclamation, Land Laws, Grazing and Stock Raising, Relations Between Rail and Water Transportation, Navigation, Power, and Conservation as a National Policy.

"The Lord thy God bringeth thee into a good land," intoned old Edward Everett Hale, the Chaplain of the Senate, *"a land of brooks of water, of fountains and springs, flowing forth in valleys and hills, a land of wheat and barley and vines and fig trees and pomegranates, a land of olive trees and honey, a land wherein thou shalt eat bread without scarceness. Thou shall not lack anything in it—a land where stones are iron and out of whose hills thou mayest dig copper."*

Roosevelt delivered the opening address.

> You have come hither at my request, so that we may join together to consider the question of the conservation and use of the great fundamental sources of wealth of this Nation. So vital is this question, that for the first time in our history the chief executive officers of the states separately, and of the states together forming the Nation, have met to consider it. It is the chief material question that confronts us, second only—and second always—to the great fundamental questions of morality.

Applause filled the room. Three days of serious discussion were only just beginning, yet already Roosevelt and Dr. Hale had sounded the conference's keynote and pedal point: that the natural endowment was a gift of God, and that utilitarianism must be subject to human and spiritual constraints.

Roosevelt remarked on the anomaly whereby man, as he progressed from savagery to civilization, used up more and more of the world's resources, yet in doing so tended to move to the city, and lost his sense of dependence on nature. Lacking that, he also lost his foresight, and unwittingly depleted the inheritances of his children. "We cannot, when the nation becomes fully civilized and very rich, continue to be civilized and rich unless the nation shows more foresight than we are showing at this moment."

Further applause interrupted the President. In the elegantly printed little program every guest had been issued, his speech bore the title: *Conservation as a National Duty.*

He reviewed the energy policy of the United States from the days of General Washington, when "anthracite coal was known only as a useless black stone" and water was practically the only source of power outside human and animal exertion. Ignorant though Washington had been of the potentials of coal and steam, he had seen clearly that the future United States could be linked in perpetuity only by a common power network. To that end, the Father of the Country had pressed for, and brought about, an interstate waterways conference between Virginia and Maryland.

"It met," said Roosevelt, allowing his listeners to make what comparisons they chose, "near where we are now meeting, in Alexandria, adjourned to Mount Vernon, and took up the consideration of interstate commerce by the only means then available, that of water; and the trouble we have since had with the railways has been mainly due to the fact that naturally our forefathers could not divine that the iron road would become the interstate and national highway, instead of the old route by water." Washington's conference had led to another, much greater one in Philadelphia, involving all the states, that "was in its original conception merely a waterways conference; but when they had closed their deliberations, the outcome was the Constitution which made the States into a Nation."

Applause again surged, acting as a drumroll to his next, thematic sentence: "The Constitution of the United States thus grew in large part out of the necessity for united action in the wise use of our natural resources."

He proceeded to catalog the irresponsibility with which Americans, over more than a century and a quarter, had successively abused water, mineral, and forest resources, leading to the loss of more than half the nation's original timber, and signs of exhaustion already visible in iron and coal reserves. The pristine waterway scheme of the Founding Fathers was now neglected, underused, and ill managed. The "soils of unexampled fertility" that had greeted pioneer farmers were leaching away through ignorance, "washed into the streams, polluting the rivers, denuding the fields, and obstructing navigation." Again, he harped on the need for "foresight," and again was applauded as his use of the word became rhythmic: "We have to, as a nation, exercise foresight . . . and if we do not exercise that foresight, dark will be the future!"

It was the duty of the Governors' Conference, he said, to formulate a national philosophy of conservation based on efficient use of finite resources and scientific management of renewable ones. For himself, he vowed to continue working through the Inland Waterways Commission, which he took pride in having created ("I had to prosecute the work by myself") and which, if Congress persisted in depriving it of funds, he would perpetuate by executive means.

This won him his loudest ovation yet, hardly quieter than the one that followed his praise of Gifford Pinchot's initiative in making conservation a national priority. Then he won bursts of laughter by quoting a recent opinion by Justice Holmes (gazing at him from only a few feet away) in favor of the right of "the State as quasi sovereign" to prevent private property owners from despoiling a waterway, even though "there are benefits from a great river that might escape a lawyer's notice."

"I have simply quoted," Roosevelt said, as the audience guffawed.

He concluded with another invocation of conservation as morality, and sat down amid cheers.

Rules were announced for orderly conduct of the conference's discussion sessions, set to begin after lunch. Experts presenting overlong statements would be subjected to the discipline of bells; governors would have chair powers; the proceedings of the conference would be recorded and published in full; a Committee on Resolutions should be organized and authorized to formulate general conclusions.

The hands of the East Room clock now stood at five minutes past noon "Gentlemen," Roosevelt called out, "I shall now have the pleasure of meeting you personally as you pass through the Blue Room."

‒‒‒

HE STAYED WITH them through Andrew Carnegie's postprandial paper on the conservation of ore. Then, having tried, and failed, to get William Jennings Bryan to speak extempore, he gracefully withdrew, explaining, "I have a good deal to do." A good deal of that good deal apparently demanded his presence on the White House tennis court, but he was conscientious thereafter in opening each session and hearing each opening paper.

The conference broke up on the afternoon of 15 May, after a "garden party" for attendees and their wives, hosted by Edith Roosevelt and hastily relocated indoors when rain descended. The governors issued a concluding declaration that upheld everything the President had said about the interrelationship of civilization and conservation, and conservation and morality, and morality and duty. They urged the "continuation and extension" of the Administration's current forest and water policies, recommended the enactment of laws against wasteful practices in mines and heavy industry, and resoundingly agreed that "this conservation of our natural resources is a subject of transcendent importance, which should engage unremittingly the attention of the Nation, the States, and the People in earnest cooperation."

‒‒‒

THUS EMPOWERED, Roosevelt promptly created a National Conservation Commission, under the chairmanship of Gifford Pinchot, instructing it to compile the inventory he had called for at Memphis. He announced that he would also call a North American Conservation Conference, to enlist the aid of Canada and Mexico in protecting the hemispheric environment. Ultimately—if not in his own presidency, then perhaps early in the next—there should be an international conference with an even larger agenda, spreading the philosophy of conservation worldwide.

Americans began to be aware of the extent to which he, often by stealth over the past six years, had used his powers (Joseph Cannon would say, misused them) to set aside an extraordinary large and varied swath of the national commons. He had created five national parks, doubling the total bequeathed to him in 1901, and struggled against mining interests to make a sixth of the Grand Canyon. Unsuccessful in that quixotic task, he had made the canyon a national monument instead, under the new Antiquities Act, effectively preserving it for future parkhood. In fewer than six months, since passage of the Act, he had proclaimed fifteen other national monuments, interpreting the latter word loosely to include environments as different as Muir Woods, California, and Gila Cliff Dwellings, New Mexico. He had initiated twenty federal irrigation projects in fourteen states under the National Reclamation Act. He had declared thirteen new national forests—a total that Pinchot intended to vastly multiply, now that "Conservation" was at last part of the American ethos.

Perhaps nearest to Roosevelt's own heart, he had created sixteen federal bird refuges, starting with Pelican Island, Florida, in an executive coup that was already part of his legend. ("Is there any law that will prevent me from declaring Pelican Island a Federal Bird Reservation? Very well, then I so declare it.") At Wichita Forest, Oklahoma, he had made the first federal game preserve. His three environmental commissions, on public lands, inland waterways, and national conservation, had embarked on the probably ill-fated but historically important task of educating corporate skeptics to an awareness of the rape of the American wilderness.

And Roosevelt had nine months left in office to expand on these beginnings, as relentlessly as he was able.

⎯⎯⎯

TWO WEEKS LATER, Congress adjourned, with no last-minute legislative largesse thrown the President's way, and its members hastened to prepare for their respective national conventions. Roosevelt remained in Washington to monitor the last few days of Taft's campaign for the Republican nomination, and quell yet another little flurry of rumors that he was hoping to be drafted for a third term. "Any man who supposes that I have been scheming for it, is not merely a fool, but shows himself to be a man of low morality," he wrote to Lyman Abbott. "He reflects upon himself, not upon me." In the midst of this protest, he could not help adding, "There has never been a moment when I could not have had practical unanimity without raising a finger."

Two West Virginia delegates elected under instructions for Taft actually announced that they were switching their votes to the President. Roosevelt was obliged to write a letter to their congressman, urging him to tell them how strongly he objected to any such pledge. He had the letter copied in case of any other defections, but doubted that he would have to use it. Taft, having managed to defeat Senator Foraker's attempt to co-opt the Ohio GOP, was now far ahead of the two other ranking candidates for the nomination, Governor Hughes and Senator Knox. Roosevelt assured Henry Adams that "Will" would get a two-thirds vote on the first ballot in Chicago. As for himself, he was "now safe out of it."

Adams had to admit, in the privacy of his own correspondence, that these words had struck a chill. For twenty years, he had pretended to detest Roosevelt, joked and gossiped about him, and mocked his every supposedly thoughtless, bull-calf blunder. But the mere thought of the President being, at last, "out of it" was enough to make Adams realize that there would soon be none left of his old Washington salon—excepting Henry Cabot Lodge, who was as much a cold stone statue, these days, as any of the capital's growing population of sculpted statesmen. Whatever else might be said of Roosevelt, he had *vigor di vita*.

"The old house will seem dull and sad," Adams wrote, "when my Theodore has gone."

CHAPTER 31

The Residuary Legatee

MR. HENNESSY	*I don't know whether th' administhration is a success or not.*
MR. DOOLEY	*Me friends differ.*
MR. HENNESSY	*Rosenfelt says it is.*
MR. DOOLEY	*Rockefeller says it isn't.*
MR. HENNESSY	*But annyhow, whether 'tis a success or not, it's been injyable.*

THE FIRST DAY OF JUNE 1908 found Theodore Roosevelt alone in the White House, with only his youngest son for company. Edith and Ethel were cruising down the Potomac in search of sea breezes, Archie had transferred to Sagamore Hill, and his elder children were gone, or half gone, along their respective roads to independence. "Until Quentin goes to bed the house is entirely lively," he wrote to Ted. "After that the rooms seem big and lonely and full of echoes. The carpets and curtains are all away, as the heat of summer has begun."

His office time was devoted largely to persuading as many still uncommitted delegates as possible to vote for Taft at the Republican National Convention, now little more than two weeks off. In doing so, he had to make fanatic Rooseveltians understand that he would not accept a draft himself, on any size of silver plate—difficult for them to believe, and depressing for him to reiterate, since the certainty that he would be elected if nominated was no less than that of Quentin growing taller.

"Q," as schoolmates called him, was an always cheerful, straight-A student with a love of long words, chopping them up patriarchally and grinning when he succeeded without stuttering. ("The Republican presidents have been most u-n-i-f-o-r-m-l-y good—but the Democrats have been, without e-x-c-e-p-t-i-o-n, *terrible.*" Some of the words were misapplied, or wholly invented; Q never let deliberation impede his eloquence.) He was ten and a half years old now, and Roosevelt noticed, with some sadness, that he was no longer interested in being read to. The White House Gang, an elite cadre of Washington's most subversive small boys, accepted Q as their leader—not because he was the son of the President, but because with his big head, cyclonic energy, and moral decisiveness he simply *was* Theodore Roosevelt in their imitative world, just as placid, plump-cheeked Charles "Taffy" Taft, unquestioningly accepting Q's orders, acted as Secretary of War in all confrontations with foreign powers, notably the District of Columbia Police Department.

As an honorary member of the Gang, which operated out of the White House attic, the President was capable of considerable mischief himself. But when Q's guerrilla activities threatened national security, he did not hesitate to exercise his authority as Commander-in-Chief. One such occasion was the Battle of the Guidon, waged on the South Lawn between two divisions of the Gang, respectively led by Q and Taffy.

The property office of the War Department having condemned a moth-eaten silk artillery pennant, Company Q decided to fight Company T for possession of it. Whichever side held the colors for three minutes (Q, like his father, was an obsessive clock-watcher) would win the privilege of dictating Gang activities for the rest of the afternoon. Taffy (like *his* father a capable deployer of military matériel) staked the guidon about five feet from the nozzle of a hose, the strategic significance of which Q did not at first appreciate.

During the ensuing battle, Taffy, by far the largest combatant, maintained his grasp of the flagstaff and ordered an aide, Edward "Slats" Stead, to spin a concealed tap. Q and his force of three men were blasted head over heels in the resultant gush of water. Enraged, Q issued a counterorder ("Keep it up! Keep it up! I'm going to sinister this, immejitly!") and disappeared. Suddenly, the gush lost its force. As the spray cleared, Q was revealed in possession of a fire ax, with which he had sliced the hose into several sections. His triumph was forestalled by a stentorian shout from the West Wing, and the President came charging through the Rose Garden, coattails flying.

TR   (*panting heavily*) Too late! Too late, by George! Quentin!—I mean Georgie Washington—come here with your i-n-c-r-i-m-i-n-a-t-i-n-g hatchet! In the heat of battle, many acts, which would not be c-o-u-n-t-e-n-a-n-c-e-d at other times, may be excusable—or at least, subject to sym-pa-thet-ic in-ter-pre-ta-tion; of course you understand that, boys?

Q   Sure. You mean that's the reason why I did it? I did it, because something had to be done, immejit-ly—

TR   That's e-x-a-c-t-l-y it! The point is always to do *something* quickly, because if you don't, the other fellow will.

Charles Evans Hughes, whose candidacy for the Republican presidential nomination had never recovered from Roosevelt's surprise attack in January, could vouch for this advice, along with Senator Foraker, Kaiser Wilhelm II, and President Marroquín of Colombia. But the President was not finished with his son:

TR You may be wrong—you were here—but you have, at least, i-n-i-t-i-a-t-e-d action. When the action is wrong, you must admit it, and correct it by some further action—

Q (*looking at the severed hose*) I don't see how *this* can be corrected.

TR Only by an entirely new garden-hose. It was Government property, still is, but also, is no longer. You cannot imagine the difficulties involved, and the things required to be done, in order to replace it. It will even cost money, part of that which I am earning—or was earning, when interrupted by a despatch regarding the progress of this war, and left hurriedly for the field—

Q Well, of course you're right; but we've learned our lesson, you know—

TR We? Don't you mean yourself? And what have you learned?

Q Not to cut up garden-hoses.

TR And not to use fire-axes on anything but a fire—

Q (*with a touch of wistfulness*) We're not so likely to have a fire.

TR Not with all this water around! You escape, Quentin, only because of the extenuating circumstances arising out of the heat of battle.

With that, he turned on his heel and marched back to the Executive Office.

To adults, as well as Gang members, Q was a freakish duplication of his father, right down to the juvenile asthma and queer, prudish chivalry. (When classmates giggled at a girl's up-folded dress, he yanked it down, trembling with anger.) He had the same physical courage, clarity of perception, and ability to concentrate totally on any task at hand. Yet, more than any of the other Roosevelt children except Alice—who in any case had a different mother—he had a large personality of his own. Henry Adams found him fascinating, as had Mark Hanna.

Q was imaginative enough to withdraw, periodically, into daydreams that seemed to elevate him in an almost physical sense. He loved heights, and the eagle's-eye perception that height endows. The famous MacMillan Commission models of Washington thrilled him. "Look down on the White House, as if you were a god! How small it looks. . . . You could drop a pebble on it and crush it, together with the p-i-g-m-y President and the State-War-Navy Department, too, by mistake!"

The last two words were an indication of Quentin Roosevelt's essentially kindly nature. Like his father, he had an aggressive urge to hurl bolts from above. Unlike his father, he thought about the consequences.

TO THE RATHER less aggressive Kermit Roosevelt, the President wrote, "I have two first-rate maps of the part of Africa we are to go to."

For some time he had been thinking of taking Kermit, who had just graduated from Groton, on a hunting trip after William Howard Taft (or William Jennings Bryan?) succeeded to the Presidency. He knew himself well enough to know that he would want to reassume control of the government (if necessary, at the head of a company of cavalry), within weeks of either man's inauguration. The stability of the country, and of his own blood pressure, might best be preserved if he withdrew to an environment as remote as possible from Washington. Newfoundland and Alaska had been presented as possibilities; but during the last few months, after a dinner with the African explorer Carl Akeley, Roosevelt had become obsessed with the idea of conducting a marathon nine-month safari through British East Africa and the uplands of the Nile.

He tried hard to pretend to Edith, when she came back from her cruise, that the trip was merely a pipe dream that could easily blow away. But to Kermit, he gave a more concrete impression:

> I think I shall get a double-barrelled 450 cordite, but shall expect to use almost all the time my Springfield and my 45-70 Winchester. I shall want you to have a first-class rifle, perhaps one of the powerful new model 40 or 45 caliber Winchesters. Then it may be that it would be a good thing to have a 12-bore shotgun that could be used with solid ball. . . . It is no child's play going after lion, elephant, rhino and buffalo.

⟶

AS HE WROTE, the Republican herd of delegates, now overwhelmingly pledged to Taft, began to converge like slow wildebeests on Chicago. ROOSEVELT STAMPEDE STOPPED ran a gratifying headline in the Washington *Evening Star.* The body copy, however, allowed that anything could still happen when they met head-to-head.

"I know that the President does not want the nomination and will not accept it," Congressman Charles B. Landis of Indiana was quoted as saying. "Of course, if the convention should nominate him and then adjourn, he would have to take it."

The ironic secret—which would have provoked the herd to a horizon-filling rout, if carried on any breeze—was that Taft did not want the nomination either. As always, when strong people around him felt strongly (Roosevelt, Mrs. Taft, Charles P. Taft, even young Taffy), he went along. His heart alone protested. A few days before the convention, he said to Senator Cullom, "If your friend Chief Justice Fuller should retire, and the

President should send me a commission as Chief Justice, I would take it now."

The hour was too late for such fantasies. At latest count, Taft had 563 delegates, Knox 68, and Hughes 54. One estimate of Taft's strength went even higher, to more than six hundred delegates. There was no question as to whose popularity, whose policies, whose rhetoric, whose patronage, and whose mastery of press relations had pumped up this formidable total. Reluctant or not, Taft could hardly avoid being seen as the inevitable successor of an irresistible party leader. The giant airship that Count Ferdinand von Zeppelin was readying for flight at Friedrichshafen, Germany, was no more shaped, stressed, powered, and dirigible.

Helen Taft's embarrassment about her husband's debt to the President was correspondingly acute. She wished he could be a candidate in his own right, and resented everything Roosevelt had done to help him, while dreading that her husband might yet suffer the indignity of having that support withdrawn.

On Tuesday, 16 June, the Convention opened at the Chicago Coliseum, where Theodore Roosevelt had been so triumphantly nominated four years before. Taft remained in Washington, headquartered in his office at the War Department, while the President worked in the West Wing, just a few dozen yards away. Both offices kept in constant telegraphic touch with floor managers in Chicago, and with each other by telephone and messenger.

At first, these communications were frequent, as a dispute about the use of injunctions in strike situations threatened the integrity of the party platform. But after Roosevelt and Taft agreed on a compromise plank, not at all to the satisfaction of the American Federation of Labor, the two power centers spoke less and less. Almost imperceptibly, a sense of separation began to develop between them.

The proceedings in the Coliseum were routine through Wednesday afternoon, when Henry Cabot Lodge, speaking as permanent chairman, described Theodore Roosevelt as "the best abused and most popular man in the United States today." This remark touched off a forty-nine-minute demonstration, nineteen minutes longer than the historic bedlam that had followed William Jennings Bryan's "Cross of Gold" speech in 1896. Twelve thousand throats, including that of an ecstatic Alice Longworth, joined in roars of *"Four more years! Four more years!"* The enormous hall, notorious for its muffled acoustics, seemed unable to hold any more noise. Lodge's black gavel rose and fell as if it were the only soundless thing. Toy bears bobbed and bowed to further shouts: *"We want Teddy! We want Teddy!"*

As soon as his voice became audible, Lodge moved to forestall what looked like an incipient stampede. "That man is no friend to Theodore Roosevelt, and does not cherish his name and fame, who now from any motive, seeks to urge him as a candidate for the great office which he has finally declined." Lodge could not help sounding oracular. But his reproof calmed the convention for the rest of the session.

Joseph Bucklin Bishop, the professional journalist, sycophant, and anti-Semite whom Roosevelt had appointed Secretary of the Panama Canal Commission, happened to be in Washington the following morning. He visited the Executive Office around eleven o'clock and found the President in the midst of yet another attempt to control fanatic third-termers in Chicago. Roosevelt never minded being observed at work, so Bishop stayed to watch and record as telegrams flashed back and forth.

The action in Chicago seemed to be off the floor, while speakers began to drone the nominations of Taft and his six rivals: Knox, Fairbanks, Foraker, Cannon, LaFollette, and Hughes. Private messages urged Roosevelt to issue another disclaimer, lest he be added to the list. He saw no reason for a man of honor to repeat himself, but was worried enough to ask for advice. Bishop persuaded him that the precautionary letter he had already issued was explicit enough.

At 1:30, the President took lunch on the South Portico with Edith, Ethel, and Quentin. Bishop and another guest joined them. The grounds were already lush with premature summer, after the loveliest spring Roosevelt could recall in Washington. Only the linden trees remained in scented bloom. Nine hundred contentious Republicans determining who might sit here in a year's time could have been a million miles away, except for further telegrams of appeal, and further, increasingly annoyed presidential refusals.

Bishop remained at the White House until around 4:00, then crossed over to the War Department to see his boss. Taft sat calmly with Mrs. Taft—not so calm—while Taffy kept scuttling in from an anteroom with slips from Chicago. Each arrived promptly enough to describe the progress of the speeches almost cheer by cheer. When at last Taft's name was announced, the telegrams tabulated the loudness and length of the ensuing ovation.

"I only want it to last more than forty-nine minutes," Helen Taft said.

She was denied her wish. The demonstration was over in less than half an hour. Oratory resumed for other candidates. Then, during a tribute to LaFollette, the President of the United States was mentioned. Taffy came in with a wire saying that the convention had "exploded." Senator Lodge was trying, and failing, to restore order; a huge American flag with Roosevelt's face on it had been unfurled on the platform. Mrs. Taft turned white, and sat in silence. Taft tapped the arm of his chair, whistling softly. Further wires reported that the flag was being circulated round the floor, amid even greater uproar. But Lodge, determined to restore order, was proceeding with the roll call of states. After about twenty-two minutes, the hubbub abated, Georgia's declaration was heard, and the convention calmed. By 5:22 P.M., the delegates had registered their choice. Taft was nominated for President of the United States by a vote of 702 to 68 for Knox, 67 for Hughes, 58 for Cannon, 40 for Fairbanks, 25 for LaFollette, and a paltry 16 for Foraker. By motion of Senator Penrose, the nomination was made unanimous, and the color returned to Helen Taft's high cheekbones.

⌐⊃⌐

AFTERWARD, WHEN CONGRESSMAN James S. Sherman of New York had been announced for Vice President, there were the usual sotto voce recriminations among those cheated of glory. Charles Evans Hughes huffed, through his wealth of beard, that he had gotten a 2:00 A.M. telegram from a White House intermediary, asking him in the names of both Roosevelt and Taft to accept the vice-presidential nomination, along with a substantial cash bonus. He had of course refused. LaFollette complained about the President's secret manipulation of the entire proceedings: "No administration in the history of this government ever gave a more flagrant example of political control of delegates than was brazenly flaunted in the face of the public at the Convention of 1908."

LaFollette was especially disturbed by Taft's choice of "Sunny Jim" Sherman, a big, bluff conservative widely seen as a stooge for Speaker Cannon. All observers were agreed, however, that the Republican ticket, at five hundred pounds and counting, was the heaviest package ever offered to American voters.

⌐⊃⌐

"THERE IS A LITTLE hole in my stomach," Q remarked to his father on the day after the convention, "when I think of leaving the White House."

Roosevelt maintained a cheerful attitude over Taft's huge win, but when writing to intimates, such as Nannie Lodge, he could not avoid imparting a similar wistfulness. "Four more years" had been so urgently, so almost compellingly, offered him, not once but day after day—years in which he could without doubt accomplish the most far-reaching reforms since Reconstruction. Declining that opportunity had, as always with him, been a matter of moral compulsion:

> It was absolutely necessary that any stampede for me should be prevented, and that I should not be nominated. . . . If I had accepted, my power for useful service would have forever been lessened, because nothing could have prevented the wide diffusion of the impression that I had not really meant what I had said, that my actions did not really square with the highest and finest code of ethics—and if there is any value whatever in my career, as far as my countrymen are concerned, it consists in their belief that I have been both an efficient public man, and at the same time, a disinterested public servant.

Ray Stannard Baker stopped by to see the President that evening, and found him in a rare reflective mood: "Well, I'm through now. I've done my work."

They talked until midnight. Baker suggested that the American people might not be through with him, and might be clamoring for his return to the White House in four years' time.

"No, revolutions don't go backwards," Roosevelt said. He seemed tired, and his voice had a note of sad finality. "New issues are coming up. I see them. People are going to discuss economic issues more and more: the tariff, currency, banks. They are hard questions, and I am not deeply interested in them: my problems are moral problems, and my teaching has been plain morality."

He stayed in Washington only long enough to accept Taft's resignation as Secretary of War, along with his profuse thanks and vows of obligation. They agreed that Luke Wright, a former Ambassador to Japan and coauthor of the Gentlemen's Agreement, should be given charge of the War Department. As to other members of the Cabinet, Taft said, in the flood of his gratitude, that he saw no reason why they should not continue to serve if he was elected President.

The President, delighted, relayed this information to all concerned. "He and I view public questions exactly alike," he wrote George Otto Trevelyan. "In fact, I think it is very rare that two public men have ever been so much at one in all the essentials of their public beliefs."

On 20 June, he left town for Oyster Bay. Taft headed in the opposite direction to work on his acceptance speech in Hot Springs, Virginia.

⌒

FOUR DAYS LATER, Grover Cleveland died. On 10 July, delegates at the Democratic National Convention in Denver, Colorado, nominated William Jennings Bryan for President. While doing so, they proved that their lungs were more leathery than those of Roosevelt's puny clique in Chicago, as they cheered the Commoner for an hour and twenty-eight minutes.

Edith was not impressed. She had met Bryan at the Governors' Conference and decided that American voters had been right in rejecting him for the presidency twice already. "A trifle too fat and oily for the fastidious," she wrote her sister-in-law.

Oily or not, Bryan was by no means unattractive to voters. He was an orator of legendary eloquence, unlike Taft, whose platform manner was awkward and gaffe-prone. (The Grand Army of the Republic had not appreciated his reminder, on Memorial Day, that General Grant had had a drinking problem.) Bryan, a genuine man of the people, was able to empathize with his audiences "one on one," whereas Taft the judge manqué always sounded as if he was handing down majority opinions.

Democratic campaign planners felt that Taft's biggest asset—his presidential backing—had counted more at the Republican Convention than it would on Election Day. By then, Roosevelt would be, ideologically, a spent force, and unless Taft built a big new political personality for himself, voters might well decide that twelve years of Republican continuity were enough.

Bryan, besides, had already had plenty of experience in leading his own party. Taft's behavior after drafting his acceptance speech indicated a certain lack of confidence after years of submitting to Roosevelt's will. Instead of heading straight home to Cincinnati to confer with his family and advisers, he took a detour to Oyster Bay, disastrously announcing that he needed "the President's judgment and criticism." Roosevelt received him at Sagamore Hill on 24 July, made a few changes to the speech, wished him well, and sent him on his way.

As Taft headed west, another visitor came to spend a few nights with the Roosevelts *en famille,* accompanied by Assistant Treasury Secretary Beekman Winthrop. Captain Archibald Butt, he of the glittering, much-befrogged soldierly presence at the Conservation Conference, had with astonishing speed become the President's closest companion. Other military and naval aides had come and gone at the Roosevelt White House—among them an extraordinarily handsome West Pointer named Douglas MacArthur—but "Archie" combined personal charm and professional efficiency to such a degree that he was already indispensable.

Large, strong, plumpish, and always beautifully turned out, whether in dress blue or mufti, he was forty-two years old, unmarried, and devoted to his widowed mother, to whom he wrote almost daily. As a youth, he had been the Washington correspondent of a small group of Southern newspapers, and shown a distinct gift for social reporting. He had carried his writing habit into the Army, with vague thoughts of one day collecting and publishing extracts from his letters for publication. To such a natural scribe, appointment to the Roosevelt White House was a privilege worthy of St.-Simon. Mrs. Butt, a Georgian lady of unreconstructed views, was finding that her son was the best-informed gossip in the United States.

JULY 25, 1908

My dear Mother:
The greatest surprise to me so far has been the utmost simplicity of life at Sagamore Hill. I am constantly asking myself if this can really be the home of the President of the United States, and how is it possible for him to enforce such simplicity in his environment. It might be the home of a well-to-do farmer with literary tastes or the house of some college professor. . . .

There was no one at the house when we got there. Mrs. Roosevelt had been out to see some sick neighbor and the President was playing tennis. They both came in together, however, he in tennis garb and she in a simple white muslin with a large white hat of some cloth material, with flowers in it, a wabbly kind of hat which seemed to go with trees and water. He welcomed us with his characteristic handshake and she most graciously and kindly. The President was so keen for us to take a swim that he did not give us time to see our rooms before we were on the way to the beach.

I do not know when I have enjoyed anything so much. I could not help remarking how pretty and young Mrs. R. looked in her bathing suit. I did not admire his, however, for it was one of those one-piece garments and looked more like a suit of overalls than a bathing suit, and I presume he did not think it dignified for the President to wear one of those abbreviated armless suits which we all think are so becoming. I confess to liking to have as much skin surface in contact with the water as possible.

Dinner was at 8:00 and we hurried home to put on evening clothes. I had asked Mrs. R. if the President dressed for dinner and she said that he always wore his dinner jacket, but to wear anything I wanted, as the only rule they had at Oyster Bay was that they had no rules or regulations. I finally wore white trousers and white waistcoat with the dinner jacket and black tie. He said it was a costume he liked more than any other for summer and that he often wore it himself. He put Mrs. Winthrop on his right, and I sat on his left. There was no special formality, and the only deference which was paid to the President was the fact that all dishes were handed to him first, then to Mrs. Roosevelt, and after that to the guest of honor, and so on.

Miss Ethel was late in coming to dinner and everyone, including the President, rose. From the conversation which followed I learned that it had always been the rule to be on time for their meals, and this remark started the Roosevelt ball rolling. The President said that he thought that Ethel ought to try to be on time, too; that he preferred that no notice be taken of him when he came to his meals late, but that since Mrs. Roosevelt (with a deferential wave of the hand toward her) insisted upon this modicum of respect being paid to the President he always tried to be on time to his meals. Mrs. Roosevelt said that she did not insist upon the mark of respect being shown to the President but to their father, whereupon all laughed, and Ethel said that she would try to be on time to all her meals except breakfast.

I was very hungry and enjoyed my dinner, being helped twice to nearly everything. We had soup, fish, fried chicken, and corn on the cob, and jelly. There was nothing to drink but water. The President asked me if I would have something, but as it was not the custom I declined.

"We often have something," the President said, "so do not hesitate to take what you want. We are not the tipplers that our friends in Wall Street would make us out, but don't mistake us for prohibitionists." . . .

I forgot to mention the fact that the fried chicken was covered with white gravy, and oh, so good! The President said that his mother had always said it was the only way to serve fried chicken; that it gave the gravy time to soak into the meat, and that if the gravy was served separately he never took it.

Ted is now grown up and, while not handsome, has a keen face and is certainly clever and has a splendid sense of humour. Kermit is very attractive in manner and in appearance, and I have an idea that he is his mother's favorite, though of course, she would deny it, just as you do when accused of favouring me over the others. Archie is the one who was so ill, and still looks very delicate. He is the pugnacious member, evidently, for he takes up the cudgel at every chance. Quentin is the youngest, and a large, bouncing youngster, who brought in his last-made kite to show his father, and who explained to me the merits of the newfangled kites for flying purposes, which controversy would not interest you in the least.

There, I have introduced you to the family, and will stop, as lunch is nearly ready, the first bell having been some ten minutes ago. By the way, the bell is a cow bell, just the kind you hear on cows in the cow lot, but sounds just as sweet as any other if one is hungry.

After lunch, the women retired to snooze, Ethel walked her dog, and the boys rowed out to spend the night on the *Mayflower*. Butt and Winthrop sat smoking on the porch with Roosevelt, gazing down the slope of Sagamore Hill to the Sound. There were no other houses to be seen anywhere, just a rich variety of trees lower down, and then nothing but water. The talk naturally drifted to Taft, his impending acceptance speech, and his prospects for election.

Roosevelt admitted to some worries on the last score. "If the people knew Taft there would be no doubt of his election. They know what he has done, but they don't know the man. If they knew him they would know that he can be relied on to carry out the policies which I stand for. He is committed to them just the same as I am and has been made the mouthpiece for them as frequently as I."

Butt said that Taft's major problem was "the residuary legatee idea." However, his legacy also included the President's popularity.

"Yes," Roosevelt said, "I think so."

CAPTAIN BUTT STAYED at Sagamore Hill for four more days, enchanted by the Roosevelt family, while they in turn found him to be unflappable, tireless, well-bred, and discreet. Like the President, he was a heroic trencherman, and matched Roosevelt plate by oversized plate, from double helpings of peaches and cream for breakfast, followed by fried liver and bacon and hominy grits with salt and butter ("Why, Mr. President, this is a Southern breakfast"), through three-course lunches and meat dinners suppurating with fat. "You think me a large eater," Butt wrote in his next letter home. "Well, I am small in comparison to him. But he has a tremendous body and really enjoys each mouthful. I never saw anyone with a more wholesome appetite, and then he complains of not losing flesh. I felt like asking him today: 'How can you expect to?' "

Between meals, there was much strenuous activity. Butt discovered during a midsummer deluge (as Ambassador Jusserand had discovered during a February snowstorm) that Roosevelt considered tennis to be a game for all seasons. The sodden ball was smashed to and fro. Swimming and water-fighting, too, were by their nature compatible with rain. When heat built up in the woods, the President was impelled to seize an ax and get in fuel for the winter. "I think Mr. Roosevelt cuts down trees merely for the pleasure of hearing them fall," Butt wrote. "Just as he swims and plays tennis merely for the pleasure of straining his muscles and shouting. Yet when he reads he has such powers of concentration that he hears no noise around him and is unable to say whether people have been in the room or not."

The President's strenuosity extended even to ghost stories. "I want ghosts who do things. I don't care for the Henry James kind of ghosts. I want real sepulchral ghosts, the kind that knock you over and eat fire . . . none of your weak, shallow apparitions."

Much of Roosevelt's library time that weekend was devoted to books and maps about Africa. He talked about it continually. "You know how you feel when you have all but finished one job and are eager to get at another. Well, that is how I feel. I sometimes feel that I am no longer President, I am so anxious to get on this trip." He hoped that by the time he came down the Nile, to meet up with Edith in Cairo, he would be "sufficiently forgotten" to return home "without being a target for the newspapers."

Winthrop asked what quarry he feared the most in East Africa. The answer came promptly: "You can kill the lion by shooting him in any part of the body, but his alertness and agility make him the most dangerous to me."

Roosevelt moved on to discuss the King of Abyssinia, Albert Beveridge's affectations, Shakespeare's "compressed thought," and the Book of Common Prayer, with interspersed witticisms that had his listeners roaring with laughter. "His humour is so elusive, his wit so dashing and his thoughts so incisive that I find he is the hardest man to quote that I have ever heard talk," Butt wrote. "In conversation he is a perfect flying squirrel, and before you have grasped one pungent thought he goes off on another limb whistling for you to follow."

Despite the President's tendency to dominate every gathering, Butt gradually became aware of "a sort of feminine luminiferous ether" at Sagamore Hill "pervading everything and everybody." Edith Roosevelt's cool discipline held the big crowded house together, as it had the White House. She made no effort to cajole or criticize her children or guests, manipulating them simply by her own quiet example. Over breakfast on Sunday morning, she announced that she and the President were going to church, but expected no one to accompany them unless "conscience" so dictated. Captain Butt, who could take religion or leave it, could also take a hint.

Knowing them both to be Protestant, he ventured an anti-Catholic remark during the automobile ride to Christ Episcopal Church. Roosevelt gave him a quizzical look.

"Archie, when I discuss the Catholic Church, I am reminded that it is the only church which has ever turned an Eastern race into a Christian people. Is that not so?"

Forty little boys saluted as the President led the way into the little church on Shore Road. Captain Butt joined him and Mrs. Winthrop in the front family pew, while Edith, Ethel, and Kermit sat behind. Butt was intrigued to see that Roosevelt, a member of the Dutch Reformed Church, bowed his head in prayer, "just as all good Episcopalians do," before the service started. He needed no prayer book, singing all the plainsong chants and the "Te Deum" by heart. He sang every hymn too, changing sometimes to a lower octave, somewhat surprising for a man whose speaking voice broke so often into falsetto. His only concession to the faith of his fathers, so far as Butt could see, was a refusal to bow his head during the Creed and again at the Gloria. "I came to the conclusion before the service was over that the President was at heart an Episcopalian, whatever his earlier training might have been."

Asked afterward what his favorite hymns were, Roosevelt listed "How Firm a Foundation," followed by "Holy, Holy, Holy," "Jerusalem the Golden," and "The Son of God Goes Forth to War."

He indulged in no sports that afternoon, explaining to Butt that although Sabbath observance meant little to him personally, it meant a lot to many Americans, and he felt an obligation, as President, to respect such common beliefs.

Butt's last day at Sagamore Hill, Tuesday, 28 July, was the eve of William Howard Taft's long-awaited acceptance speech in Cincinnati. Roosevelt again revealed that he was worried about his candidate. He sensed a general "lack of enthusiasm" for the Republican ticket, in contrast to Bryan's gathering strength. The Commoner still impressed him.

"And he is not a charlatan, either: he is a splendid politician and a wonderful leader. He has met with nothing but defeat so far, and yet he is stronger today than ever and will be the hardest man to beat, whatever the papers may say to the contrary."

President and aide sat that night on the porch in a flood of moonlight, talking about many things. Roosevelt confessed another fear, which he had entertained for the past year and a half: that of war with Japan. He did not think it would come soon, but he was sure it would one day.

"No one dreads war as I do, Archie. . . . The little I have seen of it, and I have seen only a little, leaves a horrible picture in my mind."

The surest way to postpone it, he said, was to prepare for it as much as possible, and show evidence of a steely willingness to fight. That was why he had authorized the Great White Fleet to proceed across the Pacific, stopping en route at Yokohama.

TAFT'S SPEECH SEEMED to bear out Roosevelt's belief that he intended "no backward step" from the policies of the current Administration. He pledged himself "to clinch what has already been accomplished at the White House," and said that his chief work would be "to complete and perfect the machinery by which the President's policies may be maintained."

With that, he returned to Hot Springs to complete and perfect the machinery of his golf game, which to the consternation of Republican strategists interested him much more than politics.

Now began what the veteran Philadelphia *Press* reporter Henry L. Stoddard called "a silent boycott of T.R." Roosevelt did not notice it at first, since he bombarded Taft with letters of advice almost daily, and received courteous, if not very forthcoming, replies. Only slowly, as August progressed, did he realize that no Cabinet officers were being summoned to Hot Springs. If Taft had meant what he said about wanting to work with them in future, he was not showing much present interest in their counsel. Neither was he sending for any of the President's state or national lieutenants.

Roosevelt could only assume that Taft wished, quite understandably, to counteract the "residuary legatee" factor. Plump, lovable Will must know what he was doing. If not, the rather less lovable Mrs. Taft certainly did.

THE PRESIDENTIAL CAMPAIGN of 1908 began in earnest after Labor Day. But earnestness did not translate into energy. Ideologically, the two main candidates were hampered by the fact that there was little difference between their respective platforms. The Republican Party was for the protective tariff, but not averse to reforming it; the Democratic Party wanted revision, but shrank from the idea of free trade. Both camps vowed a limited war on monopoly, called for more railroad regulation, and demanded fairer treatment for labor. Theodore Roosevelt may have been excluded physically from the campaign, but its very blandness was testimony to his *de ipse* domination of American politics: he could have written either platform himself.

He fretted, longing to get involved, as he had during his own campaign four years before. "For reasons which I am absolutely unable to fathom," he wrote Elihu Root, "Taft does not arouse the enthusiasm which his record and personality warranted us in believing he ought to arouse." A note of irritation, as of a patron taken too much for granted, colored his continuing advice to the candidate. He stopped just short of giving direct orders:

> You should put yourself prominently and emphatically into this campaign. Also I hope to see everything done henceforth to give the impression that you are working steadily in the campaign. It seems absurd, but I am convinced that the prominence that has been given to your golf playing has not been wise, and from now on I hope that your people will do everything they can to prevent one word being sent out about either your fishing or your playing golf. The American people regard the campaign as a very serious business, and we want to be careful that your opponents do not get the chance to misrepresent you as not taking it with sufficient seriousness.

Without being so tactless as to refer to the widely published image of Taft, in midswing, trying to circumnavigate his own circumference, he warned him to stay away from candid press cameras: "I never let friends advertise my tennis, and never let a photograph of me in tennis costume appear."

He tried to coach Taft in the art of personality projection. "Let the audience see you smile *always,* because I feel that your nature shines out so transparently when you smile—you big, generous, high-minded fellow." But back of the smile, there should be the aggression of a fighter for the right. "Hit at them; challenge Bryan on his record."

As September progressed, with little noticeable change in traditional party loyalties, Roosevelt calmed down. Every vote for the *status quo ante* was a vote for continued GOP dominance of all three branches of government.

Only one discord, an unresolvable one, affected Republican harmony. It was that of Brownsville. The Senate Committee on Military Affairs may have upheld the President's action, and Foraker may have been eliminated as a candidate, but the anger of black voters in such key states as Ohio and New York was potentially threatening to Taft. They did not have to give their support to Bryan to cripple his candidacy; if they were merely solid in refusing to vote at all, he could lose and lose.

Roosevelt got, if not consolation for the major mistake of his presidency, a certain grim satisfaction out of seeing Foraker totally humiliated on 17 September. William Randolph Hearst, stumping for the Independents Party, revealed the existence of letters between Foraker and Standard Oil's John D.

Archbold, going back over a period of years, that amounted to black-and-white proof of a senatorial purchase. Sums as large as fifty thousand dollars were itemized as "fees" and "payments" for vague legal services and "understandings" that clearly involved legislation.

Foraker, devastated, admitted the authenticity of the letters, but claimed that they related to law work only, which he had performed during intersessional times, and before such outside work was frowned upon by the Senate. At least one check—the largest—had been not a payment, but a loan from Standard Oil, to help a colleague buy a newspaper. Hearst had neglected to mention that Foraker had paid Archbold back within a month.

These qualifications, however, had little effect on public outrage. Foraker himself neglected to explain how $150,000 in corporate contributions toward the redecoration of his Washington mansion in no way related to his defense of corporations on Capitol Hill. He was, overnight, a dead man politically, and Roosevelt urged Taft to make the most of his demise. "I would have it understood in detail what is the exact fact, namely, that Mr. Foraker's separation from you and from me has been due not in the least to a difference of opinion on the Negro question, which was merely a pretense. . . . Make a fight openly on the ground that you stood in the Republican party and before the people for the triumph over the forces which were typified by the purchase of a United States Senator to do the will of the Standard Oil Company."

Taft, however, was not a fighter, either open or covert. Lacking aggression, all he wanted was to be loved. For the most part, this need served him well on the hustings. Audiences forgave his lackluster speaking style and warmed to his portly, always cheerful demeanor. When pressing flesh, he discharged none of Roosevelt's galvanizing energy, but instead imparted an unthreatening, gentle glow. He was everybody's favorite fat uncle from childhood, dispensing coins and lollipops.

Bryan's brazen vocal cords were worked to the limit as he crisscrossed the country, meeting large and rapturous audiences wherever he went, and saying little to tax either his or their own mental abilities. But as James Bryce sympathetically observed, "That a man who talks so much should be able to think at all is amazing."

❧

ROOSEVELT RETURNED TO Washington on 23 September and plunged into the only kind of campaign work he could do, barring a request (which never came) to tour on behalf of Taft. He fired off a series of press statements and public letters attacking every candidate in the Democratic ranks who seemed vulnerable to charges of corruption, or any other sins on the calendar of human frailty. His biggest triumph was in causing the resignation of the treasurer of the Democratic campaign, Charles N. Haskell—also on account of links to Standard Oil, which by now was equated in the public mind with Attila's Kingdom of the Huns. That the links had been first announced, again, by Hearst in no way spoiled Roosevelt's satisfaction in having deeply embarrassed Bryan. "How the President does enjoy a fight when there is need of one," James Garfield wrote in his diary.

Taft came to Washington only once, on 18 October. He was fresh from a tour of the Baptist South, and feeling somewhat bruised by the hostility of evangelicals toward his Unitarian faith. Roosevelt sympathetically went to church with him. "I did this," he wrote Kermit, "hoping that it would attract the attention of sincere but rather ignorant Protestants who support me, and would make them tend to support Taft also." It was the first time President and candidate had met since July. Roosevelt was pleased to find Taft, as ever, "just a dear," and confident of victory in a majority of states. Dixie, after all, had never been GOP territory.

The nearest thing to a campaign debate that month was that over the use of injunctions in labor disputes. Unions claimed that corporations had too much power, under existing law, to force strikers back to work, by unduly influencing judges. Samuel Gompers of the AFL castigated the Republican Party for reneging on instructions from Roosevelt himself, earlier in the year, to adopt an anti-injunction plank. But the issue appealed only to a hard core of union voters, and the President neutralized it by publishing one of his typical public letters, accusing Gompers of impugning the integrity of the courts. On 26 October, Roosevelt released another epistle, four thousand words long, summarizing Taft's fair-minded labor policies as a judge in the 1890s and as the Cabinet officer responsible for the well-being of workers in the Panama Canal Zone. He proudly identified himself as an honorary locomotive fireman, and announced that no less a personage than "the secretary-treasurer of the International Brotherhood of Steamshovel and Dredge men" was going to vote Republican.

⌒

THE FOLLOWING DAY, Theodore Roosevelt turned fifty. He celebrated with a solitary ride, jumping all the hurdles in Rock Creek Park. "That is, Roswell jumped them," he wrote Jules Jusserand. "I just sat on his back and admired the scenery."

By now, it was apparent that Taft was going to win, in a victory proportionate to his size if not his stature. Ohio black leaders announced for him, the Republican labor vote remained loyal, and Bryan's search for a last-minute, election-breaking issue failed. The President did not deny himself credit for having turned Taft into an effective campaigner. "I told him he must treat the political audience as one coming, not to see an etching, but a poster," he said to Jusserand and Archie Butt. "He must, therefore, have streaks of blue, yellow, and red to catch the eye, and eliminate all fine lines and soft colors."

Changing the subject, Roosevelt began excitedly to discuss a lecture he had been invited to give at Oxford University after he emerged from Africa. It was to be entitled "Biological Analogies in History," and would discuss the continuance and disappearance of species as illustrative of the limitations of Social Darwinism. He was already deep into paleontological and sociological research. To save time, he was dictating the lecture while Joseph De Camp painted his portrait. He wanted both it and another paper, commissioned by the Sorbonne, to be well in hand before he devoted himself entirely to safari preparations.

Jusserand, who had come to the Executive Office for tea, had to keep listening until almost eight o'clock. Captain Butt was finally permitted to escort him out.

"Was there ever such a man before?" the Ambassador asked.

CHAPTER 32

One Long Lovely Crackling Row

MR. DOOLEY   *Well, I see Congress has got to wurruk again.*
MR. HENNESSY   *Th' Lord save us fr'm harm.*

ON 3 NOVEMBER 1908, Edith Roosevelt was dismayed to hear that Pine Knot had fallen to William Jennings Bryan.

The fake telegram was sent by her husband, radiant over the election of William Howard Taft as twenty-fourth President of the United States. He regarded the vote as a vindication of his own record, and a guarantee of four more years of Rooseveltism. "We have beaten them to a frazzle!" The next morning, he arrived in the Executive Office in high good humor. James Garfield and Captain Butt were waiting to see him. "You army officers and politicians who still have futures before you may continue the struggle," he said, taking his secretary by the hand, "but Mr. Loeb and I will sing the *Nunc Dimittis.*"

Taft's Electoral College majority was overwhelming, at 321 votes over Bryan's 162. He also helped maintain the Republican control of both houses of Congress. His popular plurality was less so—1,269,606 votes over Bryan, a decisive total, but only half as impressive as Roosevelt's landslide in 1904. Missouri reverted to the Democratic Party. Other Republican losses were in Colorado, Nebraska, and Nevada, along with the new state of Oklahoma. Indiana, Minnesota, Montana, North Dakota, and Ohio chose Democratic governors. Charles Evans Hughes retained New York by the merest of whiskers, and Roosevelt began contemptuously referring to him as "the Bearded Lady."

Bryan was gracious, even self-mocking after his third failed run for the White House. He said he identified with the legendary Texan drunk who tried to get into a bar, and was escorted out. Trying again, he was hustled out; trying yet again, he was thrown out. "I guess," said the drunk, brushing dust from his clothes, "they don't want me in there."

ANY HOPES ROOSEVELT might have had that Taft would return to Washington to plot an ideologically continuous transition were disappointed when the President-elect headed straight back to Hot Springs to play golf. In his first public statement after arriving there, he announced, "I really did some great work at sleeping last night."

Meanwhile, Roosevelt was composing an early valedictory for himself, addressed to George Otto Trevelyan:

> Of course, if I had conscientiously felt at liberty to run again and try once more to hold this great office, I should greatly have liked to do so and to keep my hands on the levers of this mighty machine. I do not believe that any President has ever had as thoroly good a time as I have had, or has ever enjoyed himself as much. Moreover I have achieved a greater proportion than I had dared to think possible of the things I most desired to achieve. . . . Whatever comes hereafter, I have had far more than the normal share of human happiness. . . . But I am bound to say in addition that I cannot help looking forward to much enjoyment in the future. In fact, I am almost ashamed to say that while I would have been glad to remain as President, I am wholly unable to feel the slightest regret, the slightest sorrow, at leaving the office. I love the White House; I greatly enjoy the exercise of power; but I shall leave the White House without a pang, and, indeed, on the contrary, I am looking forward eagerly and keenly to being a private citizen again, without anybody being able to make a fuss over me or hamper my movements. I am as interested as I can be at the thought of getting back in my own house at Sagamore Hill, in the thought of the African trip, and of various things I intend to do when that is over.

He was not short of job opportunities. A large corporation offered him its presidency, at a salary of one hundred thousand dollars. The newspaperman Carr V. Van Anda offered him the editorship of a new metropolitan daily, to be formed out of a merger of the New York *Sun* and New York *Press*. The New York *World* suggested that he run for the Senate. Henry Adams thought he should emulate John Quincy Adams and become a Congressman. Philander Knox suggested he be made a bishop, to gratify his need to preach. A New York publisher made "a dazzling offer" for an exclusive on his postpresidential writings. G. P. Putnam's tried to persuade him to complete his historical saga, *The Winning of the West*. Scribner's offered him $25,000 for the story of his African adventure, *McClure's*, $72,000, and *Collier's*, $100,000. Lecture invitations came in sackfuls.

As before with the Nobel Prize, Roosevelt let his conscience, rather than greed, guide him. He had long ago been approached by the father-and-son team of Lyman and Lawrence Abbott to join their magazine, *Outlook,* as a contributing editor writing on current affairs. Lyman, an ordained clergyman with a strong social conscience, had been particularly persuasive. Although *Outlook* was not a wealthy periodical, its middle-class, mildly progressive profile appealed to Roosevelt. He gratefully remembered its support during the crises and controversies of his presidency—support that, by such a definition, had been continuous for seven years. Many magazines less loyal to him now wished to be generous, in exchange for what he could do for their circulation figures. For that reason if for no other, Roosevelt decided to accept *Outlook*'s offer. And in another gesture of loyalty, he signed a first-serial-and-book-rights deal with Charles P. Scribner's Sons for fifty thousand dollars plus 20 percent royalties. In both cases, he could easily have doubled or tripled the money elsewhere. But, as he said to his editor at Scribner's, Robert Bridges, "You have got the same standards of propriety that I have."

The Abbotts proudly announced on 7 November that "on or after the 5ᵗʰ of March, 1909, Theodore Roosevelt will be associated with the *Outlook*'s editorial staff as a special Contributing Editor." Only four days after the election, the President was having to get used to the nude look of his name shorn of any honorific.

Far from being disconcerted, he told Edith that that was how he wanted it styled on his new business cards. She thought *Mr.* would be more dignified. He thought not, and Archie Butt agreed with him.

"I might have known the true Georgians would stand together," she said, laughing. "Why should he not have '*Mr.* Theodore Roosevelt,' as any other gentleman would have on his card?"

"Because he is not like any other gentleman," Butt said.

⟳

MID-NOVEMBER BROUGHT the first snow of the season. It fell, melted a little, then froze slick enough to prevent rides in Rock Creek Park. Roosevelt continued to play singles and doubles with members of the Tennis Cabinet, or, when they were not available, with the ever-willing Archie Butt. He enjoyed the velocity of the ball off the glassy lawn, the sharp air in his lungs, and the exchange of French Revolutionary shouts with his favorite partner, Jules Jusserand. (*"Honneur au courage malheureux!" "À la lanterne!"*) But as the month progressed, he became oddly silent on court, and played with less verve. Butt surmised that he was bracing himself for the return to town of the Sixtieth Congress, and its almost certain hostility to any further attempts at reform.

If so, his pessimism was justified. His last Annual Message, issued on 8 December, was so imperious a call for enhanced executive authority that it amounted to a condemnation of the doctrine of checks and balances. "Concentrated power is palpable, visible, responsible, easily reached, quickly held to account. Power scattered through many administrators, many legislators, many men who work behind and through legislators and administrators, is impalpable, is unseen, is irresponsible, cannot be reached, can not be held to account."

His legislative requests were, for the most part, those of previous years, either strengthened or doggedly renewed: for control ("complete," now) of railroad operations, extended employer's liability and workmen's-compensation laws, an eight-hour day in all government departments, forest protection, and inland-waterway improvements.

The only really new note in Roosevelt's Eighth Message sounded so extreme, not to say eccentric, that it was criticized more as an attack on the courts than as what it really was: a deep and brilliant perception that justice is not a matter of eternal verities, but of constant, case-by-case adaptation to the human prejudices of judges. "Every time they interpret contract, property, vested rights, due process of law, liberty, they necessarily enact into law parts of a system of social philosophy; and as such interpretation is fundamental, they give direction to all lawmaking."

This suggestion that the judicial branch of government was actually a branchlet of the legislative was almost as revolutionary as Roosevelt's claim that concentration of power was democratic. Although he wrote in language considerably more thoughtful than that of his Special Message of the previous January, the mere implications of his words were enough to convince conservatives like Joseph Cannon that the best way to treat the President, as his legislative time ran out, was to ignore him.

Unless, of course, he was being deliberately and flagrantly provocative, as when he suggested, in another paragraph, that congressmen who had voted to limit the activities of the Secret Service "did not themselves wish to be investigated."

⬦

PRESIDENT-ELECT TAFT arrived in town just in time to coincide with the release of the Message and thus present an alternative image—tranquil and uncomplicated—to Roosevelt's perpetual *Sturm und Drang*. He was in reality depressed and wishing that he was headed for the Supreme Court, rather than the White House. But reporters were so beguiled by his winks and chuckles that they saw nothing strange in his unwillingness even to consider Cabinet appointments until February. "I suppose I must do it then."

Roosevelt, beguiled too, told Archie Butt, "He is going to be greatly beloved as President. I almost envy a man who has a personality like Taft's." Then, with a self-mocking leer, "No one could accuse *me* of having a charming personality."

Butt certainly could, after seven months of almost daily exposure to evidence in proof. Pondering the President's remark, he decided that the differ-

"HE WAS IN REALITY DEPRESSED AND WISHING THAT HE
WAS HEADED FOR THE SUPREME COURT."
President-elect William Howard Taft, 1909

ence between Taft and Roosevelt was that of the inanimate versus the ani-
mate. Taft's personality was soothing, "like a huge pan of sweet milk,"
whereas Roosevelt's was galvanic. "When he comes into a room and stands
as he always does for one second before doing something characteristic, he
electrifies the company and gives one just that sensation which a pointer does
when he first quivers and takes a stand on quail."

About the only trait the two men had in common was their shared love of
laughter. In company or alone, they were continually roaring with mirth, Taft
quaking from head to foot, Roosevelt so convulsed that he had to hang on to a
window frame for support. Members of the Gridiron Club had an opportunity
to see them in action on 12 December, as they sat through a skit that satirized
Roosevelt's forthcoming role as a paid-by-the-word foreign journalist.

The lights were doused, and a voice announced, "We are now in Darkest
Africa." After a medley of wild-animal noises, the lights came on again, re-

vealing a tent in a tropical jungle. From inside, came the rattle of a typewriter, punctuated regularly by the sound of a bell that registered not carriage returns, but pecuniary ones. A pair of offstage narrators kept "tab" as Author and Auditor:

AUTHOR   (*typing furiously*) The lion is a wild and ferocious animal.
AUDITOR   Eight dollars.
AUTHOR   It has a soft body and a hard face.
AUDITOR   Seventeen dollars.
AUTHOR   It is the king of beasts and its daughter is a princess.
AUDITOR   Twenty-nine dollars.
AUTHOR   The lion roars like distant thunder.
AUDITOR   Thirty-five dollars.
AUTHOR   But it is nobody's business what its religion is.
AUDITOR   Forty-four dollars.

Roosevelt and Taft guffawed throughout, even when the typed article was followed by another, more serious one, explaining that "Author" had gone to Africa to avoid any appearance of interfering with the Taft Administration.

The Gridiron's exclusively masculine, joke-heavy atmosphere was not conducive to observation of any change in the relationship of President and President-elect. As so often in situations involving transfer of power, it was women who registered the first signals of strain. Edith Roosevelt was upset to hear that Helen Taft intended to replace the White House's frock-coated ushers with liveried black footmen. Mrs. Taft let it be known that she, as a frugal housewife, did not intend to continue the Roosevelt tradition of elaborate entertainments catered from outside. Her guests would be fed out of the White House kitchen, and like it. She also felt that her husband was altogether too much seen as Roosevelt's "creature," and urged him to demonstrate his independence. Alice Longworth, who was a gifted if cruel mimic, mounted her own propaganda by driving out in the Roosevelt surrey and rearranging her face into a terrifying caricature of the toothy Mrs. Taft.

⁓

IN MID-DECEMBER, Washington's social season began with almost nightly receptions, dinners, and balls in and around the White House. The Roosevelts participated graciously, showing no signs of ennui on their eighth procession through the ritual calendar. Yet small signs of impending change darkened each event, like speckles on tired transparencies. Elihu Root announced that he was stepping down as Secretary of State, handing two months of token power over to Robert Bacon. The President's annual Cabinet dinner on 17 December was attended, as usual, by Vice President and Mrs. Fairbanks, but "Sunny Jim" Sherman showed up, too, and so did Philander Knox—no longer as a stalwart of the old Roosevelt Cabinet, but as Taft's rumored replacement for Bacon.

To the President, at least, this rumor did not suggest any abandonment of what he took to be a pledge by Taft to retain as many existing Cabinet officers as possible. He loved Bob Bacon, but the latter's appointment was strictly stopgap. And Root (having been offered a seat in the United States Senate by Republican leaders in New York) would never have stayed on at State. Afterward, talking to Archie Butt, Roosevelt gave his first hint of accepting Taft's right to proceed independently.

"I don't feel any resentment at all," he said. "Only I hope that he will take care of the men who served me here."

⟨—⟩

ALL THE ROOSEVELTS gathered in the White House for a midday Christmas dinner, along with about fifty relatives and close friends. Bamie came with her drowsy husband, now Admiral Cowles, and their son, Sheffield, whose fondness for scrapple had made him an early beneficiary of the Pure Food Law; Alice brought Nick—a rather conflicted congressman these days, being the son-in-law of the President and a protégé of the President-elect; the Lodges were accompanied by their poetic son George Cabot ("Bay") and his wife and family; the Roots were there, and various Meyers and Gardners and McIlhennys and Lowndeses and Eustaces, with their children; a few unattributable urchins, possibly gate-crashers from the White House Gang, seemed perfectly at home; and the indispensable Archie Butt, who had already been informed that the Tafts wished to keep him on, went about his business of observing and recording.

The Executive Dining Room moose looked down impassively on tables decorated with red leaves and ferns and Christmas crackers. Quentin wore a paper crown. Platters of roast turkey went round and round. Brandy-soaked plum puddings were carried in, flickering with blue flame. Little ice-cream Santas followed, each holding a tiny burning taper.

Afterward, gentlemen smoked in the Red Room while the women and children went down into the basement. There, in a specially darkened room, the White House Christmas tree stood out in colored radiance. The Jusserands and Bryces and Cabinet officers and their families came from other parties to give and exchange gifts (a volume of G. K. Chesterton's *Heretics* for Captain Butt), and the President talked politics and kissed whichever child came within reach of his bear hug.

No sooner had the debris of this party been swept up the following morning than preparations began for a much more formal event on the twenty-eighth: the debut ball of Miss Ethel Roosevelt, age seventeen. The East Room's floor was polished until it seemed to hold its own inverted chandeliers. Four hundred and forty-four places were laid at tables extending right down the length of the upper apartments. The glassed-in eastern colonnade, never used before, was turned into a luminous, flower-hung gallery. Clusters of roses perfumed the Blue Room, where expressionless Ethel would stand in her white satin gown.

A few hours before the party began, Captain Butt escorted Alice Longworth through the mansion. It looked more beautiful than either of them could remember. Time was when Alice—almost twenty-five now, filling out sexily, more poised and contemplative than in her wild teens—had made a rebellious point of staying away from the White House, but since marrying she had developed a passionate attachment to it, coming in daily for tea and gossip. Today, she had little to say, but her demeanor struck Archie as "unutterably sad."

⌒

"MR. SPEAKER, *a message from the President of the United States!*"

The traditional call echoed through the House of Representatives on 4 January 1909, in the midst of a furor prompted by Roosevelt's insinuation, one month before, that congressmen did not "wish to be investigated" by the Secret Service. That remark, coming soon after a sly reference to "the criminal classes," had been too much for Senator Aldrich, who had demanded an inquiry into whether the President should be condemned for discourtesy toward Congress. The House had simultaneously challenged Roosevelt to substantiate his words.

So far, the second session of the Sixtieth Congress had been, in Alice's words, "one long lovely crackling row between the White House and Capitol Hill." Her father's Eighth Annual Message had been, for Joseph Cannon, the last of a haystack of straws heaped on the camelback of the Constitution. The Conservation Conference and the Commission on Country Life had been bad enough, he felt; but if any of the significant centralizations of power Roosevelt called for—over the railroads, over telecommunications, over the environment—were made law, states could say good-bye to their individual rights. Progressivism would have finally replaced conservatism, with outright socialism sure to follow.

Cannon sat now, gavel in hand, as yet another Special Message was announced. It elicited such a bedlam of mocking laughter that the Speaker had to pound for order for several minutes. The Message, when read, amounted to a semi-apologetic withdrawal of Roosevelt's perceived insult to Congress. But he persisted in objecting to a House move to confine the Secret Service's activities strictly to presidential protection and the investigation of counterfeiting. Again, he said, such limitation would benefit "the criminal class."

He might also have added, but wisely did not, that the House's sudden prejudice against a venerable federal agency was due to rumors that he had been using the Secret Service for his own purposes over the years, harassing

Senators Foraker and Tillman and other political opponents, gathering espionage for political campaigns, even getting his bodyguards to fetch and carry for him.

There was some substance to these rumors, although evidence of abuse of power was lacking. As *The Atlanta Constitution* pointed out, the Secret Service had been involved in most of Roosevelt's major initiatives, from antitrust probes and peonage prosecutions to pure-food sleuthing and the grilling of Brownsville discharges. Its chief, John E. Wilkie, was a known favorite of the President. The force was tiny—only ten full-time agents—but Wilkie had funds to hire an unlimited number of private detectives for whatever purposes he deemed fit. It was these funds, and these purposes, that anti-Rooseveltians in Congress sought to restrict, conveniently focusing years of resentment against the President for his steady transfer of power away from Capitol Hill.

The Secret Service's necessarily covert nature only fueled the suspicions of conspiracists in politics and the press. Seeking, as conspiracists always do, a central intelligence behind diverse activities, these rumormongers ignored the fact that many other government departments used confidential agents not under Wilkie's or Roosevelt's direct control. The irony was that the President himself wanted to concentrate all such activities in one federal bureau of investigation, answerable to the Attorney General, if not to the general public. So, conspiracism clashed with coordination, and seven years of cumulative frustration exploded in jeers and catcalls.

The chorus unhappily coincided with a debate on the very subjects Roosevelt had raised. After seven hours of mounting rancor, the House handed him a rebuke unprecedented since the days of Andrew Jackson, voting to table his new Message as so much white paper. Thus, little more than eight weeks before the end of his Presidency, Roosevelt reached the nadir of his relations with Congress. But—to his great personal glee—the House's very action made it seem as if it was indeed afraid of an empowered Secret Service, because certain representatives might have things to hide. Effectively if not legislatively, he came out looking like a political winner.

"Nobody likes him now but the people," Ambassador Bryce remarked.

⌒

ARCHIE BUTT WAS amazed at the President's good-humored calm after his rejection by the House. While Mrs. Roosevelt chafed, her husband chuckled at Congressman Longworth's discomfiture. ("Poor Nick! What he is not suffering for love's sake these days!") He was heard laughing heartily over a newspaper transcript of Benjamin Tillman's latest anti-Roosevelt tirade in the Senate, and that night waltzed at a White House ball, happy and flushed as a boy.

Butt wrote home, "I think he sees more clearly than the rest of us do, or else he has no nerves at all."

One legislative request that Congress was powerless to deny him, because of its guarantee of last April, was an appropriation for two more all-big-gun battleships. It came through on 22 January, adding an extra glow of celebration to the White House Army and Navy Reception. Roosevelt could—and did—congratulate himself on having built up a navy second only, now, to that of Great Britain in first-class capital ships, with vastly improved design and marksmanship standards.

All that remained to complete his sense of satisfaction was the return of the Great White Fleet, scheduled for exactly one month's time.

⌒

FEBRUARY—THE MONTH in which Taft had set himself a languid deadline for the appointment of his Cabinet—found Roosevelt showing, for the first time, occasional hints of melancholy. He was saddened to hear that the Ohio Society of New York had declined to drink to his health at its recent annual banquet, presumably because the President-elect's brother was present.

"I do not believe that it was done with a view to aid in the divorcement of Taft and myself, as some friends seem to think," he said to Archie Butt. The captain thought otherwise, but kept silent.

Nothing but disillusioning news had come from the Taft camp for the past several weeks. Of all the current Cabinet, only George von L. Meyer, at latest report, stood a chance of being reappointed. So much for Taft's promise of continuity. Roosevelt, still refusing to believe the worst of his erstwhile laughing companion, went on, as if trying to convince himself: "They little realize that Taft is big enough [!] to carve out his own administration on individual lines. . . . I felt he was the one man for the Presidency, and any failure in it would be as keenly felt by me as by himself or his family." Then, in a revealing free association, he went on, "You have heard some things said against my administration, Archie, but they are nothing to what you will hear when I am completely robbed of power and in Africa. But when the history of this period is written down, I believe my administration will be known as an administration of ideals."

He cheered up in the days that followed, as carpenters invaded the upper floor of the White House and began to box up books and other Washington acquisitions for transfer to Sagamore Hill. Roosevelt went into a distributive frenzy as memento seekers, hearing that he could not resist a sad face, kept making meaningful visits. "Why, Mother," Ethel complained, "he has given away nearly everything in the study, and Aunty Corinne and every other guest in the White House have their arms full of pictures, books, and souvenirs."

Only when the carpenters transferred their hammering and sawing to Lafayette Square, and a review stand for the coming Inaugural Parade rose outside the North Gate, did the realization sink in that he was about to give away the largest memento of all: a presidency immeasurably enhanced in force, glamour, and power.

AT HAMPTON ROADS on 22 February, Roosevelt stood for the last time as Commander-in-Chief on the bridge of the *Mayflower*. He strained his one good eye through a pair of naval binoculars, trying to glimpse what everyone around him saw clearly: distant white superstructures looming through gray rain and fog. "Here they are," he eventually shouted, feeling rather than seeing, as the sound of twenty-eight ships' bands playing "The Star-Spangled Banner" grew in volume, to the rhythmic crash of cannon. The music, the gunpowder, the echelons of saluting bluejackets: all were for him, and for history.

"That is the answer to my critics," he said, his top hat glistening in the wet air. "Another chapter is complete, and I could not ask a finer concluding scene for my administrations."

"I COULD NOT ASK A FINER CONCLUDING SCENE FOR MY ADMINISTRATIONS."
The Great White Fleet returns from its round-the-world trip, 22 February 1909

4 March 1909

AT A TIME when he was still able to joke about his future, William Howard Taft used to say, "It will be a cold day when I go into the White House."

He was right, although he could not have imagined how cold. His Inauguration was the most arctic any Washingtonian could remember. For many of the visitors whose trains managed to scrabble into town, along rails carbuncled with rock-hard ice, it was the worst weather they had known in their

"I KNEW THERE WOULD BE A BLIZZARD WHEN I WENT OUT."
Roosevelt and Taft arriving at the Capitol, 4 March 1909

lives. A brutal west wind drove in billows of snow. Branchloads of ice crashed from trees, some bringing down tangled decorations. Ice sheaths snapped telephone and telegraph wires, cutting off communications with the rest of the country. Freezing rain sent automobiles careening, carriage horses sliding, and streetcars to unscheduled terminals. And the sullen sky discharged such further quantities of snow that groundsmen gave up any attempt to keep the eastern Capitol plaza clear. At eleven o'clock, spectators were told that the swearing-in ceremony was being transferred indoors. Arriving guests had to find their own way to the Senate chamber, and their own seats when they got there. The rough pine platform built for the swearing-in whitened slowly as it stood abandoned, bare of all bunting.

"I knew there would be a blizzard when I went out," said Roosevelt, with grim satisfaction.

He left the White House with Taft at ten o'clock, and they were driven to the Capitol in a twelve-team equipage whipped by flying snow. Pennsylvania Avenue was lined with empty bleachers. A few hundred well-wishers straggled along the sidewalks, walking to keep warm, easily keeping up with the presidential carriage. They cheered occasionally—"Oh, you Teddy!"—but their mood seemed more sad than celebratory. Roosevelt kept dropping his window and waving at them until the snow clouds forced him to raise it again.

Progress was so slow that the procession did not crest Capitol Hill until shortly before eleven. A small, familiar figure awaited Roosevelt and Taft at the foot of the Senate steps: that of Philander Knox, exuding triple dignity as Senator, Secretary of State–designate, and chairman of the congressional welcoming committee. He led the way to the President's Room, where a final bureaucratic duty awaited Roosevelt: the signing of a pile of bills that had been passed overnight. The Sixtieth Congress and he were going out together. There had been precious little else they had done in tandem over the last couple years.

Roosevelt's entire Cabinet was on hand to witness this ritual. Scrupulous to the last, he handed each bill out to the appropriate officer for approval before taking it back and writing his name. Taft, meanwhile, played host to politicians drifting in to pay their respects.

Toward noon, the flow of visitors slowed. Roosevelt finished his work and went to join Taft. They chatted and laughed with much of their old warmth, but a sense of strain was apparent between them. They soon ran out of conversation, and sat side by side in silence until the President got up to bid farewell to a few departing guests.

One of them was Captain Butt, already transferred to Taft's service, and not entirely happy about it. He choked as he tried to say good-bye.

"It isn't good-bye," Roosevelt said to soothe him. "We will meet again, and possibly you will serve me in a more important capacity than the one you have now."

Butt had little time to ponder this strange remark, for Vice President Fairbanks had come through the door with Sherman and announced that the "march" would begin at once.

The hands of the grandfather clock stood at 12:12 as Taft and Roosevelt followed their assigns down the corridor and into the Senate Chamber, where a sudden roar greeted them.

⎯◠⎯

OBSERVERS WERE STRUCK by Roosevelt's immobile concentration as his successor was sworn in. Those who did not know him thought that the stony expression and balled-up fists signaled trouble ahead for Taft. His sister Bamie, describing the scene to Corinne Roosevelt Robinson afterward, got only "the most wonderful feeling of dignity and strength, and people who had really not cared for him suddenly realized what a great man he was." In fact, he was making a special effort not to distract attention from the new President of the United States. An occasional curt nod indicated his approval of points made in Taft's subsequent speech.

Roosevelt's fabled vigor was apparent only at the end, when he bounded out of his seat and ran up the steps of the rostrum to shake Taft by the hand. The two men embraced briefly, then stood talking, their hands on each other's shoulders.

"There was not a dry eye in the place," Bamie wrote, "and everyone's throat contracted; as he said good-bye before anyone realized what was happening he went down the steps from the speakers desk and bowing and smiling went out of the little side door. . . . It was the simplest most dramatic exit imaginable & left the whole packed Senate with a tremor going through it."

⎯◠⎯

THE SNOW HAD stopped falling during the ceremony, and Roosevelt found a large, boisterous crowd of well-wishers waiting for him when he emerged onto the plaza outside. Mounted police tried to hold them back as they surged and roared, "Good-bye, Mr. President!" It was no longer his title, but they were clearly unwilling to give it to another.

William Loeb, Jr., was on hand (as so often before, starting at North Creek in the Adirondacks!) to escort Roosevelt to his train. A drab honor guard of about a thousand New York County Republicans formed a rectangle about the carriage and led the way toward Union Station, to thumping band music, while the crowd followed. The general mood was festive, but when the band segued into "Auld Lang Syne," a sudden valedictory pall descended. Thousands of voices swelled the chorus, and the mass of marchers began to sway to the tune's slow rhythm.

> For auld lang syne, my dear,
> For auld lang syne . . .

Roosevelt, who had been laughing and brandishing his silk hat, lapsed into quietness. Loeb furtively watched him, afraid he might break down. But by the time they arrived at the station, the band had switched to "There'll Be a Hot Time in the Old Town Tonight," and Roosevelt was as jovial as ever.

"Good-bye to you all," he shouted in his high, cracking voice, and leaped out of the carriage the moment it rolled to a halt. Before the crowd could close around him, he had disappeared.

—◦—

EDITH ROOSEVELT RECEIVED him in the new terminal's magnificent President's Room, as yet—and still—unused by any Chief Executive of the United States. Quentin was with her, looking triumphant, because he had managed to sneak into the Capitol without a pass. He and "Taffy" had watched the Inauguration together, squeezed into one seat in the Taft family row.

A special train was waiting, but ice delayed its departure for two wearying hours. Roosevelt was forced to hold an impromptu reception as hundreds of Washington friends and diplomats, including a tearful Jules Jusserand, came to wish him well and—over and over again—"good hunting." Just as frequently, he assured everyone who would listen that he had had "a bully time" as President, but was happy to lay down the burden of office.

Shortly after three o'clock, the railway north was cleared, and Roosevelt passed with his wife and son through a crowd that had swelled to several thousand. The vast station hall reverberated with roars as he waved, flashed his teeth and pince-nez, and disappeared down the platform. At 3:26 on the station register, Theodore Roosevelt officially departed Washington, D.C.

—◦—

THE STORM HAD abated, but with wires down and only hand signals operating for the next thirty miles, the train took more than two hours to get to Baltimore. By then darkness had fallen, and Roosevelt did not show himself, as if to emphasize to a small, wistful crowd that he was no longer public property.

Seven years and a hundred and sixty-nine days before, on another lowering evening, he had come south along this same track, eager to begin work as President of the United States. For all his show of grief for McKinley, and natural nervous tension, he had been happy then, as he was happy now; happy at the large things he had managed to achieve—a canal, a coal-strike settlement, a peace treaty, a national conservation conference—contented with myriad smaller triumphs, proud of his appointees, passionate about his country, in love with his wife and children; many-friended, much-honored, lusty in his physical and intellectual appetites, constantly bubbling with mirth; happy, above all, at having kept his promise not to hold on too long to power. Brownsville had been proof to many, and perhaps even a warning to himself, of the truth of Lord Acton's famous dictum.

Already, in his fifty-first year, epitaphs of him were beginning to appear, distressingly written in the past historic, from H. G. Wells's claim that he seemed "a very symbol of the creative will in man" to Henry Adams's "Roosevelt, more than any other man living within the range of notoriety, showed the singular primitive quality that belongs to ultimate matter—the quality that medieval theology assigned to God—he was pure act."

In time, no doubt, the inevitable memorial committee would form, and solemn scholars would comb his works for quotations suitable to chisel in stone. Statute books and official histories would celebrate his administrative achievements: the Monroe Doctrine reaffirmed, the Old World banished from the New World, the great Canal being cut; peace established in the Far East; the Open Door swinging freely in Manchuria and Morocco; Cuba liberated (and returned to self-government just in time for his departure); the Philippines pacified; the Navy hugely strengthened, known literally around the world; the Army, shorn of its old deadwood generals, feeling the green sap of younger replacements; capital and labor balanced off, the lynch rate declining, the gospel of cleaner politics now *actually* gospel, and enough progressive principles established, or made part of the national debate, to keep legislative reformers busy for at least ten years.

But for millions of contemporary Americans, he was already memorialized in the eighteen national monuments and five national parks he had created by executive order, or cajoled out of Congress. The "inventory," as Gifford Pinchot would say, included protected pinnacles, a crater lake, a rain forest and a petrified forest, a wind cave and a jewel cave, cliff dwellings, a cinder cone and skyscraper of hardened magma, sequoia stands, glacier meadows, and the grandest of all canyons.

Less solidly but equally enduringly, he left behind a folk consensus that he had been the most powerfully positive American leader since Abraham Lincoln. He had spent much of his two terms crossing and recrossing the country, east and west, south and north, reminding anyone who would listen to him that he embodied all America's variety and the whole of its unity; that what he had made of his own life was possible to all, even to boys born as sickly as himself. Uncounted men, women, and children who had crowded around the presidential caboose to stare and listen to him now carried, forever etched in memory, the image of his receding grin and wave.

ACKNOWLEDGMENTS

PORTIONS OF THE manuscript of *Theodore Rex* were written at the Woodrow Wilson International Center for Scholars, Washington, D.C., and in the research library of the Theodore Roosevelt Birthplace National Historic Site, New York City. The author expresses his great debt to these two institutions. He also thanks the following people for helping him in ways more than ordinary: Daniel J. Boorstin; David Burnham; Michael Cahill; William Chanler; Karen Chapel; Catherine Cook; Wallace Finley Dailey; Amanda Deaver; George Didden III; Maurice F. X. Donohue; Philip Dunne; G. Thomas Edwards; Allen Fitz-Gerald; Jeff Flannery; Stephen Fox; Rob Friedman; David Gerstner; Ann Godoff; Julie Grau; Sharon Harris, translator; Paul T. Heffron; Stephen B. Hess; Mia Kazanjian; Dave Kelly; Michael P. Lacey; Alton A. Lindsay; Robert Loomis; Henry Luce III; Margaret Fox Mandel; Thomas Mann; Albro Martin; Alison Martin; John M. Mason; Robert K. Massie; Lyle McGeoch; Bruce K. MacLaury; Charles Moose; Sylvia Jukes Morris; Angela Orcken; John Gray Peatman; Christina Rae; P. James Roosevelt; W. S. Sims; Brad Smith; Kathy Smith; Mary E. Smith; Michael D. Sternfeld; Joanna Sturm; Robert N. Walton; and John D. Weaver.

John Allen Gable is especially thanked for a scholarly review of the manuscript, and the services of Rebecca Kramer and Timothy Mennel are remembered with profound gratitude.

ARCHIVES

Unless otherwise noted, collections are held in the Library of Congress, Washington, D.C.

ABP   Alton B. Parker Papers

AC   Author's Collection, Washington, D.C.

ADW   Andrew Dickson White Papers, Olin Library, Cornell University, Ithaca, N.Y.

AJB   Albert J. Beveridge Papers

ARL   Alice Roosevelt Longworth Papers

AS   Albert Shaw Papers, Manuscript Division, New York Public Library (NYPL)

BTW   Booker T. Washington Papers

CS   Carl Schurz Papers

CSR   Cecil Spring Rice Papers, Churchill College, Cambridge, U.K.

EMH   Edwin M. Hood Papers

ER   Elihu Root Papers

ERD   Ethel Roosevelt Derby Papers, privately held (now in TRC, below)

ES   Emily Stewart Papers

EWC   Edward W. Carmack Papers, Tennessee State Library and Archives, Nashville, Tenn.

FBJ   Frances Benjamin Johnston Collection

FBL   Francis B. Loomis Papers, Hoover Institution, Stanford, Calif.

FMcC   Frank McCoy Papers

GC   Grover Cleveland Papers

GD   George Dewey Papers

GBC   George B. Cortelyou Papers

GVM   George von Lengerke Meyer Papers

GWP   George Walbridge Perkins Papers, Butler Library, Columbia University, New York, N.Y.

HBP   Harold Brayman Papers, University of Delaware Library, Newark, Del.

HH	Hermann Hagedorn Papers, TRB (below)
HJ	Henry James Papers, Houghton Library, Harvard University, Cambridge, Mass.
HKB	Howard K. Beale Papers, Mudd Library, Princeton University, Princeton, N.J.
HMD	Sir H. Mortimer Durand Papers, School of Oriental and African Studies Library, London University, U.K.
HP	Henry Pringle Papers, Houghton Library, Harvard University, Cambridge, Mass.
HW	Henry Watterson Papers
JB	John Barrett Papers
JBM	John Bassett Moore Papers
JCOL	John C. O'Laughlin Papers
JCS	John Coit Spooner Papers
JH	John Hay Papers, Hay Library, Brown University, Providence, R.I.
JHC	Joseph Hodges Choate Papers
JHW	James H. Wilson Papers
JJ	Jules Jusserand Papers, Archives of the French Foreign Ministry, Quai d'Orsay, Paris, France
JM	John Mitchell Papers, Catholic University, Washington, D.C.
JRG	James R. Garfield Papers
JSC	James S. Clarkson Papers
JTM	John Tyler Morgan Papers
KR	Kermit Roosevelt Papers
LCG	Lyman C. Gage Papers
LG	Lloyd C. Griscom Papers
LW	Leonard Wood Papers
MHM	Mark Hanna McCormick Family Papers
MHS	Massachusetts Historical Society, Cambridge, Mass.
MS	Mark Sullivan Papers, Hoover Institution, Stanford, Calif.
MST	Moorfield Storey Papers
NA	The National Archives, Washington, D.C.
NWA	Nelson W. Aldrich Papers
NYHS	The New-York Historical Society, New York, N.Y.
OSS	Oscar S. Straus Papers
PB	Poultney Bigelow Papers, Manuscript Division, NYPL
PBV	Philippe Bunau-Varilla Papers
PCJ	Philip C. Jessup Papers
PCK	Philander Chase Knox Papers
RLF	Robert M. LaFollette Papers
RO	Richard Olney Papers
RSB	Ray Stannard Baker Papers
SH	Sagamore Hill National Historic Site Archives, Oyster Bay, N.Y.

TAB	Theodore A. Bingham Papers
TD	Tyler Dennett Papers
TH	Tomás Herrán Papers, Lauinger Library, Georgetown University, Washington, D.C.
TRAF	Theodore Roosevelt Association Film Collection, Motion Picture Division
TRB	Theodore Roosevelt Birthplace National Historic Site Archives, New York, N.Y.
TRC	Theodore Roosevelt Collection, Widener and Houghton Libraries, Harvard University, Cambridge, Mass.
TRJR	Theodore Roosevelt, Jr., Papers
TRP	Theodore Roosevelt Papers
WF	Wadsworth Family Papers
WAW	William Allen White Papers
WHM	William H. Moody Papers
WHT	William Howard Taft Papers
WVD	Willis Van Devanter Papers

SELECT BIBLIOGRAPHY

The following published sources are referred to in more than
one chapter. Other sources are cited in passing.

The standard bibliographies of Theodore Roosevelt are:
Dewey W. Grantham, Jr., "Theodore Roosevelt in American
Historical Writing, 1945–1960," *Mid-America* 43.1 (1961);
Richard H. Collin, "The Image of Theodore Roosevelt in Amer-
ican History and Thought, 1885–1965" (Ph.D. diss., New York
University, 1966); Gregory C. Wilson, comp., *Theodore Roo-
sevelt Collection: Dictionary Catalogue and Shelflist*, 5 vols.,
with an important one-volume *Supplement*, Wallace Finley Dai-
ley, comp. (Cambridge, Mass., 1970, 1986); and John Allen
Gable, "Theodore Roosevelt: A Selected Annotated Bibliogra-
phy," in Natalie A. Naylor, Douglas Brinkley, and John Allen
Gable, *Theodore Roosevelt: Many-Sided American* (Interlaken,
N.Y., 1992).

DOCUMENTS

Anthracite Coal Commission. *Report to the President on the Anthracite Coal Strike of
May–October 1902*. Washington, D.C., 1903.

*British Documents on Foreign Affairs: Reports and Papers from the Foreign Office
Confidential Print*. Series C: *North America, 1837–1914*. Ed. Kenneth Bourne.
Frederick, Md., 1986–1987.

*Campaign Contributions: Testimony Before a Subcommittee of the [Senate] Commit-
tee of Privileges and Elections*. 62 Cong., sess. 2. Washington, D.C., 1913.

Conditions in the Chicago Stockyards: Message of the President of the United States.
59 Cong., sess. 1, H. doc. 873. 1906.

Die Grosse Politik der Europäischen Kabinette, 1871–1914. Berlin, 1922–1927.

Documents diplomatiques français (1871–1914). Paris, 1929–1959.

*Official Proceedings of the 13th Republican National Convention in the City of
Chicago, June 21, 22, 23, 24, 1904*. Minneapolis, 1904.

*Official Report of the Proceedings of the Fourteenth Republican National Conven-
tion*. Columbus, Ohio, 1908.

Proceedings of a Conference of Governors in the White House, May 13–15, 1908. Washington, D.C., 1909.

Proceedings of the Anthracite Coal Commission. Washington, D.C., 1903.

Republican Campaign Textbook. New York, 1904.

"Resignation of the Postmaster." 57 Cong., sess. 2, vol. 9, H. doc. 42. 1903.

Roosevelt vs. Newett: A Transcript of the Testimony Taken and Depositions Read at Marquette, Michigan, May 26–31, 1913. Privately printed, 1914 (copy in TRB).

Summary Discharge or Mustering Out of Regiments or Companies: Message of the President of the United States. Washington, D.C., 1908.

The Story of Panama: Hearings on the Rainey Resolution Before the Committee on Foreign Affairs of the House of Representatives. Washington, D.C., 1913.

United States Department of State. *Papers Relating to the Foreign Relations of the United States.* Washington, D.C., annual.

Books

Abbott, Lawrence F. *Impressions of Theodore Roosevelt.* New York, 1919.

Adams, Henry. *The Education of Henry Adams* (Boston, 1918). Modern Library edition. New York, 1996.

———. *The Letters of Henry Adams.* Ed. J. C. Levenson, Ernest Samuels, et al. Cambridge, Mass., 1982–1988.

Alfonso, Oscar M. *Theodore Roosevelt and the Philippines.* New York, 1974.

Bailey, Thomas A. *Theodore Roosevelt and the Japanese-American Crises.* Stanford, 1934.

Baker, Ray Stannard. *American Chronicle.* New York, 1945.

Barry, David S. *Forty Years in Washington.* Boston, 1924.

Bazalgette, Léon. *Théodore Roosevelt.* Paris, 1905 (copy in TRB).

Beale, Howard K. *Theodore Roosevelt and the Rise of America to World Power.* Baltimore, 1956.

Beer, Thomas. *Hanna, Crane, and the Mauve Decade.* New York, 1941.

Beisner, Robert L. *Twelve Against Empire: The Anti-Imperialists, 1898–1900.* New York, 1968.

Bemis, Samuel Flagg. *The American Secretaries of State and Their Diplomacy.* New York, 1927–1929.

Bishop, Joseph Bucklin. *Theodore Roosevelt and His Time: Shown in His Own Letters.* New York, 1920.

Blum, John M. *The Republican Roosevelt.* Cambridge, Mass., 1954.

Bolles, Blair. *Tyrant from Illinois: Uncle Joe Cannon's Experiment with Personal Power.* New York, 1951.

Bunau-Varilla, Philippe. *From Panama to Verdun: My Fight for France.* Philadelphia, 1940.

———. *Panama: The Creation, Destruction, and Resurrection.* London, 1933.

Burroughs, John. *Camping and Tramping with Roosevelt*. Boston, 1907.

Busbey, L. White. *Uncle Joe Cannon: The Story of a Pioneer American*. New York, 1927.

Butler, Nicholas Murray. *Across the Busy Years: Recollections and Reflections*. New York, 1939.

Butt, Archibald W. *The Letters of Archie Butt: Personal Aide to President Roosevelt*. New York, 1924.

Cassini, Marguerite. *Never a Dull Moment*. New York, 1956.

Chandler, Jr., Alfred P. *The Visible Hand: The Managerial Revolution in American Business*. Cambridge, Mass., 1977.

Cheney, Albert Loren. *Personal Memoirs of the Home Life of the Late Theodore Roosevelt*. Washington, D.C., 1919.

Clark, Champ. *My Quarter Century in American Politics*. New York, 1920.

Clymer, Kenton J. *John Hay: The Gentleman as Diplomat*. Ann Arbor, 1975.

Commons, John R., et al. *History of Labor in the United States, 1896–1932*. New York, 1935.

Cornell, Robert J. *The Anthracite Coal Strike of 1902*. Washington, D.C., 1957.

Croly, Herbert. *Marcus Alonzo Hanna*. New York, 1912.

Cutright, Paul Russell. *Theodore Roosevelt: The Making of a Conservationist*. Urbana, 1985.

Davis, Oscar K. *Released for Publication: Some Inside Political History of Theodore Roosevelt and His Times, 1898–1918*. Boston, 1925.

Dawes, Charles G. *A Journal of the McKinley Years*. Chicago, 1950.

Dennett, Tyler. *John Hay: From Poetry to Politics*. New York, 1933.

———. *Roosevelt and the Russo-Japanese War*. New York, 1925.

Dennis, Alfred P. *Adventures in American Diplomacy, 1896–1906*. New York, 1928.

Dorwart, Jeffrey M. *The Office of Naval Intelligence: The Birth of America's First Intelligence Agency, 1865–1918*. Annapolis, 1979.

Douglas, George William. *The Many-Sided Roosevelt: An Anecdotal Biography*. New York, 1907.

Dunn, Arthur Wallace. *From Harrison to Harding*. New York, 1922.

———. *Gridiron Nights*. New York, 1915.

Dunne, Finley Peter. *Mr. Dooley's Philosophy*. New York, 1900.

———. *Observations by Mr. Dooley*. New York, 1902.

Dunne, Philip, ed. *Mr. Dooley Remembers: The Informal Memoirs of Finley Peter Dunne*. Boston, 1963.

DuVal, Miles P. *And the Mountains Will Move*. Stanford, 1947.

———. *Cadiz to Cathay: The Story of the Long Struggle for a Waterway across the American Isthmus*. Stanford, 1940.

Dyer, Thomas G. *Theodore Roosevelt and the Idea of Race*. Baton Rouge, 1980.

Esthus, Raymond A. *Theodore Roosevelt and Japan*. Seattle, 1966.

Faulkner, Harold U. *The Decline of Laissez-Faire, 1897–1917*. New York, 1951.

Fleming, Thomas. *Around the Capitol.* New York, 1902.

Foraker, Joseph Benson. *Notes of a Busy Life.* Cincinnati, 1916.

Foraker, Julia Bundy. *I Would Live It Again: Memories of a Vivid Life.* New York, 1932.

Fowler, Dorothy Canfield. *John Coit Spooner, Defender of Presidents.* New York, 1961.

Fox, Stephen R. *John Muir and His Legacy: The American Conservation Movement.* Boston, 1981.

Gatewood, Jr., Willard B. *Theodore Roosevelt and the Art of Controversy: Episodes of the White House Years.* Baton Rouge, 1970.

Gould, Lewis L. *The Presidency of Theodore Roosevelt.* Lawrence, Kans., 1991.

———. *Reform and Regulation: American Politics, 1900–1916.* New York, 1978.

Grenville, John A. S., and George B. Young. *Politics, Strategy, and American Diplomacy: Studies in Foreign Policy, 1873–1917.* New Haven, 1966.

Griscom, Lloyd C. *Diplomatically Speaking.* Boston, 1940.

Gwynn, Stephen, ed. *The Letters and Friendships of Cecil Spring Rice: A Record.* Boston, 1929.

Hagedorn, Hermann. *The Roosevelt Family of Sagamore Hill.* New York, 1954.

Harbaugh, William H. *The Life and Times of Theodore Roosevelt.* Rev. ed. New York, 1975.

Harlan, Louis J. *Booker T. Washington: The Wizard of Tuskegee, 1901–1915.* New York, 1983.

Hay, John. *Letters and Extracts from His Diary.* Ed. Henry Adams. Privately printed, 1908.

Hays, Samuel P. *Conservation and the Gospel of Efficiency: The Progressive Conservation Movement, 1890–1920.* Cambridge, Mass., 1959.

Healy, David. *The United States in Cuba: 1898–1902.* Madison, 1963.

Hill, Howard C. *Roosevelt and the Caribbean.* Chicago, 1927.

Howe, M. A. De Wolfe. *George von Lengerke Meyer: His Life and Public Services.* New York, 1919.

———. *Justice Oliver Wendell Holmes, 1841–1882.* Cambridge, Mass., 1957–1963.

Jessup, Philip C. *Elihu Root.* 2 vols. New York, 1938.

Jusserand, Jean Jules. *What Me Befell: The Reminiscences of Jean Jules Jusserand.* Boston, 1933.

Kantrowitz, Stephen. *Ben Tillman and the Reconstruction of White Supremacy.* Chapel Hill, 2000.

Kerr, Joan Paterson, ed. *A Bully Father: Theodore Roosevelt's Letters to His Children.* New York, 1995.

Klein, Maury. *The Life and Legend of E. H. Harriman.* Chapel Hill, 2000.

Kohlsaat, Herman H. *From McKinley to Harding: Personal Recollections of Our Presidents.* New York, 1923.

Kolko, Gabriel. *The Triumph of Conservatism: A Reinterpretation of American History, 1900–1916.* New York, 1963.

LaFollette, Robert M. *LaFollette's Autobiography* (Madison, 1913). Rev. ed. Ed. Allan Nevins. Madison, 1960.

Lamoreaux, Naomi. *The Great Merger Movement in American Business, 1895–1904.* New York, 1985.

Lane, Ann J. *The Brownsville Affair: National Crisis and Black Reaction.* Port Washington, N.Y., 1971.

Lee, Arthur, Viscount of Fareham. *A Good Innings.* Privately printed, London, 1939.

Leopold, Richard. *Elihu Root and the Conservative Tradition.* Boston, 1954.

Leupp, Francis E. *The Man Roosevelt: A Portrait Sketch.* New York, 1904.

Lodge, Henry Cabot. *Selections from the Correspondence of Theodore Roosevelt and Henry Cabot Lodge, 1884–1918.* New York, 1925.

Longworth, Alice Roosevelt. *Crowded Hours: Reminiscences of Alice Roosevelt Longworth.* New York, 1933.

Looker, Earle. *The White House Gang.* New York, 1929.

Lowry, Edward G. *Washington Close-Ups: Intimate Views of Some Public Figures.* Boston, 1921.

McCullough, David. *The Path Between the Seas.* New York, 1977.

Marks, III, Frederick W. *Velvet on Iron: The Diplomacy of Theodore Roosevelt.* Lincoln, Nebr., 1979.

Martin, Albro. *James J. Hill and the Opening of the Northwest.* New York, 1976.

Merrill, Horace, and Marion Merrill. *The Republican Command, 1897–1913.* Lexington, Ky., 1971.

Miller, Donald, and Richard E. Sharpless. *The Kingdom of Coal: Work, Enterprise, and Ethnic Communities in the Mine Fields.* Philadelphia, 1985.

Miller, Stuart Creighton. *"Benevolent Assimilation": The American Conquest of the Philippines, 1899–1903.* New Haven, 1983.

Miner, Dwight C. *The Fight for the Panama Route.* New York, 1940.

Moore, J. Hampton. *Roosevelt and the Old Guard.* Philadelphia, 1925.

Morison, Elting E., ed. *Cowboys and Kings: Three Great Letters by Theodore Roosevelt.* Cambridge, Mass., 1954.

Morris, Edmund. *The Rise of Theodore Roosevelt.* New York, 1979.

Morris, Sylvia Jukes. *Edith Kermit Roosevelt: Portrait of a First Lady.* New York, 1980.

Mowry, George E. *The Era of Theodore Roosevelt, 1900–1912.* New York, 1958.

Munro, Dana G. *Intervention and Dollar Diplomacy in the Caribbean, 1900–1921.* Princeton, N.J., 1964.

O'Gara, Gordon C. *Theodore Roosevelt and the Rise of the Modern Navy.* Princeton, 1969.

Palmer, Frederick. *With My Own Eyes.* Indianapolis, 1932.

Parsons, Frances Theodora (Smith). *Perchance Some Day.* Privately printed, New York, 1951 (copy in TRC).

Pinkett, Harold T. *Gifford Pinchot: Public and Private Forester.* Urbana, 1970.

Powers, Samuel Leland. *Portraits of Half a Century.* Boston, 1925.

Pringle, Henry F. *Theodore Roosevelt: A Biography.* New York, 1931.

Putnam, Carleton. *Theodore Roosevelt: The Formative Years.* New York, 1958.

Putnam, George Haven. *Memories of a Publisher.* New York, 1915.

Richardson, James D., ed. *A Compilation of the Messages and Papers of the Presidents.* Washington, D.C., 1911.

Rippy, J. Fred. *The Caribbean Danger Zone.* New York, 1940.

Rixey, Lilian. *Bamie: Theodore Roosevelt's Remarkable Sister.* New York, 1963.

Robbins, Roy M. *Our Landed Heritage: The Public Domain, 1776–1936.* Princeton, N.J., 1942.

Robinson, Corinne Roosevelt. *My Brother, Theodore Roosevelt.* New York, 1921.

Röhl, John C. G., ed. *Kaiser Wilhelm II: New Interpretations—The Corfu Papers.* Cambridge, 1982.

Roosevelt, Kermit. *The Happy Hunting-Grounds.* New York, 1920.

Roosevelt, Theodore. *An Autobiography.* New York, 1913.

———. *California Addresses, by President Roosevelt.* San Francisco, 1903.

———. *The Letters of Theodore Roosevelt.* Ed. Elting E. Morison. Cambridge, Mass., 1951.

———. *Letters to Kermit from Theodore Roosevelt, 1902–1908.* New York, 1946.

———. *Presidential Addresses and State Papers.* New York, 1910.

———. *The Works of Theodore Roosevelt.* Memorial Edition. New York, 1923–1926. [On rare occasions, the National Edition (New York, 1926) is necessarily cited.]

Rothman, David J. *Politics and Power: The Senate, 1869–1901.* Cambridge, Mass., 1966.

Satterlee, Herbert L. *J. Pierpont Morgan.* New York, 1975.

Schirmer, Daniel B. *Republic or Empire: American Resistance to the Philippine War.* Cambridge, Mass., 1972.

Schlesinger, Jr., Arthur M., and Fred L. Israel, eds. *History of American Presidential Elections, 1789–1968.* New York, 1971.

Scott, James Brown. *Robert Bacon: Life and Letters.* New York, 1923.

Seale, William. *The President's House.* Washington, D.C., 1986.

Simkins, Francis B. *Pitchfork Ben Tillman.* Baton Rouge, 1944.

Slayden, Ellen Maury. *Washington Wife: Journal of Ellen Maury Slayden from 1897–1919.* New York, 1963.

Spector, Ronald. *Admiral of the New Empire: The Life and Career of George Dewey.* Baton Rouge, 1974.

Steffens, Lincoln. *The Autobiography of Lincoln Steffens.* New York, 1931.

Stephenson, Nathaniel W. *Nelson W. Aldrich: A Leader in American Politics.* New York, 1930.

Still, William N. *American Sea Power in the Old World: The United States Navy in Europe and Near Eastern Waters, 1815–1917.* Westport, Conn., 1980.

Stoddard, Henry L. *As I Knew Them: Presidents and Politics from Grant to Coolidge.* New York, 1927.

Straus, Oscar S. *Under Four Administrations: From Cleveland to Taft.* Boston, 1922.

Strouse, Jean. *Morgan: American Financier.* New York, 1999.

Sullivan, Mark. *Our Times.* New York, 1926–1935.

Teague, Michael. *Mrs. L.: Conversations with Alice Roosevelt Longworth.* New York, 1981.

Thayer, William Roscoe. *The Life and Letters of John Hay.* New York, 1915.

Thomas, Addison C. *Roosevelt among the People: Being an Account of the 14,000 Mile Journey from Ocean to Ocean of Theodore Roosevelt, 26th President of the United States.* Chicago, 1910.

Thompson, Charles Willis. *Party Leaders of the Time.* New York, 1906.

Thorelli, Hans B. *Federal Antitrust Policy.* Baltimore, 1955.

Tilchin, William N. *Theodore Roosevelt and the British Empire: A Study in Presidential Statecraft.* New York, 1997.

Trani, Eugene P. *The Treaty of Portsmouth: An Adventure in American Diplomacy.* Lexington, Ky., 1969.

Vagts, Alfred. *Deutschland und die vereinigten Staaten in der Weltpolitik.* New York, 1935.

Villard, Oswald Garrison. *Fighting Years: Memoirs of a Liberal Editor.* New York, 1939.

Wagenknecht, Edward. *The Seven Worlds of Theodore Roosevelt.* New York, 1958.

Washington, Booker T. *The Booker T. Washington Papers.* Ed. Louis R. Harlan. Urbana, 1972–1989.

Watson, James E. *As I Knew Them: Memoirs.* Indianapolis, 1936.

Weaver, John D. *The Brownsville Raid.* College Station, 1992.

———. *The Senator and the Sharecropper's Son: Exoneration of the Brownsville Soldiers.* College Station, 1997.

Welch, Jr., Richard E. *Response to Imperialism: The United States and the Philippine-American War, 1899–1902.* Chapel Hill, 1979.

White, William Allen. *Autobiography.* New York, 1946.

———. *Masks in a Pageant.* New York, 1928.

Willets, Gibson. *Inside History of the White House.* New York, 1906.

Wilson, Woodrow. *The Papers of Woodrow Wilson.* Ed. Arthur S. Link. Princeton, N.J., 1966–1994.

Wimmel, Kenneth. *Theodore Roosevelt and the Great White Fleet: American Sea Power Comes of Age.* Dulles, Va., 1998.

Wister, Owen. *Roosevelt: The Story of a Friendship.* New York, 1930.

Wolf, Simon. *The Presidents I Have Known from 1860–1918.* Washington, D.C., 1918.

Wood, Frederick S. *Roosevelt As We Knew Him: The Personal Recollections of One Hundred and Fifty of His Friends and Associates.* Philadelphia, 1927.

Zabriskie, Edward H. *American-Russian Rivalry in the Far East: A Study in Diplomacy and Power Politics, 1895–1914.* Philadelphia, 1946.

ARTICLES

Ameringer, Charles D. "Philippe Bunau-Varilla: New Light on the Panama Canal Treaty," *Hispanic American Historical Review* 46 (1966).

Blake, Nelson M. "Ambassadors at the Court of Theodore Roosevelt." *Mississippi Valley Historical Review,* Sept. 1955.

Burton, David H. "Theodore Roosevelt and His English Correspondents: A Special Relationship of Friends." *Transactions of the American Philosophical Society,* new series, vol. 63, pt. 2 (1973).

Friedlander, Robert A. "A Reassessment of Roosevelt's Role in the Panamanian Revolution." *Western Political Quarterly* 14 (1961).

Gow, Douglas R. "How Did the Roosevelt Corollary Become Linked to the Dominican Republic?" *Mid-America* 58 (1976).

Heffron, Paul T. "Theodore Roosevelt and the Appointment of Mr. Justice Moody." *Vanderbilt Law Review* 18.2 (1965).

Johnson, Arthur M. "Theodore Roosevelt and the Bureau of Corporations." *Mississippi Valley Historical Review,* Mar. 1959.

Livermore, Seward W. "Theodore Roosevelt, the American Navy, and the Venezuela Crisis of 1902–1903." *American Historical Review,* Apr. 1946.

Meyer, Balthazar H. "A History of the Northern Securities Case." *Bulletin of the University of Wisconsin Economics and Political Science Series* 1.3 (1904–1906).

Morris, Edmund. " 'A Few Pregnant Days': Theodore Roosevelt and the Venezuelan Crisis of 1902." *Theodore Roosevelt Association Journal,* winter 1989.

Murakata, Akiko. "Theodore Roosevelt and William Sturgis Bigelow: The Story of a Friendship." *Harvard Library Bulletin* 23.1 (1975).

Nikol, John, and Francis Holbrook. "Naval Operations in the Panama Revolution of 1903." *American Neptune* 38 (Oct. 1977).

Schoenberg, Philip E. "The American Reaction to the Kishinev Pogrom of 1903." *American Jewish Historical Quarterly,* Mar. 1974.

Schoonover, Thomas. "Max Farrand's Memorandum on the U.S. Role in the Panamanian Revolution of 1903." *Diplomatic History,* fall 1988.

Wiebe, Robert H. "The Anthracite Coal Strike of 1902: A Record of Confusion." *Mississippi Valley Historical Review,* Sept. 1961.

Ziglar, William L. "The Decline of Lynching in America." *International Social Science Review* 63 (1988).

MISCELLANEOUS

Baer, George. "Statement Regarding the Anthracite Strike," 10 June 1902. Copy in GWP.

Dunne, Finley Peter. "Remembrances." Autobiographical fragment in FPD.

Eitler, A. T. "Philander Chase Knox." Ph.D. diss. Catholic University, 1959.

Fletcher, William Glover. "Canal Site Diplomacy: A Study in American Political Geography." Ph.D. diss. Yale University, 1940.

Forman, Henry J. "So Brief a Time." Oral history conducted by Doyce B. Nunis, Department of Special Collections, Young Research Library, UCLA (1959–1960).

Hourihan, William J. "Roosevelt and the Sultans: The United States Navy in the Mediterranean, 1904." Ph.D. diss. Northeastern University, 1975.

Lacey, Michael J. "The Mysteries of Earth-Making Dissolve: A Study of Washington's Intellectual Community and the Origins of American Environmentalism in the Late Nineteenth Century." Ph.D. diss. George Washington University, 1979.

Larsen, Peter. "Theodore Roosevelt and the Moroccan Crisis, 1904–1905." Ph.D. diss. Princeton University, 1984.

Rinke, Stefan H. "Between Success and Failure: The Diplomatic Career of Ambassador Hermann Speck von Sternburg and German-American Relations, 1903–1908." M.A. thesis. Bowling Green State University, 1989.

Shoemaker, Fred C. "Alton B. Parker: The Image of a Gilded Age Statesman in an Era of Progressive Politics." M.A. thesis. Ohio State University, 1983.

Wheaton, James O. "The Genius and the Jurist: The Presidential Campaign of 1904." Ph.D. diss. Stanford University, 1964.

NOTES

The names of Theodore and Edith Kermit Roosevelt are abbreviated below as TR and EKR.

Citations of the Washington *Evening Star* often imply official, if "off-the-record" authority, because that newspaper's daily "At the White House" column amounted to a court circular for the Roosevelt Administration.

Except where otherwise indicated, all French translations are by the author. Quotations from oral sources—i.e., stenographic transcripts—have on rare occasions been repunctuated for clarity.

PROLOGUE: 14–16 SEPTEMBER 1901

3   THEODORE ROOSEVELT became   For a day-by-day chronology of TR's presidency, see the appendix of vols. 4 and 6 of TR, *The Letters of Theodore Roosevelt,* ed. Elting E. Morison (Cambridge, Mass., 1951–1954), 8 vols. (hereafter TR, *Letters*).

3   **He was bouncing**   This account of TR's descent from Mount Marcy is based on the following sources: TR to John J. Leary, Leary Notebooks (TRC); Orin Kellogg [driver] interview, unidentified news clip (TRB); Mike Cronin [driver] interview, New York *Herald,* 15 Sept., and New York *World,* 29 Sept. 1901. There are further reminiscences by these men and other contemporary witnesses in Eloise Cronin Murphy, *Theodore Roosevelt's Night Ride to the Presidency* (Adirondack Museum, N.Y., 1977), and Christina Rainsford, "A Momentous Ride," *Theodore Roosevelt Association Journal,* summer 1981. Richmond B. Williams explains the impromptu communications network that sprang up along the slope of the mountain in "TR Receives His Summons to the Presidency," *Bell Telephone Magazine,* autumn 1951. Supplemental details come from *The New York Times,* New York *Press,* and New York *Sun,* 14 Sept. 1901, and from a reconnaissance made by the author in October 1979. Route 28N, resurfaced and renamed "Roosevelt-Marcy Memorial Highway," now connects many of the places mentioned, so smoothly as to cast doubt on old accounts of the difficulties and dangers TR faced. However, a film of local wet-weather conditions, ca. 1910, preserved in the Adirondack Museum, proves these accounts were not exaggerated. (Rain had been falling continuously for three days preceding TR's ride.)

3   **Yesterday's telegrams**   Facsimile telegrams (TRB). There has been some confusion about the sequence of fifteen telegrams received by TR on Mount Marcy. A comparison of the originals with medical bulletins issued by McKinley's secretary, George Cortelyou (in GBC), makes it clear that he read the most urgent message—Elihu Root's—last. It was dispatched at 10:20 P.M. (William Loeb to Root, 13 Sept. 1901 [ER]). EKR, in her diary of 13 Sept. 1901, states that it came "between 11 and 12 when we were in bed [in the vacation cabin at Upper Tahawus]." See Sylvia Jukes Morris, *Edith Kermit Roosevelt: Portrait of a First Lady* (New York, 1980), 212–14. TR's reply (in ER) is datelined Lower Tahawus, 14 Sept. 1:32 A.M. This

helps explain TR's curious delay in leaving for Buffalo after receiving the first message, from Cortelyou, near the summit at 1:25 P.M. on 13 Sept. TR twice confirms in *An Autobiography* (New York, 1913), 364, and in the Leary Notebooks that he realized the President was dying when he saw the messenger approach. Yet the telegram stated only that McKinley's condition caused "the gravest apprehension." The next few telegrams, awaiting TR at Upper Tahawus at 5:15 or 5:30 P.M. (Murphy, *Theodore Roosevelt's Night Ride*, 18–19), indicated some improvement. Hence his remark, about 9:00 P.M., to EKR: "I'm not going unless I'm really needed" (Morris, *Edith Kermit Roosevelt*, 212). Then the telegrams became too urgent to resist.

Note on timings: An analysis of available data works out thus: dept. Upper Tahawus 11:31 P.M., 13 Sept.; arr. Lower Tahawus (ten miles) 1:31 A.M., 14 Sept.; dept. 1:35 A.M.; arr. Aiden Lair (nine miles) 3:36 A.M.; dept. 3:41 A.M.; arr. North Creek (sixteen miles) 5:22 A.M. Total: thirty-five miles covered in five hours, fifty-one minutes.

3 THE PRESIDENT APPEARS Facsimile telegram (TRB).

4 He was now A bronze tablet on Route 28N, not far north of Aiden Lair, commemorates TR's accession to the Presidency.

4 He sat alone William Allen White, *Masks in a Pageant* (New York, 1928), 294; "How the President Wears His Hat," *New York Tribune*, 29 Nov. 1901; Orin Kellogg in New York *World*, 29 Sept. 1901.

4 In his opinion TR, *Letters*, vol. 3, 141–42; *The Works of Theodore Roosevelt*, memorial edition (New York, 1923–1926), vol. 17, 96; Orin Kellogg in Murphy, *Theodore Roosevelt's Night Ride*, 21. Czolgosz did not "get away"; he was executed within weeks.

4 MEANWHILE, IN WASHINGTON New York *Press*, 4 Sept.; *Harper's Weekly*, 21 Sept. 1901; Charles Willis Thompson, *Party Leaders of the Time* (New York, 1906), 261–62, 281–82; New York *World*, 17 Sept. 1901.

4 AT ABOUT 3:30 A restored version of Aiden Lair Lodge may be seen beside Route 28N. Upper Tahawus is now a ghost town, but the Roosevelts' cabin survives. Lower Tahawus is maintained by a hunting club. North Creek station has been restored as a state historic site.

4 "Any news?" Mike Cronin interview, New York *Herald*, 15 Sept. 1901.

4 The new horses Orin Kellogg interview, New York *World*, 19 Sept. 1901; Murphy, *Theodore Roosevelt's Night Ride*, 23; Mike Cronin interview, New York *Herald*, 15 Sept. 1901.

6 SINCE PUBERTY In the half-envious words of Henry Adams, "Theodore is one of the brainless cephalopods who is not afraid." *The Letters of Henry Adams*, ed. J. C. Levenson, Ernest Samuels, et al. (Cambridge, Mass., 1982–1988), vol. 5, 349.

6 From that viewpoint For TR's presidential aspirations, see, e.g., TR, *Letters*, vol. 3, 104, 114–15, 120. According to William Allen White, *Autobiography* (New York, 1946), 327, "Even in 1899 we were planning for 1904." See also William Allen White, *Selected Letters, 1899–1943*, ed. Walter Johnson (New York, 1947), 126–27, and Henry F. Pringle, *Theodore Roosevelt: A Biography* (New York, 1931), 229–30. TR continued with his plans right through the final illness of McKinley. TR, *Letters*, vol. 3, 144 (10 Sept. 1901).

6 He had fought TR, *Works*, vol. 5, 267.

7 Yet just when See Corinne Roosevelt Robinson, *My Brother, Theodore Roosevelt* (New York, 1921), 198. TR was "very depressed" as Vice President, his daughter Alice remembered. "He thought . . . [it] was the end of his career" (Michael Teague, *Mrs. L.: Conversations with Alice Roosevelt Longworth* [New York, 1981], 112). Notwithstanding his plans for 1904, TR talked miserably of becoming a lawyer, or of writing further installments of his multivolume history, *The*

Winning of the West (George Haven Putnam, *Memories of a Publisher* [New York, 1915], 144; TR, *Letters*, vol. 3, 31, 72). The most comprehensive account of TR's prepresidential career is Edmund Morris, *The Rise of Theodore Roosevelt* (New York, 1979), to which this volume is a sequel. For a detailed study of TR's first twenty-eight years, see Carleton Putnam, *Theodore Roosevelt: The Formative Years* (New York, 1958). David McCullough, *Mornings on Horseback* (New York, 1981), covers the same period. TR's family life and second marriage are fully described in Morris, *Edith Kermit Roosevelt.*

7 **His path ran** Murphy, *Theodore Roosevelt's Night Ride,* 25.

7 **The final dash** *The New York Times,* New York *Press,* and New York *Herald,* 15 Sept. 1901. Cronin's time of 1:41 from Aiden Lair to North Creek beat his own previous record by a quarter of an hour. Later that month, a reporter attempted the same drive, at night and under similar conditions; it took him four hours (New York *World,* 29 Sept. 1901). The record still stands. Murphy, *Theodore Roosevelt's Night Ride,* 29.

7 THE PRESIDENT DIED Facsimile telegram, 14 Sept. 1901 (TRB).

7 **Looking suddenly worn** *The New York Times* and New York *World,* 15 Sept. 1901; Murphy, *Theodore Roosevelt's Night Ride,* 26–27.

7 ROOSEVELT'S FIRST WORDS New York *World,* 15 Sept., and New York *Herald,* 14 Sept. 1901; William Loeb, Jr., to author, 28 Feb. 1975 (AC).

8 **Mount Marcy's cloud banks** New York *Herald* and New York *World,* 15 Sept. 1901; Morris, *Edith Kermit Roosevelt,* 214–21.

8 **At about seven o'clock** New York *Sun,* 15 Sept. 1901.

8 **Roosevelt did not need** Ibid., 15 and 10 Sept. 1901. For an account of the anarchist phenomenon in Europe and America, 1890–1914, see Barbara Tuchman, *The Proud Tower* (New York, 1966), 63–113.

8 **Personally, Roosevelt** TR, *Letters,* vol. 3, 2. Later in the year, he dreamed of doing the same with even bigger game. "We could kill a big grizzly or silver tip with our knives, which would be great sport" (ibid., 91). See also Lloyd C. Griscom, *Diplomatically Speaking* (Boston, 1940), 221–22.

8 **His larger concern** TR specifically cited such social bacteria as William Randolph Hearst, John P. Altgeld, "and to an only less degree, Tolstoy and the feeble apostles of Tolstoy, like Ernest Howard Crosby and William Dean Howells." TR, *Letters,* vol. 3, 142.

8 **When, accepting** Ibid.; TR, *Works,* vol. 1, 43–45.

8 **Youth, size** TR was forty-two years and nearly eleven months old on acceding to the Presidency. He remains the youngest President in U.S. history, John F. Kennedy being the youngest President elected. For a classic statement of his views on "the essential manliness of the American character," as well as his attitudes toward some of the problems confronting the United States at the turn of the century, see "National Duties," the speech he delivered at the Minnesota State Fair on 2 Sept. 1901, four days before the attack on McKinley. It is a source of the ideology set forth here. TR, *Works,* vol. 15, 328–41.

9 **He refused to** Ibid., vol. 14, 235; vol. 15, 316.

9 **Roosevelt, sucking** The following survey of press reportage on 14 Sept. 1901 is taken from newspaper clippings preserved in TR scrapbooks (TRP). These volumes, assembled by William Loeb, Jr., and often contributed to by the President himself, form a reliable guide to TR's own perception of public opinion, 1901–1909.

9 **A remarkable consensus** New York *Sun,* New York *World,* New York *Herald, The New York Times,* and New York *Press,* 14–15 Sept. 1901 (originals at TRB). A typical reaction of one Wall Street executive, on hearing that TR was about to become President: "When Teddy's done with America it'll require another Christo-

pher Columbus to find what's left of it" (New York dispatch to *The Times* [London], 15 Sept. 1901). See White, *Masks in a Pageant*, 295, and Pringle, *Theodore Roosevelt*, 237ff., for the "terror" that gripped the financial community that weekend.

10 AS THE NEWS Morris, *Rise of Theodore Roosevelt*, 73, 337.

10 **In Albany, an old** Frances Theodora (Smith) Parsons, *Perchance Some Day* (privately printed, New York, 1951; copy in TRC), 120, 135–36; also Mrs. Parsons to TR, 14 Sept. 1901 (TRB); Russell B. Harrison to TR, 8 Nov. 1901 (TRP); Arthur Lee, Viscount of Fareham, *A Good Innings* (privately printed, London, 1939), vol. 1, 254; Adams, *Letters*, vol. 5, 295.

10 **Yet there was** All these achievements are described in Morris, *Rise of Theodore Roosevelt*. The best overall survey of TR's superhuman variety remains Edward Wagenknecht, *The Seven Worlds of Theodore Roosevelt* (New York, 1958).

11 THOUSANDS OF PEOPLE The following account of TR's arrival and inauguration in Buffalo is based on an October 1902 memorandum by Ansley Wilcox, preserved in the Wilcox scrapbook, Buffalo and Erie County Historical Society, N.Y.; "Story of the Wilcox House," recollections of Judge John R. Hazel in *Buffalo Evening News*, 15 Nov. 1963; and dozens of local and national news clips, 14–16 Sept. 1901, in the Wilcox scrapbook and TRB files. Incidental sources are cited below.

11 **Roosevelt's companion** Wilcox memorandum, Wilcox scrapbook.

11 **The cavalcade moved** Photographs in ibid. Julia Bundy Foraker was in Buffalo that day. "A pall hung over life. The universe lowered its voice." *I Would Live It Again: Memories of a Vivid Life* (New York, 1932), 267.

11 **Over lunch, he said** Wilcox scrapbook; *The New York Times* and New York *Herald*, 15 Sept. 1901.

11 **He would go there** Wilcox scrapbook; Mrs. Nathaniel K. B. Patch interviews, 19 Sept. 1935 and 30 Apr. 1969, t.s. in Wilcox Mansion. Mrs. Patch was the teenage girl outside the house (below).

12 **Even now** Mrs. Patch interviews, Wilcox Mansion. *The New York Times* and New York *Herald*, 15 Sept. 1901, confirm TR's burst of temper.

12 **To swelling cries** Buffalo *Courier* and Buffalo *Express*, 15 Sept. 1901; Pittsburgh *Press*, n.d., Wilcox scrapbook. Many years later, Elihu Root recalled that Hanna had snarled to him: "Now, don't you wish *you* had taken that Vice-Presidency?" (interview, 2 Sept. 1902, 1935 [PCJ]).

13 **A voice called out** TR to John J. Leary, Leary Notebooks (TRC).

13 **How often had** Philip C. Jessup, *Elihu Root* (New York, 1938), vol. 1, 423; Morris, *Rise of Theodore Roosevelt*, 677–79; Wallace G. Chessman, "Theodore Roosevelt's Personal Tax Difficulty," *New York History* 34 (1953): 54–63. See also Jessup, *Elihu Root*, vol. 1, chap. 10.

13 **Returning to his carriage** Buffalo *Courier*, 15 Sept. 1901; Wilcox scrapbook.

13 A STRANGE HOTHOUSE **glow** This library is now the centerpiece of the restored Wilcox Mansion, officially known as the Theodore Roosevelt National Inaugural Site, a public museum.

13 **The luminescence came** Wilcox scrapbook; TR, *Letters*, vol. 1, 582; Morris, *Rise of Theodore Roosevelt*, 376.

14 **They proceeded to report** For a typical reminiscence of the ceremony, see Joseph I. C. Clarke, *My Life and Memories* (New York, 1925), 373.

14 **The library clock** Buffalo *Courier*, Buffalo *Express*, and New York *Sun*, 15 Sept. 1901; Hazel, "Story." The Secretary of War's emotional struggle might have been more comprehensible to people in the room had they realized that exactly twenty years before, Root had organized another emergency inauguration—that of Chester Arthur, succeeding the assassinated James A. Garfield (Root interview, 23 Jan. 1934 [PCJ]).

14 **Roosevelt bowed** Wilcox scrapbook; *The New York Times* and New York *Sun,* 15 Sept. 1901.

14 **This speech** *The New York Times,* 15 Sept. 1901; New York *World,* 17 Sept. 1901.

14 **Roosevelt spoke with** Pittsburgh *Press,* n.d., Wilcox scrapbook. Milburn was a director of the American Express Company and Chase National Bank. Depew, in addition to being Senator, was chairman of the New York Central Railroad.

14 **Elihu Root had** Root interview, 23 Jan. 1934 (PCJ); Jessup, *Elihu Root,* vol. 1, 238. In his *Autobiography,* TR failed to mention this debt to Root. Root's advice had been preceded, earlier in the day, by similar instructions from TR's brother-in-law, Douglas Robinson, in a letter hand-delivered to the Wilcox Mansion (13 Sept. 1901 [TRP]).

14 **Judge Hazel clutched** Wilcox scrapbook; Depew in New York *Sun,* 16 Sept. 1901.

15 **Two minutes ticked by** New York *World* and New York *Herald,* 15 Sept. 1901. During these mute moments, wrote William Allen White, "youth, which he has clung to so fondly, left him, and maturity came." White, "Theodore Roosevelt," *McClure's,* Nov. 1901.

15 **"Mr. President,"** Buffalo *Courier, The New York Times,* and *Chicago Tribune,* 15 Sept. 1901.

15 **"I have witnessed"** New York *Sun,* 16 Sept. 1901.

15 ROOSEVELT REMAINED Wilcox scrapbook.

15 **A reporter was struck** Clarke, *My Life,* 373.

15 **The Cabinet meeting** Buffalo *Courier,* 15 Sept. 1901.

15 **Business completed** New York *Sun,* New York *Herald,* and Buffalo *Courier,* 15 Sept. 1901. For a detailed study of TR's security from this day on, see Richard B. Sherman, "Presidential Protection During the Progressive Era: The Aftermath of the McKinley Assassination," *Historian,* Nov. 1983.

16 **Refuge was** The following passage refers to the manuscript of TR's draft proclamation, preserved in the Wilcox scrapbook.

16 **It had always been thus** Owen Wister, *Roosevelt: The Story of a Friendship* (New York, 1930), 68.

16 AT FOUR O'CLOCK Buffalo *Courier, The New York Times,* and New York *Herald,* 15 Sept. 1901; Elmer Dover, Hanna's secretary, interviewed by J. B. Morrow, Sept. 1905 (MHM).

16 **Seated inside** Years later, TR still marveled at Hanna's toughness that afternoon. "Not a particle of subserviency . . . no worship of the rising sun!" TR interviewed by J. B. Morrow, 17 Apr. 1906 (MHM).

17 **That evening, George** Wilcox scrapbook.

17 SOMETIME AFTER MIDNIGHT *The New York Times,* 15 Oct. 1912. See also Morris, *Rise of Theodore Roosevelt,* 505–6, 824n119.

17 **Now, as he** Schrank memorandum, 15 Sept. 1912, qu. in Robert Donovan, *The Assassins* (New York, 1955), 137.

17 **"This is my murderer"** See ibid., 137–45, for an account of what happened in 1912.

17 ROOSEVELT AWOKE REFRESHED *Chicago Tribune* and New York *World,* 16 Sept. 1901.

18 VIVE LE ROI William Sturgis Bigelow and George Cabot Lodge to TR, 14 Sept. 1901 (TRP).

18 **Kohlsaat followed him** Herman H. Kohlsaat, *From McKinley to Harding: Personal Recollections of Our Presidents* (New York, 1923), 96–97; Arthur Wallace Dunn, *From Harrison to Harding* (New York, 1922), vol. 1, 135. Wilson, Professor of Jurisprudence and Politics at Princeton, was on his way home from Rosseau Falls, Ont.

Biographical Note: According to one of TR's classmates, Wilson was an "ardent" admirer of TR as early as 1883. Albert Shaw, "Reminiscences of Theodore Roosevelt," ms. (AS). Scattered references in Wilson's early papers indicate that the two men first crossed paths on the academic lecture circuit on 20 Nov. 1890. By the middle of the decade they were corresponding; they appeared on the same platform at a Reform Rally in Baltimore, 3 Mar. 1896 (*The Papers of Woodrow Wilson*, ed. Arthur S. Link [Princeton, N.J., 1966], vol. 9, 483–85; *The Baltimore Sun*, 4 Mar. 1896). Surviving correspondence dates from April 1897 (Wilson, *Papers*, vol. 10, 238). Wilson expressed public admiration for TR ("This popular, this gifted man") at Harvard on 13 Oct. 1899. TR was equally complimentary about Wilson. As Governor, he hoped the professor would visit him in Albany. "There is much I should like to talk over with you." In 1900, Wilson consulted TR about his appointment to the chair of politics at Princeton. He valued TR's advice "as showing . . . a very sane, academic side of him, not known by everybody . . . but constituting his hope of real and lasting eminence." On 18 July 1901, TR invited Wilson, as a man of "constructive scholarship and administrative ability" (TR, *Letters*, vol. 3, 277), to stay at Oyster Bay. He wished advice "on how to arouse our young college students . . . to take an active interest in politics." TR was musing on an academic career himself at this point, and had a scheme to establish student reform committees at Harvard, Yale, and Princeton. Wilson came, saw, and was conquered by TR's ebullience. Afterward, he praised the visit as "most delightful and refreshing" (Wilson, *Papers*, vol. 11, 253, 277, 352, 513–16; vol. 12, 164, 172).

18 **"I am going to make"** Kohlsaat, *From McKinley,* 97–98, 63; New York *Herald,* 15 Sept. 1901.

18 **"John Hay is"** New York *Herald,* 15 Sept. 1901; Kohlsaat, *From McKinley,* 97–98.

18 **Compounding the flattery** Kohlsaat, *From McKinley,* 99. The ultraconservative Gage was indeed nervous about having to serve under TR. Hay to Henry Adams, 19 Sept. 1901 (TD).

19 *My dear Roosevelt* Hay to TR, 19 Sept. 1901 (TRP). During the course of the day, TR also received a letter from Henry Cabot Lodge, the controlling power of the Senate Committee on Foreign Relations, beseeching him, "Above all, do nothing which could cause the retirement of Secretary Hay." Francis E. Leupp, *The Man Roosevelt: A Portrait Sketch* (New York, 1904), 54.

19 **16 SEPTEMBER DAWNED** *The New York Times* and New York *Sun,* 17 Sept. 1901; film, "President McKinley's Funeral Cortege at Buffalo," Library of Congress; Kohlsaat, *From McKinley,* 100.

20 **THE FUNERAL TRAIN** Catalogs illustrating these beautiful vehicles can be seen in GBC.

20 **Reporters were assigned** *The New York Times* and New York *Sun,* 17 Sept. 1901; Kohlsaat, *From McKinley,* 100ff.; TR scrapbooks (TRP). Loeb was subsequently appointed assistant secretary to the President. TR's decision to retain Cortelyou over him struck many Rooseveltians as opportunistic and unfeeling. McKinleyites, however, were delighted. The well-connected Cortelyou helped smooth out many transition problems between the two camps, and Loeb eventually got his delayed preferment. For a biographical sketch of Loeb, see "The Perfect Stenographer" in Louis W. Koening, *The Invisible Presidency* (New York, 1960).

20 **At 8:57** The following narrative of TR's twelve-hour, 420-mile journey to Washington is based on the firsthand observations of newspapermen who rode on the

funeral train, principally Joseph I. C. Clarke (New York *Herald*) and H. H. Kohlsaat (Chicago *Times-Herald*). Other accounts appeared in *The New York Times,* New York *Sun,* New York *World, Chicago Tribune, Buffalo Express,* and local newspapers—e.g., Harrisburg *Patriot,* 17 Sept. 1901. Some descriptions of the route traveled come from reconnaissances made by the author. Other sources cited below.

20   **What he had just**   Twelve days before, TR had spoken with pride about "this fundamental fact of American life, this acknowledgement that the law of work is the fundamental law of our being" TR, *Works,* vol. 15, 330.

20   **This first year**   London *Daily Mail Yearbook,* 1902; *Collier's Weekly,* 25 Jan. 1902; Mark Sullivan, *Our Times* (New York, 1926–1935), vol. 1, 31. Contemporary statistics, cited by an English analyst in *Collier's Weekly,* 25 Jan. 1902: The United States was the world's richest nation, worth $88 billion to Britain's $55 billion, France's $45 billion, Germany's $40 billion, and Russia's $30 billion. See also articles on United States prosperity in *Review of Reviews,* Sept. and Oct. 1901; *Success,* Oct. 1901; and New York *Evening Post,* 31 Dec. 1901. The best surveys of material America at the turn of the century are the opening chapters of Harold U. Faulkner, *The Decline of Laissez-Faire, 1897–1917* (New York, 1951), and George E. Mowry, *The Era of Theodore Roosevelt, 1900–1912* (New York, 1958).

20   **Indeed, it could consume**   Faulkner, *Decline of Laissez-Faire,* 68–69; Sullivan, *Our Times,* vol. 1, 33; *Success,* Oct. 1901; Mowry, *Era of Theodore Roosevelt,* 4; James Ford Rhodes, *The McKinley and Roosevelt Administrations, 1897–1909* (New York, 1922), 158. August's export total of $107 million was the largest in United States history (New York *Evening Post,* 31 Dec. 1901).

20   **Even if the United States**   William Woodruff, *America's Impact on the World* (New York, 1975), 115–16; *Forum,* 19 May 1902; product sampling derived from a survey of popular British periodicals, Sept.–Dec. 1901 (LC); *Success,* Oct. 1901; Frederick A. McKenzie, *The American Invaders* (New York, 1901); "The American Commercial Invasion of Europe," *Scribner's,* Jan. and Feb. 1902. For the exuberant overseas expansion of American corporations in 1901, see Mira Watkins, *The Emergence of Multinational Enterprise: American Business Abroad from the Colonial Era to 1914* (Cambridge, Mass., 1970), chaps. 4 and 5.

21   **As a result**   Andrew Carnegie, *Triumphant Democracy* (New York, 1893), 5; Faulkner, *Decline of Laissez-Faire,* 23, 87; Jean Strouse, *Morgan: American Financier* (New York, 1999), 442–43; Mowry, *Era of Theodore Roosevelt,* 4.

21   **It was hard**   Ray Stannard Baker, *American Chronicle* (New York, 1945), 89–90. See Sidney Fine, *Laissez-Faire and the General Welfare State, 1865–1901* (Ann Arbor, 1956).

21   **Trees soon barred**   Williams, "TR Receives." By 1901 the nation was making more than two billion calls annually.

22   **The foreign papers**   Clarke in New York *Herald,* 17 Sept. 1901. Foreign press quoted in New York *Sun,* 16 Sept. 1901.

22   **Continental comment was**   *World's Work,* Dec. 1901; TR scrapbooks (TRP). For a presentist French view of TR's prepresidential character, see Serge Ricard, "Théodore Roosevelt avant la présidence: analyse d'une pensée politique," *Canadian Review of American Studies* 12.2 (fall 1981).

22   **fifth in the world**   T. A. Brassey, ed., *The Naval Annual, 1902* (Portsmouth, U.K.). Great Britain led the naval ranking, followed by France, Russia, and Germany.

23   **About 9:30**   Kohlsaat, *From McKinley,* 98; Clarke in New York *Herald,* 17 Sept. 1901.

23   **For ten minutes**   Ibid.

23   **McKinley had marched**   With the exception of Grover Cleveland (who had family

responsibilities), every President since Lincoln had worn a military uniform during the Civil War. *Review of Reviews*, Nov. 1901.

23 **Powerful commercial** Faulkner, *Decline of Laissez-Faire*, 68–69; Foster Rhea Dulles, *America's Rise to World Power, 1898–1954* (New York, 1955), 46ff.

23 **They had trumpeted** *Downes v. Bidwell*, 182 U.S. Reports 244 (1901). In this decision, the Supreme Court found that the new territories were appurtenant to, rather than part of, the United States. As long as they remained thus "unincorporated" into the body politic, their inhabitants could not expect the full freedoms enjoyed by United States citizens, "only such fundamental rights as were derived from natural law" (Dulles, *America's Rise*, 56). These included rights to life, liberty, and property, but did not include guarantees of, say, uniform tariff and excise rates, nor necessarily any of democratic vote (ibid., 57). TR agreed with William Howard Taft that the Supreme Court's attitude was just: "What does well here would work ruin there [the Philippines]—trial by jury in all cases, for example" (TR, *Letters*, vol. 3, 105). Cynical observers suggested that the court's ruling had been affected by the pro-imperialism vote of 1900.

24 **The old soldiers** Frederick H. Harrington, "The Anti-Imperialist Movement in the United States, 1898–1900," *Mississippi Valley Historical Review*, Sept. 1935; see also Howard C. Hill, *Roosevelt and the Caribbean* (Chicago, 1927), 13, and Robert L. Beisner, *Twelve Against Empire: The Anti-Imperialists, 1898–1900* (New York, 1968).

24 **"World duties,"** TR, *Works*, vol. 15, 332.

24 **"So they have"** Ibid., 333.

24 **Cuba, for example** Upon arrival in Washington, the President stated emphatically that he wanted to get out of Cuba (Francis E. Leupp to Oswald Garrison Villard, 20 Sept. 1901 [CS]). "Never in recent times," TR asserted, "has any great nation acted with such disinterestedness as we have shown in Cuba" (ibid., 476–77). While repeating these sentiments twelve years later in his *Autobiography*, he admitted that in 1901 "our own direct interests were great, because of the Cuban tobacco and sugar, and especially because of Cuba's relation to the projected Isthmian Canal" (214).

24 **"Sometimes," Roosevelt** TR, *Letters*, vol. 3, 105.

24 **Clearly, a vast** *World's Work*, Sept. 1901; Richard Leopold, *Elihu Root and the Conservative Tradition* (Boston, 1954), 26–28; Alexander E. Campbell, *America Comes of Age* (New York, 1971), 94–95; Lewis L. Gould, *The Presidency of William McKinley* (Lawrence, Kans., 1989), 114–15. TR, in *Letters*, vol. 3, 209, sneers at "those amiable but very far from wise philanthropists who think that we can . . . benefit the Filipino by getting out of the Philippines and letting him wallow back into savagery." *Review of Reviews* remarked, in an article on the problems confronting Governor-General Taft: "Under the most liberal estimates, there are not over a half-million people in the islands who possess anywhere near the capacity for selfgovernment exhibited by the most ignorant negro in the black belt of our own South" (Aug. 1901). For TR's intense prepresidential interest in the Philippines (he wanted to be the first Governor-General), see Oscar M. Alfonso, *Theodore Roosevelt and the Philippines* (New York, 1974), chap. 1.

24 **President McKinley's** Leopold, *Elihu Root*, 34–35; TR, *Works*, vol. 15, 337–38. Taft disclaimed some of the rumors in a letter to Root (2 Aug. 1901 [ER]), but admitted others were true. According to Daniel B. Schirmer, *Republic or Empire: American Resistance to the Philippine War* (Cambridge, Mass., 1972), 226, 230, Filipinos were being exterminated, at the height of the insurrection, at a ratio of five dead to every one wounded. For a contemporary view of the relations between the United States and its new dependencies, see Arthur W. Dunn, "The Government of Our Insular Possessions," *Review of Reviews*, Dec. 1901.

NOTES • 581

25 THE TRAIN BEGAN *The New York Times,* 17 Sept. 1901; TR, *Letters,* vol. 3, 3, 20, 23; Alexander E. Campbell, *Great Britain and the U.S., 1895–1903* (London, 1960), 179–83; A. Northend Benjamin, "Russia in the East," *Munsey's,* June 1901.

25 **Both powers were** Frederick W. Marks III, *Velvet on Iron: The Diplomacy of Theodore Roosevelt* (Lincoln, Nebr., 1979), 4–5; Thomas A. Bailey, *A Diplomatic History of the American People,* 8th ed. (New York, 1968), 482; TR, *Letters,* vol. 3, 3, 20, 26, 112; Raymond A. Esthus, *Theodore Roosevelt and Japan* (Seattle, 1966), 8. See also A. Gregory Moore, "Dilemma of Stereotypes: Theodore Roosevelt and China, 1901–1909" (Ph.D. diss., Kent State University, 1978).

25 **Worldwide, the balance** A modern historian redefines this as "an *im*balance" favorable to the United States and Great Britain (William N. Tilchin, *Theodore Roosevelt and the British Empire: A Study in Presidential Statecraft* [New York, 1997], 49). See also Edward H. Zabriskie, *American-Russian Rivalry in the Far East: A Study in Diplomacy and Power Politics, 1895–1914* (Philadelphia, 1946), *passim.* "I think the 20th century will still be the century of the men who speak English." TR, *Letters,* vol. 3, 15.

25 **The United States acknowledged** For TR's wistfulness regarding Canada, see Morris, *Rise of Theodore Roosevelt,* 334.

25 **This was the only** TR, *Letters,* vol. 3, 21, 65–66, 109; see also TR, *Works,* vol. 15, 335–36.

26 **Roosevelt could claim** Marks, *Velvet on Iron,* 72; TR, *Letters,* vol. 2, 1209, 1186–87; Kenton J. Clymer, *John Hay: The Gentleman as Diplomat* (Ann Arbor, 1975), 177–79. See also David H. Burton, "Theodore Roosevelt and His English Correspondents: A Special Relationship of Friends," *Transactions of the American Philosophical Society,* new series, vol. 63, pt. 2 (1973): 39–42.

26 **Now there was this new** David McCullough, *The Path Between the Seas* (New York, 1977), 256–59.

26 **Roosevelt privately favored** Allan Nevins, *Henry White: Thirty Years of American Diplomacy* (New York, 1930), 156.

26 **The stupendous task** TR, *Works,* vol. 15, 273; Senator W. A. Harris to John Tyler Morgan, 29 Oct. 1901 (JTM); TR, *Public Papers of Theodore Roosevelt, Governor* (Albany, 1899–1900), 298; TR, *Letters,* vol. 3, 52; Holger Herwig, *Politics of Frustration: The United States in German Naval Planning, 1889–1941* (Boston, 1976), 70; Marks, *Velvet on Iron,* 5–6.

26 **Even so, Panama** McCullough, *Path Between the Seas,* 264–65; Campbell, *Great Britain and the U.S.,* 71.

26 **That reluctant appendix** *Review of Reviews,* Sept. 1901; TR, *Autobiography,* 528–30; *The New York Times,* 16 Sept. 1901. The first-cited periodical almost wistfully contemplated the day when the United States "should come into full authority" in Panama. "That isthmus is of no practical value to the Republic of Colombia. . . . It would be to our advantage to purchase [it] at a fair price." The author of these words was TR's friend and adviser Albert Shaw.

26 THE ALLEGHENY FOOTHILLS *Olean, City of Natural Advantages* (illustrated commercial guidebook, 1889, NYPL); *WPA Guide to New York* (1940); Sullivan, *Our Times,* vol. 1, 28, and vol. 2, 271–99.

27 **"The party of"** Qu. in Sullivan, *Our Times,* vol. 2, 250. The following account of the rise of the trusts prior to 16 Sept. 1901 is based on ibid., vol. 2, 307–37; Mowry, *Era of Theodore Roosevelt,* 6–10; Fine, *Laissez-Faire;* Hans B. Thorelli, *Federal Antitrust Policy* (Baltimore, 1955); and Naomi Lamoreaux, *The Great Merger Movement in American Business, 1895–1904* (New York, 1985).

28 **His profits were** Faulkner, *Decline of Laissez-Faire,* 167–77; Lamoreaux, *Great Merger Movement,* 159; Charles W. McCurdy, "The *Knight* Sugar Decision of

1895 and the Modernization of American Corporation Law, 1869–1903," *Business History Review Index*, autumn 1979. For a detailed study of the Sherman Act, see Thorelli, *Federal Antitrust Policy*. For statistics showing the pace of business combination prior to 1901, see Ralph L. Nelson, *Merger Movements in American Industry, 1895–1956* (Princeton, N.J., 1959).

28 **In 1898, there** Olivier Zunz, *Making America Corporate, 1870–1920* (Chicago, 1990), 68.

28 **Ideologically, Roosevelt** Nelson, *Merger Movements*, 33–34, 37; Thorelli, *Federal Antitrust Policy*, 411–16. For TR's attitude toward the trusts, see, e.g., TR, *Letters*, vol. 2, 1400, 1493–94 (comments of John M. Blum); vol. 3, 122, 159–60; and TR, *Works*, vol. 15, 315.

28 **He saw "grave dangers"** This opinion was shared by most turn-of-the-century economists (Mowry, *Era of Theodore Roosevelt*, 53). For revisionist views, see Alfred P. Chandler, Jr., *The Visible Hand: The Managerial Revolution in American Business* (Cambridge, Mass., 1977), and Albro Martin, *James J. Hill and the Opening of the Northwest* (New York, 1976). Martin helps demolish the "Robber Baron" cliché of earlier writers. Elsewhere, he views equably the tendency of a modern, multi-unit corporation to operate beyond government control ("Uneasy Partners: Government-Business Relations in 20th Century American History," *Prologue* 11 [summer 1979]). It was this antidemocratic tendency, not the growth of trusts per se, that alarmed TR in 1901.

28 **America was no longer** See H. T. Newcomb, "The Recent Great Railway Combinations," *Review of Reviews*, Aug. 1901. By now, nearly all the railroads had been consolidated into the hands of a half-dozen operators (Mowry, *Era of Theodore Roosevelt*, 7).

29 **According to a** Lewis L. Gould, *The Presidency of Theodore Roosevelt* (Lawrence, Kans., 1991), 28; Thorelli, *Federal Antitrust Policy*, 255n; Ray Stannard Baker, "John Pierpont Morgan," *McClure's*, Oct. 1901; New York *Herald*, 16 Sept. 1901.

29 ROOSEVELT LIKED MORGAN TR, *Letters*, vol. 1, 58; vol. 2, 1238, 1450; and vol. 3, 42; Herbert L. Satterlee, *J. Pierpont Morgan* (New York, 1975), 363; Lewis Corey, *The House of Morgan* (New York, 1975), 253.

29 **Leyland Steamship Lines** Baker, "John Pierpont Morgan." This purchase, made in the summer of 1901, sent shock waves of apprehension through London's financial community. Morgan sought to soothe local stockbrokers by protesting, "America is good enough for me." William Jennings Bryan's *Commoner* quipped, "Whenever he doesn't like it, he can give it back to us" (qu. in Sullivan, *Our Times*, vol. 2, 355).

29 **Control, indeed, was** William H. Harbaugh, *The Life and Times of Theodore Roosevelt*, rev. ed. (New York, 1975), 157–58; Baker, "John Pierpont Morgan"; *The New York Times*, 31 Mar. 1913; Mowry, *Era of Theodore Roosevelt*, 14; Faulkner, *Decline of Laissez-Faire*, 38, 374; *Review of Reviews*, Apr. 1901.

30 **To his mind** TR, *Autobiography*, 439–40; Chandler, *Visible Hand*, 175.

30 **"The vast individual"** TR, *Works*, vol. 15, 331–32.

30 **"I owe the public"** Corey, *House of Morgan*, 301.

30 **If they were** Ibid.; Lincoln Steffens, "The Overworked President," *McClure's* 18.6 (Apr. 1902). The latter article describes the United States government in terms of a trust much larger than United States Steel, with "the equivalent of a capital, not of a hundred millions, but a hundred billions," benefiting some seventy-six million stockholders—in effect, the greatest business organization in the world.

30 ELSEWHERE IN THE TRAIN Kohlsaat, *From McKinley*, 100–101.

30 AT FOUR MINUTES past *Buffalo Express*, 17 Sept. 1901.

31 THE STEEP CLIMB *The New York Times* and New York *Herald*, 17 Sept. 1901.

31 **Boys, youths, and old** Photographs and text in Peter Roberts, *Anthracite Coal Communities: A Study of the Demography, the Social, Educational, and Moral Life of the Anthracite Regions* (New York, 1904); John Mitchell, "The Mine Worker's Life and Aims," *Cosmopolitan,* Oct. 1901.

31 **Roosevelt knew that** Mitchell, "Mine Worker's," *passim;* Roberts, *Anthracite Communities,* 15; David Montgomery, "American Labor, 1865–1902: The Early Industrial Era," *Monthly Labor Review* 99.7 (July 1976).

31 **These boys** John R. Commons et al., *History of Labor in the United States, 1896–1932* (New York, 1935), vol. 3, 402–5; Roberts, *Anthracite Communities, passim;* Harold W. Aurand, "Social Motivation of the Anthracite Mine Workers: 1900–1920," *Labor History* 18 (summer 1977).

31 **Roosevelt understood** As early as 1897, in his review of Brooks Adams's *The Law of Civilization and Decay,* TR had publicly declared that the poverty-stricken mass "constitutes a standing menace, not merely to our property, but to our existence" (TR, *Works,* vol. 14, 135). By 1901, fewer than 4 percent of United States workers were unionized, and the cost of living was rising at a steady 7 percent. Faulkner, *Decline of Laissez-Faire,* 280, 252–54.

31 **Trade-union membership** Gould, *Presidency of Theodore Roosevelt,* 34–35; TR, *Works,* vol. 16, 509; George F. Baer, "Statement Regarding the Anthracite Strike," 10 June 1902 (GWP); Robert J. Cornell, *The Anthracite Coal Strike of 1902* (Washington, D.C., 1957), 54–57.

32 **Roosevelt had been** See TR, *Letters,* vol. 1, 100–101; Morris, *Rise of Theodore Roosevelt,* 733; TR, *Works,* vol. 15, 331. See Howard L. Hurwitz, *Theodore Roosevelt and Labor in New York State, 1880–1900* (New York, 1943), for a critical review of TR's prepresidential labor policies.

32 PILLARS OF HEMLOCK Now Elk State Forest.

32 **Roosevelt was more prone** TR, *Letters,* vol. 1, 122; Morris, *Rise of Theodore Roosevelt,* 382–85; TR, *Diaries of Boyhood and Youth* (New York, 1928), 247.

32 *Qui plantavit curabit* "He who has planted will preserve."

32 *I am sorry* Morris, *Rise of Theodore Roosevelt,* 48; WPA *Guide to Pennsylvania* (1940); *World's Work,* June and Nov. 1901; *The Forester* 7 (1901), *passim;* Sullivan, *Our Times,* vol. 1, 128; Michael Frome, *The Forest Service* (New York, 1971), 16.

32 **Descent via Emporium** TR, *Autobiography,* 325; Frome, *Forest Service,* chap. 1, *passim.*

33 **A town sign** Morris, *Edith Kermit Roosevelt,* 31; Frome, *Forest Service,* 9; Ray Stannard Baker, "What the U.S. Steel Corporation Really Is," *McClure's,* Nov. 1901.

33 **To him, *conservation*** Stephen R. Fox, *John Muir and His Legacy: The American Conservation Movement* (Boston, 1981), 108–9; TR, "How I Became a Progressive," *Outlook,* Oct. 1912. See also TR, *Letters,* vol. 2, 1421–22 (to the National Irrigation Congress, 1900), and TR, *Autobiography,* chap. 11. For the equally ominous state of the nation's fauna in 1901, see Maximilian Foster, "American Game Preserves," *Munsey's,* June 1901, and John S. Wise, "The Awakening Concerning Game," *Review of Reviews,* Nov. 1901. Michael J. Lacey's "The Mysteries of Earth-Making Dissolve: A Study of Washington's Intellectual Community and the Origins of American Environmentalism in the Late Nineteenth Century" (Ph.D. diss., George Washington University, 1979) shows that the conservation movement was in fact some twelve years old, and coming into full philosophical flower in September 1901. But the flower blushed unseen by all but very few. It remained for TR, as President, to popularize this philosophy and make it government policy.

33 IT WAS NEARLY time Washington *Evening Star,* 16 Sept. 1901. New York *World* and *Chicago Tribune,* 17 Sept. 1901.

33 **He felt at home** Leopold, *Elihu Root,* 9, 18; Jessup, *Elihu Root,* vol. 2, 503. For

another example of TR's willingness to identify himself with Root's conservative rhetoric, see his remark at the Minnesota State Fair: "It is probably true that the large majority of the fortunes that now exist in this country have been amassed not by injuring our people, but as an incident to the conferring of great benefits upon the community" (TR, *Works*, vol. 15, 332).

33 **More conservative rhetoric** New York *World* and *The Washington Post*, 17 Sept. 1901; H. Wayne Morgan, *William McKinley and His America* (Syracuse, 1963), 249.

33 **McKinley had chosen** For a profile of the American conservative at the turn of the century, see Mowry, *Era of Theodore Roosevelt*, 38–45. See also James Weinstein, *The Corporate Ideal in the Liberal State* (Boston, 1969), and Norman Wilensky, "Conservatives in the Progressive Era," *University of Florida Monographs*, no. 25 (1965).

33 **They were accustomed** The official letter-books of Gage, Hay, and Knox, e.g., are replete with acknowledgments of favors received. Sullivan, *Our Times*, vol. 3, 204; Lewis L. Gould, *Reform and Regulation: American Politics, 1900–1916* (New York, 1978), 18.

33 **They were prepared** Edward C. Kirkland, *Dream and Thought in the Business Community, 1860–1900* (Madison, 1956), 121; Gabriel Kolko, *The Triumph of Conservatism: A Reinterpretation of American History, 1900–1916* (New York, 1963), 58–59.

34 **He tended toward** Mowry, *Era of Theodore Roosevelt*, 45.

34 **Years of sweaty** See TR's review of Kidd's *Social Evolution* (1894) in TR, *Works*, vol. 14, 107–28. This volume also contains other literary essays revelatory of TR's late-nineteenth-century thought: "National Life and Character" and "The Law of Civilization and Decay." For intellectual analyses of the prepresidential TR, see John M. Blum, "TR: The Years of Decision," in TR, *Letters*, vol. 2, 1484–94; Morris, *Rise of Theodore Roosevelt*, 462–71; and Edmund Morris, "Theodore Roosevelt, President," *American Heritage* 32.4 (June–July 1981). The best overall analysis remains chap. 2, "The World of Thought," in Wagenknecht, *Seven Worlds*, 31–84.

34 **In a fundamental** TR, qu. in Blum, "TR: The Years of Decision" in TR, *Letters*, vol. 2, 1487; TR, *Works*, vol. 15, 109–10.

34 **The United States** Terence Powderley, U.S. commissioner of immigration, in *Collier's*, 14 Dec. 1901. For a selection of relevant social and economic statistics, see Gould, *Presidency of Theodore Roosevelt*, 30–39.

34 **Somehow he must** TR, *Letters*, vol. 2, 1487; vol. 3, 105.

34 **"a bully pulpit"** TR, qu. by Lyman Abbott in "A Review of President Roosevelt's Administration: IV," *Outlook*, 27 Feb. 1909.

35 **The fine white** Edward W. Bok, in *The Americanization of Edward Bok* (New York, 1922), describes in detail his relationship with TR. See also Salme H. Steinberg, *Reformer in the Marketplace: Edward W. Bok and The Ladies' Home Journal* (Bloomington, Ind., 1980), and Frank Luther Mott, *A History of American Magazines* (Cambridge, Mass., 1957), vol. 4, 539, 547, for Bok as editor, and Wagenknecht, *Seven Worlds*, 69–72, 75–76, for TR's views on the social usefulness of literature.

35 **Girls softly pelted** *Chicago Tribune*, 17 Sept. 1901.

35 **Thickening crowds** New York *World*, New York *Herald*, and *Buffalo Express*, 17 Sept. 1901.

35 **Governor William Stone** *Review of Reviews*, Sept. 1901; *Atlantic Monthly*, Oct. 1901; J. Hampton Moore, *Roosevelt and the Old Guard* (Philadelphia, 1925), 195; TR, *Letters*, vol. 3, 136.

35   **A messenger ran**   Kohlsaat, *From McKinley,* 105; New York *Evening Post* and New York *Evening World,* 16 Sept. 1901; *Commercial & Financial Chronicle,* 21 Sept. 1901. Frederick Holls met TR the next day, and wrote Albert Shaw: "He is highly gratified at the Wall Street boom and Kohlsaat has persuaded him [*sic*] to agree and keep Gage on till 1905. *That is fixed*" (17 [AS]).

36   **Roosevelt was relieved**   Kohlsaat, *From McKinley,* 105.

36   **The tolling of** Harrisburg *Patriot* and *Chicago Tribune,* 17 Sept. 1901; Kohlsaat, *From McKinley,* 102–4.

36   **Ahead, in the**   New York *Evening World,* 17 Sept. 1901.

36   THE SUN WAS   *Buffalo Express,* and Clarke in New York *Herald,* 17 Sept. 1901.

36   **Though such families**   Mowry, *Era of Theodore Roosevelt,* 12, 18–19; *Review of Reviews,* Sept. 1901; Fred A. Shannon, "The Status of the Midwestern Farmer in 1900," *Mississippi Valley Historical Review* 37.3 (Dec. 1950).

36   **Technological progress**   Shannon, "Status."

37   **Roosevelt could see**   *Chicago Tribune,* 17 Sept. 1901; Walter Wellman in *McClure's,* Sept. 1901; Shannon, "Status"; Mowry, *Era of Theodore Roosevelt,* 13. Peter J. Hill, "Relative Skill and Income Levels of Native and Foreign-Born Workers in the U.S.," *Explorations in Economic History* 12.1 (1975), shows that the general impression in 1901 of the inferiority of immigrant labor was fallacious.

37   **Not surprisingly**   John Higham, *Strangers in the Land* (New Brunswick, N.J., 1955), 137–40; White editorial, qu. in Kenneth S. Davis, "The Sage of Emporia," *American Heritage* 30.6 (Oct.–Nov. 1979).

37   **Roosevelt was not**   See Blum, "TR: The Years of Decision," in TR, *Letters,* vol. 2, 1488, and TR, "True Americanism," *Works,* vol. 15, 15–31. Thomas G. Dyer, *Theodore Roosevelt and the Idea of Race* (Baton Rouge, 1980), is the latest attempt to interpret TR's racial thought in the light of modern sensibilities, mentioning Booker T. Washington only twice.

37   **One of his favorite**   Nancy Schoenberg, "Officer Otto Raphael: A Jewish Friend of Theodore Roosevelt," *American Jewish Archives* 39.1 (1987); TR, "Ethnology of the Police," *Munsey's,* June 1897; TR, *Letters,* vol. 3, 86; Higham, *Strangers,* 105–12, 149. The League was the pet project of TR's best friend, Senator Henry Cabot Lodge. See Barbara Miller Solomon, "The Intellectual Background of the Immigration Restriction Movement in New England," *New England Quarterly* 25 (1952).

37   **Several thousand**   *Chicago Tribune* and New York *World,* 17 Sept. 1901.

37   THE CONSISTENT FEATURES   The image of the fault line is borrowed from Mowry, *Era of Theodore Roosevelt.* See ibid., 1–105, for an overall survey of the American landscape (material, intellectual, political, social, and ideological) at the turn of the century.

37   **"The extremes of"**   Qu. in Sullivan, *Our Times,* vol. 2, 243.

37   **Roosevelt thought he**   TR, *Works,* vol. 15, 314. For a survey of at least some of Everyman's feelings at the time of TR's accession, see Louis Galambos, *The Public Image of Big Business in America, 1890–1940* (Baltimore, 1975), chap. 4.

38   **"Bob" and "Tom"**   These two candidates were Robert M. LaFollette and Tom L. Johnson.

38   **Far-flung and lonely**   TR, aside from being precociously sensitive to American public opinion, had read Henry George, Edward Bellamy, and Henry Demarest Lloyd, all premature voices of Progressive protest. Faulkner, *Decline of Laissez-Faire,* 369.

   Historical Note: The word *progressive* had not yet acquired a specific political meaning in 1901. At the moment of TR's accession, the *Atlantic Monthly* predicted the rise of a new party, founded on opposition to privilege and concentrated power, "anti-corruption, anti-spoliation, dedicated to public ownership of utilities and railroads, and telegraph systems" ("The Future of Political Parties," Sept. 1901). For a concise survey of the origins of Progressivism, see Stanley P. Caine's essay in Lewis L. Gould, ed., *The Progressive Era* (Syracuse, 1974).

38 ROOSEVELT'S REVERIE *Chicago Tribune,* 17 Sept. 1901; Kohlsaat, *From McKinley,* 104; *Statistical History of the United States* (New York, 1976). For an analysis of the political, social, and economic differences between Northern and Southern blacks in 1901, see W.E.B. Du Bois, *The Black North in 1901: A Social Study* (New York, 1902; repr. 1969).

38 Census statistics such as Southern blacks contributed one third of the total convention ballot. *The Washington Post,* 12 Mar. 1902.

38 The South was Herbert Croly, *Marcus Alonzo Hanna* (New York, 1912), 298; Richard B. Sherman, *The Republican Party and Black America: From McKinley to Hoover, 1896–1933* (Charlottesville, 1973), 19–20; Horace and Marion Merrill, *The Republican Command, 1897–1913* (Lexington, Ky., 1971), 74–75; *The Booker T. Washington Papers,* ed. Louis R. Harlan (Urbana, 1972–1989), vol. 6, 336 (hereafter *Booker T. Washington Papers*).

39 "burly, coarse-fibered" TR to William Allen White, 27 Aug. 1901 (WAW). The compound adjective is incorrectly transcribed as "unterrified" in TR, *Letters,* vol. 3, 135.

39 To consolidate his TR, *Letters,* vol. 3, 149. TR reportedly talked at length about his Southern strategy on the train. H. H. Kohlsaat to editor, *The Atlanta Constitution,* 7 June 1903.

39 "Theodore" Rhodes, *McKinley and Roosevelt,* 218. Rhodes got this quotation from Hanna, who was his brother-in-law. By 1905, TR was denying that the train meeting took place. But Kohlsaat, *From McKinley,* 102–3, and Joseph L. Bristow interview, 6 Dec. 1938 (HKB), confirm it, as does Lincoln Steffens in *McClure's,* July 1905. TR's reply to Steffens suggests that he was denying the substance of the conversation, not its occurrence. TR, *Letters,* vol. 4, 1254.

39 AT TWENTY PAST *Buffalo Express,* 17 Sept. 1901.

39 There was neither *Chicago Tribune, The Washington Post,* and New York *Sun,* 17 Sept. 1901.

40 As usual in moments *The Washington Post,* 17 Sept. 1901; John Hay, *Letters and Extracts from His Diary,* ed. Henry Adams (privately printed, 1908), vol. 3, 232.

40 "Divide off" *The Washington Post,* 17 Sept. 1901.

40 "Something should be" Ibid.

40 For a moment New York *Sun, Chicago Tribune,* and *The Washington Post,* 17 Sept. 1901. EKR recorded TR's arrival at the Cowles house that evening "looking very grave and older, but not at all nervous. All the country seems behind him" (Diary, 16 Sept. 1901).

CHAPTER 1: THE SHADOW OF THE CROWN

43 *I see that* "Mr. Dooley" [Finley Peter Dunne], 28 Sept. 1901, Presidential scrapbook (TRP). See also *Mr. Dooley on Ivrything and Ivrybody,* ed. Robert Hutchinson (New York, 1963), 169–70.

43 ON THE MORNING Waldon Fawcett, "President Roosevelt at Work," *Leslie's Weekly,* n.d. Presidential scrapbook (TRP); Washington *Evening Star,* 20 Sept. 1901.

43 As the President New York *Journal,* 24 Sept. 1901.

43 A pall of EKR, speech to children at TRB, 26 Oct. 1933 (TRB); Morris, *Edith Kermit Roosevelt,* 222–23; *The New York Times Magazine,* 12 Jan. 1919.

43   **At eleven o'clock**   Unidentified Cabinet officer in Boston *Transcript,* ca. 21 Sept. 1901, Presidential scrapbook (TRP); James Wilson to W. B. Allison, 21 Sept. 1901 (HKB).

44   **"I need your advice"**   Harry Thurston Peck, *Twenty Years of the Republic, 1885–1905* (New York, 1906), 667.

44   **He interrupted**   Boston *Transcript,* ca. 21 Sept. 1901, Presidential scrapbook (TRP); James Wilson to W. B. Allison, 21 Sept. 1901 (HKB).

44   **The President's hunger**   TR, *Letters,* vol. 4, 1346; New York *Herald,* 21 Sept. 1901.

44   **"This being my"**   David S. Barry, *Forty Years in Washington* (Boston, 1924), 267.

44   **A certain code**   Ibid., 267–68.

45   **Boynton and Barry**   Ibid., 268–69.

45   MUCH LATER THAT EVENING   TR's sister lived at 1733 N Street. Her home—soon known as "the Little White House"—was to become a social hideaway for the President and his family over the next seven years. See Lilian Rixey, *Bamie: Theodore Roosevelt's Remarkable Sister* (New York, 1963).
    Chronological Note: On Tuesday, 17 Sept. 1901, TR had attended McKinley memorial services in the Capitol. He then followed the dead President's coffin to Canton, Ohio, where it was interred on the nineteenth. TR was accompanied by his entire Cabinet, with the exception of John Hay, whom he ordered to remain in Washington, "on the avowed ground," Hay wrote a friend amusedly, "that he did not want too many eggs in the same Pullman car" (William Roscoe Thayer, *The Life and Letters of John Hay* [New York, 1915], vol. 2, 267). The presidential party returned on an overnight train, arriving back in Washington early on 20 Sept.

45   **"My great difficulty"**   TR, qu. by William Allen White, "Remarks at the Roosevelt Memorial Association Dinner, 27 Oct. 1933" (HH). The following account is based on this source, with extra details from White, *Autobiography,* 338–39, and Rixey, *Bamie,* 172–76. The date of the dinner is fixed by William Allen White to TR, 17 Sept. 1901 (TRP), and the *Washington Times,* 21 Sept. 1901.

45   **Commander Cowles, replete**   White, "Remarks."

45   **"I shall be"**   Ibid. TR would in fact be fifty come March 1909.

45   **"I don't want"**   White, *Autobiography,* 339.

45   **Undisturbed by the**   Ibid; Nicholas Murray Butler, *Across the Busy Years: Recollections and Reflections* (New York, 1939), vol. 1, 312–13.

45   QUIET SETTLED   Washington *Evening Star,* 25 Sept. 1901; *Review of Reviews,* Nov. 1901.

46   **"You ought to"**   New York *World,* 23 Sept. 1901. For a man who relished publicity, TR had an odd dislike of being photographed. For a considerable time he refused even to pose formally with his Cabinet. Photo editors were reduced to exhuming group portraits of the McKinley Administration and pasting TR's head and shoulders onto those of his predecessor (Washington *Evening Star,* 5 Nov. 1901). The results were grotesque enough to persuade him eventually to relent. To the end of his life he had difficulty relaxing in front of the camera; "candid" newsreels show how quickly he froze at the sight of a lens. Consequently, his iconographic record is grim. Only a dozen or so shots survive to show that he was the most genial of men.

46   **Later, on a**   Lincoln Steffens, *The Autobiography of Lincoln Steffens* (New York, 1931), 503.

46   **"Here is the task,"**   TR to Henry Cabot Lodge, 23 Sept. 1901, *Letters,* vol. 3, 150.

46   **The presidential suite**   *The New York Times,* 24 Sept. 1901; TR, *Letters,* vol. 3, 161; Robinson, *My Brother,* 206–7.

46 **Later, when decorations** Robinson, *My Brother.* Mrs. Robinson misdates this dinner by one day.

46 TWO EVENINGS LATER John Barrett (dinner guest) to Caroline S. Barrett, 28 Sept. 1901 (JB); New York *Herald* and New York *Journal,* 26 Sept. 1901. See also Morris, *Edith Kermit Roosevelt,* chap. 18.

47 **Kermit and Ethel** New York *Herald* and New York *Journal,* 26 Sept. 1901.

47 **"It is understood"** *The Washington Post,* 28 Sept. 1901.

47 **The White House police** Ibid.

47 **Alice, naughtily** Teague, *Mrs. L.,* 62; Alice Roosevelt Longworth, *Crowded Hours: Reminiscences of Alice Roosevelt Longworth* (New York, 1933), 43.

47 DISTRACTED AS THE George Cortelyou to Booker T. Washington, 27 Sept. 1901 (BTW); Washington to TR, 1 Oct. 1901 (TRP); Louis J. Harlan, *Booker T. Washington: The Wizard of Tuskegee, 1901–1915* (New York, 1983), 307. Washington and TR had known each other since 1898. TR, *Letters,* vol. 4, 1072; *Booker T. Washington Papers,* vol. 1, 441.

47 **Washington's resistance** *Booker T. Washington Papers,* vol. 1, 439, 441; Gould, *Presidency of Theodore Roosevelt,* 23; Leupp, *The Man Roosevelt,* 215. See also Sullivan, *Our Times,* vol. 3, 128ff.

48 **State by state** C. Vann Woodward, *The Strange Career of Jim Crow* (New York, 1955), 66–68; *World's Work,* Oct. 1901. While expressing sorrow over the death of President McKinley, Washington reminded the editor of the *Montgomery,* Ala., *Advertiser* that an estimated 125,000 Americans had participated in the lynching of Negroes. Harlan, *Booker T. Washington,* 305–6.

48 **Washington, whose** Washington was not unaware of the power he would acquire as TR's race adviser. "I presume that for the mere asking I could get from President Roosevelt almost any political office within reason," he wrote privately. *Booker T. Washington Papers,* vol. 6, 216.

48 AFTER LEAVING THE Booker T. Washington to TR, 1 Oct. 1901 (TRP); *Booker T. Washington Papers,* vol. 1, 12.

48 **As his mother** Harlan, *Booker T. Washington,* 1.

48 **Blacks and whites** See, e.g., Harry Thurston Peck in *International Monthly,* 1 July 1901, and W.E.B. Du Bois, qu. in Francis L. Broderick, *W.E.B. Du Bois.*

48 **"We can be as"** Harlan, *Booker T. Washington,* 218.

49 **Washington's philosophy** *Booker T. Washington Papers,* vol. 6, 385; vol. 1, 220; Harlan, *Booker T. Washington,* 112; Harlan, "The Secret Life of Booker T. Washington," *Journal of Southern History* 37.3 (1971); TR, *Letters,* vol. 5, 227.

49 **Roosevelt, gazing at** Donald J. Calista, "Booker T. Washington: Another Look," *Journal of Negro History* 49.4 (1964).

49 NO SOONER HAD Harlan, *Booker T. Washington,* 308; Booker T. Washington to TR, 2 Oct. 1901, in *Booker T. Washington Papers,* vol. 6, 222–23.

50 **"[He] wanted to"** *Booker T. Washington Papers,* vol. 6, 224.

50 **Washington was forced** Ibid., 229.

50 **Scott delivered** Ibid.

50 **"Because my experience"** TR, *Letters,* vol. 3, 163–64. TR promised to defer further questions of Southern patronage until Hanna came back to town.

50 **Hanna wrote back** Mark Hanna to TR, 12 Oct. 1901 (TRP).

50 **Despite Hanna's concern** *Literary Digest,* 19 Oct. 1901; Sullivan, *Our Times,* vol. 3, 31; Washington *Evening Star,* 14 Oct. 1901; *Review of Reviews,* Nov. 1901. The appointment of Judge Jones bore fruit in the spring of 1903. See below and TR, *Letters,* vol. 3, 501.

50 **Encouraged, the President** Washington *Evening Star,* 10 Oct. 1901. TR's equipage eventually comprised a landau, a brougham, a basket surrey, a buggy, a phaeton, and a victoria—but no automobiles, which he felt lacked presidential dig-

nity. He owned two carriage teams and six riding horses, including two Kentucky Thoroughbreds for himself and his wife. With three additional office horses, and four more belonging to William Loeb, the White House stables were soon at capacity. See Herbert Ridgeway, *Presidents on Wheels* (Washington, D.C., 1971).

50 **He scrapped** Philander Knox to George Cortelyou, 15 Oct. 1901 (GBC); Washington *Evening Star*, 30 Oct. 1901; Stuart P. Sherman in *The Nation*, 9 Nov. 1919; Hay, *Letters*, vol. 3, 345.

50 **Roosevelt in any case** Adams, *Letters*, vol. 5, 369; TR, *Letters*, vol. 3, 164–70. See also TR's personal enunciation of Hay's "Open Door" policy on 27 Feb. 1902 (TRP). Hill, *Roosevelt and the Caribbean*, 34, notes how frequently, from now on, Hay invoked TR's authority in his diplomatic correspondence.

51 **"Teddy said"** John Hay to Henry Adams, 13 Oct. 1901 (TD).

51 **Most observers felt** 14 Oct. 1901 news clips, Presidential scrapbook (TRP).

51 **"For the moment"** Frederick A. McKenzie in unidentified news clip, ca. Oct. 1901, Presidential scrapbook (TRP).

CHAPTER 2: THE MOST DAMNABLE OUTRAGE

52 *Thousan's iv men* "Mr. Dooley" in Salt Lake City *Daily Tribune*, 10 Nov. 1901, Presidential scrapbook (TRP).

52 ON 16 OCTOBER Harlan, *Booker T. Washington*, 318–20; Presidential scrapbook (TRP); Booker T. Washington to TR, 1 Oct. 1901 (TRP).

52 **Roosevelt had a** TR, *Letters*, vol. 3, 190.

    Historiological Note: The question of whether TR was the first President to break the White House's color bar was exhaustively discussed in newspapers of the day. Research indicated that Senator Blanche K. Bruce of Mississippi, and possibly Frederick Douglass, had attended large receptions there, and probably partaken of refreshments with the general company. But neither black man ever dined with the President in intimate surroundings, as Booker T. Washington did on this occasion. Indeed, the only non-Caucasian guest to do so was Queen Liliuokalani of Hawaii, during Grover Cleveland's first administration. Cleveland himself indignantly denied, in the fall of 1901, that he had ever entertained a guest of darker hue than Her Majesty. *Chicago Tribune*, 18 Oct. 1901; *The Charlotte Observer* and Chattanooga *News* clippings, n.d., Presidential scrapbook (TRP).

52 **He received Washington** Harlan, *Booker T. Washington*, 311, errs in saying that Alice Roosevelt attended the dinner. She was still out of town.

52 **Dinner proceeded** James E. Amos, *Theodore Roosevelt: Hero to His Valet* (New York, 1927), 54; Morris, *Edith Kermit Roosevelt*, 472.

52 **The President felt** TR to Carl Schurz, qu. by Harlan, *Booker T. Washington*, 313; see also TR, *Letters*, vol. 3, 182; Maurice Francis Egan, *Recollections of a Busy Life* (New York, 1924), 213.

52 **Here, dark and** Archibald W. Butt, *The Letters of Archie Butt: Personal Aide to President Roosevelt* (New York, 1924), 68; Dyer, *Theodore Roosevelt and the Idea of Race*, 77; Charles Willis Thompson, *Presidents I've Known and Two Near Presidents* (Indianapolis, 1929), 24. Ten years after their famous dinner, TR concluded that Washington was "the highest type of all-round man I have ever met." *Booker T. Washington Papers*, vol. 1, 439.

52 **For those blacks** Dyer, *Theodore Roosevelt*, 97–98; TR, *Autobiography*, 11; TR, *Letters*, vol. 4, 1066; Wister, *Roosevelt*, 259; TR, *Letters*, vol. 5, 226.

53 **Yet Roosevelt believed** Dyer, *Theodore Roosevelt*, 92, 97; TR, *Letters*, vol. 2, 1364–65; TR in *Review of Reviews*, Jan. 1897.

54 **Sometime during the** Memphis *Commercial Appeal,* 18 Oct. 1901, in Presidential scrapbook (TRP); *The Washington Post,* 17 Oct. 1901. Leupp, *The Man Roosevelt,* 218–19, goes to extravagant lengths to describe this news leak as involuntary, and dismisses as "contemptible slander" any suggestion that TR may have authorized the announcement "for political effect." But his book, published in 1904, was a campaign biography, and Leupp himself was known to be a "mouthpiece" for the Roosevelt Administration (John Bassett Moore to J. W. Bayard, 28 Oct. 1901 [JBM]). For obvious reasons, TR would want Southern voters to think, in an election year, that the famous dinner had been an impulse on his part, never to be repeated. But in 1901 he was keen to attract what support he could from moderate Southern Republicans unbeholden to Mark Hanna. His early words to heads of press agencies quoted on pp. 44–45 make plain his strong intent to control all White House news.

54 NEITHER ROOSEVELT NOR *The Washington Post* and *New York Tribune,* 17 Oct. 1901; Harlan, *Booker T. Washington,* 313; Morris, *Rise of Theodore Roosevelt,* 264; *Booker T. Washington Papers,* vol. 6, 257; *The Washington Post,* 18 Oct. 1901. See also August Meier, *Negro Thought in America, 1880–1915: Racial Ideology in the Age of Booker T. Washington* (Ann Arbor, 1988).

54 **Whites, too,** "I thank you—I congratulate you—I pity you," a typical correspondent wrote. "I think you have done an act as brave as [the Christian martyr Hugh] Latimer's and of the same sort. You will be roasted like him, too, and like him ultimately justified with personal earthly immortality." Albion W. Tourgée to TR, 21 Oct. 1901 (TRP).

54 **But during the** *The Atlanta Constitution,* 17 Oct. 1901, Presidential scrapbook (TRP).

54 **"The most damnable"** Memphis *Scimitar,* 17 Oct. 1901, Presidential scrapbook (TRP).

55 **The word *nigger*** *New York Tribune,* 25 Oct. 1901.

55 ROOSEVELT DINES A Richmond *Dispatch,* 18 Oct. 1901; Willard B. Gatewood, Jr., *Theodore Roosevelt and the Art of Controversy: Episodes of the White House Years* (Baton Rouge, 1970), 36; *The Atlanta Constitution,* 18 Oct. 1901, Presidential scrapbook (TRP).

55 **Some of the more** Undated news clips and Presidential scrapbook (TRP). See also Theo Miller, "Booker T. Washington and Some American Writers," *Research Studies* 39.4 (1970), and Takahiro Sasaki's detailed study "Race or Individual Freedom: Public Reactions to the Roosevelt-Washington Dinner at the White House in October, 1901" (M.A. thesis, University of North Carolina, 1984).

55 **The storm squalled** William H. Lewis, TR's black classmate from Harvard, spent a night in the gubernatorial mansion, as did a stranded black baritone denied admission to local hotels. TR also entertained Booker T. Washington at Oyster Bay. Presidential scrapbook, Oct. 1901 (TRP); Pringle, *Theodore Roosevelt,* 230.

55 **Hate mail** *The Washington Post,* 19 Oct. 1901; Presidential scrapbook (TRP); Sullivan, *Our Times,* vol. 3, 136; St. Louis *Mirror,* 31 Oct. 1901. The most recent Tillman biography is Stephen Kantrowitz, *Ben Tillman and the Reconstruction of White Supremacy* (Chapel Hill, 2000). But see also Francis B. Simkins, *Pitchfork Ben Tillman* (Baton Rouge, 1944), 1–32.

55 **"At one stroke"** Richmond *News,* 18 Oct. 1901. See also Edgar G. Murphy to Booker T. Washington, 19 Oct. 1901 (BTW).

55 BY TACIT AGREEMENT *New York Tribune,* 25 Oct. 1901; *Springfield Republican,* n.d., Presidential scrapbook (TRP).

55 ON 21 OCTOBER New Orleans *Times-Democrat* and St. Louis *Republic,* 22 Oct. 1901; Harlan, *Booker T. Washington,* 317; *Booker T. Washington Papers,* vol. 6, 262; Charles P. Taft to William H. Taft, 24 Oct. 1901 (WHT).

56 **Roosevelt looked calm** New York *Herald*, 22 Oct. 1901; Platt qu. in Louis Coolidge, *An Old-Fashioned Senator: Orville H. Platt* (New York, 1910), 512; "Precautionary" [security] file, Oct. 1901 (TRP). Leon Czolgosz approached McKinley with what looked like a bandaged right hand. McKinley reached to shake his left, whereupon the "bandage" spit bullets.

56 **Shocked by this** *New Hampshire Evening Register*, 23 Oct. 1901, Presidential scrapbook (TRP); Rhodes, *McKinley and Roosevelt*, 228.

56 **Degrees were awarded** Longworth, *Crowded Hours*, 43; *The New York Times* and New York *Journal*, 24 Oct. 1901. TR was awarded an LL.D.

56 **Notwithstanding this** Frederick S. Wood, *Roosevelt as We Knew Him* (Philadelphia, 1927), 98.

56 **Twain's private** Bernard De Voto, ed., *Mark Twain in Eruption* (New York, 1940), 30–31.

56 A LARGE CROWD New Orleans *Times-Democrat*, 21 Oct. 1901; New York *Herald* and Washington *Evening Star*, 25 Oct. 1901.

57 ROOSEVELT'S QUERULOUSNESS *Booker T. Washington Papers*, vol. 6, 274–75; TR, *Letters*, vol. 3, 181, 184. In late October, Senator John L. McLaurin of South Carolina wrote a sympathetic statement explaining TR's action in terms calculated to reassure the South. But TR refused to approve it. "The President said he did not want anyone to make any explanation for him" (George Cortelyou superscript on original draft [TRP]).

57 *"My dear Mr. President"* *Booker T. Washington Papers*, vol. 6, 274.

57 **Sensing Roosevelt's need** Ibid., 263, 283.

57 **Some good, certainly** John M. Blum, *The Republican Roosevelt* (Cambridge, Mass., 1954), 44; Harlan, *Booker T. Washington*, 305, 324.

57 **"the infinite capacity"** "TR and the Press," unpublished ms. (HH).

58 **He dutifully announced** New York *Journal*, 30 Oct. 1901.

58 **"I have not been"** TR to Albion W. Tourgée, 8 Nov. 1901, *Letters*, vol. 3, 190–91.

58 **As the famous** See, e.g., TR to Carl Schurz, qu. in Harlan, *Booker T. Washington*, 321; Wister, *Roosevelt*, 254; M. A. De Wolfe Howe, *George von Lengerke Meyer: His Life and Public Services* (New York, 1919), 416, 420; TR, *Letters*, vol. 8, 981–82.

58 **And when Washington** Booker T. Washington to George Cortelyou, 20 Dec. 1901 (TRP).

CHAPTER 3: ONE VAST, SMOOTHLY RUNNING MACHINE

59 *A hard time* Finley Peter Dunne, *Observations by Mr. Dooley* (New York, 1902), 175.

59 THE NIGHT OF MONDAY Except where otherwise indicated, the following account is based on Ray Stannard Baker, "The Great Northern Pacific Deal," *Collier's Weekly*, 30 Nov. 1901; *Commercial & Financial Chronicle*, 1902, 843, 1011, 1062; and Martin, *James J. Hill*, 495ff. Additional atmospheric details from New York *Sun*, 12 and 13 Nov. 1901.

59 **three financiers conferred** The standard biographies are Martin, *James J. Hill;* Maury Klein, *The Life and Legend of E. H. Harriman* (Chapel Hill, 2000); Strouse, *Morgan;* and John A. Garraty, *Right-Hand Man: The Life of George W. Perkins* (New York, 1960).

59 **This common need** Isaac F. Marcosson, *Before I Forget* (New York, 1959), 221–24.

59 **huge damp mustache** "I never could figure out how he drank his coffee" Averell Harriman interview, 14 Feb. 1981.

59 **Decent, driven men** TR, First Annual Message to Congress, *Works,* vol. 17, 101; Faulkner, *Decline of Laissez-Faire,* 24–25, 92–93.

59 **Yet they had** Martin, *James J. Hill,* 505; Sullivan, *Our Times,* vol. 2, 347.

60 **Their meeting tonight** Balthazar H. Meyer, "A History of the Northern Securities Case," *Bulletin of the University of Wisconsin Economics and Political Science Series* 1.3 (1904–1906): 229–36; Martin, *James J. Hill,* 394–504. The panic occurred on 9 May 1901.

60 **Right now, Hill** Martin, *James J. Hill,* 504–8. Harriman had acquired the Southern Pacific earlier in the year. He also had interests in the Santa Fe.

60 **What lay before** Meyer, "Northern Securities Case," 236; Martin, *James J. Hill,* 509.

60 **Anybody could see** Meyer, "Northern Securities Case," 240; Sullivan, *Our Times,* vol. 2, 370.

60 **The flaw in** New York *World,* 15 Nov. 1901, quotes an unnamed trust expert as saying that Hill's charter was "unquestionably . . . a violation of the *spirit* of the law against combinations."

61 **But Hill was** New York *World,* 15 Nov. 1901; Thorelli, *Federal Antitrust Policy,* 445; Martin, *James J. Hill,* 511.

61 THE NEXT DAY, **Tuesday** TR to Albert Shaw, 12 Nov. 1901; TR, First Annual Message draft (TRP). See Waldon Fawcett, "How President Roosevelt Wrote His First Message," *Success,* Jan. 1902.

61 **Roosevelt worked** Washington *Evening Star,* 12 Nov. 1901.

61 ROOSEVELT HAD TAKEN The following profile of Philander Chase Knox is based on descriptions and photographs in Edward G. Lowry, *Washington Close-Ups: Intimate Views of Some Public Figures* (Boston, 1921), 194–96; New York *Herald,* 7 Apr. 1901; *The Historical Register* (New York, 1921), 54; Philadelphia *Press,* 10 June 1904; Thompson, *Party Leaders,* 310ff.; and Samuel Flagg Bemis, *The American Secretaries of State and Their Diplomacy* (New York, 1927–1929), vol. 9, 302–10.

61 **In the words of** Lowry, *Washington Close-Ups,* 194. Kate Carew in New York *World,* 10 Mar. 1904, satirizes Knox's impenetrability.

61 **Knox was the** By the late 1890s, Knox was said to be charging $250,000 for a case. A. T. Eitler, "Philander Chase Knox" (Ph.D. diss., Catholic University, 1959), 10. See also Minneapolis *Times,* 17 Jan. 1903, in Knox Scrapbook (PCK).

62 **The Attorney General** New York *Herald,* 7 Apr. 1901; Kate Carew in New York *World,* 10 Mar. 1904; Knox to Delmonico's, 13 Jan. 1902 (PCK); photographs of 1527 K Street NW (FBJ); Knox qu. in New York *Herald,* 20 June 1901.

62 **His languid, *laissez-faire*** Peck, *Twenty Years of the Republic,* 686; Adams, *Letters,* vol. 5, 232. Thorelli, *Federal Antitrust Policy,* 404–5, notes that Knox showed little spontaneous inclination to activate antitrust enforcement until galvanized by TR.

62 **A friend remarked** Thompson, *Party Leaders,* 318.

62 **Roosevelt was quick** TR qu. in Samuel Leland Powers, *Portraits of Half a Century* (Boston, 1925), 218; Washington *Evening Star,* 18 Oct. 1901; Henry Loomis Nelson, "Three Months of President Roosevelt," *Atlantic Monthly,* Feb. 1902.

62 **Knox, Roosevelt discovered** Philadelphia *Press,* 10 June 1904; Knox scrapbook (PCK); Bemis, *American Secretaries of State,* vol. 9, 309–10; Eitler, "Philander Chase Knox," 25–26, 32; Lowry, *Washington Close-Ups,* 201; White, *Autobiography,* 342.

62 **Such a truce** Hill had visited Washington at the beginning of November, and asked himself to dinner at the White House (Washington *Evening Star,* 2 Nov. 1901). Martin, *James J. Hill,* speculates: "It was time, Hill felt, to explain what the new railroad arrangements meant for the West they loved so much." For Harri-

man's and Morgan's early relationship with TR and Hill, see Klein, *Life and Legend*, 361–63.

62 **Perkins was the** TR, *Letters,* vol. 3, 159–60.

64 **"Perkins may just"** Ibid., 159–60, 177.

64 MORGAN, HILL, AND Washington *Evening Star,* 13 Nov. 1901; New York *Sun,* 14 Nov. 1901.

64 **The New York *Journal*** 14 Nov. 1901.

64 **"They are smoothing"** Ibid.

64 **"To me there is"** George Perkins to TR, 15 Nov. 1901 (GWP).

64 **In due course** New York *Sun,* 15 Nov. 1902.

64 **"Can I get some"** Mark Hanna to George Perkins, 27 Nov. 1901 (GWP).

64 **Lesser citizens** *Statistician and Economist* (New York, 1901–1902); Baker, "Great Northern Pacific Deal."

65 **"Is it possible,"** Baker, "Great Northern Pacific Deal."

65 **As if in answer** New York *Sun,* 12 Nov. 1901.

65 **"I see dynamite"** Mark Hanna to TR, 10 Nov. 1901 (TRP).

65 **He objected in** TR, First Annual Message draft (TRP); Mark Hanna to TR, 10 Nov. 1901 (TRP). Elihu Root also took "serious exception" to this part of the Message. TR to St. Clair McKelway, 21 Nov. 1901 (TRP).

65 **Other senators** Message drafts in TRP; Orville H. Platt to TR, 13 Nov. 1901 (TRP); TR to Mark Hanna, 21 Nov. 1901 (TRP). Sample language deleted: "I am firmly of the belief that a law can be framed that will enable the National Government to exercise control over the trusts. . . . It should be treated . . . as an effort, not to destroy or disarrange business, but to continue the upbuilding of our interest on foundations of justice to all. . . . *This Government must recognize the need of change.*"

65 RESTRAINED AS HE Washington *Evening Star,* 15 Oct. 1901; *World's Work,* Dec. 1901. See Wood, *Roosevelt As We Knew Him,* 473–74, on how the speed of TR's reactions exasperated Philander Knox.

66 **"Mr. President"** Boston *Transcript,* 18 Nov. 1901. The Senator was William J. Deboe of Kentucky.

66 **He would whirl** George William Douglas, *The Many-Sided Roosevelt: An Anecdotal Biography* (New York, 1907), 249–56; Walter Hines Page in *World's Work,* Dec. 1901. Both these accounts describe Roosevelt's receptions in Nov. 1901. TR was then making an average of thirty appointments a day. One alone—for Collector of Customs in Fort Worth—generated twenty-eight pounds of documents. Washington *Evening Star,* 11 Nov. 1901.

66 **Those other White** Walter Hines Page in *World's Work,* Dec. 1901; Chauncey M. Depew, *My Memories of Eighty Years* (New York, 1922), 169.

66 **There were days** Washington *Evening Star,* 23 Nov. 1901; Joseph Bucklin Bishop, *Theodore Roosevelt and His Time: Shown in His Own Letters* (New York, 1920), vol. 1, 156; James Morse diary, 24 Nov. 1901 (NYHS). See also L. T. Michener to Eugene Hay (copy in HKB).

66 **"How many men"** William Dudley Foulke, *Fighting the Spoilsmen* (New York, 1919), 55–56; *The Cincinnati Enquirer,* 25 Dec. 1901.

67 **"In El Paso"** Foulke, *Fighting,* 56.

67 ON 18 NOVEMBER See John A. S. Grenville, "Great Britain and the Isthmian Canal, 1898–1901," *American Historical Review* 61 (Oct. 1955); New York *Journal,* 21–22 Nov. 1901; Miles P. DuVal, *Cadiz to Cathay: The Story of the Long Struggle for a Waterway across the American Isthmus* (Stanford, 1940), 154.

67 **It was a big** McCullough, *Path Between the Seas,* 262. See ibid., *passim,* for background to the Isthmian Canal situation in 1901.

67 **"There are certain"** *Report of the Isthmian Canal Commission, 1899–1901,* 58 Cong., 2 sess., 1904, S. Doc. 222, 174–75.

67 **Minus that extra** Maurice Hutin to TR, 30 Nov. 1901, and John G. Walker to TR, 6 Dec. 1901 (TRP). On 4 Nov., John Hay, a Nicaragua partisan, wrote to Luis F. Corea, that country's Washington minister, warning him that "very powerful influences are at work against the Nicaragua Canal" (TD).

68 ROOSEVELT FINISHED John Hay to Joseph Bucklin Bishop, qu. in Bishop, *Theodore Roosevelt,* vol. 1, 160. Printing a Message to Congress was an innovation. TR saw no reason to perpetuate the laborious nineteenth-century custom of copying such documents in ornamental script. In a further break with tradition, he made galleys available to the press, under guarantees that the Message would be neither quoted nor summarized before it went to Congress. This gave editors plenty of time to typeset the text themselves, and TR's Message was rewarded with five times as much comment as any had enjoyed before. TR also made sure that a summary of the Message was released to European journals. See First Annual Message box and Presidential scrapbook (TRP).

68 **Twelve days still** Washington *Evening Star* and *New York Tribune,* 23 Nov. 1901.

68 BACK IN MINNESOTA Hill qu. in Martin, *James J. Hill,* 510–11.

68 WHILE THE SYLPH Washington *Evening Star,* 25 Nov. 1901; *The New York Times,* 21 Nov. 1901. A copy of the latter article was sent to the White House. Presidential scrapbook (TRP).

68 **The astrologist-author** *The New York Times,* 21 Nov. 1901.

68 **Although Roosevelt** Ibid.

68 **The President need** Ibid.

69 **The President, he** Adams, *Letters,* vol. 5, 326; Thayer, *Hay,* vol. 2, 266.

69 **Although Hay was** John Hay to Mrs. Hay, 15 Nov. 1901 (WF).

CHAPTER 4: A MESSAGE FROM THE PRESIDENT

70 *On th' wan* "Mr. Dooley" qu. in Sullivan, *Our Times,* vol. 2, 411.

70 SHORTLY BEFORE NOON *The Washington Post,* 4 Dec. 1901.

70 **Octavius L. Pruden** Washington *Evening Times,* 3 Dec. 1901; *New York Tribune,* 4 Dec. 1901.

70 **A Secret Service** The practice of presidential addresses to Congress, as opposed to messages, had ended with John Adams, and would not be revived until 1913 by Woodrow Wilson.

70 **Actually, the content** Douglas, *Many-Sided Roosevelt,* 251.

70 **Even so, Congress** Washington *Evening Times,* 3 Dec. 1901.

71 *"The Congress assembles"* The following extracts from TR's Message are taken from TR, *Works,* vol. 17, 93–160.

71 **There was an** "The sentence fell upon the House like a pall." Washington *Evening Times,* 3 Dec. 1901.

71 *"The wind is sowed"* TR, *Works,* vol. 17, 97. TR later confirmed that he was alluding to William Randolph Hearst, yellow-press lord and perennial political candidate.

71 **The House sat** The word *rapt* is that of the New York *World,* 4 Dec. 1901. See also *The New York Times,* same date.

71 **At this, the spell** New York *World,* 4 Dec. 1901.

71 THE SENATE, in Washington *Evening Times,* 3 Dec. 1901.

71 **For a quarter** New York *Sun* and New York *Herald,* 4 Dec. 1901.

71 **Mark Hanna sat** Washington *Evening Times,* 4 Dec. 1901. See John A. Garraty, *Henry Cabot Lodge: A Biography* (New York, 1953), 220–22, for Lodge's emotions during these early months of TR's Presidency.

72 As Roosevelt swung New York *World,* 4 Dec. 1901.

72 SPOONER, AT FIFTY-EIGHT This profile is based on Walter Wellman, "Spooner of Wisconsin: A Sketch," *Review of Reviews,* Aug. 1902; Thompson, *Party Leaders,* 47–51; Merrill, *Republican Command,* 32; O. O. Stealey, *130 Pen Pictures of Live Men* (Washington, D.C., 1910); Peck, *Twenty Years of the Republic,* 426–31; Dorothy C. Fowler, *John Coit Spooner, Defender of Presidents* (New York, 1961), *passim;* and photographs in various publications.

72 He was equally See, e.g., Spooner versus Senator Benjamin R. Tillman in *The Washington Post,* 28 Jan. 1902.

72 But he had Wellman, "Spooner"; Merrill, *Republican Command,* 33–34, notes the corruption of Wisconsin politics in 1901. It was difficult at that time even for honest senators to escape the taint of corruption at home, since they were not directly elected, and served at the pleasure of state legislatures.

72 His perambulation New York *World,* 4 Dec. 1901.

72 "Allison could run" TR, *Works,* vol. 17, 103.

72 This *legerdepied* Merrill, *Republican Command,* 30–31.

73 Poised in his See, e.g., Leland L. Sage, *William Boyd Allison: A Study in Practical Politics* (Iowa City, 1956), 197, 250, 292, 294, 6; David J. Rothman, *Politics and Power: The Senate, 1869–1901* (Cambridge, Mass., 1966), 47.

73 "All this is true" TR, *Works,* vol. 17, 104.

73 In the front Nathaniel W. Stephenson, *Nelson W. Aldrich: A Leader in American Politics* (New York, 1930), 136; Coolidge, *Old-Fashioned Senator,* 61.

73 There was something Coolidge, *Old-Fashioned Senator,* 65–67, 592; Thompson, *Party Leaders,* 34; George H. Mayer, *The Republican Party, 1854–1966* (New York, 1966), 277; Merrill, *Republican Command,* 27–28; Claude G. Bowers, *Beveridge and the Progressive Era* (Boston, 1932), 138–39.

73 "There is a widespread" TR, *Works,* vol. 17, 104.

73 "It is no" Ibid., 104–5.

73 If Nelson W. Barry, *Forty Years,* 152; Stephenson, *Nelson W. Aldrich,* 9, 172.

73 "The first essential" Ibid., 105.

73 Aldrich's was a Rothman, *Politics and Power,* 46; David S. Barry and Elihu Root in biographical file (NWA).

74 His power derived Merrill, *Republican Command,* 24, 28; speech cards in NWA; Barry, *Forty Years,* 153. See, e.g., James Anthony Rosmond, "Nelson Aldrich, Theodore Roosevelt and the Tariff: A Study to 1905" (Ph.D. diss., University of North Carolina, 1974).

74 Roosevelt, in contrast David S. Barry memo, biographical file (NWA).

74 As far as Aldrich Merrill, *Republican Command,* 24–25.

74 "The nation should" TR, *Works,* vol. 17, 106.

74 Aldrich believed that Barry memo, biographical file (NWA).

74 Since this was The term *Majority Leader* was not yet current. Neither was the convenient (and misleading) group term of "the Senate Four" for Aldrich, Spooner, Allison, and Platt. Although these men indeed worked closely together, they often differed on important issues—Aldrich and Allison on the tariff, e.g. Other Republican senators wielded great power in their personal fiefdoms: Henry Cabot Lodge on foreign policy, Eugene Hale on naval affairs, Hanna on labor, and so on. In a letter to his parents, written ca. Feb. 1903, the Chicago newspaper heir Medill McCormick defined the government of the United States as "an oligarchy tempered by the veto" (MHM).

74 "I believe that" TR, *Works,* vol. 17, 106.

74 THE SENATE WAS Profile of Aldrich based on biographical file (NWA); Steffens, *Autobiography,* 504; *Ainslee's Magazine,* Dec. 1901; Bowers, *Beveridge,* 313–24; Merrill, *Republican Command,* 21–26; and photographs in various publications.

74 There were a few Rothman, *Politics and Power,* 112, 136, 217, 112–15, 136, 183–86, 201.
74 Orville Platt was Stephenson, *Nelson W. Aldrich,* 203.
75 What held them Rothman, *Politics and Power,* 111, 117.
75 He granted TR, *Works,* vol. 17, 107–10.
75 Clearly, neither subject Gould, *Presidency of Theodore Roosevelt,* 12, 24–26; Merrill, *Republican Command,* 26.
76 *"The railway"* TR, *Works,* vol. 17, 116–17.
76 *"The doctrine of"* Ibid., 124.
76 *"We are dealing"* Ibid., 125.
76 FOR ANOTHER HOUR Washington *Evening Times,* 3 Dec. 1901; Paul Russell Cutright, *Theodore Roosevelt: The Making of a Conservationist* (Urbana, 1985), 93.
76 By two o'clock Washington *Evening Times,* 3 Dec. 1901; New York *World,* 4 Dec. 1901.
77 *"In the midst"* TR, *Works,* vol. 17, 160.
77 Each had an New York *World* and New York *Herald,* 4 Dec. 1901.
77 Democratic leaders, too *The Washington Post,* 4 Dec. 1901.
77 Members of the *Literary Digest,* 14 Dec. 1901. "Never in our history," commented the New York *Evening Post,* "have we had a more striking example of great responsibility upon an imperious nature." Negative comment was concentrated in the South.
77 That night, Roosevelt *Pittsburgh Times,* 4 Dec. 1901; *Review of Reviews,* Jan. 1902; Bishop, *Theodore Roosevelt,* vol. 1, 160; Washington *Evening Times,* 3 Dec. 1901, and *New York Tribune,* 4 Dec. 1901.
77 *"It is not"* Chicago *Record-Herald,* 5 Dec. 1901.
78 On 7 December Washington *Evening Star,* 7 Dec. 1901.
78 The quickest way *Review of Reviews,* Jan. 1902. On 9 Dec., TR received a letter from the black politician Ralph Waldo Tyler, forwarded by Booker T. Washington, warning him that "Senator Hanna will be candidate for President." Negro officeholders all over the South were prepared "to go to the next National convention with a solid delegation" in support of their patron. No doubt this letter added a spur to TR's own patronage plans. For his bemused reaction, see TR, *Letters,* vol. 3, 206.
78 A surprise choice Gage privately admitted that the contrast between TR's galvanic personality and that of McKinley had left him with a feeling of "chronic sadness." Gage to Charles G. Dawes, 11 Dec. 1901 (LCG).
78 Charles Emory Smith Mowry, *Era of Theodore Roosevelt,* 120; Blum, *Republican Roosevelt,* 42.
78 It did not escape Merrill, *Republican Command,* 34. See Fowler, *John Coit Spooner,* chap. 10 on the LaFollette insurgency in Wisconsin—a phenomenon that was to have enormous, if delayed, consequences for TR's political career.
78 There was further *Literary Digest,* 28 Dec. 1901; Blum, *Republican Roosevelt,* 43; Merrill, *Republican Command,* 103–5. Attrition among Hanna-backed officeholders in the Postal Service began almost immediately. See the long list of new appointments in *The Washington Post,* 28 Jan. 1902.
78 Yet another anti-Hanna James A. Kehl, *Boss Rule in the Gilded Age: Matt Quay of Pennsylvania* (Pittsburgh, 1955), 236; New York *Evening Post,* 10 Dec. 1901; L. Clarke Davis to John Hay, 10 Dec. 1901 (JH).
78 ONE UNSEEMLY INCIDENT L. T. Michener to Eugene Hay, ca. 24 Dec. 1901 (copy in HKB).
79 Roosevelt had developed Morris, *Rise of Theodore Roosevelt,* 611; James B. Martin, "The Irresistible Force and the Immovable Object: Theodore Roosevelt and Lieutenant General Nelson A. Miles," *Theodore Roosevelt Association Journal,* spring 1987. There is a comic description in Ambrose Bierce's *Devil's Dictio-*

nary of General Miles "passing in review" before two observers and nearly blinding them with his effulgence. See the definition of *story*, example 3.

79 **What angered Roosevelt** TR, *Letters*, vol. 3, 98, 241; Edward Ranson, "Nelson A. Miles as Commanding General, 1895–1903," *Military Affairs* 29.4 (1966).

79 **Secrets embarrassing** For more detail, see Jessup, *Elihu Root*, vol. 1, 243ff. In Root's later words, Miles was "a real difficulty, and must . . . be eliminated." To Philip Jessup, 26 Oct. 1934 (PCJ).

79 **Miles played into** Jessup, *Elihu Root*, vol. 1, 248. This was the famous Samson-Schley dispute. For details, see Edward L. Beach, *The United States Navy: 200 Years* (New York, 1986), 361–68.

79 **His voice rose** Annie Riley Hale, *Bull Moose Trails* (privately printed, 1912), 2–4, qu. two eyewitnesses. Ranson, "Nelson A. Miles," prints a milder version of this interview. But all contemporary accounts have TR shouting loud enough to be heard outside the White House lawn. "Poor old Miles . . . it was a brutal thing" (L. T. Michener to Eugene Hay, ca. 24 Dec. 1901 [copy in HKB]).

79 **"You have the"** Isabel McKenna Duffield, *Washington in the Nineties* (San Francisco, 1929), 48; *The Army and Navy Register*, 4 Jan. 1902.

79 PURGED, PERHAPS William Marion Reedy in St. Louis *Mirror*, 19 Dec. 1901. An extra contribution to TR's *bonhomie* at this time might have been the successful appearance, in Britain, of his latest scholarly work, a chapter on the War of 1812 in the sixth volume of William Laird Clowes's *The Royal Navy: A History from the Earliest Times to the Present* (London, 1901). A lengthy review in *The Atheneum*, 28 Dec. 1901, rated it even higher than his "excellent" *Naval War of 1812* (New York, 1882). "Twenty years ago he was remarkably fair and even-minded; now he writes from the standpoint of scientific neutrality, which conveys no hint of his nationality. . . . It is not easy to express in measured language our sense of the merit and importance of every line of this admirable essay."

80 **Yet there was** P. C. Knox to TR, 11 Dec. 1901 (TRP). See also Thorelli, *Federal Antitrust Policy*, 423.

80 **"I should say,"** William Marion Reedy in St. Louis *Mirror*, 19 Dec. 1901.

80 HOWLS OF MIRTH Joan Paterson Kerr, ed., *A Bully Father: Theodore Roosevelt's Letters to His Children* (New York, 1995), 112–13; White House press release (hand-edited by TR), 25 Dec. 1901 (TRP).

80 **The band swung** White House press release, 25 Dec. 1901 (TRP).

CHAPTER 5: TURN OF A RISING TIDE

81 *Divvle a bit* Dunne, *Observations by Mr. Dooley*, 57.

81 WALTER WELLMAN, REPORTER Chicago *Record-Herald*, 16 Jan. 1902. TR amusedly told Hay that Senator Lodge was "frantic with fury" at press reports that he was "learning to ride, so as to go out with me," qu. in Adams, *Letters*, vol. 5, 319.

81 **To Wellman and** Unidentified news clip, 21 Nov. 1901, Presidential scrapbook (TRP); Leupp, *The Man Roosevelt*, 311–13.

81 **"You must always"** Spring Rice to Valentine Chirol, qu. in Wagenknecht, *Seven Worlds*, 11.

81 **Charles William Eliot** Qu. in Richard Olney to Grover Cleveland, 14 Jan. 1902 (GC); Ecclesiastes 10:16, qu. in ibid.

82 **It was the lunches** "I feel as though I should bust," he wrote Nannie Cabot Lodge, "if I am not able to discuss at length and without my usual cautious reserve several questions—Dewey, Schley, Hanna, Foraker, Cuba, Bagehot's Shakespeare, the Hallstadt culture as connected with Homer's Acheans, the latest phase of the Monroe Doctrine, and the Boston Mayoralty elections." TR, *Letters*, vol. 8, 1442.

82 **The Washington social** For descriptions of the 1902 season, which included Alice

Roosevelt's coming-out ball, see Rixey, *Bamie*, chap. 21, and Morris, *Edith Kermit Roosevelt*, 228–38.

82   **"Theodore is never"**   Adams, *Letters*, vol. 5, 345. See also "Wanted: A President," *The Washington Post*, 1 Jan. 1902.

82   **Adams was back**   Adams, *Letters*, vol. 5, 322–23.

82   **The Fifty-seventh**   Ibid., 359; TR, *Letters*, vol. 3, 225–27.

82   **Roosevelt made it**   Amy Belle Cheney [secretary], memo, n.d. (HH); Robinson, *My Brother*, 229; TR qu. in Messmore Kendall, *Never Let Weather Interfere* (New York, 1946), 130. Koenig, *Invisible Presidency*, 151, claims that TR dictated as many as two or three hundred letters a day.

82   **He hesitated only**   See, e.g., TR, *Letters*, vol. 3, 239–40, 242. William James wrote approvingly of "the safety of his second thoughts." Henry James, ed., *The Letters of William James* (Boston, 1926), vol. 2, 232.

82   **The President was**   Lewis F. Einstein, *Roosevelt: His Mind in Action* (Boston, 1930), 104; TR, *Letters*, vol. 3, 218.

83   **"Roosevelt," declared**   George F. Parker, *Recollections of Grover Cleveland* (New York, 1911), 250.

83   ON FRIDAY, 3 JANUARY   *The New York Times*, 4 Jan. 1902; McCullough, *Path Between the Seas*, 263.

83   **Hanna said that**   Dwight C. Miner, *The Fight for the Panama Route* (New York, 1940), 125. The reader should bear in mind a distinction, in the story here beginning, between the Isthmian Canal Commission ("Walker Commission") and Senate Committee on Interoceanic Canals ("Morgan Committee").

83   **It had recommended**   *New York Tribune*, 4 Jan. 1902.

83   **At least one**   McCullough, *Path Between the Seas*, 293. Earlier that morning, Hanna had urgently summoned Spooner to a meeting behind closed doors with sympathetic members of the Isthmian Commission (JCS).

83   **On the very morning**   McCullough, *Path Between the Seas*, 266.

84   **"I want the report"**   Qu. in New York *Herald*, 17 Jan. 1902.

84   **Morgan hurried**   Hanna called to warn TR that Morgan was on his way down Pennsylvania Avenue, breathing fire (George Cortelyou telephone memorandum, 16 Jan. 1902 [TRP]). According to *The Story of Panama: Hearings on the Rainey Resolution Before the Committee on Foreign Affairs of the House of Representatives* (Washington, D.C., 1913), 166, TR summoned every member of the Commission, one by one, to his office immediately after the House vote on 9 Jan. in order to canvass their individual views. He then held a full, secret meeting at which he instructed the Commission to think again and issue a "unanimous" recommendation.

84   **Shocked and depressed**   Hill, *Roosevelt and the Caribbean*, 36; New York *Herald*, 17 Jan. 1902. Lewis M. Haupt, the most pro-Nicaragua of the ICC's eight members, held out until the report was ready for signing on Saturday. Admiral Walker then led him up and down the corridor outside the meeting room, saying that "the President was extremely anxious to have a unanimous report," in view of anti-Panama sentiment in the Senate. Haupt reluctantly signed. Haupt to John T. Morgan, 13 Sept. 1903 (JTM).

84   **The supplemental report**   New York *Herald*, 21 Jan. 1902.

84   **"The commission thinks"**   Ibid. The *Herald* was a pro-Nicaragua paper.

85   **A "Panama boom"**   DuVal, *Cadiz to Cathay*, 157; New York *Herald* and *The New York Times*, 21 Jan. 1902.

85   **Harriman began to buy**   Specifically, a total of $166,613, which he later sold for a profit of $88,447.38. Photostats in New York *World*, 17 Oct. 1910. See also Cyrus Adler, *Jacob H. Schiff: His Life and Letters* (New York, 1929), vol. 1, 207–8.

85   OF ALL THE WELL-DRESSED   Charles D. Ameringer, "The Panama Canal Lobby of

Philippe Bunau-Varilla and William Nelson Cromwell," *American Historical Review,* 68.2 (1963).

85 **Cromwell was the** New York *World,* 4 Oct. 1908; photographs in various publications; Sullivan, *Our Times,* vol. 2, 318–19; McCullough, *Path Between the Seas,* 272–73.

85 **If Cromwell's** Bunau-Varilla interviewed by Howard K. Beale, July 1936 (HKB).

85 **It was hard for Americans** Bunau-Varilla, "Confidential for Mr. Lawrence F. Abbott" (PBV); McCullough, *Path Between the Seas,* 162, 290. John Bassett Moore, who worked closely with Bunau-Varilla in 1903–1904 (see below), observed, "He is one of the cleverest men I have ever met." Moore to TR, 7 Jan. 1904 (TRP).

86 **Now forty-two** McCullough, *Path Between the Seas,* 400–401; biographical sketch of Bunau-Varilla, ca. 1903, in JBM.

86 **Bunau-Varilla therefore** *Travail pour la patrie* means *labor for the fatherland* [France], a phrase obsessively repeated by Bunau-Varilla. William Glover Fletcher, "Canal Site Diplomacy: A Study in American Political Geography" (Ph.D. diss., Yale University, 1940), 176. Fletcher interviewed and corresponded with Bunau-Varilla at length.

86 **As an engineer** "Arbitrage Entre la Compagnie Nouvelle du Canal de Panama et MM. Sullivan et Cromwell," deposition, 24 Oct. 1907 (PBV); New York *Sun,* 28 Dec. 1901; Edward P. Mitchell, *Memories of an Editor* (New York, 1924), 343.

86 ON 24 JANUARY *The Washington Post,* 26 Jan. 1902. TR's own gift was a meteorological map of the District of Columbia showing the White House to be an "Area of High Pressure."

86 AT THE END OF *Story of Panama,* 279; *The Washington Post,* 25 Jan. 1902.

86 **It was all very** *The Washington Post,* 25 Jan. 1902; McCullough, *Path Between the Seas,* 263.

86 **With new hearings** The House voted for senatorial elections, and the Senate against. Direct election of senators was to become one of the major planks of the Progressive movement.

87 **"When you come"** TR to Spooner, 28 Jan. 1902, qu. in Fowler, *John Coit Spooner,* 262. Miner, *Fight for the Panama Route,* 124–25, makes a convincing argument for TR's sponsorship of the Spooner Amendment.

87 **"He really determines"** Wilson, *Papers,* vol. 12, 262.

87 **From outer space** Cartoon by Edward Kemble in *Life,* 30 Jan. 1902.

87 A FEW DAYS TR, *Letters,* vol. 3, 229. The day before, he had been waited on by members of the Industrial Commission, who were about to publish their final report on the trusts. While favorable toward combination in general, the report did draw attention to the "vicious and intolerable" discriminatory practices of some interstate corporations, and echoed TR's call for compulsory publicity of trust workings. *Public Opinion,* 20 Feb. 1902.

87 **It was 5 February** Albert J. Beveridge to Albert Shaw, 10 Jan. 1902 (AJB); *The Washington Post,* 19 Feb. 1902.

87 **Any fool could** Eitler, "Philander Chase Knox," 61; *Review of Reviews,* Apr. 1902; H. B. Martin and Emlen H. Miller to TR, 30 Nov. and 9 Dec. 1901, Department of Justice files (NA).

88 **"Am giving it"** P. C. Knox to TR, 11 Dec. 1901 (TRB). For TR's dispatch of his overworked Attorney General to Florida, see TR to Knox, 5 Dec. 1902 (PCK). "I am not dead," Knox wrote a friend, ". . . but so far as attending to anything personal, might just as well have been." To James S. Young, 15 Jan. 1902 (PCK).

88 **Now, eight weeks** Antitrust notes, Feb. 1902, in PCK.

88 **Plunging deep into** Memorandum, "Comment on 'Underlying Laws' (in all social and industrial movements), as suggested by Kidd's *Western Civilization,*" ca. 1902, in PCK.

88 **What, then, of** *Review of Reviews,* Apr. 1902; P. C. Knox memo, 10 Feb. 1902
(PCK); McCurdy, "*Knight* Sugar Decision of 1895." TR and Knox agreed that
Kidd's revisionist allowance seemed to apply to *Knight,* which had become the enabling bible of *laissez-faire.* The Attorney General advised that the best chance to
"reverse" *Knight*'s effect would be to press a suit that challenged it technically, but
not in principle. TR ordered him to go ahead. "This [reversal] I felt it imperative to
secure." TR to Charles G. Washburn, qu. in Washburn, *Theodore Roosevelt: The
Logic of His Career* (Boston, 1916), 67–68.

88 **Knox felt that** Washburn, *Theodore Roosevelt,* 67–68.

88 **For once in** Eitler, "Philander Chase Knox," 63–64.

89 **Farther off, in** See Henry Clay Frick to P. C. Knox, 11 Nov. 1901 and 5 Feb. 1902
(PCK).

89 **a fourteen-page opinion** Draft in PCK; New York *Herald,* 10 Feb. 1902. The actual delivered opinion is now lost. Eitler theorizes (although the *Herald* reports
otherwise) that it was given to TR orally. "Philander Chase Knox," 64.

89 **"If you instruct"** Qu. by Walter Wellman in Chicago *Record-Herald,* 16 Mar.
1904 (a leak of TR's own telling of the story to his Cabinet, the day before).

89 **"Mr. Hanna,"** Martin, *James J. Hill,* 514.

89 **Hanna, preoccupied with** Ibid. *The New York Times,* 20 Feb. 1902.

89 **"The government has"** Mark Hanna to Charles E. Perkins, memorandum, 11
July 1904, qu. in Martin, *James J. Hill,* 515. Griggs was already representing Hill
in Knox's suit.

89 **"Within a very"** *The New York Times,* 20 Feb. 1902.

89 **The statement was** Thompson, *Party Leaders,* 312; Thorelli, *Federal Antitrust
Policy,* 563. The Minnesota suit indeed was rejected. *Review of Reviews,* Apr.
1902; Martin, *James J. Hill,* 512.

90 **Knox's willingness** *Literary Digest,* 1 Mar. 1902; New York *Herald, The Washington Post,* New York *Sun,* and New York *World,* 21 Feb. 1902.

90 **It had been** *The New York Times* and New York *Herald,* 21 Feb. 1902; Adams,
Letters, vol. 5, 344–45; Knox qu. in *Historical Register, 1921,* 60.

90 **Shortly afterward** *New York Tribune,* New York *World,* and Washington
Evening Star, 22 Feb. 1902.

90 **BEFORE NIGHTFALL** New York *World,* 22 Feb. 1902; *New York Tribune,* 24 Feb.
1902. For an account of the dinner, see Adams, *Letters,* vol. 5, 346.

90 **If the purpose** Adams, *Letters,* vol. 5, 346; *New York Tribune,* 24 Feb. 1902.

91 **they stood shoulder** The phrase is that of L. T. Michener to E. W. Halford, ca. 25
Mar. 1902 (copy in HKB).

91 **The Secretary of War** Adams, *Letters,* vol. 5, 345–47; William H. Taft to Mrs.
Taft, 1 Mar. 1902 (WHT); Cleveland *Plain Dealer,* 25 Mar. 1902; William H. Taft
qu. in Archibald Butt, *Taft and Roosevelt: The Intimate Letters of Archie Butt*
(New York, 1930), 2, 690. Harbaugh, *Life and Times,* 160–61, discusses TR's
probable reasons for excluding Root.

91 **Either that, or** Adams, *Letters,* vol. 5, 347.

91 **There was something** See Edward Steichen's famous 1903 portrait of Morgan, reproduced with another "take" in Strouse, *Morgan,* 496–97.

91 **Yet interlocutors** Ray Stannard Baker, "Morgan"; "J. P. Morgan," bound obitu-
aries file, 1913, NYPL. The definitive life is Strouse, *Morgan.*

91 **"That is just"** Bishop, *Theodore Roosevelt,* vol. 1, 184–85. For another interpretation of this famous dialogue, see Kolko, *Triumph of Conservatism,* 69.

91 **"send your man"** "Your man" is Knox; "my man" is Francis Lynde Stetson,
Morgan's personal attorney.

92 **Alone with Knox** Bishop, *Theodore Roosevelt,* vol. 1, 184–85.

92 THE HOUSE OF   *The New York Times,* 31 Mar. 1913, in Knox scrapbooks (PCK); Knox qu. in *New York American,* 12 Jan. 1912, Knox scrapbooks (PCK).

92 **Knox's formal complaint**   *The New York Times,* 11 Mar. 1902; James Montgomery Beck, *May It Please the Court* (New York, 1930), 333.

92 OF THE THREE   Martin, *James J. Hill,* 515–16; *The New York Times,* 21 Feb. 1902; Meyer, "The Northern Securities Case," 246–47; Joseph G. Pyle, *The Life of James J. Hill* (New York, 1917), vol. 2, 171–72.

92 **Roosevelt's action**   Adler, *Jacob H. Schiff,* vol. 1, 111; Albert Shaw in *Review of Reviews,* Apr. 1902; Robert Wiebe, *Businessmen and Reform* (Cambridge, Mass., 1902), 44; Eitler, "Philander Chase Knox," 67–68; Presidential scrapbook (TRP). TR was emphatic that his object was not to extend the applicability of *Knight* as to overturn it, and thus revitalize the necessity for some government control over business.

93 **"I am rather"**   TR, *Letters,* vol. 3, 236.

93 **He pretended to**   Lee, *Good Innings,* vol. 1, 261; TR, *Letters,* 3, 225, 237; Presidential scrapbook (TRP); TR, *Letters,* 3, 237, 239; Irwin Hoover, *Forty-Two Years in the White House,* (Boston, 1934), 293; Morris, *Edith Kermit Roosevelt,* 234; dinner plans and settings in J. E. Fenwick, compiler, "The White House Record of Social Functions" (NA). The last-named record, in thirteen volumes, offers documentary evidence of the splendor of White House entertainments in the Roosevelt Era, 1901–1909.

93 **Alice Roosevelt—debutante**   Marguerite Cassini, *Never a Dull Moment* (New York, 1956), 168–89; *Literary Digest,* 12 Apr. 1902.

94 **He regretted the**   *Literary Digest,* 12 Apr. 1902; Cassini, *Never a Dull Moment,* 194; Adams, *Letters,* vol. 5, 351; Morris, *Edith Kermit Roosevelt.* See also Rixey, *Bamie,* 196ff.

94 **Previous Presidents**   Thorelli, *Federal Antitrust Policy,* 586–87. The adverb *voluntarily* emphasizes that all of Harrison's, Cleveland's, and McKinley's antitrust suits were initiated outside their administrations, at the state or private level.

94 **For these reasons**   Wister, *Roosevelt,* 209. See also Lamoreaux, *Great Merger Movement,* 166.

CHAPTER 6:   TWO PILOTS ABOARD, AND ROCKS AHEAD

95 *It looks to me*   "Mr. Dooley," qu. in Sullivan, *Our Times,* vol. 3, 86.

95 **"CHAOS! EVERYWHERE!"**   *The Washington Post,* 15 Mar. 1902.

95 **"Both compass and"**   Ibid.

95 **On the very day**   *Washington Times,* 15 Mar. 1902.

95 **Hanna's presidential**   Adams, *Letters,* vol. 5, 349; "The Hanna Presidential Boom," *Literary Digest,* 7 June 1902, 23; *The Washington Post,* 10 Mar. 1901. "There is now in operation the most complete Bureau since 1896, and that Bureau is working day and night for Mark Hanna." L. T. Michener to Eugene Hay, ca. 24 Dec. 1901 (copy in HKB).

95 **They estimated**   Cleveland *Plain Dealer,* 13 Mar. 1902; *The Washington Post,* 15 Mar. 1902; Chairman of the New York Irish Republican League to Mark Hanna, 21 July 1902 (MHM). This last correspondent reported that in a recent poll of his membership, representing Manhattan and the Bronx, more than two thirds had expressed a preference for Hanna.

96 **Hanna dismissed the**   *Public Opinion,* 27 Mar. 1902; Volnay W. Foster, assistant treasurer of the Republican National Committee, qu. in unidentified news clip (MHM); Toledo *Blade* news clip, ca. 15 Mar. 1902 (MHM). The dinner was held in New York on 5 Mar. 1902.

96 **Deep in his** Mrs. Hanna, interviewed by J. B. Morrow, 19 May 1905 (MHM); Robert C. Rhodes, interviewed by J. B. Morrow, 17 Apr. 1906 (MHM).

96 **Yet Hanna's web** Croly, *Marcus Alonzo Hanna,* 375–76; Missouri *Post-Dispatch,* 5 Apr. 1902, news clip in MHM. Gould, *Reform and Regulation,* 40, discounts the strength of Hanna's web, finding it "fragile." That may have been the case later on, but contemporary sources are united in depicting the Senator as the GOP leader and likely nominee in 1904. He remained at this apex of power through the rest of the year.

96 **It was understood** John T. Flynn, "Mark Hanna—Big Business in Politics," *Scribner's,* Aug. 1933; Croly, *Marcus Alonzo Hanna,* 272, 344–45, 373.

96 **Such eminence** A. B. Hough, interviewed by J. B. Morrow (MHM); *The Washington Post,* 29 Mar. 1902.

97 **The Commanding General** *The Washington Post,* 15 Mar. 1902.

97 **"General Miles's most"** Boston *Herald,* 19 Mar. 1902.

97 **Not content with** TR to Nelson A. Miles, 17 Feb. 1902 (TRP; suppressed). See also TR, *Letters,* vol. 3, 245.

97 **The letter was** TR, *Letters,* vol. 3, 232, 240–42, 244–47.

98 **He had hardly** Washington *Evening Star,* 19 Feb. 1902.

98 **Root wrote separately** 57 Cong., 1 sess., 1902, S. Doc. 205, pt. 1, 1–3; Leopold, *Elihu Root,* 36; Jessup, *Elihu Root,* vol. 1, 338–39.

98 **Root's words masked** 57 Cong., 1 sess., 1902, S. Doc. 24, pt. 1, 881–85. For racism among United States soldiers in the Philippines, see Richard E. Welch, Jr., *Response to Imperialism: The United States and the Philippine-American War, 1899–1902* (Chapel Hill, 1979), chap. 8, and for their moral degeneration see Stuart Creighton Miller, *"Benevolent Assimilation": The American Conquest of the Philippines, 1899–1903* (New Haven, 1983), chap. 10.

98 **So damning was** Taft qu. in *The Washington Post,* 11 Apr. 1902. Attached to the report was the statement of a provincial official that one third of the population of Batangas—some one hundred thousand Filipinos—had died from war, disease, and famine. This document was not included in the final released text. Herbert Welsh to Moorfield Storey, 11 Apr. 1902 (MST).

98 **Root was guilty** Taft to Root, 8 Apr. 1902, in Jessup, *Elihu Root,* vol. 1, 340; John R. M. Taylor, ed., *The Philippine Insurrection Against the United States: A Compilation of Documents* (Pasay, Philippines, 1971–1973), 294–95; *Literary Digest,* 26 Apr. 1902.

98 **This measure** Jessup, *Elihu Root,* vol. 1, 240–60; William H. Carter, "Creation of the Army General Staff," 68 Cong., 1 sess., 1923, S. Doc. 119. For a review of Root's service as Secretary of War, see Leopold, *Elihu Root,* 38–46.

98 **It sought to** James B. Martin, "Irresistible Force"; Jessup, *Elihu Root,* 251; *Report of the Secretary of War* (Washington, D.C., 1902), 46–48. For an extended discussion of these changes, see Samuel P. Huntington, *The Soldier and the Statesman: Theory and Politics of Civil-Military Relations* (Cambridge, Mass., 1957). See also John A. Matzko, "President Theodore Roosevelt and Army Reform," *Proceedings of the South Carolina History Association,* 1973.

99 **Miles reminded the** Washington *Evening Star,* 19 Apr. 1902; *Washington Times,* 21 Apr. 1902.

99 **Senator Joseph Hawley** *The Washington Post,* 25 (qu. Watterson) and 26 Feb. 1902.

99 **Root's expressionless** Cleveland *Plain Dealer,* 30 Apr. 1902.

99 **Roosevelt was struggling** TR, *Letters,* vol. 3, 247–48, 271; Hale, *Bull Moose Trails,* 11–13; John C. Shaffer to TR, in Frederick S. Wood, *Roosevelt As We Knew Him: The Personal Recollections of One Hundred and Fifty of His Friends and Associates* (Philadelphia, 1927), 132–33.

99 **Perhaps, after all** Miller, *"Benevolent Assimilation,"* 258, erroneously states that Miles was sent to the Philippines "in the spring of 1902." TR did not authorize a visit until much later, when it suited his political convenience to have Miles out of the United States.

99 **"It is getting"** TR, *Letters,* vol. 3, 248.
> *Chronological Note:* TR visited Charleston, S.C., between 7 and 10 Apr. 1902. For accounts, see Rhodes, *McKinley and Roosevelt,* 231–32, and Wister, *Roosevelt,* 96ff. The trip was aimed at undoing some of the damage done to his Southern reputation by the Booker T. Washington dinner. Another purpose was to reconnoiter the extraordinarily complicated South Carolina patronage situation. From now until 1904, the state tested TR's skill in negotiating the political tightropes among Conservative, Bryan, Commercial, and Gold Democrats, not to mention Black-and-Tan (Booker T. Washington) and Lily White (Mark Hanna) Republicans. For a lucid discussion, see Willard B. Gatewood, Jr., "Theodore Roosevelt and Southern Republicans: The Case of South Carolina, 1901–04," *South Carolina History Magazine* 70.4 (1969).

99 LODGE'S COMMITTEE For extensive quotations, see *Literary Digest,* 26 Apr. 1902.

100 **"Had you any"** Major Littleton W. T. Walker court-martial, Manila, 8 Apr. 1902, transcript in NA.

100 **Waller also quoted** Ibid. For an account of the Waller case, see Miller, *"Benevolent Assimilation,"* 219–32.

100 **"A man is thrown"** 57 Cong., 1 sess., 1902 S. Doc. 331, vol. 25, no. 33, pt. 1, 1767. See Miller, *"Benevolent Assimilation,"* 213, on "this very mild form of torture," from which, apparently, "very few died."

100 **Other reports spoke** Alfonso, *Theodore Roosevelt and the Philippines,* 95; M. K. Sniffen to Carl Schurz, 22 May 1902 (CS).

100 **Amid mounting cries** 57 Cong., 1 sess., 1902, S. Doc. 331, pt. 2, 881–85. See, e.g., *Literary Digest,* 26 Apr. and 10 May 1902, and Robert W. McKee to Edward W. Carmack, 28 Apr. 1902: "A deep, half-sullen sense of mighty and most flagrant outrage against *Americanism*—[of] rape upon the holiest traditions of our land and its institutions" (EWC).

100 **He met with** Washington *Evening Star,* 14 Apr. 1902; *The Washington Post,* 15 Apr. 1902.

100 THE PRESIDENT DESIRES Full text: 57 Cong., 1st sess., 1902, S. Doc. 24, pt. 1, 1548–49. See also Jessup, *Elihu Root,* vol. 1, 342–43.

101 **Roosevelt also ordered** TR, *Letters,* vol. 3, 259; memorandum of the Secretary's movements, 1902–1904 (ER).

101 **"It is almost"** Qu. in *Literary Digest,* 10 May 1902. General Adna R. Chaffee cabled the War Department on 5 May to say that Smith was "of unsound mind" (ER). Root's final list of officers convicted or being disciplined for cruelty numbered as many as 350. Root to Henry Cabot Lodge, 4 May 1902 (ER). Although the Philippine insurrection was de facto President McKinley's war, TR was at least partly responsible for the severity of its prosecution in the early months of his Administration. After the massacre at Balangiga (26–27 Sept. 1901), he had ordered General Chaffee to use "the most stern measures to pacify Samar" (Miller, *"Benevolent Assimilation,"* 206–7, 219). Like Root, TR was disposed to be tolerant of even culpable United States soldiers. When, e.g., Lieutenant Preston Brown was sentenced by a military court to dismissal and five years' hard labor for killing a prisoner, TR commuted the sentence to loss of half pay for nine months, plus a slight downgrading of his place on the promotion list. Ibid., 218; 57 Cong., 1 sess., 1902, S. Doc. 205, pt. 1, 42–49.

101 **Roosevelt again** TR, *Letters,* vol. 3, 313–14; William H. Taft to Mrs. Taft, 1 Mar.

1902; Philadelphia *North American,* 5 May 1902; H. Welsh to Carl Schurz, 30 Apr. 1902 (CS).

101 **Like all conservatives** Jessup, *Elihu Root,* vol. 2, 503; Henry Cabot Lodge to TR, 11 July 1902 (ER); Alfonso, *Theodore Roosevelt and the Philippines,* 32; Taylor, *Philippine Insurrection,* vol. 3, 358–59; Rudyard Kipling in *McClure's,* Feb. 1899.

102 **He may be a** Sullivan, *Our Times,* vol. 1, 7.

102 **Filipinos, Taft wrote** Alfonso, *Theodore Roosevelt and the Philippines,* 44–46. See also TR, *Letters,* vol. 3, 276, for Taft attempting to restrain the President on self-determination for Filipinos.

102 **These sentiments, while** See, e.g., Woodrow Wilson in *Atlantic Monthly,* Dec. 1901: Filipinos were but "children" in "matters of government and justice." They should remain "in tutelage" to the United States, and so learn "the discipline of the law." TR's own prepresidential epithets regarding Filipinos, turned to embarrass him when Senator Edward Carmack of Tennessee wrote them into the record: "Savages, barbarians, wild and ignorant, Apaches, Sioux" (*Congressional Record,* 57 Cong., 1 sess., 1901, vol. 35, pt. 1, 4673).

102 THE PRESIDENT REMAINED David Healy, *The United States in Cuba: 1898–1902* (Madison, 1963), 202–3; Washington *Evening Star,* 29 Apr. 1902. The rumors regarding the beef trust proved accurate. Because of rising food prices, Knox's injunction, announced in May, won further popular support for the Administration, and further recriminations from corporate conservatives. Gould, *Presidency of Theodore Roosevelt,* 53; Adams, *Letters,* vol. 5, 368; Allan Nevins, ed., *Selected Writings of Abram S. Hewitt* (Port Washington, N.Y., 1965 [1937]), 402.

102 **"Theodore is a"** Adams, *Letters,* vol. 5, 378.

103 **On 24 April** TR, *Letters,* vol. 3, 242. See *Review of Reviews,* Apr. 1902, on the changeover.

103 **The little white** Clips in Presidential scrapbook (TRP); *The Washington Post,* 26 Apr. 1902. USS *Dolphin* is listed in *Jane's Fighting Ships, 1901* as a 240-foot cruiser (sixth class), commissioned in 1884.

103 **The appointments of** Gould, *Presidency of Theodore Roosevelt,* 48; TR, *Letters,* vol. 3, 242; *Review of Reviews,* Apr. 1902. Long had noticed within weeks of TR's arrival that the President intended to take personal charge of Navy policy.

103 **"big navy man"** Paul T. Heffron, "William H. Moody," in Paolo E. Coletta, ed., *American Secretaries of the Navy* (Annapolis, 1980), vol. 1, 464. Moody's service as Secretary began on 1 May 1902.

103 SPRING CAME TO Adams, *Letters,* vol. 5, 376; Thomas Fleming, *Around the Capitol* (New York, 1902), 112; TR to Joel Chandler Harris, 9 June 1902 (TRP). TR and EKR were regularly seen dining alfresco on the White House portico. Their "pleasant Continental habit of eating in the open air" soon became the vogue in Washington. New York *World,* 26 Oct. 1902.

103 **An especial closeness** Morris, *Edith Kermit Roosevelt,* 237; Rep. James Slayden in New York *World,* 30 May 1902.

103 ELIHU ROOT RETURNED Welch, *Response to Imperialism,* 142; Alfonso, *Theodore Roosevelt and the Philippines,* 103.

104 **When Lodge rose** *The Washington Post,* 5 May 1902.

104 **He began to read** Ibid.; Henry Cabot Lodge to George H. Lyman, 15 Feb. 1902 (MHS). Another imaginative Filipino technique included the slitting open of American bodies and stuffing them with United States Army mess provisions. Miller, *"Benevolent Assimilation,"* 204.

104 **Over the next** Welch, *Response to Imperialism,* 144; Some senators, notably Henry Cabot Lodge, were unenthusiastic about the bill's assembly clause, but with

Taft's powerful encouragement they eventually accepted it. Gould, *Presidency of Theodore Roosevelt*, 58.

104 **Only George F.** Thompson, *Party Leaders*, 58–71; George F. Hoar to Carl Schurz, 3 June 1902 (CS). This incident occurred on 18 May 1902. See also Hoar to TR, 15 June 1902 (TRP), and TR's moving reply in *Letters*, vol. 3, 276–77.

104 **"Everybody that"** George F. Hoar to Carl Schurz, 3 June 1902 (CS).

105 **A few seconds before noon** *Washington Times*, 20 May 1902; *The New York Times*, 21 May 1902; Leonard Wood diary, 20 May 1902 (LW).

105 **On the roof** Frank McCoy to his mother, May 1902 (FMcC); *The New York Times*, 21 May 1902; news clips and photographs in Leonard Wood scrapbook (LW).

105 **"—and I hereby"** *The New York Times*, 21 May 1902.

105 **From far across** Philadelphia *Press*, 21 May 1902; Frank McCoy to his mother, May 1902 (FMcC).

105 **By any standards** This sentence is paraphrased from one in Howard Gillette, Jr., "The Military Occupation of Cuba, 1899–1902: Workshop for American Progressivism," *American Quarterly*, Oct. 1973. See Healy, *United States in Cuba*, 179–86.

105 **A trained surgeon** Leonard Wood, transcript of speech at Williams College, 25 June 1902 (LW). See also Leonard Wood, "The Military Government of Cuba," *Annals of the American Academy of Political and Social Science* 21.30 (1903); and Gillette, "Military Occupation of Cuba."

105 **The cannons continued** New York *Herald*, 21 May 1902; Leonard Wood diary, 20 May 1902 (LW); James Hitchman, "The American Touch in Imperial Administration: Leonard Wood in Cuba, 1898–1902," *The Americas*, Apr. 1968; Healy, *United States in Cuba*, 180–82 ("By the end of 1901, free public education was a reality in Cuba"). Gillette, "Military Occupation of Cuba," suggests that Wood's experiment did much to inspire the Progressive reform movement in the United States.

106 **What protection** Leonard Wood to Elihu Root, 9 Apr. 1902 (ER).

106 **The forty-fifth** *Washington Times*, 20 May 1902; Frank McCoy to his mother, May 1902 (FMcC).

106 **There were groans** Eyewitness account in Harry Frank Guggenheim, *The United States and Cuba: A Study in International Relations* (New York, 1934), 99; New York *Herald*, 21 May 1902; Leonard Wood diary, 20 May 1902 (LW). Wood also took with him an extremely detailed, up-to-date map of Cuba, to give to the War Department, and a complete survey of Havana harbor and its environs, "including all fortifications, fieldworks, etc." Wood to Elihu Root, 18 Nov. 1902 (ER).

107 **As soon as** Leonard Wood diary, 20 May 1902 (LW); Hill, *Roosevelt and the Caribbean*, 77; New York *World*, 19 May 1902.

CHAPTER 7: GENIUS, FORCE, ORIGINALITY

108 *What's all this* Dunne, *Observations by Mr. Dooley*, 91.

108 THEODORE ROOSEVELT'S TOTAL New York *World*, 19 May 1902; Oswald Garrison Villard, *Fighting Years: Memories of a Liberal Editor* (New York, 1939), 152.

108 **Whether exercising** New York *World*, 19 May 1902.

108 **On 28 May** New York *World*, 29 May 1902; William Dudley Foulke, *A Hoosier Autobiography* (New York, 1922), 117; Leupp, *The Man Roosevelt*, 311–13; Wister, *Roosevelt*, 93–99; New York *World*, 3 May 1902. For TR's introduction to this new and exotic sport, see Akiko Murakata, "Theodore Roosevelt and

William Sturgis Bigelow: The Story of a Friendship," *Harvard Library Bulletin* 23.1 (1975).

108 **White House groundsmen** John Burroughs, *Camping and Tramping with Roosevelt* (Boston, 1907), 84; New York *World*, 30 Mar. 1902. Calvin Brice remarked that he intended in the future "to observe the President from the safe summit of some neighboring hill." Qu. in Adams, *Letters*, vol. 5, 364.

108 **Petitioners visiting** TR's current reading included a novel by the Filipino consciousness-raiser José Rizal. TR to J. C. Abrey, 31 May 1902 (TRP); Maria [Mrs. Bellamy] Storer, *In Memoriam Bellamy Storer* (privately printed, 1923), 38–39.

108 **On another occasion** New York *World*, 22 Sept. 1901. Apparently, Henry Cabot Lodge had bet him he could not do it. TR demanded, and got, the Senator's hat in settlement.

108 **He encouraged his** *Baltimore Sun*, 15 May 1902; *Washington Times*, 8 June 1902.

109 **Hay, who as** John Hay qu. in Byron Price memorandum (EMH). For a discussion of the question of presidential succession at this time, see George F. Hoar, *Autobiography of Seventy Years* (New York, 1903), vol. 2, 168–71.

109 **a permanent Census** TR, *Letters*, vol. 3, 238–39.

   Chronological Note: Until TR's Presidency, each census was conducted by a temporary "office" that went out of existence as soon as it reported. These "offices" had become sinkholes of patronage by the end of the nineteenth century; the 1900 census comprised some sixty thousand jobs, all political favors. On 6 Mar. 1902, TR signed a bill that not only created a permanent directorate, but made its appointments subject to the approval of the Secretary of the Interior. Clerkships and other administrative positions were made subject to the civil-service law. In 1903, the Bureau initiated a countrywide system of death registration and statistical reporting; in 1904, it produced the nation's first population forecasts; in 1905, the first annual reports on cotton supply and distribution, and in 1906, the first in a series of annual "inter-censual" surveys. Theodore G. Clemence, "The Early Years of the Bureau of the Census: The Politics of Appointment and the Struggle for Independence," ts. in Bureau of the Census, Washington, D.C., 8–12.

109 **Senators Aldrich and** New York *Herald*, 18 May 1902; TR to W.H.H. Llewellyn, qu. in Douglas, *Many-Sided Roosevelt*, 83.

110 **"You have wasted"** Hoar's speech is given in *Congressional Record*, 57 Cong., sess. 1, 1902, vol. 6, 5788–98.

110 **At Arlington National** The following account is based on TR, *Presidential Addresses and State Papers* (New York, 1910), vol. 1, 59–66; and Presidential scrapbook (TRP).

110 **The year's first** New York *Sun* and Washington *Evening Star*, 30 May 1902.

110 **He had been** See ms. in TRP. No previous President had delivered a Memorial Day address at Arlington.

110 **"Is it only"** TR, *Presidential Addresses and State Papers*, vol. 1, 60.

111 **Had he spat** *Literary Digest*, 7 June 1902. See also Welch, *Response to Imperialism*, 144, and, for a concise analysis of TR's antilynch policies from this moment on, William L. Ziglar, "The Decline of Lynching in America," *International Social Science Review* 63.1 (1988).

111 **Sure enough, when** Miller, *"Benevolent Assimilation,"* 250. TR finally signed it into law on 1 July 1902; *Literary Digest*, 7 June 1902. An editorial exception was the New York *Sun*, which hailed TR's speech as "a great public service . . . [that] excels anything that the President has yet delivered." Alfonso, *Theodore Roosevelt and the Philippines*, 203–5, finds the nation's press, as a whole, supportive of TR's Philippines policy.

111   **Bruised and rueful**   See TR, *Letters,* vol. 3, 268–69, for TR's attempt to explain his Philippines policy to an outraged cleric.

111   **On Wednesday, 4**   See *Congressional Record,* 57 Cong., sess. 1, 1902, vol. 35, pt. 6, 6267–80.

111   ***"Be it enacted"***   Ibid., 6267.

111   **old man's tremor**   Scholars skeptical of this detail should try to read Morgan's handwriting from 1902.

111   **He had no new**   *Congressional Record,* 57 Cong., sess. 1, 1902, vol. 35, pt. 6, 6267–80.

112   **Senator Hanna sat**   The Treaty of New Granada was basically a trade agreement intended to protect free transit (then by railway) across the Isthmus of Panama. In return for right of way, the United States guaranteed the "perfect neutrality" of the Isthmus, as well as "the rights of sovereignty and property which New Granada has and possesses over the said territory." Lawrence Beilenson, *The Treaty Trap: A History of the Performance of Political Treaties by the United States and European Nations* (Washington, D.C., 1969), 33–34.

112   **Storming on**   *Congressional Record,* 57 Cong., sess. 1, 1902, vol. 35, pt. 6, 6275.

112   **As soon as**   Ibid., 6280.

112   WHEN SENATORS RECONVENED   Washington *Evening Star,* 5 June 1902; DuVal, *Cadiz to Cathay,* 165; McCullough, *Path Between the Seas,* 319–22. The volcanic map was provided courtesy of Philippe Bunau-Varilla.

112   **Hanna entered to**   Thomas Beer, *Hanna, Crane, and the Mauve Decade* (New York, 1941), 600; *Congressional Record,* 57 Cong., sess. 1, 1902, vol. 35, pt. 6, 6317ff. All quotations from Hanna's speech come from the latter source.

112   **The chamber settled**   Beer, *Hanna.* For the "facts and conditions" behind Hanna's conversion, see Miner, *Fight for the Panama Route,* 102–4.

112   **For the next**   *The Washington Post,* 6 June 1902; *Congressional Record,* 57 Cong., sess. 1, 1902, vol. 35, pt. 6, 6317–21.

112   **"Oh, do make"**   Beer, *Hanna,* 600.

113   **Polls in smoke-filled**   The conspiracy theory was dampened by another rumor that Hanna was the agent of James J. Hill and the transcontinental railroads. He was actually conducting a filibuster, in order to have no canal at all. New York *Journal,* 17 June 1902.

113   HANNA RESUMED HIS   *Congressional Record,* 57 Cong., sess. 1, 1902, vol. 35, pt. 7, 6380; Philippe Bunau-Varilla, *Panama: The Creation, Destruction, and Resurrection* (London, 1933), 242; *Congressional Record,* 57 Cong., sess. 1, 1902, vol. 35, pt. 7, 6381. *Managua* is here a correction for Hanna's misspoken *Nicaragua.*

113   **For another hour**   *Congressional Record,* 57 Cong., sess. 1, 1902, vol. 35, pt. 7, 6377–87; Washington *Evening Star,* 6 June 1902; Bunau-Varilla, *Panama,* 248. The best account of the legislative and diplomatic struggle for the Panama Canal is in DuVal, *Cadiz to Cathay.*

113   AS LONG AS   Beer, *Hanna,* 602. The senators were Matthew Quay of Pennsylvania and Thomas Platt of New York.

113   MEANWHILE, HIS CUBAN   Guggenheim, *United States and Cuba,* 101–6; Healy, *United States in Cuba,* 196–200; TR, *Letters,* vol. 3, 288. For a detailed discussion of the reciprocity issue, see United States Tariff Commission, *The Effects of the Cuban Reciprocity Treaty of 1902,* miscellaneous series, no. 22 (Washington, D.C., 1929).

114   **Common sense**   TR, *Letters,* vol. 3, 228, 265–66; U.S. Tariff Commission, *Effects.* For evidence of TR's strong feelings on reciprocity, see his passionate reworkings of Spooner Amendment drafts in TRP.

114   **On 13 June**   Tomas Palma to TR, 12 Sept. 1902 (TRP). The text of TR's Special

Message is in James D. Richardson, ed., *A Compilation of the Messages and Papers of the Presidents* (Washington, D.C., 1911), vol. 15, 6682–84. See also Robert Freeman Smith, "Cuba: Laboratory for Dollar Diplomacy, 1898–1917," *The Historian* 28.4 (Aug. 1966).

114 **"Cuba is a young"** Washington *Evening Star*, 13 June 1902.

114 **Some senators detected** *The Atlanta Constitution*, 14 June 1902; Stephenson, *Nelson W. Aldrich*, 187; Leonard Wood to Elihu Root, 9 Apr. 1902 (ER); *World's Work*, June 1902. Embarrassingly for TR, the Message was preceded by a press revelation that Leonard Wood had used government funds for reciprocity propaganda.

114 **"My dear Mr. Cannon"** TR, *Letters*, vol. 3, 272–73.

114 **Representative Joseph** Blair Bolles, *Tyrant from Illinois: Uncle Joe Cannon's Experiment with Personal Power* (New York, 1951), 118–19, 211, 40. TR had spoken out on the subject of reclamation as early as Nov. 1900, at the National Irrigation Congress. D. Jerome Tweton, "Theodore Roosevelt and the Arid Lands," *North Dakota Quarterly* 36.2 (1968).

115 **For a quarter** Lacey, "Mysteries of Earth-Making," 372; Roy M. Robbins, *Our Landed Heritage: The Public Domain, 1776–1936* (Princeton, N.J., 1942), 325–29.

115 **Roosevelt expressed** TR, *Letters*, vol. 3, 277. Actually, Newlands and other lawmakers representing both Eastern and Western interests had been working on sketches for the Reclamation Act since 1900. But TR managed, with considerable skill, to merge the best features of all these proposals into a bill that overcame powerful Republican opposition in Congress. See TR, *Letters*, vol. 3, 317; Marc P. Reisner, *Cadillac Desert: The American West and Its Disappearing Water* (New York, 1986), 116–18; and William D. Rowley, *Reclaiming the Arid West: The Career of Francis G. Newlands* (Bloomington, Ind., 1996), 2–6, 102–4.

115 **Cannon ignored** Rowley, *Reclaiming the Arid West*, 103; P. P. Wells, "Theodore Roosevelt's Conservation Record," Oct. 1919 memorandum prepared for Joseph Bucklin Bishop (GP); Robbins, *Our Landed Heritage*, 331–33; Lacey, "Mysteries of Earth-Making," 372.

115 **"They must be"** TR to National Irrigation Congress, 15 Sept. 1903, *Letters*, vol. 3, 600. TR's role in bringing about the Reclamation Act was but a chapter in the overall story. See Samuel P. Hays, *Conservation and the Gospel of Efficiency: The Progressive Conservation Movement, 1890–1920* (Cambridge, Mass., 1959), 10–15. For the intellectual and sociological aspects of the reclamation movement, see Lacey, "Mysteries of Earth-Making"; for a view of the Reclamation Act as "the first and most durable example of the modern welfare state," see Reisner, *Cadillac Desert*, 115ff.

115 **Reclamationists spoke** Beer, *Hanna*, 595. See also *Review of Reviews*, Apr. 1902. Tweton, "Theodore Roosevelt and the Arid Lands," quotes *The Denver Post*: "For the happy termination of an endeavor which . . . appeared almost hopeless, the people of the West are indebted to President Roosevelt, without whose influence the passage of the bill would have been practically impossible." For the subsequent application of the Reclamation Act, beginning with Nevada's Truckee Dam (dedicated 17 June 1905), see Rowley, *Reclaiming the Arid West*, 1–6, and Hays, *Conservation and the Gospel of Efficiency*, 15–26.

115 **DURING THE NEXT** Beer, *Hanna*, 601; Bunau-Varilla, *Panama*, 247; McCullough, *Path Between the Seas*, 324; Miner, *Fight for the Panama Route*, 154–55. At least one bribe of ten thousand dollars in cash was offered to Senator Fred T. Dubois of Idaho, on behalf of certain "New York legal interests." John T. Morgan to Henry Watterson, 10 Dec. 1903 (JTM).

116 **By a margin** *Review of Reviews*, Aug. 1902; TR, *Letters*, vol. 3, 284. For a full

account of the passage of the Panama Canal Act, see Miner, *Fight for the Panama Route,* 125–56.

116 ROOSEVELT'S EUPHORIA Washington *Evening Star,* 21 June 1902; *Literary Digest,* 26 July 1902, qu. *Le Temps* (France); New York *Evening Post,* 14 June 1902. See also Healy, *United States in Cuba,* 201.

116 **Somewhat cheered** Boston *Herald,* 26 June 1902; Morris, *Rise of Theodore Roosevelt,* 104.

116 **Grief; disease; desire** EKR's miscarriage seems to have occurred in mid-May 1902. Morris, *Edith Kermit Roosevelt,* 237. Strangely, however, TR was still boasting about her pregnancy at the end of that month. Possibly EKR kept the news from him. A year later, she miscarried again.

116 **At the welcoming** *The Boston Globe,* 25 June 1902.

117 **"When we were"** Wister, *Roosevelt,* 7. Wister had just published his epochal Western novel, *The Virginian.* It was dedicated to TR.

117 **The President's behavior** Henry James, *Charles W. Eliot, President of Harvard University, 1869–1909* (Boston, 1930), vol. 2, 159; Wood, *Roosevelt,* 100–101. Supplementary details in the following paragraphs come from the Boston *Evening Record* and *The Washington Post,* 26 June 1902.

117 **At the Alumni** Hoar qu. in Fiske Warren diary, 2 Dec. 1903 (MST). The phrase *like an impulsive boy* is Senator Hoar's own. For evidence of TR's sincere veneration of Hoar, see TR, *Letters,* vol. 3, 276–77.

117 **Dr. Eliot began** Boston *Evening Record,* 25 June 1902; unidentified news clips in Presidential scrapbook (TRP). For TR's incomprehension of financial matters, see, e.g., TR, *Letters,* vol. 3, 691.

117 **Harvard, to Theodore** Alfonso, *Theodore Roosevelt and the Philippines,* 56–57; Boston *Evening Record* and *The Washington Post,* 26 June 1902.

117 **Hay, listening** John Hay to TR, 26 June 1902 (TRP); *The Washington Post,* 26 June 1902.

118 **He dropped back** Boston *Herald,* 26 June 1902; Rhodes, *McKinley and Roosevelt,* 232–33; Douglas, *Many-Sided Roosevelt,* 136. More than two weeks later, John Hay was still marveling. "Theodore made one of the most striking speeches I ever heard," he wrote Henry Adams on 11 July. Hay, *Letters,* vol. 3, 253.

118 **Roosevelt had to** Boston *Evening Record,* 26 June 1902, in Presidential scrapbook (TRP).

118 WASHINGTON WAS Morris, *Edith Kermit Roosevelt,* 238–39; William Seale, *The President's House* (Washington, D.C., 1986), vol. 2, 669–84.

118 **He took up** James Garfield diary, 27 June 1902 (JRG). Of the fourteen specific requests TR had made in his First Message to Congress, only three had been granted: the National Reclamation Act, the Canal Act, and the Census Act. TR's eleven failures were to get government supervision of trusts; publicity as a remedy for trust abuses; an anti-anarchism measure; stronger immigration laws; modified reciprocity; aid to American shipping; a militia law; a General Staff of the Army; a revised merit system; a Department of Commerce; and reorganizaton of the consular service.

118 **Invitations were** New York *Herald,* 15 June 1902; *Washington Times,* 30 Mar. 1902.

119 **Congress adjourned** John Hay to Henry Adams, 11 July 1902 (JH); Barry, *Forty Years,* 274–75; *The Washington Post,* 4 July 1902; *Review of Reviews,* Aug. 1902.
　　Chronological Note: The war had lasted forty-one months. 126,500 Americans had seen service in the Philippines; 4,200 had been killed, and 2,800 wounded. TR's amnesty specifically excluded the Moros of Mindanao, who, as Muslims, were fanatically determined to fight to the last man. Their terrorism was to sputter on through most of his Presidency.

Nevertheless, the former Filipino rebel leader Emilio Aguinaldo told William H. Taft that TR's peaceful gesture "was worth more than many regiments of soldiers." For the rapid moderation of American domestic argument about the Philippines after Malvar's surrender and TR's order, see Miller, *"Benevolent Assimilation,"* 245–50.

CHAPTER 8: THE GOOD OLD SUMMERTIME

120   *Th' capital iv*   Dunne, *Observations by Mr. Dooley,* 186–87.

120   SUMMER RAIN WAS   Except where otherwise indicated, the following account of TR's arrival home on 5 July 1902 is based on the *New York American,* 6 July 1902; "Oyster Bay: The Summer Capital," *Washington Times,* 13 July 1902 (text and illustrations); unidentified news clips in Presidential scrapbook (TRP); and pictures in Albert Loren Cheney, *Personal Memoirs of the Home Life of the Late Theodore Roosevelt* (Washington, D.C., 1919), *passim.* Today, the rail approach is much the same, and the "new" station of 1902 still stands, minus only its platform awnings.

120   **"There are many"**   *Boston Herald,* 3 Aug. 1902. The standard village history is Frances Irvin, *Oyster Bay: A Sketch,* rev. Jane Soames Knickerson (Oyster Bay, N.Y., 1987).

121   **The little community**   New York *World,* 6 July 1902; *New York Tribune,* 7 July 1902; *Washington Times,* 5 and 9 July 1902.

121   **The surrey splashed**   *Washington Times,* 16 July 1902; New York *Herald,* 11 Aug. 1902; New York *Evening Sun,* 7 July 1902; P. James Roosevelt to author, 4, 5, 19, 26 Apr. 1983 (AC), *Boston Herald,* 3 Aug. 1902; map preserved by Mrs. Philip Roosevelt, privately held.

121   **Turning north, the**   *Boston Herald,* 3 Aug. 1902.

121   **A private driveway**   *Washington Times,* 17 June 1902; New York *Evening Sun,* 3 July 1902; New York *Herald,* 8 July 1902.

121   RAIN GAVE WAY   TR, *Works,* vol. 3, 314.

122   **"Among Long Island"**   Ibid., 316–17.

122   **Ovenbirds fluted**   Ibid., 318.

122   **"They come up"**   Ibid.

122   **To the west**   *Boston Herald,* 3 Aug. 1902; Kermit Roosevelt, *The Happy Hunting-Grounds* (New York, 1920), 22–23.

122   **No matter how**   New York *Sun,* 8 July 1902; New York *World,* 13 July 1902 (CORDON OF GUARDS ABOUT PRESIDENT); *The Washington Post,* 11 July 1902. The President's security detail consisted of five Secret Service men and two policemen (New York *World,* 6 July 1902). Other agents were stationed twenty-four hours a day in a hotel in the village and at the station. Any given visitor was scrutinized at least three times en route to Sagamore Hill. See Walter S. Bowen and Harry E. Neal, *The United States Secret Service* (Philadelphia, 1960).

122   **a gun butt protruding**   Edna M. Colman, *White House Gossip* (New York, 1927), 284.

122   **Instead, he used**   *Washington Times,* 8 July 1902; New York *World* and New York *Sun,* 9 July 1902. Poultney Bigelow describes the sensation of one of these Cooper's Bluff plunges in *Contemporary Review* clip, ca. 1901, in Presidential scrapbook (TRP).

123   **Yet had it**   *Boston Herald,* 3 Aug. 1902; *Washington Times,* 8 July 1902; Chicago *Record-Herald,* 12 July 1902.

123   **"Cousin Theodore"**   Qu. by William E. Curtis in Chicago *Record-Herald,* 12 July 1902.

123   **Rough Riders**   *The Washington Post,* 11 July 1902. Sagamore Hill is now invisi-

ble from Oyster Bay, but a contemporary photograph in Cheney, *Personal Memoirs*, 6, shows Sagamore Hill clearly visible across the water.

123 **About once a week** Chicago *Record-Herald*, 12 July 1902.

123 **One day, he reined** *The Washington Post*, 20 July 1902, Presidential scrapbook (TRP).

124 **Unamused, the reporters** New York *Sun* and New York *Journal*, 19 July 1902.

124 **"It seems to me"** TR, *Letters*, vol. 3, 303.

124 **Dana withdrew his** Paul Dana to TR, 1 Aug. 1902 (TRP).

124 **For the younger Roosevelts** Waldon Fawcett, "The President's Summer Home at Oyster Bay," *Twentieth Century Review* clip, n.d., Presidential scrapbook (TRP). When Archibald B. Roosevelt lay dying in Florida in the summer of 1979, after a long life and much world travel, he mumbled repeatedly, "Take me home." "But you *are* home, Father." "No, no—home to Sagamore." Mrs. Archibald B. Roosevelt, Jr., interview, 20 Sept. 1981. See also Kerr, *Bully Father*, 151.

124 **The estate, with** Mrs. Philip Roosevelt interview, 24 Oct. 1982. See also Theodore Roosevelt, Jr., *All in the Family* (New York, 1929); Herman Hagedorn and Gary Roth, *Sagamore Hill: An Historical Guide* (Oyster Bay, N.Y., 1977); David H. Wallace, "Sagamore Hill: An Interior History," in Natalie A. Naylor, Douglas Brinkley, and John Allen Gable, *Theodore Roosevelt: Many-Sided American* (Interlaken, N.Y., 1992), 527–46.

124 **These haunts** Parsons, *Perchance Some Day*, 234. "He was the enchanting Pied Piper of our childhood."

124 **From early morning** Longworth, *Crowded Hours*, 6–8; Roosevelt, *Happy Hunting-Grounds*, 4–5; Nicholas Roosevelt, *Theodore Roosevelt: The Man As I Knew Him* (New York, 1967), 21–27. "My children," TR robustly told a female interviewer, "are not brought up to be cowards. They are not taught to turn the other cheek if they are struck; they are told to hit back and hit hard. I won't have any weaklings in my household. I want my boys to grow up manly and gently." He seemed to want the same for girls, encouraging them to participate in the roughest play, and saying that he liked them to be "tomboys when they are small." Boston *Sunday Record*, 3 Aug. 1902.

125 **Only when he** Archibald Roosevelt interview, 7 June 1977; research memorandum, n.d. (HH). TR's own children were supplemented, that summer, by eleven Roosevelt nieces and nephews from neighboring estates. Chicago *Record-Herald*, 12 July 1902.

125 **NO MATTER WHERE** New York *Evening Sun*, 8 July 1902; Chicago *Record-Herald*, 12 July 1902.

126 **A new magazine** "The People at Play," *World's Work*, Aug. 1902.

126 **In the good old** Sullivan, *Our Times*, vol. 3, 347; "In the Good Old Summertime" was the biggest popular hit of the early twentieth century.

126 **THE ONLY MEMBER** Alice Roosevelt diary, 21 June 1903 (ARL).

126 **Heedless on the** William E. Curtis in Chicago *Record-Herald*, 12 July 1902. It took TR just eighteen days, from 5 to 22 July, to read this mammoth work. See his report to John Hay in TR, *Letters*, vol. 3, 300.

127 **ON 14 JULY** Schirmer, *Republic or Empire*, 439.

127 **The general's fellow** TR to Albert Shaw, 1 Sept. 1902 (TRP).

127 **For a moment** TR had signed the Act into law on 1 July 1902. It was Taft's overoptimistic hope that the Philippine legislature could begin functioning as early as 1 Jan. 1904, well in advance of the next presidential election. William H. Taft to Elihu Root, 26 Mar. 1902 (ER).

127 **"I thoroughly believe"** TR, *Letters*, vol. 3, 298.

127 **Smith, however** Ibid.; Bishop, *Theodore Roosevelt*, vol. 1, 194.

127 **After dinner** *Washington Times* and New York *Sun*, 14 July 1902; TR, *Letters*,

vol. 3, 189n, 303–6. For a discussion of the Vatican holdings, see Harbaugh, *Life and Times;* 182–83.

127 **Both of them** New York *Sun,* 14 July 1902.

127 **Friends again** Ibid.; "President's Official Yacht Rivals Those of Royalty," unidentified clip, 15 July 1902 (HH); Edwin A. Falk, "USS *Mayflower,*" pamphlet in TRC.

128 **"Bully! Bully!"** New York *Sun,* 15 July 1902.

129 ROOSEVELT'S DECISION *Literary Digest,* 26 July 1902. The dismissal was announced on the sixteenth. It made TR highly unpopular with the Army, and was seen even by anti-imperialists as a stern and cathartic punishment. See, e.g., Charles Francis Adams to Carl Schurz, 31 July 1902 (CS).

129 **Even the Anti-Imperialist** League leaders protested that Roosevelt had dramatically sacrificed General Smith in order to protect hundreds of other American war criminals. On 22 July, Charles Francis Adams, Carl Schurz, Edwin Burritt Smith, and Herbert Welsh published an open letter to TR (in TRP), alleging abuses "far more general" than any he had admitted. For negative public reactions to it, see *Literary Digest,* 9 Aug. 1902.

129 **"I think he"** Charles Francis Adams to Carl Schurz, 4 and 21 Aug. 1902 (CS).

129 ALMOST UNNOTICED TR, *Letters,* vol. 3, 302; William H. Taft to TR, 27 Oct. 1902 (TRP).

129 **He dreamily informed** TR, *Letters,* vol. 3, 288.

129 **"Now . . . in the"** Ibid., 289.

130 **Having thus briskly** *The Washington Post,* 27 July 1902.

130 FOG DELAYED John A. Garraty, "Holmes's Appointment to the U.S. Supreme Court," *New England Quarterly,* Sept. 1949; G. Edward White, *Justice Oliver Wendell Holmes: Law and the Inner Self* (New York, 1993), 301.

130 **Oliver Wendell Holmes** Catherine Drinker Bowen, *Yankee from Olympus: Justice Holmes and His Family* (Boston, 1944), 120; photographs in Supreme Court Historical Society, Washington, D.C.; Oliver Wendell Holmes, Jr., *The Common Law* (Cambridge, Mass., 1963), 5.

130 **In his world** Alexander M. Bickel and Benno C. Schmidt, Jr., *The History of the Supreme Court of the United States* (New York, 1984), vol. 9, 70–71; Holmes, *Common Law,* 5. Sheldon Novick, *Honorable Justice: The Life of Oliver Wendell Holmes* (Boston, 1989), 283.

130 **Theodore Roosevelt** TR, *Letters,* vol. 3, 288.

130 **After returning to** Novick, *Honorable Justice,* 235–36; Garraty, "Holmes's Appointment."

130 **Roosevelt agreed with** Garraty, "Holmes's Appointment"; Henry Cabot Lodge to TR, 25 July 1902 (TRP). Holmes, for his part, had to admit that Roosevelt "said just the right things and impressed me far more than I had expected." Qu. in White, *Justice Oliver Wendell Holmes,* 312.

131 **"We shall have to"** Garraty, "Holmes's Appointment"; Bowen, *Yankee from Olympus,* 348. TR announced Holmes's appointment on 11 Aug. 1903.

131 *In the good old* Lyrics in Music Division, LC. In 1903, the song was sung as a waltz.

131 **Grotesque as it** Archibald B. Roosevelt interview, 7 June 1977. TR had been peripherally involved in the coal strike since early June. See, e.g., *Washington Times,* 7 June 1902.

131 **One hundred and forty-seven** Anthracite Coal Commission, *Report to the President on the Anthracite Coal Strike of May–October 1902* (Washington, D.C., 1903), 37; *Washington Times,* 7 June 1902. For background to the anthracite strike, see Donald Miller and Richard E. Sharpless, *The Kingdom of Coal: Work, Enterprise, and Ethnic Communities in the Mine Fields* (Philadelphia, 1985).

131 **A visiting British** Alexander Lowen, unidentified news clip, ca. July 1902 (JM).

131   Roosevelt concluded   Eitler, "Philander Chase Knox," 148; *Proceedings of the Anthracite Coal Commission* (Washington, D.C., 1903), vol. 28, 4377ff.

CHAPTER 9:   NO POWER OR DUTY

132   **What d'ye think**   Dunne, *Observations by Mr. Dooley*, 218–19.

132   FOR ELEVEN WEEKS   Rosamond D. Rhone, "Anthracite Coal Mines and Coaling," *Review of Reviews*, July 1902.

132   **What made Sheriff**   George E. Leighton, "Shenandoah, Pa.: Story of an Anthracite Town," *Harper's Monthly Magazine*, Jan. 1937; *Literary Digest*, 24 May and 7 July 1902; Elsie Glück, *John Mitchell: Miner* (New York, 1929), 111; Stewart Culin, *A Trooper's Narrative of Service in the Anthracite Coal Strike, 1902* (Philadelphia, 1903), 36–37. See also Victor R. Greene, *The Slavic Community on Strike: Immigrant Labor in Pennsylvania Anthracite* (Notre Dame, 1968).

132   **Only when a**   Leighton, "Shenandoah"; Walter Wellman in Chicago *Record-Herald*, 14 Sept. 1902: "Their faith in him is completely sublime."

132   **John Mitchell**   Robert H. Wiebe, "The Anthracite Coal Strike of 1902: A Record of Confusion," *Mississippi Valley Historical Review*, Sept. 1961; Leighton, "Shenandoah"; Miller and Sharpless, *Kingdom of Coal*, 254–55; Cornell, *Anthracite Coal Strike*, 116–18. This concession amounted to a personal triumph for Mitchell, who argued passionately against a national strike.

133   **Swarthy, silent**   Glück, *John Mitchell*, 106, 98; Wiebe, "Anthracite Coal Strike," 240–41.

133   **Mitchell's concessions**   Miller and Sharpless, *Kingdom of Coal*, 256; Anthracite Coal Commission, *Report to the President*, 35. See Eliot Jones, *The Anthracite Coal Combinations* (Cambridge, Mass., 1919).

133   **When the miners**   Cornell, *Anthracite Coal Strike*, 115.

133   **Roaming the anthracite**   Wiebe, "Anthracite Coal Strike," 237–38; Mark Hanna to George Perkins, 19 May 1902 (GWP).

133   **"The coal presidents"**   *The New York Times*, 30 July 1902.

133   SHENANDOAH WAS QUIET   Culin, *Trooper's Narrative, passim*; Leighton, "Shenandoah," 136.

134   **Centre Street was**   Leighton, "Shenandoah," 136; Rhone, "Anthracite Coal Mines."

134   **Shortly before 6:00**   Harrisburg *Patriot*, 31 July 1902. The deputy, Thomas Bedall, was the nephew of Sheriff S. Rowland Bedall. Their identical surnames have confused some historians—e.g., Miller and Sharpless in *Kingdom of Coal*.

134   **He was accompanied**   *The New York Times*, 31 July 1902; *Literary Digest*, 9 Aug. 1902; Leighton, "Shenandoah," 143. See also Glück, *John Mitchell*, 111ff.; Cornell, *Anthracite Coal Strike*, 151–52.

134   **guns and bayonets**   *The New York Times*, 31 July 1902; Harrisburg *Patriot* and *The Philadelphia Inquirer*, 1 Aug. 1902.

134   **This freed Roosevelt**   TR, *Letters*, vol. 3, 359; Cornell, *Anthracite Coal Strike*, 109; *Literary Digest*, 9 Aug. 1902.

134   **Ten thousand bared**   Philadelphia *Public Ledger*, 2 Aug. 1902.

135   **Few among the**   Wiebe, "Anthracite Coal Strike," 240, 235.

135   **"If you lose"**   Glück, *John Mitchell*, 94; Philadelphia *Public Ledger*, 2 Aug. 1902.

135   **For the next**   Philadelphia *North American*, 1 Aug. 1902. See Glück, *John Mitchell*, 104–5, for the visits of intellectuals to anthracite country that summer.

135   **Roosevelt began to**   William Lemke, "Teddy Downeast: The 1902 New England Tour and the Style and Substance of Roosevelt's Leadership," in Naylor et al., *Theodore Roosevelt*, 190–200.

135   **From what he heard**   Norton Goddard to TR, 12 Aug. 1902 (TRP).

135   **The feeling went**   The following account is taken from a scoop in the Philadelphia *North American,* 9 Aug. 1902.

135   **(Some years before)**   Ibid.

136   **"Will you send"**   TR to E. H. Harriman, 16 Aug. 1902 (TRP).

136   **"My day has"**   E. H. Harriman to TR, 18 Aug. 1902 (TRP).

136   **Some paragraphs**   Ibid.

137   **"The rights and"**   Facsimile in Sullivan, *Our Times,* vol. 2, 425.

137   **This pious protestation**   Cornell, *Anthracite Coal Strike,* 170–72; *The New York Times* and *New York Tribune,* 21 Aug. 1902.

137   **Roosevelt, about**   TR to Philander Knox, 21 Aug. 1902 (TRP); Eitler, "Philander Chase Knox," 148; TR, *Letters,* vol. 3, 359.

137   THE SYLPH STEAMED   Frank W. Lovering in Boston *Journal,* 23 Aug. 1902; *The New York Times,* 23 Aug. 1902; unidentified news clips, Presidential scrapbook (TRP).

137   **Three traveling aides**   For an example of TR's continuing management of press relations, see his letter to the editor of the New York *Sun,* asking for Lindsay Denison to accompany him on tour. "He is a trump, and as you know I can tell him everything" (TR to Chester S. Lord, 12 Aug. 1902 [TRP]). Denison rewarded him for this encomium with favorable *Sun* coverage and a major article, "The President on His Tours," *World's Work,* Nov. 1902.

137   **Roosevelt had grown**   Frank W. Lovering in Boston *Journal,* 4 Sept. 1902; unidentified news clip, Presidential scrapbook (TRP).

137   AT NOON THE   TR reached Providence after a night stop in Hartford, Conn., where he created a sensation by publicly associating himself with the city's blue-collar Democratic mayor. Local GOP organizers had snubbed the mayor by putting him far back in the welcoming parade. Annoyed by their discourtesy, TR mentioned the mayor by name in his speech, and afterward granted him the only private audience of his visit. This gentlemanly behavior, widely reported, was not lost on ordinary Americans. See *Harper's Weekly,* 6 Sept. 1902.

137   **Squinting against**   *The New York Times* and *Boston Herald,* 24 Aug. 1902.

138   **"We are passing"**   White House speech transcript, 23 Aug. 1902 (TRP).

138   **Human law, he**   Ibid.

138   **Roosevelt noticed**   Illustration in Frank W. Lovering, "Eyewitness Tells of TR's Pittsfield Outrage," unidentified Berkshires news clip, ca. 20 Aug. 1962 (TRB); *Boston Herald,* 24 Aug. 1902.

138   **"Where men are"**   White House speech transcript, 23 Aug. 1902 (TRP); Merrill, *Republican Command,* 21.

138   **E. H. Harriman could**   Providence *Sunday Journal,* 24 Aug. 1902. TR felt somewhat responsible for a current drought in GOP campaign contributions, brought about by the *Northern Securities* prosecution. TR, *Letters,* vol. 3, 317.

138   **His audience began**   *Boston Herald,* 24 Aug. 1902.

139   **By now, he**   Photograph and report in Denison, "The President on His Tours."

139   THERE WAS SOME   *Literary Digest,* 6 Sept. 1902.

139   PRESIDENT WOULD   *The New York Times,* 24 Aug. 1902, e.g., TR has been criticized by John M. Blum in *The Progressive Presidents: Roosevelt, Wilson, Roosevelt, Johnson* (New York, 1980), 29, for saying nothing against the trusts that had not already been said by, e.g., President McKinley's Industrial Commission. But as Galambos, *Public Image,* 258, points out, popular anger against the trusts had cooled by 1902. TR sought to rekindle it by restating old truths in his new, harsh, twentieth-century voice. For reactions to his antitrust oratory on tour, see *Literary Digest,* 6 Sept. 1902, and articles by Joseph Auer in *North American Review,* Dec. 1902, and Albert Shaw in *Century Magazine,* Jan. 1903.

139   THE PRESIDENTIAL SPECIAL   Sixty years later, Frank W. Lovering, who covered the

trip for the Boston *Journal*, was driving along Bayshore Drive in Miami and noticed an old Pullman car in a siding, silhouetted against the moonlight of Biscayne Bay. "Something impelled me . . . to cross the tracks. . . . I walked along beside the Pullman. Bright in gold leaf I read by the sputtering glow of an arc lamp, *Mayflower*. I put my hand affectionately on the polished railing of the observation platform. Time fell into retreat. It was September again in the Berkshires." Lovering, "Eyewitness."

140 **At Bangor, Maine**   Mrs. F. H. Eckstrom to C. H. Ames, 30 Aug. 1902 (TRP); Putnam, *Theodore Roosevelt*, 153ff. See also *The Washington Post*, 28 Aug. 1902. Afterward, TR invited Sewall to visit the White House with "as many of your family as you can persuade to come." For an account of their stay, see TR, *Letters*, vol. 3, 422.

140 **"Not since the"**   *Literary Digest*, 6 Sept. 1902.

140 **All Europe**   Ibid., 20 Sept. 1902. In London, the *Westminster Gazette* hailed TR as "one of the most courageous political adventurers of our time" (ibid.).

140 THE TRAIN SWUNG   Presidential itinerary (TRP).

140 **To Roosevelt, as**   Burlington *Free Press*, 2 Sept. 1902; unidentified news clip, Presidential scrapbook (TRP); John Hay to Alvey A. Adee, 30 Aug. 1902 (JH); Morris, *Rise of Theodore Roosevelt*, 738.

140 **Big Bill extra**   When the gaslights failed at a crowded Vermont reception, Craig was seen jumping "like a tiger" in front of TR. Reillumination of the room disclosed a wall of Secret Service agents around the President. *Boston Herald* and Philadelphia *Press*, 1 Sept. 1902.

140 **Brattleboro. Girls**   Boston *Journal*, 4 Sept. 1902; TR, *Presidential Addresses and State Papers*, vol. 1, 134–36, 143, 145.

141 **Wednesday. Last day**   The following account is based on Lovering, "Eyewitness"; Boston *Journal*, 4 Sept. 1902; New York *Herald*, 4 Sept. 1902; George A. Lung, "Roosevelt's Narrow Escape From Death," Brooklyn *Daily Eagle*, 9 Jan. 1919; photographs donated by W. Murray Crane (TRB); and an official report by W. T. Meyer, 1 Oct. 1902, Precautionary File (GBC).

142 **"Oh my God!"**   New York *Sun*, 4 Sept. 1902; the accident happened near the foot of Howard's Hill. See Stefan Lorant's photohistory, *The Life and Times of Theodore Roosevelt* (New York, 1959), 380.

142 ROOSEVELT LANDED   Lung, "Roosevelt's Narrow Escape." Lung tried to squeeze TR's chest to see if any ribs were broken, "but he resented the squeeze and asked to be left alone." By good fortune, TR had landed in soft earth and alluvial runoff from the hill. *The New York Times*, 4 Sept. 1902.

142 **"No, I guess not,"**   Lung, "Roosevelt's Narrow Escape"; New York *Sun*, 4 Sept. 1902; Lovering in Boston *Journal*, same date.

142 **He saw a man**   New York *Sun*, 4 Sept. 1902.

142 **"God-damned outrage"**   Lovering, "Eyewitness." Many newspapers moderated this language, extremely unusual for TR. But at least two contemporary reporters quoted it verbatim (New York *World* and Lovering), and TR himself admitted it in an impromptu interview with Lovering later that afternoon. Finley Peter Dunne recounted the incident in his next "Mr. Dooley" column. "I can't tell ye [what Roosevelt said] till I get mad. But I'll tell ye this much, a barn-boss that was standin' by and heerd it, said he niver before regretted his father hadn't sint him to Harvard." Dunne, *Observations by Mr. Dooley*, 223–25.

142 **As his heir**   John Hay to Alvey A. Adee, 4 Sept. 1902 (JH).

142 **At the time**   W. Murray Crane to Henry Cabot Lodge, 4 Sept. 1902 (HCL) ("His fighting spirit was up and he wanted to punish someone"); New York *Sun*, 4 Sept. 1902.

142 **Roosevelt did not**   New York *Sun*, 4 Sept. 1902.

143 QUENTIN WAS INDEED *The New York Times,* 4 Sept. 1902. An illustration in Lorant, *Life and Times,* 380, shows TR speaking in Lenox, Mass., just after the accident, despite the massive disfigurement of his face. He insisted on appearing also at other scheduled stops in Connecticut before returning home on the *Sylph.*

143 **He was sentenced** Judgment qu. in Pittsfield *Sun,* 22 Jan. 1903.

143 **Memories of "poor"** *New York Tribune,* 16 Sept. 1902; *Harper's Weekly,* n.d., in Presidential scrapbook (TRP).

143 **"It takes more"** *New York Tribune,* 16 Sept. 1902. Mark Hanna endorsed at least the first part of TR's statement. "You may be hung," he wrote him, "but you will certainly not be killed by a 'Trolley car,' " 4 Sept. 1902 (TRP).

Chronological Note: TR remained only one night in Oyster Bay, before proceeding south on the second of his campaign swings, a five-day trip through West Virginia, Tennessee, and North Carolina. His speeches largely echoed those of his New England trip.

143 **Only Edith knew** For a medical article arguing that the Pittsfield trauma was, at least in part, ultimately the cause of TR's death, see Robert C. Kimberley, "The Health of Theodore Roosevelt," *Theodore Roosevelt Association Journal* 5.3 (summer 1979).

CHAPTER 10: THE CATASTROPHE NOW IMPENDING

144 *It was different* Dunne, *Observations by Mr. Dooley,* 49–50.

144 THE PRESIDENTIAL EAGLE New York *Herald,* 20 Sept. 1902; TR, *Letters,* vol. 3, 326.

144 **The question was** Sage, *William Boyd Allison,* 225–27.

144 **"We favor such"** Qu. in *Literary Digest,* 16 Aug. 1902.

144 **In other words** TR to J. G. Schurman, 11 Aug. 1902 (TRP); Robert LaFollette autobiographical manuscript "B," 247 (RLF).

144 **This "Iowa Idea"** TR to J. G. Schurman, 11 Aug. 1902, and TR to Mark Hanna et al., 1 Sept. 1902 (TRP); TR, *Letters,* vol. 3, 327, 313. For a discussion of the wildly popular Iowa Idea and Western insurgency, see Fowler, *John Coit Spooner,* chap. 10.

145 **Senators Allison** Fowler, *John Coit Spooner,* chap. 10; Merrill, *Republican Command,* 117; Washington *Evening Star,* 16 Sept. 1902.

145 **But Governor Cummins's** Bolles, *Tyrant from Illinois,* 37–38; David P. Thelen, *Robert M. LaFollette and the Insurgent Spirit* (Boston, 1976), 49; "Though commercial competitors we are, commercial enemies we must not be. . . . The period of exclusiveness is past." Qu. in Alexander K. McClure and Charles Morris, *William McKinley* (New York, 1901), 309.

145 **McKinley's successor** Sereno E. Payne to TR, 15 Aug. 1902 (TRP). Carleton Putnam sagely remarks that TR was not equipped to understand tariff policy because there was no clear right or wrong to it (*Theodore Roosevelt,* 500–501). "Political economists are pretty generally agreed," TR wrote in *Thomas Hart Benton* (1887), "that protectionism is vicious in theory and harmful in practice." Yet by 1902 he saw "no reason" why Americans should not have it, if most of them wanted it. See TR, *Letters,* vol. 3, 312–13, and for a detailed study, James A. Rosmond, "Nelson Aldrich, Theodore Roosevelt, and the Tariff: A Study to 1905," (Ph.D. diss., University of North Carolina, 1974).

145 **His failure eighteen** *Literary Digest,* 27 Sept. 1902. The word *reciprocity* does not even appear in the index to the 1902 *Republican Campaign Textbook.*

145 **Tariff reform** *Literary Digest,* 16 Aug. 1902; TR, *Presidential Addresses and State Papers,* vol. 1, 192–94; Merrill, *Republican Command,* 116–20.

145 **During the next** TR, *Letters,* vol. 3, 313, 326–27; Merrill, *Republican Command,* 122–23.

146 DISEMBARKING ON *Chicago Tribune,* 20 Sept. 1902.

146 **When the train** Pittsburgh *Dispatch,* 20 Sept. 1902. Quay and his colleague Boies Penrose had met with George Baer on 3 Sept. in a vain attempt to persuade him to arbitrate (Cornell, *Anthracite Coal Strike,* 132). On the same day, TR, concerned at mounting violence in the anthracite country and criticisms of his own aloofness, released a report on the situation by Carroll D. Wright. This evenhanded document admitted a climate of "no confidence" and "distrust" on either side, but held that both had "reasonable and just" grievances that needed to be publicly adjudicated. Ibid., 109; *The Independent,* 18 Sept. 1902; TR, *Letters,* vol. 3, 327.

146 **No sooner had** New York *Sun* and Pittsburgh *Dispatch,* 20 Sept. 1902; TR, *Letters,* vol. 3, 327. Sargent is wrongly identified as Carroll D. Wright in the last-named source. For the story of Quay and Penrose's attempt to influence strike negotiations, see Cornell, *Anthracite Coal Strike,* 132–40.

146 **Roosevelt sent a** TR, *Letters,* vol. 3, 327.

146 HIS LEFT LEG Medical bulletin in Washington *Evening Star,* 24 Sept. 1902. The complete text of TR's speech, his finest trust policy statement as President, is in *Presidential Addresses and State Papers,* vol. 1, 169–83.

146 **It was the first** TR, *Presidential Addresses and State Papers,* vol. 1, 175–76, 178.

146 **Speaking lucidly** Ibid., 178.

147 **By choosing two** Ibid., 183–84.

147 **At last the audience** Cincinnati *Commercial Tribune, The Cincinnati Enquirer,* and *Detroit Today,* 21 Sept. 1902.

147 A REPORTER COVERING *Detroit Today,* 22 Sept. 1902.

147 **Actually, the main** Ibid.

147 **Early the next morning** Detroit *Evening News,* 22 Sept. 1902; Detroit *Tribune,* 23 Sept. 1902; Presidential scrapbook (TRP).

147 **Speculation that** Indianapolis *Journal,* 24 Sept. 1902; TR, *Presidential Addresses and State Papers,* vol. 1, 187–95.

147 **The tariff, for** TR, *Presidential Addresses and State Papers,* vol. 1, 191, 193.

148 **Standing awkwardly** Ibid., 194; *The Washington Post,* 24 Sept. 1902. Spooner wrote dryly to Senator Allison: "Some of it you undoubtedly recognize as familiar." Merrill, *Republican Command,* 123.

148 WITH FURTHER ROARS Washington *Evening Star,* 24 Sept. 1902. Except where otherwise indicated, the following account of the events of 23 Sept. 1902 is based on "President Roosevelt's Injury," *Indiana Medical Journal,* Oct. 1902; Indianapolis *Evening News,* 23 Sept. 1902; and *The Washington Post,* 24 Sept. 1902.

148 **From Logansport station** *The Washington Post* and Indianapolis *Evening News,* 24 Sept. 1902.

148 **"The President has"** *The Washington Post,* 24 Sept. 1902.

148 **"Elihu . . . if"** Memorandum, ca. 25 Sept. 1902 (GBC).

148 **Root paced up** Ibid.

148 **The President moved** Ibid.; "President Roosevelt's Injury"; New York *World,* 26 Oct. 1902.

149 **Dr. George H.** Medical bulletins in *The Washington Post,* 24 and 29 Sept. 1902; Dr. Lung qu. in Brooklyn *Eagle,* 9 Jan. 1919.

149 **At five o'clock** Douglas, *Many-Sided Roosevelt,* 96; *The Washington Post,* 24 Sept. 1902; Indianapolis *Evening News,* 23 Sept. 1902.

149 **Successive bulletins** Alvey A. Adee to John Hay, 24 Sept. 1902 (JH); *The Washington Post,* 29 Sept. 1902; Indianapolis *Sentinel,* 24 Sept. 1902.

149 PAINTERS AND PLASTERERS EKR Diary, 24 Sept. 1902 (TRC); *The Washington Post,* 25 Sept. 1902.

149 **She established him** Presidential scrapbook (TRP); Philander Knox to *The Washington Post,* 25 Sept. 1902; *Chicago Tribune,* 25 Sept. 1902.

149 **He regretted that** TR, *Letters*, vol. 3, 328; *The Washington Post*, 30 Sept. 1902; Merrill, *Republican Command*, 127; Willis Van Devanter to F. E. Warren, 13 May 1903 (WVD).

149 **That did not** TR, *Letters*, vol. 3, 335; New York *World*, 28 Sept. 1902; Croly, *Marcus Alonzo Hanna*, 417ff.

150 **Right now, he** TR, *Letters*, vol. 3, 335.

150 **ON SUNDAY, 28** Washington *Evening Star*, 29 Sept. 1902.
   Note: Dr. Rixey was the father of Lilian Rixey, author of *Bamie*.

150 **The President's** EKR to Kermit Roosevelt, 28 Sept. 1902 (TRC); Dr. Rixey testimony in *Roosevelt vs. Newett: A Transcript of the Testimony Taken and Depositions Read at Marquette, Michigan, May 6–31, 1913* (privately printed, 1914; copy in TRB), 66, 306–7; "President Roosevelt's Injury"; EKR to Theodore Roosevelt, Jr., ca. 29 Sept. 1902 (TRJR); Washington *Evening Star*, 29 Sept. 1902.

150 **CHILL WEATHER** George H. Gordon to John Mitchell, 27 Sept. 1902 (JM); Cornell, *Anthracite Coal Strike*, 174; Low to TR, 2 Oct. 1902 (TRP). According to Wiebe, "Anthracite Coal Strike," 244, the panic was unnecessary. If the operators had allowed their trains to haul bituminous coal (which was in plentiful supply, and which Mitchell had not embargoed), "all market demands could have been met." In any case, fairly adequate supplies of bituminous coal got through somehow. There never was, as TR believed, "a coal famine." For another account, see Arthur M. Schaefer, "Theodore Roosevelt's Contribution to the Concept of Presidential Intervention in Labor Disputes: Antecedents and the 1902 Coal Strike," in Naylor et al., *Theodore Roosevelt*, 201–20.

150 **Henry Cabot Lodge** Henry Cabot Lodge to TR, 22 and 27 Sept. 1902 (TRP).

150 **"Literally nothing,"** TR, *Letters*, vol. 3, 331. Heman W. Chaplin argues in *The Coal Mines and the Public: A Popular Statement of the Legal Aspects of the Coal Problem, and the Rights of Consumers as the Situation Exists* (New York, 1902) that TR actually was entitled to intervene under the Sherman Act (55).

150 **He suspected that** TR, *Letters*, vol. 3, 331–32.

151 **"Unfortunately the strength"** Ibid.

151 **Two days later** Washington *Evening Star*, 30 Sept. 1902; TR, *Letters*, vol. 3, 359–60; Henry Lawrence, *Memories of a Happy Life* (Boston, 1926), 156; TR to John J. Leary, Leary Notebooks (TRC).

151 **Crane suggested** Carolyn W. Johnson, *Winthrop Murray Crane: A Study in Republican Leadership, 1892–1920* (Northampton, Mass., 1967), 27–30; Cornell, *Anthracite Coal Strike*, 176; TR to John J. Leary, Leary Notebooks (TRC).

151 **Roosevelt was not** TR to Hanna, 27 Sept. 1902 (TRP); TR, *Letters*, vol. 3, 360.

151 **In the cool** Qu. in Jacob A. Riis, *Theodore Roosevelt the Citizen* (Washington, D.C., 1904), 376. Crane is generally given credit for persuading TR to hold a strike conference, but the initial idea appears to have come from John Mitchell, who wrote Mark Hanna on 8 Sept. 1902, "The strike might be brought to a close if you could have the President write the railroad presidents and our officers to meet with him and you to try to adjust our differences" (MIT).

151 **He showed them** TR, *Letters*, vol. 3, 360; Wood, *Roosevelt As We Knew Him*, 470.

152 **He got his** The following text is from the original "Memo to the President dictated by P. C. Knox as representing his views and those of Mr. Crane, Mr. Moody, and Mr. Payne," 30 Sept. 1902 (PCK).

152 **Roosevelt struck out** Ibid.; Cornell, *Anthracite Coal Strike*, 182, misdates this memorandum as 3 Oct. 1902. TR deleted the phrase *no precedent in other strikes will be created* when he made his own public statement later.

152 **THE COAL STRIKE** Horace N. Fisher to Knox, 1 Oct. 1902, and Edwin E. Hoyt to Harry Hoyt, 6 Oct. 1902 (PCK); Pottsville *Miners Journal*, 24 Sept. 1902; *Literary*

Digest, 4 Oct. 1902. Press accounts tended to exaggerate the violence, just as secretive Slavs downplayed it. John Mitchell admitted to six deaths, then seven. Stewart Culin, who spent six weeks touring the anthracite country, reported that not a day went by without "one or more" funeral procession. In the end, only three murders could be officially documented. John Mitchell to T. J. Sauerford, 1 Oct. 1902 (JM); Culin, *Trooper's Narrative,* 38–40; Anthracite Coal Commission, *Report to the President,* 73.

152 **Mark Hanna wrote**   Hanna to TR, 29 Sept. 1902 (TRP).
153 **"The present miner"**   Press statement, 29 Sept. 1902 (JM).
154 **Sentimentalities of this**   Even as TR prepared to make his "impartial" intervention in the strike, a consignment of nonunion anthracite arrived in Washington "for the exclusive use of the Executive Mansion" (Washington *Evening Star,* 22 Oct. 1902). Plenty of reserve anthracite was secretly shipped out of eastern Pennsylvania to elite customers. Culin, *Trooper's Narrative,* 28, mentions "the low roar of distant trains, moving coal under the protection of darkness."
154 **"socialistic action"**   This was no neurosis. For an example of the sort of radical activism already centering around John Mitchell, see the "Program of Reforms" drawn up by his friend Henry Demarest Lloyd, a leading socialist intellectual. The document calls for sweeping nationalizations of industry, punitive taxes on wealth, profit restrictions on private investment, and "immediate registration of all citizens." Chester Destler, *Henry Demarest Lloyd and the Empire of Reform* (Philadelphia, 1963), 472.
154 I SHOULD GREATLY   TR, *Letters,* vol. 3, 334.
154 **Duplicate telegrams**   A. J. Cassatt to TR, 2 Oct. 1902 (TRP); Cornell, *Anthracite Coal Strike,* 179.
154 **"Doesn't that just"**   New York *World,* 3 Oct. 1902. The idea that anthracite miners, by exclusively striking an exclusive resource, were a "trust" in restraint of trade was not new. Knox had received several Sherman Act petitions to that effect, including one from Willcox himself. But he rejected them on the same grounds that he disallowed antitrust prosecution of the operators. "The miners' activities are clearly restricted to production, a field in which the State [of Pennsylvania]'s power is necessarily exclusive." P. C. Knox to TR, 7 June 1902, and "Memorandum on Mr. Ross's letter," 7 Oct. 1902, both in PCK.

CHAPTER 11:   A VERY BIG AND ENTIRELY NEW THING

155 *It'll be a hard*   New York *Journal,* 17 Oct. 1902.
155 CURIOUS ONLOOKERS   Except where otherwise indicated, descriptive and atmospheric details of the coal-strike conference are based on reports in the Washington *Evening Star,* 3 Oct. 1902, and *The New York Times* and *The Washington Post,* 4 Oct. 1902.
155 **Actually, he had**   George Cortelyou interviewed by N. W. Stephenson, Aug. 1927 (NWA).
155 **For almost an**   Washington *Evening Star,* 3 Oct. 1902; visual description of Mitchell based on photographs and studio portraits in JM. Other details from "Mitchell, Leader of Men," profile in *World's Work,* 25 Oct. 1902, and Frank J. Warne, "John Mitchell: The Labor Leader and the Man," *Review of Reviews,* Nov. 1902.
156 **While George Cortelyou**   Walter Wellman, "The Inside History of the Great Coal Strike," *Collier's Weekly,* 18 Oct. 1902 (illustrated).
156 **Eben B. Thomas**   Ibid. For Markle's cruelty to employees, see Miller and Sharpless, *Kingdom of Coal,* 259, 272.
157 **"Gentlemen," said**   New York *World,* 4 Oct. 1902.

157 **"Dee-*lighted*,"**   The following account of the coal-strike conference is based on *Report of the Conference Between the President and Representatives of the Anthracite Coal Companies and Representatives of the United Mine Workers of America, October 3, 1902* (Washington, D.C., 1903). TR's own account appears in TR, *Letters*, vol. 3, 359–66. Because TR himself notes that the transcript does not include "all of the invectives of the operators," the author has also relied on a few obvious "news leaks" from participants. Cortelyou, for example, is clearly Walter Wellman's source for "Inside History." Other sources are New York *Sun* and New York *World*, 4 Oct. 1902. The latter features on-the-spot drawings.

157 **He began to**   John Mitchell interviewed by J. J. Curran, *The Survey*, 18 Jan. 1919.

157 **A yard or two**   George Cortelyou interviewed by N. W. Stephenson, Aug. 1927 (NWA).

157 **Laying down his**   *Report of the Conference*, 4; New York *World*, 4 Oct. 1902.

158 **"Mr. President, I"**   *Report of the Conference*, 4; *New York Tribune*, 4 Oct. 1902.

158 **"Before considering"**   *Report of the Conference*, 4.

158 **THE OPERATORS RETURNED**   John Markle, in Robert J. Spence, *John Markle, Representative American* (New York, 1929), 110–12, recalled being surprised and angered by the abrupt termination of the morning session. He erred, however, in saying that he protested this treatment at once. The transcript indicates he did so later.

158 **Roosevelt had**   See TR to Seth Low, 3 Oct. 1902: "I read to the operators and miners this morning the paper which you have probably seen in this afternoon's press." TR, *Letters*, vol. 3, 337.

158 **A BOWL OF WHITE**   New York *World*, 4 Oct. 1902.

158 **"Do we understand"**   *The New York Times*, 4 Oct. 1902. The following dialogue is reconstructed from accounts in ibid.; New York *World*, 4 Oct. 1902; Wellman, "Inside History"; George Cortelyou interviewed by N. W. Stephenson, Aug. 1927 (NWA).

159 **Roosevelt, perhaps**   Carroll Wright, the most unbiased man in the room, felt that the operators had some good reasons to be angry. Edward Hoyt to Harry Hoyt, 6 Oct. 1902 (PCK).

159 **Roosevelt stared**   New York *World*, 4 Oct. 1902.

159 **For five months**   *Report of the Conference*, 6.

159 **By now Baer's**   Ibid., 6.

159 **The phrase *free***   TR's face was reportedly "a study" as Baer instructed him on his "duty." Wellman, "Inside History."

159 **Baer concluded**   *Report of the Conference*, 6. Mitchell was gracious enough to acknowledge Baer's offer in the days immediately following. Baer then went further, saying that the operators would accept adjudication by any court the President cared to specify. Cornell, *Anthracite Coal Strike*, 200.

159 **Obliquely, Baer**   Carroll D. Wright, "Memo for the President: Reasons for the Appointment of the Anthracite Coal Commission," 19 Nov. 1903 (TRP); Wiebe, "Anthracite Coal Strike," 243; Baer, "Statement"; Stuyvesant Fish to TR, 3 Oct. 1902 (TRP). The latter document, urging the President not to force a settlement, lest it prevent the "legitimate extension" of the soft-coal business, afforded TR much sardonic amusement. See Henry Cabot Lodge, *Selections from the Correspondence of Theodore Roosevelt and Henry Cabot Lodge, 1884–1918* (New York, 1925), vol. 1, 541.

160 **Baer was a**   *National Cyclopaedia of American Biography*, vol. 14, 37; George Baer qu. in William N. Appel, *Addresses and Writings of George F. Baer* (privately printed, 1916), 252.

160 **Mitchell, rising**   *Report of the Conference*, 7–8; TR to Seth Low, 4 Oct. 1902 (TRP).

160 **E. B. Thomas specifically** *Report of the Conference,* 8–9.

160 **"This, Mr. President"** New York *Sun,* 4 Oct. 1902; *Report of the Conference,* 10. The cartoon, by Keppler, had appeared in *Puck,* 1 Oct. 1902.

160 **Roosevelt was fortunate** TR qu. by Thomas H. Watkins in Wood, *Roosevelt As We Knew Him,* 109 ("More amazing effrontery," he said afterward, "I have never seen"); George Cortelyou to Walter Wellman, Chicago *Record-Herald,* 4 Oct. 1902, and interviewed by N. W. Stephenson, Aug. 1927 (NWA). White House telegraph operator Colonel Benjamin F. Montgomery, who was also in the room, remarked, "It truly made me sick to listen to those men," qu. in Beer, *Hanna,* 584; see Willcox's follow-up letter to TR, 8 Oct. 1902 (PCK).

160 **It was a crucial** John Mitchell to Walter Wellman, Chicago *Record-Herald,* 4 Oct. 1902. He told the reporter that it had been the most trying ordeal of his life. TR, for his part, commented, "There was only one person there who acted like a gentleman, and it wasn't I!" Qu. in Sullivan, *Our Times,* vol. 2, 432. See also George Cortelyou interviewed by N. W. Stephenson, Aug. 1927 (NWA).

160 **"The truth of"** *Report of the Conference,* 17. A mill owner in Pennsylvania commented sourly that this was because no local jury, given UMW intimidation, "will convict any of them." Paul A. Oliver to John Bassett Moore, 21 Oct. 1902 (JBM); Cornell, *Anthracite Coal Strike,* 186–87.

160 **The air in** Wellman, "Inside History"; New York *World,* 4 Oct. 1902.

161 OUTSIDE IN LAFAYETTE *The New York Times,* 4 Oct. 1902.

161 **While doctors hovered** TR, *Letters,* vol. 3, 342.

161 **The bells of** *The New York Times,* 4 Oct. 1902.

161 **"WELL, I HAVE"** TR, *Letters,* vol. 3, 337. Wiebe, "Anthracite Coal Strike," 245, notes that TR, having "tried and failed," was risking an intervention by Hanna, who, if successful, would loom even larger as his potential rival in 1904.

161 **Aides were surprised** Beer, *Hanna,* 584; TR, *Letters,* vol. 3, 337–38, 341. See also TR to Seth Low, 4 Oct. 1902 (unmailed) (TRP).

161 **He wanted to see** *Washington Times,* 4 Oct. 1902; TR, *Autobiography,* 488. See, e.g., nearly the entire front page of the *Chicago Tribune,* 4 Oct. 1902.

161 **The national newspapers** *Literary Digest,* 11 Oct. 1902.

162 **Roosevelt tended** Brooklyn *Eagle,* 4 Oct. 1902; Cornell, *Anthracite Coal Strike,* 207–8; Walter W. Ross to TR, 5 Oct. 1902 (PCK); Frederick Holls to TR, 2 Oct. 1902 (TRC); Dwight Braman to TR, 3 Oct. 1902, and Walter W. Ross to TR, 6 Oct. 1902 (PCK); TR, *Letters,* vol. 3, 346.

162 **"the most awful"** TR, *Letters,* vol. 3, 343–44, 592.

162 **As if to reassure** Grover Cleveland to TR, 4 Oct. 1902 (TRP).

162 **This was that** Ibid.

162 **"Your letter was"** TR, *Letters,* vol. 3, 338–39. Cleveland's letter was indeed such a "help" that TR immediately leaked it to Robert Bacon at the House of Morgan.

162 **"I think I"** Ibid. TR's decision to continue negotiating split his Cabinet into two, with Root, Knox, Moody, and Payne supporting him, and Hay, Hitchcock, Wilson, and Shaw preserving a disapproving silence. Walter Wellman in *Review of Reviews,* Nov. 1902.

162 **Roosevelt did not** Cornell, *Anthracite Coal Strike,* 211; TR, *Letters,* vol. 3, 339.

162 JOHN MITCHELL RECEIVED John Mitchell to TR, 8 Oct. 1902, and Carroll D. Wright to TR, 6 Oct. 1902 (TRP).

163 ***"Dear Mr. Putnam:"*** TR, *Letters,* vol. 3, 343.

163 **Putnam obliged** Ibid., 344.

163 WHILE ROOSEVELT READ Mrs. George Dewey diary, 12 Nov. 1902 (GD); Culin, *Trooper's Narrative,* 78, 70; Edward Hoyt to Harry Hoyt, 6 Oct. 1902 (PCK); *Literary Digest,* 18 Oct. 1902; TR, *Letters,* vol. 3, 361.

163 **"He literally ran"** George H. Gordon to John Mitchell, 7 Oct. 1902 (JM). Public

leaders were beginning to talk seriously of nationalizing the anthracite industry (Carroll D. Wright to TR, 15 Nov. 1903 [TRP]).

163 **"We believe that"** John Mitchell to TR, 8 Oct. 1902 (TRP), bluntly pointed out that the President did not have the power to enforce the findings of his own commission. See Cornell, *Anthracite Coal Strike,* 196–98, for more details of TR/Mitchell negotiations at this time.

163 **His statement was** Commons, *History of Labor,* 46; *New York Tribune,* 10 Oct. 1902.

163 **"I must not be"** Lodge, *Selections,* vol. 1, 537–38; Foulke, *Hoosier Autobiography,* 129. TR was now reading E.H.R. Tatham's life of John Sobieski. See TR, *Letters,* vol. 3, 347, for the cast list of his commission.

164 **Congress was entitled** Cornell, *Anthracite Coal Strike,* 208–9; Bishop, *Theodore Roosevelt,* vol. 1, 210. Ignoring an opinion from Knox that he had no constitutional power to act, TR drafted a "posterity letter" explaining that he might invade anyway. "The first principle of civilization is the preservation of order" (TR to Carroll D. Wright, 8 Oct. 1902 [TRP]). See also his angry remark to the Washington correspondent of *The Times* of London, "If they think I am going to tolerate mob law, they will find out their mistake five minutes after they have begun" (George Washburn Smalley, *Anglo-American Memories* [New York, 1911], 376). Something about the President's smiling inscrutability at this time caused John B. Jackson, appointed envoy to Greece on 13 Oct. 1902, to feel that TR was "the most dangerous man the United States have ever seen." Jackson to Andrew D. White, 27 Mar. 1912 (ADW).

164 **"In all the"** TR, *Letters,* vol. 3, 346–47.

164 **Cleveland was** Robert McElroy, *Grover Cleveland: The Man and the Statesman* (New York, 1923), vol. 2, 310–11; Grover Cleveland to TR, 13 Oct. 1902 (TRP).

164 **Anticipating an early** This sacrifice cost the former President $2,500. McElroy, *Grover Cleveland,* vol. 2, 310–11.

164 IT WAS ELIHU Elihu Root to J. P. Morgan, 9 Oct. 1902 (ER); Cornell, *Anthracite Coal Strike,* 33–36. "Morganized" railroads controlled almost 70 percent of the region's coal output (Walter Wellman, "Inside History"). Mark Hanna had asked Morgan to help settle the strike in June. Barkis was willing, but Baer and Mitchell clung so desperately to their respective positions that the effort failed. Mark Hanna to J. P. Morgan, 3 June 1902 (GWP); Cornell, *Anthracite Coal Strike,* 124; J. P. Morgan to Mark Hanna, ca. 9 Sept. 1902 (GWP).

164 **Root told the** Elihu Root to Philip C. Jessup, 26 Oct. 1935 (PCJ).

164 **He would use** TR legal deposition, 27 May 1914, qu. in Cornell, *Anthracite Coal Strike,* 211; TR, *Letters,* vol. 3, 362; TR, *Autobiography,* 480.

164 **Far from dissenting** *New York Tribune,* 12 Oct. 1902. See Satterlee, *J. Pierpont Morgan,* 392–93, for details of Root's trip.

165 **When Mitchell** Warne, "John Mitchell."

165 THE WEATHER TURNED TR, *Letters,* vol. 3, 348; TR, *Autobiography,* 489, 491. TR has sometimes been accused of exaggerating fears of a coming catastrophe in Oct. 1902. But see the common terror of, e.g., Judge Gray in Ferdinand C. Iglehart, *Theodore Roosevelt: The Man As I Knew Him* (New York, 1919), 387; Governor Crane in Lawrence, *Memories,* 156; Charles G. Dawes, *A Journal of the McKinley Years* (Chicago, 1950), 325; and James C. Cortelyou to George Cortelyou, 7 Oct. 1902 (GBC).

165 **"I bid you"** TR deposition, qu. in Cornell, *Anthracite Coal Strike,* 211. This conversation took place at 10:00 A.M., 13 Oct. 1902. White House appointment book (TRP).

165 **Schofield must** TR had arranged through Senator Quay a means whereby Governor Stone, in response to an anonymous telegram, THE TIME FOR THE REQUEST HAS

COME, would instantly "ask" for federal military help. Bishop, *Theodore Roosevelt*, vol. 1, 212.

165   **The old soldier** Wood, *Roosevelt As We Knew Him*, 111–12. TR, *pace* the opinion of his Attorney General, considered himself empowered to send in troops by the Railroad Arbitration Act of 1888. TR to Carroll D. Wright (draft), 8 Oct. 1902 (TRP); Sullivan, *Our Times*, vol. 2, 437–38, and Dawes, *Journal of the McKinley Years*, 327–28.

165   **Then, late on** *Washington Times*, 14 Oct. 1902. Morgan was accompanied by Robert Bacon.

165   WALTER WELLMAN Walter Wellman, "The Settlement of the Coal Strike," *Review of Reviews*, Nov. 1902. The ubiquitous reporter was functioning as an unofficial conduit among TR, Mitchell, and the House of Morgan. White House appointment book, 4 Oct. 1902 (TRP); Walter Wellman to John Mitchell, 6 Oct. 1902 (JM); George Cortelyou to TR, 9 Oct. 1902 (TRP).

165   **a document capable** Beautifully bound and preserved as "Original draft of the Coal Agreement Made on Board S. Y. *Corsair* in the Autograph of Secretary Root, 11 Oct. 1902" in the Morgan Library, New York City.

    Chronological Note: Not coincidentally, Attorney General Knox was at that moment addressing the subject of Capital *v.* Government before the Pittsburgh Chamber of Commerce. His speech, entitled "The Commerce Clause of the Constitution and the Trusts," was the sharpest warning yet that the Roosevelt Administration would use the Sherman Act against any corporate combination that sought to evade regulation by Congress. He made clear that a certain coal combination was practically asking to be so disciplined. The speech caused a sensation, as TR expected. He regarded it as "the most important" one that any member of the Administration would deliver in 1902, and had personally arranged for it to be delivered on 13 Oct. Of course, TR had no advance knowledge that the operators would begin to crack that same day, but his insistence that Knox heap further propaganda on them just then illustrates his uncanny sense of political timing. TR to W. H. Keach, 7 Oct. 1902 (TRP); Keach to TR, same date (PCK).

166   **At first, Roosevelt** TR, *Letters*, vol. 3, 350, 363; Corsair Agreement, copy in ER.

166   **"An officer of"** Qu. in TR, *Letters*, vol. 3, 365.

166   **Anyone could** TR, *Autobiography*, 482–84; TR, *Letters*, vol. 3, 352; Cornell, *Anthracite Coal Strike*, 230–31.

166   **Nevertheless, Roosevelt** Wiebe, "Anthracite Coal Strike," 248, says that Morgan was responsible for including in the final published Agreement "a statement of the operators' case that excluded the possibility of recognition of the union." But the identical statement appears in the original, in Root's hand. It was, in fact, the "powerful incentive" that Root said produced "a sudden change of front" on the part of the operators (Root to Mark Sullivan, 14 July 1927 [ER]). Wiebe further accuses TR of sabotaging the UMW's primary objective—recognition—by quoting this statement in his instructions to the Commission. John Mitchell had already withdrawn recognition as a strike demand.

166   **It was also calculated** TR, *Letters*, vol. 3, 351; Bishop, *Theodore Roosevelt*, vol. 1, 205.

167   **He stopped under** *The Washington Post*, 14 Oct. 1902.

167   THE "CORSAIR AGREEMENT" George Cortelyou to John Mitchell, 14 Oct. 1902 (TRP); TR, *Letters*, vol. 3, 365, 351.

167   **Mitchell was sure** Cornell, *Anthracite Coal Strike*, 226; TR, *Letters*, vol. 3, 353.

167   **Temptingly, he** TR, *Letters*, vol. 3, 365.

167   **Roosevelt cautioned** Ibid. TR wrote a detailed memorandum of his conversation

with Mitchell to send to Morgan, but did not send it, probably because he was more confident of persuading the financier's deputies orally than Morgan himself in black and white. See ibid., 351–53.

167   GEORGE PERKINS   Lodge, *Selections*, vol. 1, 540.

168   **While they conferred**   The lightening of TR's mood is palpable after 13 Oct. 1902 in TRP, *passim*; Hay, *Letters*, vol. 3, 258.

168   THE STRIKE, HOWEVER   Lodge, *Selections*, vol. 1, 540; TR, *Letters*, vol. 3, 366.

168   **Roosevelt privately**   TR, *Letters*, vol. 3, 357, 366; Lodge, *Selections*, vol. 1, 539–40. Bacon, a former all-star athlete, had recently suffered a complete nervous and physical collapse. On doctor's orders he was soon to resign from the House of Morgan. Strouse, *Morgan*, 443.

168   **"I found"**   TR, *Autobiography*, 483 (italics added).

168   **With a straight**   TR, *Letters*, vol. 3, 366.

169   **Suspecting, perhaps**   TR, *Autobiography*, 484; TR, *Letters*, vol. 3, 366.

169   **Morgan's men**   TR, *Letters*, vol. 3, 366; Elihu Root to TR, 29 June 1903, and TR to Winthrop Murray Crane, 16 Oct. 1902 (TRP). "May Heaven preserve me from ever again dealing with so wooden-headed a set," TR wrote his sister. *Letters from Theodore Roosevelt to Anna Roosevelt Cowles* (New York, 1926), 254.

169   SOME WEEKS AFTER   Wister, *Roosevelt*, 193.

Chronological Note: It was years before Baer met Wister again and conceded, in milder mood, "About the best thing your friend ever did was to appoint the Coal Strike Commission." By that time memories of the great strike had mellowed, if not into nostalgia, then at least to mutual forgiveness.

The operators got a 10 percent increase in the price of anthracite, plus permission to go on assessing output the way they always had. The union got its 10 percent wage hike, and a reduction of one to two hours per day in its work quota. Anthracite Coal Commission, *Report to the President*, 80–87. For a summary of findings, see Cornell, *Anthracite Coal Strike*, 236–59. For a negative view of the settlement from the point of view of Mitchell and the UMW, see Joe Gowaskie, "John Mitchell and the Anthracite Mine Workers: Leadership Conservatism and Rank-and-File Militancy," *Labor History*, winter 1985–1986. The most balanced account of the arbitration is Wiebe, "The Anthracite Coal Strike," showing that on the whole it profited management more than it did labor.

The UMW had to wait more than a decade for the formal recognition it so desperately traded away, but was compensated by general public recognition. George Baer was to die rich but mocked, unable to expiate his self-anointment as God's personal representative in eastern Pennsylvania. John Mitchell could look forward to a few years of such idolatry as no labor leader had yet known in the United States, but the strain of the great strike, afflicting his heart and mind, was to lead progressively through melancholy to insomnia to alcoholism (Glück, *John Mitchell*, 92, 197ff.; Charles A. Madison, *American Labor Leaders* [New York, 1950], 171–72). He, too, would die rich—having discovered that he was by nature more a capitalist than a populist.

169   **The rest of**   Toward the end of his career, the AFL leader Samuel Gompers described the anthracite strike of 1902 as "the most important single event in the labor movement of the United States." Finley Peter Dunne, "Remembrances," unfinished autobiographical manuscript in FPD, 26.

169   **"In a most quiet"**   "Each one of the procedures [TR] used, and even those he planned to use . . . have been utilized by later Presidents confronted with similar situations," William M. Goldsmith writes. "The country waited almost fifty years

for the Supreme Court to consider the full implications of such a power, and to establish limits in its application." *The Growth of Presidential Power: A Documented History* (New York, 1974), vol. 2, 1168.

169 **At home, Roosevelt**   TR to Benjamin Odell, 22 Mar. 1903 (unsent) (ER).

CHAPTER 12: NOT A CLOUD ON THE HORIZON

170 *In this palace*   "Mr. Dooley," in *Collier's Weekly,* ca. Nov. 1902 (HH).

170 "THE PRESIDENT"   Memorandum to John Hay, 23 Oct. 1902, in TR, *Letters,* vol. 3, 367.

170 *Harper's Weekly*   Qu. in Arthur M. Schlesinger, Jr., and Fred L. Israel, eds., *History of American Presidential Elections, 1789–1968* (New York, 1971), vol. 3, 2009–10. See also "President Roosevelt's Influence in the Election," *Literary Digest,* 15 Nov. 1902. Significantly, no prominent Democrat campaigner in the current congressional elections challenged TR's Philippines policy. Welch, *Response to Imperialism,* 72.

170 **Tributes, in the**   James Wilson to TR, 21 July 1902 (TRP).

170 **At latest count**   New York *Commercial Advertiser,* 4 Oct. 1902. Actually, TR now had sixteen states, Rhode Island having pledged to him on 9 Oct. See also Rixey, *Bamie,* chap. 23; Willis Van Devanter to F. E. Warren, 13 May 1903 (WVD).

170 **"come to the front"**   Willis Van Devanter to F. E. Warren, 13 May 1903 (WVD).

171 **Roosevelt's long-term**   TR, *Letters,* vol. 3, 372; Kehl, *Boss Rule,* 240; Douglas, *Many-Sided Roosevelt,* 89.

171 **A guest at**   Helen Nicolay qu. in Morris, *Edith Kermit Roosevelt,* 251.

171 **Edith was busy**   Ibid., 245.

171 ON 4 NOVEMBER   TR, *Letters,* vol. 3, 374. TR blamed the Philippines scandal for the erosion of his popular support. "The court-martial of General Smith cost me votes—*votes!*" he growled to Herbert Welsh. Welsh to Carl Schurz, 2 Nov. 1902 (CS).

171 **Even so**   Gould, *Presidency of Theodore Roosevelt,* 71–72; *Literary Digest,* 15 Nov. 1902; Kenneth J. Martis, ed., *Historical Atlas of Political Parties in the U.S. Congress, 1789–1989* (New York, 1989), 157.

171 **Roosevelt's hopes**   TR, *Letters,* vol. 3, 373–74; Merrill, *Republican Command,* 126–33. LaFollette was re-elected Governor with a large majority. TR could not have welcomed this result, having earlier congratulated Congressman Joseph W. Babcock for fighting to prevent LaFollette's nomination. LaFollette sourly quotes this letter in *LaFollette's Autobiography* (Madison, 1913), 312. TR did, however, arrest the insurgency somewhat by persuading Governor Cummins of Iowa to abandon his "Iowa Idea" for a tax policy less hostile to big business. Gould, *Reform and Regulation,* 35–36.

171 A SIGNBOARD READING   The date was 13 Nov. 1902. Except where otherwise indicated, the following two sections are based on eyewitness reporting by an unnamed correspondent of the Associated Press and Lindsay Denison of the New York *Sun.* TR granted both men exclusive permission to accompany him. The former's coverage appeared in *The Washington Post,* 14–19 Nov. 1902, and Denison's daily reports were subsequently republished (with photographs) as "President Roosevelt's Mississippi Bear Hunt" in *Outing,* Feb. 1903. Supplementary details from Holt Collier interview, *Saturday Evening Post,* 10 Apr. 1909, and Presidential scrapbook (TRP).

171 **On one side**   TR to John L. McIlhenny, 21 Oct. 1902 (TRP); Washington *Evening Star,* 15 and 12 Nov. 1902.

172 **Among the bale-sitters**   Edgar S. Wilson in *Booker T. Washington Papers,* vol. 6, 375; Dewey W. Grantham, Jr., "Dinner at the White House: Theodore Roosevelt,

Booker T. Washington and the South," *Tennessee Historical Quarterly* 18 (1958). The repercussions of the Crum appointment (which Dr. Washington had urged upon TR) are discussed below, in chap. 14.

172 **he elsewhere favored** On 10 Nov., e.g., TR had replaced Alabama's Lily White Republican Collector of Internal Revenue with a Booker T. Washington–endorsed Gold Democrat. *The Washington Post,* 11 Nov. 1902. See also Seth M. Scheiner, "President Roosevelt and the Negro, 1901–1909," *Journal of Negro History,* July 1962.

172 **"drawing of the color"** Booker T. Washington in *Booker T. Washington Papers,* vol. 6, 547. Scheiner, "President Roosevelt and the Negro," claims that "something more than altruism" influenced TR's Southern race policy. TR always denied that his motives were political (TR, *Letters,* vol. 3, 290–91, 387–88), but Scheiner cites evidence to the contrary. It suited him, e.g., to undermine the pro-Hanna Lily Whites of Alabama, whereas he appointed them freely in North Carolina in order to win the support of Senator Jeter Pritchard's powerful machine. "His main purpose was to receive the support of Republican state organizations, not to aid or appoint Negroes."

172 **Within the depot** The ethnic composition of TR's welcoming committee—a pair of whites to a score of blacks—reflected that of the Yazoo Delta. Washington *Evening Star,* 18 Nov. 1902.

172 **George H. Helm** Gatewood, *Theodore Roosevelt and the Art of Controversy,* 96, 71; Washington *Evening Star,* 14 Nov. 1902; Denison, "President Roosevelt's Mississippi Bear Hunt"; TR, *Letters,* vol. 3, 378.

172 **Shortly before four** Gregory C. Wilson, "Bagging the First Teddy Bear," unpub. research paper, 1979, AC; Washington *Evening Star,* 13 Nov. 1902. Charles Snyder, "TR," paper read to the New England Ophthalmological Society, 13 Apr. 1959 (TRC).

172 **He stepped down** *The Washington Post,* 17 Nov. 1902.

172 **THE NEXT FIVE** Paul Schullery, ed., *American Bears: Selections from the Writings of Theodore Roosevelt* (Boulder, 1983), 10; Denison, "President Roosevelt's Mississippi Bear Hunt."

173 **"I am going"** TR to Stuyvesant Fish, 6 Nov. 1902 (TRP). The hunt, organized by Fish, otherwise consisted of seven sporting gentlemen, TR's personal physician, two Secret Service agents, and sundry guides and retainers.

173 **Embarrassingly, he** Presidential scrapbook (TRP).

173 **Paradoxically, one** Gregory C. Wilson, "The Birth of the Teddy Bear," *Bear Tracks: Official Newsletter of the Good Bears of the World,* fall 1979; Holt Collier interview, *Saturday Evening Post,* 10 Apr. 1909.

173 **No sooner had** Denison, "President Roosevelt's Mississippi Bear Hunt."

173 **Back at the** Holt Collier interview, *The Saturday Evening Post,* 10 Apr. 1909. The sex of TR's bear is a subject of debate. A hunter who has seen the skin judges it to have been that of a 246-pound female. Charles Moose interview with author, 10 Nov. 1988 (AC).

173 **"Put it out"** *The Washington Post,* 15 Nov. 1902.

174 **Whether or not** Clifford Berryman qu. in Marietta Andrews, *My Studio Window: Sketches of the Pageant of Washington Life* (New York, 1928), 172. The version of "Drawing the Line" most frequently reproduced is not the original *Washington Post* cartoon. Berryman seems to have produced a second version (with the bear as a cub), later in 1902—whether for publication or not is unclear. It is sometimes wrongly attributed to the Washington *Evening Star.* The "other" bear cartoon he drew for William E. Chandler is probably a third version, showing a pack of bear cubs joyfully escorting "Teddy" out of the forest (Presidential scrapbook [TRP]). According to Berryman, this one was "a hit." In later years, the cartoonist so iden-

tified with the Teddy Bear that he used to sign his letters with it. Andrews, *My Studio Window*, 171.

174 **Three thousand** Wilson, "Birth of the Teddy Bear"; Peggy and Alan Bialosky, eds., *The Teddy Bear Catalogue: Care, Repair, and Love* (New York, 1980), 12–21. *Historiological Note:* The most serious study of the TR/Teddy Bear phenomenon is Linda Mullins, *The Teddy Bear Men: Theodore Roosevelt and Clifford Berryman* (Cumberland, Md., 1987). See also the above-cited works of Wilson and Bialosky. Morris and Rose Michtom founded the Ideal Toy Company, largely on the strength of their stuffed-bear sales, in 1903. Family tradition claims that Michtom wrote TR asking for permission to call the bears "Teddy's Bears," and TR replied that if his name was worth anything, they were welcome to use it. The story is doubtful. There is no trace of TR's letter in his conscientiously kept copybooks, and the Michtoms do not seem to have preserved what would be its priceless original. Furthermore, TR disliked being called "Teddy," and had a strict policy of not endorsing any commercial products, even his own books, when in office. The probable truth is that the Stieff Company produced the first "Teddy Bears" (albeit modeled after bear cubs in the Stuttgart Zoo) in 1902, and that the Michtoms duplicated their design in 1902–1903. By 1904, Roosevelt "Bear Cub" associations were already noticeable in campaign tokens, and in 1906 "The Roosevelt Bears," a cartoon feature, began to run in *The New York Times*. The strip was soon parlayed by Seymour Eaton into a wildly popular series of children's books. An original 1903 Michtom thirty-inch-tall bear is now worth at least forty-five thousand dollars. With this note, the author formally withdraws from the field of Teddy Bear studies.

174 EDITH ROOSEVELT RECEIVED TR returned to Washington on 21 Nov. 1902. For EKR's extensive work with McKim, Mead & White on restoring the White House, see Morris, *Edith Kermit Roosevelt*, chap. 19.

174 **Gone were the** *Restoration of the White House: Message of the President of the United States Transmitting the Report of the Architects* (Washington, D.C., 1903), *passim;* Charles Moore, "The Restoration of the White House," *Century,* Apr. 1903; Seale, *President's House*, vol. 2, 656–84; Ellen Maury Slayden, *Washington Wife: Journal of Ellen Maury Slayden from 1897–1919* (New York, 1963), 46–47.

174 **For this improvement** *Restoration of the White House*, 17–20, 9; The work, while complete in all essentials by late November 1902, continued for another two months. Washington *Evening Star,* 31 Jan. 1903.

174 **The pavilions flanked** Moore, "Restoration"; Morris, *Edith Kermit Roosevelt,* 260.

175 **"The first impression"** Moore, "Restoration"; Wister, *Roosevelt,* 108.

175 **Roosevelt, marching** Morris, *Edith Kermit Roosevelt,* 253. Contrary to popular impression, only one of the game heads was a trophy of his.

176 **Breeding, however** Wister, *Roosevelt,* 107.

176 **Upstairs, Edith** All these apartments had en suite bathrooms. Seale, *President's House,* vol. 2, 679.

176 THE DOCUMENT WAS TR's Second Annual Message is reprinted in TR, *Works,* vol. 17, 161–95.

176 **the United States and Mexico** The dispute concerned the Pacific Pious Fund, an annual indemnity promised by Mexico "in perpetuity" to Franciscan friars, as compensation for monastic properties appropriated in 1842. Mexico stopped paying this award after the United States took over California. The Hague court found in favor of resumed payments by Mexico. *The New York Times,* 27 Dec. 1902.

176 **"As civilization grows,"** TR, *Works,* vol. 17, 175.

176 **By this he** The most exhaustive modern analysis of TR's close-to-home foreign policy is Richard H. Collin, *Theodore Roosevelt's Caribbean, the Panama Canal, the Monroe Doctrine, and the Latin American Context* (Baton Rouge, 1990).

177 **the covert diplomat** Howard K. Beale, *Theodore Roosevelt and the Rise of America to World Power* (Baltimore, 1956), 452–53; Marks, *Velvet on Iron*, 52. The *secret du roi* involved covert, personal emissaries of the king, operating often at odds with his official diplomacy. See Alfred Cobban, *A History of Modern France* (New York, 1965), vol. 1, 76, 97. TR's own preferred term was *kitchen ambassadors*. TR, *Letters*, vol. 4, 1102.

177 **Foreign policy was** TR, *Letters*, vol. 1, 409. See Nelson M. Blake, "Ambassadors at the Court of Theodore Roosevelt," *Mississippi Valley Historical Review*, Sept. 1955, and Burton, "Theodore Roosevelt and His English Correspondents." For a French view of TR's discreet diplomacy, see Serge Ricard, *Théodore Roosevelt: principes et practique d'une politique étrangère* (Aix-en-Provence, 1991).

177 **Not until after** Qu. in E. Alexander Powell, *Yonder Lies Adventure* (New York, 1932), 312; TR, *Letters*, vol. 5, 358–59.

177 **The full extent**
    Historiological Note: The best summary of archival lacunae attendant to the Venezuelan crisis is in Marks, *Velvet on Iron*, 42–47 and notes. To Marks's list might be added a corresponding gap in the dispatches of French Ambassador Jules Cambon at the Quai d'Orsay in Paris, and another (Oct.–Dec. 1902) in the normally copious correspondence between John Hay and Assistant Secretary of State Alvey A. Adee in JH. Elsewhere, this correspondence routinely refers to burnings and deletions. See also Beale, *Theodore Roosevelt*, 407–8, and Edmund Morris, " 'A Few Pregnant Days': Theodore Roosevelt and the Venezuelan Crisis of 1902," *Theodore Roosevelt Association Journal*, winter 1989. Gould, *Presidency of Theodore Roosevelt*, 78–79, dismisses the evidence of these sources and states flatly that TR in later life "came to believe that he had in fact delivered a warning."

177 ROOSEVELT HAD SEEN In 1902, sixty-two million bolivars was the equivalent of twenty-five million U.S. dollars. *The Washington Post*, 19 Nov. 1902. For a detailed background to the Venezuela crisis of 1902, see Holger Herwig, *Germany's Vision of Empire in Venezuela* (Princeton, N.J., 1986), chap. 3.

177 **These powers** D. M. Platt, "The Allied Coercion of Venezuela, 1902–1903: A Reassessment," *Inter-American Economic Affairs*, spring 1962, notes that, contrary to traditional opinion, Germany, not Britain, was the aggressor against Venezuela throughout 1902.

177 **The President sympathized** TR to Cecil Spring Rice, 13 Aug. 1897, in Stephen Gwynn, ed., *The Letters and Friendships of Cecil Spring Rice: A Record* (Boston, 1929), vol. 1, 229–30. TR could even be said to have invited the action by stating in his First Annual Message, "We do not guarantee any [Latin American] State against punishment if it misconducts itself, providing that punishment does not take the form of the acquisition of territory by any non-American power" (TR, *Works*, vol. 17, 135). But as will be seen, he expected the built-in warning to be heeded to the letter. For TR the diplomatic moralist, see Marks, *Velvet on Iron*, chap. 3.

177 **Ever the stern** TR, *Letters*, vol. 3, 116. TR was not alone in his contempt for Castro, "that unspeakably villainous little monkey." The Venezuela leader was reviled with near unanimity by contemporary diplomats, and modern historians have endorsed their verdict. See Herwig, *Germany's Vision of Empire*, 86–87.

178 **Baron von Sternburg** Emil Witte, *Revelations of a German Attaché: Ten Years of*

German-American Diplomacy (New York, 1916), 78, describes von Sternburg as "a sworn enemy of all writing." See Stefan H. Rinke, "The German Ambassador Hermann Speck von Sternburg and Theodore Roosevelt, 1889–1908," *Theodore Roosevelt Association Journal*, winter 1991, and Rinke's master's thesis, "Between Success and Failure: The Diplomatic Career of Ambassador Hermann Speck von Sternburg and German-American Relations, 1903–1908" (Bowling Green State University, 1989).

178 **When Roosevelt condoned** TR, *Works*, vol. 17, 135.

178 **a secret memorandum** Henry C. Taylor to TR, ca. late Nov. 1902 (TRP).

178 **"The first method"** Ibid.; TR, *Letters*, vol. 3, 98; Putnam, *Theodore Roosevelt*, 102–11.

178 **Part of him** TR, *Letters*, vol. 3, 98, 108; Gwynn, *Letters and Friendships*, vol. 2, 10; Morris, "'A Few Pregnant Days.'"

179 **The adjective** *temporary* Beale, *Theodore Roosevelt*, 400; Gwynn, *Letters and Friendships*, vol. 1, 246; Fritz Fischer, *Germany's Aims in the First World War* (New York, 1967), 7–21; *Review of Reviews*, Jan. 1901; John C. G. Röhl, ed., *Kaiser Wilhelm II: New Interpretations—The Corfu Papers* (Cambridge, 1982), 144. TR had been hearing from Cecil Spring Rice about German colonial ambitions in Latin America since at least 1897 (see, e.g., Gwynn, *Letters and Friendships*, vol. 1, 227). Vice Admiral Büschel, chief German naval war planner, summarized his country's 1902–1903 policy *vis-à-vis* the United States in language that requires no translation: "Feste Position in Westinden. Freie Hand in Südamerika. Aufgabe der Monroe Doktrine." Qu. in Paul M. Kennedy, ed., *The War Plans of the Great Powers, 1880–1914* (London, 1979), 57.

179 **What better place** In March 1901, John Hay, Henry Cabot Lodge, and Elihu Root had been alarmed by reports that a German gunboat was making hydrographic surveys of the Margarita Islands (Richard W. Turk, "Defending the New Empire, 1900–1914," in Kenneth J. Hagan, ed., *In Peace and War: Interpretations of American Naval History* [Westport, Conn., 1984], 189). Their scare communicated itself to TR. "The only power which may be a menace to us in anything like the immediate future is Germany," he wrote (TR, *Letters*, vol. 3, 32). In July 1901, he warned Karl Bünz, Germany's Consul General in New York, that his country must not think of acquiring "a foot of soil in any shape or way in South America." TR, *Letters*, vol. 3, 98.

179 **idea of the** *Weltpolitik* Herwig, *Politics of Frustration*, 55; Röhl, *Kaiser Wilhelm II*, 143ff.; Marks, *Velvet on Iron*, 6. The Kaiser's brother had actually intended to propose "a German sphere of influence" in South America to TR on his recent state visit, until silenced by von Bülow. J. Lepsius et al., *Die Grosse Politik der Europäischen Kabinette, 1871–1914* (Berlin, 1922–1927), vol. 17, 243.

179 **Germany, therefore** According to Herwig, *Politics of Frustration*, 46, the German high command also regarded war with the United States around this time as "a distinct possibility." See also ibid., 42–46, and John A. S. Grenville and George B. Young, *Politics, Strategy, and American Diplomacy: Studies in Foreign Policy, 1873–1917* (New Haven, 1966), 305–7.

180 **"For the first"** TR, *Works*, vol. 17, 182.

180 **Coincidentally or not** Seward W. Livermore, "Theodore Roosevelt, the American Navy, and the Venezuela Crisis of 1902–1903," *American Historical Review*, Apr. 1946.

180 SEA POWER TR, *Letters*, vol. 3, 225, 217. For TR's 1902 naval thinking, see his speech to the United States Naval Academy in TR, *Presidential Addresses*, vol. 1, 39–41; Gordon C. O'Gara, *Theodore Roosevelt and the Rise of the Modern Navy* (Princeton, N.J., 1969), 116; TR, *Letters*, vol. 3, 253–54; Beach, *United States*

Navy, 390–97. Marks, *Velvet on Iron,* 40, shows how from Dec. 1901 on TR "accompanied every step in the diplomatic confrontation with a corresponding buildup of American sea power."

180 **The most recent** *Review of Reviews,* Apr. 1902; memorandum from Office of Naval Intelligence, 11 Feb. 1903 (TRP); Charles D. Sigsbee to TR, 22 Mar. 1902 (TRP).

180 **They sat** Photograph in Ronald Spector, *Professors of War: The Naval War College and the Development of the Naval Profession* (Newport, R.I., 1977). United States Naval War College, *Rules for the Conduct of War Games* (Naval War College, R.I., 1902); Ronald Spector, "Roosevelt, the Navy, and the Venezuelan Controversy, 1902–1903," *American Neptune,* Oct. 1972.

180 **Germany, the tacticians** Livermore, "Theodore Roosevelt"; TR, *Letters,* vol. 3, 367–70.

181 HE WAS ABLE Amy S. Strachey, *St. Loe Strachey: His Life and His Paper* (New York, 1931), 142–43; Speck von Sternburg to TR, 19 Oct. 1902 (TRP); Tilchin, *Theodore Roosevelt,* 28–29; Marks, *Velvet on Iron,* 50. On 29 Oct. 1902, Henry White wrote TR that Strachey's White House invitation was "the greatest honor that has ever befallen him" (TRP).

181 **Strachey, through his** He also had the reputation of being "Germany's sharpest critic." *Review of Reviews,* Dec. 1902.

181 **Awake, however** Dewey was in full court uniform, having learned that the Roosevelts preferred their military aides that way. "They are getting to be quite a palace down there." Mrs. Dewey diary, 25 Nov. 1902 (GD).

181 **As Roosevelt reminded** TR, *Letters,* vol. 3, 275.

181 **But Dewey had** John Garry Clifford, "Admiral Dewey and the Germans," *Mid-Atlantic* 49 (1967). Like TR, Dewey had been monitoring the Venezuela situation for eleven months, in his capacity as President of the General Board of the Navy. Ronald Spector, *Admiral of the New Empire: The Life and Career of George Dewey* (Baton Rouge, 1974), 140–41.

Chronological Note: The shared concern of President and Admiral can be traced back to Germany's formation of Caribbean and South Atlantic Squadrons in 1901. The following chronology is instructive.

13 Dec. 1901: Germany notifies the United States that she might have to "coerce" Venezuela and make a "temporary occupation" of her ports. *17 Dec. 1901:* TR issues an executive order making Culebra, Puerto Rico, a naval base "in case of sudden war." *Jan. 1902:* Navy Department advises TR of a plan for emergency deployment of warships in the Caribbean; Dewey warns that Venezuela situation looks dangerous, works out defense strategy centering on Virgin Islands; TR redoubles efforts to buy the islands from Denmark; German Embassy in Washington notifies Berlin of these developments; Wilhelmstrasse strategists refocus their contingency war plans on Long Island; Navy reports German espionage team in Port of Spain, Trinidad. *February:* State Department asks information on Venezuelan landing places and roads; TR appoints young, aggressive William H. Moody to be Secretary of the Navy. *May:* Naval intelligence reports German cruiser skulking in Venezuelan waters. *June:* Forthcoming assembly of "greatest fighting fleet in U.S. history" announced in world press; TR asks Dewey to command it; State Department perfects plan for defense of Venezuelan coast. *July:* Moody orders a similar plan providing for "offense"; TR urges Speck von Sternburg, in Europe, to visit White House: "I have very much I want to say to you" (19 July [TRP]); Dewey takes personal role in plotting maneuvers; Navy Department informed that TR is "deeply interested" in same; Germany informs Great Britain of willingness for joint reclamation measures against Venezuela. *August:* Imperialist expansion pressures increase on Wilhelmstrasse. *24 Sept.:* TR has strategic conference with Dewey, and tells him "in strictest confidence—what had better not be written now" (Mrs. Dewey diary [GD]). *27 Oct.:* TR presses for new naval bases in Cuba; two days later, he sounds out Balfour on the vulnerability of Dutch Caribbean colonies and invites Strachey to make "a flying visit" to the White House. All these activities, implying an extraordinary feeling of gathering crisis, predate the Anglo-German agreement to coerce Venezuela on 12 Nov. 1902.

182   **Meanwhile, the United States** Livermore, "Theodore Roosevelt."

182   **Finally, on 1** Washington *Evening Star,* 1 Dec. 1902.

CHAPTER 13:   THE BIG STICK

183   *One good copper* "Mr. Dooley" in *The Washington Post,* 1 Feb. 1903.

183   ON THE MORNING   Morris, *Edith Kermit Roosevelt,* 224–26, 416; in 1902, the West Wing was seen as providing "temporary quarters" for White House staff, until Congress should take up the question of "a permanent, adequate, and thoroughly dignified office for the Chief Executive." Gilson Willets, *Inside History of the White House* (New York, 1906), 69.

183   **on his right** TR's Cabinet Room is now the Roosevelt Room. The Oval Office was not built until after he left the White House. The following description is taken from photographs in TRC and from William Bayard Hale, *A Week in the White House* (New York, 1908), 9–11.

184   **The room's main** A famous 1903 photograph of TR shows him with the globe in this position.

184   **There was nothing much** TR, *Letters,* vol. 8, 1108; TR to Grover Cleveland, 26 Dec. 1902, ibid., vol. 3, 398.

184   **Congress was back** Washington *Evening Star,* 1 Dec. 1902.

184   **For two and a** Ibid. When the President's Message was published the following day, its reception was equivocal. The *Harrisburg Telegraph,* clarion of Old Guard Republicanism, called it "one of the most conservative documents ever issued by the White House," while *The Washington Post* (Dem.) rejoiced that every line of the Message was "progressive."

185   **By 4 December** New York *American,* 4 Dec. 1902. The Washington newspapers' front-page coverage of the maneuvers was as warlike as TR could wish. On 5 Dec. 1902, as the "white" half of Dewey's fleet prepared to engage the "blue" half, the Washington *Evening Star* excitedly announced, ENEMY PUTS TO SEA.

185   **On 7 December** Hill, *Roosevelt and the Caribbean,* 16; TR, *Letters,* vol. 8, 1102; Henry Clay Taylor to J. B. Coghlan, 8 Dec. 1902 (GD).

185   **"We look like"** TR, *Letters,* vol. 3, 389.

185   **General Wood** Leonard Wood diary, 30 Nov. 1902 (LW).

185   *Speak softly and* TR first used the proverb publicly on 2 Sept. 1901. TR, *Works,* vol. 15, 334–35.

185   ON 8 DECEMBER   Washington *Evening Star,* 8 Dec. 1902; Beale, *Theodore Roosevelt,* 419; Marks, *Velvet on Iron,* 74; TR, *Letters,* vol. 5, 358.

185   **the most dangerous** Adams, *Letters,* vol. 5, 341, 343; Röhl, *Kaiser Wilhelm II,* 19, 158; Gwynn, *Letters and Friendships,* vol. 1, 227–30. Another of TR's early informants about Wilhelm was Speck von Sternburg.

186   **General Wood, just** Leonard Wood diary, 10 Sept. 1902 (LW); Hermann Hagedorn, *Leonard Wood: A Biography* (New York, 1931), vol. 1, 398–99. Wood had been personally received by the Kaiser, and had noted that, like TR in the 1880s, Wilhelm spoke exultantly about his country's newness and rawness and burgeon-

ing economic power. Wood also saw that he was "somewhat nervous in manner," and easily put out. All these observations were doubtless relayed to TR, between singlesticks blows.

186 **some beguiling**   Elihu Root teased TR, referring to the Kaiser as "your cousin William." Speck von Sternburg commented publicly that he had "not seen two men who are as alike." Wilhelm II himself remarked to von Holleben, "Mr. Roosevelt must in some respects be very like me." Root to TR, 15 Feb. 1904 (TRP); New York *Herald*, ca. 21 Jan. 1903; Smalley, *Anglo-American Memories*, 356–57.

186 **Only three months**   A caricature of TR and the Kaiser as twins ("Kindred Spirits of the Strenuous Life") appeared in *Punch*, 16 Nov. 1904, and was suppressed by Berlin police. See also Beale, *Theodore Roosevelt*, 441–43; Jules Jusserand to Théophile Delcassé, 9 Mar. 1904 (JJ). In youth, both men used to doodle ships and fleet dispositions, and in power, both tended to use the first-person possessive in referring to their respective navies. Wilhelm awarded himself the title of "Admiral of the Atlantic." Morris, *Rise of Theodore Roosevelt*, 142; Röhl, *Kaiser Wilhelm II*, 81; Herwig, *Politics of Frustration*, 58; Leonard Wood diary, 10 Sept. 1902 (LW); TR, *Letters*, vol. 3, 283.

186 **However, as Roosevelt**   Herwig, *Politics of Frustration*, 55. "It is absolutely impossible," Henry Adams wrote, "for anyone to be as big a fool as the Kaiser without being shut up" (Adams, *Letters*, vol. 5, 353; Röhl, *Kaiser Wilhelm II*, 18–19). Röhl quotes an example of the Kaiser's ranting against Jews: "There are far too many of them in my country. They want stamping out" (129).

186 **What made Roosevelt**   Michael Balfour, *The Kaiser and His Times* (Boston, 1964), 85; Modris Eksteins, *Rites of Spring: The Great War and the Birth of the Modern Age* (Boston, 1989), 87–88. Jules Cambon noted how "very sensitive" TR was, "in his political judgments, to questions of prestige." Geneviève Tabouis, *Jules Cambon: par l'un des siens* (Paris, 1938), 108, tr. the author. For the Kaiser's homoerotic inclinations, which included a delight in seeing his courtiers dress as poodles and ballerinas, see Isabel Hull, "Kaiser Wilhelm II and the 'Liebenberg Circle,' " in Röhl, *Kaiser Wilhelm II*.

186 **"to tell the Kaiser"**   TR, *Letters*, vol. 5, 358–59. This is TR's best, fullest, and most nearly contemporary account of the Venezuela crisis. He makes no reference to arbitration. See the chronological analysis in Morris, " 'A Few Pregnant Days.' "

187 **The tactfulness**   TR, *Letters*, vol. 8, 1102.

187 **Again von Holleben**   Even as TR met with von Holleben, the USS *Marietta* was en route to La Guiria, Venezuela, for "purposes of observation." Livermore, "Theodore Roosevelt."

187 **The Ambassador**   William Loeb to Hermann Hagedorn, n.d., and Loeb interviewed by Henry Pringle, 14 Apr. 1930 (HP).

On this same day, TR also had a conversation with George Smalley, Washington correspondent of *The Times*. His clear purpose was to have the well-connected reporter let London policymakers know just where he stood regarding Germany's threat to Venezuela. White House appointment book, 8 Dec. 1902, and Smalley to TR, 12 Dec. 1902 (TRP). "I think it desirable that you should know privately what . . . I intend to do," he quotes TR as saying, prefatory to a twenty-minute statement of great "lucidity and force" (Smalley, *Anglo-American Memories*, 350). Smalley might have been less eager to convey presidential messages had he known that TR considered him to be "a copper-riveted idiot." TR, *Letters*, vol. 3, 97.

187 THE "PACIFIC" BLOCKADE   Hill, *Roosevelt and the Caribbean*, 117; Herbert Bowen, "Roosevelt and Venezuela," *North American Review*, Sept. 1919; United States Department of State, *Papers Relating to the Foreign Relations of the United States, 1903* (Washington D.C., annual), 793 (hereafter *Foreign Relations*).

187 **John Hay relayed**   Beale, *Theodore Roosevelt*, 413; Pierre de Margerie to French

Foreign Office, 18 Jan. 1903 (JJ); Beale, *Theodore Roosevelt*, 413; Herwig, *Politics of Frustration*, 67–69; TR, *Letters*, vol. 8, 1102. TR's strategic suspicions were not unfounded. See Grenville and Young, *Politics, Strategy, and American Diplomacy*, 306.

188   IN BERLIN, Speck   Reporting back to TR on 15 Dec. 1902, von Sternburg sounded more like an American diplomat than a German. "I've told them every bit of [the truth]. . . . Fear I've knocked them down rather roughly, but should consider myself a cowardly weakling if I had let things stand as they were" (TRP).

188   Expressionless, self-effacing   Cassini, *Never a Dull Moment*, 108, 197 ("As always, Speck has three faces—one for the Russians, one for the British, and one for whomever he is stationed by"); Speck von Sternburg to TR, 15 Dec. 1902 (TRP).

188   There seemed to   Marks, *Velvet on Iron*, 50; Beale, *Theodore Roosevelt*, 422, 413. See Paul S. Holbo, "Perilous Obscurity: Public Diplomacy and the Press in the Venezuela Crisis, 1902–1903," *The Historian* 32.3 (1970), for the barrage of White House publicity during Dewey's naval maneuvers.

188   Von Bülow   Alfred Vagts, *Deutschland und die vereinigten Staaten in der Weltpolitik* (New York, 1935), 1569, tr. the author; *Die Grosse Politik*, vol. 17, 255–60; Lionel M. Gelber, *The Rise of Anglo-American Friendship* (New York, 1938), 113.

188   The ink on   Hill, *Roosevelt and the Caribbean*, 118.

188   Roosevelt continued   TR, *Letters*, vol. 8, 1102; Platt, "Allied Coercion of Venezuela."

188   Sunday, 14 December   *The Washington Post*, 15 Dec. 1902. For reasons set forth at length in Morris, " 'A Few Pregnant Days,' " Sunday, 14 Dec., must have been the date of the secret TR–von Holleben meeting. Hay's arbitration message was sent the previous day, Saturday, and von Holleben left Washington for New York on Sunday evening.

188   If Roosevelt expected   Vagts, *Deutschland*, 1569; profile in *Munsey's*, Sept. 1901; Cassini, *Never a Dull Moment*, 108; Sergei Witte, *The Memoirs of Count Witte*, ed. Sidney Harcave (Armonk, N.Y., 1990), 61, 76–77; Beale, *Theodore Roosevelt*, 422.

189   Today, von Holleben   Hill, *Roosevelt and the Caribbean*, 133; TR, *Letters*, vol. 8, 1103.

189   Controlling himself   William Loeb interviewed by Henry Pringle, 14 Apr. 1930 (HP).

189   The President said   Beale, *Theodore Roosevelt*, 414.

189   WILLIAM LOEB SAW   Marks, *Velvet on Iron*, argues that TR himself may have been initially responsible, in order not to humiliate the pathologically sensitive Kaiser. "Roosevelt's penchant for face-saving is the key to much of the mystery surrounding his foreign policy. . . . In the field of diplomacy he was nearly *always* tactful and courteous" (58–59).

189   Von Holleben   Herwig, *Politics of Frustration*, 80, 55, 69.

189   Late that evening   "At the Hotels," *The New York Times*, 15 Dec. 1902.

189   Sometime during   TR, *Letters*, vol. 8, 1104, and vol. 5, 1102; George Dewey diary, 13 Jan. 1903 (GD). Bünz, TR said years later, was "the one man who sized me up right." When the aging Consul General was arrested on espionage charges in the First World War, TR vowed to help him, "for the really valuable service he did this country as well as his own in the Venezuela matter" (TR to John J. Leary, Leary Notebooks [TRC]). See TR's exquisitely detailed expositions of the Monroe Doctrine to Bünz in *Letters*, vol. 3, 98.

189   As von Holleben   Beale, *Theodore Roosevelt*, 414; Hill, *Roosevelt and the Caribbean*, 121–22.

190   But Metternich   "If President Castro should prematurely perceive that there exists

on our part a leaning toward arbitration," Metternich opined, "he would interpret this as weakness and would certainly make no concessions." Hill, *Roosevelt and the Caribbean*, 121.

190 **It was now** TR to A. W. Callisen, 3 May 1916 (TRP); Hill, *Roosevelt and the Caribbean*, 122; Washington *Evening Star*, 16 Dec. 1902; Henry Clay Taylor to Staff Intelligence Officer, San Juan, P.R., 16 Dec. 1902 (GD). There was a flurry of nervous selling on Wall Street. New York *Herald*, 17 Dec. 1902.

190 **"Such cables,"** Henry Clay Taylor to Staff Intelligence Officer, San Juan, P.R., 16 Dec. 1902 (GD).

190 **After less than** Marks, *Velvet on Iron*, 41; New York *Herald*, 17 Dec. 1902. Livermore, "Theodore Roosevelt," notes that the fighting edge of Dewey's armada moved five hundred miles closer to Venezuela at this "critical" juncture.

190 **Throughout the crisis** Holbo, "Perilous Obscurity."

190 **By now the** *The Washington Post*, 17 Dec. 1902; "At the Hotels," *The New York Times*, 16 Dec. 1902; Marks, *Velvet on Iron*, 42, is puzzled by German Embassy letters dated 15, 17, and 18 Dec. and signed by von Holleben. There is no question that the Ambassador was out of town from 14 Dec. on: he must simply have taken official stationery with him to New York. See below.

190 **From there** *The New York Times*, 17 Dec. 1902; *The Times* (London), 18 Dec. 1902; Herwig, *Politics of Frustration*, 69.

191 **"now the cannons"** Edward B. Parsons, "The German–American Crisis of 1902–1903," *The Historian* 33 (May 1971).

191 **The reaction in** Alfred P. Dennis, *Adventures in American Diplomacy, 1896–1906* (New York, 1928), 290; George P. Gooch and Harold Temperley, eds., *British Documents on the Origin of the War, 1898–1931* (London, 1928–1931), vol. 2, 153. On 18 Dec., Hay, believing the crisis still to be acute, wasted much hot breath in a strongly worded "ultimatum" to Albert von Quadt, the German chargé d'affaires. Both men were, in a later phrase, out of the loop. The skimpy evidence surviving suggests that TR's ultimatum was received by Berlin not as a shock, but as a confirmation of repeated warnings from Bünz (June 1902) and von Sternburg (July, Oct., Nov. 1902) that the new President was not to be trifled with (Beale, *Theodore Roosevelt*, 418). Throughout the year, both von Holleben and Quadt had urged Berlin to prepare for possible war with the United States. Herwig, *Politics of Frustration*, 69, 71.

191 SO THE DEADLINE Von Bülow expressly repeated that Germany had no territorial ambitions in Venezuela. Hill, *Roosevelt and the Caribbean*, 131.

191 **"I am a sick man,"** New York *Herald* news clipping, ca. 10 Jan. 1903, John Hay Scrapbook (JH). Henry Adams, *The Education of Henry Adams* (Boston, 1918), 437; Herwig, *Politics of Frustration*, 83. Von Holleben did not return to Washington until 26 Dec. and stayed two weeks to wind up his affairs, still refusing to speak to the press. On 5 Jan. 1903, the Kaiser canceled his credentials. He left town again without saying good-bye to TR or John Hay (*New York Tribune*, 10 Jan. 1903; Pierre de Margerie to Théophile Delcassé, in *Documents diplomatiques français* [*1871–1914*], series 2, vol. 3, 24 [Paris, 1929–1959]). When he sailed home from Hoboken, N.J., on 10 Jan. 1903, "not a single member of the diplomatic corps or German official [with the exception of Karl Bünz] dared to see him off." TR, *Letters*, vol. 8, 1104, and Blake, "Ambassadors at the Court."

191 **On 19 December** Herbert W. Bowen, *Recollections Diplomatic and Undiplomatic* (New York, 1926), 261; Gooch and Temperley, *British Documents*, vol. 2, 163; Washington *Evening Star*, 20 Dec. 1902; TR, *Letters*, vol. 3, 396–98.

191 **"I suppose,"** TR, *Letters*, vol. 5, 319.

191 **Overflowing with** Washington *Evening Star*, 17 Dec. 1902; *Baltimore Sun*, 13 Feb. 1903. TR also wrote a generous letter to Grover Cleveland on 26 Dec. con-

gratulating him on "the rounding out of your Venezuela policy." TR, *Letters,* vol. 3, 398.

192 **Be yours—we** John Hay to TR, 24 Dec. 1902 (TD).

192 **Snow fell** James Garfield diary, 24 Dec. 1902 (JRG). Perhaps the brightest glow beneath TR's tree was shed by a small copper scuttle that Archie and Quentin found on the White House doorstep. It was addressed "To the President of the United States," and contained a measure of anthracite coal. Ethel Roosevelt Derby interview, 1962 (TRB). The scuttle is now in TR's library at Sagamore Hill.

Historiographical Note: Few episodes in TR's career have aroused as much controversy as the first Venezuela crisis of 1902. His secrecy about it as President, the apparent collusion of three governments in obliterating the record, and some inconsistencies in his later accounts have caused historians, beginning with Howard C. Hill in 1927, to accuse TR of faulty memory at best and boastful lies at worst. Alfred Vagts and the American diplomatic historian Dexter Perkins, apologists respectively for Nazi Germany and the New Deal, were particularly virulent in the 1930s, and contributed much to the decline in TR's reputation. They never succeeded, however, in challenging his basic honesty. Even Henry Pringle, the most iconoclastic of Roosevelt biographers, felt compelled to believe him, after an interview with William Loeb in which the former secretary testified that he was present at the two meetings with von Holleben. Loeb also described them to Hermann Hagedorn. Seward W. Livermore in 1946 and Howard K. Beale in 1956 were the first modern scholars to uncover fresh facts in support of TR's story. Since then, the historical pendulum has continued to swing his way. Edward Parsons wrote a telling essay in 1971, and Frederick W. Marks III in 1979 almost succeeded in proving an international conspiracy to deny that anything happened—when plainly, something very considerable did. The account given in this chapter is based on the author's article " 'A Few Pregnant Days.' " See also Parsons, "German-American Crisis," and, for an important conflicting view that TR's ultimatum was delivered in late January/early February 1903, see Serge Ricard, "The Anglo-German Intervention in Venezuela and Theodore Roosevelt's Ultimatum to the Kaiser: Taking a Fresh Look at an Old Enigma," in Serge Ricard and Hélène Christol, eds., *Anglo-Saxonism in U.S. Foreign Policy: The Diplomacy of Imperialism, 1899–1919* (Aix-en-Provence, 1991), 66–77. While allowing for continuing scholarly disagreement about dates, William N. Tilchin writes, "By any reasonable standard, this controversy should now be considered resolved [in TR's favor]." Tilchin, *Theodore Roosevelt,* 32.

CHAPTER 14: A CONDITION, NOT A THEORY

193 **We insist that** "Mr. Dooley" in *The Washington Post,* 1 Mar. 1903.

193 **"THE EQUILIBRIUM"** Georges Picot qu. in Jean Jules Jusserand, *What Me Befell: The Reminiscences of J. J. Jusserand* (Boston, 1933), 219; see, e.g., Jean Jules Jusserand, *The English Novel in the Time of Shakespeare* (1890), *Piers Plowman* (London, 1894); and *A Literary History of the English People* (London, 1895).

193 **Equally clearly** Jusserand, *What Me Befell,* 219; whenever TR's name was mentioned, Cambon would tap his head significantly. Storer, *In Memoriam,* 38–39.

193 **French foreign-policy** Paris correspondent of the *Chicago Tribune,* 19 Oct. 1902. For an overview of the scant French literature on TR, see Serge Ricard, "The French Historiography of Theodore Roosevelt," *Theodore Roosevelt Association Journal,* summer 1984.

193 "the proper policing"   Hay had cabled TR's refusal to arbitrate to Herbert Bowen, the American Minister in Caracas, on 27 Dec. 1902. Although tempted, TR had declined on Hay's advice, partly out of a desire to help out the court, which was atrophying through lack of business. Livermore, "Theodore Roosevelt"; Beale, *Theodore Roosevelt.*

"A great number of Frenchmen and Europeans are happy to join with me in expressing to you their gratitude for the generous, unyielding firmness you have displayed in support of international justice," a Hague delegate wrote. "The initiative of the United States, compared with the paralysis of Europe, is a sign of the times" (Baron d'Estournelles de Constant to TR, 27 Dec. 1902 [TRP]). Estournelles de Constant, like TR, was destined to win the Nobel Peace Prize. For international praise of TR, see *Literary Digest,* 3 Jan. 1903.

194 THE JANUARY ISSUE   Baker, *American Chronicle,* 168–69. *McClure's* circulation in 1903 was 350,000. This issue achieved record sales.

195 "The Oil War"   This article was the third in what eventually grew to be a nineteen-part series by Ida Tarbell.

195 "torrential journalism,"   Eric F. Goldman, *Rendezvous with Destiny: A History of Modern American Reform* (New York, 1956), 134–35; Sullivan, *Our Times,* vol. 3, 133; TR, who knew both Baker and Steffens well, was sufficiently impressed by this issue of *McClure's* to invite the two writers to visit him at Sagamore Hill in the summer of 1903. For his previous relations with them, see Baker, *American Chronicle,* and Steffens, *Autobiography, passim.* For his later response to the new journalism, see below, chap. 26.

196 "From now until"   TR, *Letters,* vol. 3, 401. The next Congress was not due until Dec. 1903. Gould, *Presidency of Theodore Roosevelt,* 26–27, points out that by statute, the second and fourth congressional sessions of any presidential four-year term had to end on 4 March. Therefore, only the first and third sessions (when Congress could sit as long as it liked) were convenient to the production of major legislation. Even the third tended to be a cautious session, in view of the upcoming presidential election. Thus, a decision to postpone tariff or reciprocity action in 1902 meant that Congress was not likely to address them again before 1905.

196 The American economy   Thorelli, *Federal Antitrust Policy,* 238–39. Sixty-three new trusts had been capitalized at more than seven figures in 1902.

196 He wanted three   Claude Barfield, Jr., "Theodore Roosevelt and Congressional Leadership: Trust Legislation in 1903," *Organization of American Historians Convention,* 1965 (Kansas City, Mo., 1965).

196 These requests   Philander C. Knox to TR, 30 Mar. 1903 (PCK); 57 Cong., 2 sess., 1903, S. doc 73, serial 4422, 15–21; specifically, Littlefield's bill gave the ICC, a semi-independent agency, subpoena powers to examine and publish the records of major companies.

196 some Rooseveltian ideas   Thorelli, *Federal Antitrust Policy,* 239–41; Merrill, *Republican Command,* 142; Powers, *Portraits of Half a Century,* 174. TR was privately advised by Knox that the Littlefield bill would be unacceptable to big business and destructive of executive authority. (Philander Knox to TR, 5 Jan. 1903 [PCK]; Arthur M. Johnson, "Theodore Roosevelt and the Bureau of Corporations," *Mississippi Valley Historical Review,* Mar. 1959). On the evening of 5 Jan., TR called in John J. Jenkins, chairman of the House Judiciary Committee, and practically dictated a bill comprising all his antitrust views. TR also took care to publish a summary of his own program in the newspapers. Whatever legislation was finally adopted would therefore seem to have been inspired by him. Jenkins to Philander Knox, 6 Jan. 1903 (PCK); *The Washington Post,* 7 Jan. 1903.

196 Corporations would not   Johnson, "Theodore Roosevelt and the Bureau of Corporations"; David B. Sickels to TR, 19 Jan. 1903 (TRP). Beer was the father of

Thomas Beer, whose impressionistic biography of Mark Hanna is cited frequently in these notes.

196 **"He was jovial"** William C. Beer to George W. Perkins, 15 Jan. 1903 (GWP).

196 JUSSERAND AND VON Except where otherwise indicated, documentary details in the following paragraphs come from the "Official Report on 1903 Diplomatic Reception," supplemented with miscellaneous news clips (TAB).

197 **"cosmic cynicism."** Adams, *Letters,* vol. 5, 319, 350.

197 **One by one** Wister, *Roosevelt,* 110.

197 **Roosevelt's strategy** John Hay to TR, 21 Jan. 1903 (TRP).

197 **The canal treaty** Herrán had been expecting an ultimatum from TR for at least a month. On 10 Jan., the Colombian Foreign Ministry granted him what he took to be carte blanche to sign the treaty. DuVal, *Cadiz to Cathay,* 196, 200; *Story of Panama,* 270–71; Miner, *Fight for the Panama Route,* 194.

197 **Downstairs, 1,800** Alice Roosevelt diary, 8 Jan. 1903 (ARL); William E. Curtis to George Cortelyou, 10 Jan. 1903 (GBC); "Official Report" (TAB).

197 **Roosevelt (attended)** Seale, *President's House,* vol. 2, 699; William E. Curtis to George Cortelyou, 10 Jan. 1903 (GBC); "Official Report" (TAB).

198 **The President, oblivious** See Wister, *Roosevelt,* 113–14, for an account of this supper, and TR's chortling recitation of "Alone in Cubia" in front of Finley Peter Dunne.

> *Chronological Note:* The Roosevelts entertained three thousand guests in the first week of the new year alone. Between the reopening of the White House in November 1902 and the beginning of Lent in 1903, their record-breaking guest numbers were as follows:

Houseguests	200
Breakfasts	50
Lunches	275
Teas	6,000
Musicales	1,800
Receptions	5,000
State dinners	270
Private dinners	720
Suppers	1,500
Total	15,815

> TR was by now spending his entire salary on entertaining. He paid the wages of twenty-three servants, the fees of musical performers, and the costs of the White House equipage. Every state dinner, down to the champagne and cigars, cost him eight hundred dollars (about sixteen thousand dollars in modern currency). When Colonel Theodore A. Bingham, Superintendent of Public Buildings and compiler of the above-cited "Official Report," criticized the Roosevelts' lavish lifestyle, he was dismissed. Washington *Evening Star,* 11 Jan. 1903; *Boston Herald,* 12 Feb. 1903; New York *Sun,* 15 Feb. 1903; New York *World,* 17 Feb. 1903; Morris, *Edith Kermit Roosevelt,* 363–65.

198 AT BREAKFAST THE next The following conversation is taken from Wister, *Roosevelt,* 116–17.

198 **William D. Crum** George Cortelyou memorandum, 31 Jan. 1903 (TRP). It is impossible to read TR's voluminous correspondence with black leaders in 1902 and early 1903 and believe that he did not realize the consequences of his Crum appointment, long before Wister challenged him. For the complex state of South Carolinian politics at this time, involving both the White House and the United States Senate, see Gatewood, "Theodore Roosevelt and Southern Republicans."

198 **Thirteen Negro** *The Washington Post,* 29 Mar. 1902. George Cortelyou memo-

randum, 31 Jan. 1903 (TRP); *Booker T. Washington Papers,* vol. 7, 28. With the exception of Crum, all TR's current black appointees were to offices already held by blacks. Most of them, indeed, were reappointments. *The Washington Post,* 26 Apr. 1903.

198 **Moreover, most had** *Booker T. Washington Papers,* vol. 2, 328.

198 **Roosevelt's argument** Gatewood, *Theodore Roosevelt and the Art of Controversy,* 91–100; TR, *Letters,* vol. 3, 383.

199 **Not until 11** Wister, *Roosevelt,* 118.

199 **WISTER FLATTERED** Ibid., 119. Wister's book, like countless others of its kind, regretfully lists the occasions when the President of the United States profited from his counsel.

199 **Mrs. Minnie Cox** For a congressional record of this affair, see "Resignation of the Postmaster," 57 Cong., sess. 2, 1903, vol. 9, H. Doc. 42.

199 **"she would get"** *Congressional Record,* 57 Cong., sess. 2, 1903, vol. 36, 853; "Resignation of the Postmaster," 33. Anselm J. McLaurin of Mississippi is not to be confused with his outgoing senatorial colleague, John L. McLaurin of South Carolina.

199 **Roosevelt's reaction** White House press releases, "1.34" (TRP).

199 **In deference** "Resignation of the Postmaster," 18, 23, 9, 12; Gatewood, *Theodore Roosevelt and the Art of Controversy,* 64. The Indianola post office eventually reopened with a white postmaster, but was downgraded to fourth-class status. Cox, meanwhile, bought a local savings bank and prospered mightily. Ibid., 88–89.

199 **ON 12 JANUARY** New York *Sun,* 13 Jan. 1903; *Booker T. Washington Papers,* vol. 1, 442. The black ADA-designate was William H. Lewis, a Harvard graduate and All-American football player.

200 **The New York Times** *The New York Times,* 29 Jan. 1903; New York *Herald,* 12 Jan. 1903; J. Henry Essen to TR, ca. 27 Jan. 1903 (TRP); Gatewood, *Theodore Roosevelt and the Art of Controversy,* 85.

200 **"a 14-karat"** Nashville *Daily News,* 15 Jan. 1903.

200 **By now, Roosevelt** A Southern Republican commented, in words that were read into the record: "Mr. McKinley so mellowed up the Southern people that they were ready to go into the Republican party by the thousands. Mr. Roosevelt is bitterly hated today by almost all Southern white men. . . . His position on the Negro question has solidified the Democrats as no other conceivable policy could have done. He has aroused the bitterest of race feeling, and it is a question of time when murders will result therefrom." *Congressional Record,* 57 Cong., 2 sess., 1903, vol. 36, pt. 2, 1188.

200 **He pointed out** TR, *Letters,* vol. 3, 431; *Booker T. Washington Papers,* vol. 7, 28.

200 **"Why the appointment"** TR, *Letters,* vol. 3, 431.

200 **Black leaders** Booker T. Washington to TR, 24 Jan. 1903, and unidentified news clip, 15 Jan. 1903, Presidential scrapbook (TRP).

    Historical Note: "No President has had the gratitude and loyal support of a race to the extent that you have it now," Booker T. Washington wrote, when TR's determination became known (*Booker T. Washington Papers,* vol. 7, 11). In Rome, Pope Leo XIII (unaware, no doubt, that he had once laid a benedictive hand on the head of eleven-year-old Teedie Roosevelt) praised the President's determination "to seek equality of treatment of all the races." Robinson, *My Brother,* 47; New York *World,* 15 Feb. 1903.

    A simultaneous pair of resolutions, by black and white groups, emphasized the paradox of the President's political situation. In Washington, the National Afro-American Council praised his commitment to "human rights," and found him "an inspiration to a people struggling heroically beneath the burden of hate" (Associated Press release, 27 Jan. 1903, Presidential scrapbook [TRP]). But in Alabama, white Republicans announced that Roosevelt had "failed absolutely" to carry out the policies of William McKinley. They demanded an extraordinary state convention "solely for the purpose of retracting the resolution endorsing him for President in 1904." The party chairman said that 95 percent of the delegates would support a presidential bid by "the greatest American statesman," Senator Mark Hanna (*The New York Times* and New York *Herald*, 27 Jan. 1903). This was an ominous development. Alabama, as Roosevelt well knew, was the first state on the national roll call. If it cast its vote for Hanna, Arkansas would be tempted to follow. But he could not, in conscience, back down. Resentfully, he told some Southern visitors that he did not understand why "so much fuss" should attend his few black appointments. Presidents Harrison, Cleveland, and McKinley had all made more than he—so far (*The New York Times*, 27 Jan. 1903; *Baltimore Sun*, 8 Feb. 1903). TR wrote privately to Booker T. Washington on 9 Feb. 1903, asking that all future black endorsements be kept "very mild," to avoid hindering him politically. *Booker T. Washington Papers*, vol. 7, 62.

200 ROOSEVELT WORKED TR, *Letters*, vol. 3, 406, 408, 412; Adams, *Letters*, vol. 5, 327; James R. Garfield diary, 17 Jan. 1903 (JRG).

201 *"Il est plus"* "He is more English than an Englishman, and more American than an American." Qu. in Pierre de Margérie to Théophile Delcassé, 12 Jan. 1903, *Documents diplomatiques*, series 2, vol. 3, 26.

201 "I see you" Gwynn, *Letters and Friendships*, vol. 1, 359; Pierre de Margérie to Théophile Delcassé, 18 Jan. 1903, *Documents diplomatiques*, series 2, vol. 3, 43–45, tr. Sharon Harris. The Kaiser confirmed, via the American diplomat Lloyd Griscom in March 1908, that he had "tried to send you a man you would like." Draft, 18 Mar. 1908, in LG.

201 This confidence Dennis, *Adventures in American Diplomacy*, 294. Italy, as a lesser creditor, was also a party to the talks.

201 "Mr. Bowen is" Pierre de Margérie to Théophile Delcassé, 18 Jan. 1903, *Documents diplomatiques*, series 2, vol. 3, 43–45.

201 "The debts will" Ibid. For British Prime Minister Arthur Balfour's early approval of the Corollary, see Tilchin, *Theodore Roosevelt*, 35.

201 "That is precisely" Tilchin, *Theodore Roosevelt*, 35. When TR voiced such patronizing sentiments publicly, as he sometimes did in reference to the Monroe Doctrine, he deeply offended Latin Americans. "If we live in disorder," Colombia's *El Porvenir* remarked, "we live in our own house, and nobody has a right to meddle with it." Qu. in Miner, *Fight for the Panama Route*, 265.

201 ON 22 JANUARY *The Washington Post*, 23 Jan. 1903.

202 Under the Spooner *Story of Panama*, 271; DuVal, *Cadiz to Cathay*, 196. Cullom was for appropriating Panama outright, on grounds of "universal public utility."

202 "I am commanded" *Story of Panama*, 322.

202 "everything might be lost" DuVal, *Cadiz to Cathay*, 203.

202 Late in the *Story of Panama*, 272.

203 Four or five New York *Sun*, 24 Jan. 1903.

203 "Pears lak us" *Georgia Social Sentry*, 13 Feb. 1903, Presidential scrapbook (TRP).

203 White reactionaries "This is about the limit," the *Richmond News* raged. *Literary Digest*, 14 Feb. 1903; Vardaman editorial in Greenwood, Miss., *Commonwealth*, 10 Jan. 1903, copy in TRP; Gatewood, *Theodore Roosevelt and the Art of Controversy*, 37.

203 This was not Senator Tillman duly appeared at the hearings, and patronized Crum so effectively ("If he were a white man he'd be all right") that a majority of the Committee voted to disapprove the nomination. Roosevelt refused to withdraw it. *The New York Times*, 23 Jan. 1903.

203 **He was lucky** Gatewood, *Theodore Roosevelt and the Art of Controversy*, 80; *The New York Times*, 25 Jan. 1903; *Congressional Record*, 57 Cong., sess. 2, 1903, vol. 36, pt. 1, 1180–81.

203 **"It is as idle"** *Congressional Record*, 57 Cong., sess. 2, 1903, vol. 36, pt. 2, 1178. The complete text of Spooner's remarks is printed in ibid., 1174–90. Even the violent Tillman praised him afterward for his "calm and dispassionate and very earnest and eloquent speech." Ibid., 2571. N.b.: Spooner used the word *duress* in the sense of *coercion* or *compulsion*.

204 **He cabled home** DuVal, *Cadiz to Cathay*, 206. Later in the year, the Colombian Minister of Foreign Affairs reportedly confirmed that Herrán's signature on the treaty was as good as his own. William Nelson Cromwell to Tomas Herrán, 5 July 1903 (TH).

204 **"Gladly shall I"** DuVal, *Cadiz to Cathay*, 206–7.

204 **IN THE LAST DAYS** *The New York Times*, 25 Jan. 1903.
Chronological Note: On 18 Jan., Germany's half-forgotten gunboats suddenly bombarded Fort San Carlos, Venezuela. Twenty-five people were killed. There was no apparent provocation, although the Reich claimed Venezuela fired first. John Hay memorandum, 21 Jan. 1903 (JH). Livermore, "Theodore Roosevelt"; Jeffrey M. Dorwart, *The Office of Naval Intelligence: The Birth of America's First Intelligence Agency, 1865–1918* (Annapolis, 1979), 76.
From Caracas came news that the allied blockade, while starving Venezuelans of bread and salt, was permitting the importation of arms by antigovernment guerrillas; it appeared that the Kaiser was deliberately fomenting unrest as an excuse to land German marines. Dennis, *Adventures in American Diplomacy*, 294.

204 **had secretly directed** *The New York Times*, 25 Jan. 1903; Parsons, "German-American Crisis." An even more secret memorandum, from the head of the Office of Naval Intelligence, noted that Germany might well be protracting the Venezuela crisis deliberately. With Dewey's ships tied down in the Caribbean, "no other objective point in the United States is now so inviting for attack as the city of Washington." Kennedy, *War Plans*, 55–56.

204 **The arbitration** Jules Jusserand to Théophile Delcassé, 7 Feb. 1903 (JJ); J. Fred Rippy, *The Caribbean Danger Zone* (New York, 1940), 189; Dennis, *Adventures in American Diplomacy*, 294.

204 **That sounded** There were additional rumors in early 1903 that the Kaiser wanted to establish a permanent Caribbean naval squadron, and bid for Panama Canal rights, should Colombia fail to ratify the Hay-Herrán Treaty.

204 **"Are people in"** Vagts, *Deutschland*, vol. 2, 1595. Public concern was also rising again in Britain. George Smalley in *The Times* (London), 24 Jan. 1903; Gelber, *Rise of Anglo-American Friendship*, 120–21. Perhaps significantly, TR's luncheon guests on 29 Jan. included the Admiral of the Navy, the Chief of the Bureau of Navigation, the Secretary of the Navy, and the Secretary of War. White House diary (TRP).

204 **He did not** Beale, *Theodore Roosevelt*, 425. "The friend of peace cannot do anything but pray for you, Mr. President. . . . Cablegrams which I have received yesterday and today convince me that the excitement in Germany has gone to an absolutely unreasonable degree" (Hugo Münsterberg to TR, 24 Jan. 1903 [TRP]). Münsterberg, a professor at Harvard, was a member of TR's *secret du roi*. He had useful private contacts on the Wilhelmstrasse.

204 **BARON VON STERNBURG** Blake, "Ambassadors at the Court." Technically, von Sternburg was not yet credentialed to the United States. He was obliged to play the face-saving fiction that he was deputizing for the "sick" von Holleben. His

proper accreditation did not arrive until the spring. Beale, *Theodore Roosevelt*, 429–30.

204 **After his first** Gooch and Temperley, *British Documents*, vol. 2, 168; Gelber, *Rise of Anglo-American Friendship*, 123; Herwig, *Politics of Frustration*, 81.

205 **Von Sternburg sent** Parsons, "German-American Crisis," 445. See also John Hay to Sir Michael Herbert, draft, 5 Feb. 1903 (JH). This was a much milder version of an earlier Hay-Roosevelt draft expressing "profound regret" at the slowness of the negotiations, and warning that "a state of unrest and anxiety exists throughout the Western Hemisphere, which if suffered to increase might bring about results which would universally be deplored" (JH).

Historical Note: On 5 Feb. 1903, TR requested a comparative analysis of United States and German naval strength in the North and South Atlantic "and the seas contiguous thereto." The answer, supplied by the Office of Naval Intelligence on 11 Feb., showed that his current temporary advantage in the Caribbean would not last long in a full war. In table form, the all-out opposition would be as follows:

	United States	Germany
Ships		
Battleships, 1st class	7	10
Battleships, 2d class	1	2
Monitors/gunboats	4	13
Guns		
Very big	32	0
Big	0	50
Smaller	110	144

From this it will be seen that TR's Big Stick was more psychological than actual. Its efficacy derived from the speed and power with which he threatened to use it.

205 **Whether it was** Dana G. Munro quotes TR as complaining about Germany's "impossible stand" as late as 9 Feb. *Intervention and Dollar Diplomacy in the Caribbean, 1900–1921* (Princeton, N.J., 1964), 73. But J. Fred Rippy shows that acquiescence began around 4 Feb.—i.e., the day after von Sternburg's urgent telegram. *Caribbean Danger Zone*, 191.

Historical Note: This brief resurgence of the Venezuela crisis provoked a purge of former von Holleben aides at the German Embassy. Albert von Quadt was recalled in mid-Feb., the chargé Baron von Ritter given just "forty-eight hours" to follow him a week later, and two other staffers reassigned. Jules Jusserand reported that they were all clearly being punished for the Kaiser's loss of "face." To Théophile Delcassé, 20 Mar. 1903 (JJ).

205 **"I am not for"** Jusserand to Théophile Delcassé, 7 and 11 Feb. 1903 (JJ).

205 **Relaxing in the** TR to James Connolly, 29 Sept. 1902 (TRP); TR, *Letters to Kermit from Theodore Roosevelt, 1902–1908* (New York, 1946), 27; Cassini, *Never a Dull Moment*, 180; Alice Roosevelt Longworth interview, 22 June 1975.

205 **The Ambassador's own** Jusserand, *What Me Befell*, 217; Jusserand to Théophile Delcassé, 11 Feb. 1903 (JJ).

205 **Beaming like a** TR to Pierre W. Coubertin, 6 Oct. 1902 (TRP); TR, *Letters to Kermit*, 27; Jules Jusserand to Théophile Delcassé, 11 Feb. 1903 (JJ). Lloyd Griscom recorded another description of TR's flooding conversational energy at this time. "He started to volley questions at me about Persia [over breakfast], but before I could answer, he launched into a monologue of the Great Empire from the rise of Genghiz Khan. He paused long enough for me to begin an account of ibex shooting, but interrupted to send for the rifle with which he had hunted in the

West; he wanted to show us the marks of a cougar's fangs on its butt. Then suddenly he switched to Japan. . . ." Griscom, *Diplomatically Speaking,* 221–22.

205 **Already, almost** Thorelli, *Federal Antitrust Policy,* 531; Strouse, *Morgan,* 452–53. The Expedition Act (which TR signed into law on 11 Feb. 1903) effectively fathered the Justice Department's modern, all-powerful Antitrust Division.

206 **Congressman Charles** TR to Gilson Gardner, unidentified news clip, 7 Feb. 1903, Presidential scrapbook (TRP); Thorelli, *Federal Antitrust Policy,* 548.

Chronological Note: When Representative Littlefield's antitrust bill first ran into trouble in the House in mid-January, Roosevelt had called a leadership conference to advance his own program (*Review of Reviews,* Feb. 1903; Johnson, "Theodore Roosevelt and the Bureau of Corporations"). He thereupon sought out the operational center between "fools" like Speaker Henderson, who opposed all business regulation, and "equally obnoxious fools" like Littlefield, who fought too hard for too much (TR, *Letters,* vol. 3, 406), and coaxed both houses and both parties into acquiescence. Henderson was promised help from George Perkins in setting up a New York law practice when he retired at the end of the session. Perkins was promised an advisory role in setting up the new Bureau of Corporations. The House Judiciary and Rules Committees at once became more hospitable to White House proposals. William C. Beer to George W. Perkins, 11 Jan. 1903 (GWP); *Review of Reviews,* Feb. 1903.

206 **Just behind came** TR, *Letters,* vol. 3, 410, and vol. 5, 334–35; Merrill, *Republican Command,* 141–42. The bill's extended title was added in order to win the support of congressmen from labor-intensive districts.

206 **Thus, Roosevelt** George Cortelyou to Philander Knox, 2 Jan. 1903 (PCK), makes plain TR's mistrust of the ICC as an agency too independent for his liking. Conservatives in Congress had the same feelings about TR.

206 **In view of** James Garfield diary, 5 Feb. 1903 (JRG); Pringle, *Theodore Roosevelt,* 341. See also *Campaign Contributions: Testimony Before a Subcommittee of the [Senate] Committee of Privileges and Elections.* 62 Cong., 2 sess., 1913, vol. 1, 18 (hereafter *Campaign Contributions*).

206 **J. D. ROCKEFELLER** *Chicago Tribune,* New York *Herald,* and *The New York Times,* 8 Feb. 1903.

206 **Both impressions** Rockefeller had just given seven million dollars for tuberculosis research. *Review of Reviews,* Mar. 1903.

207 **By publicizing these** TR, *Autobiography,* 445; L. White Busbey, *Uncle Joe Cannon: The Story of a Pioneer American* (New York, 1927), 222. Other news stories implicated three more lawmakers. Senators Aldrich, Allison, Hale, Hanna, Lodge, Teller, Quay, Platt (N.Y.), and Platt (Conn.) all denied having received Standard Oil telegrams, whereupon the New York *American* (12 Feb. 1903) published a facsimile of one addressed to Quay. Signed by John D. Archbold, the company's vice president, it protested "vexatious attacks" against big business.

Chronological Note: TR's not-to-be-attributed release of this story to the Associated Press on Saturday evening, 7 Feb., demonstrated his instinct for weekend news. Readers of Sunday-morning spreads had plenty of time to mark, learn, and inwardly digest, before firing off letters to their congressmen. Sunday-afternoon announcements were pretty sure to end up as front-page stories, because Monday morning was usually newsless.

At the time, it was assumed that TR acted on 7 Feb. after being shown one of the Rockefeller telegrams by Henry Cabot Lodge. Actually, he had been aware of Standard Oil's lobbying effort for at least three days (James Garfield diary, 5 Feb. 1903 [JRG]). He delayed his dramatic move until the day the Littlefield Bill passed the House, thus "burying" it beneath his own Sunday headlines.

207 **Subsequent articles** New York *American*, 12 Feb. 1903; Johnson, "Theodore Roosevelt and the Bureau of Corporations."

207 **The old tycoon** New York *World*, 12 Feb. 1903. Early on 10 Feb. Rep. Charles Littlefield had begged TR for help with his own bill, as promised. He received a cold message saying that the President now found it "unconstitutional and entirely too drastic." Enraged, Littlefield became the only House Republican to vote against the Commerce and Labor Bill. A mere nine Democrats joined him. Thorelli, *Federal Antitrust Policy,* 548.

207 **ON 8 FEBRUARY** *Princeton Alumni Weekly,* 14 Feb. 1903.

207 **"JUST AT PRESENT,"** TR, *Letters,* vol. 3, 423.

207 **Elihu Root's long** The Army Bill became law on 14 Feb. 1903. Internal bureaucratic conflicts kept the General Staff Corps from becoming fully effective in 1910. A quarter of a century later, Newton D. Baker described it as "the outstanding contribution made by any Secretary of War since the beginning of [U.S.] history." Leopold, *Elihu Root,* 43. See also Jessup, *Elihu Root,* vol. 1, 260ff.

207 **By agreement with** Beale, *Theodore Roosevelt,* 113.

Historical Note: With a fine disregard for the adjective *impartial,* TR chose three aggressive expansionists to be his representatives at the Alaskan Boundary Tribunal in London: Secretary of War Elihu Root and Senators Henry Cabot Lodge (R., Mass.) and George Turner (D., Wash.). The appointments were seen as deliberately provocative. Root had sent United States troops north in 1902 to secure the very frontier he would now be adjudicating. Lodge's personal shoulder-chip, in matters to do with Great Britain and its empire, amounted to a battering ram: "I do not like to be crowded, and I especially dislike being pushed by our British brother." Turner came from a community that had always regretted President Polk's failure to extend the Northwestern Territory as far as "Fifty-four Forty."

The Anglo-Canadian claim, in TR's opinion, was "an outrage pure and simple." His own big globe of the world (beside which he posed, in a photograph intended for immediate release) had been "made in London by mapmakers for the Admiralty," and showed the Alaskan boundary to be precisely where the United States said it was. Since 1825, Great Britain had understood by treaty that the line ran inland from the forty-first parallel to the Portland Channel, at a distance averaging thirty miles from the coast. This seaward strip encompassed all major inlets; when Russia sold Alaska to the United States in 1867, Canada had raised no topographical objections. Only when gold was discovered in the Klondike in 1896 had she begun to regret the ceded inlets. Canada was now suggesting— demanding—that the Alaskan boundary should be measured not from the coast, but from the extremities of islands lying far out to sea. If so, Juneau, Skagway, Dyea, the much-prized Lynn Canal, and all of Glacier Bay would be Canadian.

Roosevelt was willing to grant Canada a limited amount of inlet water, according to charts drawn up by John Hay. Strategist that he was, he suspected that the Dominion's British rulers knew their case was hopeless, and merely wanted a judicial confirmation, to quell angry local feelings. He therefore made clear to his representatives that they were not to negotiate "untenable" territorial claims, only to decide whether a boundary sanctioned by sixty years of understanding among Russia, Great Britain, and the United States was "right in its entirety or wrong in its entirety." This caused great resentment at the Alaska Boundary Tribunal. Shortly after negotiations began on 15 Sept. 1903, Oliver Wendell Holmes, Jr., visited London and sent TR private word that the British Government took an "exceedingly grave" view of his inflexible attitude. Six months later, Joseph Chamberlain was still fuming. "Our cordial neutrality and sympathy in the Spanish War followed—by what? By all that happened in regard to the Alaska Arbitration, the secret history of which is not altogether pleasant reading."

See Tyler Dennett, *John Hay: From Poetry to Politics* (New York, 1933), 357–59; Henry Cabot Lodge to Elihu Root, 27 June 1903 (ER); John Hay to Joseph H. Choate, ca. 20 Feb. 1903 (JH); TR, *Letters*, vol. 3, 287; *New York Tribune* supplement, 29 Mar. 1903, p. 1; map in *Review of Reviews*, Mar. 1903; Hill, *Roosevelt and the Caribbean*, 145; TR to Elihu Root et al., 25 Mar. 1903 (ER); Holmes to TR, 11 Oct. 1903 (TRP); Chamberlain to Poultney Bigelow, 30 Apr. 1904 (PB). For more extensive discussion, see John A. Munro, ed., *The Alaska Boundary Dispute* (Toronto, 1970); Marks, *Velvet on Iron*, 105–11; and Tilchin, *Theodore Roosevelt*, 36–48.

207 **Favorable action** Miner, *Fight for the Panama Route*, 197–98. Senatorial patience with the seventy-eight-year-old Morgan was wearing thin. "Impersonating the treaty," Mark Hanna wrote John Hay, ca. Feb. 1903, "am I not justified in killing him?" (JH).

207 **Roosevelt did not** TR, *Letters*, vol. 3, 427–28.

207 **On Saturday** *Review of Reviews*, Mar. 1903; Wiebe, *Businessmen and Reform*, 46. By midsummer, the Department of Commerce and Labor had a Washington staff of more than 1,300 and a budget of ten million dollars. George Cortelyou speech memorandum, ca. 12 Aug. 1903 (TRP).

Chronological Note: On this weekend, TR's houseguest, John Singer Sargent, was painting an oil portrait of the President pausing halfway down the White House stairway with his hand on a newel. The noticeable sadness in TR's eyes may reflect the fact that his wife, even as he posed, was suffering her second miscarriage in two years. TR, *Letters*, vol. 3, 428; Morris, *Edith Kermit Roosevelt*, 265.

207 **As a final** The agreement protocol was signed in Washington on 13 Feb. 1903. For a brief account of the negotiations, see Gelber, *Rise of Anglo-American Friendship*, 113–25.

208 THE NEXT MORNING'S *Los Angeles Times*, 14 Feb. 1903; *New York Press*, 15 Feb. 1903.

208 **"It always pays"** TR qu. in Wood, *Roosevelt As We Knew Him*, 44; TR, *Letters*, vol. 3, 450–51. See Marks, *Velvet on Iron*, 13–15, for a discussion of TR's "gentlemanly" scruples in foreign policy.

208 **It was a** Johnson, "Theodore Roosevelt and the Bureau of Corporations"; superscript on George Cortelyou memo for the President, 14 Feb. 1903 (GBC).

208 **"Say what has"** TR memo, 15 Feb. 1903, and press-release draft for New York *Herald*, 16 Feb. 1903 (PCK).

208 **The result was** *Literary Digest*, 21 Feb. 1903.

208 **Nevertheless, Roosevelt** Thorelli, *Federal Antitrust Policy*, 555–60; clip ca. Feb. 1903 in John Hay scrapbook (JH).

208 **Whether this** Nearly a century later, it has so redounded. "The year 1903 is one of the most important in the annals of antitrust. In that year, the nation became conscious for the first time of a President's taking a personal interest in the application of the law. . . . [His actions] unmistakably demonstrate the practicability and potentialities of large-scale and purposeful enforcement effort" (Thorelli, *Fed-*

eral Antitrust Policy, 560). 1903 would see only eighteen new trusts formed, as opposed to sixty-three in 1902, and forty-six in 1901.

209 GEORGE BRUCE CORTELYOU Washington *Capitol,* 21 Apr. 1900, biography file (GBC); *National Cyclopaedia of American Biography,* vol. 14; Lowry, *Washington Close-Ups,* 104, 127–28; *Review of Reviews,* Mar. 1903; George Cortelyou to R. A. Maxwell, 16 Feb. 1903 (GBC). For a later assessment, see Benjamin Temple Ford, "A Duty to Serve: The Governmental Career of George Bruce Cortelyou" (Ph.D. diss., Columbia University, 1963).

209 the elite company See, e.g., James Garfield diary, 13 Feb. 1903 (JRG).

209 **Cortelyou, despite** To TR, Garfield was "Jim," while Cortelyou was always "Mr. Cortelyou."

209 ON 18 FEBRUARY TR, *Letters to Kermit,* 30. This ride is misdated as 13 Feb. in Beale, *Theodore Roosevelt,* 426. *"Wie gut ist es doch"* the Kaiser commented, "that His Majesty's German representative goes riding *mit dem Präsidenten!" Die Grosse Politik,* vol. 17, 292.

210 **Now that Germany's** Rippy, *Caribbean Danger Zone,* 198; Hill, *Roosevelt and the Caribbean,* 145.

210 **The President's words** Marks, *Velvet on Iron,* 52–54.

210 **When Admiral Dewey** Dewey qu. in New York *Herald,* 27 Mar. 1903; Mrs. Dewey diary, 31 Mar. 1903 (GD); Frederick Palmer, *With My Own Eyes* (Indianapolis, 1932), 128–29; Bishop, *Theodore Roosevelt,* vol. 1, 239; Spector, *Admiral of the New Empire,* 145–46. According to Mrs. Dewey, TR received the Admiral privately, took his hand in both of his, and said, "My best beloved" (a habitual endearment) then, sotto voce, "Damn the Dutch!" According to Palmer, TR tapped Dewey on the wrist and said, grinning, "Admiral, consider yourself reprimanded."

210 THE FIFTY-SEVENTH Walter Wellman in Chicago *Record-Herald,* 28 Feb.–3 Mar. 1903; Stephenson, *Nelson W. Aldrich,* 210–11; Simkins, *Pitchfork Ben Tillman,* 364–65.

210 **Roosevelt's "tyrannical"** Senoia, Georgia, *Enterprise-Gazette,* 26 Feb. 1903, Presidential scrapbook (TRP); Fleming, *Around the Capitol,* 49; Sullivan, *Our Times,* vol. 3, 231–32. Dr. Crum assumed his appointment on 30 Mar. 1903.

211 *"To the Secretary"* TR to Elihu Root, 21 Feb. 1903 (ER).

211 **Treaties were** TR, *Letters,* vol. 3, 433; Walter Wellman in Chicago *Record-Herald,* 3 Mar. 1903; proclamation, 2 Mar. 1903, Presidential scrapbook (TRP).

211 **He had hardly** Chicago *Record-Herald,* 3–4 Mar. 1903; *Literary Digest,* 7 Mar. 1903.

211 **A House-Senate** The phrase *ugly with anger* is Walter Wellman's in the Chicago *Record-Herald,* 4 Mar. 1903. See also Washington *Evening Star,* same date.

211 **At 2:00 A.M.** The adjective *dilatory* is Quay's own. *Congressional Record,* 57 Cong., sess. 2, 1903, vol. 36, pt. 3, 3005–6; *The Washington Post,* 4 Mar. 1903.

211 **Outside, the moon** Washington *Evening Star,* 4 Mar. 1903; Bolles, *Tyrant from Illinois,* 8–9; *Congressional Record,* 57 Cong., sess. 2, 1903, vol. 36, pt. 3, 3058.

212 **Joseph Gurney Cannon** Thompson, *Party Leaders,* 181; *Public Opinion,* 13 Feb. 1903.

212 **Yet in this** Cannon began to speak at 3:30 A.M. He had been confirmed as Henderson's successor in January. Washington *Evening Star,* 4 and 5 Mar. 1903; Merrill, *Republican Command,* 137.

212 **Long years of** Bolles, *Tyrant from Illinois,* 8–9; Stephenson, *Nelson W. Aldrich,* 213–14.

212 **"I am in earnest"** *Congressional Record,* 57 Cong., sess. 2, 1903, vol. 36, pt. 3, 3058.

212 **When Cannon** Busbey, *Uncle Joe Cannon,* xvi; James E. Watson, *As I Knew*

Them: Memoirs (Indianapolis, 1936), 92, 99–100; Thompson, *Party Leaders,* 177–79.

212 **"I am getting"** *Congressional Record,* 57 Cong., sess. 2, 1903, vol. 36, pt. 3, 3058.

212 **Applause roared** Washington *Evening Star,* 3–4 Mar. 1903; *Congressional Record,* 57 Cong., sess. 2, 1903, vol. 36, pt. 3, 3008.

213 THEODORE ROOSEVELT'S Washington *Evening Star,* 4 Mar. 1903. The author is grateful to Brad Smith for enabling him to sit in the President's Room and revisit this moment.

213 **The naval-construction** TR, *Letters,* vol. 3, 438; *Booker T. Washington Papers,* vol. 7, 106; Gatewood, *Theodore Roosevelt and the Art of Controversy,* 112, 115. TR kept Crum in office as a recess appointee until the Senate finally confirmed him in Jan. 1905.

213 **As the hands** *Congressional Record,* 57 Cong., sess. 2, 1903, vol. 36, pt. 3, 3070; New York *Sun,* 5 Mar. 1903.

213 **Far away, at** Washington *Evening Star,* 4 Mar. 1903; Thompson, *Party Leaders,* 174–76; photographs in LC. For an analysis of the political forces Cannon harnessed in his leap to power, see Stephenson, *Nelson W. Aldrich,* 213–14.

CHAPTER 15: THE BLACK CRYSTAL

214 **We're a gr-reat** Finley Peter Dunne, *Mr. Dooley in Peace and War* (Boston, 1905), 5.

214 **"Will you take"** Pittsburgh *Gazette,* 2 Apr. 1903.

214 **The fireman stared** Pittsburgh *Gazette* and New York *Sun,* 2 Apr. 1903.
  Note: The principal source for this chapter is TR's own scrapbook, "Comment on West Coast Trip, 1903," 3 vols. (TRP). Because the scrapbook proceeds chronologically, with an abundance of overlapping information, it will be cited as a single source. The author has also relied in particular on the eyewitness daily reports of Lindsay Denison in the New York *Sun,* and TR's own narrative in *Letters,* vol. 3, 547–63. This classic, often very funny document, written at the request of John Hay, has been published separately in Elting E. Morison, ed., *Cowboys and Kings: Three Great Letters by Theodore Roosevelt* (Cambridge, Mass., 1954), 1–23. See p. 241.

214 **Free at last**
  Chronological Note: TR's official itinerary gives an idea of the rigors of presidential touring in the age before air travel and the loudspeaker. ("Whistle-stops" omitted.) APRIL 1: Leave Washington, D.C. 2: Chicago, Evanston, Ill. 3: Madison, Waukesha, Milwaukee, Wisc. 4: La Crosse, Wisc.; Minneapolis and St. Paul, Minn. 5: Sioux Falls, S.D. 6: Yankton, Mitchell, Aberdeen, S.D.; Edgeley, Fargo, N.D. 7: Jamestown, Bismarck, Mandan, Medora, N.D. 8: Livingston, Cinnabar, Mont. (Yellowstone National Park, Wyo., through 24 Apr.) 25: Billings, Mont., Alliance, Nebr. 26: Grand Island, Nebr. 27: Hastings, Lincoln, Fremont, Omaha, Nebr. 28: Shenandoah, Clarinda, Van Wert, Osceola, Des Moines, Ottumwa, Iowa. 29: Keokuk, Iowa; Quincy, Ill.; Hannibal, Clarksville, St. Louis, Mo. 30: St. Louis. MAY 1: Kansas City, Mo.; Kansas City, Lawrence, Topeka, Kans. 2: Manhattan, Junction City, Abilene, Salina, Ellsworth, Russell, Hays, Wakeeny, Sharon Springs, Kans. 3: Sharon Springs. 4: Denver, Colorado Springs, Pueblo, Trinidad, Colo. 5: Santa Fe, Albuquerque, N.M. Terr. 6: Grand Canyon, Ariz. Terr. 7: Barstow, Redlands, San Bernardino, Riverside, Calif. 8: Claremont,

Pasadena, Los Angeles, Calif. 9: Ventura, Santa Barbara, San Luis Obispo, Calif. 10: Monterey, Calif. 11: Pajaro, Santa Cruz, San Jose, Calif. 12: Palo Alto, Burlingame, San Francisco, Calif. 13–14: San Francisco. 15: Raymond, Calif. (Yosemite National Park through 18 May). 19: Carson City, Reno, Nev.; Sacramento, Calif. 20: Redding, Sisson, Calif.; Ashland, Ore. 21: Salem, Portland, Ore. 22: Chehalis, Centralia, Olympia, Tacoma, Wash. 23: Bremerton, Everett, Seattle, Wash. (by boat). 24: Seattle. 25: Ellensburg, North Yakima, Pasco, Wallula, Walla Walla, Wash. 26: Wallace, Harrison, Idaho; Tekoa, Spokane, Wash. 27: Helena, Butte, Mont. 28: Pocatello, Shoshone, Mountain Home, Nampa, Boise, Idaho. 29: Salt Lake City, Ogden, Utah; Evanston, Wyo. 30: Laramie, Cheyenne, Wyo. (on horseback). 31: Cheyenne. *JUNE* 1: North Platte, Nebr. 2: Denison, Fort Dodge, Cedar Falls, Waterloo, Dubuque, Iowa. 3: Freeport, Rockford, Rochelle, Aurora, Joliet, Dwight, Pontiac, Lexington, Bloomington, Ill. 4: Lincoln, Springfield, Decatur, Ill.; Indianapolis, Ind. 5: Return Washington, D.C. "Tour of the President to the Pacific Coast," booklet in GBC.

215 **the emotional drain** EKR was taken seriously ill at a reception on 12 Feb. 1903, and miscarried. Morris, *Edith Kermit Roosevelt*, 265.

215 **and the stress** See above, chap. 14; TR, *Letters*, vol. 3, 422; *Washington Times*, 20 Feb. 1903. Although TR's chronic respiratory problem was more or less cured by his mid-twenties, he did have occasional later attacks, usually associated with extreme fatigue or fibrous inhalation. He admitted to "asthma—occasional attacks—not severe" when applying for life insurance early in his Presidency. McCullough, *Mornings on Horseback;* Morris, *Edith Kermit Roosevelt*, 164; TR to Anna Roosevelt Cowles (TRB); New York Life policy statement, 14 Nov. 1901, New York Life Archives, New York.

215 **At Seward, he** Pittsburgh *Gazette* and New York *Sun*, 2 Apr. 1903.

215 **First, a baggage** *The Washington Post*, 3 Apr. 1903; "Comment" scrapbook. There were no women aboard the Pacific Coast Special.

215 **Last came** Ibid.

215 **AT 8:50** The following account is based on *Chicago Tribune*, 3 May 1903, and "Comment" scrapbook.

215 **"There is a homely"** TR, *Presidential Addresses and State Papers*, vol. 1, 265–66.

216 **Actually, Roosevelt** Marks, *Velvet on Iron*, 58–59. As a recent case in point, TR had instructed Senator George Turner to keep a cool negotiating head at the Alaska Border Tribunal, but to be confident that, in the event of "specious and captious objections on the part of the English, I [will] send a brigade of American regulars up to Skagway and take possession of the disputed territory and hold it by the power and force of the United States." Wood, *Roosevelt As We Knew Him*, 115.

216 **He reiterated his** TR, *Works*, vol. 13, 465, 467–68.

216 **Roosevelt continued** Dawes, *Journal of the McKinley Years*, 343–44.

216 **"His hearty greetings"** Ibid.

216 **The *Chicago Tribune*'s** "Comment" scrapbook.

216 **In Milwaukee's** New York *Sun*, 21 and 25 Apr. 1903; TR, *Presidential Addresses and State Papers*, vol. 1, 272–78.

217 **Further roars** Burroughs, *Camping and Tramping*, 10; Milwaukee *Journal* and Milwaukee *Sentinel*, 4, 3 Apr. 1903; "Comment" scrapbook.

217 **TARIFF POLICY IN** TR, *Presidential Addresses and State Papers*, vol. 1, 294–320; *Leslie's Weekly*, 30 Apr. 1903; New York *Sun*, 8 Apr. 1903; *The Washington Post*, 8 Apr. 1903.

217 **He ate a** TR, *Letters*, vol. 3, 550; Bismarck *Tribune*, 8 Apr. 1903.

217 **For the next** Burroughs, *Camping and Tramping*, 12–13; TR, *Letters*, vol. 3, 551.

217 **When the train** Burroughs, *Camping and Tramping,* 15–16; Morris, *Rise of Theodore Roosevelt,* 201, 337; TR, *Letters,* vol. 3, 551–52.

217 **Joe Ferris was** New York *Sun,* 8 Apr. 1903; TR, *Letters,* vol. 3, 552.

218 **Shortly after noon** For TR's own account of his visit to Yellowstone, see TR, *Works,* vol. 3, chap. 9.

218 **"Oom John"** *Oom* (Dutch diminutive for "old man") was TR's affectionate name for Burroughs. See also TR, *Letters,* vol. 3, 429–30.

218 **They were greeted** Cutright, *Theodore Roosevelt,* 105; Paul Schullery, "A Partnership in Conservation: Theodore Roosevelt and Yellowstone," *Montana* 28.3 (1978); New York *Sun,* 9 Apr. 1903; Burroughs, *Camping and Tramping,* 24–25.

219 **"By the way"** TR, *Letters,* vol. 3, 552–53.

219 **Hell-Roaring Bill** Herman Hagedorn, *Roosevelt in the Bad Lands* (Boston, 1921), 113–17.

219 **"I will try"** TR, *Letters,* vol. 3, 553.

219 A FEW HOURS New York *Sun* and *Baltimore American,* 11 Apr. 1903; Thorelli, *Federal Antitrust Policy,* 561; Martin, *James J. Hill,* 517; Lamoreaux, *Great Merger Movement,* 166–67.

219 **"If this decision"** Boston *Record,* 11 Apr. 1903; Satterlee, *J. Pierpont Morgan,* 401. Northern Securities stock dropped twelve points in three days after the St. Paul decision, reaching a low twenty-five points below its initial high. *The Washington Post,* 19 Apr. 1903.

219 **William Loeb asked** New York *Sun,* 10 Apr. 1903. For a popular reaction to the Circuit Court decision, see Eitler, "Philander Chase Knox," 71–73.

219 **He had also** Healy, *United States in Cuba,* 203–6; Anthracite Coal Commission, *Report to the President,* 80–87; DuVal, *Cadiz to Cathay,* 211–14.

219 **That did not** Medill McCormick to his parents, ca. Feb. 1903 (MHM); Topeka, Kans., *Herald,* 21 Mar. 1903; *The New York Times,* 22 Mar. 1903; Pittsburgh *Press,* 15 Mar. 1903; *Boston Herald,* 16 Mar. 1903.

220 **"Such a bosom"** *Literary Digest,* Apr.–June 1903, 219.

220 ROOSEVELT WAS NO George Bird Grinnell, "Theodore Roosevelt as a Sportsman," *The Country Calendar,* Nov. 1905; Robert Underwood Johnson, *Remembered Yesterdays* (Boston, 1923), 309; Cutright, *Theodore Roosevelt,* 70–73; Jeremy Johnston, "Preserving the Beasts of Waste and Desolation: Theodore Roosevelt and Predator Control in Yellowstone National Park," *George White Forum* 15.4 (1988).

220 **Or near solitude** The following account of TR's sixteen days in Yellowstone is based on Major Pitcher's diary, published in *The Washington Post,* 24 Apr. 1903; TR's own account, "Wilderness Reserves: The Yellowstone Park," *Works,* vol. 3, 266–93; Burroughs, *Camping and Tramping,* 23–75; Fred M. Davenport, "President Roosevelt in the Yellowstone," *Outlook* 142 (1926); Cutright, *Theodore Roosevelt,* 104–11; and "Comment" scrapbook.

220 **Each day, he** TR, *Letters,* vol. 3, 461–64. He made a detailed list of his natural observations to send to C. Hart Merriam of the United States Biological Survey.

220 **On 12 April** Pitcher diary, 12 Apr. 1903; TR, *Works,* vol. 3, 282–84; Burroughs, *Camping and Tramping,* 32–33.

221 **Burroughs, who** Lindsay Denison in New York *Sun,* 24 Apr. 1903; Burroughs, *Camping and Tramping,* 33; TR, *Letters,* vol. 3, 429–30.

221 **"Every man who"** TR, *Works,* vol. 3, 267–68. See also TR, *Presidential Addresses and State Papers,* vol. 1, 324–28.

221 **Roosevelt expressed** Ibid.

221 **Only once did he** TR, *Letters,* vol. 3, 463.

221 BACK IN GARDINER New York *Sun* and New York *World,* 19 Apr. 1903.

221 **Finally, on 24 April** Lindsay Denison in New York *Sun,* 29 Apr. 1903. "It was

rather a sad interview," Roosevelt wrote afterward. "The old fellow had gone to pieces, and soon after I left he got lost in a blizzard and was dead when they found him." TR, *Autobiography*, 117.

221 **Before leaving** TR, *Presidential Addresses and State Papers*, vol. 1, 324. The *Washington Post*, 25 Apr. 1903, remarked that TR's Yellowstone speech showed a new governmental attitude, "after more than thirty years of passive attention to the park."

222 **Then, with a** Except where otherwise cited, the following four paragraphs are based on stereopticon photographs by Underwood & Underwood preserved at SH; Lindsay Denison reports in "Comment" scrapbook; Addison C. Thomas, *Roosevelt Among the People: Being an Account of the 14,000 Mile Journey from Ocean to Ocean of Theodore Roosevelt, 26th President of the United States* (Chicago, 1910), copy in NYPL; and William Allen White's account of a Kansas whistle-stop in *Saturday Evening Post*, 27 June 1903.

222 **On the flatland** Burroughs, *Camping and Tramping*, 12.

222 **At whistle-stops** "Comment" scrapbook.

222 **("If I might")** TR, *Presidential Addresses and State Papers*, vol. 1, 333; TR qu. in Joseph Bucklin Bishop, *Notes and Anecdotes of Many Years* (New York, 1925), 117.

222 **Indistinguishable as** TR, *Letters*, vol. 3, 554.

223 THE "ESSENTIAL DEMOCRACY" TR, *Presidential Addresses and State Papers*, vol. 1, 328; TR, *Works*, vol. 4, 228–29. For TR's formal visit to the site of the 1904 Louisiana Purchase Exhibition in St. Louis, see, e.g., *Collier's Weekly*, 16 May 1903, and Jusserand, *What Me Befell*, 231ff.

223 **("Three cheers for")** TR, *Letters*, vol. 3, 425; Robbins, *Our Landed Heritage*, 333.

224 **In Iowa's fecund** New York *Sun*, 29 Apr. 1903; Des Moines *Register and Leader*, 29 Apr. 1903.

224 **"There were two"** TR, *Letters*, vol. 3, 554–55. In exchange for the badger, TR gave the little girls a silver-and-gold medal he had been presented in Chicago. Lindsay Denison in New York *Sun*, 4 May 1903; Des Moines *Register and Leader*, 8 June 1903.

225 **The baby badger** TR, *Works*, vol. 3, 325–6; as the journey proceeded, Josiah was joined by two bears, a lizard, a horned toad, and a horse. TR, *Letters*, vol. 3, 555.

225 NEW MEXICO TERRITORY Lindsay Denison in New York *Sun*, 6 May 1903.

225 **"Why don't the"** New York *World*, 7 May 1903; Jules Jusserand to Théophile Delcassé, 16 June 1903 (JJ).

225 **"his ancestors"** TR, *Letters*, vol. 3, 557.

225 **In the plaza** TR, *Presidential Addresses and State Papers*, vol. 1, 366; "Comment" scrapbook; photographs in *Leslie's Weekly*, 28 May 1903.

Chronological Note: TR had touched on the subject of conservation before, as Governor of New York and in his First Annual Message as President. Just before leaving Washington on 1 Apr., he had made a private speech to the Society of American Foresters at Gifford Pinchot's house (TR, *Presidential Addresses and State Papers*, vol. 1, 249–57). But his post-Yellowstone utterances at Grand Canyon on 5 May 1903 marked the first time he pronounced the gospel in plain language to the people. As will be seen, TR became increasingly obsessed with the theme of conservation as he traveled through the Southwest and California.

225 **"I don't exactly"** TR, *Letters*, vol. 3, 557. The Grand Canyon was not yet a national park in 1903. Technically a "forest reserve," it was threatened by mining and real-estate interests.

225 **"Leave it as"** TR, *Presidential Addresses and State Papers*, vol. 1, 370. For the aesthetic reaction of a later President to the Grand Canyon, see Franklin D. Roo-

sevelt: "It looks dead. I like my green trees at Hyde Park better." Fox, *John Muir and His Legacy,* 199.

226 **"I felt as"** TR, *Letters,* vol. 3, 557–58; TR, *Letters to Kermit,* 38.

226 **Fifteen hundred children** Jules Jusserand to Théophile Delcassé, 16 June 1903 (JJ); Thomas, "Roosevelt Among the People," 212–13. All TR's speeches in California have been published in *California Addresses by President Roosevelt* (San Francisco, 1903).

226 **"this plain tilled"** *California Addresses,* 24. Later, at Santa Barbara, TR exclaimed, "I do not know that I ever before so thoroughly understood the phrase, 'A garden of the Lord.' " Ibid., 36.

226 **Amid all the** TR wrote that he liked to see California girls and women riding unself-consciously astride (Kerr, *Bully Father,* 116). Every speech he made through 12 May exulted in irrigation, fertility, and beauty.

226 **For four hours** Ironically, for all this hydrological and horticultural display, Los Angeles was just beginning to realize that its swelling population and falling aquifer were incompatible. See Reisner, *Cadillac Desert,* 65ff., for how this realization led to the construction of the Owens River Aqueduct, endorsed by TR.

227 THE SIGHT OF *California Addresses,* 54; New York *Sun,* 12 May 1903.

227 **"There is nothing"** TR, *Presidential Addresses and State Papers,* vol. 1, 384. For the popular "California-as-Mediterranean" conceit of TR and his generation, see Kevin Starr, *Americans and the Californian Dream* (New York, 1973), chap. 12.

227 **In a major** TR, *Presidential Addresses and State Papers,* vol. 1, 383–90; Fox, *John Muir and His Legacy,* 124; *The Washington Post,* 9 Mar. 1903. For a case study of the largest (and most legally audacious) of TR's 1902 executive orders, see David E. Conrad, "Creating the Nation's Largest Forest Reserve: Roosevelt, Emmons, and the Tongass National Forest," *Pacific History Review,* Feb. 1977. In 1902, TR also enacted the first game laws of Alaska Territory, preventing the commercialization of deer hunting, and got an appropriation to preserve and maintain the first federal buffalo herd in Yosemite National Park. TR, *Autobiography,* 435.

227 CONCERN MOUNTED H. W. Taft to William H. Taft, 2 Mar. 1903 (WHT); TR's arrival in San Francisco after his Stanford address coincided with a guilty plea by the Federal Salt Company in another antitrust suit filed by Knox. *San Francisco Chronicle,* 13 May 1903; Thorelli, *Federal Antitrust Policy,* 427–28.

228 **A group of financiers** Chicago *Record-Herald,* 31 May 1903; speech transcript (TRB).

228 **"Before I came"** TR, *Presidential Addresses and State Papers,* vol. 1, 390–91. Elsewhere in San Francisco, he noted that the city stood "in the exact center" of the United States sphere of influence.

228 **"In the South Seas"** Ibid., 391–93.

228 **The audience** "The Manchurian War Scare," *Harper's Weekly,* 23 May 1903; A. Lincoln, "Theodore Roosevelt and the First Russian-American Crisis," *Southern California Quarterly,* Dec. 1963; Zabriskie, *American-Russian Rivalry,* 87; Beale, *Theodore Roosevelt,* 193; "Comment" scrapbook.

229 **In other disturbing** Kishinev is modern Chişinău, Moldavia. There were to be three hundred more pogroms over the next three years. Stuart E. Knee, "The Diplomacy of Neutrality: Theodore Roosevelt and the Russian Pogroms of 1903–1906," *Presidential Studies Quarterly,* winter 1989.

229 **Casualty figures** *Harper's Weekly,* 6 June 1903; *Foreign Relations 1903,* 712–15. Although Nicholas II disciplined the Governor of Bessarabia for permitting the massacre, he privately remarked, "Jews themselves . . . are to blame." Knee, "Diplomacy of Neutrality."

229 **For the first** Taylor Stults, "Roosevelt, Russian Persecution of Jews, and American Public Opinion," *Jewish Social Studies* 33.1 (1971); Philip E. Schoenberg,

"The American Reaction to the Kishinev Pogrom of 1903," *American Jewish Historical Quarterly,* Mar. 1974; John Hay to TR, 28 Apr. and 12 May 1903 (TRP); Raymond A. Esthus, *Theodore Roosevelt and the International Rivalries* (Waltham, Mass., 1970), 26.

229 **Roosevelt was constrained** TR, *Letters,* vol. 3, 474. In April alone, TR had received nearly five hundred communications, endorsed with many thousands of signatures, calling upon the Tsar to stop the persecution of Jews in Russia. Knee, "Diplomacy of Neutrality."

229 **"The inevitable march"** TR, *Presidential Addresses and State Papers,* vol. 1, 394. For an analysis of the formation of TR's Far Eastern thinking, see Beale, *Theodore Roosevelt,* 253–63.

229 **"Our place as"** Ibid., 396. Russia, preoccupied with her own problems, took little notice of TR's speech. But considerable nervousness about it was expressed in Europe, particularly in Germany (*Public Opinion,* 21 May 1903).

229 TWO EVENINGS LATER New York *Tribune,* 16 May 1903; TR, *Works,* vol. 3, 291–92.

230 **His companion was** William F. Kimes, "With Theodore Roosevelt and John Muir in Yosemite," in Westerners Los Angeles Corral, *Brand Book Fourteen* (Los Angeles, 1974), 192. This is the most detailed account of TR's visit to Yosemite. See also Fox, *John Muir and His Legacy,* 3–26.

230 **The President was** TR, *Autobiography,* 333–34; William Wordsworth, "Lucy," no. 5; Cutright, *Theodore Roosevelt,* 117; "I stuffed him pretty well regarding the timber thieves . . . and other spoilers of the forest," Muir said afterward. John L. Eliot, "TR's Wilderness Legacy," *National Geographic,* Sept. 1982.

231 **"The 'greatest number' "** Fox, *John Muir and His Legacy,* 113. See ibid. for the gradual hardening of battle lines between conservation and preservation during the Roosevelt Era.

231 **Whatever resonance** Cutright, *Theodore Roosevelt,* 117; Muir admitted afterward, "I stuffed him pretty well regarding . . . spoilers of the forest." John L. Eliot, "TR's Wilderness Legacy," *National Geographic,* Sept. 1982.

231 **For the next** James M. Clarke, *The Life and Adventures of John Muir* (San Diego, 1979), 292–93.

231 **On 17 May** "Comment" scrapbook; Muir qu. in William F. Bade, *The Life and Letters of John Muir* (Boston, 1924), vol. 2, 412.

231 **some philosophical** Fox, *John Muir and His Legacy,* 109–15; TR, *Letters,* vol. 3, 475. TR's order, which created an almost unbroken chain of mountain reserves from Mexico to British Columbia, was hailed by *Century,* Aug. 1903: "If his trip had resulted in no other public benefit, this alone would have justified it." Three years later, TR incorporated both the valley and Mariposa Big Tree Grove into Yosemite National Park.

231 **Roosevelt's next** TR, *Presidential Addresses and State Papers,* vol. 2, 414–18 (Carson City, Nev.); *California Addresses,* 40. Later, in Oregon, TR asked his new Commissioner of Public Lands, William A. Richards, to investigate that state's famously corrupt disposition of forest property to mining and lumbering interests. "The extent of the Oregon land scandal would grow over the next several years as a kind of background theme to the larger story of conservation" (Gould, *Presidency of Theodore Roosevelt,* 112). For TR's creation of the Public Lands Commission, see D. Jerome Tweton, "Theodore Roosevelt and Land Law Reform," *Mid-America* 49.1 (1967).

231 **"Well, thank"** Lodge, *Selections,* vol. 2, 17.

231 **Seattle neither** "The Day Teddy Roosevelt Arrived, 1903," Puget Sound *Enetai,* 18 Mar. 1983; Lodge, *Selections,* vol. 2, 20.

232 THE ISSUE WHICH Mark Hanna to TR, 23 May 1903 (TRP).

232 "a knockdown" TR, *Letters,* vol. 3, 482.

232 Fate—or Joseph B. Mowry, *Theodore Roosevelt,* 172.

232 Roosevelt saw James Garfield interviewed by J. B. Morrow, 14 Feb. 1906 (MHM). Hanna wanted TR to recognize that opposition to the endorsement did not signify opposition to the nomination. As Chairman of the GOP, Hanna could not favor any candidate against any other, present or future. However, as John M. Blum points out, "He had not been so patient in McKinley's behalf in 1895 or 1896." Blum, *Republican Roosevelt,* 41.

232 YOUR TELEGRAM TR to Hanna, 25 May 1903 (TRP). He adroitly refrained from giving out the text of Hanna's telegram, thus giving the impression that it had been less than respectful. Beer, *Hanna,* 613–14.

233 Hanna had no Mark Hanna to TR, 26 May 1903.The question remains, Did Hanna have any lingering presidential ambition in the spring of 1903? There is no evidence that he did, and plenty that he did not. On 20 Mar., he had sent TR a published interview in which Ohio Congressman Charles H. Grosvenor emphatically stated that the President's nomination was certain, and that anyone opposing him was committing political suicide. "That settles *me,*" Hanna joked. Just two days before TR's annihilating telegram, he had stated publicly, "I am not, and I will not be, a candidate for the presidential nomination." Croly, *Marcus Alonzo Hanna,* 424. See also John S. McCook to TR, 22 May 1903 (TRP).

233 Thus the President Washington *Evening Star,* 27 May 1903; Blum, *Republican Roosevelt,* 51; G. Thomas Edwards, "The College, the Town, and Teddy Roosevelt," *Whitman Alumnus,* Nov. 1977; Lodge, *Selections,* vol. 2, 20, 23. Having humbled Hanna, TR made an elaborate and not very convincing attempt on 29 May to explain himself. See Croly, *Marcus Alonzo Hanna,* 427, and also Beer, *Hanna,* 609–16; Blum, *Republican Roosevelt,* 50–53; and Gould, *Reform and Regulation,* 40–42.

233 ROOSEVELT ARRIVED TR, *Letters,* vol. 3, 558–59. See also Charles Dickens, *The Pickwick Papers,* chap. 13. (Mr. Pickwick: "It's always best on these occasions to do what the mob do." Mr. Snodgrass: "But suppose there are two mobs?" Mr. Pickwick: "Shout with the largest.")

233 He waited until Eyewitness account, by the Australian, in unidentified news clip, "Comment" scrapbook. See also TR, *Letters,* vol. 3, 558–59.

233 "a square deal" Ibid., TR's famous political image, although hinted at in Jamestown, N.D., on 7 Apr., had first been articulated during his Grand Canyon speech of 6 May. In that case, he applied it to American Indians, but *square deal* quickly became a metaphor for his whole domestic political program of mediation between forces. It was the rhetorical inspiration of Franklin Roosevelt's "New Deal" and Harry Truman's "Fair Deal." John Allen Gable, "Theodore Roosevelt and the Square Deal," *Theodore Roosevelt Association Journal* 17.3 (1991).

233 "My address was" TR, *Letters,* vol. 3, 559–60.

234 Roosevelt left Ibid., 561.

234 the concept of equilibrium See Morris, *Rise of Theodore Roosevelt,* 151–52, for TR's search for a fulcrum on his very first night in politics.

234 Justice separating good Kerr, *Bully Father,* 126; TR, *Letters to Kermit,* 61; New York *Sun,* 5 June 1903. The phrase, translated into Latin, was engraved on TR's inaugural medal in 1905.

234 "Envy and arrogance" New York *Sun,* 4 June 1903. "Evidently the new [twentieth-century] American would need to think in contradictions, and in spite of Kant's famous four antinomies, the new universe would know no law that could not be proved by its anti-law" (*Education of Henry Adams,* 497–98). TR's ability to "think in contradictions" both fascinated and infuriated Adams. See below, Interlude.

235 **Roosevelt was sitting** The following account comes from *Editor & Publishers*, 13 June 1903.
235 **"Guests who find"** Ibid. Beveridge and Fairbanks were arch-rivals for control of Indiana's state Republican organization in 1903, and for TR's favor as possible Vice Presidential candidates in 1904.

CHAPTER 16: WHITE MAN BLACK AND BLACK MAN WHITE

236 *Th' black has* "Mr. Dooley" in Salt Lake City *Daily Tribune*, 10 Nov. 1901.
236 SENATOR BEVERIDGE AND Washington *Evening Star*, 5 June 1903; Jules Jusserand to Théophile Delcassé, 16 June 1903 (JJ); Cleveland *Plain Dealer*, 28 May 1903. On 10 June 1903, Mark Hanna privately promised TR that he would "support him for renomination." Both men apparently regarded this pledge as "a contract." Dawes, *Journal of the McKinley Years*, 363.
236 **Roosevelt now enjoyed** *The Washington Post*, 6 June 1903. His current pledges gave him 496 committed, and possibly 730, convention votes. He needed only 493 votes to clinch the nomination.
236 **"I thank you again"** *The Washington Post*, 6 June 1903.
236 **Although the President** EKR to William Loeb, 21 Apr. 1903 (TRB); EKR to Kermit Roosevelt, 29 Apr. and 10 May 1903 (KR); *Washington Times*, 3 May 1903.
236 **Perhaps Edith had** The following catalog of calories is drawn from "Comment" scrapbook.
237 **There would be** The New York *World*, which for some reason was perennially interested in TR's weight, reported it at two hundred pounds on 14 June 1903, seventeen pounds more than at the start of his tour. The newspaper suggested that he should weigh no more than 195 pounds for his height (five feet nine inches) and frame. Modern medical opinion would put his ideal weight at about 145 pounds, and define his actual weight as obese.
237 **A younger, slimmer** Homer Davenport in *San Francisco Examiner*, 3 May 1903; TR, *Letters*, vol. 3, 391. The Encke portrait now hangs at the Sagamore Hill National Historic Site, Oyster Bay, N.Y. The famous Sargent, painted between 14 and 18 Feb. 1903, is still at the White House.
237 **He never failed** Maria Longworth Storer, *Theodore Roosevelt the Child* (privately printed, 1921), 24; TR to John Hay, John Hay diary, 8 May 1904 (JH); see, e.g., TR, *Letters*, vol. 3, 422. ("The Sewalls were here. . . . They came to the Congressional reception, and altogether they showed to great advantage. I was very proud of them.") See also chap. 9 notes, above.
238 **Although political** Wagenknecht, *Seven Worlds*, 151–52; TR, *Works*, vol. 17, 39.
238 **Yet his wife** EKR to Nannie Lodge, 14 June 1903 (HCL); Speck von Sternburg to John C. O'Laughlin, 30 June 1903 (JCOL); *The Wall Street Journal*, 8 July 1903.
238 **He would receive** Jusserand, *What Me Befell*, 240.
    Chronological Note: The Post Office investigation, quietly ordered by Postmaster General Henry C. Payne six months before, had become a press sensation during TR's Western trip, in part because of rumors that its conclusions would embarrass certain high-placed veterans of the McKinley Administration. TR was confident that his own Administration would escape unscathed (the charges were more than three years old), but he was annoyed by editorial suggestions that Payne was trying to delay and downplay the investigation. The Postmaster General had, in fact, been overeager to cooperate with reporters at twice-daily briefings. Even TR complained that Payne "talked too much," and was inviting "a newspaper trial" before all the evidence was in (James Garfield diary, 17 June 1903 [JRG]).

To that end, the President prevailed upon Payne's chief investigator, Assistant Postmaster General Joseph L. Bristow, to release at least some preliminary findings. He said he "wished nothing but the truth," and "cared not a rap who was hit." Bristow hesitated, having turned up proof that Senator Mark Hanna's closest aide at the Republican National Committee, Perry C. Heath, had used the District of Columbia Post Office as a clearinghouse for political favors.

TR promised to "protect" Bristow, and an interim report was released on 18 June. It gave Payne enough ammunition to dismiss four bureau heads, and accept many subordinate resignations. Hanna remained silent, and Heath left for a long vacation in Japan.

TR resisted renewed Democratic calls for Payne's resignation, praising him as "a singularly sweet-tempered and upright man." (He might have added that Payne had influenced his selection as McKinley's running mate in 1900.) On 22 June, he announced the appointment of two respected special counsels, Holmes Conrad and Charles Joseph Bonaparte, to assist Bristow in his probe. Bonaparte was later to become an important figure in the Roosevelt Administration.

For more details of the Post Office scandal, see Dorothy Canfield Fowler, *The Cabinet Politicians: The Postmasters General, 1829–1909* (New York, 1943), 273–77; James Garfield diary, 1903, *passim* (JRG); William W. Wight, *Henry Clay Payne: A Life* (Milwaukee, 1907), 123–41; A. Bower Sageser, *Joseph L. Bristow: Kansas Progressive* (Lawrence, Kans., 1968); Washington *Evening Star*, 18 June 1903; TR, *Letters*, vol. 3, 494–99 and *passim*.

238 **John Hay cautioned** John Hay to William Loeb, 7 June 1903 (TRP); DuVal, *Cadiz to Cathay*, 222. The Colombian Congress had not actually convened since 1898, Marroquín having seized power in 1900 by deposing another dictator, M. A. Sanclemente. TR therefore never believed that he was dealing with a republic. "[Marroquín] embodied in his own person the entire government of Colombia." TR, *Autobiography*, 532–34.

238 **There was no** *Story of Panama*, 339; *Foreign Relations 1903*, 143. See also Marks, *Velvet on Iron*, 100–101. Not one of the letters Hay sent TR on tour mentions Colombia or the treaty, although he covers lesser matters conscientiously (TRP). Hay did, however, confide his forebodings to Mark Hanna. 14 May 1903 (TD).

238 **Hay, a poet's** Elihu Root interviewed by Philip C. Jessup, 23 Jan. 1934 (ER); Jusserand, *What Me Befell*, 262, 264–65; Thompson, *Party Leaders*, 280–81; Mrs. Dewey diary, 21 Mar. 1905 (GD); Bemis, *American Secretaries of State*, vol. 9, 116–17.

239 **Roosevelt moved** Washington *Evening Star*, 8 June 1903; Jules Jusserand sagely observed that Hay, a man of "more vivacity than force," was "better able to banter than decide." *What Me Befell*, 265.

240 THE COLOMBIAN GOVERNMENT *Foreign Relations 1903*, 146.

240 **Hay acted** Thompson, *Party Leaders*, 261–62; John Hay to George Smalley, 10 July 1903 (TD); Robinson, *My Brother*, 9.

240 **At sixty-four** Hay portrait file (FBJ); John Hay profiled by James Creelman in New York *World*, 10 May 1903.

240 **The Secretary was** Ibid. Infinitely complex, graceful and cruel, warmhearted yet aloof, Hay awaits a definitive biography.

241 **With very little** Jules Jusserand to Théophile Delcassé, 16 June 1903 (JJ). See also Jusserand, *What Me Befell*, 236–40, and Morison, *Cowboys and Kings*, x. Mori-

son credits William H. Moody as the instigator of TR's monologue. But Jusserand's report, written only four days afterward, specifically states that he and Mme. Jusserand were Hay's only other guests.

241 **After dinner** Jusserand, *What Me Befell*, 240; TR to John Hay, 9 Aug. 1903 (TRP). Hay said of TR's transcript (which he bound in leather for his children), "It is a genuine nugget of life and literature, almost too valuable for any one man to own. . . . It will not lack companionship in a case which holds the Second Inaugural and the Gettysburg Address." Hay to TR, 12 Aug. 1903 (TRP).

241 THE COLOMBIAN MINISTER *Foreign Relations 1903*, 150–51; John Hay to John A. Leishman, 24 May 1904, and Hay qu. in an unidentified profile, n.d., Hay scrapbook (JH).

241 **That same day** *Story of Panama*, 344.

241 **For a half hour** White House diary, 13 June 1903 (TRP); New York *Herald*, 14 June 1903. The following account is based on William Nelson Cromwell to TR and John Hay (enclosing draft "decaration"), 14 June 1903 (JH). Supplementary details from Cromwell's easily identifiable news leaks to the New York *World*, 14 June 1903; Bunau-Varilla, *Panama*, 266; Dennett, *John Hay*, 375.

242 **Roosevelt told** New York *World*, 14 June 1903.

242 **White sails crept** *The Washington Post*, 14 June 1903.

242 **Instead, he briefed** Roger L. Farnham spoke to the *World* on condition of anonymity. Miner, *Fight for the Panama Route*, 293.

242 NEW REPUBLIC MAY New York *World*, 14 June 1903. A slightly garbled version of this article appears in *Story of Panama*, 345. Notwithstanding Cromwell's desire to keep a low profile, the *World* reported meaningfully, "William Nelson Cromwell, general counsel of the Panama Canal Company, had a long audience with the President today."

243 **One detail missing** Walter F. McCaleb, *Theodore Roosevelt* (New York, 1931), 157.

243 **Roosevelt issued** Washington *Evening Star*, 12 June, and New York *Sun*, 15 June 1903; *Story of Panama*, 280. Note that the "official" White House newspaper scooped the *World* by two days, suggesting that TR was not averse to a little leaking himself, even before he saw Cromwell.

243 ON 15 JUNE Dennett, *John Hay*, 397. See also John Hay, *Letters*, vol. 3, 310; Schoenberg, "American Reaction to the Kishinev Pogrom." Clymer, *John Hay*, 75–81, argues that Hay found Jews more amusing than threatening, unlike the virulently phobic Henry Adams. Hay made an unpublicized gift of five hundred dollars to the Kishinev relief fund.

243 **"Would it do"** TR to Hay, 25 May 1903 (TRP); John Hay to Jacob H. Schiff, 20 May 1903 (TD).

243 **Leo Levi** White House press release, 15 June 1903 (TRP); Schoenberg, "American Reaction to the Kishinev Pogrom." Russian-American relations had been cordial for most of the nineteenth century, but always fragile because of the Jewish problem. See Zabriskie, *American-Russian Rivalry*, chap. 1.

244 **Having thus expressed** White House press release, 15 June 1903 (TRP).

244 **Hay responded first** Ibid. At the end of his remarks, Hay brought tears to the eyes of the committee by reciting, "He that watches over Israel does not slumber. . . . The wrath of man now, as so often in the past, shall be made to praise him." Simon Wolf, *The Presidents I Have Known from 1860–1918* (Washington, D.C., 1918), 193, 236.

244 **"I have never"** White House press release, 15 June 1903 (TRP).

244 **"You may possibly"** Simon Wolf to TR, 3 July 1903 (TRP). *Jew policemen* was accepted usage in 1903. See in the same letter: "not a Jew petition."

244 **It was a story** TR, *Autobiography*, 191–92; Nancy Schoenberg, "Officer Otto Raphael: A Jewish Friend of Theodore Roosevelt," *American Jewish Archives* 39.1 (1987). TR particularly admired "what I might call the Maccabee or fighting Jewish type." TR, *Letters*, vol. 3, 78. See also Wagenknecht, *Seven Worlds*, 186, 230.

244 **After an hour** *The Washington Post*, 16 June 1903. Wolf, *Presidents I Have Known*, 198. A follow-up anecdote may be appended here: Later that day, TR invited Simon Wolf to join him, Ambassador von Sternburg, and Senator Louis McComas of Maryland on a trip to the German Singing Festival in Baltimore. Dense crowds surrounded their carriage, and someone slammed its door on Wolf's hand. "When the President saw what had happened he immediately put a cold bandage on my hand, went to the locker and gave me a good swig, bathed my hands and forehead like a trained nurse, and then turned round to Senator McComas and said, 'Inasmuch as Wolf has been wounded in the public service, I suggest that you introduce a bill in the Senate, pensioning him.'" Ibid., 281.

245 HIS EXCELLENCY **Arturo** *The Washington Post*, 16 June 1903.

245 **"Princess Cassini"** William H. Taft to Helen Taft, 5 Apr. 1904 (WHT); Adams, *Letters*, vol. 5, 578. In her memoir of the Roosevelt era, Marguerite Cassini explains that due to social objections on the diplomatic circuit, her mother, the singer Stefanie von Betz, was obliged to remain in Russia as Cassini's "legal but unacknowledged wife." *Never a Dull Moment*, 6, 224; Thompson, *Party Leaders*, 344.

245 **Cassini's assurances** *Education of Henry Adams*, 439; Zabriskie, *American-Russian Rivalry*, 90–91; *Foreign Relations 1903*, 153–54; Dennis, *Adventures in American Diplomacy*, 357–58.

245 **"Dealing with a"** John Hay to TR, 12 May 1903 (TRP).

245 **Roosevelt cared little** Edward B. Parsons, "Roosevelt's Containment of the Russo-Japanese War," *Pacific Historical Review*, Feb. 1969. TR remarked contemptuously of Korea that it had "an utter inability to stand by itself." TR, *Letters*, vol. 4, 1116.

245 **If the Open Door** Lucius B. Swift to TR, 2 Jan. 1904 (GBC); TR, *Letters*, vol. 3, 501.

245 **"legitimate aspirations"** TR, *Letters*, vol. 3, 497; Frederick Holls to TR, 9 May 1903 (TRP). Russia had a twenty-five-year lease on Port Arthur, not due to expire until March 1923.

245 **"Try to understand"** Cassini, *Never a Dull Moment*, 43. "Liaotung" is modern Kwangtung.

246 **He played** Cecil Spring Rice to Elizabeth Cameron, 3 June 1891 (MHS). See also Sir Mortimer Durand to Earl Grey: "The President . . . is not good at games. His eye and hand do not go together. He is very energetic and full of keenness, but not skilful. He is conscious of the fact, and deplores it." *British Documents on Foreign Affairs: Reports and Papers from the Foreign Office Confidential Print*. Series C: *North America, 1837–1914*, ed. Kenneth Bourne (Frederick, Md., 1986–1987), vol. 12, 49 (hereafter *British Documents on Foreign Affairs*).

246 **"To the left"** John L. McGrew, former TR aide, to Hermann Hagedorn, 29 Jan. 1958 (TRB).

246 **Roosevelt's favorite** James Garfield diary, 19 and 24 June 1903 (JRG); Wister, *Roosevelt*, 167.

246 ON 22 JUNE TR, *Letters*, vol. 3, 501; *Review of Reviews*, Aug. 1903. Despite all indications that Jones had an earnest desire to stamp out peonage, his sentences were usually very lenient, with the accused often being "punished" by the levying of fines. Even those that he did jail received short sentences and often had their sentences suspended and their fines modified. In one 1903 case, on the advice of Judge Jones, TR pardoned two men that Jones himself had sentenced to a year and a day

in jail. It is no surprise that this method of "pardoning everyone on a general promise of good behavior" failed to eliminate peonage. Pete Daniel, *The Shadow of Slavery: Peonage in the South, 1901–1969* (Urbana, Ill., 1990), 43–64.

246 **One hundred miles northeast** The following account is indebted to the reporting of the New York *Sun*, 23–27 June 1903, and in particular its exemplary investigatory article, "A Modern Lynching," on 28 June. White had confessed to the murder of Helen Bishop, the daughter of a local clergyman, just a few days before.

249 **Vendors hawked them** New York *Sun*, 24 June 1903. See also George M. Fredrickson, *The Black Image in the White Mind: A Debate on Afro-American Character and Destiny, 1817–1914* (New York, 1971).

CHAPTER 17: NO COLOR OF RIGHT

250 *I'll tell ye* Dunne, *Observations by Mr. Dooley*, 167.

250 **Roosevelt, child of** Jules Jusserand to Théophile Delcassé, 30 June 1903 (JJ).

250 **He poured out** Ibid.

250 **The Delaware affair** *The Washington Post*, 23–24 June 1903; 135 Americans had been lynched in 1901, 97 in 1902, but only 20 so far in 1903. The encouraging last figure, however, proved illusory. In the first week after the Delaware riot, six more lynchings occurred in the South. By year's end, the total had risen to 104. And, as Walter F. White points out, the sadism of lynchings grew steadily worse during TR's Presidency. *The New York Times*, 24 June 1903; *Public Opinion*, 2 July 1903; White, *Rope and Faggot* (New York, 1929, 1969), 19–35.

250 **On 24 June** Jusserand, *What Me Befell*, 241–43. The Savoy volumes, *Feldsüge des Prinzen Eugen von Savoyen* (Vienna, 1876–1891), had been presented to TR by the Italian Ambassador (Washington *Evening Star*, 15 June 1903). TR appears to have read, or at least browsed, a French translation of these volumes (now preserved at Sagamore Hill). He also read, in French, Arneth's three-volume biography of the Prince.

251 **"Where will it begin"** Jusserand, *What Me Befell*, 243.

251 **The next morning** *Foreign Relations 1903*, 154; Charles W. Bergquist, *Coffee and Conflict in Colombia, 1886–1910* (Durham, N.C., 1978), 216.

251 **"Out of consideration"** TR, *Letters*, vol. 3, 508.

251 CANNONS CRASHED *The New York Times*, 28 June 1903.

251 **Only Alice** Morris, *Edith Kermit Roosevelt*, 271–74; New York *World*, 24 May and 13 June 1903; TR, *Letters*, vol. 3, 484.

251 **"Father doesn't care"** Alice Roosevelt diary, 27 Jan. 1903 (ARL). In extended conversations with Michael Teague toward the end of her life, Alice Roosevelt Longworth spoke often of the ghost of Alice Hathaway Lee. Far from fading, "it became a problem" between them as she grew up. She knew that he felt her resentment of his silence about her mother, but knew also that he "could not or would not" break it. Michael Teague interview, 13 Aug. 1984. Teague's *Mrs. L.*, consisting largely of transcriptions of Alice's tea-table monologues, remains the best biographical study of this brilliant, wounded woman.

251 **"I wish she"** TR, *Letters*, vol. 3, 408.

251 **Ted, now fifteen** Endicott Peabody to TR, 1 Oct. 1903 (TRP); TR, *Letters*, vol. 3, 490.

252 **Kermit, thirteen** Morris, *Edith Kermit Roosevelt*, 298; TR, *Letters*, vol. 3, 490.

252 **Ethel, nearly** Adams, *Letters*, vol. 5, 331; TR, *Letters*, vol. 3, 408.

252 **The two smallest** Face, badger, and extremities may be viewed in Morris, *Edith Kermit Roosevelt*, 269.

253 "WASHINGTON IS NOW" Speck von Sternburg to John C. O'Laughlin, 30 June
1903 (JCOL); Francis B. Loomis to TR, 1 July 1903 (TRP).

253 **Roosevelt was mystified** Wolf, *Presidents I Have Known*, 199. Stults, "Roosevelt," notes Hay's "major reversal of policy" on Russian Jews after TR interested himself in their cause. Jules Jusserand expressed the views of much of Washington's diplomatic corps when he accused TR of currying the favor of "the influential Jewish *coterie*," and creating "a most vexatious precedent . . . a very dangerous policy." He wondered how the Administration would like it if France forwarded a petition of black Martinicans decrying lynchings in the United States. Jusserand to Théophile Delcassé, 30 June 1903 (JJ).

253 **A peremptory telegram** TR to Francis B. Loomis, 1 July 1903 (TRP).

253 **Throwing all semblance** Wolf, *Presidents I Have Known*, 200–202; Oscar S. Straus, *Under Four Administrations: From Cleveland to Taft* (Boston, 1922), 173. Cassini sailed on 8 July. New York *World*, 9 July 1903.

253 **John Hay, unaware** John Hay to TR, 1 July 1903 (TD).

254 **His letter came** New York *World*, 3 July 1903; Miner, *Fight for the Panama Route*, 387.

254 **A DAY OR TWO** *Washington Times*, 8 July 1903; John Hay to TR, 9 and 11 July 1903 (TD); Clymer, *John Hay*, 195.

254 **"I always find"** John Hay to Mrs. Hay, 4 July 1903 (TD).

254 **Sure enough,** Ibid.; New York *Sun*, 30 Aug. 1903. TR's other guests were Mark Hanna, Thomas Kearns, Charles Fairbanks, Clement Griscom, Guy Wetman Caryl, and Winthrop Chanler.

254 **When they did** John Hay to Mrs. Hay, 4 July 1903 (TD); *Foreign Relations 1903*, 155–58. The extent of Marroquín's influence on the Colombian Congress remains a matter of historical debate. In 1903, American foreign-policy experts considered him to be a strongman, but Minister Herrán complained that he was languid in comparison with TR (Herrán to Lilian H. Andrews, 8 July 1903 [TH]). Miner, *Fight for the Panama Route*, chap. 6, and Bergquist, *Coffee and Conflict*, 216, present him as essentially powerless; but see the contrary reassessment in Marks, *Velvet on Iron*, 101.

255 **President and Secretary** "We agree on all points of foreign policy." John Hay to George Smalley, 9 July 1903 (TD). See also Hay to TR, 18 July 1903: "Permit me to observe that your planet seems to be in good working order" (TRP).

255 **HAY SAID GOOD-BYE** *New York Tribune*, 9 July 1903; John Hay to TR, 13 July 1903 (TD). In this same thank-you note, Hay repeated his "trembling hope" that he might one day have TR's promised written account of his cross-country trip. TR complied on 9 Aug. 1903.

255 **On 12 July** *Story of Panama*, 346. For a detailed discussion of the political situation in Bogotá at this time, see Bergquist, *Coffee and Conflict*, 214–16.

255 **By a coincidence** New York *World*, 13 July 1903; Cromwell's aide, Roger Farnham, had given this date to the newspaper a month before. McCaleb, *Theodore Roosevelt*, 157.

255 **a desperate message** *Foreign Relations 1903*, 163.

255 **Hay prepared** Ibid., 164; TR to John Hay, 14 July 1903, qu. in Pringle, *Theodore Roosevelt*, 311.

255 **THE KISHINEV PETITION** Simon Wolf to TR, 3 July 1903 (TRP); Beale, *Theodore Roosevelt*, 197. Wolf's misgivings were shared by many Americans. A New York *World* editorial on 10 July declared that TR's "anonymous" press blast of 1 July "deprives our Kishinev interference of all moral force, degrading it into a mere bargaining trick."

255 **Oscar Solomon Straus** In 1902, TR had appointed Straus as United States Representative at The Hague.

256 **When Roosevelt heard** Wolf, *Presidents I Have Known*, 203 (facsimile of TR's draft on pp. 206–8); Marks, *Velvet on Iron*, 151.

256 **Everyone approved** Straus, *Under Four Administrations*, 172–73; John Hay to TR, 11 July 1903 (TD); TR, *Letters*, vol. 3, 517. Afterward, everybody but Straus took credit for the cable. For its text, see Cyrus Adler, *With Firmness in the Right* (New York, 1940), 268–70.

256 **Long before he** Oscar Straus to TR, 15 July 1903 (TRP); Zabriskie, *American-Russian Rivalry*, 93. The three ports were Ta-tung-kou, Mukden, and Harbin. Newchwang was already open by treaty. Zabriskie confirms that the decision to open them (made secretly on 6 and 9 July) was prompted by the Tsar's fear of "a united front of powers against Russia."

256 **Nicholas II's rejection** John Hay to TR, 14 July 1903 (TD); TR, *Letters*, vol. 3, 520. Knee, "Diplomacy of Neutrality," argues that TR's response to the Kishinev pogrom was more political than humanitarian. His main motive in cooperating with the Wolf committee was to secure New York's large Jewish vote in 1904.

256 **"If only we were"** TR, *Letters*, vol. 3, 532.

256 **One such vehicle** Ray Stannard Baker research notes (RSB). Baker subsequently reworked these notes for publication in *American Chronicle*, 170–72.

257 **A servant showed** Baker research notes (RSB). TR's study, almost unchanged, is now part of Sagamore Hill National Historic Site.

257 **Like a sudden explosion** Ray Stannard Baker to James Baker, 16 July 1903, and Baker research notes (RSB).

257 **"My dear Mr. President"** Booker T. *Washington Papers*, vol. 7, 202–3.

257 **"An old Florida"** Baltimore *Herald*, 3 July 1903.

257 **"It was a very"** Ray Stannard Baker research notes (RSB). See also Baker, *American Chronicle*, 172.

258 **Behind his jocularity** TR to Brander Matthews, 11 July 1903 (TRP); *Review of Reviews*, Aug. 1903; *Literary Digest*, 18 July 1903; Rollo Ogden to TR, 3 and 28 July 1903 (TRP). For sarcastic black reaction to the Kishinev petition, see Ziglar, "Decline of Lynching."

258 **For political reasons** Willard B. Gatewood, Jr., "A Republican President and Democratic State Politics: Theodore Roosevelt and the Mississippi Primary of 1903," *Presidential Studies Quarterly*, summer 1984.

259 **"This people is"** James Wilson to TR, 2 July 1903 (TRP).

259 **So far in 1903** *Literary Digest*, 23 May 1903; Lodge, *Selections*, vol. 2, 25; *Postal Record*, July 1903; Harrison Gray Otis to TR, 28 July 1903 (TRP). Wall Street's impression of TR as prolabor was inaccurate. His primary instinct was for social order. On 10 June 1903, he had sent federal troops to subdue some striking miners in Morenci, Arizona Territory, acting within twenty minutes of an appeal from Territorial Governor Alex Brodie. Leupp, *The Man Roosevelt*, 241; Washington *Evening Star*, 11 June 1903; TR, *Letters*, vol. 3, 593.

259 **an open shop** Frank W. Palmer to TR, 7 July 1903 (TRP).

   Chronological Note: Conditions of "intolerable tyranny" had been reported to exist in the GPO. Public Printer Palmer was accused of letting typographic and other unions create a closed and notoriously inefficient shop there, in exchange for labor peace. TR was sympathetic to an affidavit filed by a fired GPO foreman, William A. Miller, who claimed to have been penalized for raising the productivity of the bindery division by 40 percent.

   TR directed that Miller be reinstated, over Palmer's protests that such a gesture would cause the bookbinders to go on strike. He ordered George Cortelyou to investigate the situation and take whatever steps were necessary to ensure that no government union "be permitted to override the laws of the United States, which it is my sworn duty to enforce." For a full account, see Gatewood, *Theodore Roosevelt and the Art of Controversy*, 134–74.

259 **James S. Clarkson** James S. Clarkson to Benjamin F. Barnes (TR's assistant secretary), 15 July 1903 (TRP); *The Wall Street Journal* news clip, ca. 15 July 1903 (TRP).

Biographical Note: Clarkson, a notorious spoilsmaster who had fired thirty thousand Post Office appointees in a single year under Benjamin Harrison (to the extreme displeasure of Civil Service Commissioner Theodore Roosevelt), was surveyor of the Port of New York. His appointment by TR in May 1902 had, in the words of *Life* magazine, "sent cold chills down the necks of all civil service reformers." When the reformers came to the White House for an explanation, TR merely threw up his hands with a smile. "Well, the truth is, as you know, in politics we have to do a great many things that we ought not to do." To professional politicians, the appointment was both shrewd and successful: Clarkson had old scores to settle with Mark Hanna, and, grateful for his appointment, he worked energetically to elect TR in 1904. *Life*, 8 May 1902; Barry, *Forty Years*, 278–79; TR, *Letters*, vol. 3, 256–57, 262–63. See also David Crosson, "James S. Clarkson and Theodore Roosevelt, 1901–1904: A Study in Contrasting Political Traditions," *Annals of Iowa* 42.5 (1974).

259 **"Of course I will not"** TR, *Letters*, vol. 3, 519.

259 **The sun beat** *Review of Reviews*, Aug. and Sept. 1903. TR's field acreage (out of a ninety-seven-acre total) included pasture. The Sagamore Hill farm, run by a full-time superintendent and several assistants, supported five horses, six Jersey cows, eight pigs, several turkeys, and a flock of chickens. It was self-sufficient in hay, straw, milk, fruit, vegetables, and flowers. There was a windmill, an icehouse, and a machine that made gas. The President, a prodigious axman, ensured a steady supply of firewood. "Theodore Roosevelt as Farmer," *Farm Journal*, Dec. 1906.

259 **On 22 July** TR, *Letters*, vol. 3, 526.

259 **"Every morning Edie"** TR in New York *Sun*, 11 Aug. 1903; Kolko, *Triumph of Conservatism*, 69; Morris, *Edith Kermit Roosevelt*, 139. For an attempt to interest the President in the currency question, see Leslie M. Shaw to TR, 28 July 1903 (TRP), and TR, *Letters*, vol. 3, 691.

260 **The problem, apparently** John M. Mason to author, 2 Feb. 1965. Greenbacks were limited to their 1878 circulation, silver coins set at only one hundred million dollars' worth, and the volume of gold remained stable. This supply was inadequate to feed the growing prosperity of 1903.

260 **Toward the end** "Wall Street and the President," *New York Tribune*, 29 Aug. 1903; Henry Clews, *Fifty Years on Wall Street* (New York, 1908, 1973), 771–73; *The New York Times*, 31 Mar. 1903. James J. Hill suggested that *indigestible securities* might be a better phrase. Alexander D. Noyes, *Forty Years of American Finance* (New York, 1909), 309.

260 **Roosevelt referred** TR, *Letters*, vol. 3, 526; Leslie M. Shaw to TR, 24 July 1903 (TRP); Lucius Littauer to TR, 27 July 1903 (TRP). For a reassessment of Shaw's "imaginative, pragmatic, and courageous" record under TR, see Richard H. Timberlake, Jr., "Mr. Shaw and His Critics: Monetary Policy in the Golden Age Reviewed," *Quarterly Journal of Economics* 77.1 (1963).

260 **"Uncle Joe wants"** TR, *Letters*, vol. 3, 524.

260 **When the Speaker** *The Washington Post*, 23 July 1903; New York *Sun*, 30 Aug. 1903.

260 CANNON'S RUMPLED APPEARANCE The profile of Joseph Cannon is based on *Review of Reviews*, Dec. 1903; Bolles, *Tyrant from Illinois*, 6–7, 46; Thompson,

Party Leaders, 174–79; Watson, *As I Knew Them*, 92–93; and Kate Carew interview in New York *World*, 1 May 1904; TR warned Alice Roosevelt never to stand between Cannon and a cuspidor. Bolles, *Tyrant from Illinois*, 5.

261 **"a hard, narrow"** TR qu. in Moore, *Roosevelt and the Old Guard*, 219.

261 **"I could not"** Lucius Littauer to TR, 27 July 1903 (TRP).

261 **No sooner had** Noyes, *Forty Years*, 309; *Literary Digest*, 8 Aug. 1903. In retrospect, the slump of 1903 was seen as a reaction to excessive stock purchases in 1901–1902. Clews, *Fifty Years*, 771–73.

261 **Like ripples round** Faulkner, *Decline of Laissez-Faire*, 163; Leslie Shaw to TR, 24 July 1903, and James S. Clarkson to TR, 29 July 1903 (TRP). The panic moderated in Aug. TR picked the important support of *The Wall Street Journal*, which praised his "courageous advocacy of the publicity principle" in trust control, and said that if he had gotten his legislative way earlier, "the gross over-capitalization of companies" would have been restrained to the overall benefit of the economy (*The Wall Street Journal*, 12 Aug. 1903). Financial quarters remained uneasy through the beginning of November. Not until Aug. 1904 did the economy begin to expand again.

261 **So while stockbrokers** *The Wall Street Journal*, 12 Aug. 1903; New York *World*, 26 July 1903.

261 A THOUSAND MILES SOUTH Gatewood, "Republican President"; *The Washington Post*, 10 Aug. 1903.

261 **"My dear Governor"** *The New York Times*, 10 Aug. 1903; TR, *Letters*, vol. 3, 540–41.

262 **In a minority** TR, *Letters*, vol. 3, 541. This document was the first antilynching statement ever issued by an American President. Schlesinger and Israel, *History of American Presidential Elections*, vol. 2, 2013.

262 **"There are certain"** TR, *Letters*, vol. 3, 542.

262 **Rollo Odgen** Rollo Ogden to TR, 10 Aug. 1903 (TRP); Gatewood, "Republican President." Both *Harper's Weekly* and *The Atlanta Constitution* blamed TR for Vardaman's triumph, and the President unhappily admitted that "his foul-mouthed abuse of me" had drawn votes (TR, *Letters*, vol. 4, 1069). But Gatewood notes that the quiet restructuring and strengthening of the Mississippi GOP went on regardless under Governor Vardaman.

262 **Roosevelt concluded** Scheiner, "President Roosevelt and the Negro"; Vardaman editorial in Greenwood, Miss., *Commonwealth*, 10 Jan. 1903, copy in TRP. The country's largest organized black body, the National Negro Baptist Convention, commended TR for his "fearless stand" for justice at a time of high social danger. Ziglar, "Decline of Lynching."

262 BY NOW, THE State *Foreign Relations 1903*, 179, 158, 172–73.

263 **He had sent** The official explanation was that Marroquín's cable contractor was boycotting transmissions in a franchise dispute. If so, the boycott was well-timed to make Beaupré helpless, just when he was needed to lobby for the treaty. Lilian Andrews to Tomás Herrán, 21 July 1903 (TH); *The New York Times*, 7 Sept. 1903; Marks, *Velvet on Iron*, 101–2.

263 **Now there arrived** F. F. Whittekin to John T. Morgan, 20 July 1903, forwarded to TR (JTM).

263 **"I am totally"** TR, *Letters*, vol. 3, 565.

263 **"How can the"** New York *Herald*, 15 Aug. 1903.

263 **Whatever "action"** DuVal, *Cadiz to Cathay*, 264.

263 **That weekend** *The New York Times*, 18 Aug. 1903.

264 **Roosevelt came down** *New York Tribune* and New York *Sun*, 18 Aug. 1903; unidentified news clip, John Hay scrapbook (JH).

264 BOGOTÁ, AUGUST 12 *Foreign Relations 1903*, 179. See also DuVal, *Cadiz to Cathay*, 240–41, and Miner, *Fight for the Panama Route*, 323–26. Due to the va-

garies of Colombian cabling, Beaupré's wire did not reach the White House until 5:30 P.M. on Saturday, 15 Aug. It was telegraphed to John Hay on Sunday, and to TR's Oyster Bay office early the next morning.

264 ROOSEVELT WAS STILL   TR to John Hay, 17 Aug. 1903, and Hay to TR, 16 Aug. 1903 (TRP). In another memorable image, written eleven years later, TR wrote of the Colombian leaders: "You could no more make an agreement with them than you could nail currant jelly to a wall—and the failure to nail currant jelly to the wall is not due to the nail; it is due to the currant jelly." Ibid., vol. 8, 945.

264 Before replying   Francis B. Loomis to TR, 15 Aug. 1903. Moore (1860–1947) was a professor of international law and diplomacy at Columbia University. A former Assistant Secretary of State, he taught from 1891 to 1924, and wrote many scholarly works, including *History and Digest of the International Arbitrations . . .* (6 vols., Washington, D.C., 1898). At the time of his consultancy to the Roosevelt Administration, he was editing an eight-volume *Digest of International Law.*

264 Professor Moore's   Moore's memorandum, dated 2 Aug. 1903, is reproduced in its entirety in DuVal, *Cadiz to Cathay*, 508–13.

264 For almost six   Ibid., 510–11.

265 Throughout the long   Ibid., 512–13.

265 The effect upon   Miner, *Fight for the Panama Route*, 350; TR, *Letters*, vol. 3, 566–67. On 5 Sept., TR invited Moore to dine and spend the night at Sagamore Hill. He startled the professor by confiding that he would recognize Panama if it declared independence from Colombia. "Of course," he added hastily, "under proper circumstances." John Bassett Moore, "Autobiography," ms. fragment in JBM, Panama file.

265 "The fathers at"   H. A. Gudger to Francis B. Loomis, 8 Aug. 1903 (FRL), and Alvey A. Adee to John Hay, 20 Aug. 1903 (JH).

265 "The fact that"   John Hay to TR, 22 Aug. 1903 (TD). *Faire valoir* means *fully exercise.*

265 Gradually, a partial   Luis C. Rico to Tomás Herrán, 13 Aug. 1903, and J. Bidlake to Tomas Herrán, 8 Sept. 1903 (TH); Alban G. Snyder qu. in Mary X. Ferguson, "John Barrett," chap. 4, 12–13 (JB).

265 "The President will"   John Hay to Arthur Beaupré, 20 Aug. 1903 (TD).

266 "For the first"   Tomás Herrán to William Nelson Cromwell, 17 Aug. 1903 (TH).

266 AUGUST DROWSED   *The New York Times*, 1 Sept. 1903; TR, *Autobiography*, 329, 339; P. James Roosevelt to author, 24 Nov. 1984 (AC); TR, *Letters*, vol. 3, 540. By 8 Sept., three members of TR's security detail were laid up with fever. New York *World*, 9 Sept. 1903.

266 Toward the end   The following account is taken from the New York *World* and New York *Herald*, 3 Sept. 1903, plus unidentified news clips in TRB.

266 "I came to kill"   TR's would-be assassin was Henry Weilbrenner, a "paranoiac" from Syosset, New York. He said that he wanted to marry Alice Roosevelt, which, TR joked, proved that Weilbrenner was insane. Unidentified news clip (TRB).

266 The security detail   New York *World*, 4 Sept. 1904; TR, *Letters*, vol. 3, 587; TR to George Cortelyou, 25 July 1903 (TRP); Leupp, *The Man Roosevelt*, 238–39.

266 A providential invitation   Leupp, *The Man Roosevelt*, 237–38.

266 His speech there   TR, *Works*, vol. 18, 57–70; Jules Jusserand to Théophile Delcassé, 7 and 20 Sept. 1903 (JJ). A portrait of More hangs in TR's study at Sagamore Hill.

267 "Again and again"   TR, *Works*, vol. 18, 61.

267 "The line of cleavage"   Ibid., 63.

267 A civilized commonwealth   Ibid., 64–65.

268 BY MID-SEPTEMBER   Tomás Herrán to German Villa, 2 Sept. 1903 (TH); Jules Jusserand to Théophile Delcassé, 22 Sept. 1903 (JJ); TR, *Works*, vol. 20, 497–98;

Foreign Relations 1903, 264–65; Robert A. Friedlander, "A Reassessment of Roosevelt's Role in the Panamanian Revolution," *Western Political Quarterly* 14 (1961). As early as 1 Aug. 1903, the Panamanian newspaper *El Istmeno* had published a prosecession editorial, and been disciplined by Colombian authorities. H. A. Gudger to Francis B. Loomis, 1 Aug. 1903 (JH).

268 **Isthmian delegates** John Hay to TR, 7 Sept. 1903 (TD); Alban G. Snyder qu. in Ferguson, "John Barrett," chap. 4, 12–13.

268 **Desperate to keep** *Foreign Relations 1903*, 190, 362; *Story of Panama*, 354–55; Tomás Herrán to Luis Rico, 15 Sept. 1903 (TH).

268 **Proposals for a** DuVal, *Cadiz to Cathay*, 249; E. Taylor Parks, *Colombia and the United States, 1765–1934* (New York, 1968), 366. The forty-million-dollar argument was advanced by a special committee of the Colombian Senate, which argued that the Compagnie Nouvelle's last extension of its concession had been granted by executive decree in 1900, and was thus unratified. If so, the concession would be renegotiable, without any further consideration of the Compagnie, at the end of 1904. The United States need pay no more than she had already agreed to pay for canal rights, while Colombia would quadruple her expectations from the Hay-Herrán Treaty. See TR, *Autobiography*, 538.

268 **Hay ignored this** John Hay to TR, 13 Sept. 1903 (TRP). Another reason for Hay's anger toward Bogotá was that he had heard from Arthur Beaupré that Colombian negotiants had asked Germany and Britain to bid for canal rights in competition with the United States. Beaupré to Hay, 21 July 1903 (JH); TR, *Works*, vol. 20, 496.

268 **Roosevelt had already** TR, *Letters*, vol. 3, 599. See also TR, *Autobiography*, 536.

268 **so did summer** The treaty expired at midnight on 22 Sept. 1903.

268 **A harvest of tart** TR to Henry Cabot Lodge, 3 and 15 Sept. 1903, and to William Sewall, 22 Sept. 1903 (TRP); TR, *Letters*, vol. 3, 604. TR told a visitor that if people believed what was currently being written about him in the press, they would think him "the most despicable cur possible." Parsons, *Perchance Some Day*, 149.

268 **His Syracuse speech** Wayne MacVeagh to TR, 23 Sept. 1903, Henry Cabot Lodge to TR, 26 Sept. 1903, and TR to William Sewall, 22 Sept. 1903 (TRP); TR, *Letters*, vol. 3, 591; Presidential scrapbook and TR to Charles J. Bonaparte, 15 Sept. 1903 (TRP).

269 **Alaska Boundary Tribunal** The boundary negotiations had begun on 15 Sept.

269 **Roosevelt had long** Elihu Root to TR, 11 Aug. 1903 (PCJ); TR, *Letters*, vol. 3, 425.

269 **Roosevelt took** TR, *Letters*, vol. 3, 605.

269 **"I suppose few"** Ibid.

CHAPTER 18: THE MOST JUST AND PROPER REVOLUTION

270 *An autocrat's a* Finley Peter Dunne, *Mr. Dooley's Philosophy* (New York, 1900), 260.

270 THE PRESIDENT'S FIRST New York *Herald*, 30 Sept. 1903; Paul T. Heffron, "Secretary Moody and Naval Administrative Reform, 1902–1903," *American Neptune* 29.1 (1969); Wood, *Roosevelt As We Knew Him*, 95–97; William H. Moody to the Michigan Club of Detroit, 3 May 1902 (WHM). For a modern assessment, see Judith R. McDonough, "William Henry Moody" (Ph.D. diss., Auburn University, 1983).

270 **Since joining the** Washington *Evening Star*, 10 Mar. 1902; Fleming, *Around the Capitol*, 36, 256; Paul T. Heffron, "Profile of a Public Man," *Yearbook of the Supreme Court Historical Society*, 1980; *Dictionary of National Biography*. See also Wood, *Roosevelt As We Knew Him*, 95–97.

270 Emerging from the   New York *Herald,* 30 Sept. 1903.
271 "a good jolt"   TR, *Letters,* vol. 3, 514–15.
271 "In this particular"   TR to L. Clarke Davis, 21 Sept. 1903 (TRP).
271 William A. Miller   See note above, p. 659 (an open shop); also Gatewood, *Theodore Roosevelt and the Art of Controversy,* 160.
271 This apparent sanction   J. W. Basra to TR, 18 Sept. 1903, and Lynn (Mass.) Central Labor Union to William Loeb, 25 Sept. 1903 (TRP); *Washington Times,* 18 and 20 Sept. 1903; James Garfield diary, 29 Sept. 1903 (JRG); TR, *Letters,* vol. 3, 607; *The Washington Post,* 15 Sept. 1903.
271 One of them   Portrait in *The American Federationist,* Nov. 1903; New York *Herald,* 4 Sept. 1903; Glück, *John Mitchell,* 92. Mitchell, suffering from chronic alcoholism and insomnia, was heading toward a nervous breakdown. Madison, *American Labor Leaders,* 171–72.
272 Roosevelt sized Gompers   TR, *Letters,* vol. 3, 607; New York *Sun,* 30 Sept. 1903. This was not the first time TR and Gompers had met. Their acquaintance was slight, but extended back to 1884. Samuel Gompers, *Seventy Years of Life and Labor* (New York, 1925), vol. 1, 526.
272 "I thank you"   TR, *Letters,* vol. 3, 607.
272 "I ask you"   Ibid.
272 Miller's habits   Ibid.; *The Washington Post,* 30 Sept. 1903.
272 The delegation trooped   *The New York Times, The Washington Post,* and New York *Sun,* 30 Sept. 1903.
272 Editorial opinion   *Literary Digest,* 10 Oct. 1903; *The Washington Post,* 30 Sept. 1903. *The New York Times,* same date, complained only that Roosevelt had not been tough enough with labor.
272 Radical unions   New York *Sun,* 30 Sept. 1903; Gatewood, *Theodore Roosevelt and the Art of Controversy,* 164, 174; Ray Stannard Baker to TR, 15 Oct. 1903 (TRP). Baker had just begun a serialized exposé of union bossism in *McClure's.*
272 "YOU MAY HAVE noticed"   TR to Mark Hanna, 5 Oct. 1903 (TRP). Senate tinkerings with the treaty, before ratifying it in the spring, had necessitated reratification by Cuba and full consent of the new Congress. Healy, *United States in Cuba,* 205.
273 With no paved highways   Federico Boyd, *Exposición histórica acerca de los motivos que causaron la separación de Panamá de la Rep. de Colombia* [Panama, 1911?], 37; Miner, *Fight for the Panama Route,* 336.
273 The President could   Boyd, *Exposición,* 37; John Barrett to Caroline S. Barrett, 20 Nov. 1905 (JB); Marks, *Velvet on Iron,* 97–98. According to the New York *Sun,* 5 Nov. 1903, Panamanians paid higher per-capita taxes than any other Colombian citizens, yet received nothing of Bogotá's annual levy on the railroad.
273 Panama's political   Philander Knox, "Sovereignty over the Isthmus, as Affecting the Canal," 1903 memorandum (PCK); Marks, *Velvet on Iron,* 97–98; Richard H. Collin, "The Big Stick as Weltpolitik: Europe and Latin America in Theodore Roosevelt's Foreign Policy," in Naylor et al., *Theodore Roosevelt,* 296–316; TR, *Works,* vol. 17, 241–43; Parks, *Colombia and the United States,* 219–34, 397; Friedlander, "Reassessment." For a revolutionary precedent in 1885, almost identical with that of 1903, see DuVal, *Cadiz to Cathay,* 124–30.
273 "This does not"   TR to Mark Hanna, 5 Oct. 1903 (TRP). The words *therefore* and *must* do not appear in the published version of this letter. TR, *Letters,* vol. 3, 625.
273 It did not amuse   At the time TR sought to discuss Panama policy with him, Hanna was desperately trying to raise campaign money on Wall Street. Mark Hanna to John Hay, 15 Sept. 1903 (JH), and to George Perkins, ca. early Oct. 1903 (GWP); Mark Hanna to TR, 4 Oct. 1903 (TRP).
273 This advice contrasted   *Review of Reviews,* Oct. 1903. See also Lloyd J. Graybar,

Albert Shaw of the Review of Reviews: *An Intellectual Biography* (Louisville, 1974), 124–25.

274 **Roosevelt tried** TR, *Letters,* vol. 3, 625–26.

274 **"It is out of"** TR, *Autobiography,* appendix to chap. 14. Weeks later, TR quoted these words to show how considerate he had been of Congress, if not Colombia, in October 1903. Friedlander, "Reassessment."

274 **"misconduct"** TR, *Letters,* vol. 3, 626; Washington *Evening Star,* 7 Oct. 1903; William Nelson Cromwell to TR, 14 Oct. 1903 (TRP); TR qu. in Thomas Schoonover, "Max Farrand's Memorandum on the U.S. Role in the Panamanian Revolution of 1903," *Diplomatic History,* fall 1988.

274 **Philippe Bunau-Varilla** White House appointment book, 10 Oct. 1903, and Francis B. Loomis to TR, 5 Jan. 1904 (TRP). Loomis is often described as an old and close friend (and hence, wily collaborationist) of Bunau-Varilla. They had met a few times previously, but their correspondence in FBL makes plain that they did not strike up any intimacy until *after* 1904. Till then, their relations were stiffly formal. Note that Loomis's above-cited letter is a "posterity document," clearly demanded after the fact by TR.

274 **a shrewd and aggressive personality** TR to William R. Thayer, 1 Mar. 1917 (TRP); TR, *Letters,* vol. 3, 691; McCullough, *Path Between the Seas,* 162.

274 **He knew that** Schoonover, "Max Farrand's Memorandum"; Francis B. Loomis to TR, 5 Jan. 1904 (TRP); Bunau-Varilla, *Panama,* 311. TR remarked years later, "There might have been a dictograph in the room." Schoonover, "Max Farrand's Memorandum."

274 **"Mr. President"** Bunau-Varilla, *Panama,* 310–12. Bunau-Varilla, interviewed by Howard K. Beale, July 1936 (HKB), rephrased TR's question as, "What will this do to our preparations?" See also Bunau-Varilla to John Hay, 15 Oct. 1903, qu. in Bunau-Varilla, *Panama,* 318: "I [told him] the whole thing would end in a revolution" (JH).

275 **Loomis remained** Philippe Bunau-Varilla, *From Panama to Verdun: My Fight for France* (Philadelphia, 1940), 332. Bunau-Varilla (probably tipped off by Loomis) seems to have known about the professor's advisory role.

275 **"General and special"** Bunau-Varilla, *Panama,* 311.

Historiographical Note: David McCullough's inference from a third-hand source (the diary of John Bigelow) that Bunau-Varilla fully informed TR of his revolutionary plans at this meeting contradicts the testimony, on repeated occasions, of all three primary participants. It seems much more probable that Bunau-Varilla, a model of Gallic scrupulosity, gave the specifics to Loomis, to pass on to the President in executive session. This is what TR himself recalled ten years later, and does not conflict with Bigelow's contemporary diary entry, "Bunau-Varilla . . . has seen the President and the Ass't Secretary of State; unfolded to them his scheme [etc.]." Bigelow could quite well be describing separate meetings with each man. McCullough, *Path Between the Seas,* 352; Schoonover, "Max Farrand's Memorandum"; Margaret Clapp, *Forgotten First Citizen: John Bigelow* (Boston, 1947), 313.

275 **All that the President** Schoonover, "Max Farrand's Memorandum." Collin, "Big Stick," 302–3, argues that by seeking a part of the Compagnie Nouvelle's forty million dollars, Colombia—a police state corruptly ill-disposed toward both the United States and Panama—sought to reinvolve France in Latin American affairs, whereas TR wanted to take Europe out of Latin America once and for all.

275 **tremendous little foreigner** "That man would instruct Cosmos," TR told Mark Hanna. The Senator became nervous. "Never mind Cosmos. Cromwell's the man for you to listen to." John J. Leary, *Talks with TR* (Boston, 1920), 256.

275 **Bunau-Varilla, in** Bunau-Varilla, *Panama,* 310–12. See also Bunau-Varilla, *From Panama to Verdun,* 131–33. TR joked afterward, "He would have been a very dull man had he been unable to make such a guess." TR, *Letters,* vol. 3, 689.

Historiographical Note: Bunau-Varilla's interview with TR on 10 Oct. 1903 has become one of the most widely debated episodes in the Roosevelt presidency. Anglo-Saxon historians tend to dismiss Bunau-Varilla as an unreliable chronicler, given to exaggerations. However, William Glover Fletcher interviewed and corresponded with Bunau-Varilla at length in the course of researching his exhaustive dissertation, and came to the conclusion that he was an honest man (Fletcher, "Canal Site Diplomacy," 176–78).

On the day of the interview, TR wrote another letter to Albert Shaw confirming in every detail the impression that Bunau-Varilla took away (See TR, *Letters,* vol. 3, 628). TR's own accounts of the meeting (to John Bigelow in TR, *Letters,* vol. 3, 689; and to Archibald C. Coolidge in Schoonover, "Max Farrand's Memorandum") are supplemented by details provided by two mutual acquaintances. Elihu Root recalled years later: "Bunau-Varilla told me about [it]. He said that he . . . got from Roosevelt such violent expressions of opinion unfriendly to the Colombians that . . . he told his people in Panama to go ahead. . . . Roosevelt did not say a single word to him about what he intended to do, but B-V found out just what he thought from his explosive comments" (Root to Philip Jessup, 16 July 1931 [ES]).

The other item is an entry dated 16 Oct. 1903 in the journal of Bunau-Varilla's close friend John Bigelow: "Bunau-Varilla was up over Sunday [11 Oct.], has seen the President and the Ass't Secretary of State; unfolded to them his scheme for proceeding with the Isthmian Canal without much more delay. . . . It is in brief to have the Isthmians revolt from the Colombian govt. declare their independence . . . have the U.S. send vessels to protect the Railway as it did during the uprising four years ago and forbid any fighting on the Canal territory which would protect the new state from any hostility that could do it any harm, etc. &c." (qu. in Clapp, *Forgotten First Citizen,* 313).

This would appear to be damaging evidence that TR was dissembling when he stated in his Special Message of 4 Jan. 1904, "No one connected with this Government had any previous knowledge of the revolution [in Panama] except such as was accessible to any person of ordinary intelligence who read the newspapers and kept up a current acquaintance with public affairs" (TR, *Presidential Addresses and State Papers,* vol. 2, 743). But Bunau-Varilla, when shown the diary entry in 1913, remarked that "a few points . . . seem to have been confused in Mr. Bigelow's memory." He specifically disputed the allegation that Loomis and TR were fully informed of his revolutionary plans, and said that he had "strictly abstained" from giving any details that might implicate either himself or his listeners (Clapp, *Forgotten First Citizen,* 312).

As with the Venezuela episode, there seems to have been a concerted effort after the fact to create archival lacunae. Loomis's normally copious correspondence with John Hay is purged between 17 Aug. 1903 and 31 Jan. 1904 in FBL. The papers of TR, Hay, and Moody are mysteriously quiet on all matters to do with the revolution. Amador's unpublished memoir is remarkable for its deletions of what the author described as "political secrets" about the role played by the Roosevelt Administration (*Story of Panama,* 643). Fletcher saw many more documents than Bunau-Varilla was willing to deposit in his Library of Congress collection.

Cromwell's papers have vanished entirely; a small collection of his letters, once filed in the Miles P. DuVal papers at Georgetown University, have also disappeared.

TR's own comments on the meeting suggest more self-control than Bunau-Varilla remembered, but confirm that a tacit message was sent and received.

275 **"under proper circumstances"** TR on 15 Sept. 1903, qu. in Moore, "Autobiography."

275 **In the same spirit** TR, *Letters*, vol. 3, 628. TR also told Shaw that he had rejected as "underhand" a proposal in early September "to foment the secession of Panama." He did not elaborate.

275 **John D. Long could** Quoted in *Literary Digest*, 24 Oct. 1903; TR, *Letters*, vol. 3, 628–29, 631–32.

276 **Another article** *Literary Digest*, 3 Oct. 1903. See also Bunau-Varilla, *Panama*, 298–301.

276 **demolished Watterson's** Bunau-Varilla, *Panama*, 299–301.

276 **Watterson was reduced** New York *Sun*, 28 Sept. 1903; Bunau-Varilla, *Panama*, 301.

276 MANUEL AMADOR GUERRERO *Story of Panama*, 29–30; Parks, *Colombia and the United States*, 135; Philippe Bunau-Varilla, interviewed by Howard K. Beale, July 1936 (HKB).

276 **A more realistic** Bunau-Varilla had been warned by Herbert G. Squire, an intimate of Mark Hanna, not to count on the President unless there was a revolution in Panama. "TR cannot go to the electorate with a record of having broken the law." Philippe Bunau-Varilla, interviewed by Howard K. Beale, July 1936 (HKB). See also Bunau-Varilla, *Panama*, 312.

276 **Amador said that** Bunau-Varilla, *Panama*, 313.

276 **"I can provide"** Miner, *Fight for the Panama Route*, 357; Bunau-Varilla, *From Panama to Verdun*, 135.

276 **Downtown, as the** *Story of Panama*, 282; Fletcher, "Canal Site Diplomacy," 158.

277 YOUR VIRILE William Nelson Cromwell to TR, 14 Oct. 1903 (TRP).

277 BUNAU-VARILLA, **having** This section is based on Bunau-Varilla, *Panama*, 318–22. See also McCullough, *Path Between the Seas*, 354–55, and DuVal, *Cadiz to Cathay*, 310–11.

277 THAT NIGHT, **two** White House appointment book, 16 Oct. 1903 (TRP). *Story of Panama*, 367–68. See TR to Elihu Root, 14 Mar. 1903, and Samuel M. B. Young to Elihu Root, 24 Dec. 1903 (ER). The following account is based on Chauncey B. Humphrey, "History of the Revolution of Panama," unpublished ms., 5 Jan. 1923, copy in the files of the Theodore Roosevelt Association, Oyster Bay, N.Y. Supplementary details from *Story of Panama*, 367–68, and Miner, *Fight for the Panama Route*, 353–54. According to Humphrey, TR read an early draft of his ms. while still in the White House, and praised his vital role in the revolution.

278 **They confirmed** TR, *Works*, vol. 18, 428ff.; this crossing occurred on 16 Sept. 1903; Obaldía's party felt that the United States would "undoubtedly adopt the Nicaragua route." Humphrey, "History of the Revolution."

278 **He and Murphy** Humphrey, "History of the Revolution."

278 **Casting aside his** Ibid.

278 **Humphrey had declined** Ibid.

278 **"There goes our"** Grayson M.-P. Murphy, interviewed by Henry Pringle, 2 Apr. 1930 (HP).

278 ROOSEVELT SPENT White House appointment book, 17 Oct. 1903 (TRP); Putnam, *Memories of a Publisher*, 145–47.

278 **On Monday, crisp cables** TR, *Presidential Addresses and State Papers*, vol. 2,

726; DuVal, *Cadiz to Cathay,* 312–13; John Nikol and Francis Holbrook, "Naval Operations in the Panama Revolution of 1903," *American Neptune* 38 (Oct. 1977); *Story of Panama,* 429.

279 **In coincidental, yet** *Story of Panama,* 664; Morris, *Rise of Theodore Roosevelt,* 629–31.

279 **On 23 October** TR, *Letters to Kermit,* 45.

279 **On 26 October** *Story of Panama,* 380; DuVal, *Cadiz to Cathay,* 279; Miner, *Fight for the Panama Route,* 360–61.

279 **On 27 October** *Story of Panama,* 328–29; McCullough, *Path Between the Seas,* 361–62; Documents, 22 Oct. 1903, in PBV.

279 **"The only dangerous"** Bunau-Varilla, *Panama,* 324.

279 **Judging from his** Ibid., 323, 327.

280 FATE NEWS BAD Manuel Amador to Philippe Bunau-Varilla, 29 Oct. 1903, original in PBV.

280 **Some of it** Bunau-Varilla, *Panama,* 328.

280 **He was being asked** Ibid., 329.

280 **Francis B. Loomis** Bunau-Varilla, interviewed by Howard K. Beale, July 1936 (HKB); Fletcher, "Canal Site Diplomacy," 165; *Story of Panama,* 331.

280 **Riding back to New York** *Story of Panama,* 381.

280 **Newspapers aboard** *The New York Times,* 29 Oct. 1903; DuVal, *Cadiz to Cathay,* 313–14. Although he does not say so, Bunau-Varilla might have been told by Loomis that the *Nashville* had just been given (or was about to be given) its secret order to proceed at full speed to Colón. The gunboat left Kingston the following morning, Saturday, 31 Oct. Chauncey B. Humphrey states that "about Oct. 31," he heard that two Colombian battalions were on their way to relieve the garrison guard in Panama City. "I . . . informed President Roosevelt what would happen [a revolution]. He sent immediately the gunboat *Nashville* with 450 marines to Colon to prevent the landing of these two battalions." In the event, only one battalion arrived. *The New York Times,* 1 Nov. 1903; Humphrey, "History of the Revolution." See also McCullough, *Path Between the Seas,* 360.

280 ALL RIGHT Bunau-Varilla, *Panama,* 332; Fletcher, "Canal Site Diplomacy," 165–66.

280 *Ton and a half* On this day, Hay cabled Beaupré suggesting that he take "a leave of absence" from Bogotá. *Foreign Relations 1903,* 218.

280 ROOSEVELT SWATTED James Garfield diary, 29 Oct. 1903 (JRG).

281 **It was his habit** Lodge, *Selections,* vol. 2, 60–61; *Review of Reviews,* Dec. 1903.

281 **In New York** Pringle, *Theodore Roosevelt,* 339–40; Leupp, *The Man Roosevelt,* 147–55; Mark Hanna to George Perkins, ca. early Oct. 1903 (GWP); TR, *Letters,* vol. 3, 640. There is much criticism in the correspondence of Charles Francis Adams and James Wilson of TR's factional fence-straddling. Wilson, showing remarkable disloyalty for a Cabinet officer, complained on 14 Oct., "In New York he is a [Thomas] Platt man, in Pennsylvania a Quay man, and in Delaware [a John] Addicks man, and that is all there is of it" (JHW).

281 **At least there was** *The Washington Post,* 16 Oct. 1903; Tilchin, *Theodore Roosevelt,* 46–48. Ambrose Bierce's *The Cynic's Word Book* (New York, 1906), carried this definition of *boundary:* "In political geography, an imaginary line between two nations, separating the imaginary rights of one from the imaginary rights of the other."

281 **"I think you are"** Lodge, *Selections,* vol. 2, 60–61. Justice Oliver Wendell Holmes, Jr., wrote to congratulate him on scoring "a personal triumph." Holmes to TR, 21 Oct. 1903 (TRP).

281 *Master of human* A Collection of the Writings of John James Ingalls (Kansas City, Mo., 1902), 97. See also Hale, *Week in the White House,* 10.

282 **Whatever happened** TR, *Autobiography*, 526. TR told Jules Jusserand around this time that he would force canal construction "even if war resulted." Jules Jusserand to Théophile Delcassé, 17 Nov. 1903 (JJ). See also Friedlander, "Reassessment."

282 ALL DAY LONG Amador had been warned of the troopship's probable arrival by Governor Obaldía. McCullough, *Path Between the Seas*, 362.

282 **In a series** *Story of Panama*, 382.

282 **The coordinated grace** Nikol and Holbrook, "Naval Operations"; Bunau-Varilla, *Panama*, 334.

282 **the *junta* had postponed** *Story of Panama*, 382.

282 **Now the plot was** The Governor's acquiescence was taken for granted, since he lived in Amador's house. Clapp, *Forgotten First Citizen*, 314; *Story of Panama*, 385; McCullough, *Path Between the Seas*, 369.

282 **General Esteban Huertas** Huertas has been disparaged by historians because he accepted a bribe of sixty-five thousand dollars, wore a large number of feathers, and stood not much taller than his own sword. But he was strong-willed and principled enough to give the *junta* many anxious moments. See DuVal, *Cadiz to Cathay*, 321–22, 331.

282 **Huertas's battalion** Ibid., 337, 327, 307–8, 277–79; *Story of Panama*, 382–84.

283 PREVENT LANDING Miner, *Fight for the Panama Route*, 361–62. The *Dixie* received an identical cable.

283 **A similar order** *Story of Panama*, 383; *Foreign Relations 1903*, 236; McCullough, *Path Between the Seas*, 364.

283 **He was awakened** The following timings of TR's day are taken from news items covering his trip in Presidential scrapbook (TRP).

283 **Commander Hubbard sent** John Hubbard to William H. Moody, 8 Nov. 1903 (TRP); *Story of Panama*, 380, 387, 430.

283 **agreed that at all** *Story of Panama*, 388; Shaler had already transferred most of his available passenger cars to the other end of the line. McCullough, *Path Between the Seas*, 363.

283 **Hubbard's problem was** John Hubbard to William H. Moody, 8 Nov. 1903 (TRP); *Story of Panama*, 430. The number of *tiradores* was underestimated in some official communications during the day.

283 **Simultaneously, Roosevelt** Washington *Evening Star*, 3 Nov. 1903.

284 **Another, very short** Fletcher, "Canal Site Diplomacy," 166; *Story of Panama*, 340–41. The author assumes that the Panamanian jungle was as luxuriant in Nov. 1903 as it was when he crossed the Isthmus on this same railroad in 1980.

Note: Señora Amador, wife of the revolutionary leader, has been credited with the idea of separating Tovar from his troops. But Humphrey, "History of the Revolution," states that he suggested it to Ricardo Arango when plotting the revolution in early October.

284 THE PRESIDENT VOTED New York *Sun*, 4 Nov. 1903; Kerr, *Bully Father*, 134.

285 **After about a half** Kerr, *Bully Father*, 135. The "desolate emotions" referred to are conveyed not just between the lines of the letters TR wrote about this visit, but in his idiosyncratic use of the word *homesickness*. Since childhood, when a photograph of Edith Carow possessed him with "homesickness and longing for the past," he tended to conflate both emotions into a general sense of *temps perdu*. Morris, *Rise of Theodore Roosevelt*, 54.

285 AS ROOSEVELT DID SO Hubbard received his orders (misdirected to another boat in Colón harbor) at 10:30 A.M. TR came down from Sagamore Hill around that time, and left Oyster Bay at 11:15 A.M. John Hubbard to William H. Moody, 8 Nov. 1903 (TRP).

285 **The *tiradores* did** *The Washington Post*, 4 Nov. 1903; John Hubbard to William

670 • NOTES

H. Moody, 8 Nov. 1903 (TRP). Hubbard's cable, described as "mutilated" in *Story of Panama*, 289, appears to have been garbled in transmission. See Nikol and Holbrook, "Naval Operations."

285 **A certain lack** *Story of Panama*, 390; John Hubbard to William H. Moody, 8 Nov. 1903 (TRP). The *junta* had decided to advance the time of revolution to five o'clock that afternoon. Washington *Evening Star*, 4 Nov. 1903; DuVal, *Cadiz to Cathay*, 325.

285 **He cast his mind** TR, *Letters*, vol. 3, 642. The catalog of TR's reading in the following pages is taken from his letter to Butler, reproduced in *Letters*, vol. 3, 641–44.

285 **Sophocles' *Seven Against*** Actually Aeschylus.

286 REVOLUTION IMMINENT *Foreign Relations 1903*, 235. This telegram arrived at 2:35 P.M.

286 **Washington was ill** Ibid., 231; *Story of Panama*, 393.

286 **Governor Obaldía had** *Story of Panama*, 392–93.

287 **Lady Gregory's and** TR slightly misspelled some of his Irish citations (e.g., *Turin* for *Tuirean*). The Gregory and Hull titles are separate books, respectively *Cuchulain of Muirthemne* and *The Cuchullin Saga in Irish Literature*.

287 WHEN ELISEO TORRES *Story of Panama*, 440–41.

287 **Torres waxed more** Ibid.

288 **"I would be willing"** TR, *Letters*, vol. 3, 643.

288 FIVE O'CLOCK CAME *Story of Panama*, 395. Prescott had indeed been involved in revolutionary plotting since the birth of the *junta*. McCullough, *Path Between the Seas*, 342.

288 **Subsequent calls** *Story of Panama*, 394–95; John Hubbard to William H. Moody, 8 Nov. 1903 (TRP).

288 **One of their first** *Story of Panama*, 396.

288 **"Of course I have"** TR, *Letters*, vol. 3, 643–44.

288 **He dozed off** *The Washington Post*, 4 Nov. 1903; Presidential scrapbook (TRP).

289 **Refusing comment** Washington *Evening Star*, 3 Nov. 1903; *The Washington Post*, 4 Nov. 1903.

289 UPRISING OCCURRED *Foreign Relations 1903*, 231. The word *Barranquilla* refers to the troopship's port of origin.

289 **Roosevelt sent at once** Washington *Evening Star* and New York *Sun*, 4 Nov. 1903, clips in John Hay scrapbook (JH). There is hour-by-hour newspaper coverage of the revolution in this archive. The Panama dispatches to the New York *Herald* (written by the brother of a *junta* member) seem to have been especially valued by Hay, who annotated many of them.

289 **All the more** *Foreign Relations 1903*, 236.

289 **But "reason" of** Washington *Evening Star*, 4 Nov. 1903.

290 **For NASHVILLE** White House telegraph copy (unsigned), 3 Nov. 1903 (TRP). News of the instructions was leaked to the New York *Sun*.

290 **By 10:30 P.M.** *Story of Panama*, 440. A similar cable, almost directly quoting the White House draft, was sent out at 11:18 by Darling (399).

290 **The *Atlanta* had** Nikol and Holbrook, "Naval Operations."

290 **Up Pennsylvania Avenue** *The Washington Post* and Washington *Evening Star*, 4 Nov. 1903. Myron T. Herrick had been elected Governor of Ohio in a convincing victory for Hanna Republicans. The result was an immediate resurgence of the Hanna for President movement among GOP conservatives. *The Washington Post*, 5 Nov. 1903.

290 **The White House** DuVal, *Cadiz to Cathay*, 330; *Story of Panama*, 397. At 12:10 P.M., Loomis ordered Ehrman to inform the captain of the gunboat *Bogotá* "plainly" that the United States, mindful of her responsibility to maintain peace

and free transit across the Isthmus, requested him to hold any future fire. *Foreign Relations 1903*, 232.

290 **Commander Hubbard, by** *Story of Panama*, 441, 656; John Hubbard to James Shaler, and copy to Eliseo Torres, 4 Nov. 1903 (TRP). The two-way effect of Hubbard's order has been downplayed by historians seeking to blame the Roosevelt Administration for fomenting the separation of Panama (see Friedlander, "Reassessment"). While the ban on military movement undoubtedly strengthened the *junta*'s hold on Panama City, it worked to Colombia's advantage in Colón. Rebel forces, which outnumbered Colonel Torres's battalion three to one, were prevented from crossing and bloodily completing the work of revolution.

291 **Torres reacted with** *Story of Panama*, 441.

291 **The mid-morning train** John Hubbard to William H. Moody, 5 Nov. 1903 (TRP); *Story of Panama*, 439, 441.

291 **Torres went in** John Hubbard to William H. Moody, 5 Nov. 1903 (TRP).

291 **"war against the"** Ibid., and 8 Nov. 1903 (TRP).

291 **Undeterred, Torres's** John Hubbard to William H. Moody, 5 Nov. 1903 (TRP).

291 **IN WASHINGTON, the** TR, *Letters*, vol. 3, 437; Oliver Wendell Holmes, Jr., to TR, 24 Oct. 1903, and White House appointment book, 4 Nov. 1903 (TRP). Privately, as an old soldier, Holmes admitted that he came "devilishly near to believing that might makes right." For a revisionist view of the great Justice, see Albert W. Alschuler, *Law Without Values: The Life, Work, and Legacy of Justice Holmes* (Chicago, 2000), importantly countered by Jeffrey Rosen in *The New York Times Book Review*, 17 Dec. 2000.

291 **In New York** Bunau-Varilla, *Panama*, 324.

292 **"With all the"** *Story of Panama*, 446–47; Bunau-Varilla, *Panama*, 344–46. As things turned out, the rest of Bunau-Varilla's money was neither sent nor needed. See Charles D. Ameringer, "Philippe Bunau-Varilla: New Light on the Panama Canal Treaty," *Hispanic-American Historical Review* 46.1 (1966).

292 **COLONEL TORRES, closeted** *Story of Panama*, 443–44; John Hubbard to William H. Moody, 5 Nov. 1903 (TRP).

292 **Colonel Shaler undertook** *Story of Panama*, 444.

292 **A state of unnatural** DuVal, *Cadiz to Cathay*, 342; *Foreign Relations 1903*, 237.

292 **And in New York** Grenville and Young, *Politics, Strategy, and American Diplomacy*, 311. There is some evidence that TR, or at least Moody, had contemplated a punitive strike against Colombia nine days earlier. On 26 Oct. 1903, the Navy Department sent TR draft instructions for an attack on Cartagena by the Caribbean Squadron. Ibid., 310.

292 **COLONEL HUBBARD WENT** John Hubbard to William H. Moody, 8 Nov. 1903 (TRP).

293 **To popular relief** *Story of Panama*, 452–57; DuVal, *Cadiz to Cathay*, 335.

293 **Just then, at 7:05** Captain Delano (Officer Commanding, *Dixie*) to William H. Moody, 6 Nov. 1903 (TRP); *Story of Panama*, 458. The next morning, the *Atlanta* arrived, bringing United States strength in Colón to one thousand men. General Tovar and his staff were, under escort, sent back to Colombia on 12 Nov. Bishop, *Theodore Roosevelt*, vol. 2, 286.

293 **ROOSEVELT'S CABINET MEETING** *Washington Times*, 6 Nov. 1903; *Story of Panama*, 463, 467; *Foreign Relations 1903*, 239. The Frenchman's appointment was officially upgraded to "minister plenipotentiary" that evening. Bunau-Varilla, *Panama*, 348–49.

293 **There was no doubt** Bunau-Varilla, *Panama*, 349.

293 **Roosevelt and Hay** Friedlander, "Reassessment," rejects suggestions by John Hay's biographers that the Secretary was less than happy with TR's Panama policy in 1903. He quotes, e.g., Hay to John Ford Rhodes, 8 Dec. 1903: "It is hard for me

to understand how anyone can criticize our action in Panama. . . . I had no hesitation as to the proper course to take, and have had no doubt of the propriety of it since." Elihu Root was likewise supportive, insisting as late as 1931, "I have always felt that [Roosevelt's] action was right." Jessup, *Elihu Root*, vol. 1, 403.

293 **Questions were being** *The Times* (London), 5 Nov. 1903.

293 **Roosevelt did not feel** TR, "How the United States Acquired the Right to Dig the Panama Canal," *Outlook*, 7 Oct. 1911; TR, *Autobiography*, 538. In 1887, the historian George Bancroft, revered by TR, had predicted that either an international consortium, or the United States alone, "as the power most interested" in safeguarding Panama as a neutral transit zone, would elbow Colombia aside and assume "whole control for the benefit of all nations." DuVal, *Cadiz to Cathay*, 130.

293 **Colombia was clearly** Parks, *Colombia and the United States*, 406. While TR pondered his recognition decision, he very likely heard from Senator Morgan the comment of a Colombian general, just before the treaty was rejected: "It is ridiculous for the Americans to be treating with Colombia now, when we have to wait only a few years, until the French concession expires, [to] make you pay seventy, eighty, or one hundred millions." Qu. in F. F. Whitteken to John T. Morgan, 2 Nov. 1903 (JTM).

293 **"most just and proper"** TR, *Works*, vol. 20, 485.

294 THE PEOPLE OF PANAMA *Story of Panama*, 463–64.

294 ROOSEVELT ADJOURNED Straus, *Under Four Administrations*, 174–75. The question of American moral obligations had long plagued policymakers. As far back as 1864, Attorney General Edward Bates deplored the 1846 treaty, with its guarantee of Isthmian rights and sovereignty to "New Granada," as a mockery of "the wise and cautious policy of the fathers of this Republic." But since the treaty was a fait accompli, Bates felt that "honesty and good faith require us to fulfill it." He hoped that the United States would never again commit herself to "such dangerous intermeddling in the affairs of foreign nations." Qu. in Philander Knox, "Sovereignty over the Isthmus, as Affecting the Canal," 1903 memorandum (PCK).

294 **Straus suggested** TR, *Letters*, vol. 3, 648–49.

294 **Roosevelt seized** Ibid. "Your 'covenant running with the land' idea worked admirably," TR wrote Moore on 12 Nov. 1903 (TRP).

294 **That evening** *Story of Panama*, 469; copy of Hay statement, 7 Nov. 1903, in TRP.

294 **Professor John Bassett** John Bassett Moore to Oscar Straus, 11 Nov. 1903; Straus, *Under Four Administrations*, 175. Notwithstanding accusations of unseemly haste, TR did not formally recognize Panama until 13 Nov. 1903. As Moore explained to the public, he at first "merely recognized *de facto* authorities on the spot. . . . It is not an uncommon thing to recognize and hold intercourse with such authorities, pending the determination of the question of formal recognition." New York *Evening Post*, 11 Nov. 1903.

CHAPTER 19: THE IMAGINATION OF THE WICKED

295 *A man can be* Dunne, *Mr. Dooley's Philosophy*, 179.

295 **"This mad plunge"** New York *Evening Post*, 7 Nov. 1903.

295 **"It is the most"** Ibid. It was probably around this time that TR, hearing that Villard was circulating a story about Kaiser Wilhelm's ability to dismantle and reconstruct a complex Edison phonograph, ejaculated in his highest falsetto, "I *wish* that somebody would take Oswald Villard to pieces and forget to put him together again!" Villard, *Fighting Years*, 153.

296 **"Nations must strike"** Albert H. Walker to New York *Evening Post*, 10 Nov.

1903, copy in PCK. For modern historical comment, supportive of TR's Panama policy in 1903, see also Collin, "Big Stick," 302–6, 312; Friedlander, "Reassessment"; and Marks, *Velvet on Iron*, 97–105.

296 **"Nothing that Alexander"** Presidential scrapbook (TRP).

296 **However, 75** *Public Opinion*, 19 Nov. 1903; *Literary Digest*, 21 and 14 Nov. 1903; Washington *Evening Star*, 6 Nov. 1903.

296 **South American reactions** "Latin American Views of Panama and the Canal," *Review of Reviews*, Mar. 1904. See also John Patterson, "Latin American Reactions to the Panama Revolution of 1903," *Hispanic America Historical Review* 24 (1944), and E. Bradford Burns, "The Recognition of Panama by the Major Latin American States," *Americas* 26 (1969).

297 **"We have converted"** Article by "Santander A. Galofre," ca. Dec. 1903, sent to Philippe Bunau-Varilla (PBV).

297 **In Europe, as in** *The Times*, undated clipping in John Hay scrapbook (JH); Leipzig *Grenzboten*, qu. in *Literary Digest*, 26 Dec. 1903.

297 **A British visitor** Henry W. Lucy, *Sixty Years in the Wilderness* (London, 1924), 214.

Historical Note: TR's difficulties with public opinion in the aftermath of the Panama Revolution were complicated by a brief, but intense, war scare on the Isthmus. The concentration of United States warships continued as planned until, by 15 Nov., two walls of American armor effectively denied Colombia sea access to her former department. Panama City was defended by the *Boston* (7 Nov.), *Marblehead* (10 Nov.), *Concord* (10 Nov.), and *Wyoming* (13 Nov.). Several of these gunboats patrolled the new Republic's coasts, extending the limits of protection to both eastern and western borders. Colombia, meanwhile, sent a special mission to Panama, under General Rafael Reyes, with a view toward settling differences and reuniting. The *junta* refused to let Reyes land at Colón, whereupon John Hay asked that he be given "a courteous reception and considerate hearing" offshore. On 19 Nov., Reyes met with *junta* representatives aboard a French steamer. He offered them many concessions humiliating to his government, but they declared the Panama revolution to be "irrevocable." Reyes sailed north to plead, equally vainly, for an indemnity from Washington. On 3 Dec., reports that Colombian forces were advancing into Panama reached the White House. Secretary Moody ordered the *Prairie* from Guantánamo to Colón with a detachment of Marines to complement the *Dixie*'s. On 15 Dec., another detachment from the *Atlanta* tracked down a force of two thousand Colombian soldiers in Darien. Moody responded with further deployments. These actions provoked such antiwar and anticanal sentiment on Capitol Hill that TR, alarmed, ordered a radical change in policy on 21 Dec. Overriding both Moody and Root, he confined American and naval activities on the Isthmus to the canal zone only, and insisted on unaggressive behavior. "If there should come a brush with Colombia, I want to be dead sure that Colombia fires first." (TR to Moody, 21 Dec. 1903 [TRP]). By the new year, Panama's own defenses were strong enough for further reduction of United States forces. Sporadic threats of Colombian invasion continued through Jan. 1904, but when Commander Hubbard of the *Nashville* visited Cartagena on the thirty-first, he was received with resigned goodwill. Bogotá, it seemed, had accepted the inevitable. For detailed accounts, see DuVal, *Cadiz to Cathay*, chap. 15, and Nikol and Holbrook, "Naval Operations." The latter conclude: "The Navy was used by [the] Roosevelt Administration as a defensive weapon, not aggressively, in the 'taking' of Panama. The Administration made it clear to the Colombians that the Navy was defending Panama's coast and the Transit and then left it up to Colombia to force the issue."

297   ON 13 NOVEMBER White House diary (TRP); the most scholarly assessment of Bunau-Varilla's brief ministry is Ameringer, "Philippe Bunau-Varilla."

297   "It is necessary" Bunau-Varilla, *Panama*, 366. For the texts of the formal exchanges, see *Foreign Relations 1903*, 245–46.

297   Afterward, with Hay Bunau-Varilla, interviewed by Howard K. Beale, July 1936 (HKB); Bunau-Varilla, *From Panama to Verdun*, 154, 157.

297   "I shall send" Ameringer, "Philippe Bunau-Varilla"; *Foreign Relations 1903*, 235; DuVal, *Cadiz to Cathay*, 379; Bunau-Varilla, *Panama*, 157. According to Bunau-Varilla, he warned Hay, "After I go, you will have to deal with Panamanian lawyers, who are Colombian lawyers." Hay's own simile for negotiating with Latin Americans was "like holding a squirrel in your lap." Bunau-Varilla, interviewed by Howard K. Beale, July 1936 (HKB); DuVal, *Cadiz to Cathay*, 384.

297   What Bunau-Varilla Bunau-Varilla, *Panama*, 368; DuVal, *Cadiz to Cathay*, 379–80, 384. For the proffered text, see Ameringer, "Philippe Bunau-Varilla."

298   Working through the Bunau-Varilla, *Panama*, 370–75; Fowler, *John Coit Spooner*, 281; DuVal, *Cadiz to Cathay*, 382.

298   The Secretary was Bunau-Varilla, *Panama*, 376.

298   Conscious that Dr. Amador Bunau-Varilla, *From Panama to Verdun*, 159.

298   BUNAU-VARILLA WAS Bunau-Varilla, *Panama*, 378. Although Bunau-Varilla, who was more than slightly paranoiac, believed that the delegation had come to supplant him, he was empowered to act as he did. See the Panamanian dispatches qu. in Ameringer, "Philippe Bunau-Varilla." On the other hand, Amador had reason to be shocked and enraged. They had brought with them studies of "important points of the treaty from the viewpoint of Panama," and felt that they had the right to advise him in negotiating it on their behalf. Bunau-Varilla's hasty and flawed convention caused permanent damage to United States–Panama relations. See also DuVal, *Cadiz to Cathay*, 380–85.

298   Amador reeled Bunau-Varilla, *Panama*, 378.

298   Congress had convened On 9 Nov. 1903.

298   The dragging, eighteen-month For TR's second (10 Nov. 1903) Special Message to Congress on Cuban reciprocity, see TR, *Presidential Addresses and State Papers*, vol. 2, 645–48.

        Chronological Note: Due to an aggressive investment and lobbying strategy, the American Sugar Refining Company had managed in 1903 to consolidate all domestic sugar interests behind the treaty. Amid cries that opponents of reciprocity had "sold out" to the "sugar trust," the House overwhelmingly approved the treaty on 19 Nov., and the Senate followed suit on 16 Dec. Healy, *United States in Cuba*, 205–6.

299   Thanks to the "Speaker Cannon: A Character Sketch," *Review of Reviews*, Dec. 1903.

299   On 19 November *Literary Digest*, 21 Nov. and 5 Dec. 1903.

299   Cannon pointed out *Review of Reviews*, Jan. 1904; Walter Wellman in Philadelphia *Press*, 7 Dec. 1903.

299   MARK HANNA, who Hamilton Fish to TR, 21 Nov. 1903 (TRP).

299   His uncharacteristic Croly, *Marcus Alonzo Hanna*, 440–41; George Cortelyou to John Bassett Moore, 18 Apr. 1906 (JBM); Mrs. Hanna, interviewed by J. B. Morrow, 1 Nov. 1905 (MHM); Presidential scrapbook (TRP); *The Washington Post*, 5 Nov. 1903; *Literary Digest*, 5 Dec. 1903; George Cortelyou, interviewed by J. B. Morrow, 18 Apr. 1906 (MHM).

299   Morgan, no less Dawes, *Journal of the McKinley Years*, 362; Hamilton Fish to

TR, 21 Nov. 1903 (TRP); Matthew Quay to TR, 26 Oct. 1903 (TRP); Sullivan, *Our Times*, vol. 1, 598; E. H. Crowder to TR, 14 Oct. 1903; and W. A. Wadsworth to TR, 10 Dec. 1903 (TRP); New York *Evening Post*, 10 Dec. 1903; Rhodes, *McKinley and Roosevelt*, 281; Mayer, *Republican Party*, 284.

300 **When the Senator** Mrs. Hanna, interviewed by J. B. Morrow, 1 Nov. 1905 (MHM).

300 **"You can say"** New York *World*, ca. 27 Nov. 1903, in Presidential scrapbook (TRP).

300 **Roosevelt wished** *Review of Reviews*, Jan. 1903; Mark Hanna to George Perkins, 7 Dec. 1903 (GWP). Hagedorn, *Leonard Wood*, vol. 2, 378–79.

300 **In a last-minute** White House diary, 4 Dec. 1903 (TRP); TR, *Letters*, vol. 3, 664; Mark Hanna to TR, 5 Dec. 1903 (TRP); Washington *Evening Star*, 5 Dec. 1903; *Washington Times*, 6 Dec. 1903; Presidential scrapbook (TRP).

300 **Hoar began to** Shelby M. Cullom, *Fifty Years of Public Service* (Chicago, 1911), 213. Senator Cullom was an eyewitness to this interview.

300 **"I think," Philander** Knox qu. by TR in Schoonover, "Max Farrand's Memorandum." See also Lawrence F. Abbott, *Impressions of Theodore Roosevelt* (New York, 1919), 139; Jessup, *Elihu Root*, vol. 1, 414. In a speech draft ca. May 1914, Senator Knox expressed mature misgivings about TR's action in Panama. He agreed with Root that the United States was treaty-bound to be "passive" in any domestic revolution in Colombia, and "active" in maintaining Isthmian transit. But the fact remained that by behaving so in 1903, "serious damage resulted to Colombia, and corresponding benefits accrued to us." Quite apart from financial gains, the United States got "sovereignty and jurisdiction over a 10-mile zone in a dependent country as against a qualified right to occupy a 6-mile zone in an arrogant, if not unfriendly country." The American government therefore had a "moral" right to compensate Colombia "not for what she lost but what we gained." Acknowledging TR's famous bluster of 23 Mar. 1911, Knox agreed that "The fact is we *practically* [*sic*] took Panama. We did not take it from Colombia, we took it from the Panamans, and this is the only sense in which that statement is true" (PCK).

301 **Both men rallied** *Opinion* copy, 1903 (PCK); Elihu Root interviewed by Philadelphia *Press*, 2 Dec. 1903; New York *Herald*, 6 Dec. 1903; *Washington Times*, 7 Dec. 1903; Kelly Miller, "Roosevelt and the Negro" (pamphlet, ca. 1907, in Pratt Collection [TRB]), 8.

301 **"Whenever I see"** See Charles Dickens, *The Pickwick Papers*, chap. 30.

301 *I AM ENABLED* TR, *Works*, vol. 15, 235. See DuVal, *Cadiz to Cathay*, 386–95, and Bunau-Varilla, *Panama*, 387–408, for an account of the treaty's rapid, if reluctant, ratification by the Panamanian *junta*.

301 **He reviewed United States** TR, *Works*, vol. 15, 241–43.

301 **For more than half** Ibid., vol. 13, 697.

302 **"Yes, and the"** Ibid., 698.

302 **The President proceeded** TR, *Presidential Addresses and State Papers*, vol. 2, 700–704.

302 **"Under such circumstances"** Ibid., 706–7.

302 **"I don't know"** *The New York Times*, 8 Dec. 1903.

302 **"For the first time"** Ibid., 10 Dec. 1903.

303 *It is the hour* See TR to Benjamin I. Wheeler, 8 Dec. 1903 (TRP). "When the chance does come," TR had said of opportunity in 1899, "only the great man can see it instantly and use it aright." TR, *Works*, vol. 13, 420.

303 **"In this Panama"** TR, *Letters*, vol. 3, 652, 662–63.

303 **He kept such** Charles W. Dick, interviewed by J. B. Morrow, 10 Feb. 1906 (MHM); Croly, *Marcus Alonzo Hanna*, 435. For an example of the sort of alarming advisories

TR was getting at this time, see W. A. Wadsworth's letter to him of 1 Dec. 1903: "Things do not look just right. . . . Some of your political 'friends' in New York . . . are working like beavers [to ensure] that no mistake you have made or are making is lost. . . . There seems to be a systematic attempt to work up a public opinion that you . . . are liable to go off at half cock and endanger business interests" (TRP).

303 *Washington, Dec. 9* Philadelphia *Press,* 10 Dec. 1903 (italics added).

304 **Wellman said** Ibid.

304 **"He might wreck"** Ibid.

304 **"Mr. President, I"** *The Washington Post,* 12 Dec. 1903.

304 **He and Roosevelt stood** Washington *Evening Star,* 11 Dec. 1903; *The Washington Post,* 12 Dec. 1903. The following dialogue is taken from the latter source. See also Moore, *Roosevelt and the Old Guard,* 87.

304 **"I have sat"** Gamaliel: in the New Testament, a legendary leader of the Sanhedrin and teacher.

304 **Two days later** New York *Herald,* 13 Dec. 1903; Moore, *Roosevelt and the Old Guard,* 85. See also *The New York Times,* 12 Dec. 1903, *Public Opinion,* 17 Dec. 1903, and "The Passing of the Hanna Boom," *Review of Reviews,* Jan. 1904.

304 **ON 14 DECEMBER** *The Washington Post,* 16 Dec. 1903; New York *Press,* 17 Dec. 1903; Eitler, "Philander Chase Knox," 76–80. A veteran court reporter called it "the strongest address made before the Supreme Court for years." W. W. Jermane in Minneapolis *Journal,* 16 Dec. 1903. See also Barry, *Forty Years,* 250, for the reactions of Court members.

305 **All the world's** Britain announced on 24 Dec., Japan on 28 Dec. 1903. By the end of Feb. 1904, Panama was universally recognized except by Colombia.

305 **G. P. Putnam's Sons** TR to George Haven Putnam, 26 Nov. and 21 Dec. 1903 (TRP). According to the Economic History Services website (www.eh.net/hmit), thirty thousand dollars in 1903 was the equivalent of about $580,000 today. TR's two windfalls therefore netted him the modern equivalent of well over one million dollars. He remained, however, the least avaricious of men. On 5 Dec., he wrote Douglas Robinson that he thought James K. Gracie had been too generous to him, and volunteered to turn over one third of his legacy to a female relative with four children (TRP).

305 *The Works of Theodore Roosevelt* This edition, known as the "Executive Edition," was not the first, and by no means the last. It superseded no fewer than six collections, beginning with the "Sagamore Series" in 1900. Other editions published in 1901, 1902, and 1903 varied in length and quality. The Executive Edition, which grew by two additional volumes every two years, eventually totaled twenty volumes. It was itself superseded by the "Elkhorn Edition" of 1906, which grew, by 1920, to twenty-eight volumes. Other editions continued to appear throughout TR's lifetime. *The Works of Theodore Roosevelt* achieved definitive, if rather confusing, form in 1926, when two differently arranged collections appeared: the utilitarian "National Edition" (twenty volumes) and the luxury "Memorial Edition" (twenty-four volumes). The latter set is cited in this book. For a complete *Works* bibliography, see the Memorial Edition, vol. 2, 559–63.

306 **Better than money** New York *Herald,* 13 Dec. 1903; Robinson, *My Brother,* 217.

306 **THE SEVENTEENTH OF December** Washington *Evening Star,* 17 Dec. 1903.

CHAPTER 20: INTRIGUE AND STRIVING AND CHANGE

307 *Whin he does* Dunne, *Observations by Mr. Dooley,* 225.

307 **"I was stuffed"** Adams, *Letters,* vol. 5, 538–39. The following day Adams was invited to another White House party. He sent his regrets, and stayed in bed "with a pound or two of sufonal." Ibid.

Note: Adams's letters are often written in a tone of mock suffering, for humorous effect. Nor was he beyond duplicity. He frequently caricatured men like TR and Henry Cabot Lodge in private, while praising them in public. See his contrasting account of this evening in *The Education of Henry Adams,* 464.

307 **"I am glad"** Dawes, *Journal of the McKinley Years,* 364.

308 **ON THE AFTERNOON** Except where otherwise indicated, the following paragraphs are based on the William H. Taft scrapbooks in WHT; William H. Taft to Mrs. Taft, 1 Feb. 1904 (WHT); Taft interviewed by Kate Carew in New York *World,* 28 Feb. 1904. Physical descriptions are from the Carew interview, and also from White, *Masks in a Pageant,* 329–30, and Lowry, *Washington Close-Ups,* 190. ("One pair of Mr. Taft's trousers would make two suits and a short spring overcoat for Mr. Philander Chase Knox.") Donald F. Anderson, *William Howard Taft: A Conservative's Conception of the Presidency* (Ithaca, 1968, 1973), serves as an antidote to the more reverent two-volume biography by Henry Pringle, *The Life and Times of William H. Taft* (New York, 1939).

308 **Merely to look** Sullivan, *Our Times,* vol. 3, 315–16; Wister, *Roosevelt,* 146. Taft's weight in early 1904 is given at 330 pounds by Horace D. Taft in *Memories and Opinions* (New York, 1942), 114. Taft was six feet two inches tall.

308 **he was periodically** Hoover, *Forty-Two Years in the White House,* 269. Taft's scrapbooks in WHT consist largely of souvenir menus.

308 **Yet he was not** Taft, *Memories and Opinions,* 107–8; Thompson, *Party Leaders,* 308.

308 **The Supreme Court** Taft to TR, 27 Oct. 1902 (TRP); Helen H. Taft, *Recollections of Full Years* (New York, 1914), 269.

308 **"Who do you suppose"** The story of Taft's two refusals of the Supreme Court in 1902 and 1903 is told in TR, *Letters,* vol. 3, 358–59, 368, 382–83, 407, and 413. Donald Anderson, *William Howard Taft,* 10–12, advances the theory that TR wanted to eliminate Taft as a potential rival in 1904. But Taft was surely almost as far out of the way in the Philippines as he would have been on the bench. A more plausible theory is that Elihu Root (who personally recommended the Governor as his successor) was planning for a Taft presidency in 1908, as both the logical consequence of, and conservative correction to, TR's reform-minded administration. Henry W. Taft to Taft, 10 Jan. 1903 (WHT).

309 **TWO DAYS LATER** George Cortelyou memorandum of meeting, 29 Jan. 1904 (ER); Albert Shaw, "Reminiscences" (ALS); Charles Willis Thompson in New York *Sun,* 3 Nov. 1938; Wister, *Roosevelt,* 162; Elihu Root to William H. Taft, 16 Apr. 1903 (ER).

309 **Roosevelt rambled on** George Cortelyou memorandum of meeting, 29 Jan. 1904 (ER).

309 **"I thank you"** Ibid.

309 **The following evening** Montage by Clifford Berryman in *The Washington Post,* 31 Jan. 1904; Washington *Evening Star,* 1 Feb. 1904.

309 **"How is your health"** *The Washington Post,* 16 Feb. 1904; Beer, *Hanna,* 621. "I have had quite a pull with this infernal 'grip,' " Hanna had written Myron Herrick earlier in the day. "I think it [the Gridiron dinner] will brace me up." He complained that Roosevelt had been "poisoned" against him by Senator Foraker. But he added significantly, "We must organize our full strength [in Ohio] and choose the Roosevelt delegates from among our friends" (copy in TRP).

309 **The jingling cavalrymen** Hanna occupied the entire second floor of the Arlington Hotel, on Lafayette Square. *The Washington Post,* 2 Feb. 1904; Philadelphia *Press,* 27 Mar. 1905.

309 **Day followed upon** Sir Mortimer Durand to A. S. Hardy, 4 Jan. 1904 (HMD);

Cassini, *Never a Dull Moment,* 190–92, 200; Alice Roosevelt diary, 22 Jan. 1904 (ARL).

309 **Something about Alice's** Cassini, *Never a Dull Moment,* 200.

310 **Roosevelt took a** William Sturgis Bigelow to TR, 2 Feb. 1904 (TRP); Kerr, *Bully Father,* 147; TR, *Letters,* vol. 3, 706–9; *The Washington Post,* 28 Jan. 1904; Gatewood, *Theodore Roosevelt and the Art of Controversy,* 87. The white man had been recommended by Mrs. Cox.

310 **"He is not safe"** *The New York Times,* 4 Feb. 1904; *Review of Reviews,* Mar. 1904; speech copy in GBC.

310 **When Root used** Whitelaw Reid to TR, 9 Feb. 1904 (TRP); Franklin Murphy to TR, 9 Feb. 1904, and TR to Root, 4 Feb. 1904 (ER). One week after this speech, Governor Odell of New York came out strongly for TR. "It was time to set a back fire," Root wrote TR. "I do not think that I realized how far down the disaffection had gone" (15 Feb. 1904 [TRP]).

310 **Late on the evening** George Cortelyou, interviewed by J. B. Morrow, 18 Apr. 1906 (MHM); Washington *Evening Star,* 5 Feb. 1904.

310 **"My dear Mr."** Mark Hanna to TR, 5 Feb. 1904, facsimile in Croly, *Marcus Alonzo Hanna,* 452.

310 **The Senator lay** Mrs. Hanna, interviewed by J. B. Morrow, 18 May 1905 (MHM).

311 HALF A WORLD *Foreign Relations 1904,* 413. The image of "claps of thunder" is Hay's.

311 **Minister Kogoro** John Hay diary, 11 Feb. 1904 (JH); *Foreign Relations 1904,* 32–35; Cassini, *Never a Dull Moment,* 201, 215–16; James Garfield diary, 10 Feb. 1904 (JRG); Jules Jusserand to Théophile Delcassé, 16 Feb. 1904 (JJ). Zabriskie, *American-Russian Rivalry,* 103–4, points out that not only did Washington favor Japan at this stage of the war, but that Japan, heavily financed by American loans, was in effect "fighting the battle of the United States" in the Far East. As far as the Roosevelt Administration was concerned, a victorious Japan might be easier to deal with than a victorious Russia, already "overbalancing" dangerously in Manchuria. TR, *Letters,* vol. 4, 724.

311 UNCONSCIOUS The following account of the death of Mark Hanna is based on J. B. Morrow's interviews with Mrs. Hanna (18 May 1905), John Coit Spooner (10 Mar. 1905), and George Cortelyou (18 Apr. 1906), all in MHM; medical bulletins, 12–15 Feb., in Presidential scrapbook (TRP); *The Washington Post* and Washington *Evening Star,* 12–16 Feb. 1904; and Beer, *Hanna,* 622–24.

311 **The cosmopolitan curiosity** The book TR was reading was E. de Michelis's *L'Origine degli Indo-Europei* (Turin, 1903). Its Italian text gave him much difficulty, but he read it through to the end. "I have been much impressed with it, owing to the clear grasp of the author of the . . . relations between languages and races—his understanding, for instance, that Aryan is a linguistic and not a biological term." TR, *Letters,* vol. 4, 795.

311 **He had not done** Adams, *Letters,* vol. 5, 554; John T. Flynn, "Mark Hanna: Big Business in Politics," *Scribner's,* Aug. 1933. These sources give the low estimate of Hanna's wealth. According to Alfred H. Lewis in *Saturday Evening Post,* 26 Dec. 1903, "He is worth every splinter of 30 millions."

311 **"May you soon"** Croly, *Marcus Alonzo Hanna,* 454–55.

311 **Governors, generals** TR did, however, cross the square later that night to pay his respects to Mrs. Hanna. For two modern, sympathetic assessments of the great Senator, see Harvey Ploster, "Mark Hanna and the Republican Hierarchy, 1897–1904" (M.A. thesis, University of Maryland, 1964), and Gerald W. Wolff, "Mark Hanna's Goal: American Harmony," *Ohio History* 79.3–4 (1970).

312 **By now, most** *Foreign Relations 1904*, 543–51; John Hay to Elihu Root, 12 Mar. 1904 (TD). For modern support for this view, see Friedlander, "Reassessment," and Marks, *Velvet on Iron*, 96–105.

312 **The little republic** McCullough, *Path Between the Seas*, 398; Bishop, *Theodore Roosevelt*, vol. 1, 304–5.

312 **Roosevelt and his successors** *Foreign Relations 1904*, 544. Colón and Panama City were excluded from the zone, although the United States undertook to provide their sanitation, water supply, and security services. Panamanian independence was guaranteed; compensation was fixed at a ten-million-dollar initial payment, plus annual rent of $250,000, to begin after nine years.

312 **But Bunau-Varilla** Ameringer, "Philippe Bunau-Varilla."

312 **"for the honor"** Philippe Bunau-Varilla to Manuel Amador Guerrero, 23 Feb. 1904 (PBV). Amador had been inaugurated four days before.

312 AN ENORMOUS MAP Dorwart, *Office of Naval Intelligence*, 81–82; New York *World*, 27 Feb. 1904; TR, *Letters*, vol. 4, 721; Beale, *Theodore Roosevelt*, 277.

312 **Cecil Spring Rice** Spring Rice to EKR, 29 Dec. 1903 (received 4 Feb. 1904) (TRP). During the Russo-Japanese War, Spring Rice deliberately addressed some of his more outspoken letters to EKR, in order to avoid surveillance and suspicion at either end. Morris, *Edith Kermit Roosevelt*, 286.

312 **Roosevelt, replying** TR, *Letters*, vol. 4, 760–61.

313 **"very drastic"** C. S. Mellen to TR, 19 Feb. 1904 (TRP).

313 **"All I can do"** TR, *Letters*, vol. 4, 750.

313 **During the Alaska** New York *Sun*, 15 Mar. 1904; Oliver Wendell Holmes, Jr., to TR, 19 Feb. 1904 (TRP).

313 **Justice William Rufus Day** The following short biographical sketches are based on Leon Friedman and Fred L. Israel, eds., *The Justices of the United States Supreme Court, 1789–1969: Their Lives and Major Opinions* (New York, 1969–1978), vols. 2 and 3.

313 **("the last of the")** Ibid., vol. 2, 216.

313 **By noon, the** The following account is based on a detailed story (with group portrait) in the New York *Herald*, 15 Mar. 1904, and another in the Philadelphia *Press*, same date. The decision is published in *U.S. Reports*, vol. 193, 197ff. The best analysis of the proceedings remains that of Meyer, "Northern Securities Case," chap. 8.

314 **his clear, sharp voice** Fuller described Holmes's voice as "incisive as the edge of a knife" (Novick, *Honorable Justice*, 271). The Library of Congress preserves a sound recording of Holmes broadcasting to the American people, in tones unblunted by time, on his ninetieth birthday.

314 **"No scheme or"** *U.S. Reports*, vol. 193, 320–22, 327; New York *Herald*, 15 Mar. 1904.

314 **It was five** Philander Knox scrapbook (PCK); New York *Sun*, 15 Mar. 1904. TR's other lunch guests were James Cardinal Gibbons, Austrian Ambassador Baron von Hengervár Hengelmüller, and the writer William Roscoe Thayer. Thayer, *John Hay*, vol. 2, 351.

314 **The dimensions of** Lamoreaux, *Great Merger Movement*, 169.

314 **"Great cases,"** The following quotations are from *U.S. Reports*, vol. 193, 400–411. Other details from New York *Sun* and Philadelphia *Press*, 15 Mar. 1904.

315 **"I am happy"** This was the first of the great High Court dissents for which Holmes was to become famous. "The trouble with Wendell," an exasperated Bostonian friend complained, "is that he likes to play with his mind" (M. A. De Wolfe Howe, *Justice Oliver Wendell Holmes, 1841–1882* [Cambridge, Mass., 1957–1963], vol. 1, 255). As John Blum points out, TR miscalculated in thinking Holmes a reformer. The justice was "a profound skeptic" who "deeply distrusted

popular passion." In this case, Holmes felt that most of his brethren had been carried away by the temporary, and unreasoning, antitrust mood of the times. His decision not to go along was therefore "entirely in character." Blum, *Progressive Presidents*, 35.

316 **So by a margin** Knox, after leaving the Justice Department later that year, reacted dismissively to a question about the historical significance of his *Northern Securities* suit. The case was regarded as "of surpassing importance" by the press, he said, but had proved "of less real value to the government than many others that attracted no general attention." It had been, "in a sense, a test case" (*Philadelphia Ledger*, 12 June 1904). Knox's use of the phrase *real value* reflects his essentially pragmatic nature. What mattered to TR was its *symbolic* value, reaffirming the right of a federal democracy to regulate big business. Modern historical assessments, however, tend to agree with Knox. See the cynical words of Albro Martin in *James J. Hill*, 520, or the more balanced assessments in Thorelli, *Federal Antitrust Policy*, 473–74 and 562–63. Chandler, *Visible Hand*, 499, argues that *Northern Securities* led, paradoxically, to more, not less, corporate consolidation.

316 **"I could carve"** John Hay diary, 15 Mar. 1904 (JH); Harbaugh, *Life and Times*, 161–62; Lodge, *Selections*, 518. See also Adams, *Letters*, vol. 5, 564.

316 **"I have such"** Novick, *Honorable Justice*, 272. TR was writing affectionately to Holmes again by the fall of 1904 (TR, *Letters*, vol. 4, 989). Many years later, the Justice claimed that TR "looked on my dissent as a political departure (or, I suspect, more truly, couldn't forgive anyone who stood in his way)." When these words were written, TR was dead, and Holmes's tone conveys a certain octogenarian crotchetiness. Mark De Wolfe Howe, ed., *Holmes-Pollock Letters: The Correspondence of Mr. Justice Holmes and Sir Frederick Pollock, 1874–1932* (Cambridge, Mass., 1941), vol. 2, 61–62.

316 **Knox and Taft** John Hay diary, 15 Mar. 1904 (JH); A. B. Farquhar to TR, 8 Mar. 1904 (TRP); New York *World* (front page, lead article), 15 Mar. 1904; New York *Evening Post*, 15 and 16 Mar. 1904. See the vast selection of clips in Philander Knox scrapbook (PCK); also *Literary Digest*, 26 Mar. 1904. For a sample of critical opinion, see *The New York Times*, 15 Mar. 1904.

316 **The New York World** New York *World*, 15 and 20 Mar. 1904.

316 **The three men** New York *World*, 15 Mar. 1904; Pyle, *Life of James J. Hill*, vol. 2, 377; Martin, *James J. Hill*, 519; New York *Herald*, 15 Mar. 1904; A. B. Farquhar to TR, 8 Mar. 1904 (TRP).

316 **"As far as I"** Joseph Bucklin Bishop to TR, 15 Mar. 1904 (TRP).

317 **BY 1 APRIL** John Hay diary, 19 Mar. 1904 (JH); EKR to Cecil Spring Rice, 7 Feb. 1904 (CSR); Mrs. J. Borden Harriman, *From Pinafores to Politics* (New York, 1923), 83; Gould, *Presidency of Theodore Roosevelt*, 134.

317 **"He is a very"** William H. Taft to Mrs. Taft, 18 Mar. 1904 (WHT).

317 **Even so, Roosevelt's** Adams, *Letters*, vol. 5, 554; *Literary Digest*, 2 Apr. 1904; TR, *Letters*, vol. 4, 749.

317 **It was virtually** *Literary Digest*, 2 Jan. 1904. *Santo Domingo* and *Dominican Republic* were interchangeable terms in the Roosevelt Era.

317 **"Your unlimited power"** Wilhelm II to TR, 1 Feb. 1904 (TRP).

318 **The Kaiser could** *Review of Reviews*, Mar. 1902; Julius W. Pratt, *Challenge and Rejection: The United States and World Leadership, 1900–1921* (New York, 1967), 29–30.

    Historical Note: The current situation was complicated by the fact that on 1 Feb. Santo Domingo insurgents fired upon the United States cruiser *Yankee*, killing one Marine. On 5 Feb., TR ordered Rear Admiral Wise to

proceed to Santo Domingo with cruisers of the Atlantic Squadron and protect United States citizens and property (*Review of Reviews,* Mar. 1904).
There is no direct evidence that the United States feared European interference (Italy, Britain, and Belgium were owed money as well as Germany),
but the circumstantial evidence, as with the Venezuelan crisis of
1902–1903, is suggestive. At the time of the German warship scare, the
State Department was under intense pressure from the Navy Department
to allow the Mediterranean Squadron to take part in "maneuvers" in the
Caribbean (William N. Still, *American Sea Power in the Old World: The
United States Navy in Europe and Near Eastern Waters, 1815–1917*
[Westport, Conn., 1980], 163–64). Looking back on the crisis afterward,
Elihu Root said, "We went into Santo Domingo for the sole purpose of
keeping Germany from taking it" (interview, 10 Nov. 1930 [PCJ]). Ironi-
cally, Santo Domingo's financial mess had been largely caused by an American investment firm, the Santo Domingo Investment Company, in 1903.
See Douglas R. Gow, "How Did the Roosevelt Corollary Become Linked
to the Dominican Republic?" *Mid-America* 58 (1976).

319 **"I have about"** TR, *Letters,* vol. 4, 734. TR was so pleased with this image he repeated it viva voce to his Cabinet—only then the boa constrictor was an anaconda.
John Hay diary, 18 Mar. 1904 (JH).

319 TWO MONTHS AFTER TR, *Letters,* vol. 4, 772; Jessup, *Elihu Root,* vol. 1, 419;
Gould, *Reform and Regulation,* 44; TR, *Letters,* vol. 7, 615; James O. Wheaton,
"The Genius and the Jurist: The Presidential Campaign of 1904" (Ph.D. diss., Stan-
ford University, 1964), 583; TR, *Letters,* vol. 4, 785–86.

319 **In the meantime** *The Washington Post,* 3 Mar. 1904; TR, introduction to Francis
Curtis, *History of the Republican Party* (New York, 1904); TR, *Letters,* vol. 4,
771, 773; TR, *Presidential Addresses and State Papers,* vol. 3, 5–8.

319 **Cleveland fumed with** Allan Nevins, *Grover Cleveland* (New York, 1932),
750–51. The President, unabashed, was still circulating Cleveland's letter in the
fall. See, e.g., TR to C. Riggs, editor of the New York *Sun,* 2 Sept. 1904 (TRP).

319 **"Theodore thinks of"** Adams, *Letters,* vol. 5, 570.

319 **Old Guard Republicans** James S. Clarkson to William Loeb, 5 Apr. 1904.

320 **Reluctantly, in view** Kerr, *Bully Father,* 149. Marguerite Cassini recalled that her
father, Speck von Sternburg, and Jules Jusserand were "very much worried" by the
comings and goings of mysterious Japanese visitors to the White House. Cassini,
Never a Dull Moment, 198.

320 HIS SIGNATURE FINGERS William A. Day and Charles W. Russell to Philander Knox,
26 and 28 Apr. 1904 (PCK). The extraordinary series of letters and telegrams in
Knox's papers concerning the canal-rights transfer counters the doubt expressed by
revisionist historians (e.g., Henry Pringle) as to whether the Roosevelt Administration was conscientious in obtaining good title to the Canal Zone, and in ensuring
that all payments were distributed properly.

320 **the supreme adjective** Philippe Bunau-Varilla to Poultney Bigelow, 26 Feb. 1926
(PB).

320 **"I HAVE TAKEN"** TR, *Letters,* vol. 4, 788.

320 **By terms of treaty** Miles P. DuVal, *And the Mountains Will Move* (Stanford,
1947), 136–37; TR, *Letters,* vol. 4, 770.

320 **He sent Taft** TR, *Letters,* vol. 4, 786–93; the other Commission members were
William B. Parsons, Benjamin M. Harrod, William H. Burr, Carl E. Grunsky, and
Frank J. Hecker. DuVal, *And the Mountains,* 130.

320 **Roosevelt ordered Taft** TR, *Letters,* vol. 4, 790.

321 **Sanitary reform** Ibid., 791–92.

321 ON 10 MAY Wheaton, "Genius and the Jurist," 583. The following account is based primarily on Moore, *Roosevelt and the Old Guard,* 114–17.

321 **"You might as"** Ibid., 460.

321 **Shadows stole** Ibid., 117.

321 **Senator Matthew Quay** Quay's final decline had begun on 8 May.

321 **"The last consignment"** *Review of Reviews,* June 1904; New York *Sun,* 11 May 1904.

322 **businesslike light** The names of these products are taken from contemporary magazines. The shadow-free lamp of 1903 caused a revolution in American lighting.

322 **George Cortelyou** Wheaton, "Genius and the Jurist," 267; Moore, *Roosevelt and the Old Guard,* 57–58, 70.

322 **"Go see Cortelyou"** Moore, *Roosevelt and the Old Guard,* 117.

Historiographical Note: The date of this interview cannot be established with certainty. But internal evidence proves Moore was wrong in remembering it as taking place after the death of Quay (28 May 1904). His mission on behalf of Senator Penrose must have come after Bliss's rejection of the GOP chairmanship on 10 May, and before TR's announcement of the appointment of Cortelyou on 17 May.

TR's reverence for Quay, which has often embarrassed his apologists, was perfectly in character. He owed his Vice Presidency (hence, his Presidency) to him. He also admired very strong men, even if their morals were doubtful. Quay's erudition (he introduced TR to Finnish literature) was another bond. TR was so impressed by the Senator's deathbed speech that he devoted 1,500 words of his autobiography to it. See Kehl, *Boss Rule,* 226–29, TR, *Autobiography,* 158–61, and Steffens, *Autobiography,* 419–21. For more on the death of Quay and the controversy caused by TR's description of him as "my staunch and loyal friend," see *Contemporary Literature,* July 1904.

CHAPTER 21: THE WIRE THAT RAN AROUND THE WORLD

323 **"I hope ye're"** Dunne, *Mr. Dooley's Philosophy,* 87.

323 AT SIXTY-FOUR Ion Perdicaris, "In Raisuli's Hands: The Story of My Captivity and Deliverance, 18 May to 26 June 1904," *Leslie's Monthly Magazine,* Sept. 1904.

323 **This did not** Bowen, *Recollections,* 34; *Leslie's Weekly,* 23 June 1904; *Outlook,* 11 June 1904. For the diplomatic and strategic background to the story here beginning, see William J. Hourihan, "Roosevelt and the Sultans: The United States Navy in the Mediterranean, 1904" (Ph.D. diss., Northeastern University Press, 1975).

323 **He sat there** New York *Sun,* 14 June 1904; Perdicaris, "In Raisuli's Hands"; H. E. Davis, "The Citizenship of Ion Perdicaris," *Journal of Modern History* 8 (1941); *Outlook,* 11 June 1904. Ion Perdicaris was the son of a wealthy, naturalized Greek American who was appointed United States Consul General in Athens in 1837. In 1840, just after Ion's birth in that city, Perdicaris Senior returned to the United States and made a fortune in natural-gas companies. Ion was raised and educated in Trenton, N.J. After a year at Harvard, he began his divided life on both sides of the Atlantic, writing, painting, and studying the occult. Hourihan, "Roosevelt and the Sultans," 45–47.

323 **The other male** Except where otherwise indicated, the sections of this chapter detailing the kidnapping of Ion Perdicaris are based on his own three narratives: a letter written while he was being held captive, reproduced in the New York *Sun,* 14

June 1904; "Morocco, 'The Land of the Extreme West,' and the Story of My Captivity," *National Geographic*, March 1906; and "In Raisuli's Hands." Supplemental details come from Cromwell Varley, "Captured by Moorish Brigands," *The Independent*, July 1904.

324 **Just before eleven** Samuel Gummeré to Francis B. Loomis, 20 May 1904, "Dispatches-Tangier," State Department files (NA). Gummeré was an old friend of Perdicaris from Trenton, and owed his appointment to him.

324 MR. PERDICARIS Samuel Gummeré to John Hay, 19 May 1904 (NA).

325 **Conveniently, Roosevelt** Still, *American Sea Power*, 164–65; Francis B. Loomis to Samuel Gummeré, 19 May 1904, "Instructions," State Department files (NA).

325 **The last seven** Charles H. Darling to Francis B. Loomis, 19 May 1904 (NA).

326 **"It is not"** TR, *Letters*, vol. 4, 801 (italics added).

326 **"If a nation"** Ibid.

326 **"jingoism run mad"** New York *World*, 28 May 1904; John W. Blassingame, "The Press and American Intervention in Haiti and the Dominican Republic, 1904–1920," *Caribbean Studies* 9.2 (1969); Munro, *Intervention and Dollar Diplomacy*, 65; Marks, *Velvet on Iron*, 9–10, 146–47. Douglas R. Gow, "How Did the Roosevelt Corollary?" argues that Root's first enunciation of the Corollary was a political, vote-getting gesture. But he errs in saying that it had no immediate diplomatic relevance. Walter Wellman noted in *Review of Reviews* (Dec. 1904) that "the [Cuba Society] letter was written wholly as a warning to Santo Domingo." Havana also was being put on notice, as it discovered in 1906. TR enunciated the Corollary again in his Fourth Annual Message to Congress.

326 **"I ASK NOTHING"** Perdicaris, "Morocco"; Samuel Gummeré to Francis B. Loomis, 20 May 1904 (NA).

327 **A few days** Thomas H. Etzold, "Protection or Politics? 'Perdicaris Alive or Raisuli Dead?' " *The Historian*, Feb. 1975.

327 **"I had much"** TR, *Letters*, vol. 4, 821, 807. See the last-cited letter, to George Otto Trevelyan, for an expression of TR's current frame of mind. For a further sense of TR's executive maturity at this time, see his long directives on Far Eastern affairs, Panamanian cable concessions, and Philippines administration in TR, *Letters*, vol. 4, 834–43. The note of command is assured, deft, irresistible; the point of view omniscient.

327 **The odds on** Washington *Evening Star*, 20 May 1904; Bishop, *Theodore Roosevelt*, vol. 1, 322. TR had sensed Parker as his probable Democratic rival for more than a year. The *Exeter*, N.H., *News-Letter*, 6 Mar. 1903, in Presidential scrapbook (TRP).

327 **Reticence and its** Washington *Evening Star*, 21 May 1904; New York *Sun*, 27 May 1904; Newark, N.J., *Evening News*, 1 June 1904. See also TR, *Letters*, vol. 4, 804.

327 **A White House "source"** Washington *Evening Star*, 17 May 1904; TR, *Letters*, vol. 4, 797.

327 **"He wants us"** John Hay diary, 22 May 1904 (JH).

328 **Like Taft** William H. Taft to Mrs. Taft, 12 Apr. 1904 (WHT).

328 **In any case** John Hay diary, 22 May 1904 (JH); TR, *Letters*, vol. 4, 833.

328 **With less than** New York *Evening Post*, 18 May 1904; *The New York Times*, 3 May 1904; TR, *Letters*, vol. 4, 823–24, 833; Philadelphia *Press*, 4 June 1904; New York *Sun*, 18 June 1904.

328 **"Mr. President, I"** Butler, *Across the Busy Years*, vol. 1, 321. Another of TR's favorite Beveridge stories had the young Senator visiting him at night and saying with solemn urgency: "It's time now, sir, for you to govern by psychic suggestion." Wister, *Roosevelt*, 112. In the event, the temporary chairman of the 1904 Republican convention was Henry Clay Payne. Elihu Root gave the keynote speech.

328 ROOSEVELT DID NOT John Hay diary, 28 May 1904 (JH).

328 The President seemed Qu. in Peter Larsen, "Theodore Roosevelt and the Moroccan Crisis, 1904–1905" (Ph.D. diss., Princeton University, 1984), 52.

328 AT 5:30 A.M. Samuel Gummeré to Francis B. Loomis, 3 June 1904 (NA).

329 PRESIDENT WISHES Samuel Gummeré to John Hay, 8 June 1904, and Hay to Gummeré, same date (NA).

329 Before nightfall Samuel Gummeré to John Hay, 8 June 1904 (received 6:21 P.M., 9 June) (NA).

329 ON 10 JUNE Philadelphia Public Ledger, 10 June 1904.

329 Roosevelt accepted Eitler, "Philander Chase Knox," 206; TR, Letters, vol. 4, 828–29.

330 "Many great and" TR to Philander Knox, 23 June 1904 (PCK).

330 Roosevelt had grown TR, Letters, vol. 5, 782; Eitler, "Philander Chase Knox," 27, 203. Leslie Shaw once overheard Knox politely reprimanding the President that it was almost impossible to state a legal proposition to him. "Before I am halfway through stating it, you have grasped it all, and have rendered your decision before you know what my conclusions are." Wood, Roosevelt As We Knew Him, 473–74.

330 And he was quick Philadelphia Public Record, The Washington Post, and Utica, N.Y., Observer, 19 June 1904; Philadelphia American, 10 June 1904. Thorelli, Federal Antitrust Policy, 407, and Eitler, "Philander Chase Knox," 207–8, agree with Knox's sober self-assessment. "Almost without exception," Eitler remarks, "the record . . . was one of presidential leadership by Roosevelt and conservative legalistic support by Knox." As an executive pair, they separately represented the promise and the restraints of the Constitution.

330 JOHN HAY FORWARDED Foreign Relations 1904, 500; John Hay diary, 14 June 1904 (JH); Hay to TR, 15 June 1904 (TD).

330 The Secretary's desire Dennett, John Hay, 402.

330 "Our position must" TR to John Hay, 15 June 1904 (JH).

330 Hay unhappily Still, American Sea Power, 167; Jules Jusserand to Théophile Delcassé, Documents diplomatiques, series 2, vol. 25, 234; Larsen, "Theodore Roosevelt and the Moroccan Crisis," 42–44.

330 "The President's will" Jules Jusserand to Théophile Delcassé, 19 June 1904 (JJ). The French government did, however, put considerable diplomatic pressure on Morocco to settle with Raisuli. Since the Sultan was newly indebted to Foreign Minister Delcassé for a fifty-million-franc loan, he could hardly refuse. In "Perdicaris Alive or Raisuli Dead," American Heritage, Aug. 1959, Barbara Tuchman remarks of the Roosevelt/Hay approach to Jusserand: "By recognizing France's special status in Morocco, this step, consciously taken, was of international significance in the train of crises that was to lead through Algericas and Agadir to 1914." It is also possible that TR, a punctilious diplomat, was simply honoring the month-old Anglo-French Entente.

330 Similar complaints The New York Times, 17 June 1904; Dawes, Journal of the McKinley Years, 374–76; Wheaton, "Genius and the Jurist," 278–80; Howe, George von Lengerke Meyer, 92; TR, Letters, vol. 4, 838–39; Charles G. Dawes to TR, 18 June 1904 (TRP); New York Sun, 18 June 1904.

331 "Excitement is" Henry Cabot Lodge to TR, 24 June 1904 (TRP).

331 Old-timers talked The best account of TR's role in the 1884 convention is Putnam, Theodore Roosevelt, chap. 23.

331 Now, two decades The New York Times, 20 June 1904; "The Republican National Convention," Review of Reviews, Aug. 1904.

331 "From Panama on" Kerr, Bully Father, 156–57. This letter of 20 June 1904 is misdated "June 21" in TR, Letters, vol. 4, 840.

332 LONG BEFORE PROCEEDINGS The New York Times, 21 and 19 June 1904; Bolles,

Tyrant from Illinois, 45; New York *Sun,* 21 June 1904. "From beginning to end, [the convention] was ruled with an iron hand beneath a soft glove . . . the master was recognized, and loyalty to the party was simply servility to orders." *Review of Reviews,* Aug. 1904.

332 **One thing Roosevelt** New York *World,* 22 June 1904; New York *Sun,* 21–23 June 1904.

333 **A question buzzed** Wheaton, "Genius and Jurist," 283; New York *Sun,* 22 June 1904.

333 **At 12:14, another** Payne, acting chairman of the convention, died on 4 Oct. 1904. Except where otherwise indicated, the following account (including speech quotations) is based on *Official Proceedings of the 13th Republican National Convention in the City of Chicago, June 21, 22, 23, 24, 1904* (Minneapolis, 1904).

333 **Elihu Root rose** New York *Sun,* 22 June 1904.

333 **"Louder!" a voice** *The New York Times,* 22 June 1904.

333 IN WASHINGTON, it Washington *Evening Star,* 22 June 1904; Elihu Root to TR, 14 June 1904 (TRP). TR had supplied the list of "achievements" himself. See TR, *Letters,* vol. 4, 810–13, and Jessup, *Elihu Root,* vol. 1, 421–23.

333 IN TANGIER, it The exact time difference between Washington and Tangier was four hours and forty-five minutes. *World Almanac,* 1904.

333 **Today, 21 June** Samuel Gummeré to John Hay, 19 and 20 June 1904 (NA); Hourihan, "Roosevelt and the Sultans," 113; John Hay diary, 18 June 1904 (JH); Samuel Gummeré to Francis B. Loomis, 23 May 1904 (NA).

333 **Aboard the *Brooklyn*** Doris D. Maguire, ed., *French Ensor Chadwick: Selected Letters and Papers* (Washington, D.C., 1981), 362; Samuel Gummeré to John Hay, 21 June 1904 (NA). Gummeré's cable was received by the State Department at 1:40 P.M.—i.e., 6:25 P.M. Tangier time. Overnight, the Admiral changed his mind about sending Marines ashore, thus pre-empting an almost certain bloodbath. French E. Chadwick to John Hay, 24 June 1904 (JH); Hourihan, "Roosevelt and the Sultans," 115.

333 BY NOW, Root's *The New York Times,* 22 June 1904.

334 **"All except the members"** Ibid.

334 **Root did not enunciate** Ibid.

334 HAY PONDERED Larsen, "Theodore Roosevelt and the Moroccan Crisis," 65–66.

334 **Unable to confront** Dennett, *John Hay,* 402.

334 **Hunt came back** The last two sentences of this paragraph represent the author's reading of TR's attitude. Etzold, "Protection or Politics?" and Larsen, "Theodore Roosevelt and the Moroccan Crisis," 69–70, feel similarly. Although some historians have doubted that TR authorized or even knew of Hay's ultimatum in advance, TR himself was specific on 31 Dec. 1915: "I was able to secure the release of [Perdicaris] only by demanding immediate action, and making them understand that when I said action I meant it." Qu. in Maguire, *French Ensor Chadwick,* 619.

334 **Hay, drafting his** John Hay diary, 23 June 1904 (JH).

335 WE WANT PERDICARIS John Hay to Samuel Gummeré, 22 June 1904 (NA).

335 **"Then I will"** Memorandum by William D. Hassett in EMH, n.d. See also memos by Gretchen Hood and Dudley Haddock, 16 May 1943, in EMH. All three sources say Hood was the originator, in his conversation with Hay, of the phrase *Perdicaris alive or Raisuli dead.* However, Hay, never a boastful man, called the phrase his own "concise impropriety," and in his diary for the day speaks simply of "my telegram." Hood's version of the phrase was less "concise," with a superfluous *either* that Hay (a fastidious stylist) would not have permitted himself. At any rate, the journalist got the scoop.

335 **But by the time** *Foreign Relations 1904,* 503.

335 HOOD'S DISPATCH Chicago *Record-Herald,* 23 June 1904.

335   "We declare our"   Merrill, *Republican Command,* 184–86. See Wheaton, "Genius and the Jurist," 290, for Lodge's nonauthorship of the GOP platform.
335   **When Lodge finished**   Chicago *Record-Herald,* 23 June 1904.
335   *"Bulletin,"* **the clerk**   Ibid.
335   **After two days**   New York *Tribune,* 23 June 1904, used the phrase "like an electric thrill."
336   **Cannon quickly adjourned**   TR's reputation, Etzold remarks in "Protection or Politics?" has suffered from "unjust smudging" by historians who have sought to show that the Raisuli telegram was timed for political effect in Chicago, rather than diplomatic effect at Tangier. There is no evidence that TR was responsible for its timing. Hay, however, did not hesitate to share his "concise impropriety" with the press. In announcing the Scripps-McRae dispatch, Cannon said that it had been "verified," presumably in a telephone call to the State Department. Etzold comments: "The fact that Roosevelt had resolved on such a position by 15 June, before the convention even opened . . . makes it clear that the politics of conventioneering had far less to do with the message than long exasperating delays." See also Hourihan, "Roosevelt and the Sultans," 123, and Larsen, "Theodore Roosevelt and the Moroccan Crisis," 25–27.
336   **"Events are numberless"**   *Official Proceedings,* 147.
336   **It was just**   *The New York Times,* 24 June 1904.
336   **An elemental din**   Ibid.
336   THE REAL ROOSEVELT   Alice Roosevelt diary, 23 June 1904 (ARL).
337   **With kisses on**   *The New York Times,* 24 June 1904.
338   **"Thank Heaven"**   See also Ion Perdicaris to Samuel Gummeré, 29 June 1904 (NA). Taxed by an indignant Gummeré about his lapsed citizenship (which was finally confirmed in a State Department cable to Loomis on 28 June), Perdicaris said that he had traded his passport in 1861 in order to prevent the Confederacy from attaching some property he owned in South Carolina. This formality aside, "I . . . continued to consider myself an American citizen . . . both my parents being, at the time of my birth, citizens of the United States. . . . I now realize only too keenly the false position in which I have been placed by this fatal hesitation and neglect." Qu. in Larsen, "Theodore Roosevelt and the Moroccan Crisis," 67–68. Larsen cites an important, and neglected, ruling by Secretary of State Root on 27 Oct. 1905 that Perdicaris "never effectively acquired Greek, or divested himself of American citizenship." See also Etzold, "Protection or Politics?" on Perdicaris's legal entitlement to United States protection in 1904. Perdicaris was presented with a new United States passport in 1905, and spent the rest of his life in Britain.
    Raisuli, enriched by the Sultan's ransom, became a figure of legendary status in Morocco. His followers believed him to be immortal. He acquired a fleet of small ships and practiced Berber-style piracy on coastal traffic. In old age, he was captured by a younger rival, after a fierce fight. He died in April 1925, a few months after his ancient hostage.

CHAPTER 22:   THE MOST ABSURD POLITICAL CAMPAIGN OF OUR TIME

339   *I think a lot*   Dunne, *Observations by Mr. Dooley,* 225.
339   THE DIFFICULTY OF   TR, *Letters,* vol. 4, 892.
339   **So, by late June**   The most complete account of this year's campaign events is Wheaton, "Genius and the Jurist." See also Merrill, *Republican Command,* chap. 8.
339   **There was no**   William H. Harbaugh, "Election of 1904," in Schlesinger and Israel, *History of American Presidential Elections,* vol. 3, 1973–74; Thompson, *Party Leaders,* 365–66; Wheaton, "Genius and the Jurist," 315.
339   **Alton Brooks Parker**   Washington *Evening Star,* 2 May 1904; Alton Parker scrap-

book (ABP); Wheaton, "Genius and the Jurist," 109. See also Fred C. Shoemaker, "Alton B. Parker: The Image of a Gilded Age Statesman in an Era of Progressive Politics" (M.A. thesis, Ohio State University, 1983).

340 **Roosevelt had foreseen** John Hay diary, 20 Mar. 1904 (JH); Brooks Adams to TR, 22 Sept. 1902 (TRP); TR, *Letters*, vol. 4, 806.

340 **Personally, he liked** On 15 June 1900, Governor Roosevelt expressed "not merely a strong personal liking but a very high regard and admiration" for Parker, and went out of his way to secure patronage for the judge's brother, also a Democrat. Parker publicly praised TR on his retirement from Albany. There is a photograph of them sitting convivially at the same table at TR's farewell dinner. TR, *Letters*, vol. 2, 1333, and vol. 3, 1; Alton Parker, Autobiography Notes (ABP).

340 **The judge was** James Creelman, "Alton Brooks Parker: A Character Sketch," Washington *Evening Star*, 24 May 1904; M. G. Cuniff, "Alton Brooks Parker," *World's Work*, June 1904. The best assessment of Parker is Wheaton, "Genius and the Jurist," chap. 3.

340 **Eighteen years of** *Review of Reviews*, Aug. 1904; Harold F. Gosnell, *Boss Platt and His New York Machine* (Chicago, 1924), 42; *Dictionary of American Biography*; Washington *Evening Star*, 9 May 1904.

340 **And so did most** Harbaugh, "Election of 1904," 1977; Washington *Evening Star*, 6 July 1904.

340 ON FRIDAY, **a little** *The New York Times*, 9 July 1904. Parker's house, called Rosemount in 1904, is now Lamont Landing in Esopus, N.Y. Elizabeth Burroughs Kelley, *The History of West Park and Esopus* (Hannacroix, N.Y., 1978).

340 **Around sunset** The following account is taken from *The New York Times* and New York *Herald*, 10 July 1904.

341 **the achievement of his life** Nobody browsing Parker's papers in LC can doubt that his remaining twenty-two years were anticlimactic to this moment. In old age, the judge began to dictate a memoir of Saharan dryness, but words failed him when he reached 1904. Apart from a few notes, the autobiography lay unfinished.

341 **They were full** Alton Parker scrapbook (ABP); *The New York Times*, 9 July 1904.

342 **The telegram was** Washington *Evening Star*, 12 July 1904; *The New York Times*, 10 July 1904. See also Harbaugh, "Election of 1904," 1983.

342 I REGARD THE Qu. in Wheaton, "Genius and the Jurist," 343–45.

342 **An eighty-year-old** For obvious reasons, Democratic campaign literature played down the fact that the G. in Davis's name stood for *Gassaway*.

342 ROOSEVELT WAS FULL TR, *Letters*, vol. 4, 852, 858; Lodge, *Selections*, vol. 2, 89.

342 **Professionals in both** Wheaton, "Genius and the Jurist," 351–52. See, e.g., New York *Evening Post*, 11 July 1904. "For the first time, they [the Republicans] are afraid, and their fear is real." Des Portes to Théophile Delcassé, 13 July 1904 (JJ).

343 **Time would tell** Some strategists were even talking of a delay until October. See, e.g., Albert J. Beveridge to TR, 9 Aug. 1904 (AJB).

343 **Roosevelt had scheduled** Washington *Evening Star*, 2 July 1904; *The Washington Post*, 3 July 1904.

343 ON 27 JULY Except where otherwise indicated, the following account of TR's notification ceremony is based mainly on reports in *The New York Times*, New York *Sun*, New York *World*, and New York *Herald*, 28 July 1904.

344 **"That's perfectly true"** Cannon had just praised the Roosevelt Administration's actions in Panama.

344 **used the word** *power* John Hay diary, 13 July 1904 (JH). "Mr. Knox [also] thought it was touched with demagogy in its original form," TR cheerfully informed George Cortelyou. "Root agreed with Knox" (8 June 1904 [GBC]). His edited speech appears in *Presidential Addresses and State Papers*, vol. 3, 36–47.

344   She laughed with   *The New York Times* and New York *World*, 28 July 1904. The adjective *phosphorescent* is Marguerite Cassini's in *Never a Dull Moment*, 166.

344   Something flickered   *The New York Times*, 28 July 1904.

344   Roosevelt paid no   New York *World*, 28 July 1904; Alice Roosevelt diary, 21 June, 17 and 27 May ("I pray God to grant unto me a fortune"), and 9 and 13 June, 1903; 27 July 1904 (ARL). Alice called her snake "Emily Spinach." For TR's views on this pet, see below, pp. 692–93.

344   "When I come down"   Ibid., 15 June 1903 (ARL).

344   ROOSEVELT'S THOUGHTFUL   Group portrait of the GOP Notification Committee, *Leslie's Weekly*, 11 Aug. 1904.

345   Odell had proved   Richard L. McCormick, *From Realignment to Reform: Political Change in New York State, 1893–1910* (Ithaca, 1981), 166–89.

346   This brazen mixing   Wheaton, "Genius and the Jurist," 475; Gould, *Reform and Regulation*, 47; see also McCormick, *From Realignment to Reform*, 220–22.

346   It was vital   McCormick, *From Realignment to Reform*, 175; Jessup, *Elihu Root*, vol. 1, 423.

346   "The Republicans of"   TR, *Letters*, vol. 4, 677.

346   Root politely declined   Jessup, *Elihu Root*, vol. 1, 425–27.

346   ON THE DAY   *The Washington Post* and *Washington Times*, 29 July 1904; John Hay to Henry White, 2 July 1904 (TD).

347   Washington sweltered   Washington *Evening Star*, 10 Aug. and *passim* 1904; Hay, *Letters*, vol. 3, 305; John Hay to Henry White, 2 July 1904 (TD); contemporary photographs in LC.

347   Roosevelt decided   TR, *Letters*, vol. 4, 880.

347   "sweetest of all"   Morris, *Edith Kermit Roosevelt*, 351.

347   "Edith and I"   *Letters from Theodore Roosevelt to Anna Roosevelt Cowles*, 260–61.

348   In New York   Wheaton, "Genius and the Jurist," 357–58; Crosson, "James S. Clarkson."

348   A female reporter   Kate Carew, New York *World*, 12 Aug. 1904.

348   Also unlike Hanna   Wheaton, "Genius and the Jurist," 358; Dawes, *Journal of the McKinley Years*, 383. By the end of Aug., Dawes already noted "great savings" in all contract matters. "At last we have a Committee whose work is untainted by fraud of any kind."

348   The Senator softened   Dawes, *Journal of the McKinley Years*, 378.

348   Roosevelt tried once   TR, *Letters*, vol. 4, 886–87; Bishop, *Theodore Roosevelt*, vol. 1, 325.

348   ROOSEVELT HAD LONG   See Anne Venzon, "Gunboat Diplomacy in the Mediterranean," *Proceedings of the U.S. Naval Institute*, supplement, Mar. 1985.

   Chronological Note: On 27 Aug. 1903, John G. Leishman, United States Minister in Constantinople, had cabled the State Department with news of the assassination of an American diplomat in Beirut. The local government's response was inadequate and unsatisfactory. TR immediately ordered three warships to Beirut. No sooner had he done so than another cable arrived, stating that the first telegram had contained an error; the diplomat had been "shot at" rather than "shot."

   TR saw the incident as a perfect opportunity to settle several long-standing issues between the United States and the Ottoman Empire, including indifference of local officials toward the security of Christian diplomats, and discrimination and harassment suffered by American missionaries. The warships would therefore stay in Turkish waters for as long as it took to clear up such issues. On 3 Sept., Hay reported that he had told the Turkish minister "that if he does not want our ships in Turkish waters,

NOTES • 689

it is very easy to cause them to depart." The Sultan had only to settle "two or three matters which have dragged too long." However, Hay's prediction that this would take only "a few days" was not quite accurate. While satisfactory action regarding the shooting incident was taken by mid-Sept. (thanks to the appointment of a new governor in Beirut), the Ottoman government frustratingly refused to recognize that the Squadron's presence was anything other than a "friendly visit." However, TR, Hay, and Leishman continued to hope that the United States naval presence in Turkish waters would eventually persuade the Sublime Porte to deal with the relevant issues. While some minor claims were settled in Oct., nothing more substantive came about, and finally, on 1 Feb. 1904, the Squadron left Beirut (*Foreign Relations 1904*, 774; Still, *American Sea Power*, 157–64; Venzon, "Gunboat Diplomacy," 27, 30–31). For an exhaustive treatment of both the Turkish and Moroccan crises of 1903–1904, see also Hourihan, "Roosevelt and the Sultans."

349 **the Sublime Porte** The phrase *Sublime Porte* was used in 1904 much as *the Kremlin* is used today. It derived from the gate that gave access to Ottoman departments of state in Constantinople.

349 **He demanded** *Foreign Relations 1904*, 749. There is a sketch of Leishman in Lewis Einstein's memoir, *A Diplomat Looks Back* (New Haven, 1968), 30; see also Hourihan, "Roosevelt and the Sultans," *passim*.

349 **Their high hopes** Except where otherwise indicated, the following account of Parker's notification ceremony is based on news clips that the judge himself pasted into his scrapbook, and on photographs in the *Evening Mail Illustrated Sunday Magazine*, 20 Aug. 1904 (ABP).

350 **Parker received** Excerpts from Parker's speech are printed in Harbaugh, "Election of 1904," 2022–23. Ironically, the cameraman was working for a moving-pictures company.

350 AFTERWARD, LOYAL *Public Opinion*, 18 Aug. 1904; Wheaton, "Genius and the Jurist," 393–94; Washington *Evening Star*, 11 Aug. 1904.

350 **Cortelyou's textbook** Wheaton, "Genius and the Jurist," 397–400, 487–89; *Republican Campaign Textbook* (New York, 1904), *passim*.

350 **The Democratic textbook** Wheaton, "Genius and the Jurist," 395, 397–400; Schlesinger and Israel, *History of American Presidential Elections*, vol. 3, 1986.

351 **Neither party** Wheaton, "Genius and the Jurist," 399. The best that could be said about lynchings in 1904 was that the year's total of eighty-six was down from 104 in 1903. Ziglar, "Decline of Lynching in America."

351 **the most eagerly awaited** Merrill, *Republican Command*, 168. See, e.g., the *Sun's* 3 Aug. 1904 comment on TR's labor policies: "He is on the side of the men who are every day seeking to overthrow the Constitution." TR was greatly annoyed by this accusation. TR, *Letters*, vol. 4, 876–77.

351 WITHIN DAYS OF *Foreign Relations 1904*, 826; Dennis, *Adventures in American Diplomacy*, 464; Still, *American Sea Power*, 158–64. See also William J. Hourihan, "The Big Stick in Turkey: American Diplomacy and Naval Operations Against the Ottoman Empire, 1903–1904," *Naval War College Review* 34.5 (Sept.–Oct. 1981).

351 **Roosevelt hastened** TR, *Letters*, vol. 4, 885, 891; "I am well aware that I have no right to make war," he wrote on 8 Aug., "and have not the dimmest or remotest intention of doing so."

351 **Thanks to Hay's** TR, *Letters*, vol. 4, 890; *Literary Digest*, 20 Aug. 1904.

352 **For almost a month** *Review of Reviews*, Oct. 1904; *The Cambridge Modern History* (New York, 1934), vol. 12, 590–91.

352 **Farther inland** *Review of Reviews*, Oct. 1904; *Cambridge Modern History*, vol. 12, 591–92.

352 "The Russians think"   TR, *Letters,* vol. 4, 913.
352 "Unless I am"   Albert J. Beveridge to TR, 26 Aug. 1904 (AJB).
352 The "speaking"   Harbaugh, "Election of 1904," 2024–27.
352 A quieter voice   Wheaton, "Genius and the Jurist," 396; Nicholas Murray Butler to TR, 6 May 1904 (TRP); Thompson, *Party Leaders,* 81; New York *Sun,* 24 June 1904; New York *Evening Post,* 21 June 1904.
353 At six foot   Champ Clark, *My Quarter Century in American Politics* (New York, 1920), vol. 2, 281; Thompson, *Party Leaders,* 33, 81–82; Fleming, *Around the Capitol,* 228; Dunn, *From Harrison to Harding,* vol. 1, 219; Thomas R. Shipp, "Charles W. Fairbanks," *Review of Reviews,* Aug. 1904.
353 This awkwardness   New York *Sun,* 24 June 1902; Republican speaking schedule in Wheaton, "Genius and the Jurist," 599.
353 The first tests   M. Des Portes to Théophile Delcassé, 7 Sept. 1904 (JJ).
353 Both states were   *Public Opinion,* 15 Sept. 1904; *Review of Reviews,* Oct. 1904; Wheaton, "Genius and the Jurist," 373–74.
353 "Unless we throw"   TR, *Letters,* vol. 4, 919.
353 "The people need"   Joseph Pulitzer, open letter to Josephus Daniels, New York *World,* 8 Sept. 1904.
354 THE PRESIDENT CHOSE   TR, *Letters,* vol. 4, 921–43.
354 At least twelve   Wheaton, "Genius and the Jurist," 601.
354 "Our opponents"   TR, *Letters,* vol. 4, 921, 930, 939.
354 "There is not"   Ibid., 923–42.
354 "We have striven"   Ibid., 942.
354 The President's letter   Wheaton, "Genius and the Jurist," 409–10; *Public Opinion,* 22 Sept. 1904; John Hay to TR, 13 Sept. 1904 (TRP).
354 "WELL, MY PART"   TR, *Letters,* vol. 4, 945.
354 Cortelyou's first   *The Wall Street Journal,* 12 June 1903; Thorelli, *Federal Antitrust Policy,* 592–93; Merrill, *Republican Command,* 168–70.
355 When one did   George Cortelyou, interviewed by Louis Wiley, 29 June 1906, transcript in GBC.
355 "Now, Mr. Bliss"   *Campaign Contributions,* 123.
355 "You need have"   Ibid., 128. According to Archbold's testimony, this interview took place in mid-Sept. In 1912, TR vehemently denied that it took place "with my consent or knowledge" (TR, *Letters,* vol. 7, 603). "I cannot of course say whether or not it is true that Mr. Bliss asked for or received such a contribution."
355 AT 10:00 A.M.   *The New York Times,* 23 Sept. 1904.
355 The bedlam continued   Ibid.
356 Parker's next   Ibid.
356 The judge spent   Ibid., 23–25 Sept. 1904; Alton Parker scrapbook (ABP).
356 "War grows more"   John Hay to Joseph H. Choate, 1 Sept. 1904 (JHC).
356 Roosevelt, younger   Japan's special interest in Korea had been sanctioned by the Anglo-Japanese agreement of 1902. On 26 Feb. 1904, Korea agreed without protest to become a virtual protectorate of Japan.
356 "I would like"   Jules Jusserand to Théophile Delcassé, 18 Oct. 1904 (JJ).
356 "Look how long"   Ibid.
356 Jusserand, whose   Ibid. *Chronological Note:* The role of international arbiter, so different from that of Rough Rider, appealed to TR, and he was flattered to play it in preview on 24 Sept. 1904, when two hundred delegates from the Interparliamentary Union visited him at the White House. They read a resolution from their recent convention in St. Louis, where legislative officials from Europe, the British Empire, and South America had called for a peacekeeping "congress of nations" (*New York Tribune,* 25 Sept. 1904). They

begged Roosevelt to call a second Hague Conference, along the lines of the one that had established the International Court of Justice in 1899. One delegate reminded him that the first conference had postponed the vital question of arms limitation. "In applying to you we address ourselves to an earnest defender of international justice, and we bear in mind that you were the first head of state who turned governments toward the Permanent Court of Arbitration at the Hague." TR agreed to their plea, telling them, "At an early date I shall issue the call for the conference you request." Republican officials did not doubt he would choose a date "early" enough for the election. See also *Literary Digest*, 8 Oct. 1904.

356 **Joseph Pulitzer complained** New York *World*, 1 Oct. 1904.

357 **The aggregate** George Cortelyou, interviewed by Louis Wiley, 29 June 1906, transcript in GBC.

357 **Cortelyou's friends** Cortelyou's difficulties, which are amply documented in GBC, arose out of the deaths of three investors in a preparatory school he founded and headed in 1887. When the venture failed, he refused insolvency and entered the Postal Service, determined to reimburse their estates. By 1905, he was clear of all debt.

357 **Soon Democratic campaign** Wheaton, "Genius and the Jurist," 473–80.

357 **All Cortelyou said** Presidential scrapbook (TRP). "My determination to keep quiet," Cortelyou wrote the President on 2 Oct. 1904, "has been largely with the hope of drawing their fire far enough ahead of the election" (TRP).

357 **The fighter in** TR to George Cortelyou, 2 Oct. 1904 (GBC); TR, *Letters*, vol. 3, 963. Perhaps coincidentally, he wrote a few days later to praise the hunter Stewart White's prowess in killing "105 pigs in two weeks" with a knife. He doubted that he could pull off such a feat himself, although "I have a bully knife . . . with a fourteen-inch blade, and I firmly believe that one thrust would do the business . . . even against a boar." TR, *Letters*, vol. 3, 978.

357 **"Mr. Cortelyou is"** Cornelius Bliss to TR, 3 Oct. 1904 (TRP). Another professional impressed by Cortelyou's quiet, yet effortlessly thorough, performance was James S. Clarkson. "The red light is no longer a color in politics and the brass band has departed. Instead of trying to capture men in the mass, [his] system is to go to them in detail and reach them along the lines of effective influence." Clarkson to Leigh Hunt, 1 Oct. 1904 (JSC).

358 **After Elihu Root's** McCormick, *From Realignment to Reform*, 189; TR, *Letters*, vol. 4, 962.

358 **The Democratic National** James S. Clarkson to Leigh Hunt, 1 Oct. 1903 (JSC).

358 **"Pray get out"** McCormick, *From Realignment to Reform*, 191; TR, *Letters*, vol. 4, 961.

358 **"The drift here"** William D. Foulke to TR, 6 Oct. 1904 (TRP). TR had privately used the same metaphor himself. TR to George Cortelyou, 2 Oct. 1904 (GBC).

358 **At 1 Madison** *Campaign Contributions*, 685.

358 **"Who is this?"** Ibid., 685–86.

358 **"I would rather"** Long afterward, when this telephone conversation was put on the record, Scott hedged his memory of it, saying the President might have said, "Mr. Harriman is coming to see me." Whoever made the first move, each man had cause to seek the interview.

359 **Harriman was a** Harriman had also served as a delegate to the Republican National Convention (Klein, *Life and Legend of E. H. Harriman*, 363). Wheaton, "Genius and the Jurist," 494ff., suggests that Harriman's new interest in politics was an extension of his business rivalry with J. P. Morgan. TR was aware of this rivalry, and encouraged it by sedulously consulting "now the one [man], now the other" (495).

359 **"In view of"** TR, *Letters*, vol. 4, 979.
359 **"Now, my dear"** Ibid., 983.
359 **Harriman was thus** TR, *Letters*, vol. 4, 983; vol. 5, 448. Klein, *Life and Legend of E. H. Harriman*, 364, notes that this addendum also served as "evidence" that if Harriman came south to see the President, it was on his own initiative. Eight years later, TR cited it to that exact purpose. See TR, *Letters*, vol. 7, 609.
359 **When Harriman called** John Hay diary, 15 Oct. 1903 (JH); TR, *Letters*, vol. 3, 985; vol. 5, 448.
359 **Twelve thousand** New York *World* and *The New York Times*, 20 Oct. 1904. According to a survey conducted by the Odell organization, TR could expect a 96,000-vote plurality in New York State, while Higgins was trailing his Democratic opponent. Wheaton, "Genius and the Jurist," 498.
359 **Roosevelt received** E. H. Harriman to TR (telegram), 20 Oct. 1904; William Loeb to TR, 21 Sept. 1912 (TRP); EKR diary, 20 Oct. 1904 (TRC).
359 **Roosevelt spent** TR in *Letters*, vol. 7, 608; William Loeb in *Campaign Contributions*, 529; E. H. Harriman in ibid., 693; Benjamin B. Odell in ibid., 112. TR appears to have conveniently forgotten to raise the subject of railroad regulation. Another subject of great interest to Harriman that TR wished to avoid was Governor Odell's desire to have Chauncey Depew appointed United States Ambassador to France, thus making Depew's Senate seat available to himself. See text below.
359 **Whatever else** John L. Heaton, *The Story of a Page: Thirty Years of Public Service and Public Discussion in the Editorial Columns of the New York World* (New York, 1913), 317.
359 **He had a pleased** Merrill, *Republican Command*, 166; *Campaign Contributions*, 693.
359 HARRIMAN PROVED *Campaign Contributions*, 440–41.
360 **Millionaires virtually** Corey, *House of Morgan*, 370–71; Don C. Seitz, *Joseph Pulitzer: His Life and Times* (New York, 1924), 305. Gould's donation alone was worth nearly two million dollars in contemporary [2001] valuation.
360 **Other donations** Pringle, *Theodore Roosevelt*, 357–58. Heaton, *Story of a Page*, 320. TR's final fund total was $2,195,000, more than 70 percent of it from corporations. For an exhaustive, if often speculative, analysis of the corporate-financing issue, and Harriman's relations with TR, see Wheaton, "Genius and the Jurist," *passim*. Wheaton estimates that "between one-fourth and one-third [of the GOP fund] was put into the treasury in the last two weeks of the campaign" (606).
360 **"Corporate cunning"** Qu. in Sullivan, *Our Times*, vol. 2, 249–50.
360 **"It tires me"** TR qu. in *The New York Times*, 12 Jan. 1919.
360 **As one workingman** *Review of Reviews*, Nov. 1904. An oft-reproduced cartoon by Homer Davenport portrayed Parker as a sphinx in judicial robes (ABP).
360 **"Well, you are"** Alton Parker, Autobiography Notes (ABP). For another version of this anecdote, see *Campaign Contributions*, vol. 1, 899–900.
360 **The judge returned** Alton Parker, Autobiography Notes (ABP).
361 **As luck would** New York *World* and *The New York Times*, 24 Oct. 1903; Heaton, *Story of a Page*, 209.
361 **His remarks made** *The New York Times*, 24 Oct. 1903.
361 **"We are at"** Hay, *Letters*, vol. 3, 319–20.
361 ALICE LIKED TO One "posterity letter" survives in which TR, afraid that his eccentric elder daughter might cause a scandal in the waning days of the campaign, lectures her sternly over his full signature.

> Dear Alice, Do you know how much talk there has been recently in the newspapers about your betting—matching quarters at the races & c.—and courting notoriety with that unfortunate snake? . . . Do try to remember that to court notoriety by bizarre actions is underbred and unladylike. You

should not bet at all, and never in public. . . . When you do foolish things, you make it certain that worse than foolish things will be ascribed to you. To run into debt and be extravagant as to your clothes—such pointless extravagance, too—is not only foolish but wicked. Your father, Theodore Roosevelt. (28 Aug. 1904, copy in AC)

361 **Some instinct** TR, *Letters,* vol. 3, 996–97.

361 **He did not** Ibid., 995–96.

362 **By telegram, he** Ibid., 996–98. These documents, plus others written in the weeks ahead, were absorbed by TR into the longest and most vehement of all his "posterity letters," to the Senate Committee investigating campaign contributions in Aug. 1912. It is printed in ibid., vol. 7, 602–25.

362 **"I congratulate you"** Elihu Root to TR, 28 Oct. 1904 (ER).

362 IN THE LAST DAYS Wheaton, "The Genius and the Jurist," 513.

362 **"Has my request"** TR, *Letters,* vol. 3, 1004.

362 **There was no** Wheaton, "Genius and the Jurist," 530.

362 **"Although this may"** Ibid., 531; Alton Parker speech script, 31 Oct. 1904 (ABP). See also New York *World,* 1 Nov. 1904.

362 **"I have never"** EKR to Henry Cabot Lodge, ca. 1 Nov. 1904 (HCL). On this same day, Alice Roosevelt wrote in her diary, "I am positive he won't be elected. . . . I can't bear it" (ARL).

362 **The question** TR, *Letters,* vol. 3, 1013. See the whole of this strategic letter for further examples of TR's exquisite sense of press timing.

362 **Parker was tempted** Pringle, *Theodore Roosevelt,* 355.

363 **This was going** Gould, *Presidency of Theodore Roosevelt,* 143.

363 **Old-time journalists** Heaton, *Story of a Page,* 210.

363 **"Mr. Parker's accusations"** White House press statement, 4 Nov. 1904 (TRP).

363 **Roosevelt asked** Ibid.

363 **"The statements made"** Ibid. For TR's even stronger draft statement (which aides apparently toned down), see TRP.

363 **"VICTORY. TRIUMPH."** Alice Roosevelt diary, 8 Nov. 1904 (ARL). According to Wheaton, "Genius and the Jurist," 519, Parker's telegram was prompted by the collapse of his hopes in New York, and was sent to RNC headquarters at 8:30 P.M. By the time the landslide reached Chicago, most Democratic officials headed for home.

364 **Purged by his** John Hay diary, 6–7 Nov. 1904 (JH); Washington *Evening Star,* 11 Nov. 1904; Longworth, *Crowded Hours,* 64. Several observers noted TR's strange calm on this evening. He confided to his sister Corinne "that he had never wanted anything in his life quite as much as the outward and visible sign of his country's approval," and for the first time she understood how painful it had been for him to function as McKinley's "accidental" heir (Douglas, *Many-Sided Roosevelt,* 268–69; Robinson, *My Brother,* 217–18). According to Douglas, TR's disclaimer of another run was, like many of his apparently impulsive decisions, premeditated. He had discussed it several weeks before with Attorney General Moody.

364 **"On the fourth"** Washington *Evening Star,* 9 Nov. 1904. TR's final popular vote was 7,628,461, exceeding McKinley's total in 1900 by 409,970. He carried every northern and western state as well as Delaware, West Virginia, and Missouri. Parker's total of 5,084,223 fell short of Bryan's in 1900 by 1,272,511. In the Electoral College, TR scored a record 336 to Parker's 140. Republicans strengthened their domination of Congress, with a 57 to 33 division of seats with Democrats in the Senate, and 250 to 136 in the House. Altogether it was, in the words of Charles Dawes, "the greatest Republican victory on record," and, as Joseph Pulitzer's New York *World* magnanimously conceded, "the greatest personal triumph ever won by any President" (Dawes, *Journal of the McKinley Years,* 387;

Heaton, *Story of a Page,* 211). For a comprehensive analysis of voting patterns, broken down in virtually every category save hairstyle, see Wheaton, "Genius and the Jurist," chap. 13. His figures reveal some interesting negatives. For example, Democratic disillusionment with Parker (doubtless influenced by TR's pre-election tirade) had more to do with the end result than Republican enchantment with the President. Both parties lost voter support in the South, mainly because of black disfranchisement. TR personally—and surprisingly, in view of his habitual identification with the American farmer—lost votes in most rural counties across the Corn Belt. Wherever soil was poor, he gained; wherever it was rich, his support declined. His best strength was in big cities (Jews voted for him almost solidly in New York) and in areas of thriving industry. The coal-strike conference notwithstanding, TR did not do well in depressed or strike-torn counties. Wheaton concludes that the prime causes of his plurality were economic prosperity and Republican loyalty.

INTERLUDE

365   ON THE DAY   Except where otherwise indicated, the following two paragraphs are based on James J. Horgan, "Aeronautics at the World's Fair of 1904," *Missouri Historical Society Bulletin* 24.3 (1968).

366   "quite drunk"   Adams, *Letters,* vol. 5, 588.

366   "One asked oneself"   *Education of Henry Adams,* 467.

366   He had tried   See ibid., chap. 25, "The Dynamo and the Virgin."

366   The settled life   *Education of Henry Adams, passim* and 500.

366   the very personification   Ernest Samuels, *Henry Adams: The Major Phase* (Cambridge, Mass., 1964), 324.

366   "The devil is"   Adams, *Letters,* vol. 5, 537.

367   ROOSEVELT GOT TO   *Education of Henry Adams,* 468. TR was in St. Louis on 26 and 27 Nov. 1904. It was not technically his first visit to the fairgrounds, since he had stopped by and spoken there in the early planning stage, during his Western tour.

367   He came at   *Education of Henry Adams,* 468.

367   "We really had"   TR, *Letters,* vol. 3, 1047–48.

367   He stomped   Alice was convulsed when her father paused to peer shortsightedly at a statue, and pronounced it a "particularly fine Diana." As she could well see, it had all the attributes of an Apollo. Longworth, *Crowded Hours,* 65.

367   He was impressed   TR, *Letters,* vol. 3, 1048.

367   The presidential train   *The Washington Post,* 28 Nov. 1904; Robinson, *My Brother,* 220–22; TR, *Letters,* vol. 3, 1049–51. Mrs. Robinson, writing some sixteen years later, misremembers some of the details of this postmidnight session, and also, puzzlingly, recalls TR dictating another mammoth "review" of Finley Peter Dunne's views on the Irish Question. This letter was actually written previously, on 23 Nov. 1904. See TR, *Letters,* vol. 3, 1040–42. However, she may be accurate in stating that TR continued his dictation in her presence, until a porter arrived with coffee at 7:00 A.M. "Shortly after that I was assisted to my berth in a more or less asphyxiated condition, from which I never roused again until the train reached the station in Washington."

367   Nearly nineteen million   Horgan, "Aeronautics at the World's Fair"; David R. Francis, *The Universal Exposition of 1904* (St. Louis, 1913), xviii–xix.

367   As if in earnest   Horgan, "Aeronautics at the World's Fair."

367   MARGUERITE CASSINI HAD   Cassini, *Never a Dull Moment,* 215.

367   The Ambassador's choler   John Hay diary, 2 Jan. 1905 (JH); Griscom, *Diplomat-*

ically Speaking, 252. Because New Year's Day was a Sunday in 1905, official receptions were postponed by twenty-four hours.

368 **While Europe** John Hay diary, 3 Jan. 1905 (JH).

368 **Rheumatic, perpetually** Ibid., 15 and 25 Jan. 1905; Adams, *Letters*, vol. 5, 629.

368 **More and more** Jusserand, *What Me Befell*, 276.

368 **All that remained** Hay was suffering from a prostate condition and heart disease (*angina pectoris*).

368 **The Russian Baltic** The fleet, commanded by Admiral Zinovi Rozhdestvenski, had sailed from Rigal Harbor in Oct. 1904.

368 **"dealing with"** Clymer, *John Hay*, 152.

368 **Politely disapproving** John Hay diary, 4 Jan. 1905 (JH).

368 **the other his** EKR to Kermit Roosevelt, 30 Jan. 1905 (KR).

369 **"With him wielding"** *Education of Henry Adams*, 417.

369 **Roosevelt's *Energetik*** *Education of Henry Adams*, 441. *Energetik*: in German natural science, the fundamental energy of matter. In a sarcastic editorial headlined FIRMNESS—IN ROTATION, the New York *Evening Post*, 1 Feb. 1905, inquired: "Why is he never simultaneously firm on all his pet measures, but generally decided only on one at a time, in a somewhat periodic rotation?"

369 **"the darkening prairie"** *Education of Henry Adams*, 396.

369 **"always and everywhere"** Ibid., 455.

369 **"Truth was the"** Ibid., 456.

369 **ANOTHER HENRY** Henry James to William James, 14 Jan. 1903 (HJ). James had not been in Washington since the days of President Arthur. See Leon Edel, *Henry James: The Master, 1901–1916* (London, 1972), 274–76.

369 **"The President is"** Henry James to William James, 14 Jan. 1905, and to Mary Cadwalader Jones, 13 Jan. 1905 (HJ). For another account of this evening, see Lawrence, *Memories of a Happy Life*, 177.

370 **"Theodore Rex"** Henry James to Mary Cadwalader Jones, 13 Jan. 1905 (HJ). For the earlier, mutually contemptuous relations of TR and James, see Morris, *Rise of Theodore Roosevelt*, 467–68.

370 **THE IMAGINATION MUST** Bacon's aphorism 104, from his *Magna Instauratio* (1620), is given here as paraphrased by Adams (*Letters*, vol. 5, 606). The original reads, "The understanding must not therefore be supplied with wings, but rather hung with weights to keep it from leaping and flying."

370 **Here was Arthur** *Education of Henry Adams*, 437; Adams, *Letters*, vol. 5, 561; Arthur Balfour, "Reflections Suggested by the New Theory of Matter," *The Times* (London), 18 Aug. 1904.

370 **"I foresee something"** Adams, *Letters*, vol. 5, 552.

370 **Nearer home** Samuels, *Henry Adams*, 321.

370 **BOTH KANEKO** John Hay diary, 30 Jan. and 15 Feb. 1905 (JH). Kaneko, a cosmopolitan Tokyo aristocrat, had opened a discreet war public-relations bureau in New York, whence he lobbied more energetically than effectively to keep American opinion pro-Japanese through the summer of 1905. James Kanda and William A. Gifford, "The Kaneko Correspondence," *Monumenta Nipponica* 37.1 (1982); Eugene P. Trani, *The Treaty of Portsmouth: An Adventure in American Diplomacy* (Lexington, Ky., 1969), 19. For the early relationship of TR and Kaneko, see Julian Street, "A Japanese Statesman's Recollections of Roosevelt," *The New York Times Book Review*, 31 July 1921.

371 **"The weather remains"** John Hay diary, 1 Feb. 1905 (JH).

371 **Heart pain** Ibid., 28 Jan. 1905.

371 **Cassini waved** Ibid., 23 Feb. 1905.

371 **"destined to be"** Qu. in Edel, *Henry James*, 276.

371 **"Roosevelt has the"** Henry Watterson to Poultney Bigelow, 22 Feb. 1905 (PB).

CHAPTER 23: MANY BUDDING THINGS

375 *Onaisy lies th'* "Mr. Dooley" in *Collier's,* Feb. 1903.

375 THEODORE ROOSEVELT The following description is based on "TR's Inaugural Ceremony, 1905" and "TR's Inauguration, 1905," newsreel films in TRAF; the diary-letter of Matthew Hale, 4 Mar. 1905, in TRP; Lorant, *Life and Times,* 422; Washington *Evening Star,* 4 Mar. 1905; *The New York Times,* 5 Mar. 1905. Additional touches from Robinson, *My Brother,* 223–24, and Longworth, *Crowded Hours,* 67.

376 "My fellow citizens" TR, *Works,* vol. 17, 311–12.

376 The wind snatched Sir Mortimer Durand diary, 4 Apr. 1905 (HMD).

376 Nobody, with the On or about 11 Dec. 1904, TR had been sparring in the White House with a Navy aide, Lieutenant Dan Tyler Moore, and took "a hot one" to the side of the head. It ruptured a blood vessel in the left eye, and his vision immediately began to blur, degenerating into spotted half-blindness. The disability remained a secret, even from Moore, throughout TR's presidency. TR, *Letters,* vol. 4, 1065; Leary, *Talks with TR,* 20–21; Pringle, *Theodore Roosevelt,* 18–19.

376 Close observers *The New York Times,* 5 Mar. 1903; TR, *Letters,* vol. 4, 1133; Hay, *Letters,* vol. 3, 328. The ring is now in Sagamore Hill National Historic Site.

376 Hay could not Putnam, *Theodore Roosevelt,* 42. The Secretary had previously observed that TR "thought more and talked more" about Lincoln "than any one I ever met in public life" (John Hay to Norman Hapgood, 8 Aug. 1904 [TD]). TR himself admitted to "seeing" Lincoln often in the White House. "For some reason or other he is to me infinitely the most real of the dead Presidents." See also TR, *Letters, vol 3, 392.*

376 "a document which" TR, *Autobiography,* 400.

376 (which had expressed) TR, *Letters,* vol. 4, 1131.

376 "Much has been" TR, *Works,* vol. 17, 311.

377 He spoke for Ibid. Remarkably, aside from in his opening "My fellow Americans," TR did not use the personal pronoun in his address. This remains a record in inaugural oratory.

377 with a new "The Senate is determined to be 'ugly.' Their openly expressed opinion is that 'Teddy' . . . wants taking down a peg." Sir Mortimer Durand to Lord Lansdowne, 7 Mar. 1905 (HMD).

377 Afterward, Roosevelt Butt, *Letters,* 282. TR described Bacon privately as "a voluble, pinheaded creature . . . a horrid instance of the mischief that can be done by a man of very slender capacity, if only he possesses great loquacity, effrontery, and an entire indifference to the national welfare." TR, *Letters,* vol. 4, 1133.

377 So impregnable John Hay diary, 25 Feb. 1905 (JH).

377 floated an enormous Fakirs and spielers along the avenue did brisk business selling miniature replicas of this new American icon. "Take home a Roosevelt 'big stick.' " Washington *Evening Star,* 4 Mar. 1905.

377 Whatever tomorrow's TR, *Letters,* vol. 4, 491; TR to Pierre de Coubertin, 21 Nov. 1904 (TRP); Jay G. Hayden to Hermann Hagedorn, 10 Dec. 1948 (TRB); Leary, *Talks with TR,* 20.

377 "The President will" John Hay diary, 22 Oct. 1904 (JH).

377 ON 10 MARCH Ibid., 10–11 Mar. 1905.

378 He cautioned Hay Ibid., 10 Mar. 1903; Griscom, *Diplomatically Speaking,* 253.

378 Even Count Cassini John Hay diary, 16 Mar. 1905 (JH).

378 "We are condemned" Ibid.

378 Hay left Washington *The New York Times,* 18 Mar. 1905; John Hay diary, 17 Mar. 1905 (JH).

378 **Roosevelt was in** "Well, Franklin," TR said to the groom at the reception, "there's nothing like keeping the name in the family." Morris, *Edith Kermit Roosevelt*, 288–89. Some years before, as a Harvard undergraduate, Franklin had heard TR speak and "was so impressed . . . that he vowed he, too, would someday find a way to become active in the political affairs of his country." Elliott Roosevelt to John A. Gable, 7 July 1989, in *Theodore Roosevelt Association Journal*, summer 1989.

378 **Nor did he** "Uncle Ted . . . stole the show and the bridegroom and bridal party sank into an obnoxious oblivion." Corinne Robinson Alsop, unpublished autobiography, Alsop Papers (TRC), 55. See Blanche Wiesen Cook, *Eleanor Roosevelt* (New York, 1992), vol. 1, 166–67.

378 **To that end** EKR diary, 21 Jan. 1905 (TRC); Morris, *Edith Kermit Roosevelt*, 288.

378 **THE PRESIDENT TOOK** Washington *Evening Star*, 17 Mar. 1905; John Hay diary, 18 Mar. 1905 (JH).

378 **Morocco had suddenly** For the immediate background to the Moroccan crisis of spring 1905, see Beale, *Theodore Roosevelt*, 355–59, and Larsen, "Theodore Roosevelt and the Moroccan Crisis," 95–107.

378 **Kaiser Wilhelm II** John Hay diary, 7 Mar. 1905 (JH).

379 **(as Mr. Perdicaris)** See above, p. 324.

379 **If the President** Beale, *Theodore Roosevelt*, 275.

379 **and gain immensely** Ibid., 356; John Keiger, *France and the Origins of the First World War* (New York, 1981), 21. Germany's sense of exclusion in North Africa derived from the Anglo-French treaty of 8 Apr. 1904, which gave the French control of Morocco in exchange for British control of Egypt.

379 **Great Britain, in turn** TR, *Letters*, vol. 4, 1162.

379 **"The Kaiser has"** Ibid., 1150.

379 **Von Sternburg was** Ibid., 1155.

379 **April came with** Tyler Dennett, *Roosevelt and the Russo-Japanese War* (New York, 1925), 172–75.

379 **a "worthy creature"** TR, *Letters*, vol. 5, 242. Spring Rice was adjudged by his superiors to be too junior, and too likely to be manipulated by TR.

379 **who to his** Sir Michael Herbert had died prematurely on 30 Sept. 1904.

379 **"I wish the Japs"** TR, *Letters*, vol. 4, 1150.

380 **Rather than leave** Ibid.; *The New York Times*, 4 Apr. 1905.

380 **"I am not"** TR, *Letters*, vol. 4, 1156.

380 **Rumors proliferated** Dunn, *From Harrison to Harding*, vol. 1, 415; TR, *Letters*, vol. 4, 717.

380 **The President stayed**
   Chronological Note: TR's five-week hunting vacation in Oklahoma (wolves) and Colorado (bears) was preceded by a week's political tour of Kentucky, the Indian Territory, and Texas, where he attended a Rough Riders reunion. He published accounts of both his hunts in *Scribner's Magazine*, Oct. and Nov. 1905, and subsequently included them in *Outdoor Pastimes of an American Hunter* ("Wolf-Coursing" and "A Colorado Bear Hunt"). See TR, *Works*, vol. 3.

380 **THE FIRST IMPORTANT** Beale, *Theodore Roosevelt*, 283; Dennett, *Roosevelt*, 176.

380 **Tokyo did not** Dennett, *Roosevelt*, 176.

381 **Roosevelt wired back** Ibid., 178.

381 **While awaiting** TR, *Letters*, vol. 4, 1161–62.

381 **France certainly was** Keiger, *France and the Origins of the First World War*, 21.

381 **and Britain, in** TR, *Letters*, vol. 4, 1162.

381 **"I do not care"** Ibid.

381 **One little dog** TR, *Works*, vol. 3, 67.

381 **("One run was")** Kerr, *Bully Father*, 168. John "Jack" Abernathy was the sort of man TR admired. "A really wonderful fellow, catching the wolves alive by thrusting his gloved hands down between their jaws so that they cannot bite. He caught one wolf alive, tied up this wolf, and then held it on the saddle, followed his dogs in a seven-mile run and helped kill another wolf. He has a pretty wife and five cunning children."

381 **Going without lunch** TR, *Works*, vol. 3, 65. As a testament to TR's overpowering physicality, ranging from his desire to kill to his palpable love of nature in all its forms, "A Colorado Bear Hunt" makes for enlightening reading.

382 **On 24 April** TR, *Works*, vol. 3, 82–83; *Denver News*, 25 Apr. 1905; Washington *Evening Star*, 26 May 1905; TR to Philip B. Stewart, 26 Apr. 1905 (TRP). "I notice the President has got two bears," Ambassador Takahira remarked. "We would be satisfied with one!" Trani, *Treaty of Portsmouth*, 55.

382 **Then he began** TR to Philip B. Stewart, 26 Apr. 1905 (TRP).

382 **Late that evening** Benjamin J. Barnes to William Loeb, Jr., 25 Apr. 1905 (TRP).

382 **"You are hereby"** Dennett, *Roosevelt*, 179–80.

382 **Taft added, in** Ibid., 180. Henry W. Denison was Baron Komura's official American adviser in Tokyo.

382 **Loeb felt unable** The following account is taken from an interview given by Loeb to the columnist "Bob Davis," published in the New York *Sun*, 28 Mar. 1929, and later reprinted in *Roosevelt House Bulletin*, spring 1943. Loeb's movements are confirmed by the *Denver News*, 27 Apr. 1905.

382 **Before going to bed** TR to Philip B. Stewart, 26 Apr. 1905 (TRP).

383 **They treated** Alexander Lambert to TR, 18 June 1905 (TRP).

383 **"Am a good deal"** TR, *Letters*, vol. 4, 1167–68.

383 **Roosevelt spent** Pierre de La Gorce, *Histoire du Second Empire* (Paris, 1899–1905); TR, *Letters*, vol. 4, 1179; Jusserand, *What Me Befell*, 277.

383 **Roosevelt read** TR, *Letters*, vol. 4, 1174.

383 **"struck by certain"** Ibid., 1269.

383 **At least, though** Ieronim Pavlovich Taburno, *The Truth about the War* (Kansas City, Mo., 1905).

383 **WHAT NONE OF** Jusserand, *What Me Befell*, 276; TR on 7 Jan. 1905, qu. in Murakata, "Theodore Roosevelt and William Sturgis Bigelow." Bigelow, a wealthy Buddhist and connoisseur of Japanese art, was yet another member of TR's *secret du roi*. It was he who interested the President in *jujitsu*.

384 **Although Roosevelt had** Tyler Dennett believed that had TR been in Washington on 25 April, he could have "hastened the peace by a month or six weeks." *Roosevelt*, 182.

385 **"in her stomach"** TR, *Works*, vol. 3, 83.

385 **his new ambassador** "Few Ambassadors have gone to their posts with a letter so full of the mind of their ruler." John Hay diary, 5 Jan. 1905 (JH). See also TR, *Letters*, vol. 4, 1134, for the President's earlier attempts to influence the Russian government "privately and unofficially." The adroit Meyer was to become the most valuable of all his diplomatic appointments. See Howe, *George von Lengerke Meyer*.

385 **Meyer had managed** Howe, *George von Lengerke Meyer*, 145–46.

385 **The Tsarina's problem** Trani, *Treaty of Portsmouth*, 49–50; Gwynn, *Letters and Friendships*, vol. 1, 455, 465–68.

385 **"Did you ever"** TR, *Letters*, vol. 4, 1158.

385 **"my own belief"** Ibid., 1179.

385 **"As we left ever"** TR, *Works*, vol. 3, 91.

CHAPTER 24: THE BEST HERDER OF EMPERORS SINCE NAPOLEON

386 *Thim was th'* "Mr. Dooley" in *The Washington Post,* 12 Apr. 1903.
386 *"Come hither"* Wallace Irwin, "The Ballad of Grizzly Gulch," in *At the Sign of the Dollar* (New York, 1905), 32.
386 *But as he* Ibid., 34.
387 (Santo Domingo would) See Gow, "How Did the Roosevelt Corollary?"
387 the better he could Note that he does not mention a word of his involvement even to Elihu Root on 13 May. TR, *Letters,* vol. 4, 1171–72.
387 *So backward* Irwin, "Ballad of Grizzly Gulch," 35.
387 THE BATTLE OF Tsu Kenneth Wimmel, *Theodore Roosevelt and the Great White Fleet: American Sea Power Comes of Age* (Dulles, Va., 1998), 192.
387 *"a civilized"* See p. 228.
387 Although he confessed TR, *Letters,* vol. 4, 1178.
387 His cousin Wilhelm Trani, *Treaty of Portsmouth,* 47.
387 Ambassador Cassini Jusserand, *What Me Befell,* 300; TR, *Letters,* vol. 4, 1232.
387 But France, right Larsen, "Theodore Roosevelt and the Moroccan Crisis," 122–24. TR had changed his mind about staying aloof from the Moroccan squabble because he saw in it the possibility of "a world conflagration."
387 So the diplomatic

  Chronological Note: On 2 June 1905, TR initiated what Oscar Kraines calls "the first comprehensive inquiry" into federal administration (Oscar Kraines, "The President Versus Congress: The Keep Commission, 1905–1909," *Western Political Quarterly* 23.1 [1970]). On his own initiative, and without Congressional direction or confirmation, TR appointed a committee for the purpose of investigating business methods in all federal offices, with an eye toward improving efficiency and cutting costs. Headed by Assistant Secretary of the Treasury Charles H. Keep, and composed of James Garfield, Gifford Pinchot, Lawrence Murray, and Frank Hitchcock, the commission first investigated two government-agency scandals (an area technically outside their mandated province) before getting down to the stated task. Keep and his colleagues uncovered copious examples of waste and ineffective methods, and came up with some truly innovative ideas and solutions (many originated by TR himself). The Keep Commission was the first to recommend the idea of a retirement program for federal employees; to propose a classification system for federal salaries and positions; to suggest uniform regulations for work hours and leaves of absence; and to recommend the centralization of supply purchasing and distribution, as well as the reduction of unnecessary government publications and mailings. Despite the Commission's hard work, Congress refused to pass any related legislation. Kraines notes that while Congress viewed the increasing cost of government with alarm, it viewed with equal (if not greater) alarm the President's attempts to investigate and reorganize as threats to both legislative control and patronage. The Keep Commission became just another battleground between TR, who wished to expand his executive powers, and a Congress reluctant to surrender any authority. It took until 1920 for Congress to create a retirement system for federal employees.
388 ROOSEVELT PUT ALL As early as Aug. 1904, TR had considered Meyer to be Cabinet material, as well as a potential top ambassador. TR, *Letters,* vol. 4, 890.
388 Although the United States Ambassador When Meyer first met the Tsar, on 12 Apr. 1905, he was able to break the ice by saying that he had "met His Imperial Majesty's brother . . . at Kiel, when I was racing there with the Emperor of Ger-

many" (Howe, *George von Lengerke Meyer,* 142). For a modern assessment, see Wayne A. Wiegand, "George Meyer and Kaiser Wilhelm II," *Mid-America* 74.1 (Jan. 1974).

388 **The way Meyer** Howe, *George von Lengerke Meyer, passim.* Failure to "make the Porc.," as Cousin Teddy had, became a lifelong neurosis for Franklin Roosevelt. Geoffrey C. Ward, *A First Class Temperament: The Emergence of Franklin Roosevelt* (New York, 1989), 46.

388 **"I want a man"** TR, *Letters,* vol. 4, 1079.

388 **"I am not inclined"** Ibid., 1079–80.

389 **After only two** Howe, *George von Lengerke Meyer,* 157.

389 **This was not** Trani, *Treaty of Portsmouth,* 46; Dennett, *Roosevelt,* 215–16.

389 **At all costs** TR, *Letters,* vol. 4, 1203.

389 **The move was** Ibid., 1203–4.

389 **Count Lamsdorff** George von Lengerke Meyer diary, 6 June 1905 (GVM). The Tsarina's birthday is wrongly dated in Dennett, *Roosevelt,* 193.

390 **Meyer found himself** Except where otherwise indicated, the following account is taken from Howe, *George von Lengerke Meyer,* 158–62.

390 **"It is the judgment"** Telegram copy, 5 June 1905, in TRP. See also TR, *Letters,* vol. 4, 1204.

390 **As Meyer read** George von Lengerke Meyer diary, 7 June 1904 (GVM).

390 **"If Russia will"** TR, *Letters,* vol. 4, 1204.

390 **". . . and the President"** Ibid.

391 **"Mr Roosevelt's success"** London *Morning Post,* 12 June 1905.

392 **He had, in fact** *Washington Times,* 9 June 1905; TR, *Letters,* vol. 4, 1209; Morris, *Edith Kermit Roosevelt,* 289–90.

392 **"It really is"** TR, *Letters,* vol. 4, 1209.

392 **Since Edith's culinary industry** Ibid. Pine Knot, 125 miles southwest of Washington, remained TR's country hideaway throughout his second term. It is now maintained as a museum by the Theodore Roosevelt Association. See William H. Harbaugh, "The Theodore Roosevelts' Retreat in Southern Albemarle: Pine Knot 1905–1908," *Magazine of Albemarle County History* 51 (1993).

392 **"The President is"** Joseph James Matthews, *George W. Smalley: Forty Years a Foreign Correspondent* (Chapel Hill, 1973), 158.

392 **What was "going on"** TR, *Letters,* vol. 4, 1222–29; vol. 6, 234–36.

392 **"The President feels"** TR to Kogoro Takahira, 15 June 1905, qu. in *Letters,* vol. 4, 1228.

393 **There was a world** Ibid., 1230; Wood, *Roosevelt As We Knew Him,* 168.

393 **"the triumph of Asia"** TR, qu. in Wood, *Roosevelt As We Knew Him,* 168.

393 **Roosevelt had confided** Mrs. Lodge was included as an honorary member of TR's *secret du roi.* TR, *Letters,* vol. 4, 1202.

393 **As he mediated** Ibid., 1303; vol. 6, 234.

393 **Wilhelm II had** Jusserand, *What Me Befell,* 319–20. Von Sternburg asked if the President was also taking Wilhelm II's *Weltanschauung* into account in his Far Eastern negotiations. (The Kaiser had urged peace upon the Tsar, fearing that Nicholas might be assassinated after Tsu Shima.) TR truthfully replied that Meyer had used Wilhelm's name as well as his own when conversing with the Tsar. TR, *Letters,* vol. 4, 1203; Henry Cabot Lodge (qu. TR in 1905) to Philippe Bunau-Varilla, 12 July 1924 (FBL).

393 **The French Ambassador** Both the French and British governments shared TR's fear of war if the Kaiser was not thrown a sacrificial lamb. Delcassé was succeeded on 6 June 1904 by the less imperialistic Maurice Rouvier. For the text of TR's memo (which he shared with Jusserand), see TR, *Letters,* vol. 4, 1256–57. Larsen,

"Theodore Roosevelt and the Moroccan Crisis," chap. 3, provides the most detailed account of TR's parallel negotiations in 1905. For TR's own record, see TR, *Letters,* vol. 6, 231–51.

393 **Roosevelt made a point** Jusserand, *What Me Befell,* 302–3.

393 **"eight guinea-pig power"** TR, *Letters,* vol. 5, 242.

393 **A summons to** Sir H. Mortimer Durand diary, 18 June 1904 (HMD).

394 **"He told me"** Sir H. Mortimer Durand to Lord Lansdowne, 16 June 1904 (HMD).

394 **("You are the only")** TR, *Letters,* vol. 4, 1203.

394 **Lodge, in turn** Sir H. Mortimer Durand to Lord Lansdowne, 16 June 1904 (HMD). TR could not resist giving a hint to what he was doing when he told the graduating class at Clark University in Worcester, Mass., on 21 June: "No man in public position can, under penalty of forfeiting the right to the respect of those whose regard he most values, fail as the opportunity comes to do all that in him lies for peace." Transcript in TRB.

394 **Durand noted** Ibid. For TR's two June "posterity letters" to Henry Cabot Lodge, describing his activities, see TR, *Letters,* vol. 4, 1202–6 and 1221–33.

394 JUSSERAND HAD NO Jusserand, *What Me Befell,* 302–3; John Hay to TR, 16 June 1904 (TD).

394 **"I suppose nothing"** TR, *Letters,* vol. 4, 1216.

394 **In the mid-Atlantic** John Hay diary, 13 June 1904 (JH). The vision of Lincoln prompted Hay to write his own epitaph. See Thayer, *John Hay,* vol. 2, 408–9.

395 **Roosevelt was in** TR joked to Hay that "the more I saw of the Tsar and the Kaiser, the better I liked the United States Senate." TR, *Letters,* vol. 4, 1286.

395 **As they talked** John Hay to Clara Hay, 20 June 1904 (TD).

Chronological Note: On 28 June, TR attended the twenty-fifth reunion of the Harvard Class of 1880. For an excellent account, see Marian L. Peabody, "Theodore Roosevelt Visits Cambridge: Reminiscences of His Hostess's Daughter," *Harvard Alumni Bulletin,* 3 May 1958.

395 NEWS OF THE TR reacted to Hay's death with genuine grief. But he made clear that he mourned him as "a beloved friend," and not as a member of the Administration. "For two years he has done little or nothing in the State Dept. What I didn't do myself wasn't done at all" (TR, *Letters,* vol. 4, 1260—or, for harsher criticism, 1271). He attended the Secretary's funeral in Cleveland on 5 July, accompanied by past and present Cabinet officers. In a strange scene afterward, when the presidential party was picnicking on a railside lawn at Wheelock's Switch [Ohio] en route east, TR suddenly rose to his knees "and asked God's mercy" on Hay's soul. The Cabinet knelt with him for a few minutes of silence under the trees. *The New York Times,* 7 July 1905.

395 **Simultaneously, William** Washington *Evening Star,* 1 and 2 July 1905; Longworth, *Crowded Hours,* 69–70.

395 **"Elihu," the President** Emily Stewart notes, 1905 (PCJ).

395 **Root sat silent** Dunne, "Remembrances"; Elihu Root, interviewed by Emily Stewart, 13 Sept. 1932 (PCJ). According to Jessup, *Elihu Root,* vol. 1, 449, Root sacrificed an estimated $200,000 in annual income to become Secretary of State at $8,000.

395 **He exchanged glances** Emily Stewart notes, 1905 (PCJ). This conversation took place on the presidential train after Hay's funeral in Cleveland.

395 ROOSEVELT WAS QUITE Elihu Root, interviewed by Emily Stewart, 13 Sept. 1932 (PCJ).

395 **Apart from an** Japan declined TR's suggestion of an armistice. Dennett, *Roosevelt,* 205.

395 **A sense gathered** Trani, *Treaty of Portsmouth*, 83. TR did not realize that Britain needed Japan's goodwill in a secret attempt to strengthen the Anglo-Japanese Alliance *vis-à-vis* India and Korea. The allies were soon to sign a revised agreement protecting British interests in the former and Japanese aspirations in the latter. See Ian H. Nish, *The Anglo-Japanese Alliance: The Diplomacy of Two Island Empires, 1894–1907* (London, 1966).

395 **mutiny aboard** Dennett, *Roosevelt*, 205.

396 **Wilhelm II seemed** Ibid., 208.

396 **Roosevelt was reinforced** Gwynn, *Letters and Friendships*, vol. 1, 476.

396 **"Now, oh best"** TR, *Letters*, vol. 4, 1283–84.

396 **"My feeling is"** Ibid., 1284.

396 **Knowing he could** Ibid.

396 **Roosevelt's admiration** Ibid., 1233.

397 **Eight years before** Morris, *Rise of Theodore Roosevelt*, 572–73.

397 **"In a dozen years"** TR, *Letters*, vol. 4, 1233–34.

397 **The oracular tone** Esthus, *Theodore Roosevelt and Japan*, 129; Trani, *Treaty of Portsmouth*, 85. According to John Barrett, whom TR asked to report on the situation in California, anti-Japanese hysteria was largely due to propaganda put about by Michael H. De Young, owner of the *San Francisco Chronicle*, for reasons as much to do with newspaper circulation as any desire to "embarrass" the President. At any rate, the "yellow peril" propaganda was dangerously effective. John Barrett to [unknown], ca. 6 July 1905, and TR to Barrett, 15 July 1905 (JB); Thomas A. Bailey, *Theodore Roosevelt and the Japanese-American Crises* (Stanford, 1934), 10–11.

397 **He was afraid** When Cassini blustered that Russia "was fighting the battles of the white race" in the Far East, TR, thinking of the Kishinev pogrom, asked him "why in that case she had treated other members of the white race even worse than she had treated Japan." The Ambassador's reply was not recorded. TR, *Letters*, vol. 4, 1222.

397 **He asked Lloyd** Trani, *Treaty of Portsmouth*, 86. TR also vehemently protested discrimination against Chinese immigrants, with the exception of "coolies," or peasants. TR, *Letters*, vol. 4, 1235–36.

397 **HAPPILY, THE PRESIDENT** Taft's party left Washington on 30 June 1905, and sailed from San Francisco on 8 July. For varying accounts of the trip, see Ralph E. Minger, "Taft's Mission to Japan: A Study in Secret Diplomacy," *Pacific Historical Review* 30 (1961), and Stacy Rozek Cordery, "Theodore Roosevelt's Private Diplomat: Alice Roosevelt and the 1905 Far Eastern Junket," in Naylor et al., *Theodore Roosevelt*, 352–67.

399 **Roosevelt had asked** Pringle, *Theodore Roosevelt*, 384.

399 **the flare and smell** This was Alice's own phrase. Longworth, *Crowded Hours*, 70.

399 **She was, if anything** Ibid., 72–77, 68.

399 **When they arrived** Ibid., 79–84.

399 **On 27 July** William H. Taft to Elihu Root, 29 July 1905 ("Agreed Memorandum of Conversation Between Prime Minister of Japan and Myself"), cable transmission reproduced in John Gilbert Reid, ed., "Taft's Telegram to Root," *Pacific Historical Review*, March 1940 (hereafter "Taft-Katsura Memorandum"). Taft addressed himself to Root, but was communicating with TR. His cable cost the United States taxpayer just over one thousand dollars, or about $19,400 today.

399 **Although the memorandum** Esthus, *Roosevelt and Japan*, 102.
     Historiographical Note: Esthus notes the illogicality whereby conspiratorial historians have insisted, over the years, in calling this document the "Taft-Katsura Agreement." Its own title, qu. above, shows "only that the two parties agreed that the memorandum was an accurate record of what was said."

Esthus notes further that the memorandum, for all its subsequent reputation as a "secret pact" and progenitor of the myriad "executive agreements" characteristic of 20th-century diplomacy, lay forgotten for nearly twenty years, after serving its original informal purpose. TR specifically denied on 5 Oct. that there had been any quid pro quo. The memorandum was meant "merely to clear up Japan's attitude [regarding the Philippines], which had been purposefully misrepresented by pro-Russian sympathizers." Its separately numbered statements about Korea and the Anglo-Japanese Alliance stood "entirely apart" from that primary concern (TR, *Letters*, vol. 5, 46).

In further support of TR's denial, Katsura himself denied Japanese rumors of a "bargain" concerning Korea. The Prime Minister stated that United States policy toward Korea in 1905 struck him as "entirely spontaneous" (Esthus, *Roosevelt and Japan*, 105). Index entries under "Korea" in TR, *Letters*, vol. 4, *et seq.*, show that TR's own contemptuous attitude toward the Hermit Kingdom was formed long before the Taft-Katsura conversation.

For the rediscovery of the cable, see Tyler Dennett, "President Roosevelt's Secret Pact with Japan," *Current History*, Oct. 1924. For a sample modern interpretation by the conspiracy school, see Walter LaFeber, "Betrayal in Tokyo," *Constitution*, fall 1994.

399 **As the Prime Minister** Taft-Katsura Memorandum.

399 **Allowing Koreans** Ibid. For Japan's previous efforts, diplomatic and military, to colonize Korea, see Dennett, *Roosevelt*, 96–111. See also M. Hane, "Theodore Roosevelt and Korea: The U.S. Response to the Japanese Policy to Make Korea Its Protectorate," *Journal of American History* 82.4 (1996).

399 **Regarding the Philippines** Taft-Katsura Memorandum.

399 **Taft said that** Ibid. For reactions to Root's appointment, see Jessup, *Elihu Root*, vol. 1, 47–51.

400 **"If I have"** Taft-Katsura Memorandum.

400 YOUR CONVERSATION TR, *Letters*, vol. 4, 1293; Dennett, *Roosevelt*, 110–11.

400 ALICE, UNAWARE Alice Roosevelt diary, 27 July and *passim* 1905 (ARL).

400 **At a dinner entertainment** Griscom, *Diplomatically Speaking*, 259.

400 **Since her father** Teague, *Mrs. L.*, 4–5; Morris, *Rise of Theodore Roosevelt*, 122.

401 **Her last impression** Longworth, *Crowded Hours*, 85.

401 **a sketch of his daughter** Facsimile from family collection, privately held. TR's superscript reads "*Not* a posterity letter."

401 **At the time** Dennett, *Roosevelt*, 198–200.

402 **Washington was, of** TR, *Letters*, vol. 4, 1226.

402 **Only one met** Trani, *Treaty of Portsmouth*, 66. The choice of Portsmouth was announced officially on 12 July 1904.

402 **The pretty, little** Ibid., 67–70. The building (no. 86) still stands.

402 **Their respective** Trani, *Treaty of Portsmouth*, 115–16.

402 AT SIX AND A half Ibid., 74–76; Adams, *Letters*, vol. 5, 284; E. J. Dillon, "Sergius Witte," *Review of Reviews*, Sept. 1905.

402 **Henry Adams had** Adams, *Letters*, vol. 5, 284; John Hay diary, 16 Feb. 1905 (JH); Charles Hardinge to Lord Lansdowne, 4 Jan. 1905, in *British Documents on Foreign Affairs*, vol. 1A, 3, 1. The best contemporary portrait of Witte is in Smalley, *Anglo-American Memories*, chap. 30.

403 **Roosevelt had hoped** Dennett, *Roosevelt*, 42–43; TR, *Letters*, vol. 4, 1276. Ito had actually proposed a Russo-Japanese alliance in 1902, when Witte was the Tsar's finance minister.

403 **Komura was, like** Trani, *Treaty of Portsmouth*, 72; Smalley, *Anglo-American*

Memories, 398. The latter memorably describes Komura as having "an intelligent face, but of parchment written all over with hieroglyphics."

403 **Not only that** Griscom, *Diplomatically Speaking*, 225–26.

403 **The four plenipotentiaries** For a complete list of delegates to the Portsmouth Conference, see Trani, *Treaty of Portsmouth*, 72–73, 76–77.

403 **That solemn engagement** Philip G. Thompson notes (Portsmouth Conference) (HKB). The date of this visit was 27 July. *The New York Times*, 28 July 1905.

403 **a space both deep and high** The following description is based on David H. Wallace, *Historic Furnishings Report: Sagamore Hill National Historic Site* (Harpers Ferry, W. Va., 1989), vol. 1, 51–52, 246–52 (photographs taken in July 1905). See also Hermann Hagedorn, *The Roosevelt Family of Sagamore Hill* (New York, 1954), 232–35. Komura was the first VIP received by TR in the North Room.

403 **heavy Philippine hardwoods** The Roosevelts took pride in the fact that "every bit of wood or stone [in the North Room] came from the United States or her possessions." Roosevelt, *All in the Family*, 7–9.

404 **"Framed" thus in** Japan's terms are reproduced in Dennett, *Roosevelt*, 231–32. See also Trani, *Treaty of Portsmouth*, 95–96.

404 **Arrogant though these** Trani, *Treaty of Portsmouth*, 96.

404 **As for the indemnity** TR, *Letters*, vol. 4, 1293.

404 **hard numbers of yen** A member of the Japanese delegation hinted that the indemnity request might run as high as three million yen. J. J. Korostovetz, *Pre-War Diplomacy: The Russo-Japanese Problem: Diary of J. J. Korostovetz* (London, 1920), 28 (hereafter Korostovetz, *Diary*).

404 **After Komura and Takahira** TR, *Letters*, vol. 4, 1293. Philippe Bunau-Varilla to Francis B. Loomis, 27 July 1905 (FBL); Loomis to TR, 28 July 1905 (TRP).

404 **Roosevelt was worried** TR, *Letters*, vol. 4, 1293. TR here displayed acute intuition. According to Baron Rosen, Witte "would not have hesitated to consent to the payment of a war indemnity provided it could be accomplished under some plausible disguise." Roman Rosen, *Forty Years of Diplomacy* (London, 1922), vol. 1, 263–64.

404 **his friend Kentaro** See above, Interlude, p. 368.

404 **The Russian plenipotentiaries** Korostovetz, *Diary*, 31.

405 **His guests arrived** Ibid.

405 **Still less could** Trani, *Treaty of Portsmouth*, 112, quotes some of the Tsar's adamant instructions, which formed the basis of Witte's negotiating brief.

405 **Their country** Rosen, *Forty Years*, vol. 1, 263–64. Sakhalin was to remain a Russian strategic trigger-spot for most of the rest of the century: *vide* the downing of Korean Airlines Flight 007 in 1983.

405 **Paradoxically, the** Ibid., 264.

405 **Baron Rosen's suspicion** Ibid.

405 **Witte was enormous** Smalley, *Anglo-American Memories*, 386–87; TR, *Letters*, vol. 5, 61. TR's impression of Witte was not altogether pleasant, and turned to outright dislike as the peace conference progressed. TR, *Letters*, vol. 5, 22–23.

405 **"We are not"** Korostovetz, *Diary*, 31, qu. Witte's own repetition, later that day, of his words to TR.

405 **However, Witte** Ibid., 32.

406 **Witte watched** Witte, *Memoirs*, vol. 2, 442. It is probable that Witte told TR, for example, that Japan had just as many imperialistic designs in Manchuria as Russia did, and considerably more in Korea. And by her very nature, she was likely to close the Open Doors in both those countries with louder slams than any yet heard. After Portsmouth, Japan did indeed immediately close the door on Korea, and by the time TR left office she had begun to shut it in Manchuria, too. By 1938, Japan had used her military power to close off all of China to the West, and her

subsequent moves upon the Philippines, not to mention Pearl Harbor, made wastepaper of the Taft-Katsura Memorandum. It is moot, of course, whether China and Korea would have fared any better under Russian domination. See Dennett, *Roosevelt*, 238–39, for the role of public relations in formulating American attitudes in 1905.

406   **Roosevelt said**   Korostovetz, *Diary*, 35.

406   **The plenipotentiaries**   Dennett, *Roosevelt*, 240 "I have brought them to a cool spring," TR said later that afternoon. "It remains to be seen whether they will drink of it or not." Smalley, *Anglo-American Memories*, 362.

406   **Tweedledum and Tweedledee**   See above, p. 168.

406   **from next Wednesday**   When the delegations got to Portsmouth, they found that TR had made no arrangements for meetings, leaving them to construct their own schedule. Trani, *Treaty of Portsmouth*, 127.

406   **He sent two**   Korostovetz, *Diary*, 35. Except where otherwise indicated, the following is taken from this source, plus New York *Sun*, 6 Aug. 1905, and Henry J. Forman's excellent oral history of his coverage of the *Mayflower* reception for the *Sun* syndicate. Forman was one of the bright young reporters TR liked to cultivate with exclusive favors. He was given a presidential pass to remain on board during the ceremonies, and permission to dispatch bulletins ashore by rowboat shuttle (dropping them out through a porthole). A transcript of Forman's memoir, "So Brief a Time" (1959–1960), conducted by Doyce B. Nunis, is in the Department of Special Collections, Young Research Library, UCLA.

406   **glittered like a ballroom**   The simile is Forman's.

407   **From then on**   It is not likely that a peace conference ever began more noisily. The *Mayflower*'s logbook records twenty-one guns for TR, nineteen each for the plenipotentiaries, then respective honors for every Cabinet officer, admiral, and general who came aboard. O.H.M. McPherson, "The U.S.S. *Mayflower*, a Presidential Prerogative," *Yachting*, July 1992.

407   **the Stars and Stripes**   This flag now hangs at in the North Room at Sagamore Hill.

407   **Since Komura and**   Rosen, *Forty Years*, vol. 1, 265.

407   **The door to**   Witte, *Memoirs*, vol. 2, 434, 439.

407   **As the President handled**   The simile of a hostess is again that of Forman, who was stationed in the room with a notebook. It was the first decisive moment of the peace conference, a pas de deux or pas de quatre, a symbolic crossing of the threshold between formality and conviviality. The subsequent relaxation of tension was not to last.

407   **Asia and Russia**   "Two and two they came, arm in arm." Forman's original eyewitness account makes plain that TR and his senior guests did not, as often stated, enter all in a row. He led the way, as President of the United States, and the plenipotentiaries followed, "Baron Komura's shoulder touching Mr. Witte's elbow." Witte managed, by means of his longer stride, to get a foot over the threshold first.

407   **Those set aside**   Not even the punctilious Rosen recalled his orientation. "We were seated all in a group surrounding our genial host" (*Forty Years*, vol. 1, 265). Hagedorn, *Roosevelt Family*, 222, says without attribution that the principals shared a long wall seat, while TR took "the only chair in the room, facing them."

407   **To Komura, he**   Rosen tried to interpret, but was ignored.

　　　　Historical Note: TR read French easily, as indicated by his consumption of all of La Corce and Cahun's *Turcs et Mongols* in 1905 ("with such thoroughness . . . that at the end it was dangling out of the covers"). He spoke the language with equal ease ("Je le parle comme une langue touranienne"), although John Hay noticed that his grammar was "entirely lawless," and Jules Jusserand was amused by his occasional, entirely unself-conscious pauses before settling on *le mot juste* (TR, *Letters*, vol.

4, 1268; André Zardieu, "Trois Visites à M. Roosevelt," *Le Temps,* 15 Apr. 1908; Thayer, *John Hay,* vol. 2, 356; Jusserand, *What Me Befell,* 338).

According to Ethel Roosevelt Derby (interview, 1962 [TRB]), her father read German "equally well"—works of literature, history, and science, as well as poetry. In youth, he could recite stretches of the *Nibelungenlied* by heart. As President, TR often conversed in German with Germans (Dunn, *From Harrison to Harding,* vol. 1, 373; Butt, *Letters,* 116). He was less versed in Italian, although, as noted above, he read E. de Michelis's *L'Origine degli Indo-Europei* from cover to cover in 1904. For more on TR's "not inconsiderable" linguistic achievements, see Wagenknecht, *Seven Worlds,* 34–35.

408 **Other guests** *Review of Reviews,* Sept. 1905.

408 **Roosevelt went on** See TR, *Works,* vol. 18, 409.

408 **When lunch was** Rosen's position right next to the President, opposite Komura, was not accidental. As Russian Ambassador to the United States, "I was the ranking person of both delegations." Rosen, *Forty Years,* vol. 1, 265.

408 **AT TWENTY MINUTES** New York *Sun,* 6 Aug. 1905, precisely gives departure times. In what is possibly a jingoistic slip of the pen, Korostovetz has the *Dolphin* wallowing in the *Mayflower*'s wake. *Diary,* 37.

410 **"I think we"** Hagedorn, *Roosevelt Family,* 223, qu. Joseph Bucklin Bishop.

410 **The self-important** New York *Sun,* 19 Aug. 1905; Forman, "So Brief a Time," 34–35. For the negotiations up to this point, see Trani, *Treaty of Portsmouth,* 128–38. Trani's overall account of the conference is the only one based on Japanese and Russian, as well as American, primary sources.

410 **His news today** Trani, *Treaty of Portsmouth,* 137–39.

410 **Later that evening** George Meyer to TR, 18 Aug. 1905 (TRP); Trani, *Treaty of Portsmouth,* 139.

410 **Roosevelt detected** See, e.g., TR, *Letters,* vol. 4, 1222–23.

410 **A fantasy began** Lee, *Good Innings,* vol. 1, 306.

411 **He told Kaneko** Trani, *Treaty of Portsmouth,* 140.

411 **That night, Roosevelt** Beale, *Theodore Roosevelt,* 296–97.

411 **It was galvanizing** The telegram, addressed to Witte, read: "I earnestly request that you send either Baron Rosen or some other gentleman who is in your confidence to see me immediately, so that I may through him send you a strictly confidential message." Dennett, *Roosevelt,* 251–52.

411 **Roosevelt was playing** Korostovetz, *Diary,* 92.

411 **He said that three** Trani, *Treaty of Portsmouth,* 141.

411 **"We Americans"** Qu. in ibid., 142.

411 **Roosevelt seemed to know** TR was receiving regular briefs from the reporter John Callan O'Laughlin, a member of his *secret du roi* with good connections in Portsmouth. See Dennett, *Roosevelt,* 252n.

411 **He asked Rosen** Korostovetz, *Diary,* 91–92; Dennett, *Roosevelt,* 252. TR was unaware, as he talked, that Nicholas II had that day summoned the Duma (national assembly)—the first truly democratic step taken by any Russian monarch.

411 **Rosen, politely masking** The ambassador kept his anger for later (Rosen, *Forty Years,* vol. 1, 104; Korostovetz, *Diary,* 99).

411 **"If it is our"** Qu. in Beale, *Theodore Roosevelt,* 299. TR's proposal was rejected outright by Nicholas II (Trani, *Treaty of Portsmouth,* 142). Throughout the conference, the Russians felt they were being leaned on by TR, because the Japanese were rigidly silent about his equal pressure on them. He compared his own attitude

as being that of "a very polite but also very insistent Dutch uncle." TR, *Letters,* vol. 5, 1.

411 **On Monday, the President** Dennett, *Roosevelt,* 253.

412 **"I earnestly ask"** TR, *Letters,* vol. 4, 1307-8.

412 **"not an inch"** Trani, *Treaty of Portsmouth,* 138.

412 **The cable went** TR, *Letters,* vol. 4, 1306-8.

412 **"I think I ought"** Ibid., 1308-9.

412 **Then, putting** TR to Jules Jusserand, 21 Aug. 1905 (JJ). In a handwritten postscript, TR adds: "I have received a couple of brand-new pipe dreams from my constant correpondent [Wilhelm II]."

412 **"I cannot"** Adams, *Letters,* vol. 5, 707.

412 THE SIGHT OF **Sergei** Trani, *Treaty of Portsmouth,* 145.

413 **"Russia is not"** George Meyer to TR, 23 Aug. 1905, qu. in TR, *Letters,* vol. 5, 5-6. See ibid., 6-9, for more cables to and from TR during the crisis period.

413 **On the same day** For an indication of TR's frenzied activity in this period ("I am having my hair turned gray"), see Beale, *Theodore Roosevelt,* 298-302.

413 **Another year of war** TR, *Letters,* vol. 5, 1312-13.

413 **The letter was wired** Beale, *Theodore Roosevelt,* 301-2.

413 ON FRIDAY, 25 **August** For more on TR's famous dive, see Douglas, *The Many-Sided Roosevelt,* 104-5; Hagedorn, *Roosevelt Family,* 226-29.

413 **cigarette after cigarette** Smalley, *Anglo-American Memories,* 399. This dramatic story was told by Witte after the conference. Witte wrote later that he had spent the previous night "sobbing and praying." Witte, *Memoirs,* vol. 2, 440.

413 **Rumors spread over the weekend** Korostovetz, *Diary,* 102; Dennett, *Roosevelt,* 260.

414 **On Tuesday, 29 August** Korostovetz, *Diary,* 107-8.

414 **Komura sat** Dennett, *Roosevelt,* 261.

414 HENRY J. FORMAN This incident occurred on 10 Aug. 1905. Forman, "So Brief a Time," 29-31.

414 **Then Roosevelt was** Ibid., 30.

414 **"the best herder"** Adams, *Letters,* vol. 5, 719.

414 **"It's a mighty"** Harold Phelps Stokes, "Yale, the Portsmouth Treaty, and Japan," privately printed memoir, 1948 (TRC).

CHAPTER 25: MERE FORCE OF EVENTS

415 *Ye see, th' fact* Dunne, *Mr. Dooley's Observations,* 97.

415 **"Accept my congratulations"** Qu. by TR in *Letters,* vol. 5, 9. For the plaudits of other foreign government officials, see Benson J. Lossing, *Our Country* (New York, 1908), vol. 8, 2084-87.

> *Chronological Note:* On 13 Sept. 1905, in a development that greatly amused TR, Nicholas II called for a second Hague Peace Conference. TR asked the Russian Ambassador if this meant that His Majesty wished to have it appear that he (not TR in 1904) had conceived of calling a second conference. When Baron Rosen answered yes, TR told him that he was delighted to have the Tsar take the initiative in the matter, and that he would heartily back him up. While relieved that it would not fall to him, once again, to "appear as a professional peace advocate," the President did find a "rather grim irony" in the fact that the man who had so prolonged the Russo-Japanese War was now taking the lead in a "proposition toward world peace" (TR, *Letters,* vol. 5, 25-26, 30-31). The Second Hague Conference met on 15 June 1907.

415 **The Mikado's enigmatic** TR, *Letters,* vol. 5, 8–9. After the Portsmouth Peace Treaty was signed, TR sent Mutsuhito the largest of his Colorado bearskins. According to Kaneko, "His Majesty was greatly pleased with the skin, because of the emblematic nature of the gift." Street, "Japanese Statesman's Recollections."

415 **"It is enough"** TR, *Letters,* vol. 5, 1–2. Taft had, meanwhile, returned home with most of his official party.

416 **Alice had returned** Longworth, *Crowded Hours,* 106–7; TR, *Letters,* vol. 5, 15; *Review of Reviews,* Oct. 1904.

416 **This did not** "I confess that we came out from [the] Navy Yard in Portsmouth with all the booties as we could carry and cast a discreet smile on our 'wily Oriental faces.' " Kentaro Kaneko to Oliver Wendell Holmes, Jr., 7 Sept. 1905, in Kanda and Gifford, "Kaneko Correspondence," 2.

416 **After Tsu Shima** TR qu. in Wood, *Roosevelt As We Knew Him,* 168; Ferguson, "John Barrett" (JB); Grenville and Young, *Politics, Strategy, and American Diplomacy,* 313ff. Many years later, when Philip C. Jessup asked about TR's conduct of Far Eastern affairs from 1905 to 1909, Root replied dryly, "He kept them in his hands." Interview, 13 Sept. 1932 (ER).

417 **a new recruit** See James Brown Scott, *Robert Bacon: Life and Letters* (New York, 1923), 105; Jessup, *Elihu Root,* vol. 2, 455–56.

417 **Socialism was spreading** *British Documents on Foreign Affairs,* vol. 1A, 3, 162–63; Jusserand, *What Me Befell,* 322.

417 **The "odd year"** Gould, *Presidency of Theodore Roosevelt,* 26–27, points out that, by statute, the second and fourth congressional sessions of the four-year cycle had to end on 4 March. That made each a mere three months long.

417 **One issue above** Ibid.; Mowry, *Era of Theodore Roosevelt,* 198. It Is not known if TR saw Baker's earlier conspiracistic articles about J. P. Morgan and "The Great Northern Pacific Deal" in *Collier's,* Oct.–Nov. 1901. If so, he would have been able to trace the progressivist neurosis to the first weeks of his own presidency.

418 **"law-abidingness"** S. S. McClure to TR, 18 July 1905 (TRP). See also Philip Loring Allen, *America's Awakening: The Triumph of Righteousness in High Places* (New York, 1906), chap. 1.

418 **Doubtless somebody** "Somebody" by the name of Herbert Croly had indeed just begun work on what was to become the basic text of Progressivism: *The Promise of American Life* (New York, 1909). See Croly, "Why I Wrote My Latest Book," *World's Work,* May 1910, and "The Memoirs of Herbert Croly: An Unpublished Document," ed. Charles Hirschfeld, *New York History* 58.3 (1977).

418 **What particularly** S. S. McClure to TR, 18 July 1905 (TRP). The first five chapters of Mowry, *Era of Theodore Roosevelt,* remain the best survey of the rise of Progressivism in early twentieth-century America.

418 **Now here, in the** Ray Stannard Baker to TR, 9 Sept. 1905 (TRP). The page proofs are wrongly identified in TR, *Letters,* vol. 5, 25, as coming from Baker's first (Nov. 1905) article in the series. See text, below.

418 **Let Baker, Steffens** See Eugene L. Huddleston, "The Generals up in Wall Street," *Railroad History* 145 (1981), for an alternative look at Ray Stannard Baker and his work. While history has viewed Baker as one of its greatest muckrakers and a wholly impartial analyst of runaway corporate power, Huddleston maintains that Baker was neither as objective nor as well-informed as Progressives then and since have made him out to be. He claims that Baker oversimplified complex issues, fell short in command of technical data governing railroad rates, operations, and regulation, and used as his most trusted background source an outdated, fifteen-year-old book, A. B. Stickney's *The Railway Problem.* Huddleston also feels that Baker often relied on moralistic rhetoric designed to stir up emotion in an effort to disguise the fact that he had little solid evidence of wrongdoing. In Huddleston's judg-

ment, Baker's solid reputation today is based partly on the esteem accorded him by TR, who consulted with the journalist in drafting railroad-reform legislation, even including a paragraph almost exactly in Baker's words in his Message to Congress seeking such legislation. Time would demonstrate that TR used Baker to help accomplish his goal of rallying popular support for the new legislation—Baker's six-part series appeared at just the right time, November 1905–June 1906, to help the Hepburn Act through Congress—only to dismiss his brand of journalism as less than honorable. Baker's disillusionment with TR led him to ardent support of Woodrow Wilson, and he later became Wilson's official biographer.

418 **"I haven't"** TR, *Letters,* vol. 5, 25.

418 **Just how "far"** Pringle, *Theodore Roosevelt,* 359–65, shows that TR gave advance notice of his legislative intentions to the "short" Congress of 1904–1905, both in his Fourth Annual Message and in a remarkable speech to the Union Club of Philadelphia on 30 January 1905. Neither utterance had any lasting effect, due to the distraction of the Inauguration and the quick death of the Fifty-eighth Congress.

419 **On 30 September** Cheney, *Personal Memoirs,* 122–23.

419 **The President approached** New York *Sun,* 1 Oct. 1905.

419 **Two articles of his** *Scribner's,* Oct. and Nov. 1905.

419 **It supplemented** TR, *Works,* vol. 24, 559–62. TR's income from his writings in 1905 was $18,487, about $341,000 in modern dollars. Checks came from five different publishers (TRP, *passim*).

419 **livre broché** A small, sewn paperback. Léon Bazalgette, *Théodore Roosevelt* (Paris, 1905). Copy in TRB.

419 **Bazalgette admitted** Ibid., 25–26. All translations are by the author, who has occasionally repunctuated Bazalgette's ornate sentences for contemporary clarity.

420 **Perhaps the most** Ibid., 39, citing in particular the famous passage about the moonlit mockingbird in chap. 4 of *The Wilderness Hunter.* See TR, *Works,* vol. 2, 62–63.

420 **"He was able"** Bazalgette, *Théodore Roosevelt,* 29.

420 **"the supreme political"** Ibid., 5.

420 **"that most dangerous"** Morris, *Rise of Theodore Roosevelt,* 193.

420 **"The tone is resolute"** Bazalgette, *Théodore Roosevelt,* 21.

422 **"Such is the magnetism"** Ibid., 24.

422 **"When, for example"** "Lorsque l'outrance qui est dans sa nature lui fait coté le *spread-eaglism.*" Ibid.

422 **"He has only one"** Ibid., 25.

422 **an attribute Bazalgette** Another attribute that escaped Bazalgette was TR's extraordinary political caution. See Marks, *Velvet on Iron,* 144–47.

422 **the worst-beaten candidate** The phrase is Henry Pringle's, as is much of the political information in this paragraph. Pringle, *Theodore Roosevelt,* 367.

422 **Having found** Ibid., 360–61; Gould, *Presidency of Theodore Roosevelt,* 147–52. See John M. Blum, "Theodore Roosevelt and the Legislative Process: Tariff Revision and Railroad Regulation, 1904–1906," in TR, *Letters,* vol. 4, 1333–42.

423 **The most he** John M. Blum, "Theodore Roosevelt and the Hepburn Act: Toward an Orderly System of Control," in TR, *Letters,* vol. 6, 1560.

423 **Another law he** Charles C. Goetsch, *Essays on Simeon E. Baldwin* (West Hartford, Conn., 1981), 82–185; TR, *Works,* vol. 17, 253–54.

423 **That call had** Gould, *Presidency of Theodore Roosevelt,* 158; TR, *Letters,* vol. 5, 34. The nation's biggest news story in the fall of 1905 was an investigation by New York State authorities into attempts by E. H. Harriman and other financiers to speculate with the Equitable Life Assurance Company's giant pool of cash. See Sullivan, *Our Times,* vol. 3, chap. 3.

423 ONE OF THE FIRST   TR, *Works*, vol. 3, xxix–xxx. *Outdoor Pastimes of an American Hunter* contained much rewriting but only one essay previously unpublished, "At Home." This charming piece was written in the summer of 1905, no doubt as a respite from the strains of peacemaking. Unquotable out of context, its deeply disturbing last line communicates the strange blend of love and cruelty with which hunters "kill the thing they love." See Wood, *Roosevelt As We Knew Him*, 363–64.

423 "I am hurt"   TR, *Letters*, vol. 5, 86.

423 "the real spirit"   Ibid., 69.

423 Kermit had found   TR, *Letters to Kermit*, 285; TR, *Letters*, vol. 5, 1303; Mezey, *Poetry of E. A. Robinson*, xxix–xxx. According to Robinson, TR cogently proffered the Custom House job in six words: "Good salary. Little work. Soft snap!" Ibid., 196.

424 In further generosity   TR, *Works*, vol. 14, 360–64; *Outlook*, 12 Aug. 1905; Bazalgette, *Théodore Roosevelt*, 22. Interestingly, TR had rejected a suggestion that he appoint Robinson to a position in Britain, on the grounds that "our literary men are always hurt by going abroad." TR, *Letters*, vol. 5, 1155.

    Historical Note: TR's review (and strong-arming of Scribner's into acquiring and republishing *The Children of the Night*) proved something of an embarrassment to him. He was chastised by outraged literary critics for trespassing on their territory and neglecting affairs of state. Robinson's sales and professional reputation were not much enhanced. The poet spent the next four years doing nothing at the Customs House except reading the newspaper every morning. Relieved of financial worry, he continued to drink, and wrote hardly any verse. Robinson was of the poetic ilk that finds inspiration in privation. In 1910, he dedicated one of his finest collections, *The Town Down the River*, to TR, and went on to win three Pulitzer Prizes. When Robinson lay dying of cancer in 1935, Kermit Roosevelt came regularly to sit with him.

424 Tensions were high   Josephus Daniels, *Editor in Politics* (Chapel Hill, N.C., 1941), 494–95; speech typescript, 19 Oct. 1905 (TRP).

424 The floors were   Clarence Martin, *A Glimpse of the Past: The History of Bulloch Hall* (Roswell, Ga., 1987), 11.

424 "It is my very"   Speech carbon, 20 Oct. 1905 (TRB). See also John Allen Gable, "My Blood Is Half Southern: President Theodore Roosevelt's Speeches in Roswell and Atlanta, Georgia on October 20, 1905," *Theodore Roosevelt Association Journal* 17.4 (1991).

424 The farther south   Sullivan, *Our Times*, vol. 3, 144; Willard B. Gatewood, Jr., "Theodore Roosevelt in Arkansas," *Arkansas Historical Quarterly* 3.3 (1973).

425 He avoided   Gould, *Presidency of Theodore Roosevelt*, 238; TR on 12 Oct. 1905, qu. in Gable, "My Blood Is Half Southern." See also Ziglar, "Decline of Lynching in America." TR proceeded to New Orleans, whence he sailed for Washington on the USS *West Virginia*, celebrating his forty-seventh birthday at sea.

425 ROOSEVELT WAS SO   M. A. De Wolfe Howe, *James Ford Rhodes: American Historian* (New York, 1929), 119, citing Rhodes's own memo of the evening.

425 "two hundred thousand"   Rendered as digits in ibid., 120.

425 (At least Alice)   Howe, *James Ford Rhodes*, 120–21. Alice's engagement was announced on 13 Dec. 1905. Stacy A. Rozek, " 'The First Daughter of the Land': Alice Roosevelt as Presidential Celebrity, 1902–1903," *Presidential Studies Quarterly* 19.1 (1989).

426 *l'outrance qui*   Bazalgette, *Théodore Roosevelt*, 24. See the collection of imprecations amassed by Wagenknecht in *Seven Worlds of Theodore Roosevelt*, 119–29.

    Historical Note: As TR and Taft sat together on the night of 16 November 1905, Japanese guards surrounded the imperial palace in Seoul,

Korea. Emperor Kojong capitulated to them. Then, in Philip Jessup's words, "the Korean Legation in Washington transferred its archives to that of Japan, and Korea passed out of the family of nations." Jessup, *Elihu Root*, vol. 2, 6.

426   A SURPRISE RESULT   Abbott, *Impressions of Theodore Roosevelt* (New York, 1919), 96; TR, *Letters*, vol. 5, 70–71.

426   "We are at this moment"   *McClure's*, Nov. 1905 (emphasis added).

426   "Out of hopelessness"   Ibid.

427   "In our industrial"   TR, *Works*, vol. 17, 315–16.

427   The Department of Justice   Ibid., 318.

427   the law should be positive   In calling for the enactment of his program, TR used the phrase *affirmative action*. Ibid.

427   Its prime focus   Ibid., 322.

427   The President kept   Ibid., 321.

428   To Aldrich, Depew   Blum, "Theodore Roosevelt and the Hepburn Act," 1561.

CHAPTER 26: THE TREASON OF THE SENATE

429   *But now whin*   "Mr. Dooley" qu. in Sullivan, *Our Times*, vol. 3, 87.

429   "YOU AND I"   George Baer to Stephen B. Elkins, ca. Nov. 1905, memo in PCK.

429   The railroads were weary   Mowry, *Era of Theodore Roosevelt*, 123–24; Oscar D. Lambert, *Stephen Benton Elkins* (Pittsburgh, 1955), 266–67. For the complex (and ultimately inconclusive) story of TR's previous "trial run" at tariff and railroad rate reform in 1904–1905, see Blum, "Theodore Roosevelt and the Legislative Process," and TR, *Letters*, vol. 4, 1028–29. See also Gould, *Presidency of Theodore Roosevelt*, 147–53. At that time, TR traded away his demands for tariff reform in 1905 in order to gain support for rate regulation in 1906.

430   "the most popular"   Washington *Evening Star*, 17 Jan. 1906.

430   "The newspapers are"   Ibid. Tillman is here creatively misquoting *Julius Caesar*, I.ii.

430   Another weapon   Mowry, *Era of Theodore Roosevelt*, 202; Pringle, *Theodore Roosevelt*, 420; Gould, *Presidency of Theodore Roosevelt*, 166.

430   In consequence of   Gould, *Presidency of Theodore Roosevelt*, 159.

431   He was fifty   The author owes much to Sullivan, *Our Times*, vol. 3, 213ff., for this description of LaFollette. Other sources are Ray Stannard Baker, Notebook no. 2 (RSB); Mowry, *Era of Theodore Roosevelt*, 72–73; and Thelen, *Robert M. LaFollette*, which reveals among other things that the Senator subsisted on a diet of "granose biscuits, English walnuts, zwieback, butter and milk" (36). See also *LaFollette's Autobiography*, ed. Allan Nevins (Madison, 1960 [1913]).

431   "Mr. Roosevelt is"   Twain to Albert B. Paine, 9 Jan. 1906, in Mark Twain, *Autobiography* (New York, 1924), vol. 2, 290–91.

431   the outdated system   On the same day that TR welcomed LaFollette to Washington, the banker Jacob Schiff was warning the New York Chamber of Commerce that the booming American economy was destined to collapse if something was not done about the currency question. Kolko, *Triumph of Conservatism*, 152ff.

431   Elihu Root, a   These sentences closely paraphrase Root's language in an interview with N. W. Stephenson, 26 Jan. 1925, on the subject of TR *v.* Nelson Aldrich in early 1906. Copy in NWA.

431   "the radical elements"   Ibid. The New York *Herald*, early in 1906, estimated that seventy Americans were worth more than $35 million, or $630 million apiece in contemporary dollars, untaxed. Along with five thousand lesser multimillionaires, they controlled one sixteenth of the nation's wealth. The *Herald* darkly predicted "billionaires" by mid-century, unless some redistribution took place. Bolles, *Tyrant from Illinois*, 16–17.

432 **"He told me"** Sir Mortimer Durand to Sir Edward Grey, 11 Jan. 1906 (HMD).

432 **"study of Cromwell"** TR had written a biography of the Protector, *Oliver Cromwell* (New York, 1889). See Morris, *Rise of Theodore Roosevelt*, 705–7.

432 **The trouble with** George E. Mowry and Judson A. Grenier, introduction to David Graham Phillips, *The Treason of the Senate* (Chicago, 1964), 23; TR, *Letters*, vol. 5, 131.

432 **As if on** Mowry and Grenier in Phillips, *Treason*, 28.

432 **Roosevelt was not** Ibid., 26; TR, *Letters*, vol. 5, 131; Baker, *American Chronicle*, 184–85. TR looked with particular displeasure on the *Cosmopolitan* series because, six months before, Phillips had published a book of essays, *The Reign of Gilt*, mocking him for monarchical behavior.

432 IN ALGECIRAS Marks, *Velvet on Iron*, 67; TR, *Letters*, vol. 5, 145.

433 **White was under** Larsen, "Theodore Roosevelt and the Moroccan Crisis," 162–63.

433 SENATOR ELKINS TOOK Lambert, *Stephen Benton Elkins*, 268–70.

433 **On 27 January** Gould, *Presidency of Theodore Roosevelt*, 159.

433 **Tall and stately** Powers, *Portraits of Half a Century*, 219; Dunn, *From Harrison to Harding*, vol. 2, 6. See also John Ely Briggs, *William Peters Hepburn* (Des Moines, 1919).

433 **the greatest challenge** Lambert, *Stephen Benton Elkins*, 267–68.

433 **More precisely** Blum, "Theodore Roosevelt and the Hepburn Act," 1563; Sullivan, *Our Times*, vol. 3, 226.

433 **At one o'clock** The following account is taken from Ray Stannard Baker, Notebook no. 2 (RSB). See Steffens, *Autobiography*, 509–11, for another such interview.

434 **(as Elkins preferred)** Lambert, *Stephen Benton Elkins*, 275.

434 **"I do not represent"** Baker repeated these words to Lincoln Steffens that night, and Steffens said, "I gave him that yesterday" (Baker notebook no. 2 [RSB]). This is entirely possible: TR had previously borrowed the phrase *fetish of competition* from Baker. However, there is no record of Steffens visiting the White House for at least a week prior to 8 Feb. 1903, and readers of his memoirs will be familiar with his need to trump every conversational exchange. Steffens also claimed to have given TR the phrase *a square deal* in the White House: " 'That's it,' he shouted. . . . 'I'll throw that out in my next statement.' And he did" (Steffens, *Autobiography*, 506). But see p. 233 for TR's apparent coining of the phrase, with variations, on tour in the West.

434 **Even as he spoke** Mowry, *Era of Theodore Roosevelt*, 203; *LaFollette's Autobiography*, 174.

435 **One of the Senator's** Blum, "Theodore Roosevelt and the Hepburn Act," 1560, 1564.

435 **"The one thing"** TR, *Letters*, vol. 5, 56.

435 THE COSMOPOLITAN'S SERIES March issue, on sale 15 Feb. 1906; TR, *Letters*, vol. 5, 45; *La Follette's Autobiography*, 176. For a contemporary group portrait of the progressives of 1906, see Allen, *America's Awakening*.

435 **Perhaps the fiercest** *The New York Times*, 22 Aug. 1988. The original, pre-Doubleday text has been reissued as *The Lost First Edition of Upton Sinclair's "The Jungle,"* ed., Gene DeGruson (Memphis, 1988).

435 **Now, at last** *The Jungle* sold more than one hundred thousand copies in 1906, and was read by an estimated one million Americans. Christine Scriabine, "Upton Sinclair and the Writing of *The Jungle*," *Chicago History* 10.1 (1981).

435 **Senator Beveridge sent** John Braeman, *Albert J. Beveridge: American Nationalist* (Chicago, 1971), 101–10.

436 **"I recommend"** TR, *Letters*, vol. 5, 381.

436 **In requesting** Sullivan, *Our Times,* vol. 2, 483ff. This chapter of Sullivan's great saga is an exquisitely detailed piece of social history.

436 **Sinclair was but** Ibid., 479; Upton Sinclair, *The Jungle* [1906 version], ed. James R. Barrett (Chicago, 1988), 2, 334.

436 ALICE ROOSEVELT HAD Teague, *Mrs. L.,* 128; Carol Felsenthal, *Alice Roosevelt Longworth* (New York, 1988), 102–3.

437 **frenzied press activity** There are 415 large scrap albums of wedding reportage in the archives of the Martin Luther King Library in Washington, D.C.

437 **Roosevelt seemed** Felsenthal, *Alice Roosevelt Longworth,* 106; Rozek, " 'The First Daughter of the Land' "; Teague, *Mrs. L.,* 122–23. Alice's train was arranged by her cousin Franklin, who was good at that sort of thing and consequently known, among the Oyster Bay Roosevelts, as "Featherduster," and "Miss Nancy." Alsop, "Autobiography," 2; Rixey, *Bamie,* 92.

437 **"I want you"** Teague, *Mrs. L.,* 128. Alice Roosevelt Longworth frequently repeated this remark to family members, always emphasizing that it was only half humorous.

437 **"Alice—Alice"** Washington *Evening Star,* 23 Aug. 1908.

437 ROOSEVELT READ TR, *Letters,* vol. 5, 156–57. John E. Semonche, "Roosevelt's 'Muck-Rake Speech': A Reassessment," *Mid-America* 46.2 (1964), shows that TR's reaction to muckraking in 1906 was consistent with his views as early as 1901.

437 **"I need hardly"** TR, *Letters,* vol. 5, 156; see also vol. 3, 142. In 1906, Hearst was not only contesting his recent defeat as a candidate for the mayoralty of New York, but preparing to run for Governor.

437 **The pity was** Sullivan, *Our Times,* vol. 2, 531–34. Aldrich also yielded to pressure from TR and the American Medical Association.

438 **"The tone"** *British Documents on Foreign Affairs,* vol. 12, 19.

438 **If so, the** Lambert, *Stephen Benton Elkins,* 273–74; Blum, "Theodore Roosevelt and the Hepburn Act," 1564; *The New York Times,* 24 Feb. 1906.

438 **four other Republicans** Aldrich, Foraker, John Kean of New Jersey, and the former Governor of Massachusetts, Winthrop Murray Crane, appointed to the Senate in 1904 after the death of George Frisbie Hoar. Senator Tillman, who voted in favor, was the ranking Democrat on the committee.

438 **Now began** Sullivan, *Our Times,* vol. 2, 244–45; Mowry, *Era of Theodore Roosevelt,* 204–5.

438 **The issue of** Blum, "Theodore Roosevelt and the Hepburn Act," 1565–66.

439 **So, amid** For an alternative metaphor, see Sullivan, *Our Times,* vol. 2, 242: "So the battle raged until the wind-batteries had literally blown themselves out."

439 WAS ONE TO Sinclair, *Jungle* [1906], 36.

439 **(*"Eik! Eik!"*)** Ibid., 4. See TR, *Letters,* vol. 5, 178–79, for his letter to Sinclair about *The Jungle.* He wrote that, in his opinion, the author's brand of socialism would result in "the elimination by starvation" of the poor people it was supposed to save.

439 **"I would like"** TR, *Letters,* vol. 5, 176. TR's desire for secrecy proved short-lived. See James Harvey Young, "The Pig That Fell into the Privy," *Bulletin of the History of Medicine* 59.4 (1985).

439 **Roosevelt's was a** TR, *Letters,* vol. 5, 176.

439 **Sinclair's description** Sinclair, *Jungle* [1906], 124.

439 **squab stuffed** Washington *Evening Star,* 18 Mar. 1906. The menu featured no beef or pork items.

439 **" . . . the Man with"** Qu. in Sullivan, *Our Times,* vol. 3, 94. Many sources mistakenly state that TR's first "muckrake" speech took place on 27 Jan. 1906. On that earlier date, he spoke about the beginning of the construction on the Panama

Canal. The dinner of 17 March was a special celebration hosted by Speaker Joseph Cannon.

439 **Roosevelt's subsequent** Ibid.; Semonche, "Roosevelt's 'Muck-Rake Speech' ";
Victor Murdock interview, 31 Mar. 1940 (HKB); Thompson, *Party Leaders*, 160.
Thompson, who was present at the dinner, records that guests were so impressed
that they urged TR to print his speech "as a public duty."

440 **Nor was it** Semonche, "Roosevelt's 'Muck-Rake Speech' "; Baker, *American
Chronicle*, 201–2; Sullivan, *Our Times*, vol. 3, 96.

440 THE LAST THING The following account is condensed from those in Beale,
Theodore Roosevelt, 374–86, and Larsen, "Theodore Roosevelt and the Moroccan
Crisis," 167–210.

440 **With some asperity** Interview qu. in Jusserand, *What Me Befell*, 323.

440 **Roosevelt repeated** Ibid.; Jusserand to M. Bourgeois, *Documents diplomatiques*,
series 2, vol. 9, 725.

441 **Senator Knox had** A superscript on William Loeb to Philander Knox, 3 Mar.
1906 (PCK), indicates that Knox was summoned to the White House from the Be-
lasco Theater, where he had been attending a matinee, and offered Justice Brown's
seat. TR made clear that the Senator was his first choice. Knox declined (no reason
given). For subsequent events, see Paul T. Heffron, "Theodore Roosevelt and the
Appointment of Mr. Justice Moody," *Vanderbilt Law Review* 18.2 (1965) (hereafter Heffron, "Mr. Justice Moody").

441 **Unwilling as** TR, *Letters*, vol. 5, 242.

441 **"If the conference"** TR to Wilhelm II, 2 Mar. 1906 (TRP).

441 **"paltry and unworthy"** Beale, *Theodore Roosevelt*, 383. The Kaiser's more
thoughtful aides agreed with TR and Root. Chief of Staff Helmuth von Moltke
later described the Algeciras Conference as an affair Germans had to "slink out
of . . . with our tail between our legs." Isolated at the end, Germany decided never
again to trust its fortunes to international conferences. Fischer, *Germany's Aims in
the First World War*, 22.

441 **"Communicate to"** Qu. in Beale, *Theodore Roosevelt*, 384–85. TR was amused
by the elaborate flatteries he and Wilhelm II exchanged during the conference.
"How could anyone with even a glimmer of humor swallow such stuff?" he said to
his English friend Arthur Lee. "We might as well have been addressing each other
from behind ancient Greek masks. But Speck tells me the Kaiser was delighted with
it all" (Lee, *Good Innings*, vol. 1, 335). For TR's own account of the Moroccan affair, see TR, *Letters*, vol. 5, 230–51.

442 THE ARTICLE IN Phillips, *Treason*, chap. 2; *LaFollette's Autobiography*, 179;
British Documents on Foreign Affairs, vol. 12, 20.

442 **One of the weakest** The following account is taken from *LaFollette's Autobiography*, 174–75.

442 **A small group** Elihu Root interview, 30 Sept. 1930 (PCJ); Gould, *Presidency of
Theodore Roosevelt*, 160–61; Sullivan, *Our Times*, vol. 3, 233–34.

443 **The President was** Gould, *Presidency of Theodore Roosevelt*, 161; Simkins,
Pitchfork Ben Tillman, 416–17; Sullivan, *Our Times*, vol. 3, 233–34; TR, *Works*
(National Edition), vol. 13, 153.

443 **Somebody suggested** It was Henry Beach Needham, one of TR's tame reporters.
Sullivan, *Our Times*, vol. 3, 250–53. See also TR, *Letters*, vol. 5, 273–75.

443 **Tillman knew** Sullivan, *Our Times*, vol. 3, 254–55; William E. Chandler to
William Loeb, 11 Apr. 1906 (TRP).

443 BUNYAN'S NOISOME Baker, *American Chronicle*, 201; see 202–3 for Baker's attempt to head off TR's repetition of the speech.

443 **He noted** TR, *Works*, vol. 18, 576–77.

444 **"It is important"** Ibid., 578.

444 **If conservatives** The Philadelphia *Press* termed TR's inheritance-tax call "the most radical proposition ever made by a President." Presidential scrapbook (TRP).

444 **Those who had** Victor Murdock interview, 31 Mar. 1940 (HKB); Stephen E. Lucas, "Theodore Roosevelt's 'The Man with the Muckrake': A Reinterpretation," *Quarterly Journal of Speech* 59.4 (1973); Sir Mortimer Durand in *British Documents on Foreign Affairs*, vol. 12, 28. For TR's own review of the speech, see TR, *Letters*, vol. 5, 217–19.

444 **Men with muckrakes** Mowry and Grenier in Phillips, *Treason*, 40; Semonche, "Roosevelt's 'Muck-Rake Speech' "; Baker, *American Chronicle*, 204. For an extensive study of TR's relationship with Progressive journalists, see Thaddeus Seymour, Jr., "A Progressive Partnership: Theodore Roosevelt and the Reform Press—Riis, Steffens, Baker, and White" (Ph.D. diss., University of Wisconsin–Madison, 1985).

445 SENATORS TILLMAN AND Sullivan, *Our Times*, vol. 3, 256–57.

445 **A disillusioned** Nathaniel Stephenson, *Nelson Aldrich*, 314.

445 **Even Senator Elkins** Lambert, *Stephen Benton Elkins*, 274.

445 **"I love a"** *The Washington Post*, 12 May 1906. But see Blum, "Theodore Roosevelt and the Hepburn Act," 1570–71.

445 ROOSEVELT TRANQUILLY H. G. Wells, *Experiment in Autobiography* (London, 1934), 648.

445 **"He is the"** H. G. Wells, *The Future in America: A Search after Realities* (New York, 1906), 246–53. For more on this interview, see Wells, *Experiment in Autobiography*, 646–49.

446 **Having read** Wells, *Future in America*, 246–47, 250.

446 **the progressive impulse** TR had apparently expressed to Wells his concern about "the growth of monopolistic combinations" and the need for "very vigorous antitrust legislation" to combat it. Wells, *Experiment in Autobiography*, 647.

446 **Tillman railed** See Sullivan, *Our Times*, vol. 3, 264–71, for an account of the recriminations (vigorously joined in by TR) that followed news of the secret White House/Chandler/Tillman operation.

447 **had started something** Gould, *Presidency of Theodore Roosevelt*, 164, points out that although the amended bill's language on court review read vaguely enough to satisfy Senate conservatives, it enabled the Supreme Court to come down sharply, four years later, on the side of an empowered ICC.

447 **Railroad rate regulation** Lambert, *Stephen Benton Elkins*, 275–79; Sullivan, *Our Times*, vol. 3, 272–73.

447 **supplied extra details** See Young, "Pig That Fell." TR's original "first-class man" investigating the meat industry had materialized in the form of two commissioners, Charles P. Neill and James B. Reynolds. See *Conditions in the Chicago Stockyards: Message of the President of the United States*, 59 Cong., sess. 1, 1906, H. doc. 873.

447 **Apprehensive that** *British Documents on Foreign Affairs*, vol. 12, 43. See James Harvey Young, *Pure Food: Securing the Federal Food and Drugs Act of 1906* (Princeton, N.J., 1989).

447 **James W. Wadsworth** TR, *Letters*, vol. 5, 296; Young, "Pig That Fell."

447 **Again, Roosevelt** TR, *Letters*, vol. 5, 296.

448 **A pleasedly firm** Sullivan, *Our Times*, vol. 3, 459; *Review of Reviews*, Aug. 1906. The territories of Arizona and New Mexico were also offered statehood, but declined.

448 **That afternoon** Washington *Evening Star*, 30 June 1906.

448 **Still, it had** TR, *Letters*, vol. 5, 329.

448 **"Society cannot"** Qu. in Ray Stannard Baker, "The Railroad Rate: A Study in Commercial Autocracy," *McClure's*, Nov. 1905.

CHAPTER 27: BLOOD THROUGH MARBLE

449 *I'm not so* Dunne, *Mr. Dooley's Philosophy,* 217.
449 EDITH KERMIT ROOSEVELT *New York Tribune,* 2 July 1906.
449 The President emerged Ibid. Except where otherwise indicated, the following portrait of EKR in midlife is adapted from Morris, *Edith Kermit Roosevelt.*
449 To children other Alsop, unpublished autobiography, 4–5 (TRC).
450 (Archie and Quentin) Looker, *White House Gang,* 43–44.
450 New England reserve EKR was descended from Puritans and French Huguenots. See EKR, *American Backlogs: The Story of Gertrude Tyler and Her Family, 1660–1860* (New York, 1928).
450 "If they had" Morris, *Edith Kermit Roosevelt,* 559.
451 Edith was well-read Butt, *Letters,* 127. Adams, *Letters,* vol. 5, 583; Baker, notebook no. 28, Jan. 1905 (RSB); Jules Jusserand to Ministère des Affaires Étrangers 9 Mar. 1909 (JJ).
451 Whereas his For EKR's role as patroness of White House "musicales," see Elise K. Kirk, *Music at the White House: A History of the American Spirit* (Urbana, 1986), 169–88.
451 largest and worst Nicholas Roosevelt, *Front Row Seat,* 25.
451 His attitude toward Alsop, unpublished autobiography, 4 (TRC); Alice Roosevelt Longworth interview, Nov. 1954 (TRB); William Allen White, interviewed by Howard K. Beale, ca. 1936 (HKB); Wagenknecht, *Seven Worlds,* 168–69.
451 Her attitude toward Landor, "Death," qu. in Morris, *Edith Kermit Roosevelt,* 500: *I warmed both hands at the fire of life, / It sinks, and I am ready to depart.* Rixey, *Bamie,* 231.
451 HE DID NOT LOOK EKR to Corinne Roosevelt Robinson, 4 June 1906 (TRC).
452 "damned little Jew" Maurice Low, Washington correspondent of the London *Morning Post,* had reported that TR acknowledged the congratulations only of Wilhelm II after the Portsmouth peace treaty. "He spoke savagely—as he ought not have spoken to me about an Englishman" (Sir Mortimer Durand diary, 8 May 1906 [HMD]). On another occasion, TR called Low a "circumcised skunk." TR, *Letters,* vol. 5, 918.
452 William E. Chandler Leon B. Richardson, *William E. Chandler* (New York, 1940), 666–67; Watson, *As I Knew Them,* 83; J. Van Vechten Olcott, interviewed by J. F. French, 1922 (TRB). Another Roosevelt explosion is described in Mrs. Dewey's diary, 11 May 1906 (GD).
452 And Norman Hapgood TR to Hapgood, 29 June 1906 (TRP). "The usages which obtain among gentlemen leave no option in such a case; and your [refusal to name sources] both fixes your status and leads inevitably to the conclusion that you made the statement knowing it to be false."
452 But Roosevelt had TR, *Letters to Kermit,* 130; TR to Ethel Roosevelt, 17 June 1906 (TRP); Gifford Pinchot to Irving Fisher, 22 Aug. 1905 (GP). TR had been aware for at least four years that he had an eating problem. "I am rather an early Goth and eat too much and drink too much, and then trust in hard work to do away with the effects," he wrote Pierre de Coubertin, a French friend, on 21 Nov. 1902 (TRP). By "drink" he meant such liquids as milk and coffee. Apart from his bibulous evening on the night of the Cannon birthday party (which he cited years later as an aberration), TR's alcohol intake verged on that of teetotalism. See Wagenknecht, *Seven Worlds,* 92–97.
452 "It is clear" Fisher to Pinchot, 2 Sept. 1905 (GP).
452 Edith sweetly *New York Tribune,* 5 July 1906; *Oyster Bay Pilot,* 27 July 1906; *The Washington Post,* 11 July 1907. Alice teased her father that he seemed to hay "with a view to his political future." TR to Alice Longworth, 29 June 1908 (TRP).

452 *"J'ESSAIE DE"* Samuel H. Church to William Loeb, 9 Aug. 1906 (TRP). *Biographical Note:* An earlier letter (2 Aug.) from Church to Loeb states that Rodin, who was intending to visit the United States in 1907, had told Church of his "strong desire" to execute a bust or statue of TR. He felt the resulting work would convey the President's "tremendous energy and vitality," and very likely be his masterpiece. Church informed TR, through Loeb, that the Carnegie Institute would pay for the statue and subsequently exhibit it in Pittsburgh. TR agreed to pose for Rodin. For undisclosed reasons, the proposal came to nothing.

452 ("Theodore," Edith) Hagedorn, *Roosevelt Family*, 38.

453 "It is now" *The Washington Post*, 18 Aug. 1906.

453 "At a few minutes" *Summary Discharge or Mustering Out of Regiments or Companies: Message of the President of the United States* (Washington, D.C., 1908), 20–21 (hereafter *Summary Discharge*).

453 Roosevelt ordered Ibid., 20, 32. Ann J. Lane, *The Brownsville Affair: National Crisis and Black Reaction* (Port Washington, N.Y., 1971), 5–17; John D. Weaver, *The Brownsville Raid* (College Station, 1992), 29–30. The garrison's previous occupants had been white. Protests against its occupation by "nigger" troops were forwarded to Secretary Taft as early as the beginning of June.

454 As a result Weaver, *Brownsville Raid*, 30; *Summary Discharge*, 31–32.

454 Only one *Summary Discharge*, 24.

454 Some damaging Ibid., 31; Lane, *Brownsville Affair*, 18, 20.

454 Roosevelt waited *Summary Discharge*, 34. TR had also received urgent appeals from both Texas Senators to move the troops, in view of inflamed local feelings. Ibid., 29.

454 He ordered Ibid., 34.

454 Roosevelt then sent TR, *Letters*, vol. 5, 384–85; Lane, *Brownsville Affair*, 19–20.

454 It came on The complete text of Blocksom's report appears in *Summary Discharge*, 60–65.

455 "be discharged" Ibid., 64.

455 Blocksom added Ibid., 65.

455 Over the last See Gould, *Presidency of Theodore Roosevelt*, 237–38.

Biographical Note: For a definitive statement of TR's attitude toward blacks in April 1906, see TR, *Letters*, vol. 5, 226–28. It was made in response to the patrician racism propounded by his friend Owen Wister in *Lady Baltimore* (New York, 1906). TR accepted "entirely" Wister's theory that blacks were "altogether inferior to the whites," and wrote that he saw no reason why "ninety-five percent of the Negroes" in the South should be allowed to vote. He reserved his scorn for the hypocrisy of Southern whites who talked discrimination yet retained black mistresses, and, worse still, stole the votes of disfranchised blacks in order to "elect" racist members of Congress. He disagreed with Wister that Southern blacks had "become worse" since the Civil War, citing Booker T. Washington as an example of the race's power to improve itself. "I may add that I do not know a white man of the South who is as good a man as Booker Washington." See TR, *Letters*, vol. 5, 221–30.

455 His one outburst See p. 425.

455 More ominously Gould, *Presidency of Theodore Roosevelt*, 238.

455 THE PRESIDENT'S *SANGUIS* *Harper's Weekly*, 8 Sept. 1906; Cheney, *Personal Memoirs*, 83.

455 It was the greatest *Harper's Weekly*, 8 Sept. 1906; Gould, *Presidency of Theodore Roosevelt*, 123. This battleship became the *Delaware*, displacing twenty thousand

tons, and mounting ten twelve-inch guns. Wimmel, *Theodore Roosevelt and the Great White Fleet*, 195–97, 201.

456 **"the dirt fly"** TR's first use of this phrase appears to have been at the Gridiron Club on 27 Jan. 1906. "As long as I am President the dirt will fly in the Canal Zone."

456 **Having fought** Ralph E. Minger, "William H. Taft and the United States Intervention in Cuba in 1906," *Hispanic America Historical Review* 41 (1961).

456 **Roosevelt authorized** Whitney T. Perkins, *Constraint of Empire: The United States and Caribbean Interventions* (Westport, Conn., 1981), 14. See also Scott, *Robert Bacon*, 113–19.

456 **"Just at the"** TR to Henry White, 13 Sept. 1906 (TRP); TR, *Letters*, vol. 5, 401.

456 **It was particularly** John Barrett, "Elihu Root's Trip in South America," ms. in JB; Jessup, *Elihu Root*, vol. 1, 481. This grand tour was the first ever made by an American Secretary of State in office. For a detailed account, see Janice Hepworth, "A Policy of Practical Altruism," *Journal of Inter-American Studies* 3.3 (1961).

457 **a paradox of** Perkins, *Constraint of Empire*, 13. President Estrada Palma often threatened to resign, but his clear purpose in doing so was to force the United States to intervene and prop up his regime. See TR, *Letters*, vol. 5, 428.

457 **"You had no"** TR, *Letters*, vol. 5, 409. See also Christopher A. Abel, "Controlling the Big Stick: Theodore Roosevelt and the Cuban Crisis of 1906," *Naval War College Review* 40.3 (1987).

457 **His latest Secretary** Bonaparte had joined the Cabinet on 1 July 1905. For an excellent short portrait, see Eric F. Goldman, "Charles J. Bonaparte, Patrician Reformer: His Earlier Career," in *Johns Hopkins University Studies in Historical and Political Science*, series 61, no. 2. See also Walker Rumble, "Rectitude and Reform: Charles Joseph Bonaparte and the Politics of Gentility" (Ph.D. diss., University of Maryland, 1971).

457 **It was agreed** Perkins, *Constraint of Empire*, 14–15.

458 **slaughtered six hundred** Hagedorn, *Leonard Wood*, vol. 2, 65.

458 **For much of** Heffron, "Mr. Justice Moody." Moody expressed a desire to leave the Administration on 27 August, in what may have been a ploy to get TR to make up his mind. See TR, *Letters*, vol. 5, 390, 396.

458 **He was much** Lee, *Good Innings*, vol. 1, 324–26.

458 **"I would walk"** Oscar K. Davis, *Released for Publication: Some Inside Political History of Theodore Roosevelt and His Times, 1898–1918* (Boston, 1925), 54. See also Dunn, *From Harrison to Harding*, vol. 2, 38.

458 **Taft was warm** According to George Harris, a photographer assigned to the Roosevelt White House, TR decided against Root when he noticed the Secretary at a social reception, pacing alone with his hands behind his back. Elsewhere in the room, Taft jovially entertained a circle of guests. Harris in *The Washington Post*, n.d. 1952 (HKB).

458 **Roosevelt was not** "You, Mr. Speaker, will be the next President of the United States," TR told Joseph Cannon at a Sagamore Hill ceremony on 17 August. "Uncle Joe" had begun to fancy himself as the party's nominee in 1906, after hearing a few compliments too many during his recent seventieth-birthday celebrations. *The Washington Post*, 18 Aug. 1906; Bolles, *Tyrant from Illinois*, 10.

459 *The Washington Post* 28 June 1906, qu. by Durand in *British Documents on Foreign Affairs*, vol. 12, 49.

459 **JOSEPH B. FORAKER** Foraker to TR, 26 Sept. 1906 (TRP).

459 **Roosevelt could not** Taft himself, en route to Cuba, had queried TR's willingness to act unilaterally, only to be told that the President "would not dream of asking the position of Congress" in such an emergency. Nothing but "a long wrangle" would result, while the emergency worsened. A strong President must "accept re-

sponsibility to establish precedents which successors may follow even if they are unwilling to take the initiative themselves." TR, *Letters,* vol. 5, 414–15.

459 **"I am sure"** Ibid., 430–31.

459 **The Senator had** Morris, *Rise of Theodore Roosevelt,* 264–65; Weaver, *Brownsville Raid,* 24; John D. Weaver, *The Senator and the Sharecropper's Son: Exoneration of the Brownsville Soldiers* (College Station, 1997), 91. TR told Charles Dawes in Jan. 1904 that he regarded Foraker as "insincere." Dawes, *Journal of the McKinley Years,* 363.

459 **"He is a"** TR, *Letters,* vol. 5, 428–29.

460 **"I can only"** Ibid., 409. The allusion is to the court scene in *The Pickwick Papers,* wherein Sam Weller informs the judge that he spells his surname with a *v.* A confirmatory shout comes from the gallery: "Quite right too, Samivel. . . . Put it down a 'we,' my Lord, put it down a 'we.' "

460 **"Simplified Spelling"** Except where otherwise indicated, this section is based on Mark Sullivan's unsurpassed short history of spelling reform in *Our Times,* vol. 3, 162ff. See also Clyde H. Dornbusch, "American Spelling Simplified by Presidential Edict," *American Speech* 36 (1961), and John H. Vivian, "Theodore Roosevelt's Spelling Reform Initiative: The Newspaper Response," *Theodore Roosevelt Association Journal,* summer 1978.

460 *diarrhea* Sullivan himself spells this word with the Greek vowel *œ. Our Times,* vol. 3, 164.

460 *u in honor* TR was himself an excellent speller, as his autograph manuscripts attest. He nevertheless had a few quaint foibles, such as writing *Wednsday* for *Wednesday, atall* for *at all,* and inserting, for reasons best known to himself, an extra apostrophe in *did'n't.*

460 **It seemed to** TR, *Letters,* vol. 5, 390–91.

461 *addresst blusht* Office of the Public Printer, *Simplified Spelling: For the Use of Government Documents* (Washington, D.C., 1906), 15–23.

461 **Soon, the nation's** *Harper's Weekly,* Sept. 1906; TR, *Letters,* vol. 5, 389.

461 **ON 29 SEPTEMBER** Ibid., 424–26; Perkins, *Constraint of Empire,* 18; Minger, "William H. Taft," 85.

461 **In his last** TR, *Letters,* vol. 5, 435, 438.

462 **Color had become** Sullivan, *Our Times,* vol. 3, 460; *Review of Reviews,* Oct. 1906; Gould, *Presidency of Theodore Roosevelt,* 239.

462 **Only those with** Henry Cabot Lodge to TR, 13 Oct. 1906 (TRP); TR, "Legislative Actions and Judicial Decisions," *Works,* vol. 18, 83; David H. Burton, "Theodore Roosevelt's Harrisburg Speech: A Progressive Appeal to James Wilson," *Pennsylvania Magazine of History and Biography,* Oct. 1969.

462 *"If I am"* James Wilson, "On the Law of Nature," in *The Works of James Wilson,* ed. Robert G. McCloskey (Cambridge, Mass., 1967), 132–33. The author is indebted to David H. Burton for relating TR's speech to this essay. Burton argues that TR, in the fall of 1906, feared that his recent sheaf of progressive legislation might be challenged by the judiciary, which was traditionally biased in favor of property rights. Be that as it may, historians may detect in the Harrisburg speech the first signs of what was to become one of the most controversial demands of Progressivism: popular recall of judicial decisions.

462 **Propelled by** *Summary Discharge,* 178. TR's order, transmitted by the War Department, was dated 4 Oct. 1906, the day of his visit to Harrisburg. As the quoted paragraph makes clear (see the complete order for repetitive emphasis), he had already decided that the men of the Twenty-fifth were guilty.

463 **His old friend arrived** The following account is taken from Lee, *Good Innings,* vol. 1, 323–27.

463 **Lee remembered** Alan Clark, ed., *"A Good Innings": The Private Papers of Viscount Lee of Fareham, P.C.*, G.C.B., G.C.S.I., G.B.E. (London, 1974), 69–71. See 1–7 for a biographical sketch of Lee.

464 **Lee left** Lee, in *A Good Innings*, glosses over the redundancy of his visit, and is at pains to represent himself as having had to perform a painful duty in getting rid of Sir Mortimer. If he had come when TR had first summoned him, on 27 July, he might indeed have administered the coup de grâce, but illness delayed his departure until 3 October. Grey's letter recalling Durand was dispatched the following day (Durand diary, 21 Oct. 1906) (HMD). Durand subsequently heard that "the President has been complaining of me through Sir Henry White" (ibid., 12 Nov. 1906). See also Nevins, *Henry White*, 224–25, and, for TR's "appointment" letter, TR, *Letters*, vol. 5, 458. When Lee reprinted this letter, he omitted the names of two alternative ambassadors suggested by TR: Cecil Spring Rice and Munro Ferguson.

464 **Sir Mortimer was** Durand to Lord Lansdowne, 6 Dec. 1906, and to Madge Durand, 15 Dec. 1906 (HMD).

464 **Edith Roosevelt had** Durand to "Nell," 9 Aug. 1904, and to Coutts Bank, 16 Dec. 1904 (HMD).

464 **"I must try"** Durand diary, 21 Oct. 1906 (HMD). For a full account of Durand's recall, see Tilchin, *Theodore Roosevelt*, 111–13.

464 **BY NOW, TAFT** Magoon, former Governor of the Panama Canal Zone, was sworn in on 13 Oct. 1906. Although TR had told Taft to announce that elections would be held immediately, the corruption of Cuba's political process was found to be so extreme that representative government was not restored until 1908. Magoon was a popular and gentle executive who issued no death sentences and was even criticized for his leniency. The United States withdrew from Cuba by TR's outside deadline of 28 Jan. 1909. David A. Lockmiller, *Magoon in Cuba: A History of the Second Intervention* (Chapel Hill, 1938). See also Perkins, *Constraint of Empire*, 18–19; Marks, *Velvet on Iron*, 141.

464 **"It is important"** Weaver, *Senator*, 113.

464 **Ignoring him** The extraordinary care with which TR prepared for Moody's appointment belies his reputation for hasty decision making. See Heffron, "Mr. Justice Moody," and, for a parallel example at the lower federal level, Elting E. Morison, "Theodore Roosevelt Appoints a Judge," *Proceedings of the Massachusetts Historial Society* 72 (1963). Moody proved to be a distinguished but sadly short-tenured Justice, of mostly conservative opinions, whose lucid powers of expression earned the praise of both Oliver Wendell Holmes and Felix Frankfurter. A collapse of the central nervous system forced his retirement from the Supreme Court in 1910. He died, after years of torment, in 1917.

464 **General Garlington's Brownsville** See *Summary Discharge*, 178–83.

464 **He stated** Ibid., 179.

465 **Garlington had then** Ibid., 180–82.

465 **On 30 October** Harlan, *Booker T. Washington*, 309; Gould, *Presidency of Theodore Roosevelt*, 232–35; *Review of Reviews*, Dec. 1906.

465 **Charles Evans Hughes** Hughes, forty-four in the summer of 1906, had come to national attention the previous fall, when he acted as counsel to a state committee investigating the major life-insurance companies of New York. In the course of fifty-seven public hearings, he proved himself a "mental colossus," investigating fairly but with such mastery of detail that many potential witnesses left town in order to avoid his examination. His success in winning the indictments or resignations of some of New York's most powerful top executives won the admiration of TR, and propelled Hughes into public life. Even as he ran for governor, he was already being spoken of as a potential Supreme Court Justice or President. See also

Robert F. Wesser, "Theodore Roosevelt: Reform and Reorganization of the Republican Party in New York, 1901–1909," *New York History* 46.3 (1965).
465 **Washington listened** *Booker T. Washington Papers,* vol. 9, 118–19.
465 **"There is some"** Harlan, *Booker T. Washington,* 309–10.
466 **one syllable** Root, speaking in Utica, had quoted the passage in TR's First Annual Message to do with journalistic rabble-rousers who "sowed the wind" of anarchy. "I say by the President's authority that in penning these words, with the horror of President McKinley's murder fresh before him, he had Mr. Hearst specifically in mind. . . . What he thought of Mr. Hearst then, he thinks of Mr. Hearst now." *Outlook,* 10 Nov. 1906.
466 **Root's statement had** As Mark Sullivan notes, the speech also destroyed any lingering chance Root may have had of being nominated for the presidency himself. He had incurred the lifelong enmity of Hearst in his own home state. *Our Times,* vol. 3, 280.
466 **"You can not"** *Booker T. Washington Papers,* vol. 9, 118.
466 **With that, he** Emma Lou Thornbrough, "The Brownsville Episode and the Negro Vote," *Mississippi Valley Historical Review* 44 (Dec. 1957); *Summary Discharge,* 183; Weaver, *Senator,* 116; *The New York Times,* 21 Nov. 1906. Among the few empirical certainties in American history is that "Princess Alice" would not long have tolerated life in Cincinnati, Ohio.
    Historical Note: The disparity between the date of TR's order and its actual release on 7 Nov. has caused confusion in some sources. See Thornbrough, "Brownsville Episode," and Harlan, *Booker T. Washington,* 309, for contemporary anger at TR's manipulation of the election.
467 **Across the nation** Gould, *Presidency of Theodore Roosevelt,* 236; TR, *Letters,* vol. 5, 488–89.
467 **"Well, we have"** TR, *Letters,* vol. 5, 488. Optimistic as always, TR did not choose to see a conservative backlash against progressivism developing in the Republican Party, as evinced by the antilabor vote and increased majorities for Foraker and Cannon (499).
467 **"By direction of"** *Summary Discharge,* 183. See Lewis N. Wynne, "Brownsville: The Reaction of the Negro Press," *Phylon* 33 (1972).
467 **There followed** Weaver, *Senator,* 68–72; *Summary Discharge,* 183–84.
467 **For the last** *Booker T. Washington Papers,* vol. 1, 446.
467 **arrogance of tone and language** This phrase was used by Sir Mortimer Durand in a dispatch of 19 Oct. 1906. The Ambassador also quoted a telling remark by one of TR's friends: "He feels his time is short." *British Documents on Foreign Affairs,* vol. 12, 128.
468 **"The order in"** TR, *Letters,* vol. 5, 490. TR's addressee was Governor Curtis Guild, Jr., of Massachusetts.
468 HE HAD SEEN Ibid., 496; *Harper's Weekly,* 8 Dec. 1906.
    Historical Note: TR arrived off Colón on the afternoon of 14 Nov. 1906. Accompanied by his wife, doctor, and a small party of aides and press, he crossed the Isthmus the next day to inspect the Pacific approaches to the Canal Zone at La Boca. He spent the night in Panama City as the guest of President Amador. On 16 Nov., he explored the Culebra Cut, and the next day returned to Colón via Gatun (see text). The *Louisiana* left Limón Bay that evening. En route back to the United States, TR visited Puerto Rico. He arrived in Washington on 26 Nov.
468 **Imaginations less vivid** For the intensely stimulative effect of Panama on TR's fancy, see his two letters to Kermit in ibid., 495–98. See also his extraordinary, illustrated *Special Message of the President of the United States Concerning the*

Panama Canal, 17 Dec. 1906 (Washington, D.C., 1906), which shows a concern for human welfare ("I inspected between twenty and thirty water closets") never before seen in presidential documents.

468 **Roosevelt heard** Panama *Star and Herald,* 17 Nov. 1906; Palmer, *With My Own Eyes,* 266–67. For comprehensive accounts of TR's three days in Panama, see *Panama Canal Review,* Roosevelt Centennial supplement, 7 Nov. 1958, and McCullough, *Path Between the Seas,* 492–99.

468 **Food was** The author is indebted to Palmer, *With My Own Eyes,* 267–68, for the following story. Palmer accompanied TR through Culebra Cut. Extra details (including TR's "rapid-fire volley" interrogation style) come from *The New York Times,* 17 Nov. 1906, and Panama *Star and Herald,* 17 and 18 Nov. 1906.

469 **Taking the hint** TR, *Letters,* vol. 5, 498.

470 **Much of it** Ibid., 499, 504; *Panama Canal Review,* 7 Nov. 1958; McCullough, *Path Between the Seas,* 501.

470 **He could not wait** TR, *Letters,* vol. 5, 496; Panama *Star and Herald,* 18 Nov. 1906. The precipitation accompanying TR's visit was the heaviest in fifteen years.

470 "STEVENS AND HIS" TR, *Letters,* vol. 5, 497.

470 **"a big fellow"** Ibid., 495, 497.

470 **"so hardy, so efficient"** Ibid., 497. See also TR's *Special Message of the President of the United States Concerning the Panama Canal* (Washington, D.C., 1906).

471 NEW YORK William H. Taft to TR, 17 Nov. 1906 (TRP). This cable, sent to Colón, missed TR's departure for Ponce and had to be relayed there.

471 **If press reports** The reports were accurate. But on 20 November, Taft, worried at TR's unexplained failure to reply to his cable of three days before, ordered the discharges to proceed. Taft to Mrs. Taft ("The President is worked up on the subject"), 21 Nov. 1906 (WHT); Weaver, *Senator,* 118; TR, *Letters,* vol. 5, 498.

471 **While he continued** Weaver, *Senator,* 118–19. The last man discharged was also the longest to live. See *passim,* for the story of Dorsie Willis.

471 BY NOW, A Ibid.; Lane, *Brownsville Affair,* 226–28.

471 **This case was** Constitution League pressure had been the indirect cause of Taft's suspension order. See Lane, *Brownsville Affair,* chap. 2.

471 **At the end** Charles [illegible] of IRS, New York, to William Loeb, Jr., 30 Nov. 1907, warning that Stewart was likely to be "impertinent" to the President (TRP). The "communication" of Stewart to TR cited in Lane, *Brownsville Affair,* 28 and 32, is not in TRP.

471 **Beyond ambition** Joseph Benson Foraker, *Notes of a Busy Life* (Cincinnati, 1916), vol. 1, 178. See also Weaver, *Senator,* 32 and *passim.*

472 **He was so** Foraker, *I Would Live It Again,* 277.

472 **"The members of"** TR, *Works,* vol. 17, 414–15.

Historical Note: At thirty thousand words (printed "thruout" in simplified-spelling style), the Message was his longest yet. The progressive themes he had sounded a year before emerged more insistently, in calls for extended employers' liability, stronger regulation of corporations, a mandatory eight-hour day, and a drastic law against child labor. The word *conservation* appeared for the first time as a subject heading. He condemned the uncontrolled killing of seals in Alaska in language of great zoological precision, and added an income tax as well as an inheritance tax to his suggested (but not requested) revise of internal-revenue law. Elsewhere, invocations of family values and naval might represented the old Theodore Roosevelt, as did an eccentric final suggestion that rifle clubs should be established across the country, in emulation of "the little republic of Switzerland." TR, *Works,* vol. 17, 401–80.

472 **Unfortunately for** Weaver, *Senator,* 121. It was extraordinary, indeed discourte-

NOTES • 723

ous, for such a proposal to be made before the traditional reading of the President's
Message. But Foraker's hand had been forced when Senator Boies Penrose offered
a weaker resolution immediately after the convening of Congress on 3 Dec. Both
resolutions were approved, forcing both Taft and TR to document their actions.
Gould, *Presidency of Theodore Roosevelt*, 240.

472 **The resolution** Weaver, *Senator*, 121; Gould, *Presidency of Theodore Roosevelt*,
240.

472 **Roosevelt remained** TR, *Letters*, vol. 5, 521.

473 ALL IN ALL Ibid., 524. TR was the first American to win a Nobel Prize. The award
was announced on 10 Dec. 1906, but he appears to have been informed at least five
days earlier (521).

473 **He added** Ibid.
Historical Note: This project never materialized. The foundation, constituted by an act of Congress in 1907, let TR's prize money lie unused for
ten years. In July 1917, TR asked Congress to return it to him, and distributed it to various charities offering relief to victims of the Great War.
By then, the sum had grown to more than $45,482, or $818,676 in contemporary dollars. Straus, *Under Four Administrations*, 240–42.

473 **To Kermit, he** TR, *Letters*, vol. 5, 520–21.

473 **laughter seemed strained** Sir Mortimer Durand to Sir Edward Grey, 14 Dec. 1906
(HMD). TR could hardly be expected to find funny a blackface skit in which an old
Negro from Tuskegee allowed, "I had a boy in dem colored troops down at
Brownsville, but I 'spect he's on his way home now." Weaver, *Senator*, 125.

473 **"Now don't"** The author takes the liberty of inferring *damn* from the four hy-
phens in Sir Mortimer's above-cited report.

473 **"It is not"** Durand diary, 10 Dec. 1906 (HMD).
Chronological Note: Another probable reason for TR's strain this
evening was a current sensation in the press over his dismissal, earlier in
the year, of the United States Ambassador to Austria, Bellamy Storer. Mrs.
Storer, an aunt of Nicholas Longworth, had for years been monomania-
cally lobbying every person of influence in the Northern Hemisphere in behalf of a red hat for her favorite archbishop, John Ireland of St. Paul. Her
willingness to use TR's name, and even private letters from him, in efforts
to cow the Pope, ended her husband's somewhat somnolent diplomatic career. The " 'Dear Maria' Affair," as it came to be known, reached its climax on 8 Dec. 1906, after Bellamy Storer's own self-pitying account of his
dismissal, quoting other Roosevelt letters, was leaked to the *Boston Herald*. TR, more amused than annoyed, issued a devastating public response
on 10 Dec. He would have been less amused if he had known that the
paper's informant was Joseph B. Foraker. For full accounts, see Sullivan,
Our Times, vol. 3, 128, and Gatewood, *Theodore Roosevelt and the Art
of Controversy*, chap. 6.

473 **A good motto** Sir Mortimer Durand, "Report on the United States of America for
the Year 1906," in *British Documents on Foreign Affairs*, 159. The noun *rem* in
Horace's epigram is often inaccurately given as "money."

474 **a special message** The quotations from TR's first Brownsville message are taken
from Richardson, *Compilation*, vol. 10, 7710–11.

474 **As to the** Ibid., 7712.

474 "WHEN YOU TURNED" The following dialogue is taken from Wister, *Roosevelt*,
225–26. Wister does not give the date of this walk, but says that it occurred "just
in the middle of the Brownsville disturbance. This, plus TR's invitation of 5 Nov.
1906, "Do let me see you as soon as possible after I come back from Panama," suggests a White House visit before the end of the year (264).

475 **"And then jump"** According to Isabel Anderson, *Presidents and Pies* (Boston, 1920), 29, a popular riddle in Washington at this time was:
Q: Why is Roosevelt like a grasshopper?
A: Because you never know which way he'll hop, but when he does, he hops like hell.

CHAPTER 28: THE CLOUDS THAT ARE GATHERING

476 *"We've been"* "Mr. Dooley" in Washington *Evening Star,* 30 Dec. 1906.
476 **luxuriate in his Nobel** TR's Nobel Prize, the first ever won by an American, now glitters on the mantelpiece in the Roosevelt Room of the White House.
476 **note of grimness** New York *Sun,* 2 Jan. 1907. For a detailed account of this reception, see the Prologue to Morris, *Rise of Theodore Roosevelt.* TR's handshake record still stands in the *Guinness Book of World Records, 2001.*
476 **quarter of a century** See Putnam, *Theodore Roosevelt,* 249–51.
476 **Then, as ever** Ibid., 255. The dominant note of TR's Sixth Annual Message, *Literary Digest* (15 Dec. 1906) remarked, had been "a demand for greater centralization of power."
477 **On 14 January** *The New York Times,* 15 Jan. 1907. TR also withdrew his order that dischargees be denied civil employment in the government.
477 **a full investigation** Authorized by the Senate on 22 Jan. 1907.
477 **"this belief in"** TR, *Letters,* vol. 5, 631.
477 **Such an opportunity** Ibid.; Wiebe, *Businessmen and Reform,* 46–47.
477 **Judge Gary praised** Wiebe, *Businessmen and Reform,* 46–47. See also TR, *Letters,* vol. 5, 563.
478 **This was a** Wiebe, *Businessmen and Reform,* 46–47.
478 **a giant trust** Strouse, *Morgan,* 469–70.
478 IF MEMBERS OF Except where otherwise indicated, the following account is based on a reminiscence by Samuel G. Blythe, ca. Jan. 1932, in HBP and a letter of Joseph Foraker, 29 Jan. 1907, qu. in Foraker's own *Notes of a Busy Life,* vol. 2, 249–57. Other accounts appear in Arthur Wallace Dunn, *Gridiron Nights* (New York, 1915), 182–87; Watson, *As I Knew Them,* 70–73; and Clark, *My Quarter Century,* vol. 2, 443–49.
478 **a table perpendicular** The evening's seating arrangements, confused in all written accounts, are mapped out by the Washington *Herald,* 27 Jan. 1907, in Presidential scrapbook (TRP).
478 *All coons look* Blythe reminiscence (HBP).
478 **"I would like"** Ibid.
479 **"the mob"** *The Washington Post,* 29 Jan. 1907.
479 **Then, picking** Ibid.; Foraker, *Notes of a Busy Life,* vol. 2, 251.
479 **Senate debate on** Foraker, *Notes of a Busy Life,* vol. 2, 250–51.
479 **Diners from** Blythe reminiscence (HBP). Watson, *As I Knew Them,* 71, says TR's speech was "very coldly received." Blythe's earlier account ("[He] sat down amid much applause") is supported by a similar statement in *The Washington Post,* 29 Jan. 1907.
479 **"The hour for"** Foraker, *Notes of a Busy Life,* vol. 2, 249. ["I take" inferred from Foraker's "He took."] Less primary accounts have Blythe saying, "Now is the time to bridge the bloody chasm." Weaver, *Senator,* 126.
479 **(the next course)** All accounts agree that everyone remained hungry through the evening, but memories differ as to which courses did not arrive. According to *The Washington Post,* 29 Jan. 1907, there were four. In that case, diners ate just oysters and clear turtle soup. TR's speech prevented consumption of the shad, and Foraker forestalled the *filet de boeuf à la Gotham.* The terrapin *à la Maryland,* squab

stuffed with truffles, tomato salad, frozen strawberry bombe, and assorted cakes were enjoyed in menu form only. Presidential scrapbook (TRP).

479 **"all persons"** Foraker, *Notes of a Busy Life*, vol. 2, 251.

480 **He noted that** Ibid.

480 **The noise subsided** Ibid., 253. Champ Clark, writing thirteen years later, quotes TR as ranting in this rebuttal against the "bloody butchers" of Brownsville, who "ought to be hung" (*My Quarter Century*, vol. 2, 447). But he also recalls TR saying that "all talk on that subject was academic," a remark that Foraker, in his letter of 29 Jan. 1907, ascribes to the President's first speech. If TR had, at any point, used the language Clark quotes, Foraker would surely have noted it. Samuel Blythe states that TR's tone during the latter part of the evening was "neither bellicose nor belligerent." TR himself wrote on 27 Jan. that he had been "inclined to make a Berserker speech," but had decided against it. *Letters*, vol. 5, 571.

480 **"If the floor"** Blythe reminiscence (HBP). See also Watson, *As I Knew Them*, 72–73.

481 **"I call that"** Lawrence, *Memories of a Happy Life*, 157–58.

482 **a reluctant party** Lane, *Brownsville Affair*, 141–42. Taft's doughy receptivity to TR's sharp-edged impress, mentioned elsewhere in the text, is indicated by a remark to his brother Charles on 1 Jan. 1907: "I am not responsible for the Brownsville order; but I think it entirely justified" (WHT).

482 **By the time** Foraker, *I Would Live It Again*, 281–88. Mrs. Foraker's account of surveillance by the Secret Service, written in 1932, is unsupported by any other evidence, except that regarding Tillman in Dunn, *From Harrison to Harding*, vol. 2, 92. It is, nevertheless, detailed enough to give any reader pause.

482 **Roosevelt showed** TR, *Letters*, vol. 5, 559–60.

482 **A VISITOR TO** Everett Colby in Wood, *Roosevelt As We Knew Him*, 154. Colby does not give the date of his visit, except to say that the Japanese crisis had just "reached an acute stage." The only recorded visit of both Taft and Root to the Executive Office at such a moment was on the morning of 13 Feb. 1907, at the height of the first war scare. Washington *Evening Star*, same date.

482 **For the last** Esthus, *Theodore Roosevelt and Japan*, 134–35. Chinese schoolchildren already had their own schools in San Francisco. The order of 11 Oct. 1906 had been followed by a white-inspired riot, and a Japanese bank president had been killed. There were immediate calls in Japan for an anti-American boycott.

483 **Roosevelt sat** Wood, *Roosevelt As We Knew Him*, 154–55.

483 **"They don't care"** Qu. in Murakata, "Theodore Roosevelt and William Sturgis Bigelow."

483 **Some of the most** TR, *Works*, vol. 17, 452–53.

483 **This last remark** Ibid., 454–55; *San Francisco Chronicle*, 10 Dec. 1906; Bailey, *Theodore Roosevelt*, 127. Elihu Root cogently remarked to Ambassador Aoki that the antagonism of American laborers toward Japanese was not so much an assertion of superiority as an admission of inferiority. Jessup, *Elihu Root*, vol. 2, 7.

483 **Senator Tillman** *The New York Times*, 15 Jan. 1907.

483 **Tokyo's response** Jessup, *Elihu Root*, vol. 2, 9. See also Akira Iriye, *Pacific Estrangement: Japanese and American Expansion, 1879–1911* (Cambridge, Mass., 1972).

484 **The result was** Jessup, *Elihu Root*, vol. 2, 13, 15; Esthus, *Theodore Roosevelt and Japan*, 155–56. See also John R. Jenswold, "Leaving the Door Ajar: Politics and Prejudices in the Making of the 1907 Immigration Law," *Mid-America* 67.1 (1985).

484 **"Why should I"** Phillip Dunne, ed., *Mr. Dooley Remembers: The Informal Memoirs of Finley Peter Dunne* (Boston, 1963), 201–2.

484 **To win passage** Jessup, *Elihu Root*, vol. 2, 15. "Yellow Peril" Cassandras tended

to overlook the fact that many Japanese immigrants, having worked in the United States for a few years, returned home with their hard-earned dollars.

484 **"in the way"**   Root to Ambassador Luke Wright, qu. in ibid., 13.

484 **Schmitz, who**   Bailey, *Theodore Roosevelt*, 128–33, 143–44. The age scruple was not unreasonable, in that many of the immigrant "children" originally discriminated against had been twenty to thirty years old.

485 **his first term**   Frederick C. Leiner, "The Unknown Effort: Theodore Roosevelt's Battleship Plan and International Arms Limitation Talks, 1906–1907," *Military Affairs* 8.3 (1984); TR, *Letters*, vol. 5, 35.

485 **He had even**   Rebecca Kramer, "Theodore Roosevelt, Disarmament, and The Hague," t.s. monograph (AC). See notes above for chaps. 22 and 25.

485 **The idea of**   TR, *Letters*, vol. 5, 398–400.

>*Chronological Note:* With TR's encouragement, the United States at first pressed seriously for a general reduction in naval forces, insisting that the issue of arms limitation be discussed at The Hague. This proved to be an unpopular stance with Germany, which had its own strategic reasons for building up a larger navy. Britain was initially supportive of the United States, but then, in view of the Kaiser's ardent militarism, declined to negotiate away its own armed advantage. Russia and Austria also opposed the idea of disarmament (Jessup, *Elihu Root*, vol. 2, 69; *The New York Times*, 16 June 1907; TR, *Letters*, vol. 5, 357).
>
>TR himself was conflicted in his attitude. His letters on the subject earnestly contend that most arms-control proposals did not really apply to the United States, since "we have a small navy (and an army so much smaller as to seem infinitesimal) compared with the armed forces of the other great powers which in point of population, extent of territory, wealth and resources, can be put in the same category with us. Therefore we cannot ourselves reduce our forces" (TR, *Letters*, vol. 5, 358).
>
>Through most of 1906, however, he pushed for a "feasible and rational plan" of naval disarmament, declaring that limits on battleship size would reduce the rampant costs and dangers of an arms race. His proposal in Sept. 1906 that the Hague Conference should forbid the construction of any battleship larger than the *Dreadnought* was received unenthusiastically by the British and adamantly opposed by Wilhelm II. TR then wrote Sir Edward Grey in October, suggesting that an attempt should be made to limit the number of ships being built. But his temporary ardor for arms control was clearly flagging. By early 1907 he had essentially lost hope and interest in the Second Hague Conference, whose proceedings he did not even follow. It fell to Elihu Root to direct American delegates at the conference, establish the Drago Doctrine (still in force), and push for the strengthening of the Hague Permanent Court of Arbitration. This idea broke down when the countries could not agree on how the judges would be chosen. By the time the conference closed on 18 Oct. 1907, it was generally considered a failure. TR, *Letters*, vol. 5, 601; Jessup, *Elihu Root*, vol. 2, 75–79, 82. See Frederick C. Leiner, "The Unknown Effort: Theodore Roosevelt's Battleship Plan and International Arms Limitation Talks, 1906–1907," *Military Affairs* 48.3 (1984).

485 **In a letter**   TR, *Letters*, vol. 5, 528–29.

485 **Three days later**   Esthus, *Theodore Roosevelt and Japan*, 161; TR, *Letters*, vol. 5, 600–601. For Root's unenthusiastic handling of the arms-limitation issue at the Second Hague Conference, see Jessup, *Elihu Root*, vol. 2, 71ff. By February 1907, British interest in the subject had also waned, the Liberal government being at least as wary of Germany's rearmament as the Roosevelt Administration was of Japan's.

Historical Note: TR's comments on arms limitation in 1906 and early 1907 have an oddly prophetic ring. He cites, over and over again, his fear that if "free peoples" disarm too much, they will become vulnerable to "military depotisms and barbarisms" (see, e.g., TR, *Letters*, vol. 5, 366). Eighty years in advance of Ronald Reagan's cautionary motto regarding arms-control pacts, "Trust, but verify," TR was writing the British Foreign Secretary about the Hague agenda proposals, "In view of the marvelous ability certain nations have of concealing what they are doing, we would have no real idea whether or not they were keeping down their armaments even in the event of an agreement to do so." Ibid., 601.

485 AS THE END   Gould, *Presidency of Theodore Roosevelt*, 203; TR, *Letters*, vol. 5, 604.

486 *Conservation,* by itself   J. Leonard Bates, "Fulfilling American Democracy: The Conservation Movement, 1907 to 1921," *Mississippi Valley Historical Review* 44.1 (1957); Lacey, "Mysteries of Earth-Making," 386, 339.

    Historiological Note: The date at which *conservation* acquired its modern, politicized meaning is as variously debated by historians as that for *progressivism.* Bates and Lacey agree that 1907 was when conservation became a social movement, as opposed to a complex of disciplines—and as contrasted with the sentimental *preservation* of John Muir and the Sierra Club. Bates directly links conservation to progressivism. Lacey stresses conservation's scientific origins in the work of such pioneers as the explorer-geologist John Wesley Powell, the mammologist C. Hart Merriam, the forester-geographer Henry Gannett (bequeather of much data to Pinchot), and the prodigiously catholic WJ McGee. It was Gannett who first spoke of forest preservation as "almost a religion."

486 **Roosevelt had virtually**   Gould, *Presidency of Theodore Roosevelt,* 200; Harold T. Pinkett, *Gifford Pinchot: Public and Private Forester* (Urbana, 1970), 75–78; Cutright, *Theodore Roosevelt,* 216–17.

486 **There was something**   The word *hypnotic* is that of TR's childhood friend Fanny Parsons, in a description that emphasized Pinchot's extraordinary attraction for women (Parsons, *Perchance Some Day,* 127). See also Wister, *Roosevelt,* 174; *Roosevelt vs. Newett,* 196; James Garfield diary, 30 July 1904 (JRG).

487 **"Pinchot truly"**   TR qu. in Butt, *Letters of Archie Butt,* 147.

487 **A forced draft**   Mowry, *Era of Theodore Roosevelt,* 215.

487 **Thus came into**   TR's own "Memorandum on signing proclamations" appears in TR, *Letters,* vol. 5, 603–4. "Failure on my part to sign these proclamations would mean that immense tracts of valuable timber would fall into the hands of the lumber syndicates. . . . The creation of the reserves means that this timber will be kept . . . in such manner as to keep them unimpaired for the benefit of children now growing up to inherit the land."

487 **Only after the**   "The opponents of the Forest Service turned handsprings in their wrath," TR gleefully wrote in his *Autobiography* (419). The other major conservation measure of this session was TR's creation of the Inland Waterways Commission on 14 Mar. 1907. See chap. 29, below.

487 ON 4 MARCH   *British Documents on Foreign Affairs,* 171–72. For a short sketch of Ambassador Bryce, see Burton, "Theodore Roosevelt and His English Correspondents."

487 **the first Jew**   According to Straus, TR said when offering him the appointment, "I want to show Russia and some other countries what we think of Jews in this country." Straus had assumed office on 17 Dec. 1906. Straus, *Under Four Administrations,* 210.

488 **Cortelyou had been**   Sullivan, *Our Times,* vol. 3, 509; Strouse, *Morgan,* 565–66.

488   "a demonstration"   Klein, *E. H. Harriman,* 399; Adler, *Jacob H. Schiff,* vol. 1, 44–50.
488   his native Germany   Schiff was also rather deaf. An enduring joke in Rooseveltian circles was that the President, boasting at a dinner of New York notables about his appointment of Oscar Straus without any regard to ancestry or creed, turned to Schiff for corroboration ("Isn't that so, Mr. Schiff?") and got it: "Dot's right, Mr. President, you came to me and said, Chake, who is der best Choo I can put in my Cabinet?"
488   "We are confronted"   Adler, *Jacob H. Schiff,* vol. 1, 44–45.
489   Roosevelt wrote back   Klein, *E. H. Harriman,* 398; TR, *Letters,* vol. 5, 631. TR's naïveté in financial matters is indicated not only by the remark he made about Harriman, but also in his disinclination to call what might have been an important conference. He had not hesitated, seven weeks before, to invite Mayor Schmidt and the entire San Francisco school board to Washington, at government expense.
489   "This has been"   Klein, *E. H. Harriman,* 400.
489   "your stern and"   Adler, *Jacob H. Schiff,* vol. 1, 47.
489   the macabre artifact   *The New York Times,* 14 Apr. 1907.
489   More rational admirers   Adams, *Letters,* vol. 6, 55–57; Bliss Perry, *The Life and Letters of Henry Lee Higginson* (Boston, 1921), 361; TR, *Letters to Kermit,* 184.
489   Spring came   TR, *Letters to Kermit,* 186, 189.
490   In early May   James Bryce to Sir Edward Grey, *British Documents on Foreign Affairs,* 203–4; Presidential scrapbook (TRP).
490   It also revived   Ibid., 204; TR, *Letters to Kermit,* 195.
490   second elective term   Longworth, *Crowded Hours,* 148. "No one will ever know how much I wished, in the black depths of my heart, that 'something would happen' and that Father would be renominated."
490   nine tenths of him   TR made this admission on 10 Oct. 1908, long after the question of a third term had become academic. Butt, *Letters,* 125.
490   Having thus made   TR, *Letters to Kermit,* 196.
490   HE SAW THEM   TR to C. Hart Merriam, 23 May 1907 (TRP). Except where otherwise cited, the source for the following section is Alton A. Lindsey, "Was Theodore Roosevelt the Last to See the Passenger Pigeon?" *Proceedings of the Indiana Academy of Science for 1976* 86 (1977). The authoritative work on TR as ornithologist and natural historian is Cutright, *Theodore Roosevelt.*
491   He had collected   Cutright, *Theodore Roosevelt,* 78.
491   "The passenger pigeon"   Lindsey, "Was Theodore Roosevelt?" notes that the last known surviving passenger pigeon died in captivity in Ohio, on 1 Sept. 1914.
491   the last bird   William B. Mershon, *The Passenger Pigeon* (Deposit, N.Y., 1907), 223. A more recent authority cites a specimen shot in Fairfield County, Conn., in 1906. Lindsey, "Was Theodore Roosevelt?"
491   saw no evidence   See also Alton A. Lindsey, "The Sighting at Pine Knot," *Natural History,* Nov. 1977.
       Historical Note: Only after TR got back to Washington did he ponder a remark about some "wild carrier pigeons" by Dick McDaniel, the foreman of a farm adjoining Pine Knot, and realize that he had a possible supporting witness. Subsequent interviews with McDaniel, whose reliability was vouched for, established that birds matching the ones TR described had been sighted on the farm six days earlier. Lindsey, "Was Theodore Roosevelt?" subjects TR's claims to exhaustive scrutiny and concludes that he was indeed the last qualified observer of wild passenger pigeons. Nine years later, at the height of the Great War in Europe, TR wrote: "The extermination of the passenger pigeon means that mankind was just so much poorer; exactly as in the case of the destruction of the cathedral at Rheims." TR, *Works,* vol. 4, 227.

CHAPTER 29: SUCH A FLEET AND SUCH A DAY

492 **"D'ye think?"** "Mr. Dooley" in Chicago *Record-Herald*, 20 Oct. 1907.

492 **The agreeable** James R. Reckner, " 'I Had Great Confidence in the Fleet': Theodore Roosevelt and the Great White Fleet," in Naylor et al., *Theodore Roosevelt*, 383. Elihu Root remained TR's principal foreign-policy adviser, but the multilingual, much-traveled Meyer was the Administration's expert on the social aspects of diplomacy. On this date, Root was in Clinton, N.Y., recovering from illness. Jessup, *Elihu Root*, vol. 2, 23.

492 **"Nothing during my"** TR, *Letters*, vol. 5, 671–72.

493 **calling for war** Jessup, *Elihu Root*, vol. 2, 23.

493 **Elihu Root did** Ibid.

493 **Roosevelt was not so** Ibid., 6–23; Dorwart, *Office of Naval Intelligence*, 83; TR, *Letters*, vol. 7, 393. See also Abbott, *Impressions of Theodore Roosevelt*, 111; Jessup, *Elihu Root*, vol. 2, 24.

493 **The Office of** Dorwart, *Office of Naval Intelligence*, 83.

493 **He had asked** Reckner, " 'I Had Great Confidence,' " 383–84.

493 **COLONEL W. W.** Ibid., 383.

493 **Roosevelt said** Ibid.; Wimmel, *Theodore Roosevelt and the Great White Fleet*, 220. See also TR, *Letters*, vol. 5, 729–30, and James R. Reckner, *Teddy Roosevelt's Great White Fleet* (Annapolis, 1988).

493 **The idea was** Wimmel, *Theodore Roosevelt and the Great White Fleet*, 220; Dewey to TR, qu. in Jusserand, *What Me Befell*, 308. See also TR, *Letters*, vol. 5, 725–26, and Louis Morton, "Military and Naval Preparations for the Defense of the Philippines During the War Scare of 1907," *Military Affairs* 13.2 (1949).

494 **Wall Street's stock** Strouse, *Morgan*, 564–65; Adler, *Jacob H. Schiff*, 45.

494 **He had private information** TR, *Autobiography*, 564.

494 **He issued** Reckner, " 'I Had Great Confidence,' " 384.

494 **When someone asked** Wimmel, *Theodore Roosevelt and the Great White Fleet*, 221.

494 **Metcalf was authorized** Reckner, " 'I Had Great Confidence,' " 385, claims that TR bungled the announcement, first by allowing it to be leaked, then by issuing a series of conflicting statements about the fleet's true destination. According to Francis B. Loomis, TR did have some initial qualms about the possibly inflammatory consequences of his order, not only on Japanese war sentiment but on the much more truculent "yellow" newspapers of the United States. In the event, Japanese reaction was encouragingly muted, and by late July TR's resolve had hardened to a calm self-certainty. See Beale, *Theodore Roosevelt*, 332 and esp. 543–44.

495 **"a practice cruise"** TR, *Letters*, vol. 5, 709.

495 **twenty-nine million** Sullivan, *Our Times*, vol. 3, 497–98; Strouse, *Morgan*, 573–74. Rockefeller was right. The fine was canceled on appeal.

495 **Conservatives blamed** TR, *Letters*, vol. 5, 746.

495 **Roosevelt, who** Ibid., 745–46.

495 **"The present trouble"** Ibid., 747.

495 **"Please do not"** Ibid., 763. Bonaparte consulted, on TR's orders, with Herbert Knox Smith, who informed him that the Sherman Act was "an economic absurdity . . . impossible of general enforcement." On 24 September, TR instructed Bonaparte to abandon his case against International Harvester. Gould, *Presidency of Theodore Roosevelt*, 218.

495 **With that, he** TR to George Otto Trevelyan, 23 Aug. 1907 (TRP). On Wall Street, feelings of foreboding persisted, mixed with recriminations against Roosevelt for his alleged fiscal irresponsibility.

496 ONE THING THE ROMANS   Ferrero was much on TR's mind at this time. See TR, *Presidential Addresses and State Papers*, vol. 6, 1374.

496 WJ McGee, the visionary   Lacey, "Mysteries of Earth-Making," 379, nicely describes McGee's concept as "a scheme to restore the commons through water, rather than land."

496 "a comprehensive plan"   M. Nelson McGeary, *Gifford Pinchot: Forester-Politician* (Princeton, N.J., 1960), 94. See also Pinkett, *Gifford Pinchot*, 108ff., and Lacey, "Mysteries of Earth-Making," 379–82.

496 By the time   WJ McGee, ed., *Proceedings of a Conference of Governors in the White House, May 13–15, 1908* (Washington, D.C., 1909), vi–vii (hereafter *Governors' Conference Proceedings*). For TR's own account of his Mississippi cruise, see TR, *Letters to Kermit*, 216ff.

496 A sense that   TR to Archibald Roosevelt, 7 Oct. 1907 (fragment, TRB); Herbert Knox Smith, "Roosevelt's Leadership," address to Roosevelt Memorial Association, [n.d.] 1924, copy in TRB.

496 Roosevelt made his   TR, *Presidential Addresses*, vol. 6, 1432–33.

497 "There is an"   Ibid., 1431.

497 These implosions   *The Washington Post*, 16 Oct. 1907.

498 "a simultaneous deficiency"   *British Documents on Foreign Affairs*, 347.

498 "I can't go on"   Pringle, *Theodore Roosevelt*, 438.

498 "Do I look?"   Wood, *Roosevelt As We Knew Him*, 165. In 1918, shortly before his death, TR admitted that his only real regret was his misjudgment of the panic of 1907. He had acted "without a clear knowledge of business affairs." Jack Cooper interview, Oct. 1919 (TRB).

498 By now, most   Strouse, *Morgan*, 578.

499 The President was   Wood, *Roosevelt As We Knew Him*, 439. See also TR, *Letters*, vol. 5, 747–49.

499 ALTHOUGH A TOTAL   Strouse, *Morgan*, 580–84.

499 Judge Gary said   Watson, *As I Knew Them*, 69; Strouse, *Morgan*, 587–88; TR, *Letters*, vol. 5, 830–31. A congressional investigation in 1911 revealed that Gary and Frick may have taken advantage of TR's fiscal naïveté when they protested their reluctance to acquire Moore & Schley (whose name they declined to reveal to him over breakfast). What they demonstrably got, along with an assurance of anti-trust indemnity, was a bargain investment and a considerable enlargement of U.S. Steel's presence in the South. Strouse, *Morgan*, 590.

499 Gary called   Strouse, *Morgan*, 588.

499 ON 11 NOVEMBER   TR, *Letters*, vol. 5, 838–39; *Collier's*, 30 May 1908; press release file, 1908 (TRP).

501 WALL STREET'S currency   Gould, *Presidency of Theodore Roosevelt*, 248–49.

501 "I am absolutely"   TR, *Letters to Kermit*, 224.

501 "There may be"   TR, *Works*, vol. 17, 482.

501 Mr. E. H. Harriman   List copy, 25 Dec. 1907, in GBC.

502 "If there is one thing"   Barbara Tuchman, *The Proud Tower* (New York, 1966), 124.

502 "I am Commander-in-Chief"   Wimmel, *Great White Fleet*, 223.

502 "I have not"   White House press release, 12 Dec. 1907.

502 MONDAY, 16 DECEMBER   The following account is based on newspaper accounts in Presidential scrapbook (TRP), and on the detailed report of the British Embassy naval attaché in *British Documents on Foreign Affairs*, vol. 13, 6–7.

503 "By George!"   Qu. in Wimmel, *Theodore Roosevelt*, xv.

503 When the presidential   Washington *Evening Star*, 16 Dec. 1907.

503 Less audibly   Robley D. Evans, *Admiral's Log* (New York, 1910), 413–14. TR later claimed to have warned Evans that the Japanese threat was serious. "Admi-

ral, I am very fond of you, but if you or your ships are surprised in port or at sea, don't come back to me." Leary, *Talks with TR*, 11–13.

CHAPTER 30: MORAL OVERSTRAIN

504 *He's a gr'-reat* "Mr. Dooley" in Chicago *Record-Herald*, 20 Oct. 1907.
504 "THE REACTION AGAINST" Adams, *Letters*, vol. 6, 94.
504 "I find I" Leary, *Talks with TR*, 206.
505 he was insane *Current Literature*, Mar. 1907.
505 At the annual *British Documents on Foreign Affairs*, vol. 12, 246.
505 To Ambassador James Bryce James Bryce, "General Report on the United States for the Year 1907," in ibid., 349. *À outrance* = to the knife.
505 "The oppression" Ibid.
505 Bryce left vague Ibid., 350.
505 He was definite Ibid.
505 The President's initial TR, *Letters*, vol. 6, 103–4.
506 *Moral Overstrain* Written by George W. Alger (Boston, 1906).
506 Roosevelt had tried At the same time, it was noted that he had not yet given the Secretary of War a formal endorsement, so Taft remained chosen, but not blessed.
506 "Charles the Baptist" Sam McCune Lindsay, "Recollections" (manuscript memoir, 1955, in TRB). Finley Peter Dunne flatly states, "Nobody liked Hughes—nobody at all" in "Remembrances" (FPD).
506 a Special Message Davis, *Released for Publication*, 69–71, misdates Hughes's speech as 30 Jan. 1908, but is otherwise a prime source for this typical Roosevelt publicity ploy.
506 much harsher language Frank B. Kellogg, one of TR's more influential field advisers, wrote on 25 Jan. 1908 to warn him that the Special Message would be "a mistake," in that his views were already well known and did not have to be so brutally repeated. Further, he believed that the Message would "tend to alienate . . . conservative businessmen and good Republicans" from TR's candidate for the 1908 GOP presidential nomination, William H. Taft. Frank B. Kellogg Papers (LC).
506 As a result *The New York Times*, 1 Feb. 1908.
507 He demanded The complete text of TR's Special Message is reprinted in TR, *Letters*, vol. 6, 1572–91.
Historical Note: George E. Mowry remarks that historians of the Progressive Era have frequently ascribed TR's radicalization in 1910 and 1912 to the publication of Herbert Croly's *Promise of American Life* in late 1909. "A glance at his messages and speeches of 1907 and 1908 would seem to argue that Roosevelt may have had as much influence on Croly as Croly had on him" (*Era of Theodore Roosevelt*, 222). Elting E. Morison further observes that these same two messages "proposed in some detail the basic national reforms achieved under Taft and Wilson." TR, *Letters*, vol. 6, 922.
507 Roosevelt proudly Ibid., 1574–77.
507 Referring to himself Ibid., 1577–86.
508 "These new conditions" Ibid., 1588.
508 SUBSCRIBERS TO All the public comments on TR's Special Message in the following paragraphs are taken from *Current Literature*, Mar. 1907.
508 "the President is" Mark De Wolfe Howe, *James Ford Rhodes: An American Historian* (New York, 1929), 195. See also Henry Cabot Lodge to TR, 19 Sept. 1907, and TR to Lodge, 21 Sept. 1907 (TRP).

509 **"Of all your"** Nicholas Murray Butler to TR, 4 Feb. 1908 (TRP).

509 **"You regret"** TR, *Letters,* vol. 6, 925.

509 ON 7 FEBRUARY William James in *The American Magazine,* Nov. 1907; Samuel Carter III, *The Incredible Great White Fleet* (New York, 1971), 54–55.

509 **For twenty-two** Wimmel, *Theodore Roosevelt and the Great White Fleet,* 228; Carter, *Incredible Great White Fleet,* 51–52.

510 **Throughout 1907** Jessup, *Elihu Root,* vol. 2, 27–29; "Memorandum Respecting Japanese Immigration into Canada and the United States," *British Documents on Foreign Affairs,* vol. 13, 160.

510 **By 29 February** Gould, *Presidency of Theodore Roosevelt,* 262; Jessup, *Elihu Root,* vol. 2, 30. In May 1908, the Japanese monthly inflow was down to 900 from nearly 2,000 in May 1907. Bailey, *Theodore Roosevelt,* 279.

511 **He also won** Weaver, *Senator,* 131. Foraker observed that the five Democrats were prepared to find the soldiers guilty without even looking at the testimony.

511 **The dissenting members** Ibid.

511 **So did the** Ibid., 130.

511 **Roosevelt's other** Gould, *Presidency of Theodore Roosevelt,* 263–66.

512 **Sounding rather** TR, *Letters,* vol. 6, 1017–18.

512 **"But, Mr. President"** Jusserand, *What Me Befell,* 332. The following section is adapted from 332–36.

512 **"Washington and Rochambeau"** The midriver island is now Theodore Roosevelt Island, a national memorial to TR. Deep in its forested interior stands a statue modeled on the illustration on p. 141. Nan Netherton, "Delicate Beauty and Burly Majesty: The Story of Theodore Roosevelt Island," t.s. (1984), 11 (TRB).

512 **"We might meet"** For TR's version of this story, see Butt, *Letters,* 228–29.

514 **On 12 May** Wister, *Roosevelt,* 147; table plan in "Executive Mansion Social Functions," RG 42, vol. 11 (NA). This beautifully compiled scrapbook series is a monument to the social and entertainment activities of the Roosevelt White House, 1901–1909 (hereafter "Social Functions").

514 **The President sat** Some physical descriptions taken from the famous group photograph of the Governors' Conference, 13 May 1908.

514 **(in a severe sulk)** Uncle Joe's pique is mentioned in Butt, *Letters,* 45.

514 **Bryan's presence** "Conference on the Conservation of Natural Resources at the White House, May 13–15, 1908," memorandum account in "Social Functions."

514 **When wood and water** Michael Lacey notes that the Governors' Conference was not only the first but the last occasion in American history when representatives of all branches of government "gathered together to discuss a set of common issues" ("Mysteries of Earth-Making," 111). Cleveland died on 24 June.

514 **Roosevelt, wanting** "Social Functions."

514 **The dinner seating** Ibid.; Edith Kermit Roosevelt Catering Agreement, 12 May 1908, in "Letters Received" file, in ibid.

515 **"I confess to you"** Butt, *Letters,* 7.

515 **"A wonderful man"** Ibid., 91.

515 AT ELEVEN O'CLOCK *Governors' Conference Proceedings,* xix–xxxi.

516 **The "Syllabus"** Ibid., xiii–xvi.

516 **"The Lord thy God"** Ibid., 1 (Deuteronomy 8:7–9).

516 **Roosevelt delivered** The following quotations from TR's address are taken from ibid., 3–13.

517 *Conservation as a* Copy in AC. TR's speech is reprinted in TR, *Presidential Addresses and State Papers,* vol. 7, 1738–53.

518 **"the State as quasi sovereign"** See *Hudson County Water Co. v. McCarter,* 209 U.S. 349 (1908).

518 HE STAYED WITH *Governors' Conference Proceedings,* 14.

518 **The conference broke** *The Washington Post*, 16 May 1908; *Governors' Conference Proceedings*, 192–94.

519 THUS EMPOWERED Lacey, "Mysteries of Earth-Making," 391–92; TR, *Letters*, vol. 6, 1065ff.

519 **Americans began to be** The following survey of TR's conservation accomplishments through May 1908 is based on John Allen Gable, comp., "President Theodore Roosevelt's Record on Conservation," *Theodore Roosevelt Association Journal* 10.3 (fall 1983). See also Cutright, *Theodore Roosevelt, passim.*

519 **now that "Conservation"** Michael J. Lacey flatly states, "The language and aims of Conservation were invented in the spring of 1908." Lacey, "Mysteries of Earth-Making," 440.

519 **("Is there any?")** Pringle, *Theodore Roosevelt*, 469.

519 **And Roosevelt had** By the time TR left office in 1909, his conservation record had indeed expanded to include 18 national monuments, 51 federal bird reservations and 4 national game preserves, and 150 national forests (increasing the total acreage he inherited by more than 400 percent). The last-mentioned area was equal to that of all the Atlantic states from Maine to Virginia combined, with the addition of West Virginia, Pennsylvania, and Vermont. Gable, "President Theodore Roosevelt's Record."

519 **"Any man who"** TR, *Letters*, vol. 6, 1041.

520 **Two West Virginia** Ibid., 1039, 1045; Henry Adams to Mrs. Frederick Tams, 3 Apr. 1908 (JH).

520 **Adams had to** Henry Adams to Mrs. Frederick Tams, 3 Apr. 1908 (JH). Lodge's fabled *froideur*, and total lack of interest in what anybody thought of him, had finally alienated Adams. "If I told Cabot that he is personally and physically loathsome to me . . . he would not understand what I meant." Adams, *Letters*, vol. 5, 693.

CHAPTER 31: THE RESIDUARY LEGATEE

521 *I don't know* "Mr. Dooley" in Chicago *Record-Herald*, 20 Oct. 1907.

521 THE FIRST DAY TR, *Letters*, vol. 6, 1044–45.

521 **"Q," as schoolmates** For a classic memoir of Quentin Roosevelt, and an endearing boy's-eye view of his father, see Earle Looker, *The White House Gang* (New York, 1929).

521 **("The Republican")** Ibid., 44–45.

522 **The property office** The following account of the Battle of the Guidon is taken from ibid., 92–94. While writing his memoir, Looker interviewed all surviving members of the gang, save Quentin.

522 **(obsessive clock-watcher)** Q's dollar pocket-watch is a leitmotiv in Looker's descriptions of gang activities. For TR's own time consciousness, see the pseudonymous article by "K" (probably Finley Peter Dunne), "The Powers of a Strenuous President," *The American Magazine*, Apr. 1908: "No railroad engineer runs more sharply on schedule than he. His watch comes out of his pocket, he cuts off an interview, or signs a paper, and turns instantly, according to his timetable, to the next engagement. If there is an interval anywhere left over he chinks in the time by reading a paragraph of history."

522 **"Too late! Too late"** Dialogue transcribed verbatim from Looker, *White House Gang*, 94–96.

522 **Roosevelt's surprise attack** "If Hughes is going to play the game," TR had said, grinning after hogging the headlines with his Special Message, "he must learn the tricks." William Manners, *TR and Will: A Friendship That Split the Republican Party* (New York, 1969), 49.

523 **With that, he** For another presidential reprimand, involving the gang's embellishment of White House portraits with spitballs, see ibid., 16, and TR, *Letters,* vol. 6, 1004.

523 **as had Mark** Beer, *Hanna,* 586.

523 **The famous MacMillan** Looker, *White House Gang,* 120–21. "Time and again, afterwards, I have thought of these enchanting models—realizing that it was a rare privilege given me, to see the genesis of Quentin's interest in the air."

524 **"I have two"** TR, *Letters,* vol. 6, 1044.

524 **For some time** Ibid., vol. 5, 679; TR, *Letters to Kermit,* 238, 240; Carl Akeley, introduction to TR, *Works,* vol. 5, x–xi. The date of Akeley's dinner (or lunch) with TR is uncertain, but it appears to have occurred between 25 Oct. and 7 Nov. 1907, after the President's return from Louisiana. See also Wood, *Roosevelt As We Knew Him,* 224, and Kermit Roosevelt, *Happy Hunting-Grounds,* 11–14. From April 1908 on, the "note of Africa" is increasingly sounded in TR's correspondence.

524 **"I think I"** TR, *Letters,* vol. 6, 1060. Another person who got an advance indication of TR's designs on African wildlife was John Burroughs, who joined him around this time for a weekend at Pine Knot. One night after dinner, while EKR knitted, TR gave the naturalist J. H. Patterson's *The Man-Eaters of Tsavo and Other East African Adventures* (London, 1907) to read by lamplight, and himself read Cromer's *Modern Egypt* (London, 1908) at a table in the big bare room. "Suddenly Roosevelt's hand came down on the table with such a bang that it made us both jump, and Mrs. Roosevelt exclaimed in a slightly nettled tone, 'Why, my dear, what *is* the matter?' He had killed a mosquito with a blow that would have demolished an African lion." Hearing this story years later, the essayist Gamaliel Bradford commented: "He killed mosquitoes as if they were lions, and lions as if they were mosquitoes." John Burroughs, *Under the Maples* (New York, 1921), 106; Wagenknecht, *Seven Worlds,* 6. Note: Burroughs's chapter on Pine Knot contains a spurious refutation of TR's sighting of passenger pigeons there in 1907. See Lindsey, "Was Theodore Roosevelt?"

524 ROOSEVELT STAMPEDE Washington *Evening Star,* 3 June 1908.

524 **(Charles P. Taft)** was Taft's mentor-like half-brother.

524 **"If your friend"** Cullom, *Fifty Years,* 303.

525 **At latest count** Pringle, *William Howard Taft,* vol. 1, 348; Gould, *Presidency of Theodore Roosevelt,* 284.

525 **The giant airship** A photograph of the zeppelin appears on p. 537 of Sullivan, *Our Times,* vol. 3, directly opposite a paragraph on p. 536 describing the nomination of Taft.

525 **On Tuesday** Pringle, *William Howard Taft,* vol. 1, 350–51; Joseph Bucklin Bishop, *Presidential Nominations and Elections* (New York, 1916), 72.

525 **The proceedings in** *The New York Times,* 18 June 1908; Pringle, *William Howard Taft,* vol. 1, 352; Alsop, "Autobiography," 7.

525 **"That man is"** *Official Report of the Proceedings of the Fourteenth Republican National Convention* (Columbus, Ohio, 1908), 88.

526 **Joseph Bucklin Bishop** For Bishop's anti-Semitism, see, e.g., his letter to TR of 21 Oct. 1903: "I have just had the exquisite pleasure of trampling upon the Jew [newspaper editor Moses Strauss] as he crawled at my feet" (TRP). In a follow-up letter, dated 24 Oct., he warned TR against a "Jew syndicate" attempting to control the New York press. Waspish, emotional, unctuous, and conniving, Bishop was also an antifeminist. "I never met a man who had so low an opinion of women as human beings" (Villard, *Fighting Years,* 129). These traits did not dissuade TR from choosing Bishop, years later, as his authorized biographer.

526 **He saw no reason** Bishop, *Presidential Nominations,* 72–73.

526 **At 1:30** Ibid., 73; TR, *Letters to Kermit,* 250.

526 **Bishop remained** Except where otherwise indicated, the following account is taken from Bishop, *Presidential Nominations*, 74–76.

526 **She was denied** Pringle, *William Howard Taft*, vol. 1, 353.

526 **But Lodge** Ibid.; Bishop, *Presidential Nominations*, 76.

527 **a 2:00 A.M. telegram** Charles Evans Hughes, interviewed by Howard K. Beale, n.d. [ca. 1935] (HKB). The alleged bribe, apparently vouchsafed by one of Taft's rich friends, was one hundred thousand dollars, and the intermediary was identified as one Elbert Baldwin.

527 **LaFollette complained** LaFollette, "Autobiography," 247 (LC).

527 **at five hundred pounds** Mayer, *Republican Party*, 303. Progressives could hardly say that Taft had not made gestures in their direction, having tried without success to get Jonathan P. Dolliver and Albert J. Beveridge to run with him. Gould, *Presidency of Theodore Roosevelt*, 284–85.

527 **"THERE IS A"** Qu. in TR, *Letters*, vol. 6, 184.

527 **"It was absolutely"** Ibid., 183–84.

528 **"Well, I'm through"** "Roosevelt Tired," ms., 1908 (RSB). There is another version of this interview (misdated late summer 1908) in Baker, *American Chronicle*, 204–5.

528 **"No, revolutions"** "Roosevelt Tired," ms., 1908 (RSB). "I have never seen him in a more *human* mood," Baker wrote afterward, "nor have I ever been more impressed with his bigness and breadth."

528 **He stayed** Henry L. Stoddard, *As I Knew Them: Presidents and Politics from Grant to Coolidge* (New York, 1927), 341; Gould, *Presidency of Theodore Roosevelt*, 285. Wright, a Tennessee Gold Democrat, took over as Secretary of War on 1 July 1908.

528 **"He and I"** TR, *Letters*, vol. 6, 1085.

528 **Taft headed** Stoddard, *As I Knew Them*, 341.

528 **FOUR DAYS LATER** Sullivan, *Our Times*, vol. 3, 536–38.

528 **"A trifle too"** EKR to Corinne Roosevelt Robinson, 18 May 1908 (HKB).

529 **Instead of heading** *New York Tribune*, 22 and 24 July 1908; Stoddard, *As I Knew Them*, 342.

529 **Large, strong, plumpish** This description of Captain Butt is taken from references *passim* in Butt, *Letters*. See especially Lawrence F. Abbott's introduction, vii–xxviii.

529 **JULY 25, 1908** Some of Butt's letters were misdated in publication, including this one, which was begun on the twenty-fourth. Those describing his first days in the White House (pp. 1–6) should be dated May, not April. The following long quotation is from Butt, *Letters*, 62–65.

531 **smoking on the porch** TR never smoked.

532 **Like the President** Butt, *Letters*, 70–71.

532 **"I want ghosts"** Ibid., 88.

532 **"You know how"** Ibid., 85.

532 **Winthrop asked** Ibid.

532 **Roosevelt moved on** Ibid., 86–87.

533 **Despite the** Ibid., 75–76.

533 **"Archie, when I"** Ibid., 78.

533 **Forty little boys** Ibid., 79–80.

533 **Asked afterward** Ibid., 81. See also TR, *Letters*, vol. 3, 448.

533 **He indulged** Butt, *Letters*, 77.

533 **He sensed a** Ibid., 91.

533 **"And he is"** Ibid.

534 **"No one dreads"** Ibid., 92.

534 **TAFT'S SPEECH** Stoddard, *As I Knew Them*, 344.

534 **Now began what** Ibid., 342. TR was deeply saddened this month by the death, after a long battle with cancer, of his old friend Baron Speck von Sternburg.

Chronological Note: Although TR's presidential power was diminishing steadily in mid-1908, he still retained to the full his command of the executive order. On 10 August, he announced the appointment of a Commission on Country Life, a Pinchot-inspired board charged with finding out why the nation's rural population was advancing more slowly than city dwellers'.

In his letter to the Commission's chairman-designate, the agronomist Liberty Hyde Bailey, he observed that the government was subjecting farmers to too many economic coachings and cajolements, in order to increase their productivity, at the expense of consideration for their social and emotional well-being. "The great rural interests are human interests, and good crops are of little value to the farmer unless they open the door to a good kind of life on the farm."

He asked the Commission to report to him upon the present condition of country life, and to advise him as to how it could be improved, especially with regard to rural education. The children of farmers should be encouraged to grow up wanting to do what their parents did, rather than join the general querulous drift away from country to town. "There is too much belief among our people that the prizes of life lie away from the farm."

The Commission recommended in Feb. 1909 that rural areas be redeveloped using European-style communal/cooperative models. Country life should ideally offer "the four great requirements of man—health, education, occupation, society." The new doctrine of conservation should be applied so that the ravages visited on the environment by unregulated monopolies could be repaired, and the American countryside regain its beauty. TR submitted these recommendations to Congress before leaving office, but nothing was done about them. TR, *Letters*, vol. 6, 1169–70; 60 Cong., sess. 2, 1909, S. doc. 703, *Special Message from the President of the United States Transmitting the Report of the Country Life Commission.* See also George S. Ellsworth, "Theodore Roosevelt's Country Life Commission," *Agricultural History* 34 (Oct. 1960), and Lacey, "Mysteries of Earth-Making," 393–400.

535 **testimony to his** TR's Messages to Congress advocating inheritance and income taxes and stringent corporation control had deprived Bryan of much traditionally Democratic ammunition.

535 **"For reasons which"** TR, *Letters*, vol. 6, 1207.

535 **"You should put"** Ibid., 1209–10.

535 **"I never"** Pringle, *Theodore Roosevelt*, 504.

535 **"Let the audience"** TR, *Letters*, vol. 6, 1230.

535 **William Randolph Hearst** Sullivan, *Our Times*, vol. 2, 223; Weaver, *Senator*, 140.

536 **Foraker, devastated** Weaver, *Senator*, 141.

536 **These qualifications** Ibid.; TR, *Letters*, vol. 6, 1244.

536 **"That a man"** *British Documents on Foreign Affairs*, vol. 13, 147.

536 **ROOSEVELT RETURNED** Gould, *Presidency of Theodore Roosevelt*, 288–89.

537 **Taft came to** TR, *Letters*, vol. 6, 1304; Butt, *Letters*, 137. For a discussion of Taft's Unitarian problem, see Harbaugh, *Life and Times*, 340–41. See also TR's impassioned plea for religious tolerance in American public life in *Letters*, vol. 6, 1333–34. Of this letter, the Jewish leader Simon Wolf wrote to TR, "I know of no state paper in the archive of our Government, that surpasses it." Qu. in Wolf, *Presidents I Have Known*, 284–85.

537 **The nearest thing** Harbaugh, *Life and Times*, 337–39.

537 **THE FOLLOWING DAY** TR to Jules Jusserand, 27 Oct. 1908 (JJ).

537 "I told him" Butt, *Letters,* 143–44.
538 Changing the subject Ibid., 144. The De Camp portrait of TR went to Harvard University.
538 "Was there ever?" Butt seems to have been unable to answer. He had recently been treated to another Roosevelt effusion, on the subject of *Alice's Adventures in Wonderland,* in the middle of a tennis game. Ibid.

CHAPTER 32: ONE LONG LOVELY CRACKLING ROW

539 *"Well, I see"* Dunne, *Observations by Mr. Dooley,* 49.
539 The fake telegram Butt, *Letters,* 153–54. When TR's use of the word *frazzle* leaked out, to the mystification of White House correspondents, he explained, not very helpfully, "The meaning is contained in the election returns of last night." Brooklyn *Eagle,* 4 Nov. 1908. *Nunc Dimittis*—"Lord, now let us thy servants depart in peace."
539 Taft's Electoral College This election analysis closely follows that in Pringle, *Theodore Roosevelt,* 506.
539 "the Bearded Lady" Wagenknecht, *Seven Worlds of Theodore Roosevelt,* 126.
539 the legendary Texan Anecdote in memo, Nov. 1908 (JBM).
540 "I really did" Judith Icke Anderson, *William Howard Taft: An Intimate History* (New York, 1981), 114.
540 "Of course, if" TR, *Letters,* vol. 6, 1329.
540 He was not short Charles G. Washburn, *Address,* 9 Feb. 1919, reprint in Pratt Collection (TRB); Davis, *Released for Publication,* 135ff.; Heaton, *Story of a Page,* 329–30; TR, qu. in Norman Hapgood, *The Changing Years* (New York, 1930), 42; TR, *Letters,* vol. 6, 1105–6.
540 He had long Abbott, *Impressions of Theodore Roosevelt,* 12–14; TR, *Letters,* vol. 6, 1105–6, 1115, 1123.
      Note: Most of these negotiations were carried on during the summer of 1908. The amount of TR's annual retainer from *Outlook* has not been confirmed, but neither he nor the Abbotts denied that it was thirty thousand dollars. Indianapolis *Star,* 22 Oct. 1908.
541 The Abbotts proudly Abbott, *Impressions of Theodore Roosevelt,* 14.
541 She thought Mr. Butt, *Letters,* 322–23.
541 MID-NOVEMBER TR to Theodore Roosevelt, Jr., 16 Nov. 1908 (TRB).
541 French Revolutionary shouts "Honor to the unlucky brave!" and "To the lantern!" were mob calls, usually accompanying the stringing up of an aristocrat. Jusserand, *What Me Befell,* 337.
541 became oddly silent Butt, *Letters,* 175.
541 "Concentrated power" TR, *Works,* vol. 17, 586.
542 The only really new Ibid., 601.
      Historical Note: The phrase *deep and brilliant* is that of Justice Benjamin N. Cardozo, who in 1931 stated that this section of TR's 1908 Message "vindicates the title of Theodore Roosevelt to a place in the history of the jurisprudence of this country." Quoting from his own book *The Nature of the Judicial Process* (New Haven, 1921), Cardozo commended TR's profound "intuitions and perceptions," and held that contemporary critics who accused the President of "ignorance . . . of the nature of the judicial process" were themselves ignorant of the way judges thought. "Pascal's spirit of self-search and self-reproach" was not incompatible with self-doubt, but no honest judge could deny the role of self in every decision. "All these inward questionings are born of the hope and desire to

transcend the limitations which hedge our human nature. Roosevelt, who knew men, had no illusions on this score." Roosevelt Medal Acceptance Speech, 1931, transcript in TRB.

542 **"did not themselves"** TR, *Works*, vol. 17, 621.

542 **PRESIDENT-ELECT TAFT** Anderson, *William Howard Taft*, 114–15. If the reporters could have read some of Taft's private mail at this time, they might have been more concerned about his readiness for office. He confessed to a friend that questions of appointments and tariff policy left him feeling "just a bit like a fish out of water." But "my wife is the politician and she will be able to meet all these issues." Qu. in Harbaugh, *Life and Times*, 432.

542 **"He is going"** Butt, *Letters*, 232–33.

542 **Butt certainly could** Ibid., 233.

543 **The lights were** Presidential scrapbook (TRP).

544 **Roosevelt and Taft** Ibid. The "articles" in question were dispatched, respectively, to magazines named *Scribbler's* and *Lookout*.

544 **As so often** Butt, *Letters*, 205–7, 245–46; Watson, *As I Knew Them*, 128; Longworth, *Crowded Hours*, 158.

544 **The President's annual** Butt, *Letters*, 251.

545 **To the President** Ibid., 253.

545 **"I don't feel"** Ibid.

545 **ALL THE ROOSEVELTS** The following description is taken from ibid., 254–56, with minor details from Presidential scrapbook (TRP).

545 **No sooner had** Butt, *Letters*, 257–59; *The Washington Post*, 29 Dec. 1908.

546 **Time was when** Longworth, *Crowded Hours*, 137–38; Butt, *Letters*, 258.

546 **"MR. SPEAKER"** Willard B. Gatewood, Jr., "The Secret Service Controversy," in his *Theodore Roosevelt and the Art of Controversy*, 237, misdated this call as occurring on 8 Jan. See *Congressional Record*, 60 Cong., Sess. 2, 1909, vol. 43, 458–62; also TR, *Works*, vol. 17, 620; *The New York Times*, 17 Dec. 1908.

546 **So far, the** Longworth, *Crowded Hours*, 160; Harbaugh, *Life and Times*, 344.

     Historical Note: Harbaugh notes that this confrontation "served mightily to hasten" the basic swap of political philosophy between the Republican and Democratic parties in the twentieth century. TR himself accused the congressional GOP leadership of hiding behind states' rights in order to protect interstate corporations, while the Democrats, who had formerly made a shibboleth of states' rights, began to align themselves behind the President. "By the middle of the century the reversal would be relatively complete: the majority of Democrats in Congress would be wedded to the centralized welfare state; all but a small minority of Republicans would be opposed or unsympathetic to it."

546 **Cannon sat now** Gatewood, *Theodore Roosevelt and the Art of Controversy*, 237; Harbaugh, *Life and Times*, 344–45.

547 **There was some** *The Atlanta Constitution*, 11 Jan. 1909, qu. in Gatewood, "Secret Service," 238.

547 **Its chief, John** Ibid., 240–42.

547 **The Secret Service's** Ibid., 243–45, 237. When the House had first limited its Secret Service appropriation, TR and Attorney General Bonaparte transferred nine investigative agents to the Justice Department, thus forming (on 26 July 1908) the nucleus of the FBI. Ibid., 252–55.

547 **"Nobody likes him"** Butt, *Letters*, 336. See this book, *passim*, for copious anecdotes of the last days of TR's Presidency.

547 **ARCHIE BUTT was** Ibid., 278, 297, 281.

548 **One legislative request** TR, *Letters*, vol. 6, 1248; Beach, *United States Navy*,

423–26; White, *Autobiography*, 404; Sprout, *Rise of American Naval Power*, 272–73.

548   "I do not believe"   Butt, *Letters*, 314.

548   "They little realize"   Ibid.

548   "Why, Mother"   Ibid., 327–28.

549   At Hampton Roads   Washington *Evening Star*, 22 Feb. 1909; TR to Archibald B. Roosevelt, 23 Feb. 1909 (TRP); Butt, *Letters*, 353–54.

549   "That is the answer"   Butt, *Letters*, 354.

EPILOGUE: 4 MARCH 1909

550   "It will be"   Davis, *Released for Publication*, 150.

550   His Inauguration was   Except where otherwise indicated, this account of TR's departure from Washington is based on reporting in the Washington *Times* and Washington *Evening Star*, 4 Mar. 1909, plus *The New York Times* and *The Washington Post*, 5 Mar. 1909. See also Davis, *Released for Publication*, 150–55.

551   "I knew"   *The New York Times*, 5 Mar. 1909.

551   "It isn't"   Butt, *Letters*, 381. Butt wrote afterward that he felt "about as depressed as I have ever felt in parting from any one in my life, save only my own mother." Ibid.

552   OBSERVERS WERE   Moore, *Roosevelt and the Old Guard*, 222; Anna Roosevelt Cowles to Corinne Robinson, 6 Mar. 1909 (TRC).

552   "There was not"   Anna Roosevelt Cowles to Corrine Robinson, 6 Mar. 1909 (TRC).

553   did not show   *Baltimore Sun*, 5 Mar. 1909.

554   constantly bubbling   Gifford Pinchot called TR "on the whole, the happiest man I ever knew." *Roosevelt House Bulletin* 1 (1924): 3.

554   Acton's famous dictum   "Power tends to corrupt, and absolute power corrupts absolutely." Lord Acton to Bishop Mandell Creighton, 5 Apr. 1887.

554   "a very symbol"   *Harper's Weekly*, 6 Oct. 1906.

554   "Roosevelt, more than"   Adams, *Education of Henry Adams*, 417.

555   Uncounted men   For the recollection of one such child, see W. Preble Jones, memo, 24 Nov. 1924 (TRB).

ILLUSTRATION CREDITS

Unless otherwise credited, all images are from the Theodore Roosevelt Collection, Harvard College Library, Cambridge, Mass.

Frontispiece Theodore Roosevelt by Edward S. Curtis, 1904. The National Portrait Gallery, Smithsonian Institution.

INDEX

Page numbers in *italics* refer to illustrations.

EDMUND MORRIS was born in Nairobi, Kenya, in 1940. He was schooled there, and studied music, history, and literature at Rhodes University, Grahamstown, South Africa. After leaving Africa in 1964, he became an advertising copywriter in London. He immigrated to the United States in 1968 and became a full-time writer in 1972. *The Rise of Theodore Roosevelt* began life as a screenplay. It was published in 1979 and won the Pulitzer Prize and American Book Award. In 1981, Morris was appointed the official biographer of President Ronald Reagan. The resultant work, *Dutch: A Memoir of Ronald Reagan*, caused a controversy when it appeared in 1999 because of its use of a partly imaginary narrator. *Theodore Rex* is the second volume in a planned trilogy on the life of Theodore Roosevelt.

Edmund Morris lives in New York City with his wife and fellow biographer, Sylvia Jukes Morris.

This book was set in Sabon, a typeface designed by the well-known German typographer Jan Tschichold (1902–1974). Sabon's design is based upon the original letter forms of Claude Garamond and was created specifically to be used for three sources: foundry type for hand composition, Linotype, and Monotype. Tschichold named his typeface for the famous Frankfurt typefounder Jacques Sabon, who died in 1580.